I0031678

Political Developments in Contemporary Russia

Praise for Ian Jeffries' previous publications:

Socialist Economies and the Transition to the Market:

> This weighty tome can be unreservedly commended ... Students and their teachers can learn a great deal from this book ... Excellent! Ian Jeffries has done us all a service.
> (Alec Nove, *Europe-Asia Studies*)

The Countries of the Former Yugoslavia at the Turn of the Twenty-first Century: A Guide to the Economies in Transition:

> This massive volume ... should find a place in every university library.
> (Sabrina P. Ramet, *Europe-Asia Studies*)

North Korea: A Guide to Economic and Political Developments:

> Although it does not attempt to provide answers as to why events occurred as they did, it will be an indispensable source for any effort to do so.
> (Christopher Griffin, *Pacific Affairs*)

China: A Guide to Economic and Political Developments:

> This book is highly useful not only to casual China watchers ... but also to researchers and academics.
> (Marc Lanteigne, *International Affairs*)

This book provides a comprehensive overview of political developments in Russia since late 2000, following on from where the author's previous publication, *The New Russia*, left off. It covers all aspects of politics including the following: the highly centralized nature of power in Russia; central government and presidential elections; regional government and developments in the republics, including unrest in Chechnya and the other Caucasian republics; and human rights. Taking a chronological approach, it shows how politics overall has changed over the period, including how the relationship between Prime Minister (formerly President) Vladimir Putin and President Dmitri Medvedev has worked out.

The book continues – and adds to – the overview of developments in the author's *The New Russia* (2002), and is the companion volume to *Economic Developments in Contemporary Russia* (2011) – both published by Routledge.

Ian Jeffries is Honorary Professor in the Department of Economics and Centre of Russian and East European Studies at Swansea University, UK. His recent publications include *A History of Eastern Europe: Crisis and Change*, 2nd edition; and numerous books in the series, *Guides to Economic and Political Developments in Asia* (all published by Routledge).

Guides to economic and political developments in Asia

1 North Korea
A guide to economic and political developments
Ian Jeffries

2 Vietnam
A guide to economic and political developments
Ian Jeffries

3 China
A guide to economic and political developments
Ian Jeffries

4 Mongolia
A guide to economic and political developments
Ian Jeffries

5 Contemporary North Korea
A guide to economic and political developments
Ian Jeffries

6 Political Developments in Contemporary China
A guide
Ian Jeffries

7 Economic Developments in Contemporary China
A guide
Ian Jeffries

8 Political Developments in Contemporary Russia
Ian Jeffries

9 Economic Developments in Contemporary Russia
Ian Jeffries

10 Contemporary Vietnam
A guide to economic and political developments
Ian Jeffries

Political Developments in Contemporary Russia

Ian Jeffries

Routledge
Taylor & Francis Group

LONDON AND NEW YORK

First published 2011
by Routledge

2 Park Square, Milton Park, Abingdon, Oxon OX14 4RN
711 Third Avenue, New York, NY 10017, USA

Routledge is an imprint of the Taylor & Francis Group, an informa business

First issued in paperback 2016

Copyright © 2011 Ian Jeffries

Typeset in Times by Wearset Ltd, Boldon, Tyne and Wear

All rights reserved. No part of this book may be reprinted or reproduced or
utilized in any form or by any electronic, mechanical, or other means, now
known or hereafter invented, including photocopying and recording, or in
any information storage or retrieval system, without permission in writing
from the publishers.

Notice:

Product or corporate names may be trademarks or registered
trademarks, and are used only for identification and explanation
without intent to infringe.

British Library Cataloguing in Publication Data
A catalogue record for this book is available from the British Library

Library of Congress Cataloging in Publication Data
Jeffries, Ian.
Political developments in contemporary Russia/Ian Jeffries.
p. cm. – (Guides to economic and political developments in Asia; 8)
Includes bibliographical references and index.

1. Russia (Federation)–Politics and government–1991– I. Title.
JN6695.J44 2010
320.947–dc22   2010026543

ISBN 978-1-138-99506-2 (pbk)
ISBN 978-0-415-60376-8 (hbk)
ISBN 978-0-203-83446-6 (ebk)

Contents

Acknowledgements

I am much indebted to the following individuals (in alphabetical order):

At Swansea University: Robert Bideleux; Siân Brown; Diane Darrell; Michele Davies; Chris Hunt; Nigel O'Leary; Mary Perman; Ann Preece; Paul Reynolds; Kathy Sivertsen; Chris West.

Professors: Nick Baigent, John Baylis; George Blazyca, Steve Brown, Mike Charlton, Steve Cook, Phillip Hanson, Paul Hare, Lester Hunt, Michael Kaser, Phil Murphy and Noel Thompson.

Russell Davies (Kays Newsagency).

At Routledge: Louise Collins, Emma Davis, Alan Jarvis, Tracy Morgan, Jillian Morrison, Eve Setch and Peter Sowden.

Copy-editor: Liz Jones.

At Wearset: Matt Deacon, Claire Toal and Allie Waite.

While Mark Axelby expertly renovated my house, I was free to write my books.

Alexander Plekhanov of the EBRD kindly sent me the most up-to-date economic statistics on Russia before the publication of the latest *Transition Report*, while pointing out that the projected figures for 2010 may be changed.

Ian Jeffries
Honorary Professor
Department of Economics and Centre of Russian and
East European Studies, Swansea University

Introduction and summary

The chronology of political events starts on 9 December 2000, following on where *The New Russia* (see the bibliography) leaves off. *The New Russia* was wide-ranging, but there are now two separate volumes. This one on political developments has a companion volume on economic developments.

Developments in Chechnya and other Caucasian republics start on 22 January 2001.

A summary of the Russia–Georgia war of August 2008 is to be found in Appendix 1, while the heatwave of summer 2010 is dealt with in Appendix 2.

The companion volume covers Russia's difficult economic transition from a command economy, the financial crisis of August 1998 and the global financial crisis a decade later. Russia is heavily dependent on energy exports. When oil and gas prices were high economic reform took a back seat, with serious consequences when the global financial crisis hit. Specific topics covered include liberalization, privatization in the non-agricultural sectors, agriculture, direct foreign investment, macroeconomic stabilization (including hyperinflation and how it was conquered) and economic performance.

Table 1 Russia: selected economic indicators 2000–10

Economic indicator	2000	2001	2002	2003	2004	2005	2006	2007	2008	2009	2010 (projection)
Rate of growth of GDP (%)	10.0	5.1	4.7	7.4	7.2	6.4	8.2	8.5	5.2	−7.9	4.4
Inflation rate (consumer) (%)	20.8	21.6	16.0	13.6	11.0	12.5	9.8	9.1	14.1	11.7	6.6

Source: EBRD.

1 A chronology of political developments since 9 December 2000

9 December 2000. The State Duma approves the restoration of the Soviet anthem. 'The idea was proposed by Putin but opposed by Yeltsin' (*IHT*, 9 December 2000, p. 2). 'The Soviet national anthem was first broadcast nationally on 1 January 1944' (*IHT*, 20 December 2000, p. 13). The Tsarist tricolour flag (white, blue and red stripes) is made official. Also approved are the Tsarist two-headed eagle as the national coat of arms and the Soviet-era red flag (minus the hammer and sickle) as the official banner of the armed forces. (The Senate gave its approval on 20 December 2000 and the president on 26 December 2000.)

> Boris Berezovsky said he had reversed his decision to set up a trust and hand over his stake in ... ORT ... to journalists and cultured figures because he realized he could not win the battle with the government ... [He] has abandoned his effort to prevent the government from taking control of his stake in ... [the] television network.
>
> (*Guardian*, 9 December 2000, p. 23)

12 December 2000. Vladimir Gusinsky is arrested in Spain on the basis of an international warrant issued by Russia.

> The Spanish police arrested ... Vladimir Gusinsky ... acting on a warrant alleging fraud that was issued by the prosecutor here [in Moscow] through Interpol ... Interpol's headquarters announced that it has asked the Russian Interpol bureau, which is part of the interior ministry, to clarify the legal grounds of the warrant. In a statement, the headquarters, based in Lyon, said it asked the Russian bureau to verify that the case did not violate Interpol's charter, which forbids 'any intervention or activities of political, religious or racial character'.
>
> (*IHT*, 13 December 2000, pp. 1, 10)

'Moscow's warrant had not yet been sanctioned by Interpol headquarters' (*IHT*, 14 December 2000, p. 12).

'The governments of France and Britain as well as the headquarters of Interpol ... rejected ... the request by Russia's federal security service ... returning it to Moscow with a request for further evidence' (*IHT*, 19 March 2001, p. 8).

(On 22 December Gusinsky was released on bail but held under house arrest in Spain.)

13 December 2000.

> The Russian prosecutor's office announced Wednesday [13 December] that it had closed without charges a high-profile investigation into whether ... Boris Yeltsin, his daughters and a top Kremlin official had received kickbacks on contracts ... The chief investigator in the case said the prosecutor's office had terminated a probe into whether the Swiss construction company Mabetex paid kickbacks for contracts to renovate the Kremlin and other buildings. He said there was insufficient evidence to bring charges. Swiss investigators have been investigating since 1998 evidence that ... the head of Mabetex ... paid tens of thousands of dollars in credit card bills for Mr Yeltsin and his daughters, Tatiana Dyachenko and Yelena Okulova.
>
> (*IHT*, 14 December 2000, p. 4)

'Russian and Swiss authorities had been investigating allegations that Russian officials, including the former presidential property manager, Pavel Borodin, were paid millions of dollars in bribes to the Swiss-based construction firms Mabetex and Mercata Trading' (*Guardian*, 14 December 2000, p. 21).

(On 17 January 2001 Pavel Borodin was arrested in the United States on his way to the inauguration of George W. Bush as US president on 20 January. Switzerland had issued an international warrant in connection with alleged money laundering and wanted him extradited to face charges. 'Mr Borodin [is] now secretary of the nebulous Belarussian–Russian Union ... Swiss prosecutors allege he played a part in laundering $25 million in bribes ... [when he worked] as former President Boris Yeltsin's chief property manager ... [He] was once Mr Putin's boss ... The president's position is particularly awkward because it was Mr Borodin who brought Mr Putin, then a former St Petersburg city official without a job, to the Kremlin as his deputy ... Mr Putin ... dismissed Mr Borodin as the Kremlin property boss immediately after succeeding Mr Yeltsin on 31 December 1999': *IHT*, 20 January 2001, pp. 1, 6).

14 December 2000.

> President Vladimir Putin on Thursday [14 December] pardoned Edmond Pope, an American businessman and retired US Navy intelligence officer who was convicted and sentenced to twenty years for espionage ... Mr Pope was accused of spying for having obtained four reports on a high-speed torpedo, the Shkval [Squall], which Russia claimed was based on secret technology. Mr Pope's defence claimed that the technology was available in open literature and that the torpedo and its technology already existed in other countries where the missile has been sold by the Russians ... Mr Pope was arrested on 3 April and the trial started on 16 October ... He was convicted and sentenced on 2 December to twenty years in prison.
>
> (*IHT*, 15 December 2000, p. 5)

15 December 2000. 'The tax inspectorate lodged a request with a Moscow court for ... [Media-Most] to be declared bankrupt ... Court officials ... said the tax office had cited the group's "insolvency" in support of their 9 December move to liquidate Media-Most' (*IHT*, 16 December 2000, p. 4).

> Moscow tax inspectors launched a case on Friday [15 December] aimed at winding up businesses within the group, including Media-Most ZAO, part of the holding company, and NTV, its principal television station, using an obscure and rarely applied clause against insolvent traders.
>
> (FT, 18 December 2000, p. 6)

('NTV has been subject to countless ... tax audits, and it is now in financial trouble after the largest television advertising agency, controlled by media minister Lesin, refused to place any more business with it': *Business Central Europe*, February 2001, p. 15.)

21 December 2000. The State Duma approves, on first reading, a proposal by the atomic energy ministry to allow the import of other countries' spent nuclear fuel for reprocessing (*IHT*, 22 December 2000, p. 7).

> The Ministry of Atomic Energy ... is promoting a bill before parliament that may soon emasculate Russia's independent nuclear regulatory agency. The bill would transfer authority over licensing and safety inspections from the federal inspectorate for nuclear and radiation safety [GAN] ... to the ministry, known as Minatom ... The minister of atomic energy is Yevgeni Adamov ... The government supports the changes ... GAN lost its jurisdiction over Russia's nuclear navy. In 1996 the inspectorate was required to make its annual reports secret. This summer [2000] Minatom pushed through a government decree eliminating GAN's right to license any military-related nuclear activities. Now Minatom is trying to eliminate GAN's right to license and perform safety inspections in the civilian sector ... Last year [1999] GAN attempted to shut down two plutonium reactors producing electricity near Tomsk, Siberia, because they were unsafe. instead of fixing the problems, Minatom, with government collusion, kept the reactors running ... The government of President Vladimir Putin eliminated the state environmental committee earlier this year [2000].
>
> (Cristina Chuen and Elena Sokova, IHT, 22 December 2000, p. 9)

('The Duma approved [on 18 April 2001] a second reading of legislation that would allow Russia to import 20,000 tonnes of spent nuclear fuel ... over the next ten years and earn $20 billion in revenues ... In addition to reprocessing and supplying fresh nuclear fuel to other countries, the [Russian atomic energy] ministry said it would offer to store spent fuel': *FT*, 19 April 2001, p. 8.)

22 December 2000.

> The Russian authorities acknowledged Friday [22 December] for the first time that Raoul Wallenberg, the Swedish diplomat who helped save the

lives of thousands of Hungarian Jews from the Nazis, was a victim of Stalinist repression. The acknowledgement came in the form of a statement
from the Russian prosecutor's office. It said Mr Wallenberg was arrested in
January 1945 and imprisoned for two-and-a-half years on espionage charges
before he died. He was formally rehabilitated in a verdict signed by Russia's
general prosecutor. So was his chauffeur, Vilmos Langfelder, who also died
in a Soviet prison.

(*IHT*, 23 December 2000, p. 2)

Raoul Wallenberg and his driver, Vilmos Langfelder, 'were repressed by
Soviet authorities'. In Soviet-speak 'repression' refers to arbitrary arrest,
torture and murder by the secret police ... He [Wallenberg] vanished after
Soviet troops entered the city [Budapest] in January 1945, having been arrested
as a spy ... The statement ... said Wallenberg and Langfelder had been 'unjus-
tifiably arrested by non-judicial bodies and deprived of their freedom for political reasons, as socially dangerous individuals, and without being charged with
concrete offences' ... The document sheds little light on what actually happened to Wallenberg, saying only that he and Langfelder were held as suspected spies for more than two years 'until their deaths in a Soviet prison' ...
Last month [November] Alexander Yakovlev, chairman of the presidential
commission on rehabilitation of victims of political repression, said his panel
'had no doubt' that the diplomat was shot at KGB headquarters in Moscow.

(*The Independent*, 23 December 2000, p. 11)

26 December 2000. 'A Moscow court ruled Tuesday [26 December] that fraud
charges by the nation's top prosecutor against ... Vladimir Gusinsky were
unsubstantiated and illegal' (*IHT*, 27 December 2000, p. 5). ('A Moscow court
yesterday [5 January 2001] reinstated fraud charges against Vladimir Gusinsky
... The charges allege that Mr Gusinsky misrepresented his assets when obtaining a loan of $300 million last year [2000] from Gazprom ... The charges had
been struck down by a local court ... but the Moscow city court ruled yesterday
that the lower court had exceeded its powers: *FT*, 6 January 2001, p. 7.)

('Mr Gusinsky appeared late last year [2000] to have resolved a major financial dispute involving more than $470 million in debts to ... Gazprom. He agreed
to give up shares in his television and other properties to settle some of the debts.
The agreement called for Mr Gusinsky to turn over 19 per cent of the shares in
NTV as collateral for a loan, with the understanding that the shares would be
sold by Deutsche Bank to a foreign investor ... However, the agreement with
Gazprom fell apart last week ... Last week the prosecutor's office carried out
new searches of the homes and offices of Media-Most officials': *IHT*, Monday
15 January 2001, p. 5. 'Russian investigators on Monday [15 January] staged
another raid on the offices of NTV': *IHT*, 16 January 2001, p. 8. 'Gazprom ...
yesterday [17 January] launched a legal action in the Moscow courts to seize a
further 19 per cent stake in NTV ... The lawsuit in the Moscow arbitration court
follows the collapse last week of an agreement signed in November between
Media-Most and Gazprom ... Under the terms of the November deal Media-

Most was supposed to place a 19 per cent stake in NTV ... into an escrow account ahead of a sale to a third party. The money realized would be used to pay off loans coming due later this year from CSFB and guaranteed by Gazprom. However, Media-Most failed to agree the terms on which voting rights over these shares would be exercised and resisted implementing the deal. Last week in London and Gibraltar it sued Gazprom and Deutsche Bank, which agreed to attempt to find an external investor ... Russian prosecutors on Tuesday [16 January] detained ... Media-Most's finance director, on allegations of embezzlement: *FT*, 18 January 2001, p. 30.)

14 January 2001. US president-elect George W. Bush (whose term of office begins on 20 January):

> It's hard for America to fashion Russia. It just seems like to me that we don't want to be lending money and/or encourage the lending of money into a system in which the intention of the capital is never fulfilled. The intent of the capital was to encourage entrepreneurship and growth and markets ... The Chinese and the Russians know that there will be no [national missile defence] system developed in the immediate future or the foreseeable future, is a better word, that can conceivably intercept a multiple launch.
>
> (*IHT*, 15 January 2001, pp. 1, 4)

('According to the General Accounting Office, the United States has spent about $2.3 billion since 1992 promoting democracy, the rule of law and market reforms in Russia, but the annual disbursements have trailed off steeply since the Russian financial crisis of 1998. The IMF and the World Bank ... have issued loans to Russia over the same period worth approximately $30 billion': *IHT*, 15 January 20001, p. 4.)

22 January 2001.

> Russia exported $4 billion of arms last year [2000] – its best performance since the collapse of the Soviet Union ... [although] less than the $4.3 billion the government was hoping for. The recovery in exports comes as Russia plans big changes in both its defence industry and its armed forces. In November [2000] President Vladimir Putin ordered the merger of two big state arms-export agencies [Rosvooruzheniye and Promexport], creating a new export giant, Rosoboronexport, handing 90 per cent of Russian sales. Now the government is pushing ahead with a consolidation of arms manufacturing.
>
> (*FT*, 23 January 2001, p. 9)

('The Russian government completed the merger earlier this year [2001] of its two main arms trading agencies, Voosvoruzhenye and Promexport, into a single entity called Rosoboronexport': *FT*, Survey, 9 April 2001, p. v.)

23 January 2001. 'Yesterday [23 January] the prosecutor-general's office charged Media-Most financial director Anton Titov with fraud on an especially large scale': *CDSP*, 2001, vol. 53, no. 5, p. 4.)

24 January 2001.

Russia's parliament voted yesterday to impose limits on the immunity granted to Boris Yeltsin, making him liable for any serious crimes committed in office. The move, approved by 275 votes to 139 on second reading in the State Duma, is to apply to all post-Soviet Russian presidents after leaving office ... The Duma made the lifting of immunity for ex-presidents subject to a vote by both houses of parliament. Under the draft law an ex-president cannot be subject to detention, arrest, searches or interrogation for a crime not of a serious nature. Other privileges include free medical care, transport and bodyguards, the right to a dacha and a pension. Family members remain entitled to medical care, bodyguards and a pension ... A law on regional government passed on second reading, allowing some local governors to stand for a third or even fourth term.

(Daily Telegraph, 25 January 2001, p. 21)

The Duma approved a law guaranteeing generous perks and privileges to ex-presidents of the country. They include immunity from prosecution for the ex-president and his family, save only for the most serious of crimes committed when in office ... Mr Yeltsin and his immediate family will never be touched ... The new law gives immunity to his children, though not to their spouses ... The Duma voted through a law granting most regional governors the right to a third term in office, and some even a fourth, in place of the statutory two.

(FT, 27 January 2001, p. 7)

Yesterday [25 January] the [State Duma] deputies passed the law 'on guarantees for a president of the Russian Federation who has left office and for members of his family' on third and final reading ... [A president] will receive ... immunity ... But any former head of state can be 'stripped of immunity if criminal proceedings are instituted against him for committing a grave crime' ... The decision will be made by the Federation Council, with the consent of the State Duma ... If one of the chambers refuses to give its consent to strip the country's former leader of immunity, the criminal prosecution will be terminated.

(CDSP, 2001, vol. 53, no. 4, p. 11)

25 January 2001.

Gazprom ... yesterday [25 January] claimed to have acquired control of NTV ... and said it planned to call an extraordinary shareholders' meeting to change the board of directors ... Alfred Kokh, head of Gazprom Media, Gazprom's media arm which already owns 46 per cent of NTV, said yesterday that Moscow bailiffs had frozen the voting rights of a further 19 per cent of NTV held by Media-Most and Gazprom had secured majority control as a result. Media-Most immediately disputed the claim, saying that the bailiffs' actions did not respect a decision from the Moscow arbitration court earlier this month which blocked any transfer in ownership of the shares while excluding demands to freeze voting rights.

(*FT*, 26 January 2001, p. 33)

'Mr Gusinsky ... retains a 30 per cent stake directly, with a further 19 per cent frozen and pledged to Gazprom in settlement of further debts which come due in July' (*FT*, 24 April 2001, p. 26).

According to a statement made ... yesterday [25 January] by Gazprom-Media chief Alfred Kokh, his company became the owner of a controlling interest the moment that marshals of the court seized a 19 per cent stake in NTV in execution of a ruling by the Moscow arbitration court. Of the remaining 81 per cent of NTV shares, Gazprom-Media owns 46 per cent.

(*CDSP*, 2001, vol. 53, no. 5, p. 5)

He explained that the seizure of a 19 per cent stake in NTV made it impossible for anyone to vote these shares. So Gazprom-Media, as the owner of a 46 per cent interest, was now the 'controlling shareholder' of NTV ... The head of Media-Most's press office called Mr Kokh's claim to have assumed control of NTV 'hogwash'.

(p. 6)

26 January 2001. 'President George W. Bush intends to move ahead with a national missile defence plan despite objections from Russia and other countries, [US] defence secretary Donald Rumsfeld said Friday [26 January]' (*IHT*, 27 January 2001, p. 1).

5 February 2001.

Russia's energy minister and the governor of Russia's far eastern region of Primoriye both resigned yesterday [5 February] in the first significant shake-up of key political positions under President Vladimir Putin. Alexander Gavrin and Yevgeni Nazdratenko both lost their jobs after being publicly chastised by Mr Putin after the handing of the energy crisis ... Mr Gavrin is the first cabinet minister to lose his job since Mr Putin was elected president last year [2000]. He had been appointed by the president to handle the energy crisis ... Mr Nazdratenko's departure marks the first time a governor has resigned under pressure from the Kremlin. His administration has been under close scrutiny by Moscow for some years and was recently audited by several government agencies ... Discontent over massive power cuts in the far east became louder and louder ... Mr Nazdratenko will be replaced by one of his deputies, Konstantin Tolstoshein, as acting head of the region until new elections are held within six months ... Mr Putin yesterday also criticized UES, the 53 per cent state-owned electricity utility, for failing to act more swiftly to improve the situation in the far east ... Anatoli Chubais ... chief executive of the UES ... has come under recent political and investor criticism over his plan for restructuring the electricity sector.

(*FT*, 6 February 2001, p. 9)

In Siberia and the Russian far east this winter, suffering the coldest temperatures for more than fifty years, tens of thousands have been deprived of heating for days on end ... Yevgeni Nazdratenko has long been regarded as the most corrupt and vicious of all ... the regional barons ... Repeated attempts by Moscow to bring him under control came to nothing during the Yeltsin years, Now Mr Putin has succeeded.

(*FT*, 7 February 2001, p. 22)

Mr Nazdratenko once had a seemingly invincible grip on politics and industry in Primoriye ... Since early December [2000] coal and oil shortages have darkened the homes of hundreds of thousands of Primoriye residents and reduced or cut off heat to tens of thousands more ... In recent weeks citizens have mounted demonstrations against the government's failure to provide heat ... Power problems plagued other parts of Siberia and the far east as well.

(*IHT*, 6 February 2001, p. 5)

('Prime minister Mikhail Kasyanov has named Yevgeni Nazdratenko chairman of the state fisheries committee': *Vremya Novostei*, 26 February 2001, p. 1: *CDSP*, 2001, vol. 53, no. 9, p. 5. 'No one has any doubts that the president gave Nazdratenko his job for political reasons ... There is only a flimsy guarantee that the former governor will not run in the upcoming election in the Maritime Territory – nothing but Nazdratenko's oral promise to the president during an audience at the Kremlin after his notorious resignation ... The regime has decided to take some additional precautions ... Vladimir Putin proposes that governors and mayors who have resigned of their own accord or been moved from office by presidential decree be legislatively barred from running in early elections': *Nezavisimaya Gazeta*, 27 February 2001, pp. 1, 3: *CDSP*, 2001, vol. 53, no. 9, pp. 5–6). 'Mr Putin gave Mr Nazdratenko a plum consolation prize: a Moscow job as head of the state fisheries agency': *IHT*, 27 March 2001, p. 6.)

President Putin accused ... the energy minister, Alexander Gavrin ... of 'chronic incapacity to tackle the problems of the sector'. He is the first minister to be forced out since Mr Putin became acting president at the end of 1999 ... Yevgeni Nazdratenko [is] the dictatorial governor of the Pacific coastal region of Primoriye ... famed for his persecution of journalists and opponents of his rule.

(*The Independent*, 6 February 2001, p. 13)

'Primoriye is the most crime-ridden of Russia's eighty-nine regions and one of the most indebted' (*The Times*, 6 February 2001, p. 17).

Government officials quickly moved to establish control over Russia's biggest television company, ORT, after Boris Berezovsky sold his 49 per cent stake in the company ... [it was announced on] Monday [5 February] ... The government had named replacements for five board members ... The move gives all eleven seats on the board to state representatives.

(*IHT*, 6 February 2001, p. 5)

(Boris Berezovsky [10 January]: 'The sale of my shares in ORT is in its final stages. The deal is being brokered by Roman Abramovich ... Essentially these shares are coming under the control of the state ... The trustee company I planned to create would not be able to carry out its functions, would not be able to maintain ORT's independence': *CDSP*, 2001, vol. 53, no. 2, pp. 8–9. 'Boris Berezovsky ... yesterday [11 January] said he was in the process of selling his 49 per cent stake in ORT ... to the government via Roman Abramovich, his business partner ... The state already controls 51 per cent of ORT as well as 100 per cent of the rival RTR network': *FT*, 8 February 2001, p. 10. 'Berezovsky says he was tricked into the sale [of ORT] after a promise that, in exchange, the state would release his friend, Nikolai Glushkov, the former manager he appointed to run Aeroflot ... on his behalf, who has been held in custody for many months on corruption charges': *FT*, Weekend, 21 October 2001, p. iii.)

7 February 2001.

> President Vladimir Putin won first round passage Wednesday [7 February] for a bill to finance and regulate political parties ... The measure was passed by a comfortable 280-to-109 vote [in the State Duma] ... The bill ... would drastically reduce the current political menagerie of fifty-seven registered parties and more than 130 political groups. The law sets registration procedures, requiring parties to prove a membership of 10,000, with at least 100 members in half of each of Russia's eighty-nine republics, regions and administrative districts. Financing of parties by corporate sponsors and grass-roots fundraising would be banned in favour of federal financing, a step Mr Putin said would reduce corruption and criminal control of the political process. Parties that do not meet the requirements would not be able to contest elections under their own banner, but would be able to ally their forces with those that do ... The Putin bill requires prospective parties to form organizing committees and present their registration documents to the justice ministry ... The bill also does not provide for regional parties.
>
> *(IHT, 8 February 2001, p. 4)*

'[Russia has] 186 political parties' (*IHT*, 25 January 2001, p. 5).

> Under the new law only registered political parties would be allowed to field candidates in elections. To register they would have to have branches, at least 100-strong, in forty-five of Russia's eighty-nine regions, and 10,000 members. That would be far beyond most of the country's 200-odd parties.
>
> *(The Economist, 20 January 2001, p. 41)*

> The bill ... proposes allowing only parties with at least 10,000 members to register legally and to compete in national and regional elections. Registered parties would have to maintain branches of at least 100 members in at least forty-five of the country's eighty-nine regions. Parties winning more than 3 per cent of the national vote could claim state funding. At present Russia

has almost 200 political parties ... A total of twenty-six parties and alliances contested the last Duma elections in December 1999.

(FT, 15 January 2001, p. 10)

8 February 2001.

Russia pledged this week that it would finally begin to destroy 40,000 tonnes of lethal chemical weapons – the largest stockpile in the world – beginning in the summer [of 2001] ... Russia failed to accomplish first-stage tasks that envisaged elimination of 1 per cent of the chemical weapons stock – 400 tonnes – by the end of 2000 ... Though Russia signed the [Chemical Weapons] Convention in 1993, it did not come into force until 1997 ... The United States has already destroyed about 15 per cent of its chemical weapons stockpile.

(IHT, Friday 9 February 2001, p. 7)

20 February 2001.

Russia offered its alternative proposal ... for a mobile anti-missile defence system that would protect Europe ... a limited theatre-based system ... The documents were given to Nato's [visiting] secretary-general, George Robertson ... A Nato information centre in Moscow that closed down during the friction over the 1999 air war in Kosovo ... [was] reopened.

(IHT, 21 February 2001, pp. 1, 4)

The Russians not only outlined a potential system to defend Europe against missile attack ... [but] also left open the possibility that the system might eventually be adapted to protect American territory ... The [Russian] paper proposes that Western and Russian experts meet to assess the missile threats facing the continent. If a military programme is needed it proposes a land-based system that could intercept incoming warheads. The anti-missile interceptors would be cued by satellites that would make use of a centre to evaluate missile warning data that is jointly manned by Russians, Europeans and Americans ... Lord Robertson ... said his discussions in Moscow indicated that there was convergence in two respects: Moscow now accepts that some Nato allies may be confronted by a new missile threat and that the development of an anti-missile defence might be needed.

(IHT, 22 February 2001, p. 8)

Russia yesterday [20 February] outlined its proposals for an anti-ballistic defence system that Moscow says could be developed with the USA and Europe, in place of Washington's controversial National Missile Defence (NMD) system ... The plan would place an overwhelming emphasis on joint threat assessment and political solutions to ballistic missile threats, rather than building new hardware.

(FT, 21 February 2001, p. 8)

'Unlike the US plan, Mr Putin targets short-term and medium-range missiles instead of intercontinental weapons' *(IHT*, 4 April 2001, p. 4).

23 February 2001.

The Jehovah's Witnesses won a potentially far-reaching victory in a Moscow court on Friday [23 February] over prosecutors who had sought to ban the group under a 1997 law prohibiting religious sects that incite hatred or intolerance ... The ruling means that the group's 10,000 Moscow adherents can continue to practise their religion freely. But a Moscow spokesman said it would affect the 120,000 other active members throughout Russia whose local communities probably would have faced similar charges had the prosecutors won the case. It also sets a political precedent, though not a legal one, for many other religious groups outside the Russian mainstream.

(*IHT*, 24 February 2001, p. 2)

26 February 2001.

Izvestia ... claimed Monday [26 February] that a note scrawled by a sailor [Rashid Aryapov] aboard the ... *Kursk* and later found by divers ... states that the vessel sank after the apparent misfiring of a torpedo. The report ... said the note confirms 'the most unpleasant and unwanted version' of the accident, which military officers have repeatedly suggested was caused by a collision with a mine or a foreign submarine. A government commission investigating the accident reported this month [February] that an exploding torpedo, followed by several more detonations in the torpedo compartment, caused the *Kursk* to rupture ... But the military, up to and including defence minister Igor Sergeyev, has maintained that it is highly likely that the torpedo was set off by a collision ... Lieutenant Rashid Aryapov ... was one of at least twenty-three crewmen who ... survived for at least another nine hours ... [His] note attributes the disaster to 'faults in the torpedo compartment, namely the explosion of a torpedo on which the *Kursk* had to carry out tests'.

(*IHT*, 27 February 2001, pp. 1, 8)

14 March 2001.

A Communist inspired no-confidence vote in prime minister Mikhail Kasyanov's government failed ... Only 127 members voted in favour, far short of the 226 votes needed to pass in the 450-seat assembly [State Duma]. Seventy-six voted against and five abstained ... Only the Communists and their Agrarian Party allies had pledged support. The pro-Kremlin Unity Party, which had suggested that it would back the no-confidence vote as a tactical move to improve its standing in the Duma, was among those refusing to vote.

(*IHT*, 15 March 2001, p. 5)

23 March 2001. The Mir space station is destroyed in a controlled return to earth.

25 March 2001. President Putin and prime minister Yoshiro Mori of Japan meet in Irkutsk.

[They] agreed to recognize a 1956 treaty ... governing the future of the disputed islands ... known as the Kuril Islands in Russia and the Northern Territories in Japan ... The new agreement said the 1956 document would now serve as a 'starting point' for future negotiations ... Russia rescinded the 1956 agreement in 1960 after Japan revised its security treaty with the United States.

(*FT*, 26 March 2001, p. 9)

28 March 2001.

President Vladimir Putin replaced his defence and interior ministers and dismissed the atomic energy chief in the most extensive set of personnel changes in his year-old government ... Mr Putin emphasized that he was putting civilians in key posts 'as a step toward the demilitarization of society'.

(*IHT*, 29 March 2001, p. 4)

The changes are as follows:

1   Sergei Ivanov (currently secretary of the 'security council') replaces Marshal Igor Sergeyev as defence minister (Sergeyev becoming an adviser to Putin on strategic issues). Ivanov gave up his rank of lieutenant-general in the Foreign Security Service (the foreign intelligence service) in November 2000.

Lyubov Kudelina becomes deputy defence minister. She was previously a deputy finance minister. 'Lyubov Kudelina ... has been put in charge of its [the defence ministry's] financial and economic affairs' (*Daily Telegraph*, 29 March 2001, p. 20). 'Mr Ivanov drew attention to the appointment from the finance ministry of Lyubov Kudelina to the financial and economic directorate of the defence ministry as a sign that he wants to improve management and use resources more effectively' (*FT*, 30 March 2001, p. 10).

2   Boris Gryzlov (parliamentary head of the Unity Party) replaces Vladimir Rushailo as interior minister. The latter becomes secretary of the 'security council'. 'Mr Putin said yesterday [28 March] that he wanted it to focus more closely on the problems of Chechnya and the Caucasus' (*FT*, 29 March 2001, p. 10).

Mr Putin ... said the security council 'would be paying more attention' to security in the northern Caucasus, especially Chechnya. Mr Putin also said the council would focus on 'the fight against corruption, money laundering and unlawful export of capital', and he appointed the acting head of the tax police, Vyacheslav Soltaganov, as Mr Rushailo's deputy.

(*IHT*, 29 March 2001, p. 4)

'Vladimir Vasiliev ... [is] the new minister in charge of police ... Mikhail Fradkov replaces Vyacheslav Soltaganov ... [who was] in charge of the tax police' (*The Times*, 29 March 2001, p. 21).

3   'Mr Putin accepted the resignation of Yevgeni Adamov, the minister of

atomic energy ... In Mr Adamov's stead Mr Putin appointed Alexander Rumyantsev, director of the Kurchatov Institute, where the first Soviet atomic bomb was designed' (*IHT*, 29 March 2001, p. 4).

3 April 2001. President Putin gives his state of the nation speech. He emphasizes the need for economic and legal reforms.

Putin:

> The cycle of revolution and counter-revolution is over ... There will be no more reforms and counter-reforms, no more revolutions or counter-revolutions. Many of Russia's problems are rooted in the citizens' long-held mistrust of the authorities. It is the duty of the authorities to dispel this mistrust ... [There has been a] worsening of several key economic indicators ... The conditions that ensure sustained growth have unfortunately not been created ... Unless we start acting today, including on the issue of structural reform, tomorrow we may enter a prolonged period of economic stagnation. We continue to live in a predominantly rent-based economy, rather than in a production-based one ... [Government is] stifling business ... [There is an] unfavourable business climate ... Where is most of the money being made? In oil, gas, metals and other raw materials ... As a result, the structure of the economy is not being modernized and the tilt of our economy toward the extraction of raw materials is even increasing ... The system is defending its right to so-called status quo rent ... rent based on bureaucratic status. To put it in a more direct way, the right to bribes and kickbacks ... [Russia's] shadow economy [has created a] shadow judiciary [where justice is for sale] ... The period of the disintegration of Russian statehood is over ... I am against the redistribution of property ... [There is need to] make any departure from democratic liberties impossible ... I am sure if we create an acceptable business climate in the country, capital flight will stop. I do not see any point in clinging to currency restrictions that do not work. It is senseless; they do not help in any case. The time has come to re-examine the very principles of currency regulation and bring them closer to the principles generally accepted throughout the world. I believe that current restrictions on operations involving capital and real estate discriminate against Russian citizens in comparison with the citizens of other states and limit their freedom ... Our strategic priority today is to ensure the rational and fair taxing of natural resources – Russia's main source of wealth – and real estate, to steadily lower taxes on non-rent income and to finally eliminate the turnover tax ... We need to start drawing up a two-part budget. The first part should ensure the fulfilment of existing government obligations. With regard to this part, parliament should have the right to either accept or reject the government's proposal, but not change the parameters. The other part of the budget should be based on revenue sources arising from favourable external economic conditions, of the kind we have seen recently. For this part, perhaps, amendments and criticisms should be discussed ... [There is

need to] allow federation members to establish at their discretion timetables for introducing the sale of agricultural land.

(*CDSP*, 2001, vol. 53, no. 14, pp. 9–11; *IHT*, 4 April 2001, p. 4; *FT*, 4 April 2001, p. 10; *Guardian*, 4 April 2001, p. 12; *The Independent*, 4 April 2001, p. 15; *Daily Telegraph*, 4 April 2001, p. 11)

The speech ... was realistic in acknowledging the significance of favourable external conditions for the rapid growth of the Russian economy last year [2000]. The president also noted that, in spite of the good external conditions, progress with structural transformation of the Russian economy has been disappointing. Conditions for sustainable growth of the economy have not been created. Hence, according to the president, Russia continues to be a primary producing country with an economic environment that is unfavourable for development of business and investment ... The speech listed numerous tasks that must be completed in order to reform the economy ... The speech emphasized the importance of liberalization as opposed to administrative measures for solving the country's economic problems. The president also drew attention to the problems of corruption and bureaucracy ... Priority steps mentioned by the president included, among others, quick completion of remaining elements of tax reform and implementation of long-overdue land reform.

(*RET*, Monthly Update, 18 April 2001, pp. 1–2)

Gazprom ... claimed control Tuesday [3 April] over NTV, deposing its founder, Vladimir Gusinsky, and the rest of the board of directors and replacing the station's general director ... Journalists hunkered down at the station, vowing that they would not submit to the new management ... As many as 20,000 people attended a protest in Pushkin Square over the weekend [31 March] to demonstrate on behalf of NTV and freedom of speech in Russia ... Gazprom owns 46 per cent of stock in NTV and put together a coalition with a small firm that owns another 4.44 per cent at the Tuesday meeting. With that 50.44 per cent majority it then voted to replace the board of directors, including Mr Gusinsky, and installed its own panel with six of the nine members from Gazprom. The new board then voted to replace Yevgeni Kiselyov, NTV's general director ... with Boris Jordan, a Russian-American financier ... Mr Jordan then named Vladimir Kulistikov, a former NTV deputy director who was ousted last year, as editor in chief in place of Mr Kiselyov ... Until now Mr Kulistikov has been head of RIA, a government news service. Mr Jordan said he would not interfere in journalism decisions and promised that if anyone tried to interfere 'I would resign immediately' ... Mr Jordan said his main goal would be to stabilize the finances of the company ... and then bring in an international investor. He said he had talks with representatives of the CNN founder, Ted Turner, who has made a proposal to buy into NTV, but would not show preference to him ... Alfred Kokh, head of Gazprom-Media, replaced Vladimir Gusinsky as the chairman of the NTV board.

(*IHT*, 4 April 2001, p. 4)

'Yevgeni Kiselyov ... [is] NTV's most famous news anchorman and its chief editor' (*Daily Telegraph*, 6 April 2001, p. 19). 'Yevgeni Kiselyov [is] an influential commentator in his own right' (*The Economist*, 7 April 2001, p. 55).

> Boris Jordan [is] a millionaire US-born investment banker who set up Moscow's Renaissance Capital investment bank and now runs a Moscow-based investment fund ... Among the foreign investors approached by Mr Gusinsky without success was Ted Turner, the founder of CNN.
>
> > (*The Times*, 4 April 2001, p. 19)

> Ted Turner, the US media magnate, may offer more than $220 million to acquire substantial minority stakes in NTV, the Russian television network, and related companies under an outline agreement reached with leading shareholder Vladimir Gusinsky on Tuesday night [3 April] ... The bid offered hope to NTV staff trying to remain free from state control in their continued resistance to efforts by Gazprom ... to impose a new management team ... Mr Turner, in conjunction with the financier George Soros, is believed to be seeking to purchase 30 per cent or more of NTV, leaving Mr Gusinsky with a modest financial stake but requiring him to hand over the voting rights on all of his shares to bring the Turner consortium's influence to nearly 50 per cent. Mr Gusinsky has signed an agreement committing himself to the deal. Mr Turner has yet to sign the contract, and stressed that any agreement would depend on the approval of terms with Gazprom ... While Mr Gusinsky made a formal signed offer to Mr Turner on Tuesday night ... Mr Turner's consortium has stressed that its own offer would still require the agreement of Gazprom ... Capital Research and Management, a secretive Los Angeles-based fund, which holds 4.5 per cent of NTV, backed Gazprom and provided it with the necessary majority ... But Capital also has a very long-held relationship with Mr Turner.
>
> > (*FT*, 5 April 2001, p. 26)

4 April 2001.

> NTV journalists have refused to recognize what they call Gazprom's 'illegal' action, barricading themselves overnight at their headquarters ... As of late Wednesday [4 April] NTV's protests continued unhindered by the authorities, while the new Gazprom-appointed managers claimed their new titles but ruled out using violent methods to take over the network ... While Gazprom announced his [Mr Gusinsky's] ouster from NTV on Tuesday [2 April] Mr Gusinsky was cutting a deal to sell his holding company, Media-Most, to an investor group led by the CNN founder, Ted Turner. Mr Turner confirmed the deal in a statement Wednesday [3 April] and said it awaited only 'successful negotiation' with Gazprom to be complete ... The Turner group would [apparently] pay about $225 million to Mr Gusinsky for Media-Most, which includes his share of NTV, as well as other Russian media properties ... Mr Turner vowed to reach an agreement with Gazprom that would 'ensure the ongoing independence of NTV'.
>
> > (*IHT*, 5 April 2001, p. 5)

'Ted Turner ... announced that he would move to purchase nearly a third of NTV's shares' (*IHT*, 6 April 2001, p. 8).

> [NTV's journalists have] cancelled all entertainment programmes and replaced them with a message reading: 'In a sign of protest against the attempt to change illegally the management of NTV there will only be information programmes' ... [The journalists] were cheered by a crowd of 100 supporters ... [But] the Duma ... voted down a motion to debate events at NTV.
>
> (*The Independent*, 5 April 2001, p. 14)

> A member of the Russian government investigating commission, Grigori Tomchin, said in an interview that ... the Russian nuclear submarine *Kursk* ... was carrying atomic weapons ... when it sank in August [2000] ... A Norwegian engineer ... central in planning the proposed salvage of the *Kursk*, said he had also seen secret Russian documents confirming the presence of atomic weapons.
>
> (*IHT*, 5 April 2001, p. 5)

('Russian officials yesterday [5 April] denied a Norwegian television report that the *Kursk* nuclear submarine was carrying nuclear weapons when it exploded last summer and a lawmaker cited in the report said he had been misquoted': *The Independent*, 6 April 2001, p. 14.)

5 April 2001.

> Journalists ... last night [agreed] a truce with the state-backed management ... The management and the journalists at NTV agreed to set up a committee to settle the dispute. It will consist of ten journalists' representatives and ten from the new management team appointed on Tuesday [3 April]. Yevgeni Kiselyov ... said the decisions of the arbitration committee would be binding on all parties. The committee will decide who is to run the company ... By yesterday [5 April] the government had forced NTV to resume broadcasts. But the company still has two managements. The pro-Kremlin Gazprom team is led by Alfred Kokh, who was sacked as head of the state property department in the 1990s amid charges of corruption, and Boris Jordan, an American banker of Russian descent who was involved in controversial privatization deals in the same era.
>
> (*The Independent*, 6 April 2001, p. 14)

'Boris Jordan [is] an American investment banker of Russian origin, well-known for his involvement in controversial privatization deals in Russian in the mid-1990s' (*The Economist*, 7 April 2001, p. 55).

6 April 2001.

> Talks between representatives of ... Gazprom and the NTV network to decide the fate of the leadership of Russia's only nationwide independent

television network broke down Friday [6 April] in a climate of distrust. Hopes of a compromise Friday at the first meeting of a reconciliation commission died fast. After about an hour NTV journalists said Gazprom had rejected their proposal that an appeal be made jointly to the Russian supreme court to settle the differences.

(*IHT*, 7 April 2001, p. 5)

'Mr Turner ... has offered to buy 19 per cent of NTV's shares from Gazprom and 11 per cent from Media-Most' (*IHT*, 13 April 2001, p. 16).

7 April 2001. A rally takes place in Moscow supporting the NTV journalists.

The Moscow police estimated the crowd at 6,500. But NTV said that at least 25,000 showed up ... Reuters said the turnout appeared to be considerably larger than the crowd that gathered in downtown Moscow on the previous Saturday, estimated at about 10,000.

(*IHT*, 9 April 2001, p. 7)

(Some 4,000 people protested in St Petersburg the following day: *The Independent*, 9 April 2001, p. 10; *Guardian*, 9 April 2001, p. 14.)

Within hours after his arrival here [in Geneva] from New York ... Pavel Borodin was charged with money-laundering involving alleged kickbacks for renovation contracts for refurbishing Moscow buildings ... [He] was also indicted Saturday [7 April] on charges of membership in a criminal organization ... [Russia's] officials have rallied to his defence. Last week Mr Borodin ... agreed to be sent to Switzerland to face the charges ... Geneva officials suspect that he took as much as $30 million in kickbacks for awarding lucrative construction contracts involving elaborate renovations of Kremlin buildings. Two of the refurbishing firms, Mabetex and Mercata Trading, are Swiss and the money was allegedly laundered through Swiss banks ... [Mr Borodin's] lawyer has maintained that since the Moscow authorities threw out the case on grounds that no crime was committed in Russia, any prosecution of Mr Borodin will fail.

(*IHT*, Monday 9 April 2001, p. 7)

[The] Swiss investigation ... all but collapsed Thursday [12 April] after a court here [Geneva] released ... Pavel Borodin ... on $2.9 million bail, clearing the way for him to return to Russia ... The Russian Federation would pay Mr Borodin's bail ... In a hearing Tuesday [10 April] the chief prosecutor in Geneva ... outlined the charges of money laundering and membership in a criminal organization ... The principal investigator ... was able to trace the movement of 'service commissions' totalling $25.6 million from the Kremlin through Swiss bank accounts controlled by Mr Borodin. But the chief judge ... said that 'evidence of the illicit character of the commissions that Mr Borodin is accused of having received had necessarily to be established with the collaboration of the Russian authorities'. In a thinly veiled criticism of Moscow ... [the judge said] establishing such evidence would meet 'insurmountable obstacles' without Russian assistance. But she noted that the investigation ... had yielded no evidence of a criminal organization.

(*IHT*, 13 April 2001, p. 2)

'The Geneva court threw out the criminal organization charge, saying the investigation had failed to prove there had been a systematic conspiracy to launder the money in Switzerland' (*The Independent*, 14 April 2001, p. 14). 'The Swiss prosecutor insisted that ... the bribery case will go ahead' (*The Times*, 13 April 2001, p. 18).

(Borodin flew to Russia on 13 April.)

9 April 2001. President Putin (after a meeting with Mikhail Gorbachev and before meeting Chancellor Schröder of Germany in St Petersburg): 'Measures must be taken to improve the transparency and efficiency of Gazprom's activities' (*The Times*, 10 April 2001, p. 16). 'Mr Putin told Mikhail Gorbachev, the chairman of NTV's advisory board, that Russia's courts should handle the dispute' (p. 16).

'The NTV staff's united front ... [is] fragmenting. The sudden resignation of ... [a] commentator ... and ... [a] presenter ... [has] brought internal divisions to the surface' (*The Independent*, 10 April 2001, p. 14). '[They] resigned at the weekend ... Three more reporters left yesterday [9 April]' (*Daily Telegraph*, 10 April 2001, p. 15).

'[The] "St Petersburg dialogue" [is] a forum intended to bring the two countries [Russia and Germany] closer together and nurture civil liberties in Russia' (*The Independent*, 10 April 2001, p. 14).

12 April 2001. Unity (led by Sergei Shoigu) and the Fatherland-All Russia (led by Yuri Luzhkov) announce that they are to merge. A joint statement is issued: 'We are stronger together. Our merger is intended to show that responsible politicians are able to overcome the inertia of confrontation and abandon their personal ambitions for the sake of the country's high interests.'

Yuri Luzhkov ... and Sergei Shoigu ... said that Mr Putin had approved the move and that they would create a co-ordination council to pave the way for the Unity Party ... and the Fatherland-All Russia bloc to formally join forces by November.

(*IHT*, 13 April 2001, p. 5)

'The alliance will give the two centrist parties the largest number of votes in the State Duma, overtaking the Communists' (*Daily Telegraph*, 13 April 2001, p. 18).

'The leaders of Fatherland and Unity announced that the two organizations had begun the process of merger. The process will end with the formation of a single party at a unifying congress in November' (*CDSP*, 2001, vol. 53, no. 15, p. 9).

'The leader of Narodny Deputat, another central political bloc, said yesterday

[12 April] that he was also considering joining the merger' (*Guardian*, 13 April 2001, p. 12).

'A group of NTV journalists filed suit in a Moscow district court asking that the 3 April shareholders meeting be ruled illegal ... Journalists filed a similar request with the Moscow arbitration court on Wednesday [11 April]' (*IHT*, 13 April 2001, p. 16).

13 April 2001.

> A fourth Russian political party yesterday [13 April] expressed interest in merging with the powerful centrist Fatherland and Unity movements, in a move that could create a pro-Kremlin bloc with an absolute parliamentary majority. Oleg Morozov, head of Russia's Regions party, said the group would consider a coalition, after the People's Deputies party also said it wanted to combine forces with Fatherland and Unity ... Yevgeni Primakov, the former prime minister and Fatherland's choice as president, had already apparently made peace with Mr Putin, acting as an informal adviser on foreign affairs.
>
> (*FT*, 14 April 2001, p. 6)

'[The] leaders of the Russia's Regions Party and the People's Deputies faction, with 105 seats between them ... pledged their support for ... [the] proposed merger ... [of] the Unity and Fatherland parties [which] command 131 seats in the Duma' (*The Times*, 14 April 2001, p. 19).

('Four parties agreed yesterday [17 April] to form a coalition': *FT*, 18 April 2001, p. 8.)

'Boris Jordan ... an American of Russian descent ... said Friday [13 April] he had taken over control of the finances and programming of NTV' (*IHT*, 14 April 2001, p. 5).

14 April 2001.

> Gazprom physically took over NTV's headquarters on Saturday [14 April] after presenting security guards with a court order. The early morning raid culminated an eleven-day standoff, during which the broadcasters occupied the station and attracted public demonstrations of support ... On the day after the state-dominated Gazprom took over the offices of the independent NTV television network, some of the network's best known journalists were back on the air – but on another, less important channel. At least fifteen reporters and anchors, led by NTV's best known personality, Yevgeni Kiselyov, were working for TNT, a channel controlled by ... Vladimir Gusinsky, which broadcasts largely in Russia's outlying regions ... On Saturday [14 April] Channel 6 named Mr Kiselyov its director general. Mr Kiselyov planned to present his signature news programme, *Itogi*, on TNT on Sunday night [15 April]. The two channels are said to be discussing a joint news operation ... NTV ... has never made a profit. But Mr Turner has said that a mass defection of journalists could make any deal unworkable ... Mr Jordan

said Saturday that he had met with forty journalists who were still at the network ... Mr Jordan insisted that NTV would not only remain independent but would have far more freedom than it did under Mr Gusinsky ... NTV is ... one of three nationwide television networks.

(*IHT*, 16 April 2001, pp. 1, 7)

Reporters and producers who resigned en masse [up to 350 NTV personnel] when state-backed security guards arrived before dawn on Saturday [14 April] to take over NTV's offices said they were determined to set up a rival station. They rushed out three news programmes from a borrowed studio yesterday [15 April] ... Boris Berezovsky was reported to have offered Yevgeni Kiselyov ... the post of director of his TV-6 channel. Mr Kiselyov told Russian news agencies that he had accepted ... TNT [is] a second tier channel that reaches only half the Russian population. It is still controlled by Vladimir Gusinsky who ... has made TNT available as a temporary home ... Mikhail Gorbachev showed his solidarity with those who had resigned by disbanding an NTV advisory board of which he was chairman.

(*The Times*, 16 April 2001, p. 7)

The majority of its [NTV's] journalists and technical staff [went to] the studios of a smaller television station company [primarily an entertainment channel] owned by Vladimir Gusinsky ... Some 350 staff resigned ... with almost all the best known journalists going over the road to TNT. A small group of reporters stayed with the new management ... [It was] announced that NTV's old management was preparing to challenge the takeover in court next month [May].

(*Guardian*, 16 April 2001, p. 12)

16–17 April 2001. 'A spokesman for ... Vladimir Gusinsky said Monday that the police were using tax evasion charges to harass a satellite television station [NTN] carrying newscasts by rebel NTV journalists' (*IHT*, 17 April 2001, p. 4).

Two leading Russian publications linked to Vladimir Gusinsky ... were shut down yesterday [17 April] in a move seen by their journalists as fresh attacks on freedom of speech. The staff of *Itogi*, the weekly news magazine produced in conjunction with *Newsweek* of the USA, were told during the morning that they were to be dismissed as part of restructuring. Separately, the daily newspaper *Sevodnia* [edited by Mikhail Berger] failed to appear after the publisher stopped the presses on Monday evening [16 April] and said he no longer wanted it to be part of his group ... Both *Itogi* and *Sevodnia* are part of the Seven Days publishing house, set up by Mr Gusinsky but no longer controlled by him since his partner Dmitri Biryukov, the publisher, who holds 25 per cent of the shares, joined forces with Gazprom, which holds a further 25 per cent plus one share ... Mikhail Berger, *Sevodnia*'s editor, said Mr Biryukov had forged an alliance with the Kremlin and Gazprom at the end of last year [2000] ... Fresh charges of tax evasion [were] launched on Monday [16 April] against TNT.

(*FT*, 18 April 2001, p. 8)

(*Itogi* can be translated as 'results'.)

Co-owners of his [Vladimir Gusinsky's] key political magazine, *Itogi*, dismissed all the editorial staff hours after closing a sister daily [*Sevodnia*] ... Dmitri Biryukov runs the publishing house that prints *Itogi* ... Sem Dnei [Seven Days] prints *Itogi*, a joint publication with the US magazine *Newsweek* ... *Sevodnia*, a popular but money-losing liberal daily ... was closed on Monday [16 April] ... Mr Biryukov wants to keep *Itogi*, which makes a small profit ... *Newsweek* issued a statement [saying that]: 'As of now, *Newsweek* is suspending its relationship with *Itogi* and will reassess the matter when the facts are more clear; ... *Newsweek* is owned by the Washington Post Co., co-owner of the *International Herald Tribune*.

(*IHT*, 18 April 2001, p. 6)

The management of Sem Dnei recently stopped supporting Mr Gusinsky and allied itself with Gazprom Media ... The sacked *Sevodnia* editor, Mikhail Berger, said very few Russian broadsheets made money, because of the weak advertising market, and the only way serious newspapers could survive was by being adopted by publishing stables like Sem Dnei, which relied on profitable publications to subsidize their high-profile papers ... Sem Dnei plans to continue publishing *Itogi*, using an entirely new editorial team.

(*Guardian*, 18 April 2001, p. 12)

The only significant Media-Most outlet so far unaffected in the purge is Ekho Moskvy, the radio station ... Yesterday [17 April] a group of senior journalists at the TV-6 station to which most 'rebel' reporters hope to migrate announced that they would resign rather than work under Yevgeni Kiselyov.

(*The Times*, 18 April 2001, p. 13)

The editor-in-chief of Ekho Moskvy radio station, one of the few independent outlets to survive, said he did not expect to hold out against the state for very long ... Media-Most ... controlled NTV, *Itogi*, *Sevodnia* and Ekho Moskvy ... Ekho Moskvy radio station is the one part of Mr Gusinsky's empire that has still not fallen under government control. The station produces up-to-the-minute political reporting of high quality.

(*The Independent*, 18 April 2001, p. 3)

Mr Gusinsky acquired his original licence thanks to a presidential decree from Boris Yeltsin. He threw the weight of NTV, and the rest of his empire, into a totally one-sided campaign for Mr Yeltsin's re-election in 1996 and gained a twenty-four-hour broadcasting licence for less than $1,000 as an apparent reward. One year later he was outmanoeuvred by rivals in the privatization auction of Syazinvest, the telecommunications company, and he never forgave the Kremlin. By 1999 NTV was leading a campaign to expose corruption in Mr Yeltsin's entourage. It made its reputation as an 'independent' broadcaster by being the one television station to criticize conduct of the war in Chechnya.

(Quentin Peel, FT, 30 April 2001, p. 21)

Oleg Dobrodeyev ... co-founded NTV with Yevgeni Kiselyov in 1993, with support from Gusinsky ... In January 2000 Dobrodeyev was compelled to step down as general manager of NTV in favour of Yevgeni Kiselyov ... Dobrodeyev ... [is] currently in charge of the government television and radio broadcasting giant VGTRK [the All-Russia State Television and Radio Company] ... [In a critical open letter to Kiselyov he writes that] 'Right from the start the company [NTV] belonged not only to Gusinsky, but also to the Kremlin ... The first time he drew blood was in August of 1997, when Gusinsky demanded that we put out news coverage trashing the people who beat him out of a piece of the Svyazinvest pie.'

(Izvestia, 9 April 2001, p. 1: CDSP, 2001, vol. 53, no. 15, pp. 5–6)

18 April 2001.

Spain's highest court refused Wednesday [18 April] to extradite Vladimir Gusinsky ... The judges ruled two to one that there was no criminal case to answer ... The three judges noted 'questionable and peculiar circumstances, not usually seen in a judicial accusation of fraud' surrounding the extradition request. They further noted that nations were obliged 'to deny extraditions in which they have detected motives other than judicial persecution' and said the accused had claimed 'with some reason' to have identified such a motive. The ruling recognized an 'economic conflict' between Mr Gusinsky and Gazprom, but said it should be resolved in a civil not a criminal court, noting that Mr Gusinsky's actions did not amount to a crime under Spanish law.

(IHT, 19 April 2001, p. 4)

Prosecutors in Moscow alleged he [Gusinsky] was guilty of large-scale fraud. They said he had misrepresented the assets of his company, Media-Most, to obtain $300 million in loan guarantees from Gazprom in 1996. In fact, the loan guarantees were a payback to Mr Gusinsky for supporting Boris Yeltsin in the presidential election.

(Patrick Cockburn, The Independent, 19 April 2001, p. 13)

19 April 2001. 'The state prosecutor at the high court in Madrid said Thursday [19 April] that he would not appeal a ruling that rejected Russia's request to extradite Vladimir Gusinsky ... because the arguments against the extradition "are very solid" ' (*IHT*, 20 April 2001, p. 4).

'Many of the ex-NTV journalists are now moving to TV-6, a rival chain controlled by … Boris Berezovsky, while at least twenty of the TV-6 journalists have in turn walked out and said they would work for NTV' (*FT*, 24 April 2001, p. 26).

24 April 2001.

Vladimir Gusinsky left Spain last night [24 April] as … Moscow prosecutors issued a new international arrest warrant accusing him of money laundering … The Russian prosecutor's spokesman … confirmed yesterday that the new warrant had been lodged with Interpol. He said Mr Gusinsky was being accused of laundering 2.8 billion roubles. 'The charges are backed by strong evidence,' he said.

(*Guardian*, 25 April 2001, p. 16)

'On Tuesday [24 April] Russian prosecutors announced new charges, accusing Mr Gusinsky of laundering about $100 million connected with loans from Gazprom, and said they would request a new international warrant for him through Interpol' (*IHT*, 26 April 2001, p. 7).

25 April 2001.

[The State Duma] on Wednesday [25 April] ratified a European Union convention that gives the authorities more opportunities to battle money laundering and to seek the return of criminal assets hidden abroad. Under the 1990 convention, which has been signed by more than thirty countries, Russia could ask other countries for aid in seeking punitive measures against citizens and companies that spirit illegal revenues out of the country. The Russian authorities may face obstacles because foreign courts could deny asset requests believed to be politically motivated or against the law.

(*IHT*, 26 August 2001, p. 7)

1 May 2001.

President George W. Bush called Tuesday [1 May] for an ambitious anti-missile system and said that it was time to 'move beyond the constraints of' the [1972] Anti-Ballistic Missile Treaty, but he promised unilateral cuts in the US nuclear arsenal and close consultations with America's anxious allies … Mr Bush … added: 'We will reach out to other interested states, including China and Russia' … Mr Bush had telephoned President Vladimir Putin hours earlier.

(*IHT*, 2 May 2001, pp. 1, 10)

2 May 2001. Foreign minister Igor Ivanov: 'It is extremely important that the US administration does not intend to take unilateral steps, but intends to consult with its allies and friends, including Russia. Russia is ready for consultations and we have something to say' (*The Times*, 3 May 2001, p. 16).

3 May 2001. 'Geneva judicial authorities have summoned … Pavel Borodin … to return this month for further questioning' (*FT*, 4 May 2001, p. 6).

The USA is voted off the United Nations Human Rights Commission.

The United States had been a member of the commission since it was created in 1947 ... at the urging of Eleanor Roosevelt ... The vote of the Economic and Social Council, which has authority over the human rights commission, was carried out by secret ballot ... Four nations competed Thursday [3 May] to fill three Western vacancies for three-year terms on the fifty-three-member commission. France had fifty-two votes out of a possible fifty-four, Austria got forty-one and Sweden thirty-two, although there can be some overlap, as there is now. The United States trailed with twenty-nine and was eliminated. The Economic and Social Council is made up of entirely different members than the commission.

(IHT, 5 May 2001, pp. 1, 7)

4 May 2001.

Ekho Moskvy, a pioneering independent Moscow radio station [established in 1990] ... is fighting a potential takeover by ... Gazprom [which has a 25 per cent stake] ... Prosecutors swoop in regularly at the offices ... demanding documents and inside financial information ... The radio station was founded by journalists ... Five years ago the station's journalists, desperately seeking a cash infusion, made the fateful decision to team up with Mr Gusinsky's debt-ridden Media-Most holding company ... The 4 May court ruling, now being appealed, granted Gazprom another 25 per cent plus one share – enough for full control ... The [Ekho Moskvy] staff is already splitting under the pressure.

(IHT, 16 May 2001, p. 5)

14 May 2001.

Deputy prime minister Ilya Klebanov ... said Monday [14 May] that the sunken nuclear submarine *Kursk* would be raised in a three-month operation that is to be concluded by 20 September ... An agreement would be signed Monday between Russia and Dutch and Norwegian specialists.

(IHT, 15 May 2001, p. 5)

'Russia on Thursday [17 May] unexpectedly rejected a bid by a consortium of Dutch and Norwegian companies to help raise the ... *Kursk*. The contract will instead be awarded Friday [18 May] to an unnamed third party' (*IHT*, 18 May 2001, p. 5).

[On 18 May] Russia hired a firm with little experience of sea salvage ... the Dutch company Mammoet ... The international consortium that had been working since last year on plans to raise ... the *Kursk* ... was told Thursday [17 May] that its services were no longer required after it refused to begin the operation until next year and insisted on being paid in advance.

(Daily Telegraph, 19 May 2001, p. 17)

The contract with the Mammoet company calls for the submarine to be raised 110 metres (355 feet) to the surface and brought to a dock by 20 September. Russian officials said they chose Mammoet after negotiations with a consortium of Dutch and Norwegian companies because Mammoet promised to carry out the operation this year. Its methods are also more reliable, they added. Consortium officials had said they would have to wait until next year, for safety reasons, to start the operation. The last-minute switch in contractors to raise the vessel was an instant topic of debate among experts in Moscow.

(*IHT*, 21 May 2001, p. 6)

'Yesterday [18 May] Moscow dropped months of talks with a European consortium and signed a deal with a Dutch company. Critics called the move frivolous' (*Guardian*, 19 May 2001, p. 18).

The two rival Dutch bidders ... agreed yesterday [21 May] to form a joint venture to carry out the work ... Mammoet [is] the least experienced of the two ... [and] is active mainly in moving heavy equipment overland ... Smit International ... [is] a salvage expert.

(*FT*, 22 May 2001, p. 9)

18 May 2001. 'President George W. Bush and President Vladimir Putin will hold a summit meeting in Slovenia in mid-June at the end of Mr Bush's five-nation trip to Europe. It will be Mr Bush's first meeting with the Russian leader' (*IHT*, 19 May 2001, p. 3).

26–27 May 2001. There takes place the founding congress of the Union of Rightist Forces party. Its leader is Boris Nemtsov. The main parties joining forces were Yegor Gaidar's Russia's Democratic Choice, Sergei Kiriyenko's New Force, Boris Nemtsov's Young Russia, Konstantin Titov's Voices of Russia and Irina Khakamada's Common Cause (*CDSP*, 2001, vol. 53, no. 22, pp. 5–6).

Russian centre-right politicians and activists set up a new political party, the Union of Right Forces ... The new party brings together members of nine smaller movements ... It is likely to command about thirty-three of the 450 seats in the Duma ... The congress elected Boris Nemtsov, parliamentary leader of the coalition, as chairman and leader of the new party. By merging into a new single new party, the right-wing movements are anticipating legislation going through the Russian parliament, which will ban small political parties and oblige big ones to maintain nationwide branch structures.

(*FT*, 28 May 2001, p. 6)

28 May 2001.

President Vladimir Putin on Monday [28 May] completed Russia's ratification of the 1992 Open Skies Treaty, allowing other countries to conduct surveillance flights over Russian territory ... Under the pact each country is allotted a quota of flights it can make over other countries' territories using specified aircraft with sensors to monitor military activity. Russia's and Belarus's failure to ratify the treaty has kept the pact from going into effect up to now. Belarus had said it would await Moscow' ratification before taking action.

(*IHT*, 29 May 2001, p. 4)

29 May 2001. 'A Russian court on Tuesday [29 May] ordered the liquidation of the independent media company [Media-Most] in response to a suit by tax authorities' (*IHT*, 30 May 2001, p. ii, supplementary page).

A directive from the Russian Academy of Sciences orders members to report on their contacts with foreigners (*CDSP*, 2001, vol. 53, no. 22, pp. 1–4).

'Sergei Kovalyov, the veteran human rights campaigner, provoked a public debate on Thursday [1 June] after revelations that the Russian Academy of Sciences had issued instructions requiring scientists to report to the authorities any contact with foreigners' (*FT*, 2 June 2001, p. 8).

'The 24 May directive [is] entitled "The Academy of Science's Action Plan to Prevent Damage to the Russian State in the Spheres of Economic and Scientific Co-operation"' (*The Independent*, 2 June 2001, p. 15).

30 May 2001. 'A Russian court has overturned a [February 2001] legal victory for the Jehovah's Witnesses that had prevented the liquidation of the group's Moscow communities ... The group says it has at least 120,000 active members in Russia' (*IHT*, 31 May 2001, p. 7).

31 May 2001.

A senior Russian official said Thursday [31 May] that Moscow could not meet its commitment to destroy its chemical weapons arsenal, the world's largest, by 2009 and he asked international partners to move the deadline to 2012. Russia is a signatory of the 1997 Chemical Weapons Convention ... Moscow appealed in April for help to find the $8 billion to $10 billion it said was needed to pay for destruction of the arms.

(*IHT*, 1 June 2001, p. 4)

Russia said Thursday [14 June] that its plans to destroy its stockpiles of chemical weapons, the world's biggest, had fallen [five] years behind schedule because of a lack of cash ... Russia would be able to destroy only 20 per cent of its stockpile by [the original deadline of] 2007.

(*IHT*, 15 June 2001, p. 5)

1 June 2001. 'The leaders of the Customs Union (Russia, Belarus, Kazakhstan, Kyrgyzstan and Tajikistan) announced [on 1 June 2001] its transformation into the Eurasian Economic Community' (*CDSP*, 2001, vol. 53, no. 22, p. 18).

('Russia, Belarus, Ukraine and Kazakhstan ... said they planned to create a free-trade zone ... [and] promised to implement the measures this year [2003]': *FT*, 24 February 2003, p. 7.)

6 June 2001.

> The State Duma ... has given final approval to a plan to import ... as much as 20,000 tonnes ... of spent nuclear fuel in exchange for a possible $20 billion ... The waste would be put in 'temporary' storage, according to the ministry, for at least ten years, then reprocessed into fuel ... More than 90 per cent of Russia's potential spent nuclear fuel market reportedly originated at US-designed nuclear reactors and Washington retained final say over its disposition ... Public opinion polls have shown that more than 90 per cent of the Russian people oppose the plan.
>
> *(IHT,* 8 June 2001, p. 7)

> Parliament scrapped a ban on the import of spent nuclear fuel ... The bill now goes to the upper house before President Vladimir Putin signs it into law ... Opinion polls show that up to 90 per cent of Russians oppose the plan ... The USA ... has an effective veto on 90 per cent of the potential imports because countries using US-designed reactors are not allowed to export their waste to a third country without US consent.
>
> *(Guardian,* 7 June 2001, p. 12)

'Advocates say the project could earn Russia $20 billion over ten years' (*The Independent,* 7 June 2001, p. 12).

> Russian environmentalists responded with fury yesterday [11 July] to President Vladimir Putin's decision to sign legislation allowing spent nuclear fuel to be imported ... He did so in the face of overwhelming public opposition and widespread scepticism ... An opinion poll earlier this year showed that 89 per cent disapproved of the proposal ... Germany has already said it will not send radioactive waste to Russia.
>
> *(Guardian,* 12 July 2001, p. 14)

16 June 2001. President Vladimir Putin and President George W. Bush meet for the first time. The venue was Slovenia. The meeting was amicable but dealt in generalities.

> When one of the president's foreign policy advisers was asked during the [president's five-day European] trip about the impact Europeans had made thus far on plans for missile defence, his answer concerned the nomenclature of the project. For a long while Mr Bush's advisers referred to the project as national missile defence, which implied that it was designed to protect only the United States ... 'We dropped "national" [the adviser said].'
>
> *(IHT,* 19 June 2001, p. 4)

18 June 2001. Putin:

> I am confident that at least for the coming twenty-five years ... [US missile defences] will not cause any substantial damage to the national security of Russia ... [But] we stand ready [to respond to any] unilateral [US action by]

... mounting multiple warheads that will cost us a meagre sum. Thus the nuclear arsenal of Russia will be augmented manyfold.

'Vladimir Putin ... spoke of mounting multiple warheads on Russia's new generation of Topol-M missiles – a move that would breach the Start 2 agreement, whose main aim was to reduce Mirvs (multiple independently targeted re-entry vehicles)' (*The Times*, 20 June 2001, p. 17).

20 June 2001.

[The State Duma] passed an overhaul of the country's Soviet-era criminal code Wednesday [20 June], foreseeing trial by jury and a curb on prosecutors' powers ... The bill ... was passed on second reading ... The law replaces a 1960s code and foresees jury trials, now confined to a handful of regions, beginning in 2003. The bill also gives the courts the right to issue arrest or search warrants, rather than prosecutor, starting in 2004. It also lets defendants admit their guilt and avoid a court case.

(*IHT*, 21 June 2001, p. 4)

The code would introduce jury trials across Russia by the end of next year [2002] and later transfer powers of bail and detention from prosecutors to judges. It also grants greater access to lawyers to those who are accused and witnesses in police investigations.

(*FT*, 27 June 2001, p. 10)

Under the reform drafted by the Kremlin more judges would be recruited, they would be better paid, and new rules would be introduced to punish bad ones. Courtroom conditions and back-up would be improved, and the courts, not the prosecutor's office, would be responsible for issuing search and arrest warrants. Jury trials would be extended from the nine regions that currently have them to the whole of Russia.

(*The Economist*, Survey, 21 July 2001, p. 13)

By September [2001] ... the number of activities subject to licensing will be reduced by 80 per cent. New rules will restrict random visits by inspectors from the despotic health, fire, labour, trade and similar agencies. These are a big source of corruption ... From next January [2002] registering a new firm should be a question of days, not weeks, with just one point of contact with the bureaucracy, rather than ... dozens ... In the short term the chances are that the bureaucrats will simply sidestep the reforms. Clauses allowing added inspections 'in exceptional circumstances', for example, may allow the bribe-hunters to carry on as usual. The hope ... is that once the new laws are in place Russians themselves will be more prepared to take on corrupt or obstructive bureaucrats.

(pp. 12–13)

('Vladimir Putin said yesterday [9 July] he was against the death penalty ... Russia has observed a *de facto* moratorium on executions since it joined the

Council of Europe in 1996. The constitutional court ruled in 1999 that executions would be unconstitutional until trial by jury was available in all capital cases across Russia': *FT*, 10 July 2001, p. 6. There have been no executions since February 1996: *CDSP*, 2001, vol. 53, no. 25, p. 6.)

22 June 2001.

> The Financial Action Task Force ... on money laundering ... [was] set up in 1989 by the Group of Seven industrialized nations ... The FATF had proposed conditional sanctions against Nauru, the Philippines and Russia, all on the blacklist last year [2000] ... The three could face more surveillance and reporting requirements if they failed to respond to the criticism by 30 September.
>
> (*FT*, 23 June 2001, p. 7)

> The financial action task force [is] a multinational team that operates under OSCE ... A clean-up bill [is expected] to be passed by the Duma in coming weeks ... Russia ... could face potentially damaging special scrutiny and delays in aid and other international transactions ... Six other countries were targeted for new international scrutiny ... [including] Hungary.
>
> (*IHT*, 23 June 2001, p. 11)

> The Financial Action Task Force, the international money-laundering police force, has put Russia on its blacklist of worst offenders ... Russia finally ratified the 1990 Council of Europe Convention on money laundering in April [2001], along with a raft of other banking legislation. And Mr Putin signed the country's first anti-money-laundering bill at the start of June.
>
> (*Business Central Europe*, July–August 2001, pp. 34–5)

'The Russian parliament yesterday [4 July] approved new legislation to clamp down on money laundering on its second reading ... [after] the government submitted a revised draft' (*FT*, 5 July 2001, p. 10).

> Russia ... has adopted a law intended to combat money laundering ... the term for transferring illegally obtained funds through a chain of bank accounts to make the money appear legitimate ... The legislation, which was signed into law Tuesday [7 August] by President Vladimir Putin, requires banks and other financial institutions to report to the government any customer transactions of more than 600,000 roubles ($20,500). Officials say they will scrutinize cash purchases of stocks and foreign currency as well as cash transfers and cheque deposits ... But the new law does not spell out how banks are to make reports, and analysts said there was little chance of the law having much effect ... Most analysts said the new law's main benefit would be to facilitate co-operation between foreign and Russian authorities ... [The] chief economist at ... a Moscow investment bank ... estimates that some $15 billion ... is stashed abroad – or perhaps under mattresses – mainly to escape taxes and currency regulations. According to a

finance ministry official, only about 1 per cent of such hidden money is associated with criminal groups.

(IHT, 9 August 2001, p. 14)

The Financial Action Task Force, an offshoot of the Group of Seven rich countries ... [warned] Russia that it had until September to show substantial advances or face unspecified sanctions ... The [Russian] authorities unveiled the creation of a new Centre for Financial Monitoring ... designed to monitor all transactions exceeding 600,000 roubles while maintaining confidentiality ... The deputy finance minister ... estimated that 1 per cent of Russian capital in circulation may have been laundered, although others say the figures are higher.

(FT, 9 August 2001, p. 7)

29 June 2001.

Russia's upper house of parliament swiftly approved a Kremlin-sponsored bill Friday [29 June] that would reduce the number of political parties and increase their dependence on the government. The bill [was] passed in the Federation Council on a vote of 110 to three, with ten abstentions ... The State Duma also approved it this month [June] ... Russia now has more than 200 political parties, most of which exist only on paper. The bill would make parties largely dependent on government financing, with a requirement that they receive more than 3 per cent of the vote before getting aid. It would limit private donations to 3,000 roubles ($110) a year and ban contributions by foreigners and international organizations. It would also eliminate parties that do not have at least 10,000 members nationwide and at least 100 members in more than half of Russia's eighty-nine provinces.

(IHT, 30 June 2001, p. 2)

'A party must have at least 10,000 members in no fewer than forty-five of the country's eighty-nine regions' (*New York Review of Books*, 2001, vol. XLVIII, no. 13, p. 30).

The new legislation would require parties to have a minimum of 10,000 members in at least fifty of the country's eighty-nine regions ... Of Russia's more than 200 parties only twenty-six contested the 1999 parliamentary election, down from forty-three in 1995. Parties that receive more than 3 per cent of the vote would receive state financing. The bill would also oblige party officials to submit regular financial reports to the state tax service ... Among those not permitted to contribute would be foreign citizens and organizations with foreign ownership exceeding 30 per cent, as well as international organizations ... The bill ... must be approved by the Federation Council ... and signed by President Vladimir Putin.

(FT, 25 May 2001, p. 10)

30 June 2001. Colonel General Leonid Ivashev (in charge of international co-operation at the defence ministry): 'Russia does not rule out amendments to this agreement [the 1972 ABM Treaty], but what the United States is demanding will lead to the collapse of the entire accord ... We are ready to discuss missile threats' (*IHT*, 30 June 2001, p. 3; *The Independent*, 30 June 2001, p. 17).

3 July 2001.

> Vladimir Zhirinovsky ... has announced for the first time that his father was Jewish, it was reported yesterday [3 July] ... Mr Zhirinovsky said his father's side of the family were Polish Jews but he had 'no connection' to them, as they had all died in the Holocaust.
>
> (*Daily Telegraph*, 4 July 2001, p. 13)

> Mr Zhirinovsky has made a dramatic revision in his bibliography, acknowledging that his father was Jewish and saying that many of his relatives perished in the Holocaust. In an interview and a new book Mr Zhirinovsky confirmed that his father, Volf Isaakovich Eidelshtein, was a Polish Jew ... When he turned eighteen Mr Zhirinovsky said he legally changed his name from Eidelshtein.
>
> (*IHT*, 18 July 2001, p. 5)

5 July 2001.

> Top editors at Ekho Moskvy ... quit in protest over what they called the 'forced nationalization' ... One day after a court decision effectively handed control of the [news radio] station to Gazprom ... five of the station's top editors resigned ... while the editor in chief, Alexei Venediktov, sought assurances from Gazprom that the station's employees could buy enough shares from it to remain independent ... Mr Venediktov said he was also prepared to quit if Gazprom did not produce written confirmation of a tentative deal reached Wednesday [4 July] to sell 9.5 per cent of its shares to the station's workers ... On Monday [2 July] agents of the federal security service came to the station and seized the 14 per cent stake that Mr Gusinsky had agreed to give free to the station's employees ... [On 3 July] a Moscow arbitration court upheld a previous ruling that gives Gazprom full control over Mr Gusinsky's media empire, including Ekho Moskvy. Even as the court ruling appeared, Mr Venediktov was agreeing to buy back 9.5 per cent of Ekho's shares ... Gazprom told him the deal would only be good after it obtained full control over the radio station.
>
> (*IHT*, 6 July 2001, p. 10)

The State Duma approves, on first reading, a new labour code. Elements include the minimum wage, overtime, worker holidays and the problem of the late payment of wages. It will be easier for employers to dismiss employees (*CDSP*, 2001, vol. 53, p. 27, pp. 2–4).

6 July 2001.

> Scores of journalists resigned from Ekho Moskvy ... when Gazprom ... took control of the station ... On Monday [2 July] the FSB ... seized the 14

per cent stake ... that ... Vladimir Gusinsky had agreed to hand to journalists free of charge ... On Wednesday [4 July] a Moscow court ruled that
Gazprom could buy more shares than it already owns, giving it total control
over the station.

(*The Times*, 7 July 2001, p. 18)

Parliament yesterday [6 July] approved legislation banning majority
foreign ownership of national television stations ... [The legislation
involves] a ban on foreigners or Russians with dual nationality holding 50
per cent or more of networks broadcasting to more than half of the population or its regions.

(*FT*, 7 July 2001, p. 5)

10 July 2001.

Yesterday [10 July] Gazprom-Media backed out of its commitment to sell a
9.5 per cent stake in Ekho Moskvy radio to the station's staff Last week's
ruling made Gazprom the station's controlling shareholder ... Gazprom now
holds a 52 per cent stake in Ekho, while the station's staff controls a 34 per
cent share ... Alfred Kokh announced that Gazprom-Media had dropped its
plans to sell the Ekho staff a 9.5 per cent stake in the station and had begun
negotiating an arrangement with Boris Nemtsov under which Nemtsov
would receive as a gift shares in the station large enough that Gazprom-
Media would not have a controlling interest.

(*CDSP*, 2001, vol. 53, no. 28, p. 8)

11 July 2001.

Gazprom agreed yesterday [11 July] to hand over a controlling 9.5 per cent
stake in Ekho Moskvy ... to Boris Nemtsov, leader of the liberal SPS Party.
After failing to agree terms of a sale of the stake to the station's journalists,
Gazprom made the offer to allay fears it would acquire majority control
over the radio station following a court ruling earlier this week that is likely
to give it 52 per cent of the shares. Alexei Venediktov, chief editor of Ekho
Moskvy, criticized the latest Gazprom proposal.

(*FT*, 12 July 2001, p. 6)

Alexei Venediktov yesterday [11 July said that] ... Nemtsov's behaviour
could only be described as looting and corruption ... Boris Nemtsov
announced yesterday that he intends to turn over the 9.5 per cent stake ... to
'a public council made up of persons with unsullied reputations ... Our most
illustrious private radio station ought to remain independent and no single
shareholder in the company should have a controlling interest.'

(*CDSP*, 2001, vol. 53, no. 28, p. 9)

14 July 2001. The USA declares the latest test in connection with missile
defence a success. The October 1999 test was also declared a success but the
ones in January and July 2000 were failures.

15–18 July 2001. President Jiang Zemin visits Russia. On 16 July a twenty-year Good Neighbourly Treaty of Friendship and Co-operation was signed, the first being signed by China and the Soviet Union in 1950. The treaty included the following:

> [Russia and China] pledge not to use force or the threat of force in their mutual relations, not to use economic or other means of pressure against each other, and to resolve differences solely by peaceful means in accordance with the provisions of the UN Charter and other generally recognized principles and rules of international law ... In case of the emergence of the threat of aggression, the two sides shall immediately make contact with each other and carry out consultations in order to eliminate the emerging threat ... [The treaty is] not directed against third countries ... [The two sides] stand for strict observance of the generally recognized principles and norms of international law against any actions aimed at forced pressure or at interference, under any pretext, into the domestic affairs of sovereign states ... Russia and China stress the basic importance of the Anti-Ballistic Missile Treaty, which is the cornerstone of strategic stability and the basis for reducing offensive weapons, and speak out for maintaining the treaty in its current form ... The government of the People's Republic of China is the sole legitimate government representing the whole of China ... Taiwan is an integral part of China.

> The treaty promises closer economic, security and cultural ties ... The treaty bars Russia and China from concluding other treaties with third countries threatening the 'sovereignty, security or territorial integrity' of the other signatory ... The countries declare they have no 'territorial claims' on one another. They promise to resolve by negotiation remaining disagreements over two small sections of the common border ... China is already the largest export market for Russian arms ... China takes roughly a quarter of Russia's $4 billion annual arms exports. Total official two-way trade between China and Russia reached $8 billion last year [2000], though unofficial border trade may be worth half as much again.
>
> (*FT*, 17 July 2001, p. 10)

'Aside from a few disputed islands in the Amur River, which marks the border, the 2,500-mile frontier has been recognized by both countries' (*The Times*, 17 July 2001, p. 16).

> [Only] 2 per cent of the approximately 4,000-kilometre border remains in dispute. This includes two islands in the Amur River and one in the Argun. Under treaties signed by Tsarist Russia and imperial China the border ran along the Chinese bank, which meant that all of the islands were considered Russian. Under Khrushchev, however, Moscow acknowledged that this was unfair and that the border should run through the main navigating channel. Thus arose the problem of the islands.
>
> (*CDSP*, 2001, vol. 53, no. 29, p. 1)

'China's trade with Russia last year [2000] was $8 billion, while Chinese–US trade came to nearly $120 billion' (*CDSP*, 2001, vol. 53, no. 29, p. 1).

> The treaty ... covers politics, economy, trade, science and technology, culture and more ... Despite recent agreements delineating almost the entire China–Russia border, there is still deep suspicion in Russia's Far East of China's territorial ambitions ... Trade [between China and Russia] ... is worth $8 billion annually ... [but] China's trade with the USA is worth over $110 billion and climbing rapidly.
>
> (*FEER*, 26 July 2001, p. 15)

> On 16 July 2001 Russian president Vladimir Putin and Chinese president Jiang Zemin signed the Good Neighbourly Treaty of Friendship and Co-operation, replacing the outdated 1950 version that expired in 1980 ... The overall trade turnover between Russia and China was about $8 billion in 2000 and it is expected to have topped $10 billion last year [2001]. In comparison with the US–Chinese annual trade volume of $120 billion the Russian–Chinese trade activity seems puny. However, the statistics do not reflect the real cross-border 'grey economic activities' in the neighbouring regions. And one should not forget that annual US–Russian trade amounted to only $10 billion.
>
> (*Rusi Newsbrief*, 2001, vol. 22, no. 1, pp. 9–10)

[On 17 July] Russian and Chinese officials ... agreed to formulate a plan for a long-discussed oil $1.7 billion pipeline to carry oil from Siberia to north-eastern China ... The 2,400-kilometre (1,500-mile) pipeline could be completed as early as 2005 and ship 20 million tonnes (147 million barrels) a year to China.

> (*IHT*, 18 July 2001, p. 5)

22 July 2001.

> President George W. Bush and President Vladimir Putin agreed after a two-hour meeting here [Genoa] Sunday [22 July] to tie US plans for a missile defence shield to nuclear arms reductions ... The presidents met at ... the annual summit meeting of the Group of Eight ... The [joint] statement said: 'We agreed that major changes in the world require concrete discussions of both offensive and defensive systems. We already have some strong and tangible points of agreement. We will shortly begin intensive consultations on the interrelated subjects of offensive and defensive systems.'
>
> (*IHT*, 23 July 2001, p. 3)

25 July 2001.

> The United States on Wednesday [25 July] opted out of a plan to strengthen a 1972 treaty that bans biological weapons, a decision that appears to have effectively scuttled the draft pact for enforcement ... [A US spokesman] said the Bush administration still supported the germ warfare treaty ... [but]

'the draft protocol would put national security and confidential business information at risk' ... The biological weapons convention ... has been ratified by 143 countries, including the United States. It bars the development, production or possession of germ weapons ... The draft accord ... has been seven years in the making.

(IHT, 26 July 2001, p. 7)

'Though the 1972 biological weapons convention was ratified by 143 nations, it never included provisions to police it. The new arms control regime would require a new ratification process' *(FT*, 26 July 2001, p. 8).

29 July 2001. A communist, Gennadi Khodyrev, wins the election for the governorship of Nizhny Novgorod. He beat the Kremlin-backed incumbent, Ivan Sklyarov *(IHT*, 31 July 2001, p. 10). (The respective percentages of the vote were 59.8 per cent and 28.25 per cent: *CDSP*, 2001, vol. 53, no. 31, p. 11.)

After his victory Mr Khodyrev ... a Communist member of the Russian Duma ... suspended his membership of the Communist Party, apparently to avoid a clash with the government in Moscow. The Kremlin had threatened that it might transfer the capital of the Volga region to another city if a Communist became governor ... Many voters felt that the city had failed to produce the booming economy promised by market reforms and that in the past five years it had fallen behind its rival cities, including Moscow and St Petersburg ... Mr Khodyrev benefited from a dirty election campaign that had affected all candidates.

(The Independent, 31 July 2001, p. 10)

19 August 2001. The tenth anniversary of the abortive 1991 coup attempt.

'President Putin has yet to contribute to the current debate about 1991. Last year [2000] he said the plotters had gone about things the wrong way. But their aims were "noble"' *(Guardian*, 18 August 2001, p. 15).

(Gennadi Yanayev and Vladimir Kryuchkov were jailed but given an amnesty in 1994. Anatoli Lukyanov was also jailed and given an amnesty. 'General Dmitri Yazov, former Soviet defence minister, salvaged part of his reputation by refusing an order an attack on the White House. He was offered a defence ministry post by Yeltsin in 1998. Vasili Starodubtsev ... was jailed and given amnesty. This year [2001] he won re-election as the Communist governor of Tula province by a 71 per cent landslide. Boris Pugo ... shot himself and his wife when the coup collapsed. Marshal Sergei Akhromeyev ... hanged himself at the second attempt when the coup collapsed': *The Times*, Supplement, 14 August 2001, p. 2.)

3 September 2001. Yevgeni Primakov announces that he is resigning as leader of a centrist faction in the State Duma *(IHT*, 4 September 2001, p. 5).

A international task force formed to crack down on money laundering yesterday [7 September] lifted the threat of economic sanctions against Russia. The

Financial Action Task Force, a body set up by the Group of Seven leading industrialized nations ... added ... Ukraine to its list of centres with deficiencies in their money-laundering regimes ... The task force said some progress had been made but none of those already on the list had done enough work to be removed. The task force ... said it was removing its threat against Russia, which was made in June, because the government had put in place 'significant' anti-money-laundering laws. It urged Russia to act quickly to implement the new measures so that it could be removed from the blacklist.

(*FT*, 8 September 2001, p. 6)

11 September 2001. There are terrorist attacks in the United States on the World Trade Center in New York and on the Pentagon in Washington. (The USA took the war on international terrorism to Afghanistan. Bombing started on 7 October and on 19 October US special forces began the ground phase of the war in Afghanistan. The USA considered the Taleban regime to be habouring terrorists, notably the Moslem fundamentalist Osama bin Laden and his al-Qaeda ['the base'] forces. The combination of US bombing and the ground attacks of anti-Taleban forces, especially the Northern Alliance, was successful in a surprisingly rapid fashion. The Taleban regime was essentially beaten by November 2001 and a new temporary Afghan government of national unity was in place by December 2001.)

President Bush (21 October):

President Putin was the first person to call [after the 11 September terrorist attacks]. That's what a friend does, calls in a time of need ... [Russia] came to stand in solidarity with the United States ... Russia is sharing valuable intelligence on terrorist organizations, providing overflight clearance for humanitarian missions, and helping out diplomatically.

(*The Times*, 22 October 2001, p. 2)

'Within hours of the [11 September] attacks, Mr Bush told a joint press conference, Mr Putin had cancelled a Russian military exercise to "simplify our situation"' (*Guardian*, 22 October 2001, p. 2).

Vladimir Putin (11 September):

Today the United States was confronted with an unprecedented act of aggression on the part of international terrorism ... What happened today underscores once more the urgency of Russia's proposal that the international community join forces to combat terrorism, the plague of the twenty-first century. Russia knows first hand what terrorism is. And for that reason we understand the feelings of the American people more than anyone ... You have our support.

(*CDSP*, 2001, vol. 53, no. 37, p. 4)

13 September 2001. 'Moscow agreed Thursday [13 September] to work with Nato in seeking to "unite the entire international community in the struggle against terrorism"' (*IHT*, 14 September 2001, p. 4). 'Russia has officially pledged co-operation in fighting what President Vladimir Putin called a "common enemy"' (*IHT*, 15 September 2001, p. 1).

> Nato and Russia issued an unprecedented statement yesterday [13 September] denouncing the [terrorist] attacks in America ... The Nato–Russian Permanent Joint Council in Brussels said both parties would 'intensify their co-operation to defeat this scourge' ... The show of solidarity came a day after Nato ambassadors agreed this week's terrorist atrocity was an attack on all nineteen members and triggered Article 5, the collective defence clause of the Nato treaty.
>
> (*Daily Telegraph*, 14 September 2001, p. 4)

> Russia and Nato said they were 'united in their resolve not to let those responsible for such an inhuman act to go unpunished' ... [On 12 September Nato invoked] for the first time Article 5 of its charter, which says an attack against one is an attack against the alliance.
>
> (*FT*, 14 September 2001, p. 8)

14 September 2001.

> Russia on Friday [14 September] rejected participation in any US-led retaliatory strike against terrorists and said the United States should not use countries in Central Asia as a staging ground for an assault against neighbouring Afghanistan ... Tajikistan and several other countries in former Soviet Central Asia are among the few obvious launching pads against Osama bin Laden's haven in Afghanistan. Defence minister Sergei Ivanov said during a meeting in Armenia that the United States and its allies should not rely on Central Asia to stage an assault. 'I see absolutely no basis for even hypothetical suppositions about the possibility of Nato military operations on the territory of Central Asian nations," Mr Ivanov said. At the same time Russian military leaders made it clear that Russia would most likely not take part 'in the retaliatory acts' planned by the United States, said General Anatoli Kvashnin, head of the Russian General Staff ... General Kvashnin said: 'The United States armed forces are powerful enough to deal with this task alone' ... A day earlier Mr Ivanov also expressed scepticism about an active role in the US response: 'Russia is not planning any kind of military actions or strikes' ... But these statements Friday did not rule out far more extensive co-operation than in the past between Russia and the United States. Both Western and Russian sources in Moscow said that high-level talks were continuing between the two countries aimed at 'constructive' co-operation that could well go beyond sharing intelligence information ... In recent days Mr Putin and Mr Ivanov have both asserted that Mr bin Laden has given aid to the Chechen rebels ... Russia's allies in Tajikistan did not reject the possibility that the United States could use its airspace as part of an operation against Mr bin Laden ... The Tajik prime minister said [on Friday] only that he would 'definitely' consult with Russia before agreeing to such a step.
>
> (*IHT*, 15 September 2001, p. 1)

Osama bin Laden [is] the prime suspect in the terrorist attacks ... Russia ... on Thursday [13 September] offered Nato unsolicited support for a global struggle against terrorist groups ... The Russian foreign minister, Igor Ivanov ... said the attacks ... justified 'all possible means' in the fight against terrorism. But within hours the Russian military pulled back from those positions. The Russian defence minister, Sergei Ivanov, ruled out 'even hypothetical assumptions' that Russia and other former Soviet states would lend troops or bases to any Nato military action. Russian officials also warned the United States that any retaliation that caused civilian suffering would only provoke a greater terrorist response.

(IHT, 17 September 2001, p. 4)

Prime minister Akil Akilov [of Tajikistan] has said he might consider allowing Western-led forces to use its air bases against Afghanistan. But by the weekend [16 September] a spokesman for the foreign ministry said such reports had been 'groundless'.

(p. 6)

('Tajikistan ... has 20,000 or more Russian troops on its soil': *FT*, 3 October 2001, p. 20.)

Russian defence minister Sergei Ivanov yesterday [14 September] ... [said there are] 'absolutely no grounds, not even hypothetically, for speculating that some sort of Nato military operations could be undertaken on the territory of the Central Asian countries of the CIS'.

(CDSP, 2001, vol. 53, no. 37, p. 5)

15 September 2001.

'We must weigh up our decisions and make them on the basis of proven facts,' said President Vladimir Putin on Saturday [15 September]. Russia fears the instability in Central Asia that a strike on Afghanistan may provoke ... and also reaction in the Arab world where it has traditional allies.

(FT, 17 September 2001, p. 2)

17 September 2001.

Uzbekistan said yesterday [17 September] it had not ruled out offering the USA its facilities or airspace for an attack. A foreign ministry spokesman said Tashkent has received no formal request from the USA yet, but stood ready to discuss 'all possible forms of co-operation' ... Turkmenistan's insular government has been most successful in keeping the Taleban at arm's length. President Saparmurat Niyazov's policy of 'positive neutrality' keeps Turkmenistan mostly isolated, but at the same time keeps channels with Kabul open.

(FT, 18 September 2001, p. 4)

'Uzbekistan ... blames ... the Taleban ... for supporting armed Islamic rebels who have crossed into Uzbekistan in the last few years' (*The Independent*, 18 September 2001, p. 9).

18 September 2001.

> The Kazakh foreign minister ... [said that] 'Kazakhstan is prepared for the strongest possible co-operation with the United States and the world community in combating international terrorism' ... Uzbekistan has already offered to make its territory and airspace available to the United States, although it says that America has not taken up its offer. Kyrgyzstan ... [said] that 'information support' and help to the FBI were ... on offer. Tajikistan says that it will co-ordinate any help to the USA with Russia, while Turkmenistan ... has ruled out an active role ... Turkmenistan signalled its readiness to be an active part of the front line yesterday [18 September] ... The country supplies the Taleban with gas and electricity.
>
> (*The Times*, 19 September 2001, p. 10)

19 September 2001. 'The [Russian] foreign minister hinted yesterday [19 September] that US forces might be allowed to use bases in Central Asia' (*Daily Telegraph*, 20 September 2001, p. 11).

'The Pentagon let it be known Wednesday [19 September] that US combat planes were headed toward ... Uzbekistan and Tajikistan' (*IHT*, 22 September 2001, p.).

22 September 2001. 'US military transport aeroplanes landed [in Uzbekistan] on Saturday [22 September] ... Comments last week by Igor Ivanov, Russian foreign minister, echoed by President Vladimir Putin, that each country could decide for itself, seemed to signal a change' (*FT*, 24 September 2001, p. 2).

'Over the weekend several news organizations reported that up to three American transport planes had landed ... [but] Uzbekistan has not confirmed these reports ... Tajikistan has formally denied reports that American aircraft and troops have been stationed [there]' (*IHT*, 25 September 2001, p. 4).

President Nursultan Nazarbayev of Kazakhstan: 'Kazakhstan has resolutely spoken out against terrorism and is ready, in a coalition of other states, to fight it jointly because we believe that a single state, however big, cannot defeat terrorism alone' (*The Times*, 24 September 2001, p. 9).

24 September 2001. President Putin:

> Needless to say, we remain prepared to make our contribution to the war on terrorism ... We support active international co-operation through intelligence services. Russia has shared information in its possession regarding the infrastructure and whereabouts of international terrorists and terrorist training camps and will continue to do so. We are prepared to open Russian Federation airspace to aircraft carrying humanitarian cargo to the region in which the anti-terrorist operation is to be carried out. We have co-ordinated this position with our allies in Central Asia. They share this position and do not rule out the possibility of allowing the use of their airfields. Russia is also willing, if need be, to take part in international search-and-rescue operations ... We will expand our

co-operation with the internationally recognized government of Afghanistan, led by Mr Rabbani, and will provide its armed forces with additional
assistance in the form of arms and military hardware ... Russian co-
operation with the countries participating in the counter-terrorist operation could also assume other, more in-depth forms. The extent and nature
of this co-operation will be directly dependent on the overall level and
quality of our relations with these countries and on mutual understanding
in combating international terrorism ... In order to co-ordinate efforts in
all the aforementioned areas I have established a group headed by defence
minister Sergei Ivanov.

(*CDSP*, 2001, vol. 53, no. 39, p. 1)

('The Northern Alliance [is] the largest opposition movement to the ruling
Taleban in Afghanistan. The alliance is composed largely of ethnic Tajiks and
Uzbeks who are not represented in the Taleban': *FT*, 1 October 2001, p. 28.
'Russia ... has armed [the Northern Alliance] covertly since 1996': *FT*, 3
October 2001, p. 20.)

President Putin on Monday [24 September] offered the United States broad
support for anti-terrorist operations in Afghanistan, including access to its
airspace for humanitarian missions, direct participation in some search-and-
rescue operations and weapons shipments to forces opposing the ruling
Taleban movement inside Afghanistan.

(*IHT*, 25 September 2001, p. 1)

President Nazarbayev:

We are ready to support an action against terrorism with all means at our
disposal [including the use of airfields, airspace and military bases] ... We
have so far received no concrete requests for such help, but if they come
Kazakhstan will consider then positively.

(*IHT*, 25 September 2001, p. 4; *The Independent*, 25 September 2001, p. 5)

'Ukraine yesterday [24 September] cleared the way for US military cargo planes
... to fly through Ukrainian airspace' (*FT*, 25 September 2001, p. 5).

'Turkmenistan ... has no domestic fundamentalist opposition threat to worry
about' (*The Independent*, 25 September 2001, p. 5). 'The Turkmen government
has insisted on remaining neutral' (*The Times*, 25 September 2001, p. 11). 'Turkmenistan, Tajikistan and Uzbekistan [have] closed their borders to Afghanistan'
(*The Times*, 26 September 2001, p. 4).

'Turkmenistan ... proclaims a policy of "positive neutrality", which generally
translates into Turkmenistan avoiding any initiatives on a regional basis and preferring to negotiate with other countries individually' (*FT*, 26 September 2001,
p. 4). 'Turkmenistan has declared itself a neutral state ... Though retaining its
reservations, it has also been the closest to the Taleban of all five governments,
hoping to use Afghanistan one day for pipelines to export its energy resources'
(*FT*, 1 October 2001, p. 28).

25 September 2001. 'Yesterday [25 September] ... President Saparmurat Niyazov [of Turkmenistan] said that ... he had agreed to open an air corridor for US aircraft to deliver "humanitarian goods" such as food to Afghanistan, but not military supplies' (*FT*, 26 September 2001, p. 4).

President Saparmurat Niyazov was reported to have said he would open air and ground corridors to humanitarian aid. Kyrgyzstan said it had agreed to an American request to grant air corridors for aircraft involved in military opera- tions in Afghanistan ... The airport at Dushanbe, the capital of Tajikistan, 'may be offered to the US air force to carry out a retaliatory strike if the need arises' ... the Russian defence minister, Sergei Ivanov, [was quoted] as saying.

(*Guardian*, 26 September 2001, p. 6)

'India and Pakistan ... have used the crisis to secure the ending of sanctions imposed in 1998 over their testing of nuclear weapons' (*FT*, 27 September 2001, p. 22).

US co-operation with Uzbekistan is not new and has included joint military exercises. According to some officials, the country has also been used to base intelligence and other assets for US covert efforts over the last three years to track down Osama bin Laden. In his 20 September speech to Con- gress President George W. Bush named just two international groups linked to al-Qaeda: the Egyptian Islamic Jihad and the Islamic Movement of Uzbekistan (IMU), which wants to overthrow the autocratic government of President Islam Karimov and set up Islamist states elsewhere in the region.

(*FT*, 1 October 2001, p. 28)

2 October 2001.

For the first time in its fifty-two year history Nato invoked Article 5 of its treaty, obliging the alliance to give the USA assistance 'for such action as it deems necessary, including the use of armed force'. The article states that an armed attack on one or more of the allies ... 'shall be considered an attack against them all' ... But to invoke it Nato insisted on 12 September ... that Article 5 could come into play only 'if' the USA could prove the attack was directed from abroad. Yesterday [2 October] that 'if' was removed ... Lord Robertson (Nato secretary-general): 'The facts are clear and compelling. We know that the individuals who carried out these attacks were part of the worldwide terrorist network of al-Qaeda, headed by Osama bin Laden and his key lieutenants and protected by the Taleban.'

(*FT*, 3 October 2001, p. 3)

President Putin is in Brussels for talks with Nato and the EU. He again con- demns terrorism (*The Times*, 3 October 2001, p. 8).

[On 2 October] Russia signed a military co-operation agreement with Iran ... 'Russia and Iran have been the most active supporters of the Northern Alli- ance, which is opposing the Afghan Taleban movement' ... defence minister

Sergei Ivanov said ... Russia suspended arms sales to Iran in 1995 ... [There was] a decision by Moscow to restart arms sales to Teheran ... last November [2000] ... The agreement paves the way for Iran to become within five years the third largest purchaser of Russian arms after China and India.

(*IHT*, 3 October 2001, p. 2)

3 October 2001. President Putin (speaking on the second and final day of his visit to Brussels):

If Nato takes on a different shade and is becoming a political organization, of course we would reconsider our position with regard to such [Nato] expansion, if we are to feel involved in such processes. They keep saying that Nato is becoming more political than military. We are looking at this and watching the process. If this is to be so it would change things considerably ... After the tragic events of 11 September the European community has a need to look again at regional security. It is high time to come up with practical solutions.

'That positive note was slightly dampened when ... Mr Putin questioned whose security would be enhanced if the alliance enlarged' (*The Independent*, 4 October 2001, p. 2).

Lord Robertson: 'These discussions mark a major milestone in the Nato–Russia relationship ... I believe we are entering an era when substantial and practical co-operation is going to build a unique relationship between us.'

'Russia, he [Putin] said, would start holding monthly consultations with EU authorities on how to thwart terrorist financing, share intelligence on criminal suspects, track false documents and monitor movements of chemical, nuclear and biological weapons' (*IHT*, 4 October 2001, p. 1).

Yesterday [3 October] it was agreed that Russia's ambassador to the EU would be consulted on a monthly basis about COPs ... the political and security committee, which is responsible for overseeing the European Security and Defence Policy (ESDP) ... By the start of 2003 [COPs] is due to have the ESDP's 60,000-strong Rapid Reaction Force up and running ... Yesterday the EU agreed to accelerate preparatory work on Russia's accession to the WTO.

(*FT*, 4 October 2001, p. 3)

'Mr Putin secured agreement from Lord Robertson ... on the creation of a joint body for combating international terrorism' (*The Times*, 4 October 2001, p. 10).

5 October 2001.

Islam Karimov, Uzbek president, agreed during a visit by ... Donald Rumsfeld, US defence secretary ... to Tashkent to allow the use of an air base for cargo aircraft, helicopters and troops, though not as a launchpad for attacks by special forces on Afghanistan ... Mr Karimov said the base could be used for humanitarian and search and rescue operations.

(*FT*, 6 October 2001, p. 2)

President Islam Karimov: 'We are against the usage of our territory or the land operations against Afghanistan and we are against air strikes executed from the territory of Uzbekistan. Special operations forces will not be deployed in the territory of Uzbekistan' (*IHT*, 6 October 2001, p. 1).

'Most military and diplomatic observers believed such lines would be blurred in the coming weeks, or for the duration of America's campaign against the Taleban, and that US operations will be significantly more extensive' (*The Times*, 6 October 2001, p. 2).

'The United States deployed its first ground troops in the war against terrorism Friday [5 October], sending 1,000 soldiers to Uzbekistan ... The troops were en route from the United States' (*IHT*, 6 October 2001, p. 1).

7 October 2001. The USA and the UK start bombing targets in Afghanistan.

8 October 2001. 'President Vladimir Putin yesterday [8 October] strongly backed the US strikes' (*FT*, 9 October 2001, p. 9).

Vladimir Putin: 'Humankind has matured after the horrible tragedy on 11 September. I think their arrogance and self-assurance has been the terrorists' undoing. They did not expect the international community to show such cohesion in the face of a common threat' (*IHT*, 10 October 2001, p. 9).

'Yesterday [8 October] Kyrgyzstan said it could accept no more than 10,000 refugees from Afghanistan, in addition to the 1,500 it already has' (*FT*, 9 October 2001, p. 9).

The hull section of the *Kursk* nuclear submarine is raised from the sea bed. The sawn-off bow section is supposedly to be raised later. The Dutch contractors were Smit International and Mammoet. The Dutch-led salvage operation was overseen by Russia's Northern Fleet.

'Sergei Ivanov, Russia's defence minister, [has been] named ... as the country's anti-terrorist co-ordinator' (*FT*, 10 October 2001, p. 2).

'Tajikistan ... said yesterday [9 October] it had allowed in US "specialists" for "humanitarian" work in Afghanistan, but not US troops' (*FT*, 10 October 2001, p. 2). 'The USA said yesterday [10 October] it was giving Tajikistan $3 million to help private farmers. Two successive droughts have hit the country's grain harvest' (*FT*, 11 October 2001, p. 2).

('[On 16 October] the World Food Programme appealed for urgent food aid to assist around 1 million facing starvation in Tajikistan ... [which] has suffered consecutive years of drought and civil war': *Guardian*, 17 October 2001, p. 6.)

'There certainly seems little sympathy anywhere [in Tajikistan] for the Taleban' (*The Economist*, 20 October 2001, p. 76).

12 October 2001.

Yesterday [12 October] ... Uzbekistan agreed to allow US troops and aircraft to launch missions from a key Uzbek base [Khanabad] ... In yesterday's statement the Uzbek government said it agreed to provide the use of its airspace and 'necessary military and civilian infrastructure of one of its airports which could be used in the first instance for humanitarian purposes'. In return the Uzbek government has won a pledge from the USA to support the country if it faced direct threats ... The Americans would 'urgently discuss' appropriate security arrangements if Uzbekistan's territorial integrity was threatened ... The USA has also a pledge from the government in Tajikistan for its bases to be used for military operations if required.

(The Times, 13 October 2001, p. 14)

The USA and Uzbekistan said yesterday [12 October] they had signed an agreement under which Washington agreed to urgent discussions if the former Soviet republic came under threat. The joint statement referred to a classified agreement between the two sides signed on 7 October, which it said had established 'a qualitatively new relationship based on a long-term commitment to advance security and regional stability' ... Co-operation against terrorism would include 'the need to consult on an urgent basis about appropriate steps to address the situation in the event of a direct threat to the security of territorial integrity of the Republic of Uzbekistan' ... A US official said ... 'It is the first time something like this has been done with any country that was part of the Soviet Union.

(FT, 13 October 2001, p. 2)

In the [12 October] statement ... offensive operations were not explicitly ruled out, with the deal stipulating only that the Uzbek military base would be used 'in the first instance' for non-military aid purposes ... The United States and Uzbekistan have quietly conducted joint covert operations aimed at countering Afghanistan's ruling Taleban government and its terrorist allies since well over a year before the 11 September attacks, according to officials from both nations. The most significant advance came more than a year ago with stepped-up intelligence co-operation between the two countries in an effort to track and undermine ... Osama bin Laden. At the same time special forces began to work more overtly with the Uzbek military on training missions ... [The] chief spokesman for President Islam Karimov ... said significant military and intelligence joint efforts extended back 'two or three years' ... In 1998 ... [there were] terrorist attacks on the US embassies in Kenya and Tanzania.

(IHT, 15 October 2001, p. 4)

'Gazprom said yesterday [12 October] it would sell its stake in the country's only private nationwide television network [NTV] ... as well as all its other media assets' *(The Independent,* 13 October 2001, p. 18).

In addition to NTV, Gazprom owns stakes in twenty-three companies that were part of Mr Gusinsky's media conglomerate, as well as several newspapers ... Also Friday [12 October] ... Alfred Kokh resigned from his post ... [as] manager of Gazprom's media holdings ... saying he was being 'isolated from all decisions' and being turned into 'a simple fool'.

(IHT, 13 October 2001, p. 11)

21 October 2001. Presidents Putin and Bush met during the APEC (Asia-Pacific Economic forum) meeting in Shanghai.

President Putin:

> I fully agree with the position of President Bush and his action, which is measured and adequate to the threat that the United States was confronted with. If we start fighting terrorism it must be completed, otherwise terrorists would get the feeling that they are not vulnerable.
>
> (*The Times*, 22 October 2001, p. 2)

President Bush:

> President Putin was the first person to call [after the 11 September terrorist attacks]. That's what a friend does, calls in a time of need ... [Russia] came to stand in solidarity with the United States ... Russia is sharing valuable intelligence on terrorist organizations, providing overflight clearance for humanitarian missions, and helping out diplomatically.
>
> (*The Times*, 22 October 2001, p. 2)

'Within hours of the [11 September] attacks, Mr Bush told a joint press conference, Mr Putin had cancelled a Russian military exercise to "simplify our situation"' (*Guardian*, 22 October 2001, p. 2).

A statement was issued after the APEC meeting concluded:

> Leaders consider the murderous deeds [of 11 September] ... as a profound threat to the peace, prosperity and security of all people, of all faiths, of all nations. Terrorism is also a direct challenge to APEC's vision of free, open and prosperous economies.
>
> (*FT*, 22 October 2001, p. 11)

'The statement issued by the APEC leaders promised co-operation to block funds for terrorists, step up security at ports and airports, and limit the economic fallout from the attacks' (*Daily Telegraph*, 22 October 2001, p. 9). 'Leaders ... agreed to step up efforts to cut off funding for terrorists. They also called for efforts to improve aviation, maritime and energy security and to co-operate to bring the perpetrators of the 11 September attacks to justice' (*FT*, 22 September 2001, p. 11). '[The statement] pledged economic and financial measures to prevent "all forms of terrorist acts" in the future' (*Guardian*, 22 October 2001, p. 2).

The statement itself committed the nations to: 'Bring the perpetrators to justice ... [to take] appropriate measures to prevent the flow of funds to terrorists ... [and to develop] a global electronic customs network and electronic movement records' (*IHT*, 22 October 2001, pp. 1–6).

'[At the APEC meeting President Bush said that] "No government should use our war against terrorism as an excuse to persecute minorities within their borders"' (*Guardian*, 22 October 2001, p. 2).

20 October 2001. 'So far US commandos have carried out a single operation: the 20 October raid in which US commandos attacked a house used by Mullah

Mohammed Omar, the Taleban leader, and an airfield south of Kandahar' (*IHT*, 6 November 2001, p. 5).

22 October 2001. 'A new arrest warrant was issued against Boris Berezovsky ... for alleged money laundering and complicity in asset stripping at Aeroflot' (*FT*, 23 October 2001, p. 12).

25 October 2001. 'Uzbekistan has agreed to open part of its border to allow humanitarian aid into northern Afghanistan ... to allow the UN for the first time since 1998 to use the Termez river port and barges' (*FT*, 26 October 2001, p. 2).

5 November 2001.

> Tajikistan and the United States have reached a tentative agreement on military co-operation that could lead to American airstrikes against the Taleban forces from the territory of the Central Asian republic. An American inspection team has arrived in Tajikistan to examine three former Soviet bases to see whether they are usable ... The US inspection team also plans to look at bases in Kyrgyzstan and Kazakhstan ... The Tajik foreign minister said a final decision about co-operation between his country and the United States would be made after the team's assessment was complete ... Donald Rumsfeld, the US secretary of defence, stopped in Moscow [on 3 November] for talks with his Russian counterpart, Sergei Ivanov. A US defence department official said that the bases in Tajikistan were discussed and the Russians supported the use of the airfields by the United States.
>
> (*IHT*, 6 November 2001, p. 5)

11 November 2001. 'President Putin said yesterday that Russian forces would take part in the rescue of American aircrews brought down over Afghanistan' (*The Times*, 12 November 2001, p. 7).

13–15 November 2001. President Putin visits the USA.

> Mr Putin ... [had] his first meeting with Mr Bush in ... [the USA] but their fourth overall ... Their co-operation in the war against terrorism ... has proved to be a potent catalyst [to improved relations] ... [although Mr Putin made clear that they had yet to bridge their differences over US plans to develop a missile defence system ... The [US] administration recently delayed some tests.
>
> (*IHT*, 14 November 2001, p. 4)

President George W. Bush (13 November):

> The current levels of our nuclear forces do not reflect today's strategic realities. I have informed President Putin that the United States will reduce our operationally deployed strategic nuclear warheads to a level between 1,700 and 2,200 warheads over the next decade.
>
> (*IHT*, 14 November 2001, p. 4)

President Putin: '[Russia will] try to respond in kind' (*The Times*, 14 November 2001, p. 2).

'President Putin said Russia would cut its arsenal of 6,000 such weapons by at least two-thirds' (*IHT*, 17 November 2001, p. 8).

'The United States has about 7,000 intercontinental nuclear warheads to Russia's estimated 5,800' (*IHT*, 14 November 2001, p. 4).

21 November 2001.

> President Putin approved ... experimental plans to recruit a growing number of professional soldiers ... Under the latest military reform proposals, announced last November [2000], Russia will cut 600,000 jobs, a fifth of the total, over five years. Officially there are now 2.1 million uniformed personnel and 966,000 civilians in the Russian armed forces.
>
> (*FT*, 22 November 2001, p. 12)

25 November 2001. 'Juma Namangani ... the head of the Islamic Movement of Uzbekistan ... [was] reported yesterday [25 November] to have been killed [while fighting] in Afghanistan' (*FT*, 26 November 2001, p. 8).

26–27 November 2001.

> A Moscow court has ordered the dissolution of TV-6, the last major independent television station ... The court ruled that the station, owned largely by Boris Berezovsky ... was financially unsound ... Mr Berezovsky owns 75 per cent of TV-6, but he placed management responsibility in the hands of Mr [Vladimir] Gusinsky and Mr [Yevgeni] Kiselyov ... The court ... agreed with a suit filed by a minority shareholder, the Lukoil petroleum company, to liquidate the firm ... Employees suspected there had been political manoeuvring ... Lukoil deals closely with the Kremlin on important issues of export quotas and taxes ... TV-6 has six months to appeal and ... the company [said it] would do so. Theoretically the station can continue broadcasting in that period. However, the press ministry has the power to revoke the broadcaster's licence immediately.
>
> (*IHT*, 27 November 2001, p. 6)

'Lukoil ... claimed that its rights as a minority shareholder – it has 15 per cent – had been violated' (*The Times*, 27 November 2001, p. 15).

> Yevgeni Kiselyov, general director of the TV-6 network and its star commentator ... yesterday [27 November] pledged to fight a court order threatening its imminent closure, which he said was politically motivated ... His comments came after the Moscow arbitration court on Monday [26 November] upheld an earlier ruling in favour of winding up the network following a petition launched this summer by Lukoil Garant, the pension fund of the Lukoil oil group, a 15 per cent minority shareholder ... Mr Berezovsky offered Mr Kiselyov the post as general director of

TV-6 and allowed him to take many of his former colleagues and some programmes.

(FT, 28 November 2001, p. 20)

('A federal court overturned on Saturday [29 December] a three-month-old lower court ruling that ... TV-6 was insolvent and should be liquidated. The judge returned the case to the lower court for reconsideration – but the bankruptcy law underpinning the case will in any event be replaced when the new year rolls in ... a fact that elated the network's managers ... Both NTV and TV-6 have been tried under an obscure law that grants shareholders the right to liquidate a company if its net worth falls below a legally set level pegged to the value of its stock ... The managers of TV-6 have argued that the law does not apply to the network because it is showing a profit of more than $1.6 million for this year after several years of losses. Since NTV's demise TV-6 has doubled its share of the Russian television audience': *IHT*, 31 December 2001, p. 6. 'A Russian high court ordered the liquidation yesterday [11 January 2002] of the country's only independent national television station, TV-6 ... TV-6 managers say the minority shareholder, an oil company pension fund [Lukoil-Garant], was acting to please the Kremlin ... A lawyer for TV-6 said the Russian courts had ignored recent changes in law and improvements in TV-6's finances that should have staved off the liquidation order': *FT*, 12 January 2002, p. 5. 'The Moscow Higher Arbitration Court ordered the network's owners to immediately start liquidating the company ... TV-6 officially has six months to complete the liquidation ... TV-6 lawyers and managers assailed the decision, which came with unusual swiftness and was based on a law that had expired with the new year ... Legal experts say the law has not been applied in any other case of note ... They said they would appeal the ruling to Russia's constitutional court ... and perhaps to the European Court on Human Rights ... [Russia is] a nation where two of the three major television networks are state run and the third is owned by a state-controlled monopoly': *IHT*, 12 January 2002, p. 5. 'TV-6 ... stopped broadcasting at midnight on Monday [21 January] ... after a request from court bailiffs led to the company's equipment being impounded and the electricity turned off ... Mikhail Lesin, Russia's press minister, stressed that ... the existing TV-6 team of journalists and executives would be able to bid for the broadcast licence in an auction on 27 March': *FT*, 23 January 2002, p. 6). 'Russian television has a vibrant, extensive web of local and regional TV stations; not all free speech has come from Moscow. However, the attack on the national stations may well have serious effects on regional journalism, including a return to the self-censorship that was such a noticeable feature of the Soviet decades': Floriana Fossato and Anna Kachkaeva, *IHT*, 26 January 2002, p. 4.)

Russia has sent twelve transport aircraft with diplomats, humanitarian workers and de-mining experts to Kabul ... President Vladimir Putin ... [said] that the aid workers and experts had been sent at the request of Burhanuddin Rabbani, head of the internationally recognized Islamic State of

Afghanistan now installed in Kabul ... Russia's health ministry said it would be opening a field hospital in the near future at an unspecified location within Afghanistan.

(FT, 27 November 2001, p. 10)

More than 200 personnel, including support and security staff were deployed to establish a 'humanitarian centre' ... The teams deployed yesterday [26 November] were part of a ... humanitarian programme to help feed and house Afghans. They would ensure a safe route from Bagram airport to Kabul before establishing a base in the capital. The humanitarian presence will be increased ... Mr Putin said the latest move was taking place 'at the request of President Rabbani and the Islamic State of Afghanistan' and in 'close co-operation with US representatives'.

(The Times, 27 November 2001, p. 6)

Russians armed with Kalashnikovs returned here Tuesday [27 November], twelve years after the manhandled Soviet army retreated from Afghanistan in defeat, but this time they vowed only to help. A contingent of eighty-eight men from the Russian ministry of emergency situations set up a small camp on a patch of dirt ... in central Kabul ... Although officially not soldiers, the Russian dressed the part ... Russian officials said they came at the invitation of the Northern Alliance, the coalition of Afghan guerrillas now in charge of Kabul, and planned to build a medical facility and rehabilitate their long-abandoned embassy. The unexpected move made the Russians the first foreign power to publicly send armed forces into the Afghan capital since the Taleban surrendered Kabul and retreated on 13 November. When a small troop of British soldiers flew into the Bagram airbase north of Kabul the Northern Alliance expressed their displeasure ... US marines established a base near Kandahar in southern Afghanistan this week ... The Soviet Union invaded Afghanistan in December 1979 to ensure a friendly communist regime on its southern border, only to find itself mired in a devastating war that left 15,000 soldiers dead ... The last Soviet troops withdrew in disgrace in 1989, leaving behind a chaotic political situation and a civil war that has not ended ... [Russia plans to] rebuild the old embassy, which Moscow abandoned in 1992 after the fall of the communist government. The embassy has been decimated by warfare since then and now serves as home to thousands of refugees living in the rubble.

(IHT, 28 November 2001, pp. 1, 4)

[US] secretary of state Colin Powell spoke to Russia's foreign minister by phone earlier this week and urged Moscow to avoid diplomatic or military moves in Afghanistan that might undermine trust between the United States and Russia ... General Powell also said that Russia should avoid doing anything to promote its long-time ally, the Northern Alliance leader Burhanuddin Rabbani, as the official leader of a post-conflict Afghanistan.

(IHT, 30 November 2001, p. 3)

1 December 2001.

> Admiral Vyacheslav Popov was dismissed Saturday [1 December] as chief
> of staff of the Northern Fleet, as was Vice-Admiral Mikhail Motsak. Their
> new jobs were not announced. Fourteen other officers 'have been dismissed
> or received various disciplinary penalties', said the top naval commander,
> Admiral Vladimir Kuroyedov. The military chief of staff, General Anatoli
> Kvashnin, said the actions were not linked to the *Kursk* sinking ... Senior
> Russian officials ... [said] the sanctions related to 'serious failures in the
> organization of the military training activities of the fleet' ... But just hours
> before Mr Putin observed that the *Kursk* investigation 'enables us to draw a
> rather definite conclusion on the quality of preparations for, and organiza-
> tion of, military exercises and the organization of search-and-rescue opera-
> tions ... It should be admitted that, despite a large amount of work done, no
> objective evidence proving this theory [that the *Kursk* sank after colliding
> with a US submarine] has been received.'
>
> (*IHT*, 3 December 2001, p. 5)

(President Putin referred to the theory of collision with 'an unidentified subsur-
face object': *The Times*, 3 December 2001, p. 15.)

> President Vladimir Putin has demoted three senior Russian naval officers
> and fired another eleven ... [including] Vice-Admiral Oleg Burtsev ... [The
> demotions went] along with the sacking of eight other admirals and three
> senior captains ... Vladimir Ustinov, the prosecutor general ... made a pre-
> liminary report on the sinking of the *Kursk* on Saturday [1 December] ...
> Mr Putin ... refused the proffered resignations of the top navy officials,
> including Admiral Popov, at the time of the sinking pending a full
> investigation.
>
> (*FT*, 3 December 2001, p. 10)

'At the weekend ... [President Putin presided] over a congress in Moscow
that merged his own Unity Party with the Fatherland Bloc founded by Yuri
Luzhkov' (*The Times*, 3 December 2001, p. 15).

> The United Party and the Fatherland and All Russia ... have been trans-
> formed into the All-Russia Unity and Fatherland Party ... [at its] founding
> congress ... Minister for emergency situations Sergei Shoigu ... [is] to serve
> as the main co-chairman ... for an initial period, since the leadership is sup-
> posed to rotate among the three co-chairmen ... the other two being Yuri
> Luzhkov and Mintimir Shaimiev ... Sergei Shoigu: 'Our task is to unite
> society around the constructive course being pursued by the president, to
> rally everyone around the head of state.'
>
> (*CDSP*, 2001, vol. 53, no. 49, p. 6)

'The shortened version [of the party] is United Russia' (p. 7).

('This winter [2001–2] a quarter of the Union of Right Forces' thirty-two legislators walked out, charging that the party had abandoned human rights to

become a captive of big business. The defectors have since joined Liberal Russia, a new party that embraces both capitalism and civil liberties and claims to have recruited thousands of Union supporters ... [Liberal Russia's] godfather is Boris Berezovsky ... [who] fled in late 2000 to London, where he is bank-rolling Liberal Russia's startup': *IHT*, 26 March 2002, p. 5.)

3 December 2001. The United States declares that the fifth test associated with missile defence is successful, making the success rate three out of five.

5 December 2001.

> Russia said Wednesday [5 December] that it had reduced its stockpile of strategic weapons to levels required by the Start 1 arms control treaty, which was signed by the United States and the Soviet Union in 1991. The foreign ministry said the number of weapons carriers had been reduced to 1,136 and the number of nuclear warheads to 5,518, well below the ceilings established by the treaty, which were 1,600 and 6,000, respectively.
>
> (*IHT*, 6 December 2001, p. 9)

6 December 2001. '[The Kyrgyz] parliament voted Thursday to let the US-led coalition in Afghanistan use air bases in Kyrgyzstan in military and humanitarian operations for one year' (*IHT*, 7 December 2001, p. 3).

7 December 2001.

> Nato and Russia agreed Friday [7 December] ... [to create] a new council ... Since 1997 meetings have been held under a body called the Nato–Russia Permanent Joint Council, a forum originally created to ease Moscow's fears about Nato enlargement. But both sides say the council has never been satisfactory and more often than not the alliance uses it to inform Russia of positions it already has taken ... Nato officials insisted that the alliance would not be hampered by the new co-operation, and that if a decision could not be reached with Russia, Nato's governing council would make a decision without it ... Besides the struggle against terrorism Russia and Nato suggested they could work together in such areas as crisis management, non-proliferation, arms control, theatre missile defence, search and rescue at sea, military-to-military co-operation and civil emergencies ... On Thursday [6 December] the ministers told their ambassadors at Nato headquarters to start working out details of a new arrangement for regular discussions with the Russians, and ways to include them in decision-making while retaining Nato's ability to act on its own. 'The precise nature and scope of this mechanism will require substantial work over the coming months,' Lord Robertson said, but the plan is to have it in place by the next meeting of allied foreign ministers in May in Reykjavik, Iceland ... Lord Robertson said that Russia would not be able to veto Nato decisions on the new council. Lord Robertson said ... 'This is about working together more effectively when it is in all our interests to do so.'
>
> (*IHT*, 8 December 2001, p. 2)

'Lord Robertson, Nato secretary-general ... said Nato "will retain its ability to act on its own"' (*FT*, 8 December 2001, p. 8).

The new council's controversial name is 'Nato at 20', the nineteen Nato members plus Russia.

9 December 2001. The Friendship Bridge over the Amu-Darya River is opened for the first time since 1997 for aid deliveries to Afghanistan. Uzbekistan was very cautious about reopening the bridge.

12 December 2001. 'President George W. Bush informed congressional leaders Wednesday [12 December] that Washington will withdraw from the 1972 Anti-Ballistic Missile Treaty in six months ... The treaty allows either signatory to withdraw with six months' notice' (*IHT*, 13 December 2001, p. 5).

'Russian press agencies cited anonymous senior officials stating that they had already been informed of the US decision to launch the six-month notice period for withdrawal from the treaty from today [13 December]' (*FT*, 13 December 2001, p. 6).

13 December 2001. 'President George W. Bush formally announced Thursday [13 December] that the United States was withdrawing from the Anti-Ballistic Missile treaty ... Mr Bush said he had given Russia formal notice of the move on Thursday' (*IHT*, 14 December 2001, p. 1).

President Putin:

> This step was not a surprise for us. However, we consider it a mistake ... It is not a threat to the security of the Russian Federation ... We must not allow a legal vacuum in strategic stability ... One should not undermine the regime of non-proliferation of weapons of mass destruction ... I think the current level of bilateral relations between the Russian Federation and the USA should not only be retained, but also used in order to work out the new framework of strategic relationship as soon as possible.
> (*IHT*, 14 December 2001, pp. 1, 3; *Guardian*, 14 December 2001, p. 16)

14 December 2001. 'US defence secretary Donald Rumsfeld left Friday [14 December] to visit Azerbaijan, Armenia and Georgia for talks on the war on terrorism ... The three countries have offered Washington use of their airspace for military action in Afghanistan' (*IHT*, 15 December 2001, p. 4).

'During his swing through Central Asia last week Colin Powell, the US secretary of state, was offered the use of Kazakh military bases as well as overflying rights for forces involved in the military and humanitarian operations in Afghanistan' (*FT*, Monday 17 December 2001, p. 8).

16 December 2001. Yuri Luzhkov is re-elected mayor of Moscow but the 'number of voters only just exceeded the minimum quorum of 25 per cent' (*The Times*, 17 December 2001, p. 13).

18 December 2001. '[Nato] defence ministers endorsed a proposal known as

"Nato at 20" to "give new impetus and substance" to the Nato–Rusia relationship' (*IHT*, 19 December 2001, p. 8).

22 December 2001. In Afghanistan a new, interim government, headed by Hamid Karzai, is sworn in.

25 December 2001.

> A Russian military court convicted the journalist Grigori Pasko of high treason on Tuesday [25 December], handing down a four-year jail term for passing state secrets to Japan … The federal security service brought the case … Mr Pasko, a former navy captain who went free after his initial trial two years ago and who had sought to clear his name … The panel of three judges discarded nine of the ten charges against Mr Pasko but found him guilty of high treason in the form of espionage … Mr Pasko had been accused of telling Japanese news organizations where the Russian navy allegedly dumped toxic waste in the Sea of Japan. His defence was based on a law that prohibits classifying data about environmental dangers.
>
> (*IHT*, 26 December 2001, p. 7)

'Mr Pasko was accused of espionage for leaking information on Russian naval toxic dumps to the Japanese media, which officials said he did in contravention of an oath of secrecy he had sworn as a military officer' (*FT*, 27 December 2001, p. 5).

> Pasko was also stripped of his rank after being found guilty of 'intending' to pass state secrets to the Japanese media … rather than being found guilty of passing state secrets to a foreign power, as initially alleged … The case has been going on for four years … and he had already been cleared of the treason and espionage charges two years ago. On that occasion he was found guilty of the lesser charges of abuse of office and he appealed, triggering the retrial … Pasko … won his first case and was retried because he refused to accept any element of guilt and appealed against the lesser conviction – for which he received an amnesty – in 1999 … Pasko was arrested at the end of 1997.
>
> (*Guardian*, 27 December 2001, p. 15)

27 December 2001.

> After nearly a year of threatening to end programmes aimed at helping Russia stop the spread of nuclear weapons, the White House has announced that it remains committed to an effort to help Russia dispose of hundreds of tonnes of military plutonium. The Bush administration, its concerns about the availability of nuclear weapons heightened since 11 September, said it would continue a programme to reduce the dependence of some Russian cities on nuclear weapons development and to provide alternative jobs for nuclear scientists. In addition, the White House said the Pentagon would seek to speed up a project to construct a chemical weapons destruction facil-

ity at Shchuchye, 1,600 kilometres (1,000 miles) south-east of Moscow, allowing for its earlier completion ... The move marked the culmination of the Bush administration's year-long review of Clinton-era programmes designed to work with Russia to prevent the spread of nuclear weapons. Essentially it left them all intact. Early in the administration Bush administration officials criticized many of the programmes as expensive and ill conceived and had threatened to eliminate them or greatly reduce their funding ... The White House review covered thirty programmes with a combined annual budget of $750 million ... The programmes involve mostly the Pentagon, the Energy Department and the State Department and pay for the dismantling of weapons facilities and the strengthening of security at sites where nuclear, chemical and biological weapons are stored. Bush administration officials say the goal is to make the programmes more cost-efficient and better managed.

(*IHT*, 29 December 2001, p. 5)

28 December 2001. 'Yesterday [28 December] ... the president of Ingushetia, Ruslan Aushev, announced his resignation ... His decision to resign appears to have been determined by a quarrel over the timing of the next presidential election' (*Daily Telegraph*, 29 December 2001, p. 19).

The president ... resigned in protest Friday [28 December] after the supreme court ruled he must serve out his five-year term. President Ruslan Aushev ... has supported efforts to reduce the term to four years and to hold elections next year [2001]. He said he was quitting to preserve constitutional order in the republic, which borders Chechnya. Mr Aushev was elected in 1998 to a five-year term, but the parliament adopted an amendment limiting the term to four years. The amendment later was made retroactive to cut short Mr Aushev's term.

(*IHT*, 29 December 2001, p. 2)

January 2002.

The United States and its allies are building an air base in Kyrgyzstan ... as a 'transportation hub' to house up to 3,000 soldiers and to accommodate warplanes and support aircraft. Engineers are also improving runways, lighting, communications, storage and housing at bases in Uzbekistan ... [The United States is] looking to expand US military engagement by increasing technical support and training exercises with their counterparts in the region ... The [US] deputy defence secretary, Paul Wolfowitz ... said bases and exercises would 'send a message to everybody, including important countries like Uzbekistan, that we have the capacity to come back and will come back in – we're not just going to forget about them'. The willingness of the Pentagon to put a long-term footprint in Central Asia underscores a broader shift by President George W. Bush ... [about] overseas troop deployments ... But too large or too long-term a US military presence could alarm Russia and China.

(*IHT*, 10 January 2002, p. 1)

Washington does not plan to maintain a permanent military presence in former Soviet Central Asia ... the general commanding the US-led Afghan campaign said Wednesday [23 January] ... [He] said that even without a troop presence the United States would remain involved in the region as it continued its campaign against violent militants.

(*IHT*, 24 January 2002, p. 6)

The American government's decision to deploy 3,000 American and allied troops in Kyrgyzstan, at a time when the war in Afghanistan has almost come to a close, has been unpleasant news for the Russians. It will be three times the number of American soldiers based in Uzbekistan ... Kyrgyzstan has agreed to a one-year deployment of the troops near the airport of its capital Bishkek.

(*The Economist*, 19 January 2002, p. 61)

'Turkmenistan ... is [simply] allowing overflights of [US] military aircraft' (*Guardian*, 10 January 2002, p. 14).

'Turkmenistan ... has allowed humanitarian aid cargoes to use its roads and airspace' (*FT*, 22 January 2002, p. 10).

8 January 2002.

The Bush administration has told Congress that many of the warheads, bombs and intercontinental missiles involved in the president's promised two-thirds reduction of deployed strategic nuclear forces over the next ten years would be kept in reserve under its new strategic policy.

(*IHT*, 10 January 2002, p. 3)

'The [US] administration argues that it must preserve the warheads it takes off weapons during the planned reduction, thus allowing for a relatively quick build-back to a force of 4,600 warheads' (*IHT*, 14 March 2002, p. 8).

[US] secretary of state Colin Powell [has] just confirmed that the USA, in announcing a reduction of its arsenal from 6,000 to 1,700–2,200 warheads, is talking not about actually destroying them, but about 'cutting back operationally deployed strategic nuclear forces'.

(*CDSP*, 2001, vol. 53, no. 51, p. 1)

25 January 2002. 'The Russian authorities may seek the extradition of Boris Berezovsky ... for alleged financing of Chechen rebels ... "illegal armed groups" ... the federal security service said yesterday [25 January]' (*FT*, 26 January 2002, p. 6).

11 February 2002.

A quarrel between the Russian Orthodox Church and the Vatican ... which has been simmering for some time, boiled over Monday [11 February] when the Vatican created four fully fledged Catholic dioceses in Russia. Patriarch Alexei II ... immediately accused the Vatican of trespassing on Orthodox territory and renewed charges that the Catholic Church was out to poach converts.

(*IHT*, 14 February 2002, p. 3)

'Russia's Orthodox Church lambasted the Vatican for raising four "apostolic administrations" in Russia to the status of bishoprics' (*The Economist*, 16 February 2002, p. 8).

('Via a satellite link from the Vatican more than 3,000 Russian Catholics gathered in Moscow were able to receive a live blessing from ... Pope John Paul II ... for the first time in history ... The decision to air the conference in Russia infuriated the Russian Orthodox Church ... Catholics in Russia number 600,000, while there are nearly 100 million Orthodox believers': *The Times*, 4 March 2002, p. 18. 'Patriarch Alexei yesterday [3 March] denounced an appearance by the Pope on a television screen in Moscow's Catholic cathedral as "an invasion"': *Daily Telegraph*, 4 March 2002, p. 12.)

12 February 2002.

> Russia's supreme court handed a partial victory to the military journalist Grigori Pasko on Tuesday [12 February], throwing out a secrecy order that formed part of the basis for his conviction for espionage ... The court ... [annulled] a 1996 order from the defence ministry that classified certain information as secret. The court found that the order was illegal because it was itself secret, so no one could know if they were violating it ... [Whether his treason conviction will be overturned] depends partly on whether the supreme court upholds a second government order ... prosecutors used to justify the treason accusation. That order, issued in 1990, forbids military officers from engaging in contact with foreign citizens unless it is part of their duty.
>
> (*IHT*, 13 February 2002, p. 5)

13 February 2002.

> Russia's supreme court on Wednesday [13 February] dealt a further blow to the treason case against ... Grigori Pasko, striking down a 1990 order that restricted contacts between military officers and foreigners ... Pasko's lawyers said the supreme court's decisions this week ... would strengthen Pasko's hand when the supreme court ultimately considered his appeal of the conviction.
>
> (*IHT*, 14 February 2002, p. 3)

'Yesterday's court ruling found that regulations banning military personnel with access to state secrets from mixing with foreigners were illegal because they contravened a separate law' (*Daily Telegraph*, 14 February 2002, p. 19).

18 February 2002.

> Russian investigators trying to determine the cause of the explosion that sank the submarine *Kursk* acknowledged for the first time that the sinking had not been caused by a collision with another vessel. They said that an obsolete torpedo had probably caused a blast aboard the nuclear-powered ship and that the use of the weapon was being discontinued ... Russia's prosecutor-general, Vladimir Ustinov, said: 'There were no objects in a

dangerous vicinity ... There are no facts that can point to the presence near the *Kursk* of foreign ships or submarines' ... It was the first time a Russian official had publicly ruled out a theory favoured by the Russian navy: that the *Kursk*, which sank on 12 August 2000, had collided with another vessel or a World War II mine ... Investigators ... said they had not yet drawn final conclusions. Officials gave the first confirmation yet that the explosion had been caused by a failure of one of the *Kursk*'s torpedoes ... Investigators promised to release final conclusions in May after the last portion of the submarine's bow is retrieved from the crash site ... President Vladimir Putin stripped Ilya Klebanov, who oversaw the inquiry into the *Kursk* disaster, of his post as deputy prime minister for the defence industry ... He would keep his second post as minister of industry, science and technology.

(*IHT*, 19 February 2002, p. 3)

Vladimir Ustinov ... lifted the taboo on criticizing the crew, accusing it of 'traditional Russian sloppiness' in neglecting basic safety procedures. The *Kursk* ... routinely went to sea with its systems for activating an aerial and buoy in the event of an emergency switched off, he said.

(*Daily Telegraph*, 19 February 2002, p. 12)

26 February 2002.

The editor of ... Ekho Moskvy ... the first radio station to broadcast from Russia without state control ... in 1990 ... says that he and dozens of other journalists are quitting rather than work for a news outlet that was becoming another voice of the state. Alexei Venediktov ... announced his resignation less than three weeks after a subsidiary of a state-controlled monopoly moved to seize control of the station's board of directors ... The station's board remained autonomous until this month [February], when Gazprom-Media exercised its rights as majority shareholder to name five of the nine directors ... Venediktov and twelve other journalists have bid in a state auction for two radio frequencies on the same FM band as Ekho Moskvy ... [In March there will be] an auction for a television channel that formerly belonged to the independent channel TV-6.

(*IHT*, 28 February 2002, p. 5)

6 March 2002.

Pavel Borodin ... [is found] guilty of money laundering ... The [Swiss] prosecutor ... ordered him to pay a fine of 300,000 Swiss francs ($177,000) ... Borodin [who is in Russia] has not yet decided whether to accept the ruling ... [or] go to trial.

(*IHT*, 7 March 2002, p. 5)

'In Minsk yesterday [6 March] Mr Borodin, now state secretary of the Union of Russia and Belarus, denied there was any case against him' (*Daily Telegraph*, 7 March 2002, p. 18).

The Salvation Army said yesterday [6 March] it had won permission to remain in Moscow after successfully appealing against court rulings that refused it charitable status ... Russia's constitutional court ... has overruled previous decisions ... The decision ends three years of legal wrangling that began when the Salvation Army applied for reregistration in response to a 1997 change in Russian law ... Despite being recognized in the rest of Russia the application was denied by Moscow officials ... But on 7 February the constitutional court ruled that, because the body had been registered before 1997, it could not be denied reregistration on the basis of the new requirements of the 1997 law ... There are 3,500 Salvation Army members in Russia and neighbouring countries that used to form the Soviet Union.

(*The Independent*, 7 March 2002, p. 9)

'The Salvation Army was banned ... in September [2001] ... The Salvation Army has been operating in Russia since 1992' (*Guardian*, 7 March 2002, p. 16).

French Mirage 2000-D fighter jets participated for the first time in military operations in Afghanistan this week, taking off from an airbase in ... Kyrgyzstan ... The sorties were a first for France and Kyrgyzstan ... Kyrgyzstan is a signatory to the CIS's collective security agreement, which in part requires a country to gain approval with the other members – former Soviet republics – before allowing foreign troops on its soil ... [Kyrgyzstan] says that Bishkek consulted with all members of the collective security agreement, as well as the Shanghai Co-operation Forum, which includes China, and encountered 'no problems'.

(*FT*, 7 March 2002, p. 12)

15 March 2002.

President Putin urged parliament Friday [15 March] to dismiss ... central bank chief [Viktor Gerashchenko] and appoint a deputy finance minister Sergei Ignatiev] as his successor ... [There have been] difficulties with the cabinet over control of the currency market and a recent dispute over ownership of Vneshtorgbank ... The central bank owns a controlling interest in Vneshtorgbank, and Gerashchenko has reportedly resisted the government's attempts to seize control of the bank. Gerashchenko has also resisted allowing the rouble to trade freely on open markets and blamed the cabinet for its recent drop. He has also resisted a government-initiated bill that would sharply curb the central bank's powers ... His current term was to end in September.

(*IHT*, 16 March 2002, p. 11)

President Vladimir Putin's nominee to run the central bank ... [is] Sergei Ignatiev, a deputy finance minister with a reputation for honesty, competence and pragmatism ... Most recently, as first deputy finance minister, he concentrated on closing loopholes in tax and customs rules to reduce evasion.

(*IHT*, 20 March 2002, p. 18)

'Viktor Gerashchenko abruptly resigned yesterday [15 March]. His removal drew praise from analysts who had criticized the Bank of Russia for keeping a strong rouble and for sluggish banking reforms' (*FT*, 16 March 2002, p. 10).

> A newspaper known for its reports on government corruption and the war in Chechnya has been fined £1 million in two libel cases, ten times the largest libel penalty in Russia. *Novaya Gazeta* said the fine was part of an effort by the Kremlin to close it down.
>
> (*The Times*, 20 March 2002, p. 21)

> A group of influential Russian businessmen, discreetly backed by the Kremlin, yesterday [27 March] won a bitterly contested battle over the broadcasting licence of TV-6 ... Media-Sotsium ... [beat] twelve other competitors to take over TV-6's frequency ... Yevgeni Primakov, the former prime minister and head of the Russian Chamber of Commerce, joined the bidding group at the Kremlin's behest ... Media-Sotsium is headed by Yevgeni Kiselyov ... Its other leaders included Anatoli Chubais, head of UES, the Russian power company, Oleg Deripaska, head of Russian Aluminium, Roman Abramovich, the principal shareholder in the Sibneft oil group and Arkadi Volsky, head of the Russian Union of Industrialists and Entrepreneurs ... Yesterday Mr Kiselyov rejected any idea that the Kremlin in any way supported his bid and called the results a victory for the free press.
>
> (*FT*, 28 March 2002, p. 8)

> Media minister Mikhail Lesin said that an alliance comprising the TV-6 team in partnership with ... Yevgeni Primakov had won a tender for the frequency on which the old TV-6 channel had broadcast ... Local media said Primakov was part of the Kremlin's solution to its dilemma about how to calm concerns about media freedoms while keeping an eye on TV-6's independent journalists.
>
> (*IHT*, 28 March 2002, p. 5)

'Some of the financial backers Chubais recruited are well known for their Kremlin ties, including Roman Abramovich, the wealthy governor of the far eastern region of Chukotka, and Alexander Mamut, a bank owner' (*IHT*, 27 March 2002, p. 5).

'Media-Sotsium [is] the non-profit partnership established by Yevgeni Primakov and Arkadi Volsky that was joined by Yevgeni Kiselyov's team of journalists' (*CDSP*, 2002, vol. 54, no. 13, p. 5).

17 March 2002. '[The USA] successfully completed the latest "kill" above the Pacific with a prototype missile defence interceptor ... The test was the sixth of its kind and the fourth successful interception' (*The Times*, 18 March 2002, p. 14).

3 April 2002.

> The Duma voted to appoint new chairmen to seven out of nine parliamentary committees previously run by the Communists and their allies, the

Agrarian Party. The Communists and Agrarians responded by resigning from the two committee chairs left to them. They also called on Gennadi Seleznyov, a Communist Party member, to resign from his post as speaker of the Duma ... The Duma has twenty-eight committees in all, overseeing the preparation of bills.

(*FT*, 4 April 2002, p. 13)

('The Communist legislators voted, seventy-eight to fifteen, last week to demand Seleznyov's resignation ... [But on 11 April] Seleznyov bluntly rejected demands by his fellow communist to resign': *IHT*, 15 April 2002, p. 3. '[On 25 May] Russia's Communist Party expelled three leading members ... Gennadi Seleznyov, speaker of the State Duma ... Nikolai Gubenko and Svetlana Gory-acheva, the heads of two Duma committees. The three had refused a party order to give up their posts: *FT*, 27 May 2002, p. 6.)

18 April 2002. President Putin (state of the nation speech):

I have already said that Russia today needs more ambitious goals and higher rates of economic growth ... In order to give our people a decent standard of living and ensure that Russia remains an important and full member of the world community and is a strong competitor, our economy must grow at a much faster pace ... We need to make substantial changes in the actual workings of government institutions Our country's tremendous capabilities are stymied by an unwieldy, sluggish and inefficient government bureaucracy ... The way the operation of the government bureaucracy is currently organized breeds corruption ... [which is] a direct consequence of restrictions on economic freedoms. All kinds of administrative barriers are overcome through bribery ... We have taken a significant step toward modernizing the judicial and legal system. Most of the necessary decrees, acts and laws have now been adopted. The funds to implement them have been appropriated. Now we need to effectively carry out the decisions that have been made ... Our country ... is already involved in world trade, but we are barred from helping to make the rules that govern it. That is retarding the development of the Russian economy and making it less competitive. Membership in the WTO should be a tool for protecting Russia's interest in world markets ... The development of the Russian economy is possible only if we gear ourselves toward the harsh demands of the world market ... [Companies that wanted] to sit behind a fence of protectionist quotas [were] absolutely doomed strategically ... [There is need for a] single economic state [for trade and investment with the EU] ... No one is going to war with us in the modern world ... but no one is really waiting for us either, no one will help us specifically. We have to fight for our place in the economic sun ... The military stage of the conflict [in Chechnya] may be considered concluded ... Only a year ago we counted how many bandits and terrorists there were – 2,000, 5,000 or 10,000. Today it is no longer important to us how many of them there are. We must know where they are ... [Peace there continues to be] disrupted by sorties of remaining bandits.

(*CDSP*, 2002, vol. 54, no. 16, pp. 1–6; *IHT*, 19 April 2002, p. 7, and 25 April 2002, p. 6; *FT*, 19 April 2002, p. 8; *The Economist*, 20 April 2002, p. 50; *Daily Telegraph*, 20 April 2002, p. 19)

28 April 2002. Alexander Lebed, governor of Krasnoyarsk since May 1998, is killed in a helicopter crash.

In the Ingushetia election, Alikhan Amirkhanov supported by former president Ruslan Aushev. Murat Zyazikov is pro-Kremlin. Turnout was more than 60 per cent. The first round was on 7 April. 'Aushev ... resigned in December [2001] after a dispute with the Kremlin over the length of his term in office' (*IHT*, 29 April 2002, p. 3).

6 May 2002.

The United States has renounced formal involvement in a treaty creating the first permanent war crimes tribunal ... The Bush administration has no intention of approving the treaty and now considered itself 'no longer bound in any way to its purpose and objective' ... The International Criminal Court gained the necessary international backing to come into being [on 1 July] when ten nations joined fifty-six others last month [April] in announcing their ratification of the treaty, which was negotiated in Rome in 1998. President Bill Clinton signed the treaty [in December 2000] but never submitted it to the Senate for approval.

(*IHT*, 7 May 2002, p. 6)

'[On 11 April] ten nations deposited their ratifications, increasing the number of countries ratifying the treaty to sixty-six, half a dozen more than the required sixty ... A tribunal was first proposed in the ruins of World War II' (*IHT*, 13 April 2002, p. 1).

13 May 2002.

The United States and Russia said Monday [13 May] that they had agreed to slash their strategic nuclear weapons stockpiles by roughly two-thirds and would sign a binding agreement when President George W. Bush visits Russia on 24 May [the visit beginning on 23 May] ... The deal ... essentially codifies nuclear weapons reductions that the Pentagon had already decided to make and that Russia could not afford in any case to put off ... Each side [will be allowed] to 'warehouse' some of their decommissioned nuclear arms and launchers rather than dismantle them ... The new accord ... calls for both sides to reduce their arsenals of active nuclear warheads by 2012 from their current levels of about 6,000 to between 1,700 and 2,200 ... The two sides will verify that the reductions are taking place ... The treaty would allow each side flexibility in deciding how it would lower its strategic nuclear arsenal to meet new ceilings ... The reductions [are] in the form of a treaty, which requires the approval of two-thirds of the [US] Senate.

(*IHT*, 14 May 2002, p. 1)

At that point [2012] the treaty is set to expire, leaving each side free to have as many weapons as it would like unless the accord is extended ... Each side can withdraw on three months' notice ... The Russians will be free to employ new land-based missiles with multiple warheads, such as the three-warhead version of the SS-27, and to keep old ones like the SS-18.

(*IHT*, 15 May 2002, p. 5)

'Either side can give only ninety days' (instead of six months') notice of with-drawal' (*The Economist*, 18 May 2002, p. 53).

The agreement concerns the 7,295 warheads that the United States has and the 6,094 that Russia has. Under the terms of the treaty both sides will be allowed to reduce their nuclear arsenals on their own terms ... suggesting that each side had the flexibility to keep the majority of the 4,000 warheads to be taken off its weapons in storage ... That freedom gives both sides latitude to hold warheads in reserve and continue producing nuclear weapons ... A US official said some weapons would be placed in deep storage and some would be stored as 'operational spares' and the Pentagon was working on the numbers ... A new bilateral commission will be established to ensure a transparent inspection process, including on-site inspections ... The treaty would cover only the countries' strategic nuclear arsenals – those capable of striking the other's territory. It ignores an estimated 8,400 tactical nuclear weapons that the Russians are estimated to have that they could use in the battlefield ... The Centre for Strategic and International Studies ... [estimates] that both coun-tries have an inventory of close to 31,000 warheads between them, though those in day-to-day deployment may only amount to 2,000 to 3,000.

(*FT*, 14 May 2002, pp. 1, 8)

'Mr Bush was originally seeking ... [an] informal oral agreement ... In this way he would have circumvented ratification by the Senate' (*The Independent*, 14 May 2002, p. 2).

14 May 2002. The foreign ministers of Nato countries and Russia agree to form the new Russia–Nato Council to replace the Nato–Russia Permanent Joint Council (set up in 1997). (The agreement was signed on 28 May by President Putin and Nato heads of government.)

Russia will for the first time become an equal partner at the table for joint discussions and actions on a range of issues – including non-proliferation, military co-operation and civil emergency planning, and other topics as agreed to in the future by the nineteen [Nato] member nations. But those nineteen nations ... will preserve full control over membership in the alli-ance and core military decisions and use of allied troops ... The two-day meeting [14–15] also continued Nato's review of requests for new member-ship from nine nations in Eastern Europe, and added a tenth applicant, Croatia, to the list. Foreign ministers repeatedly declined to signal which candidates were favoured for membership, but in their final communiqué agreed that nations invited to join the alliance at a planned meeting in Prague this fall should all come in at once.

(*IHT*, 15 May 2002, p. 1)

'Up to seven of these [ten East European states] are expected to receive an invitation to join the nineteen allies when Nato holds its next summit meeting in Prague in November' (*IHT*, 16 May 2002, p. 8).

The declaration [by foreign ministers] covers nine policy areas for joint decision-making: counter-terrorism, crisis management (which includes peacekeeping), non-proliferation, arms control, theatre missile defence, search and rescue at sea, military-to-military co-operation and defence reform, civil emergencies and new threats and challenges.

(*The Times*, 15 May 2002, p. 16)

'The agreement leaves Nato's core functions of mutual defence, military action and membership issues untouched. Full Nato members also reserved the right to withdraw from decision-taking by the Nato–Russian council should things go awry' (*Guardian*, 15 May 2002, p. 1).

'Any member can take an issue off the Nato–Russia agenda at any time, for any reason' (*IHT*, 30 May 2002, p. 6).

(The treaty, called the Treaty of Moscow, was signed in Russia's capital by Presidents Putin and Bush on 24 May. It needed to be ratified by both the State Duma and the US Senate. The two presidents issued a joint declaration, which included co-operation in areas such as security, counter-terrorism and energy.)

29 May 2002.

The EU recognized Russia as market economy ... The European Commission president ... said Wednesday [19 May] ... The decision will smooth Russia's path to joining the WTO and require the EU to consider Russian production costs, rather than those of proxy nations, before imposing sanctions for selling goods abroad for less than production costs.

(*IHT*, 30 May 2002, p. 11)

The change is likely to be formalized by September and will clear the way for a reduction in anti-dumping cases against Russia ... Next month [June] the USA is expected to take a similar step. In exchange Russia committed itself to 'the gradual elimination of restrictions to trade and other steps aimed at liberalization of its energy markets and the gradual implementation of market principles in its energy policies', without further indications of a possible timetable ... Commitments ... include eliminating an estimated $5 billion a year in energy subsidies.

(*FT*, 30 May 2002, p. 8)

('[On 6 June it was announced] that the United States had designated Russia a market economy ... Until now Russia has been considered a non-market economy under American anti-dumping laws ... US negotiators used a "surrogate" market economy country for comparison in disputes, which was often worse for the country charged with dumping. That status has hurt certain Russian industries – in particular steel and fertilizer ... Russian companies will [now] be able to use their own cost figures ... [However, Russian] gas and electricity ... are still partly subsidized. That might cost Russian producers a penalty, albeit a lower one in dumping disputes. Russia is also waiting for the US Congress to scrap the Jackson–Vanik Amendment [at present annually waived in reality], a 1974 sanction meant to enforce communist-bloc nations to allow free emigration. The amendment is obstructing Russia's entry to the WTO': *IHT*, 7 June 2002, p. 7.)

> A Moscow regional court declared Wednesday [29 May] that the shutdown in January of TV-6 ... was illegal ... [and] that MNVK, the company that held the TV-6 licence, should resume broadcasts within three months ... The journalists, led by Yevgeni Kiselyov, won the franchise only after forming a consortium with a number of wealthy supporters of the government, as well as former prime minister Yevgeni Primakov. The move was widely seen as a devil's bargain that gave the TV-6 journalists their jobs back, but at the price of avoiding any open criticism of the government in the future.
>
> (*IHT*, 30 May 2002, p. 6)

'[In May] Mr Putin ... unveiled a new advisory body, the Council of Legislators, for speakers of the regional parliaments. This body is supposed to encourage "best practice" in local legislation' (*FT*, 10 June 2002, p. 22).

9 June 2002. About 8,000 youths rioted in central Moscow after the national side lost to Japan in the soccer World Cup. Two men were killed.

13 June 2002.

> One day after the United States formally abandoned the 1972 Anti-Ballistic Missile Treaty [on 13 June], Russia ... [said on 14 June that] it was no longer bound by the 1993 Start 2 accord that outlawed multiple-warhead missiles and other especially destabilizing weapons ... The US Congress did not approve Start 2 until 1996 and refused a protocol that would have extended its implementation deadline. Russia's parliament approved the treaty and the new deadline in 2000, but only on condition that the United States did not abandon the anti-ballistic missile accord.
>
> (*IHT*, 15 June 2002, p. 5)

19 June 2002. 'Ilya Klebanov, the trade, science and technology minister, chairman of an official investigation into the [*Kursk*] disaster ... said ... "There remains only one version – a torpedo blast. The commission discounted a collision and a mine"' (*The Independent*, 20 June 2002, p. 11).

'The final report ... said Monday [1 July] that a torpedo fuel leak caused the explosion ... Ilya Klebanov said the *Kursk* was destroyed after a second explosion set off parts of the armaments stored in the first compartment' (*IHT*, 2 July 2002, p. 4).

Ilya Klebanov ... said that investigators had made their findings after key elements from the torpedo bay were raised from the bottom of the Barents Sea last month [June]. 'A thermal explosion of the class 298A PV torpedo caused the disaster. It happened as the result of a leak of hydrogen peroxide and the ignition of materials in the torpedo tube' ... he said.

(FT, 2 July 2002, p. 7)

('[On 26 July] the general prosecutor, Vladimir Ustinov ... said that he was closing an investigation into the sinking of the *Kursk* ... and would not be bringing criminal charges against navy commanders ... His criminal investigation ... had confirmed the earlier findings of a government commission, which said that it had been caused by a torpedo fuel leak': *IHT*, 27 July 2002, p. 4. '[It was announced] that leaking torpedo fuel – and not a foreign submarine or a Second World War mine – caused the explosions that sunk the *Kursk* ... It was announced that a practice torpedo exloded in the tube': *The Independent*, 27 July 2002, p. 12.)

On 19 June a Moscow court decided to convict Mr [Anatoli] Bykov of conspiracy to murder a business associate and punish him with a mere suspended sentence. Now he is back in his home city of Krasnoyarsk, where he once dominated business and politics alike ... [He once controlled] the city's great aluminium smelter, the second biggest in Russia ... Control of his smelter passed to the Russian Aluminium group, which now dominates the industry ... He still holds ... a seat in the Krasnoyarsk parliament.

(FT, 3 July 2002, p. 9)

26 June 2002.

The former KGB general Oleg Kalugin was sentenced in absentia Wednesday [26 June] to fifteen years in a labour camp for treason and spying for the United States ... [He] moved to the United States in 1995 ... [He] is the first KGB operative to be put on trial in absentia since the collapse of the Soviet Union ... [and was] stripped of his honours.

(IHT, 27 June 2002, p. 5)

(After 1 July 2002 trials in absentia would no longer be allowed.)

27 June 2002.

A Kremlin-backed bill to fight hate crimes and attacks by fascist groups has been adopted in a final vote in ... the State Duma ... despite the concerns of some rights activists that it may give too much power to the police. The deputies voted Thursday [27 June] by 274 to 175 to pass the bill, which was recommended by President Vladimir Putin during a speech in April after a series of attacks by young Russians on people of other ethnic backgrounds ... The bill ... defines the crime of extremism more fully and sets out tougher punishments for those convicted of it. It would also allow the authorities to suspend organizations suspected of conducting such activities, even before courts decide the organization is guilty. This is the part of the bill its critics find most objectionable. The authority to suspend organizations lies with the local police and prosecutors, two groups that are little trusted by Russians ... 'The definition of extremism is too unclear' [said one critic].

(*IHT*, 29 June 2002, p. 3)

[The bill on extremism] ... allows the interior ministry to suspend an organization and freeze its assets without a court decision if the ministry believes the organization to be 'extremist'. Supporters say the bill is needed to combat a rise in racist and neo-fascist activity ... Liberals criticize the bill on extremism as a potential threat to free speech.

(*FT*, 2 July 2002, p. 7)

Vladimir Putin yesterday [28 July] signed the law 'On countering extremist activity'. Extremist activity is defined as actions aimed at forcibly altering the constitutional system, inciting ethnic, racial or religious enmity; planning acts of hooliganism or vandalism in connection with political, racial and other kinds of intolerance; and also any actions aimed at violating human and civil rights and liberties. Print and manuscript documents intended for publication or other physical carriers of information containing calls for extremist activity are deemed extremist. The law provides that if a political party or public (or religious) organization falls under suspicion of planning extremist activity, the organization shall be sent a written warning that it might be shut down. If extremist activity 'creates a real threat' of harm a 'registration agency or other governmental agency' may petition a court to ban the organization. As soon as such a petition is filed the government agency has the right 'within the bounds of its jurisdiction' to suspend the organization's activity ... Many state deputies are not happy with the bill; they detected in it a secret intent on the part of the authorities to wage a battle not against extremism, but against the political opposition.

(*Kommersant*, 29 July 2002, p. 2: *CDSP*, 2002, vol. 54, no. 30, pp. 1–2)

The United States and its Group of Eight [G8] allies agreed Thursday [27 June] to spend $20 billion helping Russia dismantle stockpiled dangerous weapons ... President George W. Bush and President Vladimir Putin of Russia sealed the ten-year pact on Russia, the newest G8 member ... The leaders ... feared that Russia's old nuclear, biological and chemical weapons stockpiles could fall into terrorist hands ... Russia would abide by a series of conditions ... The United States will spend $1 billion a year for ten years on the programme. Europe, Japan and Canada will contribute a similar amount over the same time ... Russia agreed to provide its new G8 partners access to disposal sites, such as facilities where nuclear submarines are dismantled. Moscow also assured adequate auditing and oversight authority to its partners ... Russia ... finally won ... full-fledged membership in the elite G8, made up of the United States, Britain, Canada, France, Germany, Italy, Japan and now Russia. Russia was placed in the rotation to serve as host for a summit meeting for the first time in 2006.

(*IHT*, 28 June 2002, pp. 1, 4)

28 June 2002. 'Politicians approved a bill that, for the first time since 1939, established the right of conscientious objectors to do alternative, non-military service. They must, however, serve for at least three years compared with twenty-four months for regular conscripts' (*The Times*, 29 June 2002, p. 21).

29–30 June 2002.

> Mr Zyuganov's leadership [of the Communist Party] was yesterday [30 June] the focus of an attack by the New Communist Party, a splinter group launched by Andrei Brezhnev, a businessman, political dilettante and grandson of the late Soviet leader Leonid Brezhnev. Mr Brezhnev criticized 'stagnation' at the helm of the Communist Party, which Mr Zyuganov has headed since 1992 ... In May the Communists expelled three senior members ... The Communists ... saw a potentially more serious challenge emerge on Saturday [29 June] with the founding of the 'Party of Life', a self-styled grassroots movement seeking the support of Vladimir Putin ... The new Party of Life, a movement of indistinct ideology, joins other vaguely centrist movements ... Mr Putin sent a greeting to the party's inaugural congress on Saturday in which he welcomed the party foundation as 'testimony to the formation of civil society' in Russia and 'a good sign for the country' ... Sergei Mironov, speaker of Russia's upper house of parliament and a Putin ally, [was] present at the new party's inaugural congress. He is not a member of the new party but addressed the congress as a guest.
>
> (*FT*, 1 July 2002, p. 8)

'The [New Communist] Party is being formed from three existing communist parties' (*The Independent*, 1 July 2002, p. 9).

1 July 2002. The new Criminal Procedural Code begins to operate.

> [The code] replaces one written in 1960 ... [and] governs the prosecution of criminal cases and protects the rights of those accused ... Anyone accused of a crime must now appear in court within forty-eight hours, codifying the concept of habeas corpus into Russia's system. Defendants may demand a lawyer from the moment they are arrested and, when acquitted, will no longer be subjected to double jeopardy, except in the rarest instances. The code enshrines the fundamental concept of presumption of innocence and gives new responsibilities – and, in theory, independence – to judges, while it will gradually strip prosecutors of the enormous powers they have wielded over almost every step of any prosecution, from arrest to trial. Defence lawyers will have the right to challenge the admissibility of evidence, throwing out, among other things, evidence collected by wiretaps without a warrant ... [In] Russian justice ... corruption is rife ... Russia is still a country where suspects can be detained indefinitely, where arbitrary, politically and even economically motivated prosecutions are common, where coercion of suspects is rampant, where the police can stop anyone on the street without reasonable cause ... Many of the code's most revolutionary

changes are being phased in ... By 1 January [2003] jury trials will be required for all serious cases, expanding experiments that have had mixed results in nine of Russia's eighty-nine regions since they began in 1994. By January 2004 only courts will be able to issue warrants for arrests, searches or seizures of property ... The new code is intended to introduce an adversarial process, with prosecutors required to argue the facts of any case while the defence will have new powers to challenge evidence, witnesses and procedures. Judges, who until now have worked closely with prosecutors, are supposed to act as detached arbiters ... Overcrowding [exist] in Russia's notoriously abysmal prisons, where there are today nearly 1 million prisoners.

(*IHT*, 2 January 2002, p. 10)

('The vast majority of this nation's courts have not rendered a verdict by a jury since 1917 ... The old system produced a 99.6 per cent conviction rate, partly because judges were forced to share the prosecutor's burden of proving a defendant's guilt ... No longer are judges expected to interrogate witnesses, order expert analysis and otherwise pursue the evidence if the prosecutor fails to do his job ... [In December 2002] the Duma voted to give ten of Russia's eighty-nine regions, including Moscow and St Petersburg, more time to prepare ... Judges in pilot regions say they struggle to find citizens willing to do their duty for $4 a day. Those who ignore a summons face a fine of $250 that is rarely, if ever, imposed ... In the United States ... only 5 per cent of criminal cases are tried by jury; the rest are disposed of through a plea-bargaining system that Russia has so far rejected': *IHT*, 23 December 2002, p. 4. '[On 13 December] the State Duma passed ... amendments to the new Russian Federation Code of Criminal Procedure that call for the introduction of jury trials to be phased in gradually until 2007 ... Juries were originally supposed to exist throughout the country as of 1 January 2003. However, many regions are not ready for this innovation': *CDSP*, 2002, vol. 54, no. 50, p. 9.)

Under the old system the defendant is presumed guilty almost from the moment of arrest and the conviction rate is more than 90 per cent. Those convicted, often on the basis of confessions extracted by torture, are likely to serve their sentences in a Siberian labour camp or an overcrowded prison. The collapse of communism has led to underpaid judges and police investigators taking even more bribes ... The code also recommends forms of punishment other than imprisonment. Russia has the world's largest *per capita* prison population, with more than a million held in prisons and penal colonies.

(*The Times*, 2 July 2002, p. 13)

Human rights activists say acquittals in Russian trials amount to 0.05 per cent of cases ... Jail terms are common for minor offences ... [The] prison system is disease-ridden and overcrowded ... Under the new system the detainees are entitled to a two-hour meeting with a lawyer before being questioned and can only be remanded for two days without an extension granted by a judge ... But money and corruption lie at the heart of Russia's judicial system and the new code does not solve that. A detailed study of corruption released in May found that Russians spend $274 million a year in bribes to the courts ... The government has pledged to increase the number of judges from 17,000 and to boost their low salaries.

(Guardian, 2 July 2002, p. 11)

Generally speaking, the defining characteristic of Soviet criminal procedure was its pre-trial element ... For all practical purposes the question of the guilt of the person on trial was decided during the investigative stage, if not earlier. Consequently, the courts did not acquit defendants, with very rare exceptions. (Acquittals continue to be extremely rare, accounting for just 0.4 per cent of all cases tried.) ... People sometimes turn themselves in to law-enforcement authorities or give self-incriminating testimony ... Such testimony is often beaten out of people with fists, truncheons or other improvised means. Torture has become a natural element of the investigation ... The new code states that any testimony given by a suspect or defendant in the course of a preliminary investigation without his lawyer present and that is not corroborated in court is inadmissible and has no legal validity.

(CDSP, 2002, vol. 54, no. 27, pp. 1–2)

Whereas in the past the prosecutor's office supervised and monitored the preliminary inquiry and the investigation, now it will perform only general functions with respect to overseeing these activities, as well as the task of supporting the prosecution. The prosecutor will support the prosecution in court and his main function will be to evaluate *before* the trial stage of a criminal case the evidence collected by the investigator and decide whether it is sufficient to take the case to court ... As of today [1 July 2002], at the request of the defence, any criminal case in which a person is charged with a grave crime may be tried by jury in those regions where the practice already exists and six months from now juries will be seated in all members of the Federation.

(p. 3)

The Indem Fund, a social research organization, estimates that corruption costs Russian businesses $33 billion in bribes every year. In a survey of Russians published in March by the fund, nearly half of respondents said bribery is either a necessity or makes life easier ... In June ... [Putin raised by presidential decree] the salaries of all civil servants by 50 per cent.

(IHT, 19 July 2002, p. 2)

In 2002 Georgi Satarov, an adviser to President Boris Yeltsin in the period 1992–7, published two studies.

Satarov left the government in 1997, when, in his words, being an intellectual and remaining a bureaucrat were mutually exclusive ... His
research Institute, Information for Democracy, surveyed 7,504 Russians to
piece together the first comprehensive picture of Russian graft. The
researchers estimated that Russian citizens pay about $3 billion in bribes
annually – about half of what they pay in income tax. Business owners
were found to fork over a whopping $33 billion to keep things running
smoothly, a sum just less than half of ... federal budget revenues [in
2002].

(*IHT*, 11 February 2003, p. 5)

'Prosecutor-general Vladimir Ustinov has estimated that Russia's rampant
corruption costs the country $15 billion a year' (Mark Galleotti, *The World
Today*, 2002, vol. 58, no. 8/9, p. 37).

AIDs came belatedly to Russia ... The first case was reported in 1987, but
infections did not reach epidemic proportions until the mid-1990s ... In the
last year alone the total number of registered HIV infections more than
doubled to 177,354 from 87,177 in 2000 ... Officials estimate that the
number of Russians infected may have reached 1 million.

(*IHT*, 22 July 2002, p. 5)

12 July 2002. 'Ella Pamfilova was appointed chairwoman of the Russian president's human rights commission, replacing Vladimir Kartashkin in the leadership
post ... The human rights commssion is an advisory body ... established in
1993, at which time it was headed by Sergei Kovalyov' (*CDSP*, 2002, vol. 54,
no. 28, p. 8).

The Russian atomic energy minister said Friday [12 July] that Moscow
would take back spent nuclear fuel from a Russian-built nuclear power
station in Iran. Russia is helping Iran build a 1,000-megawatt pressurized
water reactor at Bushehr in a deal worth $800 million. US officials fear
spent fuel from the project could provide Iran with weapons-grade radioactive material and bolster its efforts to develop nuclear weapons. Atomic
energy minister Alexander Rumyantsev said Russia had worked out a protocol with Iran in November 1998 specifying that Russia would take back the
spent nuclear fuel from Bushehr. But because Russia at the time did not
have a law allowing the import of such material, it could not be put in force,
he said.

(*IHT*, 13 July 2002, p. 2)

14 July 2002.

The political council of the Russia movement, led by State Duma speaker
Gennadi Seleznyov, met yesterday [14 July] ... The assembly ... voted to
form a new leftist party that has been provisionally named the Russia Social

Party ... The meeting resulted in a decision to hold the new party's founding congress in early September.

(*CDSP*, 2002, vol. 54, no. 28, p. 8)

August 2002.

A presidential decree signed this week to attack corruption could pave the way for wide-ranging civil service reform in Russia over the coming months ... President Vladimir Putin approved a document calling for legality, integrity, the elimination of conflicts of interest and the avoidance of outside influence for public servants ... [But the] measure has only voluntary status ... Legislative reforms [are] being developed by a committee led by Dmitri Medvedev, a senior Kremlin official.

(*FT*, 15 August 2002, p. 6)

The ministry of justice has put the brakes on the process of forming such a [Boris Berezovsky's] party by refusing to register the Liberal Russia movement, which the well-known entrepreneur finances and heads, as a political party ... [The] party is co-chaired by Boris Berezovsky.

(*CDSP*, 2002, vol. 54, no. 59, p. 7)

29 August 2002.

Negligence, incompetence, defective equipment and breaches of military rules and safety procedures may have contributed to the sinking of the *Kursk* ... a Russian government newspaper said yesterday [29 August] ... The report is based on the newspaper's own research and on the results of a Russian government investigation ... *Rossiskaya Gazeta* publishes both official notices and general news.

(*FT*, 30 August 2002, p. 8)

Numerous safety lapses, technical errors, bad management and simple sloppiness may have contributed to [the disaster] ... [according to a report] in the official newspaper *Rossiskaya Gazeta* ... a state mouthpiece not known for its investigative journalism ... The newspaper said [the report] was based on previously secret evidence compiled by Vladimir Ustinov's prosecutors ... Poor maintenance and inadequate training in the Russian navy played a role in the sinking ... [There were] technical problems with the torpedo's rubber gaskets [highly volatile torpedo propellant leaked and came into contact with kerosene and metal], failure to follow standard procedures and falsification of documents after the explosions ... [There were] technical mistakes, violations, negligence and defective parts.

(*IHT*, 31 August 2002, p. 3)

9 September 2002. 'The Russian navy began to blow up the front section of the *Kursk* ... to destroy military secrets such as torpedo warheads, communications equipment and computers' (*The Times*, 10 September 2002, p. 18).

22 September 2002. Alexander Khloponin wins Krasnoyarsk election (in the second round of voting) for governor to replace Alexander Lebed. (who died in a helipcopter crash in April). 'Alexander Khloponin [is] the former head of Norilsk Nickel ... For the past two years [he was] governor of the autonomous region of Taimyr [in the north]' (*FT*, 24 September 2002, p. 10). (The result was disputed. On 3 October 2002 Putin signed a decree appointing Khloponin acting governor until a fresh election could be held.)

7 October 2002. Vladimir Putin is fifty years of age.

> The three leaders of Liberal Russia [including Sergei Yushenkov] ... decided last week to boot ... Boris Berezovsky ... after he announced his latest plan to forge a 'patriotic opposition'' together with the communists and gave an interview to an extreme nationalist newspaper, *Zavtra*, urging common cause against the Kremlin. In a statement Monday [7 October] the three Liberal Russia leaders in the State Duma ... demanded that Berezovsky resign. And they threatened to oust him at a party council on Wednesday [9 October] if he refused. The tycoon's proposed alliance with the communists and nationalists was 'totally unsuitable', they said ... Berezovsky said he had no intention of quitting. He has poured 'several million US dollars' into the party, he said, and will wait and see if his allies follow through on their threat ... Berezovsky blamed the controversy on influence from the Kremlin ... 'My position has not changed at all in the last few months,' Berezovsky said. 'They know my position well, which is that I will support anyone who works against the authoritarian regime Putin is trying to create. I will work with anybody who will fight against that.' In recent months the Liberal Russia Party has been refused official registration by the Kremlin-controlled justice ministry, which the party is challenging in the courts. Berezovsky said party leaders hoped that by dumping him they could persuade the authorities to register. Without such status Liberal Russia cannot participate in next year's parliamentary election.
>
> (*IHT*, 9 October 2002, p. 3)

9 October 2002. A population census, lasting eight days, begins. The last census was in 1989. One was planned for 1999, but was postponed because of the financial crisis of August 1998.

11 October 2002.

> A task force fighting money laundering removed Russia from its blacklist of countries that fail to counter the crime ... 'As a result of the implementation of significant reforms to its anti-money laundering system, Russia was removed' from the list, the task force said ... [The] president of the [OECD] task force called the decision a 'great success for Russia and the interna-

tional community in the fight against money laundering and terrorist financing' ... The eleven countries that remain on the blacklist are; the Cook Islands, Egypt, Grenada, Guatemala, Indonesia, Burma, Nauru, Nigeria, Philippines, St Vincent and the Grenadines, and Ukraine.

(*IHT*, 12 October 2002, p. 9)

'[The task force ... [traces] movements of drugs and terrorist funds' (*The Independent*, 12 October 2002, p. 13).

14 October 2002.

An interceptor rocket destroyed a Minuteman-2 missile high above the Pacific in the latest test of the US missile defence system. The test Monday night [14 October] was the seventh such test for the Missile Defence Agency and the fourth consecutive success.

(*IHT*, 16 October 2002, p. 7)

18 October 2002.

Valentin Tsvetkov, governor of the Magadan region in the far east [of Russia] ... was assassinated [gunned down] ... in Moscow ... [He] was elected in 1996 ... Investigators said they believed the murder stemmed from conflicts the governor had had with business interests in his home region. Nikolai Petrov, a specialist on Russian regions ... said Tsvetkov had fought with regional business magnates over control of the lucrative local mineral and alcohol industries. 'Governors are less and less politicians and more and more businessmen,' Petrov said ... [Magadan is known for] its rich mineral deposits; a quarter of the country's gold is extracted there ... In the last few months alone a member of parliament, a vice-governor, a deputy railroad director, a deputy mayor and a regional lawmaker have been killed in separate incidents.

(*IHT*, 19 October 2002, p. 2)

'Valentin Tsvetkov ... is the first regional boss and the highest official to be assassinated since President Vladimir Putin came to office two years ago' (*FT*, 19 October 2002, p. 2).

Contract killings of businessmen, bankers and even politicians are common in Russia; police registered 327 last year [2001]. But Mr Tsvetkov was the first official of such rank to be killed in post-Soviet times ... It is not uncommon for high state officials in Russia to own or direct private companies in tandem with their administrative duties. Mr Tsvetkov ... owned a gold-refining plant and had reportedly been trying to bring the region's gold-mining industry under his control ... Eight parliamentary deputies have been murdered since 1992 but no case has been solved. The most recent case was Vladimir Golovlyov, shot dead near his home in Moscow in

August. Many observers believe that Mr Golovlyov's murder may also have been connected to his business dealings.

(The Independent, 19 October 2002, p. 17)

('Vladimir Golovlyov, one of the co-founders of Liberal Russia [has been shot dead]': *The Times*, 22 August 2002, p. 14. He was under investigation for embezzlement: *Guardian*, 21 August 2002, p. 14.)

23–26 October 2002. See the the section on Chechnya for the Moscow theatre siege.

30 October 2002. 'A Moscow court has issued an arrest warrant for … Boris Berezovsky in connection with the [alleged] theft of cars from Russia's biggest car maker' (*Guardian*, 31 October 2002, p. 17).

'Attempts by liberal deputies in parliament to set up a commission of inquiry were stopped by forces loyal to the government' (*New York Review of Books*, 2002, vol. XLIX, no. 20, p. 58).

5 November 2002. 'Russia has formally sought the extradition from Britain of … Boris Berezovsky, who is accused of fraud … The request … [is] based on charges issued by a Moscow court' (*The Times*, 6 November 2002, p. 16). (On 28 March 2003 his aslyum request to the British government was turned down. Berezovsky converted from Judaism to Orthodox Christianity in 1994.)

8 November 2002. The United Nations Security Council approves a resolution on Iraqi weapons of mass destruction by fifteen votes to nil.

11 November 2002. Two Russian diplomats are expelled from Sweden accused of industrial espionage (relating to the Ericsson telecommunications company). (On 2 December Russia expelled two Swedish diplomats.)

15 November 2002.

[The State Duma] by 336 votes to fifteen … approved legislation that will make Cyrillic the country's only legal alphabet. The amendments target autonomous regions such as Chechnya and Tatarstan, which has changed the written form of its dialect from Cyrillic to Roman.

(The Independent, 16 November 2002, p. 15)

19 November 2002. 'Armed men seized a Russian trawler … 400 nautical miles … [from] Vladivostok' (*IHT*, 20 November 2002, p. 1).

22 November 2002. President Bush visits Russia the day after Nato formally invited seven more countries to join as full members in May 2004. The seven were the Baltic States of Estonia, Latvia and Lithuania, Bulgaria, Romania, Slovakia and Slovenia.

16 December 2002.

Copyright and trademark owners in Russia, which has one of the highest rates of software piracy in the world, were given new protections under a law signed Monday [16 December] by President Vladimir Putin. The law, for the first time, defines counterfeit products and requires the destruction of seized bootlegged goods.

(*IHT*, 17 December 2002, p. 15)

17 December 2002.

President George W. Bush said Tuesday [17 December] that he would begin deploying a limited system to defend the United States against ballistic missiles [the initial part of the so-called Missile Defence System] ... The plan calls for ten ground-based interceptor missiles at Fort Greely, Alaska, by 2004 and an additional ten interceptors by 2005 or 2006 ... Bush said the 'initial capabilities' would also included sea-based interceptors and sensors based on land, at sea and in space ... Bush's announcement came six days after the latest test of the system failed when an interceptor rocket did not separate from its booster rocket and destroy a Minuteman-2 intercontinental missile as planned. Three of eight tests [since 1999] of the interceptors have been judged failures by the military.

(*IHT*, 18 December 2002, p. 1)

18 December 2002. The Russian foreign ministry issues a statement:

Moscow with regret follows the activation of the attempt by the United States to create a so-called 'global anti-missile defence'. Now, after taking a political decision to deploy in 2004 several strategic interceptors with support from space, the realization of these plans has entered a new destabilizing phase ... Consigning its principles to oblivion can lead only to the weakening of strategic stability, a new senseless arms race in the world, including the spread of weapons of mass destruction, and diverting resources to counter today's real challenges and threats, above all, international terrorism.

(*IHT*, 19 December 2002, p. 5)

5 January 2003. 'The Russian navy has decided to scrap about one-fifth of its ships because of a lack of funds to maintain them, its commander said in an interview published Sunday [5 January 2003]' (*IHT*, 6 January 2003, p. 3).

Admiral Vladimir Kuroyedov:

The navy will decommission ships to keep a check on unreasonable expenses ... I regret to say that it will reduce the number of navy ships by about one-fifth of their current number ... The majority of those ships will never sail again even if funding were to be boosted ... We are categorically short of money. Since 1996 the navy has received only 12 per cent of the funds needed to keep our ships afloat and technically fit.

'Russia refuses to say how many warships it has but Western estimates put the total at about 300' (*Daily Telegraph*, 6 January 2003, p. 14).

'The Russian navy ... is thought to comprise about 300 ships and is the second largest fleet after the United States' (*The Times*, 7 January 2003, p. 16).

10 January 2003. 'President Vladimir Putin and prime minister Junichiro Koizumi of Japan signed an agreement [in Moscow] on Friday [10 January] calling for an accelerated effort to resolve the long-standing territorial dispute over the Kuril Islands' (*IHT*, 11 January 2003, p. 3).

23 January 2003.

> A former navy captain-turned-journalist who was jailed after he accused the Russian navy of dumping nuclear waste at sea was freed yesterday [23 January 2003] and vowed to carry on his legal battle to clear his name. Grigori Pasko spent twenty months in prison in 1997–9 before he was cleared of treason charges, and thirteen months more before a court in Russia's far east gave him a conditional release for the remainder of a four-year sentence on espionage charges.
>
> (*FT*, 24 January 2003, p. 13)

4 February 2003. 'A man accused of masterminding a pyramid scheme ... has been charged with fraud ... Sergei Mavrodi, founder of MMM investment fund, which collapsed in 1994, could not be tried until now because he had parliamentary immunity' (*Guardian*, 5 February 2003, p. 15).

5 February 2003.

> The State Duma ... gave final approval to a law banning the use of foreign or offensive words ... The State Duma overwhelmingly approved a bill entrenching Russian as the 'state language' and barring 'offensive', 'obscene' and 'vulgar' words. Foreign words are also outlawed when Russian equivalents exist. The legislation provided no specific penalties.
>
> (*IHT*, 6 February 2003, p. 2)

> Moscow has passed a new law to protect the Russian language from ... threats of swearing, slang and, above all, English ... Anyone caught using slang or westernisms such as 'biznes', 'menedgment' or 'mirchendaizing' faces up to two months 'corrective work' – the Russian term for community service ... The law will try to purge advertising and the media of westernized words. However, the punishments for offenders are so slight that the legislation is largely symbolic. Swearing is defined as 'light hooliganism' and attracts a [light] fine or community service ... There are exceptions to the new law: journalists, for instance, may swear or use slang if this 'forms an integral part of [the] artist's intention or scheme'.
>
> (*Guardian*, 7 February 2003, p. 18)

> Although private speech is exempt, government officials, the media and the advertising industry will all be required to find Russian equivalents to

foreign words as soon as President Putin passes the bill into law. Exceptions are also allowed for artistic usage ... The new law, which envisages sentences of up to two months' community service, also aims to curb the use of swear words in the Duma.

(*The Times*, 10 February 2003, p. 16)

11 March 2003.

The Kremlin transferred control of border patrols and government communications to the federal security service, the FSB ... Power was taken from the KGB in the early 1990s ... The reforms return these old internal powers to the FSB, although the foreign reconnaissance service remains responsible for the KGB's role in foreign intelligence. The reorganization has involved abolishing two ministries, the federal agency for government communications and information ... and the federal tax police service. The defence ministry and the FSB take on the job of becoming the government's ears and eyes. The ministry of the interior takes control of the tax police's remit ... Mr Putin has created a new agency, the state committee for drug control, which will be headed by the current presidential envoy to the St Petersburg region, Nikolai Cherkesov, another former intelligence officer.

(*Guardian*, 12 March 2003, p. 15)

President Vladimir Putin abolished Russia's border guards, its tax police and a clutch of other agencies and handed their duties to cabinet-level departments ... The staff and resources of the tax police [are to be transferred] to the new State Committee for Control of Narcotic and Psychotropic Substances. Enforcing tax laws will fall to the interior ministry, which already oversees most law enforcement matters ... [and which] only recently added immigration issues to its portfolio ... [The Federal] Border Service will be folded into the Federal Security Service, Russia's domestic intelligence agency. Putin also abolished the office in charge of secure communications, the Federal Agency of Government Communications and Information, and divvied up its duties for the FSB and the defence ministry. He ordered the defence ministry to consolidate all weapons purchasing in a single new office ... In some ways Putin is undoing what President Boris Yeltsin did more than a decade ago in an attempt to shatter the KGB's pervasive power ... In Soviet times both the border service and government communications were arms of the KGB.

(*IHT*, 12 March 2003, p. 8)

The Federal Security Service (FSB) ... [has been strengthened] by presidential decree ... The FSB also took over the Border Guard, thus tripling its troop numbers to around 300,000 ... [There was a] lack of prior debate – there was absolute secrecy until the announcement ... [and] a lack of clarity over their [the decrees'] legality ... [questions about] the right to abolish state structures founded on Russian laws, which can only be amended by parliament.

(Bacon and Renz 2003: 26–7)

The FSB will now control 200,000 border troops ... The federal agency for government communications and information is being eliminated and its functions are being split between the ministry of defence and the FSB. And the defence ministry is gaining another committee, which will handle all matters related to defence contracts ... The [new] state committee for defence contracts ... has been assigned the functions of a single purchasing agent for conventional weapons ... Valentina Matvienko ... deputy prime minister for the social sphere ... will now be the president's authorized representative in the north-west district. Viktor Cherkesov, who had held that job ever since the institution of authorized representatives was created, will now head a new agency – the state committee for control of narcotic and psychotropic substances.

(*CDSP*, 2003, vol. 55, no. 10, pp. 1–5)

Until early March she ... Valentina Matvienko ... was a deputy prime minister in the federal government, the highest-ranking woman in Russian politics ... In March Mr Putin removed her from the federal government in order to name her as presidential envoy to north-west Russia, one of the seven envoys overseeing different regions of Russia. Her predecessor, Viktor Cherkesov, was named as Russia's new drugs tsar.

(*FT*, Survey, 1 April 2003, p. vi)

('Valentina Matvienko, Russia's outgoing deputy prime minister for social affairs, hinted yesterday [7 April] that she may stand for election in the region of St Petersburg, which could make her the country's first female regional governor ... Speculation about her bid for the race, which is scheduled for spring next year [2004], has intensified since her appointment last month [March] as Mr Putin's special representative for the north-west of the country ... Last week Vladimir Yakovlev, the incumbent governor, announced that he would not stand for a third term. He won re-election in May 2000 ... Mr Putin has criticized Mr Yakovlev, who beat his political mentor Anatoli Sobchak, the deceased former mayor of St Petersburg, in 1996': *FT*, 8 April 2003, p. 14.)

Eighteen judges took their seats Tuesday [11 March 2003] at the world's first permanent war crimes court ... [The court, based in The Hague, is backed by] eighty-nine countries but faces a boycott by the United States ... The court came into existence last July [2002] when the Rome Treaty was ratified by the requisite number of countries ... The administration of President Bill Clinton signed the Rome Treaty, but the signature was withdrawn by George W. Bush. Neither Russia nor China has endorsed the court ... but only the United States actively tried to block the court's creation. Bush has secured bilateral treaties with twenty-two countries granting US citizens immunity from arrest warrants issued by the international court. Congress also adopted legislation empowering the president to use 'all means necessary' to free Americans taken into the court's custody ... In the last decade the jurisprudence of war crimes has been honed in the special courts established for the former Yugoslavia, Rwanda, Sierra Leone and East Timor. The International Criminal Court will have jurisdiction to punish war crimes, including genocide, in any country that has ratified the statute – but only if that country has refused to prosecute suspects itself. Non-party states can ask the court to intervene, as can the UN Security Council.

(*IHT*, 12 March 2003, p. 3)

The United States has managed to win agreement from twenty-four countries never to surrender to the court any Americans who happen to be within their borders, offering the same in return ... [But] many of the countries that have signed such bilateral agreements have not, in fact, joined the court – and so would not be required to surrender suspects to it. No EU country has such an agreement with America. The only EU-candidate country to do so, Romania, has not submitted the agreement to its parliament for approval.

(*The Economist*, 15 March 2003, p. 40)

12 March 2003.

Russia and the United States signed an agreement that will shut down Russia's last three remaining nuclear reactors that produce weapons-grade plutonium within eight years ... Under the deal the United States would help replace the reactors, all in Siberia, with fossil-fuel plants.

(*IHT*, 13 March 2003, p. 3)

13 March 2003.

[It is reported] that the extensive art collection salvaged in Germany by Viktor Baldin, a former Soviet Army officer, would be returned from the Hermitage to the Bremen museum ... In 1997 parliament voted to declare artwork taken from Nazi collections and German state institutions, including museums, as just compensation for Russia's wartime losses and to allow the return of art only to Nazi victims and religious and charitable institutions.

(*IHT*, 15 March 2003, p. 5)

18 March 2003. 'A senior prosecutor ordered the culture ministry not to return to Germany a collection of drawings ... taken in 1945 by a Soviet army captain, saying they legally belonged to Russia' (*The Times*, 19 March 2003, p. 20).

20 March 2003. The United States starts its attack on Iraq, aided principally by British troops, without submitting a second resolution to the UN Security Council (thus saving Russia from having to make a formal decision about whether to use its threatened veto). Australia and Poland also sent troops into action. ('Poland has sent fifty-six troops': *IHT*, 3 April 2003, p. 4. 'Poland ... has fifty-four soldiers involved in ground operations in Iraq': *The Baltic Times*, 10–16 April, p. 2. 'Poland is to send 1,500 soldies there [to postwar Iraq] to keep peace and will command one of the four occupation zones': *IHT*, 30 May 2003, p. 5.) The United States insisted on referring to 'coalition' forces. The Saddam

Hussein regime effectively collapsed after three weeks, US troops entering the centre of Baghdad on 9 April, although some fighting continued.

The action of the United States deeply divided world opinion, including Nato itself. France and Germany were leading critics of the United States, suggesting that UN inspectors should have been given more time to complete their task. Russia and China (the latter less vehemently) were broadly in agreement with France and Germany.

China issued a statement on 20 March:

> We strongly urge relevant countries to immediately stop military action. They ignored the opposition of most countries and peoples of the world and went around the UN Security Council to begin military action against Iraq ... The norms of international behaviour [have been violated].
>
> (*IHT*, 21 March 2003, p. 3; *Daily Telegraph*, 21 March 2003, p. 8)

But both countries remained on relatively good overall terms with the United States.

Nevertheless, relations between Russia and the United States were aggravated by two issues in particular:

1   US accusations that Russian companies were providing weapons to the Saddam Hussein regime.

('The United States said Monday [24 March] that it had "credible evidence" that Russian companies had sold Iraq banned equipment, including anti-tank missiles, night-vision goggles and equipment to jam Global Positioning System devices ... that the coalition forces use to guide bombs, military aircraft and even troops on the ground ... [The United States] said the alleged sales had been a matter of concern "over the past year" ... [The United States] said Putin promised to look into the matter. But earlier foreign minister Igor Ivanov ... said that Russian experts had examined the matter "meticulously". He said US inquiries had begun in October [2002], that Russia had repeatedly responded as recently as 18 March and that nothing illicit had been found': *IHT*, 25 March 2003, p. 3. 'Moscow has denied that Russian companies have been selling military equipment to Iraq ... Last night [25 March] the Kremlin gave its version of the conversation between [Bush and Putin] ... in which Mr Putin insisted no such sales had taken place: *The Independent*, 26 March 2003, p. 7. 'The United States ... has provided new evidence to support its case ... In addition to providing banned technology Washington alleges that personnel from the Russian companies have been operating the equipment on the ground in Iraq ... Igor Ivanov, Russian foreign minister, yesterday [26 March] repeated denials that any transfers had taken place: *FT*, 27 March 2003, p. 5.)

2   Russian concern about US spy planes using Georgian airspace (the United States claiming that the flights were for the purposes of combating terrorism).

('[Russia] has complained about American spyplanes flying over Georgia': *The Economist*, 5 April 2003, p. 44. 'Russia criticizes US spy plane movements over Georgia': *FT*, 4 April 2003, p. 4. The flights were near the Russian border, the first being on 27 February: *CDSP*, 2003, vol. 55, no. 12, p. 5. Eduard Shevardnadze: 'Georgia's support for the United States will mean active future involvement by that country, along with Russia and other states, in resolving the conflict in Abkhazia: *CDSP*, 2003, vol. 55, no. 11, p. 7. '[On 1 April] the Georgian defence minister said ... that Georgia is prepared to provide the United States with "any form" of assistance in the operation against Iraq ... In March the Georgian parliament ratified an agreement under which the Georgian side undertook to put its military installations at the Americans' disposal and gave them permission to cross the border without visas and to import any kinds of weapons duty free: *CDSP*, 2003, vol. 55, no. 13, pp. 17–18.)

The following were significant developments:

President Putin (17 March): 'The Russian leadership continues to believe that an expansion of armed conflict is a mistake. Twenty million Moslems live in Russia. We cannot ignore their views' (*CDSP*, 2003, vol. 55, no. 11, p. 1).

President Putin (20 March):

The United States launched military action against Iraq today ... These military operations are being conducted contrary to world public opinion, and contrary to the principles and norms of international law and the UN Charter. Nothing can justify this military action, be it charges that Iraq has supported international terrorism – we have never had any information to that effect – or a desire to change the political regime in that country, something that is in direct violation of international law and is a matter that only the citizens of that country can decide. Finally, there was no need for military action to answer the main question directly posed by the international community, namely this: does Iraq have weapons of mass destruction? And if it does what must be done to destroy them and according to what timetable? Moreover, at the time the operation began, Iraq did not pose any danger to either its neighbours or other countries and regions of the world, since the country is weak both militarily and economically, especially after a ten-year embargo. And especially since international inspectors were working there. On the contrary, their efforts had recently led to significant positive changes ... [UN] Resolution No. 1441 ... did not authorize the use of force ... The military action against Iraq is a big political mistake. I have already mentioned the humanitarian aspects of the matter. But the threat of collapse of the established security system is of no less concern. If we allow international law to be supplanted by the law of 'might makes right' ... then one of the basic principles of international law – the principle of the inviolable sovereignty of states – will be called into question ... The vast hotbed of instability that arose today will grow and have negative consequences in other regions of the world ... The central role in resolving crisis situations in the world, including the Iraqi situation, should belong to the UN Security Council.

(*CDSP*, 2003, vol. 55, no. 11, p. 5)

President Vladimir Putin on Friday [28 March] called the US-led war against Iraq the most serious crisis since the end of the Cold War and warned that it threatened global stability. [Putin said] the war is 'in danger of rocking global stability and the foundations of international law … The only correct solution to the Iraqi problem is the immediate end to military activity in Iraq and resumption of a political settlement in the UN Security Council' … Russian officials have expressed concern that Russian companies, which have signed numerous contracts to develop the Iraqi oil industry, may be replaced by American companies after the war. Russia is also concerned over $8.5 billion in Soviet-era debt that is owed to Russia by [Iraq].

(*IHT*, 29 March 2003, p. 4)

'Baghdad's Soviet-era debt stands at around $8 billion and at some $16 billion if interest payments are included' (*IHT*, 12 April 2003, p. 3). ('The total value of Russia's oil contracts with Saddam Hussein is somewhere around $30 billion. Iraq owes Russia about $8 billion': *CDSP*, 2003, vol. 55, no. 13, p. 9.)

'Fewer than 5 per cent of Russians supported military intervention in Iraq' (*FT*, 8 April 2003, p. 21). 'All the opinion polls show that roughly 10 per cent of Russian citizens do support the United States' (*CDSP*, 2003, vol. 55, no. 13, p. 5).

Recent polls show a drop in the number of Russians who hold positive views of the United States, while 75 per cent see it as an "aggressor" … [Some] 71 per cent of Russians cite the United States as the main threat to world peace.

(*CDSP*, 2003, vol. 55, no. 11, p. 6)

The State Duma [on 18 March] … postponed ratification of the Russian–American Treaty on the Reduction of Strategic Offensive Potentials … [which requires] Russia and the United States to reduce and limit their strategic nuclear warheads … The deputies had planned to ratify the treaty today [19 March].

(*CDSP*, 2003, vol. 55, no. 11, p. 18)

(The treaty was not ratified by the State Duma until 14 May 2003.)

'[On 21 March] Putin told officials of the CIS … that the Iraq war could destabilize their nations. "The war against Iraq is a decision that might trigger unpredictable consequences, including increased extremism," he said' (*IHT*, 22 March 2003, p. 3).

The two top leaders of Russia's Moslems split Thursday [3 April] over the question of whether to proclaim a jihad against the United States. Supreme Mufti Talgat Tadzhuddin, the leader of an Islamic council claiming to represent all Russia, announced that the council's twenty-nine Islamic departments had voted unanimously by fax to declare a holy war ... While declaring a holy war, he did not say in detail what the council was asking ordinary Moslems to do, beyond contributing money for Iraqi war relief and weapons purchases. At the same time the Chief Mufti of Russia, Ravil Gainutdin, rejected any call for a holy war: 'Jihad against the United States has been declared by Saddam Hussein. This is enough' ... Gainutdin's Russian Council of Muftis controls nineteen Islamic departments, fewer than Tadzhuddin's, but is said to claim roughly as many adherents. The two Muftis are rivals in a long-running contest for leadership of Russia's Moslems ... Russia's justice ministry issued a statement saying that as long as the Mufti was calling on Russian Moslems to offer aid and moral support to Iraqis, 'there is nothing blameworthy' in the appeal. 'If attempts are made to hire mercenaries, buy weapons and transfer them to Iraq, this is a crime,' a senior ministry official [said] ... The number of Moslems in Russia is only roughly known. Informed estimates place the figure as between 14 million and 20 million, mostly in central Russia and in the south-western Caucasus Mountains region.

(*IHT*, 4 April 2003, p. 3)

(President Putin: 'Twenty million Moslems live in Russia. We cannot ignore their views': *CDSP*, 2003, vol. 55, no. 11, p. 1).

Talgat Tadzhuddin [said that] ... Russian Moslems ... would raise money 'to buy armaments for fighting Americans and food for the people of Iraq' ... The last time jihad was declared by Russia's Moslems was in 1941 against the Germans ... Ravil Gainutdin said that Mr Tadzhuddin represented only a tiny proportion of Russia's Moslems. Mr Gainutdin and Mr Tadzhuddin enjoy equal popularity in Russia, but represent only a small number of Moslems ... There are 3,600 registered mosques in Russia and Mr Tadzhuddin speaks for Muftis from only twenty-nine of them, but who represent several thousand Moslems.

(*The Times*, 4 April 2003, p. 2)

[Tadzhuddin declared] a jihad against the United States and Great Britain. This is just the second time Russia's Moslems, who are loyal to Russia, have declared jihad in their entire history. In 1941 Moslem leaders in the USSR declared jihad against Hitler. Tadzhuddin did not call for overt military attacks. Russia's Moslems, he said, have other means of waging jihad and are using the money to buy arms for the struggle against America and food for the Iraqi people ... He wields influence on only a third [of Moslems] ... A sizeable number of adherents of Islam in Russia are affiliated with alternative 'non-Tadzhuddinist' ecclesiastical administrations ... [A] statement from the Russian justice ministry said: 'If he [Tadzhuddin] is referring to providing moral and financial support to his co-religionists, then nothing prejudicial is at issue here. But if attempts are made to recruit mercenaries or to buy arms and send them to Iraq, then these actions are subject to prosecution under criminal law' ... Gainutdin responded with a 'counter-declaration' in which he called on Russia's Moslems to remain peaceable and wage war on no one.

(CDSP, 2003, vol. 55, no. 13, p. 7)

Talgat Tadzhuddin ... [is] chairman of the Moslem Spiritual Board, based in the city of Ufa, in Bashkortostan ... Neither they [Tadzhuddin and Gainutdin] nor anyone else can claim to speak for Russia's Moslems ... No one imam has widespread appeal ... Moslems number anywhere from 11 million to 25 million, or 7 per cent to 17 per cent of the population, including those who are culturally Moslem but do not practise the religion ... Wahhabism is a purist form of Islam founded in the eighteenth century and now prevalent in Saudi Arabia. The Soviet authorities first used the term to label all enemies in the Afghanistan war in the 1980s and it was later applied to radicals in Chechnya and other parts of the North Caucasus, whatever their religious sect. Wahhabism and extremism do exist there; but both are imports ... Radicalism has only appeared in the Caucasus in the past five years, according to Galina Yemelianova ... The desperation after years of war and poverty, she says, made some people receptive to the preaching of missionaries from the Middle East and itinerant mujahidin from Afghanistan. In other areas, she says, it is a tiny phenomenon.

(The Economist, 10 May 2003, pp. 38–9)

The prosecutor of Bashkortostan issued an official warning yesterday [4 April] to Talgat Tadzhuddin ... against making statements that 'foment religious discord' ... Bashkortostan's prosecutor ... noted that his declaration of a Moslem holy war 'foments religious discord' and cautioned him against violating the federal law 'On countering extremist activity' ... Meanwhile, the Russian prosecutor-general's office warned the leadership of the Central Ecclesiastical Administration of Moslems of Russia that any further steps along the lines of the Mufti's declaration of jihad against America would lead to the organization's dissolution.

(CDSP, 2003, vol. 15, no. 14, p. 5)

'Talgat Tadzhuddin ... has been labelled a false prophet and apostate. This was the reaction his call for a holy war drew [on 14 April] from the Council of Muftis of Russia, chaired by Tadzhuddin's long-time opponent Ravil Gainutdin' *(CDSP*, 2003, vol. 55, no. 15, p. 20).

President Vladimir Putin called Friday [11 April] for a leading role for the United Nations in postwar Iraq as the leaders of France, German and Russia met in St Petersburg ... UN general-secretary Kofi Annan cancelled his plans to attend earlier in the week. And prime minister Tony Blair of Britain ... also turned down an invitation from Putin to attend the gathering ... President Putin: 'The main task is to urgently return the Iraqi settlement process to within the framework of the United Nations ... [We] must do everything to preserve the stability of the system of international law, which is based on the supremacy of the United Nations ... It is good that the

Saddam Hussein regime has fallen. We said for a long time he had to be brought down. We did not defend him, we said it should not be done by force ... Even in its dying throes the regime did not use weapons of mass destruction. We still do not know that it had any.'

(*IHT*, 12 April 2003, p. 3)

President Putin (29 April):

Until clarity is achieved over whether weapons of mass destruction exist in Iraq, [UN] sanctions should be kept in place ... No weapons have [yet] been found ... Sanctions can only be removed if there is no suspicion, which should be subject to a Security Council vote ... It is only the Security Council that is in a position to lift those sanctions; after all they introduced them ... The question is, where is Saddam [Hussein]? Where are his arsenals of weapons of mass destruction? Perhaps Saddam is still hiding somewhere in a bunker underground, sitting on cases of weapons of mass destruction and is preparing to blow the whole thing up and kill hundreds of thousands of people. We do not know what the situation is. What we want is to ensure that there is no ambiguity and that the threat has been eliminated ... Perhaps their plan is to transfer these weapons to terrorist organizations. We simply do not know. Until we get answers to these questions we cannot feel safe and secure ... If something is found there, some empty barrels, then the UN inspectors could be summoned ... If decisions are being made by just one member of the international community and with other members being required just to subscribe to those decisions, that is something we would not find acceptable.

(*FT*, 30 April 2003, p. 1; *Daily Telegraph*, 30 April 2003, p. 4;
Guardian, 30 April 2003, p. 1)

On 22 May 2003 the UN Security Council approved a slightly modified US/UK resolution on the governance of Iraq by the occupying powers and the lifting of economic sanctions on the country.

The strongest CIS support comes from Uzbekistan, seen as tacitly seeking quid pro quo in the form of help against internal Islamic radicalism ... [The United States listed thirty countries worldwide giving it] 'unconditional support' ... [The list includes] three CIS countries – Azerbaijan, Georgia and Uzbekistan; the three Baltic States – Latvia, Lithuania and Estonia; and the former East bloc countries of Bulgaria, Hungary, Poland, Romania, Slovakia and the Czech Republic.

(*CDSP*, 2003, vol. 55, no. 11, p. 7)

Belarus was very critical of the US-led war against Iraq. President Lukashenko (16 April 2003):

[The] armed US and British invasion of Iraq [is] in contravention of international norms ... What America wanted was not Saddam Hussein, not Iraq and not even its oil, but the establishment of a new world order that gives the sole superpower special rights to use military force as it sees fit. From now on the norms of international law can no longer protect the integrity and sovereignty of a state ... The Russian press and the foreign press are asking: 'Who is next in the axis of evil?' And they point to Belarus ... Today Belarus is the only faithful and battleworthy ally of the Russian Federation.

(*CDSP*, 2003, vol. 55, no. 15, p. 21)

('Last spring [2002] the [US] State Department accused it [Belarus] of training Iraqis in the use of S-300 surface-to-air missiles': *IHT*, 21 November 2002, p. 6. 'Belarus is accused of training Iraqis in the operation of air defence missiles': *IHT*, 9 November 2002, p. 4. 'Belarus has been accused of training Iraqi military officers': *The Independent*, 16 November 2002, p. 14. 'Ukraine and Belarus have both denied providing weapons systems or sensitive technology to Iraq in violation of United Nations sanctions ... Officials in Minsk disputed assertions that Belarus had helped Iraq reconstitute its anti-aircraft defences and fuelled dual-use materials and technology that could help Saddam Hussein develop weapons of mass destruction': *IHT*, 26 September 2002, p. 6.)

A few hours after the war began Ukraine's Supreme Council dispatched to Iraq a [550-man] special battalion trained to deal with radioactive, chemical and biological contamination ... The decision ... did not come easily ... The country's president [Leonid Kuchma], who initiated the action, emphasized that 'Ukraine will not participate in the military action ... [The battalion] will provide assistance in protecting the civilian population within the area of hostilities.'

(*CDSP*, 2003, vol. 55, no. 11, pp. 7–8)

Parliament yesterday [5 June] agreed to commit more than 2,000 peacekeepers to Iraq ... [as] part of a Polish-led force of at least 7,000 troops due to go to Iraq in July to help stabilize the region between Basra and Baghdad ... Although Ukraine still opposes the US-led coalition's decision to disarm Mr Hussein by force, Kiev asked to be included in the coalition in late March, during the second week of the war.

(*FT*, 6 June 2003, p. 7)

('Relying on an analysis of clandestine tape recordings ... in which a voice believed to be Kuchma's was heard discussing smuggling the radar system to Iraq ... the United States has concluded that President Leonid Kuchma personally approved a plan in July 2000 to sell Iraq an advanced radar system that can detect approaching aircraft without their pilots' knowledge. Although there is no definitive proof that the sale was made, the government has "some indications" that the radars are now in Iraq ... The American conclusion ... led the government to suspend a $55 million-a-year aid programme to Ukraine this month, pending a review of American policy ... Other crucial assistance – for example, aid to help Ukraine dismantle its Soviet-era nuclear programmes – is unaffected by the suspension ... Over the last five years Ukraine has become the world's sixth-largest arms supplier': *IHT*, 25 September 2002, p. 8. 'Ukraine and Belarus have both denied providing weapons systems or sensitive technology to Iraq in violation of United Nations sanctions': *IHT*, 26 September 2002, p. 6. 'The United States said yesterday [24 September] ... [that it had concluded] that the Ukraine president had personally approved the sale of air defence radars to Iraq ... [and that] it was suspending aid to Ukraine's central government, worth $54 million a year, ... [But] the United States would continue aid to local and regional governments, as well as the private sector and non-government organizations ... US officials said they had concluded that a tape recording of Mr Kuchma approving the sale of radars to Iraq for $100 million was authentic': *FT*, 25 September 2002, p. 3. 'The report released Tuesday [26 November] by a team of US and British experts said a Ukrainian contract to sell the sophisticated equipment to China might have been altered to allow its resale to a third country. The experts who visited Ukraine last month [October] ruled out a direct transfer of the Kolchuga systems to Iraq. But they left open the question of whether Ukraine covertly sold the equipment to Baghdad, saying Ukrainian officials had been unco-operative and evasive': *IHT*, 27 November 2002, p. 4. 'An investigating team ... concluded that no direct sale had been made, but raised the possibility that an intermediary had been used, possibly China ... The investigators said they had been unable to track four "missing" radar systems ... The experts said Ukraine accounted for only seventy-two radars ... British and American experts said there was no evidence that Ukraine had sold the radar systems to Iraq "under openly declared contracts", but concluded that "covert or illegal arms transfers, particularly with the complicity of third parties, remained a credible possibility"': *Daily Telegraph*, 27 November 2002, p. 16. 'American and British experts have criticized Ukraine for failing to provide conclusive proof that Kiev did not sell an aircraft detection system to Iraq in breach of UN sanctions': *IHT*, 6 November 2002, p. 3.)

> Kyrgyzstan has become the only country in post-Soviet Central Asia where large-scale, well-organized protest demonstrations against the war in Iraq have been held ... Bishkek's official view remains unchanged: the situation should be put back in the hands of the UN as quickly as possible.
>
> (*CDSP*, 2003, vol. 55, no. 15, p. 22)

Prior to the actual war in Iraq, Ariel Cohen analysed the positions of the CIS countries.

> Kazakhstan and Kyrgyzstan are the two states that pay most attention to their great power neighbours [Russia and China] and take an anti-war stance ... [although] President Nursultan Nazarbayev has called on Iraq to follow Kazakhstan's experience in destroying weapons of mass destruction ... The Caucasus states have cast their lot with the Anglo-American coalition. Georgia and Azerbaijan consider Washington their main protector and benefactor. So does Uzbekistan. All three countries view Russia with suspicion ... The United States did not submit a request to Azerbaijan for the use of aerodromes which would house American airplanes should a military operation in Iraq be launched ... Azerbaijan also took pains to co-ordinate its

position with Moscow ... Armenia has traditionally excellent ties with the Arab countries and a thriving diaspora in Lebanon and Syria. Armenian foreign policy is also viewed as pro-Russian. Nevertheless, the statements of the Armenian foreign minister sound surprisingly pro-American.

(Ariel Cohen, *Rusi Newsbrief*, 2003, vol. 23, no. 3, pp. 29–30)

17 April 2003.

Sergei Yushenkov, a legislature and a co-chairman of ... [the] Liberal Party, was shot and killed on Thursday night [17 April] in front of his home in Moscow. The assassination, the second fatal shooting of a Liberal Party leader in eight months, occurred hours after Yushenkov announced that he had registered to run candidates in parliamentary elections scheduled for December ... Yushenkov had a reputation for upright behaviour ... He was known for his unyielding opposition to Russia's two wars in Chechnya ... In the Duma he was aligned first with the Union of Right Forces ... But he later quit to join the Liberal Party, a movement financed by ... Boris Berezovsky ... Its alliance with Berezovsky quickly soured last fall [2002] when it was revealed that he had quietly been courting support from the Communist Party for his opposition to Putin. The party expelled Berezovsky in October [2002] ... Eight months ago another co-chairman of the Liberal Party, Vladimir Golovlyov, was killed in what appeared to be a professional assassination ... Golovlyov had been under investigation for political corruption in connection with the privatization of state property in the mid-1990s. But in a radio interview then Yushenkov said he believed that the killing was politically inspired.

(*IHT*, 18 April 2003, p. 5)

He [Yushenkov] was the third politician to be gunned down in Moscow in seven months ... He was also fiercely critical of the security services, the FSB ... In November [2002] the governor of the far-eastern region of Magadan was assassinated ... in a central Moscow street ... Mr Golovlyov, whose body was found on 21 August last year [2002], had been under investigation for the alleged misappropriation ... of state money earmarked for social benefits and investment in the southern Ural region of Chelyabinsk, the area he represented. The murder occurred weeks after he was stripped of his parliamentary immunity from prosecution.

(*Guardian*, 18 April 2003, p. 20)

('As the head of a privatization scheme in the early 1990s, he [Golovlyov] was alleged to have embezzled large sums of money from people whose power later grew as his did not': *The Economist*, 26 April 2003, p. 37.)

Mr Yushenkov ... was the tenth national politician in the country to be assassinated in an apparent contract killing in the past decade ... Mr Yushenkov had tried to cut ties with ... Boris Berezovsky ... after Mr Berezovsky said he would support the Communist Party ... to limit votes for the pro-Kremlin United Party in the elections. Mr Berezovsky said yesterday

[18 April] that he had come to an agreement with Mr Yushenkov to continue funding Liberal Russia at a meeting in London a month ago.

(*FT*, 19 April 2003, p. 7)

Sergei Yushenkov was the tenth Russian Duma deputy to be murdered since 1994 and the second leader of the Liberal Russia Party to die in a hail of gunfire in less than a year. He had just won the right of his liberal opposition party to take part in Russia's upcoming parliamentary elections ... Russia's central electoral commission continued – until last Thursday [17 April] to deny the party the vital recognition needed to participate in the parliamentary elections in December ... Yushenkov and a few supporters attempted – and failed – to pass a Duma resolution demanding a full investigation into evidence that the FSB security service might have played a role in the ... series of devastating apartment bombs ... in the autumn of 1999 ... Like all past killings of Duma deputies, Golovlyov's murder has never been solved.

(*The Independent*, 19 April 2003, p. 22)

1 May 2003. 'Yevgeni Nazdratenko, former governor of the Primorsk region in Russia's far east, has been appointed by President Vladimir Putin, as deputy head of the state "security council", only three months after being suspended as head of the state fisheries commission' (*FT*, 2 May 2003, p. 12). ('Prime minister Mikhail Kasyanov temporarily relieved Yevgeni Nazdratenko of his duties as chairman of the state fisheries committee yesterday [14 February]': *CDSP*, 2003, vol. 55, no. 7, p. 9. '[On 14 March it came to light that he had] begun performing his official duties again. The order reinstating him was signed by Yevgeni Nazdratenko himself': *CDSP*, 2003, vol. 55, no. 11, p. 12.)

[In Moscow] on May Day thousands gathered to hear a leading figure of the Kremlin's wholly owned-and-operated political party, United Russia, denounce President Vladimir Putin's government as a tool of business moguls and its economic and social policies as 'a disgrace' ... The mayor of Moscow, Yuri Luzhkov, a founder of one United Russia faction, charged that the government had ignored the economy but was 'serving the oligarchs', a tiny and widely detested coterie of billionaire industrialists With crucial parliamentary elections in December [2003] signs are emerging that the Kremlin's hand-picked party is in trouble ... Putin's overwhelming popularity – roughly three-quarters of Russians approve of him – shows no signs of ebbing. But in opinion polls this spring [2003] United Russia has taken a beating, with its approval rating falling from nearly 30 per cent last summer [2002] to the low twenties. The Communist Party meanwhile has racked up small gains, generally matching or beating United Russia's rating. Its strategists insist that the party is gaining support among the young and among intellectuals who have been the mainstays of Putin's free-market, generally pro-Western policies ... Today United Russia is the dominant party in the powerful lower house of parliament, with 152 of its 450 seats. The Communists have eighty-two.

(Michael Wines, *IHT*, 3 May 2003, p. 4)

The second congress of United Russia opened on 29 March 2003.

The chairman of the party's supreme council, Russian minister of internal affairs Boris Gryzlov, began his report to the congress with praise for the president ... The minister followed Putin's behest to 'separate the flies from the cutlets' – in this case the government from the president ... There is nothing sensational about the minister's statement, and everyone has long been aware of United Russia's main gripes against the government: rising electricity rates, low pay for employees in the budget-funded sectors, and problems in agriculture. Moreover, Putin himself authorized criticism of the cabinet of ministers during his recent meeting with United Russia's leaders. 'You spotted the weakness of certain of the government's proposals and intervened in time,' the president told party leaders two days before the congress. Gryzlov unexpectedly took a swipe at the oligarchs as well. 'Under our constitution the party that wins an election does not form the government. Because government in our country is not party-based, influence groups linked with big capital have acquired an excessive role, appropriating political functions for themselves. But we need parties that function like corporations, not corporations that act like parties.' The topic of party affiliation for Category A government officials is a major sore point for United Russia. A bill permitting government ministers to hold executive positions in political parties has been floating around the Duma for a long time, but so far it has failed to win the 300 votes needed to pass a constitutional law. So Gryzlov and other United Russia bigwigs are having to go all this time without party membership cards.

(*Vemya Novostei*, 31 March 2003, p. 1; *CDSP*, 2003, vol. 55, no. 13, p. 10)

2 May 2003.

The United States struck another blow against the new International Criminal Court on Friday [2 May] by signing an agreement with Albania to exempt each other's citizens from prosecution ... Albania was the thirty-second country, most of them small states, to agree to the US demand ... US officials have warned countries that military aid will be cut off unless they sign the agreements by July ... Secretary of state Colin Powell ... joined the foreign ministers of Albania, Croatia and Macedonia to sign a 'US–Adriatic Partnership Charter' designed to speed the entry of the three countries into Nato.

(*IHT*, 3 May 2003, p. 4)

4 May 2003. 'A Russian Soyuz speacecraft delivered a three-man, US–Russian crew to earth yesterday [4 May] in the first landing following the [1 February 2003] Columbia space shuttle disaster [which led to the suspension of the US shuttle flights]' (*FT*, 5 May 2003, p. 8).

8 May 2003.

Russia halted some airline flights from China and crimped entries along the 4,198-kilometre Chinese border Thursday [8 May] after the authorities said that they had tentatively logged the nation's first known case of severe acute respiratory syndrome, or SARS … Federal health officials said they were 'almost certain' that a twenty-five-year-old man in Blagoveshchensk, a city of 215,000 on Russia's far eastern border with China, was ill with the disease in a hospital there … The most sweeping of the measures, which were announced on Thursday, was the temporary closing of all border checkpoints that are unable to medically screen incoming visitors. At the remaining checkpoints medical examinations will be required for visitors from nations identified by the World Health Organization as SARS hotspots.

(IHT, 9 May 2003, p. 5)

('A local man was tentatively diagnosed in early May with Russia's only known case of SARS … The border crossing points were reopened this weekend, with up to 200 tourists allowed to cross daily "under strict medical surveillance"': *IHT*, Tuesday 27 May 2003, p. 5.)

16 May 2003. President Vladimir Putin (state of the nation speech):

In the next ten years we need to at least double our GDP … We are confronted with serious threats. Our economic foundation, although it has become noticeably stronger, is still shaky and very weak. The political system is not developed enough. The state apparatus is inefficient and most sectors of the economy are uncompetitive … Everything in our country has to be competitive … Administrative reform has been stalled for too long. The government clearly needs some help. We need to cut the bureaucracy's powers by directive, not through attempts at persuasion … [There is] an acute shortage of qualified people, at all levels of government … The frequency of changes in the tax system exceeds any acceptable level, which says something about the quality of the work; the outlines of the tax system should be set and remain stable for years … The size of the population continues to diminish. Poverty is receding very slowly. A quarter of our citizens still have incomes below the subsistence level … Can Russia seriously counter these threats if our society is divided into small groups, if we are concerned only with our own narrow-minded group interests, if parasitic sentiments grow, not subside, and these sentiments are fuelled by bureaucracy's complacent attitude toward the fact the national wealth is not protected and accumulated but often wasted away … Based on the results of the upcoming elections to the State Duma, I believe it will be possible to create a professional and efficient government that will have the support of a parliamentary majority … [There is need to] strengthen the role of parties in public life, based on the outcome of the upcoming elections to the State Duma … Russia must be a country with modern, well-armed forces … The strengthening and modernization of our nuclear deterrent forces will be a significant component of the reform of our armed forces … I can inform you that at present the work to create new types of weapons, weapons of the new generation, including those regarded by specialists as strategic weapons, is in the practical implementation stage ... [Starting in 2008 the term of compulsory military service will be one year instead of two].

(*IHT*, 17 May 2003, pp. 1, 4; *FT*, 17 May 2003, p. 6; *CDSP*, 2003, vol. 55, no. 20, pp. 1–4)

[President Putin called for the modernizing of] Russia's armed forces by 2010 ... He called for full convertibility of the rouble ... President Vladimir Putin ... leant his weight to calls for a shift in power away from the Kremlin towards a parliamentary system of government ... His slightly ambiguous remarks were widely interpreted ... as suggesting that future responsibility for creating the government would be shifted from the president to the parliamentary majority ... It would reflect an electoral strategy focused on distancing responsibility for the government's actions from the Kremlin ... A stronger parliamentary system would also provide a way for Mr Putin to prolong his own ruling powers beyond the current two-term, eight-year limit as president, if he were then to be leader of the dominant party in future elections.

(*FT*, 17 May 2003, p. 6)

('President Vladimir Putin ruled out suggestions yesterday [20 June] that he would strengthen his powers by changing Russia's constitution to extend his term in office, while stressing that the country would not shift from a presidential to a parliamentary republic. He said that changes would contribute to a climate of instability which he had been fighting to overcome. The comments at a press conference damped speculation of a constitutional modification, after he had earlier said a five-year term might be better [than the current four-year term]': *FT*, 21 June 2003, p. 9.)

21 May 2003.

Russia, the EU and the United States on Wednesday [21 May] signed a nuclear safety treaty aimed at cleaning up Russia's atomic waste. The Multilateral Nuclear Environmental Programme for the Russian Federation provides a legal framework for handling spent atomic fuel from, for example, decommissioned Russian nuclear-powered submarines.

(*IHT*, 22 May 2003, p. 4)

22 May 2003. The UN Security Council approves a slightly modified US/UK resolution on the governance of Iraq by the occupying powers and the lifting of economic sanctions on the country.

Vadim Pokrovsky of the Russian Centre for AIDS prevention and Treatment ... said that at least a half-million Russians now carry the HIV virus and that the number could be as high as 1.5 million ... Russia first began recording HIV infections in the mid-1990s, fifteen years after the epidemic surfaced in the United States ... [Some] 850,000 Americans [are] believed by the US Centers for Disease Control to carry the HIV virus. The [total] US population is almost twice that of Russia ... which is about 147 million.

(*IHT*, 23 May 2003, p. 4)

27 May 2003.

St Petersburg began its 300th anniversary yesterday [27 May] ... Heads of state from around the world will be travelling to the city for a series of summits this week ... The discussions will continue as they fly to Evian [France] for a full [three-day] meeting of the G8 on Sunday [1 June].

(*FT*, 28 May 2003, p. 10)

President Putin met President Bush on 1 June.

28 May 2000.

The Federation Council ratified the accord, known as the Treaty of Moscow [Treaty on the Reduction of Strategic Offensive Potentials], in a 140-to-five vote with two abstentions ... The State Duma ratified the treaty earlier this month [on 14 May] and the US Senate approved it in March.

(*IHT*, 29 May 2003, p. 8)

('[Presidents Putin and Bush] put their final signatures to the Treaty of Moscow [on 1 June]': *Guardian*, 2 June 2003, p. 4.)

29 May 2003.

Up to 600,000 [between 200,000 and 600,000] Russians are to be moved from remote parts of Siberia and the Arctic, officials announced yesterday [29 May]. The government's programme is being partly financed by the World Bank ... The idea came in 1998 ... The project has been in a pilot phase for several years ... The effort is intended to provide assistance only to those who want to leave.

(*Guardian*, 30 May 2003, p. 18)

3 June 2003. '[At] the G8 summit [in France] ... President Vladimir Putin announced that Moscow would "stop all nuclear exports" to Iran until it signed an additional protocol with the United Nations' nuclear agency' (*FT*, 3 June 2003, p. 8).

The Additional Protocol allows UN inspectors with minimal advance notification ... Moscow has yet to heed Washington's pleas that it stop building Iran's first nuclear reactor ... Iran said Monday [2 June] that the United States could help it build reactors as a way of ensuring that Teheran kept its word not to develop atomic weapons ... US officials have already dismissed the idea, floated last week by Russia.

(*IHT*, 3 June 2003, p. 3)

16 June 2003.

[President Putin] named one of his long-standing political rivals to a senior cabinet position ... Vladimir Yakovlev, the city's [St Petersburg's] current governor, would become one of the federal government's six deputy prime ministers, in charge of housing utilities, construction and architecture ...

Yakovlev beat the late Anatoli Sobchak, Mr Putin's political mentor, to the governorship in 1996 ... [and] won re-election.

(*FT*, 17 June 2003, p. 8)

22 June 2003.

One of Russia's two main private television stations was taken off air yesterday [22 June] because of a financial crisis that made it impossible to broadcast its programmes ... TVS, whose reporting irritated the Kremlin, was replaced by a state-run sports channel, which began broadcasting yesterday.

(*FT*, 23 June 2003, p. 9)

The sole country-wide independent television channel was taken off the air yesterday ... The press ministry said it closed TVS, where many reporters worked after two other channels were closed, because it was mired in a financial and management crisis. Journalists said the move threatened objective reporting of politics.

(*The Independent*, 23 June 2003, p. 9)

The Kremlin yesterday abruptly silenced Russia's only remaining independent television station ... The debt-ridden broadcaster, one of four main territorial channels in Russia, was cut off during adverts at midnight on Saturday [21 June] ... The company's director [was] Yevgeni Kiselyov ... [Despite the financial state of the company] critics allege that the government had unilaterally shut down the remaining outlet for criticism of the Kremlin.

(*Guardian*, 23 June 2003, p. 13)

The press ministry closed the last independent television channel, TVS, citing a prolonged financial crisis that left many of its employees unpaid for weeks ... Complaining that salacious and dishonest journalism threatened to pervert the democratic process ... the State Duma voted overwhelmingly last week to amend Russia's campaign laws to allow the authorities to shut down news organizations for campaign coverage deemed to be biased ... Supporters ... said the restrictions were necessary to protect candidates from scurrilous reporting in newspapers and on television and radio – a feature of previous campaigns. In particular the amendments ... are designed to curtail the common and corrupt practice of political parties – or their financial supporters – paying journalists for articles favouring candidates or attacking their opponents. The legislation would also require that candidates or political parties report such payments as campaign expenses ... The amendments ... must be approved by the upper house, the Federation Council, and then signed by Putin ... Critics ... said the new restrictions would allow the government ... to stifle aggressive but critical coverage.

(*IHT*, 23 June 2003, p. 3)

TVS was the last independent national network ... The channel was due to go off the air the very day that the press ministry pulled the plug ... The week before parliament passed a law restricting the media's ability to pass comment on political candidates and parties or their platforms.

(*The Economist*, 28 June 2003, p. 50)

'On Wednesday [25 June] the upper house passed a bill that banned media from carrying "electoral propaganda". The vague wording of the bill has media watchhdogs worried. They fear it may be used to close any media outlet critical of the Kremlin' (*Daily Telegraph*, 27 June 2003, p. 15).

24–27 June 2003. President Putin visits the United Kingdom, the first state visit to that country by a Russian leader since Tsar Alexander II (who was assassinated in 1881) in May 1874.

The Foreign Office was claiming that the last Russian to be honoured with the pomp and ceremony of a state visit was Tsar Alexander II in 1874. He had come to watch his daughter marry Queen Victoria's son but 'there were aspects of a state visit', a British official insisted. Alexander ... liberated the serfs and got himself assassinated seven years after his trip to London. The Kremlin does not accept that was a real state visit. It says the last Russian leader to get one was Tsar Nicholas I, in 1844 ... British officials say the [Putin] visit was timed for this year because it is the 450th anniversary of diplomatic relations with Russia and the 300th anniversary of St Petersburg.

(*Guardian*, 25 June 2003, p. 6)

The UK and Russia agreed to co-operate on the planned construction of a $6 billion gas pipeline from Russia to Europe ... to run from Vyborg near St Petersburg across the Baltic Sea to Germany ... [But it was indicated that] no final commitment had been achieved from the British.

(*FT*, 27 June 2003, p. 8)

1 July 2003.

The United States on Tuesday [1 July 2003] suspended military assistance to almost fifty countries ... because they have supported the International Criminal Court and failed to exempt Americans from possible prosecutions ... President George W. Bush issued waivers for twenty-two countries ... The forty-seven countries subject to the suspension of military aid ... include ... Bulgaria, Croatia, Estonia, Latvia, Lithuania, Serbia and Montenegro, Slovakia and Slovenia ... The threat, enshrined in the American Service Members Protection Act of 2002, does not apply to the nineteen Nato members and to nine 'major non-Nato allies' ... A total of forty-four governments have publicly acknowledged signing the agreement and at least seven others have signed secret agreements, US officials say.

(*IHT*, 2 July 2003, p. 5)

2 July 2003.

[On 2 July] Russian authorities arrested a top executive at the financial group that owns Yukos Oil, Russia's largest oil company ... Platon Lebedev

[is] chairman of the board at Menatep, the company that controls Yukos. The general prosecutor's office suspects him of embezzling from a state company in 1994, an allegation he denies ... The arrest was the first of its kind since Vladimir Gusinsky ... was detained in 2000 ... There is another challenge to Putin's power. This time it comes from ... Mikhail Khodorkovsky, forty ... is the chief executive and a major holder of Yukos ... With December parliamentary elections fast approaching, Khodorkovsky began to donate money to opposition parties like Yabloko and the Union of Rightist Forces ... His supporters began talking about giving more power to Russia's parliament, implying a power shift away from the presidency ... The arrest of his close associate Lebedev was a blunt message from above to keep him in line and out of politics, said Grigori Yavlinsky ... 'It's scare tactics,' said Yavlinsky ... Khodorkovsky himself was summoned to the general prosecutor's office for questioning Friday [4 July].

(*IHT*, 4 July 2003, p. 5)

Platon Lebedev, who is a close ally of Mr Khodorkovsky and the second largest shareholder in Russia's biggest oil company, was being questioned over the transfer into private hands of a government stake in a fertilizer producer in 1994. The arrest has been widely interpreted in Moscow as part of an orchestrated campaign to curb the influence of Mr Khodorkovsky, who has political ambitions to be prime minister and possibly even president ... perhaps in 2008 ... and his powerful company, which is in the process of acquiring Sibneft ... Mr Lebedev ... is Russia's thirteenth richest man [Mr Khodorkovsky is Russia's richest] ... Mr Lebedev owns 7 per cent of the Gibraltar-registered Group Menatep, which controls 60 per cent of Yukos ... Mr Khodorkovsky recently confirmed that he used his personal wealth to back ... Yabloko and the Union of Rightist Forces ... He supports regional newspapers and has agreed to invest $100 million over ten years in Moscow Humanitarian University, a move which has been seen as an effort to bring up a new generation of political elite ... Mr Khodorkovsky has not openly stated his political intentions ... Russian police also charged the head of Yukos's security department, Alexei Pichugin, with being an accomplice in the murder of two people in 2002 ... Some analysts also linked the high-profile arrests at Yukos to the showcase arrests of policemen for alleged corruption two weeks ago.

(*FT*, 4 July 2003, pp. 8, 18)

The Russian prosecutor-general announced yesterday [2 July] that it is investigating at least three criminal cases involving the Yukos oil company and its subsidiaries and executives. Two of the cases are strictly economic – the stripping of assets from Eastern Petroleum Company, and machinations involving shares in Russia's largest producer of mineral fertilizers, the Apatit [Apatite] joint stock company (in Murmansk province). The third case appears more scandalous: a department head in Yukos's security service, Alexei Pichugin, allegedly arranged for a bomb to be set off outside the entrance to the apartment of Olga Kostina, a former public relations adviser for ... Menatep Bank ... and then killed the people who had orchestrated the bombing ... Prosecutors detained the chairman of the board of directors of the Menatep Financial Union [which owns a 61 per cent stake in Yukos], Platon Lebedev, and questioned him about his role in the Apatit fraud case ... [Mikhail Khodorkovsky, who is chief executive officer of Yukos, has been questioned] ... Yukos has a reputation as the most transparent and above-board company in Russia.

(*CDSP*, 2003, vol. 55, no. 26, pp. 6–7, 20)

'Mr Khodorkovsky is rattling nerves with his increasingly clear political ambitions ... Oleg Deripaska, an aluminium magnate, incurred the Kremlin's displeasure over his involvement with a regional election' (*The Economist*, 5 July 2003, p. 72).

4 July 2003.

Mikhail Khodorkovsky ... worth an estimated $11 billion ... was questioned by prosecutors ... Grigori Yavlinsky said: 'This is a political clean-up before the elections designed to scare off Mr Khodorkovsky and to serve as a lesson to any other large business to keep out of politics. You could start an investigation against any of the oligarchs in the country on the basis of Russian privatization, but the fact that they selectively chose Mr Khodorkovsky is a sign of the Kremlin's hand' ... Prosecutors also questioned Leonid Nevzlin, a prominent Yukos shareholder, recently installed as the head of Moscow Humanitarian University.

(*FT*, 5 July 2003, p. 6)

Mikhail Khodorkovsky ... was summoned to the general prosecutor's office to answer questions connected with the arrest of [Platon Lebedev] ... Khodorkovsky said none of the questions were connected to his company's economic activity ... The detention of Lebedev came out of an investigation requested by Vladimir Yudin, a lawmaker who is a member of the pro-Kremlin Fatherland–All Russia faction ... Grigori Yavlinsky called it a 'political, pre-election mop-up operation that is being carried out to suppress political opponents' ... Leonid Nevzlin, a former Yukos board member, was questioned [on 4 July].

(*IHT*, 5 July 2003, p. 2)

7 July 2003. 'Mikhail Khodokovsky ... sought to strike a conciliatory note with the Kremlin yesterday [7 July], saying he has no political agenda and is happy to confine himself to business at least until 2007' (*FT*, 8 July 2003, p. 8).

The charges against him [Platon Lebedev], which involve a 1994 privatization, are widely believed to be trumped up ... Most here [Moscow] see the investigation of Yukos's owners as politically motivated. The erratic application of the rule of law is one of the biggest fears of foreign investors here ... 'We are witnessing a start of a power struggle between the different parts of Vladimir Putin's entourage,' Khodorkovsky said.

(*IHT*, 8 July 2003, p. 13)

After Mr Lebedev's arrest Russia's antitrust commission said it would delay approval of the [Yukos–Sibneft] merger for another three weeks ... Just days before Mr Lebedev's arrest ... Vladimir Potanin of the Interros group made a public show of contrition for past excesses and of fealty to United Russia, the coalition in the Duma that backs the Kremlin.

(*The Economist*, 12 July 2003, p. 32)

8 July 2003.

Russia's prosecutor-general confirmed it was examining Yukos's and other oil companies' 2002 tax payments after a request from members of parliament ... Also on Tuesday [8 July] the prosecutor-general's office said it had opened an investigation into Yukos's acquisition of a 19 per cent stake in Yeniseineftegaz, a company with oil exploration licences in Siberia. The investigation was requested by the oil company Rosneft.

(*FT*, 10 July 2003, p. 8)

11 July 2003.

Armed police wearing black masks and carrying Kalashnikov rifles yesterday [11 July] raided the Moscow offices of Yukos ... and broke into the company's files and computer systems. The move followed a similar raid on the St Petersburg offices of the Menatep bank, which controls 61 per cent of Yukos.

(*FT*, 12 July 2003, p. 10)

'Yukos ... is being investigated for tax evasion, along with Sibneft, the oil company controlled by Roman Abramovich' (*Daily Telegraph*, 12 July 2003, p. 18).

Roman Abramovich ... governor of a region in north-eastern Russian called Chukotka ... [has] bought an English soccer team [Chelsea] ... Abramovich bought 50 per cent of Chelsea Village, the holding company that owns the soccer team amid the sports facility.

(*IHT*, 3 July 2003, p. 4)

'Roman Abramovich ... is one of the seventeen billionaires in [Russia] ... only three nations have more billionaires' (*The Independent*, 9 July 2003, p. 18).

Forbes magazine now lists seventeen Russians on its roster of the world's richest ... Mikhail Khodorkovsky [is] worth over $8 billion ... *Forbes* listed his [Roman Abramovich's] net worth as $5.7 billion ... As best we can tell ... Abramovich owns or controls 80 per cent of Sibneft ... [and] owns 26 per cent of ... Aeroflot, which, along with Sibneft, he took over from Berezovsky ... Abramovich has so far avoided a run-in with Putin. Even though he was originally a Berezovsky protégé, Abramovich was the one who arranged for the transfer of Berezovsky's television network to the state. He helped finance Putin's 2000 race for president ... Abramovich has taken his job of governor [of Chukotka] seriously ... [helping] to develop the province economically ... It is hard to see how he [Putin] can reconcile his suspicion of anyone with power with his role as a national leader promising greater prosperity for the country at large.

(Marshall Goldman, *IHT*, 17 July 2003, p. 9)

Roman Abramovich has also been in the line of fire, accused by Sergei Stepashin, head of the Russian parliament's accounting chamber and a close ally of Mr Putin, of evading £175 million in taxes. Mr Stepashin implied that Mr Abramovich had used the money to buy Chelsea Football Club.

(*The Times*, 18 July 2003, p. 18)

Mikhail Khodorkovsky ... [is] Russia's wealthiest man (and, according to *Forbes*, the twenty-sixth richest in the world) ... Yukos started to reveal its big shareholders, publish accounts meeting international standards and pay taxes ... Platon Lebedev ... [was arrested] on suspicion of illegally acquiring a stake in a state-owned fertilizer firm in 1994 ... It [the arrest] was followed by investigations into tax returns filed by Yukos and a delay to the antitrust commission's go-ahead for its merger with Sibneft ... Prosecutors are investigating Oleg Deripaska, an aluminium magnate, but that concerns a private dispute that began long ago.

(*The Economist*, 19 July 2003, p. 62)

Platon Lebedev was ... charged with not making the required investment for a fertilizer company ... The authorities have begun at least four other criminal investigations into people and companies affiliated with Khodorkovsky. The investigations have frightened the business community for two reasons. First, much of Russia's current economic revival came out of its corrupt privatization programme of the mid-1990s and the state could accuse any number of businessmen of past violations ... Perhaps more important is the implicit message about property rights. Russia has yet to establish an institution that protects property rights. Instead, entrepreneurs rely on connections with individual bureaucrats in the state for protection ... Investors are shaken. Russia's stock market has plunged over the past two weeks.

(Sabrina Tavernise, *IHT*, 18 July 2003, p. 11)

Russia's richest: Mikhail Khodorkovsky: chief interests Menatep and Yukos oil; he is worth $8 billion (twenty-sixth richest in the world); Roman Abramovich: Sibneft and Russian Aluminium; $5.7 billion (forty-ninth); Mikhail Fridman: Tyumen Oil; $4.3 billion (sixty-eighth); Viktor Vekselberg: Tyumen Oil; $2.5 billion (147th); Vladimir Potanin: Norilsk Nickel; $1.8 billion (222nd); Mikhail Prokhorov: Norilsk Nickel; $1.6 billion (256th); Vladimir Yevtushenkov: AFK Sistema; $1.5 billion (278th); Oleg Deripaska: Russian Aluminium; $1.5 billion (278th); Vagit Alekperov: Lukoil; $1.3 billion (329th); Alexei Mordashov: Severstal; $1.2 billon (348th) (*The Times*, 18 July 2003, p. 18).

'Roman Abramovich ... [is] probably worth more than $10 billion' (*FT*, 26 August 2003, p. 10).

17 July 2003.

Prime minister Mikhail Kasyanov … vowed that privatization could not be reversed, trying to smooth the conflict between the Kremlin and the country's top tycoons, which has shaken the Russian markets … [He said that] 'Of course, we believe and have always believed that the results of previous years' privatizations are irreversible. Our main current and past aim is clearly to improve the quality and transparency of decision-making in privatizations.'

(*FT*, 18 July 2003, p. 6)

18 July 2003.

The enquiry into Yukos … moved into a new phase yesterday [18 July] when the prosecutor's office said it was investigating seven criminal cases connected to the company, including five murders and assassination attempts … Police have arrested the head of Yukos's security, Alexei Pichugin, charging him with organizing the killing of two individuals … New investigations … include the high-profile killing of the mayor of Yukos's main production city. Vladimir Petukhov, the mayor of Nefteyugansk, who made his political career fighting Yukos, was shot dead on 26 June 1998. Prosecutors said they were also investigating the assassination attempt on a manager of East Petroleum.

(*FT*, 19 July 2003, p. 7)

22 July 2003.

Leading Russian businessmen and human rights activists urged President Putin to offer guarantees to a business community spooked by an official investigation of [Yukos] … The investigation is widely seen as politically driven. Without naming the oil company Yukos, leaders of the three business associations and several prominent rights activists said in a letter published Tuesday [22 July] that 'arbitrariness and intimidation' by the authorities threatened Russia's stability.

(*IHT*, 23 July 2003, p. 3)

24 July 2003.

[Prime minister] Mikhail Kasyanov … said the actions of prosecutors investigating it [Yukos] were hurting Russia's investment climate: 'The fact that the situation has been going on for a great length of time is not to the advantage of the country's image and investors' mood' .. Mr Kasyanov also said it was wrong to keep in prison a shareholder who is the subject of an investigation into economic crimes. His comments came a day after a Moscow court turned down an appeal to release Platon Lebedev, Yukos's key shareholder … A Yukos spokesman said the court had refused to even consider the appeal … The statement from Mr Kasyanov is a sign of an escalating struggle … between ex-KGB men brought by President Putin from his native St Petersburg and the more liberal part of the Russian government that Mr Putin inherited from the Yeltsin era, known as 'the family'. Mr Kasyanov is seen in Moscow as a representative of the 'family' side of the Russian political elite.

(FT, 25 July 2003, p. 6)

25 July 2003.

Mikhail Kasyanov ... critic of the prosecutor-general's aggressive tactics in investigating economic crimes ... using 'arm-twisting' measures in combating economic crimes ... said the tension between the Russian business world and the Kremlin 'will be resolved in the very near future'.

(FT, 28 July 2003, p. 6)

Boris Nemtsov: 'The Kremlin hates it when the oligarchs try to privatize the Duma. Besides, in a country with seventeen billionaires and 40 million poor, bashing the oligarchs is always a popular occupation, particularly before the [parliamentary] elections in December' *(FT,* 28 July 2003, p. 6).

28 July 2003.

The prosecutor-general's office filed new charges Monday [28 July] against ... Platon Lebedev ... [who] has been charged with tax evasion in a separate case ... The spokeswoman for the prosecutor-general's office ... said that statements such as [prime minister] Kasyanov's constituted 'a direct pressure on the court' and were incorrect. President Vladimir Putin has said that economic crimes must be fought without 'arm-twisting and jail cells', but has avoided making direct comments on Yukos.

(IHT, 29 July 2003, p. 4)

Roman Abramovich ... who bought Chelsea football club for £150 million ... is stepping up efforts to liquidate his investments in Russia ... say people with whom he has held talks ... Mikhail Khodorkovsky, chief executive of Yukos and its largest shareholder, said last week that the decision this spring to merge with rival oil group Sibneft – of which Mr Abramovich owns more than 90 per cent – was the trigger for the investigation.

(FT, Money and Business, 9 August 2003, p. 1)

Mikhail Khodorkovsky ... is planning to increase support for the country's liberal opposition parties ... [He] has resolved to intensify his work with Yabloko and the Union of Rightist Forces ... Mr Khodorkovsky's move comes even as Yukos is believed to be involved in discussions with senior Kremlin officials about a potential face-saving compromise that could include making a substantial payment for social programmes in Russia ... Yukos is also believed to have provided secret support to the Communist Party, which recently condemned the attacks on the company.

(FT, 11 August 2003, p. 5)

5 August 2003.

The government announced this month [August] that it plans to place its own representatives on the polling centre's board of directors. The All-Russian Public Opinion Studies, which is state-owned but receives no state money – and, until now, had no state interference – will no longer be independent.

(Vladimir Shlapentokh, *IHT*, 19 August 2003, p. 6)

The director ... Yuri Levada ... said yesterday [5 August] that the centre [created on 7 December 1987] could undergo a complete change of management ... [It] is to be converted to a joint stock company and then privatized [by the end of 2003] ... A board of directors, which is to include representatives of the ministry of labour, the ministry of property relations and the president's staff, will be formed within the next two weeks.

(*CDSP*, 2003, vol. 55, no. 31, pp. 1–2)

('A Kremlin loyalist has been appointed head [of the polling agency] ... Valeri Fyodorov ... [is] a political analyst who has previously worked on the election campaign of one of the pro-Kremlin parties ... A new board of governors has ousted ... Yuri Levada ... Mr Levada walked out, taking most of the staff with him, and announced he would set up another agency': *Daily Telegraph*, 13 September 2003, p. 21.)

12 August 2003.

Russia's anti-monopolies ministry yesterday [12 August] gave a boost to ... Yukos, saying it would approve the merger with its rival Sibneft by the end of this week ... Yukos-Sibneft [would have] ... about 30 per cent of Russian [oil] production.

(*FT*, 13 August 2003, p. 6)

14 August 2003.

The merger of ... Yukos and Sibneft received formal government approval yesterday [14 August] ... after an unusually long review of more than two months Russia's anti-monopoly ministry said it had approved the merger with a list of conditions, which analysts said appeared to be light and did not include any forced sell-offs ... The new company, to be called Yukos-Sibneft Oil Co., would have to refrain from using its dominant position in regional retail markets to force out small players. The company will also have to make it possible for other companies to participate with it in new construction projects and allow other producers access to its refineries.

(*FT*, 15 August 2003, p. 9)

'The Anti-Monopoly Policy Ministry ... insisted that Yukos-Sibneft, among other things, allow access to independent distributors in areas where the new company will dominate oil production, including parts of Siberia' (*IHT*, 15 August 2003, p. 12).

21 August 2003.

Vladimir Gusinsky ... who holds dual Russian and Israeli citizenship ... was arrested in Greece ... In Greece officials said Gusinsky has been arrested on ... [an] international warrant issued by Russia ... [The] warrant accuses him of defrauding the Russian government of $250 million, charges that stem from an audit initiated by Gazprom, the state-controlled company that eventually won control of NTV. In 2001 Russia also charged him with money laundering.

(IHT, 25 August 2003, p. 2)

'It was unclear what prompted the Greek authorities to act on a warrant dating back three years and the timing took analysts by surprise' *(FT*, 25 August 2003, p. 8).

His arrest comes as part of a bilateral deal between Greece and Russia. However, it was unclear yesterday [25 August] whether Greek authorities acted on an outstanding warrant dating back to 2000 or had a fresh request from Russian prosecutors to arrest him.

(FT, 26 August 2003, p. 6)

26 August 2003.

Russian prosecutors said yesterday [26 August] they were preparing a request to extradite ... Vladimir Gusinsky from Greece ... Mr Gusinsky had been previously arrested and later freed by Spanish authorities in connection with the same allegations. A Spanish court threw out the charges and Interpol struck out Mr Gusinsky's name from the fugitive list because of the political character of his case. His arrest in Greece appears to be carried out in the framework of Russia's bilateral agreement with Greece.

(FT, 27 August 2003, p. 8)

Some reports suggest [that] Greek airport police initially held the former media mogul because they still had a cancelled Interpol arrest warrant for him in their computer ... When a Spanish court dismissed these charges [embezzlement and fraud] as the basis for extradition the Moscow authorities came up with an accusation of money laundering against Mr Gusinsky. Interpol decided that this was 'predominantly political' and cancelled its arrest warrant.

(p. 18)

Earlier this month [August] Sergei Glazyev, a populist politician who was expected to throw his lot in with the Communists, announced that instead he is assembling a left-wing coalition (which ... he invited the Communists to join) ... Mr Glazyev, say the Communists, is just a Kremlin stooge, set up to steal their votes ... Anatoli Chubais ... has joined the race as a candidate for the reformist Union of Rightist Forces ... The People's Party peeled off from United Russia and represents members of the security services ...

After the 1999 election nearly half the Duma's single-mandate members changed party affiliation.

(*The Economist*, 30 August 2003, pp. 29–30)

29 August 2003.

Vladimir Gusinsky ... was freed on bail by a Greek court yesterday [29 August] but was ordered to remain in jail until an appeal court decides whether he should be extradited ... Russia must supply extradition documents by 1 October. If the documents have not arrived by that date Mr Gusinsky will be allowed to leave Greece.

(*FT*, 29 August 2003, p. 5)

30 August 2003.

Nine seamen were killed ... [and] one sailor was rescued ... when the K-159 ... nuclear-powered submarine sank [on Saturday 30 August] ... as it was being towed along the coast of the Kola Peninsula into a port for scrapping ... Neither of its nuclear reactors was operating ... The Russian defence minister, Sergei Ivanov, said Sunday [31 August] that radiation levels were normal in the Barents Sea where the submarine sank ... The submarine was decommissioned in 1989 and had been rusting in a submarine graveyard.

(*IHT*, 1 September 2003, p. 7)

'Russia's defence minister [Sergei Ivanov] blamed what he called his countrymen's habitual negligence and thoughtlessness' (*FT*, 1 September 2003, p. 7).

The derelict forty-year-old submarine was found on the seabed yesterday [31 August] with its hatch wide open ... Floating hulls attached to the submarine were ripped off during the fierce storm and navy sources were quoted as suggesting they had not been attached properly ... The submarine was powered by two nuclear reactors but they were shut down in 1989 when it was decommissioned. The authorities said there were no weapons on board ... But environmentalists said that the danger of radioactive contamination was much higher than official statements suggested.

(*The Independent*, 1 September 2003, p. 9)

'[The] tugboat moved faster than instructions allowed' (*The Independent*, 12 September 2003, p. 13).

'The sub was being towed to a naval scrapyard and sank with its conning tower open' (*Guardian*, 1 September 2003, p. 14).

Defence ministry officials said that the commanding officer had ignored warnings of bad weather. Early reports from diving teams also suggest that the submarine's hatch may have been open at the time of the vessel's sinking ... Russia has a multibillion-dollar programme, partly financed by the United States, to dismantle about 130 submarines by the end of the decade.

(*The Times*, 1 September 2003, p. 13)

'[The submarine was being towed to] the base where its nuclear reactors were to have been removed ... The former chief of Russia's Black Sea fleet, Eduard Baltin, questioned why there were crew aboard' (*Daily Telegraph*, 1 September 2003, p. 12).

'Of some 250 nuclear subs built by the Soviet Union, nearly four-fifths are out of service, but fewer than half of those have been scrapped. The rest, many still with fuel in their reactors, sit and rust' (*The Economist*, 6 September 2003, p. 42).

2 September 2003. 'A leak rather than a storm caused [the sinking] ... according to a naval source, who said the submarine's captain radioed the towing vessel that there was a leak' (*The Times*, 3 September 2003, p. 18).

('President Vladimir Putin has suspended ... [the] commander of the navy's Northern Fleet after the loss of the submarine': *The Independent*, 12 September 2003, p. 13.)

4 September 2003.

> A fund led by Mikhail Khodorkovsky ... said Thursday [4 September] that it had bought the influential weekly *Moskovskiye Novosti*, or *Moscow News*, and hired a major critic of President Vladimir Putin to run it. The fund, Open Russia, said it had appointed Yevgeni Kiselyov, a leading investigative journalist know for his sharp criticism of Kremlin policies, as the newspaper's editor-in-chief.
>
> (*IHT*, 5 September 2003, p. 5)

> The weekly *Moscow News*, which became synonymous with Mikhail Gorbachev's liberal reforms of the 1980s, was bought by a charity fund sponsored by Yukos shareholders ... [A] director of the fund said the decision to buy the paper was made two months ago but it was only announced this week after the anti-monopoly commission approved the deal.
>
> (*FT*, 6 September 2003, p. 9)

9 September 2003. 'Boris Berezovsky ... has been granted political asylum in Britain' (*The Independent*, 11 September 2003, p. 13).

10 September 2003. 'Dramatic allegations of a Russian-sponsored "murder plot" against Boris Berezovsky ... surfaced in a London courtrom yesterday [12 September] as his extradition case was formally halted. But there is deep scepticism in Russia over the claims' (*FT*, 13 September 2003, p. 1).

20 September 2003.

> President Vladimir Putin ... has portrayed the investigation swirling around ... Yukos Oil as an isolated criminal matter that does not signal a wholesale review of the country's privatization of state assets in the 1990s. Making his first remarks on the Yukos affair ... [he said] that as president he could not interfere with the independence of prosecutors, who he said were simply upholding the law ... Putin said accusations of Kremlin

involvement or political interference were 'utter nonsense'. And he seemed eager to reassure investors about the stability of Russia's economy.

(*IHT*, 23 September 2003, p. 14)

20–21 September 2003.

President Vladimir Putin … roundly endorsed the United Russia party, formally putting his support behind the pro-Kremlin movement … Mr Putin said his appearance at the party's final pre-election congress on Saturday [20 September] was 'exceptional' and reflected his gratitude for United Russia's support over the past four years in parliament. He added that he had voted for the party – then known as United or the Bear – in the previous elections in 1999. His attendance … comes relatively early in the electoral season. In 1999 his endorsement came just three weeks before voting, when he said that he would support the party as a personal gesture to his friend Sergei Shoigu, the minister of emergency situations, who was its leader … However, it comes in the days following controversy around Mr Putin's widely broadcast wishes of good luck to Valentina Matvienko, his preferred choice for the governor of St Petersburg, in violation of new federal election laws that demand that all candidates are granted equal media exposure … The St Petersburg race took place yesterday [21 September], following a series of legal actions launched by rival candidates over Mr Putin's endorsement of Ms Matvienko, as well as over violations including alleged forged signatures on the lists required for candidates to be nominated … Four other parties [have been] created with an explicit pro-Kremlin platform.

(*FT*, 22 September 2003, p. 8)

President Putin (20 September):

I won't conceal the fact that four years ago I voted for your party … United Russia was the force that created a powerful bloc of centrist factions in the State Duma; you fought more consistently than anyone else for the passage of laws crucial to the country … My participation in your party's congress today is an exception and I made it deliberately, to signal my gratitude.

(*CDSP*, 2003, vol. 55, no. 38, p. 7)

[United Russia] leaders … do not agree with the view that Putin violated election laws that bar government officials from backing and campaigning for specific political forces … United Russia's federal list is topped by … internal affairs minister Boris Gryzlov, emergency situations minister Sergei Shoigu. Moscow mayor Yuri Luzhkov and the president of the republic of Tatarstan, Mintimir Shaimiev.

(*CDSP*, 2003, vol. 55, no. 38, p. 8)

[In the election] only 29 per cent voted, 48.7 per cent of these for Ms Matvienko, just shy of the 50 per cent she needed to give her victory in the first vote. She will now face a run-off against her main opponent, Anna Markova, who garnered just 16 per cent of the vote. The poll campaign was laden with controversy after Mr Putin appeared on television with Ms Matvienko ... The appearance seemed to violate Russian electoral law, which forbids an official to use his post to promote political parties or election candidates. Posters across the city also depicted Ms Matvienko alongside the president ... The campaigning was also marred last week by allegations of police interference with leaflet distributions by rival candidates, and Ms Matvienko's unfair domination of the media.

(*Guardian*, 23 September 2003, p. 14)

Anna Markova [is] a former deputy governor and ally of Vladimir Yakovlev, the outgoing governor and longstanding rival of Mr Putin ... [There] was a campaign encouraging people to vote 'against everyone'. The category received 11 per cent, the third highest total.

(*FT*, 23 September 2003, p. 8)

('In the second round of voting in St Petersburg Valentina Matvienko ... won 63 per cent in a turnout of just 28 per cent': *FT*, 7 October 2003, p. 15.)

22 September 2003. 'Russia yesterday [22 September] formally requested the extradition from Greece of Vladimir Gusinsky ... on fraud and money-laundering charges' (*Daily Telegraph*, 23 September 2003, p. 16).

26–27 September 2003. President Putin has talks with President Bush in the United States.

28 September 2003.

Russia's fragile media came under fresh attack last night [28 September] after unidentified security guards attempted to take over the editorial offices of the respected Russian [weekly] newspaper *Novoe Vremya* ... Senior *Novoe Vremya* journalists locked themselves into their offices and called the police after guards from the Primex security company attempted to enter their rooms. Other journalists attempting to enter the building were refused entry by the new guards. The move follows the eviction of *Novoe Vremya*'s own three guards on Thursday night [25 September]. The new guards, who were armed with machine guns, refused to identify themselves but said the building had been legally acquired by their unknown clients. *Novoe Vremya* says it is the legal owner of the building, which has been registered in its name for forty years.

(*FT*, 29 September 2003, p. 6)

3 October 2003.

Criminal investigators conducted a new round of searches Friday [3 October] that focused on ... Yukos, a sign that the investigation that has shadowed the company since July is far from over ... Mikhail Khodorkovsky declined to discuss reports of merger talks [with Exxon Mobil] ... At least eight investigations have opened into Yukos and its subsidiaries on accusations that include fraud, tax evasion and even murder and attempted murder ... The searches ... came as Yukos announced that it had completed its merger with Sibneft ... The merger, announced Friday [3 October], valued at $45 billion, creates Russia's largest oil and gas company and the world's fifth largest private oil company. The new company will be called Yukos-Sibneft Oil, and Khodorkovsky will remain its chairman. The new company is expected to produce 2.3 million barrels of crude a day, more than a quarter of the production of Russia, the world's number two oil supplier after Saudi Arabia.

(*IHT*, 4 October 2003, p. 9)

6 October 2003.

Russia and France said Monday [6 October] that they had agreed to launch Soyuz rockets from the Kourou range in French Guyana ... Kourou, on the north-east coast of South America, is closer to the equator than Russia's base at Baikonur in Kazakhstan.

(*IHT*, 7 October 2003, p. 4)

9 October 2003.

The Russian authorities yesterday [10 October] launched more raids against individuals linked to Yukos ... in a sharp escalation of a criminal investigation widely seen as politically motivated ... Many observers argue that Yukos's approach was little different from that of other leading Russian business groups. They say Yukos was singled out because of its aggressive parliamentary lobbying, clashes with state-owned competitors and because Mr Khodorkovsky is considered a threat politically.

(*FT*, 10 October 2003, p. 7)

10 October 2003.

Defence minister Sergei Ivanov has said that his government expects the US military to withdraw from bases in ... Uzbekistan and Kyrgyzstan ... once the mission in Afghanistan is completed ... 'We have always been proceeding from the fact that those bases exist solely for the period required for the final, definitive stabilization of the situation in Afghanistan,' he said ... Ivanov also said that Russia reserved the right to intervene in former Soviet states if the human rights of ethnic Russians were violated ... [Ivanov also said that Russia] has no plans to announce a policy of nuclear pre-emption ... [Nato] officials had expressed concerns over news reports that Russia was embarking on a policy of nuclear pre-emption, but Lord Robertson, Nato's secretary general, said he had received assurances that that was not true. Russian news media reported on a speech given by Ivanov at the defence ministry last week in which he was quoted as saying that Russia reserved the right to launch pre-emptive strikes against other regions.

(*IHT*, 11 October 2003, p. 3)

14 October 2003.

A Greek court on Tuesday [14 October] rejected Russia's request for the extradition of ... Vladimir Gusinsky ... on the ground that Russian prosecutors failed to provide sufficient evidence of the alleged crimes ... allegations stemming from an investigation into a \$250 million fraud and money-laundering scheme ... The judge ... ruled that under Greek law the accusations against Gusinsky did not constitute a crime.

(*IHT*, 15 October 2003, p. 3)

'Interpol refused to hunt him [Gusinsky] because of the political nature of the case' (*FT*, 15 October 2003, p. 8).

18 October 2003.

[The State Duma] unanimously passed legislative amendments aimed at simplifying citizenship procedures that have sparked protest since they were introduced last year. The amendments to the 2002 citizenship law were introduced last month [September] by President Vladimir Putin. The amendments would waive requirements that applicants live in Russia for five years, pass a language exam and provide proof of financial solvency for former Soviet citizens who were officially registered in Russia as of 1 July 2002.

(*IHT*, 18 October 2003, p. 3)

'Russian authorities pressed tax evasion charges against a second major shareholder of Yukos ... The general prosecutor's office said it charged Vasili Shakhnovsky, a Yukos board member, with evading taxes of 29 million roubles, or \$965,000' (*IHT*, 18 October 2003, p. 14).

'Prosecutors have stepped up their attacks on Yukos ... with new tax probes of a top shareholder, an affiliated bank and Sibneft, an oil firm with which it is merging' (*The Economist*, 25 October 2003, p. 6).

'[There are] seventeen billionaires and 40 million people below the poverty line' (*IHT*, 24 October 2003, p. 10). 'In 2002 *Forbes* magazine's annual wealth survey listed seventeen billionaires from Russia, up from zero in 2000' (www.iht.com, 27 October 2003).

20 October 2003.

Russian prosecutors said ... Mikhail Khodorkovsky would be interrogated again ... [He] ranks as Russia's richest person. *Forbes* magazine estimated that his net worth more than tripled, from \$2.4 billion in 2001 to \$8 billion in 2003 ... Khodorkovsky has disagreed with the Kremlin by calling for further economic liberalization and the construction of alternative pipelines to export Russian oil ... During a trip to Asia this week President Putin made a point of saying that Russia wanted to export more oil, but has yet to decide whether it will build a pipeline from Angarsk, in Eastern Siberia, to the city of Daqing, China, or to Nakhodka on Russia's Pacific coast.

Khodorkovsky has said he expected Yukos to ship crude oil to China using rail transportation if the Russian government does not go ahead with the Angarsk–Daqing pipeline.

(*IHT*, 21 October 2003, p. 14)

23 October 2003.

Prosecutors raided one of its [Yabloko's] key political consultants, ostensibly as part of the growing investigation into Yukos. Grigori Yavlinsky criticized as 'illegal' the raid on Thursday [23 October] by prosecutors of the Agency for Strategic Communications ... Yukos ... has received significant funding from Yukos, and named three of the company's employees or core shareholders as candidates on its electoral slate.

(*FT*, 25 October 2003, p. 8)

25 October 2003.

[Forty-year-old] Mikhail Khodorkovsky was seized at gunpoint on Saturday [25 October] by government security agents and jailed on charges of fraud and tax evasion ... Mr Khodorkovsky is the first of the oligarchs to go to jail. The charges against him carry a maximum penalty of ten years' imprisonment.

(*IHT*, 27 October 2003, pp. 1, 4)

He was charged with offences including defrauding the state out of $1 billion ... An official at the prosecutor's office said: 'The head of Yukos has been charged with a series of crimes, including large-scale theft and tax evasion, both personally and by the company' ... Prosecutors argued that his detention was necessary because he had ignored a summons for questioning on Friday [24 October] ... Yukos rejected the prosecutors' claims that Mr Khodorkovsky had ignored the summons.

(www.bbc.com, 26 October 2003)

The Yukos press secretary confirmed receipt of the summons on Thursday [23] but said the company informed prosecutors that Khodorkovsky was on a business trip and would not be available until Monday [27 October] ... [The secretary said that Khodorkovsky] had been detained late Friday [24 October] in Siberia on charges that he ignored the summons.

(www.cnn.com, 26 October 2003)

'*Forbes* magazine indentified him [Khodorkovsky] last year [2002] as Russia's richest man, then worth $8 billion' (*FT*, 27 October 2003, p. 10).

[Khodorkovsky] provided millions of dollars to Yabloko ... which has four of his colleagues on its list of candidates. There was more modest support for the Union of Rightist Forces and even (though indirectly) the Communist Party, where another Yukos shareholder is standing for election.

(*FT*, 28 October 2003, p. 9)

27 October 2003. President Putin:

There will be no meetings and no bargaining whatsoever concerning the activities of law-enforcement agencies, provided, of course, that those agencies act within the framework of Russian Federation law ... In the final analysis only a court can decide that question ... whether the man [Khodorkovsky] is guilty or not ... Before the court as before the law, all must be equal: the modest clerk and the government official – even an official of the highest rank ... the ordinary citizen, the medium-level entrepreneur and the big businessman, regardless of how many billions of dollars he has in his private or corporate accounts. All must be equal before the law or we will never solve the problem of creating an economically effective and socially sound tax system, we will never teach or force people to pay their taxes and make their payments to the social-welfare and pension funds, and we will never overcome organized crime and corruption ... I consider it necessary to stress with regard to the present case that no generalizations, analogies or precedents will be drawn from it, and certainly none having to do with privatization. I would therefore ask that all speculation and hysterics on this account be stopped.

(*CDSP*, 2003, vol. 55, no. 43, p. 6)

President Vladimir Putin on Monday [27 October] backed prosecutors ... but said the case does not herald a reversal of post-Soviet privatization or threaten democracy ... Mikhail Khodorkovsky ... was arrested Saturday by special forces at a Siberian airport during a refuelling stop. He was sent back to Moscow, charged with fraud, tax evasion and forgery, and locked in one of Moscow's notoriously overcrowded jails, Matrosskaya Tishina [Sailor's Rest].

(www.iht.com, 27 October 2003)

'If convicted he [Khodorkovsky] could be sentenced to ten years in jail and face the seizure of some or all of his wealth, including, possibly, his take in Yukos' (*IHT*, 28 October 2003, p. 4).

Russia's main stock exchange, the Russian Trading System, or RTS, suspended trading for an hour at noon. Another exchange, Micex, suspended trading altogether. The rouble fell against the dollar, prompting the central bank to intervene to stabilize the currency. Prices for Russia's long-term bonds fell ... The RTS index fell 59.86 points, or 10.1 per cent, to 535.05. Yukos's stock fell 73 roubles to close at 360 roubles, or $12.04, a drop of 16.9 per cent.

(*IHT*, 28 October 2003, pp. 1, 4)

The leading RTS index closed 10.1 per cent down, its biggest one-day loss for almost three years ... since in November 2000 ... The RTS index ... [reached] a record high of 643.3 on 20 October [2003] ... Trading of Yukos shares on the Micex index ... was suspended during the morning after sharp falls.

(*FT*, 28 October 2003, pp. 1, 46)

28 October 2003. 'Russian stocks on Tuesday [28 October] reversed the sharp losses ... as top officials appealed for market stability ... The benchmark RTS index closed up 4.93 per cent at 561.45. Shares in Yukos climbed 4.2 per cent' (*IHT*, 29 October 2003, p. 13).

> Alexander Voloshin, the head of the presidential administration, threatened to resign ... According to three separate individuals with strong links to the Kremlin, Mr Voloshin ... signed his resignation letter and gave it to Vladimir Putin during the day. But it was not clear whether the president had accepted it ... Mr Voloshin's resignation, which could also undermine Mikhail Kasyanov, the prime minister, would represent a blow to a group of business leaders closely tied to Boris Yeltsin ... Mr Voloshin served in the Yeltsin administration ... Yesterday [28 October] bankers indicated that there had been fresh capital flight and the postponement of a series of big financial deals.
>
> (*FT*, 29 October 2003, p. 1)

> Mr Voloshin's departure would be a logical step in the build-up to parliamentary elections in December and a presidential election next March, which is increasingly being characterized as a struggle between a series of big business oligarchs ... and a new group of hardliners drawn from the security forces and law enforcement agencies, many from Mr Putin's native St Petersburg.
>
> (p. 10)

29 October 2003.

> Russian shares fell sharply on Wednesday [29 October] after the authorities took action against another top shareholder in Yukos ... Yukos's share price tumbled over 7 per cent on news that prosecutors had asked a court to lift the immunity of the shareholder, Vasili Shakhnovsky, who this month was charged with tax evasion. The Russian Trading System fell 25.94 points, or 4.6 per cent, to 535.51 ... Shakhnovsky was elected to the Federation Council on Monday [27 October], giving him immunity from prosecution. Earlier this month he was charged with tax evasion and ordered not to leave Moscow ... Until his election to the Federation Council from the Siberian region of Evenkiya he was Yukos's operating officer ... Also on Wednesday a leading Russian business daily reported that Putin had accepted the resignation of the chief of staff, Alexander Voloshin, who is considered the Kremlin's leading advocate of Russian big business ... Voloshin is seen as one of the most influential political supporters of the so-called oligarchs.
>
> (www.iht.com, 29 October 2003)

> Earlier this month prosecutors accused Shakhnovsky, the head of the subsidiary Yukos Moscow, of filing falsely for tax breaks but did not arrest him ... [Yukos] stock fell 2.2 per cent, closing at $12.10 a share, while ... the RTS fell 3.7 per cent.
>
> (*IHT*, 30 October 2003, pp. 1, 4)

'Vasili Shakhnovsky ... owns 4.5 per cent of Yukos' (*FT*, 30 October 2003, p. 10).

Alexander Voloshin ... submitted his resignation on Saturday [25 October] ... There were conflicting reports on whether Putin had accepted Voloshin's resignation ... Voloshin, who has been the Kremlin's strongest advocate for advancing free-market policies, is the leader of one of the two factions widely believed to be struggling for political influence under Putin ... On the other [side] are those advisers who ... served in the KGB or other security services and favour a stronger role for the state in business and other matters. This faction [is] known collectively as the *siloviki* [hawks], or chekists, after the old Soviet-era word for intelligence operatives ... Andrei Piontkovsky [a political analyst with the Centre for Strategic Studies]: 'Philosophically, he [Putin] was always close to his group. He is a chekist. They are chekists. All their philosophy – managed democracy, vertical power – is what he believes.'

(Steven Lee Myers, *IHT*, 30 October 2003, pp. 1, 4)

'Siloviki [comes] from the Russian word meaning "force"' (*The Independent*, 1 November 2003, p. 15).

'[Siloviki means] "men of power"' (*Daily Telegraph*, 6 November 2003, p. 15).

According to research by Olga Kryshtanovskaya, a sociologist at the Russian Academy of Sciences, a quarter of the country's senior bureaucrats are *siloviki* – a Russian word meaning, roughly, 'power guys', which includes members of the armed forces and other security services, not just the FSB. The proportion rises to three-quarters if people simply affiliated to the security services are included ... All important decisions in Russia, says Ms Kryshtanovskaya, are now taken by a tiny group of men who served alongside Vladimir Putin in the KGB and who come from his home town of St Petersburg ... The *siloviki* reach ... into all areas of Russian life ... [For example] Igor Sechin ... [a] deputy head of the presidential administration ... is the chairman of Rosneft.

(*The Economist*, 25 August 2007, pp. 25–6)

The name *siloviki* comes from the Russian word *sila*, meaning 'strength' or 'power' ... Olga Kryshtanovskaya, of the Russian Academy of Sciences, has studied the country's centres of power since the late 1980s ... She says: 'A quarter of the political elite are *siloviki*' ... Her definition includes not only the KGB, but also the military and other security forces ... The KGB's main successor agency is the FSB (*Federalnaya Sluzhba Bezopasnosti*, or Federal Security Service) ... Olga Kryshtanovskaya estimates that when those she describes as 'affiliated', i.e. not publicly declared, are taken into account, the figure could be as high as three-quarters.

(www.bbc.co.uk, 12 September 2007)

'"We have a regime of 'managed democracy', which means that state resources will be used to produce the desired outcomes," said Otto Latsis, the editor of *Russky Kourier*, one of Russia's few remaining independent newspapers' (*The Independent*, 1 November 2003, p. 15).

('President Putin said last month [September]: "I have been hearing allegations [about the rollback of democracy] since I became president ... If by democracy one means the dissolution of the state, then we do not need such democracy ... I do not think that there are people in the world who want democracy that would lead to chaos"': *Guardian*, 30 October 2003, p. 15.)

30 October 2003.

> Prosecutors on Thursday [30 October] froze billions of dollars' worth of stocks in [Yukos] ... by far the largest freezing of assets here in a criminal case ... even as President Putin met with major foreign investors ... [The action sent] the country's already reeling stock markets spiralling further ... The prosecutors ... announced that a court had granted their request to freeze more than 1.2 billion shares of Yukos – worth some $14 billion at the start of the day but only $12 billion after the stock plunged by more than 16 per cent ... The RTS fell more than 8 per cent ... Since Khodorkovsky's arrest Saturday the RTS index has lost 16.5 per cent of its value. Yukos has lost 28 per cent of its value on the RTS ... The shares are owned by Khodorkovsky and ... Platon Lebedev ... prohibiting them from cashing out their stocks ... The shares can still be voted and there is no change in control ... The step ... signalled intent to seize some or all of Khodorkovsky's and Lebedev's wealth as penalties if they are convicted ... [On the same day] the Yukos board of directors announced it would pay shareholders $2 billion in dividends, the company's largest ever.
>
> (*IHT*, 31 October 2003, pp. 1, 10)

> Prosecutors froze a 44 per cent block of shares in Yukos ... Menatep, the holding company that controls the shares, said most belonged to international companies [international banks and brokerage houses] and were no longer owned by Mr Khodorkovsky ... Vladimir Putin ... [held] a previously planned meeting with leading international investment institutions.
>
> (*FT*, 31 October 2003, pp. 1, 8)

> Yukos said the seized shares belonged to a wide range of individuals, including Yukos executives and senior political figures, and not Mr Khodorkovsky. Legal experts say this made the seizure questionable legally ... [Yukos] said the shares were owned by Yukos's foreign shareholders, Yukos Universal Limited and Hulley Enterprises, registered on the Isle of Man and Cyprus: 'These companies ... belong to a whole group of shareholders, most of whom have nothing to do with Mikhail Khodorkovsky.' The prosecutor's office said Hulley Enterprises ... and Yukos Universal

Limited … were subsidiaries of Gibraltar-registered Menatep Group Ltd, in which an estimated 59 per cent of shares belong to Mr Khodorkovsky.

(*IHT*, 31 October 2003, p. 3)

'Mr Putin accepted the resignation of Alexander Voloshin … [He] was replaced by Dmitri Medvedev, a Putin loyalist' (*FT*, 31 October 2003, p. 1).

'Capital flight was up sharply in the third quarter' (*The Economist*, 1 November 2003, p. 42). 'Renaissance Capital, a Moscow-based investment bank, said Lebedev's arrest in July was a "key factor" prompting Russians to send \$7.7 billion abroad in the third quarter, more than triple the amount expatriated a year earlier' (*IHT*, 6 November 2003, p. 15).

> Russia's constitutional court on Thursday [30 October] overturned sweeping amendments to election law that had severely restricted news coverage of election campaigns and had even prompted some news organizations to avoid election coverage altogether for fear of being accused of bias … [The amendments had allowed] the authorities to shut down news media after two warnings for anything deemed as biased campaign coverage … The court all but threw out the restrictions, ruling that a journalist can now be accused of unlawful bias only if the intention to support a particular candidate is proven in court … The court chairman, Valeri Zorkin, read out the decision: 'Elections are free only when the right to information and freedom of choice are truly guaranteed … In the opinion of experts, it is practically impossible to prove the presence of direct intention in the actions of a journalist.' Zorkin said the amendments adopted in June [by the State Duma] were too broad and allowed 'arbitrary application'. Many on the Central Electoral Commission [which had drafted the amendments], including President Putin, have since said that they went too far … A group including more than 100 parliamentary deputies and three journalists [including Sergei Buntman, an on-air host and deputy editor of Ekho Moskvy, a radio station known for its freewheeling commentary] had petitioned the court to strike down the amendments.
>
> (*IHT*, 31 October 2003, p. 3)

31 October 2003. Prime minister Mikhail Kasyanov:

> The arrest of shares of a private company traded on the market is a new phenomenon, the consequences of which are hard to define, since it is a new form of influence. I will refrain from estimating [the consequences], but I am deeply concerned. I hope the reshuffle in the presidential administration will not have an impact on its co-operation with the government.
>
> (*IHT*, 1 November 2003, p. 1; *Guardian*, 1 November 2003, p. 21)

Just hours after Kasyanov, widely considered the last remaining pro-business official high up in Putin's administration, spoke out in defence of Yukos, Russia's prosecutor-general freed 4.5 per cent of the 44 per cent [i.e. about 2 percentage points] of the shares in Yukos held by Mikhail Khodorkovsky that were frozen on Thursday [30 October] … Russia's benchmark

RTS index closed higher Friday [31 October], rising 1.9 per cent ... The price of Yukos stock recovered, surging 7.49 per cent to close at $11.4 per share ... Putin named the chairman of Gazprom's board, Dmitri Medvedev, as his new chief of staff, replacing Alexander Voloshin, who had resigned to protest the arrest of Khodorkovsky.

(*IHT*, 1 November 2003, pp. 1, 9)

'In 1999 Yukos became the first major Russian company to release its quarterly results in accordance with international accounting standards. Independent directors are a majority on the company's board ... Yukos gave $45 million to charity in 2002' (p. 4).

Russia's general prosecutor's office said it had lifted a freezing order on about 2 per cent [2 percentage points] of the 44 per cent of Yukos shares that it first made on Thursday. The order was designed to prevent the stake's sale by Mikhail Khodorkovsky ... Mr Putin's appointment of Dmitri Medvedev ... in Mr Voloshin's place, with Dmitri Kozak as his deputy, was welcomed by many analysts and financial institutions.

(*FT*, 1 November 2003, p. 7)

'Prosecutors ... [unfroze] 4.5 per cent [i.e. 2 percentage points] of the company's shares, accepting they "belong to private individuals having no relation to the criminal cases that are being investigated"' (*Guardian*, 1 November 2003, p. 21).

'Mikhail Khodorkovsky ... bought ... Yukos ... in 1995 for $309 million at a privatization auction run by a bank he secretly owned through offshore companies' (*The Times*, 1 November 2003, p. 25).

Khodorkovsky's [Menatep] group paid $309 million to gain control of a 78 per cent stake in Yukos ... He is ploughing money into civic good works, ranging from internet access for rural libraries to foreign exchange programmes for Russian students ... Open Russia [is] the non-profit organization he founded in 2001 to promote civil society. He publicly admitted that he and other major Yukos shareholders personally contributed to two political parties, the liberal Union of Rightist Forces and the social democrat Yabloko. He also acknowledged that some prominent Yukos shareholders supported the Communists ... His father was Jewish.

(*FT*, Magazine, 1 November 2003, pp. 17–22)

In Washington the State Department's spokesman twice expressed doubts about the fairness of Russian justice, as have officials in Europe ... The courts, whose judges serve by presidential decree, rarely challenge, let alone overrule, prosecutors, and defence lawyers have little recourse to appeal.

(Steven Lee Myers, *IHT*, 3 November 2003, p. 3)

2 November 2003.

The new Kremlin chief of staff said ... that prosecutors should have considered the economic impact of freezing a majority stake in Yukos ...

Dmitri Medvedev … also said it was not clear to him that freezing the stake of Khodorkovsky and Lebedev had been an effective move.

(*IHT*, 3 November 2003, p. 3)

Dmitri Medvedev:

How effective legally was the freezing of Yukos shares? These shares are owned offshore and can be used as compensation for damages. Our colleagues should probably consider all the economic consequences of the measures they take. The legal effectiveness of such measures is not clear.

(*The Times*, 3 November 2003, p. 15; *IHT*, 3 November 2003, p. 3)

'Mr Medvedev is seen as a liberal reformist, but he is not well disposed to … oligarchs' (*The Times*, 3 November 2003, p. 15).

'Advisers to Mr Khodorkovsky indicated that Leonid Nevzlin, his long-standing partner and key shareholder who emigrated to Israel over the summer, had taken control of his shares' (*FT*, 3 November 2003, p. 1).

Advisers to Mr Khodorkovsky say that ownership of his shares, including voting rights and the possibility of selling them to third parties, was transferred after his arrest, in accordance with a trust document that he made public last year [2002]. One adviser denied that control of his shares had passed to the influential British financier Jacob Rothschild, and indicated that it was instead held by Leonid Nevzlin, Yukos's second-latest shareholder and a long-standing partner of Mr Khodorkovsky who is now based in Israel.

(p. 7)

'The US State Department this weekend said the freezing of Yukos's assets raised "serious questions", sparking an angry response from a Russian spokesman' (*FT*, Saturday 3 November 2003, p. 19).

3 November 2003.

Mikhail Khodorkovsky … resigned Monday [3 November] as head of … Yukos, saying he wanted to protect the company from any further damage … Khodorkovsky said he planned to continue his work for the Open Russia Foundation, which he founded in 2001 … The US State Department said it [the freezing of Yukos shares] raised 'serious questions about the rule of law in Russia' … The newspaper *Gazeta* reported a major Siberian oil and gas field controlled until recently by a Yukos-affiliated company has been handed to another company. The natural resources ministry has given drilling rights to the Talakan field to Surgutneftegaz until a tender scheduled for the second quarter of 2004 … The licence held by Lenaneftegaz, which is controlled by a company majority-owned by Yukos, expired last month [October]. Gazeta said the prosecutor-general's office has ordered the ministry to determine whether Yukos is a 'conscientious user of natural resources'.

(www.iht.com, 3 November 2003)

Mikhail Khodorkovsky ... defiantly vowed to continue a public – and possibly political – campaign 'to build an open and truly democratic society in Russia' ... [He said] he was stepping aside in order to shield the company from what he and others have called a politically motivated prosecution ... Group Menatep, the financial company controlled by Khodorkovsky and Lebedev, said that Khodorkovsky had transferred control of his stocks to another Yukos shareholder, Leonid Nevzlin, who is in Israel. That leaves Nevzlin with the authority to vote on behalf of Khodorkovsky while he remains in prison ... Simon Kukes, the Russian-born American chairman of the company's board of directors, would be appointed the chief executive on Yukos on Tuesday [4 November] ... Kukes ran Tyumen Oil before joining Yukos earlier this year ... Yukos stock soared 9.3 per cent ... closing up 32.1 roubles at 379.1 roubles or $12.65 ... The RTS stock index gained 6.3 per cent.

(*IHT*, 4 November 2003, p. 1)

4 November 2003. '[It is announced that] Simon Kukos, a Russian-born American executive [who was given US citizenship in 1982] ... would succeed Mikhail Khodorkovsky as head of [Yukos] ... The RTS [closed] up 19.07 points, or 3.5 per cent, at 557.21' (www.iht.com, 4 November 2003).

5 November 2003.

President Putin disavowed a suggestion by one of his top ministers that some of the company's coveted petroleum exploration licences may be withdrawn. Putin ... stepped in quickly with words of reassurance after Russia's natural resources minister said the licences could be withdrawn. 'I expect that the government will refrain from steps of this kind,' Putin said ... 'There would be the impression that the state's goal is to discontinue the activity of the company,' he said ... The minister of natural resources, Vitali Artyukov, said that Yukos could lose the licences for its oil fields because it was not fulfilling its licensing obligations: 'If need be we will act in a pre-emptive manner. The reasons are obvious: a company which has had a controlling packet of shares frozen is hardly a suitable partner for co-operation with the federal licensing authority' ... If such steps were to be taken the government could in theory seize the oil fields and devalue the stock of Yukos ... Following what appeared to be a prearranged plan, Khodorkovsky is believed to have transferred control of his shares to Leonid Nevzlin ... Nevzlin is now in Israel, where the government said Wednesday [5 November] that it had granted him citizenship ... Khodorkovsky has a Jewish background, though he is not a practising Jew.

(*IHT*, 6 November 2003, pp. 1, 4)

(Mr Nevzlin owns 8 per cent of Yukos': *The Times*, 6 November 2003, p. 15.)

President Vladimir Putin: 'I have big doubts about the appropriateness of these steps. The state surely does not want to destroy the company' (*FT*, 6 November 2003, p. 10).

Yukos Oil's credit-ratings outlook was cut on Wednesday [5 November] by Moody's Investors Service ... Yukos shares ... fell 4.4 per cent on Wednesday ... Yukos, which planned a debut sale of $1 billion in Eurobonds this month [November], is now looking to sell the debt next year [2004].

(www.iht.com, 5 November 2003)

Yukos's shares fell 6 per cent ... Moody's, the credit rating agency, put Yukos and Sibneft ... on a 'negative watch'. The move, which normally precedes a downgrade, followed a similar decision this week by Standard & Poor's and could increase Yukos's borrowing costs ... A 42 per cent stake [in Yukos was] frozen last week.

(*IHT*, 6 November 2003, p. 10)

6 November 2003. President Putin:

People earned billions, I repeat billions, of dollars in the space of five to six years. This would not have been possible in any west European country ... I say officially that the Yukos case will not lead to revision of the Russian Federation's policy in the economic or political sphere. There are no plans of this kind. Our action is guided by the desire to instil law and order in the country and fight corruption ... Our aim is not to go after specific individuals but to establish order in the country. And we will do so in a consistent and tough fashion without regard to whatever attempts these people may make to defend themselves or even resort to blackmail. Attempts to blackmail the state authorities will fail.

(*IHT*, 7 November 2003, p. 3)

'Khodorkovsky [has] funded charitable as well as academic institutions like the Carnegie Endowment [in the United States]' (*IHT*, 7 November 2003, p. 3).

A Siberian court ... declared that his [Vasili Shakhnovsky's] election to ... the Federation Council [on 27 October] ... was invalid, stripping him of immunity from prosecution ... Russia's general prosecutor's office called on the regional court in Krasnoyarsk to declare the election void on the grounds that the Evenkia local assembly failed to respect electoral rules when it elected Shakhnovsky. The court Thursday [6 November] agreed with the prosecutor's arguments and ruled Shakhnovsky's election invalid ... Shakhnovsky last month [October] was charged with evading taxes to the tune of $1 billion between 1998 and 2000. He holds a 3.09 per cent stake in Yukos-Sibneft ... The merger is due to be finalized at a shareholders' meeting in late November.

(*IHT*, 7 November 2003, p. 3)

'It was alleged that he [Shakhnovsky] had not produced the necessary papers and had stood unopposed, which is illegal. Nor was there any obvious reason why the previous incumbent should have given up his mandate with three years to run' (*The Independent*, 7 November 2003, p. 18).

7 November 2003.

> Russia is expecting a net private capital flight of more than $13 billion in
> the last six months of this year, in contrast to the first half of the year, when
> a net $4.6 billion flowed into the country, the first sustained capital inflow
> since the collapse of communism ... Net private capital outflow reached
> $7.7 billion in the third quarter of the year and the central bank expected it
> to reach $8.6 billion for the full year ... The central bank's reserves rose by
> $100 million last week.
>
> (*FT*, 8 November 2003, p. 6)

'According to the Economist Intelligence Unit ... capital flight this year
[2003] jumped to $23 billion after falling last year to $16 billion and has started
to fell ever faster' (*The Economist*, 8 November 2003, p. 90).

('Russia's foreign exchange reserves rose $800 million last week to hit a
new high of $66.2 billion ... in a further sign that the capital flight just after
the arrest of Mikhail Khodorkovsky may be abating ... Russia had a net capital
outflow in the first half of 2003 but there was a $7.7 billion outflow in the third
quarter ... The central bank is forecasting net private capital outflows to ease
to $3 billion to $4.5 billion in the fourth quarter': *IHT*, 28 November 2003,
p. 12.)

11 November 2003.

> Shares in Yukos ... closed nearly 3 per cent lower yesterday [11 November]
> after a Moscow court refused to bail Mikhail Khodorkovsky ... The court
> rejected an appeal against Mr Khodorkovsky's continued detention in pre-
> trial custody at least until 30 December.
>
> (*FT*, 12 November 2003, p. 10)

14 November 2003.

> Prime minister Mikhail Kasyanov ... tried to rein back aggressive regional
> officials who have been probing whether ... [Yukos] has fulfilled the terms
> of its key oil production licences ... [He] said it was 'unacceptable' that the
> ministry of natural resources had created 'a threatening atmosphere around
> the company' during its inspections ... Mr Kasyanov confirmed that plans
> for administrative reform may include proposals to dilute the power of the
> prosecutor's office, handing investigations to the ministry of justice. German
> Gref, the economics minister, stressed his commitment to pursue a new pro-
> portional petroleum tax that would be levied on an oil field's maturity. The
> proposal had been fiercely resisted this summer by Yukos ... [President
> Putin told] members of the Russian Union of Industrialists and Entrepre-
> neurs that reforms would go ahead.
>
> (*FT*, 15 November 2003, p. 6)

Top Russian businessmen began to distance themselves on Friday [14 Novem-
ber] from ... Mikhail Khodorkovsky ... President Vladimir Putin reiterated

that the investigation ... did not mark return to 1990s-style privatizations. 'Any criminal case involving business prompts concern and alarm, because the question always arises: will there be a return to the past?' Putin said, referring to concerns the Yukos case signals a backtracking by the government on privatization. 'There will not be. It is impossible,' he told ... the Russian Union of Industrialists and Entrepreneurs. While the state must prosecute criminals, Putin said, 'it must also protect everybody, including and not last of all business, because that means protecting the economy of the state [country]' ... Some of Russia's tycoons were quick to avoid further confrontation ... 'The Russian president has made it perfectly clear that there should be a dividing line between business and the authorities,' said Vladimir Potanin.

(*IHT*, 15 November 2003, p. 9)

18 November 2003.

The audit chamber, the accounting watchdog of the Russian parliament, said it had conducted an enquiry of Sibneft, which recently merged with Yukos, and handed the results of its investigations to law enforcement officials ... [The chamber] accused the oil giant [Sibneft] controlled by ... Roman Abramovich of 'wrongdoings' in its tax affairs.

(*Guardian*, 19 November 2003, p. 18)

17 November 2003.

The popularity of President Vladimir Putin has risen sharply in recent days and the legal wrangle campaign against Yukos has probably contributed to the surge, a polling institute said Monday [17 November]. Approval of Putin's policies has risen to 82 per cent, compared with 73 per cent three weeks ago, the independent polling institute Vtsiom said.

(*IHT*, 18 November 2003, p. 10)

28 November 2003.

Sibneft suspended its merger with Yukos, freezing a deal that would have created the world's fourth largest oil producer. Citing 'technical difficulties' Sibneft issued a terse statement Friday [28 November] saying it had 'put on hold' a $14 billion takeover by Yukos ... The move stunned Yukos managers, who said after the announcement that the company would continue with the deal. Simon Kukes, the new chief executive of Yukos ... [said] that the deal 'is still on. It has not been suspended' ... Last month [October] Yukos became the owner of 92 per cent of Sibneft shares and Sibneft received roughly 26 per cent of Yukos shares ... Yukos acquired 92 per cent of Sibneft, paying Roman Abramovich $3 billion in cash for the first 20 per cent of his company and then swapping 26 per cent of the combined company for his other 72 per cent of Sibneft ... Before his arrest Mikhail Khodorkovsky had been negotiating for a sale of up to 25 per cent of the combined company to a major Western buyer such as Exxon Mobil or ChevronTexaco for an estimated $40 billion.

(*IHT*, 29 November 2003, pp. 1, 4)

Roman Abramovich ... called a halt to Russia's biggest corporate deal ... The companies said the decision to suspend the merger was 'mutual', but individuals close to the talks indicated that Mr Abramovich had taken the initiative after disagreements including his wish to impose Eugene Shvidler, the Sibneft chief executive, as head of the combined group ... This month [November] Yukos appointed Simon Kukes chief executive ... Mr Shvidler was set to take the less operational job of president ... If the merger fails Mr Abramovich may be forced to pay back $3 billion in cash he has received as well as a $1 billion penalty ... Sibneft and Yukos cancelled their planned merger five years ago ... It was Roman Abramovich who proposed a merger to Mikhail Khodorkovsky at the start of this year [2003].

(*FT*, Money and Business, 29 November 2003, pp. 1, 5)

Roman Abramovich blocked the ... takeover after Yukos refused to accept Eugene Shvidler, Sibneft's president, as chief executive of the merged company, people familiar with the matter said. Abramovich also asked Yukos to appoint Sibneft executives to top management posts, said the people, who asked not to be identified.

(*IHT*, 1 December 2003, p. 14)

According to *Forbes Magazine* ... Russia's headcount of billionaires is the fourth highest in the world ... Worldwide the number of billionaires year-on-year fell from 497 to 476 ... The [Russian] list burgeoned during the past year to seventeen – ten more than in 2002.

(*Transition*, 2003, vol. 14, nos 7–9, p. 14)

The 2003 list, in order of wealth in Russia and with the world ranking in brackets, is as follows:

Mikhail Khodorkovsky, $8 billion (26): Menatep/Yukos 'Khodorkovsky says he owns 6 per cent to 7 per cent of Yukos';

Roman Abramovich, $5.7 billion (49): Millhouse Capital (Sibneft/RusAl); 'Governor of the Chukotka Autonomous Region';

Mikhail Fridman, $4.3 billion (68): Alfa Group/Tyumen Oil;

Viktor Vekselberg, $2.5 billion (147): Alfa Group/Tyumen Oil;

Vladimir Potanin, $1.8 billion, (222): Interros/Norilsk Nickel;

Mikhail Prokhorov $1.6 billion (256): Interros/Norilsk Nickel;

Vladimir Yevtushenkov, $1.5 billion (278): AFK Sistema;

Oleg Deripaska, $1.5 billion (278): Base Element (RusAl);

Vagit Alekperov, $1.3 billion (329): Lukoil;

Alexei Mordashov, $1.2 billion (348): Severstal;

Leonid Nevzlin, $1.1 billion (386): Menatep/Yukos;

Eugene Shvidler, $1.1 billion (386) Sibneft;

Vladimir Bogdanov, $1.0 billion (427): Surgutneftegaz;

Mikhail Brudno, $1.0 billion (427): Menatep/Yukos;

Vladimir Dubov, $1.0 billion (427): Menatep/Yukos;

Platon Lebedev, $1.0 billion (427): Menatep/Yukos;

Vasili Shakhnovsky, $1.0 billion (427): Menatep/Yukos.

'Boris Berezovsky's name is missing from the list, although he recently estimated his fortune at $3 billion. He was declared the country's richest man in 1997' (p. 15).

7 December 2003. A general election is held.

Eighteen parties and five electoral blocs contested the 450 seats in the State Duma. There was once again a 5 per cent threshold for the 225 seats elected by proportional representation from national party lists. The other 225 seats were elected, as before, by means of single-member constituencies in a first-past-the-post system. The turnout was about 55.75 per cent (compared with 64.4 per cent in December 1995 and 61.85 per cent in December 1999). There were some 107 million eligible voters. A minimum of thirty deputies are needed to form a faction in the State Duma.

There were also other elections. For example, Yuri Luzhkov was re-elected mayor of Moscow (with 74.82 per cent of the vote). A number of regional governorships were also up for election.

Pro-Putin parties (principally United Russia, the Liberal Democratic Party, Rodina [Motherland] and the People's Party) swept to power. United Russia won almost half of the seats in the State Duma. Nationalists made major gains. The Liberal Democratic Party more than doubled its representation. The newcomers, Motherland and the People's Party, did well. In contrast, Communist Party support roughly halved. Yabloko and the Union of Rightist Forces both failed to reach the 5 per cent threshold and ended up with only a handful of constituency seats.

The 450 State Duma seats were distributed as follows (total seats, party list seats, party list percentage of vote and constituency seats, respectively:

United Russia: 222 (117, 37.57 per cent, 105);
Communist Party: 53 (41, 12.61 per cent, 12);
Liberal Democratic Party: 38 (38, 11.45 per cent, zero);
Motherland bloc: 45 (37, 9.02 per cent, 8);
People's Party 20 (zero, 1.19 per cent, 20);
Yabloko 4 (zero, 4.3 per cent, 4);
Union of Rightist Forces 3 (zero, 3.97 per cent, 4);
Agrarian Party: 3.64 per cent;
Party of Pensioners/Party of Social Justice bloc: 3.09 per cent;
Russian Revival Party/Russian Party of Life bloc: 1.88 per cent;
Unity: 1.17 per cent;
New Course/Automotive Russia bloc: 0.84 per cent;
For Holy Rus: 0.49 per cent; Greens: 0.42 per cent;
Development of Entrepreneurship: 0.35 per cent
Great Russia/Eurasian Union bloc: 0.28 per cent;
True Patriots of Russia: 0.25 per cent;
Peace and Unity Party: 0.25 per cent;

Rus: 0.24 per cent;
Democratic Party: 0.22 per cent;
Russian Constitutional Democratic Party: 0.19 per cent;
Union of People for Education and Science: 0.18 per cent;
People's Republican Party: 0.13 per cent;
None of the above (against all candidates): 4.70 per cent.
Others/independents 75?

> The nation's largest businesses – including oil giants, banks and manufac-
> turers – have not only poured money into the parliamentary elections …
> but have also filled party tickets with dozens of their own executives.
> Yukos Oil … has executives running as candidates not only for the liberal
> Yabloko party but also for the Communists and for United Russia … Two
> oil companies, TNK and Lukoil, have executives running on the party's
> ticket, as do Russian Aluminium and the steel giant Severstal. An analysis
> of United Russia's national and regional party lists by *The Moscow Times*
> showed that more than a quarter of United Russia's parliamentary candid-
> ates represented big businesses … TNK also has a spot on the Communist
> ticket, while Russian Aluminium's deputy general director is running as a
> candidate for the Liberal Democratic Party, led by Vladimir Zhirinovsky
> … The extent of executives' participation in the election has been made
> known by a new law requiring candidates to declare their incomes and
> employers. If elected, executives are required to resign from their com-
> panies, but they can keep their shares and other holdings … Leonid
> Mayevsky, a Communist deputy in the current parliament, publicly criti-
> cized the party at a news conference this month, saying that 28 per cent of
> its candidates were millionaires … He was promptly expelled from the
> party.
>
> (*IHT*, 2 December 2003, pp. 1, 4)

A lacklustre campaign produced a lacklustre turnout … The pallid turnout
appeared to reflect the indifference of voters after a campaign that lacked
great passions … United Russia offered few prescriptions for the country's ills and refused even to debate its rivals. The party relied instead on
slavish coverage by the state's television networks and on the vast
resources of regional governors and mayors … OSCE, which sent a delegation to observe the election, issued a stinging report last week citing 'a
clear bias' in media coverage and 'verified instances' of government
buildings and other resources being made available only to United Russia
… United Russia campaigned on slogans of law and order, vowing to
battle corruption and 'oligarchs' like Khodorkovsky, even though the
party has its own candidates from some of the nation's biggest businesses
… State television continued to display disproportionate coverage of Putin
and United Russia, reporting little on opposition parties as the vote continued through the day.

(Steven Lee Myers, *IHT*, 8 December 2003, pp. 1, 6)

The Communist Party ... faded badly after a bruising campaign that reflected internal divisions, challenges from breakaway parties and relentless assaults on state television ... While many in Russia and abroad have raised alarms over a steady erosion of freedoms, from the strangulation of independent media to the increasing influence of state security services, voters clearly embraced the political stability and economic development that Putin and United Russia promised to nurture.

(Steven Lee Myers, www.iht.com, 8 December 2003)

The Motherland Party [is] believed to be supported by Kremlin hardliners ... Motherland, which was created only this year [September 2003] and captured much of the Communist vote, ran on a programme that attacked the country's ... oligarchs and called for a $40 billion one-off levy to compensate the state for the cut-price privatizations from which they benefited ... It is jointly led by Dmitri Rogozin, the outspoken nationalist who heads the foreign affairs committee of the outgoing Duma and who called for Anatoli Chubais ... to be put in prison.

(*FT*, 8 December 2003, p. 8)

'Motherland launched a vociferous campaign against the oligarchs, seeking to tax the "natural rent" they make from oil and metals, and aopted nationalist rhetoric on several foreign policy issues' (*FT*, 9 December 2003, p. 10).

Rodina [Motherland] was founded four months ago by the experienced economist and former communist, Sergei Glazyev, and the Kremlin's rising star, Dmitri Rogozin. Mr Rogozin, the president's personal envoy to ... Kaliningrad, also headed the international affairs committee in parliament.

(*Guardian*, 9 December 2003, p. 14)

Motherland [is] a Kremlin-backed party ... led by Sergei Glazyev, an ex-communist, and Dmitri Rogozin, a moderate nationalist ... It did the job it was created for: snatching votes from the Communists ... Motherland and the People's Party both represent the hardline, security services wing of the Kremlin elite ... Both Motherland and the Liberal Democrats capitalized on the public's distaste for Mr Khodorkovsky by calling for increased taxes on natural resources companies, a call that even some members ... of the Union of Rightist Forces ... supported.

(*The Economist*, 13 December 2003, p. 22)

'The People's Party [is] a splinter of ... United Russia ... Motherland and the People's Party both represent the hardline, security services wing of the Kremlin elite' (*The Economist*, 13 December 2003, p. 22).

Russians can vote only in their place of permanent residence, which is usually where they were born unless they have bought property elsewhere. [The] upwardly and geographically mobile voters ... [of] Yabloko and the Union of Rightist Forces ... the people mostly likely to be living and renting in a different city ... fall foul of this. Another nail in the parties' coffin was their bitter campaign squabbles.

(The Economist, 13 December 2003, p. 23)

[Officials from OSCE] condemned the parliamentary elections in Russia on Monday [8 December], saying it fell short of international legal requirements and represented a retreat from Russia's democratic reforms ... [Bruce George, head of the parliamentary assembly for OSCE:] 'The election management on the day was superb. The major criticism was the media. Every outlet was attacking all the opposition parties. There was also an abuse of administrative resources. All governments make use of their incumbency, but there is a line past which you should not go ... [The Kremlin had] organized the machinery of government towards the goal of protecting it and its party. We have chapter and verse on that. It was the three to nine months before the election – the arrests, the cutting off of funding, the jailing of people. There was very little ballot stuffing. Much of it was subtle, but it was very effective.' George said the elections had failed to meet 'international standards' ... Extensive use of the state apparatus [and the media was to the] benefit of United Russia ... [This had] created an unfair environment for the other parties and candidates ... The enormous advantage of incumbency and access to state equipment, resources and buildings led to the election result being overwhelmingly distorted ... [The] main impression of the overall process was one of regression in the democratization of this country ... [There was] blatant fraud [in Bashkortostan and] irregularities [in Siberia and the Far East].

(Guardian, 9 December 2003, p. 3; *FT*, 9 December 2003, p. 1; *IHT*, 9 December 2003, p. pp. 1, 10)

Two groups that sent election observers, the Council of Europe and OSCE, said in a report that the results also reflected 'the extensive use of the state apparatus and the media favourable to benefit the largest pro-presidential party'. The report, based on 500 observers, offered some of the harshest European criticism, saying the vote called into question 'Russia's willingness to move towards European standards for democratic elections'.

(IHT, 9 December 2003, p. 1)

OSCE monitors found 'a clear bias in the state-owned media in support of United Russia and other pro-presidential parties ... [as well as] a selective application of registration criteria' to exclude from the ballot candidates who displeased or frightened what Russians call the party of power.

(www.iht.com, 10 December 2003)

'OSCE ... called the exercise "overwhelmingly distorted"' (*IHT*, 10 December 2003, p. 8). 'OSCE had sent a 400-member team to monitor the campaign' (www.iht.com, 8 December 2003).

OSCE ... of which Russia is a member ... said the use of the state apparatus and media to promote the programme of United Russia 'created an unfair environment for the other parties and candidates ... The main impression of the overall electoral process is of regression in the democratization process in Russia ... [The election called into question Russia's] willingness to move towards European standards for democratic elections' ... United Russia has been criticized for its leaders' use of their cabinet posts to promote the party and government facilities during the campaign.

(*Guardian*, 9 December 2003, p. 2)

('[On 26 January 2004] members of the Council of Europe in Strasbourg reiterated concern that December parliamentary elections were "free but not fair", notably as the result of heavy bias in the state media': *FT*, 27 January 2004, p. 8.)

The Bush administration expressed concern Monday [8 December] about the fairness of Russian parliamentary elections that left President Vladimir Putin in a greatly strengthened position. The administration joined its voice to that of OSCE ... which said that the election process has been 'free but certainly not fair' and had marked a retreat from democratic reforms ... The White House spokesman ... noted that OSCE expressed concerns about the fairness of the election campaign and added: 'We share those concerns.'

(*IHT*, 9 December 2003, p. 3)

The White House said it shared the concerns of OSCE, which described the conduct of the campaign as a 'regression in the democratization process of the country' ... The White House spokesman said OSCE's criticism underlined 'the importance of Russian legislators dedicating themselves to pushing through the political and economic reform agenda ... [but] based on the pre-election polling, it appears that the election results roughly reflected the views of the electorate'.

(*FT*, 9 December 2003, p. 1)

Where free elections have been held in former Soviet states they have often brought in recycled communists or fledgling tyrants. The reason is not any innate Eastern preference for dictatorship, but an inevitable frustration with the chaos and dislocation of transition.

(*IHT*, editorial, 10 December 2003, p. 8)

'The vote left United Russia with 306 seats, slightly more than the two-thirds majority required to change the constitution' (*IHT*, 6 February 2004, p. 1).

9 December 2003.

President Putin sought to dispel speculation that he planned to alter the country's constitution to extend his term of office: 'It is time for us to end all talk about the need to change the constitution. I absolutely think that the current constitution became the basis for stability in society and I believe that it has not exhausted its positive potential' ... Speculation has been rife in Moscow that Putin will try to centralize power and perhaps extend his own term. The Kremlin needed to secure 301 seats [in the 450-seat State Duma] to push through amendments to a constitution written by ... Boris Yeltsin and ratified by Russians on 12 December 1993. Russian leaders are now limited to two terms in office.

(*IHT*, 10 December 2003, p. 5)

'[A] two-thirds majority [is] needed to change the constitution ... Changing it requires the approval of most of the regional legislatures too' (*The Economist*, 13 December 2003, p. 24).

Roman Abramovich ... has called off the merger [between Sibneft and Yukos] ... people close to Sibneft said ... Mr Abramovich will have to pay back $3 billion in cash in order to get back his 92 per cent stake in Sibneft. The deal also carried a $1 billion breakup fee but people close to both companies said that would not be paid. A Yukos insider said it could take between two and three months to unwind the deal because of complex technicalities.

(*FT*, 10 December 2003, p. 1)

A source familiar with Mr Abramovich said he was prepared to pay back $3 billion and 26 per cent of Yukos shares to get back his 92 per cent in Sibneft ... It is understood that Mr Abramovich entered into a deal with Yukos on the expectations that a large stake in a new, larger company would be sold to a foreign oil group.

(*FT*, 11 December 2003, p. 12)

Yukos could demand as much as $5 billion in payments and compensation from Roman Abramovich ... Leonid Nevzlin ... said that Yukos shareholders would expect compensation for what was 'in effect an interest-free loan'. He said Yukos shareholders should also be compensated for the fall in their share prices since Mr Abramovich announced his intention to unravel the merger. Mr Nevzlin said he thought a fair fee would be $1 billion to $2 billion.

(*FT*, 12 December 2003, p. 26)

12 December 2003.

Russia's chief securities regulator said the planned merger of Yukos Oil and Sibneft should be salvaged with a Sibneft executive in charge. Igor Kostikov, chairman of the federal commission for the securities market ... is the first Russian official to publicly back the merger since it stalled last month [November].

(*IHT*, 13 December 2003, p. 15)

16 December 2003.

Yukos and Sibneft have agreed to reverse their planned merger ... reports said on Tuesday [16 December] ... The two sides signed a letter of intent over the weekend ... The process is expected to take months and approval will soon be sought from the federal securities commission ... The deal ... [is said to call for] Sibneft shareholders to return $3 billion in cash and 26 per cent of Yukos shares to [Yukos].

(www.iht.com, 16 December 2003)

Yukos and Sibneft are expected to declare on Wednesday [17 December] that they have formally ended their merger. But on Tuesday [16 December] the terms of the divorce are still not clear. At issue is whether Yukos will be paid some form of compensation by Sibneft for walking away from the planned merger ... The estimated value of the combined companies has dropped from roughly $45 billion to $30 billion since his [Khodorkovsky's] jailing. On Tuesday Yukos closed down 9.41 roubles at 290.26 roubles, or $9.90.

(*IHT*, 27 December 2003, p. 15)

17 December 2003.

Yukos Oil formally announced plans Wednesday [17 December] to reverse its merger with Sibneft ... Details are still being discussed and Yukos plans to seek interest on $3 billion in cash that it paid for part of the Sibneft stake ... But Sibneft will not have to pay a $1 billion breakup fee ... No legal documents to unwind the merger have been signed.

(www.iht.com, 17 December 2003)

'Yukos and Sibneft agreed in principle Wednesday [17 December] to dissolve the $13 billion merger agreement ... Yukos executives said the oil company would seek a payment ... reflecting interest on the $3 billion it received from its shares' (*IHT*, 18 December 2003, p. 11).

18 December 2003.

President Vladimir Putin ... confirmed Thursday [18 December] that he would run for a second term in March and dismissed suggestions that he would change the constitution to stay longer. Putin made his widely expected announcement in a three-hour televised call-in programme.

(*IHT*, 29 December 2003, p.)

President Putin:

I am going to run. I intend to make an official declaration on this matter soon ... I am against anyone, whoever he might be and however laudable his intentions might be, violating the constitution ... There is more and more talk about severe taxation of the oil industry. And I can see some sense in it. We need to balance the development of different sectors of our economy. But we need to do it very carefully.

(*IHT*, 19 December 2003, p. 3)

21 December 2003.

Yabloko ... said Sunday [21 December] that it would not field a candidate in the presidential vote next year [14 March 2004] ... Grigori Yavlinsky said the decision was made at a party congress because 'free, equitable and politically competitive elections are impossible' in Russia's current situation ... 'No one is talking about ideal democracy, but there should be certain limits. And the actions of one actor go well beyond these limits. Everything is set up to maintain complete control over the elections and the count,' Yavlinsky said ... Party delegates ... also agreed not to support Putin ... 'In the two weeks since the election we have had intensive consultations with our colleagues from Yabloko. We have unfortunately failed to find a joint candidate,' Boris Nemtsov [of the Union of Rightist Forces said] ... Yabloko and the Union of Rightist Forces spent much of the parliamentary campaign sniping at one another ... Yavlinsky also said Sunday that a party unifying the liberal opposition should be formed in the next few years and that Yabloko might be dissolved.

(*IHT*, 22 December 2003, p. 4)

'At its party congress yesterday [21 December] Yabloko said: "the parliamentary election campaign demonstrated the lack of free democratic elections in Russia" ... Yabloko also called for the release of Mikhail Khodorkovsky ... from pre-trial detention' (*FT*, 22 December 2003, p. 10).

23 December 2003.

A Moscow court extended by three months a pre-trial detention of Mikhail Khodorkovsky ... [It] ruled that Mr Khodorkovsky ... charged with fraud, tax evasion and theft ... would remain in prison at least until 25 March, after the [14 March] presidential elections.

(*FT*, 24 December 2003, p. 6)

('The collision between ... President Vladimir Putin and ... Mikhail Khodorkovsky had been brewing for months when Khodorkovsky took the step that more than any other landed him in prison – trying to sell a major stake in ... Yukos to ExxonMobil. As the story is recounted by associates and analysts, Khodorkovsky failed to consult the Kremlin adequately about a deal that would cede substantial control over a strategic Russian resource to a foreign company, and an American one at that ... Khodorkovsky's pursuit of an Exxon Mobil deal, said a senior Russian official who requested anonymity, was a "catalysing event" for the Kremlin': *IHT*, 3 January 2004, pp. 1, 8.)

'Platon Lebedev ... lost an appeal against his extended detention period' (*IHT*, 24 December 2003, p. 3).

President Vladimir Putin issued a stark warning to Russia's oligarchs yesterday [23 December] ... Speaking before the Russian Chamber of Commerce and Industry Mr Putin qualified his earlier promise not to review the results of the country's privatizations, saying this did not apply to 'people who did not follow the law' when they took place.

(*FT*, 24 December 2003, p. 6)

'President Putin ... reaffirmed his earlier stance that the government was not planning a major redistribution of assets gained through privatization of state property, but said he was referring only to those who "abided by the law" ' (*IHT*, 24 December 2003, p. 3).

President Putin:

> Those who consciously stole should not get preferential treatment compared to those who behaved well and respected the law. Yes, the laws were complicated and confusing, but you could abide by them ... It was possible to follow them completely. If five or seven or ten people broke the law it does not mean that others did the same ... Those who wanted to did so. Those who were fraudulent deliberately created better conditions from themselves than those who behaved properly. The latter may not have earned so much, but they can sleep soundly.
>
> (*The Times*, 24 December 2003, p. 14, and 29 December 2003, p. 13; *FT*, 24 December 2003, p. 6; *Guardian*, 30 December 2003, p. 11)

('Russia has announced plans to review the results of its privatization of state property ... The government's audit chamber announced the review plan in a statement after last week between Mr Putin and the top official in charge of auditing Russian firms. "Next year [2004] we plan to analyse the results of the privatization of state assets over the past ten years," the statement said': *The Times*, 29 December 2003, p. 13. '[On 29 December] the audit chamber announced it would review all privatizations from the past decade ... The announcement came a few days after President Vladimir Putin warned businessmen that the government would crack down on those who broke laws in the privatization deals ... The audit head [is] Sergei Stepashin, a former prime minister and one-time head of the FSB, Russia's security service ... The chamber is a constitutional body established by and responsible to the Duma and holds no executive power, although it makes recommendations to legislators': *Guardian*, 30 December 2003, p. 11.)

26 December 2003.

> Vladimir Zhirinovsky said Friday [26 December] that he would not run in the presidential in March ... But he added that he would 'campaign for our [Liberal Democratic Party] candidate' ... Oleg Malyshkin [is] a fifty-year-old former boxer and a complete political unknown.
>
> (*IHT*, 27 December 2003, p. 3)

> With an estimated 308 seats ... United Russia ... now holds a two-thirds majority after independents joined the pro-Kremlin faction in the wake of the parliamentary elections, party officials say. The final figure will be confirmed Monday [29 December] during the first Duma session following the election.
>
> (*IHT*, 27 December 2003, p. 3)

'A Moscow court yesterday [26 December] extended custody until 30 March [2004] of Platon Lebedev' (*FT*, 27 December 2003, p. 7).

28 December 2003.

> Gennadi Zyuganov decided not to challenge Vladimir Putin for the presidency ... [on 14 March 2004] and the Communist Party on Sunday [28 December] chose a hardliner as its candidate ... [He is] Nikolai Kharitonov ... Zyuganov, who ran in the 1996 and 2000 presidential elections, asked not to be nominated.

> (*IHT*, 29 December 2003, p. 3)

29 December 2003.

> The newly elected Russian parliament convened Monday [29 December] and, after a bit of quick horse trading, the bloc supporting President Vladimir Putin established a two-thirds majority that will allow it to pass any laws or make any constitutional changes it wishes ... Boris Gryzlov, the chairman of the president's bloc, United Russia, was elected speaker. United Russia, which is not formally a political party ... now controls at least 300 seats in the 450-seat Duma.

> (*IHT*, 30 December 2003, p. 3)

'Several independent MPs joined United Russia ... giving it 300 seats' (*Daily Telegraph*, 30 December 2003, p. 16).

> In an unusual setback for Russia's security services, a jury on Monday [29 December] acquitted a physicist who had been charged with espionage for selling information to China that he and other scientists had argued was not classified. The physicist, Valentin Danilov, who heads a research institute in Krasnoyarsk, Siberia, was arrested in September 2001 for selling information on Russia's space technology ... Human rights groups, and Danilov himself, attributed the acquittal to the fact that his trial was before a jury, a rarity in Russia, rather than before judges who could be susceptible to state pressure ... Jury trials have been held on an experimental basis over the past decade in only nine of Russia's eighty-nine regions. They are to be introduced throughout the country by 2007 ... Grigori Pasko, a military journalist who has himself been convicted of treason and is now free on parole ... [said] that the security services that succeeded the KGB were continuing a policy of fabricating spy cases ... Since he [Putin] was elected four years ago a number of scientists have been arrested and a number have been convicted on similar charges.

> (*IHT*, 30 December 2003, p. 3)

'It was the first time in recent Russian history that a jury had sat in judgement on an alleged spy' (*Daily Telegraph*, 30 December 2003, p. 16).

30 December 2003.

> Russia's tax authorities yesterday [30 December] stepped up pressure on Yukos, formally charging it with tax evasion of $3.3 billion in a move that could threaten the future of [the company] ... This is the latest and one of

the most substantial in a series of unrelenting attacks on Yukos ... Previously, the Kremlin ... had been careful to ring-fence the company from investigations into its shareholders ... Russia's tax ministry said it had conducted an investigation and concluded that Yukos had underpaid 98 billion roubles ($3.3 billion) in taxes by setting up a network of affiliated companies that claimed tax breaks described as unlawful. The charges relate to the company's activities in 2000 and exceed the company's net profit of $3.1 billion in that year. Yukos said it had paid its taxes in full ... Earlier this month Yukos had been threatened with a tax bill of $5 billion for its activities between 1998 and 2003. Analysts said the magnitude of the tax bills could threaten the very existence of the company ... Yukos is responsible for 20 per cent of the total oil production of the country. The latest attack comes at a time of further complications in the divorce negotiations between Yukos and Sibneft ... Yukos has agreed to separate, but the companies are still to work out the terms of their divorce. Sibneft is trying to reverse the agreement under which Roman Abramovich received $3 billion in cash and 26 per cent in Yukos shares in return for 92 per cent in Sibneft ... Yukos's shares fell 2 per cent yesterday [30 December] in thin trading to $10.57.

(*FT*, 31 December 2003, p. 7)

'The tax ministry ... [accused Yukos] of failing to pay 98 billion roubles, or $3.3 billion, in back taxes, fines and other penalties ... The ministry said that it had made the conclusion after checking Yukos's tax records for 2000' (www.iht. com, 30 December 2003).

Russian authorities ... accused the oil company of not paying more than $3 billion in taxes, a move analysts said could make it difficult for Yukos to survive in its current form. After months of pursuing the main owners of Yukos, the move on Tuesday [30 December] marked the first time the state had directly accused the company itself of breaking the law ... The tax ministry sent a letter to prosecutors earlier this month [December] saying Yukos might owe as much as 150 billion roubles ... Alfa Bank said Yukos's revenue for 2000 was $9 billion, on which it paid $1.9 billion in taxes, representing a 21 per cent tax burden, only slightly below the 23 per cent average for big Russian oil companies.

(*IHT*, 31 December 2003, p. 9)

The first session of the fourth State Duma [begins] ... The deputies are divided into four factions: United Russia (300 seats); Motherland (thirty-six deputies); and the Liberal Democratic Party of Russian (thirty-six deputies) ... A very small group pf independent deputies is not officially organized. Three deputies' seats remain vacant. New elections will be held on 14 March, concurrently with the presidential election. Boris Gryzlov ended up being elected speaker.

(*CDSP*, 2003, vol. 55, no. 52, p. 8)

1 January 2004.

Russian men anxious to avoid compulsory national service ... are being offered an alternative. Conscientious objectors are for the first time able to avoid two years in the military if they sign up for three-and-a-half years of social service instead ... [such as] working in a state-run orphanage or a hospital. Applicants with higher education will serve for one year and nine months, compared with a year in the armed forces ... Only about 3,000 draftees a year are expected to take up the alternative service offer, given the length of it and the fact that they must apply six months in advance ... If a conscientious objector agrees to do non-military duties on an army base, he will serve only three years ... Many families pay ... bribes to doctors to obtain medical certificates to win their sons exemption [from conscription]. Of an annual 400,000 young men who are called up experts estimate that up to a quarter manage to avoid the draft. Among the better-off middle-class families in Moscow it is rare to find a young man who has served in the military ... A four-year programme is under way to cut the army's reliance on conscripts by half. In 2008 military service is due to be reduced to one year.

(*Daily Telegraph*, 2 January 2004, p. 15)

2 January 2003.

Russia is to end conscription and fill more than half its 1.1. million-strong army by 2007. By the end of this year [2004] only full-time soldiers will be deployed in Chechnya ... Many soldiers there are conscripts on six-month or one-year contracts ... The defence minister, Sergei Ivanov, approved the scheme yesterday [2 January 2004] after inspecting the 76th Airborne Division, the first fully professional unit ... Under the previous system every Russian male between eighteen and twenty-seven was required to serve two years in the armed forces ... Under the new system the armed forces plan to recruit about 150,000 volunteers to the best units between 2004 and 2007. By then professionals should account for more than half the army ... President Boris Yeltsin [had] pledged to abolish the draft by 2000 ... The Committee of Soldiers' Mothers, a non-government organization that tracks rights abuses in the military, estimates that 3,500 conscripts die every year from physical abuse, malnutrition and disease. The defence ministry says that those figures are wildly exaggerated. There are ways to avoid conscription. University students are exempt and conscientious objectors and ethnic minorities can do their national service in hospitals, prisons and schools instead. Many others simply pay bribes or plead medical problems. But, for the rest, desertion is often the only escape.

(*The Times*, 3 January 2004, p. 18)

5 January 2004.

A former Dutch minister is to be the new Nato chief. Jaap de Hoop Scheffer, a former air force officer, takes over as Nato secretary-general from

Lord Robertson ... Mr de Hoop Scheffer, fifty-five, quit his job as Dutch foreign minister to take Nato's top job.

(*The Independent*, 5 January 2004, p. 9)

15 January 2004.

Russian police have issued arrest warrants for two key shareholders in Yukos ... Russian press agencies reported yesterday [15 January] ... Leonid Nevzlin, the second largest shareholder in Yukos, faces accusations of 27 million roubles ($935,000) in tax evasion, while Vladimir Dubov, another key lobbyist and shareholder, is under scrutiny by investigators for large-scale fraud.

(*FT*, 16 January 2004, p. 8)

'A court ... rejected a plea by ... Mikhail Khodorkovsky to be released from prison on bail ... On 23 December [2003] a court extended the detention period to 25 March [2004]' (*IHT*, 16 January 2004, p. 3).

21 January 2004. 'Boris Yeltsin has admitted that he suffered five heart attacks while in office, but that he remained "active both mentally and physically"' (*Guardian*, 22 January 2004, p. 18).

23 January 2004.

President Putin's top economic adviser has hinted that personal motives may have been behind the recent pursuit of VimpelCom, Russia's largest mobile phone operator, by the state telecommunications regulator. Andrei Illarianov said at the World Economic Forum in Davos that he could offer no comfort to investors who might conclude from the VimpelCom case that regulation in Russia was uncomfortably arbitrary. Asked if he could assure that the move against VimpelCom was neither politically nor personally motivated, he said: 'If you want assurances that the attack is not a personal attack, I could not give you such an answer.' This month [January] Gossvyaznador, the telecoms regulator, threatened to withdraw the company's operating licence by 1 February for failing to meet a technical requirement on its operating licence ... Analysts played down any direct parallels with the Yukos affair, arguing that the case against Mikhail Khodorkovsky ... was politically motivated, whereas that against Vimpel-Com was a commercial dispute linked to the private business interests of senior individuals in the Russian telecoms ministry. The dispute is believed to be related to the decision last summer [2003] of the powerful Russian conglomerate Alfa, which owns 25 per cent of VimpelCom, to acquire a 25 per cent stake in its rival Megafon, which was established with help from a company set up by Leonid Reiman, the telecoms minister. A Moscow judge on Thursday lifted the regulator's deadline pending judgement on the case ... The attacks on Yukos intensified further this week with the arrest of Rafail Zainullin, chairman of the Kuibyshev refinery, on charges of tax evasion dating from 1999 ... The Russian office of

Interpol confirmed yesterday [23 January] that arrest warrants had been issued against two of Yukos's largest shareholders, Leonid Nevzlin and Vladimir Dubov.

(*FT*, 24 January 2004, p. 8)

26 January 2004. US secretary of state Colin Powell (in an article published in *Izvestia* at the start of a two-day visit to Russia):

Russia's democratic system seems not yet to have found the essential balance among the executive, legislative and judicial branches of government. Political power is not yet fully tethered to law. Key aspects of civil society – free media and political party development, for example – have not yet sustained an independent presence ... Without basic principles shared in common our relationship will not achieve its potential ... Certain aspects of internal Russian policy in Chechnya, and toward neighbours that emerged from the former Soviet Union have concerned us. We recognize Russia's territorial integrity and its natural interest in lands that abut it. But we recognize no less the sovereign integrity of Russia's neighbours and their rights to peaceful and respectful relations across their borders.

27 January 2004.

The Russian authorities yesterday [27 January] stepped up their battle with Yukos when a top investigator said international arrest warrants had been issued against ten of its leading shareholders and managers in related companies. Yuri Biryukov, Russia's first deputy prosecutor-general, said Leonid Nevzlin, Vladimir Dubov and Mikhail Brudno, Yukos's last three core shareholders who fled abroad last year [2003], were sought on charges of 'tax evasion and other crimes'. He said another seven unnamed managers were being sought in the enquiry, in relation to alleged 'imitation' sales of oil products and other mechanisms designed to evade taxes.

(*FT*, 28 January 2004, p. 11)

Yuri Biryukov ... said that a court had placed ten of the company's shareholders or employees on international wanted lists, including some senior executives who have sought asylum in Israel ... All of the company's major shareholders are now either in prison or have fled abroad ... Nevzlin received Israeli citizenship in November [2003] and ... [it is reported that] Dubov has also applied for it ... Biryukov said they [the unnamed seven] were directors of off-shore companies 'through which tax payments were evaded'.

(*IHT*, 28 January 2004, p. 12)

30 January 2004.

The Russian government fired a warning shot across the bows of Roman Abramovich ... announcing an official audit of the remote region where he is governor. Sergei Stepashin, head of the audit chamber, announced that his department would investigate the use of federal funds in Chukotka ... Mr Stepashin claimed the audit was a routine check into the use of federal funds ... 'The purchase of Chelsea in no way influences the result of the inspection,' Mr Stepashin said. 'At the same time a natural question arises ... The charity foundation raising money for homeless children in Russia raised only $1 million over an entire year, but millions of dollars are spent on buying the soccer club' ... Mr Stepashin said he had 'moral questions' to pose to Mr Abramovich.

(*The Times*, 31 January 2004, p. 23)

'An audit official said the inspection was not linked with the Chelsea purchase ... Mr Stepashin only mentioned the "moral" element because Mr Abramovich "could have bought a Russian club, but bought Chelsea"' (*Guardian*, 31 January 2004, p. 21).

('Russian authorities stepped up the pursuit of ... the New York-listed ... VimpelCom, Russia's largest mobile telephone company, as prosecutors launched criminal investigations into the company's right to operate in Moscow ... An industry regulator last month [January] claimed the company had no right to operate in Moscow because its licence was registered in the name of its wholly-owned subsidiary rather than in its own name. However, most analysts suspect that the pursuit of VimpelCom is the result of a wider business conflict involving the interests of its shareholder Alfa Group ... Alfa, which owns a 25 per cent stake in Megafon, a rival company which is believed to be associated with senior officials at the telecommunications ministry. This has pitched Alfa against another Megafon shareholder, Telecominvest, which was set up with the help of Leonid Reiman, telecommunications minister in the early 1990s before his appointment to the government': *IHT*, 5 February 2004, p. 27.)

A Russian court on Friday [30 January] ordered a senior executive at one of Yukos's refineries released from custody. The court in the Volga Samara region threw out a criminal case against Rafail Zainullin for lack of evidence ... [The] tax authorities are claiming $3.3 billion in back taxes owed [by Yukos] from 2000.

(www.iht.com, 31 January 2004)

2 February 2004.

Yukos Oil took another step on Monday [2 February] to separate the management of the Russian oil giant from the principal shareholders ... Based on a recommendation from the company's board that 'no shareholders should interfere in the company's operational management', Mikhail Brudno was removed as acting president of Yukos RM, or Refining Marketing. Brudno was recently put on a wanted list by Russia's prosecutor-general's office. Brudno was the last large Yukos shareholder still actively involved in running day-to-day business at the company. He owns 7 per cent of a holding company called Group Menatep, which houses the financial empire of Mikhail Khodorkovsky.

(IHT, 3 February 2004, p. 11)

The largest shareholders of ... Yukos and Sibneft have signed a protocol to reverse their $13 billion merger ... [that] would have created the fourth largest oil producer in the world after Yukos dropped demands that Sibneft pay compensation for killing the deal ... Under the terms of the protocol Yukos is to return the 92 per cent stake in Sibneft it received in October [2003] and Millhouse Capital ... which represents Sibneft ... is to return the $3 billion in cash and 26 per cent stake in Yukos ... Significantly agents for Mikhail Khodorkovsky [with Group Menatep representing Yukos] and Roman Abramovich – and not the two oil companies – signed the protocol. Yukos scrapped a request for interest on the $3 billion cash payment ... Any proposal to unwind the merger would still require board approval.

(IHT, 4 February 2004, p. 13)

The agreement was signed in Moscow on Monday [2 February] ... Neither side would pay any penalty for ending the merger but would simply return each other's shares and cash payment. Yukos had demanded that Sibneft pay interest on the $3 billion that it paid on 3 October [2003] along with 26 per cent of Yukos's stock, for 92 per cent of Sibneft's shares. In theory it also had the right to demand that Sibneft pay a penalty of $1 billion stipulated for breaking off the merger ... Yukos had formally controlled Sibneft as a subsidiary since it acquired 92 per cent of the company, but its smaller rival continued to operate independently and refused to accept management appointed by Yukos ... Leonid Nevzlin, along with Vladimir Dubov and Mikhail Brudno, fellow owners of Yukos, are wanted by Russia to face charges of tax evasion and embezzlement, and are in Israel.

(www.iht.com, 3 February 2004)

'A senior Yukos executive said that no such proposal had been discussed by the company's board ... and that no simple demerger could take place' *(FT*, 4 February 2004, p. 30).

4 February 2004.

Just two months before Sotheby's was to auction the fabled Forbes family's Imperial Fabergé eggs, Viktor Vekselberg, one of the new generation of Russia's industrialists, bought the entire collection and is bringing it back to Russia. Vekselberg, the chief operating officer of TNK-BP, Russia's third largest oil company, is the fourth richest man in Russia, according to *Forbes* magazine. None of the parties would disclose the price of the private sale, which includes nine Imperial Fabergé eggs – the second largest collection after the ten in the Kremlin – along with some 180 other Fabergé objects. But experts ... say Vekselberg paid about $100 million for the collection ... Among the treasures is the 'Coronation Egg' that Tsar Nicholas II gave

Empress Alexandra for Easter in 1897 to commemorate his ascension to the throne.

(IHT, 5 February 2004, p. 3)

5 February 2004.

A Moscow court imposed a one-year suspended sentence on a former senior executive of Yukos ... in the first definitive outcome [of the investigations into the company ... Vasili Shakhnovsky, one of Yukos's key shareholders, was found guilty of dodging 28.5 million roubles [about $1 million] in taxes between 1998 and 2000 ... but was allowed to walk free 'because of the changed circumstances' ... A judge said Mr Shakhnovsky no longer posed a threat to society or worked at the company. Mr Shakhnovsky had pleaded not guilty ... However, once charged Mr Shakhnovsky had volunteered to pay 53.3 million in missed tax payments and penalties, a move that irritated President Vladimir Putin. Speaking late last year [2003] Mr Putin said: 'Such bargaining, such trading is impermissible. You should always follow the law.'

(FT, 6 February 2004, p. 6)

Under previous Russian law tax evasion could be dropped if the accused paid up what was owed. But in November [2003] parliament altered the criminal code so defendants would no longer be able to avoid prosecution by simply paying fines ... Shakhnovsky's stake in Yukos is worth an estimated $1.3 billion.

(IHT, 6 February 2004, p. 15)

Parliament on Thursday [5 February] unexpectedly scheduled a vote this month that could extend the presidential term to seven years, even though President Vladimir Putin has publicly opposed such constitutional change. The decision was made by the committee that controls parliament's legislative agenda. It put on a fast track a proposal that has languished in parliament since it was first introduced by a group of regional lawmakers in 2002. As written the legislation could allow Putin to run for two new terms, conceivably keeping him in power until 2018 ... Putin said on Thursday that he opposed the legislation ... 'This desire for stabilization must not lead to destabilizing the foundation of the state, the constitution,' he said ... Last month [January] the pro-Kremlin president of Chechnya, Akhmad Kadyrov, and ... Vladimir Zhirinovsky both said that Putin should be president for life ... Boris Gryzlov, the new parliamentary speaker ... opposed amending the constitution.

(IHT, 6 February 2004, pp. 1, 8)

6 February 2004.

Boris Gryzlov ... the speaker of [the State Duma] ... said that the pro-Kremlin majority would block a proposal to extend the presidential term to seven years from four after President Vladimir Putin criticized it. The proposal from a regional legislature was put on the house agenda ... 'I have already expressed my negative opinion on these proposals,' Putin said on Thursday [5 February] ... The legislation would have allowed Russian leaders to run for two seven-year terms. If adopted before the presidential elections the change could theoretically have kept ... [Putin] in power until 2018.

(*IHT*, 7 February 2004, p. 3)

8 February 2004.

One of Vladimir's challengers in the presidential election next month [March] has disappeared. The police and security services announced Sunday [8 February] that they had begun a search for him. Ivan Rybkin, a former speaker of parliament and national security adviser under Boris Yeltsin, has not been seen or heard of since Thursday [5 February] ... Rybkin has been one of the most unabashed critics of Putin and his policies. In polls, however, he has fared even worse than Putin's five other challengers, receiving the support of less than 1 per cent of voters ... Rybkin's Liberal Russia party has been at the centre of political intrigue and violence since its creation in 2002 ... Its patron is Boris Berezovsky ... In the last eighteen months two members of the party, Sergei Yushenkov and Vladimir Golovlyov, both members of parliament, have been shot to death on the streets of Moscow. Yushenkov split with Berezovsky shortly before his death and another party leader, Mikhail Kodanev, has been charged with his murder. Party officials say he has been falsely accused. The party election commission refused to let the party participate in parliamentary elections in December ... Rybkin, an agriculturalist and former Communist Party member, has been a prominent political figure since the collapse of the Soviet Union, first as an opponent of Yeltsin and later as a security adviser to him. He participated in the peace talks in Chechnya in 1996 and remains an advocate of peace efforts in Chechnya ... He has criticized Putin as an authoritarian ... Last month he criticized the erosion of democratic freedoms and the continued economic hardship of ordinary Russians.

(*IHT*, 9 February 2004, p. 3)

Mr Rybkin, the leader of the Liberal Russia party, has been complaining of harassment by the FSB, which he accused of searching his Moscow campaign headquarters, seizing documents and computers and detaining a staff worker ... In April last year [2003] Sergei Yushenkov, a longtime Duma deputy, Kremlin critic and the party's co-chairman, was gunned down at the entrance to his Moscow apartment building. In August 2002 another party co-chairman, Vladimir Golovlyov, was shot in an apparent contract killing while walking his dog in a Moscow suburb.

(*The Independent*, 9 February 2004, p. 9)

9 February 2004.

Moscow's prosecutor's office announced that it had opened a murder investigation in the case of Ivan Rybkin, only to have federal prosecutors close the case within an hour, saying that there was no evidence yet to suggest foul play in the disappearance.

(*IHT*, 10 February 2004, p. 3)

Boris Berezovsky ... said that Mr Rybkin had visited him in London last Tuesday [3 February] to discuss the election before flying to Moscow on Wednesday. 'He told me he [Rybkin] was being followed and watched by the FSB all the time,' he [Berezovsky] said.

(*The Times*, 10 February 2004, p. 14)

10 February 2004. Ivan Rybkin:

Last week I decided to take a break from all the bustle around me ... [I] did not tell her [my wife] ... I did not disappear anywhere. I bought a newspaper today and I was stunned. I have the right to two or three days of personal life. I went to Kiev to my friends, walked around, switched off my mobile phones, and did not watch television.

(*The Independent*, 11 February 2004, p. 26; *FT*, 11 February 2004, p. 1; *IHT*, 11 February 2004, p. 3)

'[Rybkin] later said he feared for his life ... Mr Rybkin has detailed President Vladimir Putin's business connections and accused him of being "the biggest oligarch in Russia"' (*The Economist*, 14 February 2004, p. 41).

Mr Rybkin took out a full-page ad in a Russian newspaper two weeks ago accusing the president of being 'the main oligarch in Russia' and stating: 'Power and money go hand in hand in dictatorial regimes. Putin's regime is no exception' ... The article appeared in *Kommersant*, which is owned by ... Boris Berezovsky.

(*Guardian*, 14 February 2004, p. 18)

In a full-page paid advertisement in *Kommersant* Ivan Rybkin said:

I – and I am not alone – am in possession of a large amount of concrete evidence that Putin is involved in business. The well-known [Roman] Abramovich, along with the Kovalchuk brothers [Mikhail and Yuri], [Gennadi] Timchenko and others standing in the shadows are in charge of Putin's business dealings. Shares in NTV, Channel 1, Surgutneftegaz and many other joint stock companies belong to firms and individuals over which Putin can personally exercise control. I submit that Vladimir Putin is the biggest oligarch in Russia today.

(*CDSP*, 2004, vol. 56, no. 5, p. 4)

'Later he [Rybkin] gave an incoherent explanation ... alleging he had been followed by security services and feared for his and his family's safety' (*FT*, 14 February 2004, p. 9).

13 February 2004.

Ivan Rybkin ... appeared Friday [13 February] in London and offered a new explanation for his bizarre absence, saying he had been drugged and kidnapped ... Rybkin said he had been lured to Kiev on the pretence of meeting with Aslan Maskhadov ... Rybkin, who served as a security adviser to Boris Yeltsin, was involved in the peace talks that ended the first Chechen war in 1996 and has remained an advocate of talks to end the second war, which began in 1999. After arriving at an apartment in Kiev and having sandwiches and tea, he said Friday [13 February], he had felt drowsy and then had fallen unconscious for what turned out to be four days. When he awoke, he said, two armed men showed him a compromising videotape of himself, which he refused to describe except to say that it was meant to intimidate him into silence. Rybkin suggested that his kidnapping was an effort to discredit liberal challenges to President Vladimir Putin before the presidential election on 14 March. 'I do not know who did it, but I know who have benefited from it,' he said ... He said he would not return to Moscow before the election, but would continue to run his campaign from London.

(*IHT*, 14 February 2004, p. 3)

Mr Rybkin said he flew to London last week to seek advice from Mr Maskhadov's representative, Akhmed Zakayev, who had political asylum in Britain. Mr Zakayev said he would need a week to check, but on his return to Moscow Mr Rybkin was rung again by the go-between. He decided to take the risk, without Mr Zakayev's answer.

(*Guardian*, 14 February 2004, p. 18)

'A feature of Mr Rybkin's election manifesto was a pledge to end the war with Chechnya within six months, along the lines provisionally agreed six years ago' (*The Independent*, 14 February 2004, p. 29).

A liberal opposition politician and former ambassador to the United States was appointed Friday [13 February] as the presidential human rights ombudsman and immediately criticized the 'extremely poor' situation in Russia. The lower house of parliament voted overwhelmingly to approve Vladimir Lukin, a senior figure in the Yabloko party, for the post after he was nominated by President Vladimir Putin. Lukin had been deputy speaker in the outgoing Duma.

(*IHT*, 14 February 2004, p. 6)

14 February 2004.

The death toll from the collapse of the roof of a water park here [in Moscow] on Saturday evening [14 February] rose to at least twenty-five, officials said on Sunday ... Having quickly ruled out a terrorist attack, city and federal officials focused blame on engineering flaws in the construction of the centre ... Transvaal Park opened in 2002 ... Russia's minister of emergency services ... angrily questioned the design and construction of the centre, one of several elite entertainment centres that opened in Moscow in recent years ... 'We have to put an end to this mess. When facilities like this are made there have to be controls ten times greater' ... Moscow's prosecutor announced that his office had opened a criminal investigation into the cause; the state construction department immediately suspended the licences of the centre's designer, Sergei Kiselyov & Partners, and its builder, a Turkish firm called Koscak Insaat, forcing the builder to suspend work in several regions.

(*IHT*, 16 February 2004, p. 2)

A snow-laden glass dome ... at a Moscow water park ... caved in, killing at least twenty-six people ... Emergencies minister Sergei Shoigu, saying about seventeen people, were unaccounted for, suggested that shoddy construction of the two-year-old complex of swimming pools and waterslides was to blame for the roof crashing down on bathers ... 'It is time to stop this chaos and establish control when these sites are being built,' he said, in a reference to the rush of new construction in [Moscow] ... Local media speculated that it was unlikely the roof ... simply collapsed under the weight of snow and said prosecutors had opened a criminal investigation into any possible failure to fulfil professional obligations ... 'It was not an act of terror,' the mayor [Yuri Luzhkov] told reporters. 'The moment when the roof caved in was recorded by video recorders.'

(www.iht.com, 15 February 2004)

'Several architectural experts condemned [Yuri] Luzhkov for the collapse. "Luzhkov announced a plan in 2002 to build water parks throughout Moscow, although he had not established safety controls to build these types of projects" ... [said one] expert, Grigori Revzin' (*IHT*, 17 February 2004, p. 3).

17 February 2004.

The Kremlin on Tuesday [17 February] appeared to reject an offer by major shareholders in Yukos to cede control of the company in exchange for the release of ... Mikhail Khodorkovsky and two other board members, as Russian prosecutors instead expanded charges against the jailed men. Leonid Nevzlin said that he and other major shareholders – including Khodorkovsky – were prepared to transfer their controlling $14 billion stake to the state. Khodorkovsky is in jail along with Platon Lebedev, a leading Yukos shareholder, and Alexei Pichugin, head of Yukos's security service. On Tuesday the general prosecutor's office expanded its case against Lebedev, adding a new allegation of theft of $30 million to current charges against him of fraud and tax evasion. Last week prosecutors added an allegation of large-scale personal tax evasion, accusing him of failing to pay more than 7 million roubles, or $246,000, in taxes.

(*IHT*, 18 February 2004, p. 12)

A test of two ballistic missiles in Arctic Russia, planned as part of a major military exercise attended by President Vladimir Putin, failed on Tuesday [17 February] ... The missiles failed to take off from a nuclear submarine, the *Novomoskovsk* ... A military satellite that blocked a launch signal was blamed, but no further explanation [was given].

(*IHT*, 18 February 2004, p. 4)

A malfunctioning satellite was blamed ... [A website] said one of the missiles blew up shortly after firing. The navy refused to confirm the accident ... The exercises ... Russia's biggest since the collapse of communism ... began at the end of January and are due to last until the end of this month [February].

(*Daily Telegraph*, 18 February 2004, p. 12)

18 February 2004.

On Wednesday, for the second day in a row, President Vladimir Putin oversaw one of Russia's largest strategic military exercises in years, and for a second day in a row something went wrong. An intercontinental ballistic missile fired from the nuclear submarine *Karelia* in the Barents Sea veered off course ninety-eight seconds after launching and then self-destructed ... Officials had previously described Tuesday's launches as a centrepiece of the exercise, which involve strategic nuclear forces.

(*IHT*, 19 February 2004, p. 3)

'On Tuesday [17 February] two ballistic missiles were aborted – though naval ranks insisted this was perfectly normal. And yesterday [18 February] another ballistic missile launched from a different submarine went off course and half "self-destructed" in mid-air' (*FT*, 19 February 2004, p. 5).

The main event in yesterday's exercises [17 February] was to have been the launch at sea of two RSM-54 Sineva missiles from the submerged strategic nuclear submarine *Novomoskovsk* and their flight to the Kura impact range on Kamchatka ... But the launch failed to take place ... Several hours later Internet news sites carried stories reporting that soon after launching the first missile had either been 'destroyed' or simply 'exploded' ... The launch of the second missile was scrubbed ... The government news agencies Itar-Tass and RIA Novosti put out a report about a mysterious satellite that had allegedly thwarted the missile launch. Late that same afternoon Navy Commander-in-Chief Vladimir Kuroyedov offered this altogether absurd comment: 'That operation went according to plan. Those ballistic missile launches were supposed to be "virtual" launches. That is what the submarine carried out twice' ... A week earlier [however] Colonel General Yuri Baluyevsky, first deputy chief of the General Staff, had announced ... that the coming exercise would include an actual launch at sea.

(*Kommersant*, 18 February 2004, pp. 1; 4: *CDSP*, 2004, vol. 56, no. 7, pp. 2–3)

20 February 2004.

[A] court rules that Putin can get extra television time ... Authorities ruled Friday [20 February] that President Vladimir Putin would be allowed to receive extra attention on television before the 14 March vote and rejected a complaint from his challengers that the state-controlled media were biased. The commission ruled that a televised presidential address on 12 February, at the official start of the election campaign, was legal, implying that state television had a duty to cover presidential statements in full. Russian media have been running speeches from Putin without editing or commentary.

(IHT, 21 February 2004, p. 6)

24 February 2004. President Putin:

In accordance with Article 117 of the Russian constitution, I have decided to dismiss the government. This decision has nothing to do with the government's performance, which I consider to be satisfactory on the whole. It is dictated by a desire to make clear once again my position on the question of what the course of the country's development will be after 14 March 2004 … I consider it proper to announce right now … the makeup of the state's highest executive body, which will be assuming its share of responsibility for our country's further development … I charge the present government to continue performing its duties until the new Russian Federation government is formed.

(CDSP, 2004, vol. 56, no. 8, p. 3)

President Vladimir Putin dismissed the prime minister and his entire cabinet today [24 February], saying he wanted a new team to be in place to set new policies after next month's presidential elections. Deputy prime minister Viktor Khristenko was named as acting prime minister to take over from Mikhail Kasyanov, and other members of the dismissed cabinet could potentially be reappointed after the 14 March vote … Political analysts said Putin had long expressed impatience with Kasyanov, a holdover from the days of Boris Yeltsin, whom he served as finance minister in 1996. In the Soviet era Kasyanov was a part of the state planning agency and after the collapse of the Soviet Union began to rise through the financial and economic hierarchy.

(www.iht.com, 24 February 2004)

'Putin remains overwhelmingly popular, while the government that he appointed is not' (*IHT*, 25 February 2004, p. 8).

Putin had long been expected to remove prime minister Mikhail Kasyanov, but the timing of the move … came as a surprise. Under Russian law the prime minister and his cabinet formally step down after a presidential election, though all ministers can be reappointed.

(www.iht.com, 25 February 2004)

(According to the constitution, if the prime minister is dismissed the whole cabinet must be dismissed.)

'The outgoing prime minister openly disagreed with Mr Putin several times, criticizing the criminal investigations into the owners of Yukos ... and stalling on reform of the civil service' (*FT*, 25 February 2004, p. 1). 'Viktor Khristenko [is] a broadly reformist technocrat ... One of six deputy prime ministers with a list of responsibilities including the sensitive themes of fuel and energy, he is a long-time technocrat who has shown loyalty mixed with extreme caution' (p. 10).

'Mr Putin and Mr Kasyanov ... were known to have disagreed on such issues as taxation, mortgage provision and other key elements of economic policy' (*The Independent*, 25 February 2004, p. 2).

25 February 2004.

President Putin said Wednesday [25 February] that his surprise decision to fire the cabinet ahead of next month's presidential elections was aimed at speeding up administrative reforms ... Meeting with the dismissed ministers, who remained on the job in a temporary capacity, Putin said: 'I consider it necessary to acquaint the public with the person' whom he will nominate, but did not give details. Putin said his decision to dismiss the cabinet ... was to avoid long wrangling on a new government after the election.

(*IHT*, 26 February 2004, p. 8)

27 February 2004.

Prosecutors yesterday [27 February] pressed criminal charges against a senior government official in connection with a case against shareholders in Yukos ... the first time a state official has been implicated ... Vladimir Malin, the chairman of the Russian federal property fund that manages the sale of state assets, was charged with 'abuse of office with grave consequences' in relation to the sale of Apatit. The fertilizer company's sale is at the heart of fraud charges against Platon Lebedev ... and Mikhail Khodorkovsky ... Mr Malin was allowed to go home but ordered to stay in Moscow while being investigated. The prosecutors demanded he be suspended during investigations. The charges against Mr Malin relate to the signing of an amicable agreement between the federal property fund and Volna, a company controlled by Mr Lebedev and linked to Menatep group, the largest shareholder in Yukos. In 1994 Volna won a privatization auction for a 20 per cent stake in Apatit. Under the terms of the privatization, Volna, which won the auction, was supposed to invest $283 million in Apatit within two years. Instead, Volna simply transferred money to Apatit's account for one day only, according to the prosecutors. The accounts of both companies were held in Menatep Bank, controlled by Mr Lebedev and Mr Khodorkovsky. The stake in Apatit was later sold on. In 2002 Volna's ownership of Apatit was disputed in court by the federal property fund. However, the fund allowed Volna to pay an additional $15 million for Apatit instead of demanding the full investment. Mr Malin oversaw the settlement as head of the property fund.

(*FT*, 28 February 2004, p. 9)

1 March 2004.

President Vladimir Putin followed one surprise with another on Monday [1 March] by nominating Mikhail Fradkov, a little-known former trade minister and tax police chief who is Russia's representative to the EU, to the post of prime minister … Fradkov, fifty-three, who served as a foreign trade official during the Soviet era and as Russia's trade minister twice in the 1990s, was named as the country's representative to the EU last March [2003]. He was appointed to head the tax police in March 2001, but the agency was later disbanded … Putin's nominee is subject to approval by the Duma.

(www.iht.com, 1 March 1004)

A low-profile technocrat [was named] as prime minister, a position that answers directly to the president … Mikhail Fradkov has held a number of mostly economic portfolios … Analysts described him as a competent non-political figure … In naming him Putin avoided creating an alternative centre of power or a rival for the political spotlight. Fradkov has been associated, however, with Sergei Ivanov, the defence minister and a close ally of Putin, whose name remains near the top of most lists of potential future presidents … [Putin said] that Fradkov would deal strongly with corruption because he 'knows the security structures since he was the deputy secretary of the "security council" and head of the tax police' … [Fradkov's] working relationship with the security services puts him in sync with a key power block behind the president.

(*IHT*, 2 March 2004, pp. 1, 4)

President Vladimir Putin named a little-known technocrat with ties to the security services as prime minister, mandating him to fight corruption and reform the civil service … Mr Putin … stressed Mr Fradkov's knowledge of the *siloviki*, or people closely connected with the security and law enforcement agencies, praised his 'honesty' and his 'experience in fighting corruption', and described him as a 'good, strong administrator' … Analysts argued that the appointment gave Mr Putin a free hand to implement reforms … He was minister of trade from 1999 … [He became] envoy to the EU in Brussels in March 2003.

(*FT*, 2 March 2004, pp. 1, 8)

('*Siloviki* [is] a term that includes prosecutors, police, military and members of the security services': *FT*, 24 February 2004, p. 19. '*Siloviki* literally [means] wielders of power, in other words the heads of the defence and security services': *The Economist*, 28 February 2004, p. 45.)

'President Putin said that Mikhail Fradkov … "has great experience in fighting corruption"' (*The Times*, 2 March 2004, p. 15).

Mikhail Fradkov … rose to become foreign minister under the Yeltsin government in 1997 … He was made first deputy secretary to the 'security council' in May 2000 ... [He was] promoted to head of the tax police in March 2001 ... Once the unit was disbanded in July last year [2003] he was sent to Brussels.

(*Guardian*, 2 March 2004, p. 14)

Beginning in 1984 he was named deputy director of the state committee's chief supply administration. Beginning in 1988 he served as deputy and then first deputy director of the USSR ministry of foreign economic relations' chief administration for the co-ordination of foreign economic relations. In 1991 he became a senior adviser for Russia's permanent mission to the UN office in Geneva and other international organizations in that city, as well as Russia's representative to Gatt (now the WTO). In October 1992 he became deputy minister of foreign economic relations, with responsibility for co-ordinating Russian regions' foreign economic ties ... In March 1997 he became the minister ... until 23 March [1998] ... Fradkov returned to the government in May 1999, but this time at the ministry of trade, not the ministry of foreign economic relations ... However, it was eliminated a year later ... In 2000–2001 Reserve Colonel Fradkov served as first deputy secretary of the 'security council', and in 2001–2003 he headed the federal tax police service [starting 28 March 2001] ... [He] was sent off in March 2003 to be Russia's ambassador to the EU.

(*CDSP*, 2004, vol. 56, no. 9, pp. 3–4)

2 March 2004.

Mikhail Fradkov ... asserted his determination to push ahead with economic reform and restructuring of the civil service ... He said he would name the liberally orientated politician Alexander Zhukov as his first deputy. He also said he would reduce the size of the cabinet, cutting the number of deputy prime ministers, ministers and officials ... Mr Zhukov is an English-speaking economist and experienced politician. He headed the budget and taxes committee in the previous parliament and was credited with steering through important financial reforms and defending fiscal prudence during Mr Putin's first term. Mr Zhukov was named one of several first deputy speakers in the new Duma elected last December.

(*FT*, 3 March 2004, p. 8)

3 March 2004. 'Sibneft confirmed yesterday [3 March] that the tax ministry had sent a bill for $1 billion of outstanding taxes' (*Guardian*, 4 March 2004, p. 18).

'The tax ministry accused Sibneft of underpaying its 2000–2001 bill' (*Daily Telegraph*, 4 March 2004, p. 17).

5 March 2004. The State Duma voted 352 to fifty-eight with twenty-four abstentions to confirm Mikhail Fradkov as prime minister.

'Fradkov, a long-serving bureaucrat plucked from political obscurity by President Vladimir Putin ... promised that he would streamline state services and agencies, enforce laws against corruption and tax evasion and restructure an economy heavily reliant on natural resources' (*IHT*, 6 March 2004, p. 3).

Mikhail Fradkov ... confirmed that Alexander Zhukov, the liberal former head of the tax and budget committee, would be his only deputy prime minister ... [compared with the current] six deputies ... Mr Fradkov pledged fresh reform spearheaded by a streamlined government ... Mr Fradkov stressed the need for further corporate tax cuts, and highlighted ... his priorities: promoting economic growth, fighting poverty and reforming the armed forces.

(FT, 6 March 2004, p. 6)

A group of Russian engineers aided Saddam Hussein's long-range ballistic missile programme, providing technical assistance for prohibited Iraqi weapons projects even in the years just before the war that ousted Saddam from power, American government officials say. Iraqis who were involved in the missile work told American investigators that the technicians had not been working for the Russian government but for a private company. But any such work on Iraq's banned missiles would have violated UN sanctions, even as the UN Security Council sought to enforce them ... Because some of the Russian experts were said to have formerly worked for one of Russia's aerospace design centres, which remains closely associated with the state, their work for Iraq has raised questions in Washington about whether Russian government officials knew of the experts' involvement in forbidden missile programmes ... The Iraq Survey Group, the US team that has hunted for evidence of weapons of mass destruction, also found indications that Baghdad had received assistance from sources in Belarus, Serbia and Ukraine, according to American officials ... After the war the Iraq Survey Group found evidence that, in violation of the sanctions, Iraq had agreed to pay North Korea $10 million for technical support to upgrade its ballistic missile programme. But American officials believe that North Korea never delivered anything to the Iraqis, though it apparently kept Iraq's $10 million.

(www.iht.com, 5 April 2004)

In an interim report on the progress of the Iraq Survey Group released in October [2003] ... [it was reported] that the group had found 'a large volume of material and testimony by co-operating Iraq officials on Iraq's efforts to illicitly procure parts and foreign assistance for its missile programme'. It listed several examples of assistance from foreign countries, but apart from North Korea no other countries were identified.

(IHT, 6 March 2004, p. 4).

9 March 2004.

President Vladimir Putin yesterday [9 March] unveiled a sharply streamlined cabinet that reinforced the influence of the liberal economic reformer ... He transferred Dmitri Kozak, his long-standing colleague and campaign manager, out of the Kremlin to oversee the government as head of the administration [head of government administration; chief of staff] with ministerial rank, ranked third after Mikhail Fradkov and Alexander Zhukov. The liberal-orientated Alexei Kudrin and Viktor Khristenko were formally demoted from deputy prime ministers, but retained cabinet positions in charge respectively of the ministry of finance and an enlarged ministry of industry and energy. German Gref retained his job as head of the ministry of economic development and trade. Sergei Lavrov, Russia's ambassador to the United Nations ... was appointed foreign minister ... Sergei Ivanov ... was retained in his job as defence minister.

(*FT*, 10 March 2004, p. 6)

Sergei Lavrov replaces Igor Ivanov, who will move to a less influential job as head of the president's 'security council' ... Viktor Khristenko ... was named energy minister. In the consolidated cabinet he also takes responsibility for construction, industry, arms production and nuclear power.

(*IHT*, 10 March 1004, p. 3)

'President Putin ... slashed the number of cabinet ministers from thirty to seventeen ... Mr Putin said the new government would "cease to act as a parallel shadow cabinet and become an efficient up-to-date tool for administration"' (*Guardian*, 10 March 1004, p. 18).

'Alexander Zhukov becomes deputy prime minister and overseer of economic policy as a whole ... German Gref ... keeps his job, but with far wider powers' (*The Economist*, 13 March 2004, p. 40).

The new government will be more compact, with a single deputy prime minister and only half as many ministers (before there were thirty, including the prime minister and his deputies; now there are fourteen) ... The deputy prime minister is Alexander Zhukov ... German Gref is minister of economic development and trade ... [the ministry now including the agencies that deal with state property].

(*CDSP*, 2004, vol. 56, no. 10, p. 1)

11 March 2004.

Russian prosecutors yesterday [11 March] claimed to have frozen nearly $5 billion in assets in Switzerland belonging to the crucial shareholders in Yukos ... The prosecutors' office said that the Swiss had frozen $4.8 billion in five separate banks held by twenty individuals for alleged large-scale misappropriation of state assets ... Those affected included Mikhail Khodorkovsky ... and Platon Lebedev ... Others included Leonid Nevzlin and Vladimir Dubov, both now living in self-imposed exile ... However, the Swiss authorities refused to confirm the freeze, saying that only the Russians could comment. Representatives of both Mr Khodorkovsky and Mr Nevzlin dismissed suggestions that they had any significant assets in Switzerland.

(*FT*, 12 March 2004, p. 27)

14 March 2004. In the presidential election Vladimir Putin was re-elected with 71.3 per cent of the vote. The other candidates' showings were as follows:

Nikolai Kharitonov, 13.69 per cent (a better result than expected); Sergei Galzyev, 4.1 per cent; Irina Khakamada, 3.84 per cent; Oleg Malyshkin, 2.02 per cent; Sergei Mironov, 0.75 per cent. 'None of the above' gained 3.45 per cent of the vote. The turnout was 64.39 per cent.

Julian Peel Yates (head of the joint OSCE and Council of Europe observer mission):

> The election process overall did not adequately reflect principles necessary for a healthy democratic election process. Essential elements of the OSCE commitments and Council of Europe standards for democratic elections, such as vibrant political discourse and meaningful pluralism, were lacking ... [The authorities] failed to meet important commitments regarding the treatment by the state-controlled media on a non-discriminatory basis and the principles of a secret ballot.

> The observers – representing OSCE and the Parliamentary Assembly of the Council of Europe – cited abuses of government resources, bias in state media and even instances of ballot stuffing on election day ... The observers and Putin's challengers cited biased media coverage and favouritism from election officials that, according to the international observers' report, 'reflected a lack of democratic culture, accountability and responsibility'. The report cited at least two instances of outright falsification of votes at polling stations in Moscow and Khabarovsk ... In Chechnya ... Putin received more that 92 per cent of the vote, according to official results. *The Moscow Times* quoted election officials in Grozny acknowledging that they had filled in several thousand ballots for Putin.
>
> (*IHT*, 16 March 2004, p. 3)

> A detailed study by OSCE of coverage in the Russian media over the past month showed a strong bias by the state-controlled television channels in favour of Mr Putin, who dominated news broadcasts at the expense of five rivals. Other criticisms included 'significant problems' with vote counting on polling day in more than a quarter of those counts observed.
>
> (*FT*, 16 March 2004, p. 8)

'[US] secretary of state Colin Powell said that the United States "was concerned about a level of authoritarianism creeping back into the society"' (*The Times*, 16 March 2004, p. 18).

Vladimir Putin (15 March 2004):

> Our paramount objective is to maintain economic growth ... We need to take further steps to improve the tax system and to restructure the natural monopolies. We have only just adopted framework laws on railway transportation and the electric power industry ... We are going to strengthen the multi-party system. We are going to bolster civil society and do all we can to ensure freedom of the news media. National political parties should wield real influence in the regions, and the regions, acting through those

parties, should be able to influence the highest governmental and administrative authorities of Russia as a whole ... We are going to create conditions such that neither bureaucrats hiding under the cover of national interests nor all sorts of phrasemongers hiding behind democratic rhetoric will be able to line their pockets ... Unfortunately, the government is not yet functioning effectively. We need to complete the reorganization, which will continue for several more weeks.

(*CDSP*, 2004, vol. 56, no. 11, p.)

Earlier comments and developments

Putin's main themes for his second presidency [are] doubling GDP and reducing poverty ... The need to diversify the economy is generally recognized ... He accepts the reality of American world dominance and refuses to consider it as a security threat to his country. At the same time the president's long-term objective has been reconstitution as a modern great power, raising the country's status in relation to both America and Europe ... Moscow had to conclude that partnership with the United States was impossible, while junior partnership was undesirable. Abiding confrontation with Washington, the Kremlin adopted a policy of co-operation on matters of common concern, such as terrorism, Afghanistan and the proliferation of weapons of mass destruction, while holding ground on issues where it saw the United States encroaching on its national interests – in particular in the CIS ... Protecting against an air attack is officially at the heart of the national defence effort ... The idea of integration into the West [was] popular in the late 1980s and early 1990s ... Russians ... now tend to agree that, in terms of international politics, their country should remain an international player ... Over the past decade Russians have disabused themselves of the idea of eventually acceding to the EU.

(Trenin 2004: 13–14)

Such is the state of politics in Russia today that perhaps the most prominent challenger to Vladimir Putin in the presidential election this year ... Sergei Mironov, chairman of parliament's upper house and leader of the Russian Party of Life ... accepted his party's nomination with an impassioned endorsement of the incumbent ... Putin faces nine challengers characterized mostly by degrees of deference to the Kremlin and united by the fact that none has any chance of winning. Vladimir Bryntsalov, a pharmaceutical and vodka magnate, has a photograph with Putin in his office and the symbol of the pro-Putin party, United Russia, formed in an enormous mosaic on the side of his company's headquarters ... Bryntsalov alone among Putin's challengers ran before for the presidency, in 1996. He finished tenth, behind Yeltsin and others, with less than two-tenths of 1 per cent of the vote ... Two other candidates represent Motherland, a new political party created with the tacit support of the Kremlin on the eve of parliament elections [in December 2003] ... One of them [is] Sergei Glazyev ... The lack of a significant challenge means that Putin's formidable political power has evolved into something close to absolute ... Irina Khakamada, a leader of the liberal party Union of Rightist Forces ... has begun her own presidential campaign [running as an independent] ... The Liberal Democratic Party ... increasingly loyal to the Kremlin ... nominated Zhirinovsky's former bodyguard, Oleg Malyshkin ... Putin appeared for a time to face the prospect of having no opponent at all, prompting media reports that the Kremlin was recruiting candidates like Mironov to create the appearance of a genuine race ... Putin is running as an independent. Of his nine challengers, only three are truly ideological opponents: Khakamada ... the only woman in the race ... of the Union of Rightist Forces; Nikolai Kharitonov [leader of the Agrarian Party], a former collective farmer and long-time parliamentarian nominated by the Communist Party; and Ivan Rybkin, a former parliamentary speaker and aide to Yeltsin, who participated in peace talks in Chechnya.

(Steven Lee Myers, *IHT*, 8 January 2004, pp. 1, 8)

Two of the most prominent opposition candidates, Irina Khakamada and Sergei Glazyev, have failed to win the backing of their own parties ... Glazyev came under attack last week on the state's two main television networks, which used hidden cameras to capture what they said were scenes of Glazyev's supporters in Saratov and Nizhny Novgorod paying for signatures supporting his nomination. The reports, which Glazyev denounced as slanderous, prompted the chairman of the election commission to call for a criminal investigation.

(Steven Lee Myers, *IHT*, 30 January 2004, p. 3)

Most who remain face a struggle even to register by 28 January, by which date they must have gathered 2 million signatures with not more than 50,000 from any one of Russia's eighty-nine regions ... Sergei Glazyev, the leader of the recently created Rodina (Motherland) nationalist-populist movement ... With his anti-oligarch calls for higher taxes on oil companies, tougher regulation and greater special spending, the polls put him in second place, though with just 3 per cent support. He is the only leader of a parliamentary group who is standing, which allows him to be a candidate without seeking signatures. He has decided to run independently like Mr Putin ... Oleg Malyshkin had an easier ride, as the official LDPR candidate ... while Nikolai Kharitonov is also avoiding collecting signatures by representing the Communists.

(*FT*, 17 January 2004, p. 7)

[On 6 February] the supreme court upheld a ruling by the central election commission to refuse to register the former central bank chief Viktor Gerashchenko for the race. The commission had turned Gerashchenko down

after ruling that he was nominated only by one of the parties in his nationalist Homeland bloc, instead of the entire bloc as required by law.

(*IHT*, 7 February 2004, p. 3)

'The staunch Putin loyalist Dmitri Rogozin refused to let the party [Rodina]
back Sergei Glazyev in the presidential race. Mr Glazyev was forced to run as an
independent' (*Guardian*, 13 February 2004, p. 20). 'Dmitri Rogozin persuaded
his faction to sack Mr Glazyev as Rodina's co-chairman on Sunday [15 Febru-
ary]' (*Guardian*, 20 February 2004, p. 19).

Irina Khakamada ... [is the] daughter of a Japanese communist who fled to
Russia during World War II and died disappointed in 1991 when the Soviet
Union collapsed, still embracing his Stalinist ideals of strong government
and social equality. Khakamada has a Russian mother, was born in Moscow
and speaks no Japanese.

(*IHT*, 14 February 2004, p. 3)

Irina Khakamada [January 2004):

The terrorists did not plan to blow up the Theatre Centre, but the authorities
were not interested in saving all the hostages ... [The president is creating]
a society based on lies, total secretiveness and fear ... [in which] democracy
is used as a pro forma procedure.

(*CDSP*, 2004, vol. 56, nos 1–2, p. 6)

The only chance of an upset is that the turnout falls below 50 per cent,
making the result invalid. In that case there would be another contest, with
all the original candidates barred. But the Kremlin would almost certainly
find a way of bringing its man back to power.

(*FT*, 16 February 2004, p. 16)

Ivan Rybkin, who had vowed not to return to Russia before the elections,
arrived in Moscow on Thursday night [4 March] ... and announced his
withdrawal: 'I will not participate in this farce' ... Putin now faces five
candidates ... Two of them – Sergei Mironov, the chairman of the upper
house of parliament, and Oleg Malyshkin, a member of parliament representing the Liberal Democratic Party – do not even oppose Putin ... The
others are Nikolai Kharitonov, the former collective farm boss representing the Communist Party; Sergei Glazyev, a former Communist economist who has lost the support of his own nationalist party; Irina
Khakamada.

(*IHT*, 6 March 2004, p. 3)

Concern was shown at the prospect of a low turnout, 50 per cent being the
minimum for a valid vote. President Putin made a television address on 11 March:

Each of our votes has huge significance. Taking part in the election is a
unique opportunity to influence developments in your homeland ... It is
extremely important for each of us and for the future of Russia ... Only

your support will inspire the future president with confidence in his strength.

(The Independent, 12 March 2004, p. 28; *Daily Telegraph,* 12 March 2004, p. 16; *Guardian,* 13 March 2004, p. 15)

Many politicians cynically warn that election officials will simply inflate the figures should turnout fall short. It is a sign of the Kremlin's concern about this matter that the most visible part of its campaign has been the get-out-the-vote effort ... OSCE [has] already issued an interim report criticizing shortfalls in the presidential race. The report cites state media's denial of equal access to Putin's challengers and reported abuses by local authorities, both in favour of Putin and against his opponents.

(IHT, 13 March 2004, p. 3)

[On 14 March US] secretary of state Colin Powell urged Putin to 'do a better job' of making democracy work. 'Russians have to understand that to have full democracy of the kind that the international community will recognize, you have got to let candidates have all access to the media that the president has' ... [Putin] did not campaign [or debate with the other candidates].

(IHT, 15 March 2004, p. 1)

19 March 2004.

In a ruling Friday [19 March] a Moscow court extended Mikhail Khodorkovsky's detention to 25 May ... His current detention was scheduled to end 25 March ... [The court] heeded prosecutors' claims then [December 2003] and Friday that he could flee the country or commit economic crimes.

(IHT, 20 March 2004, p. 15)

President Vladimir Putin ... [said that] over the next four years the number of poor people must be reduced from 20.5 per cent of the population to 10 per cent–12 per cent, and economic growth of at least 7 per cent a year must be attained. The rouble must be made convertible. And the question of natural resource rent must be finally decided.

(CDSP, 2004, vol. 56, no. 12, p. 5)

23 March 2004.

In a salvo of contradictory statements that could undermine trust in Russia's nuclear fleet, the head of the navy ... Admiral Vladimir Kuroyedov ... said Tuesday [23 March] that one of the nation's most advanced warship ... the *Peter the Great* [the flagship of the Northern Fleet] ... was so decrepit that it could explode at any moment. He then quickly changed directions and insisted there was no danger at all ... Kuroyedov said he had ordered the captain to fix the ship in two weeks ... Kuroyedov [later] added that some flaws in maintaining the cruiser's living quarters would be fixed within three weeks, after which the ship would become fully combat-ready.

(IHT, 24 March 2004, p. 3)

'Admiral Kuroyedov ... said the vessel was taken off the list of combat-ready ships last Thursday [18 March] and was confined to its home port near Murmansk' (*Guardian*, 24 March 2004, p. 11).

Admiral Vladimir Kuroyedov:

> The ship is in such a condition that it could explode at any moment. The situation is especially dangerous because the ship is equipped with a nuclear reactor. Everything is all right on the ship where the admirals walk around, but in the area where they do not walk around everything is in such a condition that it may blow up at any moment. I mean, in particular, the maintenance of the nuclear reactor.

Admiral Vladimir Kuroyedov (three hours later):

> There is no threat whatsoever to the ship's nuclear safety. The ship's nuclear safety is fully guaranteed in line with existing norms. However, the state of the living quarters and the general state of the ship is unsatisfactory and fails to meet requirements set down by regulations.

> Experts said that Admiral Kuroyedov was exaggerating the threat of an explosion, perhaps to try to win more funding from the Kremlin or to deflect criticism over the sinking of another submarine and the recent failure of missile tests ... Some analysts said that the decision could be linked to the trial of Admiral Gennadi Suchkov, the former head of the Northern Fleet, over the sinking of a decommissioned nuclear submarine last year [August 2003] ... Admiral Suchkov [was suspended] ... after the K159 submarine sank in stormy seas as she was being towed to a scrapyard, killing nine of the ten crew. However, Igor Kasatonov, a retired admiral, has told court hearings that Admiral Kuroyedov should bear responsibility for the disaster. Mr Kasatonov is the uncle of Rear-Admiral Vladimir Kasatonov, the commander of the *Peter the Great*, who Admiral Kuroyedov clearly blamed for the cruiser's problems ... Admiral Kuroyedov also shunned responsibility for ... [the failure in February] to perform missile launches from nuclear submarines ... saying that one of the missiles had failed because it had been stored for twice its designated length of service.

> (*The Times*, 24 March 2004, p. 16)

'Several analysts dismissed the admiral's comments as "overly dramatic", interpreting them as part of a power struggle among the navy's top brass or as a clumsy bid for more government funding' (*Guardian*, 24 March 2004, p. 11).

> Kuroyedov also faced harsh criticism for his role in the August 2000 explosion of the *Kursk* nuclear submarine in which 118 sailors died. Many expected Putin to fire Kuroyedov after that ... Kuroyedov claimed that the first of two scheduled missile launches ... during manoeuvres last month [February] ... had never been planned despite numerous earlier announcements to the contrary. On Tuesday [23 March] he said the second failed launch of an RSM-54 missile was due to its age.

> (*IHT*, 24 March 2004, p. 3)

29 March 2004. Mikhail Khodorkovsky ('The crisis of liberalism in Russia', *Vedomosti*, 29 March 2004):

Russian liberalism is going through a crisis ... The failure of the Union of Rightists Forces and Yabloko is a reality ... Putin is doubtless neither a liberal nor a democrat, but all the same he is more liberal and democratic than 70 per cent of the country's population ... [It is necessary to] abandon senseless attempts to cast doubts on the president's legitimacy. Regardless of whether we like Vladimir Putin or not, it is time to recognize that the head of state is not just an individual. The president is the institution that guarantees the country's integrity and stability. And God forbid that we should live to see the day when that institution collapses – Russia could not survive another February 1917. the country's history dictates that a poor government is better than no government ... People of liberal views who were actively engaged in public affairs – a group in which I include my errant self – were responsible for seeing to it that Russia does not stray from the path of freedom ... We screwed up. Now we need to analyse our tragic mistakes and admit our guilt, both moral and historical. Many in the first batch of Yeltsin-era liberals were people who were sincerely convinced of the historical rightness of liberalism, of the need for a 'liberal revolution' ... But having come to power the liberals approached that revolution in an excessively superficial – not to say frivolous – fashion. They were thinking of the living and working conditions of the 10 per cent of Russian citizens who were prepared for the decisive life changes that would result from the renunciation of government paternalism. They forgot about the other 90 per cent ... The time has come to ask ourselves, 'What have you done for Russia?' ... We have to, we must, admit that 90 per cent of the Russian people do not think privatization was fair, or regard those who profited from it as legitimate owners. And as long as that is the case there will always be forces – political, bureaucratic and even terroristic – that will mount attacks on private property. In order to justify privatization in the eyes of the country, where notions of Roman property law have never been strong and clear, we must force big business to share with the people – doubtless by agreeing to a reform of the tax on mineral resources and to other steps that may be none too pleasant for major property owners.

(*CDSP*, 2004, vol. 56, no. 12, pp. 1–5)

'*Forbes* magazine recently estimated [Khodorkovsky's wealth] to exceed $15 million ... Khodorkovsky's treatise [is] a time-honoured tradition from Russian exiles and prisoners' (*IHT*, 30 March 2004, p. 1).

Lawyers acting for Mr Khodorkovsky and the Menatep group of companies said yesterday [29 March] they would appeal to Switzerland's supreme court against last Friday's formal decision [26 March] by the Swiss authorities to freeze accounts worth billions of francs at Russia's request ... Russian prosecutors say the frozen cash amounts to 6.2 billion Swiss francs, although the Swiss federal prosecutor's office said only that 'several billion Swiss francs' were involved. According to Menatep's lawyers, the blocked funds include hundreds of millions of dollars in a Yukos pension fund and several operational accounts for Menatep companies.

(*FT*, 30 March 2004, p. 9)

31 March 2004.

Protests near Russian pipelines, kindergartens and official buildings and rallies that threaten 'public morality' will be banned under a new law approved by the country's parliament yesterday [31 March] ... Under the bill rallies and pickets will be forbidden near government buildings, embassies and offices of international organizations. It bans public protests near big roads, pipelines and environmentally hazardous industrial sites ... The State Duma ... backed the government-drafted bill with 294 votes for and 137 against. It is expected to become law after two more readings. The blacklist of protest sites includes schools, kindergartens, hospitals, stadium, concert halls and religious centres ... The bill states that authorities can refuse permission for a protest if it runs 'counter to the constitution of the Russian Federation and generally accepted norms of public morality'. The government says that public events near the banned sites could threaten their security.

(*The Times*, 1 April 2004, p. 18)

The Russian parliament has taken the first step toward passing a law that would ban demonstrations in most public places, narrowing one of the crucial freedoms won as the Soviet Union came to an end ... The draft law prohibits rallies outside government buildings, embassies and international organizations, on major roads, near schools, hospitals, stadiums, concert halls and religious centres, and at pipelines and environmentally hazardous sites ... Yabloko members were among the demonstrators who rallied outside parliament ... The leader of the president's parliamentary bloc, Boris Gryzlov, said there would still be plenty of places to hold demonstrations and that formal permission would no longer be required, only advance notice. The proposed law, however, contains a clause that would allow officials to block any gatherings if 'their aim contradicted the constitution, generally accepted norms of public morality and federal law'.

(www.iht.com, 1 April 2004)

1 April 2004.

Russian prosecutors asserted Thursday [1 April] that ... Platon Lebedev and ... Mikhail Khodorkovsky were part of an 'organized criminal group' that defrauded the state during privatization ... Prosecutors charge that Lebedev, Khodorkovsky and other associates fraudulently won a 20 per cent stake in Apatit, Russia's largest maker of a fertilizer, through a complex scheme involving fake bidders. The winning bid, a group backed by Lebedev, never fulfilled a pledge to invest $283 million in Apatit, prosecutors charge ... The prosecutor-general's office contends that Lebedev ... 'joined an organized group of people set up and led by Mikhail Khodorkovsky'. Their aim, the prosecution said, was to take 'possession, through deception, of shares of Russian enterprises during the period of privatization'. Prosecutors added that Lebedev, 'jointly with Khodorkovsky, was a leader of the work of that group in the process of committing crimes'.

(IHT, 2 April 2004, p. 11)

Prosecutors said they had frozen the foreign bank accounts of the two men's lawyers ... The Swiss authorities recently froze up to $5 billion in assets linked to Yukos's shareholders ... [But] Yukos yesterday [1 April] received good news when the authorities indicated that they would not revoke some of its key assets ... [The] natural resources minister said his officials had found no serious violations in the licence conditions for the oilfields Yukos operates in western Siberia and would not call for their removal.

(FT, 2 April 2004, p. 24)

2 April 2004.

After harsh criticism from civil rights and free-speech advocates ... [the State Duma] ... on Friday [2 April] agreed to amend a bill that would have banned demonstrations in most public places. In its second reading of the bill ... [the Duma] will remove language from the initial version that banned demonstrations outside government buildings, embassies and the offices of international organizations, as well as along main roads, railways and pipelines. Boris Gryzlov, leader of United Russia, backed away from supporting the bill, which his party voted for Wednesday [29 March] ... It was opposed by deputies from the Communist Party and two nationalist parties ... [Gryzlov] pledged amendments that would no longer restrict any public events held outside buildings belonging to most executive buildings, except for the president's residence ... Authorities already require political gatherings and protests to obtain permits and advance permission, and the police are generally quick to disperse unsanctioned demonstrations.

(IHT, 3 April 2004, p. 3)

Russian foreign minister Sergei Lavrov ... announced [on 2 April] an important victory for Russia in its relations with Nato [receiving] assurances from alliance secretary-general Jaap de Hoop Scheffer that Slovenia and the three Baltic countries will abide by the terms of the Treaty on Conventional Armed Forces in Europe (the CFE Treaty). Granted, he failed to mention that the alliance regards their final inclusion in the CFE Treaty as contingent upon Russia's fulfilment of the 1999 Istanbul protocols.

(CDSP, 2004, vol. 56, no. 14, p. 4)

4 April 2004.

Russia is to introduce a military television channel in an effort to improve its image and reduce the number of people trying to avoid conscription. The defence ministry hopes that *Zvezda*, or Star, will start on 23 February [2005] ... This month's call-up [April 2004] is at a record low, with 9 per cent of eligible citizens serving as conscripts. The rest avoid service through bribes or dubious ailments ... The deputy editor of the defence ministry's television studio ... [said] that 'this channel will interest all people – not just the 1 million soldiers in Russia'.

(*Guardian*, 5 April 2004, p. 15)

5 April 2004.

A researcher was found guilty of espionage on Monday [5 April] ... in a case that raised fears of a resurgence of Soviet-style tactics and alarmed the scientific community. Igor Sutyagin, a scholar at Moscow's USA and Canada Institute, has been in jail since his arrest in 1999 on charges he sold information on nuclear submarines and missile warning systems to a British company that investigators claim was a cover for the CIA. Sutyagin maintained that the analyses he wrote were based on public sources and that he had no reason to believe the British company was an intelligence cover.

(*IHT*, 6 April 2004, p. 8)

7 April 2004.

A Moscow court sentenced a Russian scientist to fifteen years at hard labour on Wednesday [7 April] for spying for the United States in a case that rights groups said harked back to Soviet-style repression. The scientist, Igor Sutyagin, an arms control expert, was found guilty of espionage Monday [5 April] for selling to a foreign company information that he and fellow scientists said was unclassified and open to the public. The sentencing is the latest step in a string of similar cases that appear to reflect concerns within the security services about contacts between Russian and foreign scientists. The FSB – the successor to the KGB security police – has stepped up investigations and prosecutions of scientists since the election in 2000 of President Vladimir Putin, who formerly headed the agency ... Sutyagin was affiliated with the prestigious USA and Canada Institute when he was arrested in October 1999. He has been in custody since ... He was accused of collecting material on nuclear submarines and missile warning systems and passing it on to a British company that prosecutors said was a cover for the CIA ... When the judge instructed the jury she made no reference to the question of whether the material was classified [said one of Sutyagin's lawyers] ... After his sentencing Sutyagin repeated his defence that he had only analysed material that was publicly available: 'The only thing I am guilty of is that I had contacts with foreigners. In fact, only newspapers, magazines and books, mostly published abroad, were the sources of my work' ... The jury trial was an innovation that has only been used once before in an espionage trial, which ended in acquittal last year [2003] for Valentin Danilov, a scientist accused of selling secrets to China.

(*IHT*, 8 April 2004, p. 8)

'[Sutyagin's lawyer] said the judge had given the jury incorrect instructions by asking them to determine whether Sutyagin had passed along the information – which the defendant did not deny – rather than whether he had passed state secrets' (*Guardian*, 8 April 2004, p. 16).

'Sutyagin's lawyers accused the judge of asking the jury to consider only whether Sutyagin had been recruited by a foreign intelligence agency and had been paid for information, not whether the information contained state secrets' (*The Times*, 8 April 2004, p. 17).

> Sutyagin, who has been detained since 1999, has been repeatedly denied bail and has already had his case heard once. That trial found the evidence inadequate and uncompelling. That jury, and the judge, were replaced and Marina Komarova, [a judge] who has a track record of trying spy cases and finding against the defendants, was brought in.
>
> (*The Independent*, 8 April 2004, p. 21)

> We learned yesterday [7 April 2004] that it was the president of Russia who gave the go-ahead for Nato to set up military bases in Kyrgyzstan, Tajikistan and Uzbekistan in 2001. The world was informed of this by Sergei Ivanov, who was in Washington on a working visit. At a press conference the Russian defence minister said for the first time that, in the wake of 11 September. Vladimir Putin had personally called Central Asian leaders and asked them to accommodate Nato troops for war in Afghanistan.
>
> (*Noviye Izvestia*, 18 April 2004, p. 4: *CDSP*, 2004, vol. 56, no. 14, p. 6)

10 April 2004.

> Russia suffered its worst mining disaster since 1997 when a methane blast tore through one of the country's newest and most efficient mines on Saturday [10 April], leaving at least forty dead … The Taizhina mine in west Siberia … dates back to 1961, but the section where the disaster occurred was new and opened only in 1998 … [It is] located in Osikinna, a small town in Russia's Kuzbass coal belt.
>
> (*FT*, 12 April 2004, p. 7)

> President Putin [in a presidential decree signed on 10 April] has raised the salaries of ministers and top state officials by between five and twelve times in a bid to combat corruption and attract more talent into government … [The decree] applied only to the top 10 per cent of the 350,000-strong bureaucracy.
>
> (*The Times*, 17 April 2004, p. 23)

> President Putin … has raised his own salary and those of his ministers by up to five times … He signed a decree on 10 April increasing the salaries of about 10 per cent of officials … [The decree] gave Mr Putin a 100 per cent pay rise. His wages last year [2003] were 70,000 roubles a month but will this year amount to 146,000 roubles. Ministers' salaries will rise five times … and some department heads will receive twelve times their present pay-packets Before his re-election campaign in March, Mr Putin declare his

entire capital assets at about 8 million roubles, as well as two small flats, some shares, and a field near Moscow ... Most bureaucrats ... benefit hugely from an array of privileges granted to them ... Russia's bureaucracy now comprises 1 per cent of the [145 million] population – double the amount employed towards the end of the Soviet era. In 1990 there were 663,000 bureaucrats. Today there are 1.25 million.

(*Guardian*, 17 April 2004, p. 14)

12 April 2004.

President Putin ... sharply condemned yesterday [12 April] a move to curb street protests in Russia ... [The State Duma] voted through a bill after a first reading that would all but ban public rallies ... With the bill yet to pass two more readings, the president firmly pointed the Duma towards watering it down, saying that as it stood it proposed 'unhealthy limitations' on citizens' rights.

(*FT*, 13 April 2004, p. 6)

14 April 2004. Mikhail Khodorkovsky (in an open letter to regional journalists):

We [liberal politicians and the business elite] have made many mistakes because of our stupidity, ambitions and the lack of understanding of what is happening in the country ... Forgive us, if you can, and allow us to redeem [ourselves] – we know how to – and if you cannot, we shall leave. And then new liberals will have almost four years to start anew.

(*FT*, 15 April 2004, p. 10)

'Simon Kukes, the Yukos chief executive, insisted on 14 April that the merger [with Sibneft] would be completed unless any "interested party" raised formal objections' (*The Economist*, 17 April 2004, p. 38). 'Yukos's management says it has had no official proposal from Sibneft or its own core shareholders' (*FT*, 20 April 2004, p. 30).

16 April 2004. 'Yukos Oil ... was banned by a Moscow court from selling any assets, ensuring the company will be able to pay $3.4 billion in tax arrears and fines if it loses a case filed by the tax ministry' (*IHT*, 17 April 2004, p. 17).

18 April 2004. 'Roman Abramovich ... has shaken up the *Sunday Times* rich list ... to become Britain's wealthiest individual ... [with] £7.5 billion ... He is the sixth richest person in Europe and the twenty-second wealthiest in the world' (*Guardian*, 19 April 2004, p. 10).

27 April 2004.

The largest shareholders ... [in Yukos] on Tuesday [27 April] nominated Viktor Gerashchenko, a Soviet-era central bank head, as the new chairman of its board ... Gerashchenko, a deputy in parliament representing the Rodina party, said he would resign his Duma seat if he is elected at the oil company's annual general meeting ... Yukos shareholders will be able to vote on the new board candidates on 24 June. Simon Kukes, the Yukos chief executive, would keep his position but give up his dual role as chief executive and chairman.

(www.iht.com, 27 April 2004)

Gerashchenko is currently a deputy ... representing Rodina, a nationalist bloc that came a surprising third in December's parliamentary elections in part of a campaign demanding higher taxes on big companies like Yukos ... [He] served as the top Soviet banker from 1989 to 1991 and he was chairman of Russia's central bank during part of the 1990s and early 2000s ... Gerashchenko's nomination was viewed by some Russians as a peace offering by Yukos to the Kremlin, since he had served with the government ... But it would seem to be an odd peace offering, given that Gerashchenko attempted to run for president against Vladimir Putin earlier this year. Gerashchenko's candidacy was rejected on a technicality ... The directors of Yukos are scheduled to approve board candidates at Wednesday's meeting [28 April] and the shareholders would then vote on the candidate list on 24 June ... [On 27 April] Yukos stock fell roughly 7 per cent following reports on Monday that a syndicate of foreign lenders had served the oil company with a notice of potential default on a $1 billion loan.

(*IHT*, 28 April 2004, p. 13)

7 May 2004. Vladimir Putin is inaugurated for his second (four-year) term of office. Unless the constitution is altered this will be his final term of office.
Vladimir Putin:

Only free people in a free country can be genuinely successful. This is the foundation for economic growth and political stability in Russia ... It is often said here that the head of state in Russia answers and will always answer for everything. That is still the case, but today, although I have a deep awareness of my own personal responsibility, I nevertheless want to emphasize that Russia's success and prosperity cannot and should not depend on one single person or one political force. We need a broad base for developing democracy in our country ... [I pledge to give citizens] a real, tangible increase in their prosperity.

(*IHT*, 8 May 2004, p. 3)

14 May 2004.

Mikhail Khodorkovsky ... faces trial without jury this summer on fraud charges totalling $1 billion after prosecutors finalized the case against him yesterday [14 May]. He is accused of membership of an 'organized group' which manipulated the privatization of the fertilizer group Apatit, non-payment of taxes and other violations in charges dating back as far as 1994 ... Separately, a Moscow commercial court began hearings yesterday on more than $3 billion in tax evasion charges against Yukos for 2000. Officials have indicated that more claims may follow for subsequent years.

(*FT*, 15 May 2004, p. 8)

('Russian deputy minister of justice, Yuri Kalinin, announced yesterday [6 April] that Mikhail Khodorkovsky … has personally disavowed authorship of the article "The Crisis of Liberalism in Russia" … Kalinin: "In an explanation addressed to the director of the pre-trial detention centre … Mikhail Khodorkovsky has stated that he did not write and did not pass to his lawyers the article concerning the fate of Russian liberalism. While Khodorkovsky denies being the author of the article, he nonetheless declares that he is in full agreement with what he says. An internal investigation is continuing" … [But one of Khodorkovsky's lawyers said that "Everyone except Kalinin understands who wrote the article" … Evidently, the attorney meant to suggest that, in disavowing authorship, Mihkail Khodorkosky, simply wanted to avoid putting his defence lawyers on the spot … Under existing legislation all correspondence by persons in detention, with the exception of official protests and statements, must pass through the pre-trial detention centre's administration and be subjected to censorship. The article in question did not pass through the Matrosskaya Tishina administration': *Izvestia*, 7 April 2004, p. 6: *CDSP*, 2004, vol. 56, no. 14, p. 12.)

19 May 2004.

The European Court of Human Rights yesterday [19 May] rebuked the Russian government for persecuting … Vladimir Gusinsky. The Strasbourg-based court ruled that the authorities had used criminal proceedings and pre-trial detention against Mr Gusinsky partly for commercial grounds beyond those permitted by Russian law, and violated his rights to liberty. It is the first time in the court's history that it has found against a member for violating Article 18 of the European convention on human rights, by using the criminal system as part of a commercial bargaining strategy. The judgement is the tenth made against Russia since it ratified the European convention on human rights, a condition for membership of the Council of Europe, the inter-governmental human rights group, in 1998. Mr Gusinsky's arrest and brief detention in June 2000 on charges of fraud were widely seen as politically motivated … The judgement said that Russia did not dispute Mr Gusinsky's claim that the authorities had offered to drop charges in exchange for him agreeing to sell his Media-Most empire to the state-backed company Gazprom … Mr Gusinsky was released after agreeing to an offer to sell his companies in exchange for the dropping of all charges. When he fled Russia and refused to sell, claiming the document had been signed under duress, fresh charges were laid.

(*FT*, 20 May 2004, p. 8)

The European Court of Human Rights … ruled partially in favour of an appeal filed by … Vladimir Gusinsky … The court held a preliminary hearing on 7 March 2002 … The court found the complaint 'partially admissible' … The court said it was impossible to consider a second part of Mr Gusinsky's appeal, which alleged that there had been 'no reasonable basis for suspecting him' of having committed any crime, citing insufficient evidence. At the same time the court handed down a preliminary ruling on the validity of Mr Gusinsky's allegation that he had been held in custody without legal cause ... The European Court ruled [on 19 May 2004] that in arresting ... [him] on 13 June 2000 and holding him for three days in pre-trial detention Russia had violated Article 5 and Article 18 of the European Convention on Human Rights ... The court ruled that the Russian prosecutor-general's office had arrested Vladimir Gusinsky not only for the purpose of trying him in court, but for 'alien reasons' as well – to pressure him into relinquishing NTV to the government-controlled Gazprom ... Russia's code of criminal procedure permits 'in exceptional circumstances' the detention of a citizen who has not yet been charged. But, as the European Court observed, it is unacceptable to have a situation in which the meaning of 'exceptional circumstances' remains completely unspecified and undisclosed by precedent cases.

(*CDSP*, 2004, vol. 56, no. 20, p. 21)

Shares of Yukos swung wildly on Wednesday [19 May] after ... [it] received another warning from its banks, followed by a rare piece of good news ... A Moscow court ruled that Russian tax authorities could not demand immediate payment of $3.4 billion they say Yukos owes in taxes and penalties – at least until after the company's appeal against the demand is heard. Before that Yukos received another 'possible event of default' notice from lenders, this time on $1.6 billion in loans. Last month [April] Yukos received a similar notice on a separate $1 billion loan.

(*IHT*, 20 May 2004, p. 13)

21 May 2004.

Russia's audit office accused a remote Arctic region run [since December 2000] by ... Roman Abramovich of serious financial abuse yesterday [21 May], saying it would send its findings to the government and to prosecutors. State auditors said the Chukotka, of which Mr Abramovich is governor, had misspent millions of dollars, was bankrupt, and awarded tax breaks to companies linked to Mr Abramovich's former oil group Sibneft that did no business there.

(*FT*, 22 May 2004, p. 10)

A Moscow court has rejected an appeal by ... Yukos to drop a tax evasion claim and close the case ... Yukos filed the appeal because the tax ministry gave the company less than two days to pay its tax bill ... $3.4 billion in back taxes for the year 2000 ... The ministry completed its investigation in mid-April and Yukos was given a deadline of 16 April to make the payment. However, Yukos won a rare court victory on Wednesday [19 May] when the Moscow arbitration court ruled that the oil company cannot be fined or made to pay any taxes until its appeal is heard. The appeal court hearing has been scheduled for 28 May.

(The Times, 22 May 2004, p. 23)

('A Moscow court on Wednesday [26 May] ordered Yukos to pay ... $3.4 billion in back taxes and fines for the year 2000 ... Yukos has a month to make an appeal and would have to begin payments only if its appeal was denied': *IHT*, 27 May 2004, p. 13.)

22 May 2004. 'Mikhail Gorbachev stepped down as leader of the Social Democratic Party of Russia' (*CDSP*, 2004, vol. 56, no. 21, p. 12).

26 May 2004. President Putin (state of the nation speech):

> Our goals are absolutely clear. They include a high standard of living in the country, with people leading secure, free and comfortable lives; a mature democracy and a well-developed civil society; and a strengthening of Russia's position in the world. But the main thing, I repeat, is a significant improvement in citizens' well-being ... The number of people with incomes below the subsistence minimum has fallen by a third ... At present about 30 million of our citizens have incomes below the subsistence minimum ... Success in achieving our top-priority national objectives depends solely on ourselves. Those objectives are well known. They include doubling our GDP in a decade [we are entirely capable of doubling our economic potential in ten years, as we said last year], reducing poverty, improving people's well-being and modernizing our military ... By no means everyone in this world would like to deal with an independent, strong and confident Russia ... Our efforts to strengthen our state system are sometimes deliberately interpreted as authoritarianism ... Our adherence to democratic values is dictated by the will of our people and the strategic interests of the Russian Federation itself ... We must now work together to solve the most urgent problems facing our country's citizens. That means, above all, the problems of the quality and affordability of housing, education and health care ... The government and regional and local authorities must set their sights on ensuring that, by the year 2010, at least a third of the country's citizens (and not a tenth, as is the case today) are able to acquire an apartment that meets present-day standards – and acquire it with their own savings and with the help of a housing loan ... We need a clear-cut legal foundation for the development of long-term mortgage lending – for both citizens and professional developers. Mortgages must become an affordable means of solving the housing problem for people with average incomes ... Our policy is to steadily reduce inflation, bringing it down to 3 per cent a year, and to create the necessary conditions for making the rouble fully convertible within the next two years. We know ... that both the government and the central bank have posed that task. But they have set more comfortable conditions for themselves – aiming for 2007 or so. Today we are capable – fully capable – of doing it

much more quickly ... A few words about the role of non-political public organization. Thousands of citizens' groups exist and are doing constructive work in our country. But by no means all of them are orientated toward upholding people's real interests. For some of these organizations obtaining funding from influential foreign foundations has become their main priority. For others the priority is to serve dubious group and commercial interests. Meanwhile the most pressing problems of the country and its citizens go unnoticed.

(*CDSP*, 2004, vol. 56, no. 21, pp. 1–6)

In a televised state of the nation speech President Vladimir Putin singled out private groups here [in Russia] that he said claim to support the welfare of the people but were in fact serving other foreign and domestic masters for pay ... Rather than defending 'the real interests of the people', Putin said, the priority of some independent groups is 'getting financing from influential foreign and domestic foundations, while others serve dubious group and commercial interests ... I have to say that when it concerns violations of fundamental human rights and infringements upon the real interests of the people, the voice of those organizations is often unheard. Actually, there is nothing strange about that. They cannot bite the hand that feeds them' ... His words ... caught human rights advocates and other civic organizations off guard, and seemed to provide a rationale for future restrictions on their activities ... For the most part, Putin's speech outlined general goals of prosperity and social well-being.

(Seth Mydans, *IHT*, 27 May 2004, pp. 1, 4)

Putin said 30 million of Russia's 144 million people live below the poverty line. 'This is a huge number, especially since the majority of poor people in the country are capable of working,' he said. He said that by 2010 one-third of all Russians should be able to buy adequate housing, as opposed to the current 10 per cent.

(p. 13)

President Putin said that the rouble could be fully convertible to other currencies within two years ... 'The policy of consistently reducing inflation must be continued, and I think that the government could attain the level of 3 per cent a year and create, in the coming two years, conditions for ensuring the rouble's convertibility' [he said] ... Russia's inflation rate is running at about 12 per cent a year ... He said the target date for the rouble's convertibility should be pushed up to 2006 from 2007 ... His speech reiterated his pledge to double its [the economy's] size, moving up the date to 2010 ... Putin said Russia's economic growth rate for the first quarter of the year [2004] totalled 8 per cent. At that rate Russia could meet his goal of doubling its GDP by 2010, rather than by 2012 as he declared during last year's address [2003] ... German Gref, the economic development and trade minister ... [has said] that a convertible rouble would greatly reduce costs for Russian business. Currently, for example, oil exporters repatriating their dollar earnings to Russia are required to keep 25 per cent of the converted currency in central bank rouble accounts for months at a time. Last year [2003], however, currency controls required deposits of 75 per cent.

(*IHT*, 27 May 2004, p. 13)

28 May 2004.

A Moscow court held preliminary hearings on $1 billion charges of fraud and tax evasion against Mikhail Khodorkovsky ... before deferring the formal opening until 8 June after a request from the tax authorities ... The court also deferred until 8 June the trial on similar charges against Platon Lebedev.

(*FT*, 29 May 2004, p. 6)

The hearing ... [was] closed to the public ... The case was postponed until 8 June because the tax authorities asked for more time to review the case ... The seven charges against Khodorkovsky range from fraud to embezzlement. They are not related to Yukos, but to the 1994 privatization of an obscure fertilizer factory called Apatit, in which Khodorkovsky's bank, Menatep, was a bidder ... Separately, the tax ministry is waging a second legal front against Yukos as a company. But prosecutors in the criminal case are expected to try to force Yukos's largest shareholders, including Khodorkovsky, to give up control of the oil producer if he is convicted ... [Among other things Khodorkovsky] had advocated higher oil exports to the West and private oil pipelines ... Yukos produced 19 per cent of the total oil extracted in Russia in 2003.

(*IHT*, 29 May 2004, p. 17)

31 May 2004.

Yukos suffered a fresh setback yesterday [31 May] as an arbitration court in Moscow upheld an earlier decision that effectively made its merger with Sibneft void. The court decided the issue of new Yukos shares, with which it paid for Sibneft, is invalid, paving the way for the divorce of the two companies. The decision could also speed up a new deal between Sibneft and one of the international majors. Yukos bought 92 per cent of Sibneft a year ago, paying with new shares, existing Treasury stock and $3 billion cash ... Yukos management refused to let Sibneft go on the same terms as it bought the company ... The ruling means that 57 per cent of Sibneft, which was purchased with new Yukos shares, should go back to Mr Abramovich. This leaves Yukos with another 35 per cent of Sibneft ... Total of France last month received preliminary approval to buy a 25 per cent stake in Sibneft. Chevron Texaco and ExxonMobil of the United States are also believed to be interested in taking a stake.

(*FT*, 1 June 2004, p. 26)

Russia on Monday [31 May] joined a US-led alliance of countries prepared to board ships and raid suspect factories to stem the tide in weapons of mass destruction ... [The] Proliferation Security Initiative is supported by more than sixty countries ... The foreign ministry statement said Russia would contribute to the initiative as long as its actions did not violate international law or its own legislation.

(*IHT*, 1 June 2004, p. 3)

2 June 2004.

One of Russia's leading independent voices on television was silenced yesterday [2 June] when the channel NTV fired the host of a current affairs programme over an interview with the widow of ... Zelimkhan Yandarbiyev ... who was assassinated earlier this year in Qatar ... Leonid Parfyonov, the host of *Namedni* (The Other Day), whose hour-long weekly broadcast was the only televised scrutiny to which the Kremlin was still subjected, is one of Russia's best known journalists ... Parfyonov was forced to drop a five-and-a-half minute segment from the programme ... The segment was broadcast in Siberia, yet withdrawn, reportedly at the request of the security services, before *Namedni* was broadcast in Moscow ... A statement on NTV's website said Parfyonov was sacked because he had broken his contract of employment which obliged him 'to support the politics of the company's leadership' ... *Namedni* was the last remaining sign of NTV's former life as the Kremlin's key critic, particularly over the war in Chechnya. The channel was bought by Gazprom in 2001 and has since begun, like all other channels, to toe the Kremlin line.

(*Guardian*, 3 June 2004, p. 18)

'Mr Parfyonov is one of Russia's most popular television presenters and his Sunday news review programme enjoyed an audience of millions' (*The Times*, 3 June 2004, p. 17).

One of Russia's most outspoken television broadcasters has been dismissed after he insisted on airing a programme against the wishes of the government ... The interview ran on Sunday [30 May] in Russia's far eastern time zones but then was pulled from the air under government pressure before it could be shown in Moscow ... NTV is the last of Russia's three national television stations to remain private. But it has become increasingly attentive to government positions since it was taken over in 2001 by the state-controlled gas monopoly Gazprom.

(*IHT*, 3 June 2004, p. 3)

The ban of the outspoken *Namedni* programme and dismissal of Leonid Parfyonov, one of the country's most prominent journalists, points to the involvement of security services in censoring information ... Mr Parfyonov

... said the decision was made under pressure from Russia's security services on the basis that the broadcast could cause problems for two Russian agents who are currently on trial in Qatar charged with the Mr Yandarbiyev's murder ... NTV, Russia's first independent channel, was taken over by Gazprom, the state-controlled gas monopoly, in a bitter row between the Kremlin and its founder Vladimir Gusinsky.

(*FT*, 3 June 2004, p. 6)

8 June 2004. 'A Moscow court ruled Tuesday [8 June] that Mikhail Khodorkovsky will be tried together with ... Platon Lebedev ... [The] district court approved a defence request to combine [the two cases] ... and scheduled the first hearing for 16 June' (*IHT*, 9 June 2004, p. 5). 'Lawyers for both men argued that it would ease the burden of building a defence' (p. 3).

9 June 2004. '[The] tax authorities have ... bundled a $700 million personal tax demand into his [Khodorkovsky's] trial for fraud and tax evasion' (*FT*, 10 June 2004, p. 11).

Russia's supreme court on Wednesday [9 June] overturned the acquittal of a physicist who had been charged with espionage, ordering a new trial in a case that has been seen as part of a crackdown on researchers and scientists working with foreigners. The ruling reversed a jury's decision last December [2003] to clear the physicist, Valentin Danilov, who had been charged with selling information on space and satellite technology to a company in China that he and other scientists argued was not classified ... In April a jury convicted Igor Sutyagin, an arms control expert accused of working with a company in Britain in a similar case that has drawn criticism from academics and human rights organizations. Sutyagin was sentenced to fifteen years in prison.

(*IHT*, 10 June 2004, p. 5)

11 June 2004.

Switzerland's supreme court ordered about $1.6 billion in assets linked to Yukos to be unfrozen ... The money [frozen since March] belongs to a subsidiary of Group Menatep, the company's biggest shareholder ... In an apparent blow to the company a Russian court on Friday [11 June] removed the judge hearing Yukos's appeal of a demand to pay more than $3 billion in back taxes. The tax ministry said the judge had demonstrated bias.

(*IHT*, 12 June 2004, p. 15)

15 June 2004.

Yukos Oil ... proposed an out-of-court settlement of the government's $3.4 billion tax claim ... Executives of Yukos ... sent a letter to prime minister Mikhail Fradkov this week asking whether the company can restructure the tax ministry's claim or sell assets to pay it off. Yukos indicated that it was willing to issue shares that could be sold to raise cash or offered as a stock settlement ... Yukos management has asked Group Menatep, which owns 44 per cent of Yukos, to approve selling new shares.

(*IHT*, 16 June 2004, p. 13)

16 June 2004.

The criminal trial of ... Mikhail Khodorkovsky and Platon Lebedev ... opened yesterday [16 June] in Moscow – only to be adjourned until next Monday [21 June] after a request for a delay on health grounds by one of the defendants' lawyers.

(*FT*, 17 June 2004, p. 9)

'[Khodorkovsky] appeared for the first time in open court' (*IHT*, 17 June 2004, p. 5).

An appellate court in Moscow on Wednesday [16 June] upheld a ban on the city's Jehovah's Witnesses ... made in March by a lower court ... The decision culminated six years of legal proceedings that began when prosecutors sought to shut down the group's activities on the ground that they threatened Russian society. Under Russia's complex laws governing minority religious groups, the Jehovah's Witnesses are registered on the national level and in nearly 400 other cities in Russia. The ban upheld on Wednesday affects only the group's activities in Moscow ... The prosecutor ... told the court's three judges that the group's Moscow chapter would be prohibited from renting buildings for religious services and from distributing religious literature ... In 2001 a court ruled in favour of the Jehovah's Witnesses, but the prosecutors reinstated the case after an appeal ... [There are] 11,000 believers in Moscow and perhaps 133,000 across the country ... Russia rehabilitated victims of Soviet religious repression in 1992.

(*IHT*, 17 June 2004, p. 3)

'Prosecutors argued that Moscow's 10,000 members of the sect endanger children by not allowing procedures such as blood transfusions. The group will no longer be allowed bank accounts or to rent premises for its activities' (*The Times*, 17 June 2004, p. 20).

18 June 2004. President Putin:

Russian authorities, the government and economic authorities are interested in the bankruptcy of such a company as Yukos. The government will do its best to prevent the collapse of the company ... As to how the process will go in the courts, that is a separate story. It is up to the courts when they come to consider the case in substance.

(*IHT*, 18 June 2004, p. 13; *IHT*, 19 June 2004, p. 13)

His [President Putin's] comments were made on the eve of a tax court hearing Friday [18 June], which Yukos said could sink the company ... Before Putin's remarks analysts had been expecting a court hearing Friday [18 June] to accept a tax ministry request for Yukos to speed up payment of the bill, raising fears that insolvency was imminent ... Yukos faces a \$3.4 billion tax claim from the tax ministry, which the company said it would be unable to pay as long as its assets remained frozen by a court order. On Thursday [17 June] the company's management wrote to prime minister Mikhail Fradkov, admitting that Yukos had underpaid taxes and asking him for help with a plan to help it pay its debts without going under. The letter said: 'The financial policies conducted in 2000–2003 by the former top management and several major shareholders led to large non-payment of taxes and have put Yukos on the edge of financial insolvency. The imminent use of all Yukos's cash resources to pay the tax ministry will lead to a complete halt in current production investments and a decline in output, which will negatively affect forthcoming tax payments. We consider it possible to solve this problem only with government participation' ... The letter ... suggested that the company could buy out Khodorkovsky's shares and offer assets to state energy companies ... Yukos has called for the restructuring of the company's tax obligations, asset sales to accumulate funds to meet those obligations and changes to ownership and management. The plan also calls for Group Menatep, Yukos's controlling shareholder, to help resolve the tax case by providing funds or shares in Yukos.

(*IHT*, 18 June 2004, p. 13)

'In the letter ... Yukos executives ... said they would be willing to issue shares that could be sold to raise cash or offered to the government as payment, to sell assets or to buy out ... Group Menatep' (*IHT*, 19 June 2004, p. 13).

18 June 2004.

An appellate court in Moscow on Friday [18 June] postponed hearings on a \$3.4 billion tax bill ... The Moscow arbitration court's appeals board put the hearings off until Monday [21 June] after rejecting a series of appeals by Yukos, which had wanted the hearings postponed until a much later date. Yukos wanted to postpone not only a judgement on the tax ministry's massive claim but also an appeal of a ruling that the company would have to pay the bill immediately.

(*IHT*, 19 June 2004, p. 1)

President Putin:

After 11 September 2001, and before the start of the military operation in Iraq, the Russian special services ... received information that officials from Saddam's regime were preparing terrorist attacks in the United States and outside it against the US military and other interests.

(*The Times*, 19 June 2004, p. 22)

President Putin said yesterday [18 June] that Russian intelligence services had told the Bush administration on several occasions that Saddam Hussein planned terrorist attacks on the United States and its interests abroad ... [President Putin] added that Russian intelligence had no proof that Saddam's agents were involved in any particular attacks ... Mr Putin said that Mr Bush had thanked one of the heads of the Russian security services for the information about possible terrorist attacks, but he said that he could not comment on how critical that information was in the US decision to go to war.

(*The Times*, 19 June 2004, p. 22)

The Interfax agency reported – citing 'a reliable source in a Russian intelligence agency' ... [that]: 'back in early 2002 Russian intelligence learned that Iraqi security services were preparing terrorist attacks against targets on US territory, as well as US diplomatic and military targets overseas. This information was repeatedly conveyed in oral and written form to Russia's American partners ... President Putin: 'It is true that after the events of 11 September and up until the beginning of the military operation in Iraq, Russian intelligence services repeatedly obtained information of this kind and passed it on to their American colleagues ... [At the same time] we had no information indicating that the Hussein regime was actually involved in any terrorist acts ... George Bush ... personally thanked the director of one of Russia's intelligence services for this information, which he considered very important ... There are certain procedures under international law that must be followed in using international affairs, and in this case [Iraq] those procedures were not followed' ... The US State Department announced that it knew nothing at all about the facts cited by Vladimir Putin ... George Bush never once cited any information from Moscow ... The White House reaction to the statement that Putin made ... remains ambiguous ... 'We have ongoing co-operation with the Russian government, including matters of intelligence. And we don't discuss specific intelligence matters publicly,' said the White House spokeswoman.

(*Kommersant*, 21 June 2004, pp. 1, 9: *CDSP*, 2004, vol. 56, no. 25, pp. 6–7)

24 June 2004.

As speculation emerged of a deep split within Yukos, the company's chief executive, Simon Kukes, stepped down on Thursday [24 June] and was replaced by Steven Theede, formerly chief operating officer ... A Russian-born American, Kukes had been in position since November [2003] ... Market analysts said ... it signalled a split within Yukos's career oil men and the majority shareholders, which include Khodorkovsky.

(www.iht.com, 25 June 2004)

29 June 2004.

A court upheld the tax service's claim of $3.4 billion in back taxes against the Yukos oil company and said it had entered force ... Yukos has three months to pay the bill of 99.4 billion roubles or it could face bankruptcy proceedings ... The court ruling followed a statement from the tax ministry that it did not want to reach an out-of-court settlement with Yukos ... The tax service says that Yukos ran up the bill in 2000 through the misuse of onshore tax havens. Yukos said that any tax strategies it used were legal and

it contested the claim. Separately, the court also decided to lower the amount
of the tax claim by the fractional amount of 32 million roubles.

(www.iht.com, 29 June 2004)

'Roughly 30 per cent of Yukos is still held by outside minority investors' (*IHT*,
30 June 2004, p. 13).

1 July 2004.

The tax ministry is demanding another $3.4 billion in back taxes from
Yukos ... The second claim is for taxes in 2001 ... The news came as bailiffs served the company papers [dated 30 June] executing the tax ministry's
original $3.4 billion tax claim against the company for 2000 ... [The bail-
iffs] said the company had five days to comply voluntarily. The order also
said the bailiffs must inventory Yukos's property and put a freeze order on
it ... According to Russian law, tax authorities can present the papers to
banks where Yukos holds accounts and demand payment within three days
... Yukos is prevented by a court order from selling its assets to raise the
money ... The company is also facing audits for 2002 and 2003.

(*IHT*, 2 July 2004, p. 13)

'Under Russian insolvency legislation the court could approve a tender for the
sale of ... assets ... Under Russia's recently modified insolvency laws tax debts
have no greater priority than other creditors' (*FT*, 2 July 2004, p. 28).

On Tuesday 29 June a court overturned Yukos's appeal against a $3.44
billion claim for back taxes for the year 2000. Though bailiffs can allow up
to five days for complying with a court order, they turned up the very next
day at the company's offices to begin enforcing it. And just a couple of
hours after they left the tax ministry announced that it will go to court with
a new and equally huge tax claim for 2001 ... To make the company pay its
taxes bailiffs can order its banks to empty Yukos's accounts. However, the
oil giant says it has only about $1 billion in cash. The bailiffs can then seize
and sell the company assets.

(www.economist.com, 2 July 2004)

'A court upheld a demand from the government that Yukos pay back taxes of
$3.4 billion [for 2000]. The oil giant offered to pay around a third of what it
owes – unpaid taxes but no fines or penalties' (*The Economist*, 3 July 2004,
p. 7).

2 July 2004. 'A court here [in Moscow] upheld a ruling barring the company
from selling any assets to cover its ... tax bills' (*IHT*, 3 July 2004, p. 11).

3 July 2004. 'Police searched the headquarters of Yukos ... and confiscated documents, safes and computer discs' (*The Times*, 5 July 2004, p. 2).

Police officers ... were looking for evidence of tax evasion by a Yukos subsidiary [Samaraneftegaz], a company spokesman said. The officers spent

several hours ... removing hard discs from the computers of Yukos's top managers and some board members ... The investigators broke into a number of file cabinets ... [and] a report on a Yukos shareholders' meeting and a large number of company tax documents were seized [the spokesman said] ... The prosecutor-general's office said that the actions were connected with a criminal fraud and tax evasion 'against structures controlled by Yukos'.

(IHT, 5 July 2004, p. 11)

3 July 2004.

On Saturday [3 July] as Gennadi Zyuganov delivered his address [to the Communist Party Congress] a breakaway communist faction was holding a separate congress ... The breakaway delegates claimed to have rounded up a quorum last week and stripped Zyuganov of power.

(IHT, 6 July 2004, p. 2)

The Russian Communist Party ... has split. After months of acrimony a faction led by the MP Gennadi Semigin has broken away from the party, accusing its leaders of corruption and inefficiency ... Two communist congresses were held in Moscow ... [The one] led by Mr Semigin was attended by around fifty candidates.

(Daily Telegraph, 6 July 2004, p. 10)

A splinter faction elected a new leader, Vladimir Tikhonov ... It accused Mr Zyuganov of links to 'oligarchic capitalism' and vowed to investigate his record since 1991 ... Mr Tikhonov, governor of the Ivanovo region, is seen [by the Kremlin] as a more compliant figure. He derives much of his support from Gennadi Semigin, a rival of Mr Zyuganov who was expelled from the Communist Party in May for collaborating with the Kremlin.

(The Times, 7 July 2004, p. 13)

('[On 17 June] Gennadi Zyuganov's opponents in the party's upper echelon – Sergei Potapov, Tatyana Astrakhanina, Alexander Shulga – presented evidence to support their accusations against [Zyuganov] ... [It] listed not only the inclusion of oligarchs and their representatives on party lists, but also contacts with the Kremlin, the party's defeat in the last federal election campaign, isolation from the party's rank and file, and "great leader syndrome and arrogance"': *CDSP*, 2004, vol. 56, no. 24, p. 8.)

[On 1 July] Zyuganov's supporters and opponents held two completely separate plenary sessions of the RFCP Central Committee ... the alternative plenum voted to terminate Zyuganov's authority and elected Ivanovo province governor Vladimir Ilyich Tikhonov to be the new chairman of the Communist Party Central Committee ... They elected him leader 'for the duration of the congress', but Tikhonov himself makes no secret of his desire to retain the post ... The Communist Party press office released a statement in which the alternative plenary session ... was termed 'another case of disinformation intended to serve as cover for the latest pre-congress attempt by a small intraparty opposition group to alter the makeup of the RFCP Central Committee leadership and turn the Communist Party into a social democratic appendage of the functionaries in the Kremlin' ... Zyuganov's opponents delivered yet another blow to the leader yesterday [1 July] by removing him from the chairmanship of the Popular-Patriotic Union of Russia (PPUR) and replacing him with Gennadi Semigin as acting chairman.

(*CDSP*, 2004, vol. 56, no. 26, p. 9)

[On 3 July] two tenth congresses of the Russian Federation Communist Party took place ... [The place] where the pro-Zyuganov RFCP congress took place experienced a power failure ... about an hour-and-a-half before the start of the activities ... Zyuganov talked about mistakes ... [including a failure] to discern the presence of 'factionalists' in the top party leadership ... [and] having accepted help from the head of the coordinating council of the Popular-Patriotic Union of Russia, 'the capitalist Mr Semigin', who succeeded during that time in acquiring influence in the party ... [At] the anti-Zyuganov congress ... RFCP Ivanovo province governor Vladimir Tikhonov was elected chairman of the RFCP (he had previously been temporarily appointed to that post by a Central Committee plenary session ... [The anti-Zyuganovs] elected their own party leadership, thereby formally punishing Zyuganov for his 'great leader complex [*vozhdism*] and arrogance', his 'ties with oligarchs' and his 'loss of contact with the party masses' ... Each of the Central Committees now has to document its legitimacy as thoroughly and quickly as possible and convince the justice ministry that its documents are the more authentic.

(*CDSP*, 2004, vol. 56, no. 27, pp. 5–6)

('The justice department decided on Tuesday [3 August] that the content of the reporting documents of the tenth congress of the Russian Federation Communist Party under Gennadi Zyuganov was closer to the truth than the contents of the analogous documents of the tenth RFCP congress chaired by Ivanovo province governor Vladimir Tikhonov': *CDSP*, 2004, vol. 56, no. 31, p. 10).

5 July 2004.

Yukos said Monday [5 July] that a syndicate of Western banks, led by Société Générale of France, had declared it in default on a $1 billion loan, and accused the government of pushing it closer to insolvency. Société Générale said the syndicate [of ten banks] was not demanding immediate repayment because it could draw on bank accounts backed by oil exports ... [Menatep Group], which lent Yukos $1.6 billion, is also not demanding repayment ... Yukos, with many bank accounts frozen, is barred from selling any assets to help pay down the loans.

(*IHT*, 6 July 2004, p. 11)

7 July 2004.

Bailiffs yesterday [7 July] visited the company registrar for Yukos ... to identify assets that could be seized to pay off a 99 billion rouble ($3.4 billion) bill for back taxes, even as ... [Mikhail Khodorkovsky] pledged his shares in an effort to stave off bankruptcy. Court officials went to the Moscow-based company that holds the share register for Yukos's operating subsidiaries ... A lawyer for Mikhail Khodorkovsky ... confirmed that his client was willing to hand over his 44 per cent stake in the company to settle its tax debts and delegate negotiating rights to the Yukos management.

(*FT*, 8 July 2004, p. 29)

'My client, Mikhail Khodorkovsky, offered the board of directors of Yukos to use the Yukos shares belonging to core shareholders to regulate the tax claims of government,' [his lawyer said] ... The police on Wednesday [7 July] raided Yukos's main shareholder registry ... and law enforcement agents also visited Yukos headquarters again to retrieve more documents.

(*IHT*, 8 July 2004, p. 1)

On Wednesday [7 July] the OECD accused the Russian government of 'highly selective law enforcement' in pursuing Yukos for alleged tax fraud. The Paris-based think-tank said the charges brought against Yukos could also be made against hundreds of other companies and millions of citizens. It decried an atmosphere in which courts 'are often subservient to the executive' and prosecutors, police and security services 'remain highly politicized'.

(www.iht.com, 7 July 2004)

The OECD (annual report on Russia):

Whether the charges against the company and its core shareholders are true or not, it is clearly a case of highly selective law enforcement ... The courts are often subservient to the executive, while the security services, the prosecutors and the police remain highly politicized. The so-called 'Yukos case' reflects these problems ... [The charges directed against Yukos and its executives could be] directed against millions of companies and citizens.

(*IHT*, 8 July 2004, p. 8)

9 July 2004.

The prosecutor-general [Vladimir Ustinov] has announced he is taking personal control of the investigation into the killing of Paul Klebnikov, the American editor of *Forbes* magazine's Russian edition ... *Forbes* started its Russian language edition in April [2004]. Klebnikov, born in the United States of Russian heritage, had previously been with the US-based *Forbes* ... Klebnikov, forty-one, was gunned down late Friday [9 July] outside the magazine's offices. Russian news reports said that ... the authorities believed the murder had probably been connected to the editor's professional activities. Klebnikov, who also wrote a book about Boris Berezovsky ... was seen as widely knowledgeable about Russia's often murky business world ... In May the magazine attracted wide attention by publishing a list of Russia's wealthiest people.

(IHT, 12 July 2004, p. 3)

'Twenty journalists have been killed in Russia [five in 2003] in the past decade for their work; fourteen since Putin became president. None of the murders have been solved' *(IHT*, 13 July 2004, p. 7).

The country's billionaires control about $110 billion, assets equivalent to a quarter of the nation's GDP, according to the magazine Klebnikov produced ... *Forbes Russia*, which first appeared in April, published a list of Russia's 100 richest people. The magazine said that Moscow was home to thirty-six billionaires, more than any city in the world.

(IHT, 19 July 2004, p. 3)

('Paul Klebnikov ... had begun investigating the killing of a prominent Russian journalist, a Moscow publisher said Friday [16 July] ... Klebnikov was looking into the 1995 shooting death of television journalist Vladislav Listyev with the aim of possibly publishing a book on the case, said Valeri Streletsky, who published two books by Klebnikov in Russian. But Streletsky said he doubted the fledgling investigation was the motive for the killing': *IHT*, 17 July 2004, p. 6.)

'Leonid Bershidsky, the publisher of the Russian edition of *Forbes*, believes he may have been murdered to show the business elite's displeasure with the magazine he edited' *(The Independent*, 12 July 2004, p. 21).

[This is] the latest in a string of violent attacks on journalists ... In 1996 Mr Klebnikov wrote a profile for *Forbes* of ... Boris Berezovsky, claiming he siphoned off hundreds of millions of dollars from Russia ... Mr Klebnikov also wrote a book on Mr Berezovsky entitled *Godfather of the Kremlin: The Decline of Russia in the Age of Gangster Capitalism*. Mr Berezovsky ... filed a libel suit against *Forbes* which was settled last year [2003] after the magazine acknowledged that it had wrongfully accused him of being involved in the murder of a television tycoon in 1995 ... Mr Klebnikov had said he had received several threats after the list [of the wealthiest people] was published [in May].

(The Times, 12 July 2004, p. 14)

Mr Klebnikov wrote an article for *Forbes* [about Boris Berezovsky] ... entitled *Godfather of the Kremlin: Boris Berezovsky and the Looting of Russia* ... Fifteen journalists have now been killed since 2000. No one has been brought to book for any of their murders.

(The Economist, 17 July 2004, p. 87)

In 1996 he [Klebnikov] wrote an article claiming Mr Berezovsky had something to do with the [unsolved March 1995] murder of ... the television journalist Vladislav Listyev ... an allegation he was forced to retract after

Forbes admitted that there was no evidence to support that. The tycoon had sued the magazine ... [Listyev] was about to take over the management of the country's main television channel ORT. The media said he had ruffled feathers by declaring a five-month moratorium on advertising on the revamped channel to stamp out corruption ... Mr Klebnikov was the fifteenth journalist to be killed since 2000 when Vladimir Putin became president.

(*The Independent*, 17 July 2004, p. 27)

11 July 2004.

President Vladimir Putin has reunified Russia's spy agencies ... twelve years after ... Boris Yeltsin ... [split] its [the KGB's] domestic and foreign security agencies ... The decree, signed on Sunday [11 July], gives Nikolai Patrushev, director of the counter-espionage service, the FSB, the status of a cabinet minister ... Founded in 1917 by Felix Dzerzhinsky ... the organization that became today's FSB began life as the Cheka ... Russia marked last month's ninetieth anniversary of the birth of Yuri Andropov, the former KGB head who preceded Mikhail Gorbachev as Soviet president, by erecting a statue to him in Petrozavodsk, north of St Petersburg.

(*Daily Telegraph*, 15 July 2004, p. 17)

12 July 2004.

Mikhail Khodorkovsky returned to the courtroom ... repeating his offer to give up his shares of Yukos [44 per cent] ... His lawyer ... denied a report that Khodorkovsky would hand over his Yukos shares for free, saying the billionaire hoped to get some kind of compensation, possibly from the company and at a future date.

(*IHT*, 13 July 2004, p. 11)

14 July 2004.

[It was reported on 7 July] that a decision had been reached to shut down some of NTV's programmes and pull them off the air. They include the *Freedom of Speech* [*Svoboda Slova*] talk show hosted by Savik Shuster, and the current affairs analysis programme *Personal Contribution* [*Lichny Vklad*], hosted by Alexander Gerasimov ... [On 9 July] the current deputy general director for news broadcasting, Alexander Gerasimov ... [was] sent on leave from which he is unlikely to return to the channel. His position has already been offered to [another person]. Consequently, *Personal Contribution* will no longer be on the air. Also [on 9 July] television viewers saw the last broadcast of Savik Shuster's programme *Freedom of Speech* ... Shuster will, however, remain at NTV as deputy general director for documentary films. The programme The *Country and the World* [*Strana i Mir*] will continue broadcasting only until this fall ... [On 10 July] Mr Gerasimov, who was regarded as the likeliest candidate for dismissal, beat his superiors to the punch by tendering his resignation ... After a month's leave owed him by his employers, neither Gerasimov himself nor his programme *Personal Contribution* will be returning to the channel ... [On 14 July] two more NTV stars were pulled off the air ... The satirical *Red Arrow* [*Krasnaya Strela*, featuring two animated puppets] ... [was] shut down.

(*CDSP*, 2004, vol. 56, no. 27, pp. 3–4)

Another anti-Kremlin voice has been silenced after ... NTV, one of only three [television] channels that cover the whole of Russia ... axed its equivalent to *Spitting Image*. *Krasnaya Strela*, or *Red Arrow*, was hosted by two puppets ... who poked fun at the powers that be, including President Vladimir Putin ... Russia's last live political talk show, *Freedom of Speech*, has been axed ... as was another political programme, *Personal Contribution*, on the same channel. A month ago Leonid Parfyonov, host of a cutting-edge analytical programme called *The Other Day*, was sacked by NTV for failing 'to support the politics of the company's leadership'. His mistake had been to interview the widow of a former Chechen rebel president, which irked the FSB, the successor organization to the KGB, accused of assassinating the man.

(*The Independent*, 16 July 2004, p. 21)

'NTV ... has in effect been taken over by the state. Its programme *Freedom of Speech*, the only balanced political talkshow on Russian television, was given a few days before Mr Klebnikov's killing [on 9 July]' (*The Economist*, 17 July 2004, p. 87).

('Yesterday [30 May] a segment of the NTV programme *Namedni* [The Other Day] that had been aired earlier in the Asian part of Russia was pulled off the air during the programme's broadcast to European Russia on the orders of NTV acting general director Alexander Gerasimov. The segment ... dealt with the trial of the Russian security service officers whom the authorities in Qatar suspect of having murdered Chechen separatist leader Zelimkhan Yandarbiyev. It showcased an exclusive interview with Mr Yandarbiyev's widow ... Leonid Parfyonov [the host of *Namedni*] admitted to *Kommersant*: "Gerasimov insisted that the special services had issued a standing request not to air anything about the trial in Qatar while the defendants' fates are still in question"': *Kommersant*, 31 May 2004, p. 3: *CDSP*, 2004, vol. 56, no. 22, p. 1. 'Alexander Gerasimov ... cited an "urgent request from the special services" ... Leonid Parfyonov has been fired from NTV. The decision was made by NTV general director Nikolai Senkevich [on 2 June]. As soon as the order was signed NTV issued a statement: "The dismissal was due to the cancellation of the *Namedni* programme, which was brought on by Leonid Parfyonov's breach of his employment contract, under which he was bound to support the policies of the station's management"': *Vremya Novostei*, 3 June 2004, p. 1: *CDSP*, 2004, vol. 56, no. 22, p. 3.)

('Russian television's last surviving independent political talk show has been axed ... The programme, *Freedom of Speech*, will be shown for the last time on NTV today [9 July], just four days after the company's chief was fired ... Vladimir Kulistikov took up the post on Monday [5 July] after Gazprom ... fired the previous chief ... [The programme] was hosted by Savik Shuster, a former Moscow bureau chief for Radio Liberty, who has often criticized the Kremlin. [On 6 July Mr Shuster was offered] a post as deputy general director ... Mr Shuster fled the Soviet Union in 1971 and became a Canadian citizen but returned to Russia in the late 1980s ... Gazprom sacked Boris Jordan, another NTV chief. Last year [2003] ... Last month [June] NTV fired a popular news anchor Leonid Parfyonov and cancelled his show ... Mr Parfyonov said he was surprised by the decision to cancel *Freedom of Speech*: "I did not expect this. There is no media freedom on television now because all the national channels are controlled by the state. Gazprom is just a pseudonym" ': *The Times*, 9 July 2004, p. 16. 'Three hours before Paul Klebnikov was gunned down [on 9 July] the last decent political programme in Russia had its final broadcast. Savik Shuster's weekly *Svodoba Slova* – "Freedom of the Word" – was pulled off NTV, the station Putin has been forcibly bringing under state control, by the newly installed director': *IHT*, 13 July 2004, p. 7.)

15 July 2004.

> At the hearing Thursday [15 July] a state prosecutor ... read through the charges against Khodorkovsky and Platon Lebedev, alleging they set up an 'organized criminal group' to fraudulently acquire 20 per cent of a large and lucrative fertilizer company called Apatit.
>
> (*IHT*, 16 July 2004, p. 11)

'The charges include embezzlement, forgery and personal tax evasion. If convicted they each face sentences of up to ten years in prison' (*IHT*, 17 July 2004, p. 11).

17 July 2004.

> Paul Peloyan, the editor of the magazine *Armenian Lane* [*Armyansky Pereulok*] was found [on 17 July] ... with severe head injuries and knife wounds ... The US-based Committee to Protect Journalists condemned the murder ... It views Russia as one of the ten most dangerous places for journalists to work ... Klebnikov was the first western [journalist to be killed].
>
> (*Guardian*, 19 July 2004, p. 12)

'Mr Peloyan edited a Russian arts and literature magazine for the Armenian community' (*FT*, 19 July 2004, p. 5).

> In contrast to the late Paul Klebnikov ... Mr Peloyan's work appears relatively uncontroversial ... Mr Peloyan's magazine was an arts publication ... [It] carried features about literature, the arts and history and included prose and poetry from Armenian writers ... It is estimated that 2 million Armenians live in Russia and the two countries have a close relationship going back hundreds of years ... The Russian media itself made far less of Mr Peloyan's murder ... Mr Peloyan is the sixteenth journalist to be murdered since 2000 when Vladimir Putin assumed the presidency. The

US-based Committee to Protect Journalists ... addressed an open letter to Mr Putin after Mr Klebnikov's killing, complaining about 'the climate of lawlessness and impunity'. 'Cases [of journalists being killed] have not been properly investigated or prosecuted, a testament to the ongoing law-lessness in Russia and your failure to reform the country's weak and politi-cized criminal justice system,' it said ... Alexei Sidorov ... died on 9 October 1993 [in Togliatti] ... [His] newspaper is known for investigative reporting on organized crime, government corruption and shady corporate deals ... Valeri Ivanov ... died on 29 April 2002 ... [He was] murdered in Togliatti after his paper exposed controversial business deals linked to organized crime and government corruption ... Natalya Skryl ... died on 9 March 2002 ... She was investigating a struggle for the control of Tagmet, a local metallurgical plant ... Eduard Markevich ... died on 18 September 2001 ... [His] paper often criticized local officials ... Igor Domnikov ... died on 16 July 2000 ... [His paper] reported on corruption in the Russian oil industry.

(*The Independent*, 19 July 2004, p. 20)

The United States-based Committee to Protect Journalists [in an open letter to Putin]: 'No one has been brought to justice in any of the slayings, creating a sense of impunity that endangers all journalists' (*The Times*, 20 July 2004, p. 15).

It emerged last week that a reporter in St Petersburg, Maxim Maximov, has been missing since 1 July ... Mr Maximov, a reporter for the St Petersburg magazine *City*, had been covering an investigation into the murder of Galina Starovoitova, a liberal politician shot in the entrance to her home in 1998.

(*The Times*, 20 July 2004, p. 15)

20 July 2004.

Bailiffs will sell off Yukos's main fuel production unit, Yuganskneftegaz ... [which] accounts for 60 per cent of production at Yukos, which as a whole pumps a fifth of Russia's oil ... Yukos faces a fire sale of assets after missing a [7 July] deadline to pay $3.4 billion in back taxes ... In a sign that Yukos's own management and shareholders are divided in the face of the intense government pressure, the company's chairman, Viktor Gerash-chenko, reacted angrily on Monday [19 July] to Khodorkovsky's calls for his dismissal. Gerashchenko, a former chairman of the Soviet and Russian central banks, was brought in to Yukos just last month [June], at the urging of others, in the hope that he could quickly broker a deal with the Kremlin. But last week Khodorkovsky said Gerashchenko had failed to open a dia-logue with the government and urged fellow shareholders to oust him. Gerashchenko, in turn, accused Khodorkovsky's allies of 'meddling' in the company's management and hurting its relations with the government.

(www.iht.com, 20 July 2004)

The Russian government took steps to seize ... the jewel in the crown of oil production at Yukos ... 'After valuation the share stake in Yuganskneftegaz will be handed over to a special organization for sale,' the justice ministry said in a statement ... Yuganskneftegaz accounts for 70 per cent of Yukos's reserves and 60 per cent of its output ... Just a decade ago in a controversial auction ... he [Khodorkovsky] won Yuganskneftegaz for just over $150 million ... Meanwhile the criminal trial of Khodorkovsky continued Tuesday [20 July], with prosecutors reading all the charges against him, including fraud, embezzlement and tax evasion in the privatization of a lucrative fertilizer factory.

(*IHT*, 21 July 2004, pp. 1, 10)

The Russian authorities ... [struck] at the heart of Yukos, the country's largest oil company, saying they will sell its main operating subsidiary to settle a $3.4 billion tax bill ... Yuganskneftegaz is valued at $30 billion on the basis of reserves and $12 billion on the basis of discounted cash flow ... A Yukos representative told one Russian news agency that Yuganskneftegaz could be sold for as little as $1.75 billion.

(*FT*, 21 July 2004, p. 1)

Mikhail Khodorkovsky paid just over $300 million for [Yukos in 1995] ... Instead of first selling the company's non-core assets as Russian law requires, the bailiffs went for Yuganskneftegaz, the main production unit of the company ... [Yukos] agreed to pay $1.3 billion in cash and volunteered to bailiffs its stake in Sibneft ... However, the bailiffs refused to seize the Sibneft stake which was later frozen by a court in Chukotka, a northern region governed by Roman Abramovich.

(p. 27)

'Yukos produces ... almost 20 per cent of Russia;s [oil] exports' (*FT*, 23 July 2004, p. 30).

26 July 2004.

A Moscow court yesterday [26 July] issued an arrest warrant on charges of murder for Leonid Nevzlin, a key shareholder in Yukos ... Mr Nevzlin fled to Israel last year [2003] ... and now has an Israeli passport ... [He has dual citizenship] ... Earlier this year he was charged with tax evasion and embezzlement. Russian prosecutors have now accused Mr Nevzlin of organizing contract killings and assassination attempts ... The prosecutor-general's office said it had gathered 'enough evidence ... that while he was a member of the Yukos board ... Mr Nevzlin conspired with Alexei Pichugin, the head of the internal and economic security department of Yukos, to kill particular individuals who represented a threat to the company as well as to Mr Nevzlin and Mr Pichugin'. Mr Pichugin, a former KGB operative who was in charge of security at Yukos, was arrested more than a year ago and accused of murder and attempted murder. Prosecutors now say he acted on the instructions of Mr Nevzlin.

(*FT*, 27 July 2004, p. 9)

28 July 2004.

Yukos ... claimed yesterday [28 July] that an order from Russia's ministry of justice barring transfer of property from its subsidiaries meant it was not allowed to sell oil [and oil products]. The ministry denied its actions were aimed at halting the work of Yukos's subsidiaries.

(*FT*, 29 July 2004, p. 1)

[A spokesman for the company said that] Yukos had written to the ministry of justice for clarification but had not heard back ... [The man] in charge of Russia's bailiffs service ... said Yukos workers would be paid: 'I declare officially that there will be no problems.'

(p. 25)

The case revolves around the establishment of companies in 'offshore zones' – regions within Russia with low tax regimes. Yukos used these companies to lower its tax burden. The charges against Yukos are based on claims that its affiliates did not do any of the things that the tax privileges were meant to encourage companies to do; they merely helped Yukos avoid taxes. I am convinced that, in an independent court, it would probably be impossible to prove these charges. A vast majority of large companies have used these methods of tax optimization and all of them, including Yukos, passed inspections by the tax services. Last year [2003] Yukos had a turnover of about $15 billion. Profits for the first nine months of 2003, according to generally accepted accounting principles, were $2.5 billion. It is almost impossible to imagine that Yukos could evade $3 billion in taxes in one year and still remain one of the largest Russian taxpayers.

(Yevgeni Yasin, economy minister 1994–7, *FT*, 29 July 2004, p. 17)

29 July 2004.

The government on Thursday [29 July] clarified a previous order freezing some assets of Yukos, which ... had warned could have shut down its oil production. The justice ministry said the company's three oil producing subsidiaries – Yuganskneftegaz, Samaraneftegaz and Tomskneft – could continue sales and production. But Yukos's property and assets remain frozen ... A top justice ministry official on Thursday denied that Yukos had been ordered to halt production ... Yukos on Thursday issued a statement saying its three production units received notification from the ministry of justice dated 28 July revoking earlier orders that prohibited 'disposal or change of assets' status'.

(*IHT*, 30 July 2004, p. 11)

The company had warned the freeze could force it to stop pumping within days ... Copies of letters from the justice ministry's bailiffs' service lifting the freezes were dated Wednesday [28 July], but it was unclear whether the letters were drafted before Yukos made its complaints public. Yukos had claimed that bailiffs' orders telling three Yukos subsidiaries to cease all sale of company property could mean a production halt in the near future ... Yuganskneftegaz was one of the three production units for which the property freeze was lifted in the letters, but it was unclear whether that indicated the state would back off its sale plan.

(www.iht.com, 29 July 2004)

4 August 2004.

Yukos has offered to sell its controlling interest in a natural gas venture with the Anglo-Russian oil company TNK-BP to help settle its huge bill for back taxes ... The sale would raise \$357 million ... TNK-BP confirmed that the company had accepted the offer to buy out Yukos's 56 per cent stake in the Rospan International gas venture. TNK-BP said the sale would be legal because Yukos's stake belongs to an offshore subsidiary and is, therefore, not part of Yukos's Russian assets, which remain frozen under a court order. A Yukos spokesman said that the company had sent a letter to the government requesting permission for the sale and was still waiting for a response.

(*IHT*, 5 August 2004, p. 11)

Yukos has written to the ministry of justice ... seeking permission to sell its controlling stake in Rospan, a Siberian gas company, to TNK-BP, which already holds the remaining 44 per cent in the joint venture ... Under a shareholder agreement TNK-BP had an option to buy Yukos's Rospan stake at any time ... However, oil analysts doubt that Yukos will be allowed to sell its stake, despite the fact that it holds it through a Cyprus-registered company that technically does not come under the asset freeze.

(*FT*, 5 August 2004, p. 26)

Yukos said the ministry of justice had told the company it could pay for its ongoing business from its bank accounts ... [A Yukos statement]: 'We welcome the decision of the ministry of justice, which lets us continue financing our ongoing business and to pay, without delay, our current taxes and our tax debt for the year 2000.'

(*FT*, 5 August 2004, p. 26)

'Yukos was yesterday [4 August] given more breathing space by the justice ministry, which allowed it to pay salaries and to continue operating' (p. 15).

5 August 2004.

The authorities rescinded an offer made just one day earlier to allow Yukos to use its frozen bank accounts to fund day-to-day operations The justice ministry went back on a decision allowing Yukos to access its current accounts to keep operations running ... The justice ministry denied in a statement that it had granted Yukos permission to use its frozen bank accounts, and said that what was made public on Wednesday night [28 July] was granted to the company by only one bailiff and was therefore illegal. The authorities then withdrew the permission and froze Yukos's accounts again ... So far court bailiffs have collected about 22 billion roubles of the 98 billion roubles, or $3.4 billion, in back taxes for the year 2000 ... Currently the government's share of Russia's 2004 estimated oil production stands at around 7.2 per cent. But if Yukos's crown jewel Yuganskneftegaz is put back under state control the government's share of oil production would grow to almost 18 per cent, making the Kremlin the second largest producer after Lukoil.

(*IHT*, 6 August 2004, p. 11)

'Yukos pumps ... about 2 per cent of the world's oil' (p. 7).

The ministry of justice said the clarification sent to Yukos a day earlier allowing it use of its revenues to pay workers, suppliers and service providers had no legal basis and therefore had to be revoked. 'All the funds that arrive to Yukos's accounts will be arrested and transferred to the budget to pay the taxes,' the ministry said ... Russian authorities said yesterday [5 August] that the flight of capital was accelerating. German Gref, the economy minister, said net capital outflows would soar from $2.9 billion in 2003 to $8.0 billion to $8.5 billion this year [2004], exceeding the central bank's forecast of $6.5 billion.

(*FT*, 6 August 2004, p. 1)

6 August 2004.

Yukos said Friday [6 August] that a Moscow court had ruled against the state's plan to seize shares of its largest oil producing unit, lifting, at least temporarily, one of the threats hanging over the company. The government last month froze the shares of Yuganskneftegaz ... The Moscow arbitration court lifted that order Friday following an appeal ... 'The court is saying the way the bailiffs went about this was illegal, but that means the bailiffs can go back and do it again properly' ... [said the] chief strategist at Alfa Bank, Russia's largest privately owned bank ... The shares of Yukos and world oil prices have swung with each turn in the case ... Yukos is awaiting the court's decision [scheduled for 9 August] on the freezing of shares in two other oil units, Tomskneft and Samaraneftegaz.

(*IHT*, 7 August 2004, p. 11)

'Yukos said bailiffs had confiscated $900 million of its revenues by yesterday [6 August], leaving its outstanding bill [for 2000] at about $2.5 billion' (*FT*, Money and Business, 7 August 2004, p. 6).

8 August 2004.

The Federation Council ... approved a controversial bill Sunday [8 August] that would end an array of Soviet-era benefits [in kind], including free transportation and medicine, for some of Russia's most impoverished and vulnerable people. The measure has sparked noisy protests ... [The upper house] approved the legislation ... by a vote of 156 to five, with one abstention. The measure had already won approval Thursday [5 August] in the lower house of parliament ... and now goes to President Vladimir Putin for his signature. The bill will replace many of the long-standing Soviet-era benefits with cash payments. About 30 million people – Russia's elderly, disabled and World War II veterans – will be affected ... The government says the move will be a boon to many and will make aid more accurately targeted – arguing, for example, that public transportation is scarce in rural areas. But many recipients are outraged ... The bill eliminates free access to urban transport, free home phone use for local calls, free provision of artificial limbs, job guarantees for the disabled and, for many, free medicine. In return they will get monthly cash payments from 1,550 roubles, or $53, down to 150 roubles, and some will have to deduct a portion of those funds to participate in a so-called 'social package' that will restore some of the lost benefits.

(IHT, 9 August 2004, p. 3)

On 5 August the Duma ... passed the bill on its third reading by 309 to 118 ... [President Putin recalled] parliament from its summer recess to ram the bill through in a matter of days ... Even those from United Russia ... seemed to have little knowledge of what they were passing. Thus nobody knows how many people will end up better off under the new system and how many will lose out. One of the law's main weaknesses is that it does not take account of the cost of living: a war veteran in the centre of Moscow will get the same paltry handful of roubles as one living in far cheaper regions. Moreover, the new law splits the burden of cash payments between regional and federal governments ... There are huge disparities between Russia's richest and poorest regions ... Though Moscow, because of its high cost of living, should contain a high concentration of people who will lose out, in fact the demonstrations never mustered more than a few hundred. Russians have become disillusioned with civil protest under Mr Putin, ever since a referendum against the import of nuclear waste which gathered 2.5 million signatures was overturned on a technicality ... In principle the reforms make sense. Russia's current welfare system lavishes many privileges on the not particularly impoverished, while many of the poorest get little or nothing. Successive governments created so many categories of beneficiaries ... that even the government is not sure how many people are entitled to the benefits. In a first step towards a fairer and more efficient welfare system the new law replaces all the existing perks with a monthly cash sum. In theory it should be good news for claimants because they will be able to spend their monthly allowance on what they really need ... Some claimants (especially the poorest) do not currently use all their entitlements: for instance, those theoretically entitled to free public transport who live in areas where there is none. These people should see the value of the benefits increase. Overall, the government is budgeting more money for the new, cash-based benefits than it currently spends on the old system. However, the protesters worry that the reforms will leave them worse off – if not straight away, after a few years when Russia's high inflation rate (currently over 10 per cent) has reduced the value of the cash benefits, Besides, can the notoriously inefficient and corrupt public bureaucracy be relied upon to distribute the cash payments on time? The main problem with Russia's welfare system [is] that most of the benefits go to the middle classes rather than the poorest.

(www.economist.com, 9 August 2004)

An estimated 30 million [are affected by the legislation, which has] ... sparked weeks of noisy demonstrations, the first since Mr Putin took power in 2000 ... An estimated 30 million pensioners, war veterans and disabled people, as well as those who have given distinguished service to the country, stand to lose: free transport passes on both city and regional transport networks; free medicines and free artificial limbs; half-rent and subsidized telephone service and electricity; annual spa treatment and transport to and from the medical centre. The cash payments to replace these will come into effect on 1 January [2005]. Many fear the new payments will in no way make up for the loss in benefits to some of Russia's most vulnerable people, including Second World War veterans ... Human rights groups delivered an 80,000-signature petition to the Kremlin on Monday [9 August] ... The cash payments under the new system start at 450 roubles a month for average pensioners, and run as high as 3,500 roubles a month for those holding government medals of honour ... Disabled Second World War veterans will receive an extra 1,550 roubles a month; survivors of the siege of Leningrad will get an extra 650 roubles, and adults with disabilities an extra 50 roubles ... In a country where salaries are often paid late and where inflation and bank crises have robbed thousands of people of their life savings, money is simply not trusted.

(*Guardian*, 12 August 2004, p. 16)

(Putin signed the bill on 29 August 2004.)

In August 2004 the president signed into law a bill that replaces most non-monetary social benefits with cash payments starting from 1 January 2005. For now the reforms exclude, among others, subsidized housing and utilities payments and all benefits to civil servants and the military.

(EBRD 2004b: 166)

'The bill leaves the federal budget responsible for some 14 million benefit recipients, while turning 20 million over to the regions, which may leave in-kind benefits in force if they cannot afford cash payment (many cannot)' (*CDSP*, 2004, vol. 56, no. 31, p. 1).

'The upper house approved, in a 142-to-nine vote with six abstentions, a new bill that will put some of Europe's toughest restrictions on beer ads' (*IHT*, 9 August 2004, p. 3).

9 August 2004.

> Crude oil prices rose to record levels on Monday [9 August] amid renewed
> concerns over output from Iraq and Russia ... Yukos said the authorities
> renewed a freeze on shares of its main Siberian oil unit, Yuganskneftegaz
> ... Yukos on Friday [6 August] won an appeal in a Moscow court contesting
> a decision last month to freeze the shares of Yuganskneftegaz. The Moscow
> arbitration court annulled the seizure of the shares, saying production assets
> could be targeted only if a debtor lacks cash or other assets to pay a tax bill.
> The apparent renewed seizure of the shares on Monday added to investors'
> confusion surrounding the government's motives.
>
> (*IHT*, 10 August 2004, p. 1)

'A court refroze shares in the company's main oil producing subsidiary ... On
Monday the unit's shares were seized again' (www.iht.com, 10 August 2004).

11 August 2004.

> Menatep ... which lent Yukos $1.6 billion ... [said Yukos] was in default
> on the loan ... The notice of default does not mean Menatep is calling for
> immediate repayment of the loan ... Last month [July] a group of Western
> banks, led by Société Générale, issued a similar 'notice of default'.
>
> (*IHT*, 12 August 2004, p. 11)

12 August 2004. 'On Thursday [12 August] the ministry of justice appointed the
investment bank Dresdner Kleinwort Wasserstein to determine the value of
Yuganskneftegaz. Analysts have estimated it could fetch from $10 billion to $20
billion' (*IHT*, 14 August 2004, p. 11).

31 August 2004.

> [A district court] upholds a request from the Russian prosecutor-general's
> office seeking to seize 76 billion roubles, or about $2.6 billion, from bank
> accounts of Yukos's operating subsidiaries and refineries ... [The] court
> froze bank accounts at production units of Yukos ... Yukos said it has paid
> just over $2 billion of a $3.4 billion bill for back taxes owed for the year
> 2000, but analysts have said the final tax bill could balloon to $10 billion.
>
> (*IHT*, 3 September 2004, p. 13)

'[The court froze] accounts belonging to two of Yukos's production facilities,
Yuganskneftegaz and Tomskneftegaz' (*FT*, 3 September 2004, p. 27).

3 September 2004.

> The tax ministry raised its tax bill for 2001 against Yukos by $700 million,
> bringing the total back-tax claims against the company to $7.4 billion. Yukos
> has already paid $2 billion of a $3.4 billion tax bill for the year 2000. But the
> tax ministry has also been pursuing back-tax claims for 2001, and initially
> sought another $3.4 billion from Yukos. The tax authorities have now raised
> the claim, saying Yukos evaded $4.1 billion in taxes through tax havens. The

2001 claim must still be upheld by a court before it can be enforced ... The tax ministry said ... that Yukos made 'fictitious' arrangements that were registered in Russian regions where taxes were low ... A court upheld a ruling allowing authorities to freeze accounts at subsidiaries of Yukos and at its refineries. Russian law enforcement officials on Thursday [2 September] said they were seizing an additional $2.4 billion from Yukos accounts, freezing the accounts of its main oil producers for the first time.

(*IHT*, 4 September 2004, p. 13)

Russian tax authorities presented Yukos with a larger than expected $4.1 billion bill for back taxes for 2001 and began to collect the bulk of it without waiting for a court order. The oil company now owes $7.5 billion in total, with further tax claims expected.

(*The Economist*, 11 September 2004, p. 7)

9 September 2004.

A court on Thursday [9 September] nullified a share swap between Yukos and Sibneft, whose former owners, led by Roman Abramovich, are trying to reverse a $13.9 billion takeover by Yukos. The arbitration court of Chukotka, an Arctic region where Abramovich is governor, ordered Yukos to return a 72 per cent stake in Sibneft to the former shareholders. They in turn must give back their stake in Yukos ... Mikhail Khodorkovsky said on his website that he had little doubt he would lose his company.

(*IHT*, 10 September 2004)

10 September 2004.

Russia's ministry of natural resources yesterday [10 September] threatened to withdraw the production licences from the main subsidiary of Yukos ... A ministry official confirmed that it was considering removing the licences from Yuganskneftegaz, Yukos's key west Siberian subsidiary, 'in the near future', because the company had failed to pay 3.6 billion roubles ($123 million) in production and other taxes ... [A] Yukos spokesman confirmed Yugansk had not paid its taxes during the past few weeks, nor other debts, but only because the Russian courts had frozen the company's bank accounts ... [He said]: 'The government wants to reduce the value of Yugansk so they can sell it cheaply.'

(*FT*, 11 September 2004, Money and Business, p. 6)

19 September 2004. 'Yukos on [19 September] confirmed that it had halted most shipments of oil by rail to China ... because of its financial difficulties' (*IHT*, 20 September 2004, p. 15). 'Yukos said that it would cut some oil exports to China because, with its accounts frozen by the government, it could not finance the rail cost of shipping the oil' (www.iht.com, 21 September 2004).

Yukos said it would suspend shipment of about 100,000 barrels a day of crude oil via rail to China National Petroleum, saying it could no longer afford the shipment costs ... The company on Monday [20 September] ...

[said] that its oil production remains constant. But as of next week 'Yukos will temporarily suspend a portion of its direct exports to China representing about 1 million tonnes until the end of 2004'.

(IHT, 21 September 2004, p. 12)

'Yukos ... said that the barrels are being exported elsewhere, so the reduction in shipments to the world market may be marginal' (www.iht.com, 22 September 2004). 'The head of Russia's state-owned railroad network announced Thursday [23 September] that a Chinese company would pay for oil deliveries by rail from Yukos in October' (www.iht.com, 24 September 2004).

30 September 2004. The government approves the 1997 Kyoto protocol to curb greenhouse gases. It now goes to the State Duma. Russia's agreement means that the industrialized countries' share of the 1990 level of global emissions exceeds the minimum 55 per cent needed for the treaty to take effect. The United States withdrew from Kyoto in March 2001.

(The State Duma approved the protocol on 22 October by 334 votes to seventy-three. The upper house did so on 29 October by 139 to one with one abstention. President Putin signed it on 4 November 2004.)

6 October 2004.

Yukos said Wednesday [6 October] that the tax authorities had sent a bill for back taxes and penalties totalling nearly $1 billion to its largest subsidiary, Yuganskneftegaz. The 2002 tax bill, for 27.8 billion roubles, or $951 million, comes in addition to the $7.5 billion in back taxes for 2000 and 2001 that Yukos already owes. Yukos has paid about $2.5 billion of that total.

(IHT, 7 October 2004, p. 11)

'The government claimed that Yukos had paid some 75 per cent of its $3.4 billion tax debt for 2000. But ... Yuganskneftegaz was handed a bill for nearly $1 billion for taxes in 2002' (*The Economist*, 9 October 2004, p. 9).

11 October 2004.

The Moscow arbitration court ruled Monday [11 October] that Yukos must pay $1.34 billion in fines and penalties as part of a $4.1 billion back-tax claim for 2001 ... The court reduced the bill slightly, saying Yukos should pay $1.34 billion instead of the original $1.39 billion.

(IHT, 12 October 2004, p. 15)

12 October 2004.

The justice ministry said on Tuesday [12 October] that it had decided to go ahead with the sale of parts of Yukos to cover billions in taxes ... The investment bank Dresdner Kleinwort Wasserstein has valued Yuganskneftegaz at $10.4 billion. The valuation would be much lower than the market expectations of between $15 billion and $17 billion.

(www.iht.com, 12 October 2004)

The government said that it would sell part of Yukos's most valuable subsidiary by the end of November ... Last week the unit was thought to be
worth $15.7 billion to $17.4 billion, according to industry estimates. Dresdner Kleinwort Wasserstein insisted that the $10.4 billion figure was at the
lower end of a range of values presented to the state – as high as $18.3
billion and as low as $10.4 billion ... The investment bank presented the
$10.4 billion price tag as a conservative, worst-case scenario ... The state
indicated that it would be selling a majority stake in Yuganskneftegaz ...
The justice ministry said that the low-end valuation represented a discount
of roughly 60 per cent, but ... said it was warranted 'considering the high
risks for a potential buyer'.

(*IHT*, 13 October 2004, p. 11)

Others who have seen the report said DrKW had characterized the $10.4
billion figure in its concluding paragraph as 'overly conservative' and recommended instead a price for the equity of Yugansk of between $15.7
billion and $18.3 billion, in line with analysts' estimates. The bank esti-
mates the full 'enterprise value', to include company debt, at a further
$2.9 billion.

(*FT*, 13 October 2004, p. 29)

13 October 2004. 'The Duma rushed through a bill that permits senior members
of the government to hold leading roles in a political party. At present senior
officials have to relinquish their party posts in order to serve in the government'
(*Guardian*, 15 October 2004, p. 20).

'The Duma voted to overturn a ban on political party leaders becoming ministers' (*The Times*, 14 October 2004, p. 19).

14 October 2004.

China and Russia settled the last of their decades-old border disputes during a
visit to Beijing by President Vladimir Putin, signing an agreement fixing their
2,700-mile-long border for the first time ... Beijing and Moscow had reached
agreements on individual border sections ... but a stretch of river and islands
along China's north-eastern border with Russia's Far East had remained in
dispute ... At one point the Soviet Union was believed to have as many as
700,000 troops on the border, facing as many as 1 million soldiers from China.

(*IHT*, 15 October 2004, p. 3)

Russia and China had reached a 'final settlement' of their border, which
stretches 3,483 kilometres, or 2,164 miles. To resolve a dispute over three
river islands controlled by Russia, one was allotted to China [Tarabarov]
and one to Russia. The largest one [Bolshoi Ussurisky Island] was split
down the middle.

(*IHT*, 22 January 2005, p. 2)

A supplementary agreement [was signed] on the eastern part of the Russian–
Chinese border, an accord that decided the fate of the disputed islands in the

Amur and Argun rivers. The agreement capped forty years of efforts to delineate the border ... In December 1999 the leaders of Russia and China signed basic demarcation documents on the western section (54.57 kilometres) and eastern section (4,195.22 kilometres) of the border. The sides divided 2,444 islands and sandbars in the border rivers roughly in half. Damansky Island went to China. That agreement did not include the islands of Bolshoi Ussurisky and Tarabarov near Khabarovsk, or Bolshoi Island in the Argun river ... The islands [of Tarabarov and Bolshoi Ussurisky] are to be transferred to China.

(*CDSP*, 2004, vol. 656, no. 42, pp. 2–4)

20 October 2004.

One of the few remaining Russian newspapers critical of Vladimir Putin's government was yesterday [20 October] hit with a record $10 million legal bill after losing a defamation case against the country's largest private bank ... Mikhail Fridman [is the] principal owner of Alfa ... Alfa sued *Kommersant* after it ran an article in July [2004] on financial difficulties at the bank, which suffered a substantial run on deposits and contributed to a mini banking crisis during the summer ... The decision of the Moscow arbitration court to award the damages to Alfa Bank was immediately condemned as politically motivated by the supporters of the *Kommersant* newspaper. Its owner [is] the exiled oligarch Boris Berezovsky ... In recent years several ... media outlets ... have been forced to close while journalists at others have been dissuaded from writing critical articles. The weekly *Novaya Gazeta* previously set the record with $1.5 million in libel damages, subsequently overturned.

(*FT*, 21 October 2004, p. 8)

Human Rights Watch publishes a highly critical report on hazing in the Russian armed services. The system is known as *dedovshchina* or 'the rule of the grandfathers' (older servicemen) (*IHT*, 21 October 2004, p. 3).

1 November 2004.

The tax ministry on Monday [1 November] served Yukos with claims for an additional $10 billion in back taxes, bringing the total tax bill to $17.5 billion ... Tax officials with the ministry finished an audit for Yukos for 2002 and ... demanded $6.7 billion for that year ... Earlier Monday Yuganskneftegaz, Yukos's main production unit, separately received a $3.3 billion back-tax claim: $2.3 billion for unpaid taxes in 2001 and $1 billion in tax owed for 2002 ... Yukos already faced total back-tax claims of about $7.5 billion for the years 2000 and 2001. The company has almost fully paid back the $3.4 billion for 2000 ... Also on Monday the detention of Mikhail Khodorkovsky ... was extended until 14 February [2005]. His detention had been due to expire on 14 November.

(*IHT*, 2 November 2004, p. 16)

5 November 2004.

> A jury in Siberia convicted a physicist of spying for China on Friday [5 November], overturning a previous jury's acquittal after a closed trial ... The jury rendered its verdict on the central espionage charge against Valentin Danilov even though the court's judges have yet to hold a hearing to decide whether the information he is accused of passing along is even secret ... Danilov, a researcher at Krasnoyarsk State University who was first charged in 2001, has acknowledged selling information about satellite technology to a Chinese company but argued that all of it was readily available from public sources. Danilov was initially acquitted last December [2003]. His trial was the first of a recent flurry of espionage cases against scientists and researchers to be decided by a jury. Jury trials are still a relative novelty in Russia, having become an option for defendants in some serious cases only in 2002.
>
> (www.iht.com, 6 November 2004; *IHT*, 8 November 2004, p. 3)

('[On 24 November] Valentin Danilov ... [was] sentenced to fourteen years in high security prison': *FT*, 25 November 2004.)

7 November 2004.

> It used to be called the day of the Great October Socialist Revolution, but it is now the Day of Accord and Reconciliation ... [Communists] were energized this year not only by revolutionary nostalgia and ideological zeal, but also by concern over a proposal that would legislate away the holiday itself ... A bill in parliament, drafted by pro-Kremlin lawmakers, would dispatch 7 November ... calling the day 'a source of tension in society'. In its place would emerge the Day of National Unity on 4 November ... It was on that day in 1612 that ... [there was] the uprising against the Polish occupation of Moscow.
>
> (*IHT*, 8 November 2004, p. 1)

'[On 4 November 1612] a people's army led by Minin and Pozharsky lieberated Kitai-Gorod [in central Moscow] from the Poles' (*CDSP*, 2004, vol. 56, no. 47, p. 13).

17 November 2004.

> President Vladimir Putin ... said on Wednesday [17 November] that the country would soon deploy new nuclear missile systems that would surpass those of any other nuclear power ... Reiterating previous statements ... Putin said Russia would continue to emphasize its nuclear deterrent ... Putin: 'We are not only conducting research and successful testing of the newest nuclear missile systems. I am certain that in the immediate years to come we will be armed with them. These are such developments and such systems that other nuclear states do not have and will not have in the immediate years to come' ... Putin did not elaborate on the new system ... The Russian military, however, is widely reported to have been trying to perfect

land- and sea-based ballistic missiles with warheads that could elude a missile defence system like the one being constructed by the Bush administration.

(*IHT*, 18 November 2004, p. 3)

19 November 2004.

The federal property fund said that the sale of a 76.79 per cent stake in Yugankneftegaz was scheduled for 19 December and that bids would be collected from now until 18 December ... [The] starting price [would be] about $8.6 billion ... Analysts [have] noted that if Yugankneftegaz were to be sold at that price – assuming that only government-approved bidders can take part and that the price is kept artificially low – the $8.6 billion would not be enough to cover Yukos's outstanding tax debts ... At $8.6 billion the starting bid price for Yugankneftegaz is well below independent and Yukos-commissioned estimates of the unit's value, which have ranged from $15 billion to as high as $22 billion ... Yukos argues that the auction is illegal under Russian law, which states that non-core assets are to be disposed of first in tax settlement cases ... In addition, the company said it had received a $6 billion tax bill for 2003 ... Before the tax bill issued Friday [19 November] Yukos was already staggering under tax arrears amounting to $18.4 billion, of which it had paid $3.9 billion.

(*IHT*, 20 November 2004, p. 1)

[The] minimum price of $8.6 billion compares with a lowest fair value of $15.7 billion placed on it by Dresdner Kleinwort Wasserstein, the government's valuer ... The terms of Yugankneftegaz's sale were denounced as 'daylight robbery' by Andrei Illarionov, Mr Putin's outspoken economic adviser.

(*FT*, 19 November 2004, Money and Business, p. 5)

'The starting price for the enterprise's voting shares is $8.65 billion' (*CDSP*, 2004, vol. 56, no. 47, p. 11).

'The senior executives of Yukos have left Russia, fearing for their safety' (*FT*, 25 November 2004, p. 1). 'Six top executives, including the American chief executive and the chief financial officer, fled the country ... Last week another tax claim left the oil company staggering under a tax debt of $24.5 billion for the years 2000 through 2003' (*IHT*, 26 November 2004, p. 1; www.iht.com, 25 November 2004).

29 November 2004.

The Dalai Lama arrived at the airport in Elista on Monday [29 November] ... making his first visit to Russia after an abrupt reversal by Moscow in its earlier refusal to grant him entry. He was to visit largely Buddhist communities in the southern republic of Kalmykia.

(*IHT*, 30 November 2004, p. 3)

The Dalai Lama last visited Russia when it was part of the Soviet Union in 1991, and Moscow had previously heeded China's objections ... [and] repeatedly refused to issue an entry visa ... Kalmykia has a Buddhist majority ... [and] is Russia's lone predominantly Buddhist republic ... Its flamboyant leader [is] Kirsan Ilyumzhino ... [There are] more than 1 million Buddhists in [Russia].

(*IHT*, 27 November 2004, p. 3)

'In Kalmykia about half of the 300,000 residents are Buddhists ... The Russian foreign ministry said it had granted him [the Dalai Lama] a visa if he limits his activities to pastoral purposes' (www.iht.com, 30 November 2004). 'Moscow said it had issued the Dalai Lama a visa because of the "strictly religious" nature of the trip, but Beijing questioned the decision' (*IHT*, 1 December 2004, p. 5).

3 December 2004.

The State Duma ... on Friday [3 December] signed off on a Kremlin-sponsored bill that replaces the popular vote for governors with a system under which the Russian president nominates gubernatorial candidates to a regional legislature. [The State Duma] voted to approve the legislation, which allows the Kremlin to pick candidates from party lists, and restricts political parties to only those with at least 50,000 members. The previous limit was 10,000.

(*IHT*, 4 December 2004, p. 5)

(The upper house approved the bill on 7 December 2004.)

13 December 2004.

The purpose of this open letter is to put the reader on notice that the forthcoming auction of OAO 'NK YUKOS' shares in OAO Yuganskneftegaz by the Russian Property Fund is illegitimate and will, we believe, be treated as invalid by an English court and other European courts applying similar principles of international law. Group Menatep Limited is the owner of the majority of shares in Yukos, which wholly owns Yuganskneftegaz. Yuganskneftegaz is not only the leading oil production company in Russia, but it constitutes Yukos's most valuable and core asset. The proposed auction is nothing more than an illegitimate attempt by the Russian authorities to expropriate Yuganskneftegaz oil and gas interests through contrived tax liabilities, compounded by improperly freezing Yukos's assets to prevent it even settling such liabilities and then seizing and selling Yukos's core asset in breach of Russian federal law on enforcement ... In addition, the Russian government has been intentionally deflating the auction price. The widely publicized Dresdner Kleinwort Wasserstein valuation established that the conservative value of the company was in the range of $17 billion to $20 billion ... We wish to make our position clear. It is that Yukos cannot be dispossessed of its ownership of Yuganskneftegaz in this way, that no purchaser will acquire any legitimate title to the shares, and no financing institution assisting the purchase will acquire any valid security over either the shares or any of the company's assets. Full legal redress will be sought from any company which acquires the shares, facilitates the purchase or deals with Yuganskneftegaz's oil or gas. Legal redress will be sought in any country applying the generally accepted principles of international law.

(*FT*, 13 December 2004, p. 11)

15 December 2004.

Yukos sought bankruptcy protection in the United States [in Houston] on Wednesday [15 December] and requested an emergency court hearing to stop the Russian government's auction of … Yuganskneftegaz [on 19 December] … [which] is being sold on to help cover more than $26 billion in back taxes.

(*IHT*, 16 December 2004, p. 13)

('A last-minute injunction [was] secured by Yukos in a court in Houston, Texas, protecting the firm's assets while it filed for bankruptcy – part of Yukos's strategy of trying to force the Kremlin into openly using extra-judicial methods': *The Economist*, 1 January 2005, p. 49.)

'The Russian government is selling Yukos assets to settle a disputed tax claim of $27.5 billion' (*FT*, 16 December 2004, p. 30).

If the government succeeds in its demands for $26 billion in back taxes – which, the company points out, is roughly equal to its annual revenues for the period – then not even the minimum amount of $8.7 billion expected from Sunday's auction [19 December] is likely to save the company from being wound up eventually … This is only slightly more than the lowest valuation of $10.4 billion put on Yuganskneftegaz by Dresdner Kleinwort Wasserstein … [whose] upper price was $17 billion … Recently, a mobile-telecoms firm was presented with a bill for $158 million in back tax, which the company contests … Mr Putin has said he wants to double the size of Russia's economy by 2010. Now that target appears to have been set back to 2015; the government has also reduced its forecast for growth this year [2004], from 6.3 per cent to 5.8 per cent.

(www.economist.com, 16 December 2004)

16 December 2004.

The Moscow arbitration court … has barred … Yukos from holding an emergency meeting … on Monday [20 December] … at which shareholders were to vote on liquidating the company … Were the board to approve Yukos's liquidation … a spokesman for Sibneft … said it would be impossible to unwind a failed merger between Yukos and Sibneft … [An official] in the Moscow arbitration court … [said] that Yukos's US bankruptcy filing would have no legal consequences in Russia.

(*IHT*, 17 December 2004, p. 13)

17 December 2004.

A US bankruptcy court judge in Houston … ordered a ten-day delay in the sale [of Yuganskneftegaz], but officials in Moscow organizing the sale rejected the ruling, and Gazprom said it would not withdraw its bid … [It was reported that] Western banks led by Deutsche Bank had frozen their planned credit to Gazprom. The US judge issued a temporary restraining order intended to block the participation of lenders and Gazprom.

(www.iht.com, 17 December 2004)

[There was] a last-minute decision by Deutsche Bank and other banks to pull out of a loan reported to be up to $13 billion … Although two other largely unknown companies have submitted bids … their presence was seen as purely an effort to make the auction seem valid. Foreign suitors, including companies from China, India and other energy investors, have been discouraged from participating in the bidding process … The sheer mountain of taxes that the government claims … Yukos now owes more than $27 billion for 2000 through 2003 – more than its entire revenue in some years … Officials have hit Russia's number two mobile phone company VimpelCommunications with a second claim for back taxes, this time for $323 million [it was reported on 17 December] … Vimpel-Communications already faces a $158 million preliminary tax bill for 2001.

(*IHT*, 18 December 2004, pp. 1, 4)

19 December 2004.

A mysterious bidder paid $9.35 billion for … Yuganskneftegaz … Baikal Finance Group, a previously unknown company … It was unclear who was behind Baikal or its finances … Moscow was rife with speculation that Baikal is a front for Gazprom … Gazpromneft, its oil arm, had declared its intention to buy Yukos's assets … Gazpromneft was the only other company present at the auction but did not bid … Some observers suggested that yesterday's auction was a face-saving exercise by the Russian government which could buy it more time to transfer the stake to Gazprom … Gazprom denied any affiliation to Baikal. Some analysts suggested that Baikal could be linked to Surgutneftegaz, an oil company which operates in the same region as Yukos. Surgut denied any knowledge of Baikal … The company paid a deposit of $1.7 billion … Baikal has fourteen working days to pay the rest of the price. If it fails to do so the shares in Yuganskneftegaz will be passed to the Russian state.

(*FT*, 20 December 2004, p. 1)

'Whatever the principal activity of a financial company named after a Siberian lake, it certainly is not pumping oil' (p. 18).

Almost nothing is known about Baikal – except that its registered address is host to a mobile phone and grocery shop in a Siberian town. It might be

Gazprom acting through a front company to dodge a ten-day sale injunction issued by a Houston court ... It could be another Kremlin-favoured company, such as Surgutneftegaz. It might even be Roman Abramovich's Sibneft, at least according to one conspiracy theory.

(*FT*, 21 December 2004, p. 20)

Baikal ... was essentially unheard of until three days ago ... The winner was ... also a complete surprise. Since Gazprom had appeared to have positioned itself to take over ... Yuganskneftegaz ... [There were] ten minutes of bidding ... The mystery surrounding ... Baikal Finans Group ... registered in Tver, a town near Moscow ... raised suspicions ... that ... [Baikal] was acting on behalf of Gazprom, or even the state itself ... It is possible that another cash-rich Russian oil company like Surgutneftegaz ... was the real bidder behind the winning company ... But analysts said it was more likely to give Gazprom time to come up with the money ... It is also possible Baikal will deliberately fail to make the full payment within the required fourteen days.

(*IHT*, 20 December 2004, p. 4)

'Baikal Finans is registered in Tver, about 100 miles, or 160 kilometres, northwest of Moscow. The building at its listed address has a liquor store, a Volga supermarket and other businesses but no sign of the buyer' (*IHT*, 21 December 2004, p. 13).

21 December 2004.

On Tuesday [21 December] a little more information surfaced about Baikal Finans ... Representatives at Baikal Finans were employees of Surgutneftegaz, a government-friendly oil company ... Baikal applied as a bidder only on Friday [17 December] ... The payment day has become increasingly flexible: the buyers now have until 11 January, not 2 January.

(www.iht.com, 21 December 2004)

Two Russian newspapers, *Gazeta* and *Vedemosti*, reported that Baikal appeared to be connected to the oil company Surgutneftegaz, Russia's fourth largest oil producer. The two representatives for Baikal who appeared at the auction were both high-level managers at Surgutneftegaz ... [which] is regarded as a conservative oil company that does not seek acquisitions.

(*IHT*, 22 December 2004, p. 8)

Vladimir Putin:

[Behind Baikal stand a] group of individuals with experience in the oil sector ... We do not rule out that the China National Petroleum Corporation would take part in the production of Yuganskneftegaz ... Gazprom and CNPC have reached an agreement about co-operation in the energy sector.

(*FT*, 22 December 2004, p. 1)

Immediately after Mr Putin's statement Gazprom said a new memorandum, signed two days before the auction, covered strategic co-operation with China in the oil sector – particularly over projects in Russia. It already has an agreement with CNPC over gas ... Surgutneftegaz operates in the same region as Yugansk ... Gazprom yesterday [21 December] said it had sold Gazpromneft in a manoeuvre to avoid the US court injunction that prevented the holding company from taking part in the auction for Yugansk.

(FT, 22 December 2004, p. 1)

22 December 2004.

Rosneft, Russia's state-owned oil company, yesterday [22 December] said that it had become the owner of Yuganskneftegaz ... in a move that in effect represents the first major renationalization of a private company since the fall of the Soviet Union. Rosneft, which is being merged with Gazprom ... said it had won the asset by buying Baikal Finance Group ... Rosneft is headed by Sergei Bogdanchikov, a sworn enemy of Mikhail Khodorkovsky.

(FT, 23 December 2004, p. 1)

'The Baikal Finans Group was a shell company that was quickly bought by Rosneft' (www.iht.com, 8 January 2005). ('Putin's deputy chief of staff, Igor Sechin, serves as Rosneft's chairman of the board': www.iht.com, 22 December 2004.)

Rosneft did not reveal what it paid for Baikal, but Yuganskneftegaz had been valued at $14 billion to $22 billion ... Rosneft is scheduled to merge sometime next year [2005] with Gazprom ... Gazprom had been expected to win, but a US court ruling on 16 December granted Yukos an injunction against the auction and its participants, scaring away Gazprom's lenders and leading to the winning bid from Baikal. Investors said Rosneft's purchase of the subsidiary might be the government's way of shielding Gazprom from further lawsuits.

(IHT, 24 December 2004, p. 13)

23 December 2004. Vladimir Putin:

You all know very well how privatization took place here in the early 1990s, and how, using various tricks and sometimes violating the laws that were in effect at the time, many market participants got hold of state property worth many billions. Today the state, using absolutely legal market mechanisms, is securing its interests. I consider this to be quite normal.

(IHT, 24 December 2004, p. 1)

26 December 2004. The tsunami strikes Asian countries around the Indian Ocean.

'Four Kuril islands [were] occupied by Soviet troops at the end of World War II ... Putin proposed in December [2004] to return the two smallest islands [to Japan], a promise that was unpopular in Russia' (*IHT*, 22 January 2005, p. 2).

27 December 2004.

> The Federation Council ... on Monday [27 December] passed legislation
> abolishing several state holidays, including the anniversary of the 1917 Bol-
> shevik Revolution, and extending the New Year holiday ... The Federation
> Council ... voted 123 to nine to back the bill, which reduces the number of
> state holidays from nine to eight ... After the 1991 Soviet collapse the [7
> November] holiday was renamed the Day of Reconciliation and Accord.
> Communists and other hardliners continue to mark the day but can no longer
> demonstrate in Red Square ... The bill replaces the 7 November commemora-
> tion with a new state holiday, to be celebrated on 4 November. The new
> holiday will mark the end of Polish intervention in Russia in 1612. The bill
> also extends New Year celebrations from 1–2 January to 1–5 January and
> scraps the 12 December Constitution Day, since it echoes a similar holiday on
> 12 June – the Day of Russia.
>
> (*IHT*, 28 December 2004, p. 3)

> President Vladimir Putin signed the bill into law [on 30 December] ... Under
> the new bill the [7 November] is replaced with People's United Day on 4
> November, the day that Polish troops marched out of Moscow in 1612,
> ending decades of civil war. But critics say the name of the new holiday
> bears too much resemblance to that of the pro-presidential party United
> Russia, originally called the Unity Party ... The act also abolishes the 12
> December Constitution Day holiday introduced by President Boris Yeltsin in
> 1993 to celebrate the adoption of Russia's current constitution ... The new
> year celebrations are extended to 5 January which, with the Orthodox Christ-
> mas on 7 January, creates a ten-day holiday ... Russia Day, the main state
> holiday, [is on] 12 June ... Victory Day, which commemorates the Second
> World War victory, [is] on 9 May ... Women's Day [is] on 8 March.
>
> (*Guardian*, 31 December 2004, p. 15)

28 December 2004. Mikhail Khodorkovsky (letter published on 27 December in
Vedomosti):

> The destruction of Yukos is almost done ... [The way chosen was] that of
> a selective application of the laws, of retroactively imposing new legal
> standards and interpretations, of a straightforward and public destruction
> of the business community's confidence in arbitration courts and any
> authority in general ... The methods used harm both the reputation of the
> authorities and the national economy ... It is probably impossible to save
> the company ... The question is what lessons the country will take from
> the Yukos affair, whose finale has become the most senseless and destruc-
> tive event for the national economy in all the time President Vladimir
> Putin has been in office ... Yukos was the second largest tax payer in the
> country (after Gazprom), accounting for almost 5 per cent of the federal
> budget ... According to experts at the ministry of taxation, Yukos should
> have paid more in taxes than it received in revenues ... The Yukos case is

not a conflict between business and state, but a politically and commercially motivated attack launched by one business, represented by officials, against another ... No true patriot would give his life for a bunch of bureaucrats who are only interested in feathering their own nests ... These small-minded people [the bureaucrats] judge everyone by their own rules. To breathe spring air, to play with children studying at an ordinary Moscow school, to read clever books – all this is much more important, right and more pleasant than multiplying wealth and settling scores ... The $15 billion fortune of which *Forbes* wrote has almost reached zero and it will soon be absolute zero ... Parting with my wealth will not be unbearably painful for me ... I have already realized that wealth, especially vast wealth, does not in itself make a person free ... I am becoming a normal person.

(*IHT*, 29 December 2004, p. 11, and 12 January 2005, p. 6; *The Independent*, 29 December 2004, p. 35; *Guardian*, 29 December 2004, p. 19; *FT*, 29 December 2004, p. 1)

'[Mikhail Khodorkovsky also] assailed Putin's efforts to strengthen government controls in Russia. He warned that the Kremlin moves to end the election of regional governors and limit economic competition and free speech would ruin the nation' (*IHT*, 29 December 2004, p. 11).

'On Tuesday [28 December] the Standard & Poor's rating agency cut its rating for Yukos's debt to default, after the oil producer missed interest payments Monday [27 December] on a $1 billion loan' (*IHT*, 29 December 2004, p. 11).

Andrei Illarionov (economic adviser to President Putin):

This year [2004], in the category of swindle of the year, the winner is the sale of Yuganskneftegaz to a mystery company ... So far we have seen these [scams] performed by street tricksters. We now see companies 100 per cent owned by the state engaging in the same techniques. This case has clearly shown that there are no rules of the game, that the rules are constantly changing depending on [someone's] current interests ... The enigma of the year ... [is to discover] where the money came from [to buy Yuganskneftegaz] ... [It] only could have come from the state budget because no other company had sufficient funds. The money was taken from the citizens of this country ... [The year 2004 has marked] a complete change of the model of economic and social development ... [illustrated by the destruction of] the best national oil company – Yukos ... The choice has been made. We live in a different country – in economic, political, ideological and other terms ... [Russia has moved to an] interventionist model of economic development, with dramatic interference from the state ... [and from its] utterly incompetent officials – some of whom have nothing to do with the economy ... The transition has taken place to an interventionist model with dramatic and utterly incompetent interference from the state ... For the past thirteen years Russia was seeking to return to the first world to which it belonged until the Bolshevik Revolution. Now we see it has preferred the third world.

(IHT, 29 December 2004, p. 11; *FT*, 29 December 2004, p. 5; *Daily Telegraph*, 29 December 2004, p. 27)

'Besides Yukos the government is seeking back taxes from companies such as VimpelCom, the second largest mobile phone company, and Volgotanker, one of the biggest river shippers' *(IHT*, 29 December 2004, p. 11).

'VimpelCom [is] a mobile phone operator listed in New York ... VimpelCom is neither a privatized company nor an energy firm ... The fracas may owe something to a rumoured spat between a government minister and a big VimpelCom shareholder' *(The Economist*, 1 December 2004, p. 49).

Shares of VimpelCommunications, the second largest phone operator by subscribers after Mobile TeleSystems, surged Wednesday [29 December 2004] after the company received a 2002 tax bill that was less than analysts had expected ... VimpelCom received a 2002 tax bill for $21 million, the company, based in Moscow, said ... The amount is less than one-tenth of what most analysts in the market had been expecting, the Nikoil brokerage firm said ... The company on 8 December said it had received a 2001 claim for $157 million ... The deputy finance minister said last week that the 2001 tax claim against VimpelCom might be significantly reduced.

(IHT, 30 December 2004, p. 13)

'[The tax bill was] cut back to $17.6 million in late December [2004]' *(IHT*, 8 February 2005, p. 14). 'VimpelCom whittled the bill down to $17 million, but only after the intervention of the Norwegian government, whose state phone company Telenor is an investor' (www.iht.com, 2 march 2005).

30 December 2004.

Yuganskneftegaz ... will not be integrated into Gazprom ... but remain as a separate state-controlled group, the government said yesterday [30 December] ... The government also said 20 per cent of the new group could be offered to China National Petroleum Corporation ... [The government] said Yuganskneftegaz, which accounts for 11 per cent of Russian oil output, would be spun off from Rosneft ... an oil company made up of leftovers from the privatization of the early 1990s ... which is being merged with Gazprom ... Viktor Khristenko (energy minister): '[The assets will be] spun off and transferred to a separate company – 100 per cent owned by the state ... Up to 20 per cent of the shares [could be acquired by CNPC].'

(FT, 31 December 2004, p. 19)

Yuganskneftegaz ... extracts 11 per cent of Russia's oil ... Baikal Finance Group bought 76.6 per cent of Yuganskneftegaz's shares on 19 December ... Russia's minister of industry and energy ... said the controlling stake in Yuganskneftegaz would be transferred to a newly created state company and would not become part of the merger between Gazprom and Rosneft.

That merger would be completed next month [January 2005], he said ...
Viktor Khristenko's statement suggested that the government hoped to
shield Gazprom from the lawsuits that Yukos's executives have vowed to
file.

(IHT, 31 December 2004, p. 1)

31 December 2004. 'Rosneft ... has taken control of Yuganskneftegaz ... and
has paid the state $9.4 billion for the asset' (*FT*, 3 January 2005, p. 18).

Russia has approved an $18 billion oil pipeline linking Siberia with the
Pacific, effectively ending dreams of a rival project to China ... [Oil will be
exported] to Japan and the United States ... Yukos had favoured a pipeline
to China ... The Pacific project will be undertaken by Transneft, the state oil
pipeline monopoly ... Japanese officials have reportedly offered to help
finance the pipeline, although Transneft said it would be able to rise sufficient funds itself ... [Of Russia's oil output] more than 70 per cent is destined for foreign markets.

(The Times, 1 January 2005, p. 44)

Russia will by May [2005] draw up detailed plans for the financing and construction of an estimated $11.5 billion oil pipeline to the Pacific following a
decision ... to adopt a Japanese-proposed route over one that would have
favoured China ... The original plan [was] to pipe oil to Daqing, China's
traditional energy centre in the north-east ... The shorter and cheaper
Daqing route, which had been supported by Yukos, would have locked
Russia into the Chinese market ... The [Pacific] pipeline ... from Taishet in
eastern Siberia to Nakhodka, near Vladivostok ... will be built by Transneft,
a Russian monopoly ... Japan is expected to provide loans for the pipeline's
construction, though it would not subsidize the project, officials said. Japanese companies were also likely to invest in upstream activities in Siberia
... Russia accepted Japan's argument that the Pacific route would enable it
to export oil to several countries in Asia as well as the west coast of the
United States.

(FT, 4 January 2005, p. 7)

'Japan had lobbied for the terminus to be at the Pacific port of Nakhodka to
ensure its access to the oil without possible Chinese interference, and it offered
$5 billion toward the cost of the pipeline as an incentive' (www.iht.com, 1
January 2005).

Transneft, the state pipeline monopoly, has been told by Moscow to find its
own financing, preferably on international markets ... Japan's development
bank could finance up to 80 per cent of the project, which would make it the
largest ever loan by the bank ... Japan offered $7 billion in soft loans for
construction of the line and billions more to help Japanese oil companies
search for and develop oil in eastern Siberia ... [Russia made a] little publicized decision in December [2004] to switch the pipeline from Vostochny,

Russia's main industrial port in the Pacific, to Perevoznaya, a tranquil bay known for its beaches and wild nature ... This winter American and European environmentalists are organizing an international campaign to persuade Moscow to go back to its original plan to build the oil pipeline to Vostochny, a modern industrial port and railhead built thirty years ago next to Nakhodka.

(*IHT*, 22 January 2005, p. 12)

3 January 2005.

President Vladimir Putin on Monday [3 January] abruptly reduced the responsibilities of a senior adviser who last week had issued a sweeping criticism of the Kremlin's leadership and expressed deep misgivings about the direction Russia is headed. In a presidential decree issued without further comment, Putin relieved Andrei Illarionov of his duties as Moscow's envoy to the G8 industrialized nations ... Illarionov, forty-three, has been an economic adviser to Putin since 2000 and at times a vocal critic of the Kremlin's course. Both the Kremlin and a spokeswoman for Illarionov said he for the moment retained his principal post ... In a long news conference last week and then in a radio interview on an independent radio station, Illarionov issued a searing and comprehensive assessment of the state of affairs in Russia, saying the country had sharply shifted direction for the worse, and risked becoming a third world state ... Illarionov described the government as both arbitrary and wrongheaded, criticizing the Kremlin's crackdown on the news media, its expropriation of the main asset of Yukos, its centralization of political power and its foreign relations ... He called the Kremlin's seizure of Yugankneftegaz the 'swindle of the year' and characterized it as 'extremely incompetent intervention in economic affairs by state officials' ... The results of the Kremlin's course, he said, were dangerous to the survival of Russia as a strong nation. By attacking a healthy company, and signalling which companies were Kremlin favourites, Illarionov said, 'financial flows are routed from the most effective companies to the least effective ones' ... Moreover, Putin's decision to do away with gubernatorial elections, and to appoint governors through the presidency, Illarionov said, ensured that political competition was undermined, to ill effect ... Illarionov: 'Limited competition in all spheres of life leads to one thing – to stagnation ... This entire [Yukos] affair regrettably demonstrates that any of the official or semi-official explanations given to the public regarding the Yukos affair do not have a leg to stand on ... We should thank the Texas judge for having done everything possible to help Russia avoid falling into the abyss they have pushed us into ... [I congratulate the Ukrainian voters and demonstrators] ... One has to pay tribute to our [Russian] colleagues, who did all they could, by making their crude, uncouth and offensive statements.'

(*IHT*, 4 January 2005, pp. 1, 8)

Andrei Illarionov:

The decline in the quality ... [of economic policy is connected to] the ruin [of Yukos] ... [The legal assault on Yukos is being carried out by] monstrously unqualified and unprofessional people ... [with] a desire to expropriate private property ... [and has] inflicted colossal damage on the country ... [The crisis in Ukraine will help Russia get over its] imperial complex ... Russia will be able to become a modern and dynamically developing country only if it stops being a formal and informal empire ... The Ukrainian electorate has helped not only themselves but also the Russians. One has to pay tribute to our [Russian] colleagues who did all they could by making their crude, uncouth and offensive statements ... [This meant that Ukrainians] who may not have intended to vote or at least did not intend to vote for Mr Yushchenko, did go to the polls and cast ballots and made Mr Yushchenko's win so convincing, so obvious and so undoubted.

(*Guardian*, 5 January 2005, p. 12; *The Times*, 5 January 2005, p. 33)

The forced sale of ... Yuganskneftegaz to Rosneft ... constituted 'expropriation of private property' and should take the prize for the 'swindle of the year' [said Andrei Illarionov] ... He added the broader charge that Russia had shifted, regrettably, to 'an interventionist model of economic development, with ... extremely incompetent intervention in economic life by state officials' ... [As regards Ukraine] he added a warning that Russia might itself be heading for a similar revolution, thanks to what he called the 'ongoing destruction ... of the whole range of civic institutions'. He cited as examples of this destruction the mass media and Russia's democratic institutions ... He hates the Kyoto Protocol on climate change, which prescribes cuts in greenhouse gas emissions: he once said that it 'can generally be compared to fascism'. In a recent interview with *The Economist*, he insisted that it was theoretically possible for Russia's GDP to double within ten years, Mr Putin's declared goal, noting that other oil producers had managed it in the past. But he added that, now that Russia has ratified Kyoto (which he calls the worst decision of 2004), it was no longer practically possible. He also said that, whereas in the early Putin years the government's economic policies had contributed positively to economic growth, they were now contributing negatively. In particular, he criticized the government's long campaign against Yukos, which he praised as the best oil company in Russia.

(*The Economist*, 8 January 2005, p. 36)

(Andrei Illarionov, commenting on the announcement on 19 November 2004 of the proposed sale of Yuganskneftegaz [Yugansk Petroleum and Gas] at a starting price of $8.65 billion for the enterprise's voting shares: '[I call it] theft in broad daylight ... The company [Yukos] expressed willingness to pay the taxes and has been paying them, so there is no need to sell any assets in order to cover the arrears': *CDSP*, 2004, vol. 56, no. 47, p. 11.)

'President Putin has described the sale of Yuganskneftegaz as a legitimate business deal and only one other senior figure, German Gref, the economic development and trade minister, has dared to contradict him' (*The Times*, 5 January 2005, p. 33).

German Gref:

> I consider direct state involvement in the oil sector unjustified. I think that both Rosneft and Yuganskneftegaz ... should be privatized ... Some people like to call themselves 'statists' ... If a statist is someone who does not have faith in his own countrymen, who wants to limit their rights and freedoms and take property for the benefit of the state ... they should be isolated from running the country because their actions cause harm ... The ineffectiveness of Gazprom is obvious. And you cannot use adminis-trative levers to make such a huge company work more effectively. The market mechanism must be turned on and that means a reform of the gas sector.
>
> (*FT*, 12 January 2005, p. 6)

10 January 2005.

> [Some] 800 elderly demonstrators in a Moscow suburb block traffic ... demanding the restoration of free public transit privileges, which were revoked on 1 January 2005 ... Muscovites had much better luck in this regard. Mayor Yuri Luzhkov gave city residents social welfare cards that allow them to ride public transportation for free ... Pensioners protested in many Russian cities ... It is becoming clear that the elimination of in-kind benefits has struck a heavy blow not just to pensioners, but to law enforce-ment personnel as well. In order to head off wholesale resignations among policemen, officials are hastily giving them rises ... Passions are seething in the armed forces as well.
>
> (*CDSP*, 2005, vol. 57, nos 1–2, pp. 1–4)

12 January 2005.

> Mikhail Khodorkovsky on Wednesday [12 January] transferred a majority stake in his investment company, which has Yukos as its main asset, to a fellow shareholder ... Leonid Nevzlin ... who lives in self-imposed exile in Israel. Khodorkovsky's holding company, Group Menatep, had held 50 per cent of Yukos in a trust, of which he was sole beneficiary ... Nevzlin already owned 8 per cent of Menatep and his stake now increases to 67.5 per cent. Menatep owns 56 per cent of Yukos. That ownership would increase to 63 per cent should Yukos ever complete a merger that has unrav-elled with Sibneft ... Khodorkovsky: 'After the sale of Yuganskneftegaz I have been relieved of the responsibility for the remaining business and the group's money in general. That is all. I see my future in public efforts to build civic society in Russia.'
>
> (*IHT*, 13 January 2005, p. 13)

[Earlier it was reported that] the transfer was triggered automatically, under an agreement with Mr Nevzlin, by last month's sale of Yuganskneftegaz … In a rare speech in court yesterday … [Khodorkovsky] denied new allegations made by state prosecutors to Russian media of embezzlement by the oil group … He insisted that he had 'no personal accounts abroad, let alone big ones'.

(*FT*, 13 January 2005, p. 9)

15 January 2005.

Demonstrations were held in … cities in the Moscow region, in the capital of Tatarstan and, for the fourth consecutive day, in Samara in central Russia. In St Petersburg several thousand demonstrators [gathered] … [The demonstrations are] the latest of a weeklong wave of protests across Russia against a new law abolishing [on 1 January 2005] a wide range of social benefits for the country's 32 million pensioners, veterans and people with disabilities … [replacing them] with monthly cash payments … Taken together the protests are the largest and most passionate since Putin came to power in 2000 … In a sign of bureaucratic inefficiency some of those eligible have yet to receive any payments … The protesters have denounced the new payments as insufficient to cover the costs of the benefits and as miserly for a country that recently reported a budget surplus of nearly $25 billion … Some local governments, most prominently the Moscow city administration, have vowed to reinstate the benefits stripped at the federal level, but few other regions are wealthy enough to afford to do so.

(*IHT*, 17 January 2005, p. 3)

Tens of thousands of pensioners took to the streets throughout Russia … In St Petersburg more than 10,000 people gathered on Saturday [15 January]. It was the biggest protest in Russia's second city for a decade … Many pensioners complain that cash payments have not been made or do not compensate for the lost benefits.

(*FT*, 17 January 2005, p. 6)

17 January 2005.

Protests often numbering in the thousands continued in cities across Russia yesterday [17 January] for an eighth consecutive day … Mr Putin ordered that pensions be raised from 1 March, a month earlier than usual, and by twice the 100 roubles per month originally planned.

(*FT*, 18 January 2005, p. 6)

President Vladimir Putin on Monday [17 January] promised to increase pensions moderately and blamed federal and regional officials for failing to properly implement the Kremlin-sponsored social reforms … [although] he defended the reform, saying its general concept was right … Putin: 'The cabinet and the regions have failed to fully implement the task we had discussed: not to worsen the position of those who need the state's help' …

Putin supported decisions by some local officials to issue subsidized travel passes and also instructed the government to add at least 200 roubles instead of an earlier planned 100 roubles to every retiree's monthly pension ... The state-run railroad said it was reinstating subsidized travel – one of the scrapped benefits – for some groups.

(*IHT*, 18 January 2005, p. 3)

[It is announced that there is to be] an early pension increase of roughly 240 roubles a month as of 1 March [2005] ... In addition, a policy decision has been made to equalize the status of federal and regional benefits with regard to urban transit services. A specific mechanism for doing this is to be worked out in the next ten to twelve days ... [It was reported that] pensions would be increased as of 1 March – rather than 1 April, as originally planned – 'by approximately 240 roubles' [per month] ... As recently as the beginning of last week the pension increase was to be only 100 roubles ... Bt the president was not satisfied with that amount.

(*CDSP*, 2005, vol. 57, no. 3, pp. 1–2)

18 January 2005. 'Pensioners continued picketing city administrations and blocking federal highways and public transit routes in various cities in protest against the monetization of benefits' (*CDSP*, 2005, vol. 57, no. 3, p. 3).

19 January 2005.

The assignment the minister received from President Vladimir Putin on Monday [17 January] to find a way to solve the problems that have arisen for benefit recipients in connection with the end of free travel was completed in two days. A draft agreement ... was sent out to the regions [on 19 January] ... The main thrust of the document is this: the central government advises the regions to introduce universal passes for all types of public transit and sell them both to people whose benefits are the responsibility of the regions ... and to those who receive federal benefits ... In keeping with the president's instructions, however, the pass is to cost no more than the minimum monthly cash compensation payment in a given region.

(*CDSP*, 2005, vol. 57, no. 3, pp. 4–5)

Russian television news has for the past ten days shown angry pensioners marching ... The protests have not been large, often numbering in the hundreds, although an estimated 10,000 to 15,000 marched on Saturday [15 January] in St Petersburg ... The demonstrations are widespread ... The protests are the biggest expression of popular discontent since Mr Putin came to power in 2000 ... The change affects 34 million pensioners, war veterans and invalids ... Yesterday [19 January] the government said it would back away from plans to scrap students' exemption from military service ... The benefits changes ... contributed to slippage in Mr Putin's ratings even before the pensioners' protests.

(*FT*, 20 January 2005, p. 6)

('[On 9 February 2005 defence minister Sergei Ivanov] dropped his proposal to end college deferments to the draft': *IHT*, 12 February 2005, p. 3.)

'Scattered protests continued across Russia yesterday [19 January] ... Authorities ... detained several organizers and political radicals, while beginning an intense public relations exercise on state television' (*The Times*, 20 January 2005, p. 44).

20 January 2005. George W. Bush is sworn in for his second term of office as president of the United States.

25 January 2005. 'President Vladimir Putin on Tuesday [25 January] sought to calm students worried by the military's push for an end to education deferments from military service. Putin said the government had not decided on the issue' (*IHT*, 26 January 2005, p. 4).

26 January 2005. Protests continue.

> The government is to give the country's entire police force a 50 per cent pay rise ... The announcement came two days after President Putin ordered the government to raise military salaries by 'a minimum of 20 per cent [instead of 10 per cent] and [this should] take place much earlier [than September]' ... [Concessions on student allowances were also announced].
>
> (*The Times*, 27 January 2005, p. 40)

27 January 2005.

> A federal law [has been drafted] increasing the baseline pension as of 1 March 2005 ... [by] 240 roubles ... The government also lent support to regional budgets yesterday [27 January] ... for the purpose of 'ensuring that transportation services in the Russian Federation are affordable and accessible to the public'.
>
> (*CDSP*, 2005, vol. 57, no. 4, p. 20)

31 January 2005.

> President Vladimir Putin nominated the first regional governor under a new law scrapping gubernatorial elections ... Putin asked the parliament of the Primorye region on the Pacific coast to approve Sergei Darkin, the incumbent and a Kremlin loyalist. Under the new law Putin can dissolve the legislature if it rejects the choice three times ... Governors have been elected since 1995.
>
> (*IHT*, 1 February 2005, p. 8)

1 February 2005.

> China lent Russia $6 billion late last year [2004] so ... Rosneft could finance the purchase of ... Yuganskneftegaz ... The borrowing was backed by Rosneft's promise of future oil deliveries over the next few years to China ... Finance minister Alexei Kudrin: 'Vneshekonombank ... borrowed $6 billion from Chinese banks to credit Rosneft' ... [This statement clears up] the

mystery of how Rosneft financed the deal ... The president of Transneft said last week that the company had started to design a pipeline to the Far East with a spur to send to China.

(IHT, Wednesday 2 February 2005, pp. 1, 8)

3 February 2005.

China issued a carefully worded denial on Thursday [3 February], saying it did not help Rosneft finance the purchase of [Yuganskneftegaz] ... capping two days of backtracking by officials and industry executives from the Kremlin and Beijing ... [But a spokesman from China] declined to say whether China had offered Russia $6 billion in loans at all ... Alexei Kudrin disavowed earlier statements that Vneshekonombank had credited money to Rosneft as part of a complex financing deal. Rosneft issued a qualified denial, saying Wednesday [2 February] that it did receive a $6 billion pre-payment as part of a long-term oil supply contract with Chinese National Petroleum Corp., but that the money was not intended to buy Yuganskneftegaz. Confusion reigned as Vneshekonombank did not deny lending money to Rosneft, and Rosneft did not deny that it had recovered the $6 billion from CNPC.

(IHT, 4 February 2005, p. 13)

4 February 2005.

[The State Duma] voted to condemn anti-Semitism after an uproar over a letter signed by some nationalists and Communist legislators demanding an investigation and even a ban on all Jewish organizations for alleged crimes ranging from inciting ethnic hatred to ritual murder ... The Duma statement: 'There should be no room for anti-Semitism or ethnic and religious hatred. Any steps aimed at inciting national or religious dissent and hatred must be stopped immediately' ... In Friday's vote nearly one in five of the deputies who voted refused to endorse the statement ... The Communist Party called for the vote to be removed from the Duma's agenda, saying: 'There is no anti-Semitism in Russia' ... The 450-member State Duma voted 306 to fifty-eight to condemn the letter, which had headings such as 'The Morality of Jewish Fascism' and 'Like a Form of Satanism', and accused Jews of collapsing the Soviet Union and controlling international capital ... Jews are accused of murdering the Reverend Alexander Men, a Russian Orthodox priest of Jewish heritage whose 1990 death has never been solved. [The letter said]: 'We underscore that many anti-Jewish actions around the world are constantly organized by Jews themselves with the goal of provocation – so as to take punitive action against patriots' ... Twenty legislators had signed the original letter, which was made public on the eve of President Putin's visit to Auschwitz for the sixtieth anniversary of the Nazi concentration camp by Soviet troops, underscoring a recent spike in anti-Semitism and xenophobia in Russia ... Fourteen of the original letter's signatories came from Rodina (Motherland), a nationalist faction that is thought to have been a Kremlin creation whipped up for the last parliamentary elections to draw votes.

(*IHT*, 5 February 2005, pp. 1, 3)

7 February 2005.

Parliament on Monday [7 February] scheduled [for 9 February] its first no-confidence vote in the government of prime minister Mikhail Fradkov ... The no-confidence vote was supported by ... Communists and the Motherland Party ... [The benefits] protests trailed off last week ... [President Putin] ordered the extra payment of ... \$4 billion to soften the impact of the change.

(*IHT*, 8 February 2005, p. 3)

8 February 2005.

Menatep ... the parent group of Yukos launched a \$28.3 billion claim for compensation from the government for alleged expropriation of its investment in Russia ... [Menatep] has brought the action under the 1994 [UN] Energy Charter Treaty, the multilateral accord designed to enforce international law in energy investments to which Russia is a signatory ... Menatep, which controls 51 per cent of Yukos through two other vehicles, says its Yukos stake was worth more than \$17 billion in October 2003, but it is now worth next to nothing ... Menatep says the shares would certainly be worth much more now.

(*FT*, 9 February 2005, p. 26)

9 February 2005.

The government survived a no confidence vote over its bungled reform of social benefits ... Only 112 parliament members [in the State Duma] supported the no confidence motion tabled by Communist, nationalist and independent deputies. That was less than half the 226 required to pass it ... Most members of the dominant ... United Russia, with 307 seats, abstained rather than vote against the motion ... Although pensioners' protests have petered out in the past ten days, a coalition styling itself the Council for Social Security is trying to organize two days of action in forty regions across Russia. It plans to picket local government buildings today [10 February] and hold demonstrations on Saturday [12 February]. The coalition includes the Russian federation of trade unions, human rights groups and a body representing clean-up workers at the Chernobyl nuclear power plant, who also lost their benefits. The government has taken steps to alleviate the effects of the benefits changes, promising to double the annual rise in pensions and restoring some free transport rights.

(*FT*, 10 February 2005, p. 6)

Twenty voted against [the motion] and four formally abstained ... Prime minister Mikhail Fradkov ... asked for six months to correct the situation with subsidized medicines and said the government would seek by

2008 to at least double the average monthly wage ... many regional authorities across Russia have restored free or subsidized transport for the elderly.

(*IHT*, 10 February 2005, p. 3)

'United Russia controls 306 of the Duma's 450 seats ... Deputies told the cabinet that it had two months to correct its mistakes or face another confidence vote' (*The Times*, 10 February 2005, p. 40).

11 February 2005. '[Yukos is] suing four Russian energy groups for more than $20 billion in damages ... The suit names names Gazprom ... Gazpromneft ... Baikal Finance Group ... and Rosneft' (*FT*, 14 February 2005, p. 29).

12 February 2005. 'Tens of thousands of Russians protested across the country [against the benefits reform] ... the most widespread in President Vladimir Putin's term. It was countered by massive demonstrations organized by the Kremlin' (*IHT*, 14 February 2005, p. 7).

An estimated quarter of a million protesters took to the streets across Russia on Saturday [12 February] in the biggest public demonstration for five years – some defending and some condemning the social benefits reform ... On Saturday the protests were countered for the first time by pro-Putin rallies ... Police said the [pro-Putin] crowd [in Moscow] numbered 5,000 to 6,000 people, but the interior ministry estimated the number at 40,000 ... The interior ministry said 245,000 Russian took part in 284 mass demonstrations at the weekend.

(*FT*, 14 February 2005, p. 8)

18 February 2005. '[President Putin] announces a visit to Iran ... Mr Putin welcomed Iran's national security chief ... to the Kremlin and declared that Tehran was not pursuing nuclear weapons, flatly contradicting repeated allegations by the United States' (*Guardian*, 19 February 2005, p. 17).

('Iran and Russia signed a nuclear fuel agreement on Sunday [27 February] paving the way for Iran to get its first reactor up and running ... The agreement [was signed] at the Bushehr nuclear power plant ... [a] $800 million complex ... Russia helped build the Bushehr plant and has agreed to provide the fuel to run it. But it wants the spent fuel returned to prevent any possibility of Tehran's extracting plutonium from it, enough of which could be used to make an atomic bomb': www.iht.com, 27 February 2005.)

24 February 2005. Presidents Bush and Putin meet in Slovakia on the fourth and final day of his visit to Europe.

President George W. Bush: 'Democracies have certain things in common. They have a rule of law and protection of minorities, a free press and a viable political opposition. I was able to share my concerns about Russia's commitment in fulfilling these universal principles' (*FT*, 25 February 2005, p. 6).

Mikhail Kasyanov, sacked as prime minister a year ago, said: 'The direction has changed. It is not the right one. The country is on the wrong track' ... He said his country had not respected any of the key democratic values over the past year ... Mr Kasyanov was installed as prime minister by Boris Yeltsin.

(*FT*, 25 February 2005, p. 6)

Mikhail Kasyanov ... [said that Russia] 'has taken the wrong turn, which harms the country's economic and social development' ... Russia's development should be based on division of power, an independent judicial system, a free press, market economy principles and freedom of entrepreneurship, he added. 'Looking at the past year I have concluded that Russia is not relying on any of these values.'

(www.iht.com, 2 March 2005)

25 February 2005.

The decision by a Houston [Texas] judge to dismiss a bankruptcy filing by Yukos has removed legal barriers for a merger between Rosneft and Gazprom ... [The US judge] upheld a challenge by Deutsche Bank against the bankruptcy filing. The bank had planned to fund Gazprom's bid for [Yuganskneftegaz] ... [The judge] said that the importance of Yukos to the Russian economy meant the dispute was best heard 'in a forum in which the participation of the Russian government is assured'.

(*FT*, Money and Business, 26 February 2005, p. 6)

Late February 2005. 'A new young people's movement called *Us* [*Nashi*: literally 'Ours'], which is being formed under the patronage of the Kremlin, held a conference' (*CDSP*, 2005, vol. 57, no. 10, p. 6).

('The head of *Nashi* (*Ours*), Vasili Yakemenko, [is] a former Kremlin bureaucrat ... the success of the Orange Revolution [in Ukraine] last December [2004] convinced the Kremlin it needed to create a stronger counterweight to groups like [Ukraine's] Pora': *The Times*, 18 July 2005, p. 28.)

2 March 2005.

Gazprom and Rosneft have finally agreed a merger ... Under the deal Yuganskneftegaz will remain a separate company headed by Sergei Bogdanchikov, the current president of Rosneft ... [Gazprom said] 'Rosneft will become a 100 per cent subsidiary of Gazprom' ... Alexei Miller, chief executive of Gazprom, said it would acquire 100 per cent of Rosneft through a share swap that would allow the government to gain majority control [raising its stake from 38 per cent to 51 per cent], a precondition for removing the ringfence mechanism that prevents foreign investors buying domestic shares in Gazprom.

(*FT*, 3 March 2005, p. 28)

Gazprom and Rosneft together will produce enough oil ... to rank as Russia's number five oil producer. Yuganskneftegaz, the stand-alone company

... would rank number four ... Kremlin fears of litigation by Yukos management and shareholders forced it to leave Yuganskneftegaz out of the merged energy giant ... The merger sets in motion a Kremlin plan to scrap the limits of foreign ownership in Gazprom. Currently foreigners are barred from buying local shares of Gazprom, and instead must purchase more expensive American depository receipts. Before it gets rid of its 'ring fence', however, the state needs to raise its ownership to a controlling 51 per cent from the current 39.3 per cent.

(*IHT*, 3 March 2005, p. 15)

15 March 2005.

Rosneft is suing Yukos for just over $11 billion, alleging that Yukos mismanaged its biggest unit [Yuganskneftegaz] and, in addition, that it still owes the state back taxes ... Rosneft confirmed that it had filed two claims against Yukos for alleged losses incurred through 'transfer pricing' from 1999 through 2003 ... Yukos and many other oil companies use transfer pricing to buy oil more cheaply from subsidiaries, sell it at market prices globally and pocket the difference. But the practice has fallen out of favour since the government's attack on Yukos.

(*IHT*, 16 March 2005, p. 13)

17 March 2005.

Anatoli Chubais ... the head of Russia's state-controlled electricity monopoly [Unified Energy Systems] ... and the architect of the country's massive post-Soviet privatization ... survived an assassination attack unhurt Thursday [17 March] when unidentified attackers detonated a powerful bomb and then fired at his car as he headed for work ... Chubais issued a brief statement saying he knew who was behind the attack but would not name them ... Chubais took over UES in 1998, and his radical restructuring of the monopoly power grid has faced massive resistance from minority shareholders, as well as business rivals and state officials ... Under the energy reform plan more than forty regional energy companies are to be split into separate generating, transmission and marketing companies, with current shareholders receiving a stake in proportion to their current share ... [In 2004] he said he had repeatedly been threatened with assassination. Chubais said he believed the reasons for the threats were his activities as Russia's privatization tsar, but some observers said the UES restructuring appeared to be the real reason behind past threats and Thursday's attack ... While presiding over UES Chubais has also continued to play a prominent role in Russia's politics as one of the leaders of the Union of Rightist Forces ... Boris Nemtsov, one of the party's leaders, said the attempt on Chubais's life appeared to have political motives. Nemtsov said Chubais's political enemies had repeatedly threatened to kill him.

(www.iht.com, 17 March 2005)

Chubais has a long list of enemies. He has said in the past that he receives many death threats and has also said he has survived three previous attempts on his life … Chubais: 'The main thing I can say today [17 March] is that I will work twice as hard on everything I have been doing to reform the nation's electricity industry and consolidate the democratic forces' … UES is the largest electricity utility in the world in terms of generating capacity, and Putin's Kremlin has strengthened control over the company by putting government representatives on its board of directors. Putin did the same at Gazprom … and at Aeroflot, the largest private airline, placing loyalists on the boards and solidifying the power of his inner circle within many of Russia's most important companies.

(*IHT*, 18 March 2005, pp. 1, 4)

[Some point to] business enemies who had bought shares in … UES in the unfulfilled expectation of gaining control of major power generating companies as the more likely organizers of the attack … The plans for a radical restructuring of UES … were adopted in February 2003, but there is uncertainty over how they will ultimately be implemented. Some analysts said that powerful industrial barons who relied on dirt-cheap electricity supplies were threatened by the electricity liberalization, which will lead to higher prices.

(www.iht.com, 18 March 2005)

'In an interview with the *FT* last November [2004] Mr Chubais said he knew at least three murder contracts had been taken out on him … Chubais: "It was purely political grounds, hatred that I sold out Russia"' (*FT*, 18 March 2005, p. 9).

18 March 2005. 'A British judge on Friday [18 March] rejected Russian government claims seeking the extradition of a Yukos accountant and a lawyer who had fled to London' (*IHT*, 21 March 2005, p. 11).

23 March 2005.

President Vladimir Putin … [says] he favours a new law limiting investigations into 1990s-era privatizations … He said it was 'possible to support' a law limiting investigations into post-Soviet privatization schemes … The law would reduce the statute of limitations on such enquiries to three years from ten.

(*IHT*, 25 March 2005, p. 1)

24 March 2005.

A court found a former top security officer of Yukos guilty of murder … Alexei Pichugin was charged with organizing a double murder in 2002, as well as an attack on the head of the Moscow mayor's communication service. The jury at the Moscow City court found him guilty … Pichugin has dismissed the charges as part of the Kremlin-instigated crackdown on Yukos and Khodorkovsky.

(*IHT*, 25 March 2005, p. 5)

A Moscow court found him guilty of organizing the murder of Sergei and Olga Gorin in 2002 ... He was also found guilty of attempting to murder a former adviser to Yukos called Olga Kostina. He allegedly had the Gorins killed because they threatened to tell police what they knew of the failed hit on Ms Kostina.

(The Independent, 26 March 2005, p. 29)

'According to prosecutors, Mr Pichugin received his orders from Leonid Nevzlin' (*FT*, 26 March 2005, p. 7).

('[On 30 March Alexei Pichugin] was jailed for twenty years for murder and attempted murder ... Pichugin was tried in camera in a Moscow court and last Thursday was found guilty by eight of the twelve jurors ... Pichugin was arrested in June 2004 ... He was charged with asking an associate, Sergei Gorin, to organize the contract killing of Olga Kostina. She had been an employee of Group Menatep, the company owning the majority of the shares of [Yukos] ... The prosecution alleged that Mr Pichugin had Mr Gorin and his wife Olga killed by a criminal gang when he threatened to expose the murder plot to police': *Guardian*, 31 March 2005, p. 16.)

28 March 2005.

In a criminal case testing the accepted boundaries of artistic expression, a court on Monday [28 March] convicted a museum director and a curator for inciting religious hatred when they organized an exhibition of paintings and sculptures that, to many, ridiculed the Russian Orthodox Church. The court, however, rejected the prosecutor's appeal to sentence them to prison and instead fined then the equivalent of $3,600 each, ruling that the exhibition was 'openly insulting and blasphemous'. The case against the exhibition, entitled 'Caution! Religion', has deeply divided Russia's religious and artistic community ever since it opened briefly in January 2004, provoking alternate charges of censorship and animosity to religious believers.

(IHT, 29 March 2005, p. 3)

Russia, angered by the growing influence of the Organization for Security and Co-operation in Europe [OSCE] in monitoring elections and human rights on its borders, is blocking this year's budget and withholding its own contribution to force changes on the organization ... It wants less of human rights and human security and more focus on military, economic and environment issues ... The issue has become so serious that a confidential EU document presented to EU ambassadors this month [March 2005] suggested that member states should step in to support the ... $240 million budget or risk a collapse of the organization ... The EU document: 'At the heart of the present crisis lies a more fundamental "values gap". Russia's main problem with OSCE concerns those things we most value in its monitoring of democracy and human rights' ... OSCE, previously called the Conference on Security and Co-operation in Europe [CSCE], was the only international grouping during the Cold War that brought together the United States, Canada, Eastern and Western Europe and the former Soviet Union. Spawned by the 1975 Helsinki Final Act, it provided a rare forum in which these countries focused on three 'baskets' for establishing confidence-building measures between two ideologically opposed camps. The first basket dealt with military and security issues, the second with economic and environmental and the third with human rights.

(*IHT*, 29 March 2005, pp. 1, 8)

Russia lifted its opposition Thursday [12 May] to a budget for OSCE, ending a bitter dispute that almost paralysed the agency's activities, which include the monitoring of elections and human rights issues in post-communist countries ... Russia agreed to the budget only on the condition that the issue of future contributions by the fifty-five members be negotiated by the end of September and that the priorities of OSCE also be reviewed ... [Russia says that] the organization was far too concerned with human rights instead of giving more attention to security and military issues ... [OSCE] was founded in 1975 as the Conference on Security and Co-operation in Europe [CSCE].

(*FT*, 13 May 2005, p. 3)

Late last week [March 2005] ... President Putin told the former Soviet republics for the first time that the CIS has accomplished its mission and that those who wish to leave it are free to do so ... It is perhaps highly symbolic that it was in Yerevan [that this was announced] ... Armenia is practically the only country that is still completely supportive of Russia ... Putin: 'Whereas in Europe countries have worked together within the framework of the EU to achieve unity, the CIS was created for the purpose of a civilized divorce. That is the difference; all the rest is a shell and idle chatter ... If anyone expected some particular achievement from the CIS there weren't any because there could not be ... [The CIS has now become a] club for sharing information and cleaning up problematic issues of a general nature ... [issues] that still remain following the collapse of the unified state and have to resolved jointly ... Deep integrative processes [are now occurring within the framework of other organizations: the Eurasian Economic Community; and the Single Economic Space established by Belarus, Kazakhstan, Russia and Ukraine in 2003].'

(*Nezavisimaya Gazeta*, 28 March 2005, p. 2; *CDSP*, 2005, vol. 57, no. 13, pp. 10–11)

29 March 2005.

Prosecutors asked ... a Moscow court to sentence Mikhail Khodorkovsky and his former partner and co-defendant, Platon Lebedev, to ten years each in prison ... Khodorkovsky served a chief executive [of Yukos] from 1997 to 2003 ... Khodorkovsky ranked as Russia's wealthiest man, with a net worth of $15 billion based on his controlling share of Yukos, according to *Forbes* magazine's 2003 survey ... In 2004 he was worth $2.2 billion, according to *Forbes* ... Khodorkovsky donated money to opposition parties and lobbied parliament to prevent changes in corporate laws that would have raised oil companies' taxes. He also advocated private oil pipelines to energy-hungry nations and increased oil exports to the West, which reportedly rankled the Kremlin. Once Russia's largest and most profitable private company, Yukos last year [2004] faced a legal onslaught from the government and is now staggering under a $28 billion back-tax claim. Its largest production unit in western Siberia ... was auctioned off last December [2004] to help pay the tax bill ... Khodorkovsky's criminal charges are unrelated to Yukos. Instead, he faces seven counts related to the 1994 privatization of a fertilizer factory named Apatit, ranging from theft of state property, tax evasion, forgery, embezzlement and money laundering, a new charge added in December [2004] ... Yuganskneftegaz, the main asset of the state oil company Rosneft, is suing its former parent Yukos for $2.2 billion, Rosneft said Tuesday [29 March]. A Rosneft spokesman said Yuganskneftegaz had filed suit at Moscow's arbitration court at the end of last week, demanding that Yukos pay for oil supplied from July to December [2004] for which Yuganskneftegaz alleged Yukos never paid. The court will hear the case on 25 April.

(*IHT*, 30 March 2005, p. 13)

30 March 2005. 'Tax authorities demanded 18 billion roubles, or $646 million, from Khodorkovsky and a co-defendant in unpaid taxes' (www.iht.com, 31 March 2005).

2 April 2005. Pope John Paul II dies.

President Putin called ... Pope John Paul II ... 'an outstanding public figure whose name signifies the whole era' ... Russia has roughly 600,000 Catholics ... Patriarch Alexei II ... ruled out a visit from the Pope ... despite invitations from Mikhail Gorbachev [who met him in 1990] ... and from Putin who met him twice.

(*IHT*, 7 April 2005, pp. 1, 8)

5 April 2005.

The Moscow arbitration court ... has ordered a freeze of the main assets still held by ... Yukos ... in response to a lawsuit brought by its former core production unit ... Yuganskneftegaz ... The former unit now [is] owned by Rosneft ... [and] is claiming $5.9 billion from Yukos in damages for allegedly paying artificially low prices for crude supplies from the oil pumping facility ... The Moscow arbitration court on 5 April issued the ruling, which bars Yukos from disposing of shares in its major remaining subsidiaries, including its top two oil production units, Tomskneft and

Samaraneftegaz, and its main refinery, Angarsk ... The Moscow arbitration court is due to examine the damages claim next month ... Rosneft alleges that the unit's former owners mismanaged the facility and are also pressing for Yukos to pay the $5.1 billion that Russia's tax authorities say Yugan-skneftegaz owes.

(www.iht.com, 19 April 2005; *IHT*, 20 April 2005, p. 16)

A Moscow court has frozen the remaining assets of Yukos ... The Moscow arbitration court froze two Yukos production facilities and three refineries in response to a $5.6 billion lawsuit filed by Rosneft. This claimed that the company had underpaid Yuganskneftegaz ... for oil supplies from 1999–2003. Yuganskneftegaz is already suing its ex-parent to recover a $5.1 billion tax demand it has received. Hearings of both cases will take place in May ... Yukos claimed that the latest court action changed little as its assets were already frozen under multiple orders.

(*FT*, 20 April 2005, p. 26)

11 April 2005.

Germany and Russia have announced an agreement to build a North European Gas Pipeline under the Baltic Sea that will allow Gazprom to deliver gas directly to Western Europe ... Russia supplies 32 per cent of Germany's energy needs and over a fifth of EU requirements.

(*IHT*, 12 April 2005, p. 1)

12 April 2005.

Vladimir Putin insisted that he will not seek a third term as president in 2008 ... Putin: 'I will not amend the basic law, and it is impossible under the constitution to be elected three consecutive times' ... He joked he might be prepared to run for a third term at a later date, but added he was 'not sure I will want to do that'.

(*FT*, 13 April 2005, p. 8)

'Mr Putin pointed out that the constitution did not ban anyone from being elected president three times if the terms were not consecutive. "True, I am not sure that I would want this," he said' (*The Times*, 13 April 2005, p. 39).

20–21 April 2005. 'Foreign ministers from Nato nations meet for their first talks in a former Soviet republic [Lithuania]' (www.iht.com, 20 April 2005).

[On 21 April] Nato signed a landmark military co-operation accord with Russia ... The 'status of forces agreement' between Nato and Moscow will make it easier for the two sides to organize joint exercises and training and, among other things, allow troops from Nato members and Russia to travel through each other's territory ... The accord, which will need the ratification of the Russian Duma, could permit Nato troops heading for Afghanistan to cross Russian territory.

(www.iht.com, 21 April 2005)

Nato moved to sign a 'status of forces' agreement with Russia that would enable it to expand joint military exercises on Russian soil, possibly for future peacekeeping operations in various trouble spots. There have been a few such joint exercises focusing on dealing with emergencies or humanitarian crises. But American and Nato officials said the new accord would widen the possibilities, making it easier to transport foreign troops across Russian soil to interdict narcotics and arms smuggling from Afghanistan and other places.

(*IHT*, 22 April 2005, p. 1)

25 April 2005. President Vladimir Putin (state of nation speech):

The collapse of the Soviet Union was the greatest geopolitical catastrophe of the century. And for the Russian people it became a real drama. Tens of millions of our citizens found themselves outside the Russian Federation ... The Russian nation's mission to bring further civilization to the Euro-Asia continent must be continued ... The main political and ideological task is the development of Russia as a free and democratic state ... [Democracy in Russia would develop] only by legal means ... Illegal methods in the fight for ethnic, religious or other interests are in contradiction with the principles of democracy. The state would react to them in a legal but tough way ... Russia will decide for itself the pace, terms and conditions of moving towards democracy ... [State television and radio must be] objective, free from any group's influence and reflect the whole spectrum of opinion ... Without liberty and democracy there can be no stability and no sustainable economic policies ... Tax agencies have no right to terrorize business by going back to the same problem again and again. We need to find ways for repaying back-taxes that preserve the state's interests while not ruining the economy or driving business into a corner ... [The state bureaucracy is] an isolated and sometimes arrogant caste which sees the civil service as just another kind of business.

(*The Independent*, 26 April 2005, p. 23; *Guardian*, 26 April 2005, p. 19; *FT*, 26 April 2005, p. 10; *IHT*, 26 April 2005, p. 8)

President Putin:

It should be recognized that the collapse of the Soviet Union was the major geopolitical catastrophe of the century. For the Russian people it was a genuine drama. Tens of millions of our fellow citizens and countrymen found themselves outside the bounds of Russian territory. What is more, the epidemic of disintegration spread to Russia itself ... To a considerable extent our bureaucracy is still a closed and sometimes downright arrogant caste that understands government service as a form of business. And, therefore, task number one for us remains the task of increasing the effectiveness of government and ensuring that public officials strictly obey the law and provide quality public service ... We need to provide incentives so that capital amassed by our citizens will be returned to our national economy. We need to allow citizens to declare in a simplified manner capital that they have accumulated in earlier years, in an earlier period. This procedure should be contingent on only two conditions: payment of the 13 per cent income tax, and deposit of the sums in question in Russian bank accounts ... Tax agencies have no right to 'terrorize' business by returning time and again to the same problems ... Russia is a country that has chosen democracy for itself ... As a sovereign country Russia is capable of determining, and will determine independently, its own timetable and conditions for moving forward on that path ... Without question the Russian nation must continue its civilizing mission on the Eurasian continent ... We must create guarantees to ensure that state television and radio are as objective as possible, free from the influence of any particular groups, and that they reflect the entire spectrum of public and political forces in the country.

(*CDSP*, 2005, vol. 57 no. 17, pp. 1–6)

President Vladimir Putin: 'The government and the regional authorities have failed to create conditions for small and medium-sized business to flourish. Everyone who opens a new business and registers a company should be given a medal for personal bravery' (www.iht.com, 25 April 2005).

27 April 2005.

The long-awaited verdict and sentencing in the trial of ... Mikhail Khodorkovsky was postponed on Wednesday [27 April] until 16 May, well after Russia's World War II commemorative holidays [9 May being the anniversary], during which the country is host to several international leaders.

(*IHT*, 28 April 2005, p. 3)

28–29 April 2005.

On the first visit by a Kremlin leader to Israel, President Putin attempted to allay Israeli fears that its security is threatened by Russia's assistance to Iran ... [which is] required to return spent nuclear fuel to Russia so it cannot be used for military purposes ... and missile sales to Syria ... No Soviet or Russian leader had ever visited Israel before Putin's visit, though Boris Yeltsin toured Israel in January 2000, days after he resigned as the Russian president ... Roughly a million Israeli citizens – more than 15 per cent of the population – have come from the former Soviet Union over the past two decades ... Putin visited Egypt before reaching Israel ... Several Russian business tycoons, who are wanted on criminal charges in Russia, have taken refuge in Israel ... The Soviet Union was a leading supporter of Arab states during the Cold War, yet Putin's visit to Egypt marked the first trip to that country by a Kremlin leader in more than forty years.

(*IHT*, 29 April 2005, pp. 1, 6)

9 May 2005. The sixtieth anniversary of 'Victory Day' in the 'Great Patriotic War' is commemorated in Moscow with international figures in attendance, including President George W. Bush of the United States. ('Victory in Europe Day', or VE Day, is celebrated on 8 May. Germany agreed to unconditionally surrender, signing on 7 May in the West and on 8 May in the East.)

It is usually reckoned that some 27 million Soviet soldiers and civilians died in the Second World War (11 million troops and 16 million civilians) (e.g. *The Times*, 10 May 2005, p. 31). 'By comparison some 10 million people [in total] perished in the First World War' (www.iht.com, 8 May 2005).

There is controversy about the question of Soviet annexations and domination in postwar Eastern Europe. President Bush visited Latvia on 6–7 May and Georgia on 9–10 May. The president of Latvia accepted Putin's invitation to attend the celebrations, but the presidents of Estonia and Lithuania did not. ('[In] 1995 none of the Baltic leaders attended the fiftieth anniversary of World War II': www.baltictimes.com, 12 May 2005.)

'[The Baltic States] were occupied by Soviet troops in 1940 and then reoccupied after the Soviet army ousted the Nazis in 1944' (www.iht.com, 8 May 2005).

President Vladimir Putin, in response to growing calls for Russia to renounce the Soviet–Nazi pact that consigned the Baltic republics to Soviet rule, said that Moscow condemned it long ago. Putin said the Soviet-era legislature, the Supreme Soviet, issued a resolution in 1989 that criticized the [August] 1939 Molotov–Ribbentrop Pact as 'a personal decision by Stalin that contradicted the interests of the Soviet people', according to the text of a German television interview published Friday [6 May] by the Kremlin ... Putin: 'I want to repeat: we already did it. What, we have to do this every day, every year?'

(*IHT*, 7 May 2005, p. 4)

President Putin:

In effect these Baltic countries were an exchange coin in world politics and that is a tragedy for these countries – one must say this outright. As for our attitude to the 1939 pact, in 1989 the Soviet Union's top representative body condemned it. It said just so: 'We condemn these agreements between Stalin and Hitler and think that this was Stalin's personal decision, contrary to the Soviet Union's nation's interests' ... The only thing we hear now is that our country must admit the illegality of these decisions and condemn them. I repeat – we have already done so. Must we do this every day of every year? That is downright senseless!

(*The Baltic Times*, 12–18 May 2005, p. 2)

[President Putin told] a German newspaper: 'Yes, of course, Stalin was a tyrant and many people call him a criminal. But he was not a Nazi. And they were not Soviet troops that crossed the German border on 22 June 1941; it was the other way around.'

(*The Times*, 7 May 2005, p. 38)

[On 7 May] the Latvian president awarded Bush the Three-Star Order, the nation's highest honour ... President Bush: '[The United States] still retained flags of your independent [Baltic] countries above your embassies during that period [of occupation by the Soviet Union]. We never recognized that occupation' ... [President Bush] stopped short, however, of saying he would encourage President Putin to recognize the occupation].

(www.baltictimes.com, 7 May 2005)

President Bush:

> The agreement at Yalta followed in the unjust tradition of Munich and the Molotov–Ribbentrop Pact. Once again, when powerful governments negotiated, the freedom of small nations was somehow expendable. Yet this attempt to sacrifice freedom for the sake of stability left a continent divided and unstable. The captivity of millions in Central and Eastern Europe will be remembered as one of the greatest wrongs of history ... The United States refused to recognize your occupation by an empire. The flags of free Latvia, Estonia and Lithuania – illegal at home – flew proudly over diplomatic missions in the United States.

> (www.baltictimes.com, 12 May 2005; *The Baltic Times*,
> 12–18 May 2005, p. 22)

'Moscow has responded that the ... [Soviet Union was] invited to march into [the Baltic States by the governments of the time]' (*IHT*, 9 May 2005, p. 1). Sergei Yastrzhembsky (the Kremlin chief of European affairs): 'There was no occupation. There were agreements at the time with the legitimately elected authorities in the Baltic countries' (www.baltictimes.com, 12 May 2005).

> [On 10 May President Putin] cuttingly said he hoped Latvia and Estonia would not make 'idiotic' territorial demands preventing the signing of formal border treaties – demands officials of both countries denied having made ... Putin: 'Today in Europe in the twenty-first century, when one country is making territorial claims against another and at the same time wants to ratify border treaties, this is complete nonsense' ... Russian has previously initialled border treaties with Latvia and Estonia but has yet to sign or ratify them ... [Putin] dismissed historical claims that Soviet forces reoccupied the Baltics after the war since by then they were already part of the Soviet Union.

> (*IHT*, 11 May 2005, p. 3)

President Putin (7 May):

> Our Baltic neighbours ... continue to demand some kind of repentance from Russia. I think they are trying to attract attention to themselves, to justify a discriminatory and reprehensible policy of their governments toward a large Russian-speaking part of their own population, to mask the shame of past collaboration ... If the Baltic countries became part of the USSR in 1939, then there is no way we could occupy them in 1941, since they were already part of the Soviet Union.

> (www.baltictimes.com, 12 May 2005; *The Baltic Times*,
> 12–18 May 2005, p. 2)

'No American president has ever visited Georgia ... President Mikheil Saakash-vili will boycott World War II commemorations on Monday [9 May] in Russia after the two countries failed to agree on dismantling two Russian military bases in Georgia' (*IHT*, 7 May 2005, p. 4).

> On 25 April the Georgian foreign minister, Salome Zurabishvili, announced that she had shaken hands with her Russian colleague, sealing an accord to start withdrawal in 2005 and close the remaining two bases by 1 January 2008. The Georgian side pressed for the signing of an official treaty. Yet the Russian foreign minister, Sergei Lavrov, never publicly confirmed that he promised to take all soldiers out by the end of 2007. Georgia is insisting on that deadline because it wants the Russians gone before parliamentary elec-tions in 2008. On 6 May, when the two foreign ministers met again, they were unable to agree on a deadline. Zurabishvili promptly announced that her president would not go to Moscow for the celebrations.
>
> (*IHT*, 10 May 2005, p. 8)

> George W. Bush [was] greeted with a huge outpouring of affection [on Tuesday 10 May in Tbilisi] ... Tens of thousands of people were gathering for a speech by the [US president]. Saakashvili said more than 150,000 people had assembled – an estimate that seemed overstated.
>
> (www.iht.com, 10 May 2005)

'The police estimated ... the crowd ... was 60,000 to 100,000' (*FT*, 11 May 2005, p. 9). (The figure of 100,000 was given by the following: *The Times*, p. 35; *The Independent*, p. 18; *Daily Telegraph*, p. 11.) The president of Abkhazia, Sergei Bagapsh: 'The Abkhaz people have already opted for an independent state at a referendum and this choice should be respected' (*IHT*, 11 May 2005, p. 1).

'Ilham Aliev [the president of Azerbaijan] boycotted the event because of the attendance of Armenia' (*Guardian*, 9 May 2005, p. 16).

> Russia ... asked whether those neighbours would have been around at all if the Red Army had not helped defeat Hitler ... Putin also ... [suggested] that the indignation from Riga to Vilnius was in aimed part at disguising a history of collaboration with the Nazis ... There can now be little debate that the exercise of communism, whatever the idealism of its origins, killed upward of 80 million people between the Soviet Union, China, Cambodia, Eastern |Europe, North Korea and Vietnam.
>
> (Roger Cohen, www.iht.com, 10 May 2005; *IHT*, 11 May 2005, p. 2)

10 May 2005.

> Russia and the EU signed a long-stalled agreement on forging close eco-nomic, political and social ties ... [but it] was more symbolic than substantive ... Negotiations over closer Russia–EU ties ... had first been proposed two years ago, then quickly stalled. In the agreement signed Tuesday [10 May] the two sides pledged to co-operate in removing barriers to trade, jointly fighting

terrorism, proliferation of weapons and organized crime and adopting uniform educational standards. The two sides failed to agree, however, on easing visa requirements – a key Russian demand – and to require Russia to accept the return of illegal immigrants detained in European nations.

(*IHT*, 11 May 2005, p. 3)

The four 'road maps' adopted at an EU–Russia summit in Moscow include promises to make visa rules simpler for travel between Russia and the EU, and commitments to step up co-ordination in international diplomacy ... The agreements also focus on Russian economic management in which Moscow will try to harmonize its laws with EU legislation – such as competition policy, intellectual property rights and the pharmaceutical and textile sectors. But the road maps – on economic integration, external security, freedom and justice, and education and research – set out ambitions for co-operation rather than marking concrete agreement. The changes to visa policy and readmission to Russia of illegal immigrants to the EU need more negotiation. The EU also failed to make progress on pushing Russia to phase out the charges European airlines pay to fly over Siberia before 2013.

(*FT*, 11 May 2005, p. 9)

13 May 2005.

Prosecutors are planning to bring fresh charges against Mikhail Khodorkovsky ... New of the prosecutors' intentions came ahead of a judgement expected on Monday [16 May] in the ten-month trial of Mr Khodorkovsky on fraud and tax evasion charges. It also came on the day a court upheld a $2.2 billion claim against Yukos ... A Moscow court upheld a claim that the company had underpaid Yuganskneftegaz ... by $2.2 billion for oil supplies ... [The former Yukos subsidiary's sale is helping] bailiffs recover $28 billion in back taxes that the authorities are claiming from Yukos ... The latest court ruling brings to $12.9 billion the outstanding claims against Yukos by Rosneft and Yuganskneftegaz ... Prosecutors indicated in January they were weighing new charges based on allegations of money laundering by senior Yukos staff ... [The prosecutors said on 13 May that] Yukos had illegally transferred more than $6 billion of crude oil revenues out of the country into companies registered in tax havens.

(*FT*, 14 May 2005, p. 6)

17 May 2005.

The government on Tuesday [17 May 2005] abandoned its efforts to gain control of Gazprom through a merger with [Rosneft] ... The government, facing claims by the main shareholders of Yukos, said that it had instead opted to raise cash to buy the needed shares of Gazprom outright and win a majority stake [from its current 39.3 per cent] in order to avoid risking lawsuits that could occupy the company for years ... Gazprom would forego the merger with Rosneft and instead create a special holding company to raise money in the capital markets. The holding company, to be called Ros-neftegaz, would first sell debt, use the cash to buy the Gazprom shares and then sell part of its stake in Rosneft through an initial public offering to pay the debt obligations ... The state will become the direct owner of a control-ling stake in Gazprom and a controlling stake in Rosneft ... Rosneft was openly against the idea of being swallowed up by its larger rival.

(IHT, 18 May 2005, p. 10)

Moscow will use cash to buy Gazprom shares held by some of its subsidiar-ies as a way of lifting the state's stake in the gas monopoly ... to 51 per cent ... Gazprom controls one-sixth of the world's gas reserves and supplies a quarter of Europe's gas ... The government will borrow internationally to fund the Gazprom share purchase. It will also place a minority stake in Rosneft on the capital market to raise capital.

(FT, 18 May 2005, p. 28)

('[On 16 June the government and Gazprom agreed a price of] $7.1 billion for the 10.74 per cent stake ... [that] will lift its [the state's] shareholding [in Gazprom] to above 50 per cent': *IHT*, 17 June 2005, p. 10.)

31 May 2005.

A court convicted Mikhail Khodorkovsky ... on criminal charges Tuesday and sentenced him to nine years in [a prison camp] ... [He] was found guilty of six charges, including fraud and tax evasion. His term will be reduced by the nineteenth months of pre-trial confinement he has already served and thus will end in 2012. Platon Lebedev was given the same sentence. Prose-cutors had asked for maximum sentences of ten years. The court also ordered the two men to pay about $613 million in taxes and fines.

(www.iht.com, 31 May 2005)

'The sentences came after judges spent ten days reading the verdict ... [Through-out the trial both men] were kept before the panel of judges in a grey metal cage' (*IHT*, 1 June 2005, pp. 1, 8).

'The chief judge said: "Khodorkovsky and Lebedev entered into an organized group with the aim of illegally appropriating other people's property and then selling the assets for their own gain"' (*The Times*. 1 June 2005, p. 29).

3 June 2005.

Gazprom announced Friday [3 June] that it had bought a 50.17 per cent stake in ... *Izvestia* ... [a newspaper] of the investment empire controlled by Vladimir Potanin ... The move has been seen as another step toward the Kremlin's control of Russia's privately held media.

(www.iht.com, 4 June 2005)

'The purchase by Gazprom ... of 50.19 per cent of ... one of Russia's most respected and aggressive newspapers ... is raising fears among some critics that the Kremlin's influence over the media might be expanding into the printed press' (*IHT*, 6 June 2005, p. 9). 'Gazprom-Media's ... media assets include three television channels, five radio stations, movie theatres, a movie studio and a publishing house' (*IHT*, 3 June 2005, p. 15).

29 June 2005.

> Russia's justice ministry has asked Lithuania and the Netherlands [where the shares are registered] to stop Yukos from selling its shares in a Lithuanian oil refinery ... Yukos holds a 53.7 per cent stake in Mazeikiu Nafta, Lithuania's only refinery, while the Lithuanian government holds a 40.6 per cent stake. The refinery, which includes a pipeline and offshore oil terminal, accounts for around 10 per cent of Lithuania's GDP ... A court-ordered freeze on its [Yukos's] assets in Russia since last year [2004] has not been applied to its controlling stake in Mazeikiu Nafta ... [Russia says] that Yukos still owed more than $2 billion in tax but was not taking active steps to settle the debt.
>
> (*IHT*, 30 June 2005, p. 15)

30 June 2005.

> Two men received long prison sentences for the [November] 1998 murder of Galina Starovoitova, one of Russia's best known champions of democracy ... in St Petersburg ... Liberal politicians immediately claimed the killing was politically motivated, but there was also speculation that it could have been linked to her efforts to expose business corruption and organized crime ... A lawyer for Ms Starovoitova's family said they were satisfied that the court 'recognized that the killing was politically motivated' ... The St Petersburg city court sentenced Yuri Kolchin to twenty years in prison for organizing Ms Starovoitova's murder and Vitali Akishin to twenty-three-and-a-half years for carrying it out.
>
> (*FT*, 1 July 2005, p. 6)

11 July 2005.

> Prosecutors said Monday [11 July] that they had opened a criminal investigation into a former prime minister, Mikhail Kasyanov, who is a potential presidential candidate and a harsh critic of President Vladimir Putin. They said they were looking into possible abuse of office and fraud in a real estate transaction by Kasyanov.
>
> (*IHT*, 12 July 2005, p. 21)

'The prosecutor-general's office said it was investigating whether Kasyanov had illegally obtained a government-owned house when he was prime minister ... and helped a friend get one' (*IHT*, 14 July 2005, p. 6).

'Prosecutors have opened a criminal investigation ... over his purchase of a luxury estate' (*The Independent*, 12 July 2005, p. 21).

'Prosecutors ... have accused Mr Kasyanov of manipulating an auction while he was prime minister, resulting in his underpaying ... for a luxury riverside villa' (*FT*, 26 July 2005, p. 8).

'Mr Kasyanov … [is accused of buying] the dacha … at a rigged auction' (*The Times*, 26 July 2005, p. 29).

13 July 2005.

> Changes to Russia's electoral laws [were] approved by the upper house of parliament yesterday [13 July] … The changes were first announced by the Kremlin last September [2004] … The new rules end the individual races that previously elected half the 450 deputies in the Duma … In future all deputies will be elected from party lists. The threshold parties must reach to enter the Duma rises from 5 per cent of the vote to 7 per cent, with parties banned from forming blocs to pass the threshold … Under the new law domestic independent observers and journalists will not be allowed to observe election counts. International observers will be permitted only by invitation. The amendments introduce electronic voting systems in some areas … They also allow people to vote in different polling stations without getting special permission from the station where they are registered.
>
> (*FT*, 14 July 2005, p. 9)

14 July 2005.

> The constitutional court … ruled that some tax crimes could be investigated beyond a three-year cut-off date … The constitutional court upheld the legality of an existing three-year time limit on tax investigations, but ruled that tax inspectors could ignore it in cases where a suspected tax dodger acted in 'bad faith'. The court did not define 'bad faith' and analysts said the ruling would encourage rigorous tax inspectors to pursue back claims unfettered by the three-year limit.
>
> (*IHT*, 15 July 2005, p. 16)

20 July 2005. Vladimir Putin: 'I am categorically opposed to foreign financing of political activities in the Russian Federation. Not a single self-respecting state permits this. And we won't permit it' (*IHT*, 21 July 2005, p. 3).

4–5 August 2005.

> Konstantin Remchukov, an assistant head of the ministry of economic development, is buying 100 per cent of the Nezavisimaya Gazeta closed-type joint stock company, which publishes the newspaper of the same name … The company has been owned by … Boris Berezovsky since 1995 … According to Konstantin Remchukov, the agreement on the sale will be signed today [5 August].
>
> (*CDSP*, 2005, vol. 57, no. 31, p. 11)

4–5 August 2005.

> A Russian mini-submarine with seven sailors aboard got caught on a fishing net and was stuck on the sea floor off Russia's Pacific Coast as oxygen supplies dwindled Friday [5 August] … The vessel's propeller became entangled

in a fishing net Thursday [4 August], trapping the craft. The mini-submarine became disabled after it was launched from a ship in a combat training exercise ... Russia asked the United States and Japan for help.

(www.iht.com, 5 August 2005)

The Russian navy worked desperately Friday to save a small military submarine that sank to the sea floor off Russia's Pacific coast. The seven sailors on board were said to have as little as a twenty-four-hour supply of air ... [But] the navy seemed unsure of the extent of its remaining air supply, with senior naval officers and spokesmen releasing estimates ... that ranged from twenty-four hours to several days ... The propeller of the vessel, which is known as *Priz* and is itself designed for undersea rescue operations, became entangled in a fishing net Thursday during a naval exercise. The submarine sank to the bottom in more than 190 metres, or 625 feet, of water off Kamchatka Peninsula ... [The Russian navy was trying to attach cables] to tow the submarine to shallow waters ... [since] the vessel was out of reach of divers and far too deep for the crew to try to escape independently ... The US Pacific Fleet said it was airlifting two remotely operated submersibles to assist in rescue efforts, while Britain said it would also send an unmanned undersea vehicle and Japan dispatched four ships to the site in response to Russian calls for help.

(*IHT*, 6 August 2005, pp. 1, 6)

There were signs yesterday [5 August] that Moscow had learned lessons from the *Kursk* crisis [of 12 August 2000]. Russia quickly sought foreign help and provided information on how the accident had happened ... During the *Kursk* incident Russian authorities refused offers of foreign help until it was too late and lied about the fate of the sailors on board.

(*FT*, 6 August 2005, p. 10)

7 August 2005.

A mini-submarine that was trapped for nearly three days under the Pacific Ocean surfaced Sunday [7 August] with all seven people aboard ... six sailors and a representative of the company that manufactured it ... alive after a British remote-controlled vehicle cut away the undersea cables that had snarled it ... Officials said the mini-submarine was participating in a combat training exercise Thursday [4 August] when it got caught on an underwater antenna assembly that is part of a coastal monitoring system ... Russia's cash-strapped navy apparently lacks rescue vehicles capable of operating at the depth where the sub was stranded. An earlier attempt to drag the vessel to shallower waters failed when cables detached after pulling it some 60 metres (65 yards). The new crisis indicated that promises by Putin to improve the navy's equipment apparently have had little effect ... The United States also dispatched a crew and three underwater vehicles to Kamchatka at Russia's request, but they were not deployed at the accident site ... The British vehicle was sent after the Russian navy made an urgent appeal for international help – unlike during the August 2000 sinking of the nuclear submarine *Kursk*, when authorities held off asking for outside assistance for days. All 118 aboard the *Kursk* died ... In an echo of the *Kursk* sinking President Vladimir Putin had made no public comment by Sunday [7 August] on the mini-sub drama. Putin remained on vacation as the *Kursk* disaster unfolded, prompting criticism that he appeared callous or ineffectual ... He was sharply criticized for his slow response to the *Kursk* crisis and reluctance to accept foreign assistance ... Defence minister Sergei Ivanov travelled to Kamchatka on Saturday [6 August].

(www.iht.com, 7 August 2005)

A small Russian submarine was freed on Sunday from its undersea entanglement by an unmanned British rescue vehicle that had cut away the nets that ensnared it ... The unmanned vessel, known as a Scorpio 45, worked for several hours trimming the material that ensnared the Russian submarine ... Uncertainties remained about how the submersible ... had become disabled and exactly what had immobilized it. Throughout the rescue operation Russian officers spoke of cables and hoses that held the craft fast, while Western naval officers said fishing nets had trapped the craft ... The rescue underscored the persistent limits of the Russian navy, which was unable to muster either a second rescue vessel or the advanced divers or unmanned vessels to free the trapped submarine on its own.

(www.iht.com, 7 August 2005)

An unmanned British submersible – accompanied on the surface by US Navy divers and a doctor – managed Sunday to cut the submarine free from fishing nets and cables that had ensnared it seventy-six hours earlier. The operation was a five-hour race against time ... Much remains uncertain, including what exactly ensnared the small submarine ... According to officials and Russian news reports, the submarine had been conducting routine maintenance on an underwater surveillance system ... The British vessel found the *Priz* entangled in netting and cables, roughly 111,000 metres, or 60 nautical miles, offshore. The Scorpio's remote-controlled arms cut through at least five cables, some made of steel nearly 1.3 centimetres, or half an inch, thick [according to the Russian Navy] ... Japan also sent a rescue team, although it arrived too late to participate ... The British and the Americans were able to dispatch help quickly because a number of nations [including Russia] formed a group to facilitate submarine rescues after the *Kursk* tragedy. The group, called the International Submarine Escape and Rescue Liaison Office, is based in Norfolk, Virginia [in the United States] ... Officials said late last week its website quickly received offers of equipment from countries like Japan, Italy and Australia ... British officials had offered assistance upon hearing of the accident Friday morning in Moscow and the Russians immediately accepted ... The British submersible – known as a Scorpio 45 – is maintained by a civilian company on contract to the British Navy ... Vyacheslav Popov, a former commander of the Northern

Fleet and now a member of the upper house of parliament said: 'Five years have passed since the *Kursk* tragedy, but we still have no means to raise the submersible trapped only 190 metres [625 feet] down' ... President Vladimir Putin, as throughout the crisis, said nothing publicly ... The Kremlin did announce, however, that Putin had expressed gratitude for the assistance and had ordered [defence minister] Sergei Ivanov to investigate the circumstances of the incident.

(*IHT*, 8 August 2005, pp. 1, 5)

'The submarine had been snagged by fishing nets and cables ... The Scorpio ... arrived Saturday and spent six hours the next day cutting away the fishing net cables that had snarled the Russian vessel and its propeller' (*IHT*, 9 August 2005, p. 3).

Initially officials said the vessel was trapped in vast fishing nets. But later reports said it was also caught up in a system of underwater antennae forming part of a military coastal surveillance system. The network was described as a two-tier antennae lattice covering an area of 750 square metres ... The managing director of the British firm involved in the rescue – Rumic – told the BBC the operation had taken several hours ... 'There were a lot of fishing nets which we had to cut away, but there were no steel cables, although some of it did look like steel. Initial reports could have suggested there were steel rather than nylon nets,' Roger Chapman told the BBC.

(www.bbc.co.uk, 7 August 2005)

'[There were] just ten hours of oxygen left to breathe ... Commander Ian Riches, who led the British rescue effort, said ... he thought the men had between ten and twelve hours of oxygen left' (*The Independent*, 8 August 2005, p. 18). Commander Ina Riches: 'According to our last estimate, there were four to six hours of oxygen left' (*The Times*, 8 August 2005, p. 4). 'The seven men aboard ... had only six hours of oxygen left ... said Commander Ian Riches' (*IHT*, 9 August 2005, p. 3).

The rescue mission was an unprecedented example of military co-operation between Russia, Britain and the United States, which sent three submersible vehicles that were not used ... Lieutenant Vyacheslav Milachevsky [was] the commander of the rescued crew ... It was not until Friday evening – more than a day after the incident – that naval officials informed the family that they were racing to save the submarine's seven-man crew before their oxygen ran out.

(*The Times*, 8 August 2005, p. 4)

The Moscow press on Monday [8 August] said the crisis once again showed the obsessive secrecy of the Russian military ... The *Kommersant* daily reported that the news leaked out only after a submariner's wife called a local radio station anonymously on Friday morning – nearly twenty-four hours after the submarine radioed an emergency signal. 'As with the *Kursk*,' the *Gazeta* daily said, 'the navy command tried to cover up information about the accident, trying to deal with it themselves. Only when the situation got critical did the navy top brass appeal to foreign countries for help.'

(www.iht.com, 8 August 2005)

'Moscow newspapers criticized the Russian Navy for having waited more than a day before revealing the submarine accident, accusing it of failing to learn the lessons of the *Kursk* disaster and not investing enough in upgrading rescue operations' (*IHT*, 9 August 2005, p. 3).

9 August 2005.

Prosecutors said Tuesday that they had opened a criminal investigation into the accident ... The deputy naval prosecutor of Russia's Pacific Fleet ... said an enquiry revealed that a series of people involved allowed negligence in the organization of the submarine's work ... [Investigators] said that people under investigation had broken fleet rules by sending out one minisub by itself, instead of two.

(www.iht.com, 10 August 2005; *IHT* 11 August 2005, p. 3)

15 August 2005.

Russia had its own underwater robot, nicknamed Venom ... [and the Russia navy] has now admitted that the Russian rescue team tried to deploy Venom at the accident site ... [But the navy has admitted that] it was 'damaged by our people'.

(*The Independent*, 16 August 2005, p. 18)

18 August 2005.

China and Russia are due to begin their most ambitious joint military exercise Thursday [18 August], with naval ships, bombers, fighter planes and 10,000 troops massing on China's north-east [Pacific] coast ... China and Russia say the exercise, named 'Peace Mission 2005', is not intended to threaten other countries but to improve their ability to thwart terrorism and separatist uprisings on their borders ... China will contribute 8,000 troops, while Russia will send 1,800, including elite paratrooper and commando forces ... [In 2004] Russia sold more than $2 billion in military equipment to China – a third of its arms exports.

(www.iht.com, 17 August 2005)

'The first-ever joint military exercises China and Russia are ... [being held] over the next eight days on China's north-eastern coast' (www.iht.com, 18 August 2005). 'Thousands of Chinese and Russian troops concluded their historic first joint military exercises Thursday [25 August] with a mock invasion by paratroopers on China's east coast. The eight-day exercises ... [involved] 7,000 Chinese troops and 1,800 Russians' (www.iht.com, 25 August 2005).

The fictional scenario ... [in the] eight-day exercise ... envisages an imaginary state engulfed in a wave of violence fuelled by 'ethnic and religious differences' ... Moscow and Beijing are keen to stress that they are rehearsing a peacekeeping mission that would be conducted under United Nations auspices.

(*The Independent*, 19 August 2005, p. 27)

'The week-long games ... [involve] Vladivostok [in Russia] and the Yellow Sea' (*Guardian*, 19 August 2005, p. 15).

'"Peace Mission 2005" ... [was] launched in ... Vladivostok and involve manoeuvres in and near China's coastal province of Shandong' (*FT*, 19 August 2005, p. 8).

'Chinese and Russian troops concluded their historic first joint military exercises Thursday [25 August] with a mock invasion by paratroopers on China's east coast ... The eight-day exercises [involved] 7,000 Chinese troops and 1,800 Russians' (www.iht.com, 25 August 2005).

23 August 2005.

Mikhail Khodorkovsky ... announced last night [23 August] that he was going on hunger strike in protest at ... Platon Lebedev ... being moved into an isolation cell ... [Khodorkovsky] launched his protest – in which he vowed to deny himself water as well as food – with an attack on President Vladimir Putin. Khodorkovsky said the recent decision to move him to a cell shared with ten others and to put Platon Lebedev in an isolation cell was punishment for his outspoken attacks on the president ... Khodorkovsky had confirmed that he would stand in a by-election to the State Duma ... expected in December ... He could be allowed to run because his appeal is pending ... He would be run as an MP in the Moscow district where President Putin is registered as a voter.

(*Guardian*, 24 August 2005, p. 13)

('Mikhail Khodorkovsky ... has ended a hunger strike as a Moscow court said it could begin hearing an appeal by Mikhail Khodorkovsky and Platon Lebedev on 14 September': *FT*, 27 August 2005, p. 6.)

31 August 2005.

Mikhail Khodorkovsky ... announced Wednesday [31 August] an improbable effort to run for elected office in a special parliamentary election in December ... Technically he has the right to run ... Under the law he can run for office because his conviction is not considered final until his appeal has been exhausted. After supporters began floating the idea of a Khodorkovsky campaign, however, the authorities announced that his first appeal would be heard on 24 September. That date is well before the filing deadline ... The chairman of the election commission ... said that Khodorkovsky could run. But ... suggested that even if Khodorkovsky were to register and win the election he would be stripped of his status as a member of parliament once his conviction was upheld and that he would have to remain in prison.

(IHT, 1 September 2005, p. 7)

4 September 2005. 'President Vladimir Putin fired the head of the navy. Admiral Vladimir Kuroyedov' (*The Independent*, 5 September 2005, p. 20).

5 September 2005. 'President Vladimir Putin has … essentially proclaimed a new social policy … [He] has announced major outlays on health care, education and housing, with a total price tag on the order of 100 billion roubles' (*Izvestia*, 6 September 2005, pp. 1–2: *CDSP*, 2005, vol. 57, no. 36, p.).

8 September 2005.

> Gazprom … agreed with E.ON and BASF on Thursday [8 September] to build a Euro 2 billion pipeline to carry natural gas from Siberia to Germany … At a meeting in Berlin between Chancellor Gerhard Schröder and President Vladimir Putin, Gazprom and the two German companies signed an accord to build the 1,200-kilometre, or 750-mile, pipeline. It will increase the amount of the fuel available in Germany by 28 per cent … Russia holds a quarter of the world's natural gas reserves … [One line [will be built] by 2010 … [and] will run from Vyborg, near St Petersburg, under the Baltic Sea to the Greifswald region in eastern Germany … The group plans to extend the pipeline to the Netherlands and Britain … The companies may build a second link with the same volume to the German market … Germany already relies on Russia for a third of its natural gas imports … E.ON [is] the largest publicly traded utility in the world … BASF [is] the largest chemical company in the world … BASF's oil and gas unit [is] Wintershall.

(IHT, 9 September 2005, p. 14)

14 September 2005. 'Mikhail Kasyanov … said Wednesday [14 September] that he would run for president in 2008' (*IHT*, 15 September 2005, p. 7).

('The prosecutor-general's office has opened criminal proceedings against former prime minister Mikhail Kasyanov … [He is accused] of abuses in the purchase of a dacha: "specifically, the matter involves the illegal transfer of the government-owned properties Sosnovka-1 and Sosnovka-2 and their sale at articially low prices to commercial organizations affiliated with M. Kasyanov"': *Nezavisimaya Gazeta*, 12 July 2005, p. 1: *CDSP*, 2005, vol. 57, no. 28, p. 1. 'The prosecutor's office drops accusations [on 12 July] … Kasyanov is to be a witness': *CDSP*, 2005, vol. 57, no. 28, p. 2.]

22 September 2005.

> A Moscow court yesterday [22 September] rejected an appeal by Mikhail Khodorkovsky against his conviction for fraud and tax evasion. However, it cut his nine-year sentence to eight years … Mr Khodorkovsky's jail sentence comes into force automatically on the rejection of his appeal and disqualifies him from

running for parliament. Mr Khodorkovsky had earlier announced he would stand in a Moscow by-election on 4 December, but his registration documents sent by post last week never reached the electoral commission.

(*FT*, 23 September 2005, p. 8)

28 September 2005.

Gazprom ... yesterday [28 September] agreed to pay $13.1 billion for Sibneft ... in the largest deal in the country's history. Gazprom said it would acquire the 73 per cent of Sibneft owned by Millhouse Capital, an offshore investment company controlled by Roman Abramovich ... The move will take Gazprom's stake to 76 per cent ... The state will now control about 30 per cent of all Russian oil production ... Sibneft had been owned by companies linked to Boris Berezovsky ... and Mr Abramovich, his then junior partner. Mr Berezovsky said he had sold his part of the business to Mr Abramovich in 2000 ... Western banks ... will provide a bridge loan to Gazprom of up to $13 billion to finance the deal.

(*FT*, 29 September 2005, p. 1)

[Gazprom said it would buy] the 72.7 per cent stake in Sibneft ... The price for the effective renationalization of Sibneft is close to its current market capitalization ... However, there is no premium for control and Sibneft would have fetched a higher price in a competitive auction.

(p. 20)

In 2003 he [Abramovich] sold the company [Sibneft] to Yukos, receiving $3 billion in cash. That deal was unwound following the prosecution of Mikhail Khodorkovsky. However, the $3 billion was never paid back and Yukos still controls 20 per cent of Sibneft ... [Abramovich] has already sold out of Rusal, the world's number three aluminium producer.

(p. 26)

Roman Abramovich ... bought the Sibneft oil company from the government in 1995 for the bargain-basement price of roughly $100 million. The sale marks the first time one of Russia's oligarchs of the 1990s has successfully cashed out their Russian holdings. The others have been hounded into exile by authorities or remain in Russia ... If the deal goes through as expected it would be the largest transaction in Russian history, topping BP's $6.15 billion purchase of half of the TNK company in 2003. Gazprom and Abramovich's British holding company, Millhouse Capital, jointly announced the sale of a 72.6 per cent stake in Sibneft for $13.09 billion. Gazprom already held a 3 per cent stake in Sibneft through its banking arm ... The purchase would put roughly one-third of the country's oil production – but most of its overall energy resources when natural gas is considered as well – under state control ... Abramovich had been shedding his Russian assets. He has already sold a stake in Russia's largest aluminium company, Russian Aluminium, and the state airline, Aeroflot ... In a possible sign of good standing with the Kremlin before the deal, Putin appointed Abramovich governor of the Chukotka territory in Russia's extreme north-east this summer. He had first been elected to the post in 2000.

(*IHT*, 29 September 2005, pp. 1, 8)

'Millhouse Capital [is] a company he [Abramovich] controls with anonymous partners. Mr Abramovich is not legally required to reveal their names' (*FT*, 30 September 2005, p. 22).

It is not known how much he will make from the Gazprom–Sibneft deal ... It is unclear how large a stake Mr Abramovich has in Millhouse and who are his other shareholders. A Sibneft spokesman says the vehicle 'manages its assets on behalf of Mr Abramovich and a group of current and former Sibneft managers'.

(p. 30)

Gazprom agreed to buy most of Sibneft, the country's fifth biggest oil firm, in what will be the biggest takeover in Russian history ... Gas will still constitute 90 per cent of its production next year [2006] ... Last year [2004] Gazprom produced 20 per cent of the world's gas. It has 60 per cent of Russia's gas reserves and 16 per cent of the world's ... [There has been a] rising independent share of total gas production (14 per cent in 2004) ... [Gazprom's] taxes in 2004 accounted for around 8 per cent of federal and regional tax revenues ... [Gazprom] is obliged to sell the bulk of its gas inside Russia at regulated prices ... The average price for industrial users in Russia during 2004 was around $29 per thousand cubic metres; for exports to western Europe the average was $140 ... Gazprom receives two-thirds of its revenue from the one-third of output that it sells abroad. It says it just about breaks even on domestic sales ... [Gazprom has a] monopoly on gas exports to countries outside the former Soviet Union ... The average price for sales to former Soviet Union countries last year [2004] was $54 per thousand cubic metres ... Almost half of the EU's gas imports come from Russia ... Last month [September] Mr Putin and Gerhard Schröder, Germany's chancellor, presided over the launch of Gazprom's latest mega-project: a Euro 4 billion ($5 billion) pipeline that will run under the Baltic Sea to Germany, Gazprom's biggest foreign customer, and thence, eventually, to Britain.

(*The Economist*, 8 October 2005, pp. 87–90)

4 October 2005.

President Vladimir Putin has promised for the first time to take back from the EU illegal immigrants from Russia and neighbouring countries who entered via its borders. At a meeting in London the EU agreed in return to relax visa restrictions for Russian diplomats, businessmen and some students.

(*Guardian*, 5 October 2005, p. 16)

The EU and Russia announced an outline agreement to ease visa rules for Russians visiting the EU, following long-standing complaints about the

costs and delays of the current system. In return Moscow will take back
travellers from third countries found trying to enter the EU illegally from
Russia – an issue of particular importance to Poland and other east European states. The deal was the main achievement of yesterday's London
summit between President Vladimir Putin and EU leaders. EU officials said
the visa deal covered all twenty-five members, except the UK, Ireland and
Denmark, which have opted out of the Schengen common travel zone.

(*FT*, 5 October 2005, p. 11)

'The bloc promised to make visa applications to eleven of its twenty-five
nations easier for Russian diplomats, students and businessmen' (www.iht.com,
5 October 2005).

7 October 2005.

Japan, concerned that China will receive most of Siberia's ... annual oil and
gas exports, will urge President Vladimir Putin of Russia in November to
accelerate plans to build an oil pipeline to Japan. Russia will build a pipeline
from East Siberia to China first, and then a smaller line to the Pacific coast
near Japan, Putin said on 5 September. Gazprom, Russia's gas exporting
monopoly, will make China a priority in Asian sales [the company said on
21 September] ... China will get two-thirds of the 30 million tonnes of oil
that Russia plans to export to Asia within four years, Putin said on 8 July ...
When Putin visits Tokyo in November Japan plans to push for an $11 billion
Siberian oil pipeline directed to the Pacific, and not to China ... [Japan] said
on 7 October that Putin would be asked to reconsider Japan's offer to fund
the proposed oil pipeline to the Pacific coast and to help develop Siberian
oil fields ... [Japan] in 2003 offered Russia $7 billion of low-interest loans
in return for an oil pipeline to the Pacific coast, enabling shipments to Japan
... Russia now directs most of its ... oil and gas exports to Europe. Japan
last year [2004] received less than 1 per cent of its oil from Russia, which
supplied 8.8 per cent of China's imports. Neither Asian nation currently
buys gas from Russia, which holds the largest reserves of the fuel ...
Rosneft, Russia's biggest oil supplier to China, said on 12 October that it
had granted China Petroleum & Chemical a 25 per cent stake in a project to
develop oil and gas fields near Sakhalin Island. Rosneft and the Chinese
company, known as Sinopec, agreed to form a venture for the Sakhalin-3
project on 1 July, the day after President Hu Jintao of China met with Putin.
Russia said this month [October] that it might cancel two planned oil pipelines to the Arctic Ocean, which could help supply the United States, to
focus on expanding sales to China and the rest of Asia.

(www.iht.com, 17 October 2005)

The [Russian] government has shelved plans to build a pipeline from West
Siberia to Murmansk ... Plans to build a pipeline to China or Japan have
been discussed for years ... At a recent meeting with foreign analysts and
journalists President Vladimir Putin confirmed that Russia would first build

a pipeline from Taishet near Lake Baikal to Daqing [in China] and only later to Japan. Oil to Japan would be carried by rail until output from East Siberia justified the second part.

(FT, Survey, 11 October 2005, p. 5)

This is a policy reversal. '[On 31 December 2004] Russia approved an ... oil pipeline linking Siberia with the Pacific, effectively ending dreams of a rival project to China ... [Oil will be exported] to Japan and the United States' *(The Times*, 1 January 2005, p. 44). 'Russia will by May [2005] draw up detailed plans for the financing and construction of an estimated $11.5 billion oil pipeline to the Pacific following a decision ... to adopt a Japanese-proposed route over one that would have favoured China' *(FT*, 4 January 2005, p. 7).

18 October 2005. Alexander Yakovlev dies.

20 October 2005. 'Mikhail Khodorkovsky has been sent to Siberia to serve his eight-year sentence ... [The camp is] near the border with China' *(IHT*, 21 October 2005, p. 1). 'Platon Lebedev ... who was also sentenced to eight years, has been sent to a prison camp above the Arctic circle' (p. 11).

21 October 2005.

Roman Abramovich ... was elected for a second five-year term as governor of the desolate region of Chukotka ... across the Bering Strait from Alaska ... Lawmakers in the regional legislature in Chukotka voted unanimously to re-elect Abramovich to head the region.

(IHT, 22 October 2005, p. 4)

'Roman Abramovich ... was sworn in yesterday for a new five-year term as governor of ... Chukotka. Before the ceremony the regional legislature confirmed Mr Abramovich's appointment, which President Vladimir Putin had proposed' *(The Independent*, 22 October 2005, p. 26).

4 November 2005.

The Day of People's Unity was marked for the first time Friday [4 November] with calls for unity in the multi-ethnic country by a government that also allowed marches by nationalists ... Renamed the Day of Reconciliation and Accord after the Soviet collapse, the 7 November holiday became an occasion for communists and others nostalgic for Soviet times ... to take to the streets ... President Vladimir Putin signed a law late last year [2004] cancelling the 7 November holiday that used to commemorate the 1917 revolution and replacing it with the Day of People's Unity, a 4 November celebration of the end of Polish intervention in 1612 ... Hundreds laid red carnations at Lenin's tomb on Sunday [6 November].

(IHT, 7 November 2005, p. 3)

Officially 4 November marks the end of the Time of Troubles – a period of chaos in the early seventeenth century when Moscow's nobility, worn out by civil conflicts, swore allegiance to Polish Prince Wladislav ... At the end of 1612 Kuzma Minin, a merchant, and Prince Dmitri Pozharsky led a militia that liberated Moscow from the Poles. The following year Mikhail Romanov was elected Tsar, founding the dynasty that ruled Russia until 1917. President Putin has often equated the period of Boris Yeltsin's rule to the Time of Troubles, when the economy was weak and the nation's unity disintegrated. 'Mr Yeltsin worked in the period of revolutions. I think Russia had enough revolutions. Now we should have a period of stability and strengthening of the state institutions,' Mr Putin declared at the beginning of his presidency.

(*FT*, 4 November 2005, p. 10)

('Felix Dzerzhinsky's statue in the front of the KGB's headquarters ... [was] toppled ... in 1991 ... But another monument ... [a] bronze bust ... has been erected outside Moscow's police headquarters ... this week': *The Economist*, 11 November 2005, p. 53.)

14 November 2005.

President Vladimir Putin yesterday [14 November] promoted Dmitri Medvedev, his chief of staff ... a former lawyer ... who is also the chairman [of the board of governors] of Gazprom ... to [the position of] first deputy prime minister ... Sergei Ivanov, the defence minister ... will assume the additional role of deputy prime minister ... Both Mr Medvedev and Mr Ivanov are allies of Mr Putin from his native town of St Petersburg ... Last month [October] Mr Putin put Mr Medvedev in charge of the Council for National Projects – a body that will oversee billions of dollars of spending on social and infrastructure projects ... The appointments of Mr Medvedev and Mr Ivanov further weakens the position of Mikhail Fradkov, the prime minister.

(*FT*, 15 November 2005, p. 9)

Defence minister Sergei Ivanov was appointed a deputy prime minister and Dmitri Medvedev, previously head of the presidential administration, was made first deputy prime minister ... [There is speculation that] Medvedev could soon replace the prime minister, Mikhail Fradkov.

(*IHT*, 15 November 2005, p. 3)

'The governor of the energy-rich Tyumen region, Sergei Sobyanin ... a relative unknown ... became Mr Putin's new chief of staff' (*Guardian*, 15 November 2005, p. 23).

16 November 2005. 'Sergei Kiriyenko ... [is named] as head of Russia's Atomic Energy Agency ... Before the reshuffle ... [he] had been the presidential envoy to Russia's key industrial Volga region' (*FT*, 17 November 2005, p. 9).

20–22 November 2005. President Vladimir Putin visits Japan for three days.

Japan won a promise Monday [21 November] from President Vladimir Putin of Russia that a planned pipeline would bring Siberian oil to the

Pacific ... Putin: 'We plan to build the pipeline to the Pacific coast with eventual supplies to the Asia-Pacific region including Japan' ... The construction calendar was set for the end of next year [2006]. Later he and prime minister Junichiro Koizumi of Japan signed preliminary accords on the pipeline, which could cost $11 billion [and] run 4,100 kilometres, or 2,550 miles ... Japan had lobbied for the pipeline to the Pacific, believing that it could cut the country's reliance on imports from the Middle East by up to 15 per cent. But last summer Putin dashed Japanese hopes for an exclusive pipeline when he announced that the first leg of the pipeline would carry oil to China. Russia's ministry of industry and energy this month [November] said that work on the China phase would start next July and would be completed by the summer of 2008.

(FT, 22 November 2005, p. 17)

President Vladimir Putin ... last visited Japan in 2000 ... The dispute over the tiny wind-swept islands known as the Northern Territories in Japan and the Southern Kurils in Russia, has marred relations between Tokyo and Moscow for much of the twentieth century and has prevented them from signing a peace treaty.

(www.iht.com, 20 November 2005)

[President Vladimir Putin has] reiterated an offer first made by former Soviet leader Nikita Khrushchev in 1956. This entails giving back the two smallest island groups of Shikotan and the Habomais in return for a peace treaty that would end the formal state of war existing between Russia and Japan since the Second World War. However, this concession amounts to a mere 7 per cent of the disputed territories.

(The World Today, 2005, vol. 61, no. 12, p. 16)

23 November 2005. The State Duma passes on first reading a bill on non-government organizations (NGOs). The voting was 370 to eighteen. Three deputies abstained, while fifty-six did not vote.

If passed into law unchanged the bill would force all NGOs to register with a state commission within a year. The commission would have broad powers to demand documents on groups' finances and activities to ensure compliance with their stated goals and Russia's constitution ... Foreign NGOs would no longer be able to operate through branch offices, but would have to register as a specific form of Russian legal entity, imposing requirements such as the need for a Russian membership that many would struggle to meet.

(FT, 24 November 2005, p. 11)

The legislation as drafted would make life difficult for all international NGOs, because they could no longer function as branch or representative offices, but would have to reregister as a specific form of Russian legal entity. That would make it difficult to receive foreign funding, and impose

244 A chronology of political developments since 9 December 2000

requirements that many would struggle to meet, such as having a board of trustees comprising only permanent Russian residents.

(FT, 26 November 2005, p. 5)

Russia moved to impose greater government controls over charities and other non-government organizations ... [The] legislation would require tens of thousands of Russian organizations to register with the ministry of justice, impose restrictions on their ability to accept donations or hire foreigners and prohibit foreign organizations from opening branches in Russia ... [There are] 450,000 non-government organizations.

(IHT, 24 November 2005, pp. 1, 10)

'[The bill] would require all non-governmental organizations to register with the justice ministry. The government would oversee the organizations' activities and financial records' (*IHT*, 25 November 2005, p. 8).

Preliminary approval [was given] to the legislation, which would force 450,000 private organizations to register under tighter rules next year [2006] ... The draft ... would force foreign organizations, including some of the world's most prominent human rights and environmental organizations, to close their offices and seek to reregister as purely Russian organizations. Even if they did they would operate under new controls ... If interpreted strictly ... the legislation would prohibit Russian organizations from accepting [foreign] grants ... The legislation's critics ... cite the Kremlin's fear that foreign and domestic support of some groups could lead to political upheaval like the unrest that toppled Ukraine's autocratic government.

(p. 3)

The legislation would, among other things, keep foreign non-profit groups from having offices in Russia and deny foreign funds to Russian organizations that are suspected of engaging in undefined 'political' activities. Even the limited grants permitted under the new law would be taxed as though they were corporate profits, at rates exceeding 40 per cent. Virtually the entire non-profit sector would be affected.

(IHT, 7 December 2005, p. 8)

[The] Kremlin-backed bill [is] designed to bring non-profit organizations under greater state control. The legislation will subject Russian non-profits, which currently number about 450,000, to much stricter oversight by the government – in large part to ensure that they do not engage in political activism – and will give the courts greater powers to close them down. They may also be forbidden to receive financial assistance from foreign sources. Meanwhile, under the current version of the legislation, foreign charitable and educational groups will be forbidden to operate in Russia unless they reregister as domestic organizations – except it is unclear if they even can ... In 2004, for the first time since the fall of the Soviet Union, Freedom House – a human rights organization that rates countries around the world on their citizens' political and personal freedoms – gave Russia the lowest of the three ratings, 'not free'. In 1990 the Soviet Union was rated 'partially free'. And in the past year things have only gotten worse.

(Cathy Young, *IHT*, 30 November 2005, p. 8)

The bill ... would force all of Russia's 300,000 NGOs to reregister in the next year and increase the government's power to close NGOs for 'political extremism', or taxation or health and safety infringements. It would also make NGOs, such as Amnesty International and Human Rights Watch, reregister as Russian organizations funded with Russian money, forcing many to close.

(*The Times*, 24 November 2005, p. 40)

President Vladimir Putin (24 November):

The continuing financing of political activity from abroad should be, I think, in the field's state of vision, especially if this financing is carried out through the state channels of other countries ... [and if the organizations] are, in fact used as a tool of the foreign policy of other states.

(*IHT*, 25 November 2005, p. 3)

('[On 9 December President Vladimir Putin] asked parliament to soften a draft law that threatens to restrict the work of foreign non-governmental organizations. Mr Putin said foreign NGOs should not be required to register as Russian entities – which would have caused many of them to close down – but would have to notify the Russian authorities of their presence and activities': *FT*, 10 December 2005, p. 8).

[On 21 December the State Duma] amended [the] legislation ... but left in place core provisions ... In the second of three required votes the lower house adopted sixty-two amendments, many of them highly technical. It backed away from the requirement that international groups register as purely Russian groups, a measure that might have forced some of the world's most prominent groups to close down in Moscow. However, under the revised legislation those organizations would face new requirements to report to the authorities to show that their work and spending did not oppose Russia's national, social or cultural interests ... Russian organizations would still be required to register with a government agency, which would be empowered to review compliance with the legislation. Groups could be shut down after a single serious violation ... The amended bill won overwhelming support, with a vote of 376 to ten ... A third vote, largely a technicality, is expected by Friday [23 December]. The legislation needs the approval of the upper house and Putin.

(*IHT*, 22 December 2005, p. 3)

(The legislation was approved on its third reading in the State Duma by 357 votes to twenty with seven abstentions.) ('Senators in the Federation Council ... backed the measure [on 28 December] by a vote of 153 to one with one abstention ... President Putin now needs only to sign it into law. Sponsors of the legislation said it was necessary to stem terrorism and extremism by ensuring the government's ability to monitor groups that could be fronts for radicals': *IHT*, 28 December 2005, p. 7.)

4 December 2005.

> The final tally in Moscow's city council election ... confirmed the expected victory of United Russia ... [which] has been sweeping local elections across the country ... The final results gave United Russia 47.25 per cent in the party list vote and swept all fifteen direct elections, giving it twenty-eight of the council's thirty-five seats. The Communist Party of the Russian Federation won 16.75 per cent of the vote, gaining four seats, and the liberal bloc running under the Yabloko party banner won 11.11 per cent, or three seats. It just crossed the 10 per cent threshold required for a party to be represented in the council ... The Union of Rightist Forces [was] the second of the two large parties in the bloc ... The vote would have held few surprises if not for the supreme court's decision Friday [2 December] to remove the nationalist Rodina party from the ballot for airing what the court ruled was a racist television campaign commercial targeting illegal migrant workers. The decision helped the Communist Party win its biggest vote in Moscow in years ... Following sweeping reforms introduced by President Putin after the Beslan school siege in 2004, the leaders of the Russian regions are no longer chosen by direct elections, but approved by local legislators. That increased the city council's powers in Moscow. Mayor Yuri Luzhkov ... has said repeatedly that he will step down when his term ends in 2007.
>
> (*IHT*, 6 December 2005, p. 3)

'Only 34 per cent of Muscovites turned out to vote' (*The Economist*, 10 December 2005, p. 46).

19 December 2005.

> Donald Evans, a former US commerce secretary and a close friend of President George W. Bush, will not accept the offer of a top job at the Russian state oil company Rosneft. Evans said Monday [19 December] that he had decided against pursuing the offer ... Evans was responsible for shaping American ties with Russia while he served in the cabinet ... President Vladimir Putin raised the possibility of a top job with Rosneft during a meeting with Evans two weeks ago in Moscow ... Putin confirmed Friday [16 December] that Rosneft was seeking a 'high class' foreign manager after reports surfaced that he had offered Evans ... the post of chairman ... [The offer came] on the heels of an announcement that Gerhard Schröder, the former chancellor of Germany, had accepted a position overseeing construction of a new Russian gas pipeline to Germany.
>
> (*IHT*, 21 December 2005, p. 19)

'Gerhard Schröder left office last month [November] and last week was appointed chairman of the company overseeing ... the North European Gas Pipeline' (*IHT*, Wednesday 14 December 2005, p. 4).

'Gerhard Schröder … was appointed [on 9 December] head of the supervisory board of a high profile Russian gas pipeline project' (*FT*, 15 December 2005, p. 9).

'Within weeks of stepping down as chancellor last month [November] … Gerhard Schröder … has taken the job of chairing the pipeline consortium's shareholder committee … BASF and E.ON [are] the two German members of the pipeline consortium' (*The Economist*, 17 December 2005, p. 40). '[The] proposed 1,200-kilometre, $5 billion pipeline along the Baltic seabed … [is planned] to be completed in 2010. It will be 30 per cent costlier than an overland version' (*The Economist*, 7 January 2006, p. 64).

27 December 2005. Andre Illarionov announces his resignation as President Vladimir Putin's economic adviser.
   Andrei Illarionov:

> I accepted the position [of economic adviser to the president] almost six years ago in order to work on creating conditions for the free development of the Russian economy and for increasing the degree of economic freedom in Russia. But during those six years the situation in the Russian economy has changed radically. It is no longer possible to conduct a policy of economic freedom in the country. Whereas previously working for the state conferred a certain potential for resisting the advance of state intervention, in the past year it has become clear that more than just the policy has changed. There has been a change in the economic model under which the country is operating. The new model is corporatism, with the dominant role being played by state-owned corporations. Although 'state' in both name and status, these corporations do not pursue state-orientated goals in even the remotest sense. This has eliminated all possibility of influencing economic policy in the country. The second reason [for my resignation] is the change in the political environment. It is one thing to work in a country that is partly free (as Russia was in earlier years) and try to help the country become freer. It is another matter when the country ceases to be politically free. The things that have happened in the past two-and-a-half years are talking the country to a different level. Qualitative changes that take away a country's freedom are reason enough in themselves for reconsidering one's relationship to the state. The very nature of the Russian state has changed. This is not the kind of state I came to work for, it is not the kind of state I signed a contract with, it is not the kind of state I swore allegiance to. Therefore, now that the state's evolution has become obvious, it has become impossible for me to continue working in my recent capacity … Before I was never subjected to any sort of restrictions. Now the freedom to speak my mind has been withdrawn, and I am no longer an adviser to the president. The freedom to speak one's mind is a person's greatest freedom … I had certain apprehensions, but I never supposed that the very nature of the state would change. A state can be foolish and irrational and pursue particular interests. But those interests will be represented as national interests. That they could evolve into corporatist and private interests to such an extent is something that I did

not foresee. And in the short term I see no possibility of changing the nature of this state.

(*Kommersant*, 28 December 2005, pp. 1–2; *CDSP*, 2005, vol. 57, no. 52, pp. 2–3)

Andrei Illarionov:

There has been a change in the political regime. It is one thing to work in a partially free country, such as Russia was six years ago. But it is quite another when the country has ceased to be politically free and democratic. I did not sign a contract with such a state and, therefore, it is absolutely impossible to remain in this post ... Six years ago, when I took up this post, I devoted my work to creating the conditions for increasing economic freedoms in Russia. In the last year it has become clear that not only has economic policy become different, but the economic model itself in the country has, too ... I considered it important to remain in this post as long as I had the possibility to do something, including speaking out ... Until recently no one put any restrictions on me expressing my point of view. Now the situation has changed.

(*IHT*, 28 December 2005, p. 1; *The Independent*, 28 December 2005, p. 19; *FT*, 28 December 2005, p. 5)

Andrei Illarionov, President Vladimir Putin's chief economic adviser ... offered his resignation yesterday [27 December], saying Russia was 'no longer free' ... His announcement came a week after a press conference in which he said Russia was moving to a 'corporatist' model, dominated by state-controlled companies chaired by government representatives which did not always function according to economic criteria. He said the 'scam of the year for 2005' had been a combination of events, including several take-overs of private companies by state-controlled giants – notably the $13.1 billion acquisition of Roman Abramovich's Sibneft by Gazprom ... he also cited the Russian state's increasing tendency to use energy as a 'weapon' in relations with other countries ... Illarionov: 'In six years the situation in the Russian economy has changed radically. There is no longer any possibility of conducting a policy of economic freedom.'

(*FT*, 28 December 2005, p. 5)

As early as 2004 Andrei Illarionov called the forced sale of the Yukos oil firm's main pumping asset the 'swindle of the year'. Shortly after that comment he was stripped of his duties as the Kremlin's envoy to the Group of 8 industrial nations. Russia is set to take over the presidency of the group on Sunday [1 January 2006]. More recently ... on 21 December ... he scolded the government for what he called a 'corporatist' model that left it out of touch with the Russian people. He also said the Kremlin played favourites, unfairly attacking some businesses with back-tax claims while supporting others. He criticized the manipulation of Russia's energy reserves not merely as an instrument of foreign policy but also as what he called 'a weapon'.

(*IHT*, 28 December 2005, p. 7)

'Andrei Illarionov joined the Kremlin as an economic adviser in 2000' (*The Times*, 28 December 2005, p. 33).

18 January 2006.

> Yukos said on Wednesday [18 January 2006] that it had received a tax claim of 107 billion roubles, renewing speculation that the Kremlin planned to seize the company's remaining assets. The demand, for $3.8 billion and related to tax payments on oil exports and 2004 operations, was received [on 27 December 2005] ... Yukos said it would contest the claim, which would raise its obligations to the government to more than $10 billion. Yukos is struggling to stay in business after the government seized and sold its biggest unit in 2004 to cover back taxes and fines that had peaked at about $28 billion ... Yuganskneftegaz, formerly the biggest unit of Yukos, now belongs to the state oil company Rosneft.
>
> (*IHT*, 19 January 2006, p. 13)

> State-run energy companies now own about a third of Russian [oil] production, up from less than 10 per cent in 2004 ... Mikhail Khodorkovsky was arrested on 25 October 2003 ... Two weeks earlier Yukos stock had reached an all-time high ... valuing the company at more than $35 billion. Its market value was about $4 billion on Thursday [19 January 2006].
>
> (*IHT*, 21 January 2006, p. 19)

23 January 2006.

> Russia's federal security service ... has attacked non-governmental organizations and human rights groups, linking then with alleged espionage by British diplomats in Moscow ... The FSB yesterday [23 January] confirmed claims made in a state television programme that it had uncovered a spying operation involving four British diplomats using a transmitter hidden in a fake rock on a Moscow street. It said the spies had also financed NGOs, including the Moscow Helsinki Group, one of the most prominent human rights campaigners in Russia.
>
> (*FT*, 24 January 2006, p. 1)

'The main message ... was that some Russian charities and human rights organizations, including a highly respected Moscow Helsinki Group and Eurasia Foundation, are financed by British intelligence services' (*FT*, 25 January 2006, p. 8).

> Russia accused four British diplomats of spying and linked some of their activities to the financing of prominent private organizations, including the Eurasia Foundation and the Moscow Helsinki Group ... The scandal [is] one the most serious in years ... The nature of the espionage was shrouded in secrecy, but the link to private organizations came amid a politically charged campaign against charities and advocacy groups, many of them financed by the United States and European countries to promote democracy, independent media and other aspects of civil society ... The relation between the

espionage charges and the organizations appeared tangential, however ...
[Russia said] that one of the diplomats ... approved grants distributed by the
British government to Russian and international organizations, even as he
was involved in covert activities ... [The UK said] that: 'All of our assistance is given openly and aims to support the development of a healthy civil
society in Russia' ... Earlier last year [2005] ... Nikolai Patrushev, the
director of the Federal Security Service ... singled out several non-
governmental organizations, including the Peace Corps and a British charity,
Merlin, as fronts for foreign espionage.

(IHT, 24 January 2006, pp. 1, 8)

'The allegations centred around the alleged illegal financing of pro-democracy
and human rights groups Moscow fears that Western-funded non-governmental
organizations could be overtly fomenting a pro-democarcy uprising like the so-
called Orange Revolution in Ukraine last year [2005]' (*IHT*, 25 January 2006,
p. 8). 'The alleged espionage was reported to have been uncovered last fall
[2005]' (*IHT*, 26 January 2006, p. 3).

25 January 2006. President Vladimir Putin: 'We see that there are attempts to
work with non-governmental organizations, with the help of special services,
and that there is financing of non-governmental organizations through the channels of foreign secret services' (*IHT*, 26 January 2006, p. 3).
      Andrei Illarionov:

> Today's Russia is not the same country it was only six years ago. Back then
> the country was unsettled, tumultuous, impoverished. But it was free. Today
> Russia is different. Richer. And not free ... We live in a different country. A
> new model of the state has taken shape and put down roots. The state has
> become a corporate enterprise ... Changes in legislation and limitations on
> political activity have effectively devalued the shares held by citizens in
> what may be described as a publicly held company called 'Russian State'.
> The company has been transformed into a privately held company which the
> nominal owners – Russian citizens – no longer control. State-owned com-
> panies have become the assault weapons of the corporate state. Having mas-
> tered the main principle of state corporatism – 'privatize profit, nationalize
> loss' – they have turned to massive intervention in the private sector. The
> victims of this corporate expansion include Yuganskneftegaz, Sibneft,
> Silovoye Mashiny, Kamov, OMZ, AvtoVaz and Eastline. Companies that
> are still in private hands resemble ever more closely their state-owned sib-
> lings. Any request from the state – whether it is a donation to a 'necessary'
> project or the sale of the company itself to 'correct' buyers – is fulfilled.
> Declining is not an option. The fate of Yukos is known to all. Another
> guiding principle of the new economic model is selectivity. One company is
> confronted with the maximum possible (and sometimes impossible) tax bill;
> another gets unique exemptions. In one case the sale of shares to foreigners
> is prohibited; in another it gets overwhelming state support (along with

financing beyond any limits set by law). In one case foreign citizens are not allowed to work for a Russian company 'for reasons of state security'; in another they are eagerly recruited. One set of buyers pay one price; another five times as much. It is not only economic freedom that has left Russia. Political freedom is also gone. Political prisoners are back ... The most important mass media are under the corporation's control ... The international organization 'Freedom House', which monitors political and civil freedoms in 150 countries, reported a qualitative change in 2005: Russia moved from the group of 'partly free' countries to the 'not free' group. Others in the group are Rwanda, Sudan and Afghanistan.

(www.iht.com, 25 January 2006; *IHT*, 26 January 2006, p. 8)

27 January 2006.

The ministry of justice is trying to shut down an umbrella organization for several prominent human rights groups ... The ministry of justice has taken the Research Centre for Human Rights to court, claiming that because it has failed to provide information about itself over the past few years it should be considered non-existent. The centre was one of the first human rights associations set up in the dying days of the Soviet Union, comprising twelve high profile human rights organizations including the Moscow Helsinki Group and the Committee for Soldiers' Mothers. The ministry of justice said the situation could be reversed if the centre provided up-to-date information about its activities ... Earlier this month [January] the UK-registered Centre for Peacemaking and Community Development [was told] to stop working in Ingushetia ... The supreme court of Ingushetia said the charity did not have proper authorization. A US NGO, International Medical Corps, is under investigation ... The Federal Security Service (FSB) ... accused four British diplomats of spying and financing NGOs ... Some eighty human rights groups, led by the Moscow Helsinki Group, yesterday [27 January] condemned the FSB's accusations as slander ... The head of the Moscow Helsinki Group said the NGOs mentioned by the security services received grants and sponsorship from the UK Foreign Office openly and transparently ... A recent session of the Council of Europe Parliamentary Assembly said Russia's law on NGOs did not comply with European norms.

(*FT*, 28 January 2006, p. 6)

3 February 2006.

A court on Friday [3 February] convicted the director of a small, American-financed human rights organization of 'inciting ethnic and religious hatred' by publishing newspaper commentaries by two Chechen separatist leaders in 2004. The court imposed only a two-year suspended sentence, however ... The criminal case [was] against Stanislav Dmitrievski, director of the Russian–Chechen Friendship Society ... [The society publishes in Nizhny Novgorod] a monthly paper, *Rights Defender*, that is one of the few sources of information on the conflict in Chechnya, especially on abuses by Russian forces there ... The United States has given the group $170,000 since 2002 through the National Endowment for Democracy. The EU and Norway have also provided grants to support the group's reporting on the Chechen conflict ... The charges turned on open letters published in 2004 by Aslan Maskhadov, the Chechen leader who was killed by Russian forces in March, and by Akhmed Zakayev, the separatist spokesman granted political asylum in Britain ... A separate claim that the group owes $35,000 in back taxes and fines has been suspended – but only until the outcome of Dmitrievski's criminal trial ... [Starting on 1 April 2006] non-governmental organizations are required to seek new registrations from the authorities ... Under the new law private organizations can be closed if their directors or sponsors have been convicted of certain crimes, including extremism and inciting hatred.

(*IHT*, 4 February 2006, p. 3)

17 February 2006.

Boris Berezovsky said Friday [17 February] that he would sell all his remaining business interests in Russia and elsewhere to a partner because of unremitting pressure from the Kremlin ... His partner ... Badri Patarkatsishvili ... is a citizen of Georgia ... The only known remaining asset of the two in Russia is the Kommersant Publishing House, owner of a respected business newspaper of the same name and current affairs and hobby magazines ... Berezovsky is accused in Russia of embezzling money from Aeroflot and from the Logovaz car dealership and of financing guerrillas in Chechnya ... Patarkatsishvili is wanted for allegedly trying to orchestrate the escape in 2001 of Nikolai Glushkov, a former vice president of Aeroflot.

(*IHT*, 19 February 2006, pp. 11, 13)

2 March 2006.

An Italian parliamentary commission concluded 'beyond any reasonable doubt' that the Soviet Union was behind the attempt in 1981 to kill Pope John Paul II – a theory long alleged but never proved – according to a draft report made available Thursday [2 March]. The commission held that the Pope was a danger to the Soviet bloc because of his support for the Solidarity movement in his native Poland. Solidarity was the first free trade union in Eastern Europe ... The draft has no bearing on any judicial investigations, which have long been closed.

(*IHT*, 3 March 2006, p. 4)

10 March 2006.

A consortium of Western banks led by Société Générale ... [and] including Deutsche Bank, ING, Citibank and BNP Paribus ... filed a lawsuit in Moscow on Friday [10 March] to declare the Yukos oil company bankrupt ... Also this week managers in Moscow were openly defying orders from the leadership – who are in self-imposed exile in London ... The company's former chairman, Mikhail Khodorkovsky, is serving a sentence in a Siberian penal colony ... The fourteen Western banks are owed $482 million ... The banks join a long list of creditors in Russia, led by the tax authorities, who have a claim of more than $6 billion. Russian law gives the state priority on any assets seized by a bankruptcy judge ... Yukos has been in talks with the banks to repay the loan from proceeds of sales of foreign assets, including a refinery in Lithuania, a pipeline in Slovakia and offices in Britain and Switzerland ... The banks have already registered claims to proceeds from sales of Yukos's foreign assets in a Dutch court ... Yukos also faces suits from tax authorities and from its former production unit, now owned by Rosneft.

(*IHT*, 11 March 2006, p. 15)

15 March 2006.

Foreign banks which last week launched bankruptcy proceedings against Yukos ... had agreed to sell their debts to ... Rosneft ... three months before taking their action, it was revealed yesterday [15 March] ... [The] group of Western banks ... yesterday confirmed the entire debt had been sold to Rosneft ... The banks ... sold their outstanding loans to Rosneft on 13 December [2005]. But some maintained the deal was only completed this week ... The hearing, scheduled to start on 28 March, is seen as the end for Yukos.

(*FT*, 16 March 2006, p. 26)

17 March 2006.

The bank accounts of a foundation led by ... Mikhail Khodorkovsky were frozen by court order on Friday [17 March], a move that strongly suggests the organization is about to be shut down ... the foundation said. The foundation, Open Russia, announced it was forced to suspend its activities ... The court action followed a crackdown on non-governmental organizations that receive foreign funding, all of which will be subject next month [April] to a law signed in January restricting their activities. Although Open Russia is a domestic organization, the new provisions seemed tailored to exclude it as well, with a clause extending the restrictions to organizations founded by citizens convicted of crimes ... Its activities have been the subject of intense government interest, including a raid on its offices last autumn [2005] and at least five tax inspections.

(*IHT*, 18 March 2006, p. 3)

24–25 March 2006.

Analysts generally agree ... [that] the Motherland political project ... was conceived by the Kremlin in 2003 as an 'alternative' to the Russian Federation Communist Party ... The party's sixth congress [was held on 25 March] ... At a meeting of the party's presidium the day before [24 March] Dmitri Rogozin announced his intention to relinquish all his posts in the party. This came less than six months after Motherland was successively disqualified from virtually every regional election, including elections to the Moscow City Duma ... Mr

Rogozin confirmed that he intends to remain a member of the party On Saturday [25 March] the delegates to the congress accepted his resignation and elected as the party's new leader businessman Alexander Babakov.

(*CDSP*, 2006, vol. 58, no. 13, p. 12)

2 April 2006.

Gerhard Schröder, Germany's former chancellor, was battling yesterday [2 April] to save his political reputation amid new revelations that his government secretly agreed to underwrite a vast loan to Gazprom. Days before leaving office last November [2005] Mr Schröder's government took the highly unusual step of guaranteeing a loan for a new gas pipeline between Russia and Germany. In the event that Gazprom was unable to pay the money back, his government agreed to pay the Russian company's debt of up to Euro 900 million ... The former chancellor now earns Euro 250,000 a year as chairman of Gazprom's supervisory board ... Mr Schröder said he knew nothing of the secret agreement and said Mr Putin had offered him the Gazprom job on 9 December – after he left office.

(*Guardian*, 3 April 2006, p. 16)

4 April 2006. 'Members of the Motherland faction [in the State Duma] yesterday [4 April] accepted the voluntary resignation of Dmitri Rogozin as faction leader. Party chairman Alexander Babakov was elected as the faction's new head for the [Duma's] spring session' (*CDSP*, 2006, vol. 58, no. 14, p. 8).

8 April 2006. 'The founding conference of a new political movement, the People's Democratic Alliance (PDA), was held on Saturday [8 April]. Former prime minister Mikhail Kasyanov was elected chairman of the movement. Political veterans Irina Khakamada and Nikolai Travkin joined the alliance' (*CDSP*, 2006, vol. 58, no. 15, p. 8).

17 April 2006. 'Russia brought into force a new law Monday [17 April] that critics say gives officials a free hand to harass charities and human rights groups that the government does not like. The law regulates the activities of nongovernmental organizations' (*IHT*, 18 April 2006, p. 3).

19 April 2006.

A Moscow court on Wednesday [19 April] sentenced a lawyer for ... Yukos to seven years in prison for embezzlement and tax evasion ... Svetlana Bakhmina has been in custody since her arrest in December 2004 in connection with an asset-stripping investigation at Yukos's Tomskneft subsidary.

(*IHT*, 20 April 2006, p. 3)

26 April 2006.

President Vladimir Putin declared on Wednesday [26 April] that an oil pipeline being built across Siberia should be rerouted away from the northern shore of Lake Baikal, one of the world's natural landmarks. Putin's unexpected edict reversed a controversial government decision last month [March] to allow the country's pipeline monopoly, Transneft, to build the line within a half mile of Lake Baikal, the world's most voluminous body of fresh water ... holding more than 20 per cent of the world's fresh water ... The pipeline, a \$11.5 billion, 2,000-mile, or 4,023-kilometre, project to pump Russia's oil to markets in Asia, prompted rare public protests following the approval of the initial route in March ... [Putin] said a new route should be charted at least 40 kilometres from Lake Baikal. That would push it outside of Baikal's watershed ... [Transneft] previously said that the planned route would be safe and that moving it could add nearly a billion dollars to the cost of the pipeline.

(*IHT*, 27 April 2006, p. 3)

10 May 2006. President Vladimir Putin delivers his seventh state of the nation address to parliament.

President Vladimir Putin:

Despite the efforts that are being made, we have still not succeeded in removing one of the most serious obstacles in the path of our development – corruption ... The goal of doubling GDP in ten years was articulated for the first time in my annual message in 2003. It is not hard to calculate that in order to achieve that result, our economy must grow at an annual rate of a little over 7 per cent ... In my annual message in 2003 I posed the task of making the rouble fully convertible ... Today I am proposing that we speed the removal of all remaining restrictions and complete that work by 1 July of this year [2006] ... And now for the most important thing ... Present-day Russia's most pressing problem [is] demography ... The average number of people living in our country is shrinking by almost 700,000 a year. We have raised this subject repeatedly, but we have really done very little about it. Solving this problem will require the following: First, a reduction in mortality. Second, an effective migration policy. And third, an increase in the birth rate ... As for improving migration, policy the priority in this area is still to attract our compatriots from outside the country. At the same time we must increasingly provide incentives for an influx of skilled immigrants ... I am proposing a programme to boost the birth rate ... I consider it necessary to drastically increase child-rearing benefits for children under the age of eighteen months ... It is necessary ... to work out a programme of financial incentives for families to adopt or foster orphans and abandoned children ... The mechanism should be launched as of 1 January 2007 ... The armed forces' mobilization resources will be upgraded. More than two-thirds of our military personnel are to be professionals by 2008. All these things are enabling us to shorten the term of conscript service to twelve months ... The armed forces stationed in the Chechen republic are manned with soldiers serving under contract. And on 1 January 2007 the internal affairs ministry troops in Chechnya will likewise shift to service under contract.

(*CDSP*, 2006, vol. 58, nos 18–19, pp. 7–10)

Putin: 'No amount of migration will solve our demographic problems unless we create the appropriate conditions and incentives to increase the birth rate here, at home, in our own country; unless we adopt efficient programmes to support mothers, children and families' (www.bbc.co, 10 May 2006).

> President Putin said Russia's population had witnessed an annual decline of 700,000 people, because of low birth rates, high mortality and migration. He outlined a ten-year programme to try to reverse the situation. One of the key elements of the programme, he said, was an increase in childcare benefits to support young mothers, especially those who had a second child. Russia's population is estimated to be just under 143 million people.
>
> (www.bbc.co.uk, 10 May 2006)

'Russia's population has been falling since before the collapse of the Soviet Union' (www.iht.com, 10 May 2006).

> President Vladimir Putin: 'The situation is critical in that sphere ... Russia's most acute problem today [is] demography' ... In 2004 for every 16 Russians who died, only 10.4 babies were born ... The average age of death for a Russian man was 58.9 years, far below other industrial nations and roughly two decades behind the average age of death of an American male.' Birth rates have also plummeted since Soviet times, falling from an average of 2.63 children per woman in 1958 and 1959 to 1.89 children per woman in 1990 and to 1.34 children per woman in 2004.
>
> (*IHT*, 11 May 2006, pp. 1, 7)

'Russia's population has fallen from 148 million when the Soviet Union collapsed to less than 143 million today' (*The Times*, 11 May 2006, p. 36).

12 May 2006.

> The head of the federal customs service, two of his deputies, three Federal Security Service (FSB) generals, two prosecutors and five internal affairs ministry investigators were simultaneously removed from their post yesterday [12 May]. None of the organizations in question explained the reasons for what had occurred. Most likely the dismissals stemmed from an investigation ... of criminal cases involving corruption in the customs service. It is already obvious, however, that the Kremlin has launched a high-visibility anti-corruption campaign; also yesterday Sergei Mironov, the speaker of the Federation Council sent requests for several regions to terminate the tenure of four senators simultaneously.
>
> (*Kommersant*, 13 May 2006, p. 1: *CDSP*, 2006, vol. 58, no. 20, p. 1)

'Sergei Mironov categorically rejected speculation that his initiative was somehow linked to the firings in law-enforcement and security organizations' (*CDSP*, 2006, vol. 58, no. 20, p. 5). 'President Vladimir Putin [has] issued a decree taking the federal customs service out of the ministry of economic development and trade and placed it under the prime minister' (p. 3).

2 June 2006.

President Vladimir Putin yesterday [2 June] … unexpectedly removed the country's hard-line chief prosecutor … Vladimir Ustinov … [He] was relieved of his duties by parliament at the request of the president … Mr Ustinov's dismissal was a serious blow to Igor Sechin, a powerful deputy head of the Kremlin administration … Analysts said Mr Ustinov's dismissal was a sign of the strengthening of Sergei Ivanov, the powerful defence minister and another candidate to succeed Mr Putin as president in 2008.

(*FT*, 3 June 2006, p. 6)

Vladimir Ustinov was appointed in 1999 by Boris Yeltsin and was the longest serving figure in this administration … Putin has dismissed relatively few high-profile officials, other than his first prime minister, Mikhail Kasyanov. But three weeks ago he removed the chief of the customs service and a dozen other officers in what was described as a newly energized fight against a deeply corrupted bureaucracy … The dismissal of Ustinov required a vote of the upper house of parliament. The vote was held without deliberation and was unanimous except for two abstentions … Along with speculation about Putin's motives, contradictory statements abounded among Putin's political allies … Ustinov was widely regarded as a hawk among Putin's advisers from security and law-enforcement backgrounds, known as *siloviki*. The faction is led by the deputy chief of the presidential administration, Igor Sechin. Another faction is made up of aides who are viewed as comparatively liberal and who are aligned with … Dmitri Medvedev.

(*IHT*, 3 June 2006, p. 3)

('President Vladimir Putin on Friday [23 June] appointed … in a decree … former chief prosecutor Vladimir Ustinov … to be Russia's new justice minister. The decision suggested that the prosecutor's removal was less dramatic a shake-up than officials close to the Kremlin initially claimed … He was replaced this week with Yuri Chaika, the justice minister he is now replacing … Some reports in the Russian media suggested that among … the *siloviki*, a cadre of security and law enforcement officials … he [Ustinov] was the preferred candidate to replace Putin when he is required to step down in 2008 … [One theory is] that Putin had sidelined Ustinov … that the prosecutor's office had grown too independent': *IHT*, 24 June 2006, p. 3.)

7 June 2006.

The government yesterday [7 June] approved the liberalization of the electricity sector from next year [2007] and cleared the way for the listing of generating assets on foreign exchanges … Anatoli Chubais, head of the Unified Energy System … masterminded Russia's most complicated industry restructuring when he took over the monopoly in 1998. His plan sees the separation of power generation from transmission and distribution networks with a subsequent sale of generating companies.

(*FT*, 8 June 2006, p. 8)

The monopoly will be split up into electricity generation companies, to be listed on foreign and Russian stock exchanges, the state-controlled grid and dispatching companies. At present the state owns 52 per cent of UES. After restructuring the government share in generating companies will fall to below 50 per cent. At the same time the government will increase its share in the grid company and dispatching units to 75 per cent plus one share. But instead of swapping assets with private investors in UES as previously suggested, the government plans to buy additional shares in the grid and dispatching units – a move implying a massive subsidy for the electricity sector.

(*FT*, 12 June 2006, p. 6)

Roman Abramovich was reported yesterday [7 June] to have bought *Kommersant*, the business daily ... [that is] the most aggressively independent news outlet in the country ... Boris Berezovsky sold it to Badri Patarkatsishvili, his Georgian business partner, in February ... Separately, Mikhail Gorbachev announced that he and a business partner had bought a significant share in *Novaya Gazeta* to try to preserve its independence ... Mr Gorbachev said that he and Alexander Lebedev had bought a 49 per cent share in the newspaper, which has a reputation for good investigative journalism but suffers chronic financial problems. The remaining 51 per cent is owned by the staff of the paper. Mr Lebedev is a wealthy businessman, a member of parliament and a prominent anti-corruption crusader.

(*The Times*, 8 June 2006, p. 31)

5–17 July 2006. The G8 summit meeting is held in St Petersburg.

[The G7] nations – the United States, Japan, Germany, France, Britain, Italy and Canada – have met annually since 1975 [following the OPEC oil price increases in the winter of 1973–4]. Russia joined in 1998, turning the G7 into the G8. The 2006 summit is to be held in St Petersburg – the first time Russia has hosted the G8. Energy security, infectious diseases and education are on Russia's [scheduled] agenda.

(www.bbc.co.uk, 15 July 2006)

Leaders of the Group of 8 nations began a full day of discussions Sunday [16 July] and issued joint declarations calling for enhancing energy security, fighting infectious diseases and improving education. But the summit was overshadowed by escalating violence in the Middle East and concerns over nuclear programmes in Iran and North Korea ... [On Saturday 15 July] President George W. Bush and President Vladimir Putin announced they had failed to come to an agreement on Russia's accession to the WTO, and aides said that the deal, which had been expected as early as this weekend, was not likely for months. Bush and Putin also expressed differences over Iraq, the state of Russia; democracy and Israel's military campaign in Lebanon ... A few positive announcements [were made] ... agreeing on initiatives to combat nuclear terrorism and share civilian nuclear material and technology ... Bush and Putin agreed to start talks to pave the way for a deal allowing nuclear waste generated from American-produced plutonium from around the world to be stored in Russia – a potential shift in US policy that would be lucrative for Russia. The United States would gain access to Russian uranium.

(www.iht.com, 16 July 2006)

Russia's bid to join the WTO stalled over its barriers to US meat exports, officials from both countries said Sunday [17 July]. Talks broke down as Russia insisted on auditing the US system for certifying livestock at pork and beef producers.

(*IHT*, 17 July 2006, p. 9)

The leaders of the G8 industrialized nations met Monday [17 July] for the final session of the three-day summit meeting ... trying to focus on the matters that had been shunted aside by the violence in the Middle East: global trade talks, debt relief and energy security.

(www.iht.com, 17 July 2006)

Russia and the United States failed on Saturday [15 July] to reach a deal on Moscow's WTO membership. The two governments have now set an October deadline for a deal that could potentially clear the way for Russia to join the 149-nation trade group by next spring [2007]. The United States is the last big partner with which Moscow has still to reach a bilateral deal after thirteen years of negotiations on WTO entry, while Russia remains the biggest economy yet to join the trade body.

(*FT*, 17 July 2006, p. 6)

The Group of 8 industrialized nations papered over their differences on energy security, declaring a general commitment to 'open, transparent, efficient and competitive' markets ... [But Russia] once again refused to ratify the Energy Charter, which would require it to open up access to its pipelines ... A law passed this month [July], awaiting President Putin's signature, legitimizes Gazprom's monopoly over export pipelines.

(*FT*, 17 July 2006, p. 6)

A G8 statement said:

'We support the principles of the Energy Charter and the efforts of participating countries to improve energy co-operation' ... The Energy Charter [is] an international rule book ... Although Russia has not ratified it, the charter is binding unless it cuts across national laws. To protect Gazprom, Russian lawmakers this month [July] wrote its monopoly into law.

(*IHT*, 17 July 2006, pp. 1, 4)

The statement issued Sunday [16 July] said the Group of 8 countries 'support the principles' of the Energy Charter, a treaty intended to integrate the oil and natural gas industries in former Soviet countries with Europe.

Russia has signed but not ratified the document, and the wording left unanswered the questions of access to Russian pipelines by independent companies or third countries ... Countries producing oil and other fossil fuels should open their energy industries to outside investment, crack down on corruption and prevent waste such as burning natural gas at oil fields, a practice called flaring and widespread in Siberia, leaders of the Group of 8 countries said.

(www.iht.com, 17 July 2006)

The International Energy Charter is important because it bars energy suppliers from interrupting or reducing energy exports as a result of transitory disputes ... Major energy players such as the United States and Norway have also signed, but not ratified, the Charter ... Russia has 34 per cent of the world's proven natural gas reserves and 13 per cent of those in oil ... Russia provides Europe with about one-third of its gas, with most of the remainder coming from Algeria and Norway ... Two-thirds of Russian hydrocarbons [are] exported to the expanding EU market.

(*Newsbrief*, July 2006, pp. 79–80)

'Leaders of China, India, Brazil, South Africa and Mexico join the summit today [17 July]' (*FT*, 17 July 2006, p. 6).

The G8 powers brought in the leaders of Brazil, China, India, Mexico and South Africa as guests. The expanded group met Monday [17 July] ... Assistance to Africa ... was also on the agenda for the session to be attended by the UN secretary-general, Kofi Annan, and the African Union.

(www.iht.com, 17 July 2006)

16 August 2006.

A Russian patrol boat opened fire on a Japanese vessel in disputed waters Wednesday [16 August], killing a fishermen and triggering a harsh protest from Tokyo ... The surviving crew and the boat was seized by Russian authorities ... The crab fisherman was shot and killed near Kaigara Island, one of several islands off the north-east of Hokkaido that are claimed by both Japan and Russia ... The four islands [are] called the Kurils in Russia and the Northern Territories by Japan ... The sparsely populated four islands – three islands and an island group – were seized by the Soviet army in the closing days of World War II. Tokyo calls the occupation illegal and wants them returned, and the territorial dispute has kept the two countries from signing a formal treaty ending wartime hostilities ... President Vladimir Putin has offered to revive a 1956 Soviet–Japanese declaration under which Moscow had agreed to return two of the islands, but Tokyo rejected the proposal as insufficient and talks on the issue are deadlocked ... While the Russian authorities have seized dozens of Japanese boats and wounded several fishermen over the years, this was the first shooting death of a Japanese since October 1956. Japanese coastguard officials said ... The Japanese fishing agency acknowledged that crab fishing in that area is illegal, though it is said it was unclear whether the boat was illegally fishing at the time of the shooting. The foreign ministry insisted the boat was in Japanese waters. A total of thirty fishing boats and 210 Japanese crew members were seized by Russia in the disputed northern waters between 1994 and 2005, and seven other fishermen were wounded when the Russian coastguard fired at them during the same period, according to the Japanese coastguard.

(www.iht.com, 16 August 2006)

30 August 2006. 'It was learned yesterday [30 August] that Alisher Usmanov, co-owner of the Metalloinvest Holding Company, has acquired the Kommersant Publishing House Closed Joint Stock Company' (*CDSP*, 2006, vol. 58, no. 35, p. 6).

4 September 2006.

Russia on Monday [4 September 2006] agreed with Greece and Bulgaria to speed up preparations for a 285-kilometre ... 175-mile ... Balkan pipeline to transport Russian oil to Europe and the United States ... The $900 million project would be signed by the three countries before the end of 2006 ... For years the countries have disagreed on central issues ... Originally drawn up in 1993, the plan envisages transporting Russian oil by sea to the Bulgarian port of Burgas, and from there by pipeline to the Greek port of Alexandroupolis on the Aegean Sea ... It expected completion [is] in 2009 or 2010 ... The pipeline is intended to reduce the expense and time of transporting Russian oil from the Caspian Sea to Europe and the United States, as well as to reduce environmental risks from spills. Oil tankers currently have to negotiate the narrow Bosphorus Strait, where increasing traffic has raised concerns over congestion. The pipeline will rival the new $4 billion Baku–Ceyhan pipeline from Azerbaijan to the Mediterranean that bypasses Russian oil ... The Baku–Ceyhan pipeline [is] a major US-backed project that was inaugurated in July [2006] by the leaders of Azerbaijan, Georgia and Turkey ... Russia supplies half of natural gas imports to Europe and a quarter of its oil ... Combined with a Turkish–Greek–Italian pipeline that is expected to start pumping natural gas from the Caspian Sea and the Middle East to Europe by early next year [2007], the pipeline would help turn Greece into a South-east European energy hub.

(*IHT*, 5 September 2006, p. 11)

5 September 2006. 'President Vladimir Putin arrived in South Africa for a two-day visit, the first ever for a Kremlin leader ... Trade between Russia and South Africa is miniscule – less than $125 million during the first nine months of 2005' (*IHT*, 6 September 2006, p. 3).

14 September 2006.

A top Russian banker who had fought to clean up the country's murky banking system died early Thursday [14 September] from gunshot wounds after being ambushed by assassins in what the police said was a contract hit. The killing of Andrei Kozlov, forty-one, respected first deputy chairman of the central bank, was the highest profile assassination in Moscow during the six years president Vladimir Putin has been in power. Kozlov had led a vigorous campaign to close banks suspected of involvement in money laundering ... Since 1995 twenty-four Russians who held senior posts in the country's banks have been assassinated ... Russia has about 1,200 banks. Many of them are tiny institutions with little capital and banking experts say allegations of malpractice are common. Contract-style killings of wealthy businessmen and bankers were common in the 1990s but they tapered off after Putin came to power in 2000. Kozlov's killing is the highest profile attack in the capital since Anatoli Chubais ... escaped unscathed from an assassination attempt in March 2005 when his motorcade was attacked.

(www.iht.com, 14 September 2006)

Andrei Kozlov ... [was] leading a campaign to clean up the country's more than 1,200 banks, some of which remain little more than fronts for illicit business or organized crime. He had withdrawn the licences of forty-four banks suspected of involvement in money laundering or other crimes already this year [2006], and fourteen last year [2005] ... Kozlov was the architect of a state-backed deposit insurance scheme, protecting depositors in the event of banks going bust, that now covers more than 900 banks. That, however, came into force only after Kozlov had helped trigger a mini banking crisis in 2004 by using new money laundering legislation to withdraw the licence of Sodbiznesbank, accusing it of laundering ransom money ... [Last week Kozlov called for] lifetime bans on bankers found guilty of banking crimes – designed to prevent those running banks that lost their licences from simply setting up new outfits and carrying on. He was widely expected to clamp down further on so-called 'pocket' banks that essentially served single oligarchs.

(*FT*, 16 September 2006, p. 6)

5 October 2006.

On 5 October President Vladimir Putin ... denounced the 'semi-gangs, some of them ethnic' that control Russia's wholesale and retail markets, where many migrants work. He said markets should be regulated 'with a view to protect the interests of Russian producers and population, the native Russian population'. Putin's remarks echoed complaints voiced widely last month [September] in Kondopoga, a small mill town in northern Russia. A bar fight there ended with the deaths of two ethnic Russians and led to a violent rampage on 2 October that destroyed markets and businesses owned by Chechens and other immigrants, who fled the town in fear. A common grievance heard afterwards was that the newcomers had criminally cornered the city's markets. Putin said a month later: 'Criminal groups play a major role in markets. And all of this results in our citizens being rightly indignant.'

(*IHT*, 23 October 2006, p. 3)

7 *October 2006.*

Anna Politkovskaya was found shot dead on Saturday [7 October] ... The forty-eight-year-old mother of two was known as a fierce critic of the Kremlin's actions in Chechnya ... Anna Politkovskaya worked for the newspaper *Novaya Gazeta* and was known for exposing rights abuses by Russian troops in Chechnya. She also acted as a negotiator with the Chechen rebels who held a siege in a Moscow theatre in 2002. She had received death threats in the past and suspicions were immediately raised that her death was a contract killing ... [She] became ill with food poisoning on her way to report on the Beslan school siege in 2004, which some believed to be an attempt on her life. In 2001 she fled to Austria after receiving email threats claiming a Russian police officer she had accused of committing atrocities against civilians wanted to take his revenge ... She was one of the few remaining high profile independent journalists in Russia.

(www.bbc.co.uk, 8 October 2006)

Anna Politkovskaya, the veteran Russian journalist and author who made her name as a searing critic of the Kremlin and its policies in Chechnya ... She was a special correspondent for the *Novaya Gazeta* newspaper and had become one of the country's most prominent human rights advocates ... [She] often spoke abroad about a war she called 'state versus group terrorism'. She was a strident critic of Putin, whom she accused of stifling civil society and allowing a climate of official corruption and brutality ... Mikhail Gorbachev, a shareholder of the newspaper where Politkovskaya worked, called her killing 'a savage crime' ... [She] had worked for *Novaya Gazeta* since 1999 and covered the second Chechen war and the terrorist siege of a Moscow theatre in 2002. One of her books, *A Small Corner of Hell: Dispatches from Chechnya*, recorded her impressions of the war's unrelenting and often macabre cruelty and the manifest corruption of many of its participants. She wrote of torture, mass executions, kidnappings to gain ransom and to eliminate rebel suspects, and the sale by Russian soldiers of Chechen corpses to their families for proper Islamic burial. Her writings cemented her place as one of the world's most vocal domestic critics ... She wrote: 'The army and police, nearly 100,000 strong, wander around Chechnya in a state of complete moral decay. And what response could one expect but more terrorism, and the recruitment of new resistance fighters?' ... At least twelve journalists have been killed in Russia in contract-style murders since 2000, according to the Committee to Protect Journalists. None has been solved, including the contract killing in 2004 of Paul Klebnikov, the American editor of *Forbes* magazine's Russian language edition. Politkovskaya had received death threats in the past, and at least once had left the country fearing for her safety. In 2004 she claimed to have been poisoned while en route on an airplane to cover the school siege in Beslan ... Vitali Yaroshevsky, the deputy editor of *Novaya Gazeta*, said that Politkovskaya had been at work on Saturday finishing an article for the Monday paper about torturers in the government of Ramzan Kadyrov, the pro-Kremlin premier of Chechnya ... In an interview in April with *The New York Times*, Politkovskaya said she had evidence of torture in Chechnya by Kadyrov's police and other gunmen, including at least one witness who had been tortured by Kadyrov himself. Kadyrov himself has always denied such allegations.

(www.iht.com, 8 October 2006; *IHT*, 9 October 2006, pp. 1, 8)

President Vladimir Putin broke two days of silence Monday [9 October] over the murder of Anna Politkovskaya ... According to a statement issued by the Kremlin, Putin told President George W. Bush in a telephone conversation initiated by the White House that 'law enforcement bodies will take all necessary measures for an objective investigation into the tragic death' ... Putin's remarks were the first [on her death].

(*IHT*, 10 October 2006, p. 3)

Anna Politkovskaya ... became the thirteenth [reporter] to be killed since Vladimir Putin became president ... There was no comment from Putin for two days after her death, and then only a brief announcement from his office that the murder would be investigated ... According to the Committee to Protect Journalists, Russia has become the third deadliest country for journalists over the past fifteen years – after Iraq and Algeria.

(p. 8)

'According to the New York-based Committee to Protect Journalists, Politkovskaya was at least the forty-third reporter killed for her work in Russia since 1993' (www.iht.com, 10 October 2006). (Anna Politkovskaya was the third journalist from *Novaya Gazeta* to be killed.)

('Colleagues of the murdered journalist Anna Politkovskaya put out a sixteen-page newspaper last week with tributes to her investigations of human rights abuses, excerpts from her writing, and a list of the 211 journalists who have been killed in Russia since 1992': *IHT*, 1 November 2006, p. 8.)

Anna Politkovskaya was best known for fearless reporting on the brutality of both Russians and Chechens in the war ... But she also probed official corruption, notably in the Russian army and was a harsh critic of the administration of Vladimir Putin, accusing it of stifling freedoms ... [She] was the thirteenth Russian journalist to die in contract killings since 2000 ... [according to] the New York-based Committee to Protect Journalists.

(*FT*, 9 October 2006, p. 6)

'Twenty-three journalists were killed in the country between 1996 and 2005, many in Chechnya, according to the New York-based Committee to Protect Journalists. At least twelve have been murdered in contract-style killings since Vladimir Putin came to power' (www.cnn.com, 8 October 2006).

There have been thirteen killings since Putin came to power in 2000 ... Anna Politkovskaya's killing was the third mob-style assassination of prominence in the last month alone ... Andrei Kozlov, the first deputy chairman of the central bank, was killed on 13 September. Less than two weeks later, Enver Ziganshin, the chief engineer of Kovytka, a potentially lucrative gas field in Siberia at the centre of a dispute with the government, was shot.

(*IHT*, 11 October 2006, p. 3)

The funeral of Anna Politkovskaya [took place on 10 October] ... Russia's ombudsman for human rights ... Vladimir Lukin ... [was] one of the few government officials to attend the funeral, though hardly one of the highest rank ... Several foreign diplomats [attended, including the US and British ambassadors] ... President Vladimir Putin, travelling in Germany, spoke about the death publicly for the first time ... Speaking without emotion Putin said: '[The] horrible [killing was] an unacceptable crime that cannot go unpunished. The killing inflicts much greater damage to the government than any of her writing. I think that journalists should know, and experts should understand, that her ability to influence political life in Russia was extremely insignificant in scale. This journalist was a sharp critic of the government in Russia, but the level of her influence on political life in Russia was very minor.'

(*IHT*, 11 October 2006, p. 3)

10 October 2006.

A manager at one of the largest Russian banks was shot and killed ... in an apparent contract killing ... Alexander Plokhin was a former low ranking government official ... The killing might have been linked to his job at a Moscow branch of the state-controlled Vneshtorgbank ... Enver Ziganshin, the chief engineer at a subsidiary of TNK-BP, was fatally shot two weeks earlier ... Andrei Kozlov was killed on 13 September.

(*IHT*, 12 October 2006, p. 15)

21 October 2006.

Ahead of her meeting with President Vladimir Putin, [US secretary of state] Condoleezza Rice met the editors and son of the murdered journalist Anna Politkovskaya ... Ms Rice had requested the meeting with Anna Politkovskaya's son, Ilya Politkovsky, and *Novaya Gazeta*'s editor-in-chief Dmitri Muratov. A [US] State Department official said the meeting was not meant as a slight to Mr Putin, but was to show support for what was left of the free media in Russia.

(www.bbc.co.uk, 21 and 22 October 2006)

27 October 2006.

Russia surpassed the United States in 2005 as the leader in weapons deals with the developing world, and its new agreements included selling $700 million in surface-to-air missiles to Iran and eight new aerial refuelling tankers to China, according to a new [US] congressional study ... delivered to members of Congress on Friday [27 October] … Those weapons deals were part of the highly competitive global arms bazaar in the developing world, which grew to $30.2 billion in 2005, up from $26.4 billion in 2004. It is a market that the United States has regularly dominated. Russian agreements with Iran are not the biggest part of its total sales – India and China are its principal buyers … Among other arms transfers described in the study was a statistic that a single, unnamed nation – but one identified separately by Pentagon and other administration officials to be North Korea – shipped about forty missiles to other nations in the four-year period ending in 2005, the only nation to have done so. Transfers of these weapons are prohibited under international agreements to control the trade of ballistic missiles … The report, *Conventional Arms Transfers to Developing Nations*, found that Russian arms agreements with the developing world totalled $7 billion in 2005, an increase from its $5.4 billion in sales in 2004. That figure surpassed the United States' annual sales agreements to the developing world for the first time since the collapse of the Soviet Union. France ranked second in arms transfer agreements to developing nations, with $6.3 billion, and the United States was third, with $6.2 billion. The leading buyer in the developing world was India, with $5.4 billion in weapons purchases, followed by Saudi Arabia with $3.4 billion and China with $2.8 billion. The total value of all arms sales deals worldwide, counting both developing and developed nations was $44.2 billion in 2005 … Russia agreed in 2005 to sell China eight of the IL-78M aerial refuelling tankers … In 2005 the United States led in total arms transfer agreements, when deals to both developed and developing nations are combined. The total was $12.8 billion, down from $13.2 billion in 2004 … France ranked second in total sales, with $7.9 billion, up from $2.2 billion in 2004. Russia was third when total sales were considered, with $7.4 billion, up from $5.6 billion in 2004.

(www.iht.com, 29 October 2006; *IHT*, 30 October 2006, pp. 1, 7)

Russia captured almost a quarter of the arms market in the developing world in 2005 … The report named China, India and Iran as the Kremlin's best customers … The report … entitled *Conventional Arms Transfers to Developing Nations* … covered government arms deals but excluded agreements by commercial dealers. France, the United States and the UK [$2.4 billion] took second, third and fourth place respectively … The biggest arms dealer [in total] remains the United States. It made arms deals last year [2005] worth a total of $12.8 billion and was involved in almost a third of all transactions.

(*The Independent*, 31 October 2006, p. 20)

15 November 2006.

President George W. Bush and President Vladimir Putin sat down Wednesday [15 November] for lunch and informal talks on ongoing nuclear disputes with North Korea and Iran, as the US leader paid an unusual visit to

Moscow en route to a summit of ... Pacific Rim leaders in Vietnam [where they will meet again].

(www.iht.com, 15 November 2006)

16 November 2006.

The government ... approved laws banning non-Russians from key sectors of the economy. From January [2007] foreigners will not be allowed to sell alcohol or medicine, and from April they will be banned from working in the retail sector. The ban extends to Russia's indoor and outdoor food and clothing markets, as well as to thousands of roadside kiosks selling anything from newspapers to cosmetics. The jobs affected are typically low paid and are often done by immigrants from former Soviet republics such as Tajikistan, Georgia and Azerbaijan. Nobody precisely knows how many people will be forced out of work, but the figure is estimated to be at least 1 million people.

(*The Independent*, 17 November 2006, p. 26)

President Vladimir Putin approved plans to bar foreigners from trading at street stalls and markets. Immigrants from former Soviet republics such as Georgia, Azerbaijan and Uzbekistan dominate markets in Russia, mainly selling fruit and vegetables ... The ban will begin with a transitional phase from 1 January [2007] when foreign small traders will not be allowed to sell alcohol and medicines.

(*Guardian*, 17 November 2006, p. 26)

17 November 2006. 'The lower house of parliament has approved a change to the electoral law that scraps a minimum turnout in elections. The move appears to be linked to voter apathy, the biggest threat to Kremlin-backed candidates' (*The Times*, 18 November 2006, p. 55).

19 November 2006.

UK police are investigating after a Russian former security agent in exile in Britain was poisoned by thallium. Alexander Litvinenko, a former KGB colonel and critic of President Vladimir Putin, fell ill on 1 November after a meeting at a London sushi bar. A clinical toxicologist said the forty-three-year-old had been given a potentially lethal dose of the poison. He is in a serious but stable condition in University College Hospital, London. He is reported to be under armed guard. Mr Litvinenko said he had been investigating the murder of Anna Politkovskaya ... Speaking to the BBC last week he said a contact had approached him to say they should talk and they arranged to meet at a restaurant ... Mr Litvinenko fled Russia and was granted political asylum in Britain in 2001 ... Mr Litvinenko had earlier alleged that members of the Federal Security Service (FSB) had plotted to kill Boris Berezovsky. In his book *Blowing up Russia: Terror from Within* [published in 2001] he alleges that FSB agents co-ordinated the 1999 apartment block bombings that killed more than 300 people.

(www.bbc.co.uk, 19 November 2006)

'Alexander Litvinenko claimed in a 2001 book ... that the Kremlin's security service had created a secret unit to hunt and kill those considered a danger to the state' (*The Independent*, 20 November 2006, p. 3).

'Alexander Litvinenko ... said a secret KGB laboratory specializing in poison was still operational in FSB. While still in the service Mr Litvinenko in 1998 told Boris Berezovsky ... that he was under orders to kill him' (*FT*, 20 November 2006, p. 6).

> The Russian authorities had no immediate comment on suggestions in media reports that the Russian secret service was behind the poisoning ... The former agent met with an Italian contact ... on 1 November ... [Alexander Litvinenko said he was handed] a four-page document ... [containing] a list of people, including FSB officers, who are purported to be connected with [Anna Politkovskaya's murder] ... At the time of the dioxin poisoning of the Ukrainian leader Viktor Yushchenko in 2004 Litvinenko said a secret KGB laboratory in Moscow was still operated by the FSB and specialized in the study of poisons.
>
> (*IHT*, 20 November 2006, p. 3)

> Alexander Litvinenko fell ill on 1 November after a meeting at a London sushi bar ... Friends of Mr Litvinenko have alleged he was poisoned because he was critical of the Russian government ... [One friend said] he actually had a couple of meetings [on 1 November] where he had drinks ... [Another said he] thought that Mr Litvinenko could have been poisoned by a Russian who met him for a tea on the day this is thought to have happened, on 1 November ... Later that day Mr Litvinenko had a sushi lunch with an Italian contact.
>
> (www.bbc.co.uk, 20 November 2006)

'Alexander Litvinenko ... was one of several Russian intelligence officers to accuse Moscow of being behind the dioxin poisoning of Ukrainian president Viktor Yushchenko during his 2004 election campaign' (www.cnn.com, 20 November 2006).

> A friend ... said both [he and Alexander Litvinenko] had received email threats days before his poisoning. Italian Mario Scaramella told a Rome press conference that he met Alexander Litvinenko the day he fell ill ... Mario Scaramella, who is involved in an Italian parliamentary inquiry into KGB activity ... said he met the Russian in a London sushi bar on 1 November to discuss the email ... The doctor treating the former spy said in the hospital's first official statement that the cause may never be found ... [He] said it was possible he may not have been poisoned by thallium, adding he could not be sure because of the time he presented himself to University College Hospital ... [A toxicologist working on the case] earlier said Mr Litvinenko may have been poisoned with a radioactive substance, thallium ... If it was radioactive thallium it would now be difficult to trace ... [He said] Mr Litvinenko had symptoms consistent with thallium poisoning but other symptoms linked to other substances.
>
> (www.bbc.co.uk, 21 November 2006)

'Initial reports said Mr Litvinenko was poisoned with the heavy metal thallium, although medical opinion has not been conclusive and the theory that some form of radioactive material was used has also been put forward' (www.bbc.co.uk, 23 November 2006). 'Initial reports that he was given the heavy metal thallium gave way to other theories including radiation poisoning' (www.bbc.co.uk, 25 November).

'Mario Scaramella ... [said] he had warned Mr Litvinenko both their names were on a hit-list connected to organized crime in St Petersburg' (*FT*, 25 November 2006, p. 6).

> Initial suspicion had focused on thallium ... But the progress of Litvinenko's symptoms over the past few days has not been typical for thallium poisoning ... The hospital statement: 'Based on results we have received today and Mr Litvinenko's clinical features, thallium poisoning is an unlikely cause of his current condition. Further tests will be carried out to establish whether or not there is a single cause for Mr Litvinenko's condition' ... Earlier Tuesday [21 November] ... a toxicologist working on the case suggested a mixture of toxins might have been used ... [Thallium] does not typically cause failure of the bone marrow. The bone marrow can be suppressed by radiation as well as by a wide variety of drugs and toxic chemicals ... Litvinenko's friends have blamed the Russian secret service, the Federal Security Service.
>
> (*IHT*, 22 November 2006, p. 3)

> First it seemed that a salt of the highly toxic metal thallium had been added to Mr Litvinenko's food or drink. Then toxicologists elaborated, suggesting that a radioactive isotope of thallium might have been used to account for the apparent symptoms of radiation sickness. But tests showed no evidence of thallium.
>
> (*FT*, 25 November 2006, p. 6)

> [The] director of clinical care at University College Hospital said [on 23 November] there had been 'a dramatic deterioration' in Alexander Litvinenko's condition overnight ... He said: 'We are now convinced that the cause of Mr Litvinenko's condition was not a heavy metal such as thallium. Radiation poisoning is also unlikely. Despite extensive tests we are still unclear as to the cause of his condition.'
>
> (www.iht.com, 23 November 2006)

Alexander Litvinenko died on Thursday evening (23 November). On 21 November he issued a statement:

> As I lie here I can distinctly hear the beating of wings of the angel of death. I may be able to give him the slip but I have to say my legs do not run as fast as I would like. I think, therefore, that this may be the time to say one or two things to the person responsible for my present condition. You may succeed in silencing me but that silence comes at a price. You have shown yourself to

be as barbaric and ruthless as your most hostile critics have claimed. You have shown yourself to have no respect for life, liberty or any civilized value. You have shown yourself to be unworthy of your office, to be unworthy of the trust of civilized men and women. You may succeed in silencing one man but the howl of protest from around the world will reverberate, Mr Putin, in your ears for the rest of your life. May God forgive you for what you have done, not only to me but to beloved Russia and its people.

(www.bbc.co.uk, 24 November 2006)

[Alexander Litvinenko's] death overshadowed a summit meeting Friday [24 November] between President Putin and EU leaders in Helsinki, which was held in hopes of reducing worsening strains over trade and energy supplies. The EU had hoped to begin talks for a new partnership with Russia to replace a 1997 deal. But a veto by Poland, which was upset over a Russian import ban on Polish meat and plant products, means those negotiations must wait ... Putin said Thursday [23 November] the EU left him no choice but to ban all EU meat imports as of 1 January [2007] as it had not consulted Moscow on plans to admit Romania and Bulgaria. A Russian ban on imports of EU meat, dairy and fish products would affect some Euro 1.7 billion, or $2.2 billion, in annual trade, according to EU figures.

(www.iht.com, 24 November 2006)

'Moscow has justified the ban on the grounds that Bulgaria and Romania, which will join the EU on that day [1 January 2007], do not have adequate food safety measures' (*IHT*, 25 November 2006, p. 3).

Police probing the death of Alexander Litvinenko have found above-normal levels of radiation at three locations in London ... at his home, a sushi bar and a hotel ... [A spokeswoman for] the [UK] Health Protection Agency ... [said] the type of death was an 'unprecedented event in the UK' ... Mr Litvinenko's death has been linked to the presence of a 'major dose' of radioactive polonium-210 in his body ... The substance, historically called radium F, is very hard for doctors to identify.

(www.bbc.co.uk, 24 November 2006)

'[A spokeswoman for the UK Health Protection Agency] said: "For someone to have had this level of radiation they would have to have eaten or inhaled it or taken it in through a wound"' (*The Independent*, 25 November 2006, p. 2).

'To poison someone much larger amounts are required and this would have to be man-made, perhaps from a particle accelerator or a nuclear reactor' (*Guardian*, 25 November 2006, p. 4).

'In the form believed to have been used in the suspected poisoning it would have required high grade technical skills and a sophisticated process to produce' (*IHT*, 25 November 2006, p. 1).

'There is no record of this extremely toxic and highly radioactive substance having been used for deliberate poisoning' (*FT*, 25 November 2006, p. 6)|.

'[The UK] had granted him [Alexander Litvinenko] citizenship a month before his death' (*The Times*, 25 November 2006, p. 20).

President Vladimir Putin: (24 November]:

> The death of a person is always a tragedy. And I convey my condolences to those close to Mr Litvinenko, to his family. Meanwhile, as far as I know, in the medical report of British doctors, there is no indication that this was an unnatural death. There is none. That means there is no reason for discussion of that kind. I hope that the British authorities will not encourage political scandals that do not have real grounds to be blown up, whatever they are.
>
> (www.bbc.co.uk, 24 November 2006)

'Kremlin officials have dismissed such allegations as "sheer nonsense"' (www.bbc.co.uk, 24 November 2006).

'[Police] officers investigating the death now regard the circumstances as "suspicious" rather than "unexplained"' (*The Independent*, 27 November 2006, p. 6).

'The British police on Sunday [26 November] ... repeated that Alexander Litvinenko's death was "suspicious" and said it was not being treated as a murder inquiry' (*IHT*, 27 November 2006, p, 3).

'[On 27 November it was reported that] radiation had also been detected in a West End office building and at a building in Mayfair' (*IHT*, 28 November 2006, p. 3).

'Police ... found traces of the radio-active metal polonium-210 in two buildings in central London [Mayfair] ... [including] a four-storey Georgian town house owned by Boris Berezovsky. It is rented to companies' (*The Independent*, 28 November 2006, p. 9).

> In yet another twist in the suspected poisoning by radiation of [Alexander Litvinenko] ... British Airways said Wednesday [29 November] that three of its planes were being tested for radioactivity. A British Airways spokesman said that two Boeing 767s had been tested at Heathrow Airport and a third would be tested in Moscow ... [It was reported that] small traces of radioactivity had been found on the two planes at Heathrow ... Yegor Gaidar has been hospitalized with a mysterious illness that his daughter and associates on Wednesday said could have been the result of poisoning ... Gaidar fell ill in Ireland on Friday [24 November], the day after Litvinenko died in London ... Doctors have not yet diagnosed the cause of his [Gaidar's] illness ... Gaidar fell ill while attending a conference [in Ireland] ... where he vomited, collapsed and lost consciousness.
>
> (*IHT*, 30 November 2006, p. 3)

('Now recovering, Yegor Gaidar – an occasional but friendly critic of Vladimir Putin – believes his ailment was part of a campaign of anti-Kremlin subterfuge': *The Economist*, 16 December 2006, p. 28).

Mario Scaramella ... has also tested positive for [polonium-210] ... Doctors said he has 'significant' amounts of the substance in his body ... Tests confirmed that an adult member of Litvinenko's family [believed to be his wife] tested positive for a small amount ... So far traces of radiation [have been found] at twelve locations. Among the sites were two British Airways airliners that had travelled between London and Moscow. A third BA plane that was grounded in Moscow was being flown back to London to undergo examinations on Friday [1 December]' (*IHT*, 2 December 2006, pp. 1, 4).

Mario Scaramella is 'well' and preliminary tests have not found any signs of illness, University College Hospital said. Officials had previously said he tested positive for traces of Polonium-210 ... [However, a friend] told the BBC that doctors had told Mr Scaramella he was going to die ... Alexander Litvinenko's wife Marina is also said to have been 'very slightly contaminated' but is not ill.

(www.bbc.co.uk, 2 December 2006)

'Doctors said ... Mario Scaramella ... was "well" with normal test results. He is said to be displaying no symptoms of radiation poisoning' (www.bbc.co.uk, 3 December 2006).

The complicating factor is the relative ubiquity of polonium-210 ... Experts initially called it quite rare, with some claiming that only the Kremlin had the wherewithal to administer a lethal dose. But public and private inquiries have shown that it proliferated quite widely during the nuclear age, of late as an industrial commodity.

(www.iht.com, 3 December 2006)

The investigation into the death of Alexander Litvinenko is broadening into an international police probe into organized crime, alleged state-sponsored murder and the activities of people who have worked for the Russian secret service. A team [of nine] from SO15, the UK's elite counter-terrorist investigation squad, are expected to fly to Moscow later today or tomorrow at the latest to interview witnesses and gather information on potential suspects ... The advice being given to [UK] ministers from police and MI5, the security service, is that the network of contacts around Litvinenko remains murky, straddling espionage, politics, criminality and business.

(*FT*, 4 December 2006, p. 2)

'The range of possible suspects, including present and former security officers, businessmen and gangsters, is wide' (p. 16).

'[One report has] quoted a Russian academic living in London ... as saying Alexander Litvinenko told her he planned to make a living blackmailing Russian billionaires and spies' (*IHT*, 4 December 2006, p. 3).

'British police have left for Moscow' (www.bbc.co.uk, 4 December 2006).

Russia will not extradite suspects in the poisoning of Alexander Litvinenko to Britain, the country's prosecutor-general has said. Yuri Chaika said any trial of a Russian citizen must take place in Russia ... Mr Chaika told a Moscow news conference that arrest of Russians by British officers would be 'impossible' under the Russian constitution ... He also dismissed the claim that the highly toxic isotope polonium-210 ... was produced in Russia ... Russian prosecutors have said they intend to question former KGB body-guard Andrei Lugovoi, who met Mr Litvinenko in London on 1 November. Mr Lugovoi has said he was expecting to meet with British police in the coming days ... Mr Lugovoi is one of three Russian businessmen reported to have met Mr Litvinenko on that date. But one of them, Vyacheslav Soko-lenko, has denied he ever had any contact with the former KGB agent ... He says Mr Lugovoi and Dmitri Kovtun met Mr Litvinenko, but he was not present, adding that he never knew the ex-spy.

(www.bbc.co.uk, 5 December 2006)

The British forensic team will be allowed to be present while the Russian police question witnesses, Yuri Chaika said, although they will have no formal authority to compel witnesses to met them ... Chaika: 'We will do the inter-viewing and they can only be present during the questioning. Of course, they can ask us for permission to conduct interviews, which we may or may not grant' ... Russia said it will not co-operate in tracing the origins of the radioac-tive polonium-210 that caused Alexander Litvinenko's death, Chaika said.

(*IHT*, 6 November 2006, p. 3)

Russian officials said that the British team would not be able to interview Mikhail Trepashkin, a former FSB agent who is serving a four-year sen-tence for disclosing state secrets. Mr Trepashkin claims to have vital information about the plot to kill Alexander Litvinenko ... The former FSB officer ... investigated the 1999 bombings of Moscow apartments ... Mr Trepashkin claimed the FSB was behind the explosions.

(*The Times*, 6 December 2006, p. 4)

Russia announced today [7 December] that it has opened its own investiga-tion into the murder of Alexander Litvinenko and the attempted murder of a Russian businessman who had met with Mr Litvinenko in London. The businessman, Dmitri Kovtun, was found to have symptoms of radioactive poisoning. He is the fourth person known to have been exposed to the radio-activity ... [There others are] Mario Scaramella and Mr Litvinenko's wife ... Andrei Lugovoi, who is in the same hospital as Mr Kovtun, has been tested but so far no results have been announced ... Russian prosecutors said they also opened a criminal case that would allow suspects to be prose-cuted in Russia ... Andrei Lugovoi said he would answer all the British investigators' questions.

(www.iht.com, 7 December 2006)

Last Sunday [3 December] *The Observer* carried an allegation by a Russian woman named Julia Svetlichnaya that Alexander Litvinenko was a black-mailer. She went on television yesterday [8 December] to repeat her claim that he had planned to make a 'substantial sum' by blackmailing an unnamed Russian oligarch. Although described as an academic, Ms Svetlichnaya is believed to have been employed as communications manager for Russian Investors, a state-owned agency in Krasnoyarsk, Siberia, which attracts investment to the Russian oil industry. Her name was on the company's website until Sunday, but was then removed.

(*The Independent*, 9 December 2006, p. 6)

The German authorities said Sunday [10 December] that they had found traces of the radioactive substance polonium in a car and two homes in Hamburg that were used by [Dmitri Kovtun] ... The discoveries were the first evidence in a tangled case that tie a specific person to the poison that killed Alexander Litvinenko and German prosecutors said they had opened a criminal investigation of Dmitri Kovtun for illegal handling of a radioactive substance. 'He may not just be a victim but could also be a perpetrator,' Martin Köhnke, Hamburg's chief prosecutor said ... Kovtun is in a hospital in Moscow and there are conflicting reports about his health ... Litvinenko fell ill after meeting in a London hotel on 1 November with Kovtun and another Russian, Andrei Lugovoi, who is now also reported to be ill with symptoms of radiation poisoning. The confirmation that traces of polonium-210, a radioactive isotope, were present in Hamburg as early as 28 October is critical because the British police have so far found no evidence of polonium contamination in London earlier than 1 November, the date of the fateful meeting in the Millennium Mayfair Hotel.

(*IHT*, 11 December 2006, p. 3)

[On 24 December] Mario Scaramella was arrested in Naples after returning from London. Rome prosecutors have accused him of arms trafficking and slander ... Last month [November] Milan daily *Corriere della Sera* published excerpts of an alleged wiretapped, January phone conversation between Scaramella and Paolo Guzzani, during which Scaramella was quoted as telling Guzzani that he could not get information that showed that Italian premier Romano Prodi had been a KGB agent. A few days later Prodi's office announced that the premier would take legal action against unnamed parties who defamed his character ... Italian Senator Paolo Guzzani [is] the former chair of a parliamentary commission that examined cases of past KGB infiltration in Italy ... Scaramella said he showed Alexander Litvinenko emails ... at a London sushi bar on 1 November ... from a confidential source identifying the possible killers of Russian investigative journalist Anna Politkovskaya and listing other potential targets for assassination – including himself and Litvinenko ... The same day that Litvinenko met with Scaramella, Alexander Litvinenko met with Andrei Lugovoi ... Dmitri Kovtun ... and Vyacheslav Sokolenko, head of a private Russian security firm, in the bar at London's Millennium Hotel ... Overall, ten people in Britain tested positive for radiation since Litvinenko died, including two staff members at the Millennium Hotel in London.

(www.iht.com, 24 December 2006)

'Mario Scaramella is being investigated in Italy for arms trafficking and violating state secrets ... [Police in London] said the arrest in Naples was not part of their investigation into Alexander Litvinenko's death' (www.bbc.co.uk, 24 December 2006).

> A former manager of Yukos could have ordered the poisoning of Alexander Litvinenko, the Russian government alleged ... In a statement released yesterday [27 December], the prosecutor-general's office said: 'A version is being looked at those who ordered these crimes could be the same people who are on an international wanted list for serious and very serious crimes, one of whom is ... Leonid Nevzlin ... [In November Leonid Nevzlin] ... who lives in Israel ... [said] that Alexander Litvinenko had given him a document related to Yukos and said he believed the former agent's killing was linked to his investigations into the company's activities.

(*Guardian*, 28 December 2006, p. 6)

'Leonid Nevzlin fled to Israel and later received Israeli citizenship' (*The Independent*, 28 December 2006, p. 16).

> The prosecutor-general's statement ... said there were indications of a link between the poisoning of Alexander Litvinenko and the attempted murder of Dmitri Kovtun – who met him in London before he fell ill – and 'the charges that several Yukos managers committed crimes against the life and health of citizens'.

(www.bbc.co.uk, 27 December 2006)

> The prosecutor-general's office of Russia ... in a statement released Wednesday [27 December] ... said its investigation indicated a link between the poisoning of Litvinenko and its continuing criminal cases against Yukos executives. It singled out Leonid Nevzlin ... who lives in self-exile in Israel and is wanted on a raft of charges in Russia ... He met with Alexander Litvinenko in the weeks before his poisoning, evidently in October. After his death Nevzlin said that Litvinenko had provided him with a dossier that 'shed light on most significant aspects of the Yukos affair' ... The contents of that dossier remain unclear, but Nevzlin said at the time that he passed them over to British investigators ... Dmitri Kovtun reportedly was hospitalized in Moscow for radiation exposure. Prosecutors in Moscow say they are investigating his exposure as an attempted murder, committed in conjunction with Litvinenko's murder. That would suggest that Kovtun was a victim of the crime, and not a suspect, as reported in Britain and Germany ... Mikhail Khodorkovsky has come under new prosecutorial scrutiny ... [He] was transferred over the weekend from the remote Siberian prison ... to a regional detention centre in Chita. On Wednesday [27 December] prosecutors preparing new

criminal charges against him questioned him and his jailed partner, Platon Lebedev ... Investigators accused him of laundering money by making contributions to Open Russia, a social and education charity Khodorkovsky founded. The authorities have since closed the charity.

(www.iht.com, 28 December 2006)

Investigators [in the UK] believe Alexander Litvinenko may have been contaminated twice, with the second attempt taking place at a central London hotel several days after the first 'hit'. Two Russian businessmen, one a former KGB officer [Andrei Lugovoi] and the other a former soldier [Dmitri Kovtun], are the focus of the investigation ... It emerged yesterday [5 January 2007] that traces of Polonium-210 were found at a restaurant that is understood to have been used by at least one of the suspects – Andrei Lugovoi ... In the latest development traces of Polonium-210 have been discovered in the Pescatori restaurant in Dover Street, Mayfair, where Mr Lugovoi is understood to have dined before 1 November.

(*The Independent*, 6 January 2007, p. 8)

'[On 1 February 2007 President Vladimir Putin] dismissed accusations by some of his own aides that Putin's enemies had killed Alexander Litvinenko. "I do not believe in conspiracy theories," he [Putin] said' (*IHT*, 2 February 2007, p. 8).

'Russian detectives investigating the death of Alexander Litvinenko have asked the Home Office for permission to come to the UK' (www.bbc.co.uk, 4 February 2007).

The widow of Alexander Litvinenko ... has written an emotional letter to President Vladimir Putin challenging him to help bring the killers to justice ... Marina Litvinenko: 'I have never said that I knew you were personally responsible. I said that if you did not make every effort to assist the UK authorities in the discovery of the perpetrators of this terrible crime, I could only assume that you must have something to hide.'

(*IHT*, 6 February 2007, p. 3)

21 November 2006. 'Gazprom is to buy Russia's biggest circulation newspaper ... *Komsomolskaya Pravda* is a tabloid with a circulation of 800,000 copies that follows a pro-Kremlin editorial line' (*FT*, 22 November 2006, p. 5).

19 December 2006. 'Nikolai Patrushev, head of the FSB state security service ... stepped up pressure on international non-governmental organizations and charities Tuesday [19 December], saying they were increasingly being used as a cover for foreign spying operations' (*IHT*, 20 December 2006, p. 3).

20 December 2006.

The Duma ... overwhelmingly ... backed a bill submitted by President Putin that will limit casinos and slot-machine halls to four remote regions of the country ... the Baltic enclave of Kaliningrad, the Promorsky region on the

Pacific coast, the Siberian region of Altai and Karsnodar-Rostov in southern Russia ... Casino operators ... must either move to the zones or close their operations by July 2009. Businesses that fail to comply ... will be ordered to shut next July [2007] ... Supporters of legislation say that much of the industry is under control of criminal gangs who use casinos and slot-machine businesses as fronts to legitimize the proceeds of illegal activities.

(*The Times*, 21 December 2006, p. 33)

27 December 2006.

Parliament yesterday [27 December] passed a law that will close casinos and slot-machine halls in most of the country ... [They] mushroomed across Russia after the collapse of the Soviet Union ... The law calls for the creation of four zones for legal gambling.

(*FT*, 28 December 2006, p. 5)

15 January 2007.

Russia began cracking down Monday [15 January 2007] on millions of illegal workers, as tough new immigration rules took effect amid a rising tide of anti-immigrant sentiment. Under the new rules, which set a quota of 6 million foreign workers for 2007, the authorities are carrying out strict checks on the estimated 10 million to 12 million foreigners who are already working in Russia, most of them illegally. The legislation relaxes stringent procedures for citizens of most former Soviet republics who enter Russia from 15 January to obtain work permits, but it also increases fines for businesses that employ illegal migrants ... Under the new regulations businesses that employ people without proper documents face fines of up to 800,000 roubles, or about $30,000, and a three-month trading suspension ... Further limiting the right of foreigners to work in Russia, a government decree that took effect on 1 January restricted the number of non-Russians in the retail trade ... Last year [2006] President Putin ordered new measures to curtail the use of foreign workers, especially at markets, saying they were crowding out native Russian producers and retailers ... The population of Russia is dropping by about 700,000 a year and has fallen below 143 million. The population decline would be even more catastrophic were it not for immigration.

(*IHT*, 16 January 2007, p. 3)

Russia introduced new laws yesterday [15 January] that experts say are intended to plug a hole in the country's labour market while discouraging foreigners from settling there permanently. The laws, passed by parliament last year [2006], are designed to streamline the red tape foreigners have to go through to live and work in Russia legally but will also reduce their numbers. One change will implement a gradual ban on foreigners working as traders in outdoor markets where immigrants dominate, causing friction with ethnic Russians.

(*FT*, 16 January 2007, p. 6)

Under new rules that came into force this week, only 40 per cent of workers at Russia's retail markets are supposed to be foreign, and none should be by 1 April ... Up to 6 million work permits are to be available this year [2007] for migrants from the poor ex-Soviet republics. That may be far fewer than the 8 million to 12 million people that the federal migration service estimates are working in Russia illegally, but it amounts to far more than have been handed out before.

(*The Economist*, 20 January 2007, p. 46)

23 January 2007.

Pro-Kremlin lawmakers Tuesday [23 January] bowed to a storm of protest by watering down a bill that would have allowed the authorities free rein to ban protests around the time of elections. The original version of the bill allowed officials to ban protests two weeks before and after elections and also barred groups and parties warned by prosecutors for extremist activities from holding rallies for six months. The two-week protest ban had been removed in an amended version of the draft law on political meetings published Tuesday.

(*IHT*, 24 January 2007, p. 10)

26 January 2007.

British police have identified ... Andrei Lugovoi from Moscow as the prime suspect in the murder of Alexander Litvinenko ... However, UK investigators believe that they do not have sufficient evidence to charge Mr Lugovoi formally, without further co-operation from the Russian authorities ... The Russian prosecutor's office said yesterday [26 January] that Mr Lugovoi could be tried in Russia, but he would not be extradited to the UK ... 'The Russian constitution prohibits the extradition of its citizens,' said one official.

(*FT*, 27 January 2007, p. 4)

27 January 2007.

The Yabloko party ... said it had been barred from local elections in St Petersburg in what analysts saw as a Kremlin signal that its leader ... Grigori Yavlinsky ... should not fight parliamentary elections later this year [2007]. The Yabloko party said the refusal by the city's electoral commission to approve its application to run in local polls due in March [11 March] was an attempt to remove political troublemakers from the pro-Kremlin council [in St Petersburg] ... Analysts said the decision at the weekend [27 January] to bar Yabloko could also be intended to persuade Grigori Yavlinsky that he should stay away from the more important parliamentary polls in December.

(*FT*, 29 January 2007, p. 8)

'Yabloko was barred from polls after the electoral commission found that more than 10 per cent of signatures on a petition it needed to be allowed to run were invalid. Yabloko is to challenge the decision in court' (*The Independent*, 29 January 2007, p. 21).

('The city [of St Petersburg] election commission disqualified Yabloko after declaring a sample of the 40,000 signatures on the party's voter registration application contained forgeries. The party was given two days to disprove a handwriting expert's conclusions by producing signed affidavits and copies of passports for hundreds of would-be voters. By early February, with the elections barely a month away [11 March], Yabloko had also been barred from the ballot in two other regions, Orel in west-central Russia and Leningrad, which surrounds St Petersburg, in what party officials called a deliberate attempt by the Kremlin to weaken it further ... The Union of Right Forces was knocked off the ballot in Volodga, Pskov and Samara. The Communist Party faced challenges in several regions, including Tyumen and Dagestan, but ultimately qualified after protests. In all, parties were denied registration in seventeen instances. The only three parties that faced no problems were United Russia, Just Russia and the Liberal Democratic Party ... Just Russia [is] a party created by the merger of three smaller parties and led by a staunch Putin supporter, Sergei Mironov':' www.iht.com, 15 February 2007; *IHT*, 16 February 2007, p. 2.)

5 February 2007.

> Prosecutors filed new charges Monday [5 February 2007] against Mikhail Khodorkovsky and his business partner ... Platon Lebedev ... in a move lawyers for the jailed tycoon said was aimed at heading off any political threat ... as parliamentary and presidential elections loom ... Khodorkovsky's lawyer ... [said] that prosecutors had indicted his client on charges of embezzling and laundering as much as $25 billion in illegal oil revenues ... Platon Lebedev had also had the same charges filed against him ... Khodorkovsky has served nearly four years of an eight-year sentence on fraud and tax evasion charges and could be eligible for parole this year [2007].
>
> (www.iht.com, 5 February 2007)

> Prosecutors brought new charges Monday ... Both Mikhail Khodorkovsky and his partner Platon Lebedev were charged with embezzlement and money laundering, which his lawyers said together could carry prison sentences of fifteen years ... Their lawyers said they had potentially qualified for parole late this year [October], upon serving half their sentences ... The new criminal charges are likely to put what remains of the company into state hands ... The charges claim Khodorkovsky and Lebedev embezzled roughly $20 billion in oil revenue through a series of internal transfers among Yukos and its subsidiaries, and then transferred the money through other accounts. A fraction of this amount is alleged to have been laundered through the Open Russia foundation, a charitable organization that Khodorkovsky founded, his lawyers said, Open Russia has also been under investigation, and its accounts frozen, since last year [2006].
>
> (*IHT*, 6 February 2007, pp. 1, 14)

The new criminal charges are likely to ease what remains of the company into state hands ... analysts and company officials said ... An attorney for Khodorkovsky said ... that prosecutors had accused Khodorkovsky of embezzling money from oil trades executed within Yukos, between company subsidiaries, in a practice known as transfer pricing. Under this practice, which he acknowledged existed, a trading arm of Yukos paid lower than world rates for oil bought from other company subsidiaries, in what the company called a legal tax-minimization strategy. These transfer pricing operations, which form the basis of the new charges, were also the source of the tax claims that bankrupted Yukos. The charges came just months before the remaining roughly $22 billion in Yukos assets were to be auctioned to cover $26 billion in tax and other claims.

(p. 13)

'Prosecutors allege that Mikhail Khodorkovsky stripped profit from Yukos by selling crude to affiliated companies at a low price, then selling it internationally and pocketing the difference' (*IHT*, 8 February 2007, p. 12).

9 February 2007.

Earlier this week defence minister Sergei Ivanov announced a big increase in military spending to fund a new generation of intercontinental ballistic missiles, nuclear submarines and aircraft carriers. Russia's defence budget would be $31 billion this year [2007], compared with $8 billion in 2001, and it would spend $189 billion over eight years on overhauling its military infrastructure. But Mr Ivanov noted yesterday [Friday 9 February] that US military spending remained more than twenty times bigger than Russia's.

(*FT*, 10 February 2007, p. 5)

10 February 2007. President Putin addresses the forty-third Munich Security Conference (founded in 1962). This is the first time he has attended the conference.
President Vladimir Putin:

The unipolar world posited after the Cold War has been a failure ... What is a unipolar world? No matter how we might adorn this term, it ultimately means just one thing in practice – a single centre of power, a single centre of force, a single centre for decision-making. It is a world in which there is one master, one sovereign. And in the final analysis this is harmful not only to all within the confines of this system, but also to the sovereign itself, because it destroys that sovereign from within. And needless to say this has nothing in common with democracy ... Everything that is going on in the world today ... is a consequence of attempts to introduce this particular concept – the concept of a unipolar world – in international affairs ... Unilateral, often illegitimate actions have not solved a single problem ... They have generated more human tragedies and new hotbeds of tension ... The number of wars and of local and regional conflicts has not diminished ... And the number of people being killed in these conflicts has not decreased but indeed decreased ... Today we see an almost totally unrestrained hyperinflated use of force in international relations – military force that is plunging the world into an abyss of conflict after conflict. As a result not enough resources are available to bring about a full-fledged solution to any of them. It is also becoming impossible to resolve them by political means. We are seeing ever-increasing disregard for the fundamental principles of international law. Moreover, certain norms – in effect almost the entire system of laws of a single state, namely the United States, of course, – have crossed over their national borders in all spheres and are being imposed on other states in the economic, political and humanitarian realms ... This is very dangerous ... It is creating a situation in which no one feels secure any more ... Because no one can hide behind international law ... Such a policy, of course, serves as a catalyst for the arms race. The dominance of the factor of force inevitably fuels the drive of a number of countries to acquire weapons of mass destruction ... I believe that it is clear that the process of Nato expansion bears no relation to modernizing the alliance itself or to safeguarding security in Europe. On the contrary it is a serious provocative factor that lowers the level of mutual trust. And we have a legitimate right to ask bluntly: Who is this expansion aimed against? And what happened to the assurances our Western partners gave after the dissolution of the Warsaw pact?

(*CDSP*, 2007, vol. 59, no. 7, pp. 1–2)

On Saturday [10 February] President Vladimir Putin accused the United States of provoking a new nuclear arms race by developing ballistic missile defences, undermining international institutions, making the Middle East more unstable through its clumsy handling of the Iraq war and trying to divide modern Europe.

(*IHT*, 12 February 2007, p. 1)

President Vladimir Putin:

[A] 'Unipolar world' [exists] ... What is a unipolar world? No matter how we beautify this term, it means one single centre of power, one single centre of force and one single centre of decision-making. This is a world of one master, one sovereign. And at the end of the day this is pernicious not only for all those within the system, but also for the sovereign itself because it destroys itself from within. It has nothing in common with democracy, of course ... Today we are witnessing an almost unconstrained hyper-use of force in international relations – military force ... One state, the United States, has overstepped its borders in all spheres – economic, political and humanitarian – and has imposed itself on other states ... Illegal [unilateral military action has plunged the world into an] abyss of permanent conflicts ... This is very dangerous. Nobody feels secure any more because nobody can hide behind international law. This is nourishing an arms race with the desire of countries to get nuclear weapons ... Local and regional wars did not get fewer, the number of people who died did not get less but increased ... [The United States has gone from] one conflict to another without achieving a full-fledged solution to any of them ... [This is a] very dangerous approach to global relations ... The process of Nato expansion has nothing to do with modernization of the alliance. We have the right to ask: against whom is the expansion directed? ... [The United States has turned OSCE] into a vulgar instrument of ensuring the foreign policy interests of one country.

(www.bbc.co.uk, 10 February 2007; *IHT*, 12 February 2007, p. 4; www.iht.com, 13 February 2007; *FT*, 12 February 2007, p. 6)

Russian defence minister Sergei Ivanov yesterday [11 February] agreed that a new Cold War was not imminent. He said Russia was spending only 2.6 per cent of GDP on defence. 'We are not spending on defence what the Soviet Union did – which was 30 per cent,' he said.

(*FT*, 12 February 2007, p. 6)

11 February 2007. 'President Vladimir Putin has arrived in Saudi Arabia at the start of a Middle East tour that will also take him to Qatar and Jordan. It is the first time a Russian head of state is to visit these countries' (www.bbc.co.uk, 11 February 2007).

15 February 2007.

Vladimir Putin promoted Sergei Ivanov [fifty-four], the defence minister, last night [15 February] in a move seen as boosting the former KGB officer's chances of succeeding Putin as president. Mr Ivanov's elevation to first deputy prime minister makes him equal in rank to Dmitri Medvedev [forty-one], the other leading contender to succeed Mr Putin ... [Dmitri Medvedev has] responsibility for multi-billion dollar social investment programmes ... The more liberal Mr Medvedev has been running slightly ahead of the tough-talking defence minister, who is seen as closer to the hardline *siloviki* faction in the Kremlin, in opinion polls. Though giving up his defence role, Mr Ivanov will retain responsibility for Russia's powerful military–industrial complex, which last year [2006] had record exports of $6 billion, as well as taking on a broader economic remit ... The surprise choice for new defence minister was Anatoli Serdyukov, who headed Russia's federal tax service.

(*FT*, 16 February 2007, p. 8)

President Vladimir Putin praised Sergei Ivanov in a television announcement ... saying his ally 'has fulfilled the tasks he faced as defence minister and fulfilled them successfully'. He said that Ivanov's duties would be broadened to include oversight of defence and some civilian industries ... Ivanov had served as one of several deputy prime ministers. Medvedev had been the only first deputy prime minister.

(*IHT*, 16 February 2007, p. 2)

2 March 2007.

On Friday [2 March] Garry Kasparov, Mikhail Kasyanov and Eduard Limonov, head of the National Bolshevik Party, led a meeting of the United Civil Front opposition group in St Petersburg. Limonov, who was arrested Saturday morning [3 March] before the march began, said the group was close to nominating Kasyanov as their candidate for president in the 2008 elections.

(IHT, 5 March 2007, p. 3)

Russian authorities are investigating the mysterious death of a prominent journalist who covered military space technology for the *Kommersant* daily. Ivan Safronov, fifty-one, fell from a fifth-floor window on Friday [2 March] at the Moscow apartment block where he lived. Prosecutors ... say they are investigating the possibility that he was 'driven to suicide'. But friends and relatives told *Kommersant* that they knew of no reason why he would commit suicide ... Safronov had irked some officials with his critical reporting and had been questioned by the Federal Security Service (FSB).

(www.bbc.co.uk, 6 March 2007)

Colleagues ... said yesterday [5 March] that they suspected foul play. A front page article in the Russian daily *Kommersant* doubted that Ivan Safronov, the military affairs correspondent who often criticized the military under Vladimir Putin could have killed himself. Mr Safronov raised hackles in the military last December [2006] when he reported the third consecutive failure to launch the new Bulava intercontinental ballistic missile.

(FT, 6 March 2007, p. 6)

Ivan Safronov ... had been threatened while working on a report claiming that Russia planned to sell sophisticated missiles to Syria and Iran, his newspaper reported Tuesday [6 March] ... Some media outlets said [the incident] could have been murder ... *Kommersant* reported Tuesday that Safronov had told his editors he was working on a story about Russian plans to sell weapons to Iran and Syria via Belarus ... Israel and the United States have strongly objected to Russian weapon sales to the two countries.

(IHT, 7 March 2007, p. 8)

Kommersant reported Thursday [8 March] that, before his death, Safronov informed his editors that he had been warned not to write about the weapons sales because 'doing so would cause an international scandal and the FSB would make charges against him of stealing state secrets stick' ... If Safronov was indeed [murdered] ... [he would be] the fourteenth journalist to be murdered in Russia since Putin came to power in 2000.

(www.iht.com, 12 March 2007)

Kommersant's editor has said he [Safronov] showed no signs of being suicidal, but the paper says it will keep an open mind. Meanwhile a report by a press watchdog has concluded that journalism in Russia has become as 'dangerous as war' ... [Safronov's] newspaper said at the time of his death he was investigating reports of alleged Russian plans to sell sophisticated missiles to Iran and fighter jets to Syria, via Belarus ... The International News Safety Institute (INSI) concluded that Russia is the second most deadly place for journalists, after Iraq. According to INSI, in the last ten years eighty-eight journalists were killed in Russia, the most common cause of these deaths being contract murders.

(www.bbc.co.uk, 7 March 2007)

Assassination has emerged as one of the most efficient tools for silencing journalists, according to a global study tracking fatalities among journalists and press staff over the last ten years ... Groups like the World Association of Newspapers and the International Federation of Journalists also track fatalities, but use different reporting methods and definitions for journalists. This report counted anyone involved in news gathering, from journalists to support employees, like translators, drivers and office personnel. The victims, overwhelmingly men, are more likely to be shot and killed while investigating local stories rather than reporting from the battlefield, according to a survey completed by the International News Safety Institute ... a Brussels-based coalition of media organizers ... It found that more than 1,000 people have died, the majority while covering local stories. Since 2000 the annual toll has steadily increased with 147 dying in 2005, followed by a record 168 fatalities last year [2006]. The three deadliest countries were Iraq, Russia and Colombia ... The number of killings, disappearances and suspicious deaths continued to mount even as the institute was preparing its final report. The latest to die in Moscow was a Russian journalist, Ivan Safronov, who covered military affairs for the *Kommersant*, newspaper. He was found dead Friday [2 March] after falling from the fifth floor of his apartment building ... The International News Safety Institute ranks Russia as the second most deadly nation for journalists, with eighty-eight fatalities over the last ten years, behind Iraq with 138.

(*IHT*, 7 March 2007, p. 3)

3 March 2007.

Police officers broke up an unusually large and unruly rally against the government of President Vladimir Putin, clashing with protesters and arresting opposition leaders. Rally organizers and the police said that more than 100 people were arrested after a mid-afternoon scuffle on Saturday [3 March in St Petersburg] ... The rally was held in advance of local elections scheduled for 11 March. Opposition events typically draw no more than several hundred people, but several thousand gathered for the rally ... Two leaders of what is left of Russia's liberal opposition, Garry Kasparov, the former chess grandmaster, and Mikhail Kasyanov, a former prime minister, spoke to the crowd. Minutes after Kasparov spoke and left the area, the police broke up the crowd, first arresting the speaker who had taken Kasparov's place.

(www.iht.com, 4 March 2007; *IHT*, 5 March 2007, p. 3)

Thousands ... as many as 5,000, according to some estimates ... marched into the city centre, defying the government ban ... It was one of the largest protests to date against the government of President Vladimir Putin ... Garry Kasparov is the chairman of the United Civil Front, an organization he created in 2005 to promote activism in a country where it has steadily disappeared ... He is also the guiding strategist behind The Other Russia, a union of groups from across the political spectrum united in their marginalization by the authorities loyal to Putin. The Other Russia has held conferences ... and staged rallies like the one in St Petersburg.

(*IHT*, 10 March 2007, pp. 1, 6)

At least 5,000 people chanted slogans against Vladimir Putin ... The opposition marched under the slogan 'Those Who Don't Agree' ... The Other Russia brings together a series of diverse opposition groups hostile to the Kremlin. They include Garry Kasparov's United Civil Front, the Popular Democratic Union, led by Mikhail Kasyanov ... and the National Bolsheviks ... [led by] Eduard Limonov.

(*Guardian*, 24 March 2007, p. 26)

('The Yeltsin government toyed with the idea of joining the EU, but the idea is now dead. In an article to mark the EU's fiftieth anniversary [established in the Treaty of Rome, signed in March 1957], Vladimir Putin stated openly that Russia has "no intention of either joining the EU or establishing any form of institutional association with it"': *Guardian*, 11 April 2007, p. 17.)

11 March 2007.

Russians were voting Sunday [11 March] in scattered regional elections marred by complaints that opposition forces were being frozen out of the country's politics. Although two mainstream parties and a smattering of smaller ones are on the ballot for legislatures in fourteen of Russia's eighty-six regions, critics say the appearance of genuine pluralism is only superficial ... The elections come amid more restrictive electoral legislation, bureaucratic measures that have flummoxed opponents and kept them off some ballots, and a new party that casts itself as the opposition but that critics say is the servant of Putin's needs. The new party, called Just Russia, is led by the speaker of parliament's upper house, Sergei Mironov, who showed his loyalty to Putin in 2004 by running against him for president and calling it a gesture of support ... United Russia [is] the party that dominates the national parliament.

(www.iht.com, 11 March 2007)

Regional elections [were] marred by complaints that Kremlin opponents had been increasingly sidelined for national parliamentary elections in

December and a vote to replace President Vladimir Putin next year [March 2008]. The elections were held under new rules that critics say restrict the ability of voters to voice discontent and that featured a new party casting itself as being in opposition but widely seen as a tool for channelling public anger at the authorities while broadening the Kremlin's base of support. While a total of fourteen political parties and their candidates competed for seats in the legislative assemblies of fourteen of eighty-six administrative regions, critics say the appearance of genuine pluralism was only superficial ... [In] St Petersburg ... some parties had been barred from the ballot – notably Yabloko, a liberal party that was shut out by a ruling that more than 10 per cent of the signatures it gathered to enter the race were invalid. Yabloko called the ruling a farce ... The liberal Union of Right Forces was barred from the ballots in four regions – in some cases, its leaders said, because candidates withdrew under pressure from threats or promises of jobs ... Voters could no longer cast ballots 'against all' and in most regions there was no longer a minimum turnout required to make the election valid.

(*IHT*, 12 March 2007, p. 3)

Voters could no longer cast ballots 'against all' and in most regions there was no longer a minimum turnout required to make the election valid. In a few regions all voting was by party, meaning no ballots could be cast for individual candidates, and the threshold parties had to clear to gain seats was increased to 7 per cent.

(*IHT*, 13 March 2007, p. 3)

Some 30 million registered voters [are eligible to take part] ... in elections in fourteen of the country's eighty-six regions ... Voters face a choice of two mainstream parties and a number of smaller ones ... Yabloko was among the parties banned from the elections [in St Petersburg] ... The elections have been marred by accusations that opposition parties are being deliberately marginalized.

(www.bbc.co.uk, 11 March 2007)

Yabloko was barred from contesting four of the nine races it wanted to enter because it failed to meet tough new election criteria ... The vote was the first test of new electoral laws introduced last year [2006]. The minimum threshold of the vote a party needs to secure seats was raised; the minimum voter turnout for elections to be valid was lowered; and the 'against all' option on ballot papers was eliminated.

(www.bbc.co.uk, 12 March 2007)

A Just Russia was formed last October [2006], with President Vladimir Putin's backing, from the merger of three smaller political groups ... United Russia ... is viewed as a right-wing pro-business faction. A Just Russia, led by Sergei Mironov, speaker of the upper house, has cast itself as a champion of social concerns facing poorer people. Critics say that it is a Kremlin invention to draw support away from the Communist Party ... Smaller opposition parties complained that they had been ignored by state-controlled media and that bureaucratic obstacles thrown up by officials who were often closely linked to United Russia had kept them off the ballot in some contests ... [Yabloko] called on supporters to spoil their ballot papers in protest yesterday [11 March] ... apart from the two pro-Kremlin parties, only the Communists and the ultra-nationalist Liberal Democratic Party competed in all fourteen regions out of fifteen registered parties. About 31 million Russians, about a third of the electorate, were eligible to vote in what was seen as a dress rehearsal for the Duma elections in December and the presidential race next March [2008] ... Parties not already represented in the State Duma had to pay a registration fee of $3.5 million or raise thousands of signatures on electoral petitions just to get on the ballot.

(*The Times*, 12 March 2007, p. 33)

Turnout was 39.1 per cent of the fourteen regions' 31 million eligible voters – about one-third of Russia's total electorate ... Yabloko was barred from contesting four of the nine races it wanted to enter because it had failed to meet tough new election criteria. It had a poor showing in the other five regions.

(www.bbc.co.uk, 12 March 2007)

'[The] campaign left the weak opposition more marginalized than ever' (www.iht.com, 12 March 2007).

Just Russia got the second highest voter support in most of those [fourteen] regions and in one actually outstripped United Russia – although United Russia retained approximately the same number of seats in regional legislatures that it had previously held ... Just Russia got the largest share of votes in the Stavropol region, 36 per cent, with 23 per cent for United Russia ... but Just Russia ended up with fewer seats in the regional assembly, half of which is chosen by party list and half by single mandate ... The Union of Right Forces reached the 7 per cent needed to win seats in one region only, and Yabloko failed to clear the threshold anywhere.

(*IHT*, 13 March 2007, p. 3)

United Russia came out on top of the vote in thirteen of fourteen regional elections for parliament. In one contest [Stavropol] Just Russia ... scored the biggest percentage ... But the Communists were the second largest party in Sunday's polls by average share of the vote ... The liberal opposition Union of Right Forces won enough votes to secure seats in several regional assemblies.

(*FT*, 13 March 2007, p. 6)

The provisional election results were as as follows: United Russia, 46 per cent; Communist Party, 16 per cent; Just Russia, 12 per cent; Liberal Democratic Party, 9 per cent; Agrarian Party, 9 per cent; Union of Right Forces, 7 per cent (p. 6).

Both parties [United Russia and Just Russia] have the president's blessing and ... both claim to be his true acolytes. 'I support him completely,' says Alexander Babakov, Just Russia's top man in the Duma. Criticizing the president, he adds, lies outside the purview of party politics. His party claims to be more social democratic than United Russia ... All their [the regions'] bosses are, in effect, now appointed by the president. The Stavropol result was probably in part a protest against an unpopular governor ... [who] is aligned with United Russia ... whom voters cannot remove directly.

(*The Economist*, 17 March 2007, p. 45)

12 March 2007.

President Vladimir Putin moved to establish a new agency that will licence media outlets and monitor their output. The new agency will have control over television, radio, newspapers and the internet ... Putin issued an order that merged the Federal Service for Media Law Compliance and Cultural Heritage and the Federal Information Technologies Agency, creating the Federal Service for Mass Media, Telecommunications and the Protection of Cultural Heritage ... The new agency is directly subordinate to the prime minister's government ... not to the [ministries] ... where the two agencies were previously housed ... The new agency will have access to personal data of internet users.

(www.cnn.com, 12 March 2007)

13 March 2007.

President Vladimir Putin removed Russia's elections chief yesterday [13 March] ... Alexander Veshnyakov, head of Russia's central electoral commission since 1999, was not among Mr Putin's five nominees to start a new four-term term in April. No explanation was given in yesterday's announcement for his exclusion ... Mr Veshnyakov has been critical of changes to electoral rules that have made life more difficult for smaller opposition parties. He has spoken in favour of freedom of choice for voters. The elections chief opposed a parliamentary bill last summer [2006] introducing additional reasons why election candidates could be denied registration, saying it could be used to block any undesirable candidate and lead to 'elections without choices, [as in] the Soviet era'. Russia should not return to the days when it had a 'sham legislature and sham elections', he [said].

(*FT*, 14 March 2007, p. 9)

Pope Benedict XVI ... met Tuesday [13 March] at the Vatican with President Vladimir Putin, in their first encounter since Benedict became Pope in April 2005 ... An aide to Putin ... said in Moscow that the two men would discuss the issue but would not broach the possibility of Benedict's visiting Russia. Putin, who met Pope Paul II in 2000 and 2003, has said he favours such a visit, though it has been opposed strongly by Russian Orthodox leaders.

(*IHT*, 14 March 2007, p. 3)

23 March 2007.

Russia's supreme court announced [on 23 March] that it had liquidated the small Republican Party, claiming it had violated electoral law by having too few members ... [The] new electoral law says that all political parties must have 50,000 members and be represented in half of Russia's provinces ... Vladimir Ryzhkov [is] the leader of the Republican Party ... [and] one of a handful of independent MPs in the Duma ... The Republican Party was formed by defectors from the Soviet Communist Party. It emerged in 1990 ... On Thursday [22 March] Moscow's prosecutor's office suspended the National Bolshevik Party ... [a] radical and previously banned anti-Kremlin group.

(*Guardian*, 24 March 2007, p. 26)

24 March 2007.

Hundreds of demonstrators are expected to gather today [24 March] at Nizhny Novgorod, Russia's fourth largest city. The Other Russia, a coalition of opposition groups, are expected to march despite attempts by pro-Kremlin officials to prevent them from demonstrating ... They have refused permission for the latest rally to go ahead and blocked the route.

(*Guardian*, 24 March 2007, p. 26)

Here in the third largest city in Russia ... Nizhny Novgorod ... barely was a banner unfurled or an anti-Kremlin slogan chanted Saturday [24 March] before a wave of heavily armoured police officers engulfed a miniscule group of demonstrators and journalists gathered for a protest against the government of Vladimir Putin ... Protest organizers said about 200 made it to Gorky Square, where the action occurred, though many simply melted into the crowd of onlookers as police ran in, making it easy for them to round up a remaining group of no more than thirty ... Protest organizers refused an offer by the city to hold a demonstration outside the city centre ... saying they would gather in the city centre in defiance of local authorities ... Saturday's was the coalition's third event ... the so-called Dissenters' Marches put on by Other Russia ... The first [was] in Moscow in December [2006] ... About 1,000 marchers held a small protest at a government-sanctioned location, closely observed by several thousand riot police officers ... [The second was] in St Petersburg on 3 March [which] defied a ban on their demonstration in the city.

(*IHT*, 26 March 2007, p. 1)

30 March 2007. 'Boris Berezovsky ... says he was interviewed at Scotland Yard [in London] by a Russian investigator in the enquiry into the poisoning of ... Alexander Litvinenko. The investigator also interviewed Akhmed Zakayev' (*IHT*, 2 April 2007, p. 3).

4 April 2007.

A law passed by Moscow city council restricts the number of people allowed to take part in political rallies to two a square metre ... Demonstrators are no longer allowed to gather in front of historic monuments, ruling out most of central Moscow. The law also restricts indoor meetings, with police given the right to break up political gatherings if there are more people than chairs ... The mayor's office insisted the law had nothing to do with politics. It was designed to prevent disruption to drivers and pedestrians, officials said ... Observers say it will be adopted in other big cities, making street protests almost impossible.

(*Guardian*, 6 April 2007, p. 27)

13 April 2007.

Anti-government protesters vowed to flout a ban on marching through Moscow centre and police promised to respond with harsh measures Friday [13 April] as tensions ratcheted up on the eve of a weekend of demonstrations in Russia's two largest cities. The so-called Dissenters' March – scheduled for Moscow on Saturday [14 April] and St Petersburg on Sunday [15 April] – would be the fourth and fifth in a series of demonstrations that have been forcibly dispersed or heavily surrounded by riot police. Garry Kasparov ... said march organizers had rejected a proposal by city authorities for demonstrators to gather in a single location for a meeting, rather than marching down one of Moscow's main avenues ... The marches are organized by Other Russia, an umbrella group that draws together disparate opposition factions, including those of former prime minister Mikhail Kasyanov and ultranationalist Eduard Limonov. But mainstream liberal parties have largely kept their distance. Grigori Yavlinsky, who heads the Yabloko Party, refused to participate, saying in a statement Friday that 'the ideological and political composition of these actions are unacceptable for Yabloko'.

(www.iht.com, 13 April 2007)

A rally in Moscow ended in scuffles and arrests ... During Saturday's march ... 170 people were arrested, including Garry Kasparov. The former chess champion was freed several hours later after being fined $40 for public order offences ... Russian authorities sanctioned the rally but banned a march ... A huge security operation, including more than 9,000 police, was launched to prevent protesters from gathering at Pushkin Square ... Garry Kasparov ... retired from chess [in 2005] to focus his efforts on defeating President Vladimir Putin ... Garry Kasparov was born in 1963 in Baku, in the then Soviet republic of Azerbaijan, to a father of Jewish decent and an Armenian mother ... [Since 2005] he has assembled a bewilderingly broad coalition, Other Russia, which includes both mainstream politicians like ... former prime minister Mikhail Kasyanov and fringe groups from both ends of the political spectrum ... Other Russia combines elements of the now weakened and fragmented democratic movement with some of their bitterest former enemies – like the National Bolshevik Party, famous for its audacious anti-government stunts and quasi-Nazi symbols, or the far-left Workers' Party, led by old-style communist firebrand Viktor Anpilov. The movement's numbers are small, but correspondents say

Mr Kasparov's high international profile is enough to persuade the Kremlin to keep a close eye on his moves ... But correspondents say the movement does not seem to enjoy genuine popular support.

(www.bbc.co.uk, 14 and 15 April 2007)

Garry Kasparov ... was arrested with nearly 200 other protesters during a rally in Moscow on Saturday [14 April] that ended in clashes with riot troops ... The rally was principally supported by ... former prime minister Mikhail Kasyanov ... and Kasparov, who lead a group called the United Civil Front ... Authorities said roughly 9,000 police and interior ministry troops, known as OMON, were deployed in Moscow on Saturday. A Moscow police spokesman said 170 people were arrested; organizers said the number was much higher.

(www.iht.com, 14 April 2007)

The Moscow protesters on Saturday ... first gathered at landmark Pushkin Square, with the aim of marching toward another square about a mile away where authorities said they could hold a demonstration. But police clamped down on Pushkin Square, detaining demonstrators ... and later scuffling with a few hundred who managed to march to the authorized square.

(www.iht.com, 15 April 2007)

Thousands of police ... 9,000 police and special forces ... brutally suppressed an unsanctioned anti-Kremlin rally in Moscow on Saturday, beating some protesters with truncheons and detaining at least 170 demonstrators ... [The numbers protesting were] estimated by organizers at about 2,000, though by some participants as only 1,000 ... Several hundred demonstrators marched across Moscow towards another venue where authorities had give permission for a rally ... But on a hill ... demonstrators clashed with a chain of special troops blocking the street, who beat back marchers with truncheons. Andrei Illarionov, former adviser to President Putin turned Kremlin critic, [was] among those leading the march ... The liberal opposition has little support among the wider population, while the president's approval ratings remain over 70 per cent.

(www.ft.com, 15 April 2007)

Riot police beat and detained protesters ... Organizers say about 2,000 demonstrators turned out ... Police officers ... beat some and detained many others ... Police say 170 people had been detained, but a Kasparov aide, Marina Litvinovich, said as many as 600 were – although about half were released quickly ... Organizers had sought permission to gather in Pushkin Square, a traditional site for protests, but city officials rejected the request. Instead, they approved Turgenev Square, about a mile east and away from the city's commercial and cultural hub ... Television newscasts on Saturday reported the protests, but gave as much or more time to a pro-Kremlin youth rally held near Moscow State University.

(www.cnn.com, 15 April 2007)

The security operation in Moscow came as Russia warned it wanted the extradition of London-based exile Boris Berezovsky. Mr Berezovsky told the UK's *Guardian* newspaper [in an interview published on Friday 13 April] that he was plotting 'revolution' to overthrow Vladimir Putin. Accusing Mr Putin of creating an authoritarian regime, the tycoon said that Russia's leadership could only be removed by force. Later he clarified his words, stating that he backed 'bloodless change' and did not support violence.

(www.bbc.co.uk, 15 April 2007)

15 April 2007.

Hundreds of anti-Kremlin demonstrators have held a rally in St Petersburg ... The participants gathered at a square in the city centre, but were encircled by a similar number of riot police and prevented from marching. Smaller groups clashed with police after the main rally finished. Several opposition leaders were arrested ... Reports say Eduard Limonov, leader of the radical National Bolshevik Party, and several other organizers were arrested ... Authorities sanctioned the rally but banned any marching.

(www.bbc.co.uk, 15 April 2007)

About 1,000 anti-Kremlin demonstrators rallied [in St Petersburg] ... Garry Kasparov was among those arrested in Moscow and was released late Saturday night after being fined $38 for disrupting public order. He did not go to St Petersburg for the Sunday 15 April] rally. Cordons of police lined the square on the edge of central St Petersburg where the rally was held, but wide-scale detentions like those in Moscow were not observed ... The crowd appeared to be less than the organizers had hoped for, filling only about half of the area marked off by metal barricades for the rally. City authorities gave permission for the rally at the square [Pioneer Square] ... but banned plans for a march after the rally that would go down the city's main avenue [Nevsky Prospekt] and then on to the city government's headquarters.

(www.iht.com, 15 April 2007)

'Police arrested more than 100 protesters' (*IHT*, 16 April 2007, p. 4).

'Club-swinging riot police clashed Sunday [15 April] with opposition supporters ... after the rally ... chasing small groups of demonstrators, beating some on the ground and hauling them into police buses' (www.cnn.com, 15 April 2007).

About 700 demonstrators gathered yesterday [15 April] ... one day after up to 2,000 gathered for an anti-Kremlin rally in Moscow ... President Putin enjoys popularity ratings of more than 70 per cent, with the majority of Russians largely apolitical and seeking stability after the tumult of the Boris Yeltsin years.

(*FT*, 16 April 2007, p. 6)

'Journalists were detained ... Police ... arrested journalists covering the event ... Two German correspondents [were arrested], one in Moscow and one in St Petersburg' (*FT*, 17 April 2007, p. 7).

17 April 2007. Dmitri Peskov (deputy Kremlin spokesman):

I think some overreaction [by the police] really took place ... but their main role was to ensure law and order in the streets ... Everybody accepts these actions were quite limited ... [in terms of] the number of participants. But, of course, the very fact of these actions draws extreme attention from foreign media. And in the foreign media a certain exaggeration took place.

(*FT*, 18 April 2007, p. 6)

19 April 2007.

EU justice and interior ministers approved a deal with Moscow Thursday [19 April] that will ease visa barriers for Russian travelling to the EU from 1 June [2007]. The agreement also commits Russia to take back any illegal migrants who enter the EU.

(www.iht.com, 19 April 2007)

23 April 2007. Boris Yeltsin died of heart failure on 23 April 2007. He was seventy-six.

Three Russian Orthodox Church bishops will officiate at what will be the first funeral for a head of state sanctioned by the Church since Tsar Alexander III's in 1894. Former US presidents Bill Clinton and George Bush Sr are expected to be among the foreign leaders attending.

(www.bbc.co.uk, 24 April 2007)

In attendance (among others) at the funeral on Wednesday 26 April were the following: Vladimir Putin; Mikhail Gorbachev; Bill Clinton; George Bush Snr; John Major (former British prime minister); Prince Andrew (Duke of York: United Kingdom); Lech Walesa (Poland).

'This was the first funeral by the Orthodox Church for a head of state since that of Tsar Alexander III in 1894' (*The Times*, 26 April 2007, p. 40).

The Church of Christ the Saviour was destroyed by Stalin in 1931 and rebuilt in the 1990s when Yeltsin was president.

'Russians had not buried a leader with Orthodox rites since 1894, and never before a democratically elected one' (*The Economist*, 28 April 2007, p. 44).

'Not since the death of Tsar Alexander III in 1894 has the Christ the Saviour Cathedral officially been used for the funeral of a Russian head of state' (*IHT*, 26 April 2007, p. 3).

In a break with the Soviet past Boris Yeltsin was buried not in the Kremlin wall along Red Square, but next to Russian writers including Bulgakov and Mayakovsky, and another political maverick, Soviet leader Nikita Khrushchev ... [in the cemetery of] the sixteenth-century Novodevichy Convent.

(*FT*, 26 April 2007, p. 6)

There ... [in] the Novodevichy cemetery ... he will lie in the company of other mavericks, cultural and political, including Soviet writers Mikhail Bulgakov and Boris Pasternak, as well as Nikita Khrushchev ... Members of the Communist Party ... refused to rise during a moment of silence held before the start of the State Duma session on Wednesday [25 April].

(*IHT*, 26 April 2007, p. 3)

26 April 2007. President Vladimir Putin (state of the union address):

There is a growth in the flow of money from abroad for direct interference in our internal affairs. There are those who, skilfully using pseudo-democratic rhetoric, would like to return to the recent past – some to loot the country's national riches, to rob the people and the state; others to strip us of political and economic independence.

(www.iht.com, 26 April 2007)

President Vladimir Putin on Thursday [26 April] declared a moratorium on the 1990 Conventional Forces in Europe Treaty, which imposed limits on conventional military equipment in Europe ... Mr Putin added that Russia might pull out of the treaty ... unless Nato countries ratified a revised version of the text agreed in 1999 ... The United States has long refused to ratify the treaty unless Russia delivers on commitments to pull out troops from enclaves in the former Soviet states of Georgia and Moldova ... Delivering an annual state of the nation address, Mr Putin said his decision was partly linked to US plans to site elements of its missile defence system in Poland and the Czech Republic. He also alleged European countries were not fulfilling their own obligations under the treaty, adding that he believed that Russia was the only country observing it ... Putin: 'This gives us full grounds to declare that our partners are, to say the least, behaving incorrectly, using this to build up military bases near our borders. Moreover, they are planning to set up elements of their anti-missile system in the Czech Republic and Poland ... and this creates a real threat to our country. In connection with this, I consider it right to declare a moratorium on Russia's fulfilment of this treaty, in any case until all countries of Nato without exception ratify this treaty.

(www.ft.com, 26 April 2007)

President Vladimir Putin announced on Thursday [26 April] that Russia would suspend its compliance with the treaty on conventional arms in Europe ... Putin said the Kremlin would use future compliance with the treaty as a bargaining point in the dispute with the United States over American proposals to install missile defences in Europe ... With its initial ambitions largely achieved, it was renegotiated in 1999 and required Russia to withdraw its forces from Georgia and Moldova, two nations where Russian forces remain ... The treaty has not been ratified by most nations, including the United States, which has withheld ratification until the Kremlin complies with the troop withdrawal commitments ... Putin abruptly called into question its future, announcing a moratorium and seizing on the proposed missile defence system and Western reluctance to ratify the latest treaty ... He did not define what he meant by 'moratorium', but suggested that Russia would withdraw completely from the treaty if he is not satisfied with negotiations with the Nato–Russia Council, an organization created in 2002 ... Putin: 'I propose discussing the problem and should there be no progress in the negotiations, to look at the possibility of ceasing our commitments under the CFE treaty.'

(*IHT*, 27 April 2007, pp. 1, 8)

President Vladimir Putin: 'In the spring of next year [2008] my duties end and the next state of the nation speech will be delivered by a different head of state' (*IHT*, 27 April 2007, p. 1).

9 May 2007.

Russia marked the anniversary [Victory Day] of the defeat of Nazi Germany ... [in] the Great Patriotic War [as the Second World War is known in Russia] ... President Vladimir Putin did not mention Estonia by name, but condemned those who 'are desecrating monuments to war heroes, and in doing that are insulting their own people and sowing enmity and a new distrust between nations and people' ... In a rare public statement of dissent for a patriotic holiday, longtime human rights activist Yelena Bonner called on Russians to acknowledge that the victory did not result in liberation for many countries, including the Baltic nations ... Yelena Bonner: 'We did not liberate anyone; we were not even able to liberate ourselves, although for four difficult years of war we hoped for it. We even said "after the war, if we survive it, all life will be different". It did not happen; not in 1945, not in 1991.'

(www.iht.com, 9 May 2007)

President Vladimir Putin:

We do not have the right to forget the causes of any war, which must be sought in the mistakes and errors of peacetime. Moreover, in our time these threats are not diminishing. They are only transforming, changing their appearance. In these new threats – as during the time of the Third Reich – are the same contempt for human life and the same claims of exceptionality and diktat in the world.

(www.iht.com, 10 May 2007)

('Victory Day has evolved into the principal holiday in Russia, replacing the Soviet-era 7 November celebration Day of the Great October Socialist Revolution. The holiday was cancelled under Putin and replaced with another, marking a 1612 uprising against Poland, celebrated on 4 November': www.iht.com, 10 May 2007.)

16 May 2007.

Ministers from the OECD agreed Wednesday to open membership talks with five countries ... Russia, Israel, Chile, Estonia and Slovenia ... The

OECD, which aims to help governments achieve sustainable economic growth, highlighted Russia as a 'special case because of its historical relationship' with the club of thirty mainly industrialized nations. Russia first requested OECD membership in 1996. The OECD issued a damning report on the Russian economy in November [2006], saying that the government's intrusion into the energy, power generation, aviation and finance sectors was a 'disturbing' phenomenon that 'bodes ill for Russia's growth prospects'. The OECD also urged Gazprom to speed up its development of reserves to meet rising domestic and European demand.

(*IHT*, 17 May 2007, p. 3)

17 May 2007.

The Russian Orthodox Church Abroad has reunited with the Russian Orthodox Church after eighty years of schism sparked by the Bolshevik revolution. The move was sealed by Patriarch Alexei II and the head of the Russian Orthodox Church Abroad, Metropolitan Lavy [Laurus], at an elaborate ceremony in Moscow ... Exiled bishops and clerics proclaimed the Russian Orthodox Church Abroad at a meeting in Serbia in 1922 – later relocating to the United States. It cut all ties with its mother church in 1927, after the leader of the church in Russia, Patriarch Sergei, declared loyalty to the Communists. The New York-based church says it has nearly 500,000 members. The Moscow Patriarchate counts nearly 70 per cent of Russia's population of about 142 million as its members.

(www.bbc.co.uk, 17 May 2007)

The signing of a canonical union [took place] at Christ the Saviour Cathedral, which was dynamited by Stalin in 1931 and rebuilt in the 1990s ... The Russian Orthodox Church Outside of Russia [is] known informally as the Russian Church Abroad ... The Russian Church Abroad was created in the 1920s by émigrés who fled Russian with the White Army ... The core of the churches' differences lay in the Russian Orthodox Church's fealty to the Soviet state, a policy known as *sergianstvo*, after Metropolitan Sergius, the acting head of the church in 1927. That year he tried to end the persecution of the church by declaring loyalty to the Soviet government, which nevertheless killed roughly 80,000 Orthodox priests, monks and nuns and destroyed churches in the 1930s.

(www.iht.com, 17 May 2007)

18 May 2007.

Police prevented ... Garry Kasparov from boarding a flight Friday [18 May] to the city of Samara, where he planned to take part in a protest march coinciding with a Russia–EU summit ... that began Thursday evening [17 May] ... Another opposition leader, Eduard Limonov, said he was also barred from the flight ... Police prevented Garry Kasparov and other opposition activists from boarding flights to Samara ... The Dissenters' March set to take place in Samara was sanctioned by the local authorities ... More than

100 protesters gathered at a square in Samara … German chancellor Angela Merkel complained that opposition activists were being prevented from travelling to a planned protest in the Volga city of Samara, near the site of the EU–Russia summit … Merkel's remark came amid a sometimes fractious exchange between President Vladimir Putin and EU leaders at the news conference over Russia's democratic freedoms and the government's treatment of critics … Merkel and European Commission president José Manuel Barroso emphasized European solidarity. 'A Polish problem is a European problem,' Barroso said, adding that the EU also fully backs its members Estonia and Lithuanian their disputes with Moscow.

(www.iht.com, 18 May 2007)

José Manuel Barroso (European Commission president):

We had occasion to say to our Russian partners that a difficulty for a member state is a difficulty for the whole European Union. It is very important if you want to have close co-operation to understand that the EU is based on principles of solidarity … The Polish problem is a European problem. The Lithuanian and Estonian problems are also EU problems … We believe there are no reasons for a ban against Polish meat. If there was a reason we would not allow Polish meat to circulate in the EU.

(*Guardian*, 19 May 2007, p. 26; *IHT*, 19 May 2007, p. 4; *FT*, 19 May 2007, p. 6)

The leaders of the EU and Russia traded sharp criticism over human rights at the summit … In a break with previous practice no joint declaration was prepared before the summit … President Vladimir Putin turned the tables on the EU, accusing members of violating the human rights of their Russian minority.

(www.bbc.co.uk, 18 May 2007)

The summit was overshadowed by arguments over Moscow's ban on imports of Polish meat, the conflict between Russia and Estonia over the removal of a Soviet war memorial and EU leaders' criticisms of a Kremlin-imposed squeeze on democratic rights in Russia.

(*FT*, 19 May 2007, p. 6)

Police … refused to allow western journalists who booked tickets through Garry Kasparov's United Civil Front movement to get on the Aeroflot plane … Only around 300 demonstrators marched through the centre of Samara … Although President Putin continues to enjoy popular support in Russia – with polls putting his personal approval ratings at around 55 per cent – opposition to his rule appears to be growing.

(*Guardian*, 19 May 2007, p. 26)

22 May 2007.

Sir Ken Macdonald … the [UK] director of public prosecutions … [said that] Andrei Lugovoi … should be charged with the murder of Alexander

Litvinenko ... Macdonald: 'I have today [22 May] concluded that the evidence sent to us by the police is sufficient to charge Andrei Lugovoi with the murder of Mr Litvinenko by deliberate poisoning ... I have instructed CPS [Crown Prosecution Service] lawyers to take immediate steps to seek the early extradition of Andrei Lugovoi from Russia to the United Kingdom, so that he may be charged with murder – and be brought swiftly before a court in London to be prosecuted for this extraordinarily grave crime' ... A spokesman for the Kremlin said Russia's constitution did not allow its nationals to be extradited.

(www.bbc.co.uk, 22 May 2007)

'In accordance with the law [in Russia] a Russian national cannot be extradited to a foreign country on criminal charges' (www.bbc.co.uk, 23 May 2007). 'The prosecutor-general's office ... [has] said Russian citizens could not be extradited to a foreign country but could appear in a domestic court "with evidence provided by the foreign state"' (www.bbc.co.uk, 28 May 2007).

'Russian prosecutors say they will refuse to extradite Andrei Lugovoi ... to London because of a constitutional ban' (www.cnn.com, 22 May 2007).

A statement issued by the Russian federal prosecutor-general's office:

A citizen of the Russian Federation cannot be extradited to another state. A citizen who has committed a crime on the territory of a foreign country can be held criminally responsible, but only on Russian territory ... A citizen who has committed a crime on the territory of a foreign state can be prosecuted with evidence provided by the foreign state, but only on the territory of Russia.

(*The Independent*, 23 May 2007, p. 4; *IHT*, 23 May 2007, p. 7)

The Russian constitution forbids the extradition of citizens, but Britain pre-emptively emphasized Russia's international commitments, including a 1957 convention on extraditions and an agreement between prosecutors from both countries (signed only days before Alexander Litvinenko died) to co-operate 'in the sphere of extradition'.

(www.iht.com, 27 May 2007)

25 May 2007.

Russian prosecutor-general Yuri Chaika: 'If the British side present us with evidence of Andrei Lugovoi's guilt and we consider it sufficient then he can be prosecuted [in Russia]' ... Lord Goldsmith, the British Attorney General, rejected the offer, saying that the trial should take place on British soil.

(*The Independent*, 26 May 2007, p. 33)

27 May 2007.

The police and riot troops Sunday [27 May] prevented a rally for homosexual rights in Moscow, detaining organizers along with European lawmakers, as members of Orthodox Christian and nationalist groups pummelled gay rights demonstrators with insults, eggs and fists ... The protest Sunday was the second attempt by organizers to hold a gay pride demonstration. A similar event a little more than a year ago ended in bloodshed ... Like last year [2006] organizers of the event Sunday violated a government ban ... Yuri Luzhkov, the Moscow mayor, referred to a gay pride parade as a 'satanic event' during an address in January [2007].

(*IHT*, 28 May 2007, p. 3)

28 May 2007. 'A formal extradition request has been made to Russia by the UK for ... Andrei Lugovoi' (www.bbc.co.uk, 28 May 2007).

29 May 2007.

Russia on Tuesday [29 May] tested [successfully] a new intercontinental ballistic missile ... the RS-24 ... that it said could break through any anti-missile defence system, and President Vladimir Putin stepped up his attacks on the proposed US shield in Poland and the Czech Republic, saying its development in Europe would turn the continent into 'a powder keg' ... The RS-24 missile was test fired from a mobile launcher ... [Russia said that it] has also successfully tested a tactical cruise missile ... The new missile is seen as eventually replacing the aging RS-18s and RS-20s that are the backbone of the country's missile forces ... Those missiles are known in the West as the SS-19 Stiletto and the SS-18 Satan ... [Russia] said the missile was a new version of the Topol-M, first known as the SS-27 in the West, modified to carry multiple-independent warheads ... The first Topol-Ms were commissioned in 1997.

(*IHT*, 30 May 2007, pp. 1, 7)

'The RS-24 was described a capable of carrying up to ten warheads ... [Russia] also watched a successful test of the Iskander cruise missile' (*FT*, 30 May 2007, p. 10).

31 May 2007. 'President Vladimir Putin has said a recent ballistic missile test was in answer to US plans to create a defence shield in Central Europe' (www. bbc.co.uk, 31 May 2007).

Andrei Lugovoi ... claimed to have evidence of British intelligence involvement in last November's poisoning of Alexander Litvinenko ... Mr Lugovoi suggested that Boris Berezovsky ... was a likely suspect in Litvinenko's death ... He also alleged Litvinenko and Berezovsky had become UK agents and British intelligence had tried to recruit him to collect material on President Vladimir Putin.

(*FT*, 1 June 2007, p. 1)

3 June 2007. 'In weekend interviews with journalists from the G8 countries, President Vladimir Putin threatened to target sites in Europe if the United States proceeded with deployment of its anti-missile shield in Poland and the Czech Republic' (*IHT*, 5 June 2007, p. 1).

President Vladimir Putin:

> If part of the strategic nuclear potential of the United States finds itself in Europe and, according to our military experts, threatens us, then we will have to take corresponding retaliatory steps. What are these steps? Of course, we will have to have new targets in Europe ... If the American nuclear potential grows in European territory, we have to give ourselves new targets in Europe. It is up to our military to define these targets, in addition to defining the choice between ballistic and cruise missiles. But this is just a technical aspect.
>
> (www.iht.com, 4 June 2007; *IHT*, 5 June 2007, p. 4)

6 June 2007.

The foreign minister of Russia withdrew a threat to pull out of a conventional arms treaty ... Last month [May] Sergei Lavrov called an emergency conference for next week in Vienna to discuss the Treaty on Conventional Force in Europe after President Vladimir Putin announced that Russia would freeze its commitments under the pact. But Lavrov said Wednesday [6 June] that Moscow was not planning to withdraw from the treaty.

(*IHT*, 7 June 2007, p. 1)

7 June 2007.

> President George W. Bush has described as 'interesting' a proposal by Russia's president for resolving the row over the panned US missile shield. Vladimir Putin said their two countries could use a radar system in Azerbaijan to develop a shield covering all of Europe during talks at the G8 summit ... The Russian leader said the threat to re-target Russian missiles could be withdrawn if Washington agreed to use the former Soviet radar base at Gabala in Azerbaijan.
>
> (www.bbc.co.uk, 7 June 2007)

> President Vladimir Putin put forth a counter-offer Thursday [7 June] to President George W. Bush's proposed missile defence plan, suggesting that instead of building radar defences in the Czech Republic the United States should use an existing system in Azerbaijan. The surprise offer came during a private meeting between the two presidents [at the G8 summit] ... Bush said the Putin plan contained 'some interesting suggestions' and the two sides agreed to form a working group of military and diplomatic experts to examine how they might co-operate on missile defence ... The Russians lease the station ... the radar station in the town of Gabala in north-east Azerbaijan ... and some Azeri politicians have objected to the arrangement, although Putin said he had already secured a pledge of co-operation from the president of Azerbaijan ... Officials from both sides said Thursday that the Russian president had not dropped his opposition to the Poland component of the shield plan, even as he put forth his own initiative for the radar.
>
> (*IHT*, 8 June 2007, pp. 1, 7)

'The Azeri radar, located in Gabala and operated by Russia under a lease, is used for early detection of launches, and is a different sort of system from the fire-control radar used to guide interceptor missies against am incoming target' (www.iht.com, 9 June 2007).

8 June 2007.

> President Vladimir Putin said Friday [8 June] that missile defence interceptors could be located in Turkey, or even Iraq or on sea platforms ... Putin: '[The interceptors] could be placed in the south, in US Nato allies such as Turkey or even Iraq ... They could also be placed on sea platforms' ... Putin said that ... interceptors could be fired from Aegis cruisers rather than from Poland ... [President Putin] proposed that Russia and the West study emerging missile threats together ... He urged the United States not to proceed with its plans until after thorough consultations with Russia on its own ideas, and suggested creating a pool of countries, including Europe, to evaluate emerging missile threats together through 2012.
>
> (www.iht.com, 8 June 2007)

11 June 2007.

> Garry Kasparov and allies ... held their latest showdown with President Vladimir Putin's government Monday [11 June], keeping up their frequent protests with a demonstration in central Moscow. Some 2,000 people gathered in a square blocked off by metal barriers and ringed by troops and police ... The protest came two days after a peaceful march and rally in St Petersburg – the first time that a demonstration led by Kasparov and his allies in a major Russian city has ended without police violence or interference ... The St Petersburg march Friday [9 June] took place as foreign executives attended a business forum and met with Putin in the same city ... Moscow authorities had granted organizers permission to protest at the site Monday but not to parade down a main street, as they requested ... City authorities also stipulated that no more than 500 people could attend the rally in a square ... The same limit was in place for Friday's march and rally in St Petersburg, but police took no action against a crowd that reached about 1,500 ... Monday was an official holiday in Russia.
>
> (www.iht.com, 11 June 2007)

A protest in Moscow led by ... Garry Kasparov and other critics of President Vladimir Putin ended peacefully Monday [11 June], in marked contrast to their last demonstration in the capital, which ended with beatings and arrest by the authorities. Interior ministry troops stood by as the crowd swelled to about 2,000. The authorities did not intervene, despite warnings by officials that no more than 500 protesters could gather at the site, near Pushkin Square in Moscow. It was only the second time that a demonstration led by Kasparov and his allies in a major Russian city had ended without police violence or other interference ... On Saturday [9 June] the authorities permitted an Other Russia march that drew 1,500 people in St Petersburg to proceed unmolested. The authorities in Moscow had granted a permit for the protest Monday, but not for a planned parade down Moscow's main street, Tverskaya. The organizers considered defying the restriction, but Kasparov said they had decided against that.

(www.iht.com, 11 June 207)

15 June 2007.

Russia's security agency said Friday [15 June] it has opened an investigation into suspected British spying, based on information from ... Andrei Lugovoi ... [who] claimed last month [May] that both Alexander Litvinenko and Boris Berezovsky had contacts with British intelligence ... The Federal Security Service (FSB) said the new investigation was based on 'Lugovoi's statement and additional information from him about intelligence activity by the British special services on the territory of Russia' ... At a news conference on 31 May Lugovoi said British intelligence services may have had a hand in Litvinenko's poisoning, but said he would only provide evidence to Russian investigators ... He said Litvinenko had tried to recruit him to work for Britain's MI6 foreign intelligence agency and gather compromising materials about Putin.

(www.iht.com, 15 June 2007)

The Russian intelligence service announced on Friday that it had opened a criminal investigation into British espionage in Russia based on statements and undisclosed evidence provided by ... Andrei Lugovoi ... [On 31 May Lugovoi] accused Britain's foreign intelligence service, MI6, of orchestrating the whole affair and of recruiting Alexander Litvinenko and Boris Berezovsky.

(*IHT*, 16 June 2007, p. 3)

A spokesman for the FSB said a criminal case had been opened based on remarks given by Andrei Lugovoi ... A statement by the FSB said a criminal case has been opened relating to allegations of espionage following an investigation into remarks made by Lugovoi.

(www.bbc.co.uk, 15 June 2007)

[On 31 May] Andrei Lugovoi claimed to have evidence that British intelligence services were linked to the murder of Alexander Litvinenko ... Mr Lugovoi also said Mr Litvinenko and Boris Berezovsky were agents of British secret intelligence and that MI6 had tried to recruit him to provide information on President Vladimir Putin.

(*FT*, 16 June 2007, p. 6)

2 July 2007.

Russian prosecutors have charged Boris Berezovsky with plotting to seize power, his lawyer said Monday [2 July] ... 'He has been charged with conspiring to seize power in a violent coup,' said Berezovsky's lawyer, Andrei Borovkov ... The charge was brought by the FSB, the Russian security agency, said the lawyer, and related to an interview the tycoon gave the *Guardian* newspaper in which he was quoted as saying that force was needed to bring about a change of power in Russia ... Berezovsky subsequently issued a state of clarification in which he said he was not advocating a violent uprising ... Alex Goldfarb, a Berezovsky associate, said that the tycoon hoped for a regime change in Russia similar to bloodless revolutions in Ukraine and Georgia ... The FSB declined to confirm that new charges had been brought against the tycoon ... In a separate case in which his lawyers declined to take part, Berezovsky is being tried in absentia on embezzlement charges. He faces up to ten years in jail if convicted of embezzling 214 million roubles, or $8.32 million, from the Russian airline Aeroflot.

(*FT*, 3 July 2007, p. 3)

Russia today [2 July] charged Boris Berezovsky with conspiring to seize power on the basis of an interview he gave to the *Guardian* ... on 13 April ... calling for a violent revolution in Russia ... In it the tycoon claimed he was plotting the violent overthrow of President Putin from his base in Britain after forging close contacts with members of Russia's ruling elite ... Mr Berezovsky claimed he was already bankrolling people close to the president who were conspiring to mount a palace coup. 'We need to use force to change this regime,' he said. 'It isn't possible to change this regime through democratic means. There can be no change without force, pressure.' Asked whether he was effectively fomenting a revolution, he said: 'You are absolutely correct'... In a separate case, Mr Berezovsky went on trial in his absence in Moscow today charged with money-laundering and embezzlement. He is accused of stealing £4.12 million from the Russian state airline Aeroflot. The case was adjourned until 12 July after Mr Berezovsky's legal team announced it was boycotting the proceedings.

(www.guardian.co.uk, 2 July 2007)

President Vladimir Putin on Monday proposed to expand his proposal for a shared missile defence system during talks [held 1–2 July] here [Kennebunkport, Maine, United States] with President George W. Bush ... Comments by Bush and Putin came near the end of a two-day visit by Putin to Kennebunkport. It was the first time the current [US] president had invited a head of state to the family home there ... [President Putin] continued his opposition to an American plan to place anti-missile facilities in Poland and the Czech Republic ... [but] proposed expanding co-operation on a missile shield to include Europe and Nato ... Putin: 'We support the idea of consultations on missile defence and believe that the number of participants should be expanded to include the European states ... [This should be done] within [the Russia–Nato council].'

(*IHT*, 3 July 2007, pp. 1, 3)

President Putin offered a second proposal on Monday [2 July]: modernize the capabilities of a Russian-operated radar in Azerbaijan, as well as link to the system a new radar facility being built in southern Russia. He also proposed making the shield more regional by bringing in Nato and setting up joint early warning missile launch centres ... The two countries pledged Tuesday [3 July] to reduce their stockpiles of long-range nuclear weapons 'to the lowest possible' level.

(www.iht.com, 4 July 2007)

Putin suggested that the United States use current or proposed radar sites in Azerbaijan and southern Russia, adding this would eliminate the need for a proposed radar site in the Czech Republic and a battery of ten interceptor missiles in Poland ... Putin last month [June] proposed that the United States share the use of a mammoth Russian-leased radar installation in Azerbaijan aimed south toward Iran, as an early warning system. He suggested that an interceptor missile site could be built only if Iran developed the capability of launching nuclear missiles ... In Kennebunkport Putin offered to modernize Gabala, as well as link to the system a new radar facility being built in southern Russia.

(*IHT*, 5 July 2007, p. 8)

President Vladimir Putin has given more details of his proposal ... for the United States to use a Russian-managed radar base in Azerbaijan as an alternative to the Czech Republic – offering to refurbish the radar to meet US requirements or even build a new facility in southern Russia.

(*FT*, 3 July 2007, p. 6)

'President Putin ... called for the establishment of joint early-warning centres in Brussels and Moscow' (*FT*, 4 July 2007, p. 8).

3 July 2007.

Mikhail Kasyanov ... has split from ... Other Russia ... The split arose because Kasyanov wanted the coalition to move quickly to choose a single candidate for the presidential vote, but Garry Kasparov and others said they needed more time ... Kasyanov is planning to run for the presidency in the 2008 election.

(*IHT*, 4 July 2007, p. 3)

'Mikhail Kasyanov said he was leaving ... Other Russia ... to form a party and pursue presidential ambitions' (*FT*, 4 July 2007, p. 7).

5 July 2007.

Russia has officially refused a UK extradition request for Andrei Lugovoi ... The Russian prosecutor-general's office said the constitution did not allow for the extradition of its citizens. However, it said it would consider the possibility that Mr Lugovoi could be put on trial in Russia ... It has taken Russia five weeks to give an official response, although prosecutor-general Yuri Chaika has repeatedly said no Russian national would stand trial in Britain.

(www.bbc.co.uk, 5 July 2007)

The prosecutor-general's office said its refusal to hand over Andrei Lugovoi was based on a constitutional ban on turning Russian citizens over to foreign countries, as well as a European convention that allows signatories to refuse to extradite their nationals ... Russian officials, including President Vladimir Putin, had emphasized that Lugovoi would not be extradited. Putin called the British request 'stupidity', saying the authorities in London should have known about the Russian constitutional ban. In a statement the prosecutor-general's office also said it would consider investigating Lugovoi as a suspect if Britain made such a request and provided sufficient evidence to justify it. Prosecutors had said earlier they would not rule out prosecuting Lugovoi ... Lugovoi said the British secret services and a self-exiled tycoon [Boris Berezovsky] could have had a hand in Alexander Litvinenko's death.

(*IHT*, 6 July 2007, p. 4)

6 July 2007.

[The State Duma] strengthened police surveillance powers Friday [6 July] and broadened the definition of extremism in legislation that Kremlin critics say will stifle freedom ahead of elections. The bill is the second such measure to be pushed through parliament in the past year ... The State Duma voted 311 to ninety to pass the [new] bill, which the government maintains is aimed at curbing nationalist and radical groups amid a surge of racist and xenophobic attacks. The measures broaden the definition of extremism by adding crimes driven by political, ideological or social hatred to the existing formula that includes racial, national and religious motives. It also allows law enforcement agencies to interpret relatively minor crimes such as hooliganism and public disturbances as extremist in some cases, and to tap phones of people suspected of extremism under the new definition. The bill also prohibits media from referring to organizations that were banned as extremist without mentioning the ban, and introduces fines for printers and publishers for disseminating literature deemed extremist. It also bars those suspected of extremism from running for government office. The bill now goes to the upper house for approval before going to President Putin ... A bill signed into law last year [2006] by Putin says slandering a government official could be treated as extremism, although a court must first issue a ruling on the statements in question and criminalizes the creation or distribution of taped, printed or other material deemed extremist – a measure critics say could affect any media reporting on extremism.

(*IHT*, 7 July 2007, p. 2)

7 July 2007.

Authorities are investigating allegations that a former Russian tax inspector spied for Britain. The Federal Security Service (FSB) said Vyacheslav Zharko was recruited by agents from Britain's M16 foreign intelligence service ... The FSB said Mr Zharko was recruited by M16 through the mediation of Alexander Litvinenko and ... Boris Berezovsky ... The FSB said Mr Zharko admitted spying for Britain after turning himself in because he feared for his life [it was reported].

(www.bbc.co.uk, 7 July 2007)

14 July 2007.

President Vladimir Putin has suspended ... the Conventional Forces in Europe Treaty (CFE) ... The suspension is not a full-scale withdrawal – but it means that Russia will no longer permit inspections or exchange data on its deployments ... The CFE agreement of 1990 ... limits the number of heavy weapons deployed between the Atlantic Ocean and the Ural mountains ... It sets strict limits on the number of offensive weapons – battle tanks, combat aircraft, heavy artillery – that the members of the Warsaw Pact and Nato could deploy in Europe, stretching from the Atlantic to the Urals. In the wake of the collapse of communism the treaty was revised in 1999, in part to address Russian concerns. But the revised treaty has never been ratified by the Nato countries who want Russia to withdraw all its forces from ... Abkhazia in Georgia and Transdniestre in Moldova.

(www.bbc.co.uk, 14 July 2007)

President Vladimir Putin signed a decree suspending Russia's participation in the CFE Treaty due to 'extraordinary circumstances ... which affect the security of the Russian Federation and require immediate measures' ... Under the moratorium Russia would halt [onsite] inspections and verifications of its military sites by Nato countries and would no longer limit the number of its conventional weapons ... The treaty was signed in 1990 and amended in 1999 to reflect changes since the breakup of the Soviet Union, adding the requirement that Moscow withdrew troops from ... Moldova and Georgia. Russia has ratified the amended version, but the United States and other Nato members have refused to do so until Russia completely withdraws.

(www.cnn.com, 15 July 2007)

The conventional forces treaty has no formal provision for a signatory nation to suspend observance. A nation can withdraw from the treaty without violating its terms, but only after notifying the other signatory countries 150 days in advance. The decree President Vladimir Putin signed on Saturday [14 July] adhered to that timeframe, but sought to apply it to suspension instead of withdrawal. The foreign ministry said this formulation complied with 'international law' ... [The] foreign ministry said that Russia would halt inspections allowed under the treaty and claimed the right to redeploy heavy weaponry along its western and southern borders, but would do so only in response to any possible Nato redeployment. It also suggested that the suspension was Russia's first official rejection of the arms limitation treaties of the Soviet Union.

(www.iht.com, 15 July 2007)

One of Moscow's central complaints [is] that the United States and its Nato allies have not even ratified a set of adaptations negotiated in 1999 to update the original pact, signed in 1990. The United States and its Western allies remain eager to ratify the adapted treaty once Moscow takes actions moving a modest number of remaining forces out of Georgia and Moldova ... [Russia says that as regards Georgia] all that remains are a few hundred Russian troops at Gudauta in Abkhazia ... In Moldova about forty-nine trainloads of Russian munitions remain, as well as about 1,300 Russian troops guarding the munitions and serving as peacekeepers in the dispute over Transdniestre ... A Kremlin statement said that Nato expansion into Eastern Europe had increased the alliance's military capabilities, in viola-tion of the original treaty. The statement also said that ... Latvia, Lithuania and Estonia were not signers of the treaty but had alliance weapons deployed on their territories. Russian officials bristle at talk from the Penta-gon of building new bases for American forces in former Warsaw Pact nations. Senior [US] administration and Nato officials counter that Western forces in Europe remain below the limits of the treaty and that few Ameri-can forces would be stationed permanently at new bases under consideration in Romania and Bulgaria, which would serve more as training stations and as springboards for deployments elsewhere.

(www.iht.com, 16 July 2007)

16 July 2007.

The UK is to expel four Russian diplomats in response to Russia's refusal to extradite ... Andrei Lugovoi ... The BBC understands they are intelligence officers ... Under the Council of Europe European Convention on Extradi-tion 1957, the Russians have the right to refuse the extradition of a citizen ... [The UK] also said co-operation with Russia on a range of issues was under review ... [The UK said that] as an initial step ... visa facilitation negotiations with Russia ... [have been suspended] ... and [that it has] made other changes to visa practice ... The British embassy in Moscow later said that the visa process would only change for applications submitted by the Russian government, not those of ordinary Russians.

(www.bbc.co.uk, 16 July 2007)

'Later the foreign ministry ... [said] a "targeted" response would take into account the interests of ordinary citizens, including business people ... The four Russian diplomats expelled by London are all middle-ranking officials uncon-nected to the Litvinenko case' (www.ft.com, 17 Juluy 2007).

'Britain's director of public prosecutions maintains that prosecutors have enough evidence to prove that Andrei Lugovoi administered a fatal dose of polo-nium-210 to Alexander Litvinenko via a pot of tea in a London hotel last November [2006]' (*IHT*, 17 July 2007, p. 1).

Britain and Russia last clashed over diplomatic expulsions in March 1996, when Moscow ordered out a number of Britons amid claims of spying.

Moscow expelled nine British diplomats in 1996 alleging that they were part of a spy ring. Britain expelled four Russians in response.

(www.iht.com, 16 July 2007)

'A waiter who was working at ... London's Millennium Hotel ... told a Britsh newspaper on Sunday [15 July] that he believed the poison had been sprayed into a pot of green tea' (www.iht.com, 18 July 2007).

'It was alleged that ... Andrei Lugovoi ... had settled an old score by spraying polonium into a pot of green tea' (*Guardian*, 17 July 2007, p. 3).

18 July 2007.

Boris Berezovsky was the target of an assassination plot, he said today [18 July] ... Boris Berezovsky: 'Three weeks ago the [British] police informed me that they were aware that an assassin had been sent from Russia to kill me ... I have over the years received many threats to my life ... All these threats bear the hallmarks of Russian security service activity and of course President Putin changed the law last year [2006] to empower agents to commit murder overseas, following an assassination by Russian agents in Qatar ... It is a joy to live in a country where the individual citizen's rights are so well protected. The most dramatic example is the Crown Prosecution Service ruling that I am free to continue my opposition to President Putin's authoritarian rule and their correct interpretation that I am not proposing a violent overthrow.'

(www.independent.co.uk, 18 July 2007)

'Boris Berezovsky said he held the Russian president responsible for the alleged plot. "It's Putin personally," he said' (www.guardian.co.uk, 18 July 2007).

Boris Berezovsky ... said the same people were behind the plan to assassinate him and the successful plot to kill Alexander Litvinenko. He said such assassinations would require the personal approval of Mr Putin. 'It's Putin personally that's behind this,' he said.

(*FT*, 19 July 2007, p. 6)

British police confirmed Wednesday [18 July] that they had arrested a man on suspicion of conspiring to murder Boris Berezovsky. The Metropolitan police said they arrested the man in central London on 21 June and handed him over to immigration officials two days later.

(www.iht.com, 18 July 2007)

'Security sources yesterday [18 July] confirmed that a Russian man was arrested ... on 21 June ... The man was questioned for two days and then handed over to the immigration services who revoked his visa and deported him (*The Independent*, 19 July 2007, p. 7).

'A man suspected of planning to murder ... Boris Berezovsky in London was deported last month [June] from the UK, police said yesterday [18 July]' (*FT*, 19 July 2007, p. 6).

19 July 2007.

Russia is to expel four UK diplomats ... [They] must leave Russia within ten days and Moscow is to review visa applications for UK officials ... Announcing the tit-for-tat response, foreign ministry spokesman Mikhail Kamynin said Moscow would not apply for any UK visas for Russian officials.

(www.bbc.co.uk, 19 July 2007)

'Mikhail Kamynin said the interest of tourists and businessmen would not be hurt. He said that on visa issues Russia would mirror Britain's actions from now on' (www.iht.com, 19 July 2007).

Mikhail Kamynin (foreign ministry spokesman):

[Russia's response is] targeted, balanced and the minimum necessary ... Until the new procedure is explained, Russian officials will not request British visas and analogous requests by British officials will not be considered ... From now on we shall act in a mirrorlike fashion in regard to all visa-related issues ... To our regret, co-operation between Russia and Britain on issues of fighting terrorism becomes impossible ... The measures declared by London recently make co-operation between Russia and the UK impossible ... in the war on terror.

(www.iht.com, 19 July 2007; *IHT*, 20 July 2007, p. 3; www.bbc.co.uk, 19 July 2007)

The nature of the reaction suggests that the Russian authorities want to avoid any escalation over the poisoning case ... In his first public comments on the tit-for-tat diplomatic expulsions, President Vladimir Putin said he believed that relations with Britain would now 'develop normally' ... Putin: 'It is necessary to measure one's actions against common sense, respect the legitimate interests of partners and everything will be all right. I think we will overcome this mini-crisis.'

(*IHT*, 20 July 2007, p. 3)

24 July 2007. 'President Vladimir Putin on Tuesday [24 July] angrily dismissed British demands for the extradition of Andrei Lugovoi ... President Putin: "What they are offering to us is a clear remnant of colonial thinking"' (*IHT*, 25 July 2007, p. 4).

30 July 2007.

Russian prosecutors said Monday [30 July] that they had asked a Moscow court to issue an arrest warrant for Boris Berezovsky in connection with a new criminal case against [him] ... The previously unknown case dates from the 1990s ... The prosecutor-general's office asked for Berezovsky's arrest on charges he stole $13 million from the SBS-Agro banking giant. It also asked the court to seize Berezovsky's property in France ... According to Berezovsky's lawyer, he is accused of suing middlemen to take out a loan from the bank in 1997, which was used to acquire a villa in southern France and never repaid ... [The lawyer said that] Berezovsky rented the villa, which was subsequently sold to a British company ... Berezovsky is currently being tried in absentia for the alleged embezzlement of millions of dollars from the state airline Aeroflot in the 1990s.

(*IHT*, 31 July 2007, p. 3)

2 August 2007.

Russian explorers have planted their country's flag on the seabed 4,200 metres (14,000 feet) below the North Pole to further Moscow's claims to the Arctic. The rust-proof titanium flag was brought by explorers travelling in two mini-submarines, in what is believed to be the first expedition of its kind ... Moscow argued before a UN commission in 2001 that waters off its northern coast were in fact an extension of its maritime territory. The claim was based on the argument that an underwater feature, known as the Lomonosov Ridge, was an extension of its continental territory, but it was rejected and Russia told to resubmit more evidence. Several countries bordering the Arctic – including Russia, the United States, Canada and Denmark – have launched competing claims to the region.

(www.bbc.co.uk, 2 August 2007)

A Russian expedition travelled Thursday [2 August] in a pair of submersibles more than 4 kilometres under the ice cap and deposited a Russian flag on the seabed at the North Pole, making a symbolic claim to the vast fields of oil and natural gas believed to be beneath the sea north of the Arctic Circle ... Five countries – Canada, Denmark, Norway, Russia and the United States – have territory in the Arctic Circle and under international convention have rights to economic zones within 320 kilometres (200 miles) of their borders ... Russian foreign minister Sergei Lavrov: 'The goal of this expedition is not to stake out Russia's rights, but to prove that our shelf stretches up to the North Pole.'

(www.iht.com, 2 August 2007; *IHT*, 3 August 2007, p. 3)

Sergei Lavrov ... [said] that the possible extension of Russia's offshore territory would be decided 'exclusively in accordance with international law' ... Lavrov: 'The goal of this expedition is not to pinpoint Russia's rights, but to prove that or [continental] shelf stretches to the North Pole.'

(*FT*, 3 August 2007, p. 8)

The five Arctic Circle countries – America, Canada, Denmark (which looks after Greenland's interests), Norway and Russia – each have a 200-mile (322-kilometre) 'economic zone' allowed by the United Nations Convention on the Law of the Sea ... The latest Russian expedition is not just collecting geological samples; on Thursday 2 August it placed the Russian flag (in titanium) on the yellow gravel 4,200 metres below the surface at the site of the North Pole.

(www.economist.com, 3 August 2007)

6 August 2007.

A court on Monday [6 August] convicted a former top security officer with the Yukos oil company on charges of involvement in several murders. Alexei Pichugin was sentenced to twenty-four years in prison on similar charges last August. But prosecutors had appealed for a life sentence last August [2006] and Russia's highest court had ordered a retrial. On Monday, at the conclusion of a new trial, the Moscow City Court ruled that Pichugin was guilty of organizing three murders and four attempted murders ... Pichugin, the former head of Yukos security service, has insisted he is innocent ... Prosecutors have charged that Mikhail Khodorkovsky's business partner Leonid Nevzlin, who lives in self-imposed exile in Israel, was linked to Pichugin.

(www.iht.com, 6 August 2007)

A court yesterday [6 August] sentenced Alexei Pichugin ... to life imprisonment in a hard labour camp for a series of murders and attempted killings. The decision upheld an earlier conviction against Mr Pichugin, who was sentenced last August [2006] to twenty-four years in prison for murder ... He had been sentenced to twenty years in a previous murder trial ... Russia's supreme court ordered the retrial in February [2007], siding with prosecutors who appealed for a tougher sentence ... Kamil Kashaev (prosecutor-general): 'I think that this sentence is a first step in the process against [Leonid] Nevzlin. The court established his participation in all the murders and attacks for which Pichugin was found guilty today' ... Crippling tax charges [have been] recently levied against Russneft, the oil group founded by Mikhail Gutseriev ... who resigned as president of Russneft last week.

(*FT*, 7 August 2007, p. 4)

7 August 2007.

A court issued a new arrest warrant Tuesday [7 August] for Boris Berezovsky ... Berezovsky is already on trial in absentia on charges of embezzling Aeroflot. Now he is accused of stealing $13 million from the SBS-Agro banking giant, a case that surfaced last month [July].

(*IHT*, 8 August 2007, p. 8)

13 August 2007.

Russia yesterday [14 August] opened a terrorist investigation into a train blast outside Moscow that left dozens injured. It was the first bomb attack outside the North Caucasus region in at least a year. No one took responsibility for the attack that derailed the Nevsky Express passenger train heading from Moscow to St Petersburg late on Monday [13 August], which left twenty-five people in hospital and injured at least thirty-five others ... Analysts said it was too early to tell whether the attack on the train was linked to the growing insurgency in the North Caucasus ... Moscow sent hundreds more troops in recent days to the worst affected region, the Ingushetia republic, which borders Chechnya ... Russian news agencies cited unnamed sources as saying investigators had found an explosive device similar to the one used to blow up a train travelling from Grozny to Moscow in 2005 which injured forty-two people.

(*FT*, 15 August 2007, p. 6)

No one was killed in the blast ... but at least six people were seriously injured ... At least sixty of the more than 230 people on board the train were injured ... [Terrorist] attacks have declined in frequency and scale since late 2004 ... Fighting has simmered again in recent weeks, however, as it often does in summer. Russia has been conducting sweep operations in Ingushetia.

(*IHT*, 15 August 2007, p. 3)

17 August 2007.

President Vladimir Putin said Friday [17 August] that he had ordered the military to resume regular long-range flights of strategic bombers ... Speaking after Russian and Chinese forces completed major war games exercises for the first time on Russian turf, Putin said a halt in regular patrols by long-range bombers after the Soviet collapse had affected Russia's security. Other nations, he said, had continued such missions – an oblique reference to the United States ... The Russian–Chinese war games ... which took place in the Ural mountains ... coincided with Russian Air Force manoeuvres involving strategic bombers that ranged far over the Atlantic, Pacific and Arctic oceans. Putin said that twenty Russian bombers had been involved in the exercise ... Putin: 'I have made a decision to resume regular flights of Russian strategic aviation ... Starting today [17 August] such tours of duty will be conducted regularly and on a strategic scale ... Starting in 1992 the Russian Federation unilaterally suspended strategic aviation flights to remote areas. Regrettably, other nations have not followed our example. That has created certain problems for Russia's security' ... In recent years Russia's bombers have resumed occasional flights to areas off Norway and Iceland, as well as Russia's north-east corner, across the Bering Strait from Alaska. However, such missions have been rare, and Putin's statement signalled that they would become more regular ... As of the beginning of the year [2007], Russia had seventy-nine strategic bombers ... At the peak of the Cold War the Soviet long-range bomber fleet numbered several hundred.

(*IHT*, 18 August 2007, p. 3)

President Putin's announcement ... came just eight days after Russian strategic bombers made their first sortie into areas patrolled by Nato and the United States since the end of the Cold War. Two Tu-95 bombers flew over a US naval base on the Pacific island of Guam on 9 August.

(*FT*, 18 August 2007, p. 6)

The BBC said Friday [17 August] that its Russian language FM broadcasts had been taken off the air by its Moscow distributor, which said its programmes were 'foreign propaganda' ... The decision by Radio Bolshoe – and similar moves by two other radio stations in the past year – leaves the BBC's Russian language services available only on medium wave and shortwave broadcasts.

(*IHT*, 18 August 2007, p. 3)

27 August 2007.

Russia's prosecutor-general said Monday that ten people had been arrested for roles in the killing last October [2006] of Anna Politkovskaya ... including a Chechen crime boss collaborating with career officers from the country's police and intelligence services ... Among those arrested was a former officer in the FSB ... But the announcement managed to raise more questions than it answered, and was denounced by Politkovskaya's former editor as a whitewash designed to deflect blame from those who had ordered the journalist's death. The controversy arose because the prosecutor, Yuri Chaika, suggested the killing had not been carried out to silence Politkovskaya ... Rather, the prosecutor said, the killing was designed to discredit the Kremlin and destabilize the Russian state ... Chaika added that the killing was ordered from abroad ... The prosecutor's description of the motive aligned neatly with President Vladimir Putin's first public statements last year [2006] about the killing ... It was swiftly criticized as an act of political convenience by Dmitri Muratov, editor in chief of *Novaya Gazeta*, the independent newspaper where Politkovskaya worked. Muratov said that he thought the ten suspects had been involved in the murder, but said Chaika's description of their motive had been tailored to the Kremlin's orders ... [Muratov] added that he had co-operated with the government's investigators on the case ... but had never found evidence supporting Chaika's claim of foreign involvement ... Muratov said that *Novaya Gazeta* had extensive evidence that 'all of the resources of the special services had been used in committing this crime' ... Chaika added that some of Politkovskaya's killers had been involved in the contract killings of Paul Klebnikov ... and perhaps of Andrei Kozlov.

(*IHT*, 28 August 2007, pp. 1, 3)

Prosecutor-general Yuri Chaika said the 7 October [2006] shooting was organized by a Chechen criminal group in Moscow that specialized in contract killings, and that among the suspects were five law enforcement officers, accused of tracking Politkovskaya and providing her killers with information.

(www.iht.com, 30 August 2007)

Prosecutor-general Yuri Chaika ... [said that] the person who ordered the crime was living outside Russia and wanted to 'destabilize the situation in the country ... and return to the previous system, when money and oligarchs decided everything' ... This would suggest either the London-based Boris Berezovsky or the former head of Yukos, Leonid Nevzlin, who lives in

Israel ... Dmitri Muratov (editor of *Novaya Gazeta*): 'We are absolutely amazed that they have openly stated they know who ordered the crime before the investigation has even been completed.'

(www.independent.co.uk, 18 August 2007)

30 August 2007.

Prosecutors have released two suspects in the contract-style killing of Anna Politkovskaya A Federal Security Service officer who had been named as among suspects was still being held, but his arrest was 'in no way' connected to Politkovskaya's killing, [a] Moscow military court spokesman ... said Thursday [30 August] ... A fourth suspect, a former police major, could not have been involved in the killing because he had been in prison from 2004 until December 2006, the *Kommersant* newspaper reported Thursday.

(www.iht.com, 30 August 2007)

'Prosecutors have released two suspects ... Russian news agencies reported Thursday, and a third is no longer linked to the case' (*IHT*, 31 August 2007, p. 6).

Two suspects, both police officers, were released ... The lawyers of a third ... [a] police lieutenant ... protested in court that his arrest had nothing to do with the case ... The *Kommersant* business daily quoted a source as saying he was in fact being held for beating a suspect. A fourth suspect, a former police major, was in jail at the time of Anna Politkovskaya's murder, *Kommersant* said ... Dmitri Muratov (editor of *Novaya Gazeta*): 'Among those suspects is the person who killed Politkovskaya. I am certain that the security forces are connected. Before her death they were carrying out surveillance on her, following her, listening to her calls.'

(*The Independent*, 31 August 2007, p. 28)

4 September 2007.

Russia said Tuesday [4 September] it had put a new prosecutor in charge of investigating the murder of Anna Politkovskaya in what her colleagues described as political interference in the case ... The prosecutor-general's office said it had added extra investigators to work on the case and was putting ... [the] head of the directorate for serious cases in charge of the investigation.

(*IHT*, 5 September 2007, p. 4)

12 September 2007.

President Vladimir Putin has accepted the resignation of prime minister Mikhail Fradkov and nominated ... Viktor Zubkov, head of the federal financial monitoring service ... a relative unknown in Russian politics ... to replace him ... The Duma is set to vote on Mr Zubkov's nomination on Friday [14 September].

(www.bbc.co.uk, 12 September 2007)

'[It was reported that] Mikhail Fradkov gave as reasons for his departure "approaching significant political events in the country and his own desire to give Russia's president full freedom of decision including staff decisions"' (www.iht.com, 12 September 2007).

> In accepting the resignation, the Russian news agency reported President Putin told his prime minister: 'indeed, the country is now approaching parliamentary elections, which will lead to a presidential election. You may be right that we all must think about how to build the power structure so that it better corresponds to the pre-election periods and prepares the country for the time after the parliamentary elections and after presidential elections.'
>
> (www.times.co.uk, 12 September 2007)

> Viktor Zubkov, sixty-five, is the head of the Federal Financial Monitoring Service ... Zubkov graduated as an economist and ran state farms in the Leningrad region before moving to St Petersburg to work in the administration there. Putin was deputy mayor at the time.
>
> (www.iht.com, 12 September 2007)

> In 1992 and 1993 Viktor Zubkov was Putin's deputy at the external relations committee of the St Petersburg mayor's office, and since 1993 he has worked as a supervisor of tax inspectors and financial crimes, first in St Petersburg, and since 2001 in Putin's federal government.
>
> (*IHT*, 13 September 2007, p. 8)

> Along with most of the other people running Russia, Viktor Zubkov's career shows no obvious traces of work in the security and intelligence services. The sixty-five-year-old worked as a collective farm boss in the 1970s and then as a Communist Party apparatchik. He was Vladimir Putin's deputy in the St Petersburg municipal foreign affairs department in the early 1990s; after that he became a senior official in the tax inspectorate, at the heart of relations between officialdom and Russia's rumbustious new business class.
>
> (www.economist.com, 12 September 2007)

'The Federal Financial Monitoring Service tracks money laundering in the Russian banking system' (www.ft.com, 12 September 2007). '[It]s main task is to combat money laundering' (www.ft,com, 14 September 2007).

'The Federal Financial Monitoring Service ... tackles tax evasion, money laundering and other financial crime' (*The Independent*, 13 September 2007, p. 26).

> [The nomination of Viktor Zubkov] confounded analysts' predictions that Putin would elevate one of the most widely favoured candidates to succeed him to the prime minister's post as a stepping stone to the top Kremlin job. That was the sequence of events under former President Boris Yeltsin, who made Putin prime minister in [August] 1999 before naming him acting president months later.
>
> (www.iht.com, 12 September 2007)

[It is reported that] the Russian air force has tested a giant fuel-air bomb which the military says is the biggest non-nuclear explosive device in the world ... [Russia claims that it] is four times more powerful ... than the [US] Moab ... [and that] its efficiency and power is commensurate with a nuclear weapon ... Such bombs are mainly designed to destroy underground targets.

(www.bbc.co.uk, 12 September 2007)

The date and location of the test were not given – Western officials said there have, in fact, been others like it – but Russia's ORT First Channel television, citing the bomb's designers, said it was bigger and better than a US mega-bomb tested in 2003. Russia described the weapon as a vacuum bomb, suggesting it fell into a category of weapons designed to create a massive fireball and a huge blast. The tested bomb appears to be a thermobaric weapons, a title derived from words meaning heat and pressure ... State television compared the Russian weapon with another US megabomb, the so-called Massive Ordnance Air Blast.

(*FT*, 15 September 2007, p. 8)

13 September 2007.

President Vladimir Putin said: 'I expect all these changes will lead to the system of government in Russia functioning without hitches in the election period and after the election period' ... Mikhail Fradkov has quarrelled publicly with other ministers ... regarded by some experts here [in Russia] as an unwelcome sign in a government that seeks to show unity as elections draw near.

(www.iht.com, 13 September 2007)

'[On Thursday 13 September Viktor Zubkov said] he would not rule out a presidential bid' (www.iht.com, 14 September 2007).

'Viktor Zubkov did not rule himself out [as a presidential candidate], saying: "If I get something done here, in this post of prime minister, then I do not exclude that"' (www.bbc.co.uk, 14 September 2007).

14 September 2007.

The State Duma ... confirmed President Vladimir Putin's choice as prime minister Friday [14 September] ... Lawmakers voted 381 to forty-seven ... [with] eight legislators abstaining ... to confirm Viktor Zubkov ... Zubkov said he would implement policies voiced by President Putin ... [Explanations for Putin's move include the idea that it is] a further indication that Putin was showing the country, especially Kremlin factions jockeying for position, that he is no lame duck and will continue calling the shots ... [Putin, it is argued] chose the option that gives the maximum possible freedom to manoeuvre.

(www.iht.com, 14 September 2007)

After his appointment Viktor Zubkov told MPs that corruption 'permeates our society' and a law was needed to fight it systematically ... Zubkov: 'We speak a lot about corruption, yet there is no clear-cut definition of what corruption is, and nobody knows how to fight it' ... He said a law was needed to set up a body like the department he once headed (Risfinmonitoring: the Federal Financial Monitoring Service) 'to deal with corruption issues regularly, on a day-to-day rather than ad hoc basis'.

(www.iht.com, 14 September 2007)

The Communist Party voted against Viktor Zubkov's confirmation ... Zubkov: 'I believe our priorities should be the strategic targets and programmes of concrete actions set out in the president's state of the nation addresses in the past few years' ... Most observers expect a limited reshuffle. Zubkov signalled on Friday [14 September] unpopular health and social affairs minister Mikhail Zurabov could be a casualty. Analysts predict that reformist economy minister German Gref could also be dropped. Markets were focusing most attention on the fate of finance minister Alexei Kudrin.

(www.ft.com, 14 September 2007)

President Vladimir Putin said there had been criticism last year [2006] that the field for the presidential election on 2 March 2008 was 'empty' ... On Friday [14 September, he said: 'Now there are a minimum of five people who can stand for president.'

(www.bbc.co.uk, 14 September 2007)

President Vladimir Putin said that there were now at least five viable presidential candidates, including Viktor Zubkov. He declined to share the others' names ... Putin: 'Currently a minimum of five people can be named who stand a real chance of running for president and getting elected. There is a real choice ... I have not decided concretely what I will do [after the next presidential election], but I will have an influence on events.'

(*IHT*, 15 September 2007, p. 3)

Putin: 'Naturally, this is a factor the next president will have to contend with. I will do everything to ensure his independence and effectiveness. I worked all these years to make Russian strong. Russian cannot be strong with a weak president' ... President Putin's ratings have never dipped below the seventies.

(www.iht.com, 16 September 2007)

'President Vladimir Putin said that ... Viktor Zubkov ... was free to stand for the presidency if he wanted to, but stressed that if he did he would be one of at least five candidates' (*The Independent*, 15 September 2007, p. 3).

President Vladimir Putin insisted yesterday that he wanted to be followed by another strong president ... but Putin said that he wanted to retain power and influence in the Kremlin after he stands down ... seemingly contradictory remarks ... Mr Putin said Russia needed a strong president who could 'ensure his own efficiency and independence', adding 'I have no interest in a weak president' ... Mr Putin declined to say whether he would stand again for the presidency in 2012, saying it was too far into the future.

(*FT*, 15 September 2007, p. 8)

President Vladimir Putin said he expected to remain an influential figure in Russian politics after he steps down next March [2008] ... He did not rule out standing for president again in 2012 or 2016 ... Mr Putin said he had not decided what to do next ... He insisted he did not want to weaken the position of his successor. And he would be the first to argue that Russia needs a strong leader. But he said his main concern was to make sure that Russian remained stable and did not veer off course. He pointedly did not rule out standing again for president in 2012 or 2016, and described himself as a factor that the next Russian president would have to take into account. He and the next president, Mr Putin said, would need to work out a way to co-exist.

(www.bbc.co.uk, 15 September 2007)

15 September 2007.

Russian investigators have arrested a former Chechen official, accusing him of organizing the contract killing of Anna Politkovskaya it was reported on 15 September] ... The suspected official Shamil Burayev, was detained in Moscow on Thursday [13 September]. Burayev was once the leader of Achkoi-Martan, one of the administrative districts of Chechnya, but was dismissed from the post several years ago. He also ran unsuccessfully for the Chechen presidency in 2003 ... One of Burayev's relatives ... [said] that Burayev was in police custody but added that 'we were told at first that he could be released soon'.

(www.iht.com, 16 September 2007)

16 September 2007.

Andrei Lugovoi (Sunday 16 September): 'I confirm LDPR leader Vladimir Zhirinovsky's announcement that I have agreed to join the party's electoral list' ... Mr Zhirinovsky announced on Saturday [15 September] Mr Lugovoi would feature in second place of the LDPR [Liberal Democratic Party] list ... If elected in December Mr Lugovoi would get immunity from prosecution.

(www.bbc.co.uk, 16 September 2007)

20 September 2007.

Samples of earth taken by Russians who left a flag on the sea bed below the North Pole last month [August] show the Arctic is Russian, the natural resources ministry argue Thursday [20 September]. The ministry said in a statement that it had received preliminary data from an analysis that confirmed that the Lomonosov Ridge 'is part of the adjoining continental shelf of the Russian Federation'.

(*IHT*, 21 September 2007, p. 4)

24 September 2007.

One of the most prominent liberals in the government, finance minister Alexei Kudrin, was promoted last night [24 September] to the role of deputy prime minister in a reshuffle seen as strengthening the position of government reformers. Mr Kudrin not only retained his finance post in spite of rumours that he might be a casualty of the shake-up, but instead saw his status enhanced. As widely flagged, German Gref, the economy minister, left the government but was replaced by a long-time deputy seen as sharing his liberal economic credentials ... The reshuffle turned out to be less sweeping than some commentators had suggested. Mr Gref, who is understood to have wanted to leave the government for some time, was replaced by Elvira Nabiullina, his deputy of the past seven years ... Mr Putin brought back into government another ally, naming Dmitri Kozak as minister of regional development. Mikhail Zurabov, who as health minister [minister of health and social development] has been a controversial figure, was sacked as expected, to be replaced by Tatiana Golikova, previously deputy finance minister.

(*FT*, 25 September 2007, p. 10)

30 September 2007.

Garry Kasparov ... [was] overwhelmingly elected as [presidential] candidate ... by the coalition Other Russia ... by 379 of 498 votes ... The coalition was choosing among six candidates who had won regional primaries ... Sergei Gulyayev, a former member of the St Petersburg legislative assembly, received fifty-nine votes and former prime minister Mikhail Kasyanov had eighteen ... [Kasparov's] candidacy still needs to be registered and could be blocked ... Other Russia also chose Kasparov to be one of three candidates to head the coalition's list in parliamentary elections in December.

(*IHT*, 1 October 2007, p. 3)

'Garry Kasparov ... beat other nominees, including former prime minister Mikhail Kasyanov and the former head of the central bank, Viktor Gerashchenko' (www.bbc.co.uk, 1 October 2007).

1 October 2007.

President Vladimir Putin has raised the possibility of becoming a future prime minister by agreeing to enter the December parliamentary polls. Mr Putin said suggestions he might seek to become prime minister were 'entirely realistic'. He told a congress of United Russia that he would head the party's list though not actually become a member. By being on the list he is guaranteed a seat in the next parliament.

(www.bbc.co.uk, 1 October 2007)

'Leading the party's ticket does not mean President Vladimir Putin will take a seat in parliament ... Putin called a proposal that he become prime minister

"entirely realistic", but added that it was still "too early to think about it" '
(www.iht.com, 1 October 2007).

7 October 2007. 'Mikhail Fradkov ... will be appointed head of the foreign intelligence service' (*FT*, 8 October 2007, p. 8).

> The independent *Novaya Gazeta* and Russian prosecutors know the identity
> of the man who killed Anna Politkovskaya ... [exactly] a year ago ...
> according to the newspaper's editor and a special report planned for publi-
> cation Monday [8 October]. But the identity of the person who ordered the
> killing has not been determined and the man who shot Politkovskaya has
> not been found and arrested, the editor ... Dmitri Muratov ... said ... The
> paper has co-operated closely with the team of investigators from the federal
> general prosecutor's office and withheld publishing many of the details of
> the prosecutors' work and the newspaper's own parallel investigation ...
> Hundreds of activists rallied in her honour.
>
> (*IHT*, 8 October 2007)

'Thousands of people across Russia held protests and vigils to mark the first
anniversary of the death of Anna Politkovskaya ... A rally of about 1,200 protesters [gathered in Moscow] ... [accusing] the authorities of failing to solve the
murder' (*Guardian*, 8 October 2007, p. 26).

'Up to 2,000 people rallied in [Moscow] ... to demand justice over the
murder of Anna Politkovskaya as President Vladimir Putin celebrated his fifty-
fifth birthday' (*The Independent*, 8 October 2007, p. 23).

8 October 2007.

> On 8 October the newspaper *Kommersant* published an open letter from
> Viktor Cherkesov, the secretive head of Russia's federal drug police and a
> close friend of the president, warning of 'war of all against all' within one of
> the Kremlin's most powerful factions. No names were mentioned, but the
> letter was seen as an indictment of two of Cherkesov's political rivals – secur-
> ity services chief Nikolai Patrushev and Putin's deputy chief of staff Igor
> Sechin. Six days before the letter appeared Patrushev's men had arrested
> Cherkesov's deputy at a Moscow airport on charges of illegally tapping
> phones. Speculation ran rampant over whose phones might have been tapped.
>
> (www.iht.com, 30 November 2007; *IHT*, 1 December 2007, p. 4)

11 October 2007.

> Boris Berezovsky sued Roman Abramovich ... Berezovsky said Thursday
> [11 October] that he had been chasing Abramovich for the past six months
> and finally served the papers after a scuffle in a boutique [in London].
> Berezovsky claims his one-time protégé forced him to sell assets cheaply ...
> In the documents Berezovsky, sixty-one, claims he and his business partner
> Badri Patarkatsishvili were forced to sell their joint stake in the three busi-
> nesses to Abramovich at a fraction of their value following a meeting in the

south of France in 2000. The pair were warned that the Russian state would seize the shares if they did not sell, the documents said. Berezovsky and Patarkatsishvili made nearly $1 billion each from the sale. Berezovsky argues that the companies were worth at least five times that amount ... In 1995, under a much-criticized loans-for-shares deal, the ... Berezovsky and Abramovich ... acquired Sibneft for $100 million. When it was sold to Gazprom Neft in 2005 Sibneft was worth nearly $16 billion.

(www.iht.com, 12 October 2007)

12 October 2007.

The Russian foreign minister Sergei Lavrov ... called for the United States to freeze plans for developing missile defence bases in Poland and the Czech Republic ... [He] insisted that the planned US missile defence bases were 'a potential threat to us'. He threatened that if the two basses were completed: 'We will have to take some measures to neutralize this threat.'

(*IHT*, 13 October 2007, pp. 1, 4)

Moscow is concerned about having US military facilities close to its borders and disagrees with the US assessment of Iranian missiles. While Russia concedes that ten missiles would not upset the strategic nuclear balance, they are concerned about possible future expansion.

(*FT*, 13 October 2007, p. 7)

16 October 2007. 'President Vladimir Putin will become the first Kremlin leader to travel to Iran since 1943 when Joseph Stalin attended the wartime summit with prime minister Winston Churchill and President Franklin Roosevelt' (*IHT*, 16 October 2007, p. 3).

'President Vladimir Putin ... went out of his way to explain that his visit was planned five years ago as part of a five-country [Iran, Russia, Azerbaijan, Kazakhstan and Turkmenistan] summit [to discuss the Caspian Sea]' (*The Economist*, 20 October 2007, p. 47).

17 October 2007. 'Nine people, including a lieutenant colonel in Russia's security service, the FSB, have been charged with involvement in the murder of ... Anna Politkovskaya ... shot in October 2006 in her apartment block' (*The Independent*, 18 October 2007, p. 31).

26 October 2007.

[At] an EU–Russian summit in Portugal ... both sides agreed to set up an early warning system in the event of disruptions of Russian oil and gas supplies to Europe ... Russia already provides 30 per cent of EU energy imports, including 44 per cent of natural gas imports ... A two-year ban on Polish meat imports has led Warsaw to veto a new agreement with Russia. But the outcome of last weekend's elections [21 October] – in which a pro-business, pro-European bloc defeated prime minister Jaroslaw Kaczynski – could ease the situation. Meanwhile, Sergei Yastrzhembsky, Russia's special envoy to the EU, told reporters that Poland had agreed to allow Russian agricultural inspectors into Polish facilities and inspections could begin next month [November].

(www.iht.com, 26 October 2007)

'[At the summit] President Vladimir Putin said: "If someone thinks that I intend to move, let's say, into the government of the Russian Federation and transfer the fundamental powers there, that is not the case"' (www.iht.com, 27 October 2007).

30 October 2007.

President Vladimir Putin has attended a memorial service near Moscow to commemorate the victims of Soviet-era oppression ... Mr Putin's decision ... now seems highly significant, since an August [2007] ceremony to erect a memorial to victims was not attended by any senior Kremlin officials.

(www.bbc.co.uk, 30 October 2007)

President Vladimir Putin on Tuesday [30 October] paid his first visit to a memorial and church built at a site ... Butovsky Poligon ... where thousands of people were executed under Stalin's regime as Russia marked the seventieth anniversary of the dictator's Great Terror and commemorated decades of Soviet repression that left millions dead ... The height of Stalin's purges [were] in 1937 and 1938 ... It was the first time Putin had joined the public commemorations of the killings. Human rights activists have criticized the president for paying little attention to the abuses of the Soviet era. He created concern this year by endorsing a new history textbook that played down Stalinist repression and praised the former dictator for industrializing the Soviet Union and winning World War II ... Soviet political prisoners held in camps in 1974 declared 30 October Political Prisoners' Day. Since 1991 the day has also been officially marked as the Day of Victims of Political Repression.

(*IHT*, 31 October 2007, p. 3)

6 November 2007.

A deal ... [was] clinched ... Tuesday [6 November] with Gasunie, the Dutch energy infrastructure company. Gasunie becomes the fourth partner in Nord Stream, joining the German companies Wintershall and E.ON Ruhrgas and Gazprom ... Under the terms of the deal signed by President Vladimir Putin and Jan Peter Balkenende, the Dutch prime minister, Gasunie will take a 9 per cent stake in Nord Stream, while the two German companies will each reduce their stakes to 20 per cent. Gazprom will retain its 51 per cent stake ... [Gazprom] has the option of acquiring from Gasunie a 9 per cent stake in the Balgzand–Bacton pipeline, which connects the Gasunie grid with Britain – a market Gazprom recently entered and where it is rapidly expanding.

(*IHT*, 7 November 2007, p. 15)

7 November 2007.

> The State Duma ... has suspended Moscow's support for ... the Conventional Forces in Europe Treaty (CFE) ... The Duma approved the bill 418 to nil ... The bill still faces approval in the upper house in December before President Vladimir Putin can sign it.
>
> (www.bbc.co.uk, 7 November 2007)

> The 1990 CFE Treaty, which originally set limits on weapons of Nato and Warsaw Pact countries, was revised in 1999 ... Russia ratified the updated treaty in 2004, but the United States and other Nato members have refused to follow suit, saying Moscow first must fulfil obligations to withdraw forces from Georgia and from Moldova's separatist Transdniestre region.
>
> (www.iht.com, 20 November 2007)

13 November 2007. President Vladimir Putin:

> If people vote for United Russia, it means that a clear majority of the people put their trust in me, and in turn that means I will have the moral rights to hold those in the Duma and the cabinet responsible for the implementation of the tasks that have been set as of today ... In what form I will do this I cannot yet give a direct answer. But various possibilities exist. If the result is the one I am counting on, I will have this possibility.
>
> (*IHT*, 14 November 2007, p. 3)

16 November 2007. 'The Senate voted unanimously to suspend the Conventional Forces in Europe (CFE) treaty' (*The Times*, 17 November 2007, p. 57).

21 November 2007.

> President Vladimir Putin likened his critics to jackals fed by foreign funding and accused the West of meddling in Russian politics, telling an election campaign rally Wednesday [21 November] ... at a sports area ... that foes at home and abroad want to weaken the country ... [He evoked] the frightening economic and political uncertainty that pervaded Russia in the years before and after the collapse of the Soviet Union.
>
> (www.iht.com, 21 November 2007)

> About 5,000 supporters gathered in a sports stadium ... Putin stressed that he had not participated in such rallies before and did not particularly like to do so ... Putin assailed unnamed former officials who adopted 'irresponsible budgets' that led to the collapse of the rouble and a debt default, and those who made 'corruption the main tool of political and economic competition'.
>
> (*IHT*, 22 November 2007, p. 3)

President Vladimir Putin:

> Our opponents want to see us disunited ... Some want to take away and divide everything, and others to plunder ... Those who confront us need a weak and ill state. They want to have a divided society, in order to do their

deeds behind its back ... Regrettably, there are those inside the country who feed off foreign embassies like jackals and count on support of foreign funds and governments, and not their own people. Now they are going to take to the streets. They have learned from Western experts and have received some training in neighbouring republics. And now they are going to stage provocations here ... If these gentlemen [of the 1990s] return back to power, they will again cheat people and fill their pockets. There should be no illusions. All of these people have not left the political arena. They want to come back, to return to power, to spheres of influence and gradually restore an oligarchic regime based on corruption and lies ... The vote on 2 December will to a large extent determine the fate of the country. By all means come to the polls and vote for United Russia ... If there is a victory in December then there will be a victory in March of next year.

(www.iht.com, 21 November 2007; *IHT*, 22 November 2007, p. 3)

22 November 2007.

Yukos has ceased to exist. A simple entry on Russia's State Companies Register on Thursday [22 November 2007] marked the company's liquidation ... Russia's Federal Tax Service confirmed on Thursday that it had completed Yukos's bankruptcy procedure and that the company has ceased to exist as a legal entity ... The treatment of Mikhail Khodorkovsky ... his lawyers said ... at times resembled a show-trial, drawing a chorus of criticism from human rights activists in Russia and abroad. Their argument remains that Mr Khodorkovsky was punished for openly pledging to finance the Russian liberal opposition and civil society. This is strongly denied by the Russian leadership, who allege Mr Khodorkovsky and the other oligarchs effectively robbed Russia during the 1990s. However, Russian justice appears to have been selective, with the oligarchs who either kept out of politics, or who chose to support Vladimir Putin, left alone. Both Mr Khodorkovsky and his business partner, Platon Lebedev, remain in a Siberian prison camp ... Over recent weeks the European Court of Human Rights has ordered Russia to pay Mr Lebedev compensation for illegal detention. And a court in the Netherlands ruled that the sale of Yukos's foreign assets was illegal and the result of a politically motivated process.

(www.bbc.co.uk, 22 November 2007)

Yukos Oil, once the biggest company in Russia, was removed from the RTS exchange Thursday [22 November], fifteen months after being declared bankrupt ... on 1 August 2006 ... Trading in Yukos stock will no longer be allowed. Yukos shares last traded at 21 cents on 11 November [2007], down from a high of $15.97 on 9 October 2003, two weeks before ... Mikhail Khodorkovsky was arrested. He was later convicted of fraud and tax evasion. The shares ceased trading on the Micex exchange, Russia's biggest by volume, more than a year ago. The Putin government dismantled Yukos after the company was hit with more than $30 billion in tax charges. Putin used assets from Yukos to help turn the state-run energy companies Rosneft and Gazprom into companies big enough to challenge BP and Royal Dutch Shell.

(IHT, 23 November 2007, p. 17)

24–25 November 2007.

Dozens of opposition activists have reportedly been detained by police ahead of a rally in St Petersburg. Police are said to have moved in when some protesters unfurled banners of the banned National Bolshevik Party. After a rally Saturday [24 November] Moscow police detained opposition activists including Garry Kasparov, who was jailed for five days ... for leading an unauthorized march ... The protesters in St Petersburg [on 25 November] are reported to have numbered about 100 – a much smaller gathering than Saturday's one in Moscow. They belong to an opposition coalition known as The Other Russia ... The officers detained young marchers from the National Bolshevik Party first and then about several dozen other protesters.

(www.bbc.co.uk, 25 November 2007)

Police have broken up an opposition rally, arresting activists for the second day running. Police detained about 150 people in St Petersburg, including opposition leader Boris Nemtsov – who was later freed ... Several hundred people took part in the St Petersburg protest – much fewer than Saturday's gathering of about 3,000 people in Moscow. Activists holding white flowers met near the headquarters of the liberal Yabloko Party, and headed to the site of the unauthorized rally. Mr Nemtsov, a leader of the opposition SPS party and a candidate in presidential elections due in March [2008], addressed the crowd. Riot police reportedly moved in when some protesters unfurled banners of the banned National Bolshevik Party and marched towards the Winter Palace ... Correspondents put the number of people taken away in police vans at about 200. Mr Nemtsov was among them – but was subsequently released from custody.

(www.bbc.co.uk, 25 November 2007)

Garry Kasparov was arrested when 2,000 people attended an anti-Kremlin protest in Moscow on Saturday ... Hundreds more demonstrators made their way to a concert hall where city authorities had sanctioned an opposition rally. But police arrested more there, saying that they were in breach of public order because their time for the rally had expired.

(The Times, 26 November 2007, p. 32)

Garry Kasparov was arrested in Moscow on Saturday when he tried to deliver a letter to the federal election authorities assailing the conduct of the election and a judge sentenced him to five days in jail. In St Petersburg on Sunday two well-known opposition politicians, Boris Nemtsov and Nikita Belykh, leaders of a mainstream liberal party, the Union of Rightist Forces, were briefly detained.

(www.iht.com, 26 November 2007)

President Vladimir Putin has reneged on a promise to deliver seats in the Duma to smaller parties if they refrained from criticizing him, according to a senior member of one of the parties. The Union of Rightist Forces began criticizing Putin this fall ... Communist and Yabloko officials said their parties had also been promised Duma seats if they vowed not to criticize Putin.

(*IHT*, 28 November 2007, p. 3)

'Police said they had detained several dozen demonstrators [in St Petersburg], but an opposition activist put the number at 200' (*IHT*, 26 November 2007, p. 3).

[Boris Nemtsov's] Union of Rightist Forces, which remains among parties approved by the Kremlin, joined Other Russia protesters for the first time after what it said was repeated harassment during its parliamentary campaign ... Yabloko says it was banned from hanging posters in [St Petersburg].

(*FT*, 26 November 2007, p. 6)

'Boris Nemtsov had on Friday [23 November] been nominated as the party's [Union of Rightist Forces] candidate [for the presidential election]' (*The Independent*, 26 November 2007, p. 18).

25 November 2007.

Former KGB chief Vladimir Kryuchkov, one of the orchestrators of the failed coup against Mikhail Gorbachev in 1991, has died, aged eighty-three ... Mr Kryuchkov signed the takeover decree after a group of hardline communists ousted Mr Gorbachev to try to halt his reform plans. The coup last three days. Mr Gorbachev appointed Mr Kryuchkov as head of the KGB in 1988.

(www.bbc.co.uk, 25 November 2007)

26 November 2007. 'Vladimir Churov ... chairman of the central election commission ... said that a president cannot step down and seek reelection while a caretaker takes his place' (*The Times*, 27 November 2007, p. 39).

28 November 2007.

Uranium seized in Slovakia on Wednesday [28 November] was enriched enough to be used in a so-called 'dirty bomb' ... [which] uses conventional explosives to scatter radioactive debris and contaminate the target area ... The uranium was found during a raid on alleged smugglers near the Hungarian border. Three people were detained. The suspects had just under 500 grams (17.6 ounces) of uranium in powder ... The radioactive uranium was even more dangerous because it was in powder form [said a senior police officer] ... Slovakian investigators believe the enriched uranium came from somewhere in the former Soviet Union ... The raid near the Hungarian border in Slovakia coincided with the arrest of one Ukrainian citizen and two Hungarians ... A police raid in the Czech Republic in 1994 uncovered an attempt to sell 2.73 kilograms (96 ounces) of enriched uranium illegally. Police in the same year confiscated 2.96 kilograms (105 ounces) of enriched uranium intended for illegal sale in the Russian city of St Petersburg.

(www.bbc.co.uk, 29 November 2007)

The uranium that two Hungarians and a Ukrainian were trying to sell was sufficiently enriched to build a nuclear bomb ... The quantity, however, was far too small to make a crude warhead ... A spokeswoman for Slovakia: 'It was possible to use this material for terrorist attacks or to build a dirty bomb' ... Western experts cautioned that uranium, even if enriched, has too little radioactivity to make a dirty bomb – a weapon that combines highly radioactive material with conventional explosives to disperse over a large area deadly dust that people would inhale. By contrast, highly enriched uranium can fuel nuclear arms ... Dirty bombs are considered more a psychological armament than a weapon of mass destruction because their radioactivity is potentially much less lethal than a bomb using conventional explosives, experts say.

(www.iht.com, 29 November 2007)

29 November 2007.

A Moscow court has sentenced Boris Berezovsky to six years in jail in absentia after finding him guilty of massive embezzlement. The court found that Mr Berezovsky had stolen nearly $9 million for the state airline Aeroflot through fraud. It ordered him to repay it ... The judge described him as part of an organized criminal group that included Aeroflot managers.

(www.bbc.co.uk, 29 November 2007)

30 November 2007. 'President Putin on Friday [30 November] signed a law suspending Russia's participation in the Conventional Forces in Europe Treaty ... Suspension of the treaty ... takes effect on 12 December' (www.iht.com, 30 November 2007). 'The [1990] treaty was first implemented in 1992' (*IHT*, 1 December 2007, p. 6).

2 December 2007. A general election is held.

In the parliamentary election on 2 December Russians will vote only for parties, not for candidates. What is more, parties now need 7 per cent of the national vote to gain seats in parliament, up from 5 per cent. They also need to submit proof that they have at least 50,000 members to be recognized as official parties, up from 10,000. It now seems possible that United Russia's advantages are so great that it will be the only party to surpass 7 per cent. In that case the constitution requires at least one other party in parliament, so some token seats will be allocated to the second most popular one.

(www.iht.com, 14 October 2007)

[On 30 October 2007] Vladimir Churov, head of the central electoral commission, said Moscow will invite 300 to 400 foreign observers to the 2

December election – a fraction of the 1,165 at the last parliamentary poll in December 2003. Russia has already left groups such as OSCE floundering to mount an effective observation mission by waiting until barely a month before the poll to issue invitations ... The total number of international observers is [to be] in the range of 300 to 400 ... The total includes monitors from OSCE's parliamentary assembly and ODIHR [Office of Democratic Institutions and Human Rights], the parliamentary assembly of the Council of Europe, former Soviet states, the Shanghai Co-operation Organization and the Nordic Council. ODIHR, usually the largest contingent among foreign observers, sent fifty long-term and 400 short-term observers to the last elections ... Russia has waged an increasingly vocal campaign against OSCE observers, accusing them of bias and focusing exclusively on elections 'west of Vienna'. It circulated proposals last month [September] to limit ODIHR missions to fifty people and bar them from making public assessments immediately after elections. Since OSCE's decision-making requires consensus, the plans are unlikely to be agreed in their entirety, although some elements could be.

(*FT*, 31 October 2007)

The system for deploying international observers to monitor elections in the states of the former Soviet Union appeared near collapse on Wednesday [31 October] after Russia formally declared its intention to cut sharply the size of the mission that will monitor its parliamentary elections in December, and European officials refused to agree immediately to the change. Russia has already made the work of this year's mission difficult by delaying the invitation to the monitoring group, and the group says this has prevented it from carrying out preliminary work. On Wednesday the group, the monitoring arm of OSCE, said it had received the invitation, but it included unprecedented restrictions. Russia said it would allow only a maximum of seventy observers to take part in a short-term mission. The group sent 400 observers for the parliamentary election four years ago ... Last month [September] Russia circulated a proposal at OSCE to limit permanently the work of the election observers in the former Soviet Union by cutting the size of missions and preventing them from issuing public statements about a government's electoral conduct in the days after citizens voted. The ODIHR has regularly dispatched observation teams to elections throughout the states of the former Soviet Union since the collapse of communism.

(www.iht.com, 31 October 2007)

'OSCE ... said Friday [2 November] that it would go ahead with plans for a "restricted" mission to monitor the parliamentary election and urged Moscow to co-operate fully' (*IHT*, 3 November 2007, p. 3).

Luc van den Brande, who is leading a team of election observers from the Council of Europe said (on 9 November): 'The ruling party almost fully controls the airwaves' ... Only eleven of eighty-five parties that wanted to stand had been allowed to do so, he said, with almost all of Russia's democratic opposition kept off the ballot paper.

(Guardian, 10 November 2007, p. 20)

OSCE ... said on Friday [16 November] that it would be unable to monitor the parliamentary elections next month [2 December] because Moscow had refused to issue visas to its observers in time ... OSCE, which organizes observer missions in fifty-six member states, said attempts to get entry visas for its experts and observers had failed ... Urdur Gunnarsdottir (a spokeswoman for OSCE's Office for Democratic and Human Rights): 'We have not received a single visa for the seventy observers. We have tried everything' ... [She] said the visas were certainly not ready by late Thursday [15 November], when the organization made the 'difficult' decision to abandon plans to monitor the elections ... She said: 'Even if the visas are there now, it is too late. We would have needed them last night' ... [She] said a 'meaningful' observation of the 2 December elections to the Duma would not be possible at this point because candidates had already registered, the media campaign was under way and there was too little time to get observers in place, she said.

(www.bbc.co.uk, 16 November 2007)

'The organization will be represented by the OSCE Parliamentary Assembly, which, together with the Council of Europe Parliamentary Assembly, is sending about 100 MPs from member countries to observe the parliamentary poll' (www.bbc.co.uk, 26 November 2007).

Urdur Gunnarsdottir: 'We have been facing delays all along the way, but what tipped the balance was the delay in issuing visas. We have not been able to deploy people to start preparations, despite repeated assurances from Russia. There have also been indications that they would attempt to limit our areas of work in Moscow. This whole situation has been extraordinary from the very beginning' ... The decision to pull out ... has split OSCE, which still plans to send observers to Russia from its Parliamentary Assembly ... Goran Lennmarker, the Assembly's president ... [was in Moscow on 16 November] to challenge the decision to limit its mission to thirty observers.

(The Times, 17 November 2007, p. 57)

All fifty-six OSCE member countries, including Russia, agreed in 1990 to invite international observers to monitor their elections. The organization [OSCE's Office for Democratic and Human Rights] has monitored elections in countries including the United States, Britain, France, Poland and Ukraine ... The president of OSCE's parliamentary assembly, Goran Lennmarker, said a team of thirty would come to Russia as planned.

(www.guardian.co.uk, 16 November 2007)

The statement ... [by] the Office for Democratic Institutions and Human Rights ... said the organization 'concludes that the authorities of the Russian

Federation remain unwilling to receive observers in a timely and co-operating manner' ... A separate mission under the auspices of OSCE, made up of members of parliament from its member countries, is still considering attending the elections.

(www.iht.com, 16 November 2007)

'The group's decision to withdraw from the monitoring mission was the first such occurrence in Russia since Moscow allowed access to election observers in 1990' (*IHT*, 17 November 2007, p. 3).

'OSCE has pulled out of poll monitoring only once before – in Albania in 1996' (*FT*, 17 November 2007, p. 8).

President Putin (26 November): '[The OSCE boycott decision] was taken on the recommendation of the American State Department. The aim is to discredit the elections, but they won't achieve their goal. We will certainly take this into account with our bilateral ties with this state' ... Urdur Gunnarsdottir (OSCE spokeswoman): '[President Putin's allegations are] nonsense. The decision was not made in consultation with any government. It was made on operational, not political grounds. Our decision did not have the aim to influence the election.'

(www.bbc.co.uk, 26 November 2007)

President Putin said: 'According to information we have, it was again done at the recommendation of the US State Department and we will take this into account in our inter-state relations with this country. Their goal is the delegitimization of the elections. But they will not achieve even this goal' ... In focusing on the supposed role of the State Department in the decision, Putin was highlighting a charge first made on 19 November by the chairman of the central election commission, Vladimir Churov. Churov noted at a news conference that the monitoring group had abandoned its mission soon after its director, ambassador Christian Strohal of Austria, visited Washington. Strohal's aide said subsequently that the timing of the visit and the decision had been coincidental ... Urdur Gunnarsdottir (spokeswoman for the election monitoring arm of OSCE, the Office for Democratic Institutions and Human Rights): '[President Putin's assertion is] nonsense. This was a decision that was simply based on the fact that we were not receiving any visas and time had run out. The only consultation that took place was within our office with the people that plan these observations and carry them through. They have 150 observer missions under their belt. They know by now what needs to be in place to do this' ... The Kremlin has in recent years chafed at the group's reports, contending that they were biased against the government ... In recent months Russian officials maintained that the monitoring group needed to be reformed.

(www.iht.com, 26 November 2007)

Russia did give visas to ... legislators belonging to the Parliamentary Assembly of OSCE ... The monitoring methods of the Parliamentary

Assembly differ sharply from those of the Office for Democratic Institutions and Human Rights. The legislators arrive just a few days in advance, whereas the latter group sends teams in advance, scrutinizes the election law, the pre- and post-election events and the role of the media ... Russia has sought to bring the Office for Democratic Institutions and Human Rights under the control of member states, a move that would give Russia a veto over where election monitors would be sent.

(*IHT*, 27 November 2007, p. 4)

Election officials have been ordered to make sure that United Russia collects double the number of votes it is expected to win in State Duma elections on Sunday [2 December] – even if they have to falsify the results, a senior election official said ... speaking on condition of anonymity for fear of reprisal ... The official heads a key regional election committee ... The official said United Russia was hoping to win big with a nation-wide campaign under which bureaucrats, doctors, teachers and other state-paid workers are being told to find ten people each to vote for the party.

(*The Moscow Times*, article reprinted in www.iht.com, 27 November 2007)

More and more people have been stepping forward saying they have been pressurized to vote in a particular way. This is even more of a concern, given how few international observers are here to monitor the vote. There are just 400 to cover almost 100,000 polling stations.

(www.bbc.co.uk, 1 December 2007)

Eleven parties are competing for place in the Duma ... [including] the Communist Party, the Liberal Democratic Party and Yabloko ... More than 100 million voters are eligible to cast ballots ... Just 330 foreign monitors will cover 95,000 polling stations ... Correspondents say more and more ordinary people have been speaking out in interviews with the mainstream media and on internet blogs about how they have been pressurized to vote for United Russia ... [The slogan is] 'Putin's Plan – Russia's Victory' ... Pro-Kremlin analyst Vyacheslav Nikonov: 'There is a liberal electorate in Russia, but only for one liberal project. During all public opinion polls the figures have been quite stable at between 8 per cent and 10 per cent. They need to unite and that is what they are not doing' ... Mr Nikonov believes the other big problem the liberal parties face is that they are still associated with the chaos of the 1990s and in particular the economic crash in 1998.

(www.bbc.co.uk, 2 December 2007)

President Vladimir Putin ... said recently at a staged meeting with road construction workers in Siberia: 'The party [United Russia] has no stable political ideology or principles for which the overwhelming majority of members are ready to fight. As a rule, being close to those in power, as United Russia is, all kinds of crooks try to latch on to it, often with success.'

(*FT*, 28 November 2007, p. 8)

'In a campaign speech for United Russia ... [President Putin said that] United Russia ... has no unifying ideology. It attracts power-seekers and "all kinds of scoundrels" [he said]' (www.iht.com, 30 November 2007).

President Vladimir (in a televised address):

> Please do not think that everything is predetermined and the pace of development we have attained, the direction of our movement toward success, will be maintained automatically by itself. This is a dangerous illusion ... I ask you to come to the polls and vote for United Russia ... [A vote for United Russia will ensure] stability and continuity ... We cannot allow the return to power of those who once tried but failed to rule the country. Today [they] would want to reshape and drown in empty talk Russia's development plans and change course supported by our nation, bringing back the times of humiliation, dependence and disintegration.
>
> (www.bbc.co.uk, 29 November 2007; *IHT*, 30 November 2007, p. 3; *FT*, 30 November 2007, p. 6)

> Authorities throughout Russia appeared determined to ensure a sizeable turnout, through pressure, persuasion and even presents ... The vote Sunday [2 December] 'meets none of the criteria of a free, fair and democratic election; in effect, it is not even an election', Andrei Illarionov, a former adviser to President Vladimir Putin, wrote in a commentary for the Cato Institute [think tank].
>
> (www.iht.com, 2 December 2007)

'United Russia leader Boris Gryzlov: "[The election was] a referendum of President Putin so I think we can say he has won a victory"' (www.bbc.co.uk, 3 December 2007).

The turnout about 63 per cent compared with 55.75 per cent in 2003.

'[There were about] 109 million eligible voters' (*The Times*, 4 December 2007, p. 31).

'[The 315 seats attained by United Russia in the 450-seat State Duma is] fourteen more than the two-thirds majority needed to pass constitutional amendments' (*Guardian*, 4 December 2007, p. 32).

A statement was made on 3 December by a joint observer team from OSCE's Parliamentary Assembly and the Council of Europe's Parliamentary Assembly:

> [The election] was not fair and failed to meet many OSCE and Council of Europe commitments and standards for democratic elections ... [It] took place in an atmosphere which seriously limited political competition ... There was not a level playing field ... [There was] frequent abuse of administrative resources, media coverage strongly in favour of the ruling party and an election code whose cumulative effect hindered political pluralism ... [It is] extremely difficult for new and smaller parties to develop and compete effectively.
>
> (www.bbc.co.uk, 3 December 2007; www.guardian.co.uk, 3 December 2007)

Luc van den Brande (head of the delegation from the Parliamentary Assembly of the Council of Europe):

> We cannot say there were fair elections ... [This was a] managed election ... [There was the] overwhelming influence of the president's office and the president ... It was not first and foremost an election of the State Duma members, but it was rather a referendum to the president ... If Russia is a managed democracy then this was a managed election.
> (www.cnn.com, 3 December 2007; *The Times*, 4 December 2007, p. 31)

Goran Lennmarker (president of OSCE's Parliamentary Assembly):

> The elections took place in an atmosphere which seriously limited political competition and with frequent abuses of administrative resources, media coverage strongly in favour of the ruling party, and an election code whose cumulative effect hindered political pluralism. There was not a level playing field in Russia in 2007 ... These elections failed to meet many of the commitments and standards we have in OSCE and the Council of Europe. Merging of the state and a political party is an abuse of power and clear violation of international standards.
> (www.guardian.co.uk, 3 December 2007; www.thetimes.co.uk, 3 December 2007)

> The independent Russian monitoring group, Golos, had earlier reported various violations during the voting, which it said amounted to 'an organized campaign'. It had claimed that in a number of cases state employees and students were pressured to vote, and those voting for United Russia were entered into a prize lottery in St Petersburg.
> (www.bbc.co.uk, 3 December 2007)

'Observers from the CIS said the election was "free and transparent"' (www. bbc.co.uk, 3 December 2007).

Nauryz Aidarov (head of the CIS observer mission): 'All necessary legal and organizational conditions for an open and free election were guaranteed in the Russian elections' (www.thetimes.co.uk, 3 December 2007).

President Vladimir Putin (3 December):

> [The election was] legitimate ... I headed the United Russia ticket and, of course, it is a sign of public trust ... It is now clear to me that Russians will never allow the country to develop along a destructive path, the way it happened in some countries in the post-Soviet space ... [The election is a] good example of domestic political stability ... This feeling of responsibility of citizens for their own country is, in my view, the most important indication that our country is strengthening, not only economically and socially but also politically.
> (www.guardian.co.uk, 3 December 2007; www.cnn.com, 3 December 2007; www.bbc.co.uk, 3 December 2007; *IHT*, 4 December 2007, p. 3)

'In Chechnya ... United Russia won 99.4 per cent of the vote, officials said ... Officials there said the turnout was 99.5 per cent' (*IHT*, 4 December 2007, p. 3).

> In Chechnya an implausible 99.2 per cent of residents backed the ruling party. Neighbouring Ingushetia, where the elections were preceded by mass protests against the government, produced an almost identical result. Observers suggested that in fact only 8 per cent of people turned out to vote there.
>
> (www.economist.com, 4 December 2007)

'United Russia barely topped 50 per cent in St Petersburg and Moscow' (Garry Kasparov, *IHT*, 7 December 2007, p. 8).

'[The Liberal Democratic Party's] candidate Andrei Lugovoi – who is wanted in the UK for the murder of Alexander Litvinenko – will be guaranteed a seat [in the State Duma, which will grant him] immunity from prosecution' (www.bbc.co.uk, 3 December 2007).

The results: percentage of the vote and number of seats, respectively, in the 450-seat State Duma:

United Russia (leader Boris Gryzlov): 64.1; 315
Communist Party (leader Gennadi Zyuganov): 11.6; 57
Liberal Democratic Party (Vladimir Zhirinovsky): 8.2;
A Fair (Just) Russia (leader Sergei Mironov): 7.8; 38

Seven parties did not attain the 7 per cent threshold to be awarded seats:

Agrarian Party: 2.3 per cent.
Yabloko: 1.6 per cent.
Civil Force: 1.1 per cent.
Union of Rightist Forces (SPS): 1.0 per cent.

10 December 2007. President Vladimir Putin endorses the candidature of Dmitri Medvedev in the 2 March 2008 presidential election. Unlike Vladimir Putin (who speaks German), Dmitri Medvedev speaks English.

'Dmitri Medvedev ... was put forward by United Russia, A Fair Russia, the Agrarian Party and Civil Force at a meeting with President Vladimir Putin' (www.bbc.co.uk, 10 December 2007).

President Vladimir Putin:

> I have known him for more than seventeen years, I have worked with him very closely all these years, and I fully and completely support this candidacy ... We have a chance to form a robust administration for the Russian Federation after the March elections ... and administration that will carry out the same policies that have brought us results for the past eight years.
>
> (www.bbc.co.uk, 10 December 2007; www.guardian.co.uk, 10 December 2007)

('President Vladimir Putin (September 2007 in a speech referring to democracy): "This road is not simple. It takes time and the right conditions. We need to ensure that our economic transformations bring about the growth of the middle class, which is the standard bearer of this ideology. This is something that takes time and cannot be achieved overnight"': *IHT*, 17 December 2007, p. 2.)

Dmitri Medvedev: born 14 September 1965 in Leningrad (St Petersburg); 1990–9 professor of law at St Petersburg State University; 1990–5 assistant to the chairman of the Leningrad City Council and analyst in the Committee for External Relations for the city of St Petersburg; 1999 deputy chief of staff for the government of the Russian Federation; 1999–2000 deputy chief of the presidential administration; 2000–3 first deputy head of the presidential administration; 2002–present chairman of Gazprom's board of directors; 2003–5 chief of the presidential administration; November 2005–present first deputy prime minister.

(www.iht.com, 10 December 2007)

'In 2000 Dmitri Medvedev took charge of Vladimir Putin's presidential campaign and in October 2003 he was appointed Kremlin chief of staff ... [He was promoted] to the post of first deputy prime minister in charge of national projects' (www.bbc.co.uk, 10 December 2007).

'As first deputy prime minister ... [Dmitri Medvedev has been] responsible for "national projects" to revive healthcare, education, housing and agriculture since 2005' (www.guardian.co.uk, 10 December 2007).

Unlike Vladimir Putin and many top officials in the Kremlin, Dmitri Medvedev appears to have no background in the KGB or its successor, the FSB, or other security agencies ... He has a reputation as a technocrat with a strong grasp of economics ... Sergei Ivanov is considered more hawkish and is a veteran of the FSB ... The decision by Putin to endorse Medvedev over Ivanov or other candidates from the security services stirred speculation in political circles that Putin had decided on a successor who could be more easily controlled from behind the scenes ... While Medvedev and Putin have different backgrounds, they are similar in one respect: both were plucked from relative obscurity and put in positions of power even though they had never before been involved in electoral politics. Putin was installed as prime minister by President Boris Yeltsin after serving in the FSB.

(Clifford Levy, www.iht.com, 10 December 2007)

The endorsement suggested that President Putin wants to turn over his office to someone who can be readily controlled as he seeks to retain influence after his term ends ... [The] relationship with Putin, fifty-five, is so close that it is sometimes likened to father and son. Medvedev, currently a first deputy prime minister, has never run for any office, and owes almost his entire career to Putin, who first hired him to work in the city government of St Petersburg in the early 1990s ... In the early 1990s Medvedev was a legal adviser to the committee on external relations in the mayor's office ... The decision to give the nod to Medvedev over candidates from the security services was seen by some in Russia as an indication that Putin did not want a strong figure to take his place ... Medvedev has a reputation as a techno-crat with a strong grasp of economics ... Putin has put him in charge of spending some of the large budget surplus ... on improving housing, health care, education and other social services ... [Spending on] what are called National Projects ... [include] agriculture, education, healthcare and afford-able housing ... Boris Gryzlov: 'We think that this is the most socially ori-entated candidate, the man who performed very well in tackling national projects' ... In contrast to Sergei Ivanov, Medvedev is considered a moder-ate with a more pro-Western bent.

(Clifford Levy, *IHT*, 11 December 2007, pp. 1, 4)

Dmitri Medvedev has no background in the state security services and virtu-ally no power base in the Kremlin and he is seen here [in Russia] as a rela-tively weak figure beholden to Putin ... If he wins election to the presidency in March, he will become Russia's youngest leader since Tsar Nicolas II assumed the throne in 1894, at twenty-six.

(Clifford Levy, www.iht.com, 11 December 2007)

'Dmitri Medvedev ... is seen as a relatively weak figure with no independent power base' (www.iht.com, 12 December 2007). 'Medvedev is seen as a moder-ate technocrat rather than a Kremlin hawk' (www.iht.com, 17 December 2007).

[President Vladimir Putin's] choice is regarded as unexpected by observers in Europe and the United States ... Should Mr Putin choose to return to the Kremlin at the next elections, Mr Medvedev could be trusted to stand aside ... Sergei Ivanov ... now first deputy prime minister ... might be less easy to manipulate once he has tasted real power as president.

(Richard Beeston, www.thetimes.co.uk, 10 December 2007)

Dmitri Medvedev [is] a relatively pro-Western liberal ... The choice of Mr Medvedev, who owes his rise entirely to President Vladimir Putin, was seen as an indication that Russia would continue along the state-managed development path established by the president – but take a more pro-business course ... The endorsement is seen by many analysts as proof of Mr Putin's determination to maintain hold of the levers of power after he steps down.

(*FT*, 11 December 2007, p. 1)

'Dmitri Medvedev ... is viewed as an economic liberal' (p. 6).

United Russia leader Boris Gryzlov: 'Dmitri Anatolievich [Medvedev] over-sees national projects. He oversees the demographic programme and we believe it is precisely the issues to do with raising standards of living that are the most important issues for the forthcoming four-year period' (www.bbc.co.uk, 11 December 2007).

11 December 2007. Dmitri Medvedev:

> I tie this offer ... to participate in the elections for the president of Russia ... to the necessity of continuing the implementation of the course our country has been moving along for eight years, the course chosen by the people during these years, the course which prevented the collapse of our economy and of the social sphere in our country, the course which prevented civil war, the course which is being conducted by President Putin. What is so dear for us today? Stability, improvement of the quality of life and the hope for durable and steady development. Education, healthcare, housing construction – we have managed to overcome the stagnation of the 1990s in these most important spheres of our life ... Our economy has strengthened considerably. We do not live in debt any more ... Our defence capacity and security has grown. The attitude toward Russia in the world is different now. We are not being lectured like schoolchildren, we are respected and we are deferred to ... But even more has to be done: we need to sharply decrease poverty, to create a modern healthcare system and education, to solve the most complicated housing problems, to achieve new living standards in rural areas. Our task is to increase the real incomes for all citizens, to ensure a decent life for the elderly, to create necessary conditions for the development of the young. It is necessary to continue reviving industries and agriculture, to secure Russia's role in international relations, and, finally, to solve the grave demographic problem. These tasks will remain relevant for decades to come. That is why it is important to continue the course which was formed at the end of the 1990s. In order to stay on this path it is not enough to elect a new president who shares this ideology. It is not less important to maintain the efficiency of the team formed by the incumbent president. That is why I find it extremely important for our country to keep Vladimir Vladimirovich Putin at the most important position in the executive power, at the post of chairman of the government.
>
> (www.iht.com, 11 December 2007)

'Dmitri Medvedev said on state television: "I call upon him [Vladimir Putin] to agree in principle to head the Russian government after the elections of the new president"' (www.cnn.com, 11 December 2007).

> [In November 2007] Dmitri Medvedev said: 'The model we are having in Russia, the socio-economic model is incompatible with the parliamentary democracy. Russia should develop as a number of major countries with strong presidential power. This is the basis for preserving the state within the existing boundaries and I think this is something difficult to argue with.'
>
> (*IHT*, 12 December 2007, p. 4)

> [Presidential candidate Dmitri Medvedev] is not in favour of the idea [of sovereign democracy] ... Medvedev: 'It would be more appropriate to talk about real democracy or just democracy in conditions of secured state sovereignty. If definitions are added to "democracy" this leaves a strange taste.

This implies that we speak about some other, unconventional democracy. Perhaps I have a more formal view on this than my colleagues.'

(www.guardian.co.uk, 11 December 2007)

The man considered the chief ideologist to President Vladimir Putin ... [is] Vladislav Surkov, a deputy Kremlin chief of staff ... Mr Surkov declined to recognize 'managed democracy' as a description of Russia's political system, although Mr Putin himself was one of the first to use the term ... 'By managed democracy we understand political and economic regimes imposed by centres of global influence – and I am not going to mention specific countries – by force and deception,' he said. Instead, Mr Surkov said Russia considered itself a 'sovereign democracy', a term he has used in recent months as the foundation of an emerging Kremlin ideology ... Surkov: 'That does not mean anything special. It means that in building an open society we do not forget that we are a free society and do not want to be ruled from outside ... We do not consider that we were defeated in the Cold War. We believe that we defeated our own totalitarian system ... Moscow did far more to democratize Eastern Europe and Central Asia than Washington or London.'

(*FT*, 29 June 2006, p. 6)

The basic idea behind the term is that Russia is a sovereign nation with its own traditions and the right to determine its own path and stand up for its interests where it feels they are threatened by the activities of other actors. The term has enjoyed the greatest vogue with those defending the Kremlin's domestic policy, countering charges that democracy is being rolled back with the argument that Russia should be allowed to develop its own version of democracy. It is a philosophy based on the pursuit and defence of national interests. But, while it definitely does send a message to outsiders that they should not interfere with internal Russian matters, it does not provide much guidance as to what the goals of internal policy should be.

(*The Moscow Times*, cited in www.iht.com, 3 September 2006)

'An essay published last November [2006] by Vladislav Surkov, a deputy chief of the presidential administration and the Kremlin's ideologist, said Russia would pursue a "sovereign democracy", in which democratic values would be subordinated to national interests' (www.iht.com, 29 June 2007).

'The Putin circle calls the new Russia a sovereign democracy – a democracy defended against hostile foreign meddling' (www.bbc.co.uk, 4 March 2008).

' "Sovereign democracy" ... touts a strong, organized state and the centre of the political machine guarding against chaos and foreign meddling' (*Guardian*, 14 August 2009, p. 23).

12 December 2007. 'Russia has gone ahead with plans to suspend its participation in ... the Conventional Forces in Europe (FCE) Treaty' (www.bbc.co.uk, 12 December 2007).

The Russian government has ordered the British Council to close down its two offices outside Moscow by the beginning of January [2008] ... Russian foreign ministry officials said the British Council had violated Russian laws, including tax regulations. But in an interview with the BBC, foreign minister Sergei Lavrov explicitly linked the order to Britain's expulsion of Russian diplomats in July. He said Russia had been left with no choice but to retaliate over the affair.

(www.bbc.co.uk, 13 December 2007)

The Russian foreign ministry said the British Council, which promotes British culture abroad, was operating illegally ... The council announced three months ago that it was closing nine regional offices by the end of the year [2007] and transferring operations to Russian partners. Those closures would leave the headquarters in Moscow, plus offices in St Petersburg and Yekaterinburg ... The council is a registered charity funded by the British government. Its state purpose is to promote British culture and education and build relationships between people in the UK and other countries.

(www.bbc.co.uk, 12 December 2007)

'Russia on Wednesday [12 December] ordered ... the British Council ... to suspend all of its operations outside Moscow at the beginning of 2008' (www. iht.com, 12 December 2007).

The Russian foreign minister. Sergei Lavrov, said in an interview with the BBC released on Wednesday [12 December] that Moscow's stance on the British Council was retaliation against Britain after the July expulsions ... In July Britain expelled four diplomats in response to Russia's refusal top extradite Andrei Lugovoi to stand trial for Alexander Litvinenko's murder. Moscow followed that by expelling four British diplomats ... Sergei Lavrov (in the BBC interview): 'The British government undertook some actions that inflicted systematic damage to our relations so we have to retaliate. This is nothing to do with anti-British sentiments. It is the law of the genre if you wish.'

(*IHT*, 13 December 2007, p. 5)

'Russia has alleged that the British Council was a for-profit operation and said its regional offices violated an international convention on consular affairs and so were operating illegally' (*IHT*, 15 December 2007, p. 6).

The [Russian] foreign ministry said the British Council had been working 'illegally' and claimed the organization had 'violated' Russian tax laws as well as the Vienna Convention ... A spokesman for the Russian foreign ministry: 'Given the lack of a legal base which could regulate the activity of the British Council in Russia, the British side was notified that the activity of all regional offices of the British Council in Russia, except for its head office in Moscow, will be suspended starting on 1 January 2008. The practical activity of the council was accompanied by violations of Russian financial, tax and other laws. The organization had also breached the Vienna

Convention on consular relations by operating out of British consulates in Russia. An abnormal situation ... has come into existence' ... The British Council has been operating in Russia since the early 1990s. It established a network of fifteen regional offices ... Tax police wearing balaclavas raided the British Council's Moscow head office three years ago. The pro-Kremlin youth group Nashi has harassed Britain's ambassador in Moscow ... since the summer of last year [2006]. It demonstrated outside the embassy last week. And in August the Kremlin closed the last FM broadcast frequency of the BBC's Russian service.

(www.guardian.co.uk, 12 December 2007)

The British Council announced in October that from 1 January [2008] it was transferring nine of its eleven regional centres in Russia to local partners such as universities ... The British Council was founded in 1934 ... [It] describes itself as 'the UK's international organization for educational opportunities and cultural relations'.

(*The Times*, 13 December 2007, p. 38)

Garry Kasparov announced on Wednesday [12 December] that he was abandoning his campaign for the presidency ... Garry Kasparov: 'My electoral campaign finishes tomorrow [13 December]. In all Moscow we have not been able to find a hall where our supporters could meet' ... Under Russian electorate law presidential contenders who are not affiliated to one of four major parties that won seats in parliament must provide the details of 2 million supporters across the country. Such contenders must also organize an 'initiative group' meeting of at least 500 supporters before a December deadline.

(www.bbc.co.uk, 12 December 2007)

14–15 December 2007.

[On 15 December] the Communist Party has nominated its leader, Gennadi Zyuganov, to run in the March presidential election ... [On 14 December] the liberal Yabloko Party nominated a Soviet-era dissident, Vladimir Bukovsky, as its candidate, in a rebuke to Grigori Yavlinsky, the party's leader.

(*IHT*, 17 December 2007, p. 2)

16 December 2007.

Russia has made its first delivery of nuclear fuel to an Iranian power station ... The United States has long been applying pressure on Russia to delay completion of the power station and until recently Russia appeared to be listening ... Construction of Bushehr has been hindered by repeated delays. Russia delayed a fuel shipment expected in March, accusing Iran of tardiness [denied by Iran] in making its monthly payments of $25 million. However, Western officials said that Russia had made the decision in part to help the West to pressure Iran into more openness on its nuclear programme.

(*IHT*, 18 December 2007, pp. 1, 8)

17 December 2007. President Vladimir Putin (addressing a conference of United Russia on 17 December):

> If the citizens of Russia show trust in Dmitri Medvedev and elect him the new president of the Russian Federation, I will be ready to continue our joint work as prime minister, without changing the distribution of authority ... We should not be ashamed or afraid to turn over the levers of control over the country, the destiny of Russia, into the hands of such a man as him.
>
> (www.iht.com, 17 December 2007; *IHT*, 18 December 2007, p. 3)

'Vladimir Putin's acceptance of Dmitri Medvedev's offer came amid reports of infighting between different factions in the Kremlin, led by rival figures tied to Russian intelligence and security agencies' (www.iht.com, 17 December 2007).

'The United Russia Party today [17 December] voted unanimously to nominate ... Dmitri Medvedev as its candidate in the 2 March [2008] presidential election' (www.guardian.co.uk, 17 December 2007).

'Party representatives voted 478 to one in favour of Dmitri Medvedev, who was the sole nominee' (*The Times*, 18 December 2007, p. 34).

> Dmitri Medvedev ... said his key policies included strengthening Russia's role in the world, and looking after the old and young ... Dmitri Medvedev: 'All this is in Vladimir Putin's strategy. I will be guided by this strategy if I am elected president.'
>
> (*Guardian*, 18 December 2007, p. 17)

> Dmitri Medvedev ... pledged yesterday [17 December] to continue Vladimir Putin's course for developing the country, and said raising living standards was a main goal. But he said Russia should strive to achieve a 'particular leadership role in the world' ... He said: 'We should build an advanced, flourishing, socially orientated Russia. That is the choice of our people and that is my choice.'
>
> (*FT*, 18 December 2007, p. 6)

19 December 2007.

> Nine independent candidates, including former prime minister Mikhail Kasyanov, and Soviet-era dissident Vladimir Bukovsky, have been registered as potential contestants in the 2 March [2008] presidential election, the central elections commission said Wednesday [19 December]. Independent candidates had until midnight Tuesday to submit documents confirming they had at least 500 voters backing their bid to enter the race.
>
> (*IHT*, 20 December 2007, p. 4)

25 December 2007.

> Russia's military on Tuesday [25 December] successfully test-fired a new intercontinental ballistic missile capable of carrying multiple nuclear

weapons – a weapon intended to replace ageing Soviet-era missiles ... such as the RS-18 and RS-20 ... The RS-24 missile was launched from the Plesetsk launch facility in northern Russia ... [Russia] said the new missile was based on the Topol-M.

(www.iht.com, 26 December 2007)

'A submarine in the Barents Sea successfully test-fired a new ballistic missile ... RSM-54 ... Tuesday, hitting a target on the Kamchatka Peninsula' (*IHT*, 26 December 2007, p. 8).

Russia has successfully tested two intercontinental ballistic missiles that are to replace ageing rockets from the Soviet era. A strategic missile know as RS-24 flew 7,000 kilometres (4,350 miles) to hit targets on the Kamchatka peninsula. Later a Russian submarine launched another new missile, hitting the same test site. It comes as Russia has again accused the United States of ignoring its concerns over a planned US missile defence system [in the Czech Republic and Poland] ... Speaking in an interview to be published later this week in the *Vremya Novostei* daily, Russian foreign minister Sergei Lavrov said it was clear the system is aimed at deterring Russia rather than Iran. The United States has said that the limited system it proposes could not threaten Russia's own missile arsenal.

(www.bbc.co.uk, 26 December 2007)

26 December 2007. 'Boris Nemtsov ... withdrew Wednesday from the presidential race, saying that the opposition needed to put forward a single candidate in the March election' (*IHT*, 27 December 2007, p. 3).

'Boris Nemtsov ... dropped out of the race ... to avoid splitting the vote with "the only other remaining candidate from the democratic opposition", former prime minister Mikhail Kasyanov' (*The Independent*, 27 December 2007, p. 25).

Russia is to supply Iran with new S-300 air defence systems ... [Iran's] defence minister ... said Wednesday [26 December] on the basis of a contract signed in the past ... The Interfax news agency quoted an unidentified source in the Russian military–industrial complex as saying that a contract for the missiles delivery had been signed several years ago and envisioned the delivery of several dozen S-300 missile systems ... Earlier this year 2007] Russia delivered twenty-nine Tor-M1 air defence missile systems to Iran under a $700 million contract signed in December 2005 ... The S-300 is a much more powerful and versatile weapon than the Tor-M1 ... Russian military officials boast that its performance beats that of US Patriot missiles.

(*IHT*, 27 December 2007, p. 3)

28 December 2007.

The federal agency overseeing Russia's military exports on Friday [28 December] denied reports that the country is planning to deliver a powerful anti-aircraft missile system to Iran ... Russia's Federal Military–Technical Co-operation Service: 'The question of deliveries of S-300 systems to Iran, which has now arisen in the mass media, is not currently taking place, is not being considered and is not being discussed at this time with the Iranian side' ... Earlier this month [December] Washington reversed course, concluding in an intelligence assessment that Iran stopped direct work on creating nuclear arms in 2003 and that the programme remained frozen through at least the middle of this year [2008].

(www.iht.com, 28 December 2007)

'The US intelligence community reported that Tehran halted its secret nuclear weapons programme in 2003' (www.iht.com, 27 December 2007).

1 January 2007. 'The British embassy said Tuesday [1 January 2008] it would defy a Russian order to close two offices of a British cultural organization [the British Council] ... in St Petersburg and Yekaterinburg' (*IHT*, 2 January 2008, p. 3).

3 January 2008.

The Russian foreign ministry told Britain on Thursday [3 January] that reopening two offices of a British cultural organization would inflame already tense relations between the countries. Russia in December ordered offices of the British Council in St Petersburg and Yekaterinburg to close as of 1 January. The offices are closed for the winter holidays in Russia, but British officials say they will defy the order and resume operations on 14 January ... The British Council is technically a non-governmental organization, but it acts as the cultural department of the British embassy. Russia contends it acts as a for-profit organization ... [A spokeswoman for the British Council] said the organization complied with Russian law, a 1994 Britain–Russia agreement and the Vienna Convention on Consular Relations ... British Council officials have been in contact with the Russian government, seeking an agreement that would allow the offices to open without incident.

(*IHT*, 4 January 2008, p. 3)

12 January 2008.

On 12 January Russia's ministry of foreign affairs told the British Council that its regional offices were operating illegally ... and that they should be closed down. But since there was no court decision Britain ... argued that the order by the ministry of foreign affairs had no legal basis and in fact broke an international convention which regulates its activities.

(www.economist.com, 19 January 2008)

14 January 2008.

The Russian foreign ministry has summoned the UK ambassador amid an escalating row over the reopening of two British Council offices ... on

Monday [14 January] despite a government ban ... A statement by the Russian foreign ministry: 'Russia views such actions as an intentional provocation aimed at inflaming tensions in Russian–British relations. The Russian side will not issue visas to new employees sent to work in the [British] consular offices of St Petersburg and Yekaterinburg to carry out British Council work' ... British ambassador Tony Brenton: '[The UK and Russia have a] serious disagreement ... [I have made a] statement of our clear view that the British Council is working entirely legally, that it will continue therefore to work, that any Russian action against it would be a breach of international law.'

(www.bbc.co.uk, 14 January 2008)

('The Russian foreign minister told [the BBC in December 2007 that] ... the closure was "retaliation" for the British government's decision to expel Russian diplomats from the UK in July': www.bbc.com, 14 January 2008.)

The British Council offices in St Petersburg and Yekaterinburg reopened after the holiday break, despite Moscow's warnings that defying orders to shut them as of 1 January [2008] would worsen already strained relations between Britain and Russia ... [The Russian foreign ministry said:] 'The [British] ambassador was told that the Russian side sees such actions as a deliberate provocation aimed at inciting tension in Russian–British relations' ... It promised 'a series of administrative and legal measures', including moves to recover what it said are back taxes owed by the British Council's St Petersburg office. In addition, Russia will stop issuing visas for new employees assigned to the British consulates in St Petersburg and Yekaterinburg, and will not renew the accreditation of current staffers ... The foreign ministry said continued operation of the St Petersburg and Yekaterinburg offices could lead to 'additional measures, including in relation to the British Council office in Moscow' ... Foreign minister Sergei Lavrov said last month [December 2007] that the British Council order was taken as a 'countermeasure' to the diplomat expulsion ... British ambassador Anthony Brenton: 'Mr Lavrov himself made it very clear that the actions that the Russian are taking against the British Council stem from the disagreement that happened at the time that we tried to extradite Mr Lugovoi. So they have made a very clear political connection. We think that connection is a mistake.'

(www.iht.com, 14 January 2008)

Russia celebrates New Year's Day and Orthodox Christmas in an extended holiday. The dispute flared again on the first Monday after the holiday period. The government has threatened to close the British Council's main office in Moscow as one of its retaliatory measures.

(*IHT*, 15 January 2008, p. 3)

'The Yekaterinburg branch quietly reopened on 9 January' (www.guardian. co.uk, 14 January 2008).

15 January 2008.

The British Council has said it is 'deeply concerned' for the safety of its staff in Russia, after they were questioned by the FSB security service ... Staff in St Petersburg were summoned for FSB interviews and visited at home late last night [15 January] ... St Petersburg office director Stephen Kinnock was followed, stopped and released by authorities on Tuesday [15 January] ... The St Petersburg British Council office closed on Wednesday [16 January] because all Russian staff have been summoned by the Russian authorities ... On Wednesday a British Council spokesman said Russian staff in St Petersburg and Yekaterinburg were 'summoned for interview by the FSB at their headquarters and subsequently visited in their homes late last night by officials of the Russian ministry of the interior' ... They have been called to more interviews on Wednesday, he said.

(www.bbc.co.uk, 16 January 2008)

'Stephen Kinnock was followed, stopped and released by the authorities on Tuesday after he had been accused of driving the wrong way up a one-way street and of smelling of alcohol' (www.bbc.co.uk, 17 January 2008).

Russia's security agency interviewed the group's Russian employees and one of its directors was stopped by law enforcement ... Russia's Federal Security Service [FSB] said it was interviewing the council's Russian employees. The FSB said it was conducting 'explanatory work' with the employees with the aim of 'protecting Russian citizens from possibly being drawn into the Britons' provocative games as tools' ... The British Council said that its St Petersburg director, Stephen Kinnock, 'was followed, stopped and subsequently released an hour later by Russian authorities' ... Russia's Interfax news agency, citing an unidentified law enforcement source, reported that Kinnock was stopped by traffic police late Tuesday [15 January] for violating a traffic sign. It said the police smelled alcohol but that Kinnock refused to undergo a test, and that the British consul arrived later and left with Kinnock ... Kinnock, who had opened the office on St Petersburg's main avenue Monday [14 January] in defiance of the Russian order, said Wednesday [16 January] that Russia's actions had prompted the office's temporary closure but that he hoped to reopen as soon as possible ... Russia's ambassador to London was summoned for talks with British officials.

(www.iht.com, 16 January 2008)

Kinnock, whose status as an accredited diplomat gives him legal protection, was not arrested or charged with any crime ... Britain closed its office in St Petersburg on Wednesday [16 January] under pressure from Russia's intelligence service, which summoned the organization's entire staff for questioning ... The closure, a British official said, was temporary.

(*IHT*, 17 January 2008, p. 3)

After an angry exchange Tuesday in which Britain's ambassador warned that action against the British Council would violate international law and Russia's foreign minister accused Britain of colonial-era arrogance, Russia's Federal Security Service [FSB] said it was interviewing the council's Russian employees. The FSB said it was conducting 'explanatory work' with the employees with the aim of 'protecting Russian citizens from possibly being drawn into the Britons' provocative games as tools' ... The director of the council's St Petersburg office was stopped for a traffic violation Tuesday night. St Petersburg police said Stephen Kinnock was stopped for violating a traffic sign and traffic police smelled alcohol but Kinnock refused to undergo testing. The British consul arrived later and left with Kinnock. The British Council said Kinnock followed global diplomatic protocol by calling the British Consulate, which instructed him not to take the test.

(www.iht.com, 17 January 2008)

'The British Council ... rejected the claim that Stephen Kinnock had been drunk. It said he appeared to be the victim of a sinister pattern of state-backed intimidation and deliberate harassment against its staff' (www.guardian.co.uk, 16 January 2008).

'Stephen Kinnock is son of the former Labour Party leader [Neil Kinnock] who is also the British Council chairman' (*FT*, 17 January 2008, p. 1). 'The Russian staff underwent a second round of questioning yesterday [16 January] by officers from the financial crimes unit of the Russian interior ministry and by the tax service' (p. 7).

While most of its $551 million budget is generated by commercial activities such as language teaching, about a third of its funding comes from the Foreign Office. The council employs 7,900 staff in about 110 countries. It opened fifteen offices in Russia after the two countries reached a 1994 cultural agreement. Stephen Kinnock ... has served with the council for more than a decade ... Neil Kinnock ... was appointed British Council chair in 2004 ... In May 2004 the council found itself in a broader political game. Russian tax police raided its offices, claiming it made 'big money' from offering English lessons and should pay tax. British officials quickly linked the case with [Boris Berezovsky and Akhmed Zakayev] ... The council eventually registered as a Russian tax-payer and in December 2005 settled back tax claims worth £1.4 million. A month later, however, Russia reopened its tax probe – after Russian secret services accused British diplomats of spying and covertly financing non-governmental organizations.

(*FT*, 18 January 2008, p. 7)

17 January 2008.

British Council chief executive Martin Davidson said on Thursday [17 January] that its St Petersburg and Yekaterinburg offices' work would have to be suspended. In a statement Mr Davidson accused the Russian government of initiating 'a campaign of intimidation against our staff' in the two offices. He said more than twenty Russian staff had been called to attend interviews with the FSB security service and ten more were visited at their homes late at night by Russian tax police ... Martin Davidson: 'The interviews had little to do with their work and were clearly aimed at exerting undue pressure on innocent individuals. Our paramount consideration is the well-being of our staff and I feel we cannot continue our work without significant risk to them. The Russian authorities have made it impossible for us to operate in St Petersburg and Yekaterinburg so I have taken the decision to suspend operations in both cities' ... UK foreign secretary David Miliband said cultural activities should not become 'a political football' so he decided not to take similar actions against Russian activities in the UK and said the British Council would continue its work in Moscow.

(www.bbc.co.uk, 17 January 2008)

British officials in Moscow said the Kremlin had used 'classic KGB-style tactics' to intimidate British Council staff ... The FSB had made numerous 'threats' against the council's staff, officials said. They included inquiring about the health of elderly relatives and warning that family pets might meet with an unfortunate accident. Tax officials had informed several staff they had a problem ... Foreign Secretary David Miliband: 'This can only make the international community more cautious in its dealings with Russia in international relations.'

(*Guardian*, 18 January 2008, p. 2)

British foreign secretary David Miliband (17 January):

We [do not] believe that cultural activities should become a political football; in fact, educational and cultural activities are important ways of bringing people together. That is why I have decided not to take similar action against Russia's cultural activities in the UK. For example, by sending back Russian masterpieces scheduled for show at the Royal Academy, or by taking measures against the two Russian diplomats at the Russian Embassy dedicated to cultural work ... The British Council will continue its work in Moscow, meeting the demand from as many as possible of the 1.25 million Russian citizens who used the Council's services last year [2007] ... Russia's actions raise serious questions about her observance of international law, as well as about the standards of behaviour she is prepared to adopt towards her own citizens. This can only make the international community more cautious in its dealings with Russia in international negotiations and more doubtful about its existing international commitments.

(www.bbc.co.uk, 19 January 2008)

'Instead of going to court the Russian ministry of foreign affairs went to the traffic police and the security services' (www.economist.com, 19 January 2008).

'Slovenia, which holds the EU's rotating presidency, issued a strongly worded statement calling on Russia to "allow the British Council to operate freely and

effectively ... and to take no further actions that might hinder its activities"'
(*The Times*, 18 January 2008, p. 8).

'The EU said it "deeply regrets in particular the harassment of British Council
staff as well as the administrative and other measures announced by the Russian
authorities"' (*IHT*, 18 January 2008, p. 3).

18 January 2008.

> Bulgaria has agreed to a gas pipeline deal with Russia ... the Bulgarian
> cabinet has agreed to allow the planned South Stream pipeline to pass through
> the country on its way from the Black Sea to southern Europe. The South
> Stream project is seen as a rival to the planned Nabucco pipeline, which is
> backed by the EU and the United States ... Russian president Vladimir Putin
> is currently on a state visit to Bulgaria ... The deal between Bulgaria and
> Russia is due to be signed shortly. The South Stream gas scheme, said to be
> worth Euro 10 billion ($14.66 billion), is being jointly developed by Gazprom
> and the Italian firm Eni. The 900-kilometre (550-mile) pipeline is expected to
> take Russian gas under the Black Sea and overland to Bulgaria to markets in
> southern Europe. Russia has offered to site a major gas hub in Serbia ... Bul-
> garia has also received an offer from the United States and EU to join the
> Nabucco project. Nabucco envisages bringing Central Asian gas to Europe, a
> move intended to reduce Europe's reliance on Russian resources ... Mr
> Putin's visit has seen Sofia sign additional agreements with Moscow on the
> construction of an oil pipeline and a nuclear power station.
>
> (www.bbc.co.uk, 18 January 2008)

> President Vladimir Putin secured the South Stream pipeline deal in tough
> talks with Bulgarian officials by offering last-minute concessions ... Tough
> bargaining over the pipeline dragged past midnight and the Bulgarian
> cabinet approved the agreement at an extraordinary meeting just hours
> before it was signed ... Bulgarian prime minister Sergei Stanishev: 'Bulgar-
> ia's interests are fully protected because the company which will be set up
> to construct and run the pipeline on Bulgarian soil will be with 50 per cent
> Bulgarian and 50 per cent Russian ownership' ... Gazprom had previously
> been offering Bulgaria a minority stake in the part of the pipeline that would
> run through Bulgaria ... The 900-kilometre (550-mile), $10 billion (Euro
> 6.8 billion) pipeline would run from Russia to Bulgaria under the Black Sea
> and could then branch off in several directions ... Gazprom has set up a
> parity joint venture with Italy's Eni to develop a feasibility study for South
> Stream ... Russia has promised to extend South Stream into Serbia and
> build a huge gas storage facility there – moves that would turn the Balkan
> nation into a major hub for Russian energy supplies to Europe. Gazprom
> CEO Alexei Miller said Gazprom and Serbian officials were close to a final
> agreement on a deal that would envisage a South Stream branch reaching
> Serbia and would also foresee Gazprom taking a controlling stake in Ser-
> bia's state oil company NIS [The EU said] it remains committed to the pro-

spective Nabucco pipeline that would deliver Caspian region gas westwards via Bulgaria, bypassing Russia ... many countries in Central and Eastern Europe have raised concerns that their growing dependency on Russian energy may make them vulnerable to attempts from Moscow to interfere in their internal affairs ... [Bulgarian and Russian] officials also signed a Euro 4 billion ($5.9 billion) contract to build Bulgaria's second nuclear plant, near the northern town of Belene. Also signed was a three-way agreement, including Greece, for a joint company to build a Burgas–Alexandroupolis oil pipeline, which will channel Russian oil from the Black Sea to the Aegean, bypassing Turkey's busy Bosphorus ... About 100 demonstrators protested Putin's visit in downtown Sofia on Thursday [18 January]. The group that organized the protest, the Anna Politkovskaya Association for Freedom of Speech, said in a statement: 'Putin is coming to Bulgaria to sign Bulgaria's total economic dependence on Russia.'

(www.iht.com, 18 January 2008)

In Bulgaria it [South Stream] will branch into two spurs: one going west to Italy, the other going north into Austria and Hungary ... The agreement [was] signed by President Vladimir Putin and his Bulgarian counterpart Georgi Parvanov ... Putin and Parvanov also signed an agreement for the construction of the Belene nuclear power plant, the first Russian nuclear plant to be built in an EU country. Construction work began in the 1980s but was cancelled in 1990. The project was revived in 2003 ... The EU intends to buy natural gas from Iran and Azerbaijan and ship it through Turkey in pipelines that will run to southern and western Europe. But failure to agree on the routes, financing and how to deal with Iran's nuclear pro-gramme has delayed the Nabucco project ... Bulgaria is also a member of Nabucco. The other countries are Austria, Turkey, Hungary and Romania ... Hungary is negotiating with Gazprom to join South Stream. Ferenc Gyurscany, the Hungarian prime minister, has repeatedly said he is commit-ted to Nabucco. But last month [December 2007], after consultations between Budapest and Moscow, it was agreed that the South Stream pipe-line would reach Hungary as well.

(*IHT*, 19 January 2008, pp. 1, 4)

Ivan Kostov (leader of Democrats for Strong Bulgaria): 'Russia is danger-ous and creates economic instability, attempting to use its heavy hand on the fledgling democracies in the Balkans' ... [The estimated cost of South Stream is] Euro 10 billion ($14.6 billion) ... [As regards the Burgas–Alex-androupolis] oil pipeline] Russian state-owned groups will own a 51 per cent stake in the new company, and the rest will be split equally between Bulgaria and Greece.

(*FT*, 19 January 2008, p. 6)

Hundreds of Bulgarians protested on Friday [18 January] against Russia's energy policy, which they fear will make their country completely dependent on Russian oil and gas. Carrying posters reading 'Stop Soviet imperialism' and 'Putin – out of Bulgaria', demonstrators marched in central Sofia to oppose energy agreements between Bulgaria's Socialist-led government and Russia that were signed during President Putin's two-day visit ... Former prime minister Ivan Kostov, who now heads the right-wing party Democrats for Strong Bulgaria, said his country depends on Russia for 90 per cent of its energy supplies and that the new agreements will turn it into 'an economic satellite of Russia'. A commemorative ceremony for Anna Politkovskaya, a Russian investigative journalist whose death many blame on Putin's regime, took place later at the memorial site for victims of communism, near the landmark National Palace of Culture.

(www.iht.com, 18 January 2008)

('[On 5 February] the Nabucco consortium said the German utility RWE would join its ranks': *IHT*, 6 February 2008, p. 15. 'The private consortium developing the Nabucco pipeline will invite Russia's Gazprom to send natural gas through the network to its European markets, consortium officials said this week. The development, which comes in response to the doubts about the project's natural gas suppliers, is a major shift in strategy. The main aim of the EU-sponosred pipeline was to reduce European dependence on Russian gas and to act as a bulwark against Gazprom's energy dominance ... [It is] unclear whether its intended suppliers, Turkmenistan, Azerbaijan and Iran, will be able to participate ... RWE Gas Midstream, a division of the German energy giant RWE, joined the consortium Tuesday [5 February], becoming the sixth member. The other five include OMV of Austria. MOL of Hungary, Transgaz of Romania, Bulgargaz of Bulgaria and Botas of Turkey': *IHT*, 7 February 2008, p. 15.)

18 January 2008.

The Russian foreign ministry on Friday [18 January] expressed satisfaction over the decision of the British government to suspend two cultural centres even as the British ambassador said he hoped the centres would reopen after further negotiations ... Anthony Brenton said that Britain planned to press Russia, through diplomacy, to allow them to resume work.

(*IHT*, 19 January 2008, p. 3)

21 January 2008.

Russia said yesterday [21 January] that the British government's cultural arm could reopen its offices if Britain restarts talks on counter-terrorism and entry visas ... [which were] suspended after the murder of Alexander Litvinenko by radiation poisoning in London in 2006.

(*The Independent*, 22 January 2008, p. 19)

22–27 January 2008. 'The prosecutor-general's office announced that a criminal investigation has been opened against the campaign of Mikhail Kasyanov for allegedly forging thousands of signatures on his nominating petitions' (www.iht.com, 22 January 2008).

> First a spokeswoman for the prosecutor-general said that irregularities in thousands of voters' signatures on behalf of Kasyanov had been uncovered in regions throughout the country. Two prosecutor offices had started investigations, she said. Then the secretary of the central election commission announced that a check of a large sample of signatures from across the country had found that 15.5 per cent were 'faked' ... Mikhail Kasyanov said last weakened [19 January] that Russia's security agencies had 'launched a special operation against me' ... His chief campaign managers issued a statement accusing the police of widespread abuse of power and violation of civil rights. The statement said that people who had signed Kasyanov's campaign documents were being threatened with home searches, arrest and dismissal from jobs ... The final list of candidates [is] to be published on Sunday [27 January].
>
> (*IHT*, 23 January 2008, p. 3)

'Prosecutors ... accuse his campaign of forging some of the 2 million signatures on his nomination papers ... Prosecutors say they suspect more than 15,000 of these are fake. And the electoral commission says it has found 62,000 forged signatures' (www.bbc.co.uk, 22 January 2008).

'If more than 5 per cent of the signatures are declared invalid, the central electoral committee will bar him [Mikhail Kasyanov] from standing' (*The Independent*, 23 January 2008, p. 19).

> Dmitri Medvedev opened his campaign on Tuesday [22 January] ... in a speech to a Kremlin-organized forum of civil-society organizations ... Medvedev: 'Russia is a country of legal nihilism at a level ... that no European country can boast of. Corruption in the official structures has reached a huge scale and the fight against it should be a national programme ... We should openly and clearly explain our plans and find allies in the world. All today's foreign policy is absolutely within the framework of international standards. Russia in the future will continue developing as a nation open for dialogue with the international community ... Modern Russia has every chance to become a successful state.'
>
> (www.ijht.com, 22 January 2008)

> Dmitri Medvedev ... emphasized continuity. 'We simply need ten years of stable development, which our country was deprived of for a long time,' he said, reiterating the Kremlin's goal of turning Russia into one of the world's five leading economies within fifteen years. Mr Medvedev emphasized the importance of the development of an 'open civil society' and functioning political institutions.
>
> (*FT*, 23 January 2008, p. 9)

> Mikhail Kasyanov's campaign said it turned in 2,067,000 signatures. But Nikolai Konkin, secretary of the central election commission, said [on 24

January that] a check of the signatures found more than 89,000 to be invalid ... Konkin: 'That means the number of reliable signatures is less than 2 million, which is the basis for the denial of registration' ... Registration can also be denied if more than 5 per cent of an aspirant's signatures were bogus in two large sample of the total submitted. On Tuesday [22 January] the prosecutor-general's office also opened a forgery case against the campaign of Kasyanov ... [Kasyanov said that] the election officials' statement about forged signatures was 'simple propaganda'. Kasyanov said that if he were kept off the ballot, Putin would be to blame ... Kasyanov: 'It is not up to the central election commission, it is up to Vladimir Putin.'

(www.iht.com, 24 January 2008)

Election officials have barred former prime minister Mikhail Kasyanov from running as an opposition candidate in the March presidential election. The central election commission said there were many invalid signatures in Mr Kasyanov's list of supporters ... [specifically] 13.36 per cent ... Russian law stipulates that no more 5 per cent of signatures in support of a candidate can be false or forged ... Mr Kasyanov has been polling about 1 per cent.

(www.bbc.co.uk, 27 January 2008)

Mikhail Kasyanov ... was barred from the ballot Sunday [27 January] by election authorities ... [The commission said that] more than 80,000 signatures were found to be bogus during the check ... [and] also pointed to other flaws in Kasyanov's documents for registration ... [The commission said] that it could ask prosecutors to investigate more evidence of alleged forgery in the campaign. If found guilty Kasyanov and members of his campaign staff could face prison terms of up to five years ... Kasyanov denounced the central election commission's ruling as politically motivated and urged voters to boycott the election, calling it a 'farce' ... Kasyanov: 'I have no doubt that Putin personally made the decision not to register my candidacy ... There has been no forgery. The authorities are afraid of the people's will. They are denying us a chance for an honest political fight' ... The latest opinion poll, released this week, had about 80 per cent of respondents saying they would vote for Medvedev ... Three others have been cleared for the race: Communist Party chief Gennadi Zyuganov, Vladimir Zhirinovsky and Andrei Bogdanov (the obscure leader of a little known party). Zhirinovsky and Bogdanov are widely seen as acting at the Kremlin's behest ... On Sunday Medvedev visited St Petersburg for ceremonies marking the anniversary of the end of the Nazis' siege of the city, which was called Leningrad during Soviet times. Medvedev promised to increase pensions and improve housing conditions for World War II veterans.

(www.iht.com, 27 January 2008)

Mikhail Kasyanov ... claimed that opinion polls showing him with a tiny faction of support had been rigged by the state and that he had actually had the support of more than a quarter of Russia's voters – enough to force a run-off campaign that could rattle the Kremlin and threaten its monopoly on power ... Andrei Bogdanov [is] the head of the small and relatively unknown Democratic Party. All three of Midvale's opponents [Gennadi Zyuganov, Vladimir Zhirinovsky and Andrei Bogdanov] have been accused of running at the Kremlin's direction or at least with its approval, to create the appearance of a contest.

(*IHT*, 28 January 2008, p. 3)

22–25 January 2008.

Serbia said Tuesday [22 January] that it had agreed a multi-billion dollar pipeline project as part of an energy deal with Russia that would increase Moscow's control over supplies to Europe. As part of the deal, the Serbian oil monopoly NIS will be sold to Russian energy giant Gazprom and Russia would route part of the South Stream gas pipeline through Serbia. The financial terms of the package and the date it would be signed were not revealed in the government statement.

(www.iht.com, 22 January 2008)

Serbia endorsed the deal just days after Russian president Vladimir Putin won Bulgaria's support for the South Stream pipeline ... Russia promised to extend the pipeline into Serbia and build a huge gas storage in the north of the country, to turn the Balkan nation into a hub for Russian energy supplies to Europe ... Russia now supplies up to 40 per cent of Europe's gas and up to a third of the oil imports of some European countries ... But the pipeline deal with Serbia apparently comes at a price. Some Serbian officials said that Russia's initial offer of $600 million (Euro 400 million) for a 51 per cent stake in NIS represented just one-fifth of the company's market value. Gazprom and Serbian officials have haggled over terms, triggering infighting in the Serbian cabinet ... Vojislav Kostunica has denied accusations by the opposition that favourable terms for Russia in the deal amounted to payback for Moscow's support over Kosovo ... [Some analysts] also said that the main pro-Western faction within Kostunica's cabinet, the Democratic Party, dropped its opposition to the deal because it needs the prime minister's support if its candidate, incumbent president Boris Attic, is to defeat an ultranationalist challenger in the country's presidential run-off on 3 February.

(www.iht.com, 22 January 2008)

Four days after signing a major pipeline deal with Bulgaria, the agreement to take a 51 per cent stake in NIS, the state-owned oil company, was yet another blow to the EU's ambitions to build its own 3,300-kilometre pipeline to bring gas to Europe from Iran and Azerbaijan via Turkey, analysts said. The EU's Nabucco pipeline project was conceived to allow Europe to reduce its dependence on Russia, which already supplies a quarter of the bloc's gas. Nabucco has been dogged by logistical delays, lack of political will and disputes over financing, the analysts said ... Gazprom, Russia's state-owned monopoly, has taken advantage of the disarray inside the EU by forging ahead with its own contracts with Italy, Bulgaria, Hungary and now Serbia, as it consolidates its presence in south-eastern Europe. Under the terms of the provisional agreement, voted Tuesday [22 January] by Serbia's cabinet, Gazprom has offered to pay $600 million, or Euro 400 million, for a 51 per cent stake in NIS, with pledges to turn Serbia into a hub for Russian energy. The contract is to be signed Friday [[25 January] in Moscow. Gazprom will also commit investments of around Euro 500 million toward modernizing Serbia's energy infrastructure. In addition, a spur from the South Stream pipeline under the Black Sea will be directed into Serbia, enhancing its role as a transit point for Russian gas. OMV, Austria's largest energy company, said it had wanted to make a bid for NIS when it was put up for sale last year [2007] but there was no official tender process ... The European Commission criticized the tender process ... The Serbian government had been divided over the deal. Prime minister Vojislav Kostunica had accepted the price, first negotiated last month [December 2007], but members of the pro-European Democratic Party had challenged it, saying it was below market value. Analysts said Tuesday the price represented only a fifth of the company's market value and the terms of the sale were not transparent. Kostunica brushed aside these criticisms. During a cabinet meeting where the deal was endorsed he said the 'strategic' deal with Russia would give Serbia a reliable supply of energy for decades. He said: 'This is Serbia's biggest economic undertaking and this agreement will guarantee our country's huge economic development' ... Vuk Jeremic, the pro-Western foreign minister, said the deal would guarantee 'secure energy supplies to Serbia and the rest of the Western Balkans' ... Given the political context, analysts said, there was a linkage between the energy deal and the presidential elections ... An EU energy expert who spoke on the condition of anonymity because of the sensitivity of the issue: 'If a pro-Western candidate were to win the election, the deal with Russia might not be signed. There was no need to rush through the NIS deal, but the cabinet did it Tuesday [22 January].'

(www.iht.com, 22 January 2008; *IHT*, 23 January 2008, p. 3)

Last month [December 2007] Gazprom offered Euro 400 million ($580 million) for NIS. The financial terms of the [22 January] deal have not yet been disclosed ... Economy minister Madman Dinky has warned that the price for NIS could have been far higher than the Russian offer.

(www.bbc.co.uk, 22 January 2008)

'Serbia gets 90 per cent of its gas from Russia' (*FT*, 23 January 20–08, p. 9).

Russia won the right Friday [25 January] to direct a major supply route for natural gas through Serbia to Europe ... The agreement [was] signed in the Kremlin ... The agreements, signed Friday by Boris Attic and prime minister Vojislav Kostunica of Serbia, gave Gazprom a 51 per cent stake in Serbia's NIS oil and natural gas company for Euro 400 million and a pledge to invest Euro 500 million more by 2012. Some analysts described the price as well below market value, giving estimates of Euro 1 billion to Euro 2 billion, although others said the NIS plant needed heavy reconstruction. NIS dominates the Serbian market, with a monopoly of refining and a network of almost 500 gas stations. The NIS deal gives Gazprom its first refinery outside Russia ... Gazprom will acquire a stake of 50 per cent in Move's natural gas hub in Austria under an agreement signed Friday ... The two will sell to Germany and Italy through the Baumgarten hub, located near a trunk pipeline from west Siberian gas fields.

(*IHT*, 26 January 2008, p. 13)

[On 25 January] Gazprom ... reached agreement to buy Serbia's oil and gas monopoly for a bargain price in return for guaranteeing Belgrade a role in shipping gas to western Europe. The state-controlled Russian gas company also agreed with OMV, the Austrian oil and gas company, to take a 50 per cent stake in a strategic gas trading hub in Baumgarten, Austria. In the Serbian deal Gazpromneft, Gazprom's oil subsidiary, will take 51 per cent of Serbia's NIS monopoly for Euro 400 million plus investment worth no less than Euro 500 million by 2012 ... After weeks of political wrangling, Gazprom did not budge from its initial offer made last month [December 2007], although some Serbian cabinet members had wanted a better deal. Most energy analysts value the company at between Euro 1 billion and Euro 2 billion. Gazprom has also secured a two-year extension on barriers against imports of oil derivatives except through NIS ... The agreement, signed in Moscow, also outlines terms for jointly building Gazprom's South Stream pipeline through Serbia. Gazprom is to hold 51 per cent of new companies for construction of gas infrastructure to be formed with Srbijagas, the local state-owned gas company. Serbia would receive Euro 200 million annual transit fees from the pipeline across its territory ... The deal announced with OMV gives Gazprom joint control of OMV's trading hub in Baumgarten, continental Europe's third biggest hub. It handles about a third of Russian gas exports to western Europe. The two companies said they aimed to develop the hub into the largest trading platform in continental Europe. They also planned to carry out joint storage projects in Austria and neighbouring counties.

(*FT*, 26 January 2008, p. 7)

28 January 2008.

Russia has invited only 400 international monitors to observe the presidential election in March, the national elections chief said Monday [28 January] – half the number that participated four years ago. The announcement by the head of the central electoral commission, Vladimir Churov, mirrors a decision officials made for the December parliamentary vote that elicited widespread criticism in the West and prompted an authoritative vote-monitoring group to refuse to send observers.

(*IHT*, 29 January 2007, p. 3)

29 January 2008.

Moscow will allow the [400] monitors to enter Russia on 28 February ... A spokesman for OSCE said: 'The invitation that we received has serious ... unprecedented ... restrictions both in terms of the number of observers and time they are allowed to observe. This doesn't allow us to perform an effective observation and thereby fulfil our mandate. We're asking the Russian side, the Russian central election commission, to reconsider these restrictions. In both cases [the December 2007 general election and the March presidential election] Russia is the only OSCE country that has ever placed any restrictions on us in terms of when we can observe and how many observers we can send.'

(www.iht.com, 29 January 2008)

Russia has said OSCE will only be allowed to send seventy observers three days before the vote ... There were 400 OSCE monitors in Russia's presidential election in 2004. Arriving just three days before the vote would mean OSCE observers could not monitor the election campaign to see if it was free and fair for all candidates. Nor could they monitor Russia media coverage to assess whether all those running for the presidency are given proper access.

(www.bbc.co.uk, 30 January 2008)

'Dmitri Medvedev has refused to meet his rivals for the presidency in live televised debates ahead of the 2 March election' (*IHT*, 30 January 2008, p. 4).

'[Dmitri Medvedev's] campaign said yesterday [29 January] that he would not participate in live debates with other candidates' (*IHT*, 30 January 2008, p. 34).

'Dmitri Medvedev has refused to take part in any live television debates during the election campaign ... Communist Party candidate Gennadi Zyuganov said the Kremlin was frightened to face its opponents' (www.bbc.co.uk, 30 January 2008).

30 January 2008.

Two leading liberal officials yesterday [30 January] warned that Moscow's increasingly aggressive foreign policy could damage inward investment, in a rare public show of dissent ... Anatoli Chubais ... head of the electricity monopoly [UES] ... told a Moscow investment conference that Russia's confrontational approach carried risks in a worsening global economic situation ... Alexei Kudrin, finance minister and a deputy prime minister, warned in the same forum: 'Our dependence on global economic ties, on our exports, is felt so strongly that in the nearest future we need to adjust our foreign policy goals to guarantee stable investment' ... Later, however, Mr Kudrin toned down his remarks, saying: '[There are] no serious mistakes in our [foreign] policy. Russia is just defending its interests.'

(*FT*, 31 January 2008, p. 8)

'The official in Alexei Kudrin's ministry, who was recently in charge of the stabilization fund, the deputy finance minister Sergei Storchak, remains in pretrial detention on fraud and embezzlement charges' (*IHT*, 31 January 2008, p. 12).

1 February 2008.

> A court has ruled that a jailed former manager of the disbanded oil group Yukos cannot be transferred to a clinic for treatment. Vasili Aleksanyan [Vaslit Alexanian] is reported to be suffering from AIDS. He was jailed in 2006 after being found guilty of embezzlement. He was deputy to ... Mikhail Khodorkovsky ... Mr Khodorkovsky says he is on hunger strike in support of Mr Aleksanyan. He says officials are punishing Mr Aleksanyan for refusing to sign false confessions ... In a letter posted on his supporters' website on Wednesday [30 January] Mr Khodorkovsky said Mr Aleksanyan had been refused medication and deliberately placed in poor conditions ... Mr Aleksanyan says he has developed serious health complications and is nearly blind.

(www.bbc.co.uk, 1 February 2008)

('A Moscow court has suspended the trial of ... a seriously ill former top executive of Russia's disbanded oil giant Yukos. But the court refused to allow Vasili Aleksanyan [Vaslit Alexanian] to undergo urgent hospital treatment for AIDS and cancer, ruling that he could be treated in prison. The thirty-six-year-old former vice president of Yukos is charged with embezzlement. He rejects the charges. Mr Aleksanyan has been in detention since 2006 ... Mikhail Khodorkovsky is on hunger strike in support of his deputy ... On Tuesday [5 February] prosecutors in Moscow charged Mr Aleksanyan with embezzlement and money laundering dating back to the late 1990s ... Last Friday [1 February] the Moscow court rejected Mr Aleksanyan's demand to be transferred to a clinic as groundless': www.bbc.co.uk, 6 February 2008. 'The court refused an application to move the defendant to a hospital, saying that he might try to escape': *The Independent*, 7 February 2008, p. 31.)

('Vasili Aleksanyan [Vaslit Alexanian] ... is to be transferred from jail to a clinic, prison officials say ... It reverses Wednesday's court ruling, which said that Mr Aleksanyan should be treated in jail': www.bbc.co.uk, 7 February 2008. 'Russia said yesterday [7 February] it would transfer Vasili Aleksanyan [Vaslit Alexanian] from prison to a specialized clinic ... In testimony before a supreme court hearing last month [January] on whether he should be released, Mr Aleksanyan claimed prosecutors had approached him three times to offer a deal in which he was to sign off on false testimony against Mikhail Khodorkovsky in return for treatment ... [He] refused, he said ... He says they have tried to force him into giving false testimony against Mikhail Khodorkovsky by withholding treatment': *FT*, 8 February 2008, p. 9. Mikhail Khodorkovsky said yesterday [11 February] he was ending a fourteen-day hunger strike after hearing Vasili Aleksanyan [Vaslit Alexanian] had been transferred from prison to a civilian hospital': *FT*, 12 February 2008, p. 6. 'Mikhail Khodorkovsky began his hunger strike on 29 January': *IHT*, 12 February 2008, p. 8.)

5 February 2008.

> [On 5 February after two days of talks] Russia offered concessions [to OSCE] ... Russia is now willing to allow a seventy-five-member mission from OSCE's Office for Democratic Institutions and Human Rights [ODIHR] to begin operating at full strength ... on 20 February ... A five-person logistical team would be welcome immediately and a twenty-member advance team could begin work Friday [8 February] ... The remaining fifty observers could start work on 20 February. Last week Russia said the mission must have no more than seventy members and could not start until 28 February ... ODIHR spokesman Curtis Budden said Monday [4 February] that he wanted to send a logistics team on Tuesday, followed by a core team Friday and the rest of the mission next week ... Budden: 'We are ready to agree to start work no later than 18 February. That means that the observers need to arrive in Russia by 15 February' ... On Tuesday [5 February] Russian news agencies quoted Budden as saying that the organization has not changed its stance.
>
> (www.iht.com, 5 February 2008)

7 February 2008.

> Europe's main election watchdog has said that it will boycott Russia's presidential election on 2 March ... Spencer Oliver (general secretary of OSCE's Parliamentary Assembly): 'We regret that circumstances prevent us from observing this election' ... OSCE's parliamentary assembly announced its decision in a letter sent to the Russian parliament ... Goran Lennmarker (assembly president): 'We unfortunately cannot accept your invitation to send a limited number of observers to Russia for the presidential election' ... Mr Lennmarker also mentioned 'other conditions and circumstances', without specifying. Separately, OSCE's election monitoring wing – the Office for Democratic Institutions and Human Rights (ODIHR) – said it would not send observers because of 'limitations' imposed by Moscow ... The ODIHR on Wednesday [6 February] rejected a commission offer designed to avert a boycott ... Monitors normally arrive in countries up to two months before voting takes place so they can observe the registration of candidates, campaigning and media coverage as well as the vote itself.
>
> (www.bbc.co.uk, 7 February 2008)

> Christian Strohal (head of ODIHR):
>
> The time frame set by the Russian authorities has already prevented us from

observing many important parts of the election process, beginning with the registration of candidates and aspects of the campaign, including the work of the media. What is true for every election is also true for this one: transparency strengthens democracy; politics behind closed doors weakens it.

(*The Times*, 8 February 2008, p. 40)

8 February 2008.

President Vladimir Putin says the world is engaged in a new arms race and Nato is failing to accommodate Russia's concerns ... He condemned Nato's expansion and the US plan to include Poland and the Czech Republic in a missile shield ... Putin: 'It is already clear that a new phase in the arms race is unfolding in the world. It is not our fault because we did not start it' ... He said other countries were spending far more than Russia on new weapons. But Russia would always respond to the challenges of a new arms race by developing more hi-tech weaponry, he said. Referring to Nato's activities in Central and Eastern Europe, Mr Putin said: 'There are many discussions on these, but ... we have still not seen any real steps towards finding a compromise. In effect we are forced to retaliate, to take corresponding decisions, Russia has, and always will have, responses to these new challenges.'

(www.bbc.co.uk, 8 February 2008)

9 February 2008.

A Russian air force bomber briefly violated Japanese airspace Saturday [9 February] over an uninhabited island south of Tokyo, prompting Japan to scramble twenty-two fighter jets ... and two airborne warning and control aircraft known as AWACs ... and to issue a protest with Moscow, Japan said. Russia denied there was an intrusion. The Russian Tupolev 95 left Japanese airspace after three minutes, following warnings by Japan air force jets over Sofugan in the Izu island chain ... Japan held an annual rally Thursday [7 February] to demand the return of a disputed island chain that Russia seized in the closing days of World War II. The disagreement over the four islands, called the Kurils in Russia and the Northern Territories in Japan, have kept the two countries from signing a formal peace treaty ... [Japan said] Russia last violated Japanese airspace in January 2006 near Rebun Island off Japan's main northern island of Hokkaido, close to the disputed northern island.

(www.iht.com, 9 February 2008)

11 February 2008.

Russia has agreed to write off $12 billion of Iraqi debt built up by the regime of former leader Saddam Hussein to buy military equipment. In return, Russian companies, including oil giant Lukoil, will be given access to invest up to $4 billion in Iraq. Lukoil is expected to develop oilfields including West Qurna, one of the country's largest ... Russia says $12 billion that Iraq owes will be written off. The outstanding amount – some $900 million – will be repaid over seventeen years ... [Russia] said the deal would involve Russian energy and electricity firms, which would be involved in the reconstruction of the country's infrastructure. Lukoil previously had a deal to develop oil deposits in Iraq, but this was ended shortly before Saddam Hussein's government was removed from power in 2003.

(www.bbc.co.uk, 11 February 2008)

Russia agreed Monday [11 February] to write off most of Iraq's $12.9 billion debt and signed a separate deal that it said opened up Iraq for $4 billion in investment from Russian companies, including the oil producer Lukoil ... Moscow had already forgiven Iraq the bulk of its debt ... The remaining $12.9 billion of Iraqi debt date back to Soviet-era supplies of military equipment ... [Russia said it] agreed to write off $11.1 billion of Iraqi debt immediately, another $900 million in the next few years and restructure another $900 million for seventeen years ... Iraq has said Lukoil would have to renegotiate the West Qurna contract, which was signed in 1997, but had already been scrapped by the government of Saddam Hussein just before he was toppled ... In 2004 the US oil company Conoco-Phillips became a strategic partner in Lukoil. It took a 20 per cent stake and agreed to work together with Lukoil in Iraq.

(*IHT*, 12 February 2008, p. 14)

The Kremlin was yesterday [11 February] accused of mounting an unprecedented attack on academic freedom after one of Russia's top universities was closed. The European University at St Petersburg (EUSP) has been forced to suspend its teaching after officials claimed that its historic buildings were a 'fire risk'. On Friday [8 February] a court ordered that all academic work cease, classrooms sealed and the university's library shut. Academics at the EUSP said the move was politically motivated and followed a row last year [2007] over a programme funded by the European Commission to improve the monitoring of Russian elections. The university accepted a three-year, £500,000 EU grant to run a project advising Russia's political parties on matters such as how to ensure elections are not rigged. Last October [2007] President Vladimir Putin launched a vitriolic attack on the EUSP – which has close links with universities in the UK and United States – accusing it of being an agent of foreign meddling. On 31 January the EUSP's academic council bowed to Kremlin pressure and abandoned the monitoring project ... The university's EC-funded project was launched in February 2007. Its aim was to develop and raise the effectiveness of electoral monitoring in Russia's regions.

(*Guardian*, 12 February 2008, p. 15)

12 February 2008.

Russia and China have proposed ... at a disarmament conference in Geneva ... a new international treaty to ban the use of weapons in outer space ... The draft treaty would prohibit the deployment of weapons in space and the use of threat of force against satellites or other craft ... The United States has long opposed being bound by such an agreement ... The 1967 Outer Space Treaty bans the stationing of weapons of mass destruction in space.

(www.bbc.co.uk, 12 February 2008)

[Russian] foreign minister Sergei Lavrov presented a joint Russian–Chinese draft of a treaty banning weapons in space Tuesday [12 February] to the United Nations Conference on Disarmament, calling for action from a body that has not produced an agreement since 1997 ... [namely] an arms control measure on chemical weapons ... Lavrov submitted a draft on 'the prevention of the placement of weapons in outer space, the threat or use of force against outer space objects'.

(*IHT*, 13 February 2008, p. 3)

'The latest Russian–Chinese draft treaty to ban weapons in space ... would not cover ground- or sea-based weapons' (*IHT*, 19 February 2008, p. 6).

15 February 2008.

Dmitri Medvedev ... gave a speech before business leaders in which he vowed to continue Russia's economic revival but also struck markedly liberal notes ... Medvedev: 'Freedom is better than non-freedom. These words are the quintessence of human experience. The talk here is about freedom in all of its manifestations: about personal freedom, about economic freedom and at last about freedom of self-expression. Freedom is inseparable from the actual recognition of the power of law by citizens' ... The courts, he said, are riddled with corruption. The state bureaucracy is weighted by indifference, predatory officials and bloat ... Medvedev: 'It is necessary to change radically the ideology of administrative procedures dealing with starting and holding a business ... [An overhaul is required] to give realistic chances for the development of small businesses, which are drowning today in a swamp of official indifference and bribes.'

(*IHT*, 16 February 2008, p. 3)

Dmitri Medvedev said that reducing the economic role of the state was among his priorities ... [He] also said he would tackle corruption if elected ... He said 'a significant share of the functions carried out by state organs should be given over to the private sector' ... Large state-owned companies should adapt to remain competitive, he said ... Medvedev: 'I think there is no reason for the majority of state officials to sit on the boards of these firms. They should be replaced by truly independent directors, which the state would hire to implement its plans' ... Mr Medvedev said he would seek to make Russia into 'one of the biggest financial centres in the world' with a stable currency, strong banking sector and reformed tax system ... He said: 'One of the key elements of our work in the next four years will be ensuring the independence of our legal system from the executive and legislative branches of power' ... Mr Medvedev also spoke of the need to mend what he called the 'law-breaking' habits of Russians ... He said: 'What kind of equal opportunity and innovative thinking can there be if everybody knows that rights only belong to those with the sharpest teeth and not those who obey the law?'

(www.bbc.co.uk, 15 February 2008)

Dmitri Medvedev said freedom – both economic and personal – would be the cornerstone of his economic policy for the next four years as president, which he said would also focus on the four 'Is' – 'institutions, infrastructure, innovation and investment' ... He repeated a call made by President Vladimir Putin last week for value-added tax to be cut and also said the government should continue to analyse whether it should be replaced by a sales tax ... Medvedev: 'Our tax system must be competitive with the tax systems of other countries. The state should collect as much tax as needed to ensure that society functions effectively and our national businesses do not flee abroad and the economy does not fail' ... He called for Russia to take advantage of the crisis in global financial markets to make the Russian rouble a regional reserve currency ... He said: 'Today the global economy is going through uneasy times. People are reviewing the role of key reserve currencies ... And we must take advantage of it ... The rouble will de facto become one of the regional reserve currencies.'

(www.ft.com, 15 February 2008)

Dmitri Medvedev has unveiled a liberal-sounding economic agenda ... [He] said he wanted to make freedoms, both economic and personal, the cornerstone of his policies, in which the rule of law and property rights would reign ... [He recommended] improvements in education and healthcare ... In a rare sign he might pursue a more liberal agenda than Mr Putin, he called for a reduction in the number of state officials on the boards of some of Russia's biggest corporations ... Vladimir Putin, who will stay largely in charge of economic policy as prime minister ... In his last annual press conference this week [given on 14 February] before he steps down as president, Mr Putin staked out a powerful role for himself to implement his development plan ... his own strategy for Russia's development strategy up to 2020 ... He said Mr Medvedev's economic programme would deal only with the four years and merely 'add detail' to his own vision ... Yevgeni Yasin (rector of Moscow's Higher School of Economics and a co-author of Mr Putin's programme in 2000): 'A great deal was not implemented. Instead, they carried out completely different tasks which the country could have done without, such as increasing the role of the state, and control over the electoral system and the media' ... Mr Yasin said the sudden inflow of oil dollars as prices soared soon after Mr Putin came to power led the Kremlin to ditch most of the plan for liberal and institutional reform that he had helped plot. Instead of cutting back on the number of state officials, under Mr Putin their number had grown, as had corruption, Mr Yasin said.

(*FT*, 17 February 2008, p. 6)

If Dmitri Medvedev is true to his word, he would have to resign from Gazprom [of which he is chairman] on his election. It would also mean that other powerful and very wealthy individuals in the Kremlin ... would have to relinquish their posts, too ... [The] list includes Viktor Ivanov, who is responsible for personnel in the Kremlin and is chairman of Almz-Antei, the armaments company, as well as Aeroflot, the Russian national airline. Then there is Andrei Fursenko, minister of education and chairman of Rosnanotekh, a corporation established last July [2007] to promote nanotechnology. Another Kremlin aide, Sergei Chemezov ... is chief of Rosoboronexport, the arms trade export agency.

(*IHT*, 21 February 2008, p. 2)

'Igor Sechin [is] deputy Kremlin chief of staff and chairman of Rosneft' (*FT*, 29 February 2008, p. 9).

17 February 2008.

Russia has accused the United States of using a plan to shoot down a broken spy satellite as a cover for testing an anti-satellite weapon ... Russia's defence ministry said the United States planned to test its 'anti-missile defence system's capacity to destroy other countries' satellites' ... A Russian defence ministry statement said: 'Speculations about the danger of the satellite hide preparations for the classical testing of an anti-satellite weapons. Such testing essentially means the creation of a new type of strategic weapon' ... [The United States] said that blowing the satellite up would disperse the hydrazine ... toxic fuel ... in space, leaving only small-scale satellite debris to fall harmlessly to earth.

(www.bbc.co.uk, 17 February 2008)

('[On 20 February] a missile interceptor launched from a US Navy warship struck a dying American spy satellite orbiting 130 miles [210 kilometres] over the Pacific Ocean ... [It was] the first time an interceptor designed for missile defence was used to attack a satellite ... China objected to the strike on the satellite, warning that the action could threaten security in outer space': *IHT*, 22 February 2008, p. 3.)

18 February 2008.

Dmitri Medvedev suggested in an interview published Monday [18 February] that the British Council and other non-governmental organizations were spying on Russia ... Medvedev: 'If you are invited into someone's home, you should behave respectfully. After all, it is known that state-financed structures conduct a mass of other activities that are not so widely advertised. Among other things, they are involved in gathering information and conducting intelligence activity.'

(*IHT*, 19 February 2008, p. 5)

20 February 2008.

> Human Rights Watch released a report from Moscow Wednesday [20 February] charging the Kremlin with using new rules to hinder the work of non-profit organizations. The group said it did not have to look far to find a fresh example of the problem: its executive director was denied a visa to travel to Moscow ... Kenneth Roth, who is based in New York, addressed a news conference in Moscow by telephone, noting that this was the first time since the fall of the Soviet Union that the Russian government had refused a visa for an official of Human Rights Watch ... Human Rights Watch said in its report ... that although the Kremlin had implemented tighter restrictions on such groups in 2006, it had not conducted a broad-based campaign to close their operations. Instead, it said, officials made it difficult to operate by forcing them to comply with onerous and bureaucratic requirements.
>
> (*IHT*, 21 February 2008, p. 3)

> Yevgeni Adamov, the former atomic energy minister accused of stealing millions in US government funds earmarked for bolstering security at Russian nuclear plants, was sentenced Wednesday [20 February] to five-and-a-half years in prison. Adamov was arrested in Switzerland and jailed for nearly six months on a US request. But Russian officials, fearing he could reveal nuclear secrets, succeeded in having him sent to Russia to face trial on similar charges. A Moscow court handed down its sentence Wednesday, a day after the court ruled that he and two others had used their positions to steal 62 per cent of the shares in a Russian–US uranium joint venture valued at $31 million. Adamov, who held his government post from 1998 to 2001, denied the charges.
>
> (*IHT*, 21 February 2008, p. 5)

26 February 2008. 'Amnesty International ... [in its] Freedom Limited report says: "The space for freedom of speech is shrinking alarmingly in Russia"' (www.bbc.co.uk, 26 February 2008).

> Freedom of expression, assembly and association [have been] seriously curtailed ... Amnesty International said in its report that: 'Human rights defenders, independent civil society organizations, political opponents and ordinary citizens have all been victims of this roll-back on civil and political rights ... The space for critical reviews and for independent media and independent organizations to operate is shrinking ... Expressing dissenting views can lead to harassment and may put people at risk of being subject to human rights violations' ... In 2006 a new law came into effect which demands that NGOs submit regular reports about their activities – 'an unduly burdensome measure', according to Amnesty ... [The Kremlin] has forced several NGOs regarded 'as a threat to the state' to close down. Additionally, the Kremlin has used a law on extremism to target organizations it does not like. The law has been used to close Rainbow House, a Siberian

NGO which promoted gay and lesbian rights and the Russian–Chechnya Society, another NGO that provided information about human rights in Chechnya. Its boss, Stanislav Dmitrievski, was convicted of extremism after he published an article by Chechen separatist leaders.

(*Guardian*, 27 February 2008, p. 19)

29 February 2008.

> President Vladimir Putin (in a televised address): 'I appeal to you to go to the election on Sunday [2 February] and vote for our future, for Russia's future.' Analysts say the Kremlin is anxious to ensure a turnout of at least 70 per cent ... Dmitri Medvedev has refused to campaign against three weaker rivals. The other candidates, by contrast, have held livelier campaigns and television debates ... Medvedev has not officially campaigned, except for one day, and has instead increased his work engagements.

(www.iht.com, 29 February 2008)

> President Vladimir Putin: 'We all understand what a great and responsible role the leader of a state such as Russia is. And how important it is for him to have the faith of his citizens. He needs it for effective and confident work in his presidential post, to ensure stability in the country' ... Voters say they are being urged, cajoled and pressured to vote ... First deputy prime minister Dmitri Medvedev has refused to debate his opponents ... [but he] has received by far the most media coverage for his official visits to schools, churches and factories.

(*IHT*, 1 March 2008, p. 2)

'President Vladimir Putin: "Every voice of yours will be important ... cast a vote for our future"' (www.bbc.co.uk, 29 February 2008).

President Vladimir Putin:

> We all understand very well how great is the role and responsibility of the head of a state like Russia. And how important for him is the trust of citizens, how necessary for his effective and confident work in the post of president, for ensuring stability in the country.

(*FT*, 1 March 2008, p. 8)

'The leader of the little known Democratic Party [is] Andrei Bogdanov. The long-haired, thirty-eight-year-old Mr Bogdanov is widely seen as a token liberal running with tacit Kremlin backing' (p. 8). '[Andrei Bogdanov is an] unknown former public relations man for United Russia' (p. 10).

2 March 2008. A presidential election is held.

'The turnout ... in parliamentary elections last December [2007 was] 63.78 per cent' (www.iht.com, 2 February 2008). 'The central electoral commission estimated turnout [on 2 March] at 67 per cent of Russia's 109 million registered voters' (*FT*, 3 March 2008, p. 6). [In Chechnya in December 2007] 99.3 per cent reportedly backed United Russia' (*FT*, 3 March 2008, p. 6).

More than 109 million are registered to vote ... Civil servants have been ordered by their managers to vote and there are reports that police and teachers are under similar pressure ... Turnout was high, at nearly 60 per cent, officials said. But there were reports that many workers were told to vote by their bosses. Various inducements were also offered to mobilize voters, including cheap food, free cinema tickets or toys.

(www.bbc.co.uk, 2 March 2008)

'Andrei Bogadanov was relatively unknown until he mysteriously produced the 2 million signatures necessary for a presidential bid' (www.cnn.com, 2 March 2008).

Kremlin critics said the [turnout] figure would be inflated by factory managers and state officials who pressure employees to vote ... Some voters complained of pressure to cast ballots in Dmitri Medvedev's favour ... Andreas Gross, head of the only Western observer mission, the Council of Europe's Parliamentary Assembly delegation, said he would travel to various Moscow polling stations, while colleagues would observe in St Petersburg and Yaroslav ... Few international observers monitored the election, in which accounts of pressure will reinforce Western concerns of backtracking on democracy under Putin ... In Chechnya president Ramzan Kadyrov predicted 95 per cent to 100 per cent turnout ... Polling stations offered enticements to voters: discounted food, office supplies, concerts and flowers ... Some polling stations set up in shopping malls. Government-paid workers and doctors across the country complained that they were being pressured to vote at their workplace under the gaze of their superiors to ensure a convincing win and a high turnout for Medvedev ... Only 300 international election observers were monitoring the 96,000 voting stations across Russia's eleven time zones.

(www.iht.com, 2 March 2008)

'[Critics claim] people have been forced to take absentee ballots and vote at their workplaces' (*IHT*, 3 March 2008, p, 4).

Turnout was high, at 69.65 per cent, officials said. But there were reports that many workers were told by their bosses to vote ... With nearly 100 per cent of the ballots counted, the election commission announced Dmitri Medvedev had won 70.23 per cent of the vote ... [His] nearest rival was Communist Party leader Gennadi Zyuganov, with 17.76 per cent of the vote. He vowed to go to court over alleged fraud ... [Vladimir Zhironovsky 9.4 per cent and Andrei Bogdanov 1.3 per cent] ... Dmitri Medvedev: '[My policies will be] a direct continuation of the path which is being carried out by President Putin' ... President Vladimir Putin [February]: 'The president is the guarantor of the constitution and sets the main domestic and foreign policy guidelines. But the highest executive power in the land lies with the government ... [whose role is not just to oversee the economy and social policy but] to create conditions to ensure defence and security.'

(www.bbc.co.uk, 3 March 2008)

The only Western observer group monitoring Russia's presidential election says the poll was flawed ... Observers from the Parliamentary Assembly of the Council of Europe (PACE) said Russia's 'democratic potential' was unfulfilled ... The PACE twenty-two members observer mission said: 'The results of the presidential election are a reflection of the will of the electorate whose democratic potential was, unfortunately, not tapped. In the elections, which had more the character of a plebiscite on the last eight years in this country, the people of Russia voted for the stability and continuity associated with the incumbent president and the candidate promoted by him. The president-elect will have a solid mandate given to him by the majority of Russians ... [But the presidential election] repeated most of the flaws [of the December parliamentary election] ... Equal access of the candidates to the media and the public sphere in general has not improved, putting into question the fairness of the election ... The European Commission, France and Germany have congratulated Dmitri Medvedev.'

(www.bbc.co.uk, 3 March 2008)

With almost 99.5 per cent of the votes counted, Dmitri Medvedev had gathered 70.2 per cent of support. He will now take over from Vladimir Putin on 7 May ... Andreas Gross, the chairman of the twenty-two-member delegation of European MPs, said today [3 May] that although the election broadly reflected the will of the Russian people it fell short on a number of crucial issues ... Gross: 'We believe there was not freedom in these elections ... Candidate registration procedures should be simplified to be more inclusive and less cumbersome for independent candidates' ... European parliamentarians called ... parliamentary elections in December [2007] ... 'to a large extent free, but not fair' ... Gross: 'It is still not free and still not fair ... [But] even if [our] concerns had been addressed, the outcome of the [presidential] election ... would have been the same ... We heard stories from professors and hospital directors that they felt under pressure' ... [Gross added] that the delegation had only visited 100 to 200 of Russia's 96,000 polling stations.

(www.guardian.co.uk, 3 March 2008)

[At Moscow's] polling station number 3065 ... your correspondent and another foreign journalist [were] violently thrown on to a nearby street, with a warning never to come back ... The incident [reflected] most probably the stuffing of a ballot box.

(www.economist.com, 3 March 2008)

Western leaders have congratulated Dmitri Medvedev ... but highlighted flaws in the election ... The UK said it would 'judge the new government on its actions' ... A White House spokesman said 'the United States looks forward to working with him [Dmitri Medvedev]', but avoided commenting on the election itself.

(www.bbc.co.uk, 3 March 2008)

Nearly final results from 99.45 per cent of precincts showed that Dmitri Medvedev received 70.2 per cent of the vote ... Gennadi Zyuganov ... with almost 18 per cent in the nearly completed results ... and Vladimir Zhirinovsky ... with 9 per cent ... alleged violations after the voting ended ... Zyuganov said he would dispute the result ... Zhirinovsky threatened to do so as well.

(www.iht.com, 3 March 2008)

With 100 per cent of the precincts reporting, Dmitri Medvedev held 70.1 per cent of the vote, the central election commission reported ... Gennadi Zyuganov was second with nearly 18 per cent and Vladimir Zhirinovsky was third with 9.4 per cent. Both men have indicated that they will question the result in court ... Golos, a Russian vote monitoring group, say it has received allegations of multiple voting papers, falsified names on electoral registers, the stuffing of ballot boxes and electoral observers and media being barred from polling stations ... British prime minister Gordon Brown congratulated Dmitri Medvedev on his election.

(www.cnn.com, 3 March 2008)

'Final official results were released Friday [7 March] ... The central election commission said Dmitri Medvedev won the election with 70.28 per cent of the vote. Turnout was 69.81 per cent' (*IHT*, 8 March 2008, p. 4).

A total of 14,070 Russian citizens residing in Latvia voted in the election, amounting to 70.35 per cent of eligible voters in the country ... Dmitri Medvedev won 85.3 per cent of the vote ... Gennadi Zyuganov came second with 11.41 per cent of votes cast in Latvia ... Only 26,500 of the 100,000 Russian voters living in Estonia voted.

(*The Baltic Times*, 6–12 March 2008, pp. 2–3)

('After December's Duma elections [2007], 113 leading candidates from the lists of the winning parties ceded their mandates to little known surrogates ... a quarter of those elected!' (Mikhail Gorbachev, www.iht.com, 4 March 2008).

3 March 2008.

Riot policemen detained opposition protesters on Monday [3 March] and pro-government youth rallied outside the US embassy ... Hundreds of young people marched through Moscow toward the US embassy to criticize American policies in Kosovo, Iraq and the Moslem world. After they rallied briefly across the street from the embassy and unfurled a banner, the police told them to leave and they dispersed. A short time later hundreds of riot police officers detained dozens of youths near a central Moscow square where opposition groups had planned an unauthorized protest against the presidential elections ... In St Petersburg Garry Kasparov and his co-leader in The Other Russia opposition coalition appeared at a simultaneous protest. Unlike in Moscow, the St Petersburg group had permission. A crowd estimated by the police at up to 3,000 gathered in a square and marched toward the heart of the city ... the police did not intervene.

(IHT, 4 March 2008)

'In Moscow, where the march went ahead without official permission, about 200 people were dispersed by police. In St Petersburg a couple of thousand protesters carried banners representing a range of civic organizations, including the Yabloko Party' (*The Independent*, 4 March 2008).

'Several hundred members of pro-Kremlin youth groups, including Nashi ("Our Own"), marched towards the US embassy in Moscow in protest over US foreign policy towards Kosovo and Iraq' (*FT*, 4 March 2008, p. 6).

April 2008. Applications for Nato membership.

> President George W. Bush expressed strong support Tuesday [1 April] for Ukrainian ambitions of joining Nato on the eve of a meeting of alliance leaders in Romania where Ukraine appears likely to be rebuffed ... Bush: 'Your country has made a bold decision and the United States strongly supports your request' ... On Monday and again Tuesday protesters gathered on Independence Square in Kiev ... The protesters represented the Communist Party of Ukraine and others, waving flags with the hammer and sickle and displaying banners that included obscenities directed against Bush and Nato ... [Bush] noted that Ukraine already contributed troops to Nato missions in Kosovo and Afghanistan, as well as to the American-led war in Iraq ... Bush: 'Ukraine is the only non-Nato country supporting every Nato mission' ... President Viktor Yushchenko said that he took heart that support for Nato in the polls had steadily climbed – to 33 per cent from 17 per cent three years ago ... Opponents of Nato include the largest opposition group, led by the former prime minister and presidential rival, Viktor Yanukovich.
>
> (www.iht.com, 1 April 2008; IHT, 2 April 2008, p. 3)

> President George W, Bush said Kiev made a bold decision to request Nato membership and the United States 'strongly supported it' ... A few thousand demonstrators shouted anti-Nato slogans in the centre of Kiev Monday evening [31 March] before President George W. Bush's arrival. A court ban on protests meant that the number had dwindled to a few hundred as his motorcade drove through the streets on Tuesday morning [1 April] ... After visiting Kiev President Bush travelled to Nato's annual summit in Bucharest to press the case for eastern expansion. He will meet President Vladimir Putin on Sunday [6 April].
>
> (www.bbc.co.uk, 1 April 2008)

> President George W. Bush said Tuesday [1 April] that both countries [Ukraine and Georgia] should be able to take part in Nato's Membership Action Plan, or MAP, which is designed to help aspiring countries meet the requirements of joining the alliance ... Bush: 'I strongly believe that Ukraine and Georgia should be given MAP.'
>
> (www.cnn.com, 1 April 2008)

President George W. Bush in Romania [on 2 April] ahead of Nato's summit in Romania: 'We must make clear that Nato welcomes the aspirations of Georgia and Ukraine for membership of Nato ... Nato membership must remain open to all of Europe's democracies that seek it, and are ready to share in the responsibilities of Nato' ... The three-day summit of leaders from the twenty-six-nation alliance is due to start in the Romanian capital, Bucharest, later. It is being billed as the most important in the alliance's fifty-nine-year history.

(www.bbc.co.uk, 2 April 2008)

Nato countries unanimously endorsed Bush administration plans for installing a missile defence system in alliance countries in Europe [in the Czech Republic and Poland] on Thursday [3 April] even as they rebuffed President George W. Bush's entreaties to extend membership of the alliance to Ukraine and Georgia ... Hopes [were dashed] of being granted a Membership Action Plan [MAP] that [would] bring them into the alliance within the next five to ten years ... The allies will also move ahead with a complementary system of short-range missile defences to cover parts of Turkey, Greece, Romania and Bulgaria that would fall outside the US shield ... The countries agreed to extend membership to Croatia and Albania, but they rejected a membership request by Macedonia, which had been championed by the United States, prompting Macedonian officials to storm out of the meeting ... Following their invitations, Croatia and Albania are expected to join Nato within the next two years, following parliamentary ratification of their entry ... [Nato] leaders argued over the exact wording of the final communiqué, in particular how to frame the rejection of Ukraine and Georgia. In the end they offered rhetorical support for these countries' aspirations, saying only that they would be members of Nato one day ... Romanian, Estonian and Latvian leaders ... supported the American position on Ukraine and Georgia ... [and] emphasized the Membership Action Plan programme involved difficult requirements for Nato membership, including internal political and military reforms and guarantees of civil liberties, and could take a decade to fulfil.

(www.iht.com, 3 April 2008)

'While Bush was supported by some half of Nato's members, including nearly all those of Central and Eastern Europe, he was opposed by Germany, France, Spain and Italy' (*IHT*, 5 April 2008, p. 6).

The alliance decided not to offer Ukraine and Georgia entry into its Membership Action Plan. Instead, after a long debate among Nato members Wednesday [3 April] Nato pledged that the two countries would become members eventually and agreed that foreign ministers would review the decision in December [2008]. Nato officials suggested that invitation to the membership might come in a year, at the next annual meeting ... or in 2010 ... Nato votes on membership were held in secret ... President George W.

Bush: 'The name issue needs to be resolved quickly so that Macedonia can be welcomed into Nato as soon as possible' ... Bush could claim success in the Nato endorsement of his missile defence plan ... and in an agreement with the Czech Republic, announced Thursday [3 April], to build a radar for the system ... The radar system will be linked to other American defence facilities in Europe and the United States ... The Czech Republic had simply requested that its defence companies be involved in some of the defence contracts, the development of the system and that there be exchange programmes for its scientists involved in the defence and security field.

(www.iht.com, 4 April 2008)

('According to polls recently conducted by the independent Democratic Initiatives Foundation in Kiev, 59 per cent of respondents would vote against joining Nato, up from 53 per cent last December [2007], and 22 per cent would vote in favour, down from 32 per cent ... Over 60 per cent want to maintain friendly relations with Russia. According to public opinion polls ... last month [May] the pro-Russian Communist Party of Ukraine announced that it had collected 1 million signatures from residents in the Crimea demanding that Russia's Black Sea Fleet remain permanently stationed there. Under an agreement between Ukraine and Russia, the fleet ... the biggest local employer ... is supposed to be withdrawn by May 2017 ... The Communist Party claims that the Black Sea Fleet would be replaced by a Nato fleet, which Nato denies ... [In] the Crimea Peninsula ... more than 60 per cent of the population is ethnic Russian. Through the Moscow–Crimea Foundation that is funded, among others, by Yuri Luzhkov, the mayor of Moscow, a strong anti-Nato movement has been established': www.iht.com, 16 June 2008.)

'More than 60 per cent of Croatians support Nato entry, a significant reversal of past scepticism' (*FT*, 31 March 2008, p. 8).

The issue was ... whether Ukraine and Georgia should be upgraded from 'intensified dialogue' with Nato to a Membership Action Plan, essentially a promise to join Nato after meeting a set of political and military benchmarks ... Macedonia had agreed to the formulation 'Republic of Macedonia (Skopje)'. Greece wanted a compound formula such as 'Upper Macedonia' or 'new Macedonia' and blocked the invitation. The allies said Macedonia would join once the issue of the name had been settled. Nato invited Croatia and Albania, boosted ties with Montenegro and Bosnia and offered Serbia a friendly hand.

(*The Economist*, 5 April 2008, p. 73)

'Bosnia and Montenegro were awarded closer ties with the alliance' (*FT*, 4 April 2008, p. 6).

Nato has confirmed it will not offer membership to Georgia and Ukraine but agreed to review the decision in December [2008] ... Georgia provides the third largest force in the US-led coalition in Iraq, after the United States and Britain. Its contingent [comprises] ... more than 2,000 troops. Georgia has seen little domestic opposition to the war in Iraq ... Only two deaths [have been] reported so far.

(www.bbc.co.uk, 3 April 2008)

'Macedonia was told it must solve a dispute over its name with Greece before becoming a member' (www.bbc.co.uk, 4 April 2008).

The Macedonian foreign minister, Antonio Milosovski, told reporters that 90 per cent of his people strongly supported membership ... Jaap de Hoop Scheffer, the Nato secretary-general, said Nato membership for Ukraine and Georgia remained a goal: 'We agree today that these countries will become member nations.'

(www.guardian.co.uk, 3 April 2008)

Skopje's rightist government has gone out of its way to provoke Athens on symbols, renaming the country's airport after Alexander the Great ... The Greek civil war saw subversive attacks launched from Macedonian soil and ended with tens of thousands of ethnic Macedonians fleeing their homes. Those Macedonians who stayed behind, like minorities in Greece, still lack fundamental rights. Property issues have never been fully resolved ... [A] compromise name proposed by the United Nations [was] 'Republic of Macedonia (Skopje)'.

(Edward Joseph, *IHT*, 1 April 2008, p. 6)

Athens is deeply offended by posters that have appeared in Skopje, which have the swastika superimposed on the Greek flag, as well as a magazine cover which depicts [Greek] prime minister Kostas Karamanlis as an SS officer. And the Greeks feel insulted by recent images of their neighbour's prime minister laying a wreath by a flag showing a map of Greater Macedonia, which includes parts of northern Greece.

(www.bbc.co.uk, 3 April 2008)

'Latvia expressed firm support for offering a Membership Action Plan to both ... Ukraine and Georgia ... Estonia confirmed [that it] has always supported issuing a MAP to Georgia' (www.baltictimes.com, 4 April 2008).

'On Friday [4 April] President George W. Bush arrived in Croatia' (www.bbc.co.uk, 4 April 2008).

Jaap de Hoop Scheffer, Nato's secretary-general, reassured Ukraine and Georgia that there was 'not a sliver of doubt' that they would join Nato before long. He said: 'These countries will become members of Nato, there can be no misunderstanding about that.'

(www.iht.com, 4 April 2008)

President Vladimir Putin has described as positive his talks with Nato members at a summit in Romania ... Russia signed an agreement to allow the transport of non-military freight to Nato forces in Afghanistan. But the deal does not include the movement of troops or air transits that Nato originally requested.

(www.bbc.co.uk, 4 April 2008)

Nato and Russia reached an agreement on Friday [4 April] to allow the transport of equipment by land across Russian territory to supply the Western alliance's peacekeeping operations in Afghanistan. The supplies that will be permitted by the deal would range from food to non-lethal military equipment ... This falls short of the alliance's hope that Russia would permit the transport of troops and munitions across the country.

(www.ft.com, 4 April 2008)

President George W. Bush visited Croatia [before meeting with President Vladimir Putin and President-elect Dmitri Medvedev in Russia on 5–6 April] ... [President Bush] met with Croatia's president and prime minister, as well as those of Albania and Macedonia ... When Bush called on Nato to open its doors not only to Macedonia but also to Bosnia-Herzegovina and Montenegro, the crowd gathered in St Mark's Square [Zagreb] cheered. When he said the same about Serbia ... the crowd remained silent ... Croatia opposed the war in Iraq, though it now has fifty military police deployed as part of Nato's mission in Afghanistan.

(www.iht.com, 6 April 2008)

President Vladimir Putin and President George W. Bush failed to resolve their differences over US plans for a missile defence system based in [the Czech Republic and Poland] ... but said they had agreed a 'strategic framework' ... the US–Russia Strategic Framework Declaration ... to guide future US–Russian relations after bilateral talks Sunday [6 April] ... In a declaration issued jointly Putin and Bush said: 'The Russian side has made clear that it does not agree with the decision to establish sites in Poland and the Czech Republic and reiterated its proposed alternative. Yet it appreciates the measures that the United States has proposed and declared that if agreed and implemented such measures will be important and useful in assuaging Russian concerns ... We are dedicated to working together and with other nations to address the global challenges of the twenty-first century, moving the US–Russia relationship from one of strategic competition to strategic partnership. Where we have differences we will work to resolve them in a spirit of mutual respect ... We agree that the foundation for the US and Russian relationship should be based on the core principles of friendship, co-operation, openness and predictability' ... This weekend's summit is the final meeting between Bush and Putin as presidents and follow both leaders' attendance at last week's Nato summit in Romania.

(www.cnn.com, 6 April 2008)

On the issue of missile defence, Russia did signal in the joint statement that while it remained opposed to the system being installed in Europe it was willing to consider co-operating with the United States and Nato on a global system of missile defence, something the Russian leader called 'the best guarantee of security of all' ... After twenty-seven previous meetings between the two leaders [President George W. Bush and President Vladimir

Putin] – one-on-one and in groups, formally and informally – their last meeting took on a reflective tone.

(*IHT*, 7 April 2008, pp. 1, 8)

15 April 2008.

President Vladimir Putin accepted an offer to become chairman of the dominant United Russia Party. Mr Putin, who steps down as president next month [7 May], told nearly 600 party delegates on Tuesday [15 April]: 'I accept the invitation of the party' ... Dmitri Medvedev declined to join United Russia, saying such a move would be 'premature' ... Putin: 'I do not believe it is sensible for a head of state, wherever his political affections are, to lead a party. Here I fully agree with Dmitri Anatolievich Medvedev. As for the chairman of the government [prime minister], a situation in which the head of the executive branch leads a party is a civilized and natural practice that is traditional for democratic states. Co-ordinated work between the government and the parliamentary majority allows us to successfully resolve the tasks of developing the economy, enhancing the quality of healthcare and education, raising the income of the population and strengthening the country's defence.'

(www.bbc.co.uk, 15 April 2008)

Surprising no one, President Vladimir Putin accepted an offer Tuesday [15 April] to lead the dominant political party [created in 2001] once he leaves office ... and takes the post of prime minister ... Until Medvedev takes office ... Putin said it would be inappropriate for him to be officially affiliated with a particular party. Once he is prime minister, he said, he sees no such problem ... Putin: 'Dmitri Medvedev, the very man I recommended to the country and the electorate, has been elected president of Russia. I have therefore accepted his proposal, one that was supported by United Russia and other parties, to head the government of the Russian Federation in accordance with the time frame stipulated in the constitution' ... Putin headed the party's ticket for the December [2007] elections, even though he was not then – and is not now – a member of United Russia ... Medvedev said that just as Putin did not join United Russia as president, he, too, should remain above the party fray for now.

(www.iht.com, 15 April 2008; *IHT*, 16 April 2008, p. 3)

Delegates had earlier changed the rules to allow a non-member to chair the party ... His candidacy was accepted unanimously by 577 voting delegates ... Vladimir Putin: 'It [United Russia] must be more open to discussion and taking voters' opinions into account. It must be debureaucratized and purged of random people trying only to profit from it.

(*FT*, 16 April 2008, p. 6)

'Delegates elected Vladimir Putin by a unanimous show of hands, even though he is not a member. United Russia changed its statutes specially on Monday [15 April] to allow this' (*The Times*, 16 April 2008, p. 8).

18 April 2008.

The number of billionaires in Russia has gone up from sixty to 110 over the past year, with Russia boasting more billionaires than any other country apart from the United States ... Roman Abramovich has slipped down from first to third place, according to *Forbes* Russia's 2008 list of the country's wealthiest individuals. His fortune is now put at $24.3 billion. Russia's richest man is the aluminium tycoon Oleg Deripaska, with a $28.6 billion fortune. The steel millionaire Alexei Mordashov is in second place with $24.5 billion, beating Abramovich for the first time.

(www.guardian.co.uk, 18 April 2008)

25 April 2008.

The State Duma ... voted Friday [25 April] ... 339 to one [on first reading] ... to widen the definition of slander and libel and give regulators the authority to shut down media outlets found guilty of publishing such material ... The bill allows authorities to suspend and close down media outlets for libel and slander – punishment that is identical for news media found to be promoting terrorism, extremism and racial hatred. It also extends the definition of slander and libel to 'dissemination of deliberately false information damaging individual honour and dignity' ... The bill's passage comes just days after a scandal involving a tabloid newspaper that had reported that President Vladimir Putin had divorced his wife and planned to marry a champion gymnast. Putin vehemently denied the report in *Moskovsky Korrespondent* and the newspaper was shut down after Moscow authorities banned its distribution and the chief editor resigned.

(www.iht.com, 25 April 2008)

28 April 2008.

Gazprom was courting Italy's departing prime minister Romano Prodi on Monday [28 April] to become boss of the new Russian–Italian South Stream pipeline ... The offer, which Prodi remarked was flattering but that he intended to reject, was made days before he was to step down as prime minister after his government's defeat this month [April] ... A spokesman for Prodi, who is a former president of the European Commission ... said Prodi 'had decided not to accept appointments of this kind' ... In late 2005, soon after Gerhard Schröder had been defeated as German chancellor by the conservative leader Angela Merkel, he was almost immediately appointed to lead the new Russian–German Nord Stream consortium ... to build a pipeline under the Baltic Sea ... South Stream will run under the Black Sea ... Prodi is close to Eni, which this month clinched a deal with Gazprom to join forces to pipe natural gas from Libya across the Mediterranean to southern Europe ... In November 2006 Gazprom and Eni reached a deal whereby Gazprom would sell 3 billion cubic metres of gas annually and directly to Italian consumers. In return Italy received guaranteed gas supplies until

2035 and would also participate in the development of Russian energy assets.

(www.iht.com, 28 April 2008; IHT, 29 April 2008, p. 9)

30 April 2008.

A official says DNA tests have solved the mystery of identifying bone shards found in a forest as those of Crown Prince Alexei, the haemophiliac heir to Russia's throne, and his sister Grand Duchess Maria. The remains of their parents, Nicholas II and Empress Alexandra, and his three siblings, including the Tsar's younger daughter Anastasia, were unearthed in 1991 and reburied in the imperial resting place in St Petersburg. The Russian Orthodox Church made all seven of them saints in 2000. Researchers unearthed the bone shards last summer [2007] in a forest near Yekaterinburg, where the royal family was killed, and enlisted laboratories in Russia and the United States to conduct the DNA tests. Eduard Rossel, governor of the region, said Wednesday [30 April] that tests done by an American laboratory had identified the shards as those of Alexei and Maria ... Nicholas abdicated in 1917 ... and he and his family were detained. They were shot by a firing squad on 17 July 1918 in the basement of a house in Yekaterinburg.

(www.iht.com, 1 May 2008)

The Tsar, his wife and three of his daughters were exhumed. They were reburied in 1998 in the Imperial crypt of the St Peter and Paul Cathedral in St Petersburg ... Patriarch Alexei II, head of the Russian Orthodox Church, has never fully accepted the authenticity ... [of] the remains in the Imperial crypt ... A spokesman for the Sverdlovsk administration said further investigations were planned to eliminate any doubt about the identity [of Alexei and Maria]: 'This testing is not final. Once these remains have been examined in the United States they will be taken to Austria.'

(Guardian, 1 May 2008, p. 21)

6 May 2008.

Russia and the United States have signed a key agreement on civilian nuclear power that will give Washington access to Moscow's nuclear technology and potentially hand Russia lucrative deals on storing spent nuclear fuel ... The new agreement will formally allow nuclear deals between US and Russian companies. The United States has similar agreements with other major economic powers, including China.

(www.iht.com, 6 May 2008)

'The United States and Russia ... agreed to co-operate in the peaceful uses of nuclear energy involving both Russian and US companies in joint ventures. Furthermore, US industries would be allowed the commercial sales of nuclear materials, reactors and major reactor components to Russia.

(www.iht.com, 14 May 2008)

Russia and the United States have signed a key agreement on civilian nuclear power that formally allows nuclear trade between US and Russian companies. It will also allow them to widen technological co-operation in areas such as storing nuclear materials ... The United States is said to be interested in developments in areas including recycling nuclear fuel, while Russia wants to establish an international nuclear fuel storage facility and have access to the lucrative US market for nuclear materials. The agreement will allow US and Russian companies to form joint ventures in the nuclear sector and will facilitate the transfer of nuclear material between the two countries.

(www.bbc.co.uk, 7 May 2008)

The [Bush] administration's argument [is] that the agreement is necessary to set up an international nuclear fuel bank in Russia. The idea of such a facility, intended to dissuade countries from developing highly sensitive nuclear technologies, has won broad international support as a non-proliferation measure.

(*FT*, 17 May 2008, p. 6)

'On Tuesday [6 May] police detained dozens of would-be protesters in advance of a planned rally by The Other Russia, an opposition group led by Garry Kasparov' (www.bbc.co.uk, 7 May 2008).

'Last month [April] he [Vladimir Putin] issued a decree ordering regional governors to submit their annual reports to the prime minister's office, rather than the Kremlin' (*The Independent*, 7 May 2008, p. 26).

Vladimir Putin has kept a pledge not to change the constitution to give himself more powers [as prime minister]. That said he has bolstered his new role through tinkering. By presidential decree Mr Putin has shifted responsibility for assessing the performance of Russia's eighty-five powerful regional governors from the Kremlin to the government ... Local governments, meanwhile, have been made directly answerable to regional governors ... Rumours suggest Mr Putin will also bring under government control seven presidential envoys he created in 2000 with responsibility for superdistricts encompassing a dozen or more regions ... United Russia boasts almost 2 million members, including about three-quarters of the regional governors.

(*FT*, 7 May 2008, p. 8)

7 May 2008. Dmitri Medvedev is sworn in as president.
President Dmitri Medvedev:

I consider my most important task to be the further development of civil and economic freedoms, the creation of new opportunities, as broad as possible for the self-realization of citizens – citizens who are free and responsible both for their personal success, and for the flourishing of the whole country ... Human rights and freedoms ... are deemed of the highest value for our society and they determine the meaning and content of all state activity ... In the last eight years we have laid a powerful foundation for long-term development, for decades of free and stable development. And we must use this unique chance to the full, so that Russia becomes one of the best countries in the world – for the comfortable, confident and secure life of our people. I will pay special attention to the fundamental role of the law, on which our state, and civil society, is based. We must achieve true respect for the law, to overcome the legal nihilism which is seriously hampering modern development.

(www.ft.com, 7 May 2008; www.guardian.co.uk, 7 May 2008; www.iht. com, 7 May 2008)

'Dmitri Medvedev repeated commitments made during his campaign to modernize Russia's economy, renew its crumbling infrastructure and establish the rule of law' (www.ft.com, 7 May 2008).

'Dmitri Medvedev ... pledged to ... modernize industry and agriculture, encourage the development of new technologies and attract investment' (www. iht.com, 7 May 2008). 'He emphasized improving living standards, education and medical care, and modernizing Russia's narrow economy' (www,iht.com, 8 May 2008).

'One of his [Dmitri Medvedev's] acts as president was nominating Vladimir Putin as prime minister. The announcement came about two hours after Medvedev took the oath of office' (www.cnn.com, 7 May 2008).

'A Kremlin spokesman said: "Medvedev has put forward Putin's candidacy for prime minister to parliament"' (www.bbc.co.uk, 7 May 2008).

'Dmitri Medvedev announced that his first foreign trip will be to China and Kazakhstan' (www.guardian.co.uk, 7 May 2008).

8 May 2008.

The State Duma ... overwhelmingly confirmed Vladimir Putin as prime minister ... receiving 392 votes in the 450-seat Duma ... He gave a forty-five-minute speech, proposing a series of domestic policy initiatives that seized many of Medvedev's campaign themes and echoed his presidential addresses over the past eight years.

(www.iht.com, 8 May 2008)

'The backing [of VladimirPutin was] by 392 to fifty-six ... with only the Communist Party voting against ... United Russia holds 315 of the 450 seats in the Duma' (*The Times*, 9 May 2008, p. 50).

Russia ordered two American military attachés at the US embassy in Moscow to leave the country following the expulsion of a pair of Russian diplomats from Washington, US officials said Thursday [8 May] ... US officials played down any linkage between the expulsion of the Americans, which were ordered out on 28 April, and US decisions to expel the Russian military attachés. One Russian military officer was ordered to leave Wash-

ington on 6 November 2007. The second was ordered to leave on 22 April
... The officials declined to discuss the reason for the expulsions, but noted
that none of the military attachés had been declared 'persona non grata' or
was accused of wrongful conduct, such as espionage.

(www.iht.com, 8 May 2008)

The two American military attachés who were expelled from Russia ... days
ahead of the Victory Day martial parade on Red Square, had made an unin-
vited visit to a military aviation factory in Siberia that Russia regards as
strategic, several American officials said. The unannounced visit occurred in
late March at the Novosibirsk Aviation Production Association ... a plant
manufacturing Sukhoi-34 fighter bombers ... It appeared, according to officials ... that the officers erred in judgement by seeking access to a military
plant without making advance arrangements.

(*IHT*, 14 May 2008, p. 3)

9 May 2008.

Tanks and intercontinental missile launchers have been paraded through
Moscow for the first time since the collapse of the USSR. The leadership
has decided to revive the communist-era custom of featuring military hard-
ware in the annual Victory Day parade ... [marking] the defeat of Nazi
Germany in 1945 ... Marching bands and 8,000 troops goose-stepped across
Red Square, and heavy weapons such as Topol-M ballistic missiles and
T-90 tanks were on display.

(www.bbc.co.uk, 9 May 2008)

The parade was the first display of armour and nuclear missile launchers
on Red Square since 1990 and was followed by a flyover of thirty-two
military planes, including strategic bombers ... Many of the heavy
weapons shown were only slightly modernized versions of equipment
developed decades ago ... Nearly 9 million Red Army soldiers are estimated to have died [in World War II] ... Russian news reports said about
3 million World War II veterans are still alive. Although veterans receive
extensive public praise, their pensions are small and many live in poor
conditions.

(www.iht.com, 9 May 2008)

12 May 2008.

Prime minister Vladimir Putin is proposing the names of ministers in his
new government ... The proposed cabinet now needs to be approved by
President Dmitri Medvedev ... Finance minister Alexei Kudrin will be
retaining his post and foreign minister Sergei Lavrov also keeps his position. Anatoli Serdyukov stays as defence minister and ex-prime minister
Viktor Zubkov is first deputy prime minister and fisheries minister ... Igor
Shuvalov is also to become first deputy prime minister and Sergei Ivanov
and Alexander Zhukov will both be deputy prime ministers ... Igor Sechin,

who was deputy head of Kremlin administration and is also head of the oil giant Rosneft, will become another deputy prime minister ... The former head of Kremlin administration, Sergei Sobyanin, also becomes a deputy prime minister as well as government chief of staff. There will be new ministries of tourism and sport, and of ecology, while the industries and energy ministry is split into two.

(www.bbc.co.uk, 12 May 2008)

Sergei Ivanov, once seen as a possible successor to Vladimir Putin as president, was modestly demoted to deputy prime minister – a step down from his previous position as first deputy premier ... The ministry of energy and industry was split into separate cabinet positions, the most major structural change to the new government. The move reflects both the growing importance of oil and gas exports to Russia's budget and concerns that the country's industrial sector is underdeveloped, making Russia vulnerable to energy price fluctuations ... In all Putin announced twenty-four positions, eight of them new. Among the new appointments were Igor Sechin and Igor Shuvalov. Sechin, formerly Putin's powerful deputy chief of staff, will have oversight of industrial development programmes as a deputy prime minister, and apparently will remain chairman of Rosneft. Shuvalov will be one of two first deputy prime ministers ... Also Monday [12 May] President Dmitri Medvedev named Nikolai Patrushev, head of the Federal Security Service [FSB], as head of the Russian security council. Alexander Bortnikov, formerly head of the agency's economic security division, becomes the new head of the FSB. The corruption-tainted telecommunications minister, Leonid Reiman, was not reappointed. A Swiss arbitration tribunal ruled in 2006 that Reiman is the true owner of a Bermuda-based fund that once controlled much of Russia's telephone industry. Reiman, a long-time Putin associate, denied any ownership of the IPOC fund, but the revelations have been seen as evidence of high level corruption in the Kremlin.

(www.iht.com, 12 May 2008)

'One new face joining the government was Alexander Avdeyev, who has been Russian ambassador in Paris, and was named culture minister ... The announcements appeared to cement further the image that Putin will retain a grip on power' (p. 3).

The most senior government newcomer was Igor Shuvalov, a liberal former Kremlin aide who was appointed first deputy premier responsible for foreign economic relations, negotiating Russia's WTO entry and development of small businesses. Analysts expect Mr Shuvalov to co-ordinate government economic policy. But they also suggested and important role as 'gatekeeper' and supervisor would be played by Igor Sechin, former deputy presidential chief of staff and a leader of the hardline *siloviki* faction of former security and intelligence personnel. Mr Sechin moves to deputy prime minister over-

seeing industrial policy and environmental questions, his first public political role. Sergei Sobyanin, formerly head of the Kremlin administration,
moved with Mr Putin to be deputy prime minister and head of the government administration ... liberal Elvira Nabiullina, economy minister, stays in
post. There was one important move in the opposite direction. Sergei Naryshkin, formerly deputy prime minister, moved to the Kremlin to become
head of the presidential administration. Biggest losers were Leonid Reiman,
who lost his job as telecommunications minister, and Viktor Cherkesov,
head of another security services clique who moved from head of the powerful anti-narcotics agency to a lesser post. The most important Medvedev ally
to enter the government was Alexander Konovalev ... He was named minister of justice.

(*FT*, 13 May 2008, p. 1)

Nikolai Patrushev, another prominent *siloviki* member, lost his position as
head of the FSB ... [It has been] suggested this was at his request owing to
health reasons. Mr Patrushev was replaced by a deputy, Alexander Bortnikov – apparently his choice as successor ... A leading adversary of the
Sechin–Patrushev group was one of the day's big losers. Viktor Cherkesov,
a former KGB general and head of a rival security services clan, lost his job
as head of the powerful federal anti-narcotics agency, shifting to head a military procurement agency.

(p. 8)

'The number of deputy prime ministers was raised from five to seven' (*The
Independent*, 13 May 2008, p. 11).

13 May 2008.

Dmitri Medvedev named a series of officials to his administration. The most
senior were all closely linked to Vladimir Putin ... Sergei Naryshkin, a
former deputy prime minister, was chosen as head of the Kremlin administration on Monday [12 may]. His deputies were named yesterday [13 May]
as Vladislav Surkov, previously a Kremlin aide and chief ideologist; Alexei
Gromov, for eight years Mr Putin's Kremlin press secretary; and Alexander
Beglov, previously a presidential aide and head of the control directorate;
Arkadi Dvorkovich, a young liberal economist seen as close to Mr
Medvedev, was named as a presidential aide.

(*FT*, 14 May 2008, p. 6)

'Konstantin Chuichenko, an old university friend ... [who] served in the KGB
... will head the Kremlin's control department, a secretive and vital job that was
once done by Vladimir Putin himself' (*The Economist*, 17 May 2008, p. 52).

15 May 2008.

Vladimir Putin on Thursday [15 May] proposed an end to weekly cabinet
meetings in favour of an inner circle of ministers, deepening his policy-

making authority ... Putin said that deputy prime ministers and selected ministers should meet weekly and the full group at least once a month ... Putin often attended ... the weekly cabinet meetings ... as president ... Putin has taken key aides with him to the government, while others dominate the new presidential administration.

(*IHT*, 16 May 2008, p. 3)

22 May 2008. 'Dmitri Medvedev arrived in Kazkahstan on Thursday [22 May] during his first trip abroad as Russia's president ... Medvedev landed in Kazakhstan on his way to China' (*IHT*, 23 May 2008, p. 6).

23 May 2008. 'President Dmitri Medvedev has arrived in Beijing ... for a two-day visit ... [China is] Russia's second largest trading partner after the EU' (www.bbc.co.uk, 23 May 2008).

'Bilateral trade rose by about one-third last year [2007] to some $48 billion, but still accounts for only 2 per cent of China's global trade. China does more than eight times as much business with the United States' (www.iht.com, 23 May 2008).

27 May 2008.

Russia's prosecutor-general has admitted that thousands of people are wrongly charged with criminal offences each year. Yuri Chaika has promised to remedy the situation. His remarks come a week after President Dmitri Medvedev said an independent court system needed to be created ... Mr Chaika's comments represent one of the first times that a senior official has publicly conceded that there are major failings in Russia's justice system. He said that in 2007 alone a total of 5,265 people were eventually exonerated after being wrongly charged ... Last week Mr Medvedev spoke of the need to make Russia's courts independent ... [He] described the current legal system as one in which decisions were reached after pressure and for money.

(www.bbc.co.uk, 27 May 2008)

29 May 2008.

Prime minister Vladimir Putin arrived in Paris ... Putin is due to meet French president Nicolas Sarkozy in a departure from usual protocol for prime ministerial visits ... Asked why Putin's agenda in France went beyond his economy brief, a Russian government source said: 'The prime minister is a member of the country's security council which has a role in formulating foreign policy' ... Dmitri Medvedev's first official trip to the West as president will be to Germany in June.

(www.iht.com, 29 May 2008)

30 May 2008.

Diplomats from 111 countries on Friday [30 May] formally adopted a landmark treaty banning cluster bombs after futile calls for participation by the weapons' biggest makers and users, particularly the United States ... The talks did not involve the biggest makers and users of cluster munitions: the United States, Russia, China, Israel, India and Pakistan. And the pact leaves the door open for new types that could strike targets more precisely and contain self-destruct technology. Participants plan to sign the treaty in Oslo in December [2008]. It would go into effect in mid-2009 ... [Norway] launched the negotiations in February 2007 ... [and said] Friday that Britain's decision to support a ban on cluster munitions had been a crucial factor in obtaining agreement from the 111 countries this week ... [Supporters argue that] the treaty would discourage ... proponents of cluster bombs from using the weapons again.

(www.iht.com, 30 May 2008; *IHT*, 31 May 2008, p. 3)

'This treaty, like the landmine treaty, will stigmatize cluster munitions and make it harder to use them' (editorial, *IHT*, 2 June 2008, p. 4).

3 June 2008.

President Dmitri Medvedev ... urged parliament Monday [3 June] to scrap a bill widely seen as restrictive to the media ... Medvedev: 'The bill's provisions could only create obstacles to the normal functioning of mass media' ... He advised the State Duma to dump the bill, which allows authorities to suspend and close down media outlets for libel and slander.

(www.iht.com, 3 June 2008)

President Dmitri Medvedev dismissed the chief of the general staff of the armed forces Tuesday [3 June], moving to tighten the Kremlin's grip of the military and its purse strings. Medvedev announced the removal of General Yuri Baluyevsky, who was loyal to the Kremlin but had become an obstacle to a campaign launched by former President Vladimir Putin to tighten control over military spending. Baluyevsky and other top brass have clashed with civilian defence minister Anatoli Serdyukov, a one-time furniture store manager Putin appointed early last year [2007] with a mandate to clean up the military's finances. While supporters say Putin appointed Serdyukov to cut waste and corruption ... critics say his brief is to ensure the Kremlin controls the money flows ... Medvedev softened the blow by giving Baluyevsky another job in Russia's elite, making him a deputy chairman of the presidential security council ... Medvedev replaced Baluyevsky with a Serdyukov ally, general Nikolai Makarov ... Medvedev stressed he was accepting Serdyukov's recommendation, seemingly warning Serdyukov's critics in the military that the Kremlin is behind him ... Generals have grumbled loudly in recent months over initiatives to sell off lucrative military land, move the navy headquarters from Moscow to St Petersburg, and use civilians in support positions such as legal and medical staff. Baluyevsky publicly criticized the proposed navy move and, as Russia's top military officer, he was seen as the representative of disgruntled generals who deeply distrust Serdyukov.

(www.iht.com, 3 June 2008; *IHT*, 4 June 2008, p. 3)

Sixty per cent of male Russians smoke ... Anti-smoking ... groups' representatives said they believed that foreign tobacco companies were responsible for a sharp increase in recent years in the number of women who smoke in Russia. The companies have focused much of their advertising on women and the percentage of Russian women who smoke has more than doubled since Soviet times ... Tobacco is hardly taxed ... President Dmitri said in June [2008] that smokers might soon have to pay more for insurance. Medvedev: 'Fifty per cent of citizens are smoking in this country. That is the highest rate in the world. I would not even mention alcohol' ... Russia has the fourth highest annual *per capita* consumption of tobacco in the world and smoking is responsible for 42 per cent of early deaths among Russian men thirty-five to fifty-nine years old, according to Euromonitor International, a consulting firm.

(www.iht.com, 7 September 2008; *IHT*, 8 September 2008, p. 2)

5 June 2008. 'President Dmitri Medvedev is starting a visit to Germany – his first trip to Europe since becoming president ... The visit to Germany follows his trip to Kazakhstan and China last month [May]' (www.bbc.co.uk, 5 June 2008).

'It was Dmitri Medvedev's second trip abroad since he was sworn in on 7 May. His first foreign trip as president was to China and Kazakhstan' (www.iht.com, 5 June 2007).

6 June 2008.

Meeting at a place outside St Petersburg on Friday [6 June] President Dmitri Medvedev of Russia and the Georgian president, Mikheil Saakashvili, said their two countries could work out their differences, including a longstanding conflict over Abkhazia, without international assistance ... Medvedev and Saakashvili met at an informal summit of leaders of the CIS ... The meeting was hosted by the new Russian president as part of the St Petersburg International Economic Forum, being held in St Petersburg this weekend ... The Konstantinovsky Palace, left in ruins after World War II, was rebuilt for Vladimir Putin to play host to world leaders.

(*IHT*, 7 June 2008, p. 3)

Corrupt Russian officials are creaming off about $120 billion a year – the equivalent of a third of the national budget, a senior prosecutor has said ... Russia's investigations committee has opened more than 1,000 corruption cases involving officials in ten months. The committee's chairman said the extent of corruption was much wider ... The committee heard that investigations included criminal cases against thirteen judges, a former regional minister and district prosecutors ... Data provided by the non-governmental Indem Foundation suggested business people spend $33 billion on bribes for officials, while low-level corruption is estimated to be worth $3 billion.

(www.bbc.co.uk, 6 June 2008)

Vasili Piskaryov (of the investigative committee of the prosecutor-general's office): 'The revenues of our bureaucrats from corrupt activity, according to experts, account for one-third of our national budget' ... On Thursday [5 June 2008] a senior official at the Russian financial watchdog Rosfinnadzor was detained for allegedly taking a Euro 13,600 bribe.

(*The Times*, 7 June 2008, p. 50)

16 June 2008.

An irreverent English language newspaper in Russia has been forced to close following an official probe, its editor said Monday [16 June]. *The Exile*, a brash monthly that criticized the Kremlin and the West in its pages – often seeking to offend – was subject to a 5 June audit, said Mark Ames, its American editor. After enquiring about the paper's links to Russia's opposition leader Eduard Limonov, inspectors issued a small fine for minor infractions such as an incorrectly printed address, Ames said. In the wake of the probe sponsors including the paper's publisher withdrew financing, forcing it to close ... Ames conceded that the technical infringements were 'absolutely valid' ... but he disagreed with ... the reasons [given by the federal agency for media and communications] behind the inspection, saying that the government apparently had lost patience after eleven years of seeing the newspaper publish Limonov's critical articles. Limonov is the leader of the banned National Bolshevik Party.

(www.iht.com, 16 June 2008)

17 June 2008.

The British Council in Moscow said it had received a punitive and 'incorrect' tax bill from the Russian authorities. Russian tax officials sent the demand in May ... The Council today [17 June] described the tax bill – which covers 2004 to 2006 – as 'incorrect'. It is taking legal action in ... court to have the bill overturned ... Council officials ... said it had already made the 'appropriate payment' in accordance with Russia's tax code.

(www.guardian.co.uk, 17 June 2008)

21 June 2008.

Grigori Yavlinsky ... who ran for president in 1996 and 2000 ... has withdrawn his candidacy for re-election as chairman of Yabloko, ending months of tension with a radical faction of the party ... Yavlinsky on Saturday [21 June] told the party congress ... that it was time for him and the party to move on. One of his deputies was then elected as chairman ... Yavlinsky, fifty-six, chose Sergei Mitrokhin, chairman of Yabloko's Moscow branch, as his successor ... Mitrokhin, forty-five, has battled corruption and unchecked real estate development ... [He gained] the votes of seventy-five of 125 delegates ... defeating Maxim Reznik and Vasili Popov ... Mitrokhin said he would continue Yavlinsky's policies ...

Yavlinsky had been accused by rival party leaders during Vladimir Putin's presidency of blocking efforts to unite and increase the chances of liberals to win election to the State Duma ... He also angered the radicals in his party by meeting in March [2008] in the Kremlin with Putin while one of them, Maxim Reznik, leader of the party's St Petersburg division, was in jail. Reznik was detained on charges of attacking a law enforcement officer and resisting arrest on the eve of an opposition march in the city. He and some other party members have allied themselves with the National Assembly, an umbrella coalition of opposition forces created by Garry Kasparov ... and Eduard Limonov, a writer who leads the National Bolshevik Party. Yavlinsky objected to such co-operation ... Yavlinsky has not revealed his plans. Some critics interpreted his Kremlin visit in March as lobbying for a government post.

(www.iht.com, 22 June 2008; *IHT*, 23 June 2008, p. 3)

24 June 2008.

A top investigative body confirmed earlier reports that bone shards unearthed last year [2007] in a Ural mountains forest were those of Tsar Nicholas II's heir and one of his daughters. The comments by the Prosecutor-General's Investigative Committee confirmed an announcement last month [May] by a regional governor.

(*IHT*, 25 June 2008.p. 4)

27 June 2008. 'Gazprom on Friday [27 June] chose Viktor Zubkov, the deputy prime minister, as its chairman. He replaces Dmitri Medvedev ... Zubkov is a former prime minister' (www.iht.com, 27 June 2008).

3 July 2008. '[On 3 July 2008] Roman Abramovich officially resigned as governor of [the Arctic region of] Chukotka ... [He] used his vast wealth to revive Chukotka ... [He assumed] the governorship in 2001' (*IHT*, 4 July 2008, p. 3).

'[Roman Abramovich's] second term as governor did not expire until 2010 ... In late 2006 Mr Abramovich told Vladimir Putin he was resigning from the post, but Mr Putin insisted he stay' (*The Independent*, 4 July 2008, p. 22).

Roman Abramovich in the remote Siberian region of Chukotka ... is seen as a saviour. It has been seven years since Abramovich began helping Chukotka, an impoverished region at the north-eastern tip of Russia that is roughly the size of two Germanys but counts just 50,600 inhabitants. In 1999 Abramovich was elected to a seat representing Chukotka in the State Duma ... He was elected governor of the region in 2001, and appointed by President Vladimir Putin last year [2005] to serve a second four-year term ... Observers suggest that he might have struck a deal with the Kremlin to govern and essentially feed the region in exchange for a guarantee that the state would not touch his wealth ... Abramovich has spent hundreds of millions of dollars of his personal wealth here. Few in Chukotka expect Abramovich ... thirty-nine ... to stay until 2009, when his current term expires ...

After Abramovich registered the trading division of Sibneft in Chukotka, taxes paid by the oil company covered nearly half of the region's annual budget of 13.5 billion roubles, or $94 million, last year. But Abramovich has since sold Sibneft to Gazprom and it has been reregistered in St Petersburg, leaving a gaping hole in the budget … 'Because taxpayers like Sibneft and Slavneft have been moved from the region, our budget is now quite shaky,' Chukotka's deputy governor, Mikhail Sobolev, a retired KGB officer and former Sibneft executive [said] … Locals do not mind that Abramovich, who lives in London, has barely shown up in Anadyr … the capital … over the past couple of years, particularly since his team of senior bureaucrats – most of whom do not live in Chukotka all year round – fly in regularly.

(Valeria Korchagina, *IHT*, 8 September 2006, p. 2)

Gennadi Zyuganov told a Roman Abramovich joke. Roman arrives in heaven only to find his way blocked by St Paul: 'Do you own Chelsea, five yachts and a 5-kilometre stretch of beach in the south of France?' Abramovich replies: 'Yes.' St Paul replies: 'I am not sure you are going to like it here.'

(*Guardian*, 19 November 2007, p. 23)

14 July 2008.

Russia announced Monday [14 July] that it is sending warships to patrol Arctic waters for the first time since the breakup of the Soviet Union … Patrols … will begin Thursday [17 July] … Russia began sending aircraft carriers to the Mediterranean Sea in December [2007] and resumed long-range bomber patrols last August [2007].

(www.cnn.com, 14 July 2008)

16–17 July 2008.

Russians attended church ceremonies Wednesday [16 July] marking ninety years since the last tsar and his family were murdered by the Bolsheviks, while investigators reaffirmed that remains unearthed last year [2007] were those of Nicholas II's only son and a daughter. Russian Orthodox churches nationwide were holding services and processions Wednesday and Thursday [17 July], some overnight, to commemorate the canonized tsar and his wife and children, who were shot dead in a basement in the Ural mountains city of Yekaterinburg on 17 July 1918. Russian investigators marked the anniversary by repeating their confirmation that bone and tooth fragments found in a shallow grave in Yekaterinburg a year ago are those of the tsar's thirteen-year-old heir Crown Prince Alexei, and one of his daughters, Grand Duchess Maria … The Investigative Committee of the Russian prosecutor-general's office said in June [2008] that the remains were those of Alexei and Maria. The finding was based on DNA and other forensic testing carried out by laboratories in Russia, the United States and other countries … The remains of Nicholas, his wife Empress Alexandra and three daughters including the youngest, Anastasia, were unearthed in Yekaterinburg in 1991 ... and later reburied in the imperial capital, St Petersburg. The remains of Alexei and Maria were not found ... The remains were discovered last July [2007] in the woods about 70 metres from the site where remains of the rest of the family were found. The church made all seven slain family members saints in 2000 ... The Russian Orthodox Church continued to express doubts about the accuracy of the scientific findings identifying the remains as those of the royal family.

(www.cnn.com, 16 July 2008)

'Vladimir Putin, who is now prime minister, was given formal responsibility this week for implementing foreign policy' (*The Economist*, 19 July 2008, pp. 72–3).

21 July 2008.

China and Russia signed an agreement Monday [21 July] to end a long-running dispute over the demarcation of their eastern border ... The tug-of-war over the eastern part of their 4,300-kilometre, or 2,700-mile, border reaches back centuries to their competition for territory as imperial China and Tsarist Russia expanded toward each other. Th struggle resulted in violent clashes in the 1960s and 1970s ... The *China Daily* reported that Russia will return Yinlong Island (known as Tarabarov Island in Russian) and half of Heixiazi Island (Bolshoi Ussurisky) to China. The 174 square kilometres of territory are on the northeast border with China ... Former Russian president Vladimir Putin signed a border agreement with China in 2004. But it is not clear how far that accord went to resolve the dispute over the stretch of river and islands along China's north-eastern border with Russia's Far East.

(www.iht.com, 21 July 2008)

The latest treaty involves a dispute over the eastern part of the [China–Russia] border ... However, China still has outstanding border issues with Japan and South Korea to the east, Vietnam to the south and India to the south-west. It has trumpeted its treaty with Russia as a new approach to border disputes. But analysts say that with energy reserves behind many of the territorial disputes, it will be many more years before China can hope to settle its borders with all its neighbours.

(www.bbc.co.uk, 21 July 2008)

'The [China–Russia] agreement settles the status of four islands in the Amur River ... The agreement itself was signed three years ago ... In 1969 a dispute over the Amur islands flared into a brief war' (*FT*, 22 July 2008, p. 6).

After decades of dispute China and Russia have at last reached agreement on where the entire length of their common border lies. On 21 July the two countries signed an accord on the last small stretch that had yet to be formally settled ... In recent years they have been tidying up the remaining odds and ends along their 4,300-kilometre (2,670-mile) frontier. The latest agreement ... resolves the niggling matter of a couple of islands at the confluence of the Amur and Ussuri rivers near the city of Khabarovsk in Russia's Far East. The two countries reached an initial accord on this problem in 2004. The deal was that Russia would hand over one of the islands, Tabarov (Yinling, as China calls it) and half of Bolshoi Ussurisky island (Heixiazi or Bear Island) ... The outcome is a compromise. Since the 1960s China had been demanding the islands in their entirety. They had been illegally taken over, they insisted, by the then Soviet Union in 1929. The Russians, who had settled on Bolshoi Ussurisky, did not want to abandon it. Now the Chinese have got the all-but uninhabited parts, where, according to rumours in the Chinese media, officials are examining the potential for tourism.

(The Economist, 26 July 2008, pp. 64–5)

'Russian officials estimate that last year [2008] there were 350,000 Chinese migrants living in the far eastern regions of the country. The native population is just over 7 million' (*IHT*, 19 August 2009, p. 14).

The United Nations predicts that the Russian population will fall to 116 million people by 2050, from 140 million now, largely because of a low birth rate and poor health habits. The government is trying to increase the birth rate by paying families to have more children ... Russia's vast and sparsely inhabited Far East has fallen in population to 6 million, from 8 million in 1991 ... Russia is trying to head off its severe population decline by luring back Russian who live abroad as well as their descendants ... Relocation and employment assistance can amount to several thousand dollars a person ... The government spent $300 million in the past two years to get the repatriation programme started, and officials estimated that more than 25 million people are eligible, many of them ethnic Russians who found themselves living in former Soviet republics after the Soviet Union collapsed in 1991 ... So far only 10,300 people have moved back under the government repatriation programme.

(IHT, 21 March 2009, p. 3)

August–September 2008. For the Russia–Georgia war, see Appendix 1.

1 August 2008.

A former top figure in Yukos has been found guilty by a Russian court of masterminding several murders. Leonid Nevzlin was tried in absentia as he now lives in Israel ... [He] fled to Israel in 2003 ... Nevzlin said the 'show trial' was mounted as part of the Kremlin's campaign against Yukos ... He was found guilty on Friday [1 August] of several counts of conspiracy to murder. They included the killing of a local mayor where the oil firm's biggest production was based ... The court heard that Nevzlin had worked with Yukos's former head of security, Alexei Pichugin, to kill people who stood in the company's way, including the owner of a building that Yukos coveted and a mayor who tried to impose local taxes. Pichugin was sentenced to twenty-four years in prison in 2006 for carrying out murders.

(www.bbc.co.uk, 1 August 2008)

The judge said that Leonid Nevzlin and Alexei Pichugin, who was sentenced to twenty-four years in prison in 2006 for carrying out murders, had organized the 1998 murder of Valentina Korneyeva, who owned a building in central Moscow that a Yukos holding firm, Menatep, wanted to buy. The judge also said Nevzlin ordered the 1998 murder of Vladimir Petukhov, the mayor of the Siberian town of Nefteyugansk, where Yukos's biggest oil production unit was based. The judge said the murder had cost Yukos $150,000.

(*IHT*, 2 August 2008, p. 3)

3 August 2008. Alexander Solzhenitsyn dies of heart failure at the age of eighty-nine.

'[Then President] Vladimir Putin travelled to Alexander Solzhenitsyn's home last year [2007] to present him with the state prize for humanitarian achievement, thanking him for 'all your work for the good of Russia' (www.thetimes.co.uk, 4 August 2008).

In 2007 Alexander Solzhenitsyn accepted a state prize from then-President Vladimir Putin – after refusing, on principle, similar prizes from Mikhail Gorbachev and Boris Yeltsin. Solzhenitsyn said in a *Der Spiegel* interview: '[Putin] inherited a ransacked and bewildered country, with a poor and demoralized people. And he started to do what was possible – a slow and gradual restoration.'

(www.iht.com, 4 August 2008)

17 September 2008. 'Russia triggered a fresh scramble for the oil wealth of the Arctic today [17 September] after President Dmitri Medvedev called on security chiefs to establish a formal border in the region' (www.thetimes.co.uk, 17 September 2008).

Russia should pass a law marking its territory in the disputed Arctic where it claims a large share of the mineral resources, President Dmitri Medvedev said today [17 September]. Medvedev said: 'We must finalize and adopt a federal law on the southern border of Russia's Arctic zone' ... Countries have until May 2009 to submit new ownership claims over the Arctic to a United Nations commission. Russia has claimed jurisdiction over much of the Arctic because an underwater ridge links Siberia to the seabed that runs underneath the North Pole.

(www.independent.co.uk, 17 September 2008)

22 September 2008.

A squadron from the Russian navy's North Sea Fleet sailed for Venezuela on Monday [22 September] ... The convoy – including the nuclear-powered guided missile cruiser *Admiral Chabanenko* – left ... to take part in joint manoeuvres with the Venezuelan navy sometime in November.

(*IHT*, 23 September 2008, p. 7)

26 September 2008. 'In his second visit to Russia in as many months Venezuelan president Hugo Chavez met with President Dmitri Medvdev on Friday [26 September] ... After the meeting the countries signed bilateral documents concerning energy co-operation' (www.cnn.com, 26 September 2008).

'The latest deal called for broader co-operation [between Russia and Venezuela] on oil and gas production' (www.bbc.co.uk, 26 September 2008).

'[Russia] signed a $1 billion military loan to [Venezuela] ... The $1 billion loan for weapons purchases and military development was announced in a Kremlin statement released Thursday night [25 September]' (*IHT*, 27 September 2008, p. 2).

> President Dmitri Medvedev announced plans to build a 'guaranteed nuclear deterrent system' to be in place by 2020. He said he wanted military chiefs to submit plans by December [2008]. He called for a programme to build new nuclear submarines as well as 'a system of aerospace defence' ... He said: '[It is necessary to build] new types of armaments ... [and to] achieve dominance in airspace ... We plan to start serial production of warships, primarily nuclear-powdered submarines carrying cruise missiles and multi-functional submarines.'
>
> (www.bbc.co.uk, 26 September 2008)

> President Dmitri Medvedev said the need for the modernization was demonstrated by last month's military conflict with Georgia. Russia responded to Georgia's attack on South Ossetia with overwhelming force and easily crushed the Georgian army, but the brief war highlighted Russia's ageing arsenal. Medvedev told military commanders: 'We must ensure superiority in the air, in carrying out precision strikes at land and sea targets and in the timely deployment of forces' ... [Medvedev] made no mention of the new Borei-class nuclear submarines, which are designed to carry a new intercontinental missile that is seen as a key future component of Russia's nuclear forces. The missile was successfully test fired last week after repeated failures. The first of the new submarines is to be commissioned later this year and two more are being built.
>
> (www.cnn.com, 27 September 2008)

'The plan would also bring all units to a state of contant combat readiness' (*FT*, 27 September 2008, p. 12).

> Somalia's notorious pirates have staged perhaps their most brazen attack yet, seizing a Ukrainian ship [bound for Kenya] in the Indian Ocean full of weapons, including dozens of battle tanks ... ammunition ... [and] grenade launchers ... The Ukrainian ship was seized Thursday evening [25 September]

... There were twenty-one people aboard, comprising seventeen Ukrainians, three Russians and a Latvian.

(*IHT*, 27 September 2008, pp. 1, 4)

'The United States Navy was in hot pursuit Friday [26 September]. And the Russians were not far behind' (www.iht.com, 27 September 2008).

'The Ukrainian ship [is] laden with thirty-three Russian-made tanks' (www.bbc.co.uk, 4 October 2008).

The US Navy says it wants to keep the arms out of the hands of militants linked to al-Qaeda in impoverished Somalia, a key battleground in the war on terrorism. To that end it has surrounded the *Fauna*, anchored off the central Somali town of Hobo, with half a dozen ships ... [A] Russian guided missile frigate is travelling to the area.

(www.cnn.com, 1 October 2008)

30 September 2008.

A Russian billionaire said Tuesday [30 September] he is teaming up with former Soviet president Mikhail Gorbachev to form a new political party that will challenge the country's recent steps away from democracy. Alexander Lebedev, a former lawmaker who has built a fortune in business and invest-ment, said he and Gorbachev would work together in a political movement tentatively named the Independent Democratic Party ... Lebedev said the new party was Gorbachev's idea ... Lebedev said the party would advocate a 'return to a normal electoral system', calling for the restoration of gubernato-rial elections, a stronger parliament, independent courts and media, and a smaller state role in the economy ... Lebedev, a major private shareholder in the Russian airline Aeroflot, joined with Gorbachev in 2006 to buy 49 per cent of *Novaya Gazeta*, an independent newspaper that has challenged the Kremlin with penetrating reporting. Anna Politkovskaya, a prominent investi-gative reporter murdered that year, worked for *Novaya Gazeta*.

(www.cnn.com, 1 October 2008)

1 October 2008.

The Russian supreme court on Wednesday [1 October] declared the last Tsar and his murdered family to be victims of political repression ... The decision by an appeals panel ends years of efforts by Tsar Nicholas II's descendants to get authorities to reclassify the killings from premeditated murder. Prosecutors and lower courts had repeatedly rejected appeals, saying the Romanov family had not been executed for political reasons. On Wednesday ... a spokesman for the court said the panel accepted the appeals of Romanov descendants to 'rehabilitate' them ... The Tsar, his wife Alex-andra and their son and four daughters were fatally shot on 17 July 1918 in a basement room of a merchant's house ... in Yekaterinburg ... The remains of Nicholas II and Alexandra and three siblings were unearthed in 1991 and reburied in the imperial resting place in St Petersburg ... Nicholas's heir,

Alexei, and his daughter, Grand Duchess Maria, remained missing for decades until bone shards were unearthed in [August] 2007 in a forest outside Yekaterinburg, not far from the place where the rest of the family's mutilated remains had been scattered. Officials said earlier this year [2008] that DNA testing had confirmed the shards belonged to Alexei and Maria. The Russian Orthodox Church made all seven of them saints in 2000. 'Rehabilitation' has legal, political and cultural significance. It recognizes that a person was a victim of political repression by the country's communist-era authorities. Many of those who were shot or sent to prison camps under Soviet rule have been rehabilitated, which also exonerates them of the crimes they were accused of at the time.

(www.cnn.com, 1 October 2008)

Last November [2007] ... the supreme court ... decided that the Romanov family was not eligible for rehabilitation because the executions had been ordered in 1918 on criminal, not political grounds ... Other members of the royal family had been rehabilitated previously. In 1999 four Romanov princes killed by the Bolsheviks, including the son of Alexander II – the Russian Tsar who was assassinated by revolutionaries in 1881 – were found not guilty of criminal wrongdoing ... The lawyer for a descendant of the Tsar said that in coming months he would file suits on behalf of other Romanovs who have yet to be rehabilitated ... The Russian Orthodox Church canonized the Romanovs as martyrs in 2000.

(*IHT*, 2 October 2008, p. 2)

The ruling is unlikely to have major legal ramifications, at least in the short to medium term, because there is no significant move to restore Russia's monarchy or compensate the royal family for its losses. There has been no material compensation for others who have been formally rehabilitated, most of them victims of Stalin-era excesses. Some historians had speculated that the Russian government was reluctant to reclassify the Tsar's killing out of fear that descendants would claim state property, such as the State Hermitage Museum, as compensation. The museum is housed in what used to be the Winter Palace. Prosecutors, lower courts and even the supreme court's main body had repeatedly rejected appeals, saying the Romanov family had not been executed for political reasons. On Wednesday [1 October] ... a spokesman for the court said the court's presidium accepted the appeals of the Romanov descendants to 'rehabilitate' the royal family, declaring them victims of 'groundless repression'. The presidium, the supreme court's highest appeal panel, has the final word for legal appeals in Russia.

(www.iht.com, 1 October 2008)

'Russia's supreme court rehabilitated Tsar Nicholas II and his family, declaring they were victims of "groundless" repression when they were murdered, at Lenin's behest, 1918. During the Soviet interregnum schoolchildren were taught that the Tsar was a criminal' (www.iht.com, 6 October 2008).

The problem that has concerned the Russian courts for the best part of a decade has been: was it a simple murder committed by a few out-of-control revolutionaries, or was it ordered from above as a political assassination? ... The Communists have been arguing that there was no direct order to execute the Tsar and it was done in the heat of the moment ... In 2005 Grand Duchess Maria Vladimirovna of Russia, representing a branch of the family, lodged an application to clear the Tsar's classification as 'state criminal'.

(*The Times*, 22 October 2008, p. 35)

Russia's supreme court yesterday [1 October] recognized that the Tsar was the victim of political repression and was unlawfully killed. By doing so it absolved the Romanovs of culpability in crimes that the Bolsheviks used to justify the Russian Revolution in 1917 and the killing by firing squad of the Tsar and his family.

(*The Times*, 2 October 2008, p. 35)

11–12 October 2008.

[On Sunday 12 October] Russia test-fired another three intercontinental ballistic missiles, a day after claiming a distance record for a missile fired from a submarine ... Russia said Saturday's [11 October] test missile ... travelled more than 11,500 kilometres (7,145 miles), an all-time distance record, the Kremlin claimed.

(www.bbc.co.uk, 12 October 2008)

Russia test-fired long-range ballistic missiles Sunday [12 October] ... The military fired a Topol intercontinental missile from the Plesetsk cosmodrome in north-west Russia at a target thousands of kilometres away in the Kamchatka Peninsula in the Russian Far East. Submarines in the Okhotsk Sea near Japan and the Barents Sea launched ballistic missiles that reached Kamchatka.

(www.iht.com, 12 October 2008)

12 October 2008. 'Roman Abramovich has been elected to parliament in the remote Chukotka region ... [He] won 97 per cent of Sunday's [12 October] vote to the regional parliament' (www.bbc.co.uk, 13 October 2008).

French police have opened an inquiry into the discovery of pellets of toxic mercury in the car of a prominent Russian human rights lawyer, Karinna Moskalenko, who became ill days before a scheduled pre-trial hearing in Moscow into the murder of one of her best known clients, Anna Politkovskaya. The metal was found in the eastern French city of Strasbourg, where Moskalenko spends much of her time pursuing cases at the European Court of Human Rights ... Apart from representing the Politkovskaya family, she has represented Mikhail Khodorkovsky ... Some of her clients have been Chechens complaining to the European Court of Human Rights in Strasbourg about alleged human rights abuses ... [Her] clients include Garry Kasparov ... and Alexander Litvinenko ... Moskalenko's husband, a chemist, discovered about ten little pellets of liquid metal Sunday [12 October] ... On Tuesday [14 October] Moskalenko complained of headaches and vomiting.

(www.iht.com, 15 October 2008)

'A police officer said the presence of mercury might have been the result of an accident before the Moskalenko family bought the car in August' (*IHT*, 16 October 2008, p. 3).

'Karinna Moskalenko ... and her family were treated for nausea and headaches' (www.bbc.co.uk, 15 October 2008).

('French police are suggesting that mercury found in the car ... was spilled accidentally ... A Paris police official says the mercury came form a barometer that broke while being transported by the car's previous owner, an antiques dealer': 24 October 2008.)

17 October 2008. A Russian court on Friday [17 October] threw out most of the tax claims filed by the authorities against the British government's cultural arm ... the British Council ... Britain sent a new ambassador this week' (*IHT*, 18 October 2008, p. 3).

21 October 2008.

The United States and Russia sent their top military officers to ... Helsinki ... for an unannounced meeting Tuesday [21 October] ... The meeting was arranged with great secrecy and was the first time that Admiral Mike Mullen, chairman of the Joint Chiefs of Staff, had met his counterpart, General Nikolai Makarov, since the Russian was appointed Chief of the General Staff this summer [2008] ... Since the Georgia crisis Mullen and [US] defence secretary Robert Gates have spoken in calm, calibrated terms of Russian military decisions and foreign policy. They have challenged the Kremlin to behave better in global affairs but have also noted that Russia's armed forces do not pose a global risk.

(www.iht.com, 21 October 2008)

'The two spoke by phone during the brief war in August between Russia and Georgia' (*IHT*, 21 October 2008, p. 3).

A senior cabinet official was ordered freed from jail Tuesday [21 October] after nearly a year in custody, but officials say he still faces attempted fraud and abuse of power charges in what observers say is a politically motivated case ... [There was no] mention of an earlier charge of attempted embezzlement ... Former deputy finance minister Sergei Storchak has been ordered to remain in Moscow ... Storchak has been in custody since his arrest in November 2007, in a case seen as the result of infighting between political factions in the Kremlin. Finance minister Alexei Kudrin hailed his deputy's release as a 'triumph of justice' ... Observers have speculated the arrest was orchestrated by veterans of Russia's security services to intimidate liberal figures in the administration such as Kudrin. Security veterans gained strong influence during the eight-year presidency of KGB veteran Vladimir Putin, who now serves as prime minister.

(www.iht.com, 21 October 2008)

30 October 2008.

The unpopular leader of Russia's violence-plagued republic of Ingushetia said Thursday [30 October] that he had resigned. President Dmitri Medvedev accepted Murat Zyazikov's resignation, the Kremlin said in a statement, clarifying earlier Russian news agency reports that suggested Medvedev had dismissed the regional leader ... Ingushetia has suffered almost daily attacks on security forces and officials in recent months, and critics had accused Zyazikov of corruption and being unable to settle the unrest. The attacks are blamed on criminal gangs, Islamist fighters and opponents of Zyazikov, fifty-one, a former KGB officer who came to power in 2002 ... Many observers fear that the growing chaos in Ingushetia is turning into a full-blown Islamic-inspired insurgency similar to the one that sent Chechnya into years of war and poverty ... Zyazikov came to international attention with the recent death of the local opposition leader Magomed Yevloyev, who had been critical of Zyazikov and ran numerous articles about him on an opposition website. Yevloyev was taken into police custody after leaving a flight from Moscow that Zyazikov had been on. Yevloyev's body was later found on the roadside near a hospital and a state investigation concluded he had been shot in the head accidentally ... Medvedev named an apparent unknown, Yunus-Bek Yevkurov, to take over as the republic's acting president.

(www.iht.com, 31 October 2008)

A career soldier has been appointed to run Russia's unstable southern republic of Ingushetia, where attacks on security forces have escalated. President Dmitri Medvedev named Yunus-Bek Yevkurov, a paratrooper, as acting president ... There are frequent attacks on officials and members of the security forces.

(www.bbc.co.uk, 31 October 2008)

8 November 2008.

An accident aboard a Russian nuclear-powered submarine making a test run in the Sea of Japan killed at least twenty people, officials said Sunday [9 November]. The nuclear reactor aboard the submarine was operating normally and radiation levels were normal after the accident Saturday [8 November], [a] Russian navy spokesman said. The accident occurred when a fire extinguishing system went into operation in error aboard the submarine ... spewing chemicals that killed at least twenty people and injured at least twenty-one others ... The victims died of poisoning from Freon gas ... Seventeen civilians and three sailors were killed ... The state-run RIA-Novosti news agency ... [said] the submarine ... is called the

Nerpa ... Construction of the *Nerpa*, an Akula II class attack submarine, started in 1991 but was suspended for years because of a shortage of funding ... It was Russia's worst naval accident since torpedo explosions sank another nuclear powered submarine, the *Kursk*, in the Barents Sea in [August] 2000, killing all 118 seamen aboard. In 2003 eleven people died when a submarine that was being taken out of service also sank in the Barents Sea.

(www.cnn.com, 9 November 2008)

[The] Russian Pacific Fleet spokesman ... said the submarine was not damaged and there had been no radiation leaks ... There were 208 people aboard at the time, eighty-one of whom were servicemen ... Twenty-one [people were] injured ... Russian news agencies say the systems on submarines used chemical fluids and the injured are reported to be suffering from various degrees of poisoning ... Freon gas [is] released by the fire extinguishing system to remove oxygen ... The *Nerpa* was due to be leased to the Indian Navy.

(www.bbc.co.uk, 9 November 2008)

'The system is designed to release Freon coolant when activated ... [An official said] at least twenty people [were killed]' (www.iht.com, 9 October 2008).

The vessel was scheduled to be commissioned in the navy later this year [2008] and most of the dead were shipbuilders on board to carry out tests. An additional 167 people on board were not hurt ... Seventeen civilians and three seamen died in the accident and twenty-one others were hospitalized ... [There was] criticism of then-President Vladimir Putin for his slow reaction to the [*Kursk*] crisis. The government's response to this incident has been notably different. Within hours of the malfunction President Dmitri Medvedev asked his defence minister for continual briefings and pledged support to victims' families. News coverage has been intense ... In 2003 a decommissioned nuclear submarine sank while it was being towed to a scrapyard, killing nine crew members aboard. In 2004 one person was killed when a holding tank on a submarine exploded during repair work. In 2005 a hurried international rescue effort brought seven Russian sailors to the surface with only three to six hours' worth of air left. And in 2006 two soldiers suffocated when a fire broke out on a nuclear submarine in the Barents Sea.

(*IHT*, 10 November 2008, p. 3)

An inquiry is under way into Saturday's gas poisoning ... An 'unsanctioned' activation of an automatic fire-fighting system released toxic Freon gas ... Freon gas removes oxygen from the air – to put out the fire – but if anyone is still trapped inside that area they face suffocation ... The accident happened in the nose of the submarine ... but the nuclear reactor, which is in the stern, was not affected and there was no radiation leak ... The submarine is due to be released to India and Indian naval personnel were due to travel to Vladivostok earlier this month to train on board the submarine ahead of its transfer ... The submarine had 208 people aboard, eight-one of whom were servicemen. However, a vessel of this type usually carries only seventy-three people.

(www.bbc.co.uk, 10 November 2008)

'Crew members carry special breathing apparatus with them at all times' (www.independent.co.uk, 10 November 2008).

('An inquiry panel has ruled that a crew member set off the fire extinguishing system ... A committee said Thursday [13 November] that the crew member "for no particular reason activated the submarine's anti-fire system" ... It added that the crew member admitted his role': www.cnn.com, 13 November 2008.)

11 November 2008.

President Dmitri Medvedev submitted a draft bill that would extend the term of Russia's president from four to six years. Medvedev said in his state of the nation address last week that he would seek constitutional change that would extend the president's term by two years. Constitutional experts say the proposed change would only apply to future presidents.

(www.cnn.com, 11 November 2008)

'President Dmitri Medvdev has proposed that the change should not apply to his current term' (*FT*, 12 November 2008, p. 8).

13 November 2008.

A Russian banker has been sentenced to nineteen years in jail for masterminding the murder of the deputy head of Russia's central bank, Andrei Kozlov, in [September] 2006 ... Earlier this year [2008] Alexei Frenkel was found guilty by a jury of hiring the gunmen who shot Mr Kozlov and his driver. On Thursday [13 November] six other defendants received terms ranging from six years in jail to life imprisonment ... [Andrei Kozlov] had headed a campaign to clean up the banking sector, during which Frenkel's VIP Bank was forced to close down in June 2006. The central bank revoked the licences of dozens of private banks, accusing them of many forms of criminal activity including money laundering.

(www.bbc.co.uk, 13 November 2008)

14 November 2008.

[The State Duma has] backed a bill to extend the presidential term from four years to six years ... The Duma passed the bill in its first reading on Friday [14 November] by 388 votes to fifty-eight. The bill will have both its second and third readings in the Duma on Wednesday [19 November]. It must then be approved by the upper house, the Federation Chamber ... The constitutional change will only apply to the next president.

(www.bbc.co.uk, 14 November 2008)

'[The State Duma] also voted to extend the Duma's term from four to five years' (www.guardian.co.uk 14 November 2008).

('Russia's upper house of parliament voted overwhelmingly on Monday [22 December] to give a final nod to a constitutional amendment extending the presidential term from four to six years. All of the 142 Federation Council senators voted to endorse a decision by Russia's regional assemblies to support a longer presidency. It is the last legislative step in the approval process. Last month [November] the State Duma and the Federation Council both passed the longer term ... The amendment will become law once President Dmitri Medvedev has signed it': www.iht.com, 22 December 2008. 'The changes needed the backing of at least two-thirds of the country's regional legislatures but were approved unanimously ... The amendment will become law once it is signed by President Dmitri Medvedev but will only take effect after the next presidential election ... The bill also extends the mandate of the State Duma from four years to five': www.bbc.co.uk, 22 December 2008. 'President Dmitri Medvedev has signed a law extending presidential terms from four years to six, the Kremlin said Tuesday [30 December] ... Medvedev's final endorsement of the legislation follows its quick approval by ... parliament and all of Russia's eighty-three provincial legislatures': www.iht.com, 30 December 2008.)

President Dmitri Medvedev ... insisted that ... this would not amount to a reform of the constitution ... Rather it was a clarification ... Before the change becomes law it must be approved by the upper house and by two-thirds of Russia's regional legislatures.

(www.economist.com, 14 November 2008)

President Dmitri Medvedev on Friday [14 November] backed away from his threat last week to deploy missiles on Europe's borders in Kaliningrad], but only on condition that President-elect Barack Obama take up a call Medvedev issued with France to hold a summit on European security by next summer [2009]. The Russian leader, who issued bellicose threats against the United States just hours after Barack Obama won the US election last week [Tuesday 4 November], argued at a summit in Nice on Friday that all countries 'should refrain from unilateral steps' before such discussions on European security take place ... the French leader supported the idea of talks on a new security architecture for Europe and suggested they could be held by OSCE next June or July.

(www.iht.com, 14 November 2008)

President Dmitri Medvedev:

Before signing a special, global treaty on European security all of us should avoid unilateral steps which affect security in Europe. Russia has never taken unilateral steps. All these measures taken by us, including the measures I announced recently, have been a response to the actions of individual countries in Europe which, without consulting anyone, have agreed on hosting new military systems on their soil.

(www.bbc.co.uk, 14 November 2008)

('The Duma voted 351 to fifty-seven on Wednesday [19 November] to pass the bill': www.cnn.com, 19 November 2008. '[On 21 November] 392 deputies voted for the constitutional changes to fifty-seven against, in the third and final reading ... The measure also has to pass the upper house ... The bill also extends the mandate of the State Duma from four to five years': www.bbc.co.uk, 21 November 2008).

20 November 2008.

> Boris Fyodorov ... who served twice as minister of finance before founding one of the country's first investment banks ... died in London on Thursday [20 November]. He was fifty. The cause was a stroke, according to the Moscow office of his investment firm, UFG Asset Management, a spin-off of the bank he founded. [He was] elected in 2000 to the board of Gazprom ... In particular he battled against restrictions on foreign ownership of shares in Gazprom ... [where] he said he had more than 7 per cent of the company's shares ... He was active in developing the '500-day plan', a sweeping economic reform plan that was tried out but never fully carried out under the Soviet president, Mikhail Gorbachev. As an adviser in that same period to Boris Yeltsin, then president of the Russian republic, he promoted laws regulating banking and market-orientated companies ... He was deputy prime minister from 1992 to 1994, at one point holding the post of finance minister at the same time. Later in the 1990s, after serving in the State Duma and creating a political party – Forward Russia – he was briefly the chief of the state tax service. In 1994, together with Charles Ryan, a Harvard-educated banker, Fyodorov created the United Financial Group, one of the country's first investment banks. Its brokerage and investment banking divisions were sold to Deutsche Bank in 2005 ... In 2003 he founded a privately financed anti-terrorist centre.
>
> (www.iht.com, 23 November 2008)

21 November 2008.

> [It was reported that] the number of registered [HIV] cases was growing 10 per cent a year despite increased federal funding ... Vadim Pokrovsky ... head of the state-funded Federal AIDS Centre ... estimated there are more than 1 million Russians infected with HIV – or almost 1 per cent of the country's 142 million population – though officially Russia has registered less than half that number at 470,000 ... The government says budget spending for HIV-related activities last year [2007] amounted to $445 million and was more than fifty times higher than in 2005.
>
> (www.iht.com, 22 November 2008)

> The International Campaign to Ban Landmines ... said Friday [21 November] ... [that] Greece, Turkey and Belarus have all violated an international treaty by not destroying landmine stockpiles, and fifteen counties (including

Britain) will miss their 2009 clearance targets … Greece and Turkey have a combined stockpile of 4.2 million anti-personnel mines, and Belarus has 3.4 million remaining to destroy under the [treaty] … also known as the Ottawa Convention … China, Russia and the United States – the countries with the largest mine stockpiles – remain outside the pact. Myanmar and Russia, neither of which are signatories to the treaty, were the only two governments reported to have used anti-personnel mines in the past year.

(www.iht.com, 22 November 2008)

28 November 2008.

President Dmitri Medvedev … arrived in Havana [Cuba] from Venezuela, where he and President Hugo Chavez signed a deal on promoting nuclear energy for civilian use … Russian and Venezuelan warships are scheduled to hold joint military exercises this week … The Russian leader travelled to Venezuela from Brazil, where he and President Luiz Inacio da Silva held talks on boosting trade and technical co-operation … Bilateral trade between Russia and Latin America could reach $15 billion this year [2008].

(www.bbc.co.uk, 28 November 2008)

2 December 2008.

The Venezuela and Russian navies have begun joint exercises in the Caribbean Sea … The three-day operation marks the first time that the Russian fleet has been in the area since the end of the Cold War … President Dmitri Medvedev recently completed a tour of Latin America … Four Russian ships and twelve Venezuelan vessels are expected to participate. Major arms deals between Russia and Venezuela since 2005 have totalled some $4.4 billion.

(www.bbc.co.uk, 2 December 2008)

5 December 2008.

Prime minister Vladimir Putin invited Nikita Belykh to his office on 5 December to make an offer. Renounce the opposition. Come to work for the Kremlin … [Nikita Belykh] was a prominent … liberal … opposition leader … Belykh, who at the age of thirty-three represented the future of the liberal opposition, said yes. He accepted an appointment as one of the Kremlin's regional governors … [namely] Kirov, an economically depressed region … The party Belykh used to lead, the Union of Rightist Forces, received only 1 per cent of the vote in the parliamentary election last year [2007] … It did not even try to run a candidate in the presidential election this year [2008]. And in October the party surrendered and disbanded. From its remains the Kremlin created a new party, the Right Cause, which is intended to espouse liberal ideas but only mildly oppose the government, if at all … Belykh did not join the Right Cause … Polls show that roughly 10 per cent to 20 per cent of Russians back the agenda of the liberals.

(*IHT*, 24 December 2008, pp. 1, 3)

A Russian warship [the *Admiral Chabanenko*] has entered the Panama Canal for the first time since World War II ... The 50-mile (80-kilometre) canal linking the Atlantic and Pacific Oceans was shut to the Soviet Union during the Cold War.

(www.bbc.co.uk, 6 December 2008)

'Alexei II, the Russian Orthodox Patriarch ... died Friday [5 December] ... [aged] seventy-nine ... [He] was named patriarch in 1990' (www.iht.com, 5 December 2008).

Alexei II was the first leader of the Russian Orthodox Church since the 1917 Bolshevik Revolution to be chosen without interference by the Soviet state ... The patriarch took the helm of the church in June 1990, just days before Boris Yeltsin was elected president of the Russian Federation ... Yeltsin had invited Pope John Paul II to visit Russia, but the Moscow Patriarchate and Alexei repeatedly charged Rome with proselytizing on the 'canonical territory' of the Russian Church and said a visit would not be appropriate ... According to a 2007 poll ... 75 per cent of Russians identify themselves as Orthodox, although polls show less than 10 per cent attend church regularly ... The church is centred in Russia ... but was founded in Kievan Rus, now Ukraine, in 988.

(*IHT*. 6 December 2008, p. 2)

'Fewer than 5 per cent of those who identify themselves as Orthodox Christians regularly go to church, according to polls' (*FT*, 6 December 2008, p. 8).

'By the time of Alexei's death the church's flock was estimated at including about two-thirds of Russia's 142 million people, making it the world's largest Orthodox Church' (www.ccn.com, 5 December 2008).

'Patriarch Alexei II ... repeatedly refused to meet the late Pope John Paul II or his successor, Benedict XVI ... The Russian Orthodox Church counts barely 70 per cent of Russia's population – about 100 million people – among its members' (www.bbc.co.uk, 5 December 2008).

'Patriarch Alexei II's ... successor will lead a growing church of around 165 million followers, including nearly 70 per cent of Russia's population' (www.bbc.co.uk, 25 January 2009). 'While some two-thirds of Russians describe themselves as Orthodox Christians, far, far, fewer regularly attend services' (www.bbc.co.uk, 27 January 2009).

('[On 6 December] the Russian Orthodox Church's top body elected a high profile bishop, Kirill, as its temporary leader ... Church leaders chose Kirill, sixty-two, in a secret ballot a day after the death of [Alexei II] ... Kirill is familiar to millions of Russian from television broadcasts and is the Church's chief envoy abroad ... Since the 1970s he has travelled abroad as an envoy of the Church and, in his current role as head of its external relations department, visited Cuba in October to consecrate a cathedral in Havana ... [Kirill's] official title is Metropolitan of Smolensk and Kaliningrad': www.bbc.co.uk, 6 December 2008. 'The Russian Orthodox Church, in a gathering Tuesday [27 January] at Moscow's ...

Christ the Saviour Cathedral ... elected an outspoken new leader to succeed Patriarch Alexei II, who died on 5 December [2008] ... Metropolitan Kirill of Smolensk and Kaliningrad, an articulate critic of declining moral values in the modern world who has been actively involved in the ecumenical movement and called for the Russian Orthodox Church to step up its outreach in secular society, was elected overwhelmingly. He has served as locum tenens, or interim patriarch, since Alexei's death. At a meeting Sunday [25 January] of the church's hierarchy, the Archbishops' Council, Kirill spoke in touching terms about threats to church unity, especially in Ukraine. The Orthodox Church in Ukraine has broken into rival groups since the collapse of the Soviet Union. The largest is still loyal to Moscow and accounts for more than one-third of the entire Russian Orthodox Church, but calls are growing for its independence, or autocephaly in church terms. Analysts have speculated that Kirill's opponent, Kilment of Kaluga and Borovsk, the Moscow Patriarch's property manager, was favoured by the Kremlin ... More than 700 delegates representing the hierarchy, clergy, monastics and laity of the church convened at Christ the Saviour Cathedral ... The original cathedral was blown up at Stalin's orders in 1931 and rebuilt in the 1990s ... The delegates were choosing from a short-list of three candidates chosen by the Archbishops' Council on Sunday. One of the candidates, Metropolitan Filaret of Minsk, who has been credited with reviving the Orthodox Church in Belarus ... withdrew his name from consideration [on 27 January]': *IHT*, 28 January 2009, p. 3. 'Metropolitan Kirill [is] seen by many as a modernizer': *FT*, 28 January 2009, p. 10. 'Kirill is widely seen as a more independent figure [than Alexei II] and a modernizer who could bring about reconciliation between the Orthodox and Catholic Churches': *Guardian*, 28 January 2009, p. 17. '[On 1 February] the Russian Orthodox Church enthroned its new leader at a ceremony in the Cathedral of Christ the Saviour in Moscow. Metropolitan Kirill of Smolensk and Kaliningrad became the sixteen leader of the Church ... Kirill is regarded as a liberal ... Kirill is a well known face in Russia, having presented religious programmes on state television for some years ... Kirill is seen by some as a modernizer ... Patriarch Kirill served as acting head of the Church after Alexei II's death and has also been the head of the Church's external relations department for the past twenty years ... Kirill's appointment was welcomed by ... the leader of the Roman Catholic Church, Pope Benedict XVI. The two churches split in 1054 and relations have been strained, with the Orthodox Church accusing the Vatican of trying to win Russian converts following the breakup of the Soviet Union. But Kirill and the Pope have met each other several times': www.bbc.co.uk, 1 February 2009.)

> Polls show that roughly half to two-thirds of Russians consider themselves Russian Orthodox, a sharp increase since the demise of the Soviet Union in 1991. Clergy frequently take part in government events, and people often wear crucifixes. But Russians remain deeply secular and most Russian say that they never attend church. About 10 to 15 per cent of Russians are Moslem, most of whom live in the south, though Moscow and other major cities have large Moslem populations. With emigration and assimilation, the

Jewish population has dwindled to a few hundred thousand people out of 140 million.

(www.iht.com, 23 September 2007)

9 December 2008.

Companies from emerging economies such as Russia and China are more likely to pay bribes when doing business in other countries, a survey claims. Anti-corruption body Transparency International interviewed 2,742 senior business executives to see which firms would pay bribes in foreign countries. Russia, China, Mexico, India, Brazil and Italy were the worst of the twenty-two economies ranked in the survey. Firms in Belgium and Canada were seen as least likely to pay bribes. The United States ranked ninth, while Britain, Germany and Japan were in joint fifth place [with the Netherlands third and Switzerland fourth] ... In the previous Bribe Payers Index (BPI), published in 2006, India was named as the worst, followed by China and Russia, while Switzerland, Sweden and Australia got the highest scores ... Russia, India and China are among the countries which have not signed the OECD's convention against bribery.

(www.bbc.co.uk, 9 December 2008)

12 December 2008.

[The State Duma] approved a bill Friday [12 December] that would end jury trials on charges of terrorism and treason ... The bill [was approved] in its final reading by a 355 to eighty-five vote. It will now go the upper house, where a swift approval is expected. The bill would strip defendants charged with crimes that include involvement in illegal armed units, violent seizure of power, armed rebellion and mass riots of the right to jury trials. Instead they would face judges .. Jury trials were reintroduced in 1993 ... In 2006, the last year for which statistics are available, only 700 of 1.2 million criminal cases were tried by a jury. Juries acquit defendants far more often than judges do.

(www.iht.com, 12 December 2008; *IHT*, 13 December 2008, p. 3)

('The upper house passed the bill Wednesday [17 December]': *IHT*, 18 December 2008, p. 4.)

14 December 2008.

Police have prevented two marches by anti-government demonstrators in Moscow and St Petersburg, detaining at least 100 protesters. Police trucks ringed two Moscow squares where protesters were to gather, and officers arrested dozens of people. In St Petersburg police blocked 100 protesters from marching on the city's main thoroughfare, arresting ten people. The protests were the latest organized by Garry Kasparov's Other Russia movement ... Among those arrested on Sunday [14 December] was Mr Kasparov's fellow leader, Eduard Limonov ... Sunday's demonstration had not been given permission ... the latest protests follow the

founding on Saturday of a new umbrella movement for Kremlin opponents, called Solidarity. It is named after the Polish trade union ... Mr
Kasparov said on Saturday [13 December] that Solidarity's goal was
'dismantling the Putin regime'. 'It is impossible to reform this regime,'
he told more than 100 delegates at the founding congress in the Khimki
area of Moscow. Other leaders include a former deputy prime minister,
Boris Nemtsov.

(www.bbc.co.uk, 14 December 2008)

Police detained ninety people at an unsanctioned political opposition rally
... The Other Russia's website said Garry Kasparov and about 200 other
opposition members met Friday [12 December] and Saturday [13 Decem-
ber] outside Moscow 'finalizing a new movement, which aims to peacefully dismantle what they describe as the illegitimate regime ruling
Russia' ... Kasparov said the country's worsening economic situation was
putting Russia 'on the edge of catastrophe' ... A spokesman for Moscow
City Hall ... [said] Kasparov and Limonov had been offered places to hold
a rally.

(www.cnn.com, 14 December 2008)

As many as 100 people were detained [in Moscow] ... The police said that
about ten people were detained during a similar protest in St Petersburg ...
The planned demonstration was meant as a demonstration against the Kremlin's handling of the financial crisis and against plans to change the constitution to extend presidential and parliamentary term limits The rally Sunday
[14 December was] called the Dissenters' March.

(www.iht.com, 14 December 2008; *IHT*, 15 December 2008, p. 3)

'Organizers said 130 people were detained, but police put the number at
ninety' (*Guardian*, 15 December 2008, p. 24).

'At least 150 people were arrested [in Moscow and St Petersburg]' (*The
Times*, 15 December 2008, p. 30).

21 December 2008.

Riot police have forcibly broken up a rally being held in the eastern city of
Vladivostok. About 500 people had gathered in the city's central square to
demonstrate against a new tax on imported cars ... Vladivostok, one of
several cities holding protests, depends heavily on car imports from Japan
and critics say the car tax could push prices up by 50 per cent. The tax is
intended to help prop up Russia's domestic car industry and prevent people
buying cheaper, imported products. Protests against it began a week ago and
have also been held in at least nine other cities in far eastern Russia ... Most
of the demonstrations were dispersed by police ... More are planned for
Moscow and other cities ... Some of the protesters were reported to have
been shouting slogans against prime minister Vladimir Putin. The protesters
were ordered to disperse by police who told them the rally was unauthorized

... Such open displays of anger are an unusual sight in Russia [said the BBC correspondent].

(www.bbc.co.uk, 21 December 2008)

Motorists staged similar rallies in thirty cities across the country ... The Pacific port of Vladivostok is a hub for imports of used Japanese cars and will be particularly hard hit ... Prime minister Vladimir Putin unveiled a $5 billion package of protectionist measures to prop up the auto industry last week including $3 billion of cheap credits for buyers of Russian cars and a $2 billion bail-out for manufacturers. Russian railways will transport new cars to the far east of the country free of charge ... Until the crisis Russia had been Europe's fastest growing auto market ... Most of the big foreign car makers have established in the past two years to cater for Russians' liking for foreign brands.

(*FT*, 22 December 2008, p. 9)

'In Vladivostok thousands demonstrated over plans to increase import duties on used foreign cars, with some carrying placards calling on Mr Putin to resign' (*FT*, 29 December 2008, p. 7).

Small demonstrations occurred in several cities over the weekend ... While each demonstration drew only a few hundred people, they have turned into perhaps the most visible evidence of discontent with the government over the financial crisis ... Imported cars are highly popular among Russians.

(*IHT*, 22 December 2008, p. 8)

'Importing used cars from Japan is a major livelihood in the far east ... Some demonstrators openly denounced Putin, Medvedev and United Russia; many angrily demanded television coverage ... Several legislatures in the far east have backed the protesters' demands' (www.iht.com, 2 January 2009).

A wave of protests over raised duties on imported cars is sweeping across Russia in the first sign of mass discontent with Kremlin measures to tackle the impact of the global financial crisis ... Measures to protect Russia's ailing motor industry by increasing duties on imported cars were announced earlier this month [December] ... The raised tariffs [are] to be introduced in January [2009] ... A gathering a week ago in Vladivostok drew 3,000 people.

(*Guardian*, 22 December 2008, p. 20)

Riot police were brutally beating up protesters and journalists in the country's far east. The immediate trigger of the protest was the government's decision to raise import duties on used foreign cars so as to protect Russian carmakers. Selling (and servicing) right-hand-drive cars imported from Japan has long been one of the economic mainstays for thousands of people. Significantly, the Kremlin could not rely on the compliance of local police (who also drive used Japanese cars). Instead, it had to fly special police units from the Moscow region to disperse the 1,000-odd demonstrators in Vladivostok.

(*The Economist*, 3 January 2009, p. 25)

23 December 2008.

Energy ministers from twelve of the world's leading exporters of natural gas met in Moscow yesterday [23 December] to create a producers' group that consumers fear could develop into an OPEC-style cartel. Russian prime minister Vladimir Putin, who chaired the meeting, warned that the era of 'cheap gas' was coming to an end and said members of the group would co-operate to make the gas market 'predictable' ... A gas producers' group could not operate in the same way as OPEC, the oil cartel, which can change its members' production from month to month to influence the market. This is because gas is generally sold under long-term contracts that are difficult to break or amend. However, the proposed group, a formal version of the Gas Exporting Forum, which has existed since 2001, could try to drive up the price of gas over the medium term. The emergence of a spot market for cargoes of liquefied natural gas, which can be sold wherever prices are highest, also creates potential for short-term market management, although those cargoes are only a small proportion of total gas sales and are likely to remain so. The gas producers' group will for the first time have a secretariat, based in Qatar [in Doha]. Russia [is] the world's biggest gas producer and the driving force behind the group.

(*FT*, 24 December 2008, p. 6)

Russian prime minister Vladimir Putin: '[The forum] will represent the interests of producers and exporters on the international market ... The time of cheap energy resources and cheap gas is surely coming to an end' ... Most countries in the Russian-backed forum are also members of OPEC, which has been at odds with Russia this autumn [2008] over the country's reluctance to reduce oil output in co-ordination with OPEC to support prices ... The sixteen nations in the forum have been meeting since 2001 as an ad hoc gathering. What was new Tuesday [23 December] was the group's adoption of a charter that would establish a permanent secretariat. The Russian government said falling energy prices had compelled the members to formalize their organization ... Natural gas prices are typically linked to the global price of oil, as power plants and other big energy users often have the capacity to switch to fuel oil as an alternative to natural gas ... The forum members are: Algeria, Bolivia, Brunei, Venezuela, Egypt, Indonesia, Iran, Qatar, Libya, Malaysia, Nigeria, the United Arab Emirates, Russia and Trinidad and Tobago, and, as observers, Equatorial Guinea and Norway.

(*IHT*, 24 December 2008, p. 11)

Vladimir Putin said the cost of extracting gas was rising sharply, therefore 'the era of cheap energy resources, of cheap gas, is of course coming to an end'. The Gas Exporting Countries Forum (GECF) meeting in Moscow agreed to a charter and plans for a permanent base ... GECF leaders agreed to establish permanent offices in Doha, Qatar ... Officials at the meeting stressed they were not trying to set up a price fixing cartel.

(www.bbc.co.uk, 24 December 2008)

31 December 2008. 'Vaslit Alexanian [Vasili Aleksanyan], the ailing jailed former executive of Yukos, has been freed after posting $1.7 million bail ... [He] has AIDS and cancer' (www.bbc.o.uk, 31 December 2008).

29 January 2009.

President Dmitri Medvedev held a surprise meeting with the editor of *Novaya Gazeta*, an independent newspaper that has established itself as one of the Kremlin's sharpest critics, ten days after it lost a twenty-five-year-old reporter in what apparently was a contract killing. Four reporters from *Novaya Gazeta* have died under mysterious circumstances since 2000. The most prominent of them was Anna Politkovskaya – a fierce critic of the Kremlin's policy in Chechnya – who in 2006 was shot to death in her stair-well, a crime that sparked worldwide outrage. Medvedev called the editor of the newspaper, Dmitri Muratov, to request a meeting, and during an hour-long conversation Thursday [29 January] expressed his 'deepest sorrow and compassion' over the death of the report, Anastasia Baburova, who was shot as she walked down a Moscow street with a human rights lawyer, Stanislav Markelov, who as also associated with the newspaper and was thought to be the primary target of the attack ... When Muratov confessed that violence against reporters had prompted him to consider closing the newspaper's doors, Medvedev's answer was 'Thank God the newspaper exists', Muratov said ... Earlier in the week Medvedev moved to scale back a bill that would expand the definition of treason, saying he had been influenced by the outcry 'in the media and society' against the proposed change. And on Wednesday [28 January] ... an anonymous military official told the Interfax news service that the Kremlin had dropped plans to deploy Iskander missiles in Kaliningrad. Official sources would not confirm the statement.

(www.iht.com, 31 January 2009)

'Some have theorized that she [Anastasia Baburova] was shot because she tried to protect him [Stanislav Markelov]' (*IHT*, 2 February 2009, p. 2).

('Legislation to expand the definition of treason ... As with existing law, the legislation would forbid actions considered detrimental to Russia's security. But the legislation, if passed, would remove qualifiers that require such actions to be "hostile" and directed against the "external security" of Russia before they are considered illegal. It addition, it would prohibit Russians from passing certain information not only to other countries, but also to foreign non-government groups': www.iht.com, 21 December 2008; *IHT*, 22 December 2008, pp. 1, 8.)

'As Anastasia Baburova tried to grab the killer he turned and shot her too' (www.bbc.co.uk, 8 February 2009).

31 January 2009.

Thousands of people have held rallies across Russia protesting against what they describe as the government's mismanagement of the economy. The biggest demonstration took place in the eastern city of Vladivostok, where protesters demanded the resignation of prime minister Vladimir Putin. In Moscow police arrested a number of people at an unauthorized gathering by a radical party ... Police detained a number of members of the radical National Bolshevik Party, including its leader, Eduard Limonov ... A small group of supporters of Garry Kasparov ... [was] attacked by unknown masked men before being arrested by police. Earlier about 1,000 supporters of the Communist Party were allowed by the authorities to hold their demonstration in the capital ... In Vladivostok the anti-government demonstration was called by the Communist Party ... The protest was joined by a local group angered by higher tariffs imposed on cars imported to the city ... Unemployment is rising rapidly, as are the prices of basic food and utilities ... Government supporters also held their rallies across the country.

(www.bbc.co.uk, 31 January 2009)

About 200 protesters from opposition groups marched down several city blocks [in Moscow], having eluded the police in a circuitous jaunt through the city subway system. The authorities had vowed to prevent the march when organizers announced it last week ... A police spokesman said that forty-one people were detained in small, unsanctioned protests throughout Moscow on Saturday [31 January]. That group included Eduard Limonov, a writer and leader of the banned National Bolshevik Party ... Several thousand people gathered in central Moscow for a demonstration organized by the main pro-Kremlin party, United Russia, in support of the government's policies ... An anti-government protest in Vladivostok was also largely peaceful ... The authorities had violently broken up a protest there in December [2008]. Tensions have escalated in the region since the government raised tariffs on the import of foreign vehicles in an effort to protect domestic auto manufacturers, which have been badly hurt by the financial crisis. Used Japanese vehicles are popular in Vladivostok, and many people make their living importing them. The tariffs have hurt the business. The federal authorities flew in riot police from Moscow for the march in December in Vladivostok ... About 1,000 participants marched through the centre of the city before holding a rally in front of a statue of Lenin, where they demanded the resignation of the government ... The regional branch of the Communist Party helped organize the event ... the authorities had approved the rally.

(www.iht.com, 1 February 2009)

The tension has shown no sign of diminishing, and in late January another demonstration in Vladivostok drew more than 1,000 people. The Communist Party ... joined in ... Even local legislators from Putin's party opposed the tariff, an unusual example of dissent that underscores the depth of feeling here [in Vladivostok] ... Dealers noted that the region's industrial base had deteriorated in recent years, and even the fishing fleet was faring poorly. They said the car industry was providing more than 100,000 jobs for people who import, maintain and transport and sell vehicles.

(www.iht.com, 16 February 2009; *IHT*, 17 February 2009, p. 3)

13 February 2009. 'A Russian heavy missile cruiser ... [the nuclear-powered] *Peter the Great* ... stopped three pirate ships off the coast of Somalia and detained ten pirates, according to a statement released Friday by [Moscow]' (www.cnn.com, 13 February 2009).

News of the Somali pirates' detention came on the same day the crew of a Ukrainian ship captured by Somali pirates arrived home at Kiev airport after a nineteen-week hijacking ordeal. The MV *Faina*, released last week, docked on Thursday 12 February] in Mombassa with its crew of seventeen Ukrainians, two Russians and one Latvian, with a cargo of tanks and munitions.

(www.bbc.co.uk, 13 February 2009)

Last week ... the ship's owners finally paid $3.2 million – in cash dropped by parachute – to free *Faina* ... Its cargo included thirty-three T-72 Soviet-era tanks, 150 grenade launchers, six anti-aircraft guns and heaps of ammunition ... The Kenyan government has insisted it still owns them and it said on Thursday [12 February] that the weapons would now be offloaded and taken to Kenyan military bases.

(www.iht.com, 12 February 2009)

24 February 2009.

Mikhail Khodorkovsky ... has been moved from a Siberian prison to Moscow for a trial on new charges of money laundering and fraud ... a court official said Tuesday [24 February]. Preliminary hearings in the new trial for Khodorkovsky and his business partner and co-defendant, Platon Lebedev, who has also been moved to Moscow, will begin on 3 March ... The two are accused of laundering $30 billion and misappropriating 350 million tonnes of oil. Khodorkovsky, who owned Yukos Oil, the largest private Russian company before it was dismantled by the government, has been serving an eight-year sentence in a Siberian prison after his conviction on tax evasion and fraud charges ... His imprisonment has been widely seen as punishment for his opposition to Vladimir Putin, who was president when he was arrested in 2003 and is now prime minister.

(www.iht.com, 24 February 2009; *IHT*, 25 February 200, p. 12)

1 March 2009.

United Russia ... has won handily in regional elections, the central election commission said ... the first electoral test ... since the economy began to turn dire ... United Russia won the majority of seats in all nine regions where local parliamentary elections were held Sunday [1 March] and nearly swept smaller municipal elections. The Communist Party, which complained of widespread violations, came in a distant second ... Some analysts pointed to a slight slip in support for United Russia of several percentage points in some regions compared with previous elections ... The Communist Party made comparatively small gains against United Russia, winning more than 20 per cent of the parliamentary seats in some regions, despite what Gennadi Zyuganov, the Communist Party leader, called major violations of election laws. Zyuganov said: 'We gained many more votes in the majority of regions even though the latest election campaign had been the dirtiest and administrative resources had been used everywhere.'

(www.iht.com, 2 March 2009; *IHT*, 3 March 2009, p. 3)

3 March 2009.

Preliminary hearings in the second trial of Mikhail Khodorkovsky began Tuesday [3 March] on Moscow ... Khodorkovsky, along with Platon Lebedev, his former business partner, is accused of laundering more than $20 billion and embezzling close to 350 million tonnes of crude oil at a time when Yukos Oil was Russia's largest private company.

(*IHT*, 4 March 2009, p. 3)

President Barack Obama sent a letter to Russia's president last month [February] suggesting that he would back off deploying a new missile defence system in Eastern Europe if Moscow would help stop Iran from developing long-range weapons, American officials said Monday [2 March]. The letter to President Dmitri Medvedev was hand-delivered in Moscow by top administrative officials three weeks ago. It said the United States would not need to proceed with the interceptor system ... if Iran halted any efforts to build nuclear warheads and ballistic missiles ... President Obama has been lukewarm on missile defence, saying he supports it only if it can be proved technically effective and affordable ... The deal with Poland included a side agreement that an American air defence battery would be moved from Germany to Poland, where it would be operated by a crew of about 100 American personnel.

(www.iht.com, 3 March 2009)

President Dmitri Medvedev:

[Russia is] working very closely with our US colleagues on the issue of Iran's nuclear programme ... [But not in the context of the missile defence plan] ... No one links these issues to any exchange, especially on the Iran issue.

(www.iht.com, 3 March 2009)

President Dmitri Medvedev (Tuesday 3 March]:

If we are to speak about some sort of exchange, the question has not been presented in such a way, because it would not be productive. Our American partners are ready to discuss this problem, and that is already positive. Several months ago we were hearing different signals ... No one is linking these issues to some kind of trade-off, particularly on the Iranian issue. We are already working in close contact with our US counterparts on the Iranian nuclear issue.

(www.bbc.co.uk, 3 March 2009)

President Dmitri Medvedev:

If we are talking about some sort of trade or exchange, then I can say that the question cannot be put that way. It is not productive ... What we are receiving from our American partners is evidence of one thing at least, that they are willing to discuss this problem, which is already good, because just a few months ago we were receiving different signals ... [Russia is] in absolute contact with our American colleagues on the problem of the Iranian nuclear programme.

(www.ft.com, 3 March 2009)

Asked Tuesday [3 March] about the letter, President Barack Obama said it was not 'some sort of quid pro quo', but a statement of fact. He said: 'What I said in the letter was that obviously to the extent that we are lessening Iran's commitment to nuclear weapons, then that reduces the pressure for or the need for a missile defence system.'

(*IHT*, 4 March 2009, p. 1)

'Yesterday President Barack Obama said that reports did not "accurately characterize" the letter and denied that he had offered "some sort of quid pro quo"' (*FT*, 4 March 2009, p. 10).

5 March 2009.

Prodded by the Obama administration [represented by US secretary of state Hillary Clinton], Nato agreed Thursday [5 March] to resume high level relations with Russia six months after they were suspended following Moscow's military offensive against Georgia ... The Nato–Russian Council ... [was] formed in 2002 as a vehicle for consultation between Russia and Nato members.

(www.iht.com, 5 March 2009)

'The [Nato] meeting in Brussels agreed to reinstate the work of the Nato–Russia Council, a consultancy body' (*Guardian*, 6 March 2009, p. 18).

The developmental model it [Russia] proposes is based on the closer relationship between the world of politics, business and crime ... In Eastern Europe the development associated with the EU and Nato is tied to hopes for an efficient, citizen-friendly state that does not constitute a threat either to its own citizens or to its neighbours.

(Slawomir Debski, *IHT*, 31 October 2008, p. 6)

17 March 2009.

President Dmitri Medvedev said Moscow will begin a comprehensive military rearmament from 2011 ... Russia will spend nearly $140 billion on buying arms up until 2011 ... Analysts say the brief war in Georgia exposed problems with outdated equipment and practices within Russia's armed forces and led to calls for modernization.

(www.bbc.co.uk, 17 March 2009)

President Dmitri Medvedev ... today [17 March] said Russia would rearm its military and boost nuclear forces because Nato is expanding towards Russia's borders. Medvedev: 'Attempts to expand the military infrastructure of Nato near the borders of our country are continuing ... [The prospect of Nato's expansion, combined with a threat of local crises and international terrorism] requires a modernization of our armed forces, giving them a modern shape ... The primary task is to increase the combat readiness of our forces – first of all our strategic nuclear forces. They must be able to fulfil all the necessary tasks to ensure Russia's security. Another task on our agenda is the transfer of all combat units into the category of permanent readiness' ... Medvedev said large-scale modernization of the army and navy would begin in 2011.

(www.independent.co.uk, 17 March 2009)

Russia is planning a 'comprehensive rearmament' of its military, President Dmitri Medvedev said Tuesday [17 March]. The 'large-scale rearmament' will begin in 2011, Medvedev said ... Medvedev said the 'most important task is to re-equip the armed forces with the newest weapons systems ... He said the process had already begun and would accelerate through 2011 ... The defence budget has 'virtually remained the same as was planned despite our current financial problems ... Defence secretary Anatoli Serdyukov said the country will aim for 70 per cent of its weaponry to be 'modern' by 2020 ... The announcement comes amid concerns in Moscow over the performance of its forces during last year's invasion of Georgia ... [said] Christopher Langton, an analyst at the International Institute of Studies in London. Langton: '[In Georgia] things they expected to perform well didn't – communications, the air force. It took five days, which is quite a long time, to suppress another country's air defences, quite a small country's' ... Former President Boris Yeltsin announced in the early 1990s that Russia would replace its conscript army with a professional force by 2010, Langton said – a target it has come nowhere close to meeting.

(www.cnn.com, 17 March 2009)

While Russia's far larger military easily triumphed over Georgia's in the conflict in August, the fighting exposed what many experts described as flaws in training, weapons and equipment ... President Dmitri Medvedev said Tuesday [17 March] that Russia would begin a 'large-scale rearming' in 2011 in response to what he described as threats to the country's security ... Mr Medvedev cited encroachment by Nato as a primary reason for bolstering the armed and nuclear forces ... He is expected to hold his first meeting with President Barack Obama in early April in London on the sidelines of the summit of the Group of 20 industrialized and developing countries ... Medvedev: 'An analysis of the military–political situation in the world shows that there are a range of regions where there remains serious potential for conflicts. Threats remain that can bring about local crises and international terrorism. Nato is not halting its efforts to widen its military infrastructure near the borders of our country. All of this demands a quality modernization of our armed forces.'

(www.iht.com, 17 March 2009; *IHT*, 18 March 2009, p. 3)

21 March 2009.

President Dmitri Medvedev replaced the governor of a north-western region [Murmansk], apparently seeking to ensure that the governing party remained in control there after it suffered a surprising defeat in local elections ... The dismissed governor, Yuri Yevdokimov, is a member of the governing party, United Russia, but had been feuding with party leaders lately, In mayoral elections this month [March] in the city of Murmansk, Mr Yevdokimov supported an independent candidate, who triumphed over United Russia's nominee ... The [Kremlin] statement said he had voluntarily resigned, but it seemed clear that if he had not done so he would have been dismissed.

(*IHT*, 23 March 2009, p. 3)

'President Dmitri Medvedev ... fired the governor of the far northern province of Murmansk after he hinted publicly that a mayoral candidate backed by United Russia had used dirty tricks in an electoral campaign' (*FT*, 30 March 2009, p. 8).

27 March 2009.

Russia plans to create a new military force to protect its interests in the disputed Arctic region, a Kremlin strategy paper says. The document outlines Russia's policy for the Arctic, which is believed to contain as much as 25 per cent of the world's undiscovered oil and gas. The paper was signed by President Dmitri Medvedev in September [2008] ... Russia, the United States, Canada, Denmark and Norway have been trying to assert jurisdiction over parts of the Arctic ... The Kremlin paper says the Arctic must become Russia's 'top strategic resource base' by the year 2020. It calls for strengthening border guard forces in the region and updating their equipment, while creating a new group of military forces 'to ensure military security under various military-political circumstances'. By 2011, it says, Russia must complete geological studies to prove its claim to Arctic resources and win international recognition of its Arctic borders ...

Moscow first submitted its claim in 2001 to the United Nations, but was rejected for lack of evidence. Russia now hopes to prove that an underwater mountain range crossing the polar region is part of Russia's continental shelf. In 2007 two Russian civilian mini-submarines descended to the Arctic seabed to collect geological and water samples and drop a titanium canister containing the Russian flag.

(www.iht.com, 27 March 2009)

'Russia, Canada, Denmark, Norway and the United States, all of whom have an Arctic coastline, dispute the sovereignty over parts of the region' (www.bbc.co.uk, 27 March 2009).

The presidential security council ... sought to play down its strategy document later on Friday [27 March], saying its emphasis was on improving the border guard service and its co-operation with other states in 'combating terrorism in the sea, seeking to prevent illicit trade and illegal migration, and in seeking to protect aquatic biological resources'.

(*Guardian*, 28 March 2009, p. 26)

31 March 2009.

Mikhail Khodorkovsky went on trial on fresh charges ... The new charges stem from accusations that he and his business partner, Platon Lebedev, who is also on trial, bribed shareholders and managers of three production units, controlled by their Yukos oil company, to sell them oil at production cost over a five-year period. The stolen money and oil was laundered through front companies, it is alleged.

(*Guardian*, 1 April 2009, p. 22)

The defence lawyers argue that the case ... ignores the universal rule [double jeopardy] that nobody can be tried for the same crime twice. And it goes over the same territory and time. In the first trial Mikhail Khodorkovsky and his partners were accused of tax evasion. Now they are charged with the embezzlement of 350 million tonnes of oil and laundering the proceeds through offshore trading companies. This is the same oil on which Mr Khodorkovsky was said not to have paid enough tax, says Vadim Klyuvgant, Mr Khodorkovsky's lawyer. Mr Klyuvgant says none of the 188 volumes of prosecution evidence explains how Mr Khodorkovsky stole Yukos's entire oil production for six years ... Yukos's former management has brought a case to the European Court of Human Rights in Strasbourg ... On 29 January the European court declared the Yukos case was admissible.

(www.economist.com, 2 April 2009; *The Economist*, 4 April 2009, pp. 35–6)

1 April 2009. '[On Wednesday 1 April] US president Barack Obama and Russian president Dmitri Medvedev ... met [for the first time] in London ahead of Thursday's G-20 summit' (www.cnn.com, 1 April 2009).

Russia and the United States are to reopen negotiations about reducing their nuclear warheads, President Dmitri Medvedev and Barack Obama have said ... In a joint statement the two leaders said they had ordered nuclear negotiators to report first results in July ... It is hoped the talks will produce a news arms control treaty to replace the Strategic Arms Reduction Treaty (Start) that expires [on 5 December 2009] ... Agreed in 1991 Start 1 limits the world's two largest nuclear arsenals to between 1,700 and 2, 200 warheads ... Mr Medvedev has invited his American counterpart to visit Moscow in July – an invitation Mr Obama has accepted.

(www.bbc.co.uk, 1 April 2009)

'Both presidents want the new deal to improve on an agreement by their prede-cessors in 2002 to cut deployed warheads to between 1,700 and 2,200 on each side by 2012' (www.bbc.co.uk, 24 April 2009).

'Negotiators from both countries will soon begin talks "to work out a new, comprehensive, legally binding agreement on reducing and limiting strategic offensive arms to replace the Start 1 Treaty", the [joint] statement said' (www. cnn.com, 1 April 2009).

'Russia has some 2,800 ... long-range nuclear missiles ... still deployed and the United States around 2,400' (*FT*, 3 April 2009, p. 12).

Presidents Obama and Medvedev have agreed to extend the Start 1 agree-ment, which ends this year [2009], and to reduce the number of warheads from 2,200, agreed in the SORT agreement by Presidents Bush and Putin in 2001, to a lower number ... [But] the criteria by which arsenals are counted differ between Start and SORT. By the rules of Start 1 missiles are counted by the number of warheads they are able to carry, not by those actually installed. SORT counts only those actually installed.

(*IHT*, 21 April 2009, p. 8)

4 April 2009.

Nato says that Danish prime minister Anders Fogh Rasmussen has been unanimously named as the alliance's new secretary-general ... All twenty-eight members must agree on the choice of a new leader ... Turkey was strongly opposed to Fogh Rasmussen before the alliance reached consensus. He infuriated many Moslems by defending freedom of speech during an uproar over a Danish newspaper's publication of cartoons in 2005 ... [He] angered Moslems by defending the right to print cartoons of the Prophet Muhammad ... He has also angered Turkey by opposing its membership in the EU. Current secretary-general Jaap de Hoop Scheffer of the Netherlands says that the decision was made unanimously Saturday [4 April] at a summit marking the sixtieth anniversary of the alliance ... The term of the alliance's current head, Dutch diplomat Jaap de Hoop Scheffer, runs out on 1 August [2009].

(www.iht.com, 4 April 2009)

5 April 2009.

President Barack Obama on Sunday [5 April] launched an effort to rid the world of nuclear weapons ... In a speech [in Prague] driven with fresh urgency by North Korea's launch just hours earlier, Obama said the United States would 'immediately and aggressively' seek ratification of a comprehensive ban on testing nuclear weapons. He said the United States would host a summit within the next year on reducing and eventually eliminating nuclear weapons and he called for a global effort to secure nuclear material ... Obama coupled his call for a nuclear-free world with an assurance that America would not unilaterally give up nuclear weapons. It must be a one-for-all, all-for-one endeavour, he said, and until that is possible the United States will maintain a big enough arsenal to serve as a deterrent ... The Comprehensive Test Ban Treaty was signed by President Bill Clinton but rejected by the Senate in 1999. Over 140 nations have ratified the ban, but forty-four states that possess nuclear technology need to both sign and ratify it before it can take effect and only thirty-five have done so. The United States is among the key holdouts, along with China, Egypt, India, Indonesia, Iran, Israel, North Korea and Pakistan ... Ratification of the test ban treaty was one of several 'concrete steps' that Obama outline as necessary to move toward a nuclear-free world. He also called for reducing the role of nuclear weapons in American national security strategy, negotiating a new strategic arms reduction treaty with Russia, and seeking a new treaty to end the production of fissile materials used in nuclear weapons ... Obama: 'Iran's nuclear and ballistic missile activity poses a real threat, not just to the United States but to Iran's neighbours and our allies. The Czech Republic and Poland have been courageous in agreeing to host a defence against these missiles. As long as the threat from Iran persists we will go forward with a missile defence system that is cost-effective and proven.'

(www.iht.com, 5 April 2009)

'President Barack Obama promised ... establish an "international fuel bank" to allow oeaceful countries access to nuclear fuel without increasing proliferation risks' (*IHT*, 6 April 2009, p. 8).

His presidency, Barack Obama declared, would see 'America's commitment to seek the peace and security of a world without nuclear weapons' ... He said: 'It is time for the testing of nuclear weapons to be banned' ... He called for the strengthening of the 1968 Nuclear Non-proliferation Treaty.

(www.guardian.co.uk, 5 April 2009)

President Barack Obama said ... North Korea's 'provocative' rocket launch earlier in the day underscored the need for action. Although his nuclear goals might not be released in his lifetime, he said he would strive to achieve them ... The number of strategic nuclear warheads: Russia 2,800; the United States 2,200; France 300; UK; China 180; UK 160 (all members of the Nuclear Proliferation Treaty); Israel 80; India 60; Pakistan 60; North Korea less than 10 (all non-members).

(www.bbc.co.uk, 5 April 2009)

President Barack Obama:

[The launch] is a clear violation of United Nations Security Council Resolution 1718, which expressly prohibits North Korea from conducting ballistic missile-related activities of any kind ... North Korea broke the rules once more by testing a rocket that could be used for a long-range missile ... With this provocative act North has ignored its international obligations, rejected unequivocal calls for restraint and further isolated itself from the community of nations. We will immediately consult with our allies in the region, including Japan and South Korea, and members of the UN Security Council and to bring this matter before the Council. I urge North Korea to abide fully by the resolutions of the UN Security Council and to refrain from further provocative actions ... Now is the time for a strong international response. North Korea must know that the path to security and respect will never come through threats and illegal weapons ... This provocation underscores the need for action, not just this afternoon at the UN Security Council, but in our determination to prevent the spread of these weapons. Rules must be binding, violations must be punished; words must mean something. Now is the time for a strong international response ... [The launch] threatens the security of nations] near and far.

(www.cnn.com, 5 April 2009; www.bbc.co.uk, 5 April 2009; www.iht.com, 5 April 2009; www.thetimes.com, 5 April 2009)

15 April 2009.

President Dmitri Medvedev chose one of the country's most Kremlin-critical publications for his first Russian newspaper interview since taking office ... Although the interview published Wednesday [15 April] did not break ground in policy matters, Medvedev's giving it to *Novaya Gazeta* had symbolic resonance. The newspaper consistently challenges the Kremlin on matters including human rights, freedom of speech and Russia's alleged backsliding on democracy. Four *Novaya Gazeta* journalists have been killed or died in suspicious circumstances over the past decade. Medvedev met privately with the newspaper's editors after the latest killing, when reporter Anastasia Baburova was gunned down on a Moscow street in January [2009] as she walked with an activist lawyer who was also killed. Many observers suspect the deaths of *Novaya Gazeta*'s reporters may be connected to Russian security agencies. Critics fault Russian leaders for not vigorously denouncing such killings. The killings were not discussed in the interview ... Asked by the newspaper whether he was aiming to 'rehabilitate democracy' in Russia, Medvedev said that was not needed. He said: 'Democracy existed, lives and will be' ... The interview was published a few hours before Medvedev was to meet in the Kremlin with representatives of his advisory council on developing civil institutions.

(www.iht.com, 15 April 2009)

President Dmitri Medvedev said democracy need not be compromised for the sake of prosperity. He said: 'Stability and a prosperous life cannot be set off against a set of political rights and freedoms' ... Amongst those killed in recent years was the investigative journalist Anna Politkovskaya ... Vladimir Putin never spoke to *Novaya Gazeta* during his eight years as president.

(www.bbc.co.uk, 15 April 2009)

21 April 2009.

Mikhail Khodorkovsky pleaded not guilty to new charges of embezzlement and money laundering ... [He] is accused of embezzling $26.4 billion and could spend twenty-two more years in prison if convicted ... His family ... accuse the government of wanting to keep him behind bars well beyond the end of his first sentence because it fears he will become the focus of an opposition movement ... Khodorkovsky and his former business partner Platon Lebedev, who was also convicted of tax evasion in 2005 and jailed, are accused of helping to embezzle some 900 billion roubles of Yukos assets and launder 500 billion roubles ($14.7 billion) between 1998 and 2003 ... Khodorkovsky: 'If I stole the oil ... and profits while the state got 40 billion roubles in taxes, what were the taxes paid for?' ... Defence lawyers also argue that Khodorkovsky and Lebedev are being tried a second time for the same alleged illegal activity they were convicted for in 2005 ... Another court in Moscow granted parole to a former Yukos lawyer imprisoned nearly four-and-a-half years ago on charges of embezzlement and tax evasion. Svetlana Bakhmina gave birth in detention in November [2008]. She was unusually denied early release twice while pregnant ... More than 95,000 people signed a petition demanding her release, along with Mikhail Gorbachev.

(www.bbc.co.uk, 21 April 2009)

Svetlana Bakhmina ... was halfway through a six-and-a-half-year sentence for embezzlement and tax evasion as deputy head of Yukos's legal department ... [She] already had two young sons when [she] gave birth to a daughter in a prison hospital last November [2008] ... The judge said: 'The court took into consideration the fact that Bakhmina admitted her guilt, committed no rule violations during her time in prison and also that she has young children' ... [There were] public calls for her release – including from prominent cultural and political figures like Mikhail Gorbachev ... Almost 96,000 people signed an online petition demanding that she be freed.

(www.iht.com, 22 April 2009)

26 April 2009. There takes place the election of mayor of Sochi (which will hold the 2014 Winter Olympic Games).

> Because regional leaders are appointed by the Kremlin, the mayors of large cities are Russia's most powerful independently elected officials. As the economic crisis deepens, some see United Russia losing its grip on power. In the seaport of Murmansk last weekend, an independent mayoral candidate, Sergei Subbotin, shocked United Russia by beating its candidate, the incumbent, with 61 per cent of the vote. The region's governor is also a member of United Russia but backed Mr Subbotin.
>
> (www.iht.com, 18 March 2009; *IHT*, 19 March 2009, p. 8)

('In March ... Anton Chumachenko ... a loyal member of United Russia ... won a seat on the local legislative council in March. Three weeks later Mr Chumachenko suddenly sent out an open letter to his voters renouncing his seat ... On election night Mr Chumachenko saw that he was sixth in a race where the top five vote-getters won seats. But when the election commission announced the results he was fifth. Four days later Mr Chumanko renounced his own election: 'I do not want to begin my political career with a cynical mockery of rights, laws and morality': www.iht.com, 9 May 2009.)

'Boris Nemtsov has registered as a candidate for mayor of Sochi ... [which] will hold the 2014 Winter Olympic Games. Mr Nemtsov claims that plans for the Games ... have already been derailed by corruption and bad management' (*IHT*, 30 March 2009).

> A court ruled Monday [13 April] that Russian tycoon Alexander Lebedev's registration as a candidate in the mayoral race in the Olympic city of Sochi is illegitimate ... His spokesman said the court ruled that Lebedev had failed to submit a financial statement required for registration ... [but his spokesman] said all required documents were submitted.
>
> (www.iht.com, 13 April 2009)

> A court in the Black Sea resort declared Alexander Lebedev's candidacy invalid, ruling that the local election committee had acted illegally when it allowed him to register as a candidate last month [March] ... Last night [13 April] Sochi's local election commission took the unusual step of condemning the judge's action ... [A] commission member said: 'As far as we are concerned he is still a candidate.'
>
> (*Guardian*, 14 April 2009, p. 20)

> Building projects for two Olympic stadiums and several other athletics facilities threaten up to 5,000 people with the loss of their homes ... Boris Nemtsov is Anatoli Pakhomov's strongest challenger ... Anatoli Pakhomov [is] the incumbent supported by United Russia ... Boris Nemtsov is campaigning on a pledge to prevent the appropriation of land.
>
> (*FT*, 25 April 2009, p. 5)

Boris Nemtsov has campaigned against Vladimir Putin's plan to stage the Olympics in Sochi, saying the massive redevelopment will destroy the Black Sea resort. He argues that several Russian cities should host the Games instead ... Six candidates made it on to the ballot from an initial list of twenty-five.

(*The Times*, 25 April 2009, p. 45)

'Polls suggest that Boris Nemtsov is running third, after Anatatoli Pakhomov and the Communist candidate, Yuri Dzaganiya' (www.iht.com, 25 April 2009).

Seven candidates were disqualified because of clerical errors in their registration forms. The remaining challengers had little space to campaign; local television blacked out news coverage and advertising of opposition candidates, and businesspeople who helped publicize their campaigns were threatened and intimidated.

(www.iht.com, 27 April 2009)

The Kremlin favourite won an overwhelming victory in the mayoral election in Sochi ... Acting mayor Anatoli Pakhomov had 76.8 per cent of the vote ... Boris Nemtsov was a distant second with 13.6 per cent of the vote ... Mr Nemtsov called the vote a fraud and vowed to challenge the result: 'This is not an election, this is fraud. This is fraud because of manipulation and censorship' ... [He] accused the authorities of pressuring vulnerable state workers to vote in early balloting for Mr Pakhomov, the candidate of United Russia. Those votes accounted for more than a quarter of the total cast ... [Yuri Dzaganiya, the candidate of the Communist Party, came third] ... Before the vote local television stations gave Mr Pakhomov ample air time and cast him in a positive light while painting Mr Nemtsov as a dangerous troublemaker and ignoring the other candidates. Several media companies refused to take paid campaign advertising and the contest was virtually invisible on streets bare of campaign posters.

(*IHT*, 28 April 2009, p. 3)

'Boris Nemtsov ... [said] the result ... was "absolutely falsified" ... International observers said 30 per cent of the votes were submitted before the election, a legal procedure but one that is open to manipulation' (*FT*, 28 April 2009, p. 8). 'The incumbent United Russia candidate won, but only at the cost of a public relations disaster. Opposing candidates were harassed and denied access to the media and ... Boris Nemtsov is suing ... to have the result invalidated' (*FT*, 30 May 2009, p. 9).

9 May 2009. 'Victory Day celebrations ... [are held to] mark the surrender of Nazi Germany' (www.cnn.com, 10 May 2009).

'A military parade [takes place] in Moscow to commemorate the victory over Nazi Germany in World War II' (www.bbc.co.uk, 9 May 2009).

9 June 2009.

A meeting of the heads of government of Russia, Belarus and Kazakhstan during a session of the executive body of the Eurasian Economic Community customs union has resulted in a joint decision to withdraw their individual bids for membership in the World Trade Organization [WTO]. The three countries' prime ministers agreed to 'proceed from the assumption that the customs union will begin functioning on 1 January 2010, and the necessary procedures will be completed as of 1 July 2011'.

(CDSP, 2009, vol. 61, no. 24, p. 1)

10 June 2009. 'Prime minister Vladimir Putin: "Why do we need nuclear weapons? If other nuclear states are ready, we are too"' (*IHT*, 11 June 2009, p. 3).

'Prime minister Vladimir Putin: "If those who made the atomic bomb are ready to abandon it, we will welcome and facilitate this process"' (*The Times*, 11 June 2009, p. 39).

26 June 2009.

A Russian court has given Boris Berezovsky, who lives in exile in Britain, a thirteen-year sentence for embezzlement. The court found the tycoon guilty of embezzling 58 million roubles from the carmaker Avtovaz and the car dealership Logovaz in the 1990s. Russia is seeking his extradition.

(The Times, 27 June 2009, p. 49)

27 June 2009.

Nato and Russia on Saturday [27 June] took another step toward rebuilding ties that were damaged by the war in Georgia last year [2008], holding a high level meeting of foreign ministers and pledging to resume full military co-operation. The ministers gathered on the Greek island of Corfu and, under the auspices of the Russia–Nato Council, discussed potential areas of co-operation, including the war in Afghanistan, nuclear proliferation, piracy, terrorism and drug trafficking ... Relations had been gradually warming this year but suffered a setback in April after Russia complained about Nato military exercises in Georgia ... When Nato would not cancel the exercises Russia responded by withdrawing its generals from a meeting with Nato military commanders. Soon after, Nato expelled two Russian diplomats from its headquarters in Brussels, saying that it had to punish Russia for spying against the alliance's members. Russia retaliated by expelling two Nato diplomats from Moscow. Throughout this period, though, Russia has continued to provide logistical assistance to Nato's military mission in Afghanistan.

(www.iht.com, 28 June 2009)

1 July 2009.

The government is shutting down every last legal casino and slot-parlour across the land, under an anti-vice plan promoted by Vladimir Putin that as recently as a few months ago was widely perceived as far-fetched ... The gambling industry says the ban will leave more than 400,000 people without work ... The government has put the figure at 60,000 people, though industry analysts say that is absurdly low ... the Kremlin has offered the gambling industry only one option: relocate to four regions in remote areas of Russia, as many as 4,000 miles from the capital ... Casinos in Russia are now to be confined to the Altai region of Siberia, the coastal area of the Far East (near the border with North Korea and China), Kaliningrad (a Russian enclave between Poland and Lithuania), and the Azov Sea region in the south ... None of the four regions are prepared for the transfer, and no casino is expected to reopen for several years. As of 1 July, not even two decades after casinos began proliferating in the free-for-all post-Soviet era, the industry's workers will be out on the street ... The law that started the whole process was introduced in 2006 by Vladimir Putin, then president and now prime minister, who spoke of the perils of [gambling] ... His plan was announced during a spy scandal between Russia and Georgia, and the timing suggested that Mr Putin was in part seeking to wound the Georgian diaspora here, which is said to have an influential role in the industry ... Some casinos said they might try to devote some space to private poker clubs, which they believe will be allowed under the law. But executives say such clubs are far less lucrative and will employ very few workers.

(www.iht.com, 29 June 2009; *IHT*, 30 June 2009, p. 2)

'Poker halls ... [and] lottery halls ... [are] two forms of gambling not banned' (*Guardian*, 30 June 2009, p. 14).

A new law has come into effect, confining gambling to four regions far from Moscow. It bans gambling on the internet and at airports, supermarkets and other sites ... From 1 July Russian gamblers are restricted to specific zones in the Kaliningrad region by the Black Sea, the Primorye region in the Far East, Altai in Siberia and a area in the south spanning the Rostov and Kras-nodar regions.

(www.bbc.co.uk, 1 July 2009)

('Poker was legally classified as a sport, giving some the prospect of curbing their losses by becoming private poker clubs. This week, though, the Kremlin said not so fast. Russian officials announced that an error was made in 2007 when poker was added to the list of official sports. As a result, poker clubs will also be illegal under the anti-gambling law': www.iht.com, 23 July 2009.)

3 July 2009.

Kremlin spokesman Alex Pavlov said Friday [3 July] ... [that] Russia will allow the United States to ship weapons across its territory to Afghanistan ... Pavlov said he does not know when the policy will take effect, but imagines the details will come out when Presidents Barack Obama and Dmitri Medvedev meet Monday and Tuesday in Moscow [6–7 July].

(www.cnn.com, 3 July 2009)

Russia will allow the United States to ship weapons across its territory to Afghanistan, a top Kremlin aide said Friday [3 July] ... The deal is expected to be signed during President Barack Obama's visit to Moscow next week, Kremlin foreign policy adviser Sergei Prikhodko said ... Russia has been allowing the United States to ship non-lethal supplies across its territory for operations in Afghanistan ... Prikhodko told reporters that the expected deal would enable the United States to ship lethal cargo and would include shipments by air and land. He said it was unclear if US soldiers or other personnel would be permitted to travel through Russian territory or airspace. He said: 'They haven't asked us for it.'

(www.iht.com, 3 July 2009)

The Russian government has agreed to let American troops and weapons bound for Afghanistan fly over Russian territory, officials on both sides said on Friday [3 July]. The arrangement will provide an important new corridor for the US military as it escalates efforts to win the eight-year war. The agreement, to be announced when President Barack Obama visits [Russia on Monday and Tuesday 6–7 July] ... Under the new arrangement, officials said, planes carrying lethal equipment and troops will be allowed to make as many as ten flights a day, or thousands a year over Russia ... President Obama has ordered 21,000 more American troops to Afghanistan. Supply routes through Pakistan have been troubled by that nation's increasing volatility. Uzbekistan evicted American troops from a base in 2005 and Kyrgyzstan threatened to do the same, until American negotiators persuaded it to reverse itself, in a deal that increases the rent ... Russian officials ... point to their suspension of the delivery of an S-300 air defence system to Iran.

(www.iht.com, 4 July 2009)

4 July 2009.

Russian delegates have walked out of an OSCE session in Vilnius after it voted for a remembrance day for the victims of both Nazism and Stalinism. The pan-European security and democracy body passed a resolution equating the roles of the Soviet Union and Nazi Germany in starting World War II. Moscow's delegation boycotted the vote after failing to have it withdrawn ... The resolution, meant to mark the twentieth anniversary of the fall of the Iron Curtain, said that Nazi Germany and Stalin's Soviet Union brought genocide and crimes against humanity to Europe. It calls for making 23 August a day of remembrance for the victims of Stalinism and Nazism. In that day in 1939 Germany and the Soviet Union signed a pact that carved up Eastern Europe between the two countries ... Out of 385 assembly members, only eight voted against the resolution. Russia's delegates to the

OSCE session were strongly opposed to the resolution and left the hall immediately after it was passed.

(www.bbc.co.uk, 4 July 2009)

5 July 2009.

Newly elected Russian Orthodox Patriarch Kirill has led Sunday prayers with Istanbul Ecumenical Patriarch Bartholomew in a show of unity ... Orthodox churches are largely autonomous, but the Istanbul-based Patriarchate is considered first among equals. The Russian Orthodox Church claims 95 million out of the world's 250 million Orthodox and is the largest in the world.

(www.iht.com, 5 July 2009)

6–7 July 2009.

[On 6 July] US president Barack Obama and Russian president Dmitri Medvedev reached an outline agreement to cut back their nations' stockpiles of nuclear weapons. The 'joint understanding' signed in Moscow would see reductions of deployed nuclear warheads to below 1,700 each within seven years of a new treaty. The accord would replace the 1991 Start 1 Treaty, which expires in December [2009].

(www.bbc.co.uk, 6 July 2009)

The United States and Russia ... reached a preliminary agreement on cutting each country's stockpile of strategic nuclear weapons ... The so-called framework agreement was put together by negotiators as President Barack Obama arrived [in Moscow] for his first Russian–American summit meeting ... Negotiators would be instructed to craft a treaty that would cut strategic warheads for each side to between 1,500 and 1,675, down from the limit of 2,200 slated to take effect in 2012 under the Treaty of Moscow signed by President George W. Bush. The limit of delivery vehicles would be cut to between 500 and 1,100 from the 1,600 currently allowed under Start. The countries would be required to meet the limits with seven years ... [There] would be a revised and extended verification system that would otherwise expire with Start in December [2009] ... The United States currently has 1,198 land-based intercontinental ballistic missiles, submarine-based missiles and bombers, which together are capable of delivering 5,576 warheads, according to its most recent Start report in January [2009]. Because not all of them are 'operationally deployed', the Arms Control Association estimates that the United States currently deploys at least 2,200 strategic nuclear warheads. Russia reported in January that it has 816 delivery vehicles capable of delivering 3,909 warheads. While the number of deployed Russian strategic warheads is not known, the Arms Control Association estimated it between 2,000 and 3,000. Both sides also have more warheads that are in storage or awaiting dismantlement and the treaty discussions do not cover thousands more tactical nuclear weapons.

(www.iht.com, 6 July 2009)

The two countries said they then wanted to build momentum for a broader agreement to be negotiated starting next year [2010] to impose even deeper cuts in their nuclear arsenals and put the world on a path toward eliminating nuclear weapons altogether.

(*IHT*, 7 July 2009, p. 3)

The Russians are pushing for deeper cuts in delivery vehicles because their missiles generally fit more warheads than American missiles. American officials said this treaty would not address warheads stored in reserve, an issue the Russians have wanted to include in the past.

(www.iht.com, 7 July 2009)

According to the framework agreement: 'Within seven years after this treaty comes into force, and in future, the limits for strategic delivery systems should be within the range of 500 to 1,100 units and for warheads liked to them within the range of 1,500 to 1,675 units' ... Estimates of current nuclear stockpiles vary but the US-based *Bulletin of the Atomic Scientists* estimated that at the start of 2009 the United States had around 2,200 operationally deployed nuclear warheads and Russia around 2,790 ... Russia also agreed to let the United States fly troops and weapons across its territory to Afghanistan ... The pact, agreed after talks in the Kremlin between visiting US president Barack Obama and President Dmitri Medvedev, allows 4,500 US military flights annually over Russia at no extra charge ... The agreement will be valid for one year with unlimited automatic extensions if both sides agree ... The pact requires ratification by the Russian parliament.

(www.independent.com, 6 July 2009)

The framework agreement was signed by President Barack Obama and President Dmitri Medvedev on the first day of a bilateral summit at the Kremlin, which also saw Moscow agree to allow the United States to fly troops and weapons across its territory to Afghanistan ... The cuts announced only take the United States and Russia twenty-five operationally deployed warheads below the 1,700 to 2,200 range which both sides agreed to reach by 2012 under a treaty from 2002.

(www.thetimes.com, 6 July 2009)

On Monday [6 July] the two sides issued a joint statement indicating that they would continue to discuss the anti-missile system. They also agreed to undertake a joint assessment of any threats presented by Iran ... President Barack Obama announced an agreement to resume military-to-military contacts, which were suspended after the Georgia war in August [2008].

(*IHT*, 7 July 2009, p. 3)

'Mr Medvedev was pleased that that Mr Obama agreed that they should talk about both offensive and defensive weapons' (www.iht.com, 7 July 2009).
    'On the contentious issue of US plans to base parts of a missile defence shield

in Eastern Europe, the presidents merely said they had agreed to a joint study into ballistic missile threats and the creation of a data exchange centre' (www. bbc.co.uk, 7 July 2009).

> President Barack Obama ... said] that it was 'entirely legitimate for our discussions to talk about not only offensive weapons systems but also defensive' ... Mr Obama acknowledged that the planned shield in Poland and the Czech Republic was a 'point of deep concern and sensitivity to the Russian government'. A review that he had ordered of whether the system 'works or not' would be ready within weeks. Mr Obama promised to pass the assessment to President Dmitri Medvedev and said that it would be 'the subject of extensive negotiations'.
>
> (*The Times*, 7 July 2009, p. 31)

'Business leaders travelling with President Barack Obama want to use the visit to boost trade and investment. Russian trade with the United States was just $36 billion in 2008, far less than with big EU states' (www.ft.com, 6 July 2009).

'US companies are expected to announce $1.5 billion in deals during President Obama's visit this week, including a $500 million investment by Deere & Co., the farm machinery maker, and a $1 billion boost to investment by PepsiCo' (*FT*, 7 July 2009, p. 8).

> PepsiCo will invest $1 billion in Russia over the next three years and open its largest bottling plant in the world outside Moscow, the company said Monday [6 July] ... Boeing agreed to buy Russian titanium parts for its wide-body Dreamliner jet, and Deere & Company, the farm equipment maker, announced plans to invest in its operations in Russia. Both companies, like Pepsi, already do business here ... Deere is the beneficiary of an agricultural renaissance in Russia, created when investors made a business of modernizing former collective farms ... Exxon Mobil, which operates an oil development on Sakhalin Island off the coast of Siberia, said it would ramp up investments in coming years.
>
> (www.iht.com, 7 July 2009)

15 July 2009.

> A prominent human rights activist, Natalia Estimirova, has been found dead in the North Caucasus. She was bundled into a van and abducted as she left her home on Chechnya on Wednesday morning [15 July] ... Ms Estimirova had been investigating human rights abuses in Chechnya for the Memorial group. She had worked in the past with the activists Anna Politkovskaya, who was shot dead in 2006, and Stanislav Markelov, who was killed in January this year [2009] ... President Dmitri Medvedev expressed 'outrage' at the murder, and ordered a top level investigation ... In recent months she had been gathering evidence of a campaign of house-burnings by government-backed militias ... In 2007 she was awarded the inaugural Anna Politkovskaya Prize, and had also received awards from the Swedish and

European parliaments … Memorial says it believes that government security services of some nature must be involved in her killing.

(www.bbc.co.uk, 15 July 2009)

Natalia Estimirova had collected evidence of human rights abuses in Chechnya since the start of the second war there in 1999 … [The] killing comes as violence spirals in Russia's North Caucasus, with Ingushetia being particularly hard hit in recent months … President Dmitri Medvedev expressed condolences to her relatives and friends.

(www.iht.com, 15 July 2009)

'President Dmitri Medvedev expressed outrage and ordered an investigation' (*IHT*, 16 July 2009, p. 3).

Unlike many voices that rose against Russia's Chechen policies, Natalia Estimirova was not enamoured with the rebels. She lived through separatist self-rule in the late 1990s. She saw they were corrupt and brutal, too. She did not choose sides. Her work pointed elsewhere: to facts.

(*IHT*, 18 July 2009, p. 3)

In the first six months of this year [2009] the Russian human rights organization Memorial, where Natalia Estimirova worked, documented seventy-four kidnappings in Chechnya, compared with forty-two for all of 2008. Human rights groups have blamed Chechnya's president, Ramzan Kadyrov, and his security forces for the bulk of the disappearances, and the killing of Natalia Estimirova … [According to Memorial] abductions have evolved from a largely successful, if brutal, counter-insurgency tactic to a form of political repression by Mr Kadyrov's government … The rise in abductions in Chechnya comes even as most reported insurgent activity in Russia's volatile North Caucasus has moved outside of Chechnya, an analysis by the Washington-based Center for Strategic and International Studies has shown. In 2008, for example, the small region of Ingushetia surpassed Chechnya in the number of reported acts of insurgency-related violence, with 350 incidents, compared with 210 in Chechnya. In Dagestan, another republic, ethnic strife and police corruption are fuelling a low-grade insurgency. Overall, the centre reported, the number of violent acts in 2008 in the North Caucasus, with a combined population of 6.1 million, was about four times larger than in Colombia, with a population of 42 million … Alu Alkhanov, an interim president who preceded Mr Kadyrov, was compelled to leave Chechnya in 2007. In 2006 Anna Politkovskaya … was shot in the entryway of her Moscow apartment building. Two brothers from a rival Moscow-based Chechen family were killed, one in his car in Moscow last year [2008] and the other in Dubai [in the United Arab Emirates] in April. In January [13 January 2009] a former Chechen government insider who had publicly accused Mr Kadyrov of torture was shot dead in Vienna.

(*IHT*, 20 July 2009, p. 3)

16 July 2009.

Oleg Orlov (chairman of the human rights group Memorial): 'I am confident about who killed Natalia Estimirova ... His name is Ramzan Kadyrov, president of the Chechen republic. Ramzan was intimidating and insulting Natalia, and considered her his personal enemy. We do not know whether it was him personally who ordered her [murder] or ... his aides who wanted to please their boss. As far as President Dmitri Medvedev is concerned, it seems that he does not mind having a murderer as head of one of the Russian regions' ... Kadyrov vowed Thursday [16 July] that he would personally oversee the investigation and assure her killers were punished ... Medvedev said Thursday the murder was 'a very sad event', adding it was 'absolutely clear ... her murder is linked to her professional activities'.

(www.cnn.com, 16 July 2009)

President Dmitri Medvedev:

It is obvious to me that this murder is linked to her professional work and this work is necessary for any normal state. She did something very useful. She spoke the truth, she had a very open and sometimes very tough evaluation of what is happening in the country. And that is the value of human rights campaigners, even if they make those in power feel uncomfortable.

(www.bbc.co.uk, 16 July 2009)

President Dmitri Medvedev on Thursday [16 July] denied that Ramzan Kadyrov had a role in the murder, calling theories about such a possibility 'most primitive and most unacceptable for authorities' ... Mr Medvedev praised Natalia Estimirova's work – in marked contrast to his predecessor, Vladimir Putin, who remained silent for three days after the 2006 murder of Anna Politkovskaya, and then belittled her work.

(www.iht.com, 16 July 2009)

President Dmitri Medvedev: 'Those who committed this evil deed counted exactly on this most primitive and most unacceptable version for the authorities being voiced' ... Lev Ponamaryov (a human rights activist): 'This is either former or current security services or people connected to Kadyrov's regime.'

(*FT*, 17 July 2009, p. 8)

'President Dmitri Medvedev ... suggested ... her killing had been committed to discredit the Kremlin' (*Guardian*, 17 July 2009, p. 19).

17 July 2009.

Yesterday [17 July] the president of Chechnya, Ramzan Kadyrov ... said that he planned to sue ... Memorial ... in order to 'defend his dignity' ... Oleg Orlov insisted that he meant Mr Kadyrov carried broader responsibility. But Mr Kadyrov rejected that explanation.

(*The Independent*, 18 July 2009, p. 35)

'Oleg Orlov, Memorial chief ... later added that he meant Ramzan Kadyrov carried broader responsibility rather than ordering the killing' (*Guardian*, 18 July 2009, p. 22).

('Ramzan Kadyrov (interviewed by Radio Free Europe on 8 August): "Why should Kadyrov kill a woman [Natalia Estimirova] who was useful to no one? She was devoid of honour, merit and conscience"': *IHT*, 12 August 2009, p. 2. 'The leader [Zarema Sadulayeva] of a charity that helped children who had been scarred physically and emotionally by the conflict in Chechnya was abducted and killed along with her husband [Alik Djabrailov], officials said Tuesday [11 August] ... The charity [is called] Save the Generation': p. 3. 'In an interview published on Wednesday [23 September] in the Russian newspaper *Zavtra*, Ramzan Kadyrov accused Natalia Estimirova of fabricating charges of rights violations, saying "she played no role in Chechnya". He called Memorial, where Ms Estimirova also worked, "an organization created for the destruction of Russia"': www.iht.com, 25 September 2009.)

('Rights worker Oleg Orlov is on trial in Moscow, accused of defamation by Ramzan Kadyrov ... Oleg Orlov accused Mr Kadyrov of creating an atmosphere in which Chechen officials, whether under orders from the president or not, can torture, kidnap and murder with impunity. Oleg Orlov: "The current situation in the Chechen republic, where horrendous crimes violating human rights go systematically unpunished, has given me every basis for believing in the unconditional political guilt of Ramzan Kadyrov in the death of Natalia Estimirova"': www.iht.com, 25 September 2009; *IHT*, 26 September 2009, p. 3. 'Ramzan Kadyrov says he has chosen and trained his own successor as president: Adam Delimkhanov, a member of parliament who was accused this spring [2009] of killing ... in the United Arab Emirates ... one of Kadyrov's rivals ... Sulim Yamadayev was shot on 31 March ... Yamadayev was once a powerful Chechen military commander, but his troops and Mr Kadyrov's guards clashed last year [2008]. Federal authorities stripped him of his command, and he left Russia for Dubai in December [2008]': *IHT*, 26 September 2009, p. 3.)

18 July 2009. 'On Saturday [18 July] Alexander Cherkasov, a director of Memorial, said the group's Grozny office would be temporariy closed because "what we have been involves mortal danger"' (www.iht.com, 19 July 2009).

'Memorial has suspended its activities in Chechnya. Alexander Cherkasov: "We cannot risk the lives of our colleagues even if they are ready to carry on their work"' (www.bbc.co.uk, 19 July 2009).

('A Chechen separatist leader and a senior representative of the regional government said Friday [24 July] they had met for talks in an effort to bring stability to the war-scarred Russian region. Rebel envoy Akhmed Zakayev and Dukuvakha Abdurakhmanov, chairman of the Chechen regional parliament, gave few details about the meetings in the Norwegian capital [Oslo] ... It was the first political talks between the two sides in eight years ... Zakayev, who lives in London, said he represents the political faction of Chechnya's separatist movement and has no connection to the military wing that is spearheading the insurgency there … The meetings had been approved by prime minister Vladimir Putin': www.iht.com, 24 July 2009. 'Further talks will be held in London in ten days time. Six months ago Ramzan Kadyrov declared that political normalization could not be achieved without the involvement of Akhmed Zakayev … Two years ago Mr Zakayev declared himself prime minister of the rebel republic of Ichkeria after the president, Doku Umarov, described Western countries as the enemies of all Moslems, and announced his intention to install sharia [law] across the region … Chechnya has in recent years been more peaceful. In April [2009] President Dmitri Medvedev ordered the end of a decade-long "counter-terrorism operation", intended to pave the way for the withdrawal of thousands of troops. But since then several attacks have taken place … Fighting has also spread to neighbouring Dagestan and Ingushetia, where a violent Islamist insurgency is growing': www.bbc.co.uk, 24 July 2009.)

20 July 2009.

> Mikhail Kasyanov, the former prime minister, has for the first time disclosed details of a closed-door conversation he claims he had with Vladimir Putin in which the then president revealed political motives for the state's legal pursuit of Mikhail Khodorkovsky … Throwing his backing behind Mr Khodorkovsky's suit in the European Court of Human Rights, Mr Kasyanov said he had laid out in a affidavit filed to the court in Strasbourg last week Mr Putin's explanation in July 2003 for the rising state pressure on Mr Khodorkovsky and his Yukos oil company … Mikhail Kasyanov: 'He told me Khodorkovsky … was financing the Communist Party without his agreement' … Mr Kasyanov said he pressed Mr Putin for an explanation many times about the July 2003 arrest of Platon Lebedev, Mr Khodorkovsky's close associate, and about mounting state pressure on Mr Khodorkovsky as prosecutors began to investigate tax claims. Mr Putin had refused to answer, he said, but at one point in July 2003 in a private meeting inside Mr Putin's office in the Kremlin Palace, the president told him that Mr Khodorkovsky had crossed a line by financing the communists without his permission even as he was financing the liberal Yabloko and Union of Rightist Forces in line with Kremlin orders. 'He did not say any more' … Mr Kasyanov's statement could add weight to Mr Khodorkovsky's appeal against the Russian government in the European Court of Human Rights claiming that his arrest in [October] 2003 was politically motivated. It could also strengthen the case lodged in the same court by Yukos shareholders claiming they had been stripped of their holdings in the oil company via the government's pursuit of multi-billion-dollar back tax claims which led to its bankruptcy. The European Court of Human Rights accepted the case in January [2009] despite the fact that Yukos had already been liquidated under Russian law, and a first set of hearings is set for November. Mr Kasyanov, now an opposition politician, has stated publicly before that he believes the case against Mr Khodorkovsky is politically motivated. But he has never before disclosed the reasons for that conviction.
>
> (www.ft.com, 22 July 2009)

('Convicted of tax evasion and fraud in 2005, Mikhail Khodorkovsky now faces a fresh set of charges that add up to the supposed theft of $30 billion ... The new indictment ... boils down to a single accusation: that Mr Khodorkovsky ... and his deputy, Platon Lebedev, were part of an "organized criminal gang" that stole 350 million tonnes of oil from their company between 1998 and 2003. If convicted, Mr Khodorkovsky, whose first sentence ends in 2011, could face an additional twenty-two years in jail ... The trial is now in its ninth month ... In 2003 Mr Khodorkovsky started to finance opposition political parties ... As Mr Khodorkovsky built Yukos, the state bureaucracy and offshore zones were exploited ... In 1998, on Mr Khodorkovsky's birthday, Vladimir Petukov, the mayor of Nefteyugansk, who had complained about Yukos's failure to pay its debts to the town and its workers, was shot and killed. Then there was the 2002 disappearance of Sergei Gorin, one-time manager of the Tambov branch of Menatep, and his wife Olga. To date their bodies have not been found, but a Moscow court has convicted one of Mr Khodorkovsky's closest partners, Leonid Nevzlin, now living in Israel, of ordering their murder. Mr Khodorkovsky, Mr Nevzlin and their lawyers deny any involvement in the crimes': *IHT*, 21 November 2009, pp. 1–2. 'Prime minister Vladimir Putin ... has recently been stepping up the criticism, comparing Mikhail Khodorkovsky to Al Capone and telling a national television call-in show that the oil executive had ordered contract murders' (www.iht.com, 22 April 2010). 'In a recent interview ... prime minister Vladimir Putin ... went out of his way to compare Mikhail Khodorkovsky to Al Capone and implicate him in a murder in the 1990s of which he has never been formally accused': www.economist.com, 22 April 2010.)

1 August 2009. Former Danish prime minister Anders Fogh Rasmussen becomes the new Nato secretary-general. Jaap de Hoop Scheffer was his predecessor.

3 August 2009.

The Kremlin replaced the commander of Russia's strategic nuclear weapons yesterday [3 August] – the latest in a series of top-level departures in the armed forces. President Dmitri Medvedev issued a decree removing General Nikolai Solovtsov as head of the missile forces. He is replaced by General Andrei Shvaichenko, fifty-six, who is currently serving as first deputy commander of the strategic missile group. The Kremlin gave no reason for the move. Analysts said it was unlikely to be connected to any larger shake-up within the missile forces since General Solovtsov had reached retirement age [sixty] in February [2009]. However, the replacement is the latest in a series of high-level departures from the top ranks of the military as the Kremlin pushes ahead with an ambitious reform to transform the military into a smaller, more mobile force able to fight three local or regional conflicts simultaneously. The plan envisages cutting the officer corps from 350,000 to fewer than 200,000 by 2012, ending conscription and modernizing equipment. There are few backers for the reform among Russia's military chiefs. Several leading opponents have already lost their jobs, most recently in April when Mr Medvedev fired the powerful head of Russia's military intelligence. Only one, General Vladimir Shamanov, commander of the airborne forces, has spoken out in public in favour of the plan ... General Solovtsov's replacement comes just weeks after Russia's long-range nuclear rocket programme was plunged into crisis by the departure of its top missile designer, Yuri Solomonov. Mr Solomonov resigned after a string of failed launches of the Bulava, a new submarine-launched missile.

(*FT*, 4 August 2009, p. 6)

A pair of nuclear-powered Russian attack submarines has been patrolling off the eastern seaboard of the United States in recent days, a rare mission ... [but] not the larger submarines that can launch intercontinental ballistic missiles ... The submarine patrols come as Moscow tries to shake off the embarrassment of the latest failed test of the Bulava missile, a long-range weapon that was test-fired from a submarine in the Arctic on 15 July. The failed test was the sixth since 2005.

(www.iht.com, 5 August 2009)

'[Russia announced on 5 August that it has] resumed the submarine patrols after restarting strategic bomber patrol flights in 2007' (www.iht.com, 5 August 2009).

The Akula-class nuclear-powered submarines, which are normally equipped with surface-loaded cruise missiles and surface-to-air missiles, have stayed in international waters ... These are not the class of submarines that can launch intercontinental nuclear missiles. It has been years since Russia operated near the seaboard, thousands of miles from home ports.

(www.cnn.com, 5 August 2009)

25 August 2009.

Russia moved to bolster its ties with Mongolia yesterday [25 August], signing deals to mine uranium and manage the railways in [Mongolia] ... Russia's president, Dmitri Medvedev, signed a five-year agreement transferring to Russia management rights to Mongolia's railways which until now have been run jointly by the two states.

(*FT*, 26 August 2009, p. 6)

Rosatom, the Russian state-owned nuclear power company whose rapid international expansion has outstripped the country's capacity to supply fuel for the power plants it builds, won a major concession Tuesday [25 August] to mine uranium in Mongolia. The deal to form a joint venture will give the company access to a deposit that could produce about a quarter of Russia's total current uranium output. The accord was struck during a state visit to Mongolia by President Dmitri Medvedev of Russia after the two countries agreed on a settlement for $150 million in Soviet-era debt ... While best known for its decade-old contract to build a nuclear power plant in Iran, the company is also active in China, India and Eastern Europe ... In 2008

Russian state-owned interests in uranium mines were consolidated into a subsidiary of Rosatom, Atomredmedzoloto (ARMZ), which is now on a buying spree. The deal Tuesday between ARMZ and a Mongolian uranium mining company, MonAtom, foresees exploration and mining in the Dornad deposit.

(IHT, 26 August 2009, p. 15)

September 2009.

Despite a recession that knocked down global arms sales last year [2008], the United States expanded its role as the world's leading weapons supplier, increasing its share to more than two-thirds of all foreign armaments deals, according to a new Congressional study. The United States signed weapons agreements valued at $37.8 billion in 2008, or 68.4 per cent of all business in the global arms bazaar, significantly up from American sales of $25.4 billion the year before [2007]. Italy was a distant second, with $3.7 billion in worldwide weapons agreements in 2008, while Russia was third with $3.5 billion in arms sales last year – down considerably from the $10.8 billion in weapons deals signed by Moscow in 2007 ... The value of global arms sales in 2008 was $55.2 billion, a drop of 7.6 per cent in 2007 and the lowest total for international weapons agreements since 2005 ... The report notes that while Moscow continues to have China and India as its main weapons clients, Russia's new focus is on arms sales to Latin America, in particular to Venezuela.

(www.iht.com, 6 September 2009)

President Hugo Chavez of Venezuela ... has visited Russia eight times as president, often seeking to procure Russian-made arms and weapons systems. Russia and Venezuela have in recent years signed agreements worth over $4 billion for deliveries of fighter jets, helicopters and automatic weapons, among other systems. In a visit last year [2008] Mr Chavez signed an agreement for a $1 billion loan from Russia for military development.

(IHT, 11 September 2009, p. 3)

President Hugo Chavez said Friday [11 September] that Venezuela had reached an agreement to buy short-range missiles from Russia ... Mr Chavez did not specify the type of Russian-made missiles that Venezuela hoped to buy, but he said that they had a range of about 186 miles ... So far this decade Venezuela has announced plans to buy more than $4 billion in weapons from Russia.

(www.iht.com, 13 September 2009)

Russia has agreed to lend Venezuela over $2 billion to purchase tanks and advanced anti-aircraft missiles ... President Hugo Chavez said on Sunday [13 September] the purchases agreed upon in a trip to Moscow last week included ninety-two tanks and an S-300 missile system [with a range of about 125 miles or 200 kilometres] that can shoot down fighter jets and cruise missiles. Two years ago Russian agreed to sell the same S-300 system to Iran but has dragged its feet over delivering the weapons amid US and Israeli concerns they will be used to defend Iran's nuclear installations ... In recent years Venezuela has bought over $4 billion in weapons from Russia including twenty-four Sukhoi jets ... Chavez said Venezuela was now buying ninety-two Russian T-72 tanks along with several types of missiles to build an air defence system ... Russia signed a contract in 2007 to supply Iran with the S-300 system. Last week Russia dismissed rumours that a ship supposedly loaded with timber that went missing in the Atlantic in July had really been carrying a cargo of S-300s for Iran.

(www.iht.com, 14 September 2009)

Over recent years Venezuela has signed over $4 billion worth of weapons contracts with Russia, including twenty-four Sukhoi fighter jets, numerous combat helicopters and 100,000 Kalashnikov assault rifles. Last November [2008] the two states held joint exercises in the Caribbean Sea, close to US territorial waters.

(www.bbc.co.uk, 14 September 2009)

11 September 2009.

President Dmitri Medvedev is ordering new restrictions on the sale of beer and similar beverages in what appears to be his first effort to battle Russia's rampant alcoholism. Medvedev has publicly decried Russia's drinking problem and its effect on the nation's well-being. The planned new restrictions would bar the sale of beer in cans or bottles larger than one-third of a litre (about 12 ounces). The new rules apply to 'light alcohol' beverages but not to wine, vodka or other hard liquors. A study published in June [2009] in *The Lancet* medical journal found that drinking has caused more than half of deaths among Russians aged fifteen to fifty-four since the 1991 Soviet collapse.

(www.iht.com, 11 September 2009)

'On Thursday [10 September] President Dmitri Medvedev published a startlingly bleak article on a Russian website, lamenting its totalitarian past, weak democracy, ineffective economy, endemic corruption and a "pandemic" of alcoholism' (www.bbc.co.uk, 12 September 2009).

President Dmitri Medvedev (10 September): 'An ineffective economy, semi-Soviet social sphere, weak democracy, negative demographic trends and an unstable Caucasus. These are very big problems even for a state like Russia ... Russia's political system will be open, flexible and complex' (*FT*, 12 September 2009, p. 6).

Prime minister Vladimir Putin has given the clearest indication yet that he might run again for the presidency. Mr Putin did not commit himself but hinted that he is thinking of coming back in 2012 when President Dmitri

Medvedev's current term expires ... Prime minister Putin (11 September): 'Did we compete against each other in 2007? No, we did not. And so we won't in 2012 either. We will reach an agreement. We are people of the same blood, with the same political views ... When it comes to 2012, we will work it out together, taking into account the current reality, our own plans, the shape of the political landscape, and the state of United Russia, the ruling party' ... In the past year the presidential term has been extended to six years.

(www.bbc.co.uk, 12 September 2009)

12–13 September 2009.

It is a symbol of global warming and a potentially lucrative new trade route between Europe and Asia. Two German container ships have successfully navigated the Russian North East Passage across Arctic waters from the Pacific for the first time ... The merchant vessel *Fraternity* passed Novaya Zemlya, regarded by Russia as the official exit point of the Northern Sea Route, at the weekend [12–13 September]. Its sister ship *Foresight* is due to follow in a few days after being delayed by bad weather in Siberia. Their journey to reach the Dutch port of Rotterdam by late September will complete a crossing that started in Ulsan, South Korea. The ships ... [with] cargo destined for a Siberian power plant ... set off for the Russian port of Vladivostok on 23 July. They arrived two days later but ... the ships waited for a month before Russian authorities gave them clearance to continue ... Ice sheets and weather patterns make the North East Passage passable to shipping for only six to eight weeks without icebreakers.

(*The Times*, 14 September 2009, p. 35)

This route is usually frozen but rising temperatures in the region caused by global warming have melted much of the ice allowing large ships through ... Both ships left South Korea in late July, negotiating the passage off north-eastern Siberia behind two Russian icebreakers ... The passage became passable without icebreakers in 2005 ... Scientists estimate that the last time that the North East Passage was as ice free as it is now was between 5,000 and 7,000 years ago.

(www.bbc.co.uk, 14 September 2009)

'Two German cargo ships broke new ground by completing much of the route with minimal icebreaker support' (www.iht.com, 16 October 2009).

17–20 September 2009.

President Barack Obama announced on Thursday [17 September] that he will scrap former President George W. Bush's planned missile defence system in Poland and the Czech Republic and instead deploy a reconfigured system aimed at intercepting shorter-range Iranian missiles ... The new system his administration is developing would deploy smaller SM-3 missiles, at first aboard ships and later probably either in southern Europe or

Turkey, officials said … The administration's four-phase plan would deploy existing SM-3 interceptors using the sea-based Aegis system in 2011, then after more testing deploy in 2015 an improved version of the interceptors both on ships and on land along with advanced sensors. A still more advanced version of the interceptors would be deployed in 2018 and yet another generation in 2020, the latter with more capacity to counter possible future intercontinental missiles. By doing so, officials said they would be getting the first defences actually in place seven years earlier than the Bush plan, which envisioned deploying in 2018 the bigger ground-based interceptors that are still being developed … Mr Obama called the leaders of both Poland and the Czech Republic before making his announcement and said he had 'reaffirmed our deep and close ties' … He also reiterated America's commitment under Article V of the Nato charter that states that an attack on one member is an attack on the entire alliance.

(www.iht.com, 17 September 2007)

'President Barack Obama … is not abandoning the two anti-missile bases built on American soil in the Bush years, one in Alaska and one in California' (www.iht.com, 18 September 2009).

The Obama administration said it planned to deploy the SM-3s in as many as three land-based sites in Europe starting in 2015 and offered Poland and the Czech Republic the chance to host those missiles … And the Obama plan calls for dozens and eventually possibly hundreds of the smaller interceptors, not just the ten larger ones included in Mr Bush's plan. Moreover, advisers to Mr Obama said they hoped to upgrade the SM-3 interceptors so that by 2020 they could be used to knock down intercontinental missiles as well as the shorter-range missiles now being encountered. And officials said they would continue to develop the ground-based interceptors from the Bush plan on the chance they might be needed later.

(www.iht.com, 18 September 2009)

After a comprehensive [sixty-day] review, President Barack Obama had decided to accept the advice of both the defence secretary, Robert Gates, and the [Joint] Chiefs of Staff … Mr Obama said that the latest intelligence suggested that threat of long-range missile attacks from Iran had receded but the threat of short- or medium-range attacks was a real one.

(www.thetimes.co.uk, 17 September 2009)

'Defence secretary Robert Gates was joined at the Thursday briefing by general James Cartwright, vice chairman of the Joint Chiefs of Staff and the point man for the missile defence shield system' (www.cnn.com, 17 September 2009).

'President Barack Obama said the [Bush] plan was scrapped, in part because … the United States has concluded that Iran is less focused on developing the kind of long-range missiles for which the system was originally developed' (www.independent.co.uk, 17 September 2009).

President Barack Obama said the change ... was based on an 'updated intelligence assessment' about Iran's ability to hit Europe with missiles ... [Iran's] 'short- and medium-range' missiles pose the most current threat, he said, and 'this new ballistic missile defence will address' that threat.

(www.cnn.com, 17 September 2009)

'America now says the Iranians are working more on short- and medium-range missiles than on long-range ones' (www.economist.com, 17 September 2009).

'The US president said "updated intelligence" on Iran's existing short- and medium-range missiles showed they were "capable of reaching Europe"' (www.guardian.co.uk, 17 September 2009).

An unspecified fresh intelligence assessment concludes that the earliest Iran could develop long-range missiles – which President George W. Bush's shield was designed to defeat – is 2018 rather than 2015 as previously reckoned. Until then the real Iranian threat comes from hundreds of short- and medium-range missiles. So instead of having a large radar in the Czech Republic and powerful interceptors in Poland, President Barack Obama says he will reconfigure the shield to establish smaller radars closer to Iran (perhaps in Turkey) and to deploy smaller interceptor missiles on board Aegis warships. By 2015 more capable interceptors would be employed at unspecified sites on land and by 2018 these would be replaced by even more capable ones that would provide coverage for all of Europe. Moreover, improvements in sensor technology and computer networks mean that the system would not need a large radar in Central Europe. Instead the sensors would be mobile and dispersed on land, at sea, on aircraft and in space.

(www.economist.com, 19 September 2009)

President Barack Obama:

Our new missile defence architecture in Europe will provide stronger, smarter and swifter defences of American forces and America's allies. It is more comprehensive than the previous programme; it deploys capabilities that are proven and cost effective, and it sustains and builds upon our commitment to protect the US homeland ... This new approach will provide capabilities sooner, build on proven systems and offer greater defences against the threat of missile attack than the 2007 European missile defence system.

(www.thetimes.co.uk, 17 September 2009; www.iht.com, 17 September 2009; www.cnn.com, 17 September)

Defence secretary Robert Gates told reporters that the news system would actually put defences in place sooner than the Bush plan and noted that land-based interceptor missiles may yet be located in Europe, including possibly in Poland and the Czech Republic. To say that the Obama administration was scrapping missile defence, Mr Gates said, is 'misrepresenting the reality of what we are doing'. He added that the new configuration 'provides a better defence capability' than the one he had recommended to Mr Bush ... The Pentagon chief was first appointed by Mr Bush.

(www.iht.com, 7 September 2009)

The new system will have 'hundreds' of missile interceptors, said General James Cartwright, deputy chairman of the Joint Chiefs of Staff and the Pentagon's main point man on the issue. It will also have mobile radars, including some in space ... The new plan includes three types of missiles to shoot down incoming threats – Patriot missiles, which defend a single location; SM-3 interceptors, which he said could protect 'a general area like the area from Philadelphia to Washington DC'; and 'large ground-based interceptors in Alaska and California'.

(www.cnn.com, 17 September 2009)

General James Cartwright, vice chairman of the Joint Chiefs of Staff, and US Defence secretary Robert Gates added that, at a later stage, the United States would be looking to Europe as a base for shorter-range interceptors than the old system proposed – and that the Czech Republic and Poland would be contenders to host them. But General Cartwright signalled that the Bush-era push to locate a radar in the Czech Republic – which he said would have 'a very deep peering capability into Russia' – would not be revived, arguing that a radar would probably be based in the Caucasus and would point firmly south. In the shorter term, he said, the United States was looking at deploying three ships with Aegis missile interceptors in the Mediterranean and the North Sea by 2011. Both men argued that the news system would cover all of Europe.

(*FT*, 18 September 2009, p. 7)

'[The Bush plan was to] install an advanced radar called X-band in the Czech Republic. The radar has the potential to "see" 360 degrees and deep into the European part of Russia, where many of its missile silos are based' (www.iht. com, 18 September 2009).

'The administration has tried to sweeten the pill by reiterating a promise to place a battery of Patriot short-range missiles to defend Warsaw' (www.economist.com, 17 September 2009).

'The Polish government has been assured by the Americans that promises of training with Patriot missile batteries and help in modernizing the Polish military remained valid' (www.guardian.co.uk, 17 September 2009).

'Defence secretary Robert Gates said the United States would base smaller SM-3 missiles on Polish soil if the Polish government still wanted them' (*IHT*, 18 September 2009, p. 3).

US officials insist that despite yesterday's decision, they will deploy Patriot missiles on Polish territory that can shoot down incoming rockets. In addition, the United States said yesterday [17 September] it wanted to go ahead with the deployment of other interceptors in Poland and the Czech Republic at a later date.

(FT, 18 September 2009, p. 7)

'Russian officials who spoke to reporters on Friday [18 September] ... did indicate that the Kremlin would withdraw its threat to base short-range missiles on Russia's western border, in Kaliningrad' (www.iht.com, 18 September 2009).

'The Kremlin cited its understanding of what the United States promised at the end of the Cold War, to not deploy weapons systems in former Warsaw Pact countries, although American officials have denied such an explicit commitment' (www.iht.com, 18 September 2009; *IHT*, 19 September 2009, p. 3).

Nato secretary-general Anders Fogh Rasmussen (18 September): 'I would like Russia and Nato agree to carry out a joint review of the new twenty-first century security challenges, to serve as a firm basis for our future co-operation ... We should explore the potential for linking the US, Nato and Russian missile defence systems at an appropriate time.'

(www.iht.com, 18 September 2009)

'The practical implications of Mr Rasmussen's comment on co-operation over missile defence were not clear. The [Nato] alliance and Russia already co-operate on short-range missile defence systems' (*IHT*, 19 September 2009, p. 3).

US Defence secretary Robert Gates:

There is now no strategic missile defence in Europe. In December 2006, just days after becoming secretary of defence, I recommended to President George W. Bush that the United States place ten ground-based interceptors in Poland and an advanced radar in the Czech Republic. This system was designed to identify and destroy up to about five long-range missiles potentially armed with nuclear warheads fired from the Middle East – the greatest and most likely danger being from Iran. At the time it was the best plan based on technology and threat assessment available ... Under the previous programme there would have been no missile defence system able to protect against Iranian missiles until at least 2017 – and likely much later. Last week President Obama – on my recommendation and with the advice of his national security team and the unanimous support of our senior military leadership – decided to discard that plan in favour of a vastly more suitable approach ... Those who say we are scrapping missile defence in Europe are either misinformed or misrepresenting what we are doing. This shift has even been distorted as some sort of concession to Russia, which has fiercely opposed the old plan. Russia's attitude and possible reaction played no part in my recommendation to the president on this issue. Of course, considering Russia' past hostility toward American missile defence in Europe, if Russia's leaders embrace this plan, then that will be an unexpected – and welcome – change of policy on their part ... I am often characterized as 'pragmatic'. I believe this is a very pragmatic proposal. I have found since taking this post that when it comes to missile defence, some hold a view bordering on theology that regards any change or any cancellation of a programme as abandonment or even breaking faith ... We are strengthening – not scrapping – missile defence in Europe.

('A better missile defence for a safer Europe', www.iht.com, 20 September 2009; *IHT*, 21 September 2009, p. 8)

'President Barack Obama told CBS television (on 20 September): "The Russians don't make determinations about what our defence posture is. If the by-product of it is that the Russian feel a little less paranoid ... then that is a bonus"' (www.bbc.co.uk, 20 September 2009).

The announcement came on 17 September, the seventieth anniversary of the Soviet invasion of Poland ... The announcement also came as Russia conducted large-scale military manoeuvres with Belarus ... Poland is now one of the very few places in Europe that prefers former President George W. Bush to President Barack Obama ... Article 5 of the 1949 North Atlantic Treaty is clear: 'The parties agree that an armed attack against one or more of them in Europe or North America shall be considered an attack against them all ... [and will trigger the] use of armed force in collective self-defence.'

(www.iht.com, 20 September 2009; *IHT*, 21 September 2009, p. 9)

Russia said Saturday [19 September] it will scrap a plan to deploy missiles near Poland since Washington has dumped a planned missile shield in Eastern Europe ... Russia's deputy defence minister Vladimir Popovkin ... [said] that President Barack Obama's move has made the deployment of Iskander short-range missiles in the Kaliningrad region unnecessary ... Popovkin later added, however, that the final decision on the subject can only be made by President Dmitri Medvedev ... Medvedev has not yet spoken on the issue ... Medvedev hailed Obama's decision as a 'responsible move'. Prime minister Vladimir Putin ... has praised Obama's decision but challenged the United States to do more by cancelling Cold War-era restrictions on trade with Russia and facilitating Moscow's entry to the WTO [in a customs union with Belarus and Kazakhstan].

(www.iht.com, 20 September 2009)

20 September 2009.

After ... the fall of the Berlin Wall ... Germany drove full-speed towards reunification. Mikhail Gorbachev was against it – and so, he learnt, were Margaret Thatcher and France's President François Mitterrand. But he discovered that the Western leaders were relying on him to block the process. He says: 'They insisted unification should not go on, that the process should be stopped. I asked them if they had any suggestions. They had only one – that somebody else should pull their chestnuts out of the fire' ... He says they wanted him to say no and send troops, then adds: 'That would be irresponsible. They were mistaken. They were mistaken [repeated].'

(www.bbc.co.uk, 20 September 2009)

9 October 2009.

United Russia's leaders convened a special meeting this month [on 9 October] with senior Chinese Communist Party officials ... in the border city of Suifenhe, China, northwest of Vladivostok ... Alexander Zhukov, a deputy prime minister and senior Putin aide, declared at the meeting: 'The practical experience they have should be intensely studied' ... Mr Zhukov invited President Hu Jintao to United Russia's convention, in November in St Petersburg. The meeting in Suifenhe capped several months of increased contacts between the political parties. In the spring [of 2009] a high level United Russia delegation visited Beijing for several days of talks, and United Russia announced that it would open an office in Beijing for its research arm.

(www.iht.com, 18 October 2009; *IHT*, 20 October 2009, p. 3)

10 October 2009.

Russia's president [on 10 October] congratulated President Barack Obama for winning the Nobel Peace Prize [on 9 October] ... President Dmitri Medvedev: 'I hope this decision would serve as an additional incentive for our common work to form a new climate in world politics and promote initiatives which are fundamentally important for global security.'

(www.iht.com, 10 October 2009)

12 October 2009.

United Russia swept regional elections across Russia, strengthening its political power nationwide while also dominating the voting for the Moscow city government ... Opposition leaders complained about electoral fraud, and disturbances were reported in the North Caucasus region of Dagestan because of problems at the voting sites ... In Derbent, in Dagestan, one-third of the polling places never opened. The town's mayor, who supports the Kremlin, won with 68 per cent of the vote ... Votes were held Sunday in seventy-five of Russia's eighty-three regions, for positions varying from mayor to representative in the local legislatures ... United Russia called its nationwide success a vote of confidence in its economic policies ... Among the more than 7,000 local elections were races conducted in Chechnya, Ingushetia and other regions of the Caucasus ... Elections to the Moscow city government were the most closely watched. With 99 per cent of the vote counted on Monday [12 October] United Russia, with 66 per cent of the vote, was poised to win thirty-two of the thirty-five seats in the legislature; the Communist Party, with 13 per cent of the vote, was expected to win three ... Yabloko did not meet the 7 per cent threshold of votes necessary for a seat. Ilya Yashin, a former youth leader of Yabloko who joined the more radical opposition movement Solidarity, was taken off the ballot in Moscow for the city Duma, the local legislature, along with other Solidarity members, including the party's leader, Boris Nemtsov, for reported irregularities.

(www.iht.com, 13 October 2009)

United Russia swept regional elections, calling it a vote of confidence in its economic policies during the financial crisis. But opposition leaders complained about electoral fraud ... Among the reports of electoral fraud being circulated by the Communist Party and Solidarity was an allegation that ballots had been stuffed by people who cast them at multiple polling sites by using the password 'Luzhkov' ... [Moscow] mayor Yuri Luzhkov [is] a member of United Russia.

(*IHT*, 13 October 2009, p. 3)

14 October 2009.

Opposition parties walked out of parliament and threatened to raise mass demonstrations in protest at local elections they say were rigged. Official results showed ... United Russia winning nearly every poll by a wide margin. Some 135 out of 450 MPs walked out of the Duma in a rare show of anger ... Vladimir Zhirinovsky, head of the ultra-nationalist Liberal Democratic Party, demanded a recount at every polling station, after accusing United Russia of having 'fraudulently appropriated' his party's votes ... The head of the Communist Party, Gennadi Zyuganov, said his members would boycott the Duma until they were granted a meeting with President Dmitri Medvedev ... The third opposition party in the Duma, Just Russia, also joined in the protest. All three parties are normally reluctant to defy the Kremlin ... In the vote for Moscow City Council, election officials said United Russia won 66 per cent of the vote, taking all but three of the council's thirty-five seats.

(www.bbc.co.uk, 14 October 2009)

'It was the first time in nine years that all factions except the main party, United Russia, had walked out in protest' (*IHT*, 15 October 2009, p. 3). 'Before the vote regional officials were told that they would be held accountable if United Russia fared poorly. They seemed to respond by doing whatever they could to ensure overwhelming victory, and preserve their jobs' (*IHT*, 24 October 2009).

16 October 2009. 'Two days after they walked out of parliament ... the Liberal Democrats and Just Russia ... returned on Friday [16 October ... The Communists did not' (www.iht.com, 17 October 2009).

A Russian-led rapid reaction force, portrayed as the Kremlin's answer to Nato, held its first war games yesterday [16 October] in Kazakhstan ... Seven thousand troops participated in the war games, the first by the force formed this year by the Collective Security Organization [CSTO], a loose security grouping between Russia, Armenia, Belarus, Kazakhstan, Kyrgyzstan, Tajikistan and Uzbekistan ... But Uzbekistan refused to join the war games ... Belarus ... was also absent ... Russia launched plans to create the rapid reaction force last year after defeating Georgia in a war [in August 2008] ... CSTO countries did not openly support Russian military action in

Georgia or follow Russia in recognizing South Ossetia and Abkhazia after the war.

(*FT*, 17 October 2009, p. 7)

('Over the past few weeks Russia, in a new burst of military assertiveness, said through the secretary of its national security council, Nikolai Patrushev, that it was lowering the threshold for the preventative use of its nuclear weapons to include, beyond big wars, "aggressors" using conventional weapons in regional or local conflicts. At the same time the State Duma ... approved a bill expanding the possibilities of using troops abroad': *IHT*, 3 November 2009, p. 2. '[A] new military doctrine authorizes the use of nuclear weapons in local wars': www.iht. com, 8 November 2009.)

21–23 October 2009.

[US] Vice President Joseph Biden ... on Wednesday [21 October] announced an agreement to station interceptors from President Barack Obama's reformulated missile defence system on the territory of [Poland] ... The deal to base here some of the smaller, mobile SM-3 interceptors [is] at the heart of Mr Obama's new missile defence plan ... Mr Biden plans to fly later in the week to the Czech Republic ... to discuss basing elements of the Obama missile shield there ... The new system envisions existing SM-3 interceptors on Aegis-equipped ships in the Mediterranean Sea and elsewhere by 2011, and on land in Eastern Europe by 2015. A more advanced system would be employed by 2018 and another generation, theoretically capable of shooting down intercontinental missiles, by 2010. The SM-3 interceptors that would be based in Poland would be deployed in 2018, according to a National Security Council official travelling with Mr Biden, roughly the same timeframe the Bush interceptors would have been stationed here ... It was too early to determine how many of the SM-3 interceptors would be deployed here. The Polish parliament needs to ratify the plan ... Mr Biden plans to fly later in the day to Romania ... and then after a day of talks will move on to Prague before returning to Washington on Friday night [23 October].

(www.iht.com, 21 October 2009)

Mariusz Handlik, chief foreign policy adviser to the Polish president, Lech Kaczynski ... said Tuesday [20 October] that the United States would supply Poland with ground-to-air Patriot missiles ... This has been a longstanding demand by Poland, which wants these missiles to upgrade its air defence.

(*IHT*, 21 October 2009, pp. 1, 3)

'Prime minister Donald Tusk has declared his country ready to take part in a revised US missile defence plan ... Poland will host a small US base equipped with short-range missiles' (www.bbc.co.uk, 21 October 2009).

The Czech Republic agreed on Friday [23 October] to host elements of the reformulated American missile defence system after Vice President Joe

Biden visited [Prague] ... Prime minister Jan Fischer said that his country would participate in the new anti-missile shield, although neither he nor Mr Biden gave details ... The US Vice President said that a senior defence team would visit Prague next month [November] to discuss how to structure that participation ... [President Barack Obama's] administration did not inform Polish and Czech leaders of the policy shift until just before the announcement ... As news of his decision was beginning to leak last month [September] Mr Obama scrambled to reach Mr Fischer by telephone to tell him first.

(*IHT*, 24 October 2009, p. 3)

'Mr Obama scrambled to reach Mr Fischer by telephone after midnight to tell him first' (www.iht.com, 23 October 2009).

22 October 2009.

Russian rights group Memorial has won the European Parliament's annual Sakharov Prize, in memory of murdered activist Natalia Estimirova ... Memorial campaigns against abuses in countries of the former Soviet Union ... The prize, named after the late Soviet dissident Andrei Sakharov, went to Memorial head Oleg Orlov and the group's activists Sergei Kovalov and Lyudmila Alexeyeva ... The Sakharov Prize for Freedom of Thought, now in its twenty-first year, comes with a cash reward of Euro 50,000 ($75,000). It will be awarded at a ceremony in Strasburg in December.

(www.bbc.co.uk, 22 October 2009)

The Russian government Thursday [22 October] dropped a $22.5 billion lawsuit against Bank of New York Mellon after the company agreed to pay $14 million to settle a decade-old money laundering case involving a former executive. The lawsuit stems from a scandal in which a Bank of New York vice president and her husband were convicted of illegally wiring $7.5 billion from Russia into accounts at the bank in the 1990s. The Russian customs service went into court in 2007 to claim lost tax revenue on those transfers, plus damages. Bank of New York, which later merged with Mellon, was never charged with any wrongdoing in the United States.

(*IHT*, 23 October 2009, p. 23)

Bank of New York Mellon has agreed without admission of liability to pay $14 million to cover the trial costs – the same amount paid by the bank to the United States in 2005 under a prosecution case related to the money laundering scandal.

(*FT*, 23 October 2009, p. 25)

28 October 2009.

The International AIDS Society urged Russia to do more to prevent the spread of HIV among an estimated 2 million drug users ... It is believed there are now at least a million people infected with HIV. This represents a dramatic increase over the past decade. The vast majority are people under the age of thirty. Most were infected because they share needles for injecting heroin. According to some estimates, there are almost 2 million intravenous drug users in the country – the results of the large quantities of heroin flowing from Afghanistan into Russia.

(www.bbc.co.uk, 28 October 2009)

30 October 2009.

President Dmitri Medvedev has made an outspoken attack on those seeking to rehabilitate Joseph Stalin. Millions of Soviet citizens died under Stalin's rule and Mr Medvedev said it was not possible to justify those who exterminated their own people. He also warned against efforts to falsify and defend repression. Some Russian politicians have recently tried to portray Stalin in a more positive light. Under President Medvedev's predecessor, current prime minister Vladimir Putin, Stalin was often promoted as an efficient leader who turned the Soviet Union into a superpower. Mr Medvedev made the unusually critical comments in a videoblog on the Kremlin's website. It appeared on the day the country is supposed to honour millions of people killed under Stalin's brutal regime ... Mr Medvedev said it was impossible to imagine the scale of repression under Stalin when whole groups of people were eliminated and even stripped of their right to be buried. The president said there were attempts to justify the repression of the past, and he warned against the falsification of history. All this flies in the face of the current trend to promote Stalin as an effective manager and a leader who transformed the Soviet Union. Under Mr Putin the order was given for school history books to be rewritten, highlighting Stalin's achievements. In Moscow there is now even a Stalin-themed café and a Metro station with one of Stalin's famous slogans on its walls. In northern Russia a historian investigating crimes committed by the former Soviet dictator was recently arrested.

(www.bbc.co.uk, 30 October 2009)

President Dmitri Medvedev on Friday [30 October] warned that Russians have lost their sense of horror over Stalin's purges and called for the construction of museums and memorial centres devoted to the atrocities, as well as further efforts to unearth and identify the dead. Mr Medvedev made the comments on his videoblog, on the occasion of a holiday devoted to the memory of victims of repression. He warned that revisionist historians risked glossing over the darker passages of the Soviet past, citing a poll that showed that 90 per cent of young people cannot name victims of the purges. Mr Medvedev said: 'Even now we can hear voices saying that these numerous deaths were justified by some supreme goals of the state. Nothing can be valued above human life, and there is no excuse for repressions' ... Though he reiterated his worry that Russia is demonized in contemporary histories of World War II, Mr Medvedev added that 'it is just as important to prevent the justification, under the pretext of putting historical records straight, of those who killed their own people' … Under Mr Medvedev's predecessor, Vladimir Putin, Russian opinions of Stalin became far rosier. Government-endorsed textbooks now balance Stalin's atrocities with praise for his achievements – especially victory over Hitler – and recent polls show that most Russians believe Stalin did more good than bad. Meanwhile, leaders have railed against Eastern European historians who paint Soviet forces as occupiers, and in May Mr Medvedev created a commission to prevent such attempts to 'falsify history' … Though Vladimir Putin spoke with compassion of Stalin's victims on the same holiday in 2007, Mr Medvedev went much further by offering concrete proposals about museums and the search for mass graves.

(www.iht.com, 30 October 2009; *IHT*, 31 October 2009, p. 4)

5 November 2009.

Investigators said Thursday [5 November] they had detained two suspects in the killing of … Stanislav Markelov and Anastasia Baburova … who were shot in central Moscow in January [2009] … [The] two suspects were … identified as Yevgenia Khasis and Nikita Tikhonov, both Moscow natives in their twenties … Law enforcement sources [were] reported [as saying] that the suspects were former members of an extreme nationalist group … Russian National Unity [is] a neo-fascist group that came to prominence in the late 1990s and is now banned in several Russian regions … Markelov had angered nationalists through his work. In 2004, around the time he was representing victims of beatings by extreme nationalists, he himself was beaten in Moscow and later received further threats from skinheads. Around the time of his death he was representing the family of a Chechen teenager killed in 2000 by a Russian officer, Colonel Yuri Budanov, who had won early release from prison. Markelov was working to put Budanov back behind bars. The officer had become a hero to nationalists during his trial.

(www.iht.com, 5 November 2009)

Prosecutors on Thursday [5 November] announced the arrest of Nikita Tikhonov and Yevgenia Khasis … The chief of the Federal Security Service said … that the killer [Tikhonov] had confessed … A man named Nikita Tikhonov was one of several neo-Nazis charged with murdering Alexander Ryukhin, an anti-fascist campaigner, in a 2006 case that Stanislav Markelov handled, although it is not clear whether that Mr Tikhonov is the same one arrested in the killings of Mr Markelov and Anastasia Baburova. The authorities said Mr Tikhonov was never arrested in the Ryukhin case because they could not locate him … [Tikhonov] was believed to be a member of a group called Unified Brigade-88, with the number meant to signify 'Heil Hitler' … Mr Tikhonov was taken into custody on National Unity Day, the 4 November holiday that has become a rallying point for

extreme nationalist and neo-Nazi groups ... Around sixty migrant workers
have been killed in nationalist attacks this year [2009], the Moscow Bureau
for Human Rights reported this week.

(www.iht.com, 6 November 2009; *IHT*, 6 November 2009, p. 3)

The man suspected of murdering ... Stanislav Markelov and Anastasia
Baburova ... in January has admitted committing the crime, saying he did it
out of 'personal enmity' for [Markelov] ... [Tikhonov's] lawyer said Friday
[6 November]. Investigators say that Nikita Tikhonov was the shooter and
that Yevgenia Khasis acted as lookout ... Mr Tikhonov intended to kill only
Mr Markelov, his [Tikhonov's] lawyer said ... Someone with the same
name as [Nikita Tikhonov] ... was considered a prime suspect in the 2006
murder of an anti-fascist campaigner. Mr Markelov, who represented a sur-
vivor of that attack, is widely credited with securing stiff prison sentences
for the accessories to that murder. Mr Tikhonov, however, was never
arrested in that case.

(www.iht.com, 7 November 2009; *IHT*, 7 November 2009, p. 3)

Nikita Tikhonov, a twenty-nine-year-old ultra-nationalist who has admitted
the murders, had been on the run since 2006, when a group of skinheads
knifed to death a nineteen-year-old anti-fascist student ... he appears to be
linked to Russian Miode, an ultra-nationalist group.

(*The Economist*, 14 November 2009, p. 52)

12 November 2009.

German prosecutors have dropped the case against a suspect in the murder
of Alexander Litvinenko in London ... Hamburg prosecutors say there is
not enough evidence to continue investigating Dmitri Kovtun ... [They said
that while traces of polonium-210 had been found in the apartment ... where
he stayed with his former wife ... there was no evidence Mr Kovtun had
taken it there.

(www.bbc.co.uk, 12 November 2009)

German prosecutors have abandoned investigations into one of the key
figures in the murder of ... Alexander Litvinenko ... in London three years
ago without bringing charges ... Dmitri Kovtun was initially suspected by
German prosecutors of illegally transporting a rare radioactive isotope,
polonium-210, through Germany and then to London where investigators
say it was used to poison Alexander Litvinenko ... The state prosecutor's
office in Hamburg said the inquiries into Mr Kovtun's activities had been
closed on 6 November because there was no evidence that Mr Kovtun illegally transported, purchased or knowingly came into contact with the radioactive isotope. Mr Kovtun was never charged by German authorities.

(www.iht.com, 12 November 2009)

'President Dmitri Medvedev has called for profound reform of the economy
in his annual state of the nation address ... Government had to become more

transparent, he said, and issues of corruption and accountability had to be addressed' (www.bbc.co.uk, 12 November 2009).

President Dmitri Medvedev called on Russian on Thursday [12 November] to refocus its economy away from Soviet-era energy and heavy industry towards information technology, telecommunications and space. Medvedev said at the start of his annual address to parliament: 'We have not managed to get rid of the primitive structure of our economy ... The competitiveness of our production is shamefully low ... Instead of a primitive economy based on raw materials, we shall create a smart economy, producing unique knowledge, new goods and technologies, goods and technologies for people ... The prestige of our homeland, the national welfare, cannot depend of the achievements of the past forever. The time has come for us – that is, today's generation of the Russian people – to make our contribution to lift up Russia to a new, higher stage in the development of our civilization' ... Noting that Russia's economy had been much harder hit by the global crisis than any other key nation, Medvedev said the country's giant state corporations had 'no prospects' and needed overhauling to improve management and competitiveness. Independent auditors should examine them and they should either be closed down or turned into companies with shareholders, he added ... He said: 'Instead of an archaic society, in which leaders think and decide for everybody, we shall become a society of intelligent, free and responsible people ... In the twenty-first century our country again requires modernization in all areas, and this will be the first time in history when modernization will be based on the values and institutions of democracy' ... He proposed some changes in election laws that he said would improve democracy at the grass roots ... He called for a more pragmatic approach to foreign relations.

(www.iht.com, 12 November 2009)

'Russia was hit harder than any other G-20 economy by the financial crisis' (*The Economist*, 28 November 2009, p. 45).

President Dmitri Medvedev painted his vision for the country's future, saying that 'modernization' was the key to its 'very survival' ... Medvedev admitted Russia is 'staying afloat' today largely thanks to its Soviet-era oil and gas facilities, nuclear weapons which protect the country and its industrial and housing infrastructure, which he admitted are 'becoming increasingly obsolete'. And Russia's 'shameful' dependence on the prices for its raw material exports, according to Medvedev, is the reason why it was hurt harder by the global economic crisis than many other countries ... In the military area Medvedev said the Russian armed forces will be re-equipped with new types of military hardware.

(www.cnn.com, 12 November 2009)

President Dmitri Medvedev: 'The nation's prestige and welfare cannot depend forever on the achievements of the past. All that has kept the country afloat, but it is rapidly ageing' ... He attacked the huge state corporations

and ordered the government to reduce the size of the state-controlled sector
– now exceeding 40 per cent – by the next presidential election in 2012.

(FT, 13 November 2009, p. 10)

'President Dmitri Medvedev proposed abolishing the current requirement for
parties wanting to register for elections to collect a large number of signatories
in support, which has hampered small parties' (*The Independent*, 13 November
2009, p. 27).

14 November 2009.

When he met President Dmitri Medvedev in April [2009], President Barack
Obama sought to open an important new supply corridor for Afghanistan by
flying American troops and weapons through Russian airspace. Visiting
Moscow in July he sealed a deal for as many as 4,500 flights a year ...
Seven months after the idea was raised and four months after the agreement
was signed, the number of American flights that have actually traversed
Russian airspace ... [is just] one ... and that was for show ... The two sides
arranged for a single test flight on 8 October, just before secretary of state
Hillary Clinton visited Moscow.

(www.iht.com, 14 November 2009)

19 November 2009.

Russia's ban on the death penalty will remain when a current legal suspension expires on 1 January [2010], the country's Constitutional Court
has ruled. It said the use of the death penalty was now impossible because
Russia had signed international deals banning it. Russia announced the
moratorium in 1996 when it joined the Council of Europe, although it
retains capital punishment in its criminal code. Opinion polls suggest that
a majority of Russians backed the death penalty. One recent survey
showed that two-thirds of Russians backed the measure ... [The court]
cited a number of international accords signed by Moscow banned the use
of capital punishment ... [and the court] also said Russia must extend the
moratorium on executions until it ratified Protocol Six of the European
Convention on Human Rights, which prohibits the use of the death
penalty in peaceful times. Russia's pledge to sign the protocol was a key
condition of its membership in the Council of Europe in 1996. However,
the country's parliament is yet to officially outlaw executions. In 1999
the constitutional court ruled that the death penalty could not be used
until jury trials had been introduced in all of Russia's eighty-nine regions.
Thursday's ruling [19 November] was its response to the country's
Supreme Court request, which had sought to clarify the future of the moratorium because the first jury trials would take place in Chechnya on 1
January [2010]. Chechnya is the only remaining part of the Russian Federation where trials by jury have never been held. Last week President
Dmitri Medvedev's representative at the Constitutional Court, Mikhail

Krotov, said that the Kremlin was in favour of the gradual abolition of the death penalty.

(www.bbc.co.uk, 19 November 2009)

The Constitutional Court effectively outlawed the death penalty Thursday [19 November], saying a moratorium on capital punishment should remain in force until the country fully banned executions ... The court said Russia must extend the moratorium on executions until it ratified a European convention banning the death penalty.

(*IHT*, 20 November 2009, p. 3)

President Dmitri Medvedev has dismissed a key aide for apparent abuse of office ... Mikhail Lesin, a media adviser and former minister, is the most senior official to leave the Medvedev administration. In 2004 he was appointed a presidential adviser by Vladimir Putin ... and he was reappointed a week after Mr Medvedev took office in May last year [2008]. The Kremlin said Mr Lesin had been 'relieved of his duties at his own request' ... However, Interfax news agency quoted a source within the government as saying he had been fired because he 'disregarded the rules and ethical principles of civil service' ... [A] newspaper said that Mr Medvedev had ordered Mr Lesin to be dismissed over conflicts of interest ... Mr Lesin founded one of Russia's leading television advertising agencies in 1990.

(*The Times*, 20 November 2009, p. 57)

21 November 2009.

President Dmitri Medvedev accused United Russia of 'backwardness' on Saturday [21 November], warning its leaders that they must learn to win elections honestly if they are to survive. Mr Medvedev's remarks [were made] at the party's annual congress in St Petersburg ... He said: '[Some regional branches of the party] show signs of this backwardness and reduce political activities to bureaucratic intrigues and games. Elections which are intended to express the national will and present competing ideas and programmes, are sometimes turned into scenarios in which democratic processes are confused with administrative ones. It is necessary to get rid of such people, and of bad political habits as well ... [members] need to learn in open contests. Democracy exists so that people can exercise their exclusive right to determine their government, to decide how their country is to be ruled, and the party is only an instrument. A very important instrument, it is true, an absolutely necessary one, but only a tool, a means to an end' ... Prime minister Vladimir Putin, also speaking at the congress, seemed eager to quiet the chatter about any disagreement by endorsing Mr Medvedev's state of the nation speech, which called for Russia to modernize its economy and break free of its economic dependence on oil and gas. Vladimir Putin: 'I am sure this call reflects the mood of all Russian society. The crisis, with all its severity, has shown how costly it is for a country to reject innovations, have low worker productivity, waste resources and have a slow bureaucracy.'

(www.iht.com, 22 November 2009; *IHT*, 23 November 2009, p. 3)

23 November 2009.

President Dmitri Medvedev called for tax incentives and other measures Monday [23 November] to assist beleaguered non-profit groups in Russia, which have come under government pressure in recent years. Mr Medvedev said in a meeting with human rights activists that new laws would not alleviate all the problems that they faced, but would certainly help ... Since taking office last year Mr Medvedev has sought to reach out to non-profit groups. He loosened the bureaucratic requirements that they face.

(*IHT*, 24 November 2009, p. 3)

24 November 2009.

President Dmitri Medvedev ordered an inquiry on Tuesday [24 November] into the death of a thirty-seven-year-old lawyer who died in pre-trial detention last week after being swept up in a battle between Russian authorities and the international investment fund he was representing. When the lawyer, Sergei Magnitsky, died of toxic shock and heart failure in a prison hospital on 16 November, interior ministry officials said they had no warning that his health was deteriorating. Mr Magnitsky's employers have released meticulous notes he took in prison that documented his numerous requests for medical care that were refused or ignored as his condition worsened ... On Tuesday Mr Medvedev ordered an inquiry not only into Mr Magnitsky's death but also into the quality of medical care in federal detention facilities. He also called for an analysis of the practice of detaining suspects after a first charge of economic crimes, and requested proposals for relevant legislation. Within hours Russia's prosecutor general announced an investigation into possible negligence and failure to provide medical treatment. Mr Magnitsky had been working as outside counsel for the Hermitage Fund, whose owner, William Browder, has openly clashed with Russian authorities. Last year [2008] Mr Browder accused Russian officials of using his companies to embezzle $230 million from the Russian Treasury. Russian authorities then accused Hermitage of failing to pay about $17.4 million in taxes. Mr Magnitsky, head of the tax practice at the law firm Firestone Duncan, was arrested with the tax evasion charge in November 2008. He was diagnosed with pancreatic and gallbladder disease in June, after six months in custody, but his medical treatment and planned surgery ended abruptly when he was transferred to a second detention centre, according to his notes. Late in August medical staff told him they were not obliged to provide him with surgery, his notes say.

(www.iht.com, 24 November 2009; *IHT*, 25 November 2009, p. 3)

'William Browder ... has been barred from Russia as an alleged security risk' (*IHT*, 26 November 2009, p. 4).

[Sergei Magnitsky's] supporters accuse prison officers of withholding medical aid to force him to provide evidence against his employer ... The death intensified the confrontation between the Russian authorities and Hermitage Capital Management, whose owner, William Browder, an American-born investor, has been charged in absentia with tax fraud. Mr Browder has lived in Britain since 2005, when, he said, he was barred entry into Russia. Last year Mr Browder accused Russian officials of illegally assuming ownership of his holding companies to embezzle $230 million from the Russian Treasury. Russian authorities then accused Hermitage of evading millions of dollars in taxes.

(www.iht.com, 26 November 2009)

Hermitage Capital Management has been accused of tax fraud by the Russian authorities and has itself charged interior ministry officials with using Hermitage-linked companies to steal $230 million in tax ... Prosecutors last week denied Sergei Magnitsky's lawyer's request for an independent autopsy, leaving Magnitsky to be buried in a hurry. The local morgue claimed refrigeration systems were failing ... Hermitage lawyers have said they believed Russian authorities worsened Magnitsky's jail conditions to force him to give false testimony.

(*FT*, 25 November 2009, p. 10)

Critics and colleagues of Mr Magnitsky ... claim that officials in the interior ministry were involved in a tax fraud worth $230 million ... Hermitage had been Russia's biggest portfolio investor until Mr Browder was denied a visa in 2005 ... After police raided Hermitage's Moscow subsidiary ... [in 2007] the interior ministry ... months after he began lobbying for permission to re-enter the country ... opened a tax evasion probe against him. After police raided Hermitage's Moscow subsidiary that year, Mr Browder alleged police officials stole company seals and charter documents. Hermitage alleges these companies were later reregistered and used in sham transactions and court cases that led to $230 million in fraudulent tax rebates. The same officials that Mr Magnitsky alleged were part of the tax fraud had then ordered his arrest [it was alleged] ... In October [2009] Mr Browder said he had uncovered another 3 billion roubles in fraudulent refunds using the same scheme, involving eight companies and sent a letter dated 13 October to Russia's audit chamber detailing the total $382 in tax fraud.

(*FT*, 28 November 2009, p. 8)

Russia has now turned into a 'criminal state', according to the man who was once its leading foreign investor. Bill Browder of Hermitage Capital was reacting to news that his lawyer had died in prison in Russia after being held for a year without charge. He told the BBC that Sergei Magnitsky had effectively been 'held hostage and they killed their hostage' ... In 2005 Mr Browder was banned from Russia as a threat to national security, after allegations that his firms evaded tax, but Mr Browder says his company was targeted by criminals trying to seize millions of pounds worth of his assets. Mr Browder says he was punished for being a threat to corrupt politicians and bureaucrats. Since then a number of Mr Browder's associates in Russia – as well as lawyers acting for his company – have been detained, beaten or robbed. Before the accusations of tax evasion were raised, for many years Mr Browder had been one of the most outspoken defenders of the Russian government and its then-president Vladimir Putin ... Sergei Magnitsky was one of the lawyers hired by Mr Browder to investigate whether fraud had been committed against his firms. Mr Browder claims that when the police raided his office they took away corporate documents which they then used to steal his companies.

(www.bbc.co.uk, 23 November 2009)

Russia's interior ministry held a rare news conference on Wednesday [25 November] to deny that its investigators had been aware of health problems that led to the death of Sergei Magnitsky at a ministry detention centre ... A spokeswoman for the interior ministry: '[The death] was completely unexpected. He never once complained to investigators about the state of his health' ... Asked whether prison officials had ever noticed problems with Mr Magnitsky's health, she said she could not comment ... William Browder's lawyers have copies of the charges against him, she said, and he has been asked to come to Russia to answer them. She said Mr Browder had never been barred from entering Russia, as he claimed, but had been refused a visa for technical reasons in 2005. She said: 'If Browder requests a visa to enter the Russian Federation he will certainly receive it. We hope that he will come and give testimony to the investigators.'

(www.iht.com, 26 November 2009)

'[The spokeswoman] said that Mr Magnitsky was detained pending his trial because he was a flight risk, based on a purchase of passport-size photographs, and because if he had been free he would have intimidated witnesses in the case' (*IHT*, 27 November 2009, p. 3).

A top Russian prison official on Thursday [26 November] acknowledged wrongdoing in the case of Sergei Magnitsky ... Alexander Smirnov, assistant director of the Federal Prison Service, said in testimony to the Public Chamber (a Kremlin advisory panel): 'We are not trying to diminish our guilt in this case – it obviously exists' ... It was the first official acknowledgment of responsibility ... Mr Smirnov said that Mr Magnitsky had been held in 'very respectable' conditions for the first eight months of his incarceration ... [but] 'then he was transferred to another detention centre' ... Mr Magnitsky's situation deteriorated when he was moved to Butyrskaya Prison, where he remained for four months until his death ... [Mr Smirnov said] that the prison service would release the results of an internal enquiry early next week.

(*IHT*, 27 November 2009, p. 3)

27 November 2009.

A bomb blast caused the train crash in which at least twenty-six people were killed, intelligence officials say. The *Nevsky Express* derailed with nearly 700 on board as it ran through remote countryside between Moscow and St Petersburg ... A spokesman for prosecutors said: 'Indeed this was a terrorist attack' ... [The] train [is] popular with government officials and business executives ... If terrorism is confirmed as the cause, observers say the derailment would represent the deadliest attack outside the volatile North Caucasus region for five years ... [There are] reports of several high ranking government and local officials among the dead ... Some reports say as many as thirty-nine people have died. The train was reported to be carrying around 650 passengers and two dozen or so staff ... In 2007 a bomb on the same line derailed a train, injuring nearly thirty passengers. Two men suspected of having links to Chechen rebels were accused of planting a bomb next to the track.

(www.bbc.co.uk, 28 November 2009)

'Officials originally said twenty-six passengers had been killed, but revised the figure down ... [to] twenty-five ... on Sunday [29 November]' (www.bbc.co.uk, 29 November 2009).

The crash happened at 9.25 p.m. when the train was 280 kilometres (174 miles) from St Petersburg. A total of 681 people – twenty of them employees – were on the *Nevsky Express* as it travelled from Moscow to St Petersburg on Friday night [27 November] ... The *Nevsky Express* is Russia's fastest train, equivalent to a bullet train ... Investigators probing the derailment of the express train found 'elements of an explosive device' at the site and believe an act of terror caused the deadly incident ... A spokesman for the investigative committee of the prosecutor's office: 'One can say with certainty that that was indeed an act of terror' ... In August 2007 an explosion on the tracks derailed the *Nevsky Express*, injuring sixty people in what authorities called a terrorist act.

(www.cnn.com, 28 November 2009)

'Eighteen people were still missing Sunday [29 November] ... after a train derailment killed at least twenty-six people' (www.cnn.com, 29 November 2009).

'The train was carrying 633 passengers and twenty railway personnel ... In 2007 an explosion on the Moscow–St Petersburg line derailed a train, injuring more than two dozen people, but the motive was unclear' (www.iht.com, 28 November 2009).

The cause of the crash of one of Russia's most illustrious trains was identified on Saturday [28 November] as a homemade bomb that went off on the tracks between Moscow and St Petersburg, killing more than twenty-five people ... Among the dead were a former senator and a senior official in the federal economics ministry ... A second, less powerful explosive went off Saturday at the site of the crash. No one was hurt.

(www.iht.com, 29 November 2009)

'The *Nevsky Express* is a preferred means of travel for the Russian elite between the country's two most important cities' (www.iht.com, 29 November 2009).

A second terrorist bomb has exploded at the site of a fatal train crash, claim officials. There was an explosion today [Saturday 28 November] near the wreckage of a derailed express train ... Russian officials say this was a second, less powerful bomb than the improvised explosive device they now believe caused Friday's crash. Russian Railways ... said the [second] bomb went off at 2 p.m. and that no one was hurt.

(www.thetimes.co.uk, 28 November 2009)

Investigators confirmed that a powerful improvised bomb caused Friday's devastating train crash in which at least twenty-six people, including several top government officials, were killed ... Officials said eighteen people were still unaccounted for ... The luxury *Nevsky Express* was carrying 682 passengers and twenty-nine crew ... It was derailed at 9.34 p.m. on Friday [27 November], close to the village of Uglova, 250 miles north-west ... According to *Ekho Moskvy*, a radical neo-Nazi group opposed to migrants from the former Soviet republics of Central Asia has claimed responsibility for Friday's crash ... Other nationalist groups later denied the report. There seems little doubt that the Kremlin will point the finger of blame at Islamist insurgents currently waging a guerrilla campaign across the North Caucasus ... Russian prosecutors said they believed Pavel Kosolapov, an ex-soldier and former associate of the late Chechen rebel leader Shamil Basayev, masterminded the previous derailment. Kosolapov is currently on the run. Prosecutors have arrested two residents of Ingushetia and charged them with helping carry out the 2006 attack. Yesterday [28 November] investigators said they had discovered a three-foot crater beneath the rails where the bomb had gone off. Reuters, however, said that its reporters at the scene had been unable to find it. Earlier Russian news agencies had quoted transport officials as saying the cause may have been an electrical fault. Russia has a poor record of serious accidents caused by Soviet-era infrastructure. Among the named dead so far were several senior Kremlin bureaucrats, including ... the head of the Federal Reserve Agency ... and a deputy head in the Federal Fishing Agency. A former St Petersburg senator ... also died.

(www.guardian.co.uk, 29 November 2009)

On Saturday [28 November] a radical neo-Nazi group, Combat 18, claimed responsibility. Other nationalist groups late denied the report ... The state-controlled television channel Vesti hinted last night that investigators were concentrating on a Chechen link. Vesti said they were looking at Pavel Kosolapov ... Prosecutors accused Kosolapov of carrying out a similar attack in 2007.

(*Guardian*, 30 November 2009, p. 18)

Pavel Kosolapov ... is believed to have converted to Islam during the 1990s and become a close associate of Shamil Basayev ... Two men from Ingushetia are standing trial for the earlier [2007] incident, and one of them admitted his guilt in court last week ... Some pundits have even doubted the official explanation of terrorism. In recent years a number of fatal accidents across Russia have been caused by decaying Soviet-era infrastructure and poor maintenance.

(*The Independent*, 30 November 2009, p. 22)

The police said they were looking for Pavel Kosolapov, a former army officer who converted to Islam and now supports Islamic fundamentalism. He was suspected of involvement in a bombing of the same train two years ago. Two of his alleged accomplices were arrested then; one pleaded guilty only two days before the second bombing.

(www.economist.com, 3 December 2009; *The Economist*, 5 December 2009, p. 42)

'Extreme nationalists were also coming under suspicion, with the attack seen as a possible reaction to a crackdown as racist and skinhead groups' (*The Times*, 30 November 2009, p. 32).

The police released a sketch and a description on Monday [30 November] of a possible suspect in the bombing of a luxury train that killed twenty-six people, as well as a description of an accomplice ... The death toll rose to twenty-six on Monday after a severely injured woman died ... In a radio interview on Monday a senior official of the state railway company suggested that people from the North Caucasus were most likely behind the bombing. Alexander Bobreshov: 'The second explosion, which occurred some time later, is the so-called double-blast method, carried out by North Caucasus sabotage groups.'

(www.iht.com, 30 November 2009)

Russia's top investigator was wounded by a bomb that went off as he and colleagues scoured the wreckage ... The last three cars of the train flew off the tracks late Friday ... Another bomb exploded Saturday as investigators scoured the wreckage ... [On Tuesday 1 December it was announced that the chief investigator] had been wounded by the bomb, which was detonated by remote control ... The wound was not serious.

(*IHT*, 2 December 2009, p. 3)

A North Caucasus Islamist group has claimed responsibility ... The website claim ... said last Friday's attack was carried out by the 'Caucasian Mujahadeen' on the orders of its leader, Doku Umarov ... It was not possible to verify the claim's authenticity ... On Tuesday [2 December] the funerals were held of some of the twenty-six who died on the *Nevsky Express* – a luxury high-speed train popular with government officials and business executives. Among those buried were ... a former

St Petersburg vice governor ... [and the] head of the Federal Agency for State Reserves.

(www.bbc.co.uk, 2 December 2009)

A statement posted on a website sympathetic to the militants said that the attack on the *Nevsky Express* ... had been 'prepared and carried out ... pursuant to the order of the Emir of Caucasus Emirate'. Doku Umarov declared himself head of a 'Caucasus Emirate' in 2007 ... There was no way to verify the claim.

(The Times, 3 December 2009, p. 45)

29 November 2009.

President Dmitri Medvedev [on Sunday 29 November] sent foreign leaders a draft of a sweeping new trans-Atlantic security treaty he has been proposing since he took office last year [2008]. The draft treaty prohibits signatories from taking any action that would damage the security of other parties to the pact.

(IHT, 30 November 2009, p. 3)

President Dmitri Medvedev has proposed a new European security agreement that could prevent the eastward expansion of Nato if the alliance harmed Russia's interests. The draft of a treaty published on the Kremlin website yesterday [29 November] would allow Russia or any party to the agreement to render military assistance to another member facing an attack without first receiving UN Security Council approval.

(FT, 30 November 2009, p. 10)

1 December 2009.

Friends and colleagues called yesterday for an investigation into the death of a television journalist who plunged from the fourteenth storey of a city centre building a day after winning a major legal case. Olga Kotovskaya, a prominent journalist in the western enclave of Kaliningrad, died on 16 November. Officials initially claimed her death was suicide, but last week opened a criminal investigation into claims she had been murdered ... Kotovskaya fell from a window a day after winning a long-running court battle to regain control of her successful Kaskad regional television channel. Founded in the early 1990s, the channel had a reputation for objective news reporting ... In 2004 a group of local bureaucrats ... seized control of the channel, which immediately stopped criticizing the enclave's administration. A day before Kotovskaya's death, a court ruled that her signature on a document giving her company to its new owners had been forged.

(Guardian, 2 December 2009, p. 15)

3 December 2009.

In an electric four-hour solo performance on live television ... on Thursday [3 December] ... prime minister Vladimir Putin ... when asked whether he will run in the next [presidential] election [in 2012] ... said: 'I will think about it, there is still enough time' ... Putin has said earlier that instead of competing against each other in 2012, he and President Dmitri Medvedev will 'sit down and decide' who will run as the elections get closer ... [Putin] offered up a virtuoso performance at the public question-and-answer session ... While Dmitri Medvedev nominally holds the higher office, he has not held such widely publicized question-and-answer sessions. He spent the day on a trip to Italy. Asked by reporters there whether he would run for re-election in 2012, he said he would decide in conjunction with Mr Putin. Mr Medvedev said: 'As we both have said, we are close to one another, we understand one another and we work together. We will be able to agree in some way without elbowing each other aside, and make a reasonable decision for our country.'

(www.iht.com, 3 December 2009; *IHT*, 4 December 2009, p. 3)

As regards Stalin, prime minister Vladimir Putin said:

It is impossible to make a general judgement. It is evident that from 1924 to 1953 the country that Stalin ruled changed from an agrarian to an industrial society ... We won the Great Patriotic War ... The positives that undoubtedly existed were achieved at an unacceptable price. Repression did take place. This is a fact. Millions of our fellow citizens suffered from this. And this way of running a state, to achieve a result, is not acceptable. It is impossible. Certainly, in this period we encountered not only a cult of personality, but a massive crime against our own people. This is also a fact. And we must not forget this.

(*FT*, 4 December 2009, p. 6; *The Times*, 4 December 2009, p. 49)

'Prime minister Vladimir Putin's annual phone appearance, which was aired live on state television ... [was] the eighth session of its kind' (www.bbc.co.uk, 3 December 2009).

[On 3 December] Russia and the Vatican agreed to establish full diplomatic relations ... Until now Moscow only had an office of representation at the Vatican. The new status means full-fledged embassies will be established in Moscow and Rome. The announcement comes after President Dmitri Medvedev met Pope Benedict XVI while on a visit to Italy ... Since 1990 the two sides have maintained representation below the level of ambassador.

(www.bbc.co.uk, 4 December 2009)

5 December 2009.

The Strategic Arms Reduction Treaty of 1991, known as Start 1, goes out of force Saturday [5 December] ... President Barack Obama and President Dmitri Medvedev had already narrowed the range for a cap on warheads to between 1,500 and 1,675 during a meeting in July [2009], down from 2,200 each side now has. They are likely to agree to lower the ceiling on delivery vehicles –

intercontinental ballistic missiles, submarine-based missiles and strategic bombers – to below 800 … although that would not result in large reductions since the United States has about 800 and Russia about 620. The most significant differences centre on verification and monitoring … If they succeed, the two sides intend to show the pact is just the beginning by announcing another round of talks next year [2010] on another treaty that would further reduce arsenals along with addressing tactical nuclear weapons and strategic warheads held in reserve … The two sides are working on a bridge agreement to continue inspections, verification and monitoring after Start 1 expires Saturday. One monitoring system, however, will not continue. The American observation station at Votkinsk, about 1,000 kilometres (600 miles) east of Moscow, will close by Saturday. Under Start 1 the station is staffed by Americans who monitor manufacturing of Topol-M ballistic missiles and other arms. The Kremlin has long chafed at the presence of an American outpost deep in its territory, since it closed its own monitoring station in the United States years ago. The Bush administration, which favoured limits on warheads but not on missiles like those produced at Votkinsk, agreed in its final months not to keep the station after Start 1 expires. When the Obama team took over, the Russian insisted it had a deal to close the station even though the new treaty will limit missiles as well as warheads. American officials hope to use electronic and other means to keep tabs on Votkinsk. Russia has taken a harder line on monitoring in part because its military and diplomatic establishment believes that a weakened Moscow in the waning days of the Cold War made concessions that infringed upon its sovereignty.

(*IHT*, 3 December 2009, pp. 1, 3)

The United States and Russia missed their deadline on Friday [4 December] to adopt a new arms control treaty, though they pledged that they would generally abide by the old one while they continued negotiating … In a joint statement the White House and the Kremlin declared their 'commitment, as a matter of principle, to continue to work together in the spirit of the Start treaty following its expiration as well as our firm intention to ensure that a new treaty on strategic arms enters into force at the earliest possible date' … [The] American monitoring post … the city of Votkinsk, 600 miles east of Moscow … was closed on Friday … According to the understanding that was announced Friday by the two counties, they might conceivably be able to send ad hoc inspection teams in this interim period. But both countries seem to be hoping that it will not come to that – that a new treaty will be signed and ratified in time for an official inspection programme to occur … At a summit meeting in Moscow in July President Barack Obama and President Dmitri Medvedev narrowed the range for a cap on warheads to between 1,500 and 1,675, down from about 2,200, which each side has now. The two countries are also expected to lower the ceiling on delivery vehicles – intercontinental ballistic missiles, submarine-based missiles and strategic bombers – to below 800, from 1,600.

(www.iht.com, 5 December 2009)

The United States and Russia say they want a new nuclear arms treaty to enter into force as soon as possible, after failing to agree a successor to the Start 1 pact. The nations uphold the 'spirit' of the 1991 treaty ... signed by Mikhail Gorbachev and George Bush senior ... despite its end, the US and Russian presidents said in a joint statement. Talks on a new accord are expecting to continue after the treaty expires, at midnight on Friday [4 December] ... Under the joint understanding signed in July, deployed nuclear warheads will be cut to below 1,700 on each side within seven years of a new treaty.

(www.bbc.co.uk, 4 December 2009)

Russian officials say the death toll from a nightclub fire in the Urals city of Perm ... on 5 December ... has risen to 152 ... Friday's statement [25 December said] that seventy-four others remain hospitalized. The blaze at the Lame Horse nightclub broke out on [Saturday] 5 December when an indoor fireworks display ignited a plastic ceiling decorated with branches. The flames spread swiftly as hundreds of customers tried to flee through a single exit. Five people, including the club's owner, have been jailed pending an investigation. The fire was Russia's deadliest since Soviet times. Russian leaders have ordered a broad review of fire regulations and urged tougher enforcement.

(www.iht.com, 25 December 2009)

9 December 2009.

An organization of natural gas exporters informally known as Gas OPEC has elected a Russian as its first secretary-general ... Leonid Bokhanovsky, a vice president at Stroitransgaz (a well connected pipeline construction company) was elected at a meeting of energy ministers from the eleven-member countries in Doha (Qatar), where the group, the Gas Exporting Countries Forum, has its headquarters. They used their inaugural meeting to address the current global natural gas glut ... The members include Algeria, Bolivia, Egypt, Equatorial Guinea, Iran, Libya, Qatar, Nigeria, Russia, Trinidad and Tobago and Venezuela, and as observers Kazakhstan and Norway.

(*IHT*, 10 December 2009, p. 17)

[On Wednesday 9 December] a Russian test launch of an intercontinental missile failed ... The submarine-based Bulava ballistic missile failed when launched from the White Sea ... At least six of thirteen previous tests also ended in failure. The Bulava can carry six individually targeted nuclear warheads. It is designed to have a range of 10,000 kilometres (6,200 miles) ... [In] Wednesday's test the third stage failed.

(www.bbc.co.uk, 10 December 2009)

The Bulava intercontinental missile suffered another in a series of failed test launchings, the Russian defence ministry confirmed Thursday [10 December], further denting Kremlin hopes that the sea-based weapon would become a cornerstone of its nuclear arsenal ... The Bulava can accommodate multiple nuclear warheads and has a range of 5,000 miles (8,000 kilometres). Officials had hoped military contracts for the submarine-launched missile could be negotiated next year [2010] ... Russian leaders have boasted about the Bulava's ability to penetrate missile defences and have described it as a crucial part of the military's future nuclear arsenal ... Of the eleven reported tests, at least six have been unsuccessful, including one on 15 July when a Bulava self-destructed after a malfunction during the first stage of its flight from the White Sea.

(*IHT*, 11 December 2009, p. 3)

11 December 2009.

President Dmitri Medvedev has dismissed the head of the Moscow prisons and numerous other prison administrators in response to the death of a lawyer in pre-trial detention, officials said on Friday [11 December] ... In all more than twenty officials lost their jobs ... Sergei Magnitsky died of toxic shock and heart failure at a pre-trial detention centre in Moscow, and Mr Medvedev reacted by ordering an inquiry into how Mr Magnitsky was treated and into the quality of medical care in the prison system ... The director of the prison system ... said Mr Magnitsky's death spurred an inquiry into medical care in the prison system and found 'violations of our requirements' ... Mr Magnitsky's death itself was still being investigated.

(www.iht.com, 12 December 2009)

13 December 2009.

The United States has begun talks with Russia and a UN arms control committee about strengthening internet security and limiting military use of cyberspace. American and Russian officials have different interpretations of the talks so far, but the mere fact that the United States is participating represents a significant policy shift after years of rejecting Russia's overtures ... The Bush administration declined to talk with Russia about issues related to military attacks using the internet ... In the last two years internet-based attacks on government and corporate computer systems have multiplied to thousands a day ... The Russians have held that the increasing challenges posed by military activities to civilian computer networks can best be dealt with by an international treaty, similar to treaties that have limited the spread of nuclear, chemical and biological weapons. The United States has resisted, arguing that it was impossible to draw a line between the commercial and military uses of software and hardware. Now there is a thaw, said people familiar with the discussions ... In addition to continuing efforts to ban offensive cyberweapons ... the Russians ... have insisted on what they describe as an issue of sovereignty calling for a ban on 'cyberterrorism'. American officials view the issue differently and describe this as a Russian effort to restrict 'politically destabilizing speech'.

(www.iht.com, 13 December 2009; *IHT*, 14 December 2009, pp. 1, 3)

15 December 2009.

President Dmitri Medvedev has fired a senior interior ministry official who is alleged to be connected to the case of a lawyer ... Sergei Magnitsky ... the Kremlin said Tuesday [15 December]. The Kremlin issued a statement with Mr Medvedev's order firing Anatoli Mikhalkin, chief of the Moscow police tax crimes department, but gave no reason for the decision.

(*IHT*, 16 December 2009, p. 3)

'The president's sacking of General Anatoli Mikhalkin ... was "indirectly linked" to a probe ordered last month [November] by President Dmitri Medvedev into the death of Sergei Magnitsky, according to a Kremlin official' (*FT*, 16 December 2009, p. 10).

16 December 2009. 'Yegor Gaidar, the architect of Russia's market reforms in the 1990s, has died aged fifty-three ... Mr Gaidar was acting prime minister in 1992' (www.bbc.co.uk, 16 December 2009).

Yegor Gaidar, the economist who oversaw the largest ever transition from communism to capitalism as the first finance minister of post-Soviet Russia ... died on Wednesday [16 December] ... He was fifty-three. The cause was likely a blood clot ... Mr Gaidar became minister of economy and finance in November 1991 ... His tenure was brief, lasting until February 1992 ... Mr Gaidar later served as acting prime minister before he was dismissed by President Boris Yeltsin in late 1992 ... After retiring from government, Mr Gaidar headed a Moscow think-tank, the Institute of Economy in Transition, until his death.

(www.iht.com, 16 December 2009; *IHT*, 17 December 2009, p. 3)

Yegor Gaidar seized the moment, first as deputy prime minister in charge of economic reform, then, briefly as finance minister, and finally as acting prime minister ... By December 1992 Mr Gaidar had lost his job at the hands of the Duma ... Mr Gaidar's dislike of Vladimir Putin's ex-KGB regime intensified over the years. When he fell ill during a trip to Ireland in 2006 he claimed he had been poisoned, though he remained coy about whom he blamed. He feared a 'Weimar Russia' in which economic collapse would provide an opening for xenophobic, authoritarian politicians. What he wanted was to root Russia in the West.

(www.economist.com, 16 December 2009)

In November 2006 Yegor Gaidar fell mysteriously ill during a trip to Dublin, prompting speculation that his affliction was connected to the recent death by poisoning of Alexander Litvinenko ... Gaidar recovered and returned to Russia, concluding in an editorial that the incident was probably engineered by adversaries of the Russian authorities to damage the relationship between the West and Russia.

(*Guardian*, 17 December 2009, p. 39)

The secretary-general of Nato held talks at the Kremlin on Wednesday [16 December] for the first time since relations soured last year [2008] ... Anders Fogh Rasmussen ... who took office in August [2009] ... met with the Russian leadership and asked for Russian helicopters for the Afghan military, as well as more help in training the Afghan police and combating drug trafficking ... [He met with] President Dmitri Medvedev ... prime minister Vladimir Putin and foreign minister Sergei Lavrov ... Russia has declined to send troops to take part in the Nato mission, though it has increasingly been willing to offer logistical support. In July it said it would allow American troops and weaponry to fly through Russian airspace to Afghanistan, although that arrangement has encountered delays ... Mr Rasmussen said: 'I believe that Afghanistan is a key element of this co-operation because we are facing the same threats – terrorism and drug trafficking – that have their roots in Afghanistan.'

(www.iht.com, 17 December 2009)

Anders Fogh Rasmussen's visit is the first by a Nato chief since relations chilled after last year's Russian–Georgian war. The three-day visit has included meetings with President Dmitri Medvedev and prime minister Vladimir Putin ... On Wednesday [16 December] Mr Rasmussen asked Moscow to provide helicopters to Afghanistan and also requested Russian help in training the Afghan air force ... Mr Rasmussen said he had presented Russian leaders with a list of 'concrete proposals' to help the Western alliance defeat the Taleban in Afghanistan – specifically requesting helicopters, helicopter training and spare parts.

(www.bbc.co.uk, 17 December 2009)

Anders Fogh Rasmussen said he spoke with President Dmitri Medvedev ... but the two did not talk about Russia sending troops, Rasmussen said ... Foreign minister Sergei Lavrov has said in the past that Russia would continue to allow cargo shipments through its territory to help supply Nato forces and maintain its training of Afghan law enforcement and counter-narcotics officials. But he said that Russia would not take on a military role in Afghanistan.

(www.cnn.com, 17 December 2009)

('Russian commercial cargo carriers have been shipping non-lethal goods out of the Middle East aboard massive Antonov 124 "Ruslan" cargo planes to Afghanistan for more than a year': www.iht.com, 4 May 2010.)

According to Olga Kryshtanovskaya ... the *siloviki* – literally 'strong guys' – hit their apogee in 2007, when they accounted for two out of every three members of the president's administration. But following the accession to the presidency of Dmitri Medvedev, they are this year [2009] down to barely one in two; their representation in other areas has fallen as well ... In 1998 only 5.4 per cent of government positions were occupied by military and KGB men. In 1993 that rose to 11 per cent; by 1999 their representation had doubled again to 22 per cent; and by the middle of Vladimir Putin's first term the proportion was 32 per cent.

(*FT*, 17 December 2009, p. 13)

22 December 2009.

The Kremlin has long been irritated by the way the United States dominates the internet, all the way down to the ban on using Cyrillic for web addresses – even kremlin.ru has to be demeaningly rendered in English. The Russian government, as a result, is taking the lead in a landmark shift occurring around the world to allow domain names in languages with non-Latin alphabets ... The decision to allow non-Latin domains was approved in October [2009] by the Internet Corporation for Assigned Names and Numbers, or Icann, the supervisory body based in the United States. More than half of the world's 1.6 billion internet users speak a native language that does not have a Latin alphabet, Icann said ... Russians themselves, though, do not seem at all eager to follow ... Computer users are worried that Cyrillic domains will give rise to a hermitic Russian web, a sort of cyberghetto, and that the push for Cyrillic amounts to a plot by the security services to restrict access to the internet ... More than 30 million Russian use the internet weekly, out of a population of 140 million, and the country's growth is among the fastest in Europe, officials said. There are 2.5 million domains with the .ru suffix, with the address written in Latin letters ... The .ru suffix will remain when Russia rolls out its Cyrillic suffix, .рФ, which stands for Russian Federation. But holders of .ru websites will have to decide whether to establish companion sites with Cyrillic addresses and the Cyrillic suffix. Many may not be enthusiastic.

(www.iht.com, 22 December 2009; *IHT*, 22 December 2009, pp. 1, 3)

23–24 December 2009.

Russia's supreme court ruled yesterday [23 December] that the arrest of ... Platon Lebedev ... was illegal ... [He] was seized by police in a Moscow hospital in June 2003 on suspicion of defrauding the government of $238 million in a privatization scam ... The supreme court's decision was a response to a European Court of Human Rights ruling in 2007 that Mr Lebedev's rights had been violated during his arrest and pre-trial detention. It ordered the Russian government to pay Mr Lebedev $14,000 in compensation.

(*FT*, 24 December 2009, p. 4)

President Dmitri Medvedev ... ordered a major overhaul of the police force on Thursday [24 December] that is to include a 20 per cent reduction in its size. Mr Medvedev said the federal government should take more control over police departments across Russia in an effort to tamp down corruption. At the heart of his proposal is a reduction in the number of officers and an unspecified increase in pay for those who remain, so they would be less susceptible to bribes. Mr Medvedev also called for scaling back the interior ministry, reducing the number of senior police officers in the provinces and adding incentives to lure higher quality recruits ... The 20 per cent reduction in the size of the police force does not take effect until 2012.

(www.iht.com, 25 December 2009)

28 December 2009.

Moscow's prisons watchdog yesterday [28 December] accused authorities of subjecting Sergei Magnitsky to 'torturous conditions' during an eleven-month detention that culminated in his death [on 17 November] ... In a damning report the Moscow Public Oversight Commission, created last year [2008] by President Dmitri Medvedev to oversee jails, criticized prosecutors, the interior ministry and prison officials for failing to prevent Magnitsky's inhumane treatment. It also accused authorities of denying him urgent medical care to coerce him to commit perjury and of deliberately working to impede the watchdog's investigation into the lawyer's death ... The report said: 'We have come to the conclusion that the circumstances that led to the death of detainee Sergei Magnitsky cannot be viewed separately from the course of the investigation of the criminal case' ... The report highlights the responsibility of a judge at a Moscow court who prolonged Magnitsky's detention four days before his death after refusing to accept written evidence of his medical condition.

(*FT*, 29 December 2009, p. 8)

A report by an independent watchdog issued Monday [28 December] found that Sergei Magnitsky, after complaining of worsening stomach pain for five days, spent the last hour of his life alone in a cell because a prison surgeon ordered a psychiatric examination rather than putting him under a doctor's care ... The inquiry, the commission wrote, 'testifies either to negligence in the performance of their duties, or to an intentional concealment of the reason for refusing the examination' ... Valeri Borshchev [was] the commission's president.

(*IHT*, 29 December 2009, p. 3)

Russia started loading Monday [28 December] the first oil tanker at Kozmino port, the terminus of the East Siberia–Pacific Ocean pipeline that aims to ease access to Asian markets The $26 billion project will give Russian producers the option ... to sell oil to eastern and western customers while helping development in East Siberia.

(*IHT*, 29 December 2009, p. 14)

29 December 2009.

President Dmitri Medvedev has signed a law banning the jailing of tax crime suspects, the Kremlin said yesterday [29 December] ... Under the new law, those who commit tax crimes for the first time but then pay their taxes and fines in full will avoid criminal liability ... [The president] separately sacked the deputy head of the federal prison system ... Alexander Piskunov.

(*FT*, 30 December 2009, p. 5)

'Presidents Dmitri Medvedev and Barack Obama have agreed to extend talks to secure a new pact ... [to replace] the 1991 Strategic Arms Reduction Treaty' (*IHT*, 14 December 2009, p. 3). 'Last July [2009] Presidents Obama and Medvedev outlined a framework for the new treaty, restricting deployed strategic warheads to between 1,500 and 1,675 while limiting the number of delivery platforms to between 500 and 1,100' (www.iht.com, 15 December 2009).

Prime minister Vladimir Putin said Tuesday [29 December] that the main obstacle to replacing the Strategic Arms Reduction Treaty is Washington's plan to build a missile shield, which he said endangers the balance of power established in the Cold War era. He said: 'If we do not develop a missile defence system, a danger arises for us that with an umbrella protecting our partners from offensive weapons, they will feel completely safe. The balance will be disrupted and then they will do whatever they want, and aggressiveness will immediately arise both in real politics and economics' ... To restore that balance, he said, Russia must develop new offensive weapons to counter the missile shield. Another solution, he said, would be for the United States to provide Moscow with data on its missile defence plans in exchange for data on Russian weapons development.

(*IHT*, 30 December 2009, p. 3)

'US officials say they have resumed talks with Russian negotiators in Geneva on a new nuclear arms reduction deal ... The Russian foreign ministry said last week that it hoped to reach an agreement in "just a few weeks"' (www.iht.com, Monday 1 February 2010).

1 January 2010.

Authorities have brought in new measures imposing a minimum price for all vodka sold in the country. The move is part of President Dmitri Medvedev's plan to tackle alcoholism. The cheapest bottle of vodka on sale will now be 89 roubles ($3) for half a litre. An average Russian earns just under 18,000 roubles ($600) per month and illegal vodka can be found for a little as 40 roubles ... Homemade vodka is highly dangerous and contributes heavily to the country's 35,000 deaths a year from alcohol poisoning.

(www.bbc.co.uk, 1 January 2010)

[On 1 January 2010] the minimum price for a half litre of vodka rose to 89 roubles (around $3) from an earlier price of $1.69. The change is part of an anti-alcoholism campaign by President Dmitri Medvedev, who said he was shaken by recent data showing that Russians consume 4.75 gallons of pure alcohol *per capita* every year, more than double the level that the World

Health Organization considers a health threat. The average American, by comparison, consumes 2.3 gallons of pure alcohol per year. A study in *The Lancet*, a British medical journal, found that more than half the deaths of Russians between the ages of fifteen and fifty-four were caused by drinking. A raft of new measures will be imposed on 1 July, including a crackdown on the production of illegal vodka, known as *samogon*. Mr Medvedev has proposed banning sales of beer from sidewalk kiosks and prohibiting the large, cheap containers of beer preferred by young Russians.

(www.iht.com, 2 January 2009)

The price of the cheapest half-litre vodka bottle will nearly double to a minimum of 89 roubles ... The cheapest vodka can be bought for 51 roubles ... Official figures showed that the average Russian drank 19 litres of pure alcohol each year.

(*The Times*, 2 January 2010, p. 40)

The new minimum price ... is aimed at pricing illegal producers out of the retail market ... Two-thirds of the public back the president, according to opinion polls ... Further measures are planned for the first half of 2010, including a single, higher, rate of excise duty for spirits, and the banning of the ubiquitous street-side kiosks where the cheapest alcohol is to be found.

(*The Independent*, 2 January 2010, p. 18)

Prime minister Vladimir Putin gave his approval Thursday [14 January] for a campaign to cut consumption of alcohol by more than half in the next ten years. He approved a series of government steps to tackle the 'national threat' of alcohol addiction, including restrictions on alcohol sales and pro-duction, higher taxation and curbs on advertising ... The strategy document said: '[Russians' health must be put ahead of] the interests of the alcohol market ... Alcohol abuse is the main reason for the rapid accumulation of demographic and social problems in Russia since the mid-1960s' ... The document said 23,000 people died each year from alcohol poisoning and more than 75,000 people from alcohol-related diseases ... Russians drink 18 litres (38 pints) of [pure] alcohol per person per year ... The goal is to cut consumption by 15 per cent by 2012 and by 55 per cent by 2020 ... In August [2009] President Dmitri Medvedev ordered tough measures to curb alcohol abuse, saying he was shocked by official consumption data. Since then Russia has moved to triple the excise duty on beer, introduced minimum prices for vodka and is considering drastic limits on where and when beer can be sold, like banning the alcohol sales at street-side kiosks. In 1985 Mikhail Gorbachev ordered major cuts in the production of wines and spirits and introduced strict controls on public consumption of alcohol. The effort led to a surge in the illegal production of low quality home-brewed alcohol.

(*IHT*, 15 January 2010, p. 3)

26 January 2010. 'Russia and Nato formally resumed military ties Tuesday [26 January] ... It was the first meeting between Nato and Russian military officials since relations broke down after the war between Russia and Georgia in August 2008' (*IHT*, 27 January 2010, p. 3).

29 January 2010.

The Russian military conducted the first successful test of its fifth-generation stealth fighter jet on Friday [29 January] ... The Sukhoi T-50 prototype [is] the first completely new fighter built by Russia since the fall of the Soviet Union ... The test, which was broadcast on Russian television, comes amid a series of failures of weapons systems that has shaken confidence in the nation's military. Russian officials hope the new fighter will one day challenge the United States Air Force's F-22 Raptor, which first flew in 1997.

(www.iht.com, 31 January 2010)

30–31 January 2010.

Up to 10,000 people rallied in the Russian Baltic enclave of Kaliningrad Saturday [30 January] demanding the resignation of prime minister Vladimir Putin over living costs and unemployment, a rare show of anger with the popular figure. Boris Nemtsov, a leader of opposition movement Solidarity, told Ekho Moskvy radio people were protesting a '25 per cent to 30 per cent' rise in utility bills and against high unemployment. He said the rally was organized by political parties, including the Communists ... Authorities traditionally increase bills for housing, transportation, water and electricity after the New Year.

(www.iht.com, 31 January 2010)

Thousands of people poured into Kaliningrad's central square Saturday, protesting higher taxes on automobile imports, cuts in social welfare programmes and high utility costs, organizers said. Numbers varied, with the police saying that no more than 6,000 attended, while organizers said there were more than 10,000. The protest, led by a loose coalition of opposition groups, was uncharacteristically large for Russia ... Much of the ire was directed at the region's governor, Georgi Boos, a former member of parliament from United Russia who is up for reappointment when his term ends later this year [2010]. In 2005, when Vladimir Putin was president, he appointed Mr Boos after doing away with direct gubernatorial elections ... The protest follows a smaller opposition rally in Kaliningrad in December [2009] ... Despite the large turnout Saturday, the authorities allowed the protest to pass peacefully, though federal channels did not cover it ... A high-ranking delegation led by Ilya Klebanov, President Dmitri Medvedev's special representative for the north-west region of Russia, has reportedly been meeting with local leaders in Kaliningrad about the protest since Monday [1 February].

(*IHT*, 3 February 2010, p. 3)

Police broke up protests in Moscow and St Petersburg yesterday [31 January] and detained scores of demonstrators, including opposition leaders. Demonstrators gathered in Moscow, defying a ban. Similar opposition was held on the last days of July, August and October. The timing is a nod to the 31st Article of the Russian constitution, which guarantees the right of assembly. Among those held were opposition leaders Boris Nemtsov and Eduard Limonov and the head of the Memorial rights group, Oleg Orlov. A similar protest in St Petersburg ... was broken up.

(*Guardian*, 1 February 2010, p. 20)

2 February 2010.

President Dmitri Medvedev sent his special envoy [Ilya Klebanov] to Kaliningrad today [2 February] ... to investigate ... after thousands of Russian took to the streets in the largest rally since the fall of the Soviet Union. The protest, staged at the weekend [30 January], saw between 10,000 and 12,000 people gather in Kaliningrad's main square to demand the resignation of the governor and shout slogans against the ruling United Russia party ... Sources suggested that the Kremlin-appointed governor Georgi Boos, was likely to be summoned back to Moscow for a dressing down ... Smaller opposition rallies were held in other towns, including Vladivostok – the scene of regular protests by car drivers over the past eighteen months – as well as Moscow and St Petersburg. Riot police violently broke up a peaceful demonstration in Triumfalnaya Square, Moscow, on Sunday [31 January], arresting 100 people ... Those arrested at Sunday's demonstrations included Oleg Orlov, the chairman of the Memorial Human Rights centre, and Boris Nemtsov, the leader of the pro-democracy Solidarity opposition movement ... Solomon Ginzburg, an opposition leader and independent deputy, said a wide coalition of residents had taken part in the [Kaliningrad] rally, including communists, liberals and ultra-nationalists. He said people were fed up with rising communal and transport charges and wanted Boos – appointed by Vladimir Putin in 2005 – to resign.

(www.guardian.co.uk, 2 February 2010; *Guardian*, 3 February 2010, p. 16)

5 February 2010.

Prime minister Vladimir Putin on Friday [5 February] warned the members of United Russia, the party he leads, that they must win back the loyalty of the people ... Mr Putin's remarks came a week after an anti-government rally in Kaliningrad drew 6,000 to 10,000 people, the largest turnout Russia has seen in years. He told party members that it was 'completely obvious, and right, that citizens turn to us with complaints about various aspects of our activities', and instructed them to pay close attention to those complaints.

(www.iht.com, 7 February 2010)

8 February 2010.

France has agreed to sell Russia an advanced amphibious warship ... the Mistral-class force projection and command vessel ... and is considering a

Russian request for three more, French defence officials said Monday [8 February]. It would be the first major arms deal between Russia and a Nato member ... Nato members and Russia have had some small, country-to-country technology deals in the past but this would be the first sale of a major piece of equipment by a Nato member to Moscow ... Mistral-class ships can anchor in coastal waters and deploy troops on land – a capacity the Russian navy now lacks. Russia's navy chief said last year [2009] that such a ship would have allowed the Russian navy to mount a much more efficient action in the Black Sea during the Georgia–Russia war. He said the French ship would take just forty minutes to do the job that the Russian Black Sea Fleet did in twenty-six hours ... Possessing a Mistral-class ship, which can carry sixteen attack helicopters and dozens of armoured vehicles, would significantly increase the Russian military's ability to launch offensives ... Some other analysts have been sceptical that buying Mistral will help the Russian navy modernize because the ship sold to Russia may be stripped of its most sensitive and valuable systems.

(www.iht.com, 8 February 2010)

'Russia first expressed interest in the French helicopter carrier after the war with Georgia exposed serious shortcomings in the Soviet-era military equipment' (*IHT*, 9 February 2010).

'The deal has not yet been signed' (www.bbc.co.uk, 8 February 2010).

US defence secretary Robert Gates told French officials Monday [8 February] that he was concerned about their plans to sell Mistral-class amphibious assault ships to Russia ... Mr Gates chose the well known diplomatic code for disagreement in describing his discussion of the arms sale with his French counterpart ... Mr Gates said: 'I think I would just say that we had a good and thorough exchange of views' ... The Pentagon press secretary said later ... [that] Mr Gates 'made our concerns very clear' on the arms sale ... Georgia fought a war with Russia [in August 2008] ... The maritime Baltic States have sought information from France about what weapons and advanced technology would be included ... Russia has been engaged in months-long negotiations [with France].

(www.iht.com, 8 February 2010)

'Last November [2009] ... the French helicopter carrier *Mistral* ... [visited] the port of St Petersburg ... Worth about Euro 500 million ($680 million) the *Mistral* can transport about eighteen helicopters, a tank battalion and 450 soldiers' (*IHT*, 13 February 2010, p. 1).

In perhaps the most poignant sign of trouble, Russia's own military is now voting with its roubles: Moscow is in talks with France to buy four Mistral-class amphibious assault ships. If agreement is reached, it would be Russia's most significant acquisition of foreign weapons since World War II. The navy's turn to France for the landing ship is 'the most salient example of the deficiencies in the Russian defence industry', said Dmitri Trenin, a military analysts at the Carnegie Moscow Center, a research group. With Moscow in the middle of a rearmament programme that runs through 2015, the inability of Russia's military contractors to meet the country's needs is causing consternation locally and globally ... The Mistral negotiations have led to geopolitical hand-wringing about what some see as France's willingness to sell out its Nato allies ... Yet opposition to the deal has been nearly as fierce inside Russia – by supporters of the weapons industry ... The $40 billion military equipment industry is showing signs of withering alongside civilian manufacturing ... Once legendary Russian weapons have shown embarrassing quality control problems. Algeria, for example, recently returned a shipment of MIG jets because of defects. An aircraft carrier refurbishment for India is four years late and hundreds of millions of dollars over budget ... The military equipment industry shrank last year [2009] to 4.28 per cent of GDP, down from 20 per cent under communism ... Like much of Russian industry ... the military industry ... was privatized haphazardly. Factories and the engineering bureaux that designed what they made, for example, were sold separately. Over time, this had a deleterious effect on quality. Big companies that inherited export contracts with China, India and the Middle East made profits on older designs and parts taken from stockpiles but did little to upgrade. The end of generous military budgets, too, caused assembly lines to creak to a halt at tank and aircraft factories across the land. More recently, the sector has suffered from an insidious economic problem known as 'Dutch disease' – when an increase in revenue from natural resources (oil and natural gas in Russia's case) pushes up a country's currency, making exports more expensive in world markets ... The rouble has risen almost 16 per cent against the dollar in the past twelve months alone. Other problems have beset Russian military contractors. Many engineers have emigrated, leaving a work force that is near retirement ... Some companies have succeeded and gone public, listing their shares on the Russian stock exchange. United Aircraft, the umbrella company for the makers of the MIG and Sukhoi fighter jets, has a market capitalization of more than $2 billion ... But domestic military spending has not been funnelled into these relatively competitive companies; instead, it has been spread to the entire gamut of military suppliers to maintain the philosophy of Russian self-sufficiency. This meant spending money on hopeless losers, like Russian makers of walkie-talkies. Meanwhile, Russia's share in total global arms sales cratered with the onset of the financial crisis in 2008, according to a US Congressional Research Service report on the international arms sales released in September. Russia sold $3.5 billion worth of weaponry that year, down from $10.8 billion in 2007. That was well behind the United States, the world's largest arms exporter, whose companies sold $37.8 billion worth of weapons – 68 per cent of the total global arms business that year. Russia's market share fell far faster than the 7.6 per cent slump in overall international weapons deals that year, the report said. In the developing world, where Russia surpassed even the United States in military exports in 2004 and

2006, its market share collapsed with the onset of the crisis. Developing-world sales were about flat in 2008, while Russia's share tumbled from 25.2 per cent of all sales to 7.8 per cent in 2008, the latest year for which figures are available ... Russian experts have contested the US figures as underestimates. Rosoboronexport, the state weapons exporting monopoly, said $15 billion in new contracts were signed in 2009 ... The policy within the industry seems to be one of trying to modernize by assimilating foreign technology – much as Russia attempted with the integration of foreign assembly plants into its automobile industry. And some Russian military manufacturers are globalizing. On the civilian side of its production, Sukhoi is in partnership with the Italian aerospace giant Finmeccanica to build the Russian Regional jet; Boeing is advising on the design and marketing. During the visit to India last week by prime minister Vladimir Putin, Russian aerospace executives said they were in talks with India to develop an export version of Russia's first stealth fighter, the Sukhoi T-50. The Indian military signed a $1.5 billion deal Friday [12 March] to buy twenty-nine carrier-based versions of the MIG-29, the same type of jet rejected by Algeria.

(Andrew Kramer, *IHT*, 13 March 2010, pp. 11, 14)

15 February 2010.

Moldova's rebel region of Transdniestre said on Monday [15 February] it was ready to host Russian [Iskander] missiles if the Kremlin were to ask ... Transdniestre linked the offer to the possible deployment of US interceptor missiles to neighbouring Romania. Both Romania and Bulgaria have offered to host elements of a reconfigured US missile shield ... On 12 February Bulgaria expressed its readiness to play a role ... Prime minister Vladimir Putin and other officials [such as foreign minister Sergei Lavrov] have called US missile defence plans an obstacle to a successor to the 1991 Start nuclear arms reduction pact, under discussion for months.

(www.iht.com, 15 February 2010)

Transdniestre leader Igor Smirnov said [on Monday 15 February] Russia had not yet asked to be a host but any request would be approved ... Over the past few days details have emerged of the US offer to Romania and Bulgaria: sea-based interceptor missiles on US ships in the Black Sea from as early as next year [2011], and land-based missiles from 2015 ... In a separate development, the Moldovan prime minister and Romanian interior minister symbolically removed the barbed wire which has stood since Soviet times, and reopened the barbed wire between the two countries.

(www.bbc.co.uk, 16 February 2010)

'Russia declined the [Transdniestre] offer' (www.economist.com, 18 February 2010).

Finans magazine ... [said] that Russia's oligarchs have bounced back from the global financial crisis ... The billionaire class jumped in size to seventy-seven this year [2010] from forty-nine in 2009 … The list of seventy-seven billionaires was the second largest since the rankings were first compiled in 2004, beaten only by the peak of 1010 names put together in 2008 … Vladimir Lisin, a steel magnate, was named Russia's richest man for the first time, with an estimated $18.8 billion, more than double the $7.7 billion he had a year ago. He overtook last year's leader, Mikhail Prokhorov, whose fortune rose to $17.85 billion from $14.1 billion. Roman Abramovich was ranked third with $17 billion, $3.1 billion more than last year. The top ten oligarchs were worth a combined $139.3 billion, up from $75.9 billion last year, but still well down on the pre-crisis total of $221 billion.

(*The Times*, 16 February 2010, p. 38)

Vladimir Lisin … owes his wealth to the Novolipetsk steel mill, one of the world's largest. He also owns an electricity firm … It is the first time that Roman Abramovich has failed to make the top two … Oleg Deripaska … is worth $13.8 billion … Alisher Usmanov (seventh) … is worth $12.4 billion.

(*Guardian*, 16 February 2010, p. 19)

18 February 2010.

President Dmitri Medvedev fired two top interior ministry officials on Thursday [18 February] and said he would eliminate thousands of ministry jobs in an effort to reform a police force widely criticized for corruption and abuse. He said some 15,000 cases of police corruption were logged last year [2009], which he said was 'just the tip of the iceberg'. He dismissed fifteen generals, including ten regional police chiefs, and told police officials that he wanted the ministry cut in half, to about 10,000 employees.

(www.iht.com, 19 February 2010)

President Dmitri Medvedev announced sweeping measures aimed at reforming the country's police force. Mr Medvedev dismissed two deputy interior ministers and sixteen police generals, as well as ordering the staff of the interior ministry police to be cut by half … On Thursday [18 February] President Medvedev castigated Russia's bloated police force for solving barely half the crimes it investigates. He said 2,000 murders and attempted murders go unsolved in Russia each year – a figure he called 'frightening'. He also alluded to the many crimes committed by the police themselves … [In Russia there are] 1.4 million officers.

(www.bbc.co.uk, 19 February 2010)

1 March 2010.

Russia has been left stunned by the worst performance of its Olympic team since the Soviet empire collapsed in 1991. The squad won just three gold medals and only fifteen medals overall [three gold, five silver and seven bronze medals] at the Winter Games in Vancouver, despite predictions that its athletes would bring home as many as thirty-one … [There are] fears that Russia will be humiliated when it hosts the next Winter Olympics in Sochi in

2014 … Russia languished in eleventh place, far below its previous worst of fifth in Salt Lake City in 2002. Sports administrators had told the Kremlin that Russia could win eleven golds in Vancouver and achieve its biggest medal haul since the last Soviet team competed in 1988 … There was particular anguish over Russia's world champion ice hockey team, the vaunted 'Red Machine' that crashed out meekly to Canada 7–3 in the quarter finals … Prime minister Vladimir Putin has put his personal authority and $12 billion in funding behind a triumphant Sochi games … Eight Russian skiers and biathletes were disqualified last year after testing positive for banned substances.

(*The Times*, 1 March 2010, p. 28)

[On Monday 1 March] President Dmitri Medvedev, angered over his country's disappointing performance at the Winter Games, began calling for athletic officials' heads … Russian athletes took home just three gold medals from Vancouver, compared with eight in the last Winter Games. Russia came a disappointing sixth place in the overall medal count with fifteen, trailing far behind the United States, which led with thirty-seven [nine gold, fifteen silver and thirteen bronze].

(www.iht.com, 1 March 2010)

Russia [is] heir to the vaunted Soviet teams that fought Cold-War proxy battles against the West every four years. On the snow and ice of the Winter Olympics especially, the Soviets dominated, winning the most gold medals of the nine times they competed … Even a large infusion of cash in the past several years has not been able to reverse the decay wrought by the Soviet collapse … The Soviet Union had about forty luge tracks … Now, Russian lugers have almost nowhere to train. After the Soviet Union fell, only four remained inside Russian proper, and those quickly crumbled into disrepair in the thin years of the 1990s. A new training track opened outside Moscow in 2008, but it still has problems with its cooling system. With few tracks or other training facilities and little money to train abroad until recently, athletes could not receive proper training … There have been problems to varying degrees across the spectrum of Olympic sports, even in areas like hockey and figure skating where Russia has traditionally excelled … In a meeting with athletic officials this month [March], prime minister Vladimir Putin said that the 2009 federal budget allocated funds to begin construction of 200 athletic facilities, though he admitted such resources did not always reach their intended recipients. Russia spent about $117 million preparing its team for Vancouver, he said, more than five times what was spent on the previous Winter Olympic Games in Turin, Italy. He said: 'A question arises. Maybe that money did not go where it was supposed to.'

(www.iht.com, 14 March 2010; *IHT*, 15 March 2010, pp. 1, 11)

'The Games in Vancouver were particularly painful for the nation because of the failures in sports such as ice hockey and figure skating' (www.bbc.co.uk, 1 March 2010).

President Dmitri Medvedev called for the resignation of the nation's top Olympic officials Monday [1 March] ... On the eve of the Games, Russian sports officials said the country could expect a place in the top three and predicted its athletes would bring home at least thirty medals ... It was in figure skating and ice hockey – the two sports where Russia has for decades been an international powerhouse – that Russia suffered its strongest and most devastating blow. In figure skating it was the first time since 1964 that a Soviet or Russian team did not win any gold. And in the hockey quarter finals the Russian national team lost to Canada for the first time in half a century of Olympic match-ups.

(www.cnn.com, 1 March 2010)

President Dmitri Medvedev decried the state of Russian athletics and called on officials to 'have the courage to submit their resignation' ... Mr Medvedev suggested that Russia's athletic system was set up to favour the 'fat cats' in charge of sports federations rather than athletes.

(www.iht.com, 3 March 2010)

The United States won the highest number of medals in total, thirty-seven (nine gold, fifteen silver and thirteen bronze). Germany was second, with a total of thirty medals (ten gold, thirteen silver and seven bronze). Canada was third, with a total of twenty-six medals (fourteen gold, seven silver and five bronze) (www.bbc.co.uk, 1 March 2010).

The head of Russia's Olympic Committee has stepped down after the nation recorded its worst performance at the Winter Games ... Leonid Tyagachyov resigned after Russia finished with just three golds in its fifteen-medal haul from Vancouver ... A former sports minister, Mr Tyagachyov had been appointed in 2011.

(www.bbc.co.uk, 3 March 2010)

'A former head trainer of the Soviet ski team, Leonid Tyagachyov was named head of the Olympic Committee in 2001' (www.iht.com, 3 March 2010).

Russian authorities have failed to take into account the environmental impact of building work ahead of the 2014 Winter Olympics, the UN says. The UN report comes after leading environmental organizations in Russia withdrew their co-operation, saying their concerns were being ignored ... Relations between environmental organizations and the authorities responsible for the massive Olympics building programme have deteriorated sharply in recent months.

(www.bbc.co.uk, 16 March 2010)

The UN Environmental Programme [UNEP] says in a report ... that impact assessments by Moscow 'did not take into account the cumulative ... effects of the various projects on the ecosystems of the Sochi region and its population' ... As constructors begin building facilities from scratch, environmental activists say the ecosystems have already suffered irreversible damage and bird and bear habitats have been destroyed ... The UNEP report was based on the body's trip to Sochi in January [2010], which involved visits to sites considered sensitive along the construction path of a road and rail link that connects coastal facilities with ones in the mountains ... In its recommendations, UNEP said a 'comprehensive assessment of the overall impact of the Olympic and tourism projects on the ecosystem' should be conducted ... The WWF [the world's leading conservation body] and Greenpeace recently suspended their co-operation as consultants for Olympstroi, the state-run constructor, in protest that their concerns were being ignored. The UNEP report urged activists and the government to continue co-operating ... The Russian government says it has taken the concerns on board and accuses activists of trying to sabotage the Games as a public relations stunt.

(www.guardian.co.uk, 16 March 2010)

Russia's Paralympians can expect a warm welcome from President Dmitri Medvedev following their triumphant showing at the Winter Games in Vancouver ... [They topped] the medal table in Canada ... Russia's thirty-two entrants won thirty-eight medals, twelve of them gold, when the competition ended on Sunday [21 March], with Germany second on twenty-four – a leading thirteen of those being gold. The Russians topped their efforts from the 2006 Turin Games, where they also topped the medal table with thirty-three in total ... Hosts Canada were third with nineteen medals, ten of them gold ... while Ukraine won five events in finishing on the same total. The United States were next with thirteen medals, including four golds.

(www.cnn.com, 22 March 2010)

The Paralympians from Russia dominated ... all without the lavish financing the government provides the main squad. The feat ... was all the more impressive considering that many disabled people here have a hard time just getting out of the front door ... [There is] a lack of ramps and elevators and minimal access to public transportation ... Despite the obstacles – or perhaps because of them – Russia's Paralympians have been wildly successful ... The Soviet collapse opened the door to competition, but with almost no support from the government or corporate sponsors, early Paralympians supported themselves, relying on hand-me-down racing wheelchairs and other equipment from western European athletes they met at competitions, athletes said. Success eventually prompted the government to take notice ... [In 1992 the team] came in third in the medal count, trailing the United States and Germany. Since then the team has been shut out of the top three only once in the Winter Games ... After the team took first place in the 2006 Winter Games in Turin, prime minister Vladimir Putin, then the president, signed a decree making cash prizes awarded by the government to medal winners equal for Olympians and Paralympians. Also under Putin ... the government increased training stipends for disabled athletes, as well as money for foreign travel.

(*IHT*, 20 May 2010, p. 14)

10 March 2010.

The exiled Russian oligarch Boris Berezovsky was today [10 March] awarded libel damages of £150,000 over 'savage' allegations that he was behind the murder of Alexander Litvinenko ... In a chaotic high court battle in London, the sixty-four-year-old tycoon successfully argued his reputation had been seriously damaged by a Russian state television broadcast in April 2007. The programme ... included an interview with a man who claimed he had been offered £40 million by Litvinenko ... to falsely claim to being a KGB hitman tasked with killing Berezovsky with a poisoned ballpoint pen ... In the programme the presenter suggested that Litvinenko, who died from poisoning with radioactive polonium in London in November 2006, was killed at Berezovsky's behest because Litvinenko was a witness to Berezovsky's fraudulent claim for political asylum. The logic was that Litvinenko would be an important witness for Russian prosecutors investigating allegations that Berezovsky's asylum was based on lies, and thus Berezovsky wanted him dead – just in case.

(www.guardian.co.uk 10 March 2010; *Guardian*, 11 March 2010, p. 17)

Boris Berezovsky ... who was granted political asylum in the UK in September 2003 ... was awarded £150,000 ($224,000) at the High Court over a claim made by Russian television channel RTR Planeta ... [Boris Berezovsky] was suing over the broadcast in April 2007. It suggested that Alexander Litvinenko had witnessed an attempt by Mr Berezovsky to avoid extradition and obtain political asylum by obtaining false evidence.

(www.bbc.co.uk, 10 March 2010)

Boris Berezovsky ... won a libel suit in London against a satellite broadcaster that had linked him to the murder in 2006 of Alexander Litvinenko, a one-time aide and former KGB operative who was poisoned with a rare radioactive isotope. Mr Berezovsky was awarded damages equivalent to $225,000 ... The broadcaster, All-Russian Television and Broadcasting, known as RTR, refused to recognize the London court's decision ... In 2007 RTR broadcast a show connecting Mr Berezovsky to the Litvinenko conspiracy ... The libel case was brought in London because, the judge said, it was probably seen by thousands of people in Britain when it was broadcast by satellite.

(www.iht.com, 10 March 2010)

In 2007 RTR broadcast a programme connecting Boris Berezovsky to the Litvinenko conspiracy ... A lawyer for the Russian broadcaster said it did not recognize the decision of the court ... The broadcaster also complained that, unusually, the trial had been conducted without a jury and that the company had not been able to defend itself without revealing the source of its reporting, which it refused to do.

(*IHT*, 11 March 2010, p. 3)

Boris Berezovsky won his claim for libel after being falsely named on Russian state television as the man behind the murder of Alexander

Litvinenko ... Mr Berezovsky was awarded £150,000 in libel damages against both the television channel RTR Planeta and Vladimir Terluk, the man who made the allegations, which were also broadcast on satellite television in the UK in April 2007 ... The central allegation in the programme *Vesti Nedeli* ... was that Mr Berezovsky was somehow responsible for the murder of Mr Litvinenko.

(*The Independent*, 11 March 2010, p. 13)

'During the hearing in London, Mr Justice Eady heard that the Russian Television and Radio Broadcasting Company (RTR), which has never suggested that what it broadcast was true, had declined to take part in the proceedings' (www. independent.co.uk, 10 March 2010).

Boris Berezovsky ... won a high profile libel action following allegations made in a Russian television programme about the murder of Alexander Litvinenko ... Mr Berezovsky ... [was] awarded £150,000 in damages against RTR Planeta, the Russian state broadcaster, and an individual called Vladimir Terluk, over allegations broadcast in April 2007 about the murder of Mr Litvinenko.

(*FT*, 11 March 2010, p. 4)

14 March 2010.

United Russia again dominated regional elections, according to preliminary results released Monday [15 March], though opposition parties made slight gains ... Voters chose new legislatures in eight regions on Sunday [14 March] and regional and municipal elections were held in seventy-six of Russia's eighty-three regions ... United Russia ... chalked up landslide victories in all eight legislature elections and won four of five mayoral races ... In some regional parliamentary elections on Sunday ... United Russia ... won over 60 per cent of the vote ... Support for United Russia, however, was significantly lower in some regions than it has been in the past, with a greater share of the vote going to the other three political parties – the Communist Party, A Just Russia and the Liberal Democratic Party. Though these opposition parties also operate to varying degrees at the behest of the Kremlin, the shift from United Russia suggests some dissatisfaction with the country's dominant political force as Russians continue to struggle with the effects of the economic crisis. The economy contracted by 8 per cent last year [2009] and unemployment rose to 9.2 per cent in January, according to official data ... In the weeks before the elections, anti-government protests were held in several cities, with demonstrators demanding an end to increases in utility prices and automobile taxes, among other complaints ... In regional elections last October [2009] ... United Russia ... trounced its opponents, gaining, for example, thirty-two out of thirty-five seats in the Moscow city legislature amid accusations of widespread fraud ... Shortly after October's elections, President Dmitri Medvedev accused United Russia of 'backwardness', admonishing the party for hamstringing elections with 'bureaucratic intrigues and games' ... On Sunday United Russia won less than half the vote in four of the eight regional parliamentary elections, and, unlike in previous elections, all four major parties won seats. In elections for the Sverdlovsk regional legislature, for instance, United Russia won just under 40 per cent of the vote compared with over 58 per cent in 2008 elections. Meanwhile, the Communist party collected about 22 per cent of the vote there on Sunday, compared with 12 per cent in the previous elections. In another blow United Russia's candidate for mayor in the Siberian city of Irkutsk ... lost to a local businessman backed by the Communist Party ... As usual, there were complaints of election law violations from all parties, though, uncharacteristically, party leaders for the most part said they were satisfied with the results. On the whole, the Communist Party, which is the only viable opposition to United Russia not completely co-opted by the Kremlin, fared well.

(www.iht.com, 15 March 2010; *IHT*, 16 March 2010, p. 3)

20 March 2010.

Russian held relatively small demonstrations across the country on Saturday [20 March] to call for the ouster of prime minister Vladimir Putin, seeking to mobilize discontent over a faltering economy, rising prices and government officials perceived as unresponsive to average people. Organizers, after weeks of appealing for support for a 'Day of Anger', had hoped to bring out tens of thousands of protesters from Vladivostok on the Pacific coats all the way to Kaliningrad on the Baltic Sea. But the turnout fell short of their predictions ... In Kaliningrad ... several hundred people [turned out] ... The Kremlin clamped down on many of the protests by using the security services to put pressure on opposition groups and by offering minor concessions. In several cities, including Kaliningrad and Moscow, the authorities refused to allow protests in central locations, though people still tried. State media gave little or no attention, and the Kremlin publicly ignored the protests ... In Kaliningrad, a Russian enclave between Lithuania and Poland that is geographically separate from the rest of the country, organizers had wanted to repeat their success of late January, when they amassed several thousand people in a protest against tax increases, cuts in social programme and utility costs ... But opposition groups have since fragmented, and a prominent one, Solidarity, cancelled the Kaliningrad protest, saying that it feared violence. Still, several hundred people gathered on a rain-soaked central square and demanded the resignation of the regional governor, Georgi Boos, who was appointed by the Kremlin ... Unlike in other cities, the police in Kaliningrad did not try to disperse or arrest protesters ... In Moscow city officials did not permit a coalition of opposition groups to conduct a demonstration on Pushkin Square, a central intersection. As is often the case, the groups announced that they would hold it anyway. Only a few hundred protesters turned out, and they were greeted by numerous police officers and journalists ... The police arrested a few dozen people before the rally dispersed.

(www.iht.com, 21 March 2010; *IHT*, 22 March 2010, p. 3)

Small street protests are not uncommon and are generally tolerated by the authorities ... But officials both ... in Kaliningrad ... and in Moscow were clearly caught off guard in January when as many as 10,000 people poured into a central Kaliningrad square to demand the resignation of the regional governor and other officials from ... United Russia ... Since then, the authorities have been scrambling to contain the damage lest the dissatisfaction in Kaliningrad spread to the rest of the country. They were able to head off another protest scheduled for last weekend [20 March], in part by making serious promises to opposition leaders to resolve their major complaints ... Though protest leaders called off a planned demonstration last week, several hundred people gathered in central Kaliningrad, shouting 'Down with Boos' ... Just a few years ago ... many were doing good business importing cars into Kaliningrad to resell to Russian farther east, one of many similar professions that thrived because import tariffs from European countries into Kaliningrad were cheaper than those for the rest of Russia. A year ago, however, the Kremlin sharply increased customs duties on imported cars.

(www.iht.com, 26 March 2010)

Thousands of demonstrators took to the streets across Russia ... to protest against the Kremlin's authoritarian policies and falling living standards. Opposition groups declared Saturday [20 March] a national protest day – the 'Day of Wrath' ... However, turnout was lower than hoped as authorities aimed to split the opposition. In most cities authorities bribed, cajoled or threatened opposition leaders to neutralize them. If that did not work, the riot police made short work of protesters. In Moscow, the most violent protest resulted in scuffles with police and thirty arrests. The authorities were anxious to avoid a repeat of January's protest in the Baltic city of Kaliningrad, where Russian leaders were taken by surprise by a 10,000-strong turnout. In Kaliningrad the opposition was split on whether to call an unsanctioned protest after authorities denied them a location in which to rally. Recriminations flew as opposition leaders called off the planned march ... Even so, 1,000 to 2,000 protesters showed up on Saturday for a 'flash mob' in a city car park ... But the rain-drenched crowd quickly dispersed ... Local governor Georgi Boos held a four-hour phone-in on Saturday, answering complaints, after which he met journalists for a combative press conference ... Rallies began in the Pacific port of Vladivostok, the scene of violent protests last year [2009], where more than 1,000 people gathered to protest against restrictive taxes on car imports. In Irkutsk, a city in east Siberia, about 1,000 protesters complained about a decision by prime minister Vladimir Putin, to reopen a factory they say pollutes Lake Baikal. They cheered loudly as Boris Nemtsov, an opposition leader, called for Mr Putin to resign ... In Moscow thirty activists were arrested as police dispersed a demonstration in the central Pushkin Square. Forty more demonstrators were detained at other rallies across the capital ... while motorists, protesting against car and road taxes, blocked part of the inner ring road.

(*FT*, 22 March 2010, p. 7)

[Protesters] descended on Kaliningrad's central square in droves. They came despite the local governor's offer of negotiations, and the driving rain. For an hour on Saturday [20 March] some 5,000 protesters called loudly for the resignations of the local governor Georgi Boos and prime minister Vladimir Putin, and bemoaned falling living standards and the lack of democracy in the country ... Across Russia the so-called 'Day of Wrath', with protests organized in fifty cities from the Baltic to the Pacific, was mostly a disappointment for the opposition. Just a few hundred people turned out in Vladivostok and Irkutsk, places where organizers had expected thousands. In Moscow there were just a few dozen protesters, many of whom were swiftly arrested ... But Kaliningrad [population 940,000] is fast becoming the vanguard of the Russian opposition movement ... Most people said they were there because they wanted systematic political change ... Protesters, male and female ranging in age from teenagers to pensioners, said they were sick of living in the present political climate ... A protest in the city in January drew more than 10,000 people and took the authorities by surprise ... In an unprecedented step, Mr Boos invited the opposition for talks ... The authorities hastily organized a farmers' market for the square on Saturday, and prominent opposition figures reported the tax police taking a sudden interest in their accounts.

(*The Independent*, 22 March 2010, p. 23)

By the beginning of 2010 unemployment ... in Kaliningrad ... had climbed to over 10 per cent – considerably higher than the Russian average ... A member of United Russia, Georgi Boos became Kaliningrad Region governor in autumn 2005 after the local parliament approved his nomination by Vladimir Putin.

(www.bbc.co.uk, 10 February 2010)

In Russian prisons the inmates are divided into barracks housing a hundred or so men without regard to the severity of their crimes ... Beginning this year [2010], however, first-time offenders may no longer have to live in fear. In the first major effort to upgrade a prison system that has changed little since Stalin established it more than seventy years ago, career criminals will be separated from the general prison population and housed in new prisons with cellblocks, rather than barracks. President Dmitri Medvedev ... is pushing the measure to first break up the culture of barracks life and then to do away with common inmate housing almost entirely ... The vast majority of Russian prisoners – 724,000 out of a total prison population of 862,000 – still live in freestanding barracks, rough-hewn, low-slung buildings of wood or brick encircled by barbed wire, usually in a remote place. Low cost and high volume, they are modest upgrades of the camps of the 1930s to 1950s and hold the second highest *per capita* inmate population in the world, trailing only the United States. The overhaul calls for a three-stage unwinding of the barracks housing system and the abolition of all 755 penal colonies, what remains of Stalin's gulag, by 2020. Under the plan some sites will be renamed 'settlement colonies', a sort of minimum security prison. Hardened prisoners will be moved to cellblocks, though only just over 2,700 inmates live in cells in Russia today ... The effort represents a departure from a long tradition of Russian correction philosophy. Correctional officers had openly – and legally until this January [2010] – used the coarse social groupings ['authorities', 'activists', 'the men' and 'the degraded'] that arose in the barracks to help run the colonies.

(www.iht.com, 23 March 2010; *IHT*, 24 March 2010, p. 17)

25 March 2010.

The Russian tycoon Alexander Lebedev has agreed to buy the money-losing British newspapers *The Independent* and *The Independent on Sunday*, the current owner said Thursday [25 March]. Mr Lebedev, who last year [2009] bought control of the London *Evening Standard*, paid £1 ($1.49) for the *Independent* papers, which lost £12.4 million last year. Independent News and Media said ... Independent News and media agreed to pay Mr Lebedev's company £9.25 million over ten months to take on the future liabilities of the newspapers ... The buyer is Independent Print, a company controlled by Mr Lebedev's family. The deal [is] expected to be completed in May ... Mr Lebedev, a former KGB agent, purchased a 75 per cent stake in the *Evening Standard* in January 2009 from the Daily Mail and General Trust. The newspaper is now the sole evening newspaper in London and is distributed free of charge.

(www.iht.com, 25 March 2010)

Alexander Lebedev first went into business in the early 1990s and built his main company, National Reserve Corporation, into a conglomerate that owns one of Russia's major banks, large stakes in Aeroflot (the airline), and Ilyushin (the aircraft maker), and holdings in several other industries. *Forbes* magazine estimates Mr Lebedev's wealth at $2 billion. His past as a spy raised eyebrows when he entered the British market in January 2009 by buying a 75.1 per cent stake in the *Evening Standard*, the only major paper for the London region. He again made waves last fall [2009] by making the *Evening Standard* free to readers, more than doubling its circulation and increasing its advertising revenue. He has not said he will do the same with *The Independent* or what role will be played in it by his son, Evgeni, who is chairman of the *Evening Standard*.

(www.iht.com, 26 March 2010)

Reports in Britain ... [have] credited the Lebedevs with keeping alive two money-losing daily papers that probably would have died without the new owners and not interfering with the *Evening Standard*'s news coverage ... Evgeni Lebedev (chairman of the *Evening Standard*): 'We have gone from a paper that was losing almost £500,000 a week [about $745,000] to now about half that or even less ... Alexander Lebedev ... began reading British newspapers in the 1980s, as part of his KGB work gathering intelligence on the British economy. For several years the agency stationed him in London. He went into business after the Soviet Union disintegrated in the early 1990s and built an empire that includes banking, airlines, hotels and manufacturing. He said his business experience, dealing with corruption in Russia and other countries, sharpened his interest in fostering openness and investigative journalism ... When other Russian tycoons were buying sports teams, Mr Lebedev invested, along with Mikhail Gorbachev, in *Novaya Gazeta*, a newspaper noted for investigative work critical of the government and powerful business interests. It is also know for its four journalists murdered in the last decade, including Anna Politkovskaya ... Early this year [2010] the airline Aeroflot, which is primarily government owned, agreed to buy back his stake in the company. Alexander Lebedev has sought public office repeatedly and served for four years in the Duma ... he has switched parties multiple times, and he and Mr Gorbachev talked of forming a reformist party ... In Russia and Britain the Lebedevs have advocated a press that is not aligned with or controlled by any political of business faction, and under them the *Evening Standard* has moved away from its former pro-Conservative stance.

(www.iht.com, 29 March 2010)

In addition to the *Evening Standard*, the Lebedevs also co-own, with Mikhail Gorbachev, *Novaya Gazeta*, one of Russia's few pro-democracy newspapers. The paper has a reputation for independence and high quality journalism. Anna Politkovskaya worked for *Novaya Gazeta* ... Alexander Lebedev also announced that he and Mikhail Gorbachev plan to establish Novaya Independent Media Foundation, a not-for-profit organization that will finance global media projects ... The *Evening Standard*'s circulation has risen from 250,000 to 600,000 ... substantially increasing its commercial revenues.

(www.independent.co.uk, 25 March 2010)

26–27 March 2010.

Supporters of Stalin opened a slander case in a Moscow court on Friday [26 March]. Stalin's grandson Yevgeni Dzhugashvili is seeking $330,000 and a retraction from the radio station Ekho Moskvy over a claim that Stalin sanctioned the execution of children as young as twelve during the 1930s purges ... Mr Dzhugashvili lost another defamation suit last October [2009] over his grandfather's memory. A Moscow judge rejected his claim that the newspaper *Novaya Gazeta* defamed Stalin's name in an article that said he personally ordered the deaths of Soviet citizens.

(www.iht.com, 27 March 2010)

Russian prosecutors have banned Adolf Hitler's 1925 book *Mein Kamp* as extremist in an attempt to combat the growing allure of far-right politics … It has been championed by some Russian far-right groups. The prosecutor's office said: 'The book justifies the destruction of non-Aryan races.'

(www.independent.com, 27 March 2010)

[Russia is] the world's largest country by land mass. This weekend Russia is cutting the number of its time zones from eleven to nine … Five Russian regions – two in European Russia and three in Siberia – will not join the rest of the country in moving the clock one hour forward to daylight saving at 2 a.m. on Sunday [28 March], thus coming a little closer to Moscow.

(www.cnn.com, 27 March 2010)

The Far East regions of Chukotka and Kamchatka will go from nine to eight hours ahead of Moscow by not switching to summer time … Moscow's time zone will absorb the Samara region and the republic of Udmurtia, abolishing a time zone one hour ahead of the capital.

(*The Times*, 27 March 2010, p. 46)

26 March 2010.

President Barack Obama and President Dmitri Medvedev … finalized a new arms control treaty with Russia on Friday [26 March] … in a morning telephone call, confirming resolution of the last outstanding details. They then announced they will fly to Prague to sign the treaty on 8 April … President Barack Obama: 'Broadly speaking, the new Start treaty makes progress in several areas. It cuts – by about a third – the nuclear weapons that the United States and Russia will deploy. It significantly reduces missiles and launchers. It puts in place a strong and effective verification regime. And it maintains the flexibility that we need to protect and advance our national security, and to guarantee our unwavering commitment to the security of our allies' … While the pact recognizes the dispute between the two countries over American plans for missile defence based in Europe, it will not restrict the United States from building such a shield. Instead, the two sides each drafted separate non-binding statements reiterating their positions on missile defence. Russia warned in its statement that it reserved the right to withdraw from the new treaty if it decided that American missile defence plans were developing in a way that threatened its security. The United States asserted in its statement that it would develop missile defence as it saw fit, but offered assurance that the programme was not aimed at Russia nor at undermining the security balance between the two countries … According to people in Washington and Moscow who were briefed on the new treaty, it will lower the legal limit on deployed strategic warheads to 1,550 each, from the 2,200 allowed as of 2012 under the previous treaty. It would lower the limit on launchers to 800 from the 1,600 now permitted. Nuclear-armed missiles and heavy bombers would be capped at 700 each. The United States currently has 2,100 deployed strategic warheads and Russia 2,600, according to the Federation of American Scientists and the Natural Resources Defense Council, so each side will have to cut hundreds within seven years after the treaty is ratified. But both sides have been cutting launchers unilaterally for years, with the United States already below 1,200 and Russia already at the 800 level permitted in the new treaty. Moreover, the treaty does not limit thousands of tactical nuclear bombs and stored strategic warheads each side has .. President Obama will be host to the leaders of as many as forty-five countries in Washington on 12 April, four days after the treaty signing in Prague, to discuss how to prevent nuclear material from falling into the wrong hands. No president has ever before gathered more than forty heads of state for a stand-alone summit meeting, according to the White House. And then a month after that world leaders will gather in New York for the regular review conference of the Nuclear Non-proliferation Treaty ... President Obama: 'The Czech Republic ... has agreed to host President Medvedev and me on 8 April, as we sign this treaty. The following week, I look forward to hosting leaders from over forty countries here in Washington, as we convene a summit to address how we can secure vulnerable nuclear materials so that they never fall into the hands of terrorists. And later this spring, the world will come together in New York to discuss how we can build on this programme, and continue to strengthen the global non-proliferation regime' ... Mr Obama also wants to negotiate a treaty on fissile materials, and plans to press the Senate to finally ratify the Comprehensive Test Ban Treaty ... Secretary of state Hillary Clinton: 'The United States and Russia still possess more than 90 per cent of the world's nuclear weapons. We do not need such large arsenals to protect our nations and our allies against the two greatest dangers we face today: nuclear proliferation and terrorism' ... defence secretary Robert Gates: 'This treaty strengthens nuclear stability. It will reduce the number of strategic nuclear weapons that both Russia and the United States are permitted to deploy by a third, and maintains an effective verification regime. America's nuclear arsenal remains an important pillar of the US defence posture, both to deter adversaries and to reassure more than two dozen allies and partners who rely on our nuclear umbrella for their security.'

(www.iht.com, 26 March 2010; *IHT*, 27 March 2010, p. 6)

[The new treaty] will establish an inspection regime to replace one that expired in December [2009] ... For a year Russia had been testing him, suspecting he was weak and certain it could roll over him ... President Barack Obama and President Dmitri Medvedev met or talked by telephone fourteen times to hash through disputes ... Mr Obama first met Mr Medvedev last

April [2009] at an economic summit meeting in London ... At a meeting on climate change in Copenhagen [7–18 December 2009] he met Mr Medvedev again ... [Among other things they agreed] they would conduct eighteen inspections a year, up from ten originally proposed by Moscow.

(www.iht.com, 27 March 2010; *IHT*, 29 March 2010, p. 2)

The preamble includes a phrase intended to mollify Russian objections by 'recognizing the existence of the interrelationship between strategic offensive arms and strategic defensive arms', a relationship that becomes 'more important' as the two sides further reduce weapons.

(www.iht.com, 10 April 2010)

'While the treaty will count the actual number of warheads deployed on land- and sea-based ballistic missiles, it will count each heavy bomber as a single warhead, even though they can carry far more' (www.iht.com, 31 March 2010).

In coming years President Barack Obama will decide whether to deploy a new class of weapons capable of reaching any corner of the earth from the United States in under an hour and with such accuracy that they would greatly diminish America's reliance on its nuclear arsenal. 'Yet even now concerns about the technology are so strong that the Obama administration has acceded to a demand by Russia that the United States decommission one nuclear missile for every one of these conventional weapons fielded by the Pentagon, That provision, the White House says, is buried deep inside the new Start treaty ... The new weapon ... [is called] Prompt Strike ... President George W. Bush and his staff promoted the technology ... In face-to-face meetings with President Bush the Russian leaders complained that the technology could increase the risk of a nuclear war, because Russia would not know if the missiles carried nuclear warheads or conventional ones ... The Pentagon hopes to deploy an early version of the system by 2014 or 2015. But even under optimistic timetables a complete array of missiles, warheads, sensors and control systems is not expected to enter the arsenal until 2017 to 2020 ... Under the administration's new concept Russia or other nations would regularly inspect the Prompt Global Strike silos to assure themselves that the weapons were non-nuclear. And they would be placed in locations far from the strategic nuclear force. Gary Samore (Barack Obama's top adviser on unconventional weapons): 'Who knows if we would ever deploy it?' ... But he noted that Russia was so focused on the possibility that it insisted that any conventional weapon mounted on a missile that could reach it counted against the new limit on the American arsenal in the treaty.

(www.iht.com, 23 April 2010)

('Ukraine's new president, Viktor Yanukovich, has offered Kiev as a location for the United States and Russia to sign a revamped nuclear arms reduction treaty, once it has been agreed to ... Russian officials welcomed the offer; the United States would prefer Prague, where President Barack Obama gave a speech on disarmament last year [2009]': www.iht.com, 17 March 2010.)

The agreement – called the Measures to Further Reduction and Limitation of Strategic Offensive Arms – replaces the Start Treaty signed in 1991 and the Moscow Treaty signed in 2001 ... [The new treaty] limits missile forces to 800 deployed and non-deployed intercontinental ballistic missile launchers, submarine-launched ballistic missile launchers, and heavy bombers equipped for nuclear weapons. The cap on deployed intercontinental ballistic missiles and submarine launched missiles is set at 700, the White House said.

(www.bbc.co.uk, 26 March 2010)

The new Strategic Arms Reduction Treaty (Start) will last ten years ... President Barack Obama told reporters at the White House: 'It puts in place a strong and effective verification regime' ... Information released by the White House says the new treaty limits both nations to 'significantly fewer strategic arms within seven years' of its signing. One of the limits: 1,550 warheads. The White House said 'Warheads on deployed ICBMs (intercontinental ballistic missiles) and deployed SLBMs (submarine-launched ballistic missiles) count toward this limit and each deployed heavy bomber equipped for nuclear armaments counts as one warhead toward this limit.' There are also limits on launchers. The treaty lays out a 'verification regime' that includes on-site inspections, data exchanges and notifications, the White House said. The White House said: 'The treaty does not contain any constraints on testing, development or deployment of current or planned US missile defence programmes or current or planned United States long-range conventional strike capabilities' ... The issue ... of missile defence ... was resolved by including non-binding language in the Start Treaty's preamble stating that there is a relationship between offensive and defensive weapons.

(www.cnn.com, 26 March 2010)

A Kremlin statement said: 'The new treaty stipulates that strategic arms will be based exclusively on the territories of each of the nations' ... The agreement must still be ratified by the [US] Senate [at least sixty-seven seats out of 100 being needed] and both houses of the Russian parliament.

(www.independent.co.uk, 26 March 2010)

'It is understood that the preamble in the treaty agreed today [26 March] will impose no limits on missile defence but will acknowledge it plays a role in fuelling the nuclear arms race' (www.guardian.co.uk, 26 March 2010).

'Another conference takes place in May [2010], under the auspices of the United Nations, for a five-yearly review of the Nuclear Non-proliferation Treaty' (www.economist.com, 27 March 2010).

Three previous arms control treaties – Start 1 (1992), Start 2 (1996) and the Moscow Treaty (2003) – were ratified [in the United States] with substantial bipartisan support ... Ratification requires a two-thirds vote in the Senate ... Start 1 expired in December [2009]. Start 2 never took effect because Russia withdrew after the Bush administration abrogated the ABM Treaty in 2002 to pursue missile defence. The Moscow Treaty set the current ceiling of 2,200 deployed warheads.

(www.iht.com, 28 March 2010)

In May [2010] the operation of the Nuclear Non-proliferation Treaty will be the subject of review in New York in which nearly all governments in the world will take part. The review that took place in 2005 ended in acrimony and some predicted the end of the treaty. Through adherence to the non-proliferation treaty that was concluded in 1970, states have committed themselves to stay away from nuclear weapons or to move away from these weapons. If all states had joined and fulfilled their commitments, the treaty would have led by now to a world free of nuclear weapons. This has not happened, of course. The number of nuclear weapons, which peaked at more than 50,000 during the Cold War, is still over 20,000 – most of them in the United States and Russia. The number of states with nuclear weapons has gone from five to nine since 1970 … [There was an] obligation of five nuclear weapons states under the treaty to negotiate toward nuclear disarmament … Israel has nuclear weapons and has refrained from adhering to the treaty … Although Iraq and Libya have been brought into compliance, North Korea has not and Iran and perhaps others might be aiming to ignore the treaty … There are many reasons for suspecting that the aim of Iran's enrichment programme is the development of a nuclear weapon in breach of treaty obligations or, at least, to move closer to the ability to make a weapon … The Comprehensive Test Ban Treaty has not entered into force because the United States, China and a number of other states have not ratified it. The negotiation of a convention prohibiting the production of enriched uranium and plutonium for weapons remains blocked at the Geneva Disarmament Conference. The Additional Protocol of the International Atomic Energy Agency for strengthened safeguards inspections remains unratified by a large number of states, including Iran … In the last few years the appeals have intensified for governments to aim, as the non-proliferation treaty does, to free the world from nuclear weapons. In January 2007 former US secretaries of state George Schultz and Henry Kissinger, former secretary of defence Bill Perry and former senator Sam Nunn published an article in which they reminded the United States and the world that the Cold War was over. They argued that if the United States, Russia and others continued to see nuclear weapons as necessary for their security, others would see the same thing and proliferation would result. They urged that the United States and Russia take the lead in a long process that would eventually result in a nuclear weapon-free world … [President Barack Obama and President Dmitri Medvedev] jointly espoused the long-term aim of full disarmament in a declaration in London in April 2009.

(Hans Blix, head of the International Atomic Energy Agency from 1981 to 1997 and chief UN arms inspector for Iraq from 2000 to 2003, www.iht. com, 4 April 2010; *IHT*, 5 April 2010, p. 8)

28 March 2010.

Thousands of people demonstrated Sunday [28 March] in the north-western city of Arkhangelsk against the high cost of living and demanded that the government quit. About 4,000 people held an unauthorized rally in biting cold at a large Lenin monument in the main square.

(*IHT*, 29 March 2010, p. 3)

2 April 2010.

Prime minister Vladimir Putin arrived at Caracas on Friday [2 April] to meet ... President Hugo Chavez and later hold talks with Bolivian president Evo Morales ... The highlight of Putin's visit will be the creation of a joint venture between Venezuela's state oil company PDVSA and a consortium of Russian firms to tap the Junin 6 field in the Orinoco oil belt ... the development will require $20 billion in investments over forty years ... The Russian companies involved ... are state giant Rosneft, private major Lukoil, Gazprom, TNK-BP and Surgutneftegaz ... PDVSA holds a 60 per cent stake in the project.

(www.iht.com, 2 April 2010)

Prime minister Vladimir Putin signed a series of key energy deals with Venezuela president Hugo Chavez during his visit to Caracas. Mr Chavez said Russia had agreed to help Venezuela with a nuclear power plant and building a space industry ... Bolivian president Evo Morales was also invited to meet Mr Putin in Caracas ... Mr Morales was expected to seek Russian loans to purchase military hardware and to discuss gas and oil exploration in Bolivia.

(www.bbc.co.uk, 3 April 2010)

5 April 2010.

President Barack Obama said Monday [5 April] that he was revamping American nuclear strategy to substantially narrow the conditions under which the United States would use nuclear weapons. But the president said in an interview [with *The New York Times*] that he was carving out an exception for 'outliers like Iran and North Korea' that have violated or renounced the main treaty to halt proliferation ... North Korea renounced the Nuclear Non-proliferation Treaty in 2003. Iran remains a signatory, but the UN Security Council has repeatedly found it in violation of its obligations ... The new strategy renounces the development of any new nuclear weapons, overruling the initial position of his own defence secretary ... For the first time the United States is explicitly committing not to use nuclear weapons against non-nuclear states that are in compliance with the Nuclear Non-proliferation Treaty, even if they attacked the United States with biological or chemical weapons or launched a crippling cyber-attack ... White House officials said the new strategy would include the option of reconsidering the use of nuclear retaliation against a biological attack, if the development of such weapons reached a level that made the United States vulnerable to a devastating strike ... The release of the new strategy, known as the Nuclear Posture Review, opens an intensive nine days of nuclear diplomacy geared toward reducing weapons. Mr Obama flies to Prague to sign a new arms control agreement with Russia on Thursday [8 April] and then will host forty-seven world leaders in Washington for a summit meeting on nuclear security ... The strategy to be released on Tuesday [6 April] is months late, partly because Mr Obama had to adjudicate among advisers who feared he was not changing American policy significantly enough, and those who fear that anything too precipitous could embolden potential adversaries ... He ended up with a document that differed considerably from the one President George W. Bush published in early 2002, just three months after the 11 September attacks. Mr Bush, too, argued for a post-Cold War rethinking of nuclear deterrence, reducing reliance on those weapons. But Mr Bush's document also reserved the right to use nuclear weapons 'to deter a wide range of threats', including banned chemical and biological weapons and large-scale conventional attacks. Mr Obama's strategy abandons that option – except if the attack is by a nuclear state, or a non-signatory or violator of the non-proliferation treaty. The document to be released Tuesday after months of study by the Defense Department will declare that 'the fundamental role' of nuclear weapons is to deter attacks on the United States, allies or partners, a narrower presumption than the past. But Mr Obama rejected the formulation sought by arms control advocates to declare that the 'sole role' of nuclear weapons is to deter a nuclear attack.

(www.iht.com, 6 April 2010)

Mr Obama on Monday described his policy as part of a broader effort to edge the world toward making nuclear weapons obsolete and to create incentives for countries to give up nuclear ambitions ... Mr Obama's strategy ... seeks to revamp the American nuclear posture for a new age in which rogue states and terrorist organizations are greater threats than traditional powers like Russia and China. It eliminates much of the ambiguity that has deliberately existed in US nuclear policy since the opening days of the Cold War ... Mr Obama said: 'We are going to want to make sure that we can continue to move toward less emphasis on nuclear weapons ... [and to] make sure that our conventional capability is an effective deterrent in all but the most extreme circumstances.'

(*IHT*, 7 April 2010, pp. 1, 4)

The Nuclear Posture Review said: 'The massive nuclear arsenal we inherited from the Cold War era of bipolar military confrontations is poorly suited to address the challenges posed by suicidal terrorists and unfriendly regimes seeking nuclear weapons. Therefore, it is essential that we better align our nuclear policies and posture to our most urgent priorities – preventing nuclear terrorism and nuclear proliferation.'

(*The Independent*, 7 April 2010, p. 19)

President Obama's administration has unveiled a defence policy to significantly narrow the circumstances in which the United States would use nuclear
arms. But its far-reaching Nuclear Posture Review warned countries breaking
the rules remain potential targets ... The Nuclear Policy Review, published on
Tuesday [6 April], outlines plans for 'achieving substantial further nuclear
force reductions' beyond the new [Start] treaty. Every president since 1991
has conducted such a review – the last one took place in 2001 at the start of
George W, Bush's administration ... For the first time the United States is
ruling out a nuclear response to attacks on America involving biological,
chemical or conventional weapons. But this comes with a big caveat: countries will only be spared a nuclear response if they comply with the Nuclear
Non-proliferation Treaty – this does not include Iran and North Korea ... The
document said America would only use nuclear arms in 'extreme circumstances', and committed it to not developing any new nuclear warheads ...
The US strategy document also raised concerns about a 'lack of transparency'
in China's nuclear programme ... The US defence department document said
China's nuclear arsenal remained much smaller than those of Russia and
America. It noted: 'But the lack of transparency surrounding its nuclear programmes – their pace and scope, as well as the strategy and doctrine that
guides them – raises questions about China's future strategic intentions' ...
The White House announced later on Tuesday that President Barack Obama
would hold talks with Chinese president Hu Jintao on the sidelines of a
nuclear non-proliferation summit ... The two-day conference begins in Washington on Monday [12 April].

(www.bbc.co.uk, 6 April 2010)

The Nuclear Policy Review said: 'The United States and China's Asian
neighbours remain concerned about the pace and scope of China's current
military modernization efforts, including its quantitative and qualitative
modernization of its nuclear capabilities' ... The US report reiterated the
Pentagon's oft-stated wish to hold a strategic dialogue with the Chinese
military that would 'provide a venue and mechanism for each side to communicate its views about the other's strategies, policies and programmes
on nuclear weapons and other strategic capabilities. The goal of such a
dialogue is to enhance confidence, improve transparency, and reduce
mistrust.'

(www.iht.com, 6 April 2010)

The document released Tuesday [6 April] declares that 'the fundamental
role' of nuclear weapons is to deter nuclear attacks on the United States,
allies or partners, a narrower presumption than the past. But Mr Obama
rejected the formulation sought by arms control advocates that the 'sole
role' of nuclear weapons is to deter a nuclear attack ... [There are an] estimated 200 tactical nuclear weapons [that] the United States still has stationed in Western Europe. Russia has called for their removal and there is
growing interest among European nations in such a move as well. But Mr

Obama said he wanted to consult with Nato allies before making such as commitment.

(IHT, 7 April 2010, p. 4)

President Barack Obama ... has committed to maintaining the safety and security of America's nuclear stockpile. He has already backed that up with an extra $624 million in next year's budget for the nuclear labs and promised ... an additional $5 billion over the next five years to build up their ageing infrastructure. Mr Obama has also promised support for more advanced conventional arms.

(www.iht.com, 7 April 2010)

'President Barack Obama's new strategy marks a break with the Bush administration's more hawkish policy laid out in its 2002 review, threatening the use of nuclear weapons to pre-empt or respond to chemical or biological attack, even from non-nuclear countries' (www.guardian.co.uk, 6 April 2010).

The Nuclear Posture Review, published after a year's work, marks one of the biggest changes in strategic thinking since the end of the Cold War and reverses policies introduced by the Bush administration. Among the changes is a pledge not to develop any new nuclear weapons, a move pushed through in the face of strong resistance by the Pentagon ... The Nuclear Posture Review shifts the focus away from a Cold War strategy that saw the main threat as coming from Russia or China, recognizing the major threat now is from nuclear proliferation or from a terrorist organization. It also regards a huge nuclear stockpile as redundant. The biggest change is recognition that the circumstances in which nuclear weapons could be used had to be narrowed. The key passage in the review says that the strategic situation has changed since the end of the Cold War and the United States has a strong enough conventional capability to deter a biological or chemical attack. As a result, the reviews says: 'The United States will not use or threaten to use nuclear weapons against non-nuclear weapons states that are party to the non-proliferation treaty and in compliance with their nuclear non-proliferation obligations' ... This contrasts with the Bush administration, which in 2001 declared that nuclear weapons would be used to deter a wide range of threats, including weapons of mass destruction and large-scale conventional military force ... North Korea pulled out of the non-proliferation treaty in 2003, while the United States claims Iran is covertly engaged in developing a nuclear weapons capability, which Iran denies ... The review allows the retention of about 200 tactical nuclear weapons held in five European countries.

(www.guardian.co.uk, 6 April 2010)

The Washington Post reported that the Pentagon is developing a weapon to plug the gap left by nuclear warheads: missiles armed with conventional warheads that could strike anywhere in the world in less than an hour. US military officials say the intercontinental ballistic missiles, known as prompt

global strike weapons, are a necessary new form of deterrence against terrorist networks.

(www.guardian.co.uk, 8 April 2010)

Russia deploys 2,600 strategic warheads while the United States deploys
about 2,100. Both sides have thousands more reserve warheads or tactical
warheads ... By contrast, China has an estimated 180 warheads, India and
Pakistan each have about seventy or eighty and North Korea just a handful.

(*IHT*, 8 April 2010, p. 4)

There are no official numbers on tactical nuclear weapons, but analysts
estimate the United States has from 150 to 250 in Germany, Belgium, the
Netherlands, Italy and Turkey. Russia may have 2,000 or more weapons,
some stored in places like the Kaliningrad region, close to Poland. These
numbers are down from their peak during the Cold War, when the United
States had some 8,000 tactical warheads and the Soviet Union had upwards
of 23,000.

(www.iht.com, 22 April 2010)

8 April 2010.

President Barack Obama and President Dmitri Medvedev signed [in Prague]
a nuclear arms control treaty on Thursday [8 April] ... Ratification requires
a two-thirds vote, or sixty-seven senators [in the US Senate] ... The Senate
has rejected an arms control agreement in recent times, refusing to ratify the
test ban treaty when it was originally brought up in 1999, Moreover, it took
three years in the 1990s to ratify the first Start follow-up treaty, known as
Start 2, which never went into force because of a dispute over Russian conditions attached during its own ratification process ... Warmer relations with
the Kremlin worry American allies in Central and Eastern Europe ... Mr
Obama plans to have dinner Thursday night [8 April] in Prague with eleven
leaders from the region, including the presidents or prime ministers of Bulgaria, Croatia, the Czech Republic, Estonia, Hungary, Latvia, Lithuania,
Poland, Romania, Slovakia and Slovenia ... Mr Obama made sure before
leaving Washington to speak by phone with President Mikheil Saakashvili
of Georgia.

(www.iht.com, 8 April 2010)

'The treaty lays out a "verification regime" that includes on-site inspections,
data exchanges and notifications, the White House said' (www.cnn.com, 8 April
2010).

7 April 2010.

Prime minister Vladimir Putin is hosting his Polish counterpart Donald Tusk in
Katyn, the site of Stalin-era massacres of Polish troops during World War II.
Putin's attendance at the Russian ceremony for 22,000 Polish prisoners of war
killed by Stalin's secret police in 1940 is an unprecedented gesture of goodwill

and reconciliation ... Putin is the first Russian leader to commemorate the Katyn massacres alongside Polish leaders, although Russia has not recognized the massacres as a war crime and Soviet archives on the matter remain sealed.

(www.iht.com, 7 April 2010)

Prime minister Vladimir Putin joined his Polish counterpart in the first joint commemoration marking the anniversary of the murder of thousands of Polish officers by the Soviet Union ... Mr Putin [becomes] ... the first Russian leader to commemorate the anniversary of the Katyn massacre. [The] site in the Katyn forest close to the city of Smolensk ... Members of the Soviet secret police executed over 20,000 Polish officers captured after the Red Army invaded Poland in 1939 ... Under President Boris Yeltsin in the 1990s Russian released archival documents showing that Stalin's Polit-buro directly ordered the massacre in March 1940 ... Last week a government-owned channel for the first time showed *Katyn*, an Oscar-nominated film by the Polish director Andrzej Wajda that portrays the mas-sacre and the Soviet cover-up. The film had previously been screened only twice in Russia. For the first time this year [2010] Russian has invited dele-gations from the Soviet Union's principal World War II allies – Britain, France and the United States – to take part in the Victory Day parade on Red Square this year, marking the sixty-fifth anniversary of Nazi Germany's defeat. Poland has also been invited.

(www.iht.com, 7 April 2010)

[Russia has failed] to declare the killings war crimes and allow Polish his-torians access to all the documents on the massacre ... Last August [2009] Mr Putin praised Polish soldiers and citizens for their bravery in resisting the Nazis at an anniversary marking the start of World War II.

(*IHT*, 8 April 2010, p. 3)

It is the first Russian ceremony to mark the murder by Soviet secret police of more than 20,000 Polish prisoners of war in April 1940 ... The Soviet Union blamed the killings on the Nazis. In 1990 President Mikhail Gor-bachev finally admitted Soviet responsibility.

(www.bbc.co.uk, 7 April 2010)

The April 1940 killings were carried out by the NKVD Soviet secret police on the orders of Stalin. They shot members of the Polish elite – officers, politicians and artists – in the back of the head and dumped their bodies in mass graves.

(www.bbc.co.uk, 7 April 2010)

The Polish parliament urged Russia on Friday [9 April] to make public all documents concerning the massacre of thousands of Polish officers by the Soviet secret police in Katyn and elsewhere in 1940. Lawmakers approved a declaration marking the seventieth anniversary of 22,000 Polish prisoners of war. Lawmakers said the attendance of the Russian prime minister, Vladimir

Putin, at a memorial ceremony Wednesday [7 April] was an 'important gesture'.

(*IHT*, 10 April 2010, p. 3)

A plane carrying the Polish president, Lech Kaczynski, and dozens of the country's top political and military leaders crashed in heavy fog in western Russia on Saturday morning [10 April], killing everyone on board. Television showed chunks of flaming fuselage in a bare forest near Smolensk, where the president was arriving for a ceremony commemorating the murder of more than 20,000 Polish officers by the Red Army as it invaded Poland. The governor of Smolensk region ... said the plane did not reach the runway but instead hit the treetops and broke apart. An official with Russia's investigative committee said possible causes were bad weather, mechanical failure and human error ... A press secretary for the governor of Smolensk said the landing took place under very bad visibility, and Russian air traffic controllers advised the crew to land in Minsk, but the crew decided to land anyway. The Polish news channel TVN24 reported that moments before the crash air traffic controllers had refused a Russian military aircraft permission to land, but that they could not refuse permission to the Polish plane ... The crash ... [killed] maybe a tenth of the country's top leadership ... The plane was a Tupolev Tu-154 designed by the Soviets in the mid-1960s. Officials in Poland have repeatedly requested that the government's ageing air fleet be replaced. Former prime minister Leszek Miller, who survived a helicopter crash in 2003, told Polish news he had long predicted such a disaster ... Among those on board ... were Mr Kaczynski, his wife Maria, former Polish president-in-exile Ryszard Kaczorowski, the deputy speaker of Poland's parliament ... the head of the president's chancellery ... the head of the National Security Bureau ... the deputy minister of foreign affairs ... the chief of the Polish army ... the president of Poland's national bank ... the commissioner for civil rights protection ... the heads of all of Poland's armed forces ... and dozens of members of parliament ... Poland's ministry of foreign affairs said eighty-eight people were on the plane. Russian emergency officials said the total number killed, including crew members, was ninety-six ... The president had been due in western Russia to commemorate the anniversary of the murder of thousands of Polish officers by the Soviet Union [in 1940] ... On Wednesday [7 April] prime minister Vladimir Putin took a major step to improve relations by becoming the first Russian or Soviet leader to join Polish officials in commemorating the anniversary ... At the ceremony Mr Putin cast the executions as one of the many crimes carried out by the 'totalitarian regime' of the Soviet Union. He said: 'We bow our heads to those who bravely met death here. In this ground lay Soviet citizens, burnt in the fire of the Stalinist repression of the 1930s; Polish officers, shot on secret orders; soldiers of the Red Army, executed by the Nazis' ... Mr Kaczynski, who was seen by the Kremlin as less friendly to Russia, was not invited to the joint Russian–Polish ceremony on Wednesday. Instead, Mr Kaczynski decided to attend a separate, Polish-organized event in Katyn on Saturday … Mr Kaczynski was elected president in December 2005 … [He] forged close relationships with Ukraine and Georgia and pushed for their accession into Nato, arguing passionately that a stronger Nato would keep Russia from reasserting its influence over Eastern Europe … According to the Polish constitution, the leader of the lower house or parliament – now acting president – has fourteen days to announce new elections, which must then take place within sixty days.

(www.iht.com, 10 April 2010)

[The] Polish ministry of foreign affairs said eighty-eight passengers were on the plane … [Those who died included] not only the famous politicians and commanding generals but also the Russian–Polish interpreter, the president's doctor … eight members of the presidential security detail … the military chaplain … [the person] in charge of the nation's monuments … Anna Walentynowicz, eighty, the former dock worker [crane operator] whose firing in [August] 1980 [from the Lenin shipyards in Gdansk] set off the Solidarity strike … [and] relatives of victims of the [Katyn] massacre … Russia halted mass production of the Tupolev Tu-154 about twenty years ago, and about 200 of them are still in service around the world … The Polish presidential jet was one of the youngest of them.

(www.iht.com, 11 April 2010)

The plane … missed the runway and snagged treetops about half a mile from the airport in Smolensk before crashing … Russian news media reported that the airplane's crew made several attempts to land before a wing hit the treetops and the plane crashed about half a mile from the runway … Prime minister Vladimir Putin had invited prime minister Donald Tusk, not President Lech Kaczynski, to ceremonies last Wednesday [7 April] marking the Katyn massacre anniversary.

(www.iht.com, 11 April 2010)

'The Russian Communist Party … insists that the Nazis, not the Soviets, were responsible for the Katyn massacre' (www.iht.com, 12 April 2010).

Polish and Russian officials said no one survived after the plane apparently hit trees as it approached Smolensk airport in thick fog. Poland's army chief, central bank governor, MPs and leading historians were among [the passengers] … Polish prime minister Donald Tusk said he would travel immediately to the site of the crash in Smolensk. Russian prime minister Vladimir Putin said he would go to Smolensk on Saturday [10 April] as well … The plane crashed at 10.56 Moscow time (06.56 a.m. GMT) … Polish officials said the delegation was eighty-eight strong … Russian officials said ninety-seven were killed in the crash, including eight crew. Russian investigators had earlier said there were 132 people on the plane … President Lech Kaczynski had suffered scares while using the plane in late 2008, when problems with the aircraft's steering mechanism delayed his departure from

Mongolia. It was then caught up in turbulence flying to Seoul ... A [Polish] government spokesman said that according to the constitution there would be an early presidential election, and the speaker of the lower house of parliament, Bronislaw Komorowski, would be acting president.

(www.bbc.co.uk, 10 April 2010)

Poland's foreign ministry said there were eighty-nine people on the passenger list but one person had not shown up ... According to the Aviation Safety Network, there have been sixty-six crashes involving Tu-154s, including six in the past five years. The Russian carrier Aeroflot recently withdrew its Tu-154 fleet from service ... Lech Kaczynski is the first serving Polish officer to die since exiled World War II-era leader general Wladyslaw Sikorski in a plane crash off Gibraltar in 1943 ... Lech Kaczynski became president in December 2005 after defeating Donald Tusk in that year's presidential vote. The nationalist conservative was the twin brother of Poland's opposition leader, former prime minister Jaroslaw Kaczynski. Kaczynski said he would seek a second term in [this year's] presidential elections ... He was expected to face an uphill struggle against parliament speaker Bronislaw Komorowski, the candidate of Donald Tusk's Civic Platform Party. According to the constitution, Komorowski would take over presidential duties.

(www.independent.co.uk, 10 April 2010)

'[The list of dead included] the army chief of staff and the heads of the air and land forces' (www.independent.co.uk, 11 April 2010).

Russian officials said the airport had been closed because of thick fog. They advised the pilot to land at Moscow or Minsk instead but he continued with the original flight plan – making three abortive attempts to land at Smolensk's Severny military airport. On the fourth attempt the Russian-built aircraft crashed ... The presidential plane was fully overhauled in December [2009] in Russia, with Russian experts today insisting it was airworthy.

(www.guardian.co.uk, 10 April 2010)

Russian officials said ninety-seven people died, including eight crew members ... The Kremlin failed to invite Lech Kaczynski to a ceremony in Katyn last Wednesday [7 April] attended by Donald Tusk and Vladimir Putin. Kaczynski organized his own separate event ... The presidential Tu-154 that crashed was twenty-six years old.

(www.guardian.co.uk, 11 April 2010)

In 1943 General Wladyslaw Sikorski, the leader of the Polish wartime government, died in a plane crash in Gibraltar. No foul play was proved there, but many Poles believe that he was murdered because of his resolute determination to expose the Katyn massacre – which the Soviet Union blamed on the Germans ... Among the ... people who died were the chief of the Polish general staff, the head of the central bank ... [and] the director of the Institute of National Remembrance (which investigates and documents crimes such as Katyn) … Many politicians from the opposition Law and Justice Party, which is led by Jaroslaw Kaczynski, the late president's twin brother, were among the delegation … The presidential elections, due to be held in October [2010], will be brought forward. Lech Kaczynski had been facing a tough challenge from Bronislaw Komorowski, a close ally of Polish prime minister Donald Tusk. Mr Komorowski is also speaker of the Sejm, the lower house of the Polish parliament. In that capacity, he now becomes acting president.

(www.economist.com, 10 April 2010)

'The Law and Justice Party lost numerous important leaders [in the crash], including its parliamentary leader. Lech Kaczynski had been trailing far behind in the polls … [covering] the presidential election' (www.iht.com, 11 April 2010).

[Speaker] Bronislaw Komorowski said he would set the date of a presidential election, which had been due in October after holding talks with Poland's political parties. Under the constitution the election must now be held by late June … Komorowski is the presidential candidate of Donald Tusk's pro-business, pro-Euro Civic Platform. Opinion polls suggest he would have defeated Lech Kaczynski in the election.

(www.iht.com, 11 April 2010)

'Lech Kaczynski had said he would seek a second term … He was expected to face an uphill struggle against the speaker, Bronislaw Komorowski' (www. guardian.co.uk, 11 April 2010).

'President Lech Kaczynski … had the support of less than a quarter of the electorate when he died and is likely to have lost presidential elections originally scheduled for this autumn' (*FT*, 16 April 2010, p. 10).

Just before his death … [President Lech Kaczynski's] approval rating was under 30 per cent, while his disapproval rating was twice that. His odds of re-election later this year were meagre. He was widely considered the worst Polish president since 1989.

(www.iht.com, 16 April 2010)

'Two parties lost their [presidential] candidates in the crash: Law and Justice, which Lech Kaczynski helped found together with his twin brother Jaroslaw, and the Democratic Left Alliance, whose nominee was Jerzy Szmajdzinski' (*FT*, 17 April 2010, p. 8).

All ninety-seven people on the jet … died … Russian officials say pilots ignored warnings they were flying too low … [They said] the pilots had ignored repeated requests from air traffic controllers to divert the flight to another airport to avoid the heavy fog around Smolensk … [On Saturday 10 April] Russian prime minister Vladimir Putin, who visited the crash site with Polish counterpart Donald Tusk, said he would oversee the investigation into the crash … Prime minister Tusk said he would, according to

Poland's constitution, set the date for a presidential election after consulting with political parties.

(www.bbc.co.uk, 11 April 2010)

Russian and Polish investigators began Sunday [11 April] to analyse evidence from the flight recorders in the crash, and prosecutors, forensic pathologists and crash investigators were working with their Russian counterparts both in Smolensk and Moscow ... A Polish government spokesman praised the co-operation with the Russian authorities on Sunday, and tried to calm Polish concerns that decisions about the investigation were being made without Polish involvement. The spokesman said: 'The Russian side did not open the black boxes but waited for the arrival of Polish experts' ... Prime minister Vladimir Putin went to Smolensk on Sunday for a ceremony to return Mr Kaczynski's body to Poland ... Russia and Ukraine have declared 12 April a day of mourning for victims of the crash.

(www.iht.com, 11 April 2010)

In August 2008, during Russia's brief war with Georgia, President Lech Kaczynski got into a dispute with a pilot flying his plane to the Georgian capital, Tbilisi, according to reports at the time. Mr Kaczynski demanded that the pilot land despite dangerous conditions, but the pilot disagreed and diverted to neighbouring Azerbaijan ... Lech Walesa ... the former Polish president ... [said] over the weekend that in these situations, the captain often sought the views of the government leaders on the plane ... On Sunday [11 April] ... an air traffic controller at the airport ... said the pilot, after trying several times to land, indicated that he wanted to try once more. He said that if he did not land then he would go to an alternative airport.

(www.iht.com, 12 April 2010)

When Russia invaded Georgia in August 2008 it was Lech Kaczynski who rushed to the rescue, leading a hair-raising trip to Tbilisi with leaders of other sympathetic ex-communist states. He tried to overrule protests by the presidential plane's pilot, that the trip into a war zone was unsafe ... The pilot later got a medal for resolutely putting his passengers' safety ahead of prestige. Mr Kaczynski may have repeated that error in the minutes before the disastrous attempt to land the presidential plane at a fog-bound on 10 April ... The Katyn massacre of 22,000 Polish officers [took place] in the spring of 1940 ... The officers, including many reservists ... [included] lawyers, doctors, teachers and intellectuals ... [and] the chief rabbi of the Polish army ... In September 2007 a Russian government newspaper, *Rossiskaya Gazeta*, published a commentary casting doubt on the idea that Katyn was a Soviet massacre. Sued by relatives of the Katyn victims in the European Court of Human Rights, the Russian government argued that blame for the massacre was unclear. The judicial rehabilitation of the victims has been blocked; the archives are still sealed ... At the joint ceremony [on 7 April] prime minister Vladimir Putin categorically acknowledged that the massacre was a crime of the Stalin regime – although he also brought up the deaths of captured Soviet officers in Polish prisoner-of-war camps twenty years earlier ... President Lech Kaczynski ... brought ... along almost the entire foreign policy leadership of his party, the commanders of the army, navy, air force and special forces, senior intelligence veterans and top historians.

(www.economist.com, 12 April 2010)

'Polls show only 19 per cent of Russians believe Stalin's secret police were responsible [for the Katyn massacre]' (www.economist.com, 15 April 2010).

Poland's chief prosecutor ... [said on 12 April] that at this stage of the investigation there was nothing to suggest pressure was put on the pilots. However, the Tu-154's black boxes were still being analysed to see 'if suggestions were made to the pilots'. The Russian government official said he could not say if such 'suggestions' had been made, adding that investigations were only at an early stage.

(*FT*, 13 April 2010, p. 10)

Traffic controller Anatoli Murayev ... part of the Russian team that handled the plane ... [said] that the crew ignored their warnings about worsening weather at the Smolensk airport. Murayev: '[The crew] started landing with confidence and with no swerving. But then the traffic controllers had doubts [about the weather]' ... He said the head controller three times ordered the plane to reattempt the landing and then advised the pilot to fly to another airport. He said: 'The crew did not listen, although the controllers warned them about bad visibility and told them to get ready to fly to a reserve airport.'

(www.iht.com, 13 April 2010)

Public discontent erupted on Tuesday [13 April] for the first time ... as hundreds of people in Krakow protested the decision to inter the president and his wife in a crypt holding the remains of many Polish kings. Opposition was building over the plan to lay President Lech Kaczynski and his wife, Maria, to rest in Wawel Cathedral in Krakow, which also holds the remains of leading historical figures like Marshal Jozef Pilsudski, the post-World War I leader of Poland, and General Wladyslaw Sikorski, leader of the government-in-exile during World War II. Those opposed to placing the often divisive Mr Kaczynski in such august company demonstrated Tuesday night [13 April] outside the Palace of Bishops, the seat of the Krakow curia.

(www.iht.com, 14 April 2010)

'Lech Kaczynski is to be the first president to be buried ... at Wawel Cathedral ... among the greatest of Polish kings, two revered romantic poets and the three great military heroes Tadeusz Kosciuszko, Jozef Pilsudski and Wladyslaw Sikorski' (www.iht.com, 16 April 2010).

Poland's chief prosecutor ... Andrzej Seremet ... said Thursday [14 April] ... there is no evidence that the pilot flying to the Katyn ceremony was pressured, and an official with Russia's investigative committee said data from the black box did not reflect that scenario ... Anatoli Murayev, an air traffic controller who was on duty that morning ... [said] that the crew had begun landing without permission when air traffic controllers warned them about the weather and recommended that they land at another airport. When the crew did not change course, he said, 'all we could do was to continue to guide the plane and watch'. Tatiana Anodina, the head of the Interstate Aviation Committee, which oversees aviation in Russia, denied published reports that the pilot made three or four attempts to land and said he made only one attempt.

(*IHT*, 16 April 2010)

Some 40,000 people have signed up to a Facebook group opposing the idea ... [of making Wawel Cathedral] the final resting place for the late President Lech Kaczynski and his wife Maria ... Poland's greatest film director Andrzej Wajda – whose father was killed at Katyn and who made an Oscar-nominated film about the massacre – called the plan 'highly unfortunate'. Mr Kaczynski, he said, was a good man but his burial in Krakow would cause the deepest split in Polish society since 1989.

(www.bbc.co.uk, 17 April 2010)

The decision to lay President Lech Kaczynski and his wife Maria to rest at Wawel has divided the nation. Thousands protested this week ... Alexander Kwasniewski, the former president and a long-time political rival of Mr Kaczynski, said ahead of the funeral that the decision to bury Mr Kaczynski at Wawel was part of an attempt by his party to mythologize him. Kwasniewski said: 'This decision has political sense, to use this catastrophe to create in an artificial way a new myth or hero. But the Polish people are too clever not to see this intention. Putting him at Wawel is a step too far' ... He said the attempt by Mr Kaczynski and his brother to turn the nation toward atavistic nationalism, scepticism of the EU, social conservatism and red-baiting has been 'extremely dangerous' ... Kwasniewski: 'Our desire for evolution proved to be correct. The Kaczynskis wanted revolution, and thank God they failed.'

(www.iht.com, 18 April 2010)

The bodies of President Lech Kaczynski and his wife Maria were flown from Warsaw to Krakow early Sunday [18 April] for burial among Polish kings and poets at a tradition-laden ceremony that will be bereft of many world leaders whose travel plans were paralysed by a plume of volcanic ash [originating in Iceland] ... Many were forced to cancel – including President Barack Obama, President Nicolas Sarkozy and Chancellor Angela Merkel – at the last minute.

(www.bbc.co.uk, 18 April 2010)

'Many world leaders could not attend due to volcanic ash grounding flights ... Russian president Dmitri Medvdev was one leader who defied the air restrictions to fly to Krakow' (www.bbc.co.uk, 18 April 2010).

'The ash also grounded British foreign secretary David Miliband and Prince Charles, who said they would be unable to attend' (www.cnn.com, 18 April 2010).

('Russia has published previously secret documents on the 1940 Katyn massacre ... The state archive said the "Packet No. 1" documents had until now only been available to specialist researchers ... The documents that the state archive published were declassified in the 1990s but had only been available to specialist researchers, reports said. They were published online on the orders of President Dmitri Medvedev. Poland has repeatedly demanded that Russia open all its files on Katyn': www.bbc.co.uk, 28 April 2010.)

('[In Moscow] aviation authorities offered new details of the plane crash ... including the revelation that two or more passengers were in the cockpit shortly before the aircraft attempted to land in dense fog ... [The] news conference [was] held by officials of Russia and Poland on Wednesday [19 May] ... The head of the [Russian] Interstate Aviation Committee ... Tatiana Anodina ... said that one of the passengers recorded in the cockpit had been identified ... but aviation rules prohibited [release of information] ... She said: "As for the influence on the decision-making of the crew, this should be investigated. This is important for the investigation and for establishing the cause [of the crash]" ... Anonymous officials in the Polish government identified one of the passengers recorded in the cockpit as the commander of Poland's air force, Andrzej Blasik ... Alexei Morozov ... another official with the Interstate Aviation Committee ... said the four-person crew ... had been assembled a few days earlier and had received minimal emergency training, ignored the warnings and requested clearance for a landing attempt': www.iht.com, 19 May 2010. 'The news fuelled widespread speculation that the pilots were pressed to land so that President Lech Kaczynski and other dignitaries would not be late for their appearance at [the ceremony] ... The aviation officials ruled out the possibility that technical failure, sabotage or terrorism led to the crash ... they said investigators were exploring whether cell-phone use on board the plane or crew inexperience were factors, and that the presence of the passengers in the cockpit was being examined ... Mr Kaczynski's delegation was an hour-and-a-half behind schedule when the plane took off from Poland for a military airfield in Smolensk in Russia': *IHT*, 20 May 2010. 'One of those in the cockpit has been identified, but the BBC has learned it was not the president': www.bbc.co.uk, 19 May 2010. 'The pilots ... received at least a dozen warnings from on-board systems to regain altitude during the last minute before the crash, according to transcripts from its cockpit recorders which were released [by the Polish government on 1 June] ... Three minutes before impact ... the transcript ... quoted an unidentified person in the cockpit as saying: "(S) he will be annoyed if ..." ': *The Independent*, 2 June 2010, p. 32. 'The crew continued to try to land in spite of more than a dozen warnings from on-board systems to regain altitude ... The transcript from the black box recorder appears to back the contention of Edmund Klich, the lead Polish investigator into the crash, that the disaster was caused by pilot error … Mariusz Kazana, a foreign ministry official, said: "We have a problem … At the moment there is no decision from the president on what to do"': *FT*, 2 June 2010, p. 8. 'About fifteen minutes before the crash, pilots told the Polish foreign ministry's diplomatic protocol chief – who was in the cockpit – that the plane was not currently able to land. "Well then we have a problem," replied the official, Mariusz Kazana. After a gap of ten minutes Mr Kazana told the pilots: "The president has not decided yet what we will do …" Three minutes before the crash the transcript shows an unidentified person in the cockpit saying: "(S)he will be annoyed if …" … Investigators revealed last week that Poland's air force chief, General Andrzej Blasik, was one of two non-crew members in the cockpit before it crashed. They said there was no evidence that General Blasik had pressurized the pilots to land in bad weather': www.bbc.co.uk, 2 June 2010. 'Russia handed over copies of the recording to the Polish interior ministry on Monday [31 May] and will keep the original recordings in Russia until the investigation is complete' (*IHT*, 2 June 2010, p. 3.)

(The prime ministers of Russia and Poland, Vladimir Putin and Donald Tusk, knelt down together in memory of the victims of Soviet state terror. Lech Kaczynski, as it turns out, was carrying a conciliatory speech on that fatal flight': Victor Erofeyev, www.iht.com, 20 April 2010; *IHT*, 21 April 2010, p. 6.)

('There is no legal basis for reopening an investigation into the Katyn massacre … a top Russian official said Monday [31 May] … The Soviet Union acknowledged responsibility for the killings in 1990, but a criminal investigation was ended in 2004 after officials said the killings were not genocide … Chief military prosecutor Sergei Fridinsky said "by law it cannot be restarted, given the expiration of the statute of limitations period" … International law generally considers that genocide has no statute of limitations': www.iht.com, 31 May 2010).

('Poland has hailed the installation of a US Patriot surface-to-air missile battery, amid criticism from Russia. Poland said the missile launchers, positioned about 60 kilometres (40 miles) from the Russian enclave of Kaliningrad, would enhance its security. The battery will be rotated in and out of Poland for the next two years, along with dozens of US troops who will train Polish counterparts to operate it. It is the first US deployment of its kind in Poland … The short-range Patriot missile battery was delivered to a military base at Morag on Sunday [23 May]. A spokesman for the US army in Europe was quoted as saying that actual missiles would not be deployed at Morag, though the US ambassador was quoted as saying they might be': www.bbc.co.uk, 26 May 2010.)

7–8 April 2010. A seven-year-old adopted Russian boy (Justin Hansen/Artyom Savelyev] was put on a plane in the United States on Wednesday 7 April and sent back to Russia, landing on Thursday 8 April.

> The case of a Russian boy who returned alone to Moscow, sent back by his adoptive mother, has focused intense attention of the pitfalls of international

adoption. But the outcry has obscured fundamental questions about why Russia has so many orphans and orphanages in the first place. In recent days senior Russian officials have begun to acknowledge how troubled their system is. The chairwoman of the parliamentary committee on family and children, Yelena Mizulina, spotlighted what she said was a shocking statistic: Russia has more orphans now, 700,000, than at the end of World War II, when an estimated 25 million Soviet citizens were killed. Ms Mizulina noted that for all the complaints about the return of the boy, Artyom Savelyev, by his adoptive mother in Tennessee, Russia itself has plenty of experience with failed placements. She said 30,000 children in the last three years inside Russia were sent back to institutions by their adoptive, foster or guardianship families ... She reeled off more figures. The percentage of children who are designated orphans is four or five times higher in Russia than in Europe or the United States. Of those, 30 per cent live in orphanages. Most of them are children who have been either given up by their parents or removed from dysfunctional homes by the authorities ... The system's defenders said that until the government figures out how to cut down on social problems like drug and alcohol abuse to improve family life, there is no alternative ... The scrutiny of the Russian system comes as Russian and American diplomats are working out new rules for adoptions ... While Russia has its share of social problems, the large number of orphans stems in part from a policy that does not place a high value on keeping families together. The Russian government spends roughly $3 billion annually on orphanages and similar facilities, creating a system that is an important source of jobs and money on the regional level – and a target for corruption. As a result, it is in the interests of regional officials to maintain the flow of children to orphanages and then not to let them leave, child welfare experts said. When adoptions are permitted, families, especially foreign families, have to pay large fees and navigate a complex bureaucracy. Boris Altshuler (who is chairman of Right of the Child, an advocacy group in Moscow, and also a member of a Kremlin advisory group) ... said that in 2008 115,000 children in Russia were designated as without parental care, typically after being removed from their homes by case workers. Only 9,000 children were returned to their parents that year. In the United States, where reuniting families is a primary goal, the percentage is far higher, he said. Overall, 13,000 children were officially adopted in 2008 – 9,000 by Russian and 4,000 by foreigners, officials said.

(www.iht.com, 4 May 2010; IHT, 4 May 2010, pp. 1, 3)

The mother said that Artyom had severe behavioural difficulties and that the Russian orphanage had lied to her about his condition when she adopted him last year [2009]. Russian officials said there was nothing wrong with him ... An American delegation was recently in Moscow to negotiate a new adoption agreement, and both sides said they hoped to have one signed relatively soon. Russian officials were said to want assurances that there would be more independent monitoring of Russian children after they have begun living in the United States. Russia was the leading source of adoptive children in the United States in 2009, with 1,586, after China and Ethiopia ... More than 50,000 Russian children have been adopted by US citizens since 1991. The adoption rate peaked at 6,000 in 2003, and then declined as bureaucratic and legal hurdles mounted. While most adoptions turn out well, cases where adoptive Russian children have been harmed or killed in the United States have drawn widespread attention in Russia, Russian officials said that of the eighteen Russian adoptive children who have been killed abroad since the Soviet collapse in 1991, seventeen were in the United States ... Andrei Fursenko, the education and science minister whose agency oversees adoptions ... [said on Tuesday 4 May] that while there have been instances of Russian children being adopted by 'inadequate' families abroad, there have been more in Russia itself.

(www.iht.com, 5 May 2010; *IHT*, 6 May 2010, p. 3)

'A Tennessee woman sent the young Russian boy her family had recently adopted back to Russia unaccompanied' (www.cnn.com, 4 May 2010).

Russia and the United States have reached a new bilateral accord on adoptions and expect to sign it within two months, a senior Russian official said Wednesday [12 May]. Russia had demanded such an accord after a seven-year-old Russian boy was sent back to Moscow alone last month [April] by his adoptive American mother, creating an uproar. American adoption officials were also horrified at the drastic action taken by the mother and angry about its possible repercussions. Russian officials say they want more control over US adoptions of Russian children and the living conditions children face in the United States ... Pavel Astakhov ... children's rights ombudsman ... confirmed Wednesday [1 May] that adoptions to the United States have not been 'legally suspended', but said they are 'effectively suspended' as Russian courts will nor rule on adoptions cases as long as there is uncertainty about the children's safety in that country. Some 1,800 Russian children were adopted in the United States last year [2009] ... Some 3,000 US families are estimated to be in various stages of adopting children now from Russia.

(www.iht.com, 12 May 2010)

'The children's rights ombudsman, Pavel Astakhov, said Friday [14 May] that Russian and US officials will work out the final draft of a deal on adoptions in mid-June' (*IHT*, 15 May 2010, p. 4).

12–13 April 2010.

Dozens of world leaders gather in Washington next week for an unprecedented meeting on nuclear security ... Forty-seven countries [will gather] ... Two nations excluded from the meeting are Iran ... and North Korea ... North Korea withdrew from the Nuclear Non-proliferation Treaty in 2003

... Iran rejects Western allegations that its atomic programme is aimed at developing weapons and refuses to stop enriching uranium ... A draft communiqué circulated to countries attending the summit ... includes a US proposal to 'secure all vulnerable nuclear material in four years'. The draft text will likely be revised before it is adopted at the end of the 12–13 April meeting.

(www.iht.com, 8 April 2010)

'The meeting ... seeks ways to better secure existing supplies of bomb-usable plutonium and highly enriched uranaium' (www.iht.com, 12 April 2010).

'North Korea and Iran ... [have not] been invited to the summit ... Syria was also left off the invitation list because the United States believes Damascus also has nuclear ambitions' (www.bbc.co.uk, 12 April 2010).

Ukraine has agreed to eliminate its entire stockpile of weapons-grade nuclear material, US officials said ahead of a key nuclear security summit. The White House said Ukraine would by 2012 get rid of enough highly enriched uranium to build 'several weapons' ... This would be removed with some technical and financial help from the United States ... The summit is all about securing stocks of highly enriched uranium and plutonium ... It is estimated that there are around 1,600 tonnes of highly enriched uranium around the world – the type used in nuclear weapons. Experts agree that virtually all of it is held by the acknowledged nuclear weapons states, most of it in Russia. There are also about 500 tonnes of the other key ingredient of nuclear weapons – plutonium. In total that is enough to make 120,000 nuclear weapons. Much international, largely US-funded, effort has attempted to clamp down on the threat of nuclear leakage from Russia in particular, but it remains a concern.

(www.bbc.co.uk, 12 April 2010)

Kiev had agreed to return nuclear warheads on its territory to Russia in 1994, but retained stockpiles of enriched uranium, some of its extracted from those weapons by Russia and returned to Ukraine ... The leaders of forty-seven countries converged on Washington for the summit meeting, the largest such assemblage since Franklin D. Roosevelt organized a meeting in 1945 to create the United Nations.

(*IHT*, 13 April 2010, p. 4)

The Nuclear Threat Initiative, a non-profit group that studies proliferation, has estimated Ukraine's stockpile at 163 kilograms, or roughly enough for seven weapons. According to a senior administration official, under the deal announced Monday [12 April] the United States will pay to secure the highly enriched uranium, which will likely be sent to Russia for conversion into low-enriched uranium for nuclear power plants. As part of the deal, the United States will also supply Ukraine with new low-enriched fuel and a new research facility.

(www.iht.com, 13 April 2010)

The head of the International Atomic Energy Authority, Yukiya Amano, said that nuclear powers needed to do more to protect nuclear materials ... He said: 'On average every two days we receive one new information on an incident involving theft or smuggling of nuclear material.'

(www.bbc.co.uk, 13 April 2010)

Before the talks President Barack Obama and President Hu Jintao agreed to step up pressure on Iran over its atomic plans. A US official ... [said] that Mr Hu had agreed to direct Chinese officials to work with their US counterparts on a UN sanctions resolution against Tehran ... A US spokesman said: 'The two presidents agreed the two delegations should work together on a sanctions resolution in New York.'

(www.bbc.co.uk, 13 April 2010)

President Barack Obama secured a promise from President Hu Jintao on Monday [13 April] to join negotiations on a new package of sanctions against Iran, administration officials said, but Mr Hu made no specific commitment ... The session with Mr Hu came just before the opening of the first summit meeting devoted to the challenges of keeping nuclear weapons and material out of the hands of terrorists ... Mr Obama laid out the details of the sanctions package for Mr Hu ... The Chinese import nearly 12 per cent of their oil from Iran ... Former President George W. Bush [made] three efforts to corral Chinese support for UN Security Council penalties ... In those cases, former American officials said, the Chinese agreed to go along with efforts to address Iran's nuclear ambitions but then used Security Council negotiating sessions to water down the resolutions that ultimately passed.

(www.iht.com, 13 April 2010)

Ukraine, Canada, Mexico and Malaysia have offered individual undertakings to tighten controls, reduce nuclear stocks or move from highly enriched to low enriched uranium fuel ... [On Monday 12 April] Ukraine said it would rid itself of all its highly enriched uranium – reportedly enough for about seven weapons – by 2012 ... President Lee Myung-Bak of South Korea said that North Korea would be welcome at the next summit meeting [in Seoul] if it made sufficient progress in the six-nation talks on its nuclear programme.

(*IHT*, 14 April 2010, p. 4)

So far only twenty-one countries have ratified the UN's Convention on Physical Protection of Nuclear Materials – far too few for it to enter into force ... President Barack Obama's goal ... [is to secure] all such material by 2013 ... Russia and the United States signed an agreement yesterday [13 April] to dispose of 34 tonnes of plutonium apiece, breaking a decade-long logjam on how to implement a deal in 2000 to do so ... Despite its record in returning risk material and its continuing nuclear power programme, Belarus ... was also not invited ... Yesterday South Korean President Lee Myung-Bak agreed to hold another nuclear security summit in his country in 2012.

(*FT*, 14 April 2010, p. 7)

Georgian security forces have foiled a criminal plot to sell weapons-grade uranium on the black market ... President Mikheil Saakashvili [said on 13 April] ... Georgian sources said the highly enriched uranium was intercepted in a sting operation carried out in March [2010] ... The Georgian president told the summit: 'The Georgian ministry of interior has foiled eight attempts of illicit trafficking of enriched uranium during the last ten years, including several cases of weapons-grade enrichment ... Ukraine and Canada said they would no longer use highly enriched uranium in research reactors. Malaysia announced it had enforced tougher controls on the shipment of nuclear equipment ... The summit's final communiqué affirmed the support of the forty-seven nations for President Barack Obama's goal of securing the stockpiles of fissile materials within four years, and called for more countries to switch from highly enriched uranium to low enriched uranium reactors. It also called on the ratification of UN conventions aimed at setting international standards for nuclear security.

(*Guardian*, 14 April 2010, p. 19)

Ending an unprecedented forty-seven-nation nuclear security summit, President Barack Obama won pledges from world leaders to take joint action to prevent terrorist groups from getting nuclear weapons ... The summit's final communiqué promised greater efforts to block 'non-state actors' like al-Qaeda from obtaining the building blocks for atomic weapons for 'malicious purposes' ... The summit communiqué included no mechanism to enforce the agreement ... South Korea would host the next nuclear security summit in 2012 ... [There is an] estimated 2,000 tonnes of plutonium and highly enriched uranium in dozens of countries. Washington and Moscow signed a deal to reduce stocks of excess weapons-grade plutonium. The United States, Canada and Mexico agreed to work together with the International Atomic Energy Agency (IAEA) to convert Mexico's research reactor from the use of highly enriched uranium to low enriched uranium fuel ... Today a Japanese expert, Yukiya Amano, leads the IAEA.

(www.iht.com, 14 April 2010)

'On Tuesday [13 April] Russia announced that it would close its ADE-2 reactor, which has been producing weapons-grade plutonium near Krasnoyarsk in Siberia for the past fifty years' (www.economist.com, 14 April 2010).

The leaders ... pledged to secure all vulnerable nuclear material within four years. US president Barack Obama said the joint action plan agreed at a summit in Washington would make a real contribution to a safer world. The plan calls for every nation to safeguard nuclear stocks and keep material out of terrorists' hands. Earlier Russia and the United States signed an agreement to dispose of 68 tonnes of surplus weapons-grade plutonium. The combined stockpiles – 34 tonnes from each country – are said to be enough to make 17,000 nuclear warheads. US officials said it would be used as fuel in civilian reactors to generate electricity. The United States will provide $400 million of the funding for the disposal of Russia's plutonium, which Moscow estimates will cost up to $2.5 billion. Several other countries – including Mexico, Chile and Ukraine – had earlier agreed to give up their stocks of highly enriched uranium ... Mexico pledged to eliminate all its highly enriched uranium. The country will work with the United States, Canada and the IAEA to convert the uranium at its research reactor into lower grade fuel ... In a joint communiqué the leaders agreed to non-binding measures to 'secure all vulnerable nuclear material in four years' and to 'prevent non-state actors from obtaining the information or technology required to use such material'. They said they would co-operate more deeply with the UN's nuclear watchdog, the International Atomic Energy Agency (IAEA), and share information on nuclear detection and ways to prevent nuclear trafficking. But increased security should 'not infringe upon the rights of states to develop and utilize nuclear energy for peaceful purposes and technology', they added. Progress is to be reviewed at a summit in South Korea in 2012 ... Iran has announced that it will hold its own nuclear summit in Tehran this weekend with the foreign ministers of fifteen countries.

(www.bbc.co.uk, 14 April 2010)

'Beyond the arms control treaty signed in Prague, the two sides [the United States and Russia] recently recommitted to a twelve-year-old agreement to dispose of 68 tonnes of plutonium, and Russia announced it would close its last weapons-grade plutonium reactor' (www.iht.com, 7 May 2010).

24 April 2010.

The State Duma ... is considering a bill that would increase the power of the Federal Security Service [FSB] ... The legislation would allow security officers to summon individuals for informal talks and issue written warnings about 'inadmissible' participation in anti-government activities like protest rallies. The warnings would be considered 'obligatory', and those who failed to follow them could face fines or fifteen days in jail. The government-drafted bill, submitted Saturday [24 April] as part of an effort to combat extremism, also appeared aimed at tightening control over the media. An explanatory note for the bill said some news organizations 'propagate the cult of individualism, violence and mistrust of the government's capacity to protect its citizens, virtually drawing the youth to extremism'. Journalists who refuse to follow the demands of security officers or who prevent them from fulfilling their duties could face charges under the legislation.

(*IHT*, 28 April 2010, p. 3)

27 April 2010.

The leaders of Russia and Norway resolved a forty-year-old dispute over dividing the Barents Sea and part of the Arctic Ocean into clear economic zones extending to the edge of Europe's northern continental shelf. The agreement could herald oil and natural gas exploration in a huge and potentially lucrative region. President Dmitri Medvedev: 'I believe this will open the way for many joint projects, especially in the area of energy' ... The agreement is subject to ratification by the legislature of each country. The Norwegian prime minister, Jens Stoltenberg, said it showed goodwill in the face of rising international anxiety over who controls the Arctic seabed, which by some estimates contains a quarter of the world's undiscovered fossil fuels ... When Russian scientists planted a flag on the seabed at the North Pole in 2007 it seemed that a 'race to the Arctic' was on, with northern nations aggressively jostling for the right to exploit resources that were previously out of reach ... Interest in shipping and offshore petroleum production may intensify if the polar ice cap continues to recede in response to warming temperatures ... The northern and Russian frontiers cap Europe's northernmost bulge ... The line approved on Tuesday [27 April] splits the disputed area nearly in half, which means the line will still run considerably closer to the Norwegian islands than the Russian ones. A number of oil or gas fields identified by Russian seismic surveys in the 1980s are thought to straddle the line ... In recent years Russia and Norway have worked closely on a shared fisheries management system.

(www.iht.com, 27 April 2010; *IHT*, 28 April 2010, p. 3)

Under the deal, each country will get roughly half of the disputed area covering 175,000 square kilometres of the Barents Sea and the Arctic Ocean. It is not known how much oil and gas is at stake, but large gas fields exist on either side of the zone ... Norwegian prime minister Jens Stoltenberg said a final pact would be signed before the end of the year ... Statoil, the Norwegian energy group, is already producing natural gas from its Snohvit field in an undisputed part of the Barents Sea, while Russia's Gasprom is developing the massive Shtokman field beneath Russian waters together with Statoil and Total of France.

(*FT*, 28 April 2010, p. 9)

'In recent years several states have launched claims to Arctic territory as climate change and technological developments have increased access to the region' (www.bbc.co.uk, 27 April 2010).

3–28 May 2010. The latest five-yearly review conference of the Nuclear Non-proliferation Treaty is held at the United Nations in New York.

The Iranian president, Mahmoud Ahmadinejad, accused the United States and other nuclear powers on Monday [3 May] of trying to intimidate non-nuclear countries and said the Americans were the 'main suspect' in the stockpiling, spread and threat of nuclear weapons. Mr Ahmadinejad took a defiant posture as the United Nations opened a conference to strengthen the forty-year-old Nuclear Non-proliferation Treaty, arguing that the world's nuclear powers needed to disarm and that there was no credible evidence that his nation was seeking to develop nuclear weapons ... In opening the conference, Secretary-General Ban Ki-moon had called on Iran to prove that its nuclear programme was solely for peaceful purposes and to accept a compromise deal offered to Tehran last fall [2009] ... Mr Ban called on Iran to comply with Security Council resolutions demanding that it stop enriching uranium and to co-operate with the IAEA in answering outstanding questions about whether its programme was peaceful or aimed at developing a nuclear weapon. Mr Ban said: 'The onus is on Iran to clarify the doubts and concerns about its programme' ... Mr Ban said the conference negotiations should focus on a few central issues: more nuclear arms cuts; greater transparency in national nuclear programmes; getting the three states outside the treaty – India, Pakistan and Israel [Israel's nuclear arsenal being estimated at 100 to 200 warheads] – to sign it; and a nuclear-free zone in the Middle East ... Mr Ban said that the need to strengthen the non-proliferation treaty remained as important as ever, given the expanding number of countries with nuclear programmes and the possible threat of nuclear terrorism ... Mr Ban also called on North Korea to return to negotiations over its nuclear programme. North Korea, which has tested nuclear devices, withdrew from the non-proliferation treaty in 2003 ... Yukiya Amano, the director-general of the IAEA, singled out Iran, North Korea and Syria for their lack of co-operation with the agency. North Korea has refused any co-operation with the agency since April 2009, he said, while Syria has refused to engage since June 2008 over questions about what officials suspect was a nuclear facility imported from North Korea and destroyed by Israel. Mr Amano said Iran needed to comply with the safeguards agreement it had signed with the agency ... One emphasis at the review conference is to persuade countries to sign up for additional inspections by the agency. Mr Amano noted that ninety-eight of the 189 parties to the treaty had signed up for the additional inspections. Iran initially accepted them, but changed its mind after its nuclear programme was referred to the Security Council. The Council has passed three rounds of sanctions against Iran and is negotiating a fourth ... Iran maintains that its nuclear efforts are for peaceful purposes, but Western nations suspect that Tehran is secretly aiming to develop a bomb ... Any agreement reached at the end of the conference on 28 May has to be adopted by consensus of all 189 members ... The last time it was held, in 2005 the nuclear non-proliferation review conference collapsed, with non-nuclear states critical of nuclear powers for not sufficiently reducing their arsenals and with extended, ineffectual bickering over how to grapple with the nuclear programmes of Iran and North Korea.

(www.iht.com, 3 May 2010; *IHT*, 4 May 2010, pp. 1, 4)

In his speech Mr Ahmadinejad said that all nuclear powers tried to intimidate countries that had no nuclear weapons, but he called the United States the 'main suspect' in fostering a nuclear arms race ... The Pentagon on Monday [3 May] declassified statistics showing that the United States now possesses 5,113 nuclear weapons, down 84 per cent from its peak of 31,255 in 1967 ... The statistics' broad outlines have been known, in general terms, for many years. The Pentagon issued gross numbers on Monday, deliberately lumping together deployed weapons, those in storage and 'inactive' warheads. The figures released for the current stockpile ... do not include several thousand retired weapons awaiting complete disarmament [waiting to be dismantled].

(www.iht.com, 4 May 2010)

'President Mahmoud Ahmadinejad of Iran accused states with nuclear weapons of threatening those who wanted to develop peaceful nuclear weapons' (www.bbc.co.uk, 4 May 2010).

The Nuclear Non-proliferation Treaty is the central element of international efforts to halt the spread of nuclear weapons. It comprises a kind of bargain in which those countries which had nuclear weapons when signing the treaty in 1970 – the United States, the former Soviet Union, China, the UK and France – agreed eventually to disarm ... All other treaty signatories agreed never to develop nuclear weapons in return for receiving full access to civilian nuclear technology ... Two nuclear weapons states – India and Pakistan – along with Israel, which has an unacknowledged nuclear arsenal, are not signatories.

(www.bbc.co.uk, 3 May 2010)

The majority of his [President Mahmoud Ahmadinejad's] thirty-five-minute speech was devoted to criticizing the massive US nuclear arsenal and suggested the US nuclear posture threatened other countries and justified their pursuit of nuclear weapons to protect themselves. He called the provision in the US Nuclear Posture Review retaining an option to use nuclear weapons against countries a non-compliance with the very treaty it accuses Iran of violating. He said: 'Regrettably, the government of the United States has not only used nuclear weapons [in World War II], but also continues to threaten to use such weapons against other countries, including Iran.'

(www.cnn.com, 4 May 2010)

4 May 2010.

President Dmitri Medvedev today [4 May] ordered an urgent inquiry into why a prisoner who died last week in custody was refused medical treatment ... Medvedev said criminal charges would be brought against investigators who permitted the death of Vera Trifonova, a fifty-three-year-old businesswoman. She was arrested last December [2009] and locked up in Moscow's notorious Matrosskaya Tishina pre-trial detention centre. Trifonova died on Friday [30 April] despite repeated requests for her release. She had been suffering from severe diabetes and kidney failure. She was almost blind and only able to breathe with one lung. When she complained of breathlessness, doctors advised her to sleep 'standing up' ... This follows the death in the same detention centre of Sergei Magnitsky last November [2009], a thirty-seven-year-old lawyer working for Hermitage Capital, the asset management fund. Hermitage accused the interior ministry of defrauding the company of $230 million in a large-scale tax scam allegedly involving sixty senior Russian officials. The same officials then arrested Magnitsky and kept him in prison for nearly a year without charge. He died after he was refused treatment for an embolism. Medvedev issued guidelines that defendants accused of economic crimes should automatically be given bail. Prosecutors claim Trifonova, who ran a successful real estate business, tried to sell a seat in Russia's upper chamber federation council for $1.5 million. Trifonova dismissed the charge as ludicrous ... Medvedev ordered criminal charges to be brought against Sergei Pysin, the chief investigator in the case, who had opposed Trifonova's numerous petitions for bail ... So far nobody has been prosecuted in connection with Magnitsky's death.

(www.guardian.co.uk, 4 May 2010; *Guardian*, 5 May 2010, p. 26)

Vera Trifonova ... was suffering from severe diabetes. One kidney had already failed and her lungs were filled with so much fluid that there was a danger she could drown in her sleep, her lawyers said ... Ms Trifonova was finally granted permission to go to the hospital on 29 April, but it was too late. The next day she died of heart failure in the medical ward of a Moscow pre-trial detention facility ... President Dmitri Medvedev ordered an investigation on Saturday [1 May] ... On Tuesday [4 May] the lead investigator in the fraud case against Ms Trifonova, Sergei Pysin, was charged with negligence in connection with the death. At least two other officials at the department were fired ... Ms Trifonova, head of a real estate company, was arrested on 16 December [2009] and charged with involve-ment in a scheme to sell a seat in Russia's upper house of parliament for $1.5 million to the head of a Russian bank, an accusation she denied. Although suffering from health problems even before her arrest, she refused an offer from Mr Pysin, the lead investigator, to confess in exchange for release from custody, said her lawyer ... Russian law allows for investigators to set the terms of imprisonment, a tool that is frequently used to extract confessions from people in pre-trial confinement ... The lawyer Sergei Magnitsky died of toxic shock and heart failure in November [2009] ... President Dmitri Medvedev quickly signed a law easing punish-ment for economic crimes, including allowing for suspects to post bail rather than remain in prison in certain cases ... No one has been held legally accountable.

(*IHT*, 5 May 2010, p. 4)

9 May 2010.

As Russians prepare to celebrate the sixty-fifth anniversary of the defeat of Nazi Germany [on Sunday 9 May] ... a major question still looms: what should be done about Stalin? ... Plans to mark the anniversary with the display of wartime propaganda posters bearing Stalin's image have reopened this sore ... President Dmitri Medvedev (Friday 7 May): 'Stalin committed massive crimes against his own people. Despite how hard he worked and the successes achieved under his leadership, what he did to his own people cannot be forgiven ... The regime built in the Soviet Union can be called nothing other than totalitarian. Unfortunately, it was a regime where elementary rights and freedoms were suppressed ... In no case is it possible to say that Stalinism is returning to our daily lives, that the symbols are returning, the posters or anything else' ... Still, a few of the posters have already been displayed, and a city bus painted with a portrait of Stalin in military garb began ferrying passengers along St Petersburg's streets ... Mr Medvedev denounced Stalin's treatment of returning soldiers, many of whom were sent to prison camps on suspicion of collaborating with the Nazis. He said: 'One thing is absolutely obvious. The Great Patriotic War was won by our people, not Stalin' ... On a holiday devoted to the victims of Soviet repression last October [2009] ... President Dmitri Medvedev ... warned that Russians had begun to forget the millions killed under Stalin and criticized some historians for trying to whitewash the atrocities ... For the first time troops from the United States, France and Poland have been invited as representatives of the anti-Hitler coalition to march across Red Square in Moscow in the victory parade on 9 May.

(www.iht.com, 8 May 2010)

For the first time since Stalin began commemorating the Soviet Union's victory over Nazi Germany, serving US, British, Polish and French troops joined over 11,000 Russian soldiers to parade past the Kremlin's red walls. The opposition Communists and some Soviet war veterans condemned the move ... Seventy troops from the US 170th Infantry Brigade [took part] ... German chancellor Angela Merkel, Chinese president Hu Jintao and other world leaders looked on ... Prime minister Vladimir Putin hosted a meeting and dinner at his country retreat for President Hu Jintao ... President Barack Obama [was] unable to come to Moscow because of a scheduling clash ... Russia's Communists, still the country's biggest opposition party, held a demonstration after the parade, chanting 'Glory to the great Stalin' ... Most of the Soviet war veterans attending the parade seemed unconcerned by the presence of Nato soldiers, though they did not applaud when they marched past ... A poll by the independent Levada Centre last month [April] showed that 55 per cent of Russians were wholly or partly positive about Nato troops at the parade, with only 28 per cent against ... Defence minister Anatoli Serdyukov said this year's commemorations would be among the biggest, with over 102,000 troops marching across the country ... French president Nicolas Sarkozy and Italian prime minister Silvio Berlusconi cancelled their attendance at the last minute to deal with the crisis surrounding the Euro ... Prime minister Vladimir Putin revived two years ago a Soviet-era tradition of parading tanks, missiles and military vehicles across the square and flying aircraft overhead. This year's parade included 127 helicopters, fighters, bombers and refuelling planes.

(www.iht.com, 9 May 2010)

Invitations [were given] to troops from the countries known here as the anti-Hitler coalition ... Beethoven's 'Ode to Joy' ... an EU anthem ... [was played] by a military band ... President Dmitri Medvedev: 'It was a common victory. All peoples of the former USSR struggled for it. And today soldiers of Russia, the former Soviet countries and the anti-Hitler coalition states march together triumphantly. A single rank is evidence of our common readiness to defend peace' ... Communists and nationalists have held protests, saying that the presence of ... Nato soldiers ... was an insult ... [But] it was hard to find a critical word among the veterans who were in the grandstands ... Roughly 25 million people in the Soviet Union died in the [Second World] War, historians say.

(*IHT*, 10 May 2010, p. 3)

'President Dmitri Medvedev said it was "absolutely out of the question" to permit the revival of Stalin's personality cult by erecting street posters in his honour for Victory Day as Moscow City Council officials had wanted' (*The Times*, 8 May 2010, p. 5).

Prime minister Vladimir Putin has snubbed both the Prince of Wales and the US vice president Joe Biden by refusing to allow them to attend a parade in Red Square marking the sixty-fifth anniversary of the end of the Second World War ... Russia invited Gordon Brown and other heads of state to attend the Kremlin's celebrations on Sunday [9 May] – the biggest ever. But with the [UK] prime minister unable to attend because of the general election [held on 6 May], the Foreign Office suggested Prince Charles instead. Last week, however, the prince quietly stood down after Putin made it clear that he did not want him there – apparently a sign of his continuing annoyance with the UK over its failure to extradite Boris Berezovsky ... Putin has apparently not forgiven what he regards as an earlier betrayal by [the then UK prime minister] Tony Blair, who failed to telephone him when Berezovsky was granted asylum in 2003. Ever since Putin has declined offers to meet senior British representatives ... Biden is close to Mikheil Saakashvili, Georgia's president. President Barack Obama told President Dmitri Medvedev he was unable to attend but had confidently offered Biden as his replacement ... For the first time troops from Britain, France and the United States – the Soviet Union's wartime allies – are taking part in the victory parade, marching alongside 10,500 Russian soldiers. More than twenty-five foreign leaders will attend, including France's president, Nicolas Sarkozy, and Germany's chancellor, Angela Merkel. But there will be no senior British figure. Both the UK and the United States will be represented by their respective ambassadors.

(www.guardian.co.uk, 8 May 2010)

Troops from four Nato countries have marched for the first time in Russia's annual parade to mark victory in World War II. Soldiers from Britain, France, Poland and the United States marched through Moscow's Red Square ... Along with 10,000 Russian troops, the parade included tanks, ballistic missiles and a fly-past of 127 aircraft. It was the largest display of Russia's military hardware since the collapse of the Soviet Union ... France was represented at the parade by the Normandie-Niemen squadron ... The United States [was represented] by a detachment from the 2nd Battalion, 18th Regiment ... Poland [sent] seventy-five service personnel representing the Polish army, air force and navy ... Britain was represented by seventy-six soldiers from the 1st Battalion Welsh Guards ... German chancellor Angela Merkel was among some two dozen world leaders attending the sixty-fifth anniversary ... Western allies mark Victory in Europe Day every year on 8 May, but Russia celebrates the event a day later as it was 9 May in Moscow when the Nazi surrender came into force.

(www.bbc.co.uk, 9 May 2010)

'President Dmitri Medvedev emphasized that the victory was achieved together with the other allies – although of course the Soviet Union played a decisive role ... Beethoven's Ninth Symphony [was] played by the international military band' (www.iht.com, 14 May 2010).

11 May 2010.

President Barack Obama has revived a civilian nuclear energy pact with Moscow, which was shelved in the wake of Russia's 2008 conflict with Georgia. Mr Obama resubmitted the pact to Congress ... The agreement would allow the transfer of technology and equipment, including reactors ... The pact had been signed in 2007 by President George W. Bush and President Vladimir Putin. But the conflict in Georgia meant the deal was never put to a Senate vote.

(www.iht.com, 11 May 2010)

Prime minister Vladimir Putin delivered an icy reproach Monday [17 May] to the management of the Raspadskaya coal mine in Siberia, where about ninety miners and rescue workers were killed in twin methane explosions [on Saturday 11 May], expressing bafflement that its director had not been dismissed after several safety violations. Spitting out statistics about worker fatalities in Russian mines, Mr Putin said the death toll had roughly held steady since 1998, even as expenditures for the safety of workers increased nine-fold, and asked: 'Where exactly is this money going – for whose safety, and to which workers? The question arises, what is going on here?' ... The dressing down of management came three days after several protest actions in the city of Mezhdurechenensk, where workers complained that financial incentives pressure workers to tolerate safety risks. Two hundred protesters blocked a set of railroad tracks on Friday night [14 May], pelting the riot police with stones and bottles when they forcibly dispersed the crowd. The authorities detained twenty-eight protesters, and said seventeen policemen were hurt in the melee. The regional governor, Aman Tuleyev, blamed outside provocateurs for the disorders, telling Mr Putin that police have 'traced two British, four Ukrainian and four Moscow websites bent on agitating the populace'. Still ... Mr Putin echoed complaints that union officials have voiced in recent days, to an audience that included ... Roman Abramovich, one of the owners of the steel giant Evraz, which owns 40 per cent of the Raspadskaya Coal Company, and Gennadi Kozovoy, the coal company's general director. Mr Putin recommended a 70 per cent increase in pay for coal miners and excoriated management for risking workers' lives. In particular, he cited a report from the state safety inspector, Rostekhnadzor, that reported finding 1,401 violations at the mine in 2009 and the first four months of 2010. Mr Putin said the company had been penalized only 1.5 million roubles (about $50,000) for those violations, and that inspectors had failed in repeated attempts to dismiss Igor Volkov, the mine's director, for violations ... Mr Putin: 'There was no reaction. Citizen Volkov is working even now, and is sitting in the hall with you' ... Mr Putin recommended that Rostekhnadzor's powers be expanded to include temporarily shutting mines and dismissing mine officials ... The coal company said Mr Volkov would resign before the end of the day.

(www.iht.com, 17 May 2010; *IHT*, 18 May 2010, p. 4)

The Raspadskaya Coal Company announced on Tuesday [18 May] that Igor Volkov, the director of the mine where ninety people were killed in twin methane explosions, has left his post after a public reproach from prime minister Vladimir Putin, who said the mine's management should be held accountable for safety violations ... He recommended an increase in basic pay for coal miners so they could depend less on incentives paid for making quotas, a step he said would 'minimize miners' motivation to increase extraction at any price'. In recent days miners have said they routinely ignore or distort methane readings in order to reach production quotas.

(www.iht.com, 18 May 2010)

Protesters blocked railroad tracks at the site of a western Siberian mine disaster on Friday night [14 May], demanding to meet with the management of the Raspadskaya Coal Company and complaining that low salaries and financial incentives were pressurizing miners to cut corners on safety ... financial incentives [which] could compel the workers to circumvent or disable the [methane] detectors.

(www.iht.com, 14 May 2010)

18 May 2010.

Senior Barack Obama administration officials urged the Senate on Tuesday [18 May] to approve a new arms control treaty with Russia ... Defence secretary Robert Gates responded [to a senator's question] that while Russia is already below the treaty limit in terms of launchers, it currently has more warheads than would be allowed: He said: 'They will be reducing the number of warheads' ... The treaty would permit fewer inspections than the original Strategic Arms Reduction Treaty of 1991 ... Each side could conduct twenty-eight inspections a year, and the United States maintained a full-time inspection team at the Votkinsk missile production factory in Russia. The new treaty does not renew the Votkinsk team and calls for just eighteen inspections a year. The Obama officials said the new inspections would cover twice as much ground as the old ones, and that American inspectors would have to monitor only twenty-seven facilities in Russia today, compared with the seventy-three that were being monitored in the old Soviet Union.

(www.iht.com, 18 May 2010; *IHT*, 19 May 2010, p. 3)

The two sides included non-binding language in the treaty preamble 'recognizing the existence of the inter-relationship between strategic offensive arms and strategic defensive arms', basically a rhetorical nod at Russian concerns without actually limiting American plans. The only binding restriction in the treaty bars the United States from using old intercontinental missile silos for missile defence interceptors, something the administration did not intend to do anyway.

(www.iht.com, 19 May 2010)

'Mikhail Khodorkovsky declared a hunger strike to protest a court decidion made earlier this month [May] that extended his term in custody ... Mr Khodorkovsky said the decision violated amendments to Russian law recently signed by President Dmitri Medvedev' (www.iht.com, 19 May 2010).

Mikhail Khodorkovsky began a hunger strike yesterday [18 May] to draw attention to what he says is the abuse of the criminal justice system ... Last week a Moscow judge extended Mr Khodorkovsky's detention by three months while he is tried on fresh charges of money laundering and fraud that could mean a further twenty-two year sentence. In a letter to Russia's supreme court, Mr Khodorkovsky said the ruling went against the legislation initiated by President Dmitri Medvedev forbidding the pre-trial detention of people who stand accused of economic crimes ... Mr Medvedev proposed the law last year [2009] after Sergei Magnitsky died in jail as he awaited trial for tax evasion.

(*FT*, 19 May 2010, p. 10)

Mikhail Khodorkovsky ... said that the decision to keep him locked up violated a decree by President Dmitri Medvedev stating that people accused of economic crimes should not be held in pre-trial detention facilities. The former Yukos boss said that his hunger strike would be 'indefinite' until he received confirmation that Mr Medvedev had received 'comprehensive information' about the way the law was being violated ... Given that Mr Khodorkovsky is still serving his first prison term, he would still have remained behind bars even if the judge had ruled in his favour ... [But he] said that he wanted to draw attention to the flaws in the system as a whole. This is the third time he has announced a hunger strike.

(*The Independent*, 19 May 2010, p. 31)

('Mikhail Khodorkovsky yesterday [19 May] ended a two-day hunger strike held to draw the Kremlin's attention to a court ruling that he claimed was illegal': *IHT*, 20 May 2010, p. 8.)

21 May 2010.

As it sought support for international sanctions on Iran, the Obama administration gave Moscow two concessions: lifting American sanctions against
the Russian military complex and agreeing not to ban the sale of Russian
anti-aircraft batteries to Tehran. The administration dropped the sanctions
on Friday [21 May] against the Russian state arms export agency and three
other Russian entities previously found to have transferred sensitive technology or weapons to Iran. The move came just three days after the United
States and Russia agreed on a package of UN sanctions against Iran. Russian
and American officials also said Friday that while the UN resolution would
ban many weapons sales to Iran, it would not prohibit Moscow from
completing the sale of S-300 anti-aircraft missiles to Tehran, a contract that
Russia has suspended but not cancelled. The sophisticated defence system
could help Iran shoot down American or Israeli warplanes should either try
to bomb its nuclear facilities. Russia has invented a series of reasons to
delay delivery of the systems, under strong American pressure ... Other provisions of the sanctions, urging countries to exercise caution in what they
deliver to Iran, would give Washington the ability to continue to urge Russia
never to deliver the systems. Iran, in frustration, announced recently that it
was developing a similar system that would be domestically manufactured,
but outside experts said that would take years ... The civilian nuclear plant
built by Russia ... [is] set to open this year [2010] ... [Obama] administration officials said there was no evidence of current arms or technology transfers involving the companies freed of sanctions on Friday. Rosoboronexport,
the state arms export corporation, was sanctioned in 2008 for arms sales to
Iran, while the Dmitri Mendeleyev University of Chemical Technology, the
Moscow Aviation Institute and the Tula Instrument Design Bureau were all
originally sanctioned in 1999. Earlier this year the administration lifted
sanctions on two other Russian entities, Glavkosmos and the Baltic Technical University, both sanctioned in 1998 for helping Iran's missile and
weapons programmes.

(www.iht.com, 22 May 2010)

27 May 2010.

President Barack Obama's first formal National Security Strategy ... lays
out a vision of a 'stable, substantive, multi-dimensional relationship with
Russia', but promises to 'promote the rule of law, accountable government
and universal values' within Russia and 'support the sovereignty and territorial integrity of Russia's neighbours'.

(*IHT*, 28 May 2010, pp. 1, 6)

28 May 2010.

Hard-fought negotiations over the future of the Nuclear Non-proliferation
Treaty ended on Friday [28 May] with 189 nations reaffirming their com-

mitment to eliminating all nuclear weapons and setting a new 2012 deadline for holding a regional conference to eliminate unconventional weapons from the Middle East.

(www.iht.com, 29 May 2010)

8 June 2010.

Four Russian soldiers assigned to guard the still-smouldering remains of a Polish airliner and the ninety-six people who died in the crash collected bank cards from an official who died in the crash, said Vladimir Markin, a spokesman for the Investigative Committee of the Russian general prosecutor. Over the weekend Russia's interior ministry emphatically denied Polish allegations that the police had taken valuables from the dead ... But on Tuesday [8 June] Moscow acknowledged that four soldiers had been caught with stolen bank cards. The four conscripts, who were manning a cordon around the crash site, admitted their guilt and are co-operating with investigators, Mr Markin said ... Between one and three hours after the crash, about $1,700 was withdrawn from a bank card belonging to Andrzej Przewoznik, who oversaw war memorials and commemorations in Poland, according to Warsaw prosecutors ... Late on Tuesday a lawyer who represents the families of several crash victims said prosecutors are investigating attempts to use bank cards from another victim, parliamentarian Alexandra Natalii-Swiat ... [Her] cards were blocked by the bank on the day of the crash so no money was taken ... [Russian] Investigators said on Tuesday that the suspects took five cards and managed to steal 60,345 roubles (approximately $1,890) ... News of the theft first broke Saturday [5 June] in ... a daily newspaper in Poland.

(www.iht.com, 8 June 2010)

About 6,000 zloty was withdrawn on the cards ... Three of the four soldiers had previous criminal convictions, including robbery and counterfeiting, the Russian prosecutor's office said. The soldiers have already admitted their involvement, a spokesman was quoted as saying ... The men had been responsible for sealing off the crash site at Smolensk airport. The Polish government plane crashed on 10 April.

(www.bbc.co.uk, 8 June 2010)

President Dmitri Medvedev has ordered the government to prepare plans to cut up to 20 per cent of government staff. The move comes after Kremlin initiatives to cut the size of the army and the police force by similar ratios ... Russia's bureaucracy grew sharply during oil-fuelled growth years under the former president, now prime minister, Vladimir Putin. From 1999 to 2009, according to Rosstat, the statistical service, the number of federal employees grew from 866,000 to 1.5 million ... Boris Gryzlov, chairman of the Duma, said in January that a 20 per cent cut would save about 50 billion roubles ($1.6 billion) a year. Russia's bureaucracy [is[notorious for inefficiency and corruption.

(*FT*, 9 June 2010, p. 9)

9 June 2010.

The UN Security Council voted in favour of fresh sanctions against Iran over its nuclear programme. The council voted twelve to two, with one abstention, in favour of a fourth round of sanctions, including tight finance curbs and an expanded arms embargo ... The Security Council resolution was opposed by Turkey and Brazil. They had earlier brokered a deal with Iran on uranium enrichment. Lebanon abstained. The new sanctions were passed after being watered down during negotiations with Russia and China ... There are no crippling economic sanctions and there is no oil embargo ... Those passed include prohibiting Iran from buying heavy weapons such as attack helicopters and missiles. They also toughen rules on financial transactions with Iranian banks and increase the number of Iranian individuals and companies that are targeted with asset freezes and travel bans ... Three earlier rounds of UN sanctions blocked trade of 'sensitive nuclear material', froze the financial assets of those involved in Iran's nuclear activities, banned all of Iran's arms exports and encouraged scrutiny of the dealings of Iranian banks.

(www.bbc.co.uk, 9 June 2010)

The new sanctions [represent] a modest increase from previous rounds ... China and Russia were adamant that the sanctions will not affect Iran's day-to-day economy ... The sanctions require countries to inspect ships or planes headed to or from Iran if they suspect banned cargo is aboard, but there is no authorization to board ships forcefully at sea ... China is believed to have surpassed the EU as Iran's major trade partner with exchanges surpassing the EU's $35 billion. China imports some 11 per cent of its oil needs from Iran and has signed more than $120 billion in oil industry deals in recent years. At one point Iran imported some 40 per cent of its refined gasoline needs, but it has been reducing that through deals with China to expand its refining capacity and by signing agreements with countries like Venezuela.

(www.iht.com, 9 June 2010)

A fourth round of sanctions ... ban the sale of heavy weapons, extend travel bans and asset freezes on Iranian companies and officials, and give countries the right to examine suspect Iranian cargoes at their ports and airports ... Russia has found endless pretexts to delay the commissioning of a nuclear reactor that it has built at Bushehr, on Iran's southern coast, and stall delivery of a sophisticated missile defence system. The Iranians also suspect Russia of holding up their application to join the Shanghai Co-operation Organization, a six-country mutual security outfit led by China, Russia and Kazakhstan.

(*The Economist*, 12 June 2010, p. 66)

'[According to the Security Council resolution] officials will allow individual countries to take more draconian steps to stamp on the trade supporting Iran's programme ... Countries that have long wanted to be tougher can now be so' (p. 17).

Russia has said its long-standing contract to supply surface-to-air missiles to Iran will not be affected by new UN sanctions. Russia agreed to supply Iran with S-300 systems several years ago but has not delivered them. Foreign minister Sergei Lavrov stressed the missiles were not subject to the limits set by the UN on co-operation with Iran. He said Moscow was in talks on building further nuclear reactors in Iran. The United States and Israel are concerned with the S-300 missiles, designed to counter both aircraft and cruise missiles, might be used to protect Iran's nuclear facilities from possible attack ... Russian officials pointed out on Thursday [10 June] that the new UN Security Council resolution affected only 'missiles or missile systems as defined for the purpose of the UN Register of Conventional Arms'. The register's section on missiles states that it 'does not include ground-to-air missiles' ... Sergei Lavrov: 'As far as military-technical co-operation is concerned, the resolution introduces limits to co-operation with Iran on offensive weapons and defensive weapons do not fall under these limits' ... Mr Lavrov said Moscow was in talks on building nuclear reactors in Iran in addition to the Bushehr site, due to open in August after years of delay.

(www.bbc.co.uk, 11 June 2010)

Prime minister Vladimir Putin has said Moscow will freeze the sale of surface-to-air missiles to Iran, according to French officials ... Russia's foreign minister said President Dmitri Medvedev will decree which weapons cannot be sold to Iran. Sergei Lavrov earlier [Thursday 10 June] said the missiles were not subject to fresh UN sanctions ... But on Friday [11 June] he said: 'According to our practice, the UN Security Council resolution is implemented through the decrees issued by the Russian president. A decree to this effect will be prepared.'

(www.bbc.co.uk, 11 June 2010)

17 June 2010.

Russian and US negotiators have agreed to set up licensed adoption agencies and allow monitors to visit the homes of adopted children as part of a new accord, Russia's children's rights ombudsman said Thursday [17 June] ... A breakthrough occurred after US negotiators gave in to Russia's demand that the accord be retroactive so that it protects children already adopted.

(*IHT*, 18 June 2010, p. 3)

The fresh EU sanctions approved in Brussels on Thursday [17 June] include a ban on investments and technology transfers to Iran's key oil and gas industry – measures that go further than the latest UN sanctions. Only a day earlier the United States announced sanctions that ban Americans from trading with a number of firms and individuals, including Iran's Post Bank, its defence minister and the air force and missile command of the Revolutionary Guard Corps ... President Dmitri Medvedev (17 June): 'We did not

agree to this when we discussed the joint resolution at the United Nations ...
A couple of years ago that would have been impossible. We should act collectively. If we do we will have the desired result.'

(www.bbc.co.uk, 18 June 2010)

24 June 2010.

President Dmitri Medvedev and President Barack Obama have hailed an
improvement in relations between Washington and Moscow ... Mr Obama
said the United States was backing Russia's ascension to the WTO. Moscow
would also allow the United States to resume poultry exports to Russia after
a ban of almost six months ... Mr Medvedev had visited California before
travelling to Washington ... Russia wants to join the WTO but the United
States insists Moscow must do more to safeguard intellectual property
rights. Mr Medvedev began his visit to the United States by touring high-
tech companies in California's Silicon Valley, which he wants Russia to
emulate. He signed up for micro-blogging service Twitter with the username
KremlinRussia. Mr Medvedev also visited the computer equipment manu-
facturer Cisco, which is investing $1 billion in Russia over the next ten
years. The Russian president welcomed the investment, saying he wanted
his country to be a place where quality of life was ensured by intellectual,
rather than natural resources.

(www.bbc.co.uk, 24 June 2010)

Russia and the United States ... [fear] that the south [of Kyrgyzstan] ... will
fall prey to Islamist extremists if the country disintegrates. Meeting in
Washington this week President Barack Obama and President Dmitri
Medvedev issued a joint statement pledging to 'continue to work jointly
with Kyrgyzstan to counter the threat of drug trafficking and terrorism'.

(*FT*, 26 June 2010, p. 8)

27 June 2010.

On Monday [29 June] federal prosecutors accused eleven people of being
part of a Russian espionage ring, living under false names and deep cover in
a patient scheme to penetrate what one coded message called American
'policy-making circles'. An FBI investigation that began at least seven years
ago culminated with the arrest on Sunday [27 June] of ten people in
Yonkers, Boston and northern Virginia. The documents detailed what the
authorities called the 'Illegals Programme', an ambitious, long-term effort
by the SVR [External Intelligence Service], the successor to the Soviet
KGB, to plant Russian spies in the United States to gather information and
recruit more agents. The alleged agents were directed to gather information
on nuclear weapons, American policy toward Iran, CIA leadership. Congressional politics and many other topics, prosecutors say. The Russian
spies made contact with a former high ranking American national security
official and a nuclear researcher, among others. But the charges did not

include espionage, and it was unclear what secrets the suspected spy ring – which included five couples – actually managed to collect … So-called illegals [are] spies operating under false names outside of diplomatic cover … Prosecutors said the 'Illegals Programme' extended to other countries around the world … The defendants were charged with conspiracy, not to commit espionage, but to fail to register as agents of a foreign government, which carries a maximum sentence of five years in prison; nine were also charged with conspiracy to commit money laundering, which carries a maximum penalty of twenty years. They are not accused of obtaining classified materials.

(www.iht.com, 29 June 2010)

An eleventh suspect remains at large, according to the US Department of Justice … [which] has made clear that none of the information at stake was classified … Investigators say some of the agents had been using false identities since the early 1990s.

(www.bbc.co.uk, 29 June 2010)

'According to US court papers, most of those arrested purported to be citizens of the United States or Canada' (www.bbc.co.uk, 30 February 2010).

An eleventh suspect … was arrested on Tuesday [29 June] on the Mediterranean island of Cyprus, police there said. They said he was arrested at Larnaca airport as he tried to leave for Budapest and was release on bail pending US extradition proceedings. He is wanted in the United States on suspicion of espionage … A statement by the Russian foreign ministry on Tuesday said of the allegations: 'In our opinion such actions are groundless and pursue unseemly aims. In any case, it is highly deplorable that all of this is happening against the background of the reset in Russia–US ties announced by the US administration itself.'

(www.bbc.co.uk, 29 June 2010)

The Russian foreign ministry issued a statement calling the arrest 'baseless' and 'unseemly'. It accused American prosecutors of acting 'in the spirit of the spy passions of the Cold War period'. The statement said: 'We would like to note only that this type of information has happened more than once in the past, when our relations were on the rise. In any case, it is deeply regrettable that all this is taking place on the background of the "reset" in Russian–American relations declared by the US administration itself' … Cells of undercover operatives, masked as ordinary citizens, are know in Russian as 'illegals' and they occupy a storied position in Soviet culture … Illegals, unlike most spies, live in foreign countries without the benefit of a diplomatic cover, which would have offered them immunity from prosecution if they were caught, Soviet intelligence services began training a corps of these agents shortly after the October Revolution in 1917, when few countries had diplomatic relations with the Soviet Union, and it came to be seen as a particular Soviet speciality.

(www.iht.com, 29 June 2010)

'On Tuesday night [29 June] the Russian foreign ministry issued another state-ment acknowledging that the suspects were Russian citizens: 'They have not conducted any activities against the interests of the United States' (www.iht.com, 29 June 2010)

> American officials said they believed that most of the accused spies had been born in Russia and had been given sophisticated training before reset-tling in the United States, posing as married couples ... None of the eleven people accused in the case face charges of espionage, because in all those years they were never caught sending classified information back to Moscow ... None was caught accepting documents from government offi-cials ... At a meeting with former President Bill Clinton on Tuesday [29 June] prime minister Vladimir Putin and a former spy himself said: 'Your police have gotten carried away, putting people in jail. I really expect that the positive achievements that have been made in our intergovernmental relations lately will not be damaged by the latest events.'
>
> (www.iht.com, 30 June 2010)

> [On Wednesday 30 June] Moscow played down the arrest of alleged Russian spies in the United States ... A Russian foreign spokesman: 'We expect that the incident involving the arrest in the United States of a group of people suspected of spying for Russia will not negatively affect Russian–US relations. In this connection, we take note of the statement of White House official representative Robert Gibbs' ... On Tuesday [29 June] Mr Gibbs said: 'I think we have made a new start to working together on things like the United Nations, dealing with North Korea and Iran. I do not think that this will affect those relations' ... US Assistant secretary of state for European Affairs Phil Gordon echoed Mr Gibbs, saying: 'We're moving towards a more trusting relationship. We're beyond the Cold War; our rela-tions absolutely demonstrate that ... I don't think anyone was hugely shocked to know that some vestiges of old attempts to use intelligence are still there.'
>
> (www.bbc.co.uk, 30 June 2010)

> The eleventh suspected member ... has disappeared ... Late Wednesday [30 June] a police spokesman ... [said] the suspect had failed to report as required ... A local court ordered his release on bail of around $25,000 on the condition that he surrendered his passport while arrangements were made for his extradition to the United States. The island's long political division could offer a fugitive certain advantages, including the absence of international extradition treaties in the Turkish-controlled north.
>
> (www.iht.com, 1 July 2010)

> This case should be easier to overcome without tit-for-tat expulsions because the suspected spy ring did not seem to achieve any serious breach of national security ... Much of the Russian commentary suggested that the arrests were an effort by dark forces in the American government to under-

mine President Barack Obama's reset policy … The charges … include money laundering, conspiracy and failure to register as foreign agents. According to criminal complaints, the Russian government planted them as spies in the United States to collect information about nuclear weapons and others sensitive programmes.

(www.iht.com, 1 July 2010)

'One of the suspects … admitted that he worked for Russia's intelligence service, federal prosecutors say … The suspect known as Juan Lazaro made a "lengthy post-arrest statement on 27 June"' (www.cnn.com, 2 July 2010).

The judge said Vicky Pelaez could be released on a $250,000 personal recognizance bond, and must wear an electronic ankle bracelet and remain in home incarceration. In contrast to the other defendants, he said, she apparently was not a trained agent and had not used ay false names.

(www.iht.com, 2 July 2010)

On Thursday [1 July] journalist Vicky Pelaez was granted bail in New York after the judge said she was a US citizen and did not appear to have been trained as a spy. However, the judge ordered that she should not be freed before Tuesday [5 July], allowing time for a possible appeal by prosecutors. She will remain under house arrest under a $250,000 bond and will be electronically monitored … Her husband, who goes under the name Juan Lazaro, is said to have admitted to prosecutors that he works for Russia's intelligence service.

(www.bbc.co.uk, 2 July 2010)

'Three suspected Russian spies held by the United States have been denied bail … Six suspects were earlier denied bail … An eleventh suspect is on the run in Cyprus' (www.bbc.co.uk, 3 July 2010).

Federal prosecutors in Manhattan say that two more of the suspected Russian agents arrested last weekend gave statements to the FBI … and admitted to being Russian citizens who had been living under false identities in the United States The two [were] living under aliases of Michael Zottoli and Patricia Mills.

(www.iht.com 2 July 2010)

The mother of a Russian scientist convicted of spying for the United States said Wednesday [7 July] that her son had been moved from a penal colony to Moscow in preparation for a possible trade involving the Russian spy suspects detained last month [June] in the United States … Igor Sutyagin was arrested in 1999 and accused of passing nuclear submarines and missile warning systems secrets to a British company that prosecutors said was a front for the CIA. Mr Sutyagin, who was convicted in 2004 and sentenced to fifteen years in prison, had maintained his innocence … Svetlana Sutyagina (his mother): 'He said they made him sign a confession of guilt, and that there was not much time, as they should accuse those detained in

America tomorrow' ... ... Mr Sutyagin was arrested in the late 1990s and early part of this decade during a string of detentions of Russian scientists, on accusations of selling military or scientific secrets to American and other foreign intelligence agencies. After the fall of the Soviet Union and the shrinking of state subsidies for science, many scientists found work in research and other activities for foreign companies. Mr Sutyagin, an arms control researcher working for the Institute of USA and Canada, a research group in Moscow, had argued during his trial that he could not be convicted of espionage as he had no access to state secrets ... Svetlana Sutyagina said that her son had an appeal pending before the European Court of Human Rights in Strasbourg, but that he was compelled to abandon it by signing an admission of his guilt.

(www.iht.com, 7 July 2010)

Ten people accused of espionage for Russia have pleaded guilty in a New York court to spying for a foreign country ... The ten pleaded guilty to 'conspiracy to act as an unregistered agent of a foreign country' ... It was the first time the ten are appearing in public together since they were arrested last week ... A federal indictment against them, along with an eleventh suspect who went missing after being released on bail in Cyprus, was unsealed on Wednesday [7 July].

(www.bbc.co.uk, 8 July 2010)

The United States has deported ten Russian agents as part of a prisoner exchange deal with Moscow. A flight carrying the five men and five women left New York after a judge ordered their expulsion during a court hearing at which they admitted spying for a foreign country ... The ten Russian agents pleaded guilty to 'conspiracy to act as an unregistered agent of a foreign country'. More serious money laundering charges against them were dropped ... The New York court appearance was the first time they had all appeared in public together since being arrested last month [June] ... The Peruvian [Vicky Pelaez] may want to go back to her country [Peru] but the others now face starting all over again in a country that some have not seen for ten or even fifteen years ... Meanwhile, President Dmitri Medvedev has pardoned four people convicted of espionage in Russia. They reportedly submitted a plea for pardon admitting their guilt. The Kremlin named the four as: Igor Sutyagin ... Sergei Skripal ... Alexander Zaporozhsky ... [and] Gennadi Vasilenko.

(www.bbc.co.uk, 9 July 2010)

The glamorous Anna Chapman appears to have spent more time flogging private planes to Russian oligarchs ... They have all been offered a Moscow flat and a $2,000 [monthly state pension ... The timeline of the spy ring case in the United States suggests American intelligence agencies were tracking the Russian agents for up to a decade.

(www.bbc.co.uk, 10 July 2010)

Senior [US] administration officials said the agents agreed never to return to the United States without permission from the US government ... Authorities have lost track of an eleventh suspect, who was detained in Cyprus, released on bail and then failed to check in with authorities as he had promised to do ... President Dmitri Medvedev signed a decree Friday [9 July] pardoning the four individuals imprisoned for alleged contact with Western intelligence agencies ... [The Russian press secretary said that] all four appealed to the Russian president to free them after admitting their crimes against the Russian state ... An attorney for Vicky Pelaez said his client does not want to take up residence in Russia and would prefer to ultimately live in her native Peru or in Brazil where she has family ... Pelaez and her husband, both naturalized Americans, were stripped of their citizenship as a part of a plea deal.

(www.cnn.com, 9 July 2010)

In the first step of a carefully choreographed swap, the ten Russian agents pleaded guilty Thursday [8 July] in a New York court to charges against them and were immediately deported. Then, around midnight local time, President Dmitri Medvedev signed a decree pardoning four spies serving jail terms in Russia on charges of spying for the West ... All bar one of the fourteen agents are Russian citizens.

(www.iht.com, 9 July 2010)

News reports on Friday [9 July] said that the American plane had landed at a British military base in central England [RAF Brize Norton in Oxfordshire] and later that the Russian plane had arrived in Moscow ... The ten sleeper agents had pleaded guilty to conspiracy before a federal judge in Manhattan after revealing their true identities. All ten were sentenced to time served and ordered deported ... Within hours of the New York court hearing, the Kremlin announced that President Dmitri Medvedev had signed pardons for the four men Russia considered spies after each of them signed statements admitting guilt. The Kremlin identified them as: Igor Sutyagin, an arms control researcher held for eleven years; Sergei Skripal, a colonel in Russia's military intelligence sentenced in 2006 to thirteen years for spying for Britain; Alexander Zaporozhsky, a former agent with Russia's Foreign Intelligence Service who has served seven years of an eighteen-year sentence; and Gennadi Vasilenko, a former KGB major who was arrested in 1998 for contacts with a CIA officer but eventually released only to be arrested again in 2005 and later convicted on illegal weapons [and explosives] charges ... All but three – Anna Chapman [a Russian, Anya Kushchenko, who was once married to an Englishman with the surname Chapman], Mikhail Semenko and Vicky Pelaez ... [A US administration official said that] some of the four Russians to be freed are in ill health.

(www.iht.com, 9 July 2010)

Four men [were taken to the UK] ... Two of them, Igor Sutyagin and Sergei Skripal, got off there, and the remaining two, Alexander Zaporozhsky and Gennadi Vasilenko, flew on to [the United States] ... ... For several years in the 1990s, Mr Zaporozhsky, a colonel in Russian intelligence who became deputy chief of the American Department, was secretly working for the CIA, one of the highest ranking American moles in history, Russian prosecutors say ... Igor Sutyagin, working at a Moscow think-tank, did contract research work for a British company that may or may not have been a front for Western intelligence. He has maintained his innocence, and human rights activists have defended him ... American officials demanded precisely these four Russians as soon as talks about a swap began ... A lawyer for Mr Skripal said he had diabetes ... [Russia says that] the four men who flew west on Friday are free to return when they wish ... The children of the sleeper agents all left with their parents or were preparing to join them ... The FBI had been monitoring the Russian sleeper agents as far back as a decade.

(www.iht.com, 10 July 2010)

Amnesty International warned [8 July] that sending ... Igor Sutyagin ... abroad as part of the swap could amount to forcible exile, a violation of international law. His mother told Amnesty International he had been forced to confess to spying in order to be freed from prison in a remote Arctic region of Russia ... US Attorney General Eric Holder said none of the ten had passed classified information and therefore none had been charged with espionage.

(www.cnn.com, 11 July 2010)

Anna Chapman ... has been deprived of her British citizenship ... Exclusion is expected to follow ... She is expected to be 'formally excluded' ... meaning she cannot travel to the UK ... Last week her lawyer said she would like to come to the UK as she has a UK passport through a previous marriage ... It is understood steps are being taken to permanently exclude Ms Chapman from travelling to the UK in the future ... Earlier this month [July] Briton Alex Chapman ... talked to a newspaper about his four-year marriage to the twenty-eight-year-old Russian ... Ms Chapman, who is also known as Anya Kushchenko, is the daughter of a Russian diplomat. Until the Home Office's decision she had dual Russian–UK nationality.

(www.bbc.co.uk, 13 July 2010)

'[The Home Office] carried out the actions under a [2002] law that provides for the revocation of British citizenship from dual nationals when to do so would be "conducive to the public good"' (www.iht.com, 14 July 20010).

Igor Sutyagin insists he is not a spy. And his friends warn him not to go home again ... Mr Sutyagin has had a decade to think about where he went awry, how sending foreigners information about the Russian military gleaned from newspapers could be taken for treason ... Over the course of seven hours of interviews in London this week, Mr Sutyagin denied any espionage. He said: 'No, of course I am not a spy' ... .He described the pressure to sign a statement admitting otherwise last month [July] when the Americans requested his release. He said: 'It is a very simple deal: you give your honour in exchange for your freedom. If it were not for my family, I would have stayed' ... He did not want to sign a clemency request that included an admission, and he did not want to leave Russia ... He has a valid Russian passport and a presidential pardon so there is no legal obstacle to his return – only the dire warnings of friends ... The [US] State Department said flatly that Mr Sutyagin was not an American spy, an exoneration it did not provide the other three ... Was the mysterious British company a CIA front even if he did not know it? He said: 'I am not a counter-intelligence specialist so I cannot tell you ... What kind of intelligence service is it that is interested in information that six months ago was published in *The Washington Post*?' ... Over the years Mr Sutyagin said the authorities acknowledged privately to him that the case was bogus. He quoted an intelligence officer telling him: 'Of course I realize. But if we admit that and let you go we'll take your place behind bars.'

(www.iht.com, 12 August 2010; *IHT*, 14 August 2010, pp. 1, 3)

July–August 2010. For the summer heatwave and its effects, see Appendix 2.

Speaking after arriving in the Ukrainian capital, Kiev, US secretary of state Hillary Clinton said: 'Ukraine is a sovereign and independent country that has the right to choose its own alliances and Nato's door remains open' ... She will travel to Armenia, Georgia and Azerbaijan ... as well as visiting Poland.

(www.bbc.co.uk, 2 July 2010)

'During a visit to Ukraine US secretary of state Hillary Clinton said: "We're committed to building a new and positive relation with Russia. We're looking toward the future"' (www.bbc.co.uk, 2 July 2010).

US secretary of state Hillary Clinton is to arrive shortly in Poland, where she is expected to sign a controversial missile defence shield agreement ... Mrs Clinton will also discuss Poland's shale gas deposits ... If Poland is found to have large deposits it could radically alter energy security in Europe, which currently depends heavily on Russian gas.

(www.bbc.co.uk, 3 July 2010)

[On Saturday 3 July US secretary of state Hillary Clinton] signed an agreement with the Poles on missile defence, allowing the deployment of American mobile rockets on Polish soil. They are expected to be capable of intercepting missiles from 2018 ... Saturday's signing was an amendment to a previous agreement, taking into account changes approved by President Barack Obama.

(www.bbc.co.uk, 4 July 2010)

Azerbaijan urged the United States on Sunday [4 July] to help solve the Nagorno-Karabakh dispute and US secretary of state Hillary Clinton pressed its authoritarian government on human rights ... Baku in April [2010] accused the United States of siding with Armenia over Nagorno-Karabakh ... As a result of the strains in the relationship, including the absence of a US ambassador for more than a year, Baku threatened to 'reconsider' its ties with the United States ... Azerbaijan has been a key supply route for US troops in Afghanistan but ties have been frayed by multiple issues. While seeking to improve relations and make some headway on Nagorno-Karabakh, Clinton also pressed Azerbaijan to show greater respect for civilian liberties and said she had raised the case of two jailed opposition bloggers ... Last month four ethnic Armenian troops and an Azeri soldier died in an exchange of fire near Nagorno-Karabakh ... Clinton is the second top US official to visit Azerbaijan in a month, following Defence Secretary Robert Gates's early June trip designed to smooth ruffled feathers and to guarantee US supply lines for Afghanistan.

(www.iht.com, 4 July 2010)

'In mid-June an exchange of gunfire along the front lines near Nagorno-Karabakh killed four ethnic Armenian troops and one Azerbaijani soldier' (www.iht.com, 8 July 2010). 'US secretary of state Hillary Clinton ... made the one-hour flight to Armenia' (*IHT*, 5 July 2010, p. 3).

'[In Azerbaijan US secretary of state Hillary Clinton met] youth groups but not opposition parties. In private she discussed two bloggers who were jailed after ridiculing state officials' (www.economist.com, 8 July 2010).

US secretary of state Hillary Clinton ... used her toughest language yet to condemn Russia's 'invasion and occupation of Georgia' during a visit on Monday [5 July] to Tbilisi, Georgia's capital ... US vice president Joseph [Joe] Biden delivered the same message in the same capitals ... [Hillary Clinton] said in her visit to Krakow [Poland], 'We must be wary of the steel vice in which many governments are slowly crushing civil society and the human spirit', including Russia on a list alongside Zimbabwe, Congo, Ethiopia, Egypt and China. She said Washington will continue to fund non-governmental organizations in the region ... and to stand up for independent journalists who are being harassed or persecuted.

(www.iht.com, 5 July 2010; *IHT*, 6 July 2010, p. 3)

The [Russian] foreign ministry criticized US secretary of state Hillary Clinton on Wednesday [7 July] for using the word 'occupation' in referring to Russian forces in Abkhazia and South Ossetia. Russia says its military was invited to deploy troops in the regions, which it considers sovereign countries. A ministry statement said: 'Therefore, Secretary of State Clinton's use of the word "occupation" has no basis. There is not a single Russian serviceman on Georgian territory' ... Mrs Clinton made the remarks in Georgia on Monday [5 July] challenging Russia to abide by a French-brokered ceasefire agreement that would require it to withdraw its forces to prewar positions. Most countries – except Russia, Venezuela, Nicaragua and Nauru – consider the region is part of Georgia.

(www.iht.com, 8 July 2010)

2 July 2010.

The State Duma has approved a complete ban on drink driving. President Dmitri Medvedev called for the ban on 1 December [2009]. He said allowing a small amount of alcohol in the blood encouraged drivers to consume more. The measure is expected to be approved in the upper house and become law ... Heavy drinking is seen as one of the main reasons why one in three Russian men dies before retirement age. Russia has one of the world's highest rates of traffic accidents related to drink driving. In Russia last year [2009] more than 2,000 people were killed and around 18,000 people injured in road accidents linked to drink driving ... A total ban was in force until July 2008, when the law was amended to allow alcohol content of 0.3 grams per litre of a driver's blood. That is the equivalent to half a litre of beer, 40 grams of vodka or a glass of white wine consumed by a person weighing 80 kilograms (176 pounds). Duma deputy Tatiana Yakovleva, who is a doctor, said a driver with even the legal limit of alcohol was twice as likely to have a serious road accident, compared with an alcohol-free driver. Opponents of the ban say most traffic accidents in Russia are due to poor roads, with drivers swerving into oncoming traffic as they try to avoid potholes.

(www.bbc.co.uk, 2 July 2010)

12 July 2010.

Two men who organized a controversial art exhibition in Moscow in 2007 have been found guilty by a court of inciting hatred. Andrei Yerofeyev and Yuri Samodurov had set up the Forbidden Art exhibition at the Sakharov Museum in Moscow. The show provoked condemnation from the Russian Orthodox Church, among others, for artworks that included a depiction of Jesus Christ with the head of Mickey Mouse. Both men were ordered to pay a fine. The exhibition featured several images of Jesus Christ. In one painting of the crucifixion, the head of Jesus Christ was replaced by the Order of Lenin medal. There was also a spoof ad for Coca-Cola with the slogan 'This is my blood' that visitors looked at through peep holes. Mr Yerofeyev, an art expert, and Mr Samodurov, the former director of the Sakharov Museum, said they organized the exhibition to fight censorship of art in Russia. But prosecutors opened an investigation after an ultra-nationalist Orthodox group filed a complaint against the show. The court fined Mr Samodurov 200,000 roubles (£4,300) and Mr Yerofeyev 150,000 roubles (£3,200). The trial began in April 2009 and was fiercely criticized by rights activists and artists ... In a letter sent to the Russian Orthodox Church last month [June] Mr Yerofeyev apologized if the show unintentionally offended Christians. But the Council of the People, the group who brought the complaint, defended the legal actions

... Mr Samodurov has been convicted of inciting religious hatred before. He was fined in 2005 for an exhibition called 'Caution: Religion! At the Sakharov Museum.

(www.bbc.co.uk, 12 July 2010)

A Russian art exhibition was ruled offensive and its curators fined by a Moscow court yesterday [12 July] in one of the biggest censorship cases to hit the country's art world since the end of the communist era. Art expert Andrei Yerofeyev and Yuri Samodurov, former museum director, were found guilty of 'actions aimed at inciting hatred' with the 2007 'Forbidden Art' exhibition at the Sakharov Museum. Some of the works portrayed Jesus Christ as Mickey Mouse and Vladimir Lenin and provoked the ire of the People's Council, the extreme nationalist Orthodox religious group that filed the accusations. The court fined the two men the equivalent of $6,500 but did not give them a prison term ... This was apparently the first time that a 2002 law to prevent extremism was applied to artists and museum directors.

(*FT*, 13 July 2010, p. 9)

President Dmitri Medvedev: 'Iran is moving closer to possessing the potential which in principle could be used for the creation of nuclear weapons' ... It is one of the first times Moscow has publicly recognized that Iran might be moving towards a nuclear weapon ... [Moscow] has recently adopted a tougher stance towards Tehran's nuclear drive, and backed the fourth round of UN sanctions that was imposed last month [June].

(www.bbc.co.uk, 12 July 2010)

The exhibition consisted of works which were previously barred from other exhibitions ... The Russian minister of culture intervened saying this was no matter for criminal justice and a spokesman for Kirill, the Patriarch of the Russian Orthodox Church, said that a jail sentence would be wrong.

(www.economist.com, 13 July 2010)

Yuri Samodurov ... and Andrei Yerofeyev ... were fined 200,000 roubles (about $6,500) and 150,000 roubles (about $4,900), respectively, on charges of inciting religious and ethnic hatred with an exhibition called 'Forbidden Art–2006', which displayed works of contemporary art that had been banned by Russian museums ... Mr Samodurov was convicted and fined on similar charges in 2005 for a 2003 exhibition at the museum called 'Caution, Religion!' He has filed with the European Court of Human Rights to have that conviction overturned.

(*IHT*, 14 July 2010, p. 4)

'Andrei Yerofeyev was fired two years ago as curator of contemporary art at the prestigious Tretyakov Gallery after he had organized a show of Soviet kitsch' (*IHT*, 17 July 2010, p. 6).

13 July 2010.

One of Russia's last remaining regional strongmen said Tuesday [13 July] that he would retire at the end of his term next year [2011], signalling the passing of a muscular group of leaders who survived the fall of the Soviet Union and retained a share of autonomy from the Kremlin. The retiring leader, Murtaza Rakhimov, seventy-six, has led the oil-rich south-western republic of Bashkortostan since 1990 ... Liberals criticized him for police crackdowns and heavy-handed control – but also delighted in his caustic criticism of Kremlin policies ... A year ago Mr Rakhimov told a Moscow newspaper that Russian politics were more centralized than they had been in Soviet days, showing 'distrust and disrespect' toward regional populations. He also said the leadership of United Russia ... 'have never commanded three chickens' ... News of his retirement when his term expires in October 2011 raised some speculation that he could leave before then ... At a regional gathering a month ago, Mr Rakhimov said the appointment of an outsider to lead the republic would be 'a humiliation to all Bashkirs' ... Soon after, state-controlled media began airing blistering exposes accusing Mr Rakhimov and his family of corruption ... In recent months the Kremlin has shown increasing confidence in replacing the so-called 'heavyweight' governors – among them Eduard Rossel, of Sverdlovsk Oblast, and Mintimir Shaimiev, of Tatarstan, both of whom have been in office since 1991. The last of the 'heavyweight' group is Yuri Luzhkov, who has been mayor of Moscow since 1992.

(www.iht.com, 13 July 2010; *IHT*, 15 July 2010, p. 2)

14 July 2010.

Russia's energy minister announced a broad programme of co-operation with Iran in the oil, natural gas and petrochemical industries on Wednesday [14 July] that appeared to invite Russian companies to contravene sanctions the Obama administration adopted just two weeks ago. The sanctions were meant to be an additional means of punishing Iran for refusing to unwind its secretive nuclear programme ... Australia, Canada and Europe also decided to put additional measures against Iran in place. While clearly intended to discourage the type of investment the Russian minister had in mind, the US sanctions law provides a presidential waiver for companies in countries otherwise seen as co-operating in discouraging Iran from obtaining nuclear weapons ... The American sanctions impose penalties on foreign entities that sell refined petroleum to Iran or assist Iran with its domestic refining capacity ... President Dmitri Medvedev voiced opposition to adding any sanctions beyond those imposed by the United Nations, and the foreign ministry warned the United States against trying to punish Russian companies under the new unilateral sanctions. On Wednesday Russia's minister of fuel and energy ... Sergei Shmatko ... took the most overt stance against the American sanctions so far, announcing the plans for closer co-operation between Russian and Iranian petroleum interests.

(www.iht.com, 15 July 2010; *IHT*, 15 July 2010, p. 5)

15 July 2010.

President Dmitri Medvedev said the authorities had identified ... Natalia Estimirova's ... killer and were searching for the person who ordered her murder ... President Medvedev: '[It is] false to say there is no investigation. We have established and positively identified the perpetrator of this murder – the killer. Now we have an investigation to find not only the killer, who is already the target of a manhunt, but also the person who ordered this grave crime' ... Mr Medvedev did not offer details, but investigators claim Ms Estimirova was killed by an anti-government militant in retaliation for her research into his group, according to an internal document made public this week ... A lawyer representing Ms Estimirova's sister, Svetlana, said the government primary suspect is a member of a militant group, Alhazur Bashayev – who was reported killed during a counter-terrorism raid last fall [2009] ... Ms Estimirova's colleagues and relatives rejected this explanation on Thursday [15 July], urging authorities to investigate the theory they have put forward – that she was killed by forces linked to the Chechen government who were unhappy with her inquiries into police abuses.

(www.iht.com, 15 July 2010)

'On Wednesday [14 July] ... [Natalia Estimirova's] colleagues and family accused the authorities of ignoring vital leads in the investigation' (www.bbc. co.uk, 15 July 2010).

Russia will invest $800 million into a new spaceport in the country's Far East, prime minister Vladimir Putin has announced. The move is meant to ease the dependence on the Baikonur launch site in Kazakhstan, built during the Soviet era. The future cosmodrome will be built near the town of Ugke-gorsk in the Far Eastern Amur region, close to the border with China. It is planned to be mostly used for civilian launches and should be operational by 2015. Prime minister Vladimir Putin: 'The government had made a decision to earmark 24.7 billion roubles ($809 million) over the next three years for the start of the full-blown construction of the Vostochny [Eastern] cosmodrome ... I very much expect that Vostochny will become the first national cosmodrome for civilian purposes and will guarantee Russia full independence of space activities' ... It will be smaller than Baikonur, which Russia rents from Kazakhstan ... [and which] is the largest and oldest space launch facility in the world ... Russia plans to build a new generation of space vessels that could also be used for interplanetary flights – in particular for a voyage to Mars ... The Russian segment of the International Space Station should be completed by 2015 ... In early 2011 the Russian Soyuz launch vehicle will start operating at ESA's [European Space Agency's] French Guiana Space centre in Kourou. Later, the Phobos-Grunt Russian interplanetary spacecraft will put a Chinese space probe in orbit around Mars ... With the US shuttle programme being phased out in February

2011, the only means to get to the International Space Station will be by the Soyuz rocket.

(www.bbc.co.uk, 20 July 2010)

22 July 2010. Judge Hisashi Owada (president of the International Court of Justice in The Hague, the UN's highest court): 'The court considers that general international law contains no applicable prohibition of declaration of independence. Accordingly it concludes that the declaration of independence of 17 February 2008 [by Kosovo from Serbia] did not violate international law' (www.iht. com, 22 July 2010).

> Legal experts warned [that the ruling] could spur separatist movements around the world. But legal experts emphasized that while the court had ruled that Kosovo's declaration of independence was legal, it had scrupulously avoided saying that the state of Kosovo was legal under international law, a narrow and carefully calibrated compromise that they said could allow both sides to declare victory in a dispute that remains raw even eleven years after the war there. Political analysts said the advisory opinion, passed in a ten–four vote by the court judges, is likely to spur other countries to recognize Kosovo's independence, which has thus far been recognized by sixty-nine countries, including the United States and a majority of EU nations, but has failed to attain recognition by two-thirds of the UN General Assembly ... Serbia was adamant that it would never recognize what it has previously called a false state, while Russia, one of its staunchest allies, insisted the court's decision did not provided a legal basis for Kosovo's independence ... Kosovo's declaration of independence from Serbia on 17 February 2008 marked the culmination of a showdown between Serbia and the West and a majority of European nations argued that Serbia's violent repression of Kosovo's majority ethnic Albanians under former Serbian president Slobodan Milosevic had forfeited Serbia's moral and legal rights to rule the territory. Belgrade and its ally Moscow countered that the declaration of independence by Kosovo was a reckless breach of international law that would inspire separatists everywhere. Last year [2009] the UN General Assembly, at Serbia's urging, referred Kosovo's declaration to the court ... Hearings began in December [2009]. Analysts said that the legal legitimacy conferred on the independence declaration could have profound consequences for global geopolitics by potentially being seized upon by secessionist movements in places as diverse as Northern Cyprus, Somaliland, Nagorno-Karabakh and Transdniestre. But legal experts stressed that the court's studious avoidance of ruling on the legal status of Kosovo as a state had been calculated to avoid encouraging nationalist movements and left the issue of a territory's independence at the discretion of the countries that chose to recognize it ... Major European powers and the United States have been at pains to characterize Kosovo as a special case that should not serve as a precedent for other groups hoping to declare independence. But in hearings last December in The Hague Spain, Russia and China – all of

which face secessionist movements in their own borders – argued forcefully that Kosovo should remain a part of Serbia ... In the Balkans the ruling could fortify separatist elements in the Serb half of Bosnia.

(www.iht.com, 22 July 2010)

President Boris Tadic of Serbia: 'Serbia will never recognize the unilaterally proclaimed independence of Kosovo' ... The judges on the panel – split almost evenly between countries that have recognized Kosovo's independence and those that have not – have a history of narrow and conservative judgements ... The ruling came just one day after another court at The Hague ordered the former prime minister of Kosovo, Ramush Haradinaj, to be retried on charges of murder, rape and torture, because it said witnesses had been intimidated ... Five of the twenty-seven EU countries – Spain, Romania, Greece, Slovakia and Cyprus – have refused to recognize Kosovo – fearing that to do so would set a dangerous precedent for other secessionist movements in their own countries.

(*IHT*, 23 July 2010, p. 3)

('A UN diplomat, speaking on condition of anonymity before the announcement, said that if the court says the declaration was legal, the main significance will likely be that more countries will recognize Kosovo's independence – and once that number tops 100, its full statehood can be established': www.iht.com, 22 July 2010.)

'Serbia put forward a resolution to ask the International Court of Justice for an advisory opinion, and members states [of the UN General Assembly] voted overwhelmingly in favour of it in October 2008' (www.cnn.com, 22 July 2010).

So far sixty-nine of the UN's 192 countries have recognized Kosovo as independent – they include the United States, the UK, neighbouring Albania and Croatia. Those opposed include Russia, China and Bosnia ... The EU is not united on the issue – Spain and Greece are among five of its twenty-seven members to be opposed.

(www.bbc.co.uk, 22 July 2010)

Serbian President Boris Tadic said after the ruling: 'Serbia will never recognize the unilaterally proclaimed independence of Kosovo' ... Mr Tadic, a reformer, stressed that Serbia would not resort to violence and would prefer to negotiate a compromise with Kosovo's ethnic Albanian leaders. He acknowledged the ruling was 'a difficult decision for Serbia' but said Belgrade would continue to try for a UN resolution that would urge both sides to start a dialogue.

(www.bbc.co.uk, 23 July 2010)

'To date sixty-nine countries have recognized Kosovo's independence, including the United States and twenty-two of the twenty-seven EU member states. But Russia, Brazil, India and many other important countries have refused to follow suit' (www.economist.com, 22 July 2010).

[Countries] such as Spain and China have been opposed to recognition on the grounds that it will legitimize an act of secession, with implications for ethnic minority issues within their own states … Kosovo has diplomatic relations with sixty-nine countries and needs a total of 100 to be recognized at the UN.

(*FT*, 23 July 2010, p. 5)

In the wake of the opinion the Serbs complained that the International Court of Justice did not examine Kosovo's right to secede. This is because the Serbs did not ask it to; their question was simply whether the declaration was legal.

(www.economist.com, 29 July 2010)

Kosovo police have arrested the central bank governor Hashim Rexhepi in an anti-corruption investigation. The EU's rule of law mission Eulex said the probe concerned suspected bribes, tax evasion, influence-peddling and money laundering. Eulex said Mr Rexhepi was among four suspects whose homes were searched … The EU has some 1,900 law enforcement officials deployed across Kosovo to strengthen law and order, in the Eulex mission launched in December 2008. They have the power to take on cases that the local judiciary and police find difficult to handle … Friday's [23 July] operation in Pristina follows other high profile searches by Eulex and Kosovan police. In April [2010] the offices of Kosovo's transport minister, Fatmir Limaj, were raided as part of a probe into the construction of a major highway. Earlier this month [July] four companies suspected of fraud over the issuing of a mobile phone licence were also searched … To achieve international recognition Pristina knows it has to present itself as a more functional government, able to combat the corruption and organized crime that have flourished in Kosovo since the war of the 1990s.

(www.bbc.co.uk, 23 July 2010)

23 July 2010.

France has agreed to build two advanced warships for the Russian navy … The ships are part of a deal – which alarmed France's Nato allies – to supply Mistral-class vessels. Costing $388 million each [they] can carry troops or helicopters and are used in amphibious assaults. In February [2010] it was announced that France had agreed to build one vessel and Russia had requested three others … The deal, which is the first of its kind between France and its Cold War enemy, has caused alarm in Nato as there are fears it will give Russia more cutting-edge technology. In February a US official told reporters the United States 'had questions' for France about the order.

(www.bbc.co.uk, 23 July 2010)

24 July 2010.

Prime minister Vladimir Putin [during a visit to Ukraine] said Saturday [24

July] that he had met with Russian agents swapped in an exchange with the United States this month, and promised them a good future in Russia ... Mr Putin did not say where he met the agents.

(www.iht.com, 25 July 2010)

Prime minister Vladimir Putin says he sang a patriotic song with the Russian spies who were expelled from the United States and promised them a 'bright' future ... [He] said he recently met with the ten sleeper agents, without saying when or where ... [He said] the spies ... were uncovered by a betrayal.

(www.iht.com, 25 July 2010)

During a recent meeting prime minister Vladimir Putin provided encouragement and sang patriotic songs with ten agents expelled from the United States this month ... Putin said that betrayal allowed the spy network to be uncovered, adding that he knew the names of those responsible.

(www.cnn.com, 25 July 2010)

26 July 2010.

Tensions between Russia and Iran appeared to grow on Monday [26 July] over Russian support for sanctions approved last month [June] by the UN Security Council. The Russian foreign ministry criticized the Iranian president, Mahmoud Ahmadinejad, over his recent comments about President Dmitri Medvedev. Mr Ahmadinejad had said that Mr Medvedev was becoming a 'mouthpiece' for Iran's enemies ... In a statement on Monday the Russian foreign ministry described as Ahmadinejad's comments as unacceptable, saying that he was using 'pointless and irresponsible rhetoric' ... Russia has long sought to maintain warm ties with Iran, in part because the two countries are neighbours, and the Kremlin does not want Iran to stir up trouble with Russia's Moslem regions.

(www.iht.com, 26 July 2010)

27 July 2010.

Russia said Tuesday [27 July] that new EU sanctions on Iran undermined international efforts to resolve concerns over its nuclear programme ... EU foreign ministers on Monday [26 July] approved a range of extra restrictions on Iran that went beyond UN sanctions agreed last month [June], including a ban on dealing with Iranian banks and insurance companies as well as steps to prevent investment on Tehran's lucrative oil and gas sector. The foreign ministry said in a statement: 'This not only undermines our joint efforts to seek a political and diplomatic settlement around Iran's nuclear programme, but also shows disdain for the carefully calibrated and co-ordinated provisions of the US Security Council resolutions' ... The use of sanctions outside of the UN Security Council framework is 'unacceptable', the statement said ... In addition to the EU sanctions, the statement criticized unilateral US sanctions approved by Congress on 24 June aimed at squeezing Iran's energy and banking sectors. The statement said: 'We regret to say that all the recent steps by the EU and the United States to build pressure on Iran display their disdain for the principles of collaboration.'

(www.iht.com, 27 July 2010)

The EU measures go beyond the fourth set of UN sanctions adopted on 9 June. They include a ban on dealing with Iranian banks and insurance companies, as well as steps to prevent investment in Tehran's oil and gas sector ... Iran is under four sets of UN sanctions over its refusal to heed repeated Security Council ultimatums to suspend uranium enrichment, the most controversial part of its nuclear programme. Tehran says it is enriching uranium purely for peaceful purposes, but Western powers accuse it of trying to develop a nuclear weapon ... Similar measures [were] adopted by the US Congress on 24 June.

(www.bbc.co.uk, 27 July 2010)

31 July 2010.

Police have detained two opposing leaders and dozens of other activists trying to hold rallies in Moscow and St Petersburg ... Opposition figures Boris Nemtsov and Sergei Udaltsov were among those detained ... Reports say the crackdown in St Petersburg was particularly harsh, with some demonstrators injured ... Protesters brandished the number 31, after the article of the constitution guaranteeing the right to public gatherings. The date of the protests – 31 July – was symbolic ... In Moscow the square where activists had planned to meet was sealed off for a rally-car and quad-bike display ... But a handful of opposition members did manage to mix into the small crowd watching the motor show and then started shouting their slogans for freedom of assembly. They were quickly tackled by the police who dragged them away.

(www.bbc.co.uk, 1 August 2010)

Police arrested anti-Kremlin opposition leader Boris Nemtsov and at least ninety-five others on Saturday [31 July] at demonstrations in cities across Russia against restrictions on freedom of assembly. In St Petersburg sixty of about 200 people were arrested in what Reuters witnesses said was one of the most violent recent crackdowns on protesters ... Opposition activists traditionally stage demonstrations on the 31st day of those months that have thirty-one days to defend Article 31 of the constitution, which guarantees the right to public gathering. Activists say this gives them the right to hold protests without permission, which is regularly denied to opposition groups. Police habitually break up rallies not approved by the authorities. In Moscow, along with Nemtsov, the police arrested Left Front opposition leader Sergei Udaltsov and at least thirty-five others ... On Saturday Moscow's unsanctioned protesters disappeared in a crowd of several hundred people that gathered in Triumfalnaya Square in the city's centre to watch a car and motorcycle show ... The eighty-two-year-old veteran human rights activist Lyudmila Alexeyeva said the organizers will try next times to co-ordinate the protest with city hall … Earlier in Vladivostok about thirty people protested and no arrests were made … In the cities where the rallies took place activists chanted 'Russia will be free', which by now has become a symbolic chant.

(www.iht.com, 1 August 2010)

2 August 2010.

A UN convention banning the use of cluster bombs comes into force: 107 countries have signed the convention and thirty-seven have ratified it. America, Russia and China have all declined to sign. Those who oppose the convention tend to argue that it gives an unfair advantage to non-state groups such as the Taleban. Campaigners retort that there would be fewer cluster bombs for the Taleban to use if more countries signed up and agreed to stop making them.

(www.economist.com, 2 August 2010)

3 August 2010. 'A [US] Senate committee on Tuesday [3 August] shelved the treaty … called New Start … until fall, when it faces an uncertain future in the midst of a hotly contested election season' (www.iht.com, 4 August 2010).

7 August 2010.

Russia's foreign ministry released a report on Saturday [7 August] accusing the United States of violating dozens of provisions of nuclear, chemical and biological weapons treaties going back about a decade, apparently in a retort to American critics of a new arms treaty, who have been accusing Russia of violating past agreements. The ten-page report detailed lapses in security at Los Alamos National Laboratory, cited reports on security threats posed by private laboratories in the United States conducting research on potential military pathogens and noted what it called failures by the United States to provide telemetry on test missile launchings. It also rekindled complaints that the United States and other Nato nations had disregarded a 1997 agreement with Russia limiting the deployment of forces in former Eastern bloc countries, and noted that the American missile defence programme employed decoy rockets seemingly belonging to a class of missiles banned under a treaty on intermediate range nuclear weapons … The [US] Senate is considering ratification of … New Start … and opponents had pointed to a State Department report that says Russia violated past arms control treaties, at times denying access to inspectors. The report cited several compliance disputes but said Russian had lived up to the treaty's 'central limits' … The Russian report cited a number of complaints against policies of the Bush administration. The United States, it said, had converted B-1 bombers to carry conventional weapons, rather than destroying them to meet treaty obligations. And assurances that such weapons could not be quickly retooled for nuclear bombs were inadequate. Citing the Department of Agriculture's own reports, it said control over laboratories studying plant pathogens was weak.

(www.iht.com, 8 August 2010; *IHT*, 9 August 2010, p. 3)

12 August 2010.

Ceremonies are being held in Russia and on board its naval vessels to commemorate the tenth anniversary of the *Kursk* nuclear submarine disaster. The submarine, one of the Russian navy's most advanced vessels, sank in the Barents Sea on 12 August 2000, with the loss of all 118 people on board. An explosion of fuel from an old torpedo caused the disaster. Moscow's response to one of the greatest disasters in Russian naval history was widely criticized ... The initial response to the disaster in 2000 was shambolic ... After radio contact was lost there was a still unexplained delay before a search and rescue mission was launched. Although the submarine was lying just 100 metres below the surface of the sea, attempts to locate it and reach it repeatedly failed. It was days before the authorities informed relatives that something was wrong and the then President Vladimir Putin initially remained on holiday. Russia eventually accepted international assistance, but when the Norwegian divers opened the *Kursk*'s hatch ten days later they found the boat flooded and everyone dead. Many had died within seconds of the initial explosion, but others survived for several hours, a report found. Russian officials originally suggested the submarine may have collided with a foreign ship or with a stray mine. But it emerged that an explosion was caused by fuel that had leaked from a torpedo. This started a fire, which subsequently caused all ammunition on board to detonate. The boat was raised and the bodies recovered in 2001.

(www.bbc.co.uk, 12 August 2010)

13 August 2010.

Russia says it will undertake a key step next week towards starting up a reactor at Iran's first nuclear power station. Russia's state atomic corporation, which is building the plant, said engineers will begin loading the Bushehr reactor with fuel. However, it could be six months before the reactor is fully operational. Russia has been helping build the plant since the mid-1980s, amid tensions over Iran's nuclear programme. Spokesman Sergei Novikov said: 'The fuel will be charged in the reactor on 21 August. From that moment, Bushehr will be considered a nuclear installation' ... The project was started under the Shah ... Russia will run the plant, supply the fuel and take away the fuel waste.

(www.bbc.co.uk, 13 August 2010)

Russia will load fuel into Iran's first nuclear power plant next week despite US demands to prevent Iran obtaining nuclear energy until the country proves that it is not pursuing a weapons capacity, officials said Friday [13 August]. Uranium fuel shipped by Russia will be loaded into the Bushehr reactor on 21 August, beginning a start-up process that will last about a month and end with the reactor sending electricity to Iranian cities, Russian and Iranian officials said. Sergei Novikov (a spokesman for the Russian nuclear agency): 'From that moment the Bushehr plant will be officially considered a nuclear-energy installation' ... Russia signed a $1 billion contract to build the Bushehr plant in 1995 but has dragged its feet on completing the project. Moscow has cited technical reasons for the delays, but analysts say Moscow has used the project to press Iran to ease its defiance over its nuclear programme ... The uranium fuel used by Bushehr plant is enriched to a level too low to be used in a nuclear weapon. Iran is also producing uranium enriched to that level – about 3.5 per cent – and has started a pilot programme of enriching uranium to 20 per cent. Iran claims it needs the 20 per cent enriched uranium to produce fuel for a medical research reactor, but the move has further heightened international concerns to its nuclear programme. Uranium must be enriched to over 90 per cent to be used in a nuclear warhead ... Iran's semi-official ISNA news agency quoted Vice President Ali Akbar Salehi, who is also the head of the Atomic Energy Organization of Iran, as saying that the country had invited the IAEA experts to watch the transfer of fuel, which was shipped about two years ago, into the Bushehr reactor ... Russia has said that the Bushehr project has been closely supervised by the UN nuclear watchdog, which declined to comment Friday. It also says Iran has signed a pledge to ship all spent uranium from Bushehr back to Russia for reprocessing, excluding a possibility that any of it could be used to make nuclear weapons.

(www.iht.com, 13 August 2010)

The atomic energy agency of Russia ... said that technicians would move tonnes of low-enriched uranium fuel from a storage site into the reactor on 21 August, the first of three steps in a months-long process for starting it up. The agency said: 'The event will symbolize that the period of testing is over and the stage of physical start-up has begun' ... The United States had asked Russia to hold off moves to start the plant until Iran assuaged concerns that it is using its civilian nuclear programme to also build a bomb. The construction and start-up of the plant ... have been plagued by dozens of delays since Russian took over the work there in the mid-1990s. Russian officials ... had long appeared to use the plant construction schedule and the drawn-out start-up process as leverage with Iran's leaders and in wider Russian diplomacy in the Middle East. Often, delays for ostensibly technical reasons have come just days after a Russian leader makes a political statement critical of Iran ... From the Iranian perspective, the start-up has been possible since roughly February 2009, when the reactor core was successfully tested. In the first step, set for 21 August, fuel will be shifted from storage to the reactor chamber. The second involves loading the fuel into the hardened steel core. The final step is bringing the fuel rods together to begin the nuclear reaction. Once the fuel is irradiated in the final step of the start-up, it will begin to generate plutonium that could be used in an atomic weapon, which is why Russia had insisted on its return as a condition of completing and fuelling the plant. The process will not introduce new nuclear material into Iran; Russia delivered the shipment of low-enriched uranium fuel under an agreement that would require Iran to send the spent fuel back to Russia for disposal. The Russian fuel has been kept under IAEA seal. In fact, the United States under a policy put in place by the Bush administration has supported the Russian fuel shipments, though not the decision to start the plant. The Russian fuel meets all the needs for the Bushehr plant, largely removing the rationale for an enrichment programme. The critics of co-operation with Iran say the Russian contract at Bushehr, held by the state company Atomstroiexport, gives the Iranian government a justification to enrich uranium. The Russians counter that the reactor itself is harmless if looked at separately from the effect to enrich uranium fuel. The Russians also dismiss criticism that they are exposing Israel, Europe and possibly the United States to nuclear risk for a narrow commercial interest, as nuclear officials here [in Moscow] say the $1 billion Bushehr contract, signed in the early 1990s, is no longer even profitable. Iran says its nuclear programme is intended to generate electricity and medical isotopes, not for weapons development.

(www.iht.com, 13 August 2010)

'President Barack Obama's spokesman ... said Friday [13 August] that the loading of the fuel by Russia demonstrated that Iran did not need to pursue uranium enrichment in order to have a peaceful nuclear power programme' (*IHT*, 14 August 2010, p. 4).

Sergei Novikov (spokesman for the Russian Atomic Agency): 'This event will symbolize that the period of testing is over and the stage of physical start-up has begun' ... Novikov said the fuel's arrival does not mean the plant is ready to begin producing energy ... he said that will take about six more months ... He said: 'The IAEA inspectors will remove the seals from containers with nuclear fuel and examine it. The fuel will then be transferred into a special storage facility. And when the Iranian nuclear watchdog gives its permission, the fuel will be loaded into the reactor.'

(www.cnn.com, 13 August 2010)

'Russia agreed in 1995 to build the plant on the site of a project begun in the 1970s by [the German company] Siemens' (*FT*, 14 August 2010, p. 4).

The [US] Treasury Department released new regulations on Friday [13 August] that could bar foreign banks or companies from accessing the financial system in the United States if they did business with entities or people subject to US and US sanctions. The regulations grew out of legislation Congress passed in June ... The Treasury regulations prohibit or impose strict conditions on the use of American bank accounts by any institution that engages in activities associated with Iran's nuclear and missile programmes.

(www.iht.com, 14 August 2010)

16 August 2010.

Russia's leaders appeared to make a rare bow to popular pressure on Monday [16 August], denying a second term to a governor on the grounds that he lacked public support in a region where a huge anti-government protest broke out earlier this year. With opposition leaders in the region, Kaliningrad, vowing another major protest later this week, United Russia, the governing party, led by prime minister Vladimir Putin, decided not to submit the governor, Georgi Boos, for reappointment ... Governors were popularly elected in Russia until a 2004 decree by Mr Putin, then president, that gave the president responsibility for appointing them. The president now selects governors beholden to the Kremlin from a list of candidates drawn up by the governing party. Critics have charged that the practice has made governors beholden to the Kremlin and insensitive to the popular sentiments in the regions they govern. President Dmitri Medvedev said on Monday that popular support for local governors was a priority regardless of how they were selected. He said: 'I have repeatedly stated that despite changes in the system of vesting powers with governors, we do care about what kind of authority any particular candidate has: they must be people who gain the unconditional respect and trust of citizens living in any particular region' ... The inability to elect governors was one of the central grievances when as many as 10,000 protesters took to the streets of Kaliningrad last January [2010] to call for Mr Boos's ouster. It was the largest anti-government demonstration in years, and appeared to take both Mr Boos and his former backers by surprise.

(www.iht.com. 16 August 2010; *IHT*, 17 August 2010, p. 3)

18 August 2010.

President Dmitri Medvedev on Wednesday [18 August] offered Pakistan support in dealing with catastrophic floods as he hosted the leaders of Afghanistan, Pakistan and Tajikistan for talks on efforts to stabilize the region ... The four-way talks at Medvedev's seaside residence will also focus on fighting terrorism and drugs spreading from Afghanistan. The Russian president has previously held similar talks, seeking to strengthen Russia's clout in the volatile region ... Nato has urged Russia to provide helicopters and training for the Afghan air force and to train more local police. Moscow has responded that it is willing to help – fearing that a return to power by Taleban extremists would destabilize ex-Soviet Central Asia and threaten Russia's security – but not for free and suggested that Nato pay the costs. Russia's foreign minister Sergei Lavrov told reporters Wednesday that Russia is currently negotiating the sale of about twenty helicopters to Afghanistan and expects Nato to foot the bill ... Lavrov also said that Moscow would provide a free shipment of firearms for the Afghan interior ministry and step up training of its personnel. Russian officials previously said that they planned to train about 200

Afghan policemen this year ... The Russian support for Nato- and US-led operations so far has been limited to offering transit for railway shipments of non-lethal supplies and air corridors for weapons supplies, as supply routes through Pakistan have come under increased Taleban attack. Russian officials have also strongly urged Nato and US forces to do more to stem a flow of drugs from Afghanistan to Russia ... Afghanistan provides more than 90 per cent of the heroin consumed in the world, and the bulk of it flows through ex-Soviet Central Asia and Russia. The problem of drug abuse is of vital concern to Russia – where cheap, abundant Afghan heroin has helped fuel a surge in addiction rates, and injection drug use has been a key factor in the spread of the virus that causes AIDS.

(www.iht.com, 18 August 2010)

Russians are negotiating to refurbish more than 140 Soviet-era projects, including hydroelectric stations, bridges, wells and irrigation systems, in deals that could be worth more than $1 billion. A Russian helicopter company, Virtol, has contracts with Nato and the Afghan government to fly Mi-26 heavy lift helicopters throughout the country ... Russia's foreign minister, Sergei Lavrov, said Afghan officials had invited Russia to take part in a new project: an effort to lay a north-to-south electrical line across their country, intended to supply Pakistan with electricity from abundant sources of hydroelectric power in Tajikistan ... Mr Lavrov conceded that the idea existed only on paper, but that Russia would be eager to take part.

(*IHT*, 19 August 2010, p. 3)

Moscow authorities have cut the daily sales for beverages with more than 15 per cent alcohol, making it illegal to buy such beverages in stores between 10 p.m. and 10 a.m. ... The move, which reduces by three hours a day the time those beverages can be sold in stores, will go into effect at the beginning of September ... The tightened limits on alcohol sales also prohibit local prefectures from issuing twenty-four-hour sales permits to shops. The cut in sales does not affect bars, restaurants or night clubs in Moscow, which can still obtain twenty-four-hour liquor licences and serve beer, wine or bottled cocktails with less than 15 per cent alcohol ... The new law will only affect the Moscow region because there is no nationwide alcohol sales regulation, leaving alcohol available on store shelves twenty-four hours a day throughout the rest of the country.

(www.cnn.com, 19 August 2010)

Shops and other outlets in Moscow had been banned from selling alcohol over 15 per cent in strength between 11 p.m. and 8 a.m. but a legal loophole allowed them to acquire permission for twenty-four-hour sales from district authorities. Establishments serving food are not affected.

(*Guardian*, 19 August 2010, p. 21)

19 August 2010.

Russia is marking the fiftieth anniversary of the space flight of two mongrel dogs – Belka [Squirrel] and Strelka [Arrow] – who became the first living creatures to circle the Earth and come back alive. The August 1960 mission helped test the equipment which was used to carry the first human, Yuri Gagarin, into space on 12 April 1961 ... Belka and Strelka ... followed Laika, a dog that flew into space on 3 November 1957 but was not meant to survive and died.

(www.iht.com, 19 August 2010)

The mission by Belka and Strelka on 19 August 1960 was a major step in preparations for the flight of Yuri Gagarin ... Laika became the first dog to orbit Earth in a non-returnable capsule but died of overheating after her 1957 launch. Two other dogs died in a July 1960 launch when their rocket exploded seconds after blastoff.

(*IHT*, 20 August 2010, p. 3)

21 August 2010.

Iranian and Russian engineers began loading fuel into Iran's first nuclear power plant on Saturday [21 August] ... Moscow says it believes the Bushehr project is essential for persuading Iran to co-operate with international efforts to ensure Iran does not develop the bomb. The United States, while no longer formally objecting to the plant, disagrees and says Iran should not be rewarded while it continues to defy UN demands to halt enrichment of uranium ... On Saturday a first truckload of fuel was taken from a storage site to a fuel 'pool' inside the reactor building. Over the next ten days 163 fuel assemblies ... will be moved inside the building and then into the reactor core ... It will be another two months before the 1,000-megawatt light-water reactor is pumping power to Iranian cities ... Of greater concern to the West, however, are Iran's stated plans to build ten new uranium enrichment sites inside protected mountain strongholds. Iran said recently it will begin construction of the first one in March [2011] in defiance of the UN sanctions ... [Also] at a news conference inside the plant ... [was] the head of Russia's state-run nuclear corporation, Sergei Kiriyenko ... Russia began shipping fuel for the plant in 2007 and carried out a test-run of the plant in February 2009. Iran says it plans to build other reactors and says designs for a second reactor in south-western Iran are taking shape. The Bushehr project dates back to 1974, when Iran's US-backed Shah Mohammed Reza Pahlavi contracted with the German company Siemens to build the reactor. The company withdrew from the project after the 1979 Islamic Revolution toppled the Shah. The partially built plant later sustained damages after it was bombed by Iraq during its 1980–8 war against Iran. Before making the Russian deal to complete Bushehr, Iran signed pacts with

Argentina, Spain and other countries only to see them cancelled under US pressure.

(www.iht.com, 21 August 2010)

'Russia also announced what seemed to be a new safeguard. Its technicians will jointly operate the station for two to three years under an agreement signed Saturday before the opening ceremony ... gradually handing over controls to the Iranians' (*IHT*, 23 August 2010, p. 3).

('[On 3 September] Japan imposed new sanctions on Iran over its nuclear programme. The measures – which go beyond those imposed by the UN Security Council – ban transactions with some Iranian banks, and also target energy-related investments ... Japan is a major importer of Iranian crude oil, but did not impose any restrictions on oil imports from Iran ... The United States, the EU, Canada and Australia have also announced additional sanctions, which have been opposed by Russia and China. China is now Iran's closest trading partner, with major energy interests in the country': www.bbc.co.uk, 4 September 2010.)

> Viktor Bout ... a Russian businessman [was extradited from Thailand to the United States on Friday 20 August] ... Mr Bout ... is suspected of running a large-scale trafficking organization that provided weapons to governments, rebels and insurgents across the globe ... Russia, which has been seeking to prevent Mr Bout from being placed in the American legal system, reacted angrily ... The United States began pursuing Mr Bout in the 1990s after officials became alarmed that he was making conflicts more deadly by showering warring parties with weapons on an unprecedented scale, including weapons as sophisticated as attack helicopters ... Mr Bout was arrested in March 2008 at a hotel in Bangkok to sell millions of dollars' worth of arms to undercover agents for the United States Drug Enforcement Administration posing as rebels for the Revolutionary Forces of Columbia (Farc).
>
> (www.iht.com, 21 August 2010)

'In the United States ... officials say he supplied arms to warlords, al-Qaeda and the Taleban' (www.bbc.co.uk, 21 August 2010).

24 August 2010.

> Moldovan police have seized 1.8 kilograms of uranium-238 in the capital, Chisinau ... Seven people were arrested, including former interior ministry officials ... The smugglers had reportedly been trying to sell the material on the European black market for Euro 9 million ... A nuclear expert has told the BBC that this form of uranium is of no use for making nuclear weapons. He told BBC News that the amount was 'trivial', and could safely be held in a person's hand ... But investigator Oleg Putintica told Moldova's ProTV Chisinau channel the material could be used 'both in the civilian nuclear industry and for military purposes to produce weapons of mass destruction'. The source and intended destination of the uranium was not clear, he said. Uranium-238 is the most commonly found, naturally occurring form of the

substance. It is the type needed for nuclear fuel and weapons, for which it needs to be enriched ... There were seven suspects, some of whom had previous convictions for possessing radioactive materials in Moldova, Russia and Romania.

(www.bbc.co.uk, 24 August 2010)

The authorities in Moldova said Wednesday [25 August] that they had arrested two former police officers and one other person on trafficking charges in connection with the transfer of 1.8 kilograms (4 pounds) of uranium-238. Uranium-238 can be enriched into the fissile material of nuclear warheads or converted into plutonium, also used to arm nuclear missiles.

(*IHT*, 26 August 2010, p. 3)

The material ... was sufficient to have been turned into a devastating dirty bomb, a nuclear expert with Greenpeace said. Two former policemen and another man were arrested on 20 July ... A fourth is being sought. The uranium had been smuggled into Moldova and has been sent to a German laboratory to establish its country of origin ... The campaigns director for Greenpeace Russia and an expert on nuclear materials, said cases of uranium and plutonium smuggling had taken place regularly after the collapse of the Soviet Union, but had tailed off over the past decade.

(*Guardian*, 26 August 2010, p. 19)

26 August 2010.

President Dmitri Medvedev has ordered the suspension of controversial plans to build a new motorway through a forest outside Moscow. Mr Medvedev said construction of the road from the capital to St Petersburg, via the Khimki forest, would be halted until a public hearing had been held. The decision came after appeals from environmental groups and, surprisingly, the governing United Russia Party. On Sunday [22 August] some 2,000 people attended a concert to protest against the road. Environmentalists say there are several options for the route to bypass the forest, which they say is a unique ecosystem that is home to centuries-old oak trees and many species of wildlife ... Mr Medvedev said he had ordered the suspension because 'our people, from the governing United Russia Party to united opposition groups to circles of experts, are saying this demands more analysis'. He said: 'I order the government to halt implementation of the orders to build the road in question and hold additional public and expert discussions' ... Boris Gryzlov (chairman of United Russia): 'United Russia has turned to the president of Russia ... with the request to halt the construction of the highway through the Khimki forest. We have different opinions within United Russia about this question. But the situation does not look simple.'

(www.bbc.co.uk, 26 August 2010)

For years environmentalists have risked arrests and sometimes beatings by the police and masked plainclothes thugs in their efforts to halt the construction of a highway linking Moscow to St Petersburg that they say would destroy the Khimki forest, one of the few remaining in the Moscow region ... During protests in the forest this summer, gangs of masked men attacked environmentalists, beating several. The police have detained others. Mikhail Beketov, an investigative journalist and outspoken opponent of the highway, was savagely attacked by unidentified men in November 2008 and is now severely brain damaged. At issue is the fate of a 2,500-acre oak forest. North of Moscow, in the town of Khimki. Vladimir Putin ... signed an order for the construction of a new highway traversing the forest when he was still president. Top officials in the federal government and the powerful governor of the Moscow region have backed the idea as the simplest and most cost effective way to strengthen transportation links between Moscow and St Petersburg ... Few dispute the need. Currently the trip by car is a treacherous 430-mile drive ... Environmentalists have called for building the new highway close to the existing road, which runs through an industrial zone. Building the highway through the forest, they say, would disrupt the ecological balance of Moscow, which depends on a shrinking belly of green space around it to help filter air pollution ... This summer's 100-degree temperatures, along with the huge wildfires that blanketed Moscow and the surrounding region with noxious smoke, seem to have persuaded officials to look anew at the arguments of environmentalists, especially since their calls to save the forest seem to have resonated with many residents of this city [Moscow] and beyond. More than 2,000 people gathered in central Moscow for a protest against the construction plans last weekend, an exceptionally large turnout here. And last month [July] hundreds of people raided the Khimki mayor's office, throwing rocks and smoke bombs in retaliation for earlier attacks on environmentalists defending the forest.

(www.iht.com, 27 August 2010)

The [Khimki] forest was being cleared to pave the way for a much-needed new road between the Russian capital and St Petersburg. Environmental campaigners and anti-Kremlin political activists contended there were other less damaging routes that could have been chosen. They also alleged that the authorities had scorned normal procedures to fast track the project, riding roughshod over public opinion in the process. The movement against the forest's destruction ... first hit the headlines in 2008 when a local journalist campaigning against the new road was savagely beaten in front of his own home. Mikhail Beketov, editor of a local newspaper, was pummelled with metal poles by an unknown number of attackers and left for dead. Doctors later had to amputate one of his legs and he lay in a critical condition for months. The brutality of that attack, which was, unusually, given wide coverage in state-controlled media, radicalized other activists. They organized numerous protest meetings, and, before long, Russia's tiny and enfeebled anti-Kremlin opposition co-opted the issue, farming it as a test of Mr Medvedev's pledges to foster a stronger civil society. The protests culminated in a lively demonstration on Moscow's Pushkin Square last Sunday [22 August] featuring an impromptu performance from veteran rocker Yuri Shevchuk. Mr Shevchuk, the front man for a band called DDT, became a pin-up for the anti-Kremlin opposition earlier this year when he confronted prime minister Vladimir Putin in a meeting, during which he asked him a series of awkward questions about the state of democracy in Russia.

(www.economist.com, 27 August 2010)

30 August 2010.

Prime minister Vladimir Putin disparaged Russian dissidents in crude street language during an interview Monday [30 August] and said they would keep getting beaten if they continued to hold unauthorized rallies ... He said: 'You will be beaten upside the head with a truncheon' ... Opposition groups plan to rally Tuesday evening [31 August] ... The opposition holds protests on the last day of every month with thirty-one days to call attention to Article 31 of Russia's constitution, which guarantees freedom of assembly.

(*IHT*, 31 August 2010, p. 3)

Prime minister Vladimir Putin dismissed protests against his regime as 'provocations' and said anyone who took part in unsanctioned street rallies against the Kremlin should expect a 'whack on the bonce' ... Anti-Putin rallies are due to take place for the first time outside the Russian consulate ... in London, and in New York, Helsinki, Berlin and Tel Aviv.

(*Guardian*, 31 August 2010, p. 22)

('[On 6 September prime minister Vladimir Putin] was scathing about opposition protesters, who have been holding meetings both in Russia and abroad – including in London last week – on the 31st of each month. Picking up from an interview with *Kommersant* newspaper, when he said demonstrators deserved a 'whack on the bonce', Putin dismissed those rallying as a marginal force. He said everybody had a right to express their views, but added that some people deliberately provoked a police beating to capture the media's attention. He said: 'Some people want to be beaten by truncheons. They lack patience. They hold private ambitions. Those groups are behaving in such a way that they are not a political force in the country'': *Guardian*, 7 September 2010, p. 22).

31 August 2010.

The Moscow police detained about seventy anti-government demonstrators on Tuesday [31 August] ... though they failed to prevent opposition groups from holding a planned demonstration against what protesters say are violations of their constitutionally guaranteed rights of assembly. It was the latest in a series of similar demonstrations in Moscow and other cities on the last day of each 31-day month. Riot police officers hauled off opposition leaders and packed anyone caught waving political signs into buses ... The Moscow government rarely allows opposition groups to hold demonstrations.

(www.iht.com, 1 September 2010)

'Police detained more than 100 people including prominent opponents of prime minister Vladimir Putin at anti-Kremlin protests yesterday [31 August] ... In Moscow police detained Boris Nemtsov ... and dozens of other protesters' (*The Independent*, 1 September 2010, p. 24).

The venue is Triumph Square, Moscow, near a statue of Vladimir Mayako- vsky, the poet, which was a gathering spot for dissidents during the Soviet era. In an attempt to head off the protest, the Moscow city government fenced off the entire square on 17 August, saying it was going to build an underground car garage. But protesters confronted police in a narrow plaza just off the square. About a thousand people crammed into the space, roughly a third of them demonstrators, a third policemen and a third journal- ists and cameramen.

(*FT*, 1 September 2010, p. 7)

7 September 2010.

For more than two years, the mayor of a Siberian village was held in pre- trial detention centre after she filed complaints against the successor agency [the FSB] to the Soviet-era KGB. But on Tuesday [7 September], with her case attracting widespread attention, she was unexpectedly given a reprieve. A judge in the regional centre of Irkutsk convicted the mayor, Tatiana Kaza- kova, on felony charges and sentenced her to six years in prison, but then suspended the sentence. She was also barred from holding public office for two-and-a-half years. Ms Kazakova's lawyers said the decision indicated that the authorities were seeking a face-saving way to end the case without admitting that it had been falsified. The charges against Ms Kazakova were the subject of an article in *The New York Times* [and in *The International Herald Tribune*] in July [2010]. Her defenders said the public attention influenced how the authorities handled the case ... In late 2007 she repeat- edly clashed with the director of a local resort that is owned by the FSB ... She said the resort had been carrying out illegal construction that threatened the village's heating system ... Officials denied that their inquiry had any- thing to do with Ms Kazakova's dispute with the resort ... After her arrest in March 2008, she was confined to a pre-trial detention centre for more than two years and denied virtually all contact with her family ... In late June [2010], after *The New York Times* made repeated inquiries to the agency about the charges against Ms Kazakova, the judge in the case ... reversed previous decisions and released her on bail ... Ms Kazakova ... would appeal the convictions.

(www.iht.com, 7 September 2010; *IHT*, 8 September 2010, p. 3)

10–11 September 2010.

An unprecedented Kremlin-sanctioned documentary accused ... Mos- cow's mayor Yuri Luzhkov ... of caring more about his bee collection than the people of his city. The film, screened on Friday [10 September] ... [by] the pro-Kremlin NTV channel ... recalled how Luzhkov went on holiday to Austria in August as Moscow's citizens were struggling to breathe in choking smog while forest fires enveloped Russia. On his return the mayor, a bee enthusiast, gave more money to beekeepers than to smog-affected Muscovites, it said. The programme's title sequence asked: 'Why did Moscow choke while the mayor rescued his bees? How did his wife become the richest woman in Russia? And why does his deputy have a watch worth more than $1 million? ... The film attacked Luzhkov's opulent lifestyle and that of his wife, Yelena Baturina, the world's third richest woman ... It is the first time such frank criticism has been aired on federal television. NTV returned to the attack on Saturday [11 September] with another anti-Luzhkov programme ... Last week Luzhkov criticized the president's decision to freeze construction of a new Moscow–St Petersburg highway after a public outcry over the demolition of the capital's Khimki forest ... On Friday President Dmitri Medvedev hit back ... On Friday Yuri Luzhkov insisted he would see out his term of office, which is due to finish in June.

(*Guardian*, 13 September 2010, p. 15)

President Dmitri Medvedev criticized Yuri Luzhkov in a speech on Friday [10 September], telling him to 'either help build institutions or join the opposition' ... Mr Luzhkov has high approval ratings ... ruling Moscow since 1992 ... He originally opposed the rise of Vladimir Putin, backing his competitor Yevgeni Primakov in the 2000 presidential election ... He insists he will not step down until his term ends next year [2011].

(*FT*, 14 September 2010, p. 10)

13 September 2010.

Moscow mayor Yuri Luzhkov says he will sue several state-linked television channels after they ran documentaries that were critical of him. The programmes alleged that Mr Luzhkov used his position to further the business interests of his wife, Russia's richest woman. They also criticized him for holidaying during a wildfire crisis this summer ... The construction company, Inteko, which is owned by Mr Luzhkov's wife, Yelena Baturina, said it was also planning to sue several channels ... Last week the seventy-three-year-old mayor wrote an article in which he criticized a decision by President Dmitri Medvedev to suspend a road-building project and said the mood in Russian society was 'difficult' ... On Friday [10 September] NTV ran a programme entitled *The Cap Affair*, a reference to Mr Luzhkov's habit of wearing a flat cap. The documentary berated him for remaining outside Moscow during a heatwave this summer when the capital was engulfed in smog. It also accused him of failing to tackle the city's traffic problems, as well as promoting his wife's business interests.

(www.bbc.co.uk, 13 September 2010)

15 September 2010.

It has been almost six years since a Russian defence minister set foot inside the Pentagon ... Defence Secretary Robert Gates devotes Wednesday [15 September] to hosting his Kremlin counterpart, Anatoli Serdyukov ... In parallel Mr Gates and Mr Serdyukov have declared war on their expensive, inefficient bureaucracies ... Mr Gates is trying to cut defence department spending on overheads to scrounge up more money for troops in the field and investment in new weapons ... In Russia, after his appointment as defence minister in 2007, Mr Serdyukov, who had more experience in the furniture industry than with the military, announced the largest overhaul in decades of his massive armed forces ... Mr Gates has ruffled feathers with his call to cut the ranks of Pentagon contractors, reduce his civilian management staff and trim the roster of generals and admirals by fifty or more. But that pales in comparison with Mr Serdyukov's goals: eliminating nearly 200,000 officers, including 200 generals; reducing the central headquarters staff by 60 per cent; and adopting a streamlined command structure that, like the United States Army, focuses on deployable rather than larger division structures. Russian troop levels will drop by 130,000 to about 1 million by 2016, in an attempt to transform the military from a lumbering Cold War relic into a more nimble force ... The Russian defence and military establishment has suffered from years of gross neglect and chronic corruption ... [Mr Gates is] a former CIA director who has served six presidents of both parties in a long career of public service. In contrast, Mr Serdyukov is the first Russian defence minister without a security background and has not cut as dramatic a figure across the global policy stage as his predecessor, Sergei Ivanov ... [who was] a career intelligence officer ... fluent in English ... In recent years much of the dialogue with the Russian military ... has been carried out by Admiral Mike Mullen, chairman of the Joint Chiefs of Staff, who has established a solid working relationship with his counterpart, General Nikolai Makarov, chief of the Russian general staff.

(www.iht.com, 14 September 2010; *IHT*, 15 September 2010, p. 3)

Norway and Russia have agreed on where their Arctic border should be drawn ... The two nations have been locked in a dispute over a 175,000 square kilometre (67,000 square mile) area in the Barents Sea for forty years ... The treaty, signed by the foreign ministers, will now be submitted to the countries' parliaments for ratification. Russia and Norway are among the countries eager to exploit the Arctic. The region's reserves of oil and gas are becoming more accessible due to ice melting. The disputed area, half the size of Germany, lies to the north off the two countries' coastlines ... President Dmitri Medvedev and Norway's prime minister Jens Stoltenberg attended the signing ceremony in Murmansk ... [Norway's foreign minister said] that the treaty secured the continued co-operation on fishing between the two countries, and regulated oil and gas offshore exploration in the border zone ... A Kremlin source told Russian news agency Interfax:

'Engagement in this area will be regulated by the principle of shared handling of all mineral deposits, crossed by the delimitation line.'

(www.bbc.co.uk, 15 September 2010)

The two countries have been negotiating their maritime boundary since 1970 … [The area] has become the focus recently on intense interest from oil and natural gas companies. The disputed area between Novaya Zemlya on the Russian side and the Svalbard archipelago on the Norwegian side is now seen as valuable territory in the rush to develop petroleum deposits under the Arctic Ocean … With the polar ice cap receding as global temperatures rise … [this makes] development seem far more feasible … The treaty … settles one of several disputes by the five countries with coasts along the Arctic – Russia, the United States, Canada, Denmark and Norway – and diplomats hailed it as a model for applying international law to the scramble for resources in the north … The resolution of the Russian–Norwegian boundary dispute, however, is unrelated to the central issues in the most contentious claim, a Russian staking out of territory that includes the North Pole. That is based on an assertion that an undersea mountain range forms part of Russia's continental shelf. It also governs drilling in any oil or gas fields that may be straddling the new border; they will be developed jointly … The dispute left about 67,600 square miles of open sea, an area the size of Florida, contested for four decades … The new boundary, one of the longest in what is still geographically part of Europe, roughly splits the difference between the country's claims. Legally, it is based on a calculation taking into consideration the longer Russian coastline, the Norwegian negotiator said.

(www.iht.com, 15 September 2010)

'The deal clears the way for the lifting of a thirty-year moratorium on oil and gas extraction in the disputed region' (www.cnn.com, 15 September 2010).

Russian prosecutors say they will seek to recover $465 million in foreign assets from fugitive UK-based tycoon Boris Berezovsky. Chief prosecutor Yuri Chaika said his office would actively work towards repatriating the assets, which he said were kept in Europe and elsewhere. Berezovsky has twice been convicted in Russia of embezzlement, and sentenced in absentia to nineteen years in prison. He says the proceedings were politically motivated. Granted political asylum in the UK in 2003, a couple of years after leaving Russia, the Yeltsin-era oligarch became a fierce critic of the Kremlin after Vladimir Putin took power. At the end of August [2010] he was seen taking part in a political rights protest outside the Russian embassy in London, holding a placard which simply read: 'I made you, I'll remove you too.' In November 2007 he was sentenced to six years in jail in his absence for stealing millions of dollars from the Russian airline Aeroflot in the 1990s. He described the verdict by a Moscow court as 'a farce'. Then in June 2009 he was sentenced to thirteen years in his absence for stealing thousands of cars from Avtovaz, also in the 1990s.

(www.bbc.co.uk, 15 September 2010)

2   Human rights

Moscow joined ... the Council of Europe ... in 1996 ... The European Court of Human Rights in Strasbourg [is] the judicial body of the Council of Europe ... It has become a court of last resort for Russians seeking justice and compensation for abuses, usually at the hands of the police or military. In 2006 Russians filed 10,596 cases, 22 per cent of the court's caseload. Nearly half were found inadmissible, but the court found against the Russian authorities in 102 cases that year.

(www.iht.com, 27 May 2007; *IHT*, 28 May 2007, p. 3)

Documents ... [of] the European Court of Human Rights ... show that as of 1 January 2007 of some 90,000 cases pending in the court, approximately 20,000 now originate in Russia. More than 10,500 applications were logged in 2006 alone, double the 2003 figure and an increase of 400 per cent over 2000 ... The list of Russian cases heard by the court is heavily dotted with accusations of extrajudicial executions, disappearances, torture and unlawful detention – most of which originate in the turbulent North Caucasus republics. Among the decisions reached in 2006 Russian cases made up approximately a third of all the grave violations of the right to life and prohibition of torture. The most frequent remedy ordered by the European rights court is payment of compensation to victims and their families ... The Russian government usually pays – albeit grudgingly ... Russia's foreign minister Sergei Lavrov: 'We consider some rulings of the European court to be politicized ... but despite the fact that we do not agree with certain rulings of the court in principle, we do comply with them.'

(*IHT*, 11 August 2007, p. 4)

Reporters from around the world who will gather in Moscow next week are poised to stand up for their colleagues in a country where journalism and journalists are increasingly under attack. The 1,000 news media representatives plan to establish a commission to finally investigate the growing number of unsolved murders of journalists in Vladimir Putin's Russia. Russia is now the third deadliest country for journalists, after Iraq and Algeria, according to the Committee to Protect Journalists. Since the year 2000, when President Vladimir Putin was first elected, at least fourteen journalists have been murdered because of their work. None of these murders have been solved ... The radio correspondents for the Russian News Service, the main source of news for radio stations, resigned earlier this month [May 2007] to protest censorship by new owners. And the Russian Union of Journalists, a strong voice against the march to silence any independent reporting, was ordered to leave its Moscow headquarters just days before the international conference ... The definition of extremism has been expanded to include media criticism of state officials. That can mean jail time for the reporter and the shutting down of the news outlet.

(*IHT*, 25 May 2007, p. 8)

A Russian court has convicted seven men in the 2000 murder of journalist Igor Domnikov – one of more than a dozen cases of journalists being killed during President Vladimir Putin's years in power. The Domnikov case represented the first time suspects were prosecuted in a journalist's killing since Putin became president in 2000. Domnikov wrote extensively on official corruption for the newspaper *Novaya Gazeta* ... The New York-based Committee to Protect Journalists says at least fourteen journalists have been killed since 2000 in reprisal for their reporting ... CPJ executive director Joel Simon: '[The verdict in Domnikov's case is] a groundbreaking step in the fight against impunity in the killing of journalists ... [but the Russian authorities need] to go further [and find and prosecute the mastermind of Domnikov's murder]' ... The convicted gang's leader ... who was sentenced to life ... told the court that Domnikov's killing had been ordered by former deputy governor of western Lipetsk region Sergei Dorovsky for a series of critical articles on his policies, said Andrei Lipsky, the deputy editor of *Novaya Gazeta*. Dorovsky has denied involvement and has never been charged.

(www.iht.com, 31 August 2007)

Russian have been able to appeal to the European Court of Human Rights [in Strasbourg] since their country ratified the European Convention on Human Rights in 1998. Russians now file more complaints with the court than citizens of any other country; many are Chechens.

(*IHT*, 18 January 2008, p. 3)

The journalist Magomed Yevloyev annoyed the authorities in Ingushetia, a predominantly Moslem region ... [He was] critical of corruption among the region's bosses and their violent repression of political opponents ... On 31 August [2008] Yevloyev flew into the region's capital on the same plane as Ingushetia's governor, Murat Zyazikov ... When he debarked he was shoved into a police car and driven off. He was found soon after at the road-side, with a bullet in his head. The authorities put out a story about an 'incident', a far-fetched tale of an accidental shooting after Yevloyev allegedly grabbed for the gun of one of his police captors ... Since 1990 at least 291 journalists have been killed or disappeared in Russia and only a few cases have resulted in convictions.

(editorial, *IHT*, 12 September 2008, p. 6)

Russia began taking part in the European Court of Human Rights in the late 1990s. In 2000 the court received 1,987 appeals against Russia, or 8 per cent of the total ... At the end of 2008 the number of cases filed against Russia had risen to 27,250, or 28 per cent of the total, far more than any other country, and out of proportion to its population.

(*IHT*, 30 March 2009, p. 4)

'At least sixteen journalists have been killed in Russia since 2000, according to the Committee to Protect Journalists. Only one of those killings has led to a conviction and none of the organizers have been found' (*IHT*, 26 June 2009, p. 3).

'The New York-based Committee to Protect Journalists ranks Russia as the world's third most dangerous place for reporters, after Iraq and Algeria. It says fifty reporters have been killed in Russia since 1992' (www.iht.com, 7 August 2009).

The New York-based Committee to Protect Journalists said in a report that seventeen journalists in Russia had been killed in retaliation for their work since 2000, making Russia the third most dangerous country for the press, after Iraq and Algeria. In only one of the seventeen cases have the killers been punished, the report said ... The committee said the journalists became targets because they were scrutinizing powerful people by reporting on corruption or other misconduct ... The committee said President Dmitri Medvedev and prime minister Vladimir Putin had a moral responsibility to address what the committee said was a culture of impunity ... The report maintained that fear of violence had led to a growing climate of self-censorship, with many journalists reluctant to carry out investigative reporting.

(www.iht.com, 15 September 2009)

Each year the European parliament awards a Sakharov Prize for Freedom of Thought, named after the Russian scientist and human rights activist Andrei Sakharov ... In a ceremony this week the prize was given to Memorial, a human rights group from Sakharov's native country ... Memorial suspended its operations in Chechnya after the murder ... of Natalia Estimirova last July ... but reopened them this month [December].

(*IHT*, 21 December 2009)

The State Duma ... on Friday [15 January] reversed its longstanding opposition to reforms in the European Court of Human Rights ... Legislators in the lower house voted 392 to fifty-six to ratify the reforms ... The international human rights court, based in Strasbourg (France) has been clogged in recent years with a backlog of complaints, nearly one-third of them filed against Russia. The reform plan, Protocol 14, aimed to speed up the court's work, in part by reducing the number of judges necessary to make major decisions. Since 2004 Russia has been the only one of forty-seven participating states to refuse to ratify Protocol 14. Moscow's opposition seemed coloured by its overall suspicion of the court, which has found Russian officials guilty of corruption, torture and other misconduct. But Dmitri Vyatkin, who serves on parliament's legislative committee, said European ministers had finally addressed Russian complaints about the proposals, in part by guaranteeing that Russian judges would be involved in reviewing complaints against Russia ... Strasbourg has provided an international platform for hundreds of cases damaging to the government. One of the most damaging had been expected to grab attention on Thursday, the day of the first hearing in a $100 billion lawsuit filed by the former managers of Yukos ... The court said Tuesday [12 January] that the hearing would be delayed for a third time, until 4 March ... Thomas Hammarberg ... the human rights commissioner at the council ... [said] Russia will be held to the same rules that apply to other members, and no changes were made to the protocol during negotiations ... But Mr Vyatkin said the council had provided written commitments on the Russians' main fears. He aid he was reassured that Russian judges would be included in reviews of potential cases against Russia, that the court would not begin investigating complaints before cases were formally accepted and that the court would not have new powers to force rulings to be carried out ... The Council of Europe established the human rights court.

(www.iht.com, 15 January 2010)

Russian leaders have long been unhappy with the court, and a raft of rulings have found officials guilty of corruption, torture and other misconduct ... Since the late 1990s, when Russia began taking part, complaints against Russia have come to constitute a third of the cases before the court. The court has found the Russian military responsible for killing and abducting scores of Chechen civilians. It was due Thursday to hear a lawsuit filed by the former managers of Yukos ... who are seeking $100 billion in damages for the firm's seizure and bankruptcy ... Mr Vyatkin said the council had provided written commitments addressing specific fears. Deputies have been assured [for example] that a Russian judge would be included in the three-judge panels reviewing potential cases against Russia ... [There is the argument that] after the Orange Revolution in Ukraine, the view swept through Russia's ruling classes that the court was one of many Western organizations intent on fomenting a similar uprising in Russia.

(*IHT*, 15 January 2010, p. 3)

Protocol 14 is part of the European Convention for the Protection of Human Rights ... Ratification in the upper house, the Council of the Federation, is expected to be a formality. Russia faces the largest number of cases pending before the court – 28 per cent of the total ... After a Council of Europe meeting on 14 December [2009] Duma speaker Boris Gryzlov said the Council had agreed that a Russian judge would participate in any decisions concerning Russia. Protocol 14 would cut down the number of judges on panels charged with deciding issues such as the admissibility of cases. It also paves the way for new rules to ensure that states implement fundamental changes to national laws or practices, as ordered by the court ... Experts say the changes would speed up the handing of cases by up to 25 per cent ... [Russia] said that of the 112,000 cases currently before the European Court 27,000 were filed by Russian citizens.

(www.bbc.co.uk, 15 January 2010)

The Council of Europe has announced plans to streamline procedures at the European Court of Human Rights to help deal with a backlog of 120,000 cases. Ministers from the Council's forty-seven member states agreed at a meeting in the Swiss city of Interlaken. They provide for one judge to decide on a case's admissibility, and for cases similar to those previously brought to be heard by a panel of three judges. Russia, the origin of 27,000 pending cases, initially resisted the reforms. All members of the Council of Europe have had to incorporate the European Convention on Human Rights into their national laws, accepting that the court's rulings are final and must be obeyed ... At the end of the two-day conference in Interlaken, ministers agreed that 'additional measures are indispensable and urgently required'. Under Protocol 14, one judge rather than three will decide on a case's admissibility, and cases which are similar to ones previously brought will be decided by a three-judge panel, rather than the original seven-member chamber. Judges will be able to strike off the record cases with similarities to those already decided, as well as cases where an applicant has suffered no 'significant disadvantage'. The Protocol will also allow the Committee of Ministers, which is charged with supervising the enforcement of judgements, to work more effectively with national governments to ensure compliance ... One sticking point was Russia, most of whose cases relate to alleged abuses by the country's security forces in Chechnya – including extra-judicial killings, torture and disappearances – or conditions in prisons. Moscow was at first unwilling to agree to measures that would bring these cases before the court more quickly. It only agreed at the last minute when a provision was included to allow a Russian judge to participate in any decisions concerning the country.

(www.bbc.co.uk, 21 February 2010)

A police officer who shot and killed a prominent journalist in Ingushetia ... was released on Tuesday [2 February] ... after serving three months of a two-year sentence for involuntary manslaughter. The journalist. Magomed Yevloyev, a critic of the Ingush leader at the time, Murat Zyazikov, was shot in the head after being detained at the local airport. His death provoked large protests, prompting the Kremlin to replace Mr Zyazikov with Yunus-Bek Yevkurov.

(*IHT*, 4 March 2010)

On Thursday [4 March] the European Court of Human Rights in Strasbourg will hear the case that they ... former Yukos executives, shareholders and creditors ... are owed $98 billion ... because their rights to property and a fair trial were violated under a treaty to which Russia is a party ... The damage claim of $98 billion ... equivalent to about 10 per cent of Russia's GDP ... is an estimate of what Yukos would have been worth had its most valuable properties not been stripped away in 2007, when the company was struck from the register of Russian companies and effectively ceased to exist ... It is the largest claim for damages ever filed with the court, which enforces human rights in the forty-seven countries in the Council of Europe. The court is often used by Russian claimants in instances of disappearances in Chechnya, police abuse and disputes over payments of pensions ... The Yukos plaintiffs argue that the Putin government selectively applied tax laws for political reasons, leading to the company's demise ... The judges are expected to publish their rulings within several months ... Many thousands of applications are never accepted by the court. But once admitted, most cases are decided in favour of claimants. Of the 219 cases from Russia the court took up last year [2009], for example, judges ruled against the Russian government 210 times. The court exonerated the government six times and three cases were settled out of court.

(*IHT*, 4 March 2010, p. 18)

The European Court of Human Rights has begun hearing a complaint from Yukos against the Russian government ... [The court] agrees to hear about one in twenty applications it receives ... The firm claims that it was 'targeted' by the Russian authorities and illegally driven out of business. Yukos representatives first filed the claim with the European Court of Human Rights in 2004 ... Yukos claims that the Russian government's action were 'unlawful, disproportionate, arbitrary and discriminatory, and amounted to disguised expropriation' of the company ... Russian authorities began pursuing Yukos in 2002.

(www.bbc.co.uk, 4 March 2010)

Reporters Without Borders has named the leaders of China, Russia and Rwanda as some of the world's worst 'predators of freedom'. The report, marking World Press Freedom Day, lists what the Paris-based group regards as the forty worst offenders against the freedom of the press. North Korea's leader Kim Jong Il and the head of Burma's military government Than Shwe are also on the list ... Russian prime minister Vladimir Putin has 'promoted a climate of pumped-up national pride that encourages the persecution of dissidents and freethinkers'.

(www.bbc.co.uk, 3 May 2010)

The Committee to Protect Journalists says that thirty-two journalists have been murdered since 1992 ... President Barack Obama ... this week signed the Daniel Pearl Freedom of the Press Act, requiring the State Department to identify countries that allow or participate in attacks on journalists.

(www.iht.com, 20 May 2010)

To the surprise of human rights activists and their own colleagues, European delegates to the Council of Europe's Parliamentary Assembly on Tuesday [22 June] approved a harshly critical draft resolution on Russia's policy in the North Caucasus, which says 'human rights violations and the climate of complete impunity were found to foster the rise of extremist movements' ... This is hardly the first time the assembly ... has issued a damning assessment of human rights in the North Caucasus ... But never in fourteen years of membership has Russia's delegation voted to approve one, much less praised it as objective and balanced. Delegates hailed the vote – 132 in favour with six abstentions – as a historic moment, and the author of the resolution called it a 'major signal' of a shift in Russia's approach to the region ... The author, Dick Marty, [is] a former prosecutor from Switzerland who visited Chechnya, Ingushetia and Dagestan in March [2010]. He said: 'I think it shows that they understand the situation must change, and that they actually want to change something. We are far from having found a solution, but I believe we are entering a new era, a period where dialogue might be possible' ... The resolution cites findings by the European Court of Human Rights that the authorities in the region employed torture and extrajudicial killings, and says Russia's failure to punish these crimes feeds 'the nefarious cycle of violence'. It levels particular criticism at the president of Chechnya, Ramzan Kadyrov, saying he has nurtured 'a climate of pervading fear'. An accompanying report zeroes in on the killing of Umar Israilov, who was shot in Vienna in January of 2009 as he prepared to testify against Mr Kadyrov. Mr Marty offers some evidence that a key witness in the murder, refused protection by the Austrian authorities, was killed after his return to Russia, and that a second witness was killed in Azerbaijan ... As the Tuesday vote approached Russian delegates said they had negotiated to remove the resolution's harshest language, including a section that characterized Mr Kadyrov's rule as a 'cult of personality' ... Two Russian delegates abstained from the Tuesday vote [out of eight] ... Mr Marty was effusive in his thanks to Russian delegates who assisted him during his research ... Some of his toughest comments Tuesday were directed at European governments that he said were hesitant to challenge Russia on its human rights record ... Austria's response to Mr Israilov's murder in Vienna , he said 'shows the degree to which authorities in European countries are willing to act in a way that is not consistent with the elegant pronouncements on human rights which they emit so often.'

(*IHT*, 23 June 2010, p. 3)

'Parliament ... is in the process of approving legislation that would allow FSB agents to warn people that their activities were "unacceptable" and leading toward a crime. The KGB once enjoyed a similar practice against Soviet dissidents' (www.iht.com, 4 July 2010).

The State Duma ... approved a bill Friday [16 July] that would widen the powers of the Federal Security Service ... The bill would allow ... the FSB

... to issue warnings to people suspected of preparing crimes against Russia's security. Critics say this power could be used to intimidate government opponents and stifle protests ... The bill was approved by a vote of 354 to ninety-six. Members of the Communist and A Just Russia parties voted against it ... President Dmitri Medvedev, when asked at a news conference Thursday [15 July] about the proposed law, said it was his initiative and said the country has 'the right to improve its own legislation'. Opposition groups are frequently denied permission to hold rallies or are allowed to hold them only in out-of-the-way neighbourhoods. Riot police often break up unsanctioned rally attempts swiftly and brutally ... The liberal party Yabloko said three of its activists were arrested outside the Duma as they protested the bill that was about to be voted on.

(www.iht.com, 16 July 2010)

[The State Duma] passed a draft law on Friday [16 July], which will allow the FSB to officially warn citizens that their activities could lead to a future violation of the law, reviving a Soviet-era KGB practice that was often used to chasten dissidents. The legislation was proposed during the tense weeks after two suicide bombers blew themselves up on the Moscow subway and its stated goal was to staunch the growth of radicalism among Russian young people. Twenty leading human rights representatives condemned it as a blow to 'the cornerstone principles of law: the presumption of innocence and legal certainty' in a letter made public on Thursday [15 July]. When asked about the bill by a German reporter during a meeting with German chancellor Angela Merkel on Thursday, President Dmitri Medvedev said: 'What is going on is the result of my direct instructions. The law on the FSB is our domestic bill. Every country has the right to perfect its laws, including laws on special services' ... The final version is somewhat weakened from its earlier form, which prescribed punishment for individuals who ignored such warnings from the FSB ... The legislation leaves vague what actions would prompt FSB warnings, or what measures will be used to enforce them. Other provisions in the bill impose fifteen-day sentences or fines of 500 roubles to 1,000 roubles (around $16.50 to $33) on citizens who obstruct the work of an FSB agent. Previously, such administrative fines applied to police or prison officials.

(www.iht.com, 16 July 2010)

A law allowing the Federal Security Service (FSB) to issue warnings to people 'whose acts create the conditions for a crime' was passed yesterday [19 July] by the Federation Council, the upper house of parliament. Rights activists and opposition parties argue that it gives FSB officers the right to crack down on people simply for expressing dissent, on the grounds that it could lead to extremism or an act of terrorism. They accuse the FSB of reviving powers given to its predecessor, the KGB, in 1972 to warn Soviet dissidents against 'antisocial activities that contradict national security'. Civil rights groups have sent an open letter to President Dmitri Medvedev challenging him to veto the legislation as contrary to his pledges to uphold the supremacy of law in Russia. It said: 'Today it depends precisely on you whether to stop the passage of the bill ruining the cornerstone principles of law: the presumption of innocence and legal certainty' ... Powers for FSB officers to issue fines and jail people for fifteen days for refusing to obey the warnings were dropped after a public outcry. Opponents say that the bill will allow the security service to intimidate activists who are critical of the Kremlin in the run-up to the presidential election in 2012 ... The bill does not define what acts would trigger warnings from the FSB ... The Kremlin justified the law as part of the fight against terrorism after the suicide bombings in the Moscow Metro that killed forty people in March.

(*The Times*, 20 July 2010, p. 29)

The bill passed yesterday [19 July] by the upper house of parliament allows the FSB ... to issue warnings to people suspected of planning crimes. Another provision in the bill allows for fines or short jail sentences to be imposed on anyone who obstructs the work of FSB agents ... After a public outcry the bill was watered down from an initial draft that would have forced those whom the FSB wanted to 'warn' to present themselves for an interview, with the penalty of a jail sentence if they did not comply. The revised version says that the FSN can warn a person that they are 'on the boundary' of committing a crime, but does not specify what further measures can be taken.

(*The Independent*, 20 July 2010, p. 27)

The FSB ... can now officially warn citizens against 'creating the conditions' for crimes. Anyone obstructing an FSB officer or refusing to obey a legal request made by an FSB officer faces either a fine or up to fifteen days' detention ... President Dmitri Medvedev signed the amendments to the law on the FSB after it passed both houses of parliament where ... it provoked unusually strong debate. Sergei Mironov, speaker of the upper house – the Federation Council – said the security services had quite enough power already without the new legislation. Russian human rights organizations had urged President Medvedev not to sign the bill, arguing that its wording was too vague and open to abuse. Of particular concern was the section of the law granting the FSB the right to 'warn officially an individual about the admissibility of actions that create the conditions for the commission of crimes' ... The Memorial human rights organization accused the FSB of seeking 'preventative' powers like those used by the KGB to persecute dissidents ... Officially the FSB's focus has been on fighting domestic terrorism, particularly that emanating from Chechnya and other parts of the North Caucasus, but critics believe it has been used to intimidate legal opposition to the Kremlin.

(www.bbc.co.uk, 29 July 2010)

One of Russia's most senior human rights campaigners has resigned from her position as head of an advisory council to President Dmitri Medvedev. Ella

Pamfilova, head of the president's council on human rights and civil society for six years, gave no reason. But a colleague told the BBC she had been dismayed by the lack of support she had received from the president. She had, her colleague said, been under attack from groups associated with hardline members of the government ... The sudden resignation ... was accepted by Mr Medvedev on Friday [31 July] ... The youth group Nashi ... has frequently called for her resignation and is currently trying to sue her for slander after she criticized it last week ... She proposed economist Alexander Auzan as her replacement ... [He] said he had not been approached by the Kremlin ... Ella Pamfilova, a veteran politician who served as MP in the dying days of the USSR and stood for president in 2000, was appointed to her advisory post in 2002 under President Vladimir Putin. In March [2010] she told EU officials that Russia's democratic institutions were underdeveloped and that she had not seen any significant changes in the civil rights area.

(www.bbc.co.uk, 31 July 2010)

One of the authorities' newest tactics for quelling dissent: confiscating computers under the pretext of searching for pirated Microsoft software. Across Russia the security services have carried out dozens of similar raids against outspoken advocacy groups or opposition newspapers in recent years. Security officials say the inquiries reflect their concern about software piracy, which is rampant in Russia. Yet rarely if ever do they carry out raids against advocacy groups or news organizations that back the government ... In politically tinged inquiries across Russia, lawyers retained by Microsoft have staunchly backed the police ... Microsoft ... has promised to review its policies in Russia ... Microsoft also says it has a programme in Russia to provide free and low-cost software to newspapers and advocacy groups so that they are in compliance with the law.

(Clifford Levy, www.iht.com, 12 September 2010 *IHT*,
13 September 2010, pp. 1, 4)

Microsoft announced on Monday [13 September] that it would essentially prohibit its Russian division from taking part in software privacy cases against government opponents, responding to criticism that it was assisting the authorities in a crackdown on dissent. The security services in recent years have seized computers from dozens of outspoken advocacy groups and opposition newspapers in raids that all but paralysed their operations. Officials claim they are merely investigating the piracy of Microsoft software, but the searches typically happen when these groups are seeking to draw attention to a cause or event ... [Microsoft said it] would thwart such piracy inquiries by offering advocacy groups and opposition newspapers a blanket software licence that would automatically cover them, without having to apply for it. In other words, Microsoft would formally declare that the programmes on their computers were legal, making it all but impossible for the authorities to charge these groups with stealing Microsoft software ... The policy is intended to last until 2012 but could be extended ... In the meantime ... Microsoft [said it] would step up efforts to ensure that non-profit groups have access to a programme that provides free and low-cost Microsoft software ... The company indicated that ... the policy ... would apply to other countries as well, though it did not identify them. Microsoft was reacting to an article in *The New York Times* [and *The International Herald Tribune*] on Sunday [12 September] that detailed how lawyers retained by the company in Russia had strongly supported prosecutors and the police in piracy cases against advocacy groups and opposition news-papers. The lawyers made formal declarations that the company was a victim and asserted that criminal charges should be pursued, according to interviews and a review of law enforcement documents. The article described the case of a prominent environmental group in Siberia, Baikal Environmental Wave, which was raided by the police in January [2010] just as it was planning protests against a decision by prime minister Vladimir Putin to reopen a paper factory that had long polluted Lake Baikal. Plain-clothes officers took twelve computers from Baikal Wave and immediately charged the group with piracy, even though its leaders said they had only licensed Microsoft software. Leaders of Baikal Wave said they had been disappointed that Microsoft had rebuffed their pleas for help in defending themselves against the inquiry.

(Clifford Levy, www.iht.com, 13 September 2010; *IHT*,
14 September 2010, p. 4)

After police seized a dozen computers from a Siberian environmental group, the group said all its software was legally licensed and asked Microsoft to confirm this. Microsoft would not. The police used this information from the computers to track down and interrogate some of the group's supporters. Before changing policy on Monday [13 September], Microsoft executives said the company was required under Russian law to take part in such inquiries.

(editorial, www.iht.com, 15 September 2010)

3 Developments in Chechnya and other Caucasian republics since 22 January 2001

22 January 2001.

> President Vladimir Putin effectively downgraded Russia's war in Chechnya on Monday [22 January] from a military to a counter-terrorist operation, saying that he plans to cut Russia's 80,000-man force in the province by nearly three-quarters in coming months ... [The plan was] combined with an order turning control of Chechen operations to his domestic intelligence agency, the Federal Security Service ... 'This does not mean the end of the counter-terrorist operation,' Mr Putin said ... 'On the contrary it will be continued and not less intensively but with the use of different means and forces and with a different emphasis' ... Mr Putin announced the change in strategy on national television ... While he gave no timetable he and his aides said the government intended to reduce forces there to a 15,000-man army division and 7,000 troops from the interior ministry. Other officials said the army alone now keeps about 40,000 troops in Chechnya ... A spokesman for the Federal Security Service said that the agency's existing forces would be strengthened with more special operations and searches for rebel forces, but that traditional military operations would continue.
>
> (*IHT*, 23 January 2001, p. 5)

> President Vladimir Putin yesterday [22 January] ordered troop withdrawals from Chechnya and a shift in command from military leaders to the FSB domestic security service ... His decision came after the appointment last week of Stanislav Illyasov as prime minister for Chechnya and government pledges to prepare a 15 billion rouble reconstruction programme for the republic during the current year. The moves reflect a growing emphasis on reducing the role of the armed forces in the region and re-establishing a civilian administration ... Mr Putin indicated that at least 22,000 troops would remain permanently in the southern part of Russia, which includes Chechnya.
>
> (*FT*, 23 January 2001, p. 9)

> Officials said that the number of uniformed soldiers in Chechnya would be cut from 80,000 to 22,000. Large numbers of security service agents would be moved into the province to join an operation run by Nikolai Patrushev,

who succeeded Mr Putin as head of the service ... The FSB has been given until 15 May to produce results.

(The Times, 23 January 2001, p. 14)

General Yuri Baluyevsky, deputy chief of staff, said ... that the rebels now had only 1,000 men in the field compared with 20,000 at the start of the war and that the Russian army had about 40,000 men and 170 tanks in Chechnya. For several months most of the fighting has been done by interior ministry troops.

(The Independent, 23 January 2001, p. 13)

[President Putin said] 'I have decided today on a partial withdrawal from the republic. This does not mean the end of the counter-terrorism operation. On the contrary it will be continued, but with different means and forces and with a different emphasis ... [The war would now be waged by] FSB and interior ministry special units. ... By the official tally, widely seen as too low, the Russians are being killed at the rate of more than 160 a month, with almost 500 being wounded as the rebels use ruthless hit-and-run tactics.

(Guardian, 23 January 2001, p. 3)

President Vladimir Putin yesterday [22 January] signed a decree ... From now on Federal Security Service director Nikolai Patrushev will be in command of the counter-terrorist operation in Chechnya ... The military presence in Chechnya will be limited to the Forty-Second Motorized Infantry Division and an internal troops brigade, which are to be stationed there on a permanent basis. This means the Joint Group of Forces will be reduced by about half.

(CDSP, 2001, vol. 53, no. 4, p. 6)

Overall command will now be exercised by FSB director Nikolai Patrushev instead of defence minister Igor Sergeyev ... Special operations to suppress the last centres of resistance will be carried out under FSB supervision. At the same time 14 billion roubles is being allocated to restore normal civilian life in Chechnya. Seven billion roubles was allocated in 2000.

(p. 7)

'The Russian government yesterday approved Chechen chief administrator Akhmad Kadyrov's 2001 economic reconstruction programme for Chechnya ... The previously quoted sum of 16.4 billion roubles was pared down to 14.4 billion roubles' (p. 6).

5 February 2001. A bomb explodes in one of Moscow's busiest underground stations. Injuries but no deaths are reported. There is speculation whether Chechen terrorists or criminal elements are to blame.

7 February 2001.

A mission from OSCE will soon return to Chechnya after pulling out more than three years ago ... OSCE's new chairman, Mircea Geoană, said the 'assistance group' would return after technical issues were resolved and praised 'modest steps in the right direction' to reach a political settlement in Chechnya ... 'The group will return to Chechnya in the near future.'

(*IHT*, 8 February 2001, p. 4)

24 February 2001. A mass grave is discovered on the outskirts of Grozny. There is speculation that Russian security forces are to blame.

19 March 2001.

A Russian court on Monday [19 March] convicted six men in the [4] September 1999 bombing in the republic of Dagestan. Two of them were sentenced to life terms ... The trial ... is the first court proceeding brought by Russian prosecutors to pin responsibility for the wave of apartment bombings ... All of ... the six defendants ... [were] described by prosecutors as Islamic extremists who were under the command of Chechen rebel leaders Shamil Basayev and Khattab ... The six men were part of a group of nine accused of planning and setting off the explosion that destroyed a residential building that housed Russian military personnel and their families in the Dagestani town of Buinaksk ... The explosion ... was followed by two blasts that destroyed apartment blocks in Moscow and another in the southern city of Volgodonsk ... Nine-year sentences were handed down [to two] ... [Another] two of the defendants ... received three-year sentences, but they were immediately set free under a standing amnesty programme for short sentences.

(*IHT*, 20 March 2001, p. 7)

21 March 2001. 'An announcement [is made in the United States] that Ilyas Akhmadov, foreign minister of the rebel Chechen regime, would be received by an assistant secretary in a White House building this weekend' (*Daily Telegraph*, 22 March 2001, p. 17).

Moscow accused the Bush administration of ... [an] 'explicitly unfriendly act' by announcing that a senior representative from the rebellious Chechen republic would be invited for high-level consultations in Washington this week ... A state department announcement [on 21 March said that] a senior American official would meet with Ilyas Akhmadov, described as foreign minister of the separatist Chechen leadership.

(*IHT*, Friday 23 March 2001, p. 4)

('Russia denounced as "immoral" yesterday [27 March] a meeting between a senior US official and an envoy of the rebel government. Ilyas Akhmadov, foreign minister of the separatist leadership, met [the] acting US special adviser for newly independent states ... in Washington': *The Independent*, 28 March 2001, p. 14.)

24 March 2001. Three nearly simultaneous car bombs in southern Russia kill twenty-four people. The blasts took place in Mineralvye Vody (at a local market), Yesentuky (near a police checkpoint) and near a checkpoint in

Karachayevo-Cherkesya. 'The Russian prosecutor ... asserted that ... the attack was organized by the Jordanian-born Chechen commander known as Khattab ... A spokesman for ... Aslan Maskhadov denied any responsibility for the violence' (*IHT*, 26 March 2001, p. 7).

13 June 2001.

> The OECD prepared to re-establish a presence in the region on Friday [15 June] ... The organization ... that quit in 1998 ... was set to reopen a permanent office in Znamenskoye in the north ... The European agency has agreed to pay the Russian ministry for a twenty-five-man protection squad for its team.
>
> (*IHT*, 15 June 2001, p. 4)

9 July 2001.

> Russian troops have unleashed a massive 'cleansing' operation in Chechnya, prompting new allegations of brutality and so angering the Kremlin's administrator that he accused the military of 'a large-scale crime against civilians'. As new details emerged about the violent roundup of more than 1,000 male civilians in several Chechen villages over the weekend, Akhmad Kadyrov, a Moslem cleric who is Moscow's ... administrator, unexpectedly rebuked the Russian military Monday [9 July] ... A group of local officials appointed by Moscow quit in protest over the roundups.
>
> (*IHT*, 11 July 2001, p. 5)

> Akhmad Kadyrov ... accused the military of 'criminal conduct' during a sweep through three villages in western Chechnya last week ... The systematic ransacking started ... on 3 July said ... [a member of] the human rights organization Memorial ... The Russian army in Chechnya ... has not previously arrested the entire male population of villages.
>
> (*The Independent*, 10 July 2001, p. 12)

'Five men ... not Chechens ... accused of the bombing of apartment blocks in Moscow that killed 200 people in 1999 ... have gone on trial in southern Russia ... in a penal colony outside Stavropol' (*The Independent*, 11 July 2001, p. 13).

11 July 2001.

> The commander of Russian forces in Chechnya said on Wednesday [11 July] that his soldiers had committed 'widespread crimes' when, after mine blasts killed [as many as eleven] Russian soldiers nearby, they inflicted beatings and electric shocks on 1,500 civilians and looted homes in two villages. General Vladimir Moltensky, acting commander of Russian forces in the northern Caucasus ... [said]: 'Those who conducted the searches did so in a lawless fashion, committing numerous outrages and then pretending that they knew

nothing about it' ... The general said he was making the statement because 'numerous crimes' had been committed. He instructed his subordinate commanders to respond to every citizen complaint filed with prosecutors as a result of the 'mopping up' operations on 3 and 4 July ... The soldiers ... arrested every Chechen male between the ages of fifteen and fifty-five ... On Tuesday [10 July] in Moscow Sergei Yastrzhembsky, an aide to President Vladimir Putin, acknowledged that soldiers might have committed offences in the villages. He said the matter was under investigation.

(*IHT*, 12 July 2001, p. 5)

In an unprecedented criticism of his own army, General Vladimir Moltensky ... admitted yesterday [11 July] that his men had committed 'widespread crimes' in searching two villages last week ... Some 1,500 villagers were beaten and tortured, the Russian media and human rights groups reported. Many were only released after they paid bribes to soldiers. This is the first time such a degree of official contrition has been shown by army commanders for the behaviour of troops during the present Chechen war.

(*The Independent*, 12 July 2001, p. 13)

19 July 2001.

Russia's top official in Chechnya demanded Thursday [19 July] that top army commanders be held responsible for alleged human rights abuses ... Akhmad Kadyrov, head of Chechnya's administration within the Russian government, said he wanted military commanders brought to book in addition to six soldiers who have been accused of crimes against civilians during recent searches ... [Mr Kadyrov]: 'The case should not be limited to the arrest of six servicemen. Generals should be held responsible, too. Heads should roll here, in Moscow. Only then can we restore the people's faith.'

(*IHT*, 20 July 2001, p. 11)

7 September 2001. President Putin:

We are ready for any contacts, with whoever. Talks are always better than actions involving the use of force ... All bandit formations must disarm without fail, unconditionally and without delay. Especially odious bandits whose hands are up to their elbows in the blood of the Russian people must be handed over to the federal authorities.

(*FT*, 8 September 2001, p. 8; *IHT*, 8 September 2001, p. 2)

His comments ... came in response to recently renewed calls from Boris Nemtsov ... for discussions with Aslan Maskhadov ... [In July there had been] a call by Mr Maskhadov for talks in an open letter to leaders of the G8 nations during the Genoa summit.

(*FT*, 8 September 2001, p. 8)

11 September 2001. There are terrorist attacks on the United States.

18 September 2001.

Russian troops fanned out across Chechnya on Tuesday [18 September] ... The drive came after ... Gudermes came under a strong rebel attack. Large areas of Gudermes fell into guerrilla hands Monday [17 September] when up to 300 rebels entered the town in their biggest assault in months ... The pro-Russian Chechen government ... [said] Tuesday that the town was quiet ... The guerrillas [said they] remained largely in control of the town ... The assault on Gudermes [was] coupled with a string of smaller attacks throughout Chechnya ... Defence secretary Sergei Ivanov last week repeated assertions that the Chechen rebels were linked with Osama bin Laden, the Afghan-based Saudi dissident named by the United States as the chief suspect in the terrorist attacks [on 11 September] on the World Trade Center [in New York] and the Pentagon [in Washington].

(*IHT*, 19 September 2001, p. 8)

All the main rebel commanders remain at large, including the Jordanian-born Khattab, one of the handful of outsiders on the Chechen side and reputedly a close friend of Osama bin Laden's. Russian intelligence said this week that one of the suicide attackers in America was a veteran of the Chechen war.

(*The Economist*, 22 September 2001, p. 38)

'Moscow issued a new demand to Georgia to give up suspected guerrillas sheltering in its territory' (*Guardian*, 19 September 2001, p. 15).

'Russia sent a tough diplomatic note to Georgia demanding the extradition of the "hundreds" of Chechen fighters supposedly sheltering there, as well as the closure of a Chechen information centre in Tbilisi' (*The Economist*, 22 September 2001, p. 38).

Russian prosecutor general Vladimir Ustinov has announced that ... Osama bin Laden ... has been actively supporting Khattab and Basayev in their fight against the 'infidels' ... In a recent interview Russian defence minister Sergei Ivanov ... [said] 'We have reliable, confirmed reports that Khattab is a close aide to Osama bin Laden and does his best to link his operations with the Taleban's plans.'

(*Trud*, 20 September 2001, p. 3: *CDSP*, 2001, vol. 53, no. 38, p. 4)

The Russian foreign ministry yesterday [18 September] sent Tbilisi an unprecedentedly harsh note accusing Georgia of abetting terrorism ... In it Moscow states that 'despite numerous requests from Russia hundreds of terrorists' ... have not been handed over. Russia demands the 'immediate extradition of those responsible for terrorist attacks, bombings of civilian facilities, hostage-taking and armed resistance to the authorities'. The Pankisi Gorge is termed a 'logistics base for international terrorists', while the 'mission and information centre of the Chechen Republic of Ichkeria' operating in Georgia are described as 'rebel supply' channels ... Boris

Nemtsov ... late last week ... said since Georgia was incapable of solving the problem itself, it should agree to allow Russian servicemen to take part in operations ... Georgia declared categorically that it would 'not allow its territory to be used for military operations by foreign states'. That was on Friday [14 September]. But on Monday Georgia's leaders said that they were willing to make their military bases available to the United States.

(CDSP, 2001, vol. 53, no. 38, p. 20)

24 September 2001. President Putin:

Events in Chechnya cannot be viewed out of the context of international terrorism. At the same time we realize that these events have their own unique causes and background. I believe that there may still be people in Chechnya who took up arms under the influence of false and misguided values. At a time when the civilized world has taken a stance on terrorism, each individual has to determine where he stands. This opportunity must also be given to those who have yet to lay down their arms in Chechnya. I therefore call on everyone serving in illegal armed units as well as those who call themselves political leaders to break off all contact with international terrorists and their organizations at once. These people should contact official representatives of the federal authorities within seventy-two hours to discuss the following procedures whereby the illegal armed units and groups will disarm, and procedures whereby these individuals may join civilian life in Chechnya ... These contacts will be handled by Viktor Kazantsev, the Russian Federation president's authorized representative in the Southern Federal District, which includes Chechnya.

(CDSP, 2001, vol. 53, no. 39, p. 1)

The president's offer brought a positive reaction from Aslan Maskhadov, the elected president of Chechnya, who named Akhmad Zakayev, the deputy prime minister of his separatist government, as a negotiator with Viktor Kazantsev ... President Vladimir Putin's special representative for the region.

(FT, 27 September 2001, p. 12)

25 September 2001. Chancellor Gerhard Schröder of Germany (speaking during a visit to Germany by President Putin): 'Regarding Chechnya, there will and must be a more differentiated evaluation in world opinion' (*IHT*, 26 September 2001, p. 6).

26 September 2001. President George W. Bush: 'To the extent that there are terrorists in Chechnya, Arab terrorists associated with the al-Qaeda organization, I believe they ought to be brought to justice. We do believe there are some al-Qaeda folks in Chechnya' (*IHT*, 28 September 2001, p. 3).

A spokesman for President George W. Bush:

The Chechen leadership, like all responsible political leaders around the world, must immediately and unconditionally cut all contact with international terrorist groups such as Osama bin Laden and the Qaeda organization ... The United States has always said that only a political process can resolve the conflict in Chechnya and we welcome the steps by the Russians to engage the Chechen leadership. Respect for human rights and accountability for violations on all sides are crucial to a durable peace.

(*IHT*, 27 September 2001, p. 4)

('Last week it [the Bush administration] delivered a tough message to the exiled Chechen foreign minister demanding that the rebel leadership break off relations with two Chechen commanders who represent the movement's radical Islamic faction. And this week it is telling the visiting president of Georgia, Eduard Shevardnadze ... that he must ... [take] action against Chechen militants in Georgia': *IHT*, Friday 5 October 2001, p. 8. 'Georgia is handing over thirteen people detained on its northern border who Russia claims are Chechen fighters': *The Economist*, 6 October 2001, p. 42.)

Nato secretary-general George Robertson ... made a sympathetic remark last week after a meeting of Russian and Nato defence ministers. Although Chechnya was not discussed at the meeting, he said 'there has always been an understanding' in the West for Russia's predicament.

(*IHT*, Tuesday 2 October 2001, p. 8)

'Russia ... has consistently linked the insurgency with Islamic militancy, portraying the rebels as "terrorists" trained and funded from abroad' (*IHT*, 27 September 2001, p. 4).

27 September 2001. 'Chechen rebel envoys have contacted the Russian authorities about possible talks on disarmament ... Viktor Kazantsev ... said he had spoken with representatives of ... Aslan Maskhadov' (*IHT*, 28 Septemebr 2001, p. 4).

'Russian officials have increasingly stressed the role of foreign Islamic fundamentalists in supplying funds and fighters in Chechnya ... Although others suggest that such contributions are modest' (*FT*, 28 September 2001, p. 12).

3 October 2001. President Putin (speaking in Brussels):

For us there are obvious links between international terrorism and those who have taken up arms to resolve whatever problems there might be in the Northern Caucasus, above all in Chechnya ... [The bombings of Russian apartment blocks in 1999 bore] the same signature as the suicide plane attacks on New York and Washington.

(*Guardian*, 4 October 2001, p. 8)

'The EU dropped a sentence evoking its concerns on human rights in Chechnya from its joint declaration with Russia' (*The Times*, 4 October 2001, p. 10).

'The official EU statement yesterday [3 October] simply called for a "political solution" to the conflict' (*Daily Telegraph*, 4 October 2001, p. 10).

'A year ago 24 per cent of Russians named policy towards Chechnya as one of the things they admired most about Mr Putin. Early this year [2001] that figure had fallen to 7 per cent' (*FT*, 6 October 2001, p. 13).

24 October 2001.

> A top aide to ... Aslan Maskhadov ... proposed Wednesday [24 October] to open talks with the Kremlin on disarming the rebels and ending the two-year-old war ... Viktor Kazantsev said he had received the offer by telephone Wednesday ... Mr Kazantsev said ... that the proposal came without conditions and that he expected discussions to be held in Moscow within ten days ... But ... Sergei Yastrzhembsky ... said talks with Mr Maskhadov's government did not rise to the level of a dialogue between the warring sides ... Privately the United States is known to have sent Mr Maskhadov a blunt message in recent weeks: either renounce the extremists who have seized control of the Chechen rebellion and, Russia charges, his political structure, or face American isolation as well ... [The Russian army has] suspended a number of officers in Chechnya after surveys of some sixty military checkpoints on the province's roads uncovered widespread extortion and abuse of civilians ... Last week the military named a new commander for its armed forces in Chechnya, General Vladimir Moltenskoi, who drew praise as someone 'who strictly follows the letter and spirit of the law' from the head of the pro-Russian Chechen regional government.
>
> (*IHT*, 25 October 2001, p. 7)

'Viktor Kazantsev ... said he had been approached by Akhmed Zakayev ... with a request for a meeting in Moscow to discuss disarmament. But Mr Zakayev said that Russia's demand for the rebels to disarm before peace talks had not been accepted' (*The Times*, 25 October 2001, p. 21).

'Russia dropped all preconditions for talks with Chechen rebels and opened negotiations Sunday [18 November] ... A Maskhadov envoy, Akhmed Zakayev, flew from Istanbul and met ... Viktor Kazantsev [in Moscow]' (*IHT*, 19 November 2001, p. 5).

'Chechen rebels and the Russian authorities met yesterday [18 November] for their first official talks since the war between them began two years ago' (*Guardian*, 19 November 2001, p. 14).

[This was] the first serious dialogue ... since 1999' (*FT*, 19 November 2001, p. 6).

> President Putin [on 17 November] ... said 500 mercenaries 'from Arab countries' had already been killed in Chechnya, many of them already reliably identified; and that a further 500–700 'from different Islamic states' were still fighting there ... Northern Alliance commanders [in Afghanistan] have estimated that several hundred Chechens have been fighting on the side of the Taleban ... Five men allegedly trained by Khattab were convicted of plotting bomb attacks on Russian cities, but the trial, in Stavropol, took place behind closed doors.
>
> (*FT*, 19 November 2001, p. 6)

Nato's secretary-general, Lord Robertson [said on 23 November 2001 on a visit to Moscow that] 'We have certainly come to see the scourge of terrorism in Chechnya with different eyes' ... adding that the West still 'disagreed' with Russia over its handling of the Chechnya war.

(*Guardian*, 24 November 2001, p. 6)

14 December 2001.

[Boris] Berezovsky accused Russia's secret services of organizing the Moscow apartment explosions in 1999 which triggered the second Chechen war and helped Mr Putin win the election as president. He had in previous interviews said he had no evidence of any such link.

(*FT*, 18 December 2001, p. 14)

25 December 2001.

Salman Raduyev, a Chechen warlord, was jailed for life by a court in Makhachkala, the capital of Dagestan ... after being convicted of terrorism and taking hostages. In 1996 he led an armed raid on a hospital in Kizlar in which seventy-eight people were killed.

(*The Times*, 26 December 2001, p. 12)

9 January 2002.

Russia said Wednesday [9 January 2002] that its troops had killed ninety-two rebels in a month-long crackdown in Chechnya, one of the bloodiest ... for more than a year ... [Russia] said five Russian servicemen were killed ... in the crackdown, which targeted a host of settlements south-east of ... Grozny.

(*IHT*, 10 January 2002, p. 6)

Yesterday [9 January] one of the biggest engagements for months was completed by Russian special forces. Acting on intelligence that terrorist attacks were planned for New Year's Eve, federal forces conducted operations in four areas ... culminating in the blockade of Argun ... The rebels say that they have lost no fighters but more than fifty Russians were killed.

(*The Times*, 10 January 2002, p. 14)

22 January 2002.

Russian soldiers beat, robbed and tortured civilians in the Chechen village of Tsotsin-Yurt in a four-day spree of lawlessness over the New Year's holiday that left at least three villagers dead, according to a new report by Memorial, Russia's leading human rights group. Six other villagers arrested by the Russian troops are missing, according to the report, which was issued Tuesday [22 January] ... What the army termed its 'mopping up operation' in Tsotsin-Yurt began 30 December [2001] and ended 3 January [2002] ... A Kremlin spokesman said Russian soldiers had killed more than ninety rebels ... As of April [2001] Russian prosecutors had opened 358 investigations into alleged human rights violations committed against Chechen civilians, according to Human Rights Watch, a New York-based organization ... But only about one-fifth of those cases are being actively investigated and very few have resulted in charges against soldiers, according to the group.

(*IHT*, 23 January 2002, p. 6)

24 January 2002.

Russia stepped up its diplomatic offensive Thursday [24 January] ... accusing the United States of taking an 'unfriendly step' by receiving a separatist envoy ... Moscow earlier this week denounced a meeting between a British Foreign Office official and an envoy from ... Aslan Maskhadov.

(*IHT*, 25 January 2002, p. 5)

Russian troops are killing civilians in a campaign of executions and looting that takes place alongside military operations aimed at destroying rebel forces, according to Chechen police officials ... On a visit to Paris this month [January] President Vladimir Putin asserted that Russian troops were being held accountable for violence against Chechen civilians. 'About twenty servicemen have already been brought to justice,' he said.

(*IHT*, 25 January 2002, p. 2)

27 January 2002.

A Russian deputy minister and thirteen others were killed Sunday [27 January] when a military helicopter carrying senior police officials crashed in Chechnya ... There was immediate speculation, unconfirmed by the Kremlin, that it could have been hit by a missile fired from the ground ... 'The exact reason for the explosion has not yet been established' ... [the] head of the federal security service in Chechnya was quoted as saying ... The helicopter carried General Mikhail Rudchenko, a deputy interior minister responsible for security in southern Russia ... [who] headed interior ministry forces for the region and was Russia's top police official for Chechnya ... [Included among the dead were] two interior ministry generals and three colonels ... A contact between the Kremlin and a rebel representative last November [2001] at a Moscow airport failed to produce concrete results.

(*IHT*, 28 January 2002, p. 5)

The Council of Europe last week condemned Russia's slow progress in prosecuting troops and officers for suspected war crimes against civilians, in particular for alleged mass killings ... Akhmed Zakayev, special envoy of ... Aslan Maskhadov, addressed the council and urged it to press Moscow back to the talks. Moscow also protested after Mr Zakayev talked to British officials in London ... Mr Zakhayev led the Chechen side last November [2001] ... Akhmed Zakhayev: 'Viktor Kazantsev, President Putin's representative, had just one message: to lay down our weapons. We proposed an immediate ceasefire, an end to Russia's armed "sweeps" through populated areas and the establishment of a joint Chechen–Russian commission to continue the talks. The Russians merely asked us to give up our weapons. We cannot accept capitulation. Kazantsev said further meetings could be held. However, since then we have heard nothing and we believe hardliners in the army convinced Putin to give them time to finish the war off. The sweeps have intensified since November. After 11 September we had a meeting with US officials and told them we were ready to co-operate in the search for terrorists and would hand over any who are in Chechnya. There has been a lot of talk of Chechen volunteers in Afghanistan but not one Chechen has been found, dead or alive, as part of al-Qaeda or Taleban forces.'

(*Guardian*, 28 January 2002, p. 14)

1 February 2002.

Boris Berezovsky [in London] says that he is just weeks away from laying out documentary evidence that Russia's security services were involved in apartment-house explosions in September 1999 that killed more than 300 people ... He said his investigation of the bombings, for which separatists in Chechnya were blamed and which triggered a full-scale invasion [of Chechnya] ... was the reason Nikolai Patrushev, Russia's intelligence chief, accused him last week of providing financial support to Chechen 'terrorists' ... Mr Patrushev said ... that his bureau had information that Mr Berezovsky was involved in financing Chechen rebels ... Though dozens of arrests were made no one has been convicted of direct complicity in the unsolved bombings.

(*IHT*, 2 February 2002, p. 2)

5 March 2002.

Boris Berezovsky [in London] ... said Tuesday [5 March] that President Putin knew that the country's special services were involved in the bombing of apartment houses in Moscow and other cities in September 1999 in which nearly 300 people died ... [But] he offered extremely sketchy and circumstantial evidence suggesting that the authorities were behind the bombings to get Putin elected.

(*IHT*, 6 March 2002, p. 5)

Boris Berezovsky:

I am sure the bombings were organized by the FSB [federal security service]. It's not just speculation. It's a clear conclusion. I am not saying Mr Putin gave an order to blow up those buildings. I'm saying that at least he knew the FSB was involved ... At a minimum he knew, he was aware of the FSB's participation.

(*Guardian*, 6 March 2002, p. 16; *IHT*, 6 March 2002, p. 5)

At a block of flats in Ryazan [in 1999] ... a resident alerted police after seeing three suspicious people unloading bags into a basement a few days after the first explosion in Moscow. The next day the interior minister said the police had defused a timing device after finding explosives in the bags.

But when the new FSB chief said the bags contained sugar and had been planted as a drill to test police vigilance, the hunt for suspects was called off ... Officials say they know who carried out the bombings and maintain they were 'Chechen terrorists', but the only two suspects to come to court are non-Chechens. They were acquitted last year [2001].

(*Guardian*, 6 March 2002, p. 16)

No one has been convicted for the attacks, but suspicions of an official cover-up were raised after ... [the Ryazan incident]' (*The Times*, 6 March 2002, p. 20).

The Chechen rebel leadership is pushing for the creation of a war crimes tribunal to deal with alleged atrocities by Russian forces, a senior Chechen representative said Friday [8 March] ... 'Those who committed genocide against the Chechen people must answer for their crimes,' said Akhmed Zakayev, chief envoy of ... Aslan Maskhadov.

(*IHT*, 9 March 2002, p. 3)

12 March 2002. 'Mary Robinson [UN High Commissioner for Human Rights] accused Russia on Tuesday [12 March] of failing to meet international demands for "credible" investigations of possible killings, torture and looting by its forces in Chechnya' (*IHT*, 13 March 2002, p. 4).

15 March 2002.

Russian lawmakers have opened a new dialogue with Chechen political figures in hopes of setting terms for direct talks between President Putin and rebel leaders ... Informal talks [are to take place] in Moscow this month ... The new dialogue ... was organized by the Council of Europe's parliamentary assembly ... The forum, called the Chechen Consultative Council, is made up of pro-Russian Chechens, Chechens living abroad, intellectuals and pro-independence militants. It met for the first time in the Russian parliament building on 15 March and was attended by some Chechens who supported the rebellion.

(*IHT*, 16 March 2002, p. 5)

2 April 2002.

Russia's foreign ministry summoned a senior US diplomat on Tuesday [2 April], saying that plans of Radio Liberty – funded by the United States – to broadcast to Chechnya amounted to propaganda and endangered improving relations. Radio Liberty, whose anti-communist programmes Moscow repeatedly jammed during Soviet days, said it would broadcast starting Wednesday [3 April] in local languages.

(*IHT*, 3 April 2002, p. 3)

19 April 2002.

The [UN's] annual Commission on Human Rights ... absolved Russia from accusations of widespread abuses in Chechnya on Friday [19 April] ... [It thus] reversed its stance of the past two years and rejected an EU resolution condemning Moscow for alleged summary executions, torture and other violations by just one vote. The defeated text, co-sponsored by countries including the United States, also condemned abuses by Chechen fighters.

(*IHT*, 20 April 2002, p. 3)

'The defeated text, co-sponsored by the EU and the USA, also condemned "all terrorist attacks, kidnappings and executions" by Chechen fighters' (*FT*, 20 April 2002, p. 6).

25 April 2002. Russia claims that Khattab (Omar ibn al-Khattab) was killed in March. The claim was initially denied by the rebels but later confirmed. Khattab died after opening a poisoned letter. 'Khattab [was] a Saudi national born in Jordan' (*FT*, 1 May 2002, p. 6).

28 April 2002.

A bomb tore through a market [in Vladikavkaz] ... Sunday [28 April], killing seven people ... The bombing was the latest in a series of market blasts that have killed about seventy people in this [southern Russian] city over the last three years.

(*IHT*, 29 April 2002, p. 3)

(Once again it was uncertain whether the blast was linked with Chechen rebels or local criminals.)

'Putin has recently scrapped his token offer of negotiations with the Chechen rebel leadership' (*IHT*, 30 April 2002, p. 8).

1 May 2002. 'Russia's military says it has killed Shamil Basayev ... But it said that "so far" Basayev's body had not been found' (*IHT*, 2 May 2002, p. 4).

9 May 2002. A bomb explodes in Kaspiisk (Dagestan) during a military parade commemorating Victory Day (over the Nazis). At least thirty-four people are killed, including at least twelve children. President Putin blamed Chechen rebels, but no one claimed responsibility. (The death toll was later put at forty-one, including twenty-one servicemen playing in a band and at least thirteen children.) In November 1996 sixty-eight residents of a military block of flats were killed in an explosion in November 1996.

25 June 2002.

Sergei Ivanov, Russia's defence minister, yesterday [25 June] ruled out a fresh offer of a peace plan with rebel leaders ... as he accused them of planning an attack on Grozny. Aslan Maskhadov ... called on the leaders of the world's leading economic nations to intervene in an effort to launch political negotiations.

(*FT*, 26 June 2002, p. 8)

Russia turned down an offer by ... Aslan Maskhadov on Tuesday [25 June] for talks to end almost three years of war, saying it had seized documents linking him to international terrorism. The independent radio station

Ekho Moskvy reported that it had received a letter from Maskhadov to President Vladimir Putin proposing fresh contacts and a ceasefire on 15 July.

(*IHT*, 26 June 2002, p. 12)

'[On 24 June President Putin] noted that efforts were under way to hold a constitutional referndum to end the conflict in Chechnya' (p. 3).

A respected Russian polling firm says that 62 per cent of Russians support entering into negotiations with the Chechen resistance, a dramatic turnaround from just two years ago, when only 22 per cent favoured talks and 72 per cent supported continuation of the war.

(Zbigniew Brzezinski, Alexander Haig and Max Kampelman, *IHT*,
25 June 2002, p. 6)

25 July 2002.

Alexander Litvinenko ... a former Russian security agent ... [said] in Britain, where he was granted asylum last year [2001] ... [discusses what he says is a] statement from Achimez Gochiyayev, who Russian authorities claim was paid $500,000 by a Chechen warlord to organize bombings in Moscow in 1999. The purported statement includes Gochiyayev's admission that he rented space in the two Moscow apartment buildings that were bombed, at the request of a childhood friend he now suspects was an agent with the Russian Security Service, to store goods the friend was selling. This implied that some of the stored items may have included materials for the bombs.

(*IHT*, 26 July 2002, p. 10)

Alexander Litvinenko, a [former] Federal Security Service lieutenant-colonel, sought political asylum in Britain in 2000 ... Last month [June] a military court sentenced him to three-and-a-half years' imprisonment after trying him in absentia ... [He claimed on 18 July] to have located and received information from Achimez Gochiyayev, the man named by the FSB as chief suspect in the bombings case. The FSB has been hunting Mr Gochiyayev for two years, describing him as the leader of a Chechen terrorist band. Mr Litvinenko ... [said] that Mr Gochiyayev has 'explained in detail what had happened in Moscow', where the worst bombings took place ... Mr Litvinenko fled Russia after claiming the FSB ordered him to kill Boris Berezovsky ... [who] has accused the FSB of organizing the 1999 bombings to create a climate of fear and so help Mr Putin, an ex-KGB officer, to win the presidency.

(*FT*, 20 July 2002, p. 6)

29 July 2002. 'The United Nations said it was indefinitely suspending its humanitarian operations in Chechnya, following the kidnapping there of a Russian aid worker employed by a local organization' (*IHT*, 30 July 2002, p. 5).

'The regional head of the Russian charity Druzhba (Friendship) was seized on 23 July' (*Guardian*, 30 July 2002, p. 10).

'The only [UN] programme that will not be suspended is one that provides fresh water to ... Grozny' (*The Times*, 30 July 2002, p. 16).

19 August 2002. A huge Russian military transport helicopter is shot down near Grozny by Chechen rebels. It landed in a minefield. The death toll was 116, including an army nurse and her child. Twenty-eight people, including the crew of five, survived. (The final death toll was 127: *IHT*, 8 May 2003, p. 3.)

> [This was] the single largest loss of life suffered by the Russians since they went to war in the breakaway republic three years ago ... [Official figures show that] 114 people died in the crash out of a total of 147 aboard a helicopter built to carry eighty [eighty-two] ... All five crew members were among the thirty-three survivors ... The previous worst day in the war was in February 2000 when eighty-four paratroopers were ambushed and killed while fighting in the Argun Gorge.
>
> (*IHT*, 21 August 2002, pp. 1, 4)

'The Mi-26 transport helicopter was carrying almost twice as many people as its capacity, with 147 on board, including one child and three women, compared with a maximum of eighty-five for which it was designed' (*FT*, 21 August 2002, p. 5).

'[This was] Russia's worst military aviation disaster ... [The helicopter was] carrying mostly officers' (*The Independent*, 21 August 2002, p. 9).

> President Vladimir Putin [on 22 August] sharply criticized Russia's military commanders ... bluntly blaming dereliction of duty for the catastrophic crash ... [He] disclosed that the defence ministry had banned the use of helicopters like the one that crashed from transporting troops in 1997, limiting them to cargo flights ... 'How could it happen that, despite a defence ministry order banning the use of helicopters from carrying people, people were still being carried?' Putin asked.
>
> (*IHT*, 23 August 2002, p. 3)

> Well before the helicopter crash it was clear the Chechen war was flaring up, not cooling down. On 15 August guerrillas attacked eight villages simultaneously. Their hit-and-run attacks have been killing a dozen soldiers a week ... Aslan Maskhadov last month [July 2002] ... [named] an old rival, the fiery Shamil Basayev, to head his defence council.
>
> (*The Economist*, 24 August 2002, p. 34)

26 August 2002.

> Chechen rebels ... asked yesterday [26 August] for peace talks with the Kremlin and said they would accept direct rule from Moscow. Akhmed Zakayev, the representative of ... Aslan Maskhadov, disclosed that the Chechen leadership had called for the introduction of direct presidential rule during talks with federal authorities last autumn [2001] ... Mr Zakayev [said]:

'Direct presidential rule is needed at least for now, when no laws are effective in Chechnya, neither Russian nor international. Lawlessness is rampant.'

(*Daily Telegraph*, 27 August 2002, p. 12)

9 September 2002.

The United Nations said yesterday [9 September] it was resuming its humanitarian programmes in Chechnya after a six-week suspension in protest at the kidnapping of an aid worker. The UN halted relief operations on 29 July following the kidnap of … [the] head of Druzhba, a non-governmental organization that works with the body. During the suspension the UN continued its clean water programme for residents of Grozny.

(*FT*, 10 September 2002, p. 10)

4 October 2002.

President Vladimir Putin on Friday [4 October] repealed the [27 August 1991 presidential] decree granting the US-funded Radio Liberty special permission to operate in Russia, culminating years of tension over the station's unstinting coverage of the bloody war in Chechnya. The revocation of the decree … will not force Radio Liberty to leave and may have little practical effect as the station can still operate under normal laws governing foreign news organizations … The dispute escalated with the start of Chechen-language broadcasts in April … Russian authorities arrested a Radio Liberty reporter, Andrei Babitsky, 2000 … only to release him later.

(*IHT*, 5 October 2002, p. 3)

23–26 October 2002. Over fifty Chechen rebels, heavily armed and threatening to use explosives, take over a 1,100-seat theatre in Moscow, demanding the withdrawal of Russian troops from Chechnya. Nearly 800 were in the audience.

Some hostages were allowed to leave, including children under fifteen and some women, Moslems and foreigners. There were about seventy-five foreigners among the audience. The Chechens gave the authorities a week to negotiate and then set a 6 a.m. 26 October deadline for the withdrawal of Russian troops to begin. Otherwise hostages would start being executed.

President Putin (24 October): '[The incident was planned by] foreign terrorist centres … The same people planned the terrorist act in Moscow [i.e. those who planned the terrorist acts in Bali – Indonesia – and the Philippines recently]' (*FT*, 25 October 2002, p. 1; *IHT*, 25 October 2002, p. 10).

There followed a pre-dawn attack by Russian special forces on Saturday 26 October An initially unrevealed sedative gas was used to flood the theatre before the attack. (It was not until 30 October that it was officially revealed that the gas was an opiate-based narcotic used as an anaesthetic.)

Five hostages were killed by gunfire (including one woman who tried to enter the theatre after the siege started). The rest of the 129 hostages (including eight foreigners) who did not survive died because of the effects of the gas. The 646 hostages who were rescued were hospitalized and even doctors were not initially told the name of the gas. The hostages were kept in seclusion. Forty-one rebels (including nineteen women) were killed, but several were captured or escaped. The surviving rebels did not detonate their explosives. No members of the Russian special forces were killed.

Although popular opinion in Russia generally rallied strongly around President Putin, there was criticism about the use of the gas (especially in such vast quantities), the initial secrecy surrounding the exact type of gas, the seeming lack of medical preparedness to treat those affected and the danger that the rebels would still have time to use their explosives if they so wished. There was also the issue of how such a large band of rebels were not detected before they reached the Moscow theatre.

> Much of the criticism ... has centred on the secrecy around the use of the gas and the failure to have enough of a proven antidote ready. All the ambulances carried the drug, called Naloxone, but were soon overwhelmed by the number of victims.
>
> (*IHT*, 2 November 2002, p. 2)

> While many in the theatre were put to sleep immediately, some surviving hostages have said they noticed a smell or a mist at least a minute or so before passing out. That would mean that the guerrillas had enough time to detonate their explosives but did not.
>
> (*IHT*, 1 November 2002, p. 3)

> One of the hostages suddenly rose from his seat and lunged forward ... A guerrilla opened fire and the man was struck in the eye. The guerrillas called the command centre and asked the medics to evacuate the man. Fatefully, however, the gunmen did not make clear that the shooting had been a spontaneous eruption of violence and not the beginning of executions ... Not all of the guerrillas succumbed to the gas. There was intense fighting ... Several grenades exploded, but none of the guerrillas' explosives
>
> (*IHT*, 2 November 2002, p. 2)

President Putin thanks international leaders for 'support in the fight against our common enemy – international terrorism'.

Aslan Maskhadov said he felt responsible for those 'who resorted to self-sacrifice in despair' though the rebels had nothing to do with official policy. He rejected 'terror as a method of reaching any goals'. His spokesman said: 'We cannot come down to the level of our [Russian military] opponents, targeting innocent people.'

Aslan Maskhadov: 'There is no military solution ... There is one reasonable, correct step – to sit down at the negotiating table. All the rest is death, blood, hostages and the death of absolutely innocent people' (*The Times*, 29 October 2002, p. 13).

A spokesman for Aslan Maskhadov: 'Maskhadov, as before, is ready without any preconditions, to sit down at the negotiating table. It is up to the Russian leadership' (*IHT*, 29 October 2002, p. 5).

President Putin (28 October):

> International terrorism is becoming bolder, acting more cruelly, and here
> and there around the world threats of the use of means comparable to
> weapons of mass destruction are heard. If anyone tries to use such means in
> relation to our country, Russia will answer with measures adequate to the
> threat to the Russian Federation – in all places where the terrorists, the
> organizers of these crimes or their ideological or financial sponsors are
> located. I emphasize: wherever they may be.
>
> (*Guardian*, 29 October 2002, p. 4)

> The war between the Russian and the Chechens has been going on since
> 1783, when Catherine the Great proclaimed the Caucasus to be Russia's,
> and Russian troops began to try to enforce that claim in what until then had
> been a region of tribal societies and tribal authority ... The Chechens and
> their Ingush minority were Catherine's most ferocious opponents. They
> fought conquest until 1859 ... [and] fought Russian occupation until 1917.
>
> (William Pfaff, *IHT*, 31 October 2002, p. 5)

29 October 2002.

> [The arrest takes place] in Denmark of Akhmed Zakayev, the top European
> representative of Aslan Maskhadov ... Mr Zakayev was ... the main speaker
> at the World Chechen Congress [in Copenhagen] ... The Danish police were
> acting on an Interpol warrant issued at Russia's request in October last year
> [2001]. A Danish judge ordered Mr Zakayev to be held in custody for thirteen
> days while he studied the huge dossier provided by the Russian authorities.
> The police said that the Russians had accused Mr Zakayev of helping to
> prepare last week's theatre seizure in Moscow and of taking part in other 'ter-
> rorist' acts between 1996 and 1999 ... The long-planned Chechen Congress
> ... was moved to Denmark after Turkey gave in to Russian pressure not to
> allow it ... President Putin responded this week by cancelling a state visit to
> Denmark and persuading the EU to move its summit meeting with Russia
> next month from Copenhagen to Brussels. Denmark holds the EU presidency.
>
> (*Guardian*, 31 October 2002, p. 16)

'Mr Zakayev is a senior aide to Aslan Maskhadov ... Both men have condemned the raid in Moscow as the work of an extremist rebel faction' (*The Independent*, 31 October 2002, p. 14).

> Mr Zakayev was quicker to condemn the theatre assault than Mr Maskhadov
> and had long spoken out against terrorist attacks on civilian targets. A senior
> US diplomat indicated in Moscow this week he had independent informa-
> tion connecting Mr Maskhadov to Shamil Basayev.
>
> (*FT*, 31 October 2002, p. 8)

> Mr Maskhadov over the summer did what many think was inevitable: he
> reunited the rebel factions and gave government posts to radical command-

ers. That step ... lost him all stock with the Russian government – and the American one, which publicly distanced itself from him. The hostage-takers claimed that Mr Maskhadov took part in the planning, or at least knew of it ... Mr [Shamil] Basayev ... was named by the hostage-takers as their 'supreme military emir'.

(*The Economist*, 2 November 2002, p. 31)

('[On 3 December] Denmark freed [Akhmed Zakayev] ... "Taking into account the character and the content of the witnesses' statements, as well as the circumstances in relation to these statements, the Danish Ministry of Justice has found the evidence [presented by Russia] to be insufficient in order to allow for extradition," the statement said ... The four-page report said that Russian prose-cutors had initially linked Zakayev to the [theatre] siege ... based primarily on the fact that he had granted interviews to the media during the crisis. It also said that prosecutors interviewed witnesses of crimes he was accused of committing only after he had been arrested, even though the alleged crimes took place between 1996 and 1999. And it said that those interviews suffered "from lack of precision" about the crimes themselves, let alone Zakayev's role in them, and that they appeared to rely heavily on hearsay': *IHT*, 4 December 2002, p. 3. 'In an interview after his release [in Denmark] he [Zakayev] called the siege a tragedy that scuttled quiet efforts to negotiate an end to the conflict. "It brought to naught, for all practical purposes, all the work I had done for a year and a half," he said ... Zakayev has not been in Chechnya since early 2000, when he was badly injured in a car accident ... At the time he was commander of a special military brigade organized by Maskhadov. After he recovered, in 2001, Maskhaov appointed him his chief envoy and spokesman in exile. In November 2001, two months after Russia issued an international warrant for his arrest, he met with a Kremlin envoy, General Viktor Kazantsev, at an airport in Moscow. This year he has met unofficially with other Russian officials in Liechtenstein and Switzerland, including Chechnya's only deputy in parliament, Aslambek Aslakhanov, and the former chairman of Russia's security council, Ivan Rybkin': *IHT*, 10 December 2002, p. 8. On 6 December Akhmed Zakayev was arrested in London and then quickly released on bail.)

31 October 2002.

Phone calls between guerrillas inside the theatre and compatriots in Chech-nya and elsewhere during the siege 'clearly indicate that Mr Maskhadov was fully informed about what was happening', said Sergei Yastrzhembsky, a special assistant for Chechen affairs to President Vladimir Putin. 'And the people who were in the concert hall also acted with his being aware of what they were doing' ... One tape played Thursday [31 October] purportedly captured Movsar Barayev, the leader of the hostage-takers, speaking to an ally [named as Zelimkhan Yandarbiyev] in Qatar during the siege ... Accord-ing to the Russian translation of the conversation in the Chechen language, the men said the operation was being conducted 'with the recognition of

Shamil [Basayev]' and that 'when the operation was prepared Aslan and Shamil were present'.

(*IHT*, 1 November 2002, p. 3)

Russian officials played crackly tapes of intercepted telephone conversations ... In one ... a man identified as ... Movsar Barayev said 'Shamil' ... was present during preparations for the hostage-taking raid. 'Shamil was acting on Aslan's instructions,' the voice said.

(*The Independent*, 1 November 2002, p. 14)

[On 1 November] a Chechen website published what it claimed to be a statement in which ... Shamil Basayev assumed responsibility for directing the theatre raid ... Basayev claimed the attack was planned without the knowledge of Maskhadov ... He asked Maskhadov's forgiveness for preparing the raid in secret and said he would resign from all posts in the rebel hierarchy ... Moscow has alleged that he [Basayev] planned the attack with the approval of Aslan Maskhadov.

(*IHT*, 2 November 2002, pp. 1–2)

'Maskhadov had appointed him [Basayev] the head of the Chechen military committee in August, apparently in an effort to unify factions fighting the Russians' (*IHT*, 10 December 2002, p. 8).

1 November 2002.

The State Duma] approved tough new media curbs during 'anti-terrorist' operations, giving the authorities greater control over coverage of crises such as the Moscow theatre siege. The measure ... passed its third reading by a vote of 231 to 106 ... The changes [were] submitted well before the hostage crisis ... The new media rules bar dissemination of information seen as hampering anti-terrorist operations, endangering lives, remarks judged as propaganda or justifying resistance to counter-terrorist measures. The new rules also specifically prevent the media from publishing information about technology, arms, ammunition and explosives used in anti-terrorist operations ... Since the siege the Kremlin has been angry that some media outlets accused authorities of failing to pursue talks with the guerrillas before launching a raid to free about 800 hostages. Critics also questioned the use of a knockout gas ... The authorities banned the private NTV channel from broadcasting a statement by Movsar Barayev.

(*IHT*, 12 November 2002, pp. 1–12)

The Russian Duma ... [allowed] the government to ban all reporting on terrorism and the war in Chechnya ... [The new law] imposes rule on the coverage of any 'anti-terrorist operation which poses a threat to people's lives and health' and gives the Kremlin the power to judge what exceeds the new definition ... Under the new rules the media cannot report the nature of the gas used, nor speculate on whether special forces caused hostage deaths by excessive use … The law prevents the media investigations of human rights abuses at home and in … Chechnya.

(*Daily Telegraph*, 2 November 2002, p. 24)

'Legislative amendments … will curb news coverage of anti-terrorist operations and prohibit the media from carrying rebel statements' (*The Independent*, 2 November 2002, p. 12).

The additions to the law prohibit the media from disseminating information 'about the technology of manufacturing weapons, ammunition, explosives and explosive devices' … They forbid the disclosure of 'special techniques and tactics for conducting a counter-terrorist operation'. Television and newspapers also may not provide information that would hinder such an operation, or print or broadcast statements by individuals seeking to hinder such an operation or 'advocating or justifying resistance' to it. Finally, they are forbidden to reveal any information about people involved in such an operation (on the federal side) without those people's permission.

(*CDSP*, 2002, vol. 54, no. 44, p. 9)

('Russia's parliament has approved [13 November] a draconian new law increasing restrictions on reporting [of the war in Chechnya] … The new law … [which still needs] formal approval from President Putin … would bar the media from carrying reports deemed to hinder anti-terrorist operations and … ban comments "justifying resistance to a counter-terrorist operation"': *The Times*, 14 November 2002, p. 21.)

('Meeting with a group of media executives yesterday [25 November], President Vladimir Putin told them he had vetoed the recently passed amendments to the law on the news media … proposing that a conference committee be set up to "work on the language" … Late last week [20 November] the leaders of Russia's leading media organizations had requested the veto in a special appeal to the president. The president called for striking a balance between restrictions on the press during the crisis and the need to inform the public fully about actions taken by government authorities "so that the state does not start thinking it is infallible". Mr Putin spoke in favour of professional behaviour in crisis situations': *Vremya Novostei*, 26 November 2002, p. 2: *CDSP*, 2002, vol. 54, no. 48, p. 1. Critics expressed doubt that any substantial changes would be made.)

('[In 2002] the Duma began debating amendments to the media law to restrict reporting of "anti-terrorist" events. These would include a ban on reporting "statements of people trying to stop an anti-terrorist operation". Critics feared this would be used as an excuse to strangle all coverage of … the war in Chechnya … [As a result of the Moscow theatre siege] the changes to the media law were quickly passed. Fearing outright censorship, leading editors banded together and, at the press minister's suggestion, petitioned President Vladimir Putin to veto the amendments. He agreed … [A] committee of journalists, MPs and officials has been set up to write an entirely new media law … Given the way the authorities already behave, it is doubtful what difference either the original amendments or a new media law would make in practice': *The Economist*, 11 January 2003, pp. 33–34.)

3 November 2002.

> Sergei Ivanov, the defence secretary, said yesterday [3 November] that Russia was temporarily suspending plans to cut its military presence in Chechnya. 'From today the group of forces in Chechnya has launched broad-scale, tough and targeted special operations in all Chechnya's regions,' he said.
>
> (*The Independent*, 4 November 2002, p. 8)

> Defence minister Ivanov announces [on 3 November] a halt to troop cut-backs ... [and] the start of a new republic-wide 'special operation' ... All told, according to the official figures, the federal forces in the Chechen republic number 70,000 to 80,000 men. The true number could actually be as high as 100,000.
>
> (*CDSP*, 2002, vol. 54, no. 45, p. 1)

> Russia has cancelled plans to cut its troop strength in Chechnya ... His comments seem to reverse orders he outlined after President Vladimir Putin met his senior security chiefs after the end of the Moscow hostage siege ... Russia would withdraw 'excess' troops, Mr Ivanov said then. The interior minister, Boris Brylov, also confirmed plans last week to set up a Chechen police force to take over from Russian police troops ... Unofficial estimates put the number of Russian troops in Chechnya as high as 80,000 ... Access to Chechnya by Russian and foreign correspondents is only permitted under the Kremlin's control.
>
> (*Guardian*, 4 November 2002, p. 15)

> President Vladimir Putin has insisted as recently as this summer that Russia's three-year war in Chechnya was essentially won and that the government could soon begin turning over peacekeeping duties to local forces ... By most estimates about 75,000 to 80,000 Russian forces are in Chechnya, facing a guerrilla army of 2,000 or more. The Kremlin has announced plans to withdraw so-called surplus troops at least three times in the last two years, but the number of federal forces has remained essentially unchanged.
>
> (*IHT*, 4 November 2002, p. 10)

> The Russian authorities earlier this year [2002] pledged to reduce troop numbers within and around Chechnya from the current 80,000, but have already backtracked on such promised reductions several times during the three-year conflict ... Over the past few months there have been several apparent suicide bombings by Chechen women against federal targets, and up to eighteen with explosives strapped to their bodies were present during the Moscow siege.
>
> (*FT*, 4 November 2002, p. 11)

10 November 2002. President Putin: 'Those who choose Maskhadov choose war. Instead of talks he has chosen the path of terror' (*Guardian*, 11 November 2002, p. 15).

11 November 2002. President Putin: '[Chechen rebels are] religious extremists and international terrorists ... [who are determined] to kill all non-Moslems ... all Americans and their allies. If you are a Christian your life is threatened.'

13 November 2002. '[The State Duma] rejected two proposals to create an independent commission to investigate the [theatre] siege' (*IHT*, 14 November 2002, p. 1).

6 December 2002.

> The EU commissioner for humanitarian affairs, accused Russia of a 'serious neglect of humanitarian concerns' in closing camps for Chechens who had fled the conflict into ... Ingushetia 'with no alternative accommodation proposed, in the middle of a harsh winter' ... The US ambassador to Moscow also voiced his concern at reports that those in the camps were returning to Chechnya 'involuntarily', in spite of Russian assurances to the contrary.
> (*FT*, 7 December 2002, p. 7)

> Chechen refugees living in two camps in Ingushetia have been told that the camps will be closed, an activist ... from the Chechen Committee for National Salvation said ... Immigration officers and officials from Grozny gave the warning when they visited the camps yesterday [9 December] ... At least 8,000 people live in the two camps, which will be closed by 20 December ... Last week the US ambassador to Russia said he feared refugees were being coerced into returning when it was unsafe to do so.
> (*The Independent*, 10 December 2002, p. 10)

('Russian forces have begun [26 November] to eject at least 1,000 Chechen refugees from a south-western tent city [in Ingushetia], according to human rights observers ... The government had set a deadline of 21 December for clearing the area of refugees': *IHT*, 29 November 2002, p. 3.)

14 December 2002. 'Salman Raduyev, a Chechen warlord who was serving life ... has died in prison' (*The Times*, 16 December 2002, p. 14). 'He was sentenced to life imprisonment last December [2001]' (*The Independent*, 16 December 2002, p. 8). 'Officials said Raduyev died ... [of] natural causes ... [He] was captured in March 2000' (*IHT*, 16 November 2002, p. 3).

16 December 2002. 'A Russian colonel who admitted murdering [in March 2000] an eighteen-year-old Chechen woman ... [was judged to be] temporarily insane at the time of the killing' (*The Times*, 17 December 2002, p. 14).

'[The colonel] will probably not be jailed' (*Guardian*, 17 December 2002, p. 11).

'Colonel Yuri Budanov [is] the first senior Russian officer to go on trial for crimes against civilians in Chechnya' (*IHT*, 17 December 2002, p. 10).

('Colonel Yuri Budanov ... the first Russian military officer to be charged with abuses in Chechnya ... was pronounced [temporarily] insane and absolved of criminal responsibility by a court yesterday [31 December]. Budanov admitted strangling Elza Kungayeva ... He said he suspected her of being a rebel sniper who had killed some of his comrades ... Military authorities initially accused Budanov of rape and murder, but he was officially charged with murder and abduction. During the trial psychiatrists made four evaluations of Budanov's health. The first team ruled he was sane, the second ruling was never made public and the two most recent examinations concluded he was temporarily insane at the time of the murder ... Also on trial was Lieutenant Ivan Fyodorov, who was found guilty yesterday of abuse of authority for participating in the beating with Budanov of another officer. He was sentenced to three years in jail, but was expected to be freed under an amnesty for people sentenced to three years or less': *The Independent*, 1 January 2003, p. 7. 'Colonel Budanov ... admitted killing Elza Kungayeva ... but he pleaded temporary insanity. The military court accepted his plea and ordered him to undergo psychiatric treatment': *The Times*, 1 January 2003, p. 14.)

18 December 2002.

President Putin dismissed the top general in Chechnya this week. General Troshev left his post as commander of the North Caucasus military district on Wednesday [18 December], apparently for refusing to accept a posting in Siberia. Observers say this could be seen as an attempt by Mr Putin to wrest control from General Troshev, an ethnic Russian who comes from Chechnya. Some reports indicate that the general may want a career in politics ... United Nations officials expressed hope this week that Russia had decided not to close all Chechen refugee camps in Ingushetia by 31 December. But Russian authorities were still said to be urging refugees to leave.

(*FT*, 31 December 2002, p. 6)

27 December 2002.

Suicide bombers ploughed two explosives-laden vehicles through a military perimeter Friday [27 December] and blew up the headquarters of Chechnya's pro-Russian government in Grozny, killing at least forty-six people ... The regional government office, opened ... barely twenty months ago, was among the most heavily protected buildings in the region ... The building was bombed in September 2001, less than five months after it opened, when an explosive left in a women's restroom killed a cleaning lady ... An official of Russia's emergencies ministry said the toll could reach 200 because the blast had heavily damaged a nearby canteen, where as many as 200 people were said to work ... The head of Chechnya's civil administration, Akhmad Kadyrov, and the new prime minister, Mikhail Babich, were both out of the building and were not wounded ... Twenty-two died ... in October ... when a bomb destroyed a police station in Grozny.

(*IHT*, 28 December 2002, pp. 1, 4)

The final death toll was seventy-two (*CDSP*, 2003, vol. 55, nos 1–2, p. 12).

'Aslan Maskhadov ... has denied responsibility and said he rejects suicide bombings as a way of achieving the guerrillas' aims' (*IHT*, 31 December 2002, p. 5).

1 January 2003. 'Russia has refused to extend the mandate of human rights monitors in ... Chechnya. OSCE failed to win an extension for its mission, which expired on 31 December [2002]' (*FT*, 2 January 2002, p. 4).

> Russia has announced that it is shutting down the mission in Chechnya of OSCE, ending any permanent international monitoring in the republic ... Russian officials insisted they would ... renew the mission, which opened in 1995 ... only if its mandate were limited to providing relief aid.
>
> (*IHT*, 2 January 2003, p. 3)

10 January 2003.

> Russia announced Friday [10 January] that it would hold a constitutional referendum in Chechnya on 23 March ... The vote on the new constitution will be followed by presidential and parliamentary elections ... Chechnya will have its own president, but will remain firmly under Moscow's rule. The fifty-page document was published in December [2002] ... [Critics] say the government approved a version that allowed less autonomy than in ... [republics] like Tatarstan.
>
> (*IHT*, 11 January 2003, p. 2)

> Vladimir Putin's plan [is] to hold a referendum on a proposed new constitution in March, followed by new presidential and parliamentary elections ... The idea that a fair test of Chechen opinion can be carried out in the present climate of intimidation is ludicrous. Doubts about the real nature of this exercise have been reinforced by the news that the petition authorizing the referendum obtained the required number of signatures only by including Russian soldiers stationed in Chechnya.
>
> (*IHT*, editorial, 15 January 2003, p. 8)

16 January 2003. 'The European Court of Human Rights agreed Thursday [16 January] to hear six complaints filed by inhabitants of Chechnya who claim the Russian military tortured and indiscriminately killed their relatives ... Russia joined the continent's top human rights watchdog in 1996' (*IHT*, 17 January 2003, p. 3).

Law suits by survivors or relatives of those who died are launched against the Moscow city government for compensation over the Moscow theatre siege. ('Under Russia's 1998 anti-terrorism law it is forbidden to sue the security forces': *The Independent*, 17 January 2003, p. 12.)

16–17 January 2003.

> Boris Jordan ... the American financier who runs Russia's often-embattled NTV television network said Friday [17 January] that he had been dismissed

by the network's state-controlled owner ... Boris Jordan said he had been fired Thursday from his job as chief executive officer of Gazprom Media, a holding company that owns some of Russia's best-known media properties, including NTV and the popular Ekho Moskvy newsradio station. He said he was also told that he would be removed as director-general of NTV, a separate job in which he managed the business affairs of Russia's third-largest broadcast network ... Jordan said ... that he was not told why he had been dismissed, but he made it clear that he believed the move was driven by domestic politics. 'There is an election coming up at the end of the year and NTV takes a very independent position on these things,' he said. Russia's 450-seat lower house of parliament holds elections in December and President Vladimir Putin is widely expected to seek a second term in the spring 2004 presidential election ... Official attitudes towards Jordan appeared to shift dramatically in October [2002], after guerrillas seized hundreds of hostages in a Moscow theatre and NTV aired twenty-four-hour coverage of the crisis and its climax ... The Kremlin accused NTV of endangering the hostages' lives by broadcasting the movements of special forces as they prepared to storm the theatre. Jordan replied that videotapes of the network's coverage proved that the accusation was false.

(*IHT*, 18 January 2003, p. 2)

'And Gazprom ... was said to be unhappy about the network's coverage of corruption in Russia's oil and gas business in Kazakhstan' (*IHT*, 24 January 2003, p. 10).

Mr Jordan, a US citizen, promised an independent editorial line at NTV and surprised many by maintaining news coverage that periodically criticized the government. Its twenty-four-hour coverage of the storming by Russian forces of the Moscow theatre held by Chechens – including interviews with angry relatives of the 129 who died – was widely picked up by foreign and domestic media ... [Jordan's] dismissal sparked fresh concerns for the country's fragile freedom of speech in the buildup to parliamentary elections over the next fourteen months ... Boris Nemtsov, the leader of the liberal SPS party, said yesterday: 'With parliamentary elections this year and presidential elections next year the state is using its influence to control the media.'

(*FT*, 17 January 2003, p. 8)

24 January 2003.

Lord Frank Judd, head of ... the parliamentary assembly of the Council of Europe, the inter-governmental human rights organization ... warned last Friday [24 January 2003] that the situation was not calm enough to allow for a democratic debate on the referendum [on the new constitution for Chechnya to be held on 23 March], and that no observers should be sent for fear of lending authenticity to a process he called 'meaningless'.

(*FT*, 28 January 2003, p. 8)

30 January 2003.

> The Council of Europe's chief negotiator with Russia has offered to resign ...
> Lord Judd, the council's rapporteur on Chechnya, said yesterday [30 January]
> that he would resign from his post if a referendum on the republic's constitu-
> tion went ahead on 23 March: 'The security situation is such that there is no
> way people can meet to discuss [this new constitution]. In the Chechen refugee
> camps in Ingushetia I did not find a single person who has even seen a copy of
> the constitution. If the referendum goes ahead on that date I cannot see any
> way I can remain' ... After a visit to Chechnya last week, Lord Judge said that
> a 'climate of impunity' still reigns in the republic. He pointed out that mass
> killings and abductions by Russian troops had not been investigated properly.
>
> (*Guardian*, 31 January 2003, p. 20)

31 January 2003.

> Yesterday [31 January] his [Lord Judd's] most vocal Russian opponent,
> Dmitri Rogozin ... a senior Russian MP ... said he would resign from the
> ... joint working group set up to engineer a peaceful solution to the conflict
> in Chechnya ... The decision seriously undermines the group's viability ...
> Mr Rogozin resigned and called for the group's dissolution after hearing
> rumours that Lord Judd may reconsider.
>
> (*Guardian*, 1 February 2003, p. 20)

8 February 2003. The Moscow theatre, scene of the Chechen siege, is reopened,
'Mikhail Babich, the recently appointed prime minister, [has] resigned' (*FT*, 10
February 2003, p. 4).

'The man appointed in November [2002] to head the Chechen administration,
Mikhail Babich, said he had resigned ... Babich has had a dispute with his supe-
rior, Akhmad Kadyrov, over personnel issues' (*IHT*, 10 February 2003, p. 4).

10 February 2003.

> Anna Politkovskaya, a Russian journalist ... a reporter with *Novaya Gazeta*
> ... known for her balanced reporting in Chechnya, has won the 2003 Prize
> for Journalism and Democracy, awarded by OSCE ... [She] was asked to
> mediate by Chechen rebels during the siege of a theatre in Moscow in
> October [2002].
>
> (*The Independent*, 11 February 2003, p. 11)

28 February 2003. 'The [US] State Department ... after months of discussion ...
designated three Chechen militant groups as terrorist organizations subject to
American sanctions' (*IHT*, 1 March 2003, p. 5).

> The supreme court has overturned a much-criticized lower court ruling that
> ... Colonel Yuri Budanov ... was not criminally responsible for the killing
> ... of a Chechen woman ... and sent the case for retrial ... [He] is confined
> to a psychiatric hospital by the court ruling in December [2002].
>
> (*Guardian*, 1 March 2003, p. 19)

3 March 2003.

> Russia's defence ministry announced on Monday [3 March] a small troop withdrawal from Chechnya ... More than 1,000 servicemen and 200 pieces of equipment would be leaving ... It was the first clear indication of troop reductions since the ministry announced that Moscow was suspending a planned withdrawal from Chechnya after [the Moscow theatre siege].
>
> *(IHT,* 4 March 2003, p. 6)

'[There is] a rebel attack on the motorcade of the pro-Moscow mayor of Grozny ... Akhmed Kadyrov' *(Guardian,* 4 March 2003, p. 14).

4 March 2003.

> A resolution overwhelmingly adopted by the legal and human rights committee of the Council of Europe's parliamentary assembly said it would consider setting up an ad hoc tribunal modelled on the International Criminal Court for the former Yugoslavia if the Russian authorities did not do more to prosecute war crimes.
>
> *(FT,* 5 March 2003, p. 7)

23 March 2003. A referendum on a new constitution for Chechnya is held.

> The average level of support for all three questions that were put to a vote (concerning the constitution and laws on parliamentary and presidential elections in Chechnya) was around 95 per cent ... On Sunday [23 March] as of 6 p.m. 79.63 per cent of those eligible to vote had cast their ballots ... The referendum was monitored by fifty observers, twenty-eight of them foreigners.
>
> *(CDSP,* 2003, vol. 55, no. 12, p. 12)

'What they [ordinary Chechens] want – above all – is peace and security. That is why, despite the flaws, many were willing to support the referendum: any chance of positive change seems better than none' (Andrew Jack, *FT,* Survey, 1 April 2003, p. vi). 'Many people hope that the adoption of a constitution and the creation of a legal framework will in fact put a stop to lawlessness and restore peace to the republic' (Bakhtiyar Akhmedkhanov, *Vremya MN,* 25 March 2003, pp. 1–2: *CDSP,* 2003, vol. 55, no. 12, p. 11).

'Nearly 90 per cent of voters turned out for a referendum on a new constitution and over 95 per cent of these backed it. So official sources said' *(The Economist,* 29 March 2003, p. 8).

> The authorities declared that 477,000 people turned out ... That would have been 88 per cent of registered voters ... Chechnya's voters (or their phantoms) overwhelmingly approved laws for electing the president and parliament ... Last October's census [2002], according to preliminary figures, found nearly 1.1 million people in Chechnya – a shade more than when the war began – but in the same month the Danish Refugee Council, the aid

agency most active in Chechnya, which does regular population surveys, estimated 785,000.

(pp. 43, 46)

'Chechens [were] drawn by promises from President Putin of compensation for lost homes and handouts to young mothers' (*The Times*, 24 March 2003, p. 16). 'Mr Putin has promised the prospect of financial compensation, amnesties for rebel fighters and significant autonomy' (*FT*, 24 March 2003, p. 9). 'The government suggested that an amnesty for some fighters might be possible' (*IHT*, 24 March 2003, p. 7).

'Some 540,000 people were registered to vote in Chechnya and camps in Ingushetia, including 28,000 of an estimated 80,000 troops stationed in the republic' (*FT*, 24 March 2003, p. 9).

> Only adult Chechens registered within the republic ... which officials of ... Akhmed Kadyrov, the Kremlin-appointed president of Chechnya ... put at just over 500,000 ... will vote. This excludes refugees and the diaspora in other parts of Russia, but includes more than 20,000 Russian soldiers 'permanently' stationed in Chechnya.
>
> (*FT*, 28 January 2003, p. 8)

'An estimated 110,000 Chechens are still in ... refugee camps in Ingushetia, only about half of whom were eligible to vote ... according to the Chechen election commission' (*The Independent*, 24 March 2003, p. 15).

> 'Internally displaced persons' are now facing a new problem: obtaining documents ... A large proportion of refugees simply do not have them – none of any kind. People had to leave their homes so quickly that they were unable to grab and take along their [internal] passports or documents that could be used to get new ones issued – birth certificates, for example ... They will not be able to participate in the referendum because they do not have documents proving their identity ... The issuing of documents ... is done at their place of permanent residence, i.e. in the Chechen republic ... Residents of refugee camps [are] the people who are the most dissatisfied with the authorities.
>
> (*CDSP*, 2003, vol. 55, no. 6, p. 13)

'The Chechen diaspora in Russia are unhappy ... In their opinion ... the [proposed] referendum arrangements ... mean that only people living in the republic would be able to vote' (*CDSP*, 2003, vol. 55, nos 1–2, p. 12).

> A deputy Russian defence minister ... said that a 'maximum of 20,000' troops would cast ballots ... A Putin aide, Sergei Yastrzhembsky, said last month [February] that 37,000 Russian soldiers whose units are permanently stationed in Chechnya would be entitled to vote in the referendum, making up about 7 per cent of Chechnya's approximately 538,000 eligible voters.
>
> (*IHT*, 7 March 2003, p. 5)

[The new constitution] envisages a federal-style presidential system, in a republic of rival clans ... [There have also been criticisms of] the speed with which the constitution has been drafted and the refusal to grant even the degree of autonomy given to some of Russia's other ethnic republics.

(*FT*, 28 January 2003, p. 8)

'The new constitution has automatically excluded any figures with separatist inclinations' (*FT*, Survey, 1 April 2003, p. vi).

'The proposed constitution offers Chechnya "wide autonomy" ... [but] "The territory of the Chechen republic is indivisible and is an integral part of the territory of the Russian Federation"' (*The Independent*, 24 March 2003, p. 15).

The draft republic constitution ... would for the first time officially establish the republic's name as Chechnya. It declares Russian and Chechen to be the official state languages. The highest institution of government would be the People's Assembly. The republic's highest official would be a president, elected for a maximum of two five-year terms ... Some 13,200 signatures were collected in support of the referendum.

(*CDSP*, 2003, vol. 55, nos 1–2, p. 12)

[The] new constitution declares it [Chechnya] once more an 'autonomous republic' of the Russian Federation ... [but] the Kremlin will have the right to dismiss Chechnya's president at any time, unlike those of other autonomous republics ... Memorial, a Russian human rights organization ... has refused to legitimize it [the referendum] by sending observers; so too have OSCE (though it will send a small group of 'fact finders') and the Council of Europe ... There have been press reports of people being forced to register to vote, on pain of losing food aid ... Aslan Maskhadov ... has called for a boycott.

(*The Economist*, 22 March 2003, p. 44)

'The new constitution allows the Russian president to sack the Chechen one without giving a reason' (*The Economist*, 29 March 2003, p. 46).

The foreign minister of ... [the] rebel government, Ilyas Akhmadov, unveiled an alternative peace plan last week in Washington, which would defer the republic's quest for statehood until genuine peace was achieved. The rebel plan calls for international peacekeeping troops to take over security functions from Russian troops, on the model of recent UN-backed operations in Kosovo and East Timor.

(*The Independent*, 24 March 2003, p. 15)

3 April 2003. 'The Council of Europe has demanded a Hague-style war crimes tribunal set up by the UN to prosecute key Russian and Chechen leaders as war criminals responsible for systematic murders and disappearances in Chechnya' (*Guardian*, 4 April 2003, p. 13).

8 April 2003.

> European nations formally submitted a resolution to the United Nations Human Rights Commission in Geneva yesterday [8 April] accusing Russia of violations in ... Chechnya. The resolution, put forward by the fifteen EU members and seven other nations, cites forced disappearances, summary executions and torture.
>
> *(The Independent,* 9 April 2003, p. 11)

11 April 2003. 'The [US] State Department said Friday [11 April] that it would break with past practice and decline to sponsor a resolution criticizing Russia when the Chechnya conflict comes before the UN Human Rights Commission this week' *(IHT,* 15 April 2003, p. 9).

16 April 2003.

> The fifty-three-country UN Commission on Human Rights ... rebuffed a bid by the EU to censure Russia for alleged violations in Chechnya. The EU had urged the annual meeting to express 'deep concern' at the reported violations, which it said included 'forced disappearances, extrajudicial, summary or arbitrary executions, torture, ill treatment as well as alleged violations of international humanitarian law' by Russian forces in Chechnya. But the resolution, which was backed by the United States, was rejected by fifteen votes in favour to twenty-one opposed, with seventeen countries abstaining. A similar motion in 2002 failed by one vote ... The United States-based Human Rights Watch, which says that the situation in Chechnya is getting worse, accused the EU of having backtracked on earlier tougher demands for an international investigation into allegations of abuses.
>
> *(IHT,* 17 April 2003, p. 8)

17 April 2003.

> About 300 Russian servicemen are under investigation for their part in the 'disappearances' of hundreds of people amid guerrilla fighting in Chechnya last year [2002], Chechnya's prime minister said Thursday [17 April] ... But Anatoli Popov, the Moscow-appointed prime minister, added that he was unaware of an official document reportedly tabled before the Russian government saying 1,132 civilians had been killed in Chechnya in 2002 and that seventy-six people were murdered and 126 abducted in the first two months of 2003.
>
> *(IHT,* 18 April 2003, p. 5)

30 April 2003.

> The office of the Russian prosecutor-general has unexpectedly closed its investigation into the three apartment bombings in September 1999, which killed 243 people ... The prosecutor's office announced that nine Russian and foreign Islamic fighters carried out the bombings – two in Moscow and one in the southern city of Volgodonsk ... None of the accused

appeared to be Chechens. Rather, they were Moslems from other regions
... While dozens of arrests were made and suspects identified, no one has
yet to be tried, let alone convicted of direct complicity ... Five of those
accused Wednesday [30 April] are already dead, including a Jordanian-
born leader known as Khattab, who was killed in Chechnya last year
[2002], reportedly by a poisoned letter sent by the Russian security service
... The announcement ... will do little to answer accusations – never substantiated – that the bombings were carried out by Russia's security
service, the FSB.

(*IHT*, 2 May 2003, p. 6)

12 May 2003. A suicide attack (involving a lorry packed with explosives) on a
government complex in Znamenskoye (near Chechnya's northern border) kills
sixty people.

'Russian officials blamed the attack on Monday [12 May] on Abu Walid, a
Saudi-born warlord thought to be a follower of the fundamentalist Wahhabi
school of Islam, which is a powerful force in Saudi Arabia' (*The Times*, 15 May
2003, p. 21).

14 May 2003. Another suicide bombing takes place, this time at a religious
(Moslem) festival organized by United Russia and held in a village east of
Grozny. The festival was attended by Akhmad Kadyrov, the pro-Moscow head
of Chechnya's local administration and apparent target. He escaped injury but
eighteen died.

'Foreign-born militants were also blamed [by Russian officials] for yesterday's [Wednesday's] attack' (*The Times*, 15 May 2003, p. 21).

'Russian security officials alleged that a Saudi citizen, Abu Walid, had trained
suicide bombers in Chechnya. His involvement in yesterday's [Wednesday's] –
or Monday's attack – however, had yet to be determined, they added' (*Guardian*, 15 May 2003, p. 14).

16 May 2003.

President Vladimir Putin on Thursday [15 May] proposed granting
amnesty to Chechen separatists who agreed to lay down their arms by 1
August, but the offer would exclude anyone accused of murder, rape, kidnapping or other crimes ... The amnesty would cover any fighters who
rebelled against Russia beginning in August 1993, a year before the first
Chechen war began ... Amnesty would be granted to neither Aslan
Maskhadov ... nor any commanders suspected of organizing suicide
bombings or other terrorist acts ... A few thousand Chechen rebels, at
most, are believed to remain active in or near the republic, fighting beside
an unknown number of foreign mercenaries ... The remaining fighters,
however, have only intensified their attacks since the March referendum
... Unable to control territory or fight Russian forces head-on, they have
also increasingly resorted to suicide attacks.

(*IHT*, 16 May 2003, p. 4)

The amnesty ... would not cover foreigners or Russian citizens who were guilty of murder, kidnapping, rape or other grave crimes. The amnesty also denies pardon to all those who made an attempt on the lives of federal police officers and servicemen – a provision that makes it meaningless, according to critics.

(*IHT*, 21 May 2003, p. 5)

'The amnesty ... also applies to Russian troops in Chechnya ... The amnesty does not pardon rebels or Russian soldiers who have committed particularly grave crimes – such as premeditated murder, rape and hostage-taking – or foreigners' (*IHT*, 7 June 2003, p. 2). 'Guerrilla leaders have rejected the amnesty as a ploy to clear scores of Russian soldiers who face punishment for crimes and human rights abuses' (*IHT*, 6 June 2003, p. 3).

Yesterday [6 June] the State Duma adopted on third and final reading a resolution [on the amnesty] ... Russian presidential adviser Sergei Yastrzhembsky did not rule out the possibility that even Aslan Makhadov might take advantage of the amnesty: 'The resolution contains a section on "armed revolt" and the main criminal charge against Maskhadov is in fact participation in an armed revolt.'

(*CDSP*, 2003, vol. 55, no. 23, p. 11)

5 June 2003. In North Ossetia a suicide bomb attack on a bus travelling to an airbase results in twenty deaths (including civilians).
5 July 2003.

Two female suicide bombers allegedly from Chechnya blew themselves up at the gates to an open air rock festival at Tushino airfield on the outskirts of Moscow ... The double suicide bombing in Moscow on Saturday [5 July] killed at least thirteen people ... Nobody claimed responsibility for the bombing but the Russian authorities blamed separatist forces in Chechnya ... This is the first time Chechen militants [have] used ... suicide bombing in Moscow ... Most Chechen suicide bombers appear to be women, often the widows of Chechen fighters and victims of violence committed by Russian military forces ... The attack came a day after Mr Putin issued a decree ordering presidential elections in Chechnya on 5 October ... President Putin yesterday [6 July] cancelled trips to Malaysia and two former Soviet republics [Azerbaijan and Uzbekistan].

(*FT*, 7 July 2003, p. 6)

Two female suicide bombers killed themselves and at least thirteen others ... The political wing of the Chechen separatist movement, led by ... Aslan Maskhadov, denied involvement ... Russian officials blame foreign-backed terrorist organizations – including al-Qaeda – for much of the violence, saying the groups are funnelling money and expertise into the province. Most outside experts say that the guerrilla war there has at least some popular support, but that most Chechens are so desperate for peace that they would accept any reasonable solution.

(IHT, 7 July 2003, p. 7)

(The final death toll was seventeen, including the two suicide bombers.).

7 July 2003. 'President Putin ... [said that] rebel fighters in Chechnya "were not only linked with international terrorist organizations but also have become an integral part of them, perhaps the most dangerous part"' (*FT*, 8 July 2003, p. 8).

> The two women believed to have blown themselves up at a Russian rock concert on Saturday belonged to a group of thirty-six suicide bombers trained by separatists, Russian media reported yesterday [7 July] ... In May the Chechen interior ministry had warned that the thirty-six had been trained by Shamil Basayev.

(Guardian, 8 July 2003, p. 15)

10 July 2003.

> A security agent was killed early Thursday [10 July] while defusing a bomb that had been carried by a woman identified by the authorities as a [would-be] suicide bomber from the northern Caucasus. The woman was stopped by security guards while trying to enter a restaurant in a fashionable area of central Moscow.

(IHT, 11 July 2003, p. 4)

(The woman was arrested.)

25 July 2003.

> A Russian [military] court yesterday [25 July] sentenced an army colonel to ten years in prison for the murder of a Chechen woman. Colonel Yuri Budanov, the highest-ranking Russian officer to face charges for abuses in Chechnya, admitted strangling eighteen-year-old Elza Kungayeva during an investigation on 27 March 2000, but was initially let off on an insanity plea ... But the initial ruling last year [2002] required Colonel Budanov to undergo psychiatric treatment.

(IHT, 26 July 2003, p. 6)

> In his first trial [in a military court], which ended last New Year's Eve with an acquittal on the ground that he was temporarily insane ... Russia's supreme court threw out that verdict in February [2003] ... Budanov admitted ... strangling her to death, but he said he did so in an emotional rage, believing she was a sniper who had killed his soldiers ... A specialist's conclusion that Kungayeva had been raped was removed from an autopsy report and a rape charge was dropped.

(IHT, 26 July 2003, p. 5)

27 July 2003.

> A woman died of wounds she suffered in a suicide bombing that the authorities said had been aimed at the son of Chechnya's administration chief, officials said Monday [28 July] ... A woman detonated explosives Sunday [27 July] outside the base of a security force commanded by Ramzan Kadyrov.
>
> (*IHT*, 29 July 2003, p. 6)

29 July 2003. 'Russia moved control of the Chechen military campaign from the security services Tuesday [29 July] and handed it to the regular police ... [transferring] power from the federal security service to the interior ministry' (*IHT*, 30 July 2003, p. 8).

1 September 2003. 'By the official deadline of 1 September ... only 150 rebels had turned themselves in – along with 220 Russian soldiers wanting to shake off war crimes allegations' (*The Economist*, 8 September 2003, p. 8).

> The amnesty, announced in June ... was ostensibly aimed at around 2,000 Chechen fighters ... [But] only around 150 Chechens took up the offer. Some reports suggested that they were fighting on the Russian side. More than 220 Russian troops ... have applied for amnesty.
>
> (*Daily Telegraph*, 3 September 2003, p. 13)

> In three months only 171 rebel fighters took advantage of [the amnesty] ... Over the same period 226 soldiers and policemen were also amnestied ... The amnesty covered individuals who had committed dangerous acts with the borders of the former Chechen–Ingush republic in the period from 12 December 1993 to the day the resolution went into effect ... The amnesty also covered servicemen, internal affairs agency personnel and correctional employees. The amnesty did not apply to persons who had committed murder, kidnapping, rape, robbery or other grave and especially grave crimes ... According to law enforcement agencies' figures, the total number of armed rebels in Chechnya is currently somewhere between 1,500 and 3,000.
>
> (*CDSP*, 2003, vol. 55, no. 35, p. 10)

1 August 2003. A suicide attack on a Russian military hospital in Mozdok (North Ossetia) involving a vehicle packed with explosives kills at least fifty people.

3 September 2003.

> At least five people were killed ... when two bombs exploded under a passing commuter train ... near a small station on the outskirts of Kislovodsk ... near Chechnya. Although officials did not immediately blame Chechen rebels, the bombings followed a recent string of attacks attributed to rebels.
>
> (*IHT*, 4 September 2003, p. 5)

'Six people were killed ... Reports discounted any connection with the Chechen conflict' (*FT*, 4 September 2003, p. 13).

11 September 2003.

> The only two serious opponents of the Moscow-backed incumbent dropped out [of the election race] ... Aslambek Aslakhanov, a member of the Russian parliament and one of the favourites, withdrew his candidacy saying he had chosen instead to become a Kremlin aide. The other leading candidate, Malik Saidullayev, a businessman, was barred from standing by a court ruling in Chechnya. Earlier Mr Saidullayev had said: 'I got a suggestion from officials in Moscow that I should do the same [as Mr Aslakhanov], but I refused.'.

> (*Daily Telegraph*, 12 September 2003, p. 18)

'Aslambek Aslakhanov ... was expected to gain nearly a quarter of the vote, nearly double that of the Kremlin's favourite, Akhmad Kadyrov, the Chechen administration head' (*Guardian*, 12 September 2003, p. 18).

> Malik Saidullayev, a Moscow-based Chechen businessman, was struck off the candidates' list by the local election commission last Thursday [11 September] after it allegedly found that many of the signatures to support his candidature had been falsified. On the same day Aslambek Aslakhanov, the current Chechen representative in [the State Duma] ... and ranked highly in opinion polls ... withdrew his candidature ... [after he] had been appointed as an adviser to the Kremlin on policy towards the country's southern districts. Several other potential rivals also pulled out in recent weeks, and Ruslan Khasbulatov, the Chechen academic and former speaker of the Russian parliament who has long called for talks with ... Aslan Maskhadov, decided not to stand. Chechens have long expressed concerns that Mr Kadyrov has failed ... to create broad consultative mechanisms or to broaden appointments of officials beyond people close to him. They accuse his staff of intimidating rival candidates and have criticized his decision to eliminate the regional press ministry and to merge its functions under the control of a close ally.

> (*FT*, 16 September 2003, p. 7)

> Ten candidates were in the race until this week, when the two most dangerous challengers to the incumbent, Akhmad Kadyrov, were forced by the government to withdraw ... The election, in the view of many analysts, has been stage-managed by Moscow, as part of an exit strategy from an unending, unwinnable, horribly destructive war ... The Kremlin's exit strategy is part of a very real election, but it is not the race for the presidency of Chechnya. It is the Russian parliamentary elections in December and the presidential vote next March ... Kadyrov himself is a potential threat. A former Islamic leader, he was chosen three years ago by Moscow to run Chechnya. He commands a private army of his own. Frightened residents who demand

anonymity say it has become a new source of terror, carrying out killings, kidnappings and torture. It could become a dangerous third force if the Russians fail to assure his victory ... At the moment there are 40,000 troops in the republic, about half the peak deployment in 1999 said [a Russian military spokesman] ... He said that number was to be drawn down to a standing 25,000 ... [He said] that full-scale military operations had ended in June ... [The spokesman said there are] about 3,000 fighters he called bandits dispersed into small groups ... In a report this month [September] ... the International Campaign to Ban Landmines ... said explosives laid by both sides killed 5,695 people last year [2002], compared with 1,286 in Afghanistan ... Two months ago ... President Putin ... reported progress: 'We have practically brought to an end the so-called counter-terrorist operation and are handing over to the interior ministry responsibility to the interior ministry for maintaining public order.'

(Seth Mydans, *IHT*, 19 September 2003, p. 2)

A consortium of twelve human rights group issued a statement last month [September] that they would not participate as observers at the election. Many residents and human rights group here [in Chechnya] said that Kadyrov's private army has been threatening and kidnapping opposition workers and terrorizing entire villages in advance of the vote ... [Kadyrov] has 30,000 ready-made constituents among the 545,000 eligible voters ... Russian troops stationed here who have been added to the election rolls. Once the votes are in ... the ballot boxes will be held overnight in the hands of Kadyrov government officials before counting begins next morning.

(*IHT*, Seth Mydans, 4 October 2003, p. 3)

15 September 2003. At least five people were killed (including the two suicide bombers) when a truck bomb exploded outside the regional headquarters of the Federal Security Service in Magas, the capital of Ingushetia. There was no immediate claim of responsibility.

27 September 2003.

The prime minister in Chechnya's Moscow-backed government, Anatoli Popov, has been hospitalized for food poisoning, officials said ... in what may have been an attack on his life ... Popov was admitted to hospital Saturday evening [27 September] after complaining of pain as his motorcade was returning to Grozny from Gudermes ... [He] had been in Gudermes for a ceremony opening a new gas line ... Officials were investigating the possibility that poison may have been deliberately slipped into something Popov ate or drank in an attempt on his life.

(*IHT*, 29 September 2003, p. 3)

'Investigators tried to determine if it was a deliberate attack against [Popov] ... or food poisoning ... A military source said early evidence suggested spoiled curd cheese might have been the cause' (*FT*, 29 September 2003, p. 10).

Mr Popov, who was appointed prime minister of Chechnya this year [2003] ... took over as acting president during the campaign for next Sunday's presidential poll ... Mr Popov is not running in the election ... The Moscow Helsinki Group, Russia's oldest human rights watchdog, has cancelled plans to send 300 observers to monitor the voting. Four of the main candidates have mysteriously withdrawn or been rejected. In September armed members of Mr Kadyrov's 2,000-man security force, headed by the leader's son Ramzan, occupied the offices of Chechnya's only television station and all eight of the republic's newspapers.

(*The Independent*, 29 September 2003, p. 8)

5 October 2003. In the presidential election seven candidates ran. Official figures put the turnout at 87.7 per cent and Akhmad Kadyrov's share of the vote at 80.84 per cent.

Akhmad Kadyrov's main opponents have either been excluded from – or persuaded against – running, meaning his election is guaranteed ... The remaining candidates are little more than names on a list. One candidate, Said Selim Tsuyev, is a close aide to Mr Kadyrov. There is little attempt to make the election campaign appear fair, despite Moscow's fury at the US State Department for denouncing the vote as rigged ... No reputable international organization will observe Sunday's election; they say it will not be free or fair ... Many Chechens ... fear Mr Kadyrov's 40,000-strong private army will then [after the election] make a move against anyone considered opposition ... Locals – and some aid workers – fear Mr Kadyrov will use his electoral 'mandate' to unleash what one resident called 'the third military campaign against the Chechens' ... Many fear that the Kremlin's strategy will lead to a Russian-backed civil war among the Chechens ... A former rector of the Islamic Institute in Chechnya ... Mr Kadyrov, fifty-three, fought against the Russian army in 1994, later becoming a religious leader. Then, in 1999, he approached the Kremlin, saying he sought a better life for his country. Vladimir Putin made him head of the Russian administration in Chechnya. His 'betrayal' means he is, perhaps, one of the most hated men in [Chechnya] ... Grozny is covered with posters of Mr Kadyrov shaking Mr Putin's hand ... No promotion of other candidates is tolerated.

(*Guardian*, 1 October 2003, p. 17)

Mr Kadyrov controls a private army of up to 7,000 ... [There have been] months of violent electioneering by Mr Kadyrov and his men, many of whom are former rebels ... Relatives of opponents have been kidnapped or even murdered ... Chechnya knows that Mr Kadyrov's victory is a foregone conclusion. Over the past two weeks Moscow has removed the only other serious candidates from the list: Malik Saidullayev, Aslambek Aslakhanov and Khusain Dzabrailov. The first was tripped by alleged violations in the signature lists for his application, the second accepted a top-ranking job in Putin's administration and the third was threatened with a court case over compromising material by a member of the administration. The six remaining candidates are too weak to pose a real challenge to Mr Kadyrov. International observers have refused to attend the election, as have human rights activists ... Mr Kadyrov, a formal rebel under Aslan Maskhadov, swapped sides in October 1999 when he handed over Gudermes to the Russians. He was appointed head of Chechnya's temporary administration in June 2000.

(*The Times*, 4 October 2003, p. 18)

Although seven candidates are running for the presidency, analysts say Mr Kadyrov's six surviving rivals are nonentities. Four serious contenders – all of whom were performing better than Mr Kadyrov in independent opinion polls – have quit since July ... The Moscow Helsinki Group, a Russian human rights watchdog, last month [September] cancelled plans to send 300 election monitors. Most international organizations, including the Council of Europe and OSCE, declined to send observers ... Critics say Mr Kadyrov has stacked local administrations with his cronies and employed his personal security force – led by his son Ramzan – to intimidate rivals and seize control of all the republic's media outlets.

(*The Independent*, 6 October 2003, p. 11)

Observers from the Council of Europe and OSCE did not attend ... ostensibly on security grounds. Observers from the CIS declared the voting to be democratic and there were few reports of disruption or violence ... [Critics warn] that Mr Kadyrov's election risked triggering a civil war.

(*FT*, 6 October 2003, p. 6)

'Human rights groups and many independent analysts said they doubted the fairness of the election and the credibility of the vote count' (*IHT*, 7 October 2003, p. 3).

'[The] election [was] marred by violence and allegations of vote-rigging. Eyewitnesses said polling stations were often half-empty' (*Daily Telegraph*, 7 October 2003, p. 16).

Mr Kadyrov said he would ask the Russian parliament to renew an amnesty that was offered to rebels during the summer and expired in September. He said that 171 fighters had surrendered under the amnesty and that many were now serving in his security service.

(*The Independent*, 7 October 2003, p. 13)

Malik Saidullayev ... was persuaded to run by Sergei Yastrzhembsky, an aide to Mr Putin. But by September another Kremlin official was pressing Mr Saidullayev to withdraw. He refused. A court then disqualified him, because some voters who signed his candidacy petition had not put 'Chechen republic' in their addresses ... Government workers tell of being ordered to vote for Mr Kadyrov or lose their jobs. Polling station officials known to have opposition sympathies were visited at home, with grimmer threats. People were told to support Mr Kadyrov if they wanted their pensions or pay-outs from a fund set up to compensate war victims. Mr Kadyrov is said to have given cars to local officials. Television stations virtually ignored other candidates; the new election law requires equal coverage for all, but the courts refused to consider their complaints ... On election day Grozny's streets were empty compared with the days before and after, even though both were holidays ... The official turnout attained Soviet-style absurdity. Turnout in the deserted capital was 98 per cent ... Abdullah Bugayev, one of the remaining opposition candidates, got 6 per cent overall, but barely more than 1 per cent in the north-western Nadterechny district, one of his supposed strongholds ... A referendum in March ... [was] also rigged (though perhaps unnecessarily).

(*The Economist*, 11 October 2003, p. 44)

22 October 2003.

One year after Moscow's Dubrovka theatre siege [which began on 23 October 2002] Russian prosecutors have launched international arrest warrants for three men they accuse of organizing the Chechen hostage-taking ... [They are] Shamil Basayev, Hasan Zakayev and Gerihan Dudayev ... The federal and city authorities jointly paid one-off compensation of up to 110,000 roubles ($3,700) for each victim and 60,000 roubles to relatives of those killed.

(*FT*, 23 October 2003, p. 10)

'Families are banned from suing the federal government and the Moscow city authority, which can be sued, has argued successfully in court that it is not responsible' (*Daily Telegraph*, 23 October 2003, p. 17).

'Courts have rejected sixty-four moral compensation suits filed by survivors and relatives of the victims' (*IHT*, 24 October 2003, p. 3).

13 November 2003.

An English court yesterday [13 November] refused to extradite Akhmed Zakayev ... saying the prosecution was politically motivated ... In a damning commentary of Russian justice Senior District Judge Timothy Workman ... said it would be 'unjust and oppressive' to return him for trial to Russia, where there was 'a substantial risk' that he might be tortured. He said he was 'quite satisfied' that the events in Chechnya in 1995–6 amounted to an 'internal armed conflict' and he dismissed four of the thirteen charges as non-extraditable offences, because similar conduct in such circumstances would not amount to a crime in the UK. As for the remaining charges of murder and conspiracy to murder, the judge said there had been a seven-year delay in bringing the proceedings as well as delays in proper investigation of the alleged offences.

(*FT*, 14 November 2003, p. 9)

Judge Timothy Workman said: 'It would be unjust and oppressive to return Mr Zakayev to stand his trial in Russia. I have come to the inevitable conclusion that if the authorities are prepared to resort to torturing witnesses, there is a substantial risk that Mr Zakayev would himself be subject to torture' ... Workman said he believed Moscow sought the extradition to 'exclude him from continuing to take part in the peace process'. The judge said he had concluded that fighting in Chechnya was a war, not an 'anti-terrorism operation' ... Workman also said he believed a witness who testified that he had been held in a pit and tortured for six days, including with electric shocks, in order to provide Moscow with a statement then used against Zakayev.

(IHT, 14 November 2003, p. 3)

Timothy Workman said ... 'If the Russian authorities are preparing to resort to torturing witnesses, there is a substantial risk that Mr Zakayev would be subjected to torture. I am satisfied that such punishment would be by the reason of his nationality and his political opinions.'

(The Independent, 14 November 2003, p. 15)

The judge said ... 'I am satisfied that, more likely than not, the motivation of the government of the Russian Federation was and is to exclude Mr Zakayev from continuing to take part in the peace process and to discredit him as a moderate' ... The judge found that Russia has 'carpet-bombed' Grozny ... and was quite confident that events in Chechnya between 1995 and 1996 amounted in law to an internal armed conflict: 'I was unable to accept the view expressed by one witness that the actions of the Russian government in bombing Grozny were counter-terrorist operations.'

(Guardian, 14 November 2003, p. 6)

Timothy Workman highlighted evidence of other leading Chechens who had died in prison after receiving long sentences. It was, he said, 'at best an unfortunate coincidence, at worst unlawful killing' ... Judge Workman said he was 'quite satisfied' that the Russian Federation was involved in an 'internal armed conflict', effectively a war, there ... He said the crimes which involved Mr Zakayev allegedly using armed force against combatants were not extraditable because they took place in a war situation. However, he could not discharge counts that involved the alleged murder of civilians. But he ruled that it would be 'unjust or oppressive' to extradite Mr Zakayev.

(Daily Telegraph, 14 November 2003, p. 12)

21 November 2003.

Russia will send investigators to Chechnya next year [2002] to investigate allegations of extensive embezzlement of aid money ... More than thirty cases of financial abuse have been opened after a preliminary audit by the Russian audit chamber of the use of budget money allocated to Chechnya for reconstruction in 2003.

(IHT, 22 November 2003, p. 4)

5 December 2003.

A suicide bomber blew himself up inside a crowded commuter train in southern Russia, killing at least forty-one people in what President Putin denounced as a terrorist act intended to disrupt parliamentary elections [on 7 December] ... While there was no immediate claim for responsibility for the bombing ... the federal security service said ... that it bore all the characteristics of terrorist acts by Chechnya's separatist fighters ... [The FSS] said the bomber appeared to work with three accomplices, all women. Two of them are believed to have leapt from the train shortly before the explosion. A third, whom it said might have detonated the explosive by remote control, was badly wounded and not likely to survive ... In recent months the attacks appeared to wane. The last occurred in early September when a bomb exploded on a train on the same commuter line as the attack on Friday [5 December], killing six people ... Officials have attributed the attacks ... as well as the [Moscow theatre siege] ... to Chechens aided by international Islamic extremists. [They] said that intelligence reports suggested that separatist fighters in Chechnya continued to receive financial support from abroad, including Islamic charities in Saudi Arabia.

(*IHT*, 6 December 2003, pp. 1, 5)

'The bomb expoded ... in the Stavropol region, not far from the Chechen border' (*The Times*, 6 December 2003, p. 18).

President Putin: 'This is clearly an attempt to destabilize the country on the eve of the elections. International terrorism, which has presented a challenge to many countries, continues to remain a serious threat to our country' (*Guardian*, 6 December 2003, p. 1).

'A senior Russian security source ... [said] the blast was probably the work of radical groups with links to al-Qaeda' (*Guardian*, 6 December 2003, p. 1).

(The final toll was forty-six.)

9 December 2003.

A suicide bomber blew herself up Tuesday [9 December] outside a historic hotel in the centre of Moscow, officials said, killing at least five others ... only steps away from the Kremlin ... The National Hotel [is] one of the city's landmarks ... an elegant century-old building where Lenin stayed in 1918 after moving the new Bolshevik capital to Moscow from St Petersburg ... Officials said the bombing might have involved a second female terrorist ... Moscow's mayor, Yuri Luzhkov, said two women might have taken part in the attack and might not have been directing it at the National Hotel ... Luzhkov said that witnesses reported hearing two women ask for directions to the parliament, which stands just across Tverskaya Street, one of the city's commercial arteries ... No group immediately claimed responsibility for the bombing, though officials linked it to Chechen terrorists.

(*IHT*, 10 December 2003, pp. 1,4)

15 December 2003.

> A group of Chechen rebels crossed into ... Dagestan, not far from Russia's border with Georgia ... killed nine border troops and seized four [civilian] hostages ... including two hospital workers ... on Monday [15 December] before disappearing ... The rebels, estimated to number between two dozen and four dozen, appeared to have stumbled into a firefight with federal forces ... None of the rebels were reported killed.
>
> (*IHT*, 16 December 2003, p. 3)

16 December 2003. 'Chechen rebels who fought their way into the neighbouring Dagestan region and occupied a village released all their [eleven] hostages and fled, avoiding capture' (*IHT*, 27 December 2003, p. 4).

> Up to 120 fighters have been in Dagestan since Monday [15 December], when they ambushed border guards, killing eight young conscripts and an officer. Local officials said an attack helicopter had tracked down the rebels and killed eight of them ... Yesterday [17 December] three rebels briefly seized the village of Gaalatli, where they took seven hostages, in addition to the four they took on Monday ... Russia's defence minister, Sergei Ivanov, said six rebels had been killed in the latest action.
>
> (*Guardian*, 17 December 2003, p. 12)

12 January 2004.

> A Moscow court on Monday [12 January 2004] sentenced two men to life in prison for their involvement in a series of apartment house bombings that incited the second war in Chechnya. Russian officials quickly blamed the blasts on Chechen rebels, though rebel leaders denied involvement and some critics even suggested that Russia's Federal Security Service, or FSB, had engineered the attacks to justify the military campaign. Yusuf Krymshamkhalov and Adam Dekkushev were convicted on charges of terrorism, murder, illegal possession and trafficking of explosives and other crimes in relation to the 1999 bombings in Moscow and Volgodonsk, which killed 246 people. Prosecutors said the pair made explosives, packed them in sugar sacks and drove them to Moscow and Volgodonsk on the order of Chechen rebels. According to the charges, the two, who are residents of Karachayevo-Cherkessia, west of Chechnya, drove a truckload of explosives right to the wall of the apartment building that was blown up in Volgodonsk. Their two-month trial was closed to the public ... The authorities have said that another six suspects were killed during the fighting in Chechnya and that two suspects remain at large ... Following the verdict a group of victims' relatives released an open letter raising questions about the murky circumstances of the bombings, which they said were left unanswered in the trial. Last month [December 2003] the Russian authorities seized thousands of copies of a book that accuses the FSB of staging the explosions. The book's co-author, Alexander Litvinenko, a former FSB

agent who had received political asylum in Britain, based his charges on an incident in the city of Ryazan in September 1999 shortly after the bombings. The police there discovered what they took to be explosives in an apartment building basement and ordered an evacuation. The FSB said that they were not explosives but sacks of sugar planted as an anti-terrorism drill, but Litvinenko and other critics insist the explosives were real and used in a pattern that resembled the explosions in Moscow and Volgodonsk. Litvinenko is associated with Boris Berezovsky ... who made similar charges ... in Britain, where he also received political asylum ... Vladimir Putin, a former FSB chief ... was named prime minister just weeks before the explosions.

(*IHT*, 13 January 2004, p. 3)

Dekkushev was quoted as telling the court he had not wanted to cause any casualties and had been in favour of attacking other targets rather than an apartment block. Krymshamkhalov said he had not been aware he had been carrying explosives ... Russian media quoted investigators as saying they believed the blasts had been masterminded by two foreign guerrilla leaders, Ibn al-Khattab and Abu Umar, who had fought for the Chechen rebels. Al-Khattab, a Jordanian, and Abu Umar, born in Saudi Arabia, are now dead.

(*Guardian*, 13 January 2004, p. 16)

Senior military and intelligence officers have claimed that a parallel invasion of Dagestan ... by Chechen warlord Shamil Basayev was tacitly encouraged by the FSB. 'I myself heard tapes of officials from Moscow speaking with Basayev to discuss arrangements for the attack,' an FSB officer told the *Daily Telegraph* ... On 22 September 1999 locals in the regional town of Ryazan saw three men emerging from the cellars of a block of flats who later turned out to be FSB officers. When local police checked the cellars they found sacks of high explosive wired up to a detonator. The FSB later attempted to explain away the incident by claiming that the entire operation had merely been a drill and the explosive was in fact sugar, despite a test that proved the contrary ... They rewarded the three locals who notified the authorities with colour television sets.

(*Daily Telegraph*, 13 January 2004, p. 12)

Since the election of President Akhmad Kadyrov ... Chechens seem to have taken over what was previously Russian work: the 'clean-up operations' where suspected rebel sympathizers are abducted and then interrogated, tortured or even murdered ... His private army of 4,000 is led by his police captain son ... Ramzan is the president's son and security chief.

(*Guardian*, 13 January 2004, p. 16)

13 January 2004.

Russian authorities have set a deadline of 1 March [2004] to close tent camps sheltering thousands of refugees ... The Kremlin has been pressing refugees in neighbouring Ingushetia to go home since launching a peace plan last year [2003] ... Human rights groups and the United Nations are concerned that refugees are being forced to return to Chechnya ... The director of the Moscow office of Human Rights Watch said: 'The Russian authorities are trying to give the impression that the situation in Chechnya is normalizing and it is safe to return. That is not the case' ... The United Nations estimates that there are 67,000 refugees in Ingushetia, including 7,000 living in tent camps. The rest live in disused farmhouses and other temporary shelters, or with relatives.

(*The Times*, 14 January 2004, p. 17)

('[Some] 65,000 Chechen refugees live in neighbouring Ingushetia ... Russian officials now say they will close ... the tent camps by 1 March ... The Chechen government has set up temporary accommodation for returning refugees and is offering 350,000 roubles in compensation to each for lost homes and property. But refugees who have returned say they receive little government support': *The Times*, 21 February 2004, p. 21.)

14 January 2004.

Russia's leading opposition presidential candidate yesterday [14 January] blamed the Kremlin for the deaths of 130 hostages during Moscow's [October] 2002 Nord-Ost theatre crisis, saying the Chechens who seized the building had no intention of blowing it up ... In an open letter to the Russian media Irina Khakamada ... said the authorities did not want to negotiate. She also said Alexander Voloshin, former head of the presidential administration, had told her not to interfere. Ms Khakamada, who had talked to the hostage takers, accused Vladimir Putin of lying when he said the gas used by special services did not kill any hostages. She questioned why all the Chechens were shot during the raid, when some carried no explosives.

(*FT*, 15 January 2004, p. 7)

29 January 2004.

A March deadline to close tent camps housing Chechen refugees has been scrapped, the chief of UN humanitarian affairs said on Thursday [28 January] ... [An announcement had been made] that all tents near the region should be closed by 1 March ... The camps house about 7,000 of the 70,000 refugees in Ingushetia.

(*IHT*, 30 January 2004, p. 8)

1 February 2004.

Assailants wielding guns and hand grenades killed five members of ... [Akhmad Kadyrov's] security force Sunday [1 February] ... As many as ten attackers burst into the home of the local commander ... [He] and four other members of the force died ... One assailant was killed.

(*IHT*, 2 February 2004, p. 8)

3 February 2004.

A car bomb exploded Tuesday [3 February] near the central market in Vladikavkaz, a southern Russian city [the capital of North Ossetia] near the Chechen republic, killing two people ... One civilian and one soldier [were killed] ... and eight wounded: four interior military police cadets and four civilians ... A truckload of interior ministry servicemen was passing by ... The explosion took place in a parking area ... The market and others in the city have been hit by a series of bombings in the last five years ... [A spokesman for North Ossetia] said there was no immediate indication whether the blast was related to the Chechen war or to criminal groups.

(*IHT*, 4 February 2004, p. 3)

6 February 2004.

At least thirty-nine people were killed ... after an explosion ripped through a busy underground train in central Moscow during the morning rush hour ... The Moscow Metro system is used by 9 million people a day ... No group has so far claimed responsibility ... President Putin: 'We do not need any indirect confirmation. We know for certain that Maskhadov and his bandits are linked to this terrorism. Russia does not negotiate with terrorists, it destroys them' ... Akhmed Zakayev, a spokesman for Mr Maskhadov, denied the accusation and condemned the attack: 'It is a horrific crime which cannot be justified by any cause. We condemn any form of terrorism whoever stands behind it' ... The Chechen problem ... did not feature as an issue in the parliamentary elections last year [2003] and is unlikely to be raised in next month's presidential elections.

(*FT*, 7 February 2004, p. 6)

Akhmed Zakayev (spokesman for Aslan Maskhadov): 'These actions in Moscow against citizens are in no way of benefit to us' (*IHT*, 7 February 2004, p. 4).

Aslan Maskhadov, through his spokesman Akhmed Zakayev, declared that official forces of Ichkeria [Chechnya] had nothing to do with the incident, and that he himself condemned such actions. On the other hand, security agents reminded a *Kommersant* correspondent, Shamil Basayev has threatened repeatedly to bomb the Moscow subway.

(*CDSP*, 2004, vol. 56, no. 6, p. 3)

'The kavkazcenter.com website has posted a statement by a certain Lom-Ali Gazavat (Fighters of the Holy War), claiming responsibility for the 6 February bombing in the Moscow subway ... Nothing was heard even from Shamil Basayev, who has readily claimed responsibility for all major terrorist acts that have occurred recently both in Chechnya itself and in other parts of the country. And spokesmen for Aslan Maskhadov categorically declared that 'those are not our methods'.

(*Kommersant*, 3 March 2004, p. 5: *CDSP*, 2004, vol. 56, no. 9, p. 12)

'An explosion ripped through a subway car in the Moscow Metro during rush hour Friday morning, killing at least thirty people in what authorities were investigating as the latest in a series of terrorist attacks' (www.iht.com, 6 February 2004).

'Shamil Basayev ... has claimed responsibility for a string of attacks, including the Dubrovka theatre siege in 2002 ... and the suicide bombing on the Moscow Metro in February that killed forty people' (*The Times*, 1 April 2004, p. 18).

(The final death toll was forty-one.)

13 February 2004.

> Former President Zelimkhan Yandarbiyev of Chechnya was assassinated Friday [13 February] in an explosion that destroyed his car [in Doha, the capital of the Gulf state of Qatar] ... Yandarbiyev was acting president of Chechnya from 1996 to 1997. Russia had been seeking his extradition from Qatar, where he lived for at least three years, accusing him of ties to kidnappers and international terrorists. Last year [2003] the United Nations put Yandarbiyev on a list of people with links to al-Qaeda. The US government also put Yandarbiyev on a list of international terrorists who are subject to financial sanctions. Yandarbiyev was considered a key link in the Chechen rebels' finance network, channelling funds from abroad. He himself had denied that the Chechen rebels had ties to al-Qaeda ... Yandarbiyev, who was born in 1952, became vice-president of Chechnya under separatist President Dzhokhar Dudayev. In 1996 he led the rebel delegation in peace negotiations with President Boris Yeltsin, and prime minister Viktor Chernomyrdin.
>
> (*IHT*, 14 February 2004, p. 3)

'Zelimkhan Yandarbiyev ... contested the presidential election in 1997 ... but was defeated by Aslan Maskhadov ... Mr Yandarbiyev had opened a Chechen embassy in Kabul and a consulate in Kandahar during the reign of the Taleban' (*The Times*, 14 February 2004, p. 19).

> A senior FSB source claimed that Mr Yandarbiyev was 'a representative of al-Qaeda' ... [and that he] had also helped to finance the Nord-Ost theatre siege ... An FSB source had previously told the *Guardian* that financiers in Qatar were supplying Mr Yandarbiyev and other leading Chechens in Doha with $2 million to $3 million a month for 'Islamic extremism'.
>
> (*Guardian*, 14 February 2004, p. 18)

> Moscow has repeatedly requested Mr Yandarbiyev's extradition from the Gulf state over the past sixteen months, accusing him of organizing Chechen guerrilla operations, including the Moscow theatre siege ... and of acting as an important fundraiser ... He took refuge in Doha ... three years ago ... The Russians claim to have intercepted a telephone conversation between Mr Yandarbiyev and the leader of the Chechen hostage-takers during the

Nord-Ost theatre siege ... But the tape they produced only demonstrated that Mr Yandarbiyev was seeking information about events; it did not prove he was directing them ... Mr Yandarbiyev took over as acting president of Chechnya in April 1996, after his predecessor Dzhokhar Dudayev was assassinated.

(The Independent, 14 February 2004, p. 37)

26 February 2004.

Qatar has arrested two Russian secret agents and charged them with the murder of ... Zelimkhan Yandarbiyev ... prompting a sharply worded rebuke on Thursday [26 February] that accused the Qatari authorities of violating international law ... [The Russian foreign office statement] denied any involvement in the death ... [The statement] was the first public acknowledgement that two men arrested by the authorities in Doha last week were not only Russian citizens but members of the secret services. 'They were legally assigned to the Russian embassy in Qatar, conducting work in connection with countering international terrorism, without violating local legislation in any way' [the statement said] ... A third Russian agent who was arrested has been released because he carried a diplomatic passport ... [the statement] demanding that the others be released as well. It was an unusual public acknowledgement that an intelligence agent served under diplomatic disguise ... Russian officials attributed the bombing to internal feuds among Chechens.

(IHT, 27 February 2004, p. 3)

'The Russian citizens, one of whom has a diplomatic passport, are members of the Russian special services ... linked to the battle against international terrorism' [the Russian statement said] ... The SVR, the Russian foreign intelligence service, said it had not killed anyone abroad since 1959.

(The Times, 27 February 2004, p. 23)

1 March 2004. 'Russia claimed yesterday [1 March] that it had killed Ruslan Gelayev ... Unsubstantiated reports of Mr Gelayev's death have been reported several times' (*The Times*, 2 March 2004, p. 15).

('A man killed in a clash with border guards in the Dagestan region ... was Ruslan Gelayev, one of Chechnya's most powerful rebel warlords, [Russian] officials said': *The Independent*, 3 March 2004, p. 23. 'Russian special services yesterday [2 March] officially confirmed a report of the death of Ruslan Gelayev, one of the three main leaders – along with Shamil Basayev and Aslan Maskhadov – of the Chechen separatists. It has been established for certain that it was indeed Gelayev who was killed on 29 February during a spontaneous exchange of gunfire ... in Dagestan': *CDSP*, 2004, vol. 56, no. 9, p. 12).

11 March 2004.

Médecins sans Frontières has accused Russian officials of involvement in the kidnapping of one of their aid workers, who was abducted near Chechnya in August 2002 and is thought to be still alive ... [It is alleged] that the aid worker, Arjan Erkel, had been abducted in Dagestan by a group that has links to an MP in the local parliament ... [who] has superiors in the federal parliament in Moscow who are also involved ... The Russian authorities have denied involvement.

(*Guardian*, 12 March 2004, p. 17)

1 April 2004. 'One of the last two Chechen refugee camps in Ingushetia was closed on Thursday [1 April] ... Residents of the tent camp who do not want to return have to seek private accommodation in a region with already poor housing' (*IHT*, 2 April 2004, p. 4).

2 April 2004.

> Stealing in Chechnya has reached unprecedented proportions. Out of 22 billion roubles appropriated from the federal budget last year [2003] to rebuild the republic's economy, more than 2 billion was embezzled ... These shocking figures were made public by Vladimir Yakovlev, the president's authorized representative in the Southern Federal District ... In other words, one of every ten roubles earmarked for rebuilding Chechnya's economic and social infrastructure was stolen ... Accounting office officials also found that 45 million roubles had been used for purposes other than those intended, and 344 million roubles had been used ineffectively ... The authorized representative touched on another sore subject as well: compensation payments for lost homes, and the problem of internal refugees. Here, too, not all is well. Some 70,000 families have filed claims for compensation, but only 1,806 individuals have received any money. For the sake of fairness, it must be said that the slow rate of payment is due in large part to false claims discovered during the audit. Last year [2003] the authorities suspended the transfer of funds when they came across instances of people being put on housing compensation lists illegally. Nevertheless, the presidential representative declared the results of the compensation effort unsatisfactory.

(*CDSP*, 2004, vol. 56, no. 14, p. 13)

6 April 2004.

> Murat Zyazikov, president of ... the southern republic of Ingushetia ... that borders Chechnya ... narrowly escaped an assassination attempt Tuesday [6 April] when a car exploded next to his motorcade ... No group took responsibility for the attack and officials did not immediately identify any suspects ... Zyazikov, a former officer in the KGB security police and its successor, the Federal Security Service, is a political ally of President Vladimir Putin.

(*IHT*, 7 April 2004, p. 3)

'Mr Zyazikov, who was appointed by President Vladimir Putin, has implemented the Kremlin's hard-line policies in the region, in an attempt to halt the growing influence of separatists and repatriate the thousands of Chechen refugees in the republic' (*Guardian*, 7 April 2004, p. 12).

> The attack came the day after a court in Moscow convicted a Chechen woman of Ingush descent of an attempted suicide bomb attack on a restaurant in Moscow ... Ingush officials said that there was no evidence of a link between the attack yesterday [6 April] and the trial of Zarema Muzhakhoyeva, a Chechen resident of Ingush descent, who was arrested outside a Moscow restaurant in July [2003] and accused of planning to detonate a bomb in her bag. A bomb disposal expert was killed trying to defuse the device. On Monday [5 April] the court found her guilty of terrorism and prosecutors recommended that she be sentenced to twenty-four years in prison.
>
> (*The Times*, 7 April 2004, p. 13)

8 April 2003.

> Zarema Muzhakhoyeva ... was sentenced to twenty years in prison ... [She] was arrested in July [2003] after her behaviour attracted the attention of security guards at a central Moscow restaurant ... On Monday [5 April] a jury found her guilty of terrorism, attempted murder and illegal possession of explosives.
>
> (*IHT*, 9 April 2004, p. 4)

15 April 2004. 'In a twenty-three to twelve vote the United Nations Human Rights Commission rejected a resolution submitted by European countries saying that Moscow must do more to end abuses by its troops in Chechnya' (*IHT*, 16 April 2004, p. 4).

> Eighteen countries abstained ... [in the vote of the fifty-three-country commission] ... While condemning terrorist acts by Chechen separatists, the resolution cited cases of abductions, extrajudicial killings and torture by the Russian military. It said that although Russian authorities had taken steps to punish military personnel for crimes against civilians, Chechens still faced difficulties in getting officials to investigate alleged human rights abuses. The resolution also called on Russia to provide better access to Chechnya for humanitarian groups and to co-operate with international bodies that want to monitor the situation ... It is the third year running that Russia has escaped criticism over Chechnya.
>
> (*The Independent*, 16 April 2004, p. 21)

18 April 2004.

> The Saudi commander of Arab fighters in Chechnya, Abdul Aziz al-Ghamdi, who is also known as Abu Walid, has been killed ... a family member said Sunday [18 April]. Ghamdi is said by the Kremlin to be among those behind the bombing of the Moscow subway in February. Ghamdi's brother said the family ... had received news of his death Sunday morning,

but did not say how the thirty-four-year-old guerrilla had died. The Saudi website Islam Today said Ghamdi had 'been hit in the back' while preparing for prayers on Friday. The incident happened at one of the camps of mujahidin fighting the Russian government, it said. A brother of Ghamdi ... said Abu Walid, who was married to a Chechen, had been in Chechnya for the past six years and had also fought then-Soviet forces in Afghanistan during the 1980s ... Ghamdi succeeded the Arab warlord known as Khattab, who was also Saudi-born, after he was killed ... in March 2002 ... According to Chechen rebels, Khattab died five minutes after receiving a poisoned letter, which had been delivered by a messenger.

(*IHT*, 19 April 2004, p. 3)

'Ghamdi ... was killed a few days ago, his brother said yesterday [18 April] ... Islamist websites prominently featured news of [his death] ... and some said he had been betrayed by companions while he was preparing to pray' (*The Independent*, 19 April 2004, p. 21).

9 May 2004.

President Akhmad Kadyrov ... was killed Sunday [9 May] when an explosion tore through a stadium [the Dynamo stadium] in ... Grozny ... where he was attending Victory Day observances marking the defeat of the Nazis in World War II ... The blast ... [was] believed to have been a land mine planted under the stadium's VIP section ... A top Russian military commander, Colonel-General Valeri Baranov, was also at the stadium and there were conflicting reports on whether he had died or was seriously wounded ... A second land mine was found near the VIP seats ... There was no immediate claim of responsibility, but suspicion inevitably fell on the rebels ... Kadyrov was a rebel commander during the separatists' 1994–6 war that ended with Russian forces withdrawing. However, he became disenchanted during the period of Chechnya's de facto independence, complaining of the growing influence of the Wahhabi sect of Islam in the republic ... He broke with Aslan Maskhadov, who had been elected president in 1997, and in 2000 the Kremlin appointed him the republic's top civilian administrator. He was elected president last October [2003] in a vote widely criticized as fraudulent ... Refugees who have returned to Chechnya say that Kadyrov's administration has withheld promised compensation for six months or more and many Chechens complain of seizures of civilians under his administration. Kadyrov's son Ramzan runs a security force that is widely blamed for civilian disappearances ... Chechen prime minister Sergei Abramov would become the republic's acting president ... as called for in the republic's new constitution, until new elections are held.

(www.iht.com, 9 May 2004)

The explosion, reportedly caused by a bomb planted inside a concrete pillar, occurred as Kadyrov and other Russian and Chechen leaders attended a parade and concert in Grozny commemorating the fifty-ninth anniversary of victory over Nazi Germany ... The explosion ... tore a gaping hole beneath the grandstand's central VIP section ... Khussein Isayev, chairman of the republic's state council under Kadyrov, was also killed in the blast ... Colonel-General Valeri Baranov, commander of the Russian military in the northern Caucasus since late 2002, was gravely wounded ... There were conflicting reports of the death toll ... Some reports said as many as thirty-two died, though officials ... said that only fourteen deaths, including Kadyrov's, had been confirmed ... Kadyrov won [the October 2003 presidential election] after the Kremlin orchestrated the removal of his most prominent challengers ... Kadyrov dominated politics and power in Chechnya ... He once served as the republic's chief Mufti, or Islamic religious leader.

(*IHT*, 10 May 2004, pp. 1, 4)

After a decade of war the exhausted people of Chechnya had allowed themselves to hope for normalcy under Moscow's handpicked president ... His killing ... struck all the harder at people who had begun to let down their guard and imagine the possibility of another kind of life ... Kadyrov had begun to win grudging respect with his heartfelt manner, his hints of defiance towards Moscow and the small improvements he was bringing ... Along the fringes of the wreckage tiny shops and cafés have appeared ... People say there seems to be less gunfire at night.

(Seth Mydans, *IHT*, 24 May 2004, p. 3)

'The bomb appeared to have been embedded in the concrete structure of the stadium during recent renovation and detonated by remote control. A second land mine was later found' (*The Times*, 10 May 2004, p. 1).

The explosion appeared to have been concealed in the stadium's concrete underpinning ... A second bomb was reported to have been detected minutes later and successfully defused ... The Chechen separatist website ... raised the possibility that the attack may have been the work of a female suicide bomber or 'black widow'.

(*The Independent*, 10 May 2004, p. 19)

Kadyrov was elected deputy Mufti of Chechnya's Moslems in 1993 ... [and Mufti in 1995] ... He was seen by the separatist movement as a turncoat, and by most moderates as a gangster (his militia was routinely involved in kidnapping, extortion and looting).

(*Daily Telegraph*, 10 May 2004, p. 23)

'In recent weeks reports surfaced that Kadyrov had been holding talks with Aslan Maskhadov ... Such discussions ... were denied by Kadyrov' (*Guardian*, 10 May 2004, p. 13).

[The blast] came after a period of relative calm following the arrest, killing or surrender of leading rebel figures ... Mr Kadyrov had been resented by many Chechens for his strong-arm rule, which triggered accusations of human rights abuses by forces headed by his son, Ramzan ... [There were] local people who accused him of co-ordinating a reign of terror ... [He has a] centralized style, with little power-sharing ... [He put] his own trusted people in all key positions.

(*FT*, 10 May 2004, p. 6)

10 May 2004.

Hours after [the burial of Akhmad Kadyrov] ... his violent son Ramzan [twenty-seven] was appointed first deputy prime minister, placing him second in command in [Chechnya] ... He is head of the notorious presidential security service, made up of several thousand armed men, many of them former rebels, which critics accuse of acting as a private army. Witnesses testify to Ramzan's personal involvement in interrogation and torture ... It is unlikely that President Putin will abandon his policy of 'Chechenization', which encourages Chechens to rule themselves, or plans for the eventual removal of Russian troops ... Russian media reported that the toll from the explosion stood at six ... while Chechen authorities said that thirty-two had been killed ... The blast was caused by an explosive device made from two artillery shells, one of which did not detonate.

(*The Times*, 11 May 2004, p. 11)

The president, Akhmad Kadyrov, fifty-two, was buried Monday [10 May] ... just seven months after being elected in a stage-managed vote that was intended to demonstrate that the war had become a manageable, localized conflict ... Kadyrov's private army ... of 2,000 to 3,000 fighters ... including a number of rebel fighters ... was maintaining its grip through a campaign of kidnappings and terror, according to local residents and human rights groups ... The fighters, known as Kadyrovtsy, are under the command of Kadyrov's son, Ramzan. He was named Monday [10 May] to be the first deputy head of the regional government ... The Russian forces, which numbered 40,000 when Kadyrov was elected, have also been implicated in kidnappings and brutal killings The number of people who were killed ... varies from one official report to another ... On Sunday [9 May] two officials said the overall toll was at least fourteen ... Aslan Maskhadov denied any involvement.

(*IHT*, 11 May 2004, p. 3)

'The official death toll ranges from six to thirty' (*The Independent*, 11 May 2004, p. 22).

11 May 2004.

President Vladimir Putin paid a lightning visit to [Grozny] ... Mr Putin's trip, characterized by such tight security that his persistent claims that life in the province is returning to normal may have been undermined, was only announced upon his return to Moscow. There had been no visible sign of his presence in Grozny ... It was his first trip to Chechnya since 2000, when he flew into the republic in a fighter jet as Russian forces completed their military campaign ... Mr Putin told his government to add 1,125 police to the region's force by the end of the day, a move that will be largely symbolic in a country already held in the grip of 70,000 Russian troops and thousands of pro-Moscow Chechen police and security forces.

(Guardian, 12 May 2004, p. 15)

Mr Putin pledged to send another 1,000 police officers to the area, on top of about 70,000 troops already in place and called on his cabinet to redouble its efforts to reconstruct the ruined city and rebuild the republic ... Mr Putin posthumously decorated Mr Kadyrov as a hero of the Russian Federation.

(FT, 12 May 2004, p. 12)

After drawing down Russia's security forces in the region and attempting to transform the decade-long separatist war into a local conflict, Putin announced Tuesday [11 May] a plan to bolster the local police force by at least 1,000 officers. He said he would send a high-level team to look at the region's underlying social and economic problems ... Putin: 'We need to look again at the reconstruction of Grozny. Despite all that is being done, it looks horrible from a helicopter.'

(IHT, 12 May 2004, p. 3)

Mr Kadyrov was loathed by the various Chechen separatist warlords as a turncoat ... The brutal suppression of suspected rebels by a militia run by his son, Ramzan, was making Mr Kadyrov more enemies by the day ... The Chechen leader was also strongly opposed by some Russian nationalists, who complained that Mr Putin was handing too much power to him and his militia. Mr Kadyrov was also recently said to have made foes among the Russian forces occupying Chechnya, by muscling in on some of their lucrative scams ... Britain's *Daily Telegraph* reported on Monday [10 May] that he had infuriated some Russian military chiefs in Chechnya by seizing some illegal oil wells that they had been using to line their pockets ... He had been making enemies on the Russian side by demanding that most Russian troops withdraw from Chechnya ... Under his rule Chechnya had begun to show a few signs of a return to peace – but only at the cost of brutal repression by his son's 2,000-strong militia. They killed, kidnapped and looted with impunity, adding their own reign of terror to those maintained by the Russian army and the rebel groups. Young men who refused to join the militia had a tendency to disappear ... [But] even human rights workers admit that in the past few months there have been small signs of improvement in people's lives. Cafés and shops have started appearing in Grozny; universities and schools have reopened; and refugees from the war have begun to get the compensation payments that the government had promised them (minus the bribes they had to pay to the officials handing them out).

(www.economist.com, 11 May 2004)

For Vladimir Putin ... the task of Mr Kadyrov was to validate the policy of 'Chechenization': the idea that putting the region in Chechen hands, with a bit of autonomy (not independence), could succeed where brute force failed ... He was said to have alienated the local Russian garrison, by muscling in on some of the scams – such as illicit oil refining ... Under Mr Kadyrov's heavy hand, a thin veneer of normality had started to return ... There were fewer explosions and rebel attacks ... The Kadyrovtsy ... estimated to number anywhere from 1,500 to 5,000 ... are a nasty mixture of convicts, ex-rebels and ex-soldiers.

(*The Economist*, 15 May 2004, pp. 37–8)

12 May 2004. 'Ramzan Kadyrov ... will not be able to run for president because he is three years under the legal minimum age of thirty, Russian officials said' (*IHT*, 13 May 2004, p. 4).

17 May 2004. 'Shamil Basayev issued a statement yesterday [17 May] in which he claimed full responsibility for the recent assassination of Akhmad Kadyrov' (*The Independent*, 18 May 2004, p. 21).

Basayev claimed responsibility for the 9 May terrorist attack at the Dynamo stadium in Grozny that killed six people including Chechen President Akhmad Kadyrov. Moreover, for the first time since the war in Chechnya began Basayev threatened Russian president Vladimir Putin and his family.

(*CDSP*, 2004, vol. 56, no. 20, pp. 2–3)

30 May 2004.

A passenger train left Grozny ... en route to Moscow for the first time in five years on Sunday [30 May] under tight security a day after an explosion derailed seven cars of a train in a region [North Ossetia] adjacent to Chechnya ... Passenger train travel to Grozny had been cut off early in the war, which began in Chechnya in September 1999 ... Passenger trains between Moscow and Gudermes, Chechnya's second largest city, have been running for some time.

(*IHT*, 31 May 2004, p. 3)

4 June 2004.

An explosion tore through an outdoor market in the southern city of Samara [a city of roughly 1.2 million near the border with Kazakhstan] ... killing at least nine ... the Kremlin said, although some news agencies reported that eleven had died. Several of the injured were said to be wounded critically and the death toll seemed likely to rise ... The blast was initially reported as an accident caused by exploding gas or oxygen cylinders, but within hours the authorities said they had found evidence of a bomb ... It was not clear who had placed the bomb or what the motive was ... [Samara] has not had a history of terrorism related to [Chechnya] ... [and] the prosecutor's office had not ruled out the possibility that the bomb resulted from a dispute between criminal gangs.

(*IHT*, 5 June 2004, p. 2)

21–22 June 2004.

Thousands of Russian troops streamed into a southern city Tuesday [22 June] in pursuit of suspected Chechen rebels who launched a series of brazen attacks ... The fighters seized the interior ministry in Nazran, the largest city in Ingushetia, and attacked border guard posts there and in two villages near the border with Chechnya shortly before midnight Monday [21 June] ... [The] insurgents staged co-ordinated attacks on the police and security buildings in at least three cities ... By late Tuesday morning [22 June] thousands of Russian soldiers and anti-terrorism troops were moving into Nazran and most of the fighters had retreated ... [Russia] blamed Chechen rebels for planning the attacks, but the raids ... involved fighters from both Chechnya and Ingushetia ... Chechnya's interior minister, Alu Alkhanov, the Kremlin-supported candidate in Chechnya's upcoming presidential elections ... [said] that he believes ... Shamil Basayev ... was behind the foray into Ingushetia.

(www.iht.com, 22 June 2004)

An audacious overnight raid by heavily armed militants in ... Ingushetia ... killed as many as seventy-five people ... before the fighters withdrew with minimal losses [an estimated two dead] and a cache of captured weapons ... The raid, which began late Monday night [21 June] with a series of attacks against police and security posts across Ingushetia, was the largest attack by Chechnya's separatist rebels outside Chechnya since 1999 ... The death toll remained unclear by Tuesday night [22 June], but among the dead were at least forty-seven local police or security officers ... At least twenty-eight civilians also died ... The fighting killed Ingushetia's acting interior minister ... and his deputy. Two criminal investigators and four prosecutors died ... At least 100 militants seized the interior ministry's headquarters for several hours and destroyed several other security posts around Nazran and two other cities before breaking off the raid and retreating early Tuesday ... In all about 200 militants were believed to have participated in the attacks ... New fighting was reported on Tuesday afternoon near Galashki, a small village in Ingushetia, where at least some of the militants appeared to be making their way ... to Chechnya ... Only last week Chechnya's interior minister and the [presidential] front-runner ... Major General Alu Alkhanov ... said that no more than 500 rebels were still resisting federal and local forces in Chechnya. In Grozny on Tuesday General Alkhanov blamed ... Aslan Maskhadov, who last week ... [said] that the rebels would change tactics and focus on larger attacks.

(*IHT*, 23 June 2004, pp. 1, 8)

Russia blamed Aslan Maskhadov ... Akhmed Zakayev denied it ... But Mr Maskhadov had told Radio Free Europe/Radio Liberty that the rebels were changing tactics from 'acts of sabotage' to 'launching big attacks'. The day before the attack Mr Zakayev confirmed to *Kommersant* that such a decision had been adopted by field commanders on 14 June – among them Shamil Basayev ... [There were] reports that some raiders spoke Ingush, not Chechen, and that the man authorities claim led the raid is an Ingush ... The attackers seemed to come from several directions.

(The Economist, 26 June 2004, p. 46)

'Skirmishes were also reported in Dagestan' *(FT,* 23 June 2004, p. 6).

Ninety-two people were killed ... Sixty-seven of the dead were members of law enforcement agencies [There were] simultaneous attacks on fifteen sites ... The fighting raged ... for approximately four hours ... Chechen interior minister Alu Alkhanov said that the attacks had been led by an Ingushetia-based rebel leader, Magomed Yevloyev.

(www.iht.com, 23 June 2004)

The death toll ... climbed to ... ninety-five ... on Wednesday [23 June] ... most of them security personnel, including the region's interior minister, as well as several dozen civilians. The rebels had only two confirmed casualties Between 200 and 300 fighters simultaneously struck three towns in Ingushetia, firing on police stations, government buildings and checkpoints with automatic weapons and rocket-propelled grenades. The attacks also claimed the life of a local UN worker.

(IHT, 24 June 2004, p. 3)

23 June 2004.

While the report [by Amnesty International] also criticized Chechen separatist rebels for human rights abuses and for the targeting of policemen and government officials, the majority of its findings focused on Russian troops and the Moscow-backed local militia run by Ramzan Kadyrov ... [The report said]: 'Russian federal and security forces continue to carry out human rights violations such as extra judicial executions, "disappearances", arbitrary detentions, ill-treatment and torture, including rape, with impunity ... Women have increasingly been targeted' ... Amnesty said that similar abuses were starting to be perpetrated by Russian forces in neighbouring Ingushetia.

(The Independent, 24 June 2004, p. 25)

24 June 2004.

President Vladimir Putin said Thursday [24 June] that Russia would increase its military presence in the troubled Caucasus region ... Troops [are] now unofficially reported at some 80,000 around the region ... [President Putin] confirmed the deployment of a new regiment in Ingushetia ... Ninety-eight were confirmed killed ... Between 200 and 300 fighters simultaneously struck three towns.

(IHT, 26 June 2004, p. 3)

Nearly two-thirds [of those killed were] from the ranks of law enforcement or military agencies ... At each checkpoint along the roads they replaced the dead or retreating police officers with men in similar uniforms and began coolly checking the documents of each car that approached. Almost everyone who displayed a police or military identification was promptly killed ... Chechen officials say that the force that overwhelmed Ingushetia was principally composed of Ingush fighters and led by an Ingush emir ... Ingush officials ... say they were attacked from Chechnya by a mixed force of Chechen, Ingush and Russian fighters, perhaps with Arab jihadists among them.

(*IHT*, 26 June 2004, p. 6)

[The attacks] left at least ninety-eight people dead ... Who mounted the attacks and why they did remains unclear. Some saw the incident as related to the war in neighbouring Chechnya, while others thought the attacks on law enforcement buildings were linked to abductions.

(*IHT*, 28 June 2004, p. 3)

'[The] ninety-eight deaths included sixty-seven officers from the Russian army, MVD, and the Federal Security Service (FSB) Border Guard Service' (*Rusi Newsbrief*, 2004, vol. 24, no. 8, p. 92).

28 June 2004.

Russian forces on Monday [28 June] said they had killed Magomed Yevloyev, the leader of a rebel group that rampaged through the Ingushetia region bordering Chechnya ... After the raids ... refugees are in motion once more, saying they are being blamed for the guerrillas' success and must leave or face retaliation in the night. They are deeply afraid ... Thousands of Chechens, heeding what they regard as an implicit message, are fleeing Ingushetia for Grozny ... To stay, they say, is to risk their lives ... Estimates of the number of Chechen refugees who remain in Ingushetia ... range from 40,000 to 80,000.

(*IHT*, 29 June 2004, p. 3)

30 June 2004.

A Qatari court found two Russian intelligence agents guilty of assassinating Zelimkhan Yandarbiyev ... on 13 February ... in a car bombing that the judge said had been approved by 'Russian leadership' ... Both men were sentenced to life imprisonment, which in Qatar means twenty-five years ... [The judge] said the plot ... had been carried out with the approval of the 'Russian leadership' and co-ordinated between Moscow and the Russian embassy in Qatar ... Russia has denied involvement in the killing and has said the defendants were agents gathering intelligence about terrorism.

(*IHT*, 1 July 2004, p. 3)

'The Russian leadership issued an order to assassinate ... Yandarbiyev. The plan was discussed at Russian intelligence headquarters in Moscow,' the judge said ... A life sentence is twenty-five years in Qatar ... [but the judge]

said that Qatari law allowed judges to reduce sentences under certain circumstances ... [He] said that a third Russian, who had diplomatic status and
was expelled from Qatar before the trial, helped to plot the attack.

(*The Times*, 1 July 2004, p. 18)

13 July 2004.

A remotely detonated bomb struck the motorcade of Chechnya's acting
president ... Sergei Abramov ... on Tuesday [13 July] in Grozny, killing a
presidential guard ... Sergei Abramov narrowly escaped injury ... [He] has
not declared an intention to run [in the presidential election] ... Last week a
militant group calling itself the Military Council Majlis Al-Shura of Ingushetia declared a jihad in Ingushetia against Russia and also against local
people who co-operate with the Russian government ... Both Chechnya and
Ingushetia are overwhelmingly Moslem. Chechnya's southern mountains
are occupied by militants; Ingushetia harbours pockets of underground
fighters with separatist views. The forces are thought to be at least loosely
aligned.

(*IHT*, 14 July 2004, p. 3)

19 July 2004.

President Vladimir Putin has fired three of Russia's top generals and a
senior state security official yesterday [19 July] after suffering a series of
humiliating setbacks in Chechnya. The main casualty was the chief of the
general staff, General Anatoli Kvashnin. His post as commander of the
Russian forces was weakened last month [June] when parliament passed a
law giving operational control of the army to the defence minister, Sergei
Ivanov. The deputy head of the security services, the FSB, Anatoli Yezhkov,
who was in charge of their operations in the North Caucasus, was also
sacked, along with the head of Russia's interior ministry troops, Vyacheslav
Tikhomorov, and his deputy Mikhail Labunets.

(*Guardian*, 20 July 2004, p. 12)

Moving to quell a feud for control of the Russian military and simultaneously reacting to a stinging military setback last month [June], President
Vladimir Putin dismissed four senior military and security officers ...
Among the dismissed were General Anatoli Kvashnin, the chief of Russia's
general staff ... Russian news media reported that the veteran officer had
refused the new job [a lesser post] and would retire. Putin also removed a
slate of officials responsible for security in the Caucasus, including the
commander of interior ministry forces, as well as the region's top military
commander and a deputy leader of the Federal Security Service [FSB] ...
Kvashnin had been mired in a bureaucratic quarrel with Sergei Ivanov, the
defence minister and one of Putin's confidants. Last month Putin trimmed
Kvashnin's role by a presidential decree that reorganized the military's
leadership, making the general staff subordinate to the ministry of defence

and responsible for analysis and planning rather than operational command. Outspoken and brash, Kvashnin has been prominent in Russian military circles since he commanded the Russian army's armoured thrust into Grozny in the winter of 1995. Hundreds of Russian soldiers died ... Kvashnin assumed the post of Russia's senior military officer in 1997, under President Boris Yeltsin, and had presided over a second war in Chechnya ... In the last years of the Soviet Union the military had more than 4 million members. Today it musters little more than a quarter of that ... Training budgets are small enough that Kvashnin said in an interview last year [2003] that many Russian pilots, who require at least 100 hours of flight time each year to maintain their skills, were flying as little as six hours a year.

(www.iht.com, 20 July 2004)

Anatoli Kvashnin ... had spent most of his seven years in the job in conflict with people meant to be his bosses ... A few weeks ago ... the Duma passed a law handing operational control of the army to the defence ministry and leaving the generals in charge only of strategy ... In the end he [Kvashnin] asked to go ... General Kvashnin's replacement, Yuri Baluyevsky, is seen as the opposite of his mercurial, stubborn ex-boss.

(*The Economist*, 24 July 2004, p. 34)

Talk of Anatoli Kvashnin's inevitable dismissal was first heard a month ago. On 14 June the State Duma gave its virtual unanimous approval to amendments to the federal law on defence on third reading. As a result of those amendments the general staff ceased to be the principal agency for operational command and control of the Russian Federation armed forces. Command of the army and navy was completely transferred to the defence minister. This essentially put an end to divided authority ... In the opinion of many experts the biggest mistake made by the former chief of the general staff was that he was unwilling and unable to appreciate the fact that the armed forces have to be prepared to fight wars of a completely new kind – noncontact wars. Until very recently Kvashnin planned and conducted exercises for conventional forces – motorized infantry and tank forces. During his tenure not a single military higher educational institution began training specialists who could maintain our country's defensive capability under modern-day conditions, in an era when wars will be waged exclusively with high-precision weapons.

(*CDSP*, 2004, vol. 56, no. 29, p. 8)

2 August 2004.

Aslan Maskhadov has claimed responsibility for a violent June raid into southern Russia that appeared to bury hopes for a settlement of a five-year war through political dialogue. 'I approved this operation,' the internet site run by the rebels quoted Maskhadov as saying.

(*IHT*, 3 August 2004, p. 4)

6 August 2004.

Russia accused the United States yesterday [6 August] of undermining the fight against global terror by offering asylum to a leader of Chechen rebels ... Ilyas Akhmadov, 'foreign minister' in Chechnya's separatist leadership, gained asylum this week after the US Department of Homeland Security scrapped an appeal against an earlier decision to grant him asylum. US official said the appeal was dropped because there was not enough evidence to connect the rebel leader to international militant groups.

(FT, 7 August 2004, p. 6)

22 August 2004.

Vladimir Putin made a short trip to Chechnya yesterday [22 August] [visiting] the grave of Akhmad Kadyrov ... Mr Putin was accompanied on the trip by Ramzan, Mr Kadyrov's son ... and Alu Alkhanov, the interior minister, who is favourite to win this week's elections ... The president's visit was his second this year ... Seven candidates on the ballot ... Mr Alkhanov, who always supported the Russian Federation authorities throughout the past decade ... has said he does not rule out negotiations with Aslan Maskhadov ... on condition he renounces separatism.

(FT, 23 August 2004, p. 7)

'The visit [was] Mr Putin's second since the killing ... of Akhmad Kadyrov ... and the third of his presidency' (*Guardian,* 23 August 204, p. 11).

17 August 2004.

Two passenger jets crashed nearly simultaneously ... only minutes apart late Tuesday night [around 11 p.m. local time] ... [They had taken off from] Domodedovo International Airport [in Moscow], Russia's most modern ... President Putin cut short a vacation to return to Moscow ... One of the planes that crashed was a Tupolev 154 on its way to the Black Sea port of Sochi, where Putin was having his vacation ... The other plane, Volga AviaExpress Flight 1303, a Tupolev 134 on the way to Volgograd.

(IHT, 26 August 2004, p. 1)

Federal Security Service [FSB] officials yesterday [25 August] stubbornly rejected the theory that terrorists were responsible for the plane crashes ... The head of the FSB's public relations centre: 'According to preliminary findings of investigative teams working at the crash sites, no evidence of terrorist acts or explosions has been found. There are also no grounds as yet for saying that the aircraft might have been hijacked.'

(Kommersant, 26 August 2004, pp. 1, 3: *CDSP,* 2004, vol. 56, no. 34, pp. 2–3)

Russia's security service announced Friday [27 August] that investigators had found traces of explosives in the wreckage of one of the two passenger airliners ... and declared it a terrorist act. The announcement was made as an Islamic extremist group claimed its fighters had hijacked the two planes to avenge the deaths of Moslems in the war in Chechnya and elsewhere. The evidence of explosives aboard one of the planes – Sibir Airlines Flight 1047 – was the strongest indication yet that both crashes, which killed eighty-nine people [forty-six on Flight 1047 and forty-three on Flight 1303], had been deliberate acts, not the results of human or mechanical errors, as Russian officials initially suggested ... Officials said that investigators were focusing on two women with Chechen names – one aboard each plane ... The website of a group calling itself the Islambouli Brigades of Al-Qaeda claimed responsibility for both crashes, though it described two hijackings and made no mention of any bombings ... [The group] had not previously been known to operate in Russia. Earlier this month [August] the group claimed to have carried out an attempt to assassinate ... Pakistan's prime minister-designate ... The group apparently takes its name from Khaled Islambouli, the leader of a group of Egyptians who assassinated President Anwar Sadat of Egypt in Cairo in 1981 ... The website threatened new attacks in Russia, citing the war in Chechnya and what it called Russian involvement in other Moslem countries. The latter might be a reference to the killing of Zelimkhan Yandarbiyev [in Qatar] ... [The website stated]: '[The] first strike ... will be followed by other operations in a campaign aimed at helping our Moslem brothers in Chechnya and other Moslem countries enduring Russia's atheism' ... After the crash representatives of Aslan Maskhadov ... denied any involvement in the crashes.

(IHT, 28 August 2004, pp. 1, 4)

Ninety people [were killed n the two crashes] ... In the hours after the crash ... [there came] swift claims from the [FSB] ... that terrorism was an unlikely explanation. These met widespread scepticism in Russian media and provoked questions of a cover-up ... [The seeking of] information on two Chechen women who died in the crashes ... raised suspicions of the possible use of female suicide bombers [so-called 'black widows'] ... Islamic Bridges ... with reported links to al-Qaeda ... suggested that as many as five suicide bombers might have been present on each flight ... Officials began discussions yesterday [27 August] on transferring responsibility for airport security to the interior ministry.

(FT, 28 August 2004, p. 7)

'[The] obscure Islamist group called the Islambouli Brigades ... threatened more bloodshed yesterday "until the killing of our Moslem brothers in Chechnya ceases"' (*The Independent*, 28 August 2004, p. 28).

'The Russian media has heavily criticized the government for rebutting the theory of a terrorist attack; it has been alleged that the Kremlin did not want to blame terrorists until after the [presidential] election' (*Guardian*, 28 August 2004, p. 14).

18 August 2004.

> Two policemen were killed ... during a fierce battle Wednesday afternoon [18 August] near Nalchik, the capital of Kabardino-Balkaria ... [Although it was not] certain whom the policemen had been fighting ... the heads of the local special services declared that ... 'this criminal group has a terrorist bent'.
>
> (*CDSP*, 2004, vol. 56, no. 33, p. 11)

27 August 2004.

> [Chechen] authorities have ordered anyone wearing a mask or a balaclava to be shot on sight after an incident in which separatist rebels infiltrated Grozny disguised as mask-wearing policemen ... which unconfirmed reports say left up to seventy people dead. Dressed as mask-wearing policemen, the rebels set up fake checkpoints, murdering anyone they found carrying security ID.
>
> (*The Independent*, 28 August 2004, p. 28)

'The local administration issued an order banning Chechens from wearing masks on threat of being shot, in an effort to cut down on the number of disappearances of local people in raids by unknown groups' (*FT*, 31 August 2004, p. 9).

28 August 2004.

> Investigators found traces of explosives on the second of two passenger aircraft ... Volga AviaExpress Flight 1303 ... confirming that they consider the two air disasters to be terrorist acts ... Investigators searching the wreckage of Flight 1303 also said they had found the remains of a forty-fourth passenger, possibly that of a suicide bomber. That raised the death toll to ninety in Russia's worst act of air terrorism.
>
> (*IHT*, 30 August 2004, p. 3)

> It took two-and-a-half days for Russia's security service to announce what virtually everyone else believed from the moment two domestic passenger airlines plunged to earth simultaneously ... If history repeats itself, Russians may never know how or who or why. Some of the deadliest attacks in recent years remain shrouded in the miasma of Russia's endless conflict in Chechnya, and, critics say, in the penchant for secrecy that has been a hallmark of the presidency of a former KGB colonel, Vladimir Putin. Some of the attacks have been solved, at least nominally, in that officials have announced arrests and even held trials in a handful of cases. The trials were closed. Many more cases have not been solved ... The FSB officially closed its investigation into the [1999] bombings last year [2003], declaring that nine Russian and foreign Islamic fighters had carried them out, presumably to advance Chechnya's separatist cause, though none of the nine were Chechens. Some Russians still believe that the FSB was behind the bombings, trying to build momentum for another unpopular war in Chechnya.

The suspicion was fuelled by the discovery of FSB agents with explosives in the basement of a fourth apartment building. It was a training exercise, officials hurriedly explained ... After the Nord-Ost siege ... in October 2002 ... the lower house of parliament voted against investigating what exactly happened. In the days after the crashes last week officials discounted the possibility of terrorism, suggesting that human or mechanical errors were the cause. By Friday [27 August], however, the FSB announced that explosives had been found in the wreckage of one of the two airliners that crashed.

(Steven Lee Myers, *IHT*, 31 August 2004, p. 3)

29 August 2004. The presidential election is held. As expected, Alu Alkhanov won easily.

Malik Saidullayev, thirty-nine ... [is] a Chechen businessman ... Of the seventeen candidates registered for the election he is probably the most popular, analysts believe ... His popularity is derived largely from his charity ... [But] when he tried to run in last year's election [2003] he was disqualified on a technicality. A few days before, he says, a Kremlin official had visited his office to try to persuade him to pull out ... [Saidullayev's] money comes from the business empire he built up after moving from Grozny to Moscow in 1991 ... [He] decided to enter politics after his sister and brother were kidnapped in 1998 and 1999. Both were released, but his brother was shot and needed seventeen operations ... As for his politics, Mr Saidullayev is neither radically pro-Moscow nor separatist. He advocates negotiating a truce with rebels and re-establishing the rule of law in Chechnya, but keeping the region within the Russian Federation ... So far, Mr Saidullayev says, no one has explicitly asked him to withdraw from the race. But he had to sell the Russian lotto ... Russia's most popular televised lottery ... after the television station broadcasting it threatened to take it off the air. He said that Russian reporters have been warned not to interview him.

(*The Times*, 5 July 2004, p. 14)

Malik Saidullayev ... has been barred from running in Chechnya's presidential election on a technicality ... Chechnya's election commission said that ... [his] passport had an inaccuracy that ruled him out of the poll ... His passport said he was born in 'Alkhan-Yurt Chechnya', which, at the time of his birth was called 'the autonomous Soviet Chechen–Ingush republic'.

(*The Times*, 23 July 2004, p. 18)

'The election commission said Saidullayev's application contained errors, including his reported use of the word Chechnya instead of Chechen–Ingush republic, as the region was known when he was born' (*IHT*, 2 August 2004, p. 3).

[The election is held] under heavy security and with few voters in this hushed and abandoned capital [Grozny] ... Major General Alu Alkhanov, the republic's interior minister, has been endorsed by Vladimir Putin ... [whose] policy [is one] of gradually turning over the republic to Chechen proxies ... The official republic-wide turnout rate was more than 79 per cent before polls closed ... [but] that number did not square with the silent streets.

(*IHT*, 30 August 2004, p. 3)

Voting [was] marred by at least one death and allegations of improper conduct ... One man approached a voting station in Grozny and ran away when challenged by soldiers, before explosives he was carrying blew up, killing him [but no one else] ... By mid-afternoon election officials claimed that more than 60 per cent of Chechnya's 587,000 registered voters had already come to vote, and up to 90 per cent of the 27,000 servicemen stationed in the republic who are eligible had attended ... Yesterday's [29 August] official turnout figures conflicted with anecdotal reports from observers within Chechnya that it was low. There was also widespread criticism from human rights groups about techniques used to disbar rival candidates and provide disproportionate media coverage for Mr Alkhanov. Andreas Gross, from the Council of Europe ... who travelled to the Caucasus ahead of the vote, called the elections 'a farce' ... Aside from possible vote-rigging, high support from many Chechens is likely simply as the most pragmatic way to benefit from Russian co-operation, including pledges of compensation for their destroyed houses ... Aslan Maskhadov ... warned recently of larger scale attacks against Russian forces, and threatened to open a new front against the pro-Russian forces in Georgia's breakaway republic of South Ossetia.

(*FT*, 30 August 2004, p. 8)

'Ballot-stuffing and vote manipulation is rife and Mr Alkhanov's main competitor, Malik Saidullayev, was barred from running ... leaving only a handful of unknowns or Kadyrov loyalists to present a nominal challenge to Mr Alkhanov' (*Guardian*, 30 August 2004, p. 10).

The election was overshadowed by terrorist attacks that downed two airliners and a major rebel assault on Grozny last week ... Last weekend some 250 rebels attacked Grozny, leaving up to 120 people dead ... The Chechen capital was a virtual ghost town ... Mr Alkhanov is a career police officer ... Kadyrov's twenty-eight-year-old son Ramzan ... embarrassed Moscow by proposing to send troops to the breakaway Georgian region of South Ossetia.

(*The Times*, Monday 30 August 2004, p. 12)

The six other candidates were virtual unknowns; the only serious contender ... Malik Saidullayev ... had been barred from standing on a spurious technicality ... A bloody rebel incursion into Grozny the week before left up to seventy dead ... More than 585,000 people are registered to vote in the republic of over 1 million people ... [Some] 75 per

cent of the population [are] unemployed, reliable electricity and telephone services [are] largely non-existent and hundreds of people [are]
kidnapped every year.

(The Independent, 30 August 2004, p. 19)

The election was widely seen as rigged ... Officially the turnout passed 30
per cent at midday, the threshold for the election to be declared valid ... In
the past week guerrilla raids have killed about fifty pro-Moscow security
personnel in the capital, Grozny ... Many war-weary Chechens are now
willing to accept Moscow's rule if it means more security.

(Daily Telegraph, 30 August 2004, p. 12)

Major General Alu Alkhanov, the republic's top police officer ... received
nearly 74 per cent of the vote ... said the Chechen elections commission
head ... Other candidates complained of widespread violations in a vote that
was shadowed by violence ... Election officials reported a turnout of about
85 per cent. However, little activity was seen at some polling stations.

(www.iht.com, 30 August 2004)

The Russian government's choice for president of Chechnya was declared
the winner Monday [30 August] of an election that was overshadowed by
possible fraud and violence ... Other candidates complained of widespread
violations in a vote that was marred by violence, including a man who blew
himself up near a polling station in Grozny ... The Chechen elections commission chairman ... [said that the] turnout was about 85 per cent, even
though attendance at many polling stations appeared sparse ... The International Helsinki Federation for Human Rights and its Russian affiliate said
that 'minimum international standards for holding free and fair elections do
not exist in Chechnya' and that Russian electoral authorities kept competitors out to ensure Alkhanov's victory. The group's director, Aaron Rhodes,
said that 'manipulating democracy to produce a predetermined outcome is
neither fair nor a solution' to Chechnya's problems ... Officials in the
Moscow-backed Chechen government barred Alkhanov's only serious challenger from running in the election. Alkhanov had received widespread
coverage on local television and radio, while the six other candidates were
seen little. Chechnya's more than 1 million residents live in a deeply troubled region. Nearly three-quarters of the population is jobless, electricity
and telephone services are largely non-existent, and tens of thousands of
people have fled while hundreds have disappeared in kidnappings blamed
on rebels, Russian forces and allied paramilitaries ... On 21 August some
thirty people were reported killed in a night of attacks on police stations and
patrols in Grozny.

(IHT, 31 August 2004, p. 3)

The bombings followed a night of rebel raids on 21 August in Grozny that
went virtually unreported by officials and the state media. Chechen rebels
attacked polling stations and seized several checkpoints in the heart of the

city, stopping police officers or soldiers who worked for the pro-government forces and shooting them. Officially twenty-two federal or local troops died, but in Chechnya officials said the death toll reached fifty.

(*IHT*, 1 September 2004, p. 3)

Alu Alkhanov ruled out talks with separatists and said that President Vladimir Putin had backed him in his demands to take back control of regional oil export revenues, in exchange for preventing corruption ... Mr Alkhanov yesterday [30 August] reiterated his opposition to negotiations with rebel leaders unless they renounced separatism, saying that the only chance for Aslan Maskhadov ... was to seek forgiveness from his people for the suffering they had undergone ... Government observers claimed the ballot was clean, although others, including at least one of Mr Alkhanov's six rivals for the post, argued that it was marred by violations.

(*FT*, 31 August 2004, p. 9)

'The EU said it had noted concerns that the elections were not free and fair, while the US State Department ... said they had failed to meet democratic standards' (*FT*, 1 September 2004, p. 8).

Alu Alkhanov [forty-seven] yesterday [30 August] ... demanded that ... Aslan Maskhadov should face trial and apologize to the Chechen people ... The election [was] considered a farce by many observers ... [There was] a serious attack on the capital by militants the previous Saturday [21 August] ... Mr Alkhanov yesterday dismissed the idea of negotiations with Mr Maskhadov as 'not necessary' ... Mr Alkhanov was installed to keep supporters of Akhmad Kadyrov loyal to Moscow, yet the clan's key strongmen have reportedly begun to bicker.

(*Guardian*, 31 August 2004, p. 9)

The election commission said that more than 85 per cent of the electorate voted, but reporters who toured polling stations saw few voters and the Chechen capital was almost deserted ... A Russian newspaper ... *Izvestia* ... reported that two Chechen women suspected of blowing up two aircraft were friends who disappeared from the Caucasus with two other women days before the aircraft went down. The suspects ... shared an apartment in Grozny with ... [one of the suspect's sister and another woman].

(*The Times*, 31 August 2004, p. 14)

The two prime suspects in last week's explosions have been identified as Chechens ... Both had lost brothers in Chechnya's hostilities ... All four women ... were either divorced or single and worked as market traders in Grozny's central market ... [Izvestia] interviewed the two dead women's relatives in Chechnya, who suggested that they had been murdered and their passports used by real suicide bombers.

(*The Independent*, 31 August 2004, p. 23)

31 August 2004. A car bomb is exploded by a female suicide bomber in Moscow. Ten died.

'An Islamic group claimed responsibility for the bombing' (*The Independent*, 1 September 2004, p. 21).

'The group Islambouli Brigades had also claimed responsibility for the plane bombings' (*Daily Telegraph*, 1 September 2004, p. 14).

'The Federal Security Service announced Tuesday [31 August] that a bombing at a bus stop in Moscow on the night the airliners crashed was a terrorist act, possibly related to the airline bombings, and not hooliganism as first reported' (*IHT*, 1 September 2004, p. 3).

'Law enforcement officials on Wednesday [1 September] circulated a photograph of a young Chechen woman they suspect blew herself up ... [They] said she was the sister of ... [the woman] suspected of detonating the blast on board [flight 1303]' (*IHT*, 2 September 2004, p. 3).

1 September 2004.

> Heavily armed insurgents, some with explosives attached to their bodies, seized a school in southern Russia Wednesday [1 September], herded scores of school children, parents and teachers into its gymnasium and threatened to kill them. More than a dozen guerrillas, both men and women, stormed Middle School No. 1 in the town of Beslan in the republic of North Ossetia, not far from Chechnya ... Gunfire erupted in the seizure and afterward. At least two police officers died in the initial raid, while an unknown number of people might have died inside the school ... The rebels were demanding a withdrawal of Russian troops from Chechnya and the release of insurgents jailed after a series of rebel raids in Ingushetia in June that killed nearly 100 people, most of them local police officials. The guerrillas threatened to destroy the school if any attempt was made to free the hostages, and vowed to kill fifty children for each guerrilla killed ... The exact number of hostages remained unclear – estimates ranged from 130 to nearly 400 ... President Vladimir Putin, for the second time in eight days, disrupted his working vacation in the Black Sea resort of Sochi and returned to Moscow ... [The school] has nearly 900 students, ages six to sixteen, and some sixty teachers. It was not immediately clear how many guerrillas were involved, though officials said there appeared to be fifteen to seventeen fighters, at least two of them women and fifty-nine teachers ... The man who answered the phone at the school said he represented the Second Group of Salakhin Riadus Shakhidi, a rebel contingent believed to be headed by ... Shamil Basayev.
>
> (*IHT*, 2 September 2004, pp. 1, 8)

> [On 1 September] 130 children and their parents were taken hostage ... Skirmishes during the morning killed at least eight civilians and one member of the terrorist gang. But up to fifty pupils escaped and another fifteen were later released during the day ... North Ossetia is one of the

republics that has until now been relatively free from rebel or terrorist activity. Some reports said the gang numbered up to thirty and as many as 400 people were being held ... Russia called an emergency session of the United Nations Security Council to condemn the siege – an unusual step for a country that has treated violence in the Caucasus as an internal matter.

(*FT*, 2 September 2004, p. 1)

'Up to 350 people – pupils aged from seven to seventeen, their parents and teachers [were taken hostage] ... [The militants demanded the] release of twenty-four prisoners, militants captured in a recent raid' (*Guardian*, 2 September 2004, p. 1).

2 September 2004.

Two explosions rocked the area around a school where heavily armed militants ... were holed up for a second day Thursday [2 September] with about 350 hostages ... More than half [of the hostages are] children ... The attackers inside the school – believed to number as many as thirty-five or forty – have threatened to kill the hostages ... A series of explosions was heard near the school ... followed by intermittent gunfire from inside, but the soldiers and security officers did not return fire ... The attackers ... described as Chechen, Ingush and at least one local fighter – seized Middle School No. 1 as the first day of the school year began on Wednesday [1 September] ... Officials now say the attackers are linked to the separatists that have been fighting forces in Chechnya ... On Wednesday one of the attackers inside the school ... said the fighters represented a contingent led by Shamil Basayev.

(www.iht.com, 2 September 2004)

Thirty-one hostages were released on 2 September. They were women and children, some of them only babies.

'Fifteen children ... [had been] set free shortly after the start of the siege' (www.economist.com, 2 September 2004).

At least one Ossetian militant is among [the fighters] ... They have threatened to kill fifty hostages for every militant killed and twenty hostages for every militant injured ... At least twelve people had died in the initial shootout ... [As regards the] attackers inside the school ... their exact number is unknown, but estimates include sixteen to as many as forty.

(*IHT*, 3 September 2004, p. 1)

The UN Security Council issued a statement expressing determination to combat 'all forms of terrorism' ... A key demand of the hostage-takers is that Russia release the dozen or so gunmen arrested and imprisoned after a Chechen raid ... in Ingushetia in June.

(*Guardian*, 3 September 2004, p. 4)

'Reports suggest that the hostage-takers demand the release of thirty men detained after the June attack' (*FT*, 3 September 2004, p. 5).

'The hostage-takers in Beslan have claimed allegiance to Shamil Basayev ... The UN Security Council condemned the hostage-taking "in the strongest terms"' (*The Economist*, 4 September 2004, p. 40.

> Ingushetia, which used to be fairly free of the arbitrary kidnappings that are common in Chechnya, has suffered at least fifty of them since the start of 2003, according to Memorial, a human rights group ... In June an all-night raid by Chechen rebels in Ingushetia claimed dozens of lives. The terrorists apparently bribed their way through a series of checkpoints, and, according to a foreign aid agency official in Nazran, federal troops based nearby mysteriously failed to come to the aid of besieged local Ingush forces until about ten hours after the attackers had melted away.
>
> (www.economist.com, 2 September 2004)

> The Chechens' capacity to strike is enhanced by the fact that some two-thirds of the population live outside Chechnya in neighbouring republics, in Moscow and elsewhere ... There are also signs of unrest in Kabardino-Balkaria, an ethnic republic north-west of Chechnya, where at least two police recently died fighting a group of armed men they described as 'bandits'. And in Dagestan, which borders Chechnya to the east, feuding clans are struggling for control of the republic.
>
> (*FT*, 3 September 2004, p. 5)

> Russian authorities are working on the assumption that ... Shamil Basayev ... and Doku Umarov, who took part along with Mr Basayev in a raid on police stations in Ingushetia ten weeks ago ... are behind the seizure of the school in Beslan ... Aslan Maskhadov ... has an uneasy relationship with Mr Basayev. He publicly approves of some of his actions while denouncing others. His spokesmen say that while Mr Basayev belongs to Chechnya's overall 'defence council' he does not fully co-operate with Mr Maskhadov ... Although the Ingush have kept largely clear of the Chechen uprising ... tens of thousands of Chechen refugees live in Ingushetia in miserable conditions. The previous Ingush president, Ruslan Aushev, gave them protection and often called on the Kremlin to negotiate with the leaders of the independence movement. But he was replaced by a former FSB security services general, Murat Zyazikov, last year [2003]. President Zyazikov launched a roundup of Ingush suspected of sympathizing with the Chechen resistance, provoking widespread anger and resentment. Other Ingush have been kidnapped by unknown gunmen, possibly linked to the authorities.
>
> (Jonathan Steele, *Guardian*, 3 September 2004, p. 4)

'The Russian assault on Chechnya has fragmented the rebel groups, undermining the central authority of Aslan Maskhadov, who has tried to distance himself from the siege by publicly condemning it' (*FT*, 4 September 2004, p. 7).

'Only about 20 per cent of Chechens support the Islamist groups fighting Russia, while the remaining population supports secular groups' (*FT*, 4 September 2004, p. 7).

'The conflict with Moscow dates to the nineteenth century, when Tsarist forces struggled for sixty years to incorporate the mountainous territory into the Russian empire' (*FT*, 4 September 2004, p. 7).

> Nationalism has been a driving force in the Caucasus since the eighteenth century. The Chechens fought Tsarist imperial expansion from 1818. After 1917 they fought the Bolsheviks. They rose again when the German offensive reached Chechnya in 1942, and in revenge Stalin deported many to Central Asia [in 1944] ... Hundreds of thousands of deportees died of cold and hunger. Those who tried to stay behind were executed.
>
> (*IHT*, 4 September 2004, p. 6)

> Extremists ... gained an ascendancy in Chechnya ... during the period of its de facto independence from 1996 to 1999. After the Russian withdrawal in 1996 these radical forces revolted against the democratically elected government of President Aslan Maskhadov and turned Chechnya into a base for a monstrous wave of kidnapping and murder against Russians, Westerners and fellow Caucasians. In alliance with radical Islamists linked to al-Qaeda they launched a campaign to drive Russia from the whole of the northern Caucasus and united it with Chechnya in one Islamic republic. President Maskhadov failed completely to suppress these groups.
>
> (Anatol Lieven, *IHT*, 9 September 2004, p. 6)

> One of his [Stalin's] cruellest acts was the deportation of thousands of Chechen civilians in cattle trucks in the winter of 1994 – an entire nation banished from its homeland in the northern Caucasus for alleged collaboration with the German army. According to popular Chechen memory, at least 500,000 perished. Even Soviet police records admit to 200,000.
>
> (*FT*, 9 September 2004, p. 19)

> President Vladimir Putin has mistakenly (or culpably) assigned an international cause to his crisis ... The source of terrorism in Russia since the late 1990s has been the ethnic nationalist uprising in Chechnya that Russian authorities have brutally been trying to stop. Today there certainly are international reinforcements fighting for the Chechens, and there are increasing numbers of radical Islamic teachers and clerics in the Caucasus. Like Iraq the region has become a battlefront in the war of Islamic radicals against the infidels. But to hold them responsible for what has happened in Chechnya is like insisting that 'regime remnants and foreign terrorists' are the only ones doing the fighting in Iraq.
>
> (William Pfaff, *IHT*, 9 September 2004, p. 6)

'Though there is some evidence of links between al-Qaeda and Chechen rebels, the conflict in Chechnya is essentially a home-grown problem in need of a home-grown solution' (www.economist.com, 9 September 2004).

The verified links between Chechen terrorists and al-Qaeda are few and tenuous. Intelligence sources doubt that the Islambouli Brigades that claimed responsibility for the two aircraft bombings last month [August] actually did the deed ... Russia's conflict in Chechnya is homegrown, nurtured in a republic that has been systematically destroyed in the struggle for power. Russia has tried to wipe out Chechnya's separatists, first through direct military force, and more recently through 'Chechenization', i.e. foisting the problem on to a local strongman ... But the result has been to breed an anarchy in which soldiers and separatists alike kidnap and murder the innocent with impunity. Crackdowns on rebels hiding in neighbouring republics have simply spread the lawlessness ... Top to bottom corruption makes a joke of existing controls.

(*The Economist*, 11 September 2004, p. 9)

Chechnya's militant separatists have received money, men, training and ideological inspiration from international Islamic organizations, but they remain an indigenous and largely self-sustaining force motivated by nationalist more than Islamic goals, Russian and international officials and experts say ... The relationship between the separatists and Islamic terrorists abroad remains only an element in a far more complicated war ... the officials and experts said ... The number of foreign fighters is thought to be small – from a dozen to 200 – though most estimates fall on the lower end ... The number of separatist guerrillas is estimated at several hundred to a couple of thousand ... Alu Alkhanov, who was elected 29 August ... said in a recent interview that battlefield losses had reduced them to 400 or 700. By all accounts the number of foreigners among them is small.

(*IHT*, 13 September 2004, p. 2)

Khassan Baiev (head of the International Children of Chechnya, a non-profit group):

Our nation is small, a third of the size of Belgium, with a prewar population of 1 million. In the recent ten-year war with Russia 250,000 people died, fully a quarter of the population. Of those deaths an estimated 42,000 were children ... In the nineteenth century the Tsarist government exiled us to Turkey, Jordan and Syria. In 1944 Stalin herded our whole population into cattle cars and shipped us to Siberia. A third of us perished on the journey or in the harsh conditions of exile.

(*IHT*, 13 September 2004, p. 8)

3 September 2004. The school is stormed, but this was not planned. There was heavy loss of life.

The siege of the school ... ended Friday [3 September] in panic, violence of death ... fifty-two hours after it began ... Two large explosions set off pitched battles ... Other officials, in Moscow and North Ossetia, said that Russian forces had not instigated the firefights but were forced to return fire,

then storm the school after the first explosions, which occurred at 1 p.m. ...
A spokesman for North Ossetia's president: 'Taking advantage of the panic,
hostages began to escape. The bandits began shooting them in the back. The
special forces on our side had to cover the fleeing hostages' ... The dizzying
events of Friday began when the captors invited emergency workers to take
away the dead. Explosions went off, which some hostages took as a signal
to flee. Their captors sent bullets whizzing after them ... Chaos ensued ...
There were conflicting accounts of the source and the reason for the explosions. Some witnesses and officials ... said the attackers had mishandled a
bomb; some said two female fighters had detonated explosive belts wrapped
around their bodies; the spokesman for Russia's FSB ... said the explosions
might have been staged by the attackers in an attempt to sow confusion and
escape ... He and others said that some of the guerrillas ... fired on those
who fled.

(*IHT*, 4 September 2004, pp. 1, 8)

A police bomb expert said that bombs hung in basketball hoops had
exploded ... Emergency workers approached the school with agreement
from the militants to retrieve bodies of dead hostages. Explosions were
heard and militants opened fire on a group of fleeing hostages.

(*FT*, 4 September 2004, pp. 1, 7)

'A terrorist bomb went off accidentally' (*The Independent*, 6 September 2004,
p. 30). (Two bombs in total went off accidentally. These were among others
strung up between basketball hoops in the gym.)

'On Friday [3 September] Alexander Dzasokhov, North Ossetia's president
... [said the fighters] refused offers of safe passage and refused to allow food or
water into the school' (*IHT*, 4 September 2004, pp. 1, 8).

On Friday [3 September] Alexander Dzasokhov, North Ossetia's president ...
said the authorities had turned to Chechnya's separatist leaders to help negotiate a peaceful solution. He also said he had received instructions to open a
channel to Aslan Maskhadov ... Dzasokhov and Ruslan Aushev, the regional
political leader [former president of Ingushetia] who negotiated the release of
twenty-six hostages on Thursday [2 September], both called Maskhadov's
chief representative abroad, Akhmed Zakayev, on Thursday evening and again
on Friday morning. That appeared to reverse the Kremlin's policy never to
negotiate with men whom Putin has denounced as terrorists. After the assault a
Kremlin spokesman, Alexander Smirnov, distanced Putin from the contacts,
saying they were 'the personal initiative' of Aushev ... [Zakayev said] that he
and Maskhadov were prepared to assist: 'I assured them that President
Maskhadov was as distraught as they were. He is ready without any conditions
to make all efforts to save these children and resolve the crisis.'

(*IHT*, 4 September 2004, pp. 1, 8)

Aslan Maskhadov hurried to distance himself from the killings, saying: 'There
can be no justification for terror against innocent citizens.' He took the

opportunity, though, to put the blame on Putin, who inaugurated the second round of the war in 1999 and has pursued it single-mindedly, and at great human cost.

(www.iht.com, 6 September 2004)

'The roof of the gymnasium had collapsed and burned' (*IHT*, 4 September 2004, pp. 1, 8).

On Friday [3 September] a presidential adviser said for the first time that as many as 1,200 hostages might have in fact been held' (*IHT*, 4 September 2004, pp. 1, 8).

'Finally, the government put the number at 1,181' (*IHT*, 7 September 2004, p. 8).

'[There were] more than two dozen masked and camouflaged fighters … The fighters had been said to number sixteen to forty and include Chechens, Ingush and at least one Ossetian' (*IHT*, 4 September 2004, pp. 1, 8).

'The director of North Ossetia's branch of the FSB said that half the dead fighters [i.e. ten out of twenty] were foreigners, apparently from Arab countries' (*IHT*, 4 September 2004, pp. 1, 8).

The head of the FSB for North Ossetia … said that ten of the hostages who had been killed were foreign – nine of them Arab and one African. Other local security officials said Shamil Basayev and Abu Omar As-Seif, a radical Islamic Wahhabite financier, had backed the operation, which was led by Magomed Yevloyev.

(*FT*, 4 September 2004, pp. 1, 7)

Prosecutors … [said on 5 September] that thirty of the thirty-two hostage-takers had been found, and that they were Chechen, Ingush, Kazakh, Arabic and Slav in origin. The whereabouts of the suspected leader, Magomed Yevloyev, was unknown … Aslan Maskhadov … said his movement bore no responsibility for the takeover of the school and … that his independence movement would not target innocent civilians.

(*Guardian*, 6 September 2004, p. 1)

'President Putin did not immediately address what unfolded' (*IHT*, 4 September 2004, pp. 1, 8).

4 September 2004.

President Vladimir Putin … warned in a national television address that corruption in the law enforcement agencies, neglect of defence and security issues and a lack of professionalism had allowed the terror attack … Mr Putin called for the creation of a crisis-management system for Russia.

(*FT*, 6 September 2004, p. 1)

President Putin: 'This is a challenge to all of Russia, to all our people. This is an attack against all of us' … He ordered North Ossetia's borders sealed, apparently a confirmation that at least some of the captors had managed to escape … He criticized corruption in the judiciary, the inefficiency of law enforcement and the difficult transition to capitalism that he acknowledged had left few resources to secure Russia's borders in a changing and dangerous epoch ... [He demanded] that security and law enforcement agencies work more efficiently to counter the threat of terrorism. He also suggested that Russian society itself needed to develop to succeed in the fight: 'Events in other countries prove that terrorists meet the most effective rebuff where they confront, not only the power of the state, but also an organized and united civil society' ... He said he would soon propose measures to strengthen the nation's unity, to co-ordinate the political and security structures of Russia's Caucasian republics, and to create a new emergency management system ... He did not mention the war in Chechnya.

(IHT, 6 September 2004, p. 3)

President Vladimir Putin:

Today we live in conditions that took shape after the collapse of an enormous and great state. A state that, unfortunately, turned out to be unviable in a rapidly changing world ... [As Russia] we proved to be totally unprepared for many of the changes that occurred in our lives ... It must be confessed that we failed to understand the complexity and danger of processes occurring in our own country and in the world as a whole. At any rate we failed to react properly to them. We showed weakness. And the weak are trampled on. Some people want to tear off a 'juicy morsel' from us, and others are helping them ... It would appear that we have a choice: to rebuff them [terrorists] or to ... allow them to destroy Russia and pull it apart bit by bit ... As president ... [I] swore an oath to defend the country and its territorial integrity ... I am convinced that in actually we do *not* have a choice ... We are dealing with direct intervention against Russia by international terrorism ... We must create a much more effective security system and demand that our law enforcement agencies take actions commensurate with the level and magnitude of the new threats that have emerged ... A set of measures aimed at strengthening the country's unity will be prepared in the very near future ... I consider it imperative to create a new system of interaction among the forces monitoring and controlling the situation in the North Caucasus ... It is imperative to create an effective system for managing and averting crises, including fundamentally new approaches to the work of law enforcement agencies.

(CDSP, 2004, vol. 56, no. 36, pp. 5–6)

'President Putin ... failed to mention Chechnya at all ... and suggested that Russian was now being confronted with an international terrorist threat rather than a simple Chechen rebellion' (*The Times*, 6 September 2004, p. 4).

President Vladimir Putin: 'What we are facing is direct intervention of international terror directed against Russia ... We showed ourselves to be weak and the weak get beaten' (*The Economist*, 11 September 2004, p. 9).

Rather than focus on Chechnya specifically ... [President Putin] spoke about Russia as a target of global terrorism. Ever since the attacks on the United

States of 11 September 2001 Mr Putin has sought to place terrorist acts in a similar category ... In his address [on 4 September he claimed] that the siege at Beslan was 'an all-out attack' on Russia and a 'direct intervention on international terror against Russia' ... [He said that Russia was] a desperately weakened country, afflicted by 'intense internal conflicts and inter-ethnic contradictions' that in Soviet times were 'harshly suppressed by the prevailing ideology' ... President Putin: 'We have failed to pay due attention to questions of defence and security, we have allowed corruption to tarnish the judiciary and law and order' ... Russia [he said] now found itself undefended simultaneously 'from West and East'.

(*The Independent*, 6 September 2004, p. 8)

6 September 2004.

Public criticism increased yesterday [6 September] of the Russian authorities' handling of the Beslan school siege, as the country continued to bury the victims. The Russian media were highly critical of the management of the siege ... Raf Shakirov, editor of ... *Izvestia*, controlled by the businessman Vladimir Potanin, resigned after a dispute over the newspaper's critical coverage of the siege ... The former head of the neighbouring republic of Ingushetia, who mediated with the hostage-takers, Ruslan Aushev, indicated that armed locals were the first to shoot at the school, suggesting that Russian forces failed to cordon off the surrounding area ... The federal security services ... said one hostage-taker was captured alive, while the remaining thirty-two were killed. Russian authorities showed their captive ... on television, claiming the operation was ordered by Shamil Basayev and Aslan Maskhadov.

(*FT*, 7 September 2004, p. 6)

'In the predominantly Christian republic of North Ossetia the widespread belief that Ingush were among the Beslan hostage-takers has inflamed old rivalries' ((p. 19). ('A fighter captured ... [said]: "When we asked the Colonel [one of the leaders of the hostage-takers] why we must do it, he said: 'Because we need to start war in the entire territory of the North Caucasus'"': *The Independent*, 8 September 2004, p. 25.)

Criticism mounted ... newspapers and independent commentators said the government had failed to protect citizens from a mounting campaign of terrorism or to be honest about its roots ... Putin found himself facing the most direct criticism of his presidential tenure ... *Kommersant* said the emphasis in his speech on the evils of international terrorism was a dodge that 'allows governments all over the world not to assume their responsibilities for the deaths of their citizens'. 'It is as if the children did not die because of the war in Chechnya that has been going on for ten years, but because international terrorism has been on the attack,' the newspaper said ... The newspaper *Vedemosti*, too, wrote: 'It is strange the president neglected the question of Chechnya in his address ... [trying instead] to shift responsibility to the people who divided up the country in 1991' ... Even state tele-vision, which had dutifully played down the extent of the hostage-taking, conceded Sunday [5 September] that the government had a duty to keep the public better informed. 'At such moments society needs the truth,' said Sergei Brilyov, a commentator on the Rossia television station ... The editor-in-chief of *Izvestia*, Raf Shakirov, announced his forced resignation after he published an extraordinary front page on Saturday [4 September] that carried nothing but a huge harrowing photograph of a man carrying a wounded child.

(IHT, 7 September 2004, pp. 1, 8)

Russian newspapers unleashed a barrage of criticism of the government's handling of the siege and accused officials of concealing the truth from the public ... *Izvestia* printed a devastating point-by-point rebuttal of the official version of events yesterday [6 September] despite the sacking of its editor over the paper's coverage ... [For example]: The carnage was triggered not, as officials said, by an explosion detonated by the militants, but by shots fired by one of the vigilantes who had flocked to the school to prevent the authorities storming it. The militants fired back ... Several newspapers remarked on the 'bizarre' coverage of Russian state television's main channel, the only one received across the country ... *Novaya Gazeta* reported that two journalists ... Anna Politkovskaya and Andrei Babitski ... were mysteriously prevented from travelling to Beslan to cover the siege.

(The Independent, 7 September 2004, p. 7)

7 September 2004. 'Tens of thousands of Russians attended a rally against ter-rorism in Moscow yesterday [7 September], but the turnout was lower than state organizers expected and many criticized their own government. Officials had said they were expecting 100,000 people' *(FT*, 8 September 2004, p. 8).

'More than 130,000 people converged on Red Square' *(The Independent*, 8 September 2004, p. 1).

A spokesman for the Kremlin ... said Tuesday [7 September] that despite earlier assertions by security officials no Arabs had yet been found among the dead terrorists. The FSB ... had earlier reported that the bodies of nine Arabs had been found ... [The spokesman] said thirty bodies were con-firmed as terrorists ... He said there could be one more. He also said only one of the attackers had been captured alive, rather than the three reported earlier ... He denied reports that twenty Russian commandos had been killed in the attempt to rescue hostages, saying that ten had died on the scene and one later. He said investigators were coming to the conclusion that the explosion that set off the violence after a two-day standoff was accidental.

(IHT, 8 September 2004, p. 8)

The Russian defence minister, Sergei Ivanov, said yesterday [7 September] that 'not a single Chechen' had been identified among the bodies of the thirty hostage-takers. He said there was one Ingush among the dead hostage-takers, half of whom have now been identified.

(*The Independent*, 8 September 2004, p. 2)

Ruslan Aushev, the former president of Ingushetia, who negotiated with the hostage-takers, told yesterday's *Novaya Gazeta* newspaper that an explosion triggered accidentally by one of the terrorists prompted the local militia ... [a third force of] armed locals ... to open fire ... The hostage-takers then activated other explosives.

(*The Times*, 8 September 2004, p. 16)

('Ruslan Aushev ... the official sent by the Kremlin to negotiate ... said the attackers gave him a handwritten list of demands ... Though the demands were extreme, he said, they could at least have formed the basis for negotiations if they had been addressed more quickly and if explosions and gunfire on the third day had not brought the siege to a violent end. The main demand was for a withdrawal of Russian troops from Chechnya, for the inclusion of Chechnya as a separate state within the commonwealth of former Soviet states, for the maintenance of the rouble as currency and for the federal government to restore order in the region. The demands were addressed "To his Excellency, President of the Russian Federation, from the servant of Allah, Shamil Basayev" ... Basayev has claimed responsibility for the school takeover ... Aushev said he persuaded the terrorists to release fifteen babies and eleven women: "But as far as I know one of those women returned, because there were other children, her children inside" ... He said that the authorities had made plans to storm the school but that no order for storming was given before two bombs exploded and wild shooting began. He said the rebels began shooting first, but he blamed local militiamen for much of the violence ... [He] warned Tuesday [29 September] of an explosion of violence that could cause the Caucasus region of southern Russia "to go up in flames" ... "The situation is balanced between war and peace," said Aushev ... "If Ingushetia gets drawn into a conflict with Ossetia, it will be a mess ... There is Georgia, there is South Ossetia, there are Abkhazia, Kabardino-Balkaria and Dagestan. It is a big pot where everyone will seek to solve his own problems"': www.iht.com, 29 September 2004.)

8 September 2004.

Russia's Federal Security Service [FSB] offered a reward of 300 million roubles ... about $10.3 million ... for information that could help 'neutralize' the Chechen leaders Shamil Basayev and Aslan Maskhadov. Russia is also prepared to make pre-emptive strikes on 'terrorist bases' anywhere in the world ... General Yuri Baluyevsky, the chief of staff, said: 'With regard to preventive strikes on terrorist bases, we will take any action to eliminate terrorist bases in any region of the world. But this does not mean we will carry out nuclear strikes ... [Russia's choice of action] will be determined by the concrete situation wherever it may be in the world ... Military action is the last resort in the fight against terrorism' ... Russian officials have accused Basayev and Maskhadov of masterminding the attack last week on the school in the city of Beslan ... Prosecutor-general Vladimir Ustinov ... said 326 hostages had been killed and 727 wounded in the takeover ... He said 210 bodies had been identified and forensic workers were also trying to identify thirty-two body fragments. The death toll could rise, Ustinov said ... Ustinov said the approximately thirty attackers, including two women, had met in a forest early on the morning of 1 September ... People who had gathered to mark the first day of school were forced into the gym by the militants, some of whom voiced objections to seizing a school. The detainee, Nur-Pasha Kulayev, said the group's leader, who went by the name Colonel, had shot one of the attackers and said he would do the same to any other militants or hostages who did not show 'unconditional obedience'. Later that day he detonated the explosives worn by two female attackers, killing them, to enforce the lesson. One of the militants was stationed with his foot on a button that would set off the explosives, Ustinov said; if he lifted his foot the bombs strung up around the school gymnasium would detonate, he said. On Friday [3 September] the militants decided for unknown reasons to change the arrangement of the explosives and appear to have set off one bomb by mistake. That set off panic. Hostages tried to flee and the attackers opened fire.

(www.iht.com, 8 September 2004)

Prosecutor-general Vladimir Ustinov ... in a televised report to President Vladimir Putin ... said that not all the attackers had realized that their mission was to seize a school and that one of them was shot when he objected to kidnapping children. Two women hostage-takers were killed, as a gesture of intimidation, when the bombs strapped to their bodies were detonated by remote control, Ustinov said ... Colonel-General Yuri Baluyevsky, chief of the military's general staff: 'As for carrying out preventative strikes against terrorist bases, we will take all measures to liquidate terrorist bases in any region of the world ... [though that would be] an extreme measure' ... The government has blamed them [Aslan Maskhadov and Shamil Basayev] for the hostage-taking, although Basayev has denied involvement.

(*IHT*, 9 September 2004, p. 3)

('Chechen rebels responded to the FSB's bounty offer with a statement posted on separate websites promising to pay $20 million to anyone helping them capture President Putin': *The Times*, 10 September 2004. 'Mr Maskhadov's followers then offered $20 million for Mr Putin': *The Economist*, 11 September 2004, p. 6.)

Thousands demonstrated in North Ossetia ... They called for the resignation of Alexander Dzasokhov, the republic's president, whom they accuse of failing to make sufficient efforts to prevent the deaths. M Dzasokhov said he would fire his government but made no mention of himself.

(*FT*, 9 September 2004, p. 6)

'The senior official in North Ossetia ... told 1,000 angry demonstrators outside parliament that his government would step down amid heavy criticism for its handling of the siege' (*Daily Telegraph*, 9 September 2004, p. 17).

> Beslan is a small town in North Ossetia, which is the only mainly Orthodox Christian province in the otherwise Moslem North Caucasus region ... The bereaved families of Beslan have been directing much of their anger at the people of Ingushetia – another neighbouring mainly Moslem province – who are seen as sympathetic to the Chechen rebels. This follows reports that some of the hostage gang were Ingushes ... A Moscow radio station quoted a senior official of the FSB (Federal Security Service) as claiming that the school hostage-takers had coerced local police into helping them.
>
> (www.economist.com, 9 September 2004)

> In the news media ... 'black widows' [are] women prepared to kill and die to avenge the deaths of fathers, husbands, brothers and sons in Chechnya ... In Russia the women are known as *shakhidki*, the feminine Russian variant for the Arabic word meaning holy warriors who sacrifice their lives.
>
> (*IHT*, 10 September 2004, p. 1)

9 September 2004. 'Security officials have said that ten of the raiders ... have been identified and that six came from Chechnya ... They said that four others came from Ingushetia' (*The Independent*, 10 September 2004, p. 25).

> Security officials identified six of the militants who seized the school as being from Chechnya ... The other four militants who have been identified came from Ingushetia, which is sandwiched between North Ossetia and Chechnya and was targeted in brazen co-ordinated attacks against police that killed ninety people in June. The presence of Ingush raiders threatens to inflame long-standing tensions between Ingush and ethnic Ossetians ... None of those identified so far were Arabs ... Putin and Russian investigators have said about ten of the roughly thirty attackers were Arabs, but authorities have not publicly provided evidence of the assertion. Officials ... made no mention of Arabs being among the militants. Russian officials have repeatedly cast the military campaign in Chechnya as part of a war against international terrorism – a battle they say Western countries have hindered by granting asylum to Chechen figures and questioning Kremlin policy in Chechnya. To push the point that Russia is a victim of international terror – and not just of violence spawned by the Chechen conflict, which critics say Kremlin policies have aggravated ... foreign minister Sergei Lavrov met Rudolph Giuliani, mayor of New York during the 11 September attacks ... [Lavrov] did not name specific countries, but Russia was particularly angered by Britain's granting of refugee status to Akhmed Zakayev ... and by US asylum for Ilyas Akhmadov, whom Aslan Maskhadov named his foreign minister while he was Chechnya's president in the late 1990s.
>
> (www.iht.com, 10 September 2004; *IHT*, 11 September 2004, p. 4)

'Of the dead suspects identified so far all came from Ingushetia or were ethnic Chechens, including some who raided the police and other security garrisons in Ingushetia, killing nearly 100 people' (*IHT*, 13 September 2004, p. 2).

> North Ossetia and Ingushetia fought a bloody five-day war in 1992 in which up to 800 people were killed. Relations between the two have been strained since ... Most North Ossetians are Orthodox Christians, while the Ingush are Sunni Moslems. Ingush and Chechen students studying at Vladikavkaz University have already been bussed out 'for their own safety' and in the days after the attack a huge crowd headed for the Prigorodny district of Northern Ossetia, where many Ingush live The [authorities] stopped them before violence erupted, but tensions are still running high. The Prigorodny district ... was the scene of the first ethnic conflict in the former Soviet Union. Ingush fighters tried to seize it from North Ossetia in 1992 and were only repelled after bloody clashes that left hundreds dead. The land used to be part of Ingushetia but was given to North Ossetia by Stalin in 1944 after he decided to exile the entire Ingush and Chechen people to Central Asia on the spurious grounds that they were minded to collaborate with the Nazis. The Ingush and the Chechens were eventually allowed to return in the 1950s by the Soviet leader Nikita Khrushchev, but when they got back to Prigorodny they found their homes inhabited by North Ossetians.
>
> (*The Independent*, 11 September 2004, p. 32)

'Stalin deported the Ingushis and Chechens to Central Asia in 1944 and gave parts of Ingushi land to the Ossetians' (*IHT*, 21 September 2004, p. 3).

10 September 2004.

> President Vladimir Putin agreed Friday [10 September] to a parliamentary enquiry [by the upper house into the Beslan siege] ... after having previously said none was necessary. Putin had already agreed to an internal investigation into the attack ... Russian officials say one of the bombs wired in the gym blew accidentally and some of the hostages tried to flee. The attackers opened fire and Russian special forces assaulted the building.
>
> (www.iht.com, 10 September 2004)

> Putin might have agreed to an enquiry to appease critics angered by his comments this week demeaning the value of a parliamentary investigation ... A seven-year-old boy died on Friday, bringing the death toll, including eleven members of the special forces and at least thirty militants, to at least 368.
>
> (*IHT*, 11 September 2004, p. 1)

'North Ossetia's parliament approved a new prime minister ... President Alexander Dzasokhov dismissed the [previous] regional government but did not step down himself' (*IHT*, 11 September 2004, p. 4).

11 September 2004. 'On Saturday [11 September] he [Putin] dismissed the interior minister and security chief of North Ossetia' (*IHT*, 14 September 2004,

p. 8). 'Putin ordered the firing of North Ossetia's interior minister and the regional head of the FSB, the agency that is supposed to spearhead anti-terrorist efforts' (www.iht.com, 13 September).

13 September 2004.

> President Vladimir Putin announced Monday [13 September] a series of far-reaching initiatives aimed at combating terrorism, which would significantly strengthen the Kremlin's control over the country's political life ... Putin said top down control from the central government was key, and that strong political parties must become one of the tools for mobilizing the entire society to conduct the fight against terrorism. He recommended changing the system of electing the State Duma to a purely proportional system. That would eliminate the individual races that currently fill half the chamber's seats, and would further increase the clout of the pro-Kremlin faction and its allies, who already enjoy an overwhelming majority. Putin also said he would propose legislation to the State Duma before the end of the year providing for regional governors to be elected by regional legislatures on the recommendation of the head of state ... Putin said that he had ordered the country's security services to increase their international co-operation, and that Russia needed a new federal agency to co-ordinate the fight against terror ... He proposed setting up a new structure called the Public Chamber to engage non-governmental organizations and other groups to mobilize society in the fight against terror and to strengthen public oversight of the government and actions of law enforcement agencies.
>
> (www.iht.com, 13 September 2004)

> President Vladimir Putin ordered a sweeping overhaul of Russia's political system in what he called an effort to unite the country against terrorism ... His proposals would strengthen the Kremlin's already pervasive control of the legislative branch and regional governments ... Putin outlined what would be the most significant political restructuring in more than a decade – one that critics immediately said would violate the constitution and stifle what political opposition remains. Under Putin's proposals, which he said required only legislative approval and not constitutional amendments, the governors or presidents of the country's eighty-nine regions would no longer be elected by popular vote but rather by local parliaments – and only on the president's recommendations ... In last December's election [2003] those [district] races accounted for all of the independents and liberals now serving in the Duma ... A direct proportional election would give the advantage of incumbency to those parties in power and eliminate local grassroots campaigns that have provided the handful of dissenting voices heard on the Duma floor ... Putin demoted his representative in the Southern Federal District, Vladimir Yakovlev, who had overseen Chechnya and the rest of the North Caucasus. In his place Putin appointed one of his most

trusted aides, Dmitri Kozak, who since March has served as chief [of staff] of the government.

(IHT, 14 September 2004, pp. 1, 8)

'Putin ... proposed stripping citizens of the right to elect their own regional executives (governors in most regions and presidents in the ethnic republics)' (*IHT*, 18 September 2004, p. 4). 'Putin's decree, signed late Monday [13 September], gave the government one month to draw up proposals' (www.iht.com, 14 September 2004).

> On paper the changes in the federal parliament appear to move Russia towards a Western-style system with a handful of political parties. In practice they will mean the elimination of independent candidates who owe their election to local people ... Vladimir Yakovlev ... will run a new ministry of regions and nationalities, a post abolished during the president's first term.
>
> *(FT*, 14 September 2004, pp. 1, 8)

'The new system could in theory give smaller parties seats in parliament, but the current rules let only parties with more than 7 per cent of the vote take seats' (*Guardian*, 14 September 2004, p. 15).

'The Kremlin will propose regional governors whose appointments will be voted on by regional legislatures. It is unclear what will happen if the Kremlin candidate is rejected' (*Daily Telegraph*, 14 September 2004, p. 11).

'The new legislation would give Putin the authority ... to disband regional legislatures if they rejected his appointees twice' (*IHT*, 5 October 2004, p. 2).

'[President Putin] has ended the free election of regional governors ... [This] is an opportunistic lunge at the separate problem of wealthy industrialists buying into regional political fiefdoms' (*The Times*, editorial, 15 September 2004, p. 21).

President Putin:

> I believe that in the present situation, under the present circumstances, the country's system of executive power should not merely be adapted to work in crisis situations but be fundamentally restructured for the purpose of bolstering the country's unity and preventing crises. We have no right to forget that, in their far-reaching plans, those who aspire, organize and carry out acts of terrorism are striving to split the country apart; they are seeking the break-up of our state, the collapse of Russia. I am convinced that national unity is the principal condition for victory over terror ... One way of ensuring real dialogue and interaction between the public and the authorities in their struggle against terror should be national political parties ... The socio-economic picture in the North Caucasus region remains pitiful ... The executive branch is to blame for this situation ... The North Caucasus is a highly important strategic region of Russia ... For all practical purposes we have achieved no visible results in our efforts to combat manifestations of terror. We have particularly failed to achieve visible results in our efforts to eliminate its sources. But the roots of terror lie in the continuing mass unemployment in the region ... the level of unemployment there is several times higher than the

national average ... in the lack of an effective social policy, and in the low level of education of the younger generation – sometimes the absence of any opportunity to get an education at all. All these things constitute a rich culture medium for extremist propaganda, for the growth of hotbeds of terror and the recruitment of any supporters of terrorism ... A number of countries that have encountered the threat of terrorism have long since created unified security systems that are responsible for providing comprehensive domestic security and combating terrorism. We in Russia need the same kind of organizational effort and the same kind of organization of the work of the national security system that is capable not only of halting terrorist acts and overcoming their consequences, but also of working to prevent terrorist attacks and acts of sabotage and man-made disasters perpetrated by terrorists. It must work to forestall and destroy the criminals in their own lairs, as they say, and, if circumstances require it, to get them and bring them back even from abroad.

(*CDSP*, 2004, vol. 56, no. 27, pp. 1–3)

14 September 2004.

Russia is to spend an additional 157 billion roubles ($5.4 billion) on security ... Russia's security agencies will split an additional 50 billion roubles. The defence ministry will receive an extra 107 billion roubles. It was not clear whether the government was earmarking new funds or highlighting increases already in the draft 2005 budget.

(*FT*, 15 September 2004, p. 6)

Russia's main security agencies – the FSB, interior ministry, border guards service and foreign intelligence service – will split an additional $1.71 billion in funding, The defence ministry will receive an additional $3.66 billion ... It was not clear, however, whether the government was earmarking new funds or if ... [the finance minister] was highlighting increases that had already been put in the draft 2005 budget ... A finance ministry press officer said that ministry officials themselves did not know. About $18.1 billion had already been earmarked for defence in 2005, a 28 per cent increase over this year [2004] and $13.6 billion had been set aside for national security and law enforcement, a 20 per cent increase ... [The finance minister] had already committed $68.5 million in next year's budget to a new anti-terrorism programme that would be used to increase security in public places, including Moscow's subway system.

(*IHT*, 15 September 2004, p. 3)

'An extra $1.7 billion had already been pledged last month [August], after two aircraft were blown up by suicide bombers' (*The Economist*, 18 September 2004, p. 51).

15 September 2004.

The suicide bombers who destroyed two passenger jets over Russia last month [August] had been detained in the airport shortly before boarding, both were released by a police supervisor, and one swiftly bribed her way onto the aircraft she would destroy ... prosecutor-general Vladimir Ustinov ... said Wednesday [15 September] ... The prosecutor said the bribe paid to an agent for boarding one doomed jetliner – Sibir Airlines Flight 1047, with forty-five people on board – was 1,000 roubles, equivalent to \$34 ... The women received help from a man ... who took an amount in roubles worth roughly \$68 from one woman and \$103 from the other ... Ustinov's remarks did not shed light on how the second woman boarded the plane she is thought to have destroyed.

(www.iht.com, 16 September 2004)

The prosecutor-general, Vladimir Ustinov, said the two suicide bombers ... had bribed their way on board. The two women were flagged as security risks after arriving from the southern city of Makhachkala and taken in for questioning. But a police captain let them go without a search, and a ticket seller accepted 4,000 roubles for himself and another 1,000 roubles for an Air Sibir employee to help them get on their next flights without further checks. Corruption among officials had reached 'dangerous' levels, said Mr Ustinov. The thirty-two hostage-takers in the Beslan siege are believed to have travelled from outside the republic, passing several military check-points. But apparently their trucks full of weapons were not challenged ... Aslambek Aslakhanov, Mr Putin's Chechnya adviser ... estimated that as much as 80 per cent of government money meant to help rebuild Chechnya had been siphoned off by corrupt officials.

(*Guardian*, 17 September 2004, p. 19)

16 September 2004. Boris Yeltsin:

We should not allow ourselves to step away from the letter – or the spirit – of a constitution that the country adopted in a national referendum in 1993. The strangling of freedoms, the roll-back of democratic rights – this can only mean that the terrorists won. Only a democratic country can success-fully lead a fight against terrorism and count on standing shoulder to shoul-der with all of the world's civilized nations.

(*IHT*, 17 September 2004, p. 3; *Guardian*, 18 September 2004, p. 15)

'[Yeltsin] has at times criticized Putin's policies, but his latest comments, though veiled, were some of his sternest yet against the new regime' (*IHT*, 17 September 2004, p. 3).

Mikhail Gorbachev:

Unlike the president I believe that the terrorist attacks of recent weeks are directly connected with the military actions in the Caucasus ... Once again we must seek political solutions, enter into negotiations with moderate rebels, and cut them off from implacable extremists ... Under the banner of combating terrorism proposals are being made to drastically restrict demo-cratic freedoms and deprive citizens of the right to directly express their opinions of the government in free elections. We are being asked to consent to what amounts to the appointments of governors and to give up elections in single-seat districts. And this at a time when we already have predominantly 'tame' parties ... Such a system will definitely not help combat terrorism.

(*CDSP*, 2004, vol. 56, no. 37, p. 6)

The media freedom watchdog of the fifty-five-nation OSCE ... said Thursday [16 September] that Russia's failure to provide full and timely information of the Beslan school siege and Russian television's weak reporting had hurt democracy and fanned public mistrust ... [The report said that] there had been cases of detention and harassment of journalists covering the siege ... [OSCE's media freedom representative]: 'Even more importantly the government did not provide in a timely manner truthful information on the handling of the crisis' ... A result in Beslan was a 'triple credibility gap' between the government and news media, between the news media and citizens and between the government and its people, the report said. 'This is a serious drawback for a democracy,' it said. The report also singled out the three nationwide television broadcasters, the main source of information in a country spread across eleven time zones. All are controlled directly or indirectly by the state ... [The representative] said: '[The national broadcasters] underperformed ... Television itself, the journalists, applied self-censorship, probably out of feelings of responsibility but also probably because of lack of understanding.

(*IHT*, 17 September 2004, p. 3)

Boris Gryzlov, Duma speaker, said Thursday [16 September] that Russia would open a second parliamentary enquiry into the [siege] ... a further retreat by the authorities who initially ruled out a probe. The State Duma will investigate the event separately from the upper house, which announced its enquiry last week. The investigations mark a U-turn by Putin, who originally said any parliamentary probe could turn into a 'political show' and ruled out a public enquiry.

(*IHT*, 17 September 2004, p. 3)

Aslambek Aslakhanov, Mr Putin's Chechnya adviser ... [said the president] had been prepared to release terrorists detained in Ingushetia and offered to swap up to 700 adults for the children ... Aslakhanov: 'I had 700 people ready to replace the hostages [including Olympic champions and political leaders] ... We were ready to release detained terrorists from Ingushetia. We were bargaining over the number of children that would be released.'

(*Guardian*, 17 September 2004, p. 19)

'Official claims [are that of the] ... thirty-two hostage-takers one was captured' (*The Times*, 17 September 2004, p. 17).

A deputy to the transport minister for North Ossetia ... [has said] that 1,347 people had been taken hostage – a figure that contradicts the ministry of interior's total of 1,189 and the general-prosecutor's total of 1,156. A local newspaper last week printed a preliminary list of 1,388 people.

(*Guardian*, 20 September 2004, p. 14)

17 September 2004.

Shamil Basayev claimed responsibility Friday [17 September] for the Beslan school siege in a statement on a rebel website ... Basayev had previously denied involvement. On Friday he expressed regret for the deaths of ... hostages ... and blamed the outcome on the Kremlin. He made clear there would be no let-up in rebel attacks in the future in the campaign for an independent Chechnya, threatening further attacks by any means he saw fit. Basayev's statement appeared a day after President Vladimir Putin ruled out negotiations, linking the Chechen rebels with al-Qaeda. Basayev also confirmed Russian suspicions that his group had masterminded suicide bomb blasts that brought down two passenger planes over Russia on 24 August with the death of ninety people as well as two other bomb attacks in Moscow. Basayev said armed units of the Riyadus-Salakhin group that he heads carried out the Beslan attack ... Most official versions say a bomb broke loose and exploded in the gymnasium where most of the hostages were being held, and some hostages seized the chance to flee. They were shot down by the gunmen, provoking the storming by security services, the authorities say. Basayev said the hostage-takers had told intermediaries that the hostages would be given food and water and the youngest released if the Russian side began to meet their demand for the withdrawal of Russian forces from Chechnya or, in the absence of this, the resignation of Putin.

(www.iht.com, 17 September 2004)

Although its authenticity could not be confirmed, in the past the website, believed to be operated in part from Lithuania, has carried exclusive material from Basayev, and the posting provoked a stinging reaction from Russian and other officials, who acted upon it as if it were real ... Lithuania has announced that it will move to shut the website ... Shamil Basayev ... listed the attacks that have unnerved the nation since they began on 24 August: two bombs in Moscow, the in-flight destruction of two passenger jets and the siege of Middle School No. 1 in Beslan ... [He] insisted that his fighters had not shot them [the hostages] or used them for cover. He blamed the deaths on Russian forces and their bungled attack ... [The statement] said that thirty-three militants had seized the school in Beslan, including two Arabs ... Basayev used the slang 'Russnya' for 'Russia', a sneering and derogatory form he has used in the past.

(*IHT*, 18 September 2004, pp. 1, 6)

'Shamil Basayev ... wrote an email signed with his *nom de guerre*, Abdullah Shamil' (*The Times*, 18 September 2004, p. 18).

Basayev insisted that the Kremlin was lying and had stormed the school. He even offered to co-operate with Russian investigators to prove as much, and demanded that the UN and the EU conduct independent enquiries ... He said a thirty-three-strong martyrs' brigade ... had occupied the school on his orders and that he had personally trained the fighters ... The group included twelve Chechen men, he said, two Chechen female suicide bombers and nine Ingush men, as well as three Russian men, two Ossetians and two Arabs among others. Basayev boasted that the entire operation had cost him $8,000 and that all of the weapons and transport had been stolen from Russian forces ... He added that the suicide bombing of the two airliners had cost him $4,000 while the Moscow Metro bombing and a bus-stop bomb had set him back $7,000.

(*The Independent*, 18 September 2004, p. 31)

Mr Basayev alleged that emergency ministry workers sent to collect bodies of hostages killed early in the siege were really security service officers, and the explosions went off only after they shouted at hostages to run out of the school ... Mr Basayev also disputed official claims that the hostage-takers made no clear demands. He confirmed earlier reports that they had demanded the withdrawal of Russian troops from Chechnya and, failing that, the resignation of Mr Putin ... Mr Basayev said the thirty-three attackers included ... five other Russian citizens from various groups. Russian authorities said there were thirty-two attackers, all but one of whom was killed.

(*The Times*, 18 September 2004, p. 18)

Shamil Basayev (Abdullah Shamil):

They are fighting us without any rules, with the direct connivance of the whole world, and we are not bound by any circumstances, or to anybody, and we will continue to fight as is convenient and advantageous to us, and by our rules ... A terrible tragedy occurred in the city of Beslan; the Kremlin vampire destroyed and wounded 1,000 children and adults, giving the order to storm the school for the sake of imperial ambitions and the preservation of his [Putin's] own throne ... We declare Russian special forces stormed the school. It was planned from the very beginning ... Putin is trying to pin all this on us in the most impudent fashion, labelling us international terrorists and asking the whole world to help. We regret what happened in Beslan. It is simply that the war, which Putin declared on us five years ago, which has destroyed more than 40,000 Chechen children and crippled more than 5,000 of them, has gone back to where it started from ... The operation ... in the town of Beslan [was carried out by] the second battalion of martyrs under the command of Colonel Orstkhoyev ... [The Riyadus-Salakhin Reconnaissance and Sabotage Battalion of Chechen Martyrs has] carried out a number of successful operations on the territory of Russia ... I do not know Osama bin Laden. I do not get any money from him, but I would not turn it down ... Chechens

fight only against Russnya for their freedom and independence ...
Chechens are fighting Russians only ... for now.

> (*FT*, 18 September 2004, p. 6; *IHT*, 18 September 2004, pp. 1, 6;
> *The Times*, 18 September 2004, p. 18; *Guardian*, 18 September 2004, p. 15;
> *The Independent*, 18 September 2004, p. 31)

'Mikhail Gorbachev (*Moskovski Novosti*, 17 September 2004): "How can you
stamp out corruption without a normal parliament or press? Without control on
the part of society? But there is no movement in this direction. The reverse is
happening"' (*Guardian*, 18 September 2004, p. 15).

'Mikhail Gorbachev called for negotiations with moderate Chechen fighters
and warned that the Kremlin's plans to change voting for parliament and
regional governors would "dramatically curtail democratic freedoms"' (*FT*, 18
September 2004, p. 6).

Martin Wolf: 'The bombings that preceded his first election and then as con-
veniently ceased gave him [Putin] the presidency' (*FT*, 22 September 2004, p. 21).

24 September 2004. Aslan Maskhadov:

> Unfortunately, in the conditions of the current ongoing war, the trial of those
> responsible for the recent terrorist acts is practically impossible. At the same
> time I declare that at the end of the military phase the guilty will be taken to
> court, including Shamil Basayev.
>
> (*Guardian*, 25 September 2004, p. 20)

> Mr Maskhadov ... reportedly made him [Basayev] his commander in chief
> in August 2002 to quieten resistance ahead of peace talks. Yet since the
> Moscow theatre siege in October of that year Mr Basayev has taken the lead
> in organizing attacks against Russian civilians.
>
> (*Guardian*, 25 September 2004, p. 20)

President Vladimir Putin (addressing media agencies):

> There will be no turnabout in the country's life. Russia made its choice
> ten years ago for a democratic, free market, socially orientated state ...
> For Russia democracy and stability are of equal importance. We are man-
> aging to build a system under which Russia will have democracy and
> stability ... It is obvious that the struggle against terrorism cannot be an
> excuse to infringe upon the freedom and independence of the press. But
> you yourselves, as professionals, should develop a model of work that
> would allow media to become an effective instrument in the struggle
> against terror.
>
> (*The Times*, 25 September 2004, p. 22;
> *Guardian*, 25 September 2004, p. 20)

'Parliament rejected a bill to ban all television and radio coverage of
hostage crises until they had been resolved' (*Guardian*, 25 September 2004,
p. 20).

5 October 2004. 'Alu Alkkhanov ... is sworn into office' (www.iht.com, 6 October 2004).

> Short on hope, options and resources, an increasing number of the nationalist guerrillas are turning to the Islamists. At the start of this year [2004] the latter accounted for perhaps a third of the approximately 1,000 active full-time fighters – and almost none of the 3,000 to 4,000 part timers who occasionally join major and opportunistic attacks. But as Maskhadov's forces dwindle, desert and fail to recruit new manpower, the split will be nearly even by the end of the year.
>
> (Mark Galeotti, *The World Today*, 2004, vol. 60, no. 11, p. 18)

12 November 2004.

> About 1,000 troops are to be withdrawn from Chechnya and conscripts will no longer be used in the war, defence minister Sergei Ivanov said ... but the 42nd Motorized Division, the main military unit, 'will stay there forever' ... Russia has 70,000 armed forces in the rebel region.
>
> (*The Times*, 13 November 2004, p. 50)

('[President Putin declared] that in future only volunteers, not conscripts, would be sent to Chechnya': *The Independent*, 31 August 2004, p. 30.)

23 December 2004.

> [It was announced on 23 December that] two Russian intelligence agents jailed for life [in June] in Qatar for killing ... Zelimkhan Yandarbiyev ... on 13 February ... will be sent back to Russia to serve out their sentences ... Russia at the time denied that the men were responsible but admitted that they were intelligence agents. The Qatari court said the killing had been carried out with the backing of 'Russian leadership' and co-ordinated between Moscow and the Russian embassy in Qatar.
>
> (*IHT*, 24 December 2004, p. 3)

29 December 2004. 'Ramzan Kadyrov, the Chechnya deputy prime minister ... has been awarded the Hero of the Russian Federation title by President Putin' (*The Times*, 30 December 2004, p. 35).

31 December 2004.

> The Moscow-backed president of Chechnya, Alu Alkhanov, said yesterday [31 December] that Russia's invasion of the republic on New Year's Eve 1994 was a 'mistake'. It united the ... [republic] behind the rebel leader, Dzhokhar Dudayev, and led to a decade of war.
>
> (*Daily Telegraph*, 1 January 2004, p. 14)

1 January 2005.

> For ex-Soviet citizens Russia will require international passports for entry as of 1 January 2005 ... Citizens of Commonwealth countries ... will be

able to enter Russia only if they hold international passports. And Russian citizens got a present, too: a statement by the Russian foreign ministry yesterday [12 October 2004] advises all ... to apply for international passports 'in short order' ... As of 1 January 2005 'internal passports, birth certificates and various types of government-issued identification documents will no longer be valid for crossing the border'.

(CDSP, 2004, vol. 56, nos 40–1, p. 4)

28 January 2005. 'Three Russian human rights advocates were awarded [in Stockholm] the Olaf Palme Prize for their efforts to promote democracy in Chechnya. The winners were Anna Politkovskaya, Ludmilla Alexayeva and Sergei Kovalev' (*The Independent*, 29 January 2005, p. 26).

2 and 7 February 2005.

Aslan Maskhadov urged Moscow on Monday [7 February] to open peace talks in response to his unilateral ceasefire, but the Kremlin insisted it would not negotiate with 'terrorists' ... He ordered a temporary truce in the republic until 22 February ... Other rebels are observing the ceasefire ... A source in the pro-Russian Chechen government said Monday [7 February] that there had been a virtual halt to Chechen rebel attacks since the truce was announced on Wednesday [2 February].

(IHT, 8 February 2005, p. 3)

'[The] unilateral ceasefire will last for one month ... The radical wing of the fighters, which is controlled by Shamil Basayev, accepted the ceasefire' (Akhmed Zakayev, *IHT*, 16 February 2005, p. 6).

22 February 2005. 'The ceasefire called by Aslan Maskhadov expired ... late Tuesday [22 February] ... Wednesday [23 February is] the sixty-first anniversary of the Stalin-era deportation of Chechens to ... Central Asia ... Russian officials naintained that rebels kept up their attacks' (*IHT*, 24 February 2005, p. 4).

24 February 2005.

The European Court of Human Rights in Strasbourg found Russian authorities had committed serious breaches of human rights during offensives in Chechnya – including breaches of the right to life and failure to carry out adequate investigations ... Claims [were] brought by six Chechens who blamed Moscow for deaths of relatives ... In the claims decided yesterday [24 February 2005] two residents of Grozny had alleged torture and murder of their relatives by the Russian military in 2000. Another case centred on complaints about the indiscriminate Russian bombing of civilians who were fleeing Grozny in late 1999. A third focused on the bombing of Katyr-Yurt village in late 2000 ... Lawyers say 'well over' 100 cases involving alleged abuse by the Russian military during their crackdown on separatist rebels ... are stacked up in the Strasbourg court.

(FT, 25 February 2005, p. 6)

'The six cases were the first of at least 120 concerning the Chechen conflict submitted to the court ... [There were] seven judges, one of them Russian' (*Daily Telegraph*, 25 February 2005, p. 13).

> [The court ordered Russia] to pay compensation of more than 135,000 Euros ... in damages and legal costs ... to the families of eleven civilians killed by federal troops ... [Russia is] a signatory to the European convention ... the complaints were first lodged in Strasbourg in April 2000 and accepted as admissible in December 2002 ... About 150 ... further complaints ... are already registered with the court ... Russia will either have to obey the judgement or take the drastic step of leaving the Council of Europe.
>
> (*Guardian*, 25 February 2005, p. 17)

25 February 2005.

> The Union of Committees of Soldiers' Mothers (UCMS) signed [in London] a 'road to peace' proposal ... [with] Akhmed Zakayev, envoy of Aslan Maskhadov ... [They agreed] that the decade-old conflict in Chechnya could not be settled by force. They blamed the growth of terrorism [in Chechnya] ... on the 'short-sighted and criminal policies' of the Russian government ... The peace proposal [is] understood to centre around a gradual cessation of violence by rebels ... Yesterday's meeting [was] organized by European parliament members ... [Maskhadov] recently called a three-week ceasefire and urged President Vladimir Putin to start peace talks. The Russian authorities ignored the offer, dismissing Mr Maskhadov as a terrorist who was not in control of all Chechen forces.
>
> (*FT*, 26 February 2005, p. 8)

8 March 2005.

> Aslan Maskhadov ... [was killed on 8 March 2005 in a raid by] Russian special forces ... [on the] village of Tolstoy-Yurt only 19 kilometres, or 12 miles, from Grozny ... Maskhadov's imminent capture or death has been reported before, but officials showed little doubt that it was Maskhadov who died in the raid ... One of his most prominent aides, Akhmed Zakayev, said [in London] that he also had confirmation of Maskhadov's death from sources inside Chechnya ... Earlier this year he was reported to have offered a month-long ceasefire, which ended on 23 February. Attacks in Chechnya did seem to slow, but Russian officials denounced the gesture as a stunt, refusing, as before, to hold any negotiations with him or any other separatist leaders ... Zelimkhan Yandarbiyev died in a car bombing in February 2004 while in exile in Qatar. A court there convicted two Russian secret agents and sentenced them to life in prison, though they later released them to the Russian authorities.
>
> (*IHT*, 9 March 2005, pp. 1, 8)

The spokesman for the Russian forces in the North Caucasus ... [said that Maskhadov] died ... apparently by accident, in an explosion ... Akhmed

Zakayev [said that] ... he was killed 'in a fight, a shootout' ... Ramzan Kadyrov ... [said that Maskhadov] had been killed by a careless shot fired by his bodyguards ... Last week Aslan Maskhadov was calling for peace talks with President Vladimir Putin, asserting that a half-hour tête-à-tête would be enough to settle a decade of war in Chechnya.

(Guardian, 9 March 2005, p. 12)

Earlier this year [2005] he [Aslan Maskhadov] proclaimed, and broadly enforced, a three-week end to hostilities. He insisted that if he were given just half an hour with Mr Putin, and allowed to explain what was really happening, the war would end quickly.

(The Economist, 12 March 2005, p. 104)

10 March 2005.

Chechen rebels have appointed a little known Islamic cleric to replace Aslan Maskhadov ... In a show of unity moderates and radicals said they supported the appointment of Abdul Khalim Saidullayev, the former head of Chechnya's Islamic court ... [Maskhadov's] replacement was announced on a rebel website by Shamil Basayev ... The appointment was also supported by more moderate Chechens in the West, including Akhmed Zakayev.

(Daily Telegraph, 11 March 2005, p. 17)

The underground separatist government of Chechnya appointed a little known fighter and religious leader as a successor to Aslan Maskhadov ... Shamil Basayev publicly committed himself to Saidullayev ... Basayev was said to have turned the formal leadership post down ... Abdul Khalim Saidullayev, an Islamic judge ... [who] had been essentially unknown as a rebel ... [He is] believed to be a native Chechen ... [and is] thirty-five to thirty-eight years old ... His appointment was announced on two websites, used by Chechen rebels and terrorists, which said he had been next in line to the leadership since 2002, when Maskhadov decreed that if he was ever captured or killed Saidullayev would assume his post ... [It is said that] Saidullayev had been based in the town of Argun with perhaps a few dozen fighters and was more of a religious figure than fighter; his wife was killed at a military checkpoint not long ago.

(IHT, 11 March 2005, p. 3)

'Chechen rebels denied that Mr Saidullayev was a Saudi national [as a Russian website had claimed] ... Shamil Basayev ... commands at least half the estimated 1,500 to 5,000 rebels still fighting against Russian rule' *(The Times,* 11 March 2005, p. 38). 'Russian officials say there are about 1,500 rebels active in Chechnya, divided into 100 groups and about half are commamded by, or co-operating with, Mr Basayev' *(The Times,* 10 March 2005, p. 39).

'Russia paid $10 million for information that helped track down ... Aslan Maskhadov ... The Federal Security Service also said it would offer the same reward for Shamil Basayev' *(IHT,* 16 March 2005, p. 3).

12 June 2005.

> A suspected terrorist bomb derailed a train travelling from Chechnya to
> Moscow on Sunday [12 June] ... Trains started travelling between the
> Chechen and Russian capitals only a year ago after a five-year interruption
> due to war in Chechnya ... The train, which takes two days to make the trip,
> travels twice a week.
>
> (www.iht.com, 12 June 2005)

19 August 2005. 'Elections to a regional parliament in Chechnya will take place
on 27 November ... Parliament will consist of two chambers – the Council of
the Republic with twenty-one members and the Popular Assembly with forty
members' (*IHT*, 20 August 2005, p. 5).

26 August 2005.

> Shamil Basayev ... has been appointed deputy leader of Chechnya's separa-
> tists ... [He] is the new first deputy prime minister in Chechnya's separatist
> government ... in charge of the 'ministries of force' ... Basayev was forced
> out of the movement's leadership in 2002 after Aslan Maskhadov said his
> methods were too extreme. Maskhadov was killed by Russian forces in
> March and replaced by a Moslem cleric, Abdul Khalim Saidullayev.
>
> (*IHT*, 27 August 2005, p. 3)

'Abdul Khalim Saidulleyev has named him first deputy chairman of his
cabinet, overseeing national security and internal affairs' (*FT*, 27 August 2005,
p. 6).

'Maskhadov had marginalized Basayev and promised to prosecute him for the
Beslan massacre if he retook Chechnya from the current administration ... Saidullayev also appointed Akhmed Zakayev to the post of culture minister in his
new cabinet' (*Guardian*, 27 August 2005, p. 21).

> According to the Russian government, 331 people were fatally injured here
> [Beslan] last year [2004] from 1 September through 3 September, including
> 186 children. More than 700 were wounded ... [Russia says] that thirty-two
> terrorists seized the school – thirty men with automatic rifles and two
> women wearing suicide bombs. Thirty-one of them died, according to this
> account. They are not counted among the 331 victims.
>
> (*IHT*, 26 August 2005, pp. 1, 4)

'[In Beslan the terrorists took] 1,128 people hostage' (*Guardian*, 1 September
2005, p. 15).

'On the morning of 1 September the terrorists took nearly 1,200 hostages. It
ended ... on 3 September: 331 people died, including 186 children. More than
700 other people were wounded' (*IHT*, 1 September 2005, p. 7).

2 September 2005.

> President Putin met Friday [2 September] with relatives of the victims of
> last year's school siege in Beslan ... The meeting Friday [in Moscow]

came in the middle of three days of commemoration and mourning, which have included exhibitions, vigils and rallies across Russia, both for and against Putin's government ... Protest ... [has been] led by a group calling itself the Beslan Mothers Committee. It has questioned the official version of events and accused the government of covering up a botched rescue attack and failing to punish any officials for wrongdoing. They even told Putin that he would not be welcome in Beslan during the memorials.

(IHT, 3 September 2005, p. 6)

'President Vladimir Putin ... declared that 3 September ... would be a day of "solidarity with victims of terrorist acts"' *Guardian*, 3 September 2005, p. 15).

13 October 2005.

Islamic militants launched a major attack on police facilities and government buildings in ... Nalchik, the capital of the republic of Kabardino-Balkaria ... Chechen rebels claimed responsibility for the offensive ... Originally a separatist movement, the rebel struggle has melded increasingly with Islamic extremism and spread far beyond Chechnya's borders ... The [Caucasus] region has suffered a growing wave of violence ... The Kavkaz Centre website, seen as a voice for rebels loyal to Shamil Basayev, said it had received a short message claiming responsibility for the attack on behalf of the Caucasus Front. It said the group is part of the Chechen rebel armed forces and includes Yarmuk, an alleged militant Islamic group based in Kabardino-Balkaria.

(IHT, 15 October 2005, pp. 1, 8)

'Dagestan ... has seen a sharp rise in violence this year [2005], with bomb attacks and clashes between the police and fighters of uncertain affiliation reported almost daily' (www.iht.com, 14 October 2005).

Violence once confined to Chechnya ... has spread across the entire North Caucasus region ... The tactics used ... [by] the local and federal authorities ... in Chechnya and then in nearby Ingushetia have been applied in Kabardino-Balkaria, too, with predictable alienating results.

(The Economist, 15 October 2005, p. 48)

'In February a three-day siege [in Nalchik] ended with the deaths of seven alleged perpetrators of a murderous attack on a government agency some months beforehand' (www.economist.com, 13 October 2005).

The violence [in Chechnya] has been fast spreading into neighbouring Moslem republics, including Kabardino-Balkaria, Dagestan and Ingushetia ... Both Chechen and Russian sources said the assault had involved local Islamists in Nalchik, who had joined forces with their fellow Moslems from Chechnya as they have in Ingushetia and Dagestan.

(FT, 14 October 2005, p. 8)

Hardly a day goes by without some kind of rebel attack in Russia's northern Caucasus republics ... Yet while Chechnya's declaration of independence from Russia in 1991 led to the two wars that have devastated the republic, locals say there is little popular separatism elsewhere ... Nor is Islamic extremism itself a driving force, though all the republics except North Ossetia are predominantly Moslem. Experts say social and economic factors are pushing people into rebel groups that have forged links with international Islamic terrorism ... poverty ... unemployment ... corruption ... and ethnic and land disputes ... [There is a] tangle of clan, ethnic and religious rivalries across the seven republics [in the Caucasus region: Adygeya; Karachayevo-Cherkessia; Karabardino-Balkaria; North Ossetia; Ingushetia; Chechnya; and Dagestan].

(*FT*, 29 August 2005, p. 6)

Akhmed Zakayev [is] the UK-based Chechen rebel spokesman ... [who was] recently appointed a deputy prime minister in the rebel Chechens' 'shadow government' ... Zakayev: 'This was a legitimate military operation which took place in the framework of the Caucasus Front ... [Russia should] definitely [expect more attacks].'

(*FT*, 15 October 2005, p. 8)

After the seizure of a theatre in Moscow by Chechen terrorists in 2002 and a large raid in the nearby city of Nazran and school hostage siege in Beslan in 2004, survivors of those events said hostages needlessly died or terrorists escaped because of a range of problems among the Russian security services, including ineptitude. But in this attack in the republic of Karbardino-Balkaria the outcome was different. After being initially surprised and outgunned, the Russians moved reinforcements into the city and fought back, closing off many escape routes and killing scores of insurgents.

(www.iht.com, 16 October 2005)

On the surface the attack in Nalchik, in which authorities said ninety-two Islamist militants and twenty-four civilians died, was reminiscent of an incursion last year [2004] by rebels from Chechnya into ... Ingushetia. But there was an important evolution: the attack in Nalchik appeared to reflect a recent change of leadership and tactics among Chechen rebels, and their ability to rely upon local discontent in the republics of the North Caucasus ... In a statement on a website Chechen rebels called the Nalchik attack a 'successful operation' by 'forces of Mujahidin of the Caucasus Front (the Kabardino-Balkaria sector and units of other sectors)' ... [There was an] effective response from its [the federal government's] forces, which relatively quickly brought Nalchik under control.

(*FT*, 17 October 2005, p. 9)

'[The] fighting left at least 130 people, including ninety-four alleged attackers, dead, according to official tallies' (*IHT*, 17 October 2005, p. 3).

[On 17 October] Shamil Basayev ... claimed he was behind militant attacks last week in ... Nalchik that officials say left at least 137 people dead ... Basayev said that the attacks were carried out by militants affiliated with the Chechen rebels, but that Chechen fighters were not involved ... Basayev: 'I carried out the general operative management.'

(*IHT*, 18 October 2005, p. 4)

Shamil Basayev hailed the attack on Nalchik as a success but claimed his fighters had sustained heavy losses because of a 'serious' information leak five days before the attack. The leak allowed the Russian forces to draft in an extra 1,000 special forces in preparation, he said. Basayev claimed to have been in 'overall command' of the operation ... He claimed that forty-one of his fighters had died but said they had killed about 140 members of the law enforcement authorities and destroyed several helicopters. The Russians say they killed ninety-one gunmen, captured another thirty-six, and lost thirty-five of their own men and nine civilians. Basayev said that 217 'mujahidin' took part in the assault ... Yesterday [17 October] it was reported that most of the gunmen who took part in last Thursday's attack were not Chechens but disgruntled locals from the republic of Kabardino-Balkaria.

(*The Independent*, 18 October 2005, p. 23)

'Two more civilians died of their wounds ... taking the official toll for non-combatants to eleven' (*The Independent*, 19 October 2005, p. 22).

After two days of fighting Russian special forces overcame the rebels ... The following Tuesday [18 October] more gunfights were reported ... Violence once confined to Chechnya ... has spread across the entire North Caucasus region ... [In] Ingushetia and Dagestan ... shoot-outs and killings abound ... The tactics used ... [by] the local and federal authorities ... in Chechnya and then in nearby Ingushetia have been applied in Kabardino-Balkaria, too, with predictable., alienating results. In the past year large groups of 'suspects' have been rounded up and brutalized; the security services harass and torture with impunity.

(www.economist.com, 20 October 2005)

The fighting in Nalchik killed at least 138, including thirty-five security officers and fourteen civilians, the republic's coroner said ... Under a law adopted in the wake of the siege of a Moscow theatre in 2002 ... the bodies of those considered terrorists have been deemed unworthy of family burials. They are buried instead in anonymity and in undisclosed locations.

(www.iht.com, 31 October 2005; *IHT*, 1 November 2005, p. 3)

27 November 2005. Elections take place in Chechnya for the fifty-eight-seat, two-chamber parliament. A turnout of at least 25 per cent is needed for the election to be valid.

Chechens voted Sunday [27 November] in their first parliamentary elections since Russian troops reinvaded abut six years ago. Few international observers, however, were monitoring the election for the flaws that had marred three previous votes ... Electoral authorities announced a turnout of more than 60 per cent ... but the pro-independence Kavkaz Centre website claimed that the turnout was ... 5 per cent to 7 per cent.

(*IHT*, 28 November 2005, p. 3)

'OSCE ... declined to send observers' (*The Independent*, 28 November 2005, p. 30).

The election commission put [the turnout] at about 60 per cent ... Preliminary results ... [show that] United Russia, a pro-Kremlin party, won 61 per cent of the vote, followed by the communists with 12 per cent. The Union of Right Forces, a liberal party, did significantly better than expected, winning 10 per cent ... Alu Alkhanov, the president of Chechnya: 'I will soon go to Brussels to meet with members of the Maskhadov regime.'

(*FT*, 29 November 2005, p. 7)

The official turnout was over 60 per cent and United Russia, the Kremlin's pet party, took around 60 per cent of the votes ... There are few credible, moderate leaders left. A few recently demobbed separatists ran in the election; one, Magomed Khambiyev, is said to have turned himself in after several relatives were kidnapped. Mr Khambiyev stood for the Union of Right Forces, a liberal party whose strongish showing was the election's only semi-surprise. But no active separatists took part ... President Putin's policy of 'Chechenization' has meant outsourcing most of the violence to local militias – especially the *kadyrovtsy* ... henchmen of Ramzan Kadyrov ... first deputy prime minister ... On most estimates [the *kadyrovtsy*] number around 7,000 ... Russian soldiers in Chechnya say that the *kadyrovtsy* already clash often, and violently, with federal troops, as well as with official Chechen police ... In a pre-election poll 2 per cent of Chechens said the election results would be determined by the voters; 9 per cent said by Mr Putin; 72 per cent said by Ramzan Kadyrov. Next year [2006], when he turns thirty – the age that Chechnya's constitution prescribes as the minimum for its president – Mr Kadyrov's de facto power may become official ... [President] Alu Alkhanov ... said this week in Grozny that he was willing to meet followers of Aslan Maskhadov.

(www.economist.com, 1 December 2005; *The Economist*, 3 December 2005, pp. 41–2)

12 December 2005.

President Vladimir Putin attended the opening session of Chechnya's newly elected parliament on Monday [12 December], pledging to help rebuild [Grozny] ... and urging the authorities to combat rampant abductions ... Putin promised that rebuilding Grozny would be a top priority for the government. Nearly 1,700 people have been abducted in Chechnya and are still missing, a committee said this year [2005].

(*IHT*, 13 December 2005, p. 10)

14 December 2005.

Chechen deputies voted on Wednesday [14 December] to rename ... Grozny ... in honour of their assassinated president, raising the prospect of a third name for the city in ten years ... The speaker of the region's parliament said the Kremlin had been asked to change the name of Grozny to Akhmadkala, in memory of Akhmad Kadyrov, the pro-Moscow president who was killed in a rebel bombing in 2004. Grozny was renamed Dzhokhar after a pro-independence leader, Dzhokhar Dudayev, by the de facto independent government of Chechnya before Russian troops returned in 1999. The rebels still call the city Dzhokhar.

(*IHT*, 15 December 2005, p. 8)

'Dzhokhar Dudayev was killed by a Russian bomb in 1996 ... Grozny [was] named by Cossacks in the nineteenth century' (*The Independent*, 15 December 2005, p, 21).

4 March 2006.

Ramzam Kadyrov [twenty-nine] ... [is] appointed as the republic's prime minister ... Kadyrov, who had been deputy prime minister, replaces Sergei Abramov, who resigned last week for medical reasons after being injured in a car accident in November [2005] ... While his predecessor was recovering Kadyrov was Chechnya's interim head of government, issuing decrees restricting alcohol sales and supporting polygamy.

(*IHT*, 6 March 2006, p. 3)

'Ramzan Kadyrov ... turns thirty later this year [October 2006] and becomes eligible for the highest office ... the Chechen presidency' (*The Independent*, 1 March 2006, p. 19).

26 May 2006.

A Russian court on Friday [26 May] sentenced a terrorist who participated in the siege at a public school to life imprisonment, pointedly sparing the man execution only because of a moratorium on capital punishment ... which has been Kremlin policy since 1996 [when Russia joined the Council of Europe]. The convicted man, Nur-Pasha Kulayev, a young Chechen carpenter, was caught during a final battle at School Number One in Beslan in 2004. Some 331 civilians and Russian servicemen died in the siege, including 186 children. The death count does not include the thirty-one terrorists that Russia says were killed. Kulayev has been presented to the Russian public as the sole surviving terrorist taken from the ruins of the school on 3 September 2004, two days after it was seized by a Chechen terrorist group. He was charged with several crimes, including terrorism and murder ...

Many bereaved families supported a call [for the death penalty]. Other former hostages and families who lost relatives, however, while agreeing that Kulayev was guilty, said he should not be executed. They have cited various reasons, including the belief that he was a minor player in the siege, that capital punishment debases the government, and that secrets about the siege held by Kulayev would be lost with his death ... Many survivors have treated the trial as both a source of fascination and a distraction from what they regard as official culpability in loss of life.

(IHT, 27 May 2006, p. 2).

Nur-Pasha Kulayev was [also] found guilty ... of inflicting material damage worth $1.3 million' (www.iht.com, 26 May 2006).

The Beslan siege claimed a greater toll of human life than all but one act of modern terrorism, the destruction of the World Trade Center. The terrorists' actions and the bungled rescue efforts [in Beslan] ended with the deaths of 331 people, not counting the thirty-one terrorists the Russian government says were killed. Among the deaths were 186 children and ten members of Russia's Special Forces ... More than 700 other people were injured.

(IHT, 29 May 2006, p. 2)

The judge ... said Kulayev's actions had in part led to the killing of sixteen hostages by the attackers and he had detonated a bomb at School Number One that had injured hostages and government troops. He was also found guilty of shooting children and other hostages who tried to escape the school on the third day of the crisis.

(www.bbc.co.uk, 27 May 2006)

17 June 2006.

[On 17 June Russia said that its] special forces have killed the leader of Chechnya's separatists ... Abdul Khalim Saidullayev died in a raid in a Chechen village in which two Russian soldiers were also killed ... Argub [is] a village that is close to Grozny and is believed to have been his home town ... Saidullayev, who was believed to be in his thirties, was a little known fighter, religious figure and Islamic judge when he was appointed in March 2005 to replace Aslan Maskhadov ... Ramzan Kadyrov said Saidullayev had been betrayed by an informer bought for the price of a dose of heroin ... Shamil Basayev and another prominent rebel commander, Doku Umarov, remain at large.

(IHT, 19 June 2006, p. 3)

'A rebel website ... said the new rebel leader or "president" would be Doku Umarov, a field commander' *(FT*, 19 June 2006, p. 6).

As vice-president of 'Ichkeria' ... Doku Umarov was automatically elevated to the post of new president upon the death of Abdul Khalim Saidullayev, thirty-nine, on Saturday [17 June] ... Ramzan Kadyrov described how the militant leader was betrayed by 'a close associate' ... [for] a dose of heroin ... costing 1,500 roubles (£30).

(Guardian, 19 June 2006, p. 19)

10 July 2006.

> Shamil Basayev ... was killed early Monday [10 July] in what the director of Russia's security service described as a special operation that began by tracking shipments of weapons and explosives from abroad ... Nikolai Patrushev said that the operation had disrupted plans for a terrorist attack in southern Russia intended to coincide with a meeting of the Group of 8 leaders ... which is to begin Saturday [15 July] in St Petersburg ... A website that often carries statements by Basayev ... announced his death Monday evening and said Basayev had died by accident, not during an operation by Russian forces ... Patrushev and other officials said that Basayev had died shortly after midnight Monday when an enormous explosion destroyed a truck stopped on the outskirts of a village in Ingushetia [Ekazhevo] ... Basayev was standing nearby, accompanied by other fighters travelling in three automobiles, a [Russian spokesman said] ... Basayev repeatedly claimed responsibility for planning the [Beslan] siege. Russia placed a $10 million reward on his head ... The last period of intensive and sustained separatist operations was in the summer of 2004.

(IHT, 11 July 2006, pp. 1, 4)

'Another rebel leader, Doku Umarov, pledged last month [June] that rebels would step up their attacks against Russian forces' (www.iht.com, 10 July 2006).

> The Russian FSB security service said that Shamil Basayev was killed when a consignment of explosives was deliberately detonated yards from where he was sitting in a parked car ... The FSB said that the operation was planned over six months and that Basayev was located due to surveillance of foreign countries that were supplying the separatists with arms ... The rebels allege that Basayev and three other fighters were killed by an 'accidental spontaneous' explosion of the consignment.

(The Independent, 11 July 2006, p. 18)

'A Chechen rebel website ... confirmed Shamil Basayev's death but said it was caused by an accidental explosion' (*FT*, 11 July 2006, p. 1). 'Only days ago Shamil Basayev had been named "vice president" in the rebel Chechen leadership by its new head ... Doku Umarov' (p. 4).

'The Kremlin said he [Shamil Basayev] was killed in a special operation. His own people and some local officials insist he died in an accidental explosion' (*The Economist*, 15 July 2006, p. 5).

> Shamil Basayev's death has become the latest of Russia's public mysteries ... The means and even the timing of his death have become subjects of disagreement, fuelled since the first hours by contradictory official statements, a climate of secrecy and opposing reports from the government, the separatists and Russian news sources. According to the official version, Russian

special services officers killed Basayev ... by causing an explosion near him as he stood beside a stopped truck and cars. The separatists have disputed this, saying Basayev died when a truck in his convoy hit a pothole, accidentally detonating explosives the separatists were moving ... *Kommersant* has since suggested that he was killed by rivals from Dagestan.

(*IHT*, 21 July 2006, p. 3)

At first the press service of the FSB's [Federal Security Service's] Administration for Ingushetia announced that the militants had been using the KamAZ truck to carry explosives intended for a terrorist attack, and that the truck had detonated spontaneously ... Not until the evening did FSB director Nikolai Patrushev announce that in fact the KamAZ had exploded not by itself but as a result of a special operation.

(*CDSP*, 2006, vol. 58, no. 28, p. 1)

So the explosives-packed KamAZ did not 'hit a pothole'. In other words, counter-intelligence agents had found people in certain countries who were trusted by the 'arms buyers'. The arms had been collected, packed up and shipped in the knowledge that they would 'detonate' at the appropriate time.

(p. 3)

The European Court of Human Rights ruled Thursday [27 July] that Russian military forces were responsible for the disappearance and presumed death of a young man during the war in Chechnya six years ago, and awarded his mother Euro 35,000 ($44,000) in damages. In an important decision the court also ruled that Russia violated the European Convention on Human Rights by unlawfully detaining the man during a takeover of a Chechen village by Russian troops and by failing to properly investigate the incident ... [In television footage an] officer orders soldiers to shoot her son ... The officer ... was questioned about the incident by Russian authorities but never prosecuted ... Russia has three months to appeal Thursday's verdict, the first in a Chechen disappearance case. Some 200 similar cases are still pending in the Strasbourg court ... [There was] unanimity of the decision [of the court], including the Russian judge.

(www.iht.com, 27 July 2006)

The European Court of Human Rights on Thursday [27 July] found Russia responsible for the disappearance and presumed death of a prisoner detained in Chechnya ... Kahdzhi-Murat Yandiyev ... an ethnic Ingush ... was detained in February 2000 ... It ruled that Russia had failed to conduct a proper investigation into complaints that the man had been summarily executed on orders from a Russian general ... Colonel General Alexander Baranov [is] one of the country's most senior military officers ... Baranov has been awarded the Hero of Russia medal and promoted. He now serves as the head of Russian military forces in the North Caucasus ... [The court] found that Russia was liable for Yandiyev's death and noted that Russia had neither investigated the disappearance in a timely manner nor provided his mother an explanation for his disappearance. It also noted that Yandiyev had never been logged into the appropriate custody records, obscuring the trail from the beginning ... About 200 more cases of grave human rights abuses in Chechnya are before the court.

(*IHT*, 28 July 2006, p. 3)

'The authorities issued a $180 million back-tax bill this month [July 2006] to the International Protection centre, which has also helped people to take Chechen-related cases to the European Court' (*The Times*, 28 July 2006, p. 35).

August 2006.

The humiliation of Malika Soltayeva, a pregnant Chechen woman suspected of adultery, was ferocious and swift ... The torture of Soltayeva, recorded on a video obtained by *The New York Times*, and other recent brutish acts and instances of religious policing, raise questions about Chechnya's direction. Since 2004 the war in Chechnya has tilted sharply in the Kremlin's favour, as open combat with separatists has declined in intensity and frequency. Moscow now administers the republic and fights the remaining insurgency largely through paramilitary forces led by Ramzan Kadyrov ... Kadyrov's police and security forces, known as *kadyrovsty*, are staffed mostly with uneducated young men, some of whom have been fighting for years, including many former rebels who have changed sides.

(C.J. Chivers, www.iht.com, 30 August 2006; *IHT*,
31 August 2006, pp. 1, 8)

15 February 2007. 'Ramzan Kadyrov was named [by President Vladimir Putin as] acting President of Chechnya in place of Alu Alkhanov, who was made Russia's deputy justice minister' (*The Times*, 16 February 2007, p. 41).

1 March 2007.

President Vladimir Putin on Thursday [1 March] appointed Ramzan Kadyrov ... to be the new president of ... Chechnya ... The senior human rights official for Europe, Thomas Hammarberg, visited Grozny and denounced 'a real widespread pattern of serious ill-treatment and many cases of torture against those who have been arrested'. Hammarberg was attending a government-organized conference on human rights that the most prominent Russian human rights groups boycotted as a sham ... The appointment requires the endorsement of the republic's parliament, but that is a formality.

(*IHT*, 2 March 2007, p. 3)

2 March 2007. 'Ramzan Kadyrov ... won fifty-six votes in the fifty-eight-seat Chechen legislature' (*IHT*, 3 March 2007, p. 5).

'The European Commissioner for Human Rights, Thomas Hammarberg, called for an independent commission to investigate the disappearance of an estimated 2,600 people in Chechnya since 1994' (*FT*, 3 March 2007, p. 5).

Of the fifty-eight deputies present fifty-five voted in his favour, two spoiled their ballot papers, and only one unnamed politician dared to cast his vote against ... Parliament is packed with Kadyrov supporters ... Thomas Hammarberg, the Council of Europe's human rights commissioner, said yesterday [2 March] he had found evidence of 'widespread torture' in Chechnya following a recent fact-finding trip ... Mr Hammarberg also raised concerns about the number of people who have disappeared in recent years, abducted from their homes or from the streets. He said the official figure was 2,600 and called for a truth-and-reconciliation commission to be set up to ascertain precisely what happened to the missing.

(*The Independent*, 3 March 2007, p. 30)

8 March 2007.

The first regularly scheduled civilian passenger flight since [March] 1999 arrived at Chechnya's main airport Thursday [8 March] ... Also Thursday Ramzan Kadyrov said he had nominated Odes Baisultanov, a first deputy prime minister who oversaw the rebuilding of the airport, to be prime minister.

(*IHT*, 9 March 2007, p. 3)

5 April 2007. Ramzan Kadyrov is inaugurated as president of Chechnya.

The European Court of Human Rights awarded over Euro 50,000, or about $67,000, in damages on Thursday [5 April] to a woman from Chechnya whose husband disappeared during a sweep by Russian troops – the sixth time in a row it has found against Russia in a case related to Chechnya.

(www.iht.com, 5 April 2007)

25 June 2008.

Though violence in Chechnya has decreased markedly in recent years, fighting between Moslem insurgents and Russian troops threatens to engulf a neighbouring region, a human rights group said in a report Wednesday [25 June]. The group, Human Rights Watch, asserted that a recent spike in insurgent attacks in the region, Ingushetia, has provoked a spate of kidnappings, torture and arbitrary killings of innocent civilians by law enforcement reminiscent of earlier rights abuses in Chechnya ... Ingushetia, a tiny Moslem republic on Chechnya's western border, has long been considered a relatively peaceful enclave in the North Caucasus ... Recently, however, it has become a haven for rebels fleeing a brutal counter-insurgency in Chechnya ... A total of sixty-five servicemen were killed in the republic in 2007 ... Violence against civilians has sparked raucous street protests that have rankled the authorities.

(www.iht.com, 25 June 2008)

Further developments

The deaths of prominent figures such as Anna Politkovskaya (7 October 2006) and Natalia Estimirova (15 July 2009) are dealt with in the political chronology.

In a statement on Thursday [16 April] Russia's National Anti-terrorist Committee issued a statement: '[The Committee has] cancelled the decree imposing an anti-terrorist operation on the territory of Chechnya, effective from midnight [of Thursday 16 April: 20.00 GMT Wednesday]. This decision aims to create conditions to further normalize the situation in the region, to restore and develop its economic and social infrastructure.'

(www.bbc.co.uk, 16 April 2009)

'President Boris Yeltsin ordered the counter-terrorist operation in 1999' (www.cnn.com, 16 April 2009).

The committee did not mention troop withdrawals ... Russian officials said they would have more legal leeway to scale down the number of federal military and security forces in Chechnya ... An unnamed law enforcement official told the Interfax news agency that as many as 20,000 troops under Moscow's control could eventually leave the republic.

(www.iht.com, 16 April 2009)

('Three districts in Chechnya have been officially designated zones of counter-terrorist activity only a week after Russia said it had ended its decade-long military campaign against separatist rebels: www.bbc.co.uk, 24 April 2009.)

The construction minister in Russia's violence-plagued Ingushetia was shot to death in his office Wednesday [12 August], the latest in a series of high profile attacks on top officials ... [The] Ingush security council secretary ... said investigators believe the killing could be related to recent audits of construction projects that turned up building violations and misuse of funds. Ingushetia, which borders Chechnya, in recent months has seen near-daily attacks on police or police operations against fighters variously believed to be militants inspired by Chechnya's separatists or connected with criminal clans. In June Ingush president Yunus-Bek Yevkurov was seriously injured in a suicide car-bomb attack on his convoy. Two weeks earlier a justice of the republic's supreme court was shot to death as she dropped off her children at a kindergarten. Dagestan, on Chechnya's eastern border, is similarly troubled by violence. The republic's top law enforcement official was killed by a sniper in June, and attacks on police are frequent.

(www.iht.com, 12 August 2009)

More than twenty people were killed in violent clashes in Russia's North Caucasus [in Dagestan and Chechnya] ... The clashes were among the bloodiest to hit the region in recent months, though bloodshed occurs almost daily, particularly in Chechnya, Dagestan and Ingushetia ... Most of the violence centres on fighting between the police and various radical Islamist or more secular separatist organizations in the region, some of which are remnants of the militant groups that fought federal forces in Chechnya's two wars. Also common is violence among organized crime groups and competing ethnic clans.

(www.iht.com, 14 August 2009; *IHT*, 15 August 2009, p. 3)

A suicide bomber exploded a truck at a police station in ... the city of Nazran in Ingushetia ... At least twenty people were killed ... It was the bloodiest single attack to hit Ingushetia in some time, though violence against police and government officials in this and other North Caucasus republics occurs almost daily ... Ingushetia's Kremlin-appointed president, Yunus-Bek Yevkurov, was badly wounded in a suicide bombing in June and has not yet returned to his duties ... Yevkurov blamed Chechen separatist warlord Doku Umarov for staging June's suicide attack on his convoy ... Mr Yevkurov had vowed to take a softer approach in dealing with rebel violence than Ramzan Kadyrov, the president of Chechnya. A former intelligence officer and a devout Moslem. Mr Yevkurov reached out to opposition leaders as well as militant commanders in an attempt to ease the bubbling tensions in Ingushetia. But the violence has continued, fuelled in part by the arrival of militants fleeing Mr Kadyrov's brutal counter-insurgency in Chechnya ... Mr Kadyrov has sent Chechen commanders to Ingushetia to conduct counter-terrorism operations there ... While large-scale fighting from the two wars that ravaged Chechnya since 1994 has ended, Islamic militants continue to mount hit-and-run attacks and skirmishes. Bloodshed has surged in recent months and increasingly spilled into Chechnya's neighbours.

(www.iht.com, 17 August 2009)

The blast occurred in a heavily populated area, not far from several banks and government buildings ... [A spokesman for Mr Yevkurov said] ten of the wounded were children ... In response to the bombing, President Dmitri Medvedev fired Ingushetia's interior minister ... Dmitri Medvedev: 'I suggest that this is not just the result of problems connected with terrorism, but also the result of unsatisfactory work by law enforcement agencies in the republics' ... A former intelligence officer and a practising Moslem, Mr Yevkurov has reached out to opposition leaders as well as to militant commanders in an attempt to ease tensions in Ingushetia. But the violence has continued, fuelled in part by local militants as well as by the arrival of separatist fighters fleeing Ramzan Kadyrov's brutal counter-insurgency in Chechnya.

(*IHT*, 18 August 2009, p. 3)

The blast, which injured 118 – including women and children – led to President Dmitri Medvedev sacking the Ingush minister of the interior, saying the atrocity could have been prevented ... Yunus-Bek Yevkurov (who was injured in a suicide attack in Nazran): 'Arab fighters [were fighting alongside local rebels in Ingushetia] ... I have stressed this [before] and am saying again now: the West will strive not to allow Russia to revive its former Soviet might' ... He moved to end the abuse of civilians by security forces that human rights activists said swelled the ranks of insurgents while Murat Zyazikov, the former Ingush president, was in power ... Russia has fought two wars against separatists in Chechnya since the Soviet Union dissolved in 1991, but claimed this year that it had pacified the region, lifting its designation of Chechnya as 'a counter-terrorist operation' zone. But insurgency has recently intensified in the North Caucasus with increasingly audacious attacks on high profile targets.

(*FT*, 18 August 2009, p. 6)

'The attack was the bloodiest in Ingushetia since ninety-two people were killed when Chechen rebels took over the centre of Nazran in 2004' (*Guardian*, 18 August 2009, p. 18).

'Yunus-Bek Yevkurov: "I am far from believing that Arabs are behind all of this. We can see in whose interest this is – the United States, Great Britain and Israel"' (*The Independent*, 18 August 2009, p. 18).

'The death toll from the suicide truck bombing of a police station ... has risen to twenty-one, and nine police officers are still missing. More than 130 people were wounded' (*IHT*, 19 August 2009, p. 3).

'According to the most recent government figures ... the blast killed at least twenty-five people and wounded around 280' (www.iht.com, 21 August 2009).

President Dmitri Medvedev said at a meeting of top law enforcement officials on Wednesday [19 August]: 'A short time ago there was a growing impression that the situation in the Caucasus as regards terrorism had substantially improved. Unfortunately, recent events have shown that this is not so. If our work stops we will begin to see more serious incidents.'

(www.iht.com, 21 August 2009)

Suicide bombers killed at least four police officers in separate attacks in Grozny on Friday [21 August] ... capping off a week of violence in Russia's North Caucasus region that has left dozens of people dead, most of them law enforcement officials ... The bloodshed has spiked this summer, with almost daily attacks on police and government officials ... In late July a suicide attack in Grozny killed six people, including four police officers who tried to stop the bomber from entering a theatre ... Also on Friday [21 August] a Russian jihadist group said in a letter posted to a Chechen separatist website that it had used an anti-tank grenade to cause an accident at the Sayano-Shushenskaya hydroelectric plant in Siberia on Monday [17 August]. At least thirty people died in the accident and some forty-five are still missing. The Russian government has dismissed the claims, saying that no evidence of explosives has been found at the accident site ... On Monday morning Russia's biggest hydroelectric dam was crippled by a surge of water through the machine room.

(www.iht.com, 21 August 2009)

'At least forty-seven died in the [hydroelectric plant] accident and twenty-eight are still missing' (*IHT*, 22 August 2009, p. 3).

'[The] statement posted ... [was] by the "Battalion of Martyrs" on a rebel website yesterday [21 August]' (*The Independent*, 22 August 2009, p. 20).

> The death toll from Monday's accident at Russia's largest hydroelectric plant has risen to sixty-seven ... eight people are still missing after a massive surge of water in the turbine hall at the Sayano-Shushenskaya plant in Siberia ... The cause of the accident at the plant on the Yenisei River remains unclear and an investigation has been launched ... There have been claims from Chechen websites that Islamist militants were responsible for the accident. These suggestions have been rejected by Kremlin sources as 'idiotic' and investigators have reportedly found no traces of explosives at the site. Previous reports suggested a transformer exploded during repairs, destroying three generating units and leading to the flooding of a turbine hall. Prime minister Vladimir Putin visited the site on Friday [21 August]. He promised relatives of the victims to pay 1 million roubles ($30,000) each in compensation. Mr Putin also compared the current state of Russia's infra-structure to that of a wartime front, and promised to match the company's payouts with government compensation ... The plant's owner [is] RusHy-dro ... The dam ... opened in 1978 ... [was] undamaged by the blast.
>
> (www.bbc.co.uk, 22 August 2009)

> Russian authorities were reportedly warned that Siberia's massive Sayano-Shushenskaya hydroelectric power plant had fallen into serious neglect and was unsafe more than a decade before last week's deadly accident. The death toll rose to sixty-six yesterday [22 August] as rescuers continued to drain the dam's destroyed turbine room. They recovered nineteen more bodies ... Nine workers are still missing ... Prime minister Vladimir Putin, who toured the crippled plant on Friday [21 August], has acknowledged that Russia must plan for the regular upgrade of 'vital parts of the infrastructure'.
>
> (www.independent.co.uk, 23 August 2009)

'In an August accident ... [in which the turbine room of the giant Sayano-Shushenskaya hydroelectric dam in Siberia [was] damaged ... seventy-five [were killed]' (www.iht.com, 3 December 2009).

> A suicide bomber today [25 August] killed four policemen in ... Mesker-Yurt, a village twelve miles from Grozny ... Suicide operations became a gruesome hallmark of the second war in Chechnya, with frequent attacks between 2000 and 2004. But the tactic was dropped after the Chechen rebel commander Shamil Basayev was killed in 2006. This spring [2009], however, the veteran Chechen guerrilla leader Doku Umarov claimed he was reviving Basayev's notorious Riyadus-Salikhin group, known as the Reconnaissance and Sabotage Battalion of Chechen Martyrs. The battal-ion, whose name means Garden of Martyrs, was behind the 2004 Beslan

school massacre, in which 334 people, mainly children, died, and other atrocities. Earlier this summer [2009] Russian law enforcement officers announced Umarov had been killed, but in a subsequent telephone call to Radio Free Europe–Radio Liberty Umarov said he was alive and well, and shuttling between armed rebel groups on the Chechnya and Dagestan border ... The Kremlin has been unable to contain a spiralling insurgency in the Moslem republics of Ingushetia, Chechnya and Dagestan ... In April [2009] the Kremlin officially discontinued its counter-terrorist regime in Chechnya.

(www.guardian.co.uk, 25 August 2009)

Explosions and shootings have been a daily occurrence in the region all summer. Between June and August [2009] 436 people have been killed, compared with 150 during the same months in 2008. And the number of attacks jumped to 452 from 265, according to statistics compiled by the Center for Strategic and International Studies, a private research group based in Washington ... Suicide bombings have returned to Chechnya after a pause of several years. Two militants blew themselves up Friday [28 August] to escape capture, making it a total of three suicide bombings in the region in just the past week ... Ramzan Kadyrov blames Wahhabis and other Islamic extremists for the attacks and has repeatedly charged that they are financed and trained by Western countries.

(www.iht.com, 29 August 2009; *IHT*, 31 August 2009, p. 3)

'Russian forces have killed an al-Qaeda militant in Dagestan, officials say ... The Algerian national ... was killed when police stormed a house on Sunday night [30 August]' (www.bbc.co.uk, 31 August 2009).

'In the republic of Dagestan on Tuesday [1 September] a passer-by was killed and thirteen people wounded when a man detonated explosives in a car at a traffic police post' (www.iht.com, 1 September 2009).

Thousands are gathering in Beslan to mourn the hundreds of people who died five years ago in Russia's worst terrorist attack. Mourners on Tuesday [1 September] are filling the gymnasium of Beslan's School No. 1, where more than 1,000 hostages were held for nearly three days without food or water by thirty-two heavily armed militants. The ordeal ended on 3 September 2004 in a botched rescue attempt that resulted in the deaths of 334 people, more than half of them children, in the North Caucasus town. In the attack's aftermath the Kremlin made sweeping changes to the country's electoral system, tightening its grip on power.

(www.iht.com, 1 September 2009)

Thirty-two heavily armed militants – Chechens and others – seized the school on 1 September 2004, herding more than 1,000 men, women and children into the gymnasium and demanding that Russian forces withdraw from war-wracked Chechnya ... With violence spiking through the North Caucasus, few survivors or relatives of victims believe much has changed since then. Few are satisfied with the official investigations, which largely absolved police of blame for not preventing the attack. Many also maintain that law enforcement agencies botched the rescue, using flame-throwers, grenade launchers and heavy guns that only made the situation worse. Survivors insist the explosions that sparked the chaos came from outside the building ... The only attacker know to have survived, Nur-Pasha Kulayev, was sentenced to life in prison in 2006.

(www.iht.com, 1 September 2009)

'Russia is marking the fifth anniversary of the Beslan siege ... [The] school was seized by Chechen rebels [in 1 September 2004] ... The siege ended when security forces stormed the building. Those killed in the ensuing battle included 186 children' (www.bbc.co.uk, 1 September 2009).

Thirty-two heavily armed militants took more than 1,200 people – children, parents and teachers – hostage on the first day of school in 2004 ... Officials say a militant set off a bomb on the third day of the siege, prompting special forces to respond with a barrage of gunfire ... However, some relatives of the victims, as well as human rights organizations, say the bloodshed began with a government sniper firing at a militant ... In an address Tuesday [1 September] marking the first day of the school year, President Dmitri Medvedev made no mention of the Beslan massacre ... Coverage of the anniversary was also overshadowed by media attention to the seventieth anniversary of the beginning of World War II.

(www.cnn.com, 1 September 2009)

'A roadside bomb blast ripped through a police car in southern Ingushetia on Friday, killing three officers' (www.iht.com, 4 September 2009).

The spectre of suicide bombers penetrating into the heart of Moscow came back to haunt Russia today [5 September] after authorities said they had shot dead five militants, two of whom had explosive belts and tickets to the capital. Chechen security forces said they had killed two rebel fighters in the republic's second city of Gudermes during a shootout on Friday night [4 September]. The insurgents were found to have explosive strapped to them, hand grenades and train tickets to Moscow, officials said. Law enforcement agents also said they shot dead three men during a gun battle in the neighbouring republic of Ingushetia, including the senior rebel commander Rustam Dzortov ... On 22 June a suicide bomber rammed into Ingushetia's Kremlin-appointed president Yunus-Bek Yevkurov's heavily armoured Mercedes, leaving him seriously injured. Officials say Dzortov was behind the attack ... Yesterday [4 September] human rights activists said a new generation of radicalized teenage fighters had gone off to join the rebels in the forests and mountains of Chechnya. They said the wanton behaviour of local law enforcement agencies, responsible for a string of 'disappearances' and for reprisals against the rebels' families, had made the situation worse ... In April

[2009] the Kremlin cancelled its counter-terrorist regime in Chechnya, increasing the power of Ramzan Kadyrov.

(www.guardian.co.uk, 5 September 2009)

'Violence in the North Caucasus led to at least nine dead over the weekend' (*IHT*, 14 September 2009, p. 3).

Ramzan Kadyrov on Tuesday [6 October] won a defamation lawsuit against a rights activist who had blamed him for the killing of a colleague ... The court in Moscow ordered the activist, Oleg Orlov, chairman of the rights group Memorial, to retract his statement that Mr Kadyrov was responsible for the death of the colleague, Natalia Estimirova ... Mr Orlov has never said he had evidence of Mr Kadyrov's direct involvement in Ms Estimirova's killing but has repeatedly blamed him for it, citing an atmosphere of lawlessness and impunity that he said the powerful leader had fostered. Mr Orlov vowed to appeal ... Mr Kadyrov sought 10 million roubles ($330,000) in damages, but the judge ruled that Memorial and Mr Orlov should pay only 70,000 roubles ... The ruling came after a defence witness, Alexander Cherkasov, testified that Ms Estimirova had feared for her safety after a March 2008 conversation with Mr Kadyrov.

(*IHT*, 7 October 2009, p. 3)

After Russia finally took control of Chechnya, extremist rebels proclaimed an Islamic Emirate of the North Caucasus and spread the fight into Russia's other mainly Moslem republics, like Ingushetia ... More than 200 people have been killed so far this year [2009], the same figure for the whole of 2008. More and more young men are going 'into the hills', as joining the rebels is known. Some may do so out of religious belief, yet Magomed Mutsolgov of human rights NGO Mashr believes that at least 80 per cent leave home because of revenge.

(www.bbc.co.uk, 7 October 2009)

A prominent opposition activist on Ingushetia was shot and killed today [25 October] by unidentified gunmen in at least the third such killing in Russia's North Caucasus region in just over three months ... Makshirop Aushev died when several assailants sprayed his vehicle with automatic gunfire from a passing car. A woman travelling with him was badly wounded in the attack on a road in neighbouring Kabardino-Balkaria ... Aushev's murder follows the killing in July of Natalia Estimirova ... who was found shot dead in Ingushetia after being kidnapped in Chechnya. And in August Zarema Sadulayeva, a Chechen woman who helped injured children, and her husband were kidnapped and killed ... Aushev became involved in rights activities after his son and nephew were kidnapped in 2007. Aushev later got them released. He started working in human rights in Ingushetia and tried to combat abductions ... Aushev had worked with Magomed Yevloyev, a journalist, lawyer and opposition activist who was detained and killed by police in August 2008. Police said at the time that

Yevloyev was shot and killed after he tried to grab a weapon from one of the officers ... Yunus-Bek Yevkurov pushed for an investigation into Yevloyev's killing, and a court ruled last November [2008] that his detention by police was illegal.

(www.guardian.co.uk, 25 October 2009)

Makshirop Aushev, a businessman from a prominent family, was killed and a passenger wounded when they were shot from a passing vehicle in the neighbouring republic of Kabardino-Balkaria ... Mr Aushev's life turned a corner several years ago, after his son and nephew were kidnapped. He blamed state security forces for the abductions and threw his considerable clout behind organizing public protests against then president Murat Zyazikov, something virtually unheard in Ingushetia at the time ... The Kremlin last October [2008] removed Mr Zyazikov and installed Yunus-Bek Yevkurov ... In August Zarema Sadulayeva, who ran the charity Save the Generation, was found shot dead in the trunk of her car after being seized in her office. Mr Aushev survived a kidnapping attempt in September ... His colleagues said he remained at odds with Mr Zyazikov's relatives and continued to criticize the tactics of Russian special forces stationed in the region.

(www.iht.com, 25 October 2009)

The Kremlin last October removed Mr Zyazikov and installed Yunus-Bek Yevkurov, who actively reached out to internal dissidents and seemed to offer them a degree of protection. Mr Aushev was supportive of Mr Yevkurov, and felt optimistic enough to take a position on an official human rights council set up by Russia's federal ombudsman.

(*IHT*, 26 October 2009, p. 3)

President Yunus-Bek Yevkurov ... an appointee of President Dmitri Medvedev who has made a point of reaching out to internal dissidents ... said Monday [27 October] that ... Makshirop Aushev ... might have been killed by law enforcement officers ... Yevkurov: 'We understand that law enforcement structures could have taken part in this. Law enforcement representatives sometimes take part in criminal feuds. But that does not mean the authorities ordered it' ... President Yunus-Bek Yevkurov also said the killing was a direct challenge to his authority ... Makshirop Aushev had mostly withdrawn from opposition activities since Mr Yevkurov was appointed, though he continued to accuse security forces of abducting and killing citizens in their efforts to control Islamic militant groups in Ingushetia.

(www.iht.com, 27 October 2009)

The first international flight to leave Chechnya in fifteen years has taken off from the airport in Grozny. The Boeing 757 left with 200 pilgrims travelling to Moslem holy sites in Saudi Arabia ... An official statement said seven aircraft would carry 2,000 pilgrims to Saudi Arabia, and regular international flights would begin soon ... Moscow decided to lift all restrictions on international flights from Grozny earlier this month [November]. The move followed Moscow's announcement in April [2009] that anti-terrorist operations in Chechnya were to end as stability had returned.

(www.bbc.co.uk, 16 November 2009)

A suicide bomber killed ... six policemen ... on Wednesday [6 January 2010] ... on the outskirts of Dagestan's capital Makhachkala ... by detonating a car packed with explosives at a traffic police depot ... The bombing took place as 150 officers lined up outside for a roll call ... The police spotted the suspicious car and rammed it from the side after which the explosion took place ... [The police said that] the officers who died took action to prevent far greater devastation ... Those killed were at the gate, including the three officers in a police jeep that blocked the attacker's path ... Police [said they] had received information about a planned attack.

(www.iht.com, 6 January 2010)

A suicide car bomber killed six police officers Wednesday ... The bombing came five days after the police said they had killed a militant leader. Officials said the death toll could have been far higher; the driver was stopped at a checkpoint just outside a traffic police station, where officers were mustering for roll call in the yard. The driver apparently realized he could not get past the checkpoint and instead detonated the bomb as a truck carrying police officers happened to drive past, a spokesman for the investigating committee of the prosecutor's office said.

(*IHT*, 7 January 2010, p. 3)

Five policemen were killed yesterday [6 January] ... The driver of a jeep tried to enter a police compound ... It hit a truck carrying five policemen that was leaving the compound ... Experts estimate that at least 100 policemen and an even higher toll of civilians have been killed by bombings and shootings in the past year in Ingushetia, Dagestan and Chechnya.

(*FT*, 7 January 2010, p. 8)

A day after the kidnapping and murder of Natalia Estimirova in Grozny, President Dmitri Medvedev called accusations that security forces were involved 'primitive' and 'unacceptable'. He said: 'It is deliberate provocation' ... Rights groups say Moslem separatists attack civilians in the Caucasus, often on religious grounds. There have been assaults on fortune-tellers, prostitutes and merchants selling alcohol, while a rebel website has threatened school principals and teachers with death if they ban head scarves or seat girls next to boys. But rights advocates also accuse the government of forced disappearances, illegal detentions, extra-judicial killings and house burnings. In a report last month [December 2009] the human rights organization Memorial, based in Moscow, called for an end to 'the massive and systematic human rights violations by the security agencies' ... Dozens of people who once monitored rights violations have stopped working or fled.

(*IHT*, 11 January 2010, p. 3)

President Dmitri Medvedev has appointed a new special envoy to the North Caucasus ... Alexander Khloponin will be given the specific task of promoting economic development ... Mr Khloponin is not from the Caucasus, but is a former governor in Siberia ... The former businessman will be responsible for the newly created North Caucasus federal district, which includes Chechnya, Dagestan and Ingushetia, as well as four other regions: Kabardino-Balkaria, Karachai-Cherkessia, North Ossetia and Stavropol. The Kremlin says one of his top priorities will be to build up the local economies and create new jobs. Experts say many young men in the region have joined a hard core of Moslem militants to fight for independence as a result of poverty and widespread abuses by the security forces, including kidnapping and torture.

(www.bbc.co.uk, 20 January 2010)

A bomb exploded on the tracks beneath a railroad maintenance engine in St Petersburg on Tuesday [2 February], slightly wounding the vehicle's operator ... The blast produced a crater over three feet wide, but caused little other damage ... The head of the regional investigation unit covering transportation ... [said] that the bombing was probably a terrorist attack. In November [2009] a bomb exploded beneath a luxury train travelling between Moscow and St Petersburg, killing over twenty-five people. Officials have named no suspects in that attack.

(www.iht.com, 3 February 2010)

'Prime minister Vladimir Putin has ordered officials in the North Caucasus to ensure what he called the "normal work" of human rights activists operating in the region' (*IHT*, 25 January 2010, p. 3). 'President Dmitri Medvedev appointed former metals executive Alexander Khloponin to head the North Caucasus Federal District to try to target corruption, unemployment and poverty that is seen as threatening an area important to the security of energy transit' (www.iht.com, 12 February 2010). ('Alexander Khloponin ... [is a] businessman ... not a general or a veteran of the FSB security service ... [He was given] the task of creating new jobs ... At a meeting with senators last month [February] Mr Khloponin publicly challenged Ramzan Kadyrov, saying he travelled internationally as if he were the president of an independent country. Mr Khloponin asked: "Did he think Saudi Arabia was going to give him money? We have a foreign ministry for that kind of negotiation"': www.iht.com, 31 March 2010.)

Pressure has been steadily rising in Dagestan, where clan wars intersect with a growing Islamic fundamentalism and a deepening sense of public alienation. All these threats factor into a question the Kremlin has to answer in the coming days. Who will bring peace if he is named president? ... A year of rising violence in the [Caucasus] region has made it clear that Moscow's control is more tenuous than it seemed. Nowhere is this more obvious than in Dagestan, where militants have stepped up their attacks while clan groupings have fought, sometimes murderously, over the republic's resources ...

Dagestan, one of the most heavily subsidized of Russia's regions, should be able to support itself. It has oil and gas reserves, like neighbouring Azerbaijan, and once lucrative vineyards and fisheries. The sandy coastline, stretching 250 miles along the Caspian Sea, should be a money-maker ... But the beaches around Makhachkala, a city of 466,000, offer a primer in what has gone wrong. Tycoons have chopped up much of the coast for private mansions, and local residents complain that the public beaches are too dirty and ill-kept to enjoy ... There has always been competition for power in Dagestan [population 2.5 million], which is cobbled together out of more than thirty ethnic groups, but with the Soviet collapse it turned violent ... The first term of Dagestan's president, Mukhu Aliyev, ends on 20 February [2010]. At the time of his appointment, Mr Aliyev raised great hopes in a populace furious over corruption; a long-time Communist Party figure, he was known for steadfastly refusing bribes and lived, famously, in a modest three-room apartment. But four years later Mr Aliyev's critics say he has been too weak to control the factions beneath him. It is clear that the calm of his early presidency is gone. Three hundred people died in violent attacks in Dagestan in 2009 – more than in either the nearby republics of Ingushetia or Chechnya – and the number of attacks were more than double the 2008 figure ... President Dmitri Medvedev could reappoint Mr Aliyev, sixty-nine, or choose a new face like Magomed Abdullayev, forty-eight, a deputy prime minister who, like Mr Medvedev, studied and lectured at the law department of St Petersburg University. Uncertainty over the question has gripped Makhachkala since mid-November, and some complain that it fuelled a spike in violence in December and January ... [There is the view that] public disgust over corruption is driving young people to embrace fundamentalism ... [To] disappear into 'the forest' ... [is the term] people here ... [use to describe] underground militant networks.

(www.iht.com, 31 January 2010; *IHT*, 1 February 2010, p. 3)

President Dmitri Medvedev on Monday [8 February] ... Magomedsalaam Magomedov to be the next president of Dagestan ... Magomedsalaam Magomedov is an economist and businessman who rose to prominence thanks to his father Magomedali Magomedov, who led Dagestan from 1987 until 2006. That year Mukhu Aliyev was appointed to succeed him, amid a push to fight corruption in the republic. Though violence and corruption seemed to ease during the early years of Mr Aliyev's presidency, last year [2009] saw a number of armed attacks more than double, and some blamed the president's weak grip over Dagestan's combative clan groupings. The nomination of Mr Magomedov, a seasoned manager and industrialist, falls in line with the appointment of a new presidential envoy, Alexander Khloponin, who is launching a campaign to bring order to the Caucasus through economic means, said Grigori Shvedov, the editor-in-chief of the web-based news service Caucasian Knot. It also suggests the Kremlin wants to see significant changes, since Mr Magomedov has been a persistent critic of Mr Aliyev's government ... Mr Shvedov added that for decades leading up to Mr Aliyev's presidency, leaders in Moscow secured the loyalty of the most powerful of Dagestan's clans by allowing them to profit off lucrative, tax-free businesses ... Mr Medvedev appointed four new governors on Monday, but the decision on Dagestan was the most anxiously awaited.

(www.iht.com, 8 February 2010; *IHT*, 9 February 2010, p. 5)

Militants have killed five Russian soldiers in Chechnya ... The gunfight broke out on Thursday night [4 February] in forested mountains south-west of Grozny ... Five insurgents were also killed ... Russian forces have fought two wars against separatists in Chechnya since 1994. The conflicts claimed more than 100,000 lives.

(www.bbc.co.uk, 5 February 2010)

At least five soldiers were killed ... in a fight with rebels that began late Thursday night [4 February] in Chechnya ... At least five militants were also killed in the fighting, which continued into Friday ... On Thursday at least six rebels were killed by military forces in Chechnya in another operation.

(www.iht.com, 7 February 2010)

President Ramzan Kadyrov backed down Tuesday [9 February] from a conflict with human rights defenders and journalists, withdrawing several libel suits at the request, aides said, of his mother ... The lawsuits were prompted by accusations that the Chechen leader has used kidnapping, torture and murder ... [His spokesman added] that prominent Chechen cultural figures and clergy had also advised him to drop the suits ... Oleg Orlov [is] director of the rights group Memorial ... Mr Kadyrov sued Mr Orlov last autumn [2009], asking prosecutors to open a criminal case after Mr Orlov accused the president of complicity in the July murder of his colleague, Natalia Estimirova. Although the criminal suit has been dropped, Mr Orlov and Memorial must still pay Mr Kadyrov about $2,200 after losing a civil suit in October ... Mr Kadyrov also dropped claims against Lyudmila Alexeyeva, an eighty-two-year-old human rights worker, and journalists with *Novaya Gazeta* ... Russia's leaders have appeared of late to be shifting their strategy in Chechnya and the Caucasus region from war to economic development, and, his mother's wishes aside, Mr Kadyrov's move seems more the result of Kremlin pressure, observers said.

(*IHT*, 10 February 2010, p. 3)

Russian security forces said Friday [12 February] that they had killed at least twenty insurgents in Ingushetia ... The death toll included ten deaths on Thursday [11 February] in a continuing operation in a mountainous area near the border with Chechnya ... Islamist militancy overlaps with the activity of criminal groups and clan and ethnic rivalries ... Local leaders in Ingushetia, with a population of some 300,000, say poverty and unemployment are fuelling the insurgency, though Russia's security services say links to al-Qaeda also play a part ... Security measures have been strengthened to prevent the violence from crossing into neighbouring Chechnya, President Ramzan Kadyrov said Thursday [11 February].

(www.iht.com, 12 February 2010)

The Federal Security Service launched the sweep on Thursday [11 February]. Fighting by Moslem militants against Russian rule has stepped up in the past two years in Ingushetia and Dagestan ... President Dmitri Medvedev says violence in the North Caucasus remains Russia's biggest domestic problem.

(www.bbc.co.uk, 12 February 2010)

Memorial, a group that advocates for human rights, said Monday [15 February] that four civilians who were killed during recent operations against Islamist militants in the North Caucasus region had not been accidentally caught in a cross-fire, as Russian authorities have contended. Memorial said in a report that the four had been abducted, tortured and killed ... An unofficial Islamist website ... said Monday that fourteen civilians had been killed during the clashes.

(www.iht.com, 16 February 2010)

A lead investigator in the murder of Natalia Estimirova, a human rights worker who was abducted and shot to death in Chechnya last July [2009], said the authorities know who shot her but that they have been unable to arrest the suspect or identify the person who ordered the killing. Igor Sobol, head of the investigative committee for the Southern Federal District prosecutor's office, confirmed an account given to the Interfax news service on Thursday [25 February]. He said the gun used to kill Ms Estimirova had been found in a weapons cache, and that there are 'objective grounds to identify a group of people' behind her killing. He said the authorities could not arrest the suspect because he was in hiding, and said he could give no more information out of fear of harming the investigation ... Ms Estimirova was leaving for work when several men pushed her into a white car. Her body was found about 50 miles away, by the side of a highway in the neighbouring republic of Ingushetia, with gunshot wounds to the head and chest ... [In January] Ramzan Kadyrov said he believed the exiled tycoon Boris Berezovsky was behind Ms Estimirova's killing, as well as the murders of journalist Anna Politkovskaya and dissident Alexander Litvinenko.

(www.iht.com, 25 February 2010; *IHT*, 26 February 2010, p. 3)

After federal forces descended on ... the farming village of Ekazhevo on Tuesday [2 March] ... in Ingushetia, Russian authorities said Friday [5 March] that they had retrieved a burnt corpse, possibly of Alexander Tikhomorov, a charismatic militant leader. He has been linked to a series of bloody bombings in the last year, including one of a luxury train to St Petersburg in November [2009] that killed twenty-six people A spokesman for federal forces in the North Caucasus said the body had been found with a passport registered to Mr Tikhomorov … who adopted the nom de guerre of Said Buryatsky after he converted to Islam and joined the insurgency … He is seen as a compelling recruiter of suicide bombers. In a video posted on the internet last August [2009] he took responsibility for a bombing that killed twenty people at an Ingushetia police station … The police also suspect Mr Tikhomorov of involvement in a June attack on Ingushetia's president, Yunus-Bek Yevkurov, and the November train bombing. But many responded warily to the announcement on Friday, because reports of Mr Tikhomorov's death have circulated widely before, so much so that in September [2009] he posted a video insisting he was still alive. Tuesday's raid in Ekazhevo was the most powerful federal blitz in recent years, local residents said, resulting in six reported deaths. It was the same village where the renowned Chechen warlord Shamil Basayev was killed in a special operation in 2006.

(www.iht.com, 6 March 2010)

Russia confirmed Saturday [6 March] that its forces had killed Alexander Tikhomorov, who under the name Said Buryatsky is believed to have trained suicide bombers in the North Caucasus. And Russian officials said they had proof that his organization was behind the bombing of a luxury train … the *Nevsky Express* … in November [2009] … [Russia said] eight fighters were killed and ten detained during the federal raid, which sealed off the village of 25,000 before dawn on Tuesday [2 March] … Violence in the North Caucasus has sharply risen in the past year.

(www.iht.com 7 March 2010; *IHT*, 8 March 2010, p. 3)

In Dagestan … fifty-eight police officers were killed in attacks last year [2009], according to the republic's interior ministry … Last month alone [February 2010], according to press reports, thirteen officers were killed in bombings and gangland-style shootings. The gunmen [are] some combination of Islamist militants, alienated young people, ordinary criminals and foot soldiers in private armies … As the number of attacks doubled, to 201 last year from 100 in 2008, the authorities tried to offer relief. The blue stripes were removed from most police cars and officers were told they no longer had to wear uniforms on their way to work … Every traffic officer in Makhachkala, the capital city, is now backed up by a riot policeman in camouflage, Kalashnikov assault rifle at the ready … [In] the North Caucasus occasional clashes with militants have intensified into something closer to guerrilla war. Russia has been trying to wipe out the militant underground since the late 1990s, when separatists moved into Dagestan from bases in neighbouring Chechnya … [Recently two cars] pulled up beside the police chief, Akhmed Magomedov, opened fire on two bodyguards in an escort and then strafed the chief's Volga with armour-piercing bullets, leaving him and a driver to bleed to death.

(www.iht.com, 21 March 2010; *IHT*, 22 March 2010, p. 2)

This month [March] federal forces carried out a series of major raids and claimed to have killed two major figures in the insurgency: Alexander Tikhomorov, who is said to have recruited and trained waves of young suicide bombers, and Anzor Astemirov, who is believed to have planned major attacks on federal forces in 2004 and 2005.

(www.iht.com, 29 March 2010)

'Counter-terrorist operations in March killed four high ranking members of the Caucasus Emirate, a militant Islamist group led by Doku Umarov … Sayd Buratski … Abu Khaled (a militant commander of Arab origin) … Salambek Akhmadov … [and] Anzor Astemirov' (*FT*, 30 March 2010, p. 5).

On Monday [29 March] two … huge explosions during morning rush hour in two subway stations in central Moscow … The causes of the blasts were not immediately clear, but the government said it suspected suicide bombers … The first explosion occurred in the Lubyanka subway station [which takes its name from the infamous Lubyanka prison that also served as the former headquarters of the KGB, the Soviet-era secret police] … About forty minutes later another explosion occurred … at the Park Kultury station.

(www.iht.com, 20 March 2010)

Officials said they suspected that the attack … at the Lubyanka station … was intended to send a message to the security forces, which have helped lead the crackdown in Chechnya and other parts of the Caucasus region … The subway system … known as the Metro … carries as many as 10 million people a day.

(www.iht.com, 29 March 2010)

(The exact times of explosions local time were 7.56 a.m. and 8.37 a.m.: www.guardian.co.uk, 30 March 2010; 8 a.m. local time is equivalent to 04.00 GMT: www.cnn.com, 30 March 2010.)

Authorities in the capital have declared it a 'terrorist' incident … No one has yet claimed responsibility, but the explosions do appear to have been co-ordinated. Moscow's Metro is one of the world's most used underground railways in the world, carrying some 5.5 million passengers a day.

(www.bbc.co.uk, 29 March 2010)

The Lubyanka station … is underneath the building that houses the main offices of the Federal Security Service [FSB], the KGB's main successor agency … The Park Kultury station area … is next to the city's renowned Gorky Park … The Moscow subway system is one of the world's busiest, carrying around 7 million passengers on an average workday.

(www.independent.co.uk, 29 March 2010)

'London's Underground network carries more than 3 million commuters daily' (www.cnn.com, 29 March 2010).

Moscow mayor Yuri Luzhkov: 'It was a terrorist act carried out by female bombers [according to the FSB]' … Alexander Bortnikov of the FSB: 'Our preliminary assessment is that this act of terror was committed by a terrorist group from the North Caucasus region. We consider this the most likely scenario, based on investigations conducted at the site of the blast. Fragments of the suicide bombers' bodies found at the blast, according to preliminary findings, indicate that the bombers were from the North Caucasus region' ... An estimated 500,00 people were riding trains throughout the capital at the time of the attacks ... Monday's bomb attacks on the Moscow subway bear the hallmarks of an operation carried out by female suicide bombers called 'black widows', according to security analysts ... The 'black widows' are believed to be made up of women whose husbands, brothers or fathers or other relatives have been killed in the conflict. The women are often dressed head-to-toe in black and wear the so-called 'martyr's belt' filled with explosives. They have been involved in a number of attacks in Russia and first came to prominence in 2002 when they were part of a group of separatists who threatened to blow up a Moscow theatre.

(www.cnn.com, 29 March 2010)

'In December 2003 a woman bomber blew herself up in central Moscow, killing six people ... She was identified as the widow of a Chechen guerrilla commander, and the female bombers soon became known in Russia as the "black widows"' (www.iht.com, 29 March 2010).

In the past decade [in Russia] ... women ... committed at least sixteen bombings, including two on board planes ... The first female suicide member was a sixteen-year-old Palestinian girl who drove a truck into an Israeli army convoy in 1985 ... Suicide bombing was a tactic that came late to Chechnya and was nearly unknown during the first war from 1994 to 1996, but once it arrived, in 2000, in an attack that killed twenty-seven Russian special forces soldiers, it quickly became associated with women.

(*IHT*, 30 March 2010, p. 3)

Chechen rebels first used female suicide bombers in 2000, when two women blew themselves up at a Russian army base in Alkhan-Yurt, a village in Chechnya that had been the scene of a massacre carried out by Russian troops the previous year.

(www.independent.co.uk, 30 March 2010)

At least thirty-eight people were killed ... in two suicide bomb attacks on the Moscow Metro during the morning rush hour ... The system was partially disrupted following the attacks, but damage to the stations was minimal and both had reportedly reopened by the evening rush hour ... FSB chief Alexander Bortnikov said its investigators believed the attacks had been carried out by 'terrorist groups related to the North Caucasus'. He said: 'This is likely to be our main conclusion, because fragments of the bodies of two female suicide bombers were found earlier at the scene of the incident and examinations show that these individuals came from the North Caucasus region'... Federal prosecutors said they had opened an investigation into 'suspected acts of terrorism'.

(www.bbc.co.uk, 29 March 2010)

'Other Metro lines remained open, with trains running regularly' (www.economist.com, 29 March 2010).

'Both [the affected] stations reopened around 5 p.m. Monday [29 March]' (www.cnn.com, 30 March 2010).

'The Kremlin controls the major television networks ... In the first few hours after the subway bombings ... the national channels ... barely mentioned or ignored altogether the news, instead broadcasting cooking programmes, detective movies or the usual fare' (www.iht.com, 4 April 2010; *IHT*, 5 April 2010, p. 3).

> Moscow is holding an official day of mourning for the thirty-nine people killed ... Inside the Lubyanka Metro station twenty-three people died ... [In] the Park Kultury station a second explosion left twelve people dead. Another four people died in hospital, and officials have warned that the death toll could rise.
>
> (www.bbc.co.uk, 30 March 2010)

'The *Kommersant*, newspaper yesterday [30 March] claimed the authorities had been warned Chechen terrorists were planning a suicide attack on the capital's Metro' (*FT*, 31 March 2010, p. 9).

> Citing security sources, *Kommersant* reported that Said Buryatsky, a leading terrorist ideologue who was killed by Russian security forces earlier this month [2 March], had prepared a bridge of thirty potential suicide bombers. The women had been sent to Turkey for training, and then returned to the Caucasus for personal instruction from Buryatsky. Nine of the women have already been deployed in terror acts, mostly in the North Caucasus, but twenty-one remain unaccounted for.
>
> (*The Times*, 31 March 2010, p. 25)

> Agents from the FSB believe that the women were avenging the death of Said Buryatsky, the leading ideologue of the Islamic rebels in the North Caucasus Buryatsky, a Moslem convert who was born Alexander Tikhomorov, was among six militants killed in an FSB operations in Ingushetia on 2 March [2010].
>
> (*The Independent*, 31 March 2010, p. 25)

> A source in the General Prosecutor's Investigative Committee told the newspaper *Kommersant* that Alexander Tikhomirov had recruited thirty potential suicide bombers, who were sent for training at a madrasa in Turkey and then returned to Mr Tikhomirov's authority. The investigator said, according to his data, nine of those women had already carried out attacks.
>
> (www.iht.com, 1 April 2010)

Investigators believe that one of the two female suicide bombers in the subway attacks that killed thirty-nine people in Moscow was a seventeen-year-old girl ... who was the widow of an insurgent leader, officials said on Friday [2 April] ... Dzhennet Abdurakhmanova had been married to Umalat Magomedov, who was ... killed in a security operation on 31 December 2009 ... The *Kommersant* newspaper showed a photo of the two, both holding weapons ... Ms Abdurakhmanova, whose last name has also been reported as Abdullayeva, is believed to have carried out the first suicide blast on Monday [29 March] ... She was from Dagestan ... and supposedly first established contact with the insurgents on the internet, *Kommersant* reported ... The woman who carried out the other attack, at the Park Kultury station, has not yet been identified, officials said ... President Dmitri Medvedev has been an advocate of addressing what he has termed the 'root causes' of terrorism in the Caucasus, including poverty and corruption ... On Thursday [1 April] Mr Medvedev reiterated that the government needed to improve living conditions in the Caucasus, but he also tended to sound more like Vladimir Putin ... Mr Medvedev said federal forces must embrace a broader range of tactics.

(www.iht.com, 2 April 2010)

Kommersant ... reported today [2 April] that one of the two female suicide bombers who attacked Moscow's subway was the seventeen-year-old widow of a slain Islamist rebel from the North Caucasus ... The report ... identified the second bomber as twenty-year-old Markha Ustarkhanova from Chechnya. On Thursday [1 April] it said she was the widow of a militant leader who was killed last October [2009] while preparing to assassinate Chechen President Ramzan Kadyrov.

(www.independent.com, 2 April 20010)

Police in southern Russia confirmed to the BBC that they had given Moscow colleagues information about Dzhennet Abdurakhmanova from Dagestan ... A police spokesman said Abdurakhmanova had been married to a leading Islamist militant, Umalat Magomedov ... He would not confirm that she was definitely one of the Metro bombers ... The second suspected bomber has not yet been identified.

(www.bbc.co.uk, 2 April 2010)

Dzhennet Abdurakhmanova ... and her husband Umalat Magomedov were foot soldiers in a shadowy grouping, the Caucasus Emirate, which on Wednesday [31 March] claimed responsibility for the [Moscow] blasts. Like al-Qaeda and other Islamist terror groups, it is less of an organization and more of a brand name for loosely affiliated movement of warlords, bound by little more than ideology and hatred. Its leader [is] Doku Umarov ... His declared objective is liberation of the entire North Caucasus region from Russian rule and establishment of an Islamic caliphate ... Mr Umarov created the emirate in 2007 ... The parliament of Chechnya has even tried to legislate it out of existence ... in the resolution ... last October [2009] ... Security officials believe the second [Moscow] bomber ... was Markha Ustarkhanova, a widow of Chechen militant Said Khizriyev, who was killed last October [2009] by the security forces of Chechen President Ramzan Kadyrov. She made contact with Islamist radicals over the internet, according to her parents, who spoke to Russian newspaper *Kommersant* ... Mr Umarov's father, wife and son were kidnapped by Russian security forces in 2005, and have disappeared. Shortly thereafter he formed the Caucasian Emirate, an alliance of Chechen separatists and Islamists ... The Russian government says that Mr Umarov is funded mainly from abroad, by Islamist sympathizers in the Middle East and friendly overseas intelligence services who want to stir up trouble in Russia. Experts say that while Mr Umarov has claimed many successful terror attacks, including Monday's blast [in Moscow], it is unclear how much real authority he holds.

(*FT*, 3 April 2010, p. 6)

'Twin suicide bombings in Moscow's Metro killed at least forty' (www.iht. com, 4 April 2000).

'The blasts ... killed forty people' (www.bbc.co.uk, 5 April 2010).'The last time Moscow was hit by a confirmed terrorist attack was in August 2004 when a suicide bomber blew herself up outside a subway station [in Moscow]' (www. independent.co.uk, 29 March 2010).

'[On 31 August 2004] a suicide bomber killed at least nine other people ... outside the Rizhskaya subway ... [On 6 February] of that same year a women carrying a bomb destroyed another subway car, killing at least forty-one people' (www.iht.com, 20 March 2010).

In the early part of the decade, the subway system was subjected to several attacks related to the terrorist war in Chechnya ... In February [2010] a Chechen rebel leader, Doku Umarov, threatened in an interview on a website to organize terror acts in Russian population centres.

(www.iht.com, 29 March 2010)

'Doku Umarov: "If Russians think that the war is happening only on television, somewhere far off in the Caucasus, and it will not touch them, then we are going to show them that this war will return to their homes"' (www.iht.com, 20 March 2010).

In February [2010] the Chechen rebel leader Doku Umarov warned in an interview on a rebel-affiliated website that: 'The zone of military operations will be extended to the territory of Russia ... The war is coming to their cities' ... Umarov claimed his fighters were responsible for the November [2009] bombing of a Moscow to St Petersburg train in which twenty-six people were killed.

(www.guardian.co.uk, 29 March 2010)

Chechen rebel leader Doku Umarov warned in February [2010] that: 'The zone of military operations will be extended to the territory of Russia ... The war is coming to their cities' ... Last November [2009] he said his Caucasian Mujahadeen had carried out a bombing that killed twenty-six people on board an express train travelling from Moscow to St Petersburg.

(www.bbc.co.uk, 29 March 2010)

Doku Umarov fought in both of Chechnya's separatist wars with Russia ... and served as its security minister during its brief spell of independence. The security services have repeatedly proclaimed him to have been killed, most recently last June [2009], but he continues to elude them. He once rejected attacks on civilians but shifted tack recently, saying: 'We try to avoid civilian targets but for me there are no civilians in Russia. Why? Because a genocide of our people is being carried out with their consent.'

(*The Independent*, 31 March 2010, p. 25)

'A suicide attack in 2003 [5 July] killed fifteen people at a Moscow concert' (www.cnn.com, 29 March 2010).

Chechnya has been relatively calm in recent years ... But violence has spread to neighbouring republics, particularly Ingushetia and Dagestan, both of which have descended into a state resembling civil war ... In Ingushetia corrupt officials have paid off insurgents to keep their lucrative fiefs ... Big terrorist attacks have in the past been used by the Kremlin to justify tightening its grip on power and curbing the opposition. The second war, in 2000, which helped to propel Vladimir Putin into his presidency, was accompanied by a move to bring Russian television under Kremlin control. In 2004, after the school siege in Beslan, North Ossetia, Mr Putin scrapped regional elections.

(www.economist.com, 29 March 2010)

Sergei Arutyunov, a Caucasus expert at the Russian Academy of Sciences, estimates the number of militants at 500 to 1,000. He said: 'They are educated intelligentsia. They can remain in the shadows if they want. They could be officials who can live a double life, or they could be in the police force ... Mr Arutyunov, who has studied the response to the insurgency in Dagestan, asserted that no more than 10 per cent of the people there support insurgent groups like the one headed by Doku Umarov ... But if militants are seeking to replenish the ranks of suicide bombers, he said, they will find a vast pool of young men and women who lost siblings or friends in counter-terrorist operations. He said: 'To find candidates is very easy. There are 100,000 people here who are furious with the authorities.'

(*IHT*, 7 April 2010, p. 3)

For many years Moscow has routinely portrayed Chechen bombers as Islamic extremists, many of them foreign, who want to make Islam the world's dominant religion. Yet however much Russia may want to convince the West that this battle is part of a global war on terrorism, the facts about who becomes a Chechen suicide attacker – male or female – reveal otherwise. The three of us, in our work for the Chicago Project on Security and Terrorism, have analysed every Chechen suicide attack since they began in 2000, forty-two separate incidents involving sixty-three people who killed themselves. Many Chechen separatists are Moslem, but few of the suicide bombers profess religious motives. The majority are male, but a huge fraction – over 40 per cent – are women. Although foreign suicide attackers are not unheard of in Chechnya, of the forty-two for whom we can determine place of birth, thirty-eight were from the Caucasus. Something is driving Chechen suicide bombers, but it is hardly global jihad ... On 7 June 2000 two Chechen women, Khava Barayeva and Luiza Magomadova, drove a truck laden with explosives into a Russian special forces building in Alkhan-Yurt, Chechnya; while the Russians insist two soldiers were killed, the Chechen rebel claim of more than two dozen fatalities seems more likely. This was the first Chechen suicide attack and showed the many advantages of female suicide bombers ... Ms Barayeva is considered responsible for inspiring a movement of 'black widows' – women who have lost a husband, child or close relative to the 'occupation' and killed themselves on missions to even the score. In total twenty-four Chechen females ranging in age from fifteen to thirty-seven, including the most deadly – the co-ordinated bombings of two passenger flights in August 2004 that caused ninety deaths (according to Russian authorities), the subway blasts on Monday [29 March] that killed nearly forty ... Chechen women have carried out eight of the ten suicide attacks in Moscow. Although we are still learning the details of Monday's bombings, there were warnings that a major attack in Russia was coming. Twice this year [2010] one of Chechnya's leading rebel commanders, Doku Umarov, issued video statements warning of attacks in Russia proper. He said: 'The Russians think the war is distant. Blood will not only spill in our towns and villages but also it will spill in their towns ... Our military operations will encompass the entirety of Russia' ... He also made clear that his campaign was not about restoring any Islamic caliphate, but about Chechen independence. He said: 'This is the land of our brothers and it is our sacred duty to liberate these lands' ... The trajectory of Chechnya's suicide campaign reveals a stark pattern: twenty-seven attacks from June 2000 to November 2004; no attacks until October 2007; and eighteen since. What explains the three-year pause? The answer is loss of public support in Chechnya for the rebellion, for two reasons. The first was the revulsion against the 2004 Beslan school massacre in which Chechen rebels murdered hundreds of Russian children ... Second, Russian pursued a robust hearts-and-minds programme to win over the war-torn population. Military operations killed significantly fewer civilians. Amnesty was granted to rebel fighters and nearly 600 Chechen separatists surrendered in 2006 alone. Unfortunately, the Russians then over-reached. Starting in late 2007,

Moscow pressured the pro-Russian government of Ramzan Kadyrov to stamp out the remaining militants ... Why did the current wave of Chechen suicide attacks gain force in the spring of 2009 after Russia announced an end of all its military operations in Chechnya? Because the Kadyrov government's counter-terrorism measures had grown so harsh that some had actually begun to view Moscow as a moderating force in the region. Still, the picture is clear: Chechen suicide terrorism is strongly motivated by both direct military occupation by Russia and indirect military occupation by pro-Russia Chechen security forces.

(Robert Pape, Lindsey O'Rourke and Jenna McDermit, www.iht.com, 31 March 2010; *IHT*, 1 April 2010, p. 6)

At least twelve people, including a top police official, have been killed in two suicide bombings in the town of Kizlyar in Dagestan ... A total of nine police officers were among the dead ... A car bomb was detonated at about 08.30 (10.30 GMT) outside the offices of the local interior ministry and the FSB security service. Another bomber ... wearing a police uniform ... then blew himself up twenty minutes later as a crowd gathered.

(www.bbc.co.uk, 31 March 2010)

'Such attacks, which are not uncommon in the [Caucasus] region, typically target police and government officials' (www.iht.com, 31 March 2010). 'In Dagestan on Wednesday [31 March] the first of the bombs exploded in a parked car ... As rescue workers and police officials gathered at the scene, a man wearing a police uniform walked up and set off his explosives' (www.iht.com, 31 March 2010).

A suicide bomber in a car detonated explosives when the police tried to stop the car ... As investigators and residents gathered around the scene of the blast, a second bomber wearing a police uniform approached and set off explosives, killing the town's police chief, among others.

(*IHT*, 1 April 2010, p. 3)

'Twelve people were killed ... Most of the dead and wounded were police officers' (www.cnn.com, 1 April 2010).

The rebel leader Doku Umarov ... took responsibility on Wednesday [31 March] for the double bombing that killed thirty-nine people on the Moscow subway system ... and he warned that he was plotting more attacks in revenge for what he called the repressions against Chechens ordered by prime minister Vladimir Putin. The statement ... was posted via internet video hours after another double bombing that killed at least twelve people in Dagestan ... That attack appeared aimed at the police, according to the Russian prosecutor's office. Mr Umarov said the Moscow attacks were meant to avenge a February [2010] anti-terror raid that killed both civilians and militants in a wooded area near the border between Chechnya and Ingushetia. Doku Umarov (on the video dated 29 March, the day of the

Moscow bombings): 'You Russians hear about the war on television and the radio, and that is why you are quiet, this is why you do not react to the atrocities committed by the bandit group that is led by Putin. I promise you the war will come to your streets, and you will feel it in your own lives and on your own skin ... [The subway attacks] were carried out on my orders, and they are not the last ones, with God's will.'

(www.iht.com, 31 March 2010)

'Doku Umarov: "On 11 February 2010 officers of the criminal formation known as the FSB carried out an operation to destroy peaceful citizens"' (www.iht.com, 1 April 2010).

Kavkaz Centre, a website that regularly carries messages from the rebels, released a video in which Doku Umarov said he was behind the Monday [29 March] attacks. The attacks were revenge for what Umarov called a 'massacre conducted by the Russian occupiers against the poorest residents of Chechnya and Ingushetia' ... According to the site, the video was taped on the same day as the attacks. The incident Umarov referred to is a February special operation by Russian forces, after which there were accusations of Russians killing innocent civilians. In the video Umarov said the victims were simply gathering garlic to make a living.

(www.cnn.com, 31 March 2010)

Doku Umarov ... said the Moscow attacks were an act of revenge for the killings of poor Chechen and Ingush civilians by the Russian security forces near the town of Arshty on 11 February [2010]. He said the civilians were 'massacred by Russian occupiers' as they were gathering wild garlic to feed their families. The rebel, who styles himself as the Emir of the Caucasus Emirate, said the attacks on Russian soil would continue ... [He said the video] was recorded on Monday [29 March] – just hours after the Metro attacks. Earlier on Wednesday [31 March] Doku Umarov's spokesman [Shemsettin Batukaev] had told Reuters that his militant group 'did not carry out the attack in Moscow, and we do not know who did it'.

(www.bbc.co.uk, 31 March 2010)

Nikolai Patrushev (secretary of Russia's security council): 'We have had information that individual members of Georgian special forces support contacts with terrorist organizations in the Russian North Caucasus' ... Dmitri Rogozin (Russia's envoy to Nato): 'Georgian special forces have really been working on this issue.'

(*The Times*, 1 April 2010, p. 45)

President Dmitri Medvedev made an impromptu visit on Thursday [1 April] to Dagestan ... He said federal forces must embrace a broader range of tactics that would be 'more effective, but also tough, severe and preventative' ... The police said they killed one of Doku Umarov's associates on Wednesday [31 March] in a neighbouring republic, Kabardino-

Balkaria ... The insurgents lacked a central figurehead, a role that Mr Umarov now seems determined to seize for himself. Grigori Shvedov, the editor of the web-based news service Caucasian Knot, said Mr Umarov, forty-five, had long been influential as a guerrilla fighter but has traditionally depended on younger, more charismatic protégés to communicate with the public ... After the collapse of the Soviet Union he left a career as a construction engineer to fight with the Chechen separatists. In 1997, when Russian troops had withdrawn from Grozny, he was appointed the head of the fledgling government's security council. But within ten years Russia had crushed the separatist movement and killed its most charismatic leaders ... In 2007 Mr Umarov ... declared himself the Emir of the Caucasus Emirate, which aimed to establish a shariah-based state independent of Russia. With him came many of the former separatist fighters. Last April [2009] Mr Umarov took another decisive step by announcing the revival of Riyadus-Salikhin, or the 'Garden of Martyrs', a suicide formation once led by Shamil Basayev that had lain dormant for five years. The battalion took responsibility for a 2002 hostage-taking at a Moscow theatre. Since 17 May suicide bombings have been recorded, Mr Shvedov said ... Some experts argue that the militant underground in the Caucasus has become so dispersed in recent years that neither Mr Umarov nor anyone else could emerge as its leader ... [that the] movement [is] made up of widely dispersed warlords.

(www.iht.com, 1 April 2010)

President Dmitri Medvedev made a surprise visit to Dagestan on Thursday [1 April] ... Mr Medvedev's visit came as a Russian newspaper named one of the female bombers who took part in Monday's attacks on the Moscow Metro as Markha Ustarkhanova, a widow of a Chechen militant ... killed in an October [2009] gun battle with the security forces of Chechen president Ramzan Kadyrov. The Metro bomber made contact with Islamist radicals over the internet, according to her parents. The newspaper claimed the parents had notified police after her marriage ... and since last summer she had been listed as missing ... Mr Medvedev is holding a summit of security officials and the heads of the North Caucasus autonomous regions ... [the] scene of a growing civil war in which 900 people died last year [2009]. Mr Medvedev said in an annual address to the Federal Assembly last November [2009] that violence in the North Caucasus was the worst problem Russia faces.

(www.ft.com, 1 April 2010)

Two bombs exploded in Dagestan on Sunday [4 April], derailing a freight train ... Nobody was wounded ... The pre-dawn blasts on a rail line from Moscow to Azerbaijan caused nine wagons of a train carrying construction materials to derail ... After the first blast derailed eight of the wagons, a second device went off ... A source in the regional transport police said: 'The device was placed near the railway track twenty-five metres from the first one and was meant to be blown up when police and investigators arrived on the scene' ... A passenger train from Siberia to Azerbaijan's capital Baku was stranded on the track by the damage.

(www.iht.com, 4 April 2010; *IHT*, 5 April 2010, p. 3)

A suicide bomber killed at least two police officers ... on Monday [5 April] ... in Ingushetia ... A suicide bomber blew himself up next to a police car in the town of Karabulak ... Three police officers were taken to hospital ... Two of them died ... The bomber's car exploded later, wounding an investigator.

(www.iht.com, 5 April 2010)

'A Russian newspaper reported Monday [5 April] that the second Moscow suicide bomber may have been a twenty-eight-year-old teacher from Dagestan. *Novaya Gazeta* quoted the woman's father saying he recognized her in a photograph' (www.iht.com, 5 April 2010).

'The woman's father, Rasul Magomedov, told *Novaya Gazeta* that he recognized his daughter Mariam Sharipova in a photograph circulated on the internet ... She lived ... in Dagestan ... with her parents, both of whom are teachers' (www.bbc.co.uk, 5 April 2010).

'Russian officials have confirmed the identity of the second suicide bomber to attack the Moscow Metro, a twenty-eight-year-old woman from Dagestan. Mariam Sharipova is the wife of Islamist rebel commander Magomedali Vagapov, the officials said' (www.bbc.co.uk, 6 April 2010).

'Ms Sharipova's father, Rasul Magomedov, first contacted the authorities last week ... He acknowledged that he had been told by Russian security officials before the bombing that an insurgent leader, Magomedali Vagapov, had secretly married Ms Sharipova' (www.iht.com, 6 April 2010).

'A woman strapped with explosives barged through a line of police officers Friday [9 April] as they fought militants in Ingushetia, shot an officer to death and then blew herself up ... The militants also reportedly blew themselves up' (*IHT*, 10 April 2010, p. 3).

A Dubai court convicted two men Monday [12 April] of involvement in the 2009 assassination of Chechen military commander Sulim Yamadayev, and handed them a life sentence ... [The men were from Tajikistan and Iran] ... Dubai police named Adam Delimkhanov, an advisor to Ramzan Kadyrov, as the person who masterminded the murder. Delimkhanov has repeatedly denied any involvement.

(www.iht.com, 12 April 2010)

A court in Dubai jailed two men – an Iranian and a Tajik – for twenty-five years over their role in the assassination of ... Sulim Yamadayev ... a rival of Chechen President Ramzan Kadyrov ... on 28 March 2009 ... In 2005 Yamadayev was named a Hero of Russia ... Last year [2009] Interpol issued arrest warrants for seven Russians in connection with the killing ... It is alleged that the Iranian handed over a briefcase containing the murder weapons. The Tajik was accused of collecting intelligence for the assassination and of helping the killers flee the UAE ... In September 2008 Yamadayev's brother was shot in Moscow.

(www.bbc.co.uk, 12 April 2010)

Umar Israilov, a whistle-blower living in hiding after accusing ... Ramzan Kadyrov ... of personally participating in torture, kidnapping and murder, was gunned down ... in Vienna ... last year [2009] ... He had received asylum in Austria and was taking his evidence against Mr Kadyrov to the European Court of Human Rights ... A fifteen-month Austrian investigation into the crime has uncovered links between the suspected killers and one of Mr Kadyrov's close advisers ... [namely] Shaa Turlayev ... The new evidence raises questions about Mr Kadyrov's denial and whether Chechnya's president or government played a direct role in the killing, one of a string of contract-style slayings – in Chechnya, Azerbaijan, Turkey, Moscow, Europe and the Middle East – that have silenced the Chechen president's critics or rivals ... Adam Delimkhanov ... since 2007 ... has been a member of Russia's Duma, the lower house of parliament. Mr Delimkhanov, a member of the political party led by prime minister Vladimir Putin, is wanted on an international arrest warrant for his suspected role in ordering the killing in the United Arab Emirates of Sulim Yamadayev.

(www.iht.com, 26 April 2010; *IHT*, 27 April 2010, pp. 1, 4)

A military strike by Russia against Islamist militants in the North Caucasus region is much more likely this year [2010] than last [2009] and would threaten the lives of scores of civilians, a report showed Monday [26 April] ... Minority Rights Group International said in a report: 'The combination of circumstances is dangerously close to those that prevailed in 1999 before the start of the second Chechen war, which caused the deaths of at least 25,000 civilians' ... The report forms part of its annual index of countries where civilians are most at risk of genocide, mass killings or violent repression. In those three turbulent regions of Russia, at least 862 people were killed last year [2009] in clashes, bombings and gun battles, according to internet news agency Caucasian Knot. Russia has jumped up seven places to rank sixteenth in the 2010 index of seventy countries, calculated on the basis of ten indicators such as measures of conflict, governance and economic risk.

(www.iht.com, 27 August 2010)

Chechnya's president, Ramzan Kadyrov, ordered the kidnapping of a Chechen whistle-blower in Vienna last year [2009], in which the man was fatally shot, Austria's counter-terrorism department concluded after a year-long investigation. The nation's public prosecutor's office released the news on Tuesday [27 April]. Mr Kadyrov has denied any role in the killing of the whistle-blower, Umar Israilov ... But the Austrian government's investigators concluded that Mr Kadyrov ordered that Mr Israilov be kidnapped, and that the group of Chechens who tried to snatch Mr Israilov from a Viennese street botched the job. One of them shot Mr Israilov after he broke free and tried to escape, the investigators found. Their conclusions, pointed and direct but based largely on circumstantial evidence, shift the focus now to Austria's prosecutor's office, which has been preparing indictments. Three Chechen exiles are in custody in the case … The fourth suspect … left Austria and returned to Russia after the killing … He is suspected of shooting Mr Israilov three times with a pistol.

(www.iht.com, 28 April 2010; *IHT*, 29 April 2010, p. 3)

Violence broke out in two north Caucasian republics on Saturday [1 May] as militants attacked gatherings on May Day, a revered Soviet holiday that still draws flocks of Russian to public celebrations. A bomb went off … in a hippodrome in Nalchik, the capital of the republic of Kabardino-Balkaria, killing a 104-year-old war veteran … The bomb was planted near the VIP box and was detonated not long before a delegation of regional leaders was due to arrive … The blast wounded the ministers of the interior and culture … Ten minutes before the Nalchik blast an armed man was killed trying to enter a sports complex where dignitaries were gathered in the city of Nazran, in neighbouring Ingushetia … Ingushetia's president, Yunus-Bek Yevkurov, was inside the complex.

(www.iht.com, 2 May 2010)

Three men involved in the Moscow subway bombings in March were killed when they fought back during an attempt to arrest them, the director of the Federal Security Service told the Russian president Thursday [13 May] … One of the three killed had accompanied the two female suicide bombers from Dagestin to Moscow and guided one of them to the subway, Alexander Bortnikov told President Dmitri Medvedev. Bortnikov said: 'They offered a bitter armed resistance and were eliminated. Active measures have been taken to hunt down the other members of the gang.'

(www.cnn.com, 13 May 2010)

All those involved in the bombings have now been identified, officials said … Alexander Bortnikov [head of the Federal Security Service): '[The deaths occurred during] an attempt to detain three members of an illegal group. To our great regret we were unable to detain them alive because they put up such fierce armed resistance and were killed' … Mr Bortnikov said the suspects included a man who had escorted the suicide bombers to Moscow and another man who had accompanied one bomber to the station … The FSB head said that efforts to find other identified planners of the attacks were continuing.

(www.bbc.co.uk, 13 May 2010)

A bombing outside a planned performance by a dance company from Chechnya left four people dead … on Wednesday [26 May] … The bomb went off outside a community centre in the south-western city of Stavropol … The blast happened … fifteen minutes before the Chechen dance company Vainakh was scheduled to perform ... Early reports indicate the bomb was detonated by remote control.

(www.cnn.com, 26 May 2010)

A bomb has killed at least six people ... outside a concert hall in Stavropol ... Five women and a girl of twelve were killed when it exploded in the street minutes before a Chechen dance troupe were due to perform inside the building ... The bomb exploded on the busy street about fifteen minutes before Chechnya's Vainakh state ensemble was due to perform indeed the hall ... The ethnically Russian city lies close to the troubled North Caucasus but has largely escaped militant violence.

(www.bbc.co.uk, 27 May 2010)

Four policemen and five gunmen have been killed in a shoot-out in Dagestan ... In a separate incident four suspected militants were killed by security forces after refusing to stop their car' (www.bbc.co.uk, 16 June 2010).

Six policemen and eight militants were killed Wednesday [16 June] in separate shootings in the North Caucasus region ... In Dagestan ... four [police] officers were killed ... during a siege that left five militants dead ... In a separate incident four gunmen were killed after they refused police orders to pull over and opened fire on officers ... Two officers died in other attacks – one in Dagestan and another in nearby Kabardino-Balkaria.

(*IHT*, 17 June 2020, p. 3)

'Russian interior ministry officials announced this spring [2010] that 'terrorist crime' in the North Caucasus was up by 60 per cent in 2009 compared to 2008' (*IHT*, 23 June 2010, p. 6).

Russia on Thursday [24 June] hailed a decision by the United States to designate the Caucasian insurgent leader Doku Umarov a terrorist, a step announced on the eve of President Dmitri Medvedev's visit to the White House. The State Department late Wednesday [23 June] released a statement describing Mr Umarov, a Chechen separatist commander, as being part of a radical jihadist movement that poses a threat to the United States as well. Ambassador Daniel Benjamin, the State Department's counter-terrorism co-ordinator, said that Mr Umarov's recent attacks on Russian targets 'illustrate the global nature of the terrorist problem we fight today'. Western governments have historically been reluctant to consider Caucasian militants in the same light as organizations like al-Qaeda, in part because they evolved out of a secular push for independence that followed the break-up of the Soviet Union ... In 2007 Mr Umarov pronounced himself emir of the Caucasus Emirate, which aims to establish a pan-Caucasian state independent of Russia and based on Islamic law. He revived a dormant Chechen suicide battalion, Riyadus-Salikihn, just as the tactic surged back in the North Caucasus ... Anatoli Safonov, Mr Medvedev's representative on terrorism, said the State Department designation would help Russia in its efforts to stamp out the insurgency, by imposing international sanctions on anyone who aids Mr Umarov or his associates ... Mr Umarov is the latest on a list of eighty-three entities identified by the president or secretary of state under an executive order introduced by President George W. Bush after the 11 September attacks. Four other designations sprang from the conflict in Chechnya and were passed in 2003, as Mr Bush sought Russian backing for the war in Iraq ... Ramzan Kadyrov, the president of Chechnya, said the decision should have come earlier, when Mr Umarov commanded a powerful force. Ramzan Kadyrov: 'There remain just a few individuals in the forest – most have found a way back into peaceful life. Umarov is a sick, toothless, pitiful thing.'

(www.iht.com, 24 June 2010; *IHT*, 25 June 2010, p. 3)

'The US State Department said the listing, approved by Secretary of State Hillary Clinton, would help to stem the flow of funds to Doku Umarov' (*FT*, 25 June 2010, p. 6).

'A suicide bomber blew himself up ... in Grozny ... on Wednesday [30 June] wounding three police officers and two civilians' (*IHT*, 1 July 2010, p. 3).

Europe's top human rights body has strongly criticized Chechen leader Ramzan Kadyrov for calling rights campaigners 'enemies of the people'. Dick Marty, a rapporteur on human rights for the Council of Europe, said the comments were 'unacceptable'. Mr Kadyrov was speaking in a television interview in which he also praised people who fire paintballs at women not wearing Islamic headscarves. Rights group Memorial says it had recorded several such attacks recently. Since the beginning of June unidentified men with paintball guns have been driving round the centre of Grozny shooting at girls with uncovered heads, Memorial said. In his interview, which was broadcast on 3 July, Ramzan Kadyrov launched a stinging attack on human rights campaigners. He said: 'They are getting big salaries from the West and in order to report on their activities they write all kinds of nonsense and filth in the internet. That is why they are not my opponents. They are the enemies of the people, enemies of the law, enemies of the state' ... Mr Marty called the remarks 'unacceptable and unworthy'. Mr Marty said: 'Such words, similar to those uttered by Mr Kadyrov against Natalia Estimirova, a member of Memorial's staff subsequently murdered last summer, are barely disguised threats' ... He also appealed to the Russian government 'to ask the Chechen authorities to ensure the protection of human rights defenders' ... On the paintball attacks, Mr Kadyrov referred to the women as 'naked', adding that they should be 'ashamed'.

(www.bbc.co.uk, 10 July 2010)

Russian security services have broken up what they described as a terrorist cell in ... Dagestan ... that was preparing female suicide bombers for attacks on major Russian cities, officials announced Monday [12 July]. They said six women had been arrested who had already written 'farewell letters' as they were being prepared for deployment ... Two men were also arrested, including one said to have played a role in attacks by two female suicide bombers on two subway stations in Moscow in March, which killed forty people ... The National Anti-terrorism Committee, a federal body, said the six women ranged in age from fifteen to twenty-nine years, adding that four of them were widows whose husbands had died in security operations ... Officials indicated on Monday that they believed that the arrests of the six women prevented another attack by so-called 'black widows' – young women from the Caucasus region who are turned into human bombs in Russian cities.

(www.iht.com, 13 July 2010; *IHT*, 14 July 2010, p. 3)

Three Chechens have been charged in France in connection with a conspiracy to commit terror attacks in Russia ... The suspects are believed to be linked to a rebel group that said it was responsible for attacks on the Moscow Metro on 29 March, when forty people died. Arrests last week in the Sarthe area of western France came after a tip-off from Russian authorities ... Those charged are accused of having links with a man arrested in Russia on terrorism charges.

(www.bbc.co.uk, 16 July 2010)

Officials in ... Dagestan say a Christian bishop has been shot to death by unknown attackers ... The victim of Thursday evening's shooting [15 July] in Makhachkala, the capital, was Artur Suleimanov, the bishop in Dagestan for the Russian evangelical denomination Osanna. Dagestan, which is about 90 per cent Moslem, is plagued by insurgent violence, with many of the militants inspired by or affiliated with Islamic separatists in neighbouring Chechnya ... [Also on Thursday] two militants were killed by police in a clash in the town of Khasavyurt.

(www.iht.com, 16 July 2010)

The fight continues in many parts of Russia's mainly Moslem North Caucasian autonomous republics. Dagestan, the most populous of the republics, is the epicentre of the conflict, in which sixty-five policemen have been killed so far this year [2010], up by a third from the same period last year [2009]. Several dozen militants have also been killed. Many observers reckon it is the last civil war in Europe.

(*FT*, 17 July 2010, p. 5)

A bomb and gun attack on a hydroelectric power station in Russia's Kabardino-Balkaria region has killed two guards ... Four bombs caused a fire in the Baksan plant's engine room which was later extinguished ... Supplies to the electricity grid were not affected, according to the state-run RusHydro company ... RusHydro said ... that explosions had hit the plant ... on Wednesday [21 July]. The attackers detonated four explosive devices ... while a fifth failed to go off ... Two cars carrying half a dozen assailants had attacked the plant ... The same group are believed to have earlier opened fire on a police station in the town of Baksan.

(www.bbc.co.uk, 21 July 2010)

Militants attacked a hydroelectric power plant in Russia's North Caucasus region on Wednesday [21 July], killing two guards before setting off several bombs that forced the facility to be shut down. Between three and five armed men raided the Baksanskaya station, a small plant in the Kabardino-Balkaria region ... They shot the two guards, then broke into the plant's engine room ... The militants then set and detonated at least four bombs, which destroyed three generators, but failed to cause a breach in the dam ... A fire caused by the explosions had been extinguished by midday, and no power failures were reported in the region ... Investigators have yet to identify those responsible ... An unidentified source in the Federal Security Service ... [said] that a local militant leader was suspected of masterminding the attack ... Attacks on infrastructure have been rare ... In May [2010] militants sabotaged a cellphone tower in Dagestan ... and killed several repair workers who were sent to fix it.

(www.iht.com, 21 July 2010)

Gunmen opened fire on security guards at a provincial food market in the southern Russian city of Samara on Saturday [24 July], killing a least two ... At least six attackers arrived at the market in three cars and opened fire before fleeing ... Even the smallest of Russian enterprises employs security guards, who are often in the line of fire when business disputes turn violent ... The Samara market was changing ownership ... Three soldiers in Dagestan were killed when assailants attacked their convoy in a drive-by shooting ... Around the same time, the top official in a village in Dagestan ... was in a separate attack ... In Ingushetia a well known businessman shot dead a university official to whom he was related ... The attacker was killed along with two other people – also relatives – in a shootout when police cornered him.

(www.iht.com, 24 July 2010)

Three militants broke into the home of a senior investigator ... in Makhachkala, the capital of Dagestan ... on Sunday [1 August] and shot him dead ... In Chechnya three unknown men armed with Kalashnikovs ambushed a police patrol early Sunday in Grozny and killed two officers.

(www.iht.com, 2 August 2010)

Chechen leader Doku Umarov ... is said to be resigning. In a video released online a man appearing to be Mr Umarov, forty-six, says he is handing over to a younger colleague. The speaker says a man seated next to him, named as Aslambek Vadalov, can lead 'more energetically' ... Doku Umarov served as security minister in the separatist government from 1996 to 1999. The Russian state regards him as a notorious terrorist, head of the self-styled

Caucasus Emirate – an armed Islamist movement seeking control of the mainly Moslem territories in the Russian North Caucasus. He is also officially described as a terrorist by the US State Department ... Aslambek Vadalov [is] a native Chechen. He is said to have taken part in the first Chechen war of 1994 to 1996 and fought Russian forces in the 1999 war under Khattab, the foreign-born warlord killed in 2002 ... Aslambek Vadalov ... swore an oath of allegiance to Mr Umarov in 2007.

(www.bbc.co.uk, 2 August 2010)

A grainy video of a man resembling Doku Umarov, the self-described leader of a militant insurgency network based in Russia's North Caucasus region, has surfaced on the internet in recent days and shows him announcing his retirement in favour of an energetic young man ... In the video, which has not been authenticated, the man who claims to be Mr Umarov said he had grown tired, but would continue to play an advisory role in the insurgency ... The man says in accented Russian: 'We have unanimously decided that I will leave my post. This does not mean that I am leaving the jihad' ... The video ... was dated summer 2010 ... In June [2010] the United States officially designated Mr Umarov as a terrorist, linking him to other international organizations that it considers terrorist groups, and asserting that he posed a threat to the United States. Russian officials have long accused Mr Umarov of maintaining ties with groups like al-Qaeda ... Mr Umarov, forty-six, was part of the insurgent group that drove Russian troops from Chechnya in the war there in the mid-1990s. After Russian forces launched a second offensive against Chechnya, killing a succession of rebel commanders, he recast himself as the leader of a pan-Caucasus jihadi movement. In recent years he has stepped up recruiting efforts in the North Caucasus, reviving a force of prospective suicide bombers that had been dormant for years. After the suicide bombings that killed forty people in Moscow's subway in March [2010] Mr Umarov, speaking in a similar video, vowed more attacks in the Russian heartland. No similar attacks have occurred, through violence has continued unabated in the North Caucasus. In the most recent video a man resembling Mr Umarov, bearded and wearing fatigues, is shown seated in a wooded area between two other fighters. He names one of them, a bearded, camouflaged insurgent identified as Aslambek Vadalov, as his successor ... Doku Umarov: 'I think that our brother Aslambek is younger, more energetic and will bring different results.'

(www.iht.com, 2 August 2010; *IHT*, 3 August 2010, p. 3)

A man recognizable as Doku Umarov says in the grainy footage that was posted late on Sunday [1 August] that he is handing over command of the group of fighters known as the Caucasus Emirate, which experts say has links to al-Qaeda and related terrorist groups ... [Umarov] appeared frail ... He said: 'Today I am leaving my post, but it does not mean that I am leaving jihad. As an old veteran I will be doing my best to help with words and deeds' ... [The] government of Chechnya has claimed that Umarov was seriously wounded in June 2009 and nearly died in July [2010] after a federal intelligence agent poisoned his food. Chechen President Ramzan Kadyrov said yesterday [2 August] that Umarov had stepped down due to deteriorating health.

(*The Independent*, 3 August 2010, p. 19)

Doku Umarov ... said in an internet posting that he would not step down as leader of an Islamist insurgent network ... reversing an earlier announcement. He said in a video posted to a separate website on Wednesday [4 August]: 'Given the current situation in the Caucasus, I believe that it is impossible to resign from my post' ... In his earlier statement he claimed to have been in poor health. But in the latest video, with his arm resting on the barrel of an automatic rifle, he said: 'My health, thanks to Allah, by the will of Allah, is good.'

(www.iht.com, 5 August 2010)

A gunman strode into the Eastern Fairy Tale café in the southern Russian city of Nazran on Wednesday [4 August] and emptied his pistol into two men. Dead on the spot was Ibragim Yevloyev, a police officer who was involved in a notorious killing two years ago ... Mr Yevloyev had confessed to fatally shooting an opposition leader, Magomed Yevloyev, in the head while he was being driven to police headquarters for questioning. (The two men share a last name but were not related.) The opposition leader was at fierce odds with Murat Zyazikov, the then-leader of Ingushetia, and protesters called for senior officers to be investigated in the killing. Two months later the Kremlin replaced both Mr Zyazikov and the head of the police force. By this spring [2010] the only formal suspect in the case was Ibragim Yevloyev, a low-level interior ministry employee, and he wound up with a mild punishment – two years under a relaxed form of house arrest. State investigators described the shooting as an accident, and it was prosecuted under a charge often used in medical malpractice cases ... The lawyer for Mr Yevloyev said he may have been killed in revenge. Even as he celebrated his victory in court this spring [the lawyer said] ... Mr Yevloyev's fears shifted to the centuries-old Caucasian tradition of the blood feud declared against a killer by his victim's family ... Three weeks after the opposition leader's death, an unsigned note on the website he founded ... declared a blood feud against thirteen officials it said were involved in his death. Among the names listed were those of Ibragim Yevloyev and Beslan Albogachiev, reportedly the second officer killed in Wednesday's attack.

(www.iht.com, 5 August 2010; *IHT*, 6 August 2010, p. 3)

A suicide attack on a police checkpoint ... on Tuesday [17 August] killed at least one officer ... The attack occurred in North Ossetia, a mostly Christian region of the North Caucasus, where violence in recent years has been rare ... A man in his twenties blew himself up when he was stopped by police at a checkpoint close to the border with Ingushetia ... In the early 1990s a bloody ethnic conflict erupted over a territorial dispute between North Ossetia and Ingushetia in the border area between both regions ... North Ossetia has been relatively quiet for some years, compared with neighbouring regions where there are daily reports of bloodshed. A suicide attack in 2008 in North Ossetia's capital, Vladikavkaz, killed about a dozen people. North Ossetia saw its worst bout of violence in 2004 when militants from neighbouring Chechnya raided a school in Beslan taking more than 1,000 children, parents and teachers hostage. More than 300 were killed when bombs wired by the militants exploded and Russian forces raided the school.

(www.iht.com, 17 August 2010)

At least sixteen people have been injured after an explosion outside a café in the volatile North Caucasus region of southern Russia ... The blast left two of those injured in a critical condition ... The blast happened in the spa town of Pyatigorsk, in the Stavropol region, wounding café customers and passers-by ... The cause of the explosion has not yet been confirmed. However, an official ... said a car parked outside the café had exploded. Pyatigorsk is the capital of the North Caucasus Federal District, which includes the restive republics of Dagestan, Chechnya and Ingushetia.

(www.bbc.co.uk, 17 August 2010)

The man suspected of organizing twin suicide bombings that killed forty people in the Moscow subway system in March was killed in a shootout with Russian security forces on Saturday [21 August] ... Magomedali Vagabov and four others were killed in a gunfight with special forces in the Dagestan region ... The National Anti-terrorism Committee told Russian news agencies that Mr Vagabov was effectively the second in command of an Islamist insurgent network in the Caucasus. The chief, Doku Umarov, claimed responsibility for the subway bombings, which were carried out by two women ... He announced this month that he was stepping down as his network's leader, but later backtracked.

(www.iht.com, 22 August 2010)

Over the weekend a Chechen detonated explosives as policemen tried to detain him, the police said Sunday [22 August], killing himself and one officer ... In Dagestan three unknown men firing Kalashnikovs from a car window killed one police officer as he was walking home Saturday night [21 August] ... The attackers also shot three local residents, killing two of them and badly wounding the third.

(*IHT*, 23 August 2010, p. 3)

One Russian border guard was killed and another who disappeared with him remained missing ... Police said Monday [23 August]. The border guards were serving in Dagestan ... The two border guards were last seen late Saturday [21 August] when they drove from their post's headquarters ... At least three people were wounded in attacks carried out Monday, while four suspected militants died when explosives they were transporting by car unexpectedly blew up ... The deputy mayor of the Dagestani city of Kizlyar was badly wounded when he was attacked by unknown gunmen outside the city administration building ... A five-year-old girl and nineteen-year-old woman were wounded in the city of Derbent when a nearly police post came under automatic weapons fire.

(www.iht.com, 23 August 2010)

Prosecutors in Austria said Tuesday [24 August] that they had filed a formal indictment against three men in connection with the killing of a Chechen whistle-blower last year [January 2009]. But the prosecutors said they did not have enough evidence to charge Ramzan Kadyrov, who had earlier been implicated in the crime. In April Austria's public prosecutor's office, citing circumstantial evidence, announced after a year-long investigation that the whistle-blower, Umar Israilov, had been fatally shot during a botched kidnapping ordered by Mr Kadyrov ... On Tuesday ... a spokeswoman for the public prosecutor's office in Vienna said that an indictment against three men charged as accessories in the murder has been sent to the Regional Court of Vienna, but there was 'not enough proof' to bring charges against Mr Kadyrov ... Investigators believe that a fourth suspect, Lecha Bogatirov, who fled to Russia after the murder, fired the three shots that killed Mr Israilov.

(www.iht.com, 24 August 2010; *IHT*, 25 August 2010, p.3)

More than two dozen prisoners, including organizers of an alleged coup plot, escaped ... from a detention centre in Dushanbe after a bloody shoot-out and are being pursued by security forces. President Imomali Rakhmon has ordered a manhunt for twenty-five or more fugitives, who authorities say killed at least five guards while breaking out of the prison and then fled toward the Afghan border. Sources within the security forces told Reuters the escaped prisoners included citizens of Tajikistan, Afghanistan and Russia who were among those sentenced last week on accusations of organizing a coup ... Tajikistan, which shares a 1,340-kilometre (840-mile) border with Afghanistan, has imprisoned more than 100 members of banned groups this year [2010] alone, including thirty-six members of Hisz ut-Tahrir and twenty-five members of the Islamic Movement of Uzbekistan. Dressed in camouflage, the prisoners fled in the direction of Afghanistan after breaking out ... All were originally arrested in July 2009 in eastern Tajikistan, the scene of fierce civil war battles in the 1990s. The Russians were sentenced to between nineteen and thirty years and others received terms ranging from ten years to life.

(www.iht.com, 23 August 2010)

More than two dozen prisoners with suspected ties to Islamist militants have escaped from a detention centre in Tajikistan, killing five prison guards, officials there said Monday [23 August]. Among the twenty-five prisoners who managed to flee, according to officials, were militants from Russia's North Caucasus region and members of the Islamic Movement of Uzbekistan, a terrorist group with links to the Taleban in Afghanistan. Concerns about Islamic militancy are high in Tajikistan, an impoverished, mostly Moslem former Soviet republic of about 7 million people that shares a large, porous border with Afghanistan. Many of those believed to have escaped were among the dozens sentenced last week to long prison terms after being convicted by Tajikistan's supreme court of planning to overthrow the government, officials said ... Prisoners were somehow able to overpower their guards late Sunday night [22 August] at a detention centre in Dushanbe, Tajikistan's capital ... They changed into camouflaged uniforms before fleeing the prison with stolen weapons ... The escapees included citizens of Afghanistan and Russia, as well as Tajikistan. The organizers of the escape were identified as two Tajik citizens, Ibrokhim Nasriddinov and Khikmat Azizov, as well as Magamed Akhmedov, a Russian citizen from the North Caucasus region of Dagestan, a hotbed of Islamic violence ... A statement on the [Tajik] president's website described the escaped prisoners as 'especially dangerous criminals' who were arrested last year on a host of charges, including terrorism and drug trafficking. The statement also said that the men were part of a militant group that had been planning a coup. In the 1990s Islamist and nationalist groups fought a bloody civil war in Tajikistan with forces loyal to the former Soviet authorities. Tens of thousands were killed, though the country has been relatively stable for years. Still, the government expressed growing fears about the rise of fundamentalist Islam, and has made the elimination of what it calls Islamist extremist groups a priority. The government touted the arrest and conviction of many of those who escaped on Sunday night as a success in this effort. But critics have caused the government of using the extremist label to brand opponents as criminals in an effort to stifle dissent.

(www.iht.com, 23 August 2010)

'Twenty-five prisoners sentenced on terrorism charges escaped from jail in the Tajik capital after a dramatic assault that left at least five guards dead' (*IHT*, 24 August 2010, p. 4).

Twenty-five prisoners, including several Islamic militants, have escaped from a prison in Tajikistan, reports say. The break-out took place in Sunday night [22 August] in Dushanbe. The group is said to have killed at least five prison guards as they fled ... Tajikistan had a five-year civil war between the Moscow-backed government and Islamist-led opposition. The war ended in 1997 ... [One report] said that the escapees included Russian and Afghan citizens, as well as members of an Islamist militant group.

(www.bbc.co.uk, 23 August 2010)

At least fourteen militant suspects and two police officers have been killed in three raids in the North Caucasus region, the police said Saturday [28 August]. Nine suspects were killed in two separate shoot-outs with the police in the Kabardino-Balkariya republic late Friday [27 August] ... Two of those killed were suspected of organizing a bombing in May that killed one man and wounded dozens of others ... Separately, five militant suspects and two police officers were killed in a shoot-out Friday in the Dagestan republic ... The men are suspected of belonging to a group led by the warlord Magomedali Vagabov, who was behind the Moscow subway bombings in April that killed forty people ... Mr Vagabov, whose wife carried out one of the suicide attacks, was killed last week in a shoot-out with security forces in Dagestan ... Militants say they seek an Islamic emirate across the North Caucasus in southern Russia.

(www.iht.com, 29 August 2010)

A shoot-out between the Chechen president's personal protection detail and a group suspected of being separatist insurgents left at least nineteen people dead Sunday [29 August], including five civilians, officials and media reports said. At least twelve of the suspected insurgents and two security officers were killed when the rebels entered Tsentoroi, the home village of President Ramzan Kadyrov, according to his spokesman ... Television reports said that five civilians had been killed in the crossfire. Mr Kadyrov, who is thought to regularly supervise security operations in the field, was in the village at the time and directed the counter-offensive [his spokesman said] ... In a separate incident Sunday security forces in Dagestan shot and killed four suspected militants travelling in two cars when they refused to stop at a police checkpoint.

(*IHT*, 30 August 2010, p. 3)

Five civilians were among nineteen people killed today [29 August] in a shoot-out between the Chechen president's security guards and suspected separatists ... At least twelve insurgents and two security officers were killed when the rebels entered Tsentoroi, Ramzan Kadyrov's home village ... Five civilians were killed in the crossfire. Kadyrov, who is thought to regularly supervise security operations, was in the village at the time and directed the counter-offensive ... Police averted a possible assassination attempt on Kadyrov in 2009 ... In a separate incident today security forces in Dagestan province shot dead four suspected militants. On Saturday [28 August] nine suspected militants were killed in two separate shoot-outs with police in Kabardino-Balkariya republic, while five suspected militants and two police officers were killed in another shoot-out in Dagestan.

(www.guardian.co.uk, 29 August 2010)

The main website used by the rebels ... claimed sixty 'mujahidin' had stormed Ramzan Kadyrov's village ... destroying two checkpoints and blowing up an armoured personnel carrier. It said five of its fighters from three units were 'martyred' ... The rebels claim they carried out a 'sweep' of the village, occupying it for one hour and burning down ten houses. They also seized ammunition and communications equipment, the website said.

(*Guardian*, 30 August 2010, p. 18)

Ramzan Kadyrov ... [said] he headed the operation to fight off the attack on the village of Tsentoroi, although it was not clear whether Mr Kadyrov was in the village at the time of the attack, or directing operations from Grozny, 40 miles away ... The government said thirty rebels attacked the village early yesterday morning [29 August] and only a few rebels shooting a video of the raid managed to escape ... An Islamic website ... [said] at least fifteen of Mr Kadyrov's security officers were killed, while a total of sixty insurgents attacked the village. Five rebels were also killed, it said ... The website [said the insurgents] ... torched ten houses it described as belonging to 'Kadyrov confidants'. It was not clear whether Mr Kadyrov's own house was also set ablaze, it said. Mr Kadyrov has been the target of a number of assassination attempts in the past ten years, and Tsentoroi was raided by insurgents back in 2004, in what Mr Kadyrov said was an attack aimed at killing him.

(*The Independent*, 30 August 2010, p. 2)

A car bomb in Dagestan killed a driver and injured a government official and his two bodyguards on Saturday [4 September] ... Dagestan's minister of national policy, information and external relations received minor, non-threatening injuries ... Similar attacks in 2003 and 2005 killed his two predecessors ... Investigators said the victims were headed to work in two cars from the minister's apartment in Makhachkala, the region's capital, when a device at the bottom of one of the vehicles exploded.

(www.cnn.com, 4 September 2010)

'Dagestan's minister for national, religious and foreign affairs ... was wounded in a car bombing in Makhachkala, along with two bodyguards. His driver was killed' (www.bbc.co.uk, 5 September 2010).

A suicide car-bomber killed three soldiers ... in an attack on a military base in Dagestan on Sunday [5 September], officials said. The attack took place at about 1 a.m. [local time] at the base in the city of Buinaksk ... about 50 kilometres (30 miles) west of Makhachkala ... After the blast a roadside bomb hit a car taking investigators to the scene, but there were no reported injuries reported in that explosion ... Dagestan is gripped by near-daily violence between police and soldiers and insurgents believed to be inspired by separatists in neighbouring Chechnya. The attack came almost eleven years after a car bomb outside an apartment building in Buinaksk housing the families of military officers killed sixty-four people. The 4 September 1999 attack was the first of four apartment bombings in Russia over a two-week period that killed a total of more than 290 people and that Russian officials cited as justification for launching the second war against Chechen rebels. All the 1999 bombings were blamed on Chechen rebels, who had recently launched an incursion into Dagestan to try to establish an Islamic state. But suspicions persist that the bombings were orchestrated by Russian officials to justify the beginning of that war. Former Federal Security Service agent

Alexander Litvinenko, who was fatally poisoned with a radioactive substance in exile in Britain in 2006, co-authored a book making those allegations ... In Kabardino-Balkariya ... a policemen was shot to death Sunday by a man whom he had stopped for a document check.

(www.iht.com, 5 September 2010)

The suicide bomber barrelled through the gates of a firing range ... The Kremlin has struggled to crack down on the insurgency, calling for both harsh measures and new policies to address what it acknowledges is pervasive poverty and other problems that can give rise to terrorism.

(*IHT*, 6 September 2010, p. 3)

'Gunmen killed a Russian judge in a North Caucasus province ... the authorities said Wednesday [8 September]. The district judge ... was shot several times outside his home in Kabardin-Balkaria late on Tuesday [7 September]' (*IHT*, 9 September 2010, p. 3).

A car bomb exploded in North Ossetia on Thursday [9 September], killing at least seventeen people – including an eighteen-month-old baby. The vehicle blew up near a market in Vladikavkaz ... The republic's leader, Taimuraz Mamsurov: 'Information that I possess indicates that the explosion in Vladikavkaz was organized by a suicide bomber, who drove a Volga 3102 car near the entrance to the market' ... The market has seen other terrorist attacks in the past. In November 2008 a suicide bomber blew up a bus at a nearby bus station, killing twelve people ... An explosion killed more than fifty people ... in March 1999.

(www.cnn.com, 9 September 2010, and 10 September 2010)

Vladikavkaz market has been repeatedly targeted. It was bombed in 1999, killing fifty-five people. In 2001 six people were killed in a bombing, and another died in a 2004 attack ... Experts believe rival militant groups may be vying for supremacy in the region.

(www.bbc.co.uk, 9 September 2010)

The blast occurred in North Ossetia, a mostly Orthodox Christian area where major acts of violence have been rare in recent years compared with Moslem majority republics in the region, such as Chechnya or Dagestan ... Police disarmed a second explosive device found near the market entrance ... The attack came after an Islamist website said a fire that knocked a hydroelectric power plant in Dagestan out of commission this week was caused by bombs planted by rebels. Nobody was hurt and supplies were not affected ... On Wednesday [8 September] [the website] said two bombs had detonated ... while a third was caused by an accident. But Russian news agencies, citing a local law enforcement source, reported on Thursday [9 September] that a bomb had been found at the plant and defused. Interfax cited a security official as saying traces of explosives were found where the fire broke out.

(www.iht.com, 9 September 2010)

Clashes between police and alleged militants left six people dead in the North Caucasus region a day after a suicide bomb killed seventeen ... In the republic of Dagestan police were said to have killed four militants after a raid in the village of Makhargi. A policeman and prison warden were shot in separate incidents.

(*The Times*, 11 September 2010, p. 49)

'A senior security police officer was shot and killed by unknown gunmen in Dagestan on Sunday [12 September] ... [The] head of the North Caucasus's Federal District's Anti-extremism police department was killed in his car in Makhachkala' (*IHT*, 13 September 2010, p. 4).

Akhmed Zakayev has been warned by Poland that he faces arrest on a Russian warrant if he visits the country this week. Mr Zakayev, who has been living in the UK since receiving political asylum in 2003, says he means to attend a Chechen congress opening in Poland on Thursday [16 September] ... The World Chechen Congress ... is expected by its organizers to attract some 200 delegates from the Chechen diaspora ... A spokesman for Poland's chief prosecutor: 'The warrant automatically requires all Interpol member states to arrest the person for whom the warrant is issued. If Mr Zakayev comes to Poland, even though he is not wanted by our country, the police still have the obligation to detain him and bring him before public prosecutors and a court that will rule on his eventual extradition' ... Russia regards him as a terrorist and has an international warrant lodged against him through Interpol ... President Dmitri Medvedev is due to visit Poland before the end of this year [2010], at the invitation of the new Polish president, Bronislaw Komorowski ... Mr Zakayev has served as a representative of the Chechen rebel government in the West since it was ousted by Russian military action in 2000. The former rebel culture minister is accused by Russia of armed rebellion, murder and kidnapping.

(www.bbc.co.uk, 15 September 2010)

Akhmed Zakayev has been arrested in Poland ... He had earlier been warned by Polish authorities he faced arrest because of a Russian warrant issued through Interpol ... Before travelling to Warsaw he said he had received his Polish visa ... Speaking yesterday [16 September] Polish prime minister Donald Tusk said that if the Chechen separatist leader were to be arrested, the courts might not agree to extradite him to Russia.

(www.bbc.co.uk, 17 September 2010)

Russia accuses the fifty-one-year-old ... Akhmed Zakayev ... of kidnapping and murder during a separatist war in Chechnya in the 1990s. Zakayev and his supporters have said the allegations are trumped up and that he represents the political faction of Chechnya's separatist movement and has no connection to the military wing spearheading the region's insurgency ... [A] national police spokesman ... said that detailed information from Russia with dates and places where Zakayev would be in Poland triggered the arrest. On previous visits to Poland Zakayev moved freely ... [The conference organizer] noted that

Zakayev had frequently visited Poland in the past ... Zakayev entered politics in 1994, when as an actor he was named culture minister by Chechnya's first separatist president just months before the Russian army rolled in to crush the tiny mountainous region's independence bid. The war ended in a ceasefire and a humiliating Russian withdrawal that left Chechnya de facto independent and largely lawless. When the Russian army marched back into Chechnya in 1999, Zakayev was a top assistant to separatist President Aslan Maskhadov. Zakayev was wounded and left Chechnya, becoming Maskhadov's top envoy abroad ... [Zakayev] has said he represents the Chechen separatist political faction, and distanced himself from radical Islamist rebels. This year [2010] he denounced the militant leader who claimed responsibility for the Moscow subway bombings in March, which he described as a 'monstrous crime'.

(www.iht.com, 17 September 2010)

A former actor and rebel commander, Akhmed Zakayev has sought to distance himself from such violence, and has long been viewed as a moderate voice among Chechnya's separatist leaders. While he continues to insist on independence for Chechnya, his years of exile have made him a largely irrelevant figure there ... Ramzan Kadyrov: 'We ask countries that are sheltering refugees who have committed grave crimes in the Chechen republic to arrest and return them to Russia, where they will be punished in accordance with the law.'

(www.iht.com, 17 September 2010)

Akhmed Zakayev was a brigade general of the Chechen rebel forces during the 1995–6 war. He served as culture minister, foreign minister and deputy prime minister in Chechnya's separatist government in the three years when it enjoyed independence from Russia between 1996 and 1999. After Russia crushed rebel rule during a second war with Chechnya that started in 1999, Zakayev emigrated to Europe, where he has been the head of the Chechen government in exile. Russia issued an international warrant for Zakayev's arrest in October 2001.

(www.cnn.com, 17 September 2010)

[Akhmed Zakayev has visited] Poland three times this year already, including three weeks ago ... Last year [2009] ... Ramzan Kadyrov tried to persuade Zakayev to return home, offering him a job as theatre director in Grozny. Zakayev held a series of discussions in Europe with Kadyrov's trusted aide Dukuvakha Abdurakhmanov about political reconciliation. The plan fell through after Russia refused to drop outstanding terrorist charges against him. At the same time Chechnya's current Islamist rebel leadership denounced Zakayev as a traitor and announced their intention to kill him. Today Kadyrov said Zakayev should be handed back to Russia and then sentenced to life in prison ... [Zakayev] has said he represents the Chechen separatist political factions, and distanced himself from radical Islamist rebels. This year [2010] he denounced Doku Umarov who claimed responsibility for the Moscow subway bombings in March. Zakayev called the attack a 'monstrous crime'.

(www.guardian.co.uk, 17 September 2010)

'Akhmed Zakayev's case will be heard by an independent court, but the extradition request also has to be approved by the justice minister' (*FT*, 18 September 2010, p. 6).

In its ruling late on Friday [17 September] ... a Polish court released Akhmed Zakayev ... He had been detained earlier in the day on an international death warrant issued by Russia ... The court said Mr Zakayev was being released from custody pending a decision on his extradition ... Earlier on Friday a Polish police spokesman said Warsaw had had no choice but to detain Mr Zakayev because Interpol had put him on its most-wanted list, at Russia's request ... Earlier this year [2010] he called for negotiations with Russia, describing Chechen independence as 'not an end in itself'. A sharia court formed by ... Doku Umarov declared him an apostate last year [2009] and sentenced him to death.

(www.bbc.co.uk, 18 September 2010)

Akhmed Zakayev ... was released from custody Friday evening [17 September], several hours after he was detained. A judge in Warsaw denied a prosecutor's request to arrest [him] ... The court press secretary said: '[Akhmed Zakayev] is at large and may leave the country' ... A prosecutor could appeal the court's decision [the secretary said] ... After the ruling Zakayev told reporters he would travel to address the World Chechen Congress in Pultusk, about 60 kilometres (40 miles) north of Warsaw ... Russia issued an international warrant for Zakayev's arrest in October 2001. A year later he was detained in Denmark but the Danish justice ministry rejected Russia's demand for Zakayev's extradition. Then in December 2002 he moved to the United Kingdom, where another extradition request was turned down. Political asylum was granted to Zakayev in November 2003 and he has been living in London ever since. A Polish judge cited that decision in Friday's ruling. The judge said: 'Beyond all doubt, a decision of one [EU] member country is valid for the whole of the EU.'

(www.cnn.com, 18 September 2010)

'Akhmed Zakayev ... has returned to London after a Polish court rejected a Russian warrant for his arrest for kidnapping, murder and terrorism' (*The Times*, 21 September 2010, p. 37).

The toll

Ilyas Akhmadov (foreign minister of Chechnya in 1999): 'During this decade-long war more than 200,000 individuals – one quarter of the Chechen population – have lost their lives, including thousands of children. Roughly 300,000 Chechens have fled' (*IHT*, 25 February 2005, p. 7).

'Some 10,000 Russian soldiers by official figures (or 20,000 by conservative unofficial estimates) have died in the two wars. Chechen losses have been far worse: 50,000 to 200,000 out of a population of 1 million' (*The Economist*, 15 January 2005, p. 38).

> The official Russian death toll from the war stands at more than 4,700 sol-diers, although independent observers say the true toll may be three times higher ... The human rights organization Memorial reported that up to 5,000 Chechens have been abducted in the last five years.
>
> (*IHT*, 8 February 2005, p. 3)

> Two wars in Chechnya have left [up to] 160,000 combatants and civilians dead, a top official in the local government loyal to Russia said Monday [15 August 2005] ... [the range being] between 150,000 and 160,000 ... Between 30,000 and 40,000 ethnic Chechens have died ... About 100,000 of the dead were ethnic Russian servicemen and civilians [according to the official] ... He did not explain the gap of at least 20,000 in his tally ... Offi-cial [Russian] military death tolls for the two wars come to about 10,000 Russian soldiers, although independent estimates are at least twice that ... The Russian human rights organization Memorial said that following the first war the state statistics office published an estimate of 30,000 to 40,000 civilians killed. Memorial estimates the figure at 50,000 ... Figures from the US organization Human Rights Watch and from Memorial show that in the second war about 25,000 civilians have been killed ... The [Russian] gov-ernment has never published conclusive figures of military losses in the second Chechnya campaign.
>
> (*IHT*, 16 August 2005, p. 3)

'An estimated 100,000 civilians, soldiers and rebels have died in two wars in Chechnya since ... 1994' (*IHT*, 28 November 2005, p. 3).

'An estimated 100,000 civilians, soldiers and insurgents have died in Chech-nya in the two conflicts since 1994. Human rights groups have also reported mass disappearances, blaming them on pro-Moscow Chechen security forces and Russian troops' (www.iht.com, 27 July 2006).

'The human rights organization Memorial estimates that as many as 5,000 people have vanished after detention or round-ups during the war. Almost all are presumed dead and Chechens blame Russian forces or their pro-Kremlin local proxies' (*IHT*, 28 July 2006, p. 3).

'Up to 5,000 people have disappeared in Chechnya since 1999' (*The Times*, 28 July 2006, p. 3).

'Russian forces have fought two wars against separatists in the mainly Moslem republic of Chechnya since 1994. The fighting claimed 100,000 lives' (www.bbc.co.uk, 21 August 2009).

> The Human Rights and Security Initiative [is] at the Center for Strategic and International Studies in Washington ... A recent CSIS report shows that the number of suicide bombings in the North Caucasus in 2009 nearly

quadrupled compared to the previous year. Most of the attacks occurred in Chechnya. Ambushes, shootings, and roadside bombings are also on the increase across the region: last year [2009] more than 900 people were killed there, almost double from the year before ... Eighty-six abductions [were] documented in one-third of Chechnya in the first nine months of last year by the human rights group Memorial ... many of these 'disappeared' later turned up dead.

(*IHT*, 20 March 2010, p. 6)

A report by the Centre for Strategic and International Studies said 916 people died in the North Caucasus in 2009 in violence related to the clashes, up from 586 in 2008. Another monitoring group, the Caucasian Knot, reported the region suffered 172 terrorist attacks last year [2009], killing 280 people in Chechnya, 319 in Ingushetia and 263 in Dagestan.

(*IHT*, 1 April 2010, p. 3)

Appendix 1

The Russia–Georgia war of August 2008

The Tagliavini report

The Independent International Fact-Finding Mission on the Conflict in Georgia was created in December [2008], under the leadership of the Swiss diplomat Heidi Tagliavini. It was scheduled to present its conclusions at the end of July [2009] ... The release was postponed two months because investigators received new documents, organizers have said.

(IHT, 24 September 2009, p. 4)

After a lengthy enquiry, investigators commissioned by the EU are expected to conclude that Georgia ignited last year's war with Russia by attacking separatists in South Ossetia, rejecting the Georgian government's explanation that the attack was defensive, according to an official familiar with the investigators' work. But the report is expected to balance this conclusion with an equally weighty one: if Georgia fired the first shot, Russian created and exploited the conditions that led to war ... In the years preceding the conflict, Russian encouraged separatist movements in Abkhazia and South Ossetia, training their military forces and distributing Russian passports ... The report's contents will be presented to the EU's Council of Ministers at noon on Wednesday [30 September] and then released to the public ... The enquiry will break ground by determining who started the war. The president of Georgia, Mikheil Saakashvili, has said he had no choice but to order the shelling of Tskhinvali, the South Ossetian capital, variously explaining that it was necessary to stop attacks on Georgian villages, to bring the region under control or to deter a Russian invasion already in progress. Georgia has already released telephone intercepts from Ossetian border guards that purport to show that a Russian armoured regiment crossed into South Ossetia a full day before Georgia's attack on Tskhinvali.

(www.iht.com, 29 September 2009)

A much anticipated EU enquiry into last August's war in Georgia concludes that Georgia ignited the conflict by attacking separatists in South Ossetia, but that Russia had provoked violence in the enclave for years and exploited its consequences. The report finds no evidence that there was a Russian invasion under way on 7 August, when Georgia ordered the shelling of the South Ossetian capital, Tskhinvali. It says Georgia broke international law by using force against Russian peacekeepers stationed in the city, and that Russia's army had legal grounds to defend the peacekeepers. But the report says Russia 'went far beyond the reasonable limits of defence' in undertaking a drive outside South Ossetia that violated international law and was 'not even remotely commensurate with the threat to Russian peacekeepers'. Investigators also found that Russia allowed 'ethnic cleansing' in Georgian villages, dismissed Russian allegations that Georgia was carrying out genocide and said that Russia had acted illegally by distributing passports and by recognizing South Ossetia and Abkhazia as sovereign ... The report's author Heidi Tagliavini said: 'While the onus of having actually triggered off the war lies with the Georgian side, the Russian side, too, carries the blame for a substantial number of violations of international law' ... The report documented that some Russian regular troops were illegally present in South Ossetia before the war.

(www.iht.com, 30 September 2009; *IHT*, 1 October 2009, p. 3)

Heidi Tagliavini:

A year ago the EU helped mediate an end to a war that left 850 Georgians (including South Ossetians) and Russians dead and 138,000 displaced ... The war of August 2008 had several causes. The proximate cause was the shelling by Georgian forces of the capital of the secessionist province of South Ossetia, Tskhinvali, on 7 August 2008, which was followed by a disproportionate response of Russia. Another factor was the lack of progress, for more than fifteen years, in the resolution of the two 'frozen conflicts' of Abkhazia and South Ossetia ... Russia systematically gave passports to residents of Abkhazia and South Ossetia, asserting responsibility for Russians in what it called its 'near abroad' without any consultation with Georgia, whose territorial integrity was thus increasingly challenged. Meanwhile Georgia was pressing to accelerate its accession to Nato, and embarking, with the support of the United States and Israel, on a major modernization of its armed forces. Georgia's military budget grew from 1 per cent of GDP to 8 per cent, and military bases near Abkhazia and South Ossetia were modernized. In 2007 and the first half of 2008 ceasefire arrangements made after the first Georgia war came under increasing strains. Russian forces did not refrain from shooting down Georgian drones over Abkhazia, and dangerous incidents provoked by both sides occurred more and more frequently ... At a time when preventative diplomacy is rightly seen as a priority, it must be said that the conflict of 2008 was predictable and preventable ... More than 35,000 people are in forced displacement for an indefinite future.

(www.iht.com, 30 September 2009; *IHT*, 1 October 2009, p. 7)

The war in Georgia last year was started by a Georgian attack that was not justified by international law, an EU-sponsored report has concluded.

However, the attack followed months of provocation, and both sides violated international law ... The report said about 850 people were killed in the August 2008 war, and that more than 100,000 fled their homes, about 35,000 of whom are still displaced ... The report says: 'The shelling of Tskhinvali by the Georgian armed forces during the night of 7–8 August 2008 marked the beginning of the large-scale armed conflict in Georgia ... There is the question of whether [this] use of force ... was justifiable under international law. It was not' ... [The report] also says Georgia's claim that there had been a large-scale Russian military incursion into South Ossetia before the outbreak of war could not be 'sufficiently substantiated', though it said there was evidence of a lower level military buildup. The report states that while Russia's initial actions in fighting back against attacks on its personnel in South Ossetia were justified, its subsequent actions in pushing far into Georgia 'went far beyond the reasonable limits of defence' and was 'in violation of international law' ... The report says: 'Furthermore, continued destruction which came after the ceasefire agreement was not justified by any means' ... The report's author said Russia's recognition [of South Ossetia and Abkhazia] 'must be considered as being not valid in the context of international law, and as violations of Georgia's territorial integrity and sovereignty'.

(www.bbc.co.uk, 30 September 2009)

[The report said] that the Russians had moved mercenaries and paramilitary forces into South Ossetia in apparent preparation for armed hostilities before President Mikheil Saakashvili launched the offensive ... South Ossetian irregular forces violated the rules of war in attacks on Georgian villages and that Russian peacekeeping forces 'would not or could not' control them ... The report said: 'There is the question of whether the force by Georgia during the night of 7–8 August was justifiable under international law. It was not ... It is not possible to accept that the shelling of Tskhinvali with Grad multiple rocket launchers and heavy artillery would satisfy the requirements of having been necessary and proportionate' ... The report also said Georgian attacks on Russian peacekeepers in South Ossetia 'in the initial phase of the conflict' were unjustified ... The report said: 'There was no ongoing armed attack by Russia before the start of the Georgian operation. Georgian claims of a large-scale presence of Russian armed forces in South Ossetia prior to the Georgian offensive could not be substantiated ... It could also not be verified that Russia was on the verge of such a major attack.'

(www.guardian.co.uk, 30 September 2009)

The report said Georgian armed forces shelled Tskhinvali the night of 7 August. While that action was seen as the start of the conflict, the report said 'it was only the culminating point of increasing tensions, provocations and incidents' ... The report said: 'The conflict has deep roots in the history of the region, in people's national traditions and aspirations as well as in age-old perceptions or rather misperceptions of each other, which were never mended and sometimes exploited' ... Any evaluation of the conflict should take that into account, along with mounting tensions in the months and weeks leading up to it, the report said, as well as 'years of provocations, mutual accusations, military and political threats and acts of violence both inside and outside the conflict zone' ... The report said: 'It has to consider, too, the impact of a great power's coercive politics against a small and insubordinate neighbour, together with the small neighbour's penchant for overplaying its hand and acting in the heat of the moment without careful consideration of the final outcome, not to mention its fear that it might permanently lose important parts of its territory through creeping annexation' ... A total of about 850 people were killed on all sides, the report said, and untold numbers of others were wounded or went missing. About 100,000 civilians fled their homes, and about 35,000 have been unable to return.

(www.cnn.com, 30 September 2009)

The report said: 'The risk of a new confrontation remains serious' ... The authors acknowledged that Russian troops – other than official peacekeeping forces – were already in South Ossetia before the Georgian shelling. But they rejected Tbilisi's claims that this was 'a large-scale Russian military incursion' ... The report condemned Moscow's policy of establishing spheres of influence in its neighbourhood as 'irreconcilable with international law''.

(*FT*, 1 October 2009, p. 9)

'In 2002 Russia changed its citizenship law to allow a massive distribution of passports to people in both regions. This later became a pretext for defending "Russia's citizens"' (*The Economist*, 3 October 2009, p. 48).

Earlier findings

Newly available accounts by independent military observers at the beginning of the war between Georgia and Russia this summer call into question the longstanding Georgian assertion that it was acting defensively against separatists and Russian aggression. Instead, the accounts suggest that Georgia's inexperienced military attacked Tskhinvali on 7 August with indiscriminate artillery and rocket fire, exposing civilians, Russian peacekeepers and unarmed monitors to harm. The accounts are neither fully conclusive nor broad enough to settle the many lingering disputes over blame in a war that hardened relations between the Kremlin and the West. But they raise questions about the accuracy and honesty of Georgia's insistence that its shelling of Tskhinvali was a precise operation, which it has variously defended since as necessary to stop heavy Ossetian shelling of Georgian villages, bring order to the breakaway region or counter a Russian invasion ...

The observations [were made] by the monitors ... [who] included a Finnish major, a Belarussian airborne captain and a Polish civilian.

(*IHT*, 7 November 2008, pp. 1, 3)

('Monitors, who were on the ground in South Ossetia when hostilities commenced the night of 7 August, reported seeing Georgian artillery and rocket launchers assembling just outside South Ossetia at 3 p.m. that day, well before any Russian convoy had crossed into the enclave': www.iht.com, 11 November 2008.)

President Mikheil Saakashvili of Georgia

President Mikheil Saakashvili (in an article in the *FT*):

Moscow says it invaded Georgia to protect its citizens in South Ossetia. Over the past five years it cynically laid the groundwork for this pretence by illegally distributing passports in South Ossetia and Abkhazia, 'manufacturing' Russian citizens to protect ... Yesterday [27 August] on this page, Mr Medvedev asserted that Georgia attacked South Ossetia. In fact, our forces entered the conflict zone after Russia rolled its tanks on to our soil, passing through the Roki Tunnel into South Ossetia, Georgia ... Moscow also counts on historical amnesia. It hopes the West will forget ethnic cleansing in Abkhazia drove out more than three-quarters of the local population – ethnic Georgians, Greeks, Jews and others – leaving the minority Abkhaz in control. Russia also wants us to forget that South Ossetia was run not by its residents (almost half were Georgian before this month's ethnic cleansing) but by Russian officials. When the war started South Ossetia's de facto prime minister, defence minister and security minister were ethnic Russians with no ties to the region.

(*FT*, 28 August 2008, p. 13)

Recognition of the independence of Abkhazia and South Ossetia

Abkhazia declared today [20 August 2008] that it would ask Russia to recognize its independence ... The Abkhaz parliament said it would send a formal request for recognition to President Dmitri Medvedev in Moscow tomorrow [21 August] ... Mr Medvedev has already pledged 'to make the decision which unanimously supports the will of these two Caucasus peoples' ... Nato declared its support for 'Georgia's independence, sovereignty and territorial integrity' at yesterday's [19 August] emergency meeting of foreign ministers ... President Mikheil Saakashvili has long argued that any declaration of independence by Abkhazia is meaningless because at least 200,000 ethnic Georgians were expelled from the region after the war sixteen years ago and remain refugees.

(www.thetimes.co.uk, 20 August 2008)

Lawmakers in Abkhazia approved the request from President Sergei Bagapsh ... to recognize independence ... The president also called for a friendship and mutual assistance treaty, which would call for maintaining Russian peacekeepers in the region ... Bagapsh: 'I propose that the Russian Federation recognize the Republic of Abkhazia as a sovereign and independent state and establish diplomatic relations between Abkhazia and Russia.'

(www.cnn.com, 21 August 2008)

South Ossetia President Eduard Kokoyev (25 August 2008): 'We have more political-legal grounds than Kosovo to have our independence recognized. When I say "we" I mean both South Ossetia and Abkhazia' ... Kosovo declared independence from Russia's historical ally Serbia in February [2008].

(www.cnn.com, 25 August 2008)

'Abkhazia's President Sergei Bagapsh said: "Neither Abkhazia nor South Ossetia will ever again live in one state with Georgia"' (www.thetimes.co.uk, 25 August 2008).

President Dmitri Medvedev (Tuesday 26 August):

The night-time execution-style bombardment of Tskhinvali by the Georgian troops resulted in the deaths of hundreds of our civilians. Among the dead were Russian peacekeepers ... The most inhuman war was chosen to achieve the objective – annexing South Ossetia through the annihilation of a whole people ... In 1991 President Gamsarkhurdia of Georgia ... ordered attacks on the cities of Sukhumi and Tskhinvali ... Our country came forward as a mediator and peacekeeper insisting on a political settlement. In doing so we were invariably guided by the recognition of Georgia's territorial integrity. The Georgian leadership chose another way ... Russia continually displayed calm and patience. We repeatedly called for returning to the negotiating table and did not deviate from this position of ours even after the unilateral proclamation of Kosovo's independence. However, our persistent proposals to the Georgian side to conclude agreements with Abkhazia and South Ossetia on the non-use of force remained unanswered. Regrettably they were ignored also by Nato and even at the United Nations. It stands quite clear now: a peaceful resolution of the conflict was not part of the Tbilisi plan. The Georgian leadership was methodically preparing for war, while the political and material support provided by their foreign guardians only served to reinforce the perception of their own impunity. Tbilisi made its choice during the night of 8 August 2008. Saakashvili opted for genocide to accomplish his political tasks. By doing so he himself dashed all hopes for the peaceful co-existence of Ossetians, Abkhazians and Georgians in a single state. The peoples of South Ossetia and Abkhazia have more than once spoken in referenda supporting the independence of their republics. We understand that after what happened in Tskhinvali and what has been planned for Abkhazia they have the right to decide their destiny by themselves ... Considering the freely expressed will of the Ossetian and Abkhaz peoples and being guided by the provisions of the UN Charter, the 1970 Declaration of the Principles of International Law Governing Friendly Relations between States, the CSCE Helsinki Final Act of 1975 and other fundamental international instruments, I have signed decrees on the recognition by the Russian Federation of the independence of South Ossetia and the independence of Abkhazia. Russia calls on other states to follow its example. That is not an easy choice to make, but it represents the only possibility to save people's lives.

(www.ft.com, 26 August 2008; www.bbc.co.uk, 26 August 2008; www.cnn.com, 26 August 2008; www.independent.co.uk, 26 August 2008; www.iht.com, 26 August 2008)

[On Sunday 31 August 2008] President Dmitri Medvedev said: '[Russia will defend] the life and dignity [of Russian citizens] no matter where they are located … Russia, like other countries in the world, has regions in which it has privileged interests. There are countries in these regions with which we are traditionally connected by friendly, good neighbourly relations … We will very attentively work in these regions and develop friendly relations with these states, with our close neighbours.'

(*FT*, 1 September 2008, p. 5)

President Dmitri Medvedev (Sunday 31 August 2008): 'Russia, like other countries in the world, has regions where it has privileged interests. These are regions where countries with which we have friendly relations are located' … Asked whether this sphere of influence would be the border states around Russia, he answered: 'It is the border region, but not only.'

(www.iht.com, 1 September 2008)

'The notion of a "sphere of privileged interests" first appeared in Russian diplomatic parlance as early as 1939' (www.iht.com, 30 October 2008).

President Daniel Ortega of Nicaragua (2 September 2008): 'The government of Nicaragua recognizes the independence of the republics of South Ossetia and Abkhazia and we are completely with the Russian government's position' (www.iht.com, 5 September 2008).

President Hugo Chavez of Venezuela … on Thursday [10 September] announced that his country would become the third to recognize the independence declared by Abkhazia and South Ossetia … Until Thursday only Nicaragua had followed [Russia] … President Chavez: 'Starting today [10 September] we will recognize these republics' … Mr Chavez has visited Russia eight times as president, often seeking to procure Russian-made arms and weapons systems. Russia and Venezuela have in recent years signed agreements worth over $4 billion for deliveries of fighter jets, helicopters and automatic weapons, among other systems. In a visit last year [2008] Mr Chavez signed an agreement for a $1 billion loan from Russia for military development.

(*IHT*, 11 September 2009, p. 3)

[On 14 December 2009] the tiny atoll nation of Nauru ... in the South Pacific ... [said it would] recognize Abkhazia and South Ossetia ... Russia is preparing to give Nauru $50 million in humanitarian aid. In return Nauru will establish diplomatic relations with Abkhazia and South Ossetia ... Nauru is eight square miles in size [and] home to 11, 320 citizens.

(*Guardian*, 15 December 2009, p. 20)

The tiny, destitute Pacific island nation of Nauru on Tuesday [15 December] became the fourth country to formally establish diplomatic relations with Abkhazia, effectively recognizing its sovereignty ... In meetings with Russian officials ... Nauru secured a pledge of $50 million for 'urgent social and economic projects' on the island ... Nauru, which measures 9 square miles (23 square kilometres), is home to about 14,000 people ... Abkhazia has a population of about 215,000 ... It was not clear whether Nauru would make a similar announcement regarding South Ossetia, which [Nauran foreign minister] Kieren Keke visited over the weekend.

(*IHT*, 16 December 2009, p. 3)

'So far only Venezuela, Nicaragua and the tiny Pacific island of Nauru have joined Russia in recognizing the independence of the two regions' (www.bbc.co. uk, 11 August 2010).

The toll

'Russian investigators have released a list of 311 names of South Ossetians killed during the five-day war with Georgia. Initially Russian and South Ossetian authorities had estimated at least 1,400 fatalities' (www.bbc.co.uk 8 September 2008).

The war [in August 2008] ... was over in four days but about 1,000 people died, including perhaps 600 civilians. Of 138,000 who fled, about 30,000 have not returned, mostly ethnic Georgians from South Ossetia and Abkhazia. Many now live in central Georgia in aid-funded prefabricated buildings ... South Ossetia, where the parliament, university and 40 per cent of housing were destroyed, still resembles a war zone ... Abkhazia escaped lightly last year but still bears the scars of fighting with Georgia in the early 1990s ... In Georgia rapid economic expansion has ended in recession, with the economy forecast to shrink this year [2009] by 1.5 per cent. Only a $4.5 billion (Euro 3.2 billion) international aid plan, worth about $1,000 per head, prevents a social crisis ... The United States and the EU have concluded that Mikheil Saakashvili contributed to his own misfortune by letting himself be provoked.

(*FT*, 3 August 2009, p. 7)

'Russia and Georgia fought a five-day conflict in 2008 ... A total of about 850 people were killed on all sides and untold numbers of others were wounded or left missing, an EU fact-finding mission concluded last year [2009]' (www.cnn.com, 11 August 2010).

Implications for Russia

President Dmitri Medvedev said the need for the modernization was demonstrated by last month's military conflict with Georgia. Russia responded to Georgia's attack on South Ossetia with overwhelming force and easily crushed the Georgian army, but the brief war highlighted Russia's ageing arsenal. Medvedev told military commanders: 'We must ensure superiority in the air, in carrying out precision strikes at land and sea targets and in the timely deployment of forces' ... [Medvedev] made no mention of the new Borei-class nuclear submarines, which are designed to carry a new intercontinental missile that is seen as a key future component of Russia's nuclear forces. The missile was successfully test fired last week after repeated failures. The first of the new submarines is to be commissioned later this year and two more are being built.

(www.cnn.com, 27 September 2008)

Background to Abkhazia and South Ossetia

'Abkhazia (the name means "country of the soul") came under Tsarist rule in 1810' (*The Independent*, 29 September 1993, p. 13).

The declaration of 'sovereignty' by Abkhazia on 26 July 1992 (actually the 27 July 1925 constitution was referred to) was followed by an invasion by Georgian troops in mid-August (though officially at first on the grounds of releasing kidnapped ministers). [Russian President] Boris Yeltsin helped produce an agreement involving a ceasefire (effective 5 September 1992), a partial withdrawal and a peacekeeping force that would include Russian troops. But the fighting did not cease.

(Jeffries 1993: 108)

Eduard Shevardnadze (who was Communist Party boss 1972–85) returned to Georgia on 7 March 1992 and three days later was made president of the State Council. Fighting continued in South Ossetia over its desire to join North Ossetia in Russia, but Russia and Georgia agreed to send in a joint peacekeeping force in mid-July 1992.

(p. 83)

'In August 1992 defence minister Tengiz Kitovani invaded Abkhazia without the approval of Eduard Shevardnadze. Georgian troops engaged in wholesale looting, raping and killing' (*IHT*, 9 June 1994, p. 6).

Before hostilities broke out ethnic Georgians accounted for 45 per cent of Abkhazia's population and Abkhaz about 15 per cent. Today Georgians make up no more than 20 per cent of the population and most live in Gali district next to the Georgian border.

(*CDSP*, 1997, vol. XLIX, no. 27, p. 16)

'The conflict in Abkahzia cost 10,000 lives and caused 300,000 people to flee their homes' (*FT*, 28 July 1997, p. 2). 'About 10,000 people were killed and some 150,000 ethnic Georgians made refugees' (*Guardian*, 16 August 1997, p. 11).

> Only 200,000 people live in Abkhazia. Before the war in the early 1990s only 18 per cent of them were Abkhaz; even today they make up no more than 45 per cent of the people, the rest being Armenians, Russians and Georgians. More than 200,000 Georgians from Abkhazia are refugees in Georgia ... Georgians accuse the Abkhaz of ethnic cleansing. The Abkhaz say they have reclaimed what was lost by deportations to Turkey in the nineteenth century and to Siberia in the twentieth century, as well as through later Georgian settlement (Stalin was Georgian) ... South Ossetia is a tiny patchwork with perhaps as few as 50,000 inhabitants in the Ossetian-controlled part. Much of the land is controlled by Georgians. It is linked to Russia by a tunnel through the mountains; on the other side is the autonomous Russian republic of North Ossetia.
>
> (*The Economist*, 1 December 2007, pp. 52, 54)

When the Bolsheviks occupied Georgia, Abkhazia was given the status of a Soviet republic. Only in 1931 did Stalin (a Georgian) turn Abkhazia into an autonomous region of Georgia. Later his secret police chief, Beria (also a Georgian, born in Abkhazia), resettled Georgians from the western part of the country in Abkhazia, tipping its ethnic balance in favour of Georgians. Abkhaz schools were shut and the language was banned ... In August 1992 Georgia, itself in near anarchy, began a war in Abkhazia ... The tide of war changed ... The Abkhaz [were] helped by Chechens and Russian mercenaries ... Some 250,000 of the pre-war Georgian inhabitants (who accounted for 45 per cent of the total population) were forced out through ethnic cleansing.

(*The Economist*, 5 July 2008, p. 60)

The Ossetians are a distinct ethnic group originally from the Russian plains just south of the Don River. In the thirteenth century they were pushed southwards by Mongol invasions into the Caucasus Mountains, settling along the border with Georgia ... Ethnic Georgians are a minority in South Ossetia, accounting for less than one-third of the population. But Georgia rejects even the name South Ossetia, preferring to call it by the ancient name of Samachablo, or Tskhinvali, after its main city ... As far as Georgia is concerned, the use of the word 'north' in North Ossetia is misleading. In Tbilisi's eyes the region of Russia which bears that name is only Ossetia. It prefers to call South Ossetia, which is part of the Georgian province of Shida Kartl, by the ancient name of Samachablo or, more recently, Tskhinvali region. The Ossetians are believed to be descended from tribes which migrated into the area from Asia many hundreds of years ago and settled in what is now North Ossetia ... By tradition the Ossetians have had good relations with Russians and were regarded as loyal citizens, first of the Russian empire and later of the Soviet Union. They sided with the Kremlin when Bolshevik forces occupied Georgia in the early 19920s and, as part of the carve-up which followed, the South Ossetian Autonomous Region was created in Georgia and North Ossetia was formed in Russia.

(www.bbc.co.uk, 9 August 2008)

A chronology of historical events is provided by the *Guardian* (www.guardian.co.uk 8 August 2008):

1237–40: Mongols invade Russia, forcing Ossetians to migrate south over the Caucasus Mountains to present-day Georgia;

eighteenth and nineteenth centuries: the Russian empire extends to the Caucasus, provoking strong resistance from the people of the North Caucasus – the South Ossetians do not join the uprising, some preferring to side with the Russian army;

1801: South Ossetia and Georgia are annexed by Russia and absorbed into the Russian empire;

1918: Georgia declared independence following the Russian Revolution;

1921: the Red Army invades – the South Ossetians are accused of siding with the Kremlin;

1922: Georgia becomes a founder member of the Soviet Union – the South Ossetian Autonomous Oblast (district) is created with Georgia in April 1922.

'South Ossetia is a tiny patchwork of villages – Georgian and South Ossetian – ... It is head by a thuggish former Soviet official, Eduard Kokoyev, and run by the Russian security services. It lives off smuggling and Russian money' (www.economist.com, 17 August 2008).

In the early 1990s, when Georgia was barely a state, its nationalistic leaders committed atrocities in South Ossetia and Abkhazia. But it is also true that 200,000 Georgians were driven out of Abkhazia ... Abkhazia has the trappings of a nascent state, but South Ossetia is a chessboard of villages (Georgian and Ossetian) which suffered under a Moscow-sponsored, thuggish and corrupt regime.

(www.economist.com, 28 August 2008)

'South Ossetia has a population of about 70,000' (www.cnn.com, 11 August 2010).
   'South Ossetia is inhabited mostly by ethnic Ossetians, who speak a language remotely related to Farsi. Georgians account for less than one-third of the population' (www.bbc.co.uk, 25 August 2008).

Since the collapse of the Soviet Union … South Ossetia … has had no
economy to speak of, except for apple orchards and illegal trade in drugs,
armaments and counterfeit hundred-dollar bills … One industry that continued to thrive was the smuggling through the Roki Tunnel, which cuts through
the huge ridge of the Caucasus. Consumer goods poured south from Russia,
avoiding Georgian duties, and crime rings transported drugs from Central
Asia and Afghanistan … [The Georgian interior ministry] estimates that
Russia financed 95 per cent of … [South Ossetia's] budget in 2007 … In Abkhazia separatist leaders have adamantly demanded independence. In South
Ossetia, by contrast, most people want to become part of Russia. The South
Ossetians are part of a larger ethnic group that settled on both sides of the
Caucasus. They dream of reuniting with the North Ossetians to restore Alania,
an ancient kingdom they believe was home to their ancestors, the Scythians
… In 1990 Georgia's president, Zviad Gamsakhurdia, abolished autonomous
regions, stripping South Ossetia of the self-determination it enjoyed in Soviet
days. A war broke out in which about 1,000 people were killed, and the once-
friendly relations between Georgians and South Ossetians turned poisonous.

(www.iht.com, 26 August 2008)

'More than half of South Ossetia's 70,000 citizens are said to have taken up
Moscow's offer of Russian citizenship' (www.bbc.co.uk, 2 September 2008).

'Up to 90 per cent of South Ossetia's non-Georgian population carry Russian
passports' (www.guardian.co.uk 8 August 2008).

Stalin … designed the Soviet Union using his knowledge of Caucasian
ethnic feuds to create republics within republics, including Ossetia and Abkhazia, as Russia's Trojan horses, and they have outlived Stalin's great
project. I've spent a great deal of time in the Caucasus since 1991, always
analysing the long-standing Russian game of undermining and controlling
Georgia by Stalinist means. Russia's recent policy of encouraging rebel
skirmishing in South Ossetia and offering Russian passports to its citizens
was a classic trap. As colonial puppeteer and a successful restorer of Russia
as imperial superpower, Putin is Stalin's consummate heir.

(Simon Sebag Montefiore, *IHT*, 26 August 2008, p. 6)

The Georgia conflict [of August 2008] marks the first war between countries
with majority Orthodox Christian populations since the Second Balkan War
in 1913 pitted Serbia, Greece, Montenegro and Romania against Bulgaria in
a prelude to World War II … Georgia has fewer than 5 million people, but it
is one of the most ancient Christian countries in the world. Its church dates
back to the fourth century, far outpacing the Russian church, which dates its
founding to the Baptism of Rus in 988, when Prince Vladimir of Kiev
brought Orthodoxy to the banks of the Dnieper River. Russia annexed
Georgia, which was seeking protection from Persia, in 1801, absorbed its
church, which was restored – in name, at least – only after the Bolsheviks
came to power … When Russia annexed Georgia at the beginning of the

nineteenth century, it abolished the patriarch in 1811 [and] it persecuted the Georgian language at all levels, including the church.

(*IHT*, 6 September 2008, p. 2)

The kind of ethnic standoff has repeatedly arisen across the former Soviet Union. These clashes – in Georgia, Azerbaijan, Moldova and elsewhere – are often referred to as frozen conflicts because they have not been resolved over many years. They entangle the major powers, as in the case of the 2008 war between Russia and Georgia over the renegade enclave of South Ossetia.

(www.iht.com, 18 June 2010; *IHT*, 19 June 2010, pp. 1, 3)

More recent developments

President Dmitri Medvedev made an unscheduled visit to Abkhazia, his first to the breakaway Georgian region since the brief war between Russian and Georgia two years ago. He held talks with Abkhazia's leader [Sergei Bagapsh] and promised to develop economic, political and security relations ... During his visit, Mr Medvedev pledged more financial support to the two regions [Abkhazia and South Ossetia] ... Russia has used the anniversary of the conflict [8 August] to emphasize the strength of its ties with the two ... Last year [2009] prime minister Vladimir Putin visited Abkhazia for the first anniversary of the conflict and announced Moscow would pay for part of the country's defence infrastructure.

(www.bbc.co.uk, 8 August 2010)

President Dmitri Medvedev pledged Sunday [8 August] to provide further support to South Ossetia and Abkhazia on the second anniversary of the Russian–Georgian war. Mr Medvedev arrived Sunday [8 August] in Abkhazia to hold talks with the government there. He said Moscow would increase investment in Soviet-era resorts to turn Abkhazia into a magnet for Russian tourists. Mr Medvedev addressed Russian troops stationed in the Black Sea port of Gudauta in Abkhazia.

(*IHT*, 9 August 2010, p. 3)

Russia announced Wednesday [11 August] that it had deployed and advanced a surface-to-air missile system in Abkhazia ... General Alexander Zelin, the commander of Russia's air force, said the system, called the S-300, was deployed to protect Russian military facilities in the enclave and to prevent 'violations of government borders' ... General Zelin said different air defence systems had been sent to protect the skies over South Ossetia ... Russia signed a military pact with the separatist Abkhaz government in February [2010], establishing an army base on the territory. The agreement called for the deployment of about 1,700 Russian troops for a minimum of forty-nine years. The S-300, called the SA-20 in the West, is one of Russia's most advanced air defence systems.

(www.iht.com, 11 August 2010)

Russian air force commander Colonel Alexander Zelin [said Wednesday 11 August that] ... the S-300 system will help 'ensure the security' of Abkhazia and South Ossetia ... It is also designed to protect the Russian military base in Abkhazia ... he said.

(www.cnn.com, 11 August 2010)

Air force commander-in-chief Alexander Zelin said the role of the missiles would be 'anti-aircraft defence of the territory of Abkhazia and South Ossetia'. The self-styled Abkhaz 'foreign minister', Maxim Gvinjia, later contradicted General Zelin, telling the BBC that the general's statement on the S-300s had been 'misinterpreted'.

(www.bbc.co.uk, 11 August 2010)

Appendix 2

The summer 2010 heatwave and its effects

A blistering heatwave has ... dried out millions of hectares of wheat before it could ripen on the stems, setting back an agricultural revival that was just reaching its stride after years of faltering reforms ... Relentless sun, in a region where summer showers are the norm, caused grain crops on some of the world's most fertile land to wither on a vast scale, just as Russia was staging a revival in farming ... In some parts of the agricultural belt, sometimes called the Black Earth or the breadbasket of Europe, not a drop of rain has fallen since April [2010] ... The Grain Union on Monday [19 July] lowered its forecast for the harvest to 81.5 million tones from 85 million tonnes. By comparison, the fields yielded 97 million tonnes last year [2009]. This unusually bountiful zone was sown in recent years not only with seeds but also with huge investments in agricultural machinery, soils and grain-carrying railroad cars in new efforts to finally revive production and help meet steadily rising global demand for food. But irrigation is impossible in the huge fields, and farmers depend as they always have on Mother Nature ... Agriculture, as it always has in Russia, depends on the whim of rain clouds ... So far seventeen regions in Russia where crops depend on rain have declared states of emergency. But Russia went into the drought with silos overflowing with bumper crops last year and the year before – the payoff from a policy of privatizing collective farms to attract investment – so the country will be able to meet its own needs, with a few million tonnes left over for export ... Russia is now a net importer of food, if meat is taken into consideration.

(www.iht.com, 20 July 2010; *IHT*, 21 July 2010, p. 3)

It is estimated that a fifth of Russia's wheat crop has now died because of the lack of rain in what is thought to be the country's worst drought for more than a century ... Forest fires are raging in central Russia as a heatwave grips much of the country ... [The capital Moscow had] a record temperature of 39 Celsius (102 Fahrenheit) on Thursday [29 July 2010] and warnings from health experts of pollution levels ten times higher than normal safety limits. A thick layer of smoke [came] from peat bogs burning in the surrounding region.

(www.bbc.co.uk, 30 July 2010)

Fires have been raging in five regions as Russia endures dry weather and one of the hottest months on record. Thursday [29 July] saw Moscow reach 102 Fahrenheit (39 Celsius), the highest temperature since records began in 1879 … Temperatures across much of western and central Russia have topped 95 Fahrenheit (35 Celsius) during the past five weeks … The month of July is expected to break the record for the hottest month ever recorded in Moscow.

(www.cnn.com, 30 July 2010)

When the heatwave hit Russia, agriculture seemed the first to fall victim across much of the country, with officials predicting that grain production could decline by as much as 25 per cent … July has been the hottest month since the city [Moscow] began taking such measurements under the Tsars, 130 years ago.

(www.iht.com, 30 July 2010)

Stoked by parched forests, dried-out swamps and the hottest summertime temperatures ever recorded in Russia, wildfires burned down several villages in the central part of the country, killing about two dozen people, government officials said Friday [30 July] … Russia, like much of the northern hemisphere, has been baking in a heatwave this summer. Thursday [29 July] was the hottest day in Moscow since record keeping began there under the Tsars, 130 years ago, topping out at 100 degrees [Fahrenheit] … Thousands of acres of wheat and barley crops have dried up, and twenty-seven agricultural regions have declared states of emergency because of crop failures.

(www.iht.com, 31 July 2010)

'Much of western and central Russia is suffering a severe drought, thought to be the worst since 1972, in what has been the hottest summer since record-keeping began 130 years ago' (www.iht.com, 2 August 2010).

At least twenty-five people have been killed and thousands left homeless by wildfires sweeping through western Russia, authorities said Saturday [31 July] … The blazes are among the worst ever to hit the region … A hot dry summer has been a key factor in the fires, drying out large parts of land and igniting the peat bogs that lie all over central Russia … The fires are the worst ever to hit the European part of Russia, the region west of the Ural Mountains … Temperatures across much of western and central Russia have topped 95 Fahrenheit (35 Celsius) during the past five weeks.

(www.cnn.com, 31 July 2010)

'At least twenty-eight people have been killed and thousands left homeless by wildfires sweeping through western Russia, authorities said Saturday [31 July]' (www.cnn.com, 1 August 2010).

'Wildfires have killed at least thirty people, officials say … Temperatures [are] forecast to hit 40 Celsius (104 Fahrenheit) in some areas' (www.bbc.co.uk, 1 August 2010). 'This July was the hottest on record, with Moscow, which sees an average high of 23 Celsius on the summer months, sweltering in heat of 37.8 Celsius last Thursday [29 July]' (www.bbc.co.uk, 1 August 2010).

'The discovery of two more bodies ... brought the number of dead to thirty-three, including three firefighters' (*The Times*, 2 August 2010, p. 29).

> President Dmitri Medvedev has declared a state of emergency in seven Russian regions because of wildfires fuelled by a heatwave. The death toll from the fires has risen to at least thirty-four ... Emergency officials say the heat and drought are the main cause of the fires, but they also blame human carelessness [e.g. a cigarette thrown from a car window] and urged people to use extreme caution when walking or driving in the woods or countryside ... Russians are bracing themselves for another week of high temperatures, with forecasts of up to 40 Celsius (104 Fahrenheit) for central and southern regions.
>
> (www.bbc.co.uk, 2 August 2010)

'Emergencies minister Sergei Shoigu ... confirmed that many of the fires were caused by human negligence' (www.bbc.co.uk, 4 August 2010).

> Authorities have imposed a state of emergency around 500 towns and villages because of wildfires ... Most of the fires were started accidentally by people dropping garbage, dropping cigarettes, or failing to extinguish campfires or barbecues properly ... [said the] emergency situations ministry [The ministry said] thirty-four people have been confirmed dead.
>
> (www.cnn.com, 2 August 2010)

> Fires were being fought in fourteen regions, stretching to the Ural Mountains and beyond, including Kamchatka in the far east ... President Dmitri Medvedev's emergency declaration restricts movement and activity in the affected areas and calls for the military to help fight the fires. According to the declaration, the regional authorities are granted the right to determine the length of the state of emergency. As of Monday evening [2 August] forty people had died in the fires ... Last week, as the fires spun out of control, prime minister Vladimir Putin said that local officials who had failed to take the necessary fire prevention measures should resign ... And on Monday Mr Putin said that Russia's regional governors, who are appointed by the Kremlin, would also be held accountable.
>
> (*IHT*, 3 August 2010, p. 3)

> Wheat prices have seen the biggest one-month jump in more than three decades on the back of a severe drought in Russia ... European wheat prices jumped 8 per cent yesterday [2 August] to Euro 211 a tonne, the highest in two years. Wheat prices have risen nearly 50 per cent since late June [2010] ... The rally comes as the worst heatwave and drought in more than a century continues to devastate grain crops in Russia, Ukraine and Kazakhstan. The trio is among the world's top ten wheat exporters ... Executives and traders fear the three countries could restrict their grain exports or even

impose an export ban in an effort to keep their local market well supplied and prices low ... Grain controls [were introduced by Russia] ... during the 2007–8 crisis ... Wheat traders and analysts said Russia's wheat production could drop in 2010–11 to 45 million to 50 million tonnes, down as much as 27 per cent from last season's 61.7 million tonnes. Ukraine and Kazakhstan would also produce less.

(*FT*, 3 August 2010, p. 1)

Traders in Chicago's grain pits have just seen the largest monthly wheat process surge in nearly forty years ... US futures prices topped $7 a bushel yesterday [2 August], a two-year high that comes just weeks after a nine-month low ... The former Soviet Union has transformed itself from an agricultural basket case back to breadbasket, producing 15 per cent of the world's wheat. This understates its importance as it is a far bigger exporter than some larger producers ... [But] the United States ... [has] a near record crop.

(p. 12)

About a fifth of Russia's grain crop has been destroyed and there was another big rise in the price of wheat on international markets on Monday [2 August] ... Wheat prices have hit a twenty-two-month high after a severe drought and ensuing wildfires in Russia devastated crops. Chicago Board of Trade wheat for delivery in September broke through the $7 a bushel level in US trade for the first time since September 2008 before falling back to $6.93. Prices have risen 50 per cent since late June ... Russia was the world's fourth largest wheat exporter in the twelve months to June behind the United States, the EU and Canada, according to the US Department of Agriculture ... Along with other former Soviet Republics such as Kazakhstan, it accounted for about 25 per cent of the world's wheat exports ... Wheat prices dropped back slightly from their highs after deputy agriculture minister Alexander Belayev said there was no need for Moscow to restrict its grain exports at the moment ... Russia has high levels of grain in reserves and will start using those. But Mr Belayev said that production levels would be lower than forecast. He said: 'We will manage to produce 70 to 75 million tones, I think' ... The ministry of agriculture had forecast the grain crop to come in below 85 million tonnes, compared with 97 million tones in 2009 ... [According to one estimate] the crop declines in the former Soviet Union ... [may be of the order of] 20 to 25 per cent drops in production leading to equivalent declines in exports. But ... there are still big exportable surpluses in other parts of the world, particularly the United States.

(www.bbc.co.uk, 4 August 2010)

Russia has cut its 2010 grain crop forecast as damage from the worst drought in more than a century spreads, but the big cereal supplier said it would not curb exports for now. Russia may harvest 70 to 75 million tonnes of grain this year ... [said] deputy minister Alexander Belayev on Tuesday [3 August], down from a previous official forecast of less than 85 million tonnes, and 97 million tonnes last year. But he said there was no need to restrict grain exports. Russia introduced high grain export tariffs for several months in 2004 and 2008 to keep grain at home, and it sold grain from its stocks on the domestic market to keep prices down. The worsening drought in Russia helped propel US wheat futures to twenty-two-month highs on Monday [2 August], but on Tuesday [3 August] they were little changed.

(*IHT*, 4 August 2010, p. 17)

Moscow acted to prevent panic in the market, saying its grain exports would be stable ... because of plentiful stocks ... Wheat prices yesterday [Tuesday 3 August] fell slightly from Monday's two-year high, but trading was frenetic. European milling wheat in Paris dropped nearly 1.7 per cent to Euro 204.25 a tonne, after touching an intraday high of Euro 211 a tonne on Monday [2 August].

(*FT*, 4 August 2010)

President Dmitri Medvedev [said on Tuesday 3 August that] the government ... would rely on help from nations such as Ukraine and Azerbaijan, which have offered to donate military aeroplanes and helicopters ... The Kremlin has scrambled to respond to the wildfires, which have run out of control in part because of shortages in proper fire-fighting equipment and poor planning by local authorities ... Investment in firefighting equipment has shrivelled since the collapse of the Soviet Union and the government employs a decreasing number of specialists to protect forests ... Yesterday [3 August] prime minister Vladimir Putin promised that the government would flood peatlands in the future.

(*FT*, 4 August 2010, p. 6)

'President Dmitri Medvedev has interrupted his holiday to hold emergency talks on wildfires raging across central Russia. The death toll from the disaster has reached forty-eight' (www.bbc.co.uk, 4 August 2010).

President Dmitri Medvedev has sacked several top military officials for failing to stop wildfires from destroying a naval base outside Moscow ... Last Thursday [29 July] flames tore through the naval logistics base in Kolomna, 100 kilometres south-east of Moscow, destroying office buildings and warehouses and equipment. Mr Medvedev said commanders of the base were absent when the fire occurred and that it was 'unclear where they were'. As a result, Mr Medvedev formally reprimanded the head of the navy Admiral Vladimir Vyotsky, and his deputy Alexander Tatarinov, accusing them of a lack of 'professional responsibility' over how the fire was handled. He also said he had ordered the sacking of a swathe of officers, including the head of the navy's logistics division ... and ... the head of the navy's aviation arm. Mr Medvedev said many other military sites across Russia were also threatened by the wildfires, and warned that if they were not property protected by the military there would be more sackings.

(www.bbc.co.uk, 4 August 2010)

'President Dmitri Medvedev yesterday [4 August] broke off his holiday and ordered an investigation into the wildfires that have swept across the country, blaming local and military authorities for mismanagement' (*FT*, 5 August 2010, p. 6).

'[The] emergency has now claimed fifty lives ... Foreign reinforcements are arriving, including two Canadian water-bombing planes from Italy. Ukraine and Belarus are also sending firefighters' (www.bbc.co.uk, 5 August 2010).

Russia announced Thursday [5 August] that it would ban grain exports through the end of the year [2010] ... The ban ... helped propel wheat prices in the United States toward their highest levels in nearly two years ... The ban is in force from 15 August to 31 December ... Prime minister Vladimir Putin said that Russia had sufficient stockpiles of grain but that blocking exports was an appropriate response to the worst drought in decades. He said: 'We need to prevent a rise in domestic food prices, we need to pre-serve the number of cattle and build up reserves for the next year.'

(www.iht.com, 5 August 2010)

The decision caused an immediate and sharp rise in the already high global price of wheat. It rose more than 8 per cent in early trading on the Chicago Board of Trade, having increased about 90 per cent since June because of the drought in Russia, Ukraine, Kazakhstan and parts of the EU, and flood in Canada ... Large, multinational grain trading companies that operate in Russia had lobbied for the ban as a means to claim a legal exemption from futures con-tracts struck before the drought, when prices were far lower. A Russian subsidi-ary of Glencore, the Swiss-based commodities trading company that has close ties to the Russian government, pressed hard as the scope of the drought's dev-astation became clear. This company, International Grain Company, is the largest wheat exporter in Russia. Mr Putin said that the government could con-sider extending the ban if the harvest yields less even than the current grim forecasts. The Russian harvest is now projected to yield about 70 million tonnes of grain, according to the Russian Grain Union, a lobbying group for farmers, about equal to the country's internal demand including for animal fodder of about 71 million tonnes per year. The group was sharply critical of the decision ... Owing to a bumper crop last year, Russia currently holds about 24 million tones in reserves in grain elevators, the group said ... Russia, by some esti-mates, has the largest potential anywhere to meet mounting demand for food from a growing and hungry world population, as Russia possesses the greatest reserve of fertile land that is now fallow, while its own population is shrinking.

(www.iht.com, 5 August 2010)

The price of wheat rose more than 8 per cent Thursday [5 August] on the Chicago Board of Trade on the news, after already rising about 90 per cent since June because of the drought in Russia, Ukraine, Kazakhstan and other parts of the EU, and floods in Canada.

(*IHT*, 6 August 2010, p. 1)

'Wheat prices have soared by about 90 per cent since June ... and the [export] ban pushed prices even higher. Exports from Ukraine, another major exporter, are down sharply this year' (www.iht.com, 6 August 2010).

'Prime minister Vladimir Putin: "I think it is expedient to temporarily ban exports of grain and grain products from Russia" ... Russia is the world's third largest wheat exporter' (www.cnn.com, 5 August 2010).

> Wheat prices immediately jumped 60 cents to $7.85 a bushel – the highest since September 2008 ... Prices have surged from a low of $4.25 earlier this year [2010], although they remain well below the peak of the last surge in the cost of wheat, which hit $13.49 a bushel in February 2008 ... Crops are expected to be bumper in the United Kingdom ... Despite the ban Russian farmers have little incentive to export anyway because prices have been rising even faster in Russia than in world markets.
>
> (www.independent.com, 5 August 2010)

'Heavy rainfall is taking its toll on Canadian output' (www.economist.com, 5 August 2010).

> 'Prime minister Vladimir Putin: "I think it advisable to introduce a temporary ban on the export from Russia of grain and other agricultural products made from grain" ... Russia, one of the biggest producers of wheat, barley and rye, exported a quarter of its 2009 grain out. Mr Putin's announcement sent wheat prices to a twenty-three-month high ... However, many commodity analysts insist there is currently a surplus of wheat in global markets following record harvests in 2008 and 2009. They say that speculators have been driving wheat prices artificially high because they are hoping to make a profit from the worries over Russian exports ... The United States – the world's number one exporter – is predicting a bumper harvest of its current crop ... Russia is banning the export of grains including wheat, barley, rye ... from 15 August to 31 December ... Russia will also ask its regional customs union partners – Kazakhstan, another leading grain exporter, and Belarus – to follow suit. Mr Putin said that grain from the state reserves would not be auctioned but would be distributed to regions with the greatest need. The prime minister said: 'The aim in this case is not to make more money, but to aid those farmers that need help today' ... He added that the government would provide 10 billion roubles ($335 million) in subsidies and another 25 billion roubles in loans to agricultural companies affected by the drought ... Russia produces a soft type of wheat that is unsuitable for making the traditional loaf of bread seen in the United Kingdom. As a result, Britain only buys a nominal amount of Russian wheat. Russia, instead, sends most of its wheat exports to the Middle East, where it is

used to make unleavened flatbreads. Egypt is its largest export market, followed by Turkey, Syria, Iran and Libya.

(www.bbc.co.uk, 5 August 2010)

[On 5 August] wheat prices rose more than 12 per cent to hit a peak of Euro 236 a tonne on record trading volumes. US wheat futures jumped and are up more than 80 per cent since mid-June, the fastest rally in nearly forty years ... Traders at Glencore, the world's largest commodity trading company, on Tuesday [3 August] warned the [Russian grain] crop could fall to about 65 million tonnes.

(*FT*, 6 August 2010, p. 1)

The International Grains Council predicted Russia would export 6 million to 7 million tonnes less wheat than expected this year as a result of the export ban. That compares with US inventories, which are forecast to hit a two-decade high of almost 30 million tonnes on the back of a bumper crop, according to the US Department of Agriculture's July predictions ... US farmers, who traditionally are the world's exporters of last resort on the grain market, are sitting on almost 30 million tonnes of wheat, up from just 8 million tonnes in 2007–8. Inventories of rice, corn and other crops are also above the level of three years ago ... Australia and Argentina will harvest their wheat crops in December ... The 2007–8 crisis, the first in three decades, saw the cost of agricultural commodities from corn to rice surge to record highs.

(p. 4)

'A new Forest Code in 2006 dismantled a federal forest safety system and trans-ferred responsibility to regional authorities and forest tenants, such as logging companies, which have preformed badly' (*FT*, 7 August 2010, p. 4).

A Russian presidential aide criticized local officials over the handling of hundreds of wildfires across the country that have so far claimed at least fifty lives, according to news reports published Friday [6 August]. Mayors will face a 'debriefing' and those who are found to have lagged in response to battling the fires 'will be brought to justice' ... Local officials in Russia have faced accusations of not doing enough to prevent fires and of failing to respond adequately to the blazes. Last week prime minister Vladimir Putin called for the resignations of local leaders who had not adequately dealt with the crisis ... The heatwave began in mid-June, and no relief was in sight on Friday as temperatures in Moscow were forecast to remain slightly above 100 degrees Fahrenheit (about 38 degrees Celsius). The average daytime high for Moscow in early August is in the mid-70s Fahrenheit ... The wildfires could still pose a threat of nuclear contamination if not con-tained, a Russian official said on Thursday [5 August]. Heat from the fires in the Bryansk region ... located about 250 miles south-west of Moscow ... could release into the air harmful particles that have remained since contam-ination more than twenty years ago from the Chernobyl nuclear disaster, emergencies ministry Sergei Shoigu was quoted as saying. He said: 'In the event of a fire there, radionuclides could rise together with combustion particles, resulting in a new pollution zone' ... Firefighters from various European nations and former Soviet republics were arriving in Moscow to help firefighters battle the blazes.

(www.iht.com, 6 August 2010)

Russia struggled Friday to gain control of wildfires raging across the country that have claimed at least fifty lives, clogged the skies with a stinging smog, snarled air travel and forced the military to transfer weapons away from a base near Moscow ... Earlier this week material was transferred away from a nuclear research facility in Sarov in the Nizhny Novgorod region, about 310 miles east of Moscow, as fires approached that location.

(www.iht.com, 6 August 2010)

Wildfires ... have claimed fifty-two lives, clouded Moscow in smoke and on Friday [6 August] forced the military to transfer rockets away from a garrison near the capital ... Most [wildfires are in] western and central parts of the country ... Temperatures have been spiking since mid-June and there was no relief in sight on Friday, when temperatures in Moscow were forecast to exceed 100 degrees Fahrenheit, about 25 degrees higher than usual ... By 1.40 p.m. the city's environmental protection agency said the concentrations of carbon monoxide were five times higher than acceptable levels, while particulate pollution was three times higher. The heavy smoke disrupted flights into Moscow ... President Dmitri Medvedev fired five military officers last week for allowing a fire to burn through hangars at an air force base near the capital, and he has upbraided governors and other lower level officials ... Mr Medvedev has declared a state of emergency in seven regions, while another twenty-eight regions have declared an emergency for farmers whose crops are failing in a severe drought.

(www.iht.com, 6 August 2010)

There is growing alarm that fires in regions coated with fallout from the Chernobyl nuclear disaster twenty-four years ago could now be emitting plumes of radioactive smoke. Several fires have been documented in the contaminated areas of western Russia, including three heavily irradiated sites in the Bryansk region, the environmental group Greenpeace said in a statement released Tuesday [10 August]. Bryansk borders Belarus and Ukraine ... Officials from Russia's federal forest protection service confirmed that fires were burning at contaminated sites on Tuesday, and expressed fears that lax oversight as a result of recent changes in the forestry service could increase the chances that radioactive smoke would waft into populated areas ... The danger comes from radioactive residue still coating large areas of Ukraine, Belarus and Russia, years after the explosion of Reactor No. 4 at the Chernobyl nuclear power plant on 26 April 1986, in what was then the Soviet republic of Ukraine ... It took days for the Soviet government to inform its people of the Chernobyl explosion, leaving thousands unknowingly exposed to deadly radiation ... The forest protection service has identified seven regions where dozens of fires have been burning in contaminated zones, with attention focusing on Bryansk, one of the regions most heavily contaminated by the Chernobyl disaster ... Little official information has been made available about the radioactive threat. Responding to the Greenpeace statement on Tuesday, Gennadi Onishenko, Russia's chief sanitary doctor, played down the danger. He said: 'There is no need to sow panic. Everything is fine.'

(www.iht.com, 11 August 2010)

The death toll from the fires since the end of July is fifty-two ... Daytime temperatures in Moscow remain close to 40 Celsius (104 Fahrenheit) with little sign of relenting in the next few days. The smog has been affecting the capital for a week, and appeared to have been easing – before it worsened on Friday [6 August] ... The level of CO_2 in Moscow's air is more than three times higher than normal, officials say. According to some experts, inhaling the polluted air is as dangerous as smoking several packets of cigarettes a day.

(www.bbc.co.uk, 6 August 2010)

Wheat prices held just below a two-year high Friday [6 August] ... The introduction of the export ban from 15 August to the end of the year may be reversed depending on the results of the harvest season, first deputy prime minister Igor Shuvalov said Friday ... US wheat futures on the Chicago Board of Trade fell 5 per cent Friday after surging more than 20 per cent earlier in the week to a two-year high. The price had nearly doubled since early July, to $8.41 a bushel. The increase has revived memories of the surge in prices in early 2008, when US wheat rose above $13 a bushel ... But analysts played down the possibility of a similar spike, saying that world supplies had grown steeply during the past couple of years, which had the biggest wheat crops in history ... China and India, both big consumers, are largely insulated from rising prices by large wheat reserves. Russia was the world's third largest wheat exporter last year [2009] ... [According to one estimate] there is going to be something like 5 million tonnes that are not going to be available for export.

(*IHT*, 7 August 2010, p. 8)

[According to one forecast] there is still going to be the third largest wheat crop in world history, even with the Russian shortfall ... On Friday [6 August] the futures prices [for wheat] fell again, this time hitting the lower limits on all three exchanges, on tentative reports that Russia might honour some of its export contracts after all or at least postpone the embargo until after its wheat harvest ... First deputy minister Igor Shuvalov: 'The decision to ban exports can be adjusted, depending on the harvest' ... By close of trading on Friday, wheat futures for September delivery on the Chicago

Board of Trade had dropped 60 cents, to \$7.25 a bushel, still sharply higher than a few weeks ago ... In 2007 worldwide stocks had already fallen sharply. By 2008 they had fallen to the lowest level in thirty years because of falling production and higher consumption ... Stocks had recovered by May 2010 ... Russia represents only 11 per cent of the world's wheat exports and any shortfall could be met by major wheat exporters like the United States, Australia or Canada.

(www.iht.com, 7 August 2010)

Russian news media reported that firefighters had discovered access roads to the forest were overgrown and in poor repair, ponds intended to provide water for refilling their tanks were filled with sludge and their fire trucks were frequently broken down. Local officials also blame a revised 2006 forest code that allowed logging companies to contract out firefighting operations. When the fires broke out, the contractors were woefully unprepared and inadequately equipped, said Viktor Sorokhin, a deputy head of administration for the Orekhovo-Zuyeva district, about 50 miles east of Moscow. The new code also cut the number of foresters in the district by half, he added, to 150 from 300 ... Russians typically suffer far more from fires than people in most developed countries. In 2006 more than 17,000 people died in fires, nearly thirteen for every 100,000 people – more than ten times the rates in Western Europe and the United States.

(www.iht.com, 8 August 2010; *IHT*, 9 August 2010, pp. 1, 3)

'A new Forest Code in 2006 dismantled a federal forest safety system and transferred responsibility to regional authorities and forest tenants, which have performed badly' (*FT*, 9 August 2010, p. 6).

SovEcon, a leading agricultural analyst, said on Monday [9 August] that Russia's wheat crop might be about one-third smaller than last year's – dropping to 43 million tonnes from 61.7 million tonnes in 2009. Russia's main sugar lobby warned on Monday that the drought may hamper this year's beet sugar output, reducing it from the earlier expected 4 million tonnes to 3.2 to 3.5 million tonnes. The downgraded sugar beet forecast is not expected to change Russia's import needs as it has large domestic reserves. Almost all sugar produced in Russia is consumed domestically.

(www.iht.com, 9 August 2010)

Moscow's health chief has confirmed the mortality rate has doubled as a heatwave and wildfire continue to grip the capital. There were twice the usual number of bodies in the city's morgues, Andrei Seltsovsky told reporters ... He said: 'On normal days between 360 and 380 die – now it's around 700' ... Mr Seltsovsky did not give a time frame but earlier reports had spoken of the death rate in Moscow for July rising by up to 50 per cent compared with the same period last year [2009] ... Mr Seltsovsky did not attribute the rise in the mortality rate to the heatwave or smog but doctors, speaking off the record, have talked of morgues filling with victims of heat stroke and smoke ailments ... Reuters news agency reported on Sunday [8 August] that one Moscow doctor had written on his anonymous blog – since deleted – of the stench from bodies piling up in the basement of his clinic where the fridges were full. The blogger wrote: 'We cannot give that diagnosis [heat stroke and smoke ailments] – we do not want to be sacked. We have families to feed' ... Another doctor at a major hospital, speaking on condition of anonymity, told Reuters that staff had been instructed by senior management not to link patients' illnesses to the heatwave ... Soon after Mr Seltsovsky gave his information, Russia's health minister. Tatiana Golikova, demanded a formal clarification of his data. Her ministry said it was 'puzzled by the unofficial figures quoted at the briefing' ... The head of the state weather service, Alexander Frolov, said on Monday [9 August] that the heatwave of 2010 was the worst in 1,000 years of recorded Russian history ... A state of emergency has been declared around a nuclear reprocessing plant in the southern Urals because of nearby wildfires ... Some of the land around the Mayak plant being threatened by the wildfires was the site of Russia's worst nuclear disaster in 1957. Some of the land around the Mayak plant in the town of Ozersk (known in Soviet times as Chelyabinsk-40) is believed to be still contaminated from the disaster, in which a tank of radioactive waste exploded. Several leaks of radioactive waste have been reported from the plant in recent years ... There was a new warning over shortfalls in Russia's grain harvest. Prime minister Vladimir Putin said this year's harvest ... would be worse than previously forecast. Currently expected to be 65 million tonnes, it could be as low as 60 million tonnes, Mr Putin said. Mr Putin also said that a ban on grain exports could be extended beyond the end of 2010 because of shortages for domestic markets.

(www.bbc.co.uk, 9 August 2010)

The mortality rate in Moscow has 'doubled recently' ... Andrei Seltsovsky, the head of the city health department told news agencies Monday [9 August] ... The ministry said twenty-two out of the country's eighty-three regions, mostly in central Russia, are affected by wildfires ... Alexander Frolov, who heads Roshyrdomet ... the Russian meteorological service ... appeared live on Russian state television on Monday. He said high levels of pollutants in the Moscow air pose a serious danger to Muscovites' health. He said: 'The highest levels were registered on 7 and 8 August, with the concentration of particulate dust exceeding the permitted level by 3.4 times. It is very harmful for the human body as it accumulates and is virtually not excreted' ... Frolov said carbon monoxide and ozone levels were significantly higher than the permitted norm ... Roshyrdomet forecasts a 30 per cent drop in Russia's harvests due to the drought, he said ... Frolov said: 'One can say that neither we nor our ancestors observed or registered anything like it, in terms of heat, within a 1,000-year period since the foundation of our country. This phenomenon is absolutely unique. There is no record of such cases' ... At Monday's government meeting broadcast on state television prime minister Vladimir Putin said the order [to impose a ban on grain exports] was prompted by uncertainty over this year's farm production. A decision on the timeframe for the grain export ban will happen only after the results of the harvest are known, Putin said ... The prime minister said Russia would need 78 million tonnes of grain to support its people this year, but because of the drought the country might produce only 60 to 65 million tonnes, forcing it to dip into its 'state intervention fund'.

(www.cnn.com, 9 August 2010)

[Moscow's] normal daily death toll has nearly doubled in recent days ... [the capital's] chief health official said Monday [9 August], pointing to the lengthy heatwave rather than the factor most people here fear: the choking cloud of wildfire smoke. The acknowledgement at once confirmed a flurry of rumours that bodies were beginning to pile up in morgues and gave rise to yet more: that authorities, possibly trying to ward off a panicked exodus, had engaged in a Soviet-style whitewash of the health risks of the smoke. In any case, people are leaving ... After denying statements from morticians and doctors last week that the morgues were filling. Andrei Seltsovsky essentially confirmed them.

(www.iht.com, 9 August 2010)

'Andrei Seltsovsky cited heat stroke, rather than smoke-related ailments, as the main culprit ... In Andrei Seltsovsky's comments on Monday it was unclear when, exactly, the mortality rate had spiked to double the normal rate' (*IHT*, 10 August 2010, p. 3).

Andrei Seltsovsky ... Moscow's health department chief ... [said] heat-stroke was the main cause of the increase [in the city's death rate], although bronchial problems, heart disease and strokes were also soaring ... Tatiana Golikova, Russia's health minister, questioned Mr Seltsovsky's comments and asked for more data.

(*FT*, 10 August 2010, p. 8)

'Roshydromet ... the federal environmental monitoring agency ... has asked factories in Moscow to temporarily cut emissions by up to 40 per cent' (*Guardian*, 10 August 2010, p. 12).

'Global climate change is partly to blame for the abnormally hot and dry weather in Moscow ... say researchers ... Environmentalists say the number of personnel employed to spot wildfires has been slashed by over a half' (www. bbc.co.uk, 10 August 2010).

Seemingly disconnected ... far-flung disasters are reviving the question of whether global warming is causing more weather extremes. The collective answer of the scientific community can be boiled down to a single word: probably ... Russia has long played a reluctant, and sometimes obstructionist, role in global negotiations over limiting climate change, perhaps in part because it expected economic benefits from the warming of its vast Siberian hinterland. But the extreme of heatwave, and accompanying drought and wildfires, in normally cool central Russia seems to be prompting a shift in thinking. President Dmitri Medvedev told the Russian security council this month [August]: 'Everyone is talking about climate change now. Unfortunately, what is happening now in our central region is evidence of this global climate change, because we have never in our history faced such weather conditions in the past' ... It will be a year or two before climate scientists publish definitive analyses of the Russian heatwave and the Pakistani floods, which might shed light on the role of climate change. Some scientists suspect they were caused or worsened by an unusual kink in the jet stream, the high altitude flow of air that helps determine weather patterns, though that itself might be linked to climate changes. Certain recent weather events were so extreme that a few scientists are shedding their traditional reluctance to ascribe specific disasters to global warming.

(www.iht.com, 15 August 2010; *IHT*, 16 August 2010, pp. 1, 4)

Russia is the third biggest emitter of greenhouse gases globally, behind only China and the United States. Yet Russia's attitude to climate change to date has been cavalier, at best. Indeed, until recently its leaders seemed to believe climate change would be beneficial. Warmer weather would open up the Arctic's mineral wealth, create new shipping routes along its northern coast, and extend agriculture into infertile areas. At a conference in 2003 Vladimir Putin, then president, even said global warming would merely mean that 'we Russians will spend less on fur coats' ... No one can say with certainly that the fires were influenced by climate change. Yet they are the sort of disasters that lie ahead if warming is not held in check. Russia, by virtue of its size and variable continental climate, is unusually vulnerable to the extreme weather that climate change will bring. Flooding, in particular, will be a problem for cities such as St Petersburg. Changes in the flow of rivers, storms, melting ice and many other hazards will cause difficulties, too. Russia's leaders had slowly begun to change their tone even before this summer. A climate plan was endorsed by the government in 2009. President Dmitri Medvedev announced in the run-up to the climate change meetings in Copenhagen that Russia would accept a target of reducing its carbon emissions by 15 to 20 per cent below 1990 levels, later elevated to 20 to 25 per cent. Critics correctly point out, however, that even these higher figures would see Russian carbon emissions increase, once the effects of the collapse of heavy industry are taken into account. Mr Medvedev may have agreed to them in part because, as yet, little follows from their acceptance. Even so, they mark an encouraging shift of emphasis. Mr Medvedev has also recently stressed the importance of achieving greater energy efficiency, an important step given the profligate way Russia uses energy. In a recent speech he also explicitly linked the heatwave to climate change ... The emissions permits Russia already holds as a result of signing up to Kyoto could be put to good use, to fund more environmentally responsible policies. This would build on the moves in July [2010] when – finally starting to make use of its carbon credits – the government endorsed fifteen clean energy projects. The rest of the world has a further strong interest in helping Russia: limiting the damage likely to result from the effects of global warming upon Russia's frozen peat bogs. As they melt, these huge sinks of carbon will release vast amounts of methane into the air – and methane is a greenhouse gas many times more potent than CO_2.

(Anthony Giddens, *FT*, 27 August 2010, p. 9)

Moscow's daily death rate is now twice what it would be normally for the time of year. While officials have been careful not to link this to the heat and smog, doctors have been doing so off the record ... The extreme weather conditions and smog have also led to some factories closing down production lines temporarily ... The head of Moscow region's forestry directorate, Sergei Gordeichenko, has been sacked by the government. He remained on holiday even when a state of emergency was declared in the region because of the wildfires. President Dmitri Medvedev, who cut short his own summer holiday, said earlier that forestry service chiefs who had failed to return to work from holiday in spite of the fires should be sacked. Yuri Luzhkov, the mayor of Moscow, has come under Kremlin criticism for failing to return from holiday sooner. An unnamed Kremlin official said it was good that he had returned on Sunday [8 August] but he should have returned earlier. Prime minister Vladimir Putin summoned Mr Luzhkov on Tuesday [10 August] for a report on the situation. Mr Putin also spent part of the day aboard a fire-fighting plane dropping water on forest fires in the Ryazan region.

(www.bbc.co.uk, 10 August 2010)

'An inquiry by prosecutors in one area showed that the local authorities did not have even basic firefighting equipment and that officials did not co-ordinate efforts properly' (*IHT*, 11 August 2010, p. 3).

Economists warned that the wildfires and disastrous summer harvest could wipe as much as 1 per cent [1 percentage point] off the country's economic growth ... Economists have predicted that Russia's economy will grow by about 4 per cent this year [2010] ... Industrial enterprises, including Avtovaz and GAZ, Russia's biggest car makers, closed assembly lines this month, claiming high temperatures made working conditions unbearable on factory floors ... Surging grain prices are likely to stoke inflation, economists say, undermining the government's success in driving down inflation to record post-Soviet levels. Renaissance Capital, a Moscow investment bank, recently raised its inflation forecast from 6.3 per cent to 7 per cent to 7.5 per cent.

(*FT*, 11 August 2010, p. 5)

Prices of basic foodstuffs have soared, prompting accusations that farmers are hoarding grain ... Russian flour and cereal prices rose by more than 9 per cent in July, doubling the expected inflation rate ... President Dmitri Medvedev ordered law enforcers to clamp down on food price speculators last week, saying the failed harvest was affecting the 'most sensitive foodstuffs', including bread and milk ... If drought prevents the sowing of winter wheat, Russia could be forced to turn to world markets to fulfil its grain needs next year.

(*FT*, 16 August 2010, p. 7)

Russia is mounting extra patrols to fight wildfires in a region hit by nuclear fallout from Chernobyl, amid fears that radiation could spread. Crews put out several fires in Bryansk, the emergencies ministry said, amid concern that wind or fire could whip up radioactive particles in the soil. Officials say they are assessing the danger and there is no need to panic. The chief of the forest protection service said his agency had increased patrols around the forests in Bryansk, the part of Russia that suffered the most from the Chernobyl disaster in what was then Soviet Ukraine. Agency chief Vladimir Rozinkevich: 'There is a danger, but we are controlling the situation' ... Environmental groups, including Greenpeace, have warned that radioactive particles which settled into the soil after the 1986 disaster could be thrown up into the air once again by wildfires and blown into other areas by the wind.

(www.bbc.co.uk, 11 August 2010)

Officials from Russia's national forest protection service confirmed that fires were burning at contaminated sites and expressed fears that lax oversight as a result of recent changes in the forestry service could increase the chances that radioactive smoke would waft into populated areas. It is unclear what health risks the radiation could pose, or to what extent radioactive particles have spread in the weeks that wildfires have been raging throughout Russia, consuming villages and blanketing huge tracts of land with thick smoke.

(*IHT*, 12 August 2010, p. 3)

[Moscow mayor] Yuri Luzhkov left for holidays and 'treatment for a serious sports injury' ... on 2 August and did not return until Sunday [8 August] ... [He has been] in office since 1992 ... Prime minister Vladimir Putin greeted the tanned-looking mayor in a televised meeting yesterday [10 August], saying: 'You were quite right to return from your vacation. Your timing is perfect' ... Observers interpreted the comments as disapproval.

(www.guardian.co.uk, 11 August 2010)

The skies cleared and air quality significantly improved for a second straight day in Moscow on Thursday [12 August] ... The wind shifted direction to blow the smoke out of the city beginning Wednesday [11 August], and firefighters have succeeded in extinguishing a number of forest fires burning near the capital. In central Russia improved conditions led to the lifting of the state of emergency in three regions. The state of emergency was still in effect in Moscow and other areas, and forecasters, however, warned that smoke could periodically waft back over the capital for weeks, with the main culprits hard-to-extinguish fires in dried-out peat bogs ... The authorities said Thursday they had detected no increase in radiation levels in Moscow or elsewhere after wildfires burned some forests that had been contaminated after the 1986 Chernobyl disaster.

(www.iht.com, 12 August 2010)

'The levels of carbon monoxide and fine particles, the worst air quality offenders, had declined to well within acceptable levels [in Moscow] by Thursday [12 August], officials said. Traffic picked up, and more foreign embassies reopened' (*IHT*, 13 August 2010, p. 3).

A quarter of Russian crops have been lost in the recent drought, leaving many farms on the brink of bankruptcy, President Dmitri Medvedev said Thursday [12 August]. The government should prevent increases in the price of grain and fodder, which will eventually affect the prices of food products like flour, bread, meat and milk, Medvedev said at a government agriculture meeting in the southern region of Rostov ... He said government authorities should closely monitor food prices on a daily basis: 'Otherwise there will always be someone who would want to capitalize on this situation. There are such cases already' ... Alexander Frolov, who heads the meteorological service Roshydromet, said this week that virtually no rain is forecast in Russia this month. The situation is so bad in some regions that there is 'no reason' to start planting winter crops, Frolov said ... Prime minister Vladimir Putin [said that] ... some regions won't be sowing winter grains at all this year ... On Thursday President Medvedev lifted the state of emergency in three of seven regions most affected by wildfires.

(www.cnn.com, 12 August 2010)

'The crisis ... has killed at least forty-three people' (www.economist.com, 12 August 2010).

Doctors in Moscow are being told not to diagnose heatstroke as a cause of death after a jump in the mortality rate during the heatwave, Russia media say ... The number of people said to have been killed by the fires directly stands at fifty-four ... But little has been revealed officially about the number of people who succumbed to temperatures approaching 40 Celsius (104 Fahrenheit) and choking smog from the fires ... While wildfires continue to burn, temperatures are starting to drop ... While wildfires continued to burn up to 100 kilometres (60 miles) away from the site of the Chernobyl nuclear accident in Ukraine, experts said there was little danger of serious radioactive contamination ... President Dmitri Medvedev said the fires had destroyed a quarter of the agricultural land where cereals are grown.

(www.bbc.co.uk, 13 August 2010)

Russia has imposed a ban on grain exports until the end of the year ... Agriculture ministry data has revealed that this year's crop is unlikely to meet even domestic demand ... Russians eat bread with practically everything and rising bread prices is an issue which has traditionally had the power to stoke popular unrest ... Prime minister Vladimir Putin said that this year's crop could be as low as 60 million tonnes, well below last year's 97 million tonnes, and Russia needs almost 80 million tonnes for the Russian consumer. The Kremlin says talks on the issues will be held in October. Last year Russia exported a quarter of its 2009 grain output ... On Saturday [14 August] heavy rain cooled the capital.

(www.bbc.co.uk, 15 August 2010)

'The poisonous smog ... returned to Russia's capital today [Sunday 15 August]' (www.guardian.co.uk, 15 August 2010).

Firefighters have succeeded in pushing back wildfires while an advancing cold front is expected to finally put an end to a two-month heatwave, officials said Monday [16 August] ... Meteorologists say that a cold front advancing from the north-west will hit the Moscow region Monday, bringing heavy rains and colder temperatures ... The authorities have insisted that all wildfires in the Bryansk region and other Chernobyl-affected areas have been quickly dealt with ... The regional branch of the emergencies situations ministry said on Monday there are no fires burning now in the area and radiation levels have remained normal.

(www.iht.com, 16 August 2010)

Russia's record-breaking heatwave looks set to come to a dramatic end, with a severe storm now heading for Moscow after battering St Petersburg ... Moscow is expected to be hit later. Temperatures there dropped to 25 Celsius on Monday [16 August] after nearing 40 Celsius for weeks ... The emergencies ministry said the area affected by peat and forest fires was down to 45,800 hectares, compared to a peak of almost 200,000 hectares ... More than fifty people have died in the forest fires, but the wider death toll is much larger ... More people perished from the direct effects of the heat, or from drowning while trying to escape it, or from the smog that has blanketed Moscow and other regions during the fires. The smog has returned to Moscow, despite the lower temperatures and reduced fire area, but is expected to be dispersed by the coming winds ... Environmentalist and regional legislator Lyudmila Kolmogortseva warned that radioactive material near Bryansk still posed a threat. She said: 'Almost a million cubic metres of dead radioactive wood pose serious danger if the fires spread. The forest is practically impenetrable, and we practically have no aviation so we'll have nothing to fight the fires if they spread' ... Officials said any fires that had reached the area so far have been extinguished.

(www.iht.com, 16 August 2010)

Ukraine may cut grain exports for the remainder of 2010, following the impact on crops of a severe drought. The move would follow Russia's ban on grain exports on Sunday [15 August] because of drought and a spate of wildfires. Ukraine's cabinet will discuss whether to cut exports at a meeting on Wednesday [18 August] ... The news sent wholesale wheat prices higher ... Over the last decade the Black Sea region has emerged as a key exporter of grain to global markets. Ukraine is the world's largest exporter of barley and the sixth biggest of wheat. The country exported 21 million tonnes of grain in the year to June. But Mykola Prysyazhnyuk, Ukraine's agricultural policy minister, said: 'We are proposing to allow the export of 2.5 million tonnes from now until the end of the year' ... One million tonnes currently held in ports would also be exported, he said. Russia [was] the world's third largest wheat exporter last year [2009] ... An EU spokesman said on Tuesday [17 August] that the EU has plenty of grain stocks and export bans will not hurt supplies.

(www.bbc.co.uk, 17 August 2010)

Ukraine, one of the world's largest grain producers, is set to impose quotas on its grain exports to protect national food supplies after poor weather damaged crops, government officials said yesterday [17 August] ... [In] the 2007–8 food crisis countries from India to Argentina imposed trade restrictions ... Citing the need to secure Ukraine's 'food security', Mykola Prysyazhnyuk, the agriculture minister, said his government would decide today [18 August] on final quota levels after discussions with grain traders. Ukraine is traditionally the world's largest exporter of barley, with a 35 per cent market share, as well as being a big supplier of wheat to North Africa and the Middle East. Wheat prices have risen more than 50 per cent since June, while the price of barley – used for feeding animals and brewing beer – has more than doubled ... Officials and traders said Ukraine would seek to limit exports of milling wheat to 500,000 tonnes, feed wheat to 1 million tonnes, and barley to 1 million tonnes. That would mark a sharp drop from the 9.3 million tonnes of wheat and 6.2 million tonnes of barley the country exported in 2009–10, according to US government data. Quotas were not expected on other crops. Wheat prices were little moved by the news, with European wheat futures remaining at a historically high level of Euro 208 ($268) a tonne, but below the recent peak of Euro 230. Some fear Kazakhstan, the sixth largest wheat exporter, may also impose some form of export restriction, although the government has said it has no such plans ... Kiev is conscious of the need to keep bread prices low for citizens recovering from the economic recession. To achieve this, the government wants to buy millions of tonnes of milling wheat for its state reserves. Traders said the quotas, expected to be introduced in September, were a compromise from the Ukrainian government after weeks of tense negotiations ... Traders have accused Kiev of informally freezing exports through administrative means, and called for a formal ban. This would shelter them from penalties for failing to meet export obligations as they could cite force majeure clauses. Ukrainian officials accused traders of manipulating the market and sparking panic to push up prices.

(*FT*, 18 August 2010, p. 6)

Ukraine ... unexpectedly put off a decision to introduce grain export quotas yesterday [18 August], saying it needed more time to study how much wheat and barley have already been shipped overseas. Wheat prices declined following Ukraine's decision to postpone the export limits.

(*FT*, 19 August 2010, p. 6)

'[Wheat] prices hit a two-year high recently, up 57 per cent in less than three months. And on Thursday [19 August] the price of wheat spiked again ... on reports that Russia may have to import millions of tonnes of wheat' (ww.iht.com, 19 August 2010).

Muscovites are finally in the clear ... Overnight rains helped clear the smoke, and showers over the next few days could help keep the air clean. Worries that wildfires in areas contaminated by the 1986 Chernobyl nuclear disaster would send up plumes of radioactive smoke also seem to have been unfounded ... The number of acres burning in Russia's central regions fell precipitously in the last twenty-four hours ... the Emergency Situations Ministry said Thursday [19 August] ... Only about 20 acres continued to burn in the Moscow region. Overall, nearly 28,000 acres were still burning across Russia ... down from a high of about 44,500.

(www.iht.com, 20 August 2010)

'Prime minister Vladimir Putin yesterday [Friday 20 August] sacked Russia's forestry chief, who was crticized over the failure to prevent the summer's devastating wildfires. Mr Putin dismissed Rosleskhoz head Alexei Savinov' (*The Independent*, 21 August 2010, p. 25).

Prime minister Vladimir Putin has sacked the head of the forestry agency for failing to deal adequately with the recent wildfires ... Mr Putin replaced Alexei Savinov with his deputy, Viktor Maslyakov ... During the recent crisis Mr Savinov had faced criticism that he kept a low profile and had failed to make efficient use of government funds allocated for fire prevention. On Friday [20 August] President Dmitri Medvedev lifted a state of emergency around Moscow, Nizhny Novgorod and Mordovia. Heavy rain has brought respite to the capital with temperatures falling from 32 Celsius (89.6 Fahrenheit) to 9 Celsius (48 Fahrenheit) in two days.

(www.iht.com, 21 August 2010)

Drought in Russia will cut economic growth up to 0.8 percentage points this year while pushing inflation up above target levels, Andrei Klepach, the country's deputy economy ministry said Tuesday [24 August]. The rouble, on the other hand, should be largely unaffected, as Russia will retain its trade surplus and reserves, he said.

(*IHT*, 25 August 2010, p. 17)

Early reports from Russia's harvest are showing that yields of wheat and barley are down drastically ... The harvest [is] about half over ... Across Russia the harvest has been diminished by more than 30 per cent, according to the ministry of agriculture. Russia will certainly produce less grain than it consumes for the first time since 2004, and may import wheat for the first time in a decade ... Russia, one of the world's largest grain exporters last year, may become a net importer this year ... On Friday [27 August] prime minister Vladimir Putin took another swipe at rising bread prices, saying that 'someone is simply cashing in on the circumstances' ... Prosecutors have raided bakeries in Moscow on accusations of price gouging, and a shortage of buckwheat led to panic buying throughout the country.

(*IHT*, 28 August 2010, p. 15)

The [US] Department of Agriculture is predicting that world wheat production will reach the same level this year – 645 million tonnes – that helped bring prices down from their astonishing $13.50 a bushel peak in February 2008 ... [That] episode of market volatility ... two years ago ... led to food riots in many parts of the world ... At present prices for December [2010] wheat are about $6.95 a bushel, down over 50 cents from a month ago, but up since early June [2010] ... Canada's wheat harvest may be off by 36 per cent this year, because of too much rain. Australia is unlikely to fill the Russian export gap because it is in the midst of extreme drought. Wheat and corn stockpiles could drop to their lowest since 2008, despite a very good wheat and corn harvest in the United States.

(www.iht.com, 28 August 2010)

The UN Food and Agricultural Organization (FAO) says that world food prices have risen to their highest level in two years. It says the increase is partly due to drought in Russia and to government export restrictions which have brought about a surge in the price of wheat. The Rome-based agency says that its food price index shot up 5 per cent between July and August. However, this is 38 per cent down from its peak in June 2008 ... The FAO now thinks that world cereal production will be 1.8 per cent lower than its June forecast. The wheat production forecast has been revised for the second time in a month. It is expected to be 5 per cent lower than in 2009. But despite these falls, world cereal and wheat production levels would still be the third highest on record, the UN agency said.

(www.iht.com, 1 September 2010)

Russia will consider lifting its grain export ban only after the next harvest has been reaped, prime minister Vladimir Putin has said ... Global wheat prices have risen by 1.4 per cent on Thursday [2 September], after gaining more than 3 per cent during the previous session ... Mr Putin said that the ban was extended to 'provide stability and predictable conditions for all market participants' ... In 2009 Russia exported a quarter of its annual grain output of 97 million tonnes. This year's crop could be as low as 60 million tonnes, but Russia needs almost 80 million tonnes just to cover domestic consumption.

(www.bbc.co.uk, 2 September 2010)

Prime minister Vladimir Putin announced Thursday [2 September] that Russia's ban on grain exports ... would be extended well into next year [2011] because of continued uncertainty over production. The government had been scheduled to review the ban toward the end of this year [2010], but Mr Putin indicated at a meeting of senior officials that to ensure stability in the domestic grain market, grain exports should be halted for considerable longer than that. Mr Putin said: 'I believe that we must make clear that we can examine the cancellation of the ban on exports only after next year's harvest is gathered and there is clarity regarding grain levels. There should be no frantic movement here' ... The ban was intended to last until 31 December [2010] and it was not entirely clear from Mr Putin's comments on Thursday exactly how much longer it would be prolonged. But he seemed to be suggesting that it would go through autumn 2010. Analysts estimate that this year's harvest will fall by roughly a third. Last year Russia was the world's third largest wheat exporter, behind the United States and Canada. In his remarks Thursday Mr Putin also demanded that officials crack down on food speculators, seeking to calm a public that has grown jittery because of rising prices for meat, flour, pasta and other staples.

(www.iht.com, 3 September 2010)

'A new wave of wildfires killed one person and destroyed at least sixty buildings Thursday [2 September] in the Volgograd region' (*IHT*, 3 September 2010, p. 3).

At least four people have died in a new outbreak of wildfires ... In the south of the country fire swept through villages and towns, destroying hundreds of homes and other buildings ... While temperatures have eased in much of Russia, they are still high in the south, reaching almost 40 Celsius ... At least fifteen villages and towns have been affected in the Volgograd and Saratov regions, some 1,000 kilometres (600 miles) south-east of Moscow ... East of Moscow, although there has been heavy rain and much cooler temperatures recently, peat fires are still burning, and firefighters are still hard at work trying to prevent another major outbreak of fires near the capital.

(www.bbc.co.uk 3 September 2010)

'Eight people were killed and more than 400 homes were destroyed by fresh wildfires ... in Volgograd and Saratov provinces' (*The Times*, 4 September 2010, p. 39).

A UN food agency said Friday [3 September] it has called a special meeting on the recent spike in food prices, responding to fears of a repeat of the shortages that led to riots in parts of the world two years ago. The announcement by the Rome-based Food and Agriculture Organization followed Russia's decision to extend its ban on wheat exports. The ban has been held as partly responsible for the 5 per cent increase in food prices worldwide over the last two months, to their highest level in two years ... [A spokesman for the FAO] said the meeting of the inter-governmental committee on grains will be held on 24 September ... He said a large number of member countries had expressed concern about a possible repeat of the 2008 food crisis. Mozambique saw deadly riots this week triggered in part by an increase in the price of bread. There has also been anger over rising prices in Egypt and Serbia, while in Pakistan – where floods destroyed a fifth of the country's crops – the prices of many food items have risen by 15 per cent. However, agency officials and other experts have been stressing that the conditions are different from 2008, when high oil prices and growing demand for biofuels pushed world food stocks to their lowest levels since 1982. Drought in Russia – and the country's subsequent restrictions on wheat exports – forced a sudden sharp rise in wheat prices, the agency said. Higher sugar and oilseed prices were also factors in the higher index. Russian prime minister Vladimir Putin went on television Thursday [2 September] to announce he has extended Russia's ban on wheat exports until next year's harvest to ensure it has bounced back from the drought and wildfires that destroyed 20 per cent of the crop this year.

(www.iht.com, 3 September 2010)

Food prices rose 5 per cent globally in August, according to the United Nations, spurred mostly by the higher cost of wheat, and the first signs of unrest erupted as ten people died in Mozambique during clashes ignited partly by a 30 per cent leap in the cost of bread ... After two days of rioting set off by price increases for bread and utilities like electricity and water, the streets in Maputo, the capital of Mozambique, were largely calm on Friday [3 September] ... Harvest forecasts in Germany and Canada are clouded by wet weather and flooding, while crops in Argentina will suffer from drought, as could Australia's, according to agricultural experts ... Food prices are still some 30 per cent below the 2008 levels ... said Abdolreza Abbassian, an economist at the FAO ... when a tripling in the price of rice among other staples led to food riots in about a dozen countries and helped topple at least one government. The wheat crop this year globally is the third highest on record, according to the FAO ... In June Russia was predicting a loss of just a few million tonnes due to hot weather, but by August it announced it would lose about one-fifth of its crop. Wheat prices more than doubled in that period ... A decade ago, the area around the Black Sea – mainly Russia, Ukraine and Kazakhstan – used to supply just about 4 per cent of the wheat traded internationally. But most of the growth in demand globally has been supplied from there, and the region now produces about 30 per cent of the wheat traded internationally, said Mr Abbassian. This is the first time a supply crisis has originated from that area, he noted ... Prime minister Vladimir Putin announced Thursday that the ban on grain exports would extend into 2011.

The price of wheat jumped again, and that has had a spillover effect into other grains like corn and soybeans. The forecast for the global rice harvest has also dropped, although it is still expected to be higher than in 2009 and should be a record, the FAO said. Mr Abbassian: 'If you look at the numbers globally, the Americans, the Europeans and Australians can make up the supply. There is no reason for this hype, but once the psychological thing sets in it is hard to change that perception, especially if Russia keeps sending bad news … People still remember what happened a few years ago, so it is a combination of psychology and the expectation that worse may come. There are critical months ahead' … As with any commodity, questions of wheat shortages spur speculation and hoarding, and experts expect both are at play in the current market.

(www.iht.com, 4 August 2010; *IHT*. 6 September 2010, pp. 1, 5)

Russia's grain export ban will be lifted as soon as it is clear how much has been harvested, President Dmitri Medvedev has said. It contradicts prime minister Vladimir Putin, who said last week that the ban could be lifted only after next year's harvest has been reaped. Usually, Russia's harvest results become clear in October … Mr Medvedev said on Monday [6 September]: 'The grain embargo is a forced temporary measure. As soon as it is clear how much we have harvested, all sorts of embargoes will be lifted, you do not need to doubt that.'

(www.bbc.co.uk, 6 September 2010)

In the earlier crisis … of 2007–8 … violent protests shook many countries, including Egypt, Haiti, Côte d'Ivoire, Uzbekistan and Bolivia … [Wheat] prices now are still more than 40 per cent below those record highs … The FAO estimates world wheat production this year at 646 million tonnes, 5 per cent down on 2009's bumper crop but still the third highest on record, thanks to excellent harvests in America and Canada. Australia is also set for a weighty crop, having successfully dealt with a threatened plague of locusts. Last year's bonanza replenished stocks, which stood at a seven-year high at the beginning of the year. By 2011 these inventories will be run down to around 181 million tonnes but this is still a lot more than the 144 million tonnes of wheat stocks at the height of the food crisis … Countries such as Russia and Ukraine used to be insignificant exporters: better farming there means they supply some 30 per cent of the world's wheat. Other growers in the northern hemisphere have planted less. Abdolreza Abbassian of the FAO thinks that the variable weather in the region around the Black Sea makes it inherently less suited to cereal cultivation … During the previous food crisis several countries, including Argentina and India as well as Russia, reacted to the spiralling price of food crops with export bans.

(www.economist.com, 9 September 2010; *The Economist*, 11 September 2010, pp. 61–2)

'Moscow has set a target to plant 18 million hectares of winter wheat this year as part of a plan to boost grain production to 80 to 90 million tonnes in

2010–11. But analysts believe the goal is unrealistic because dry weather will prevent some winter wheat crops from thriving' (*FT*, 1 October 2010, p. 3).

Official data on the devastation will not be known until next month [November] but with the harvest almost complete, the Institute of Agricultural Markets, an agriculture consultancy in Moscow, estimates 23 per cent of the area sown with grain was destroyed and with other areas suffering damage, more than a third of the crop was lost ... The export ban not only drew international criticism, it failed to halt a surge in food prices as Russians, haunted by memories of Soviet-era shortages, hoarded supplies ... Prime minister Vladimir Putin is determined to revive agriculture and ensure Russia's food self-sufficiency, ending what he calls a "humiliating dependence on foreign bread" ... The global food crisis of 2007–8 prompted the Kremlin to draw up a food security doctrine setting a goal for Russia to produce at least 80 per cent of the cereals, meat and milk it needs by 2010. Since the drought, Mr Putin has raised the bar, calling for Russia to become a net food exporter, relying on foreign markets only for exotic products such as "tropical fruit" ... Despite some of the world's most fertile soil, grain yields in the Black Earth region are a third of those in Western Europe. Grain storage and transport bottlenecks hamper deliveries to shoppers and ports. Analysts believe many small farmers, who account for half of Russian food production, could be bankrupted by the drought. But larger agricultural groups will not curtail their investment plans.

(*FT*, 5 October 2010, p. 11)

Ukraine has set quotas for grain exports following a severe drought in the summer ... The quota would remain in place until the end of the year [2010]. The government will allow the export of 2 million tonnes of maize, 500,000 tonnes of wheat and 500,000 tonnes of barley ... In August Ukraine's government reduced its forecast for the year's grain harvest to 39 million tonnes from 46 million tonnes in 2009. Ukraine, the world's top producer of barley, was hard hit by this summer's heatwave.

(www.bbc.co.uk, 7 October 2010)

Russia's death rate rose by more than a quarter during August's heatwave and forest fire crisis, official data show. According to the state statistics office, 41,262 more people died during the same month of 2009. The highest rise in mortality was recorded in Moscow and other regions badly affected by the heat such as Samara and Voronezh. Reports of an alarming rise in the death rate back in August were slapped down by the Kremlin. But the data published on the state statistics office website show that 191,951 people died across Russia in August 2010, compared to 150,689 in August 2009. In the city of Moscow 15,016 people died compared to 8,905 the previous year. Russian demographer Sergei Zakharov told the BBC's Russian service that no data was available on causes of death but he accepted that "the intense heat and smog [from burning peat bogs] could have led to a rise in the death rate". Asked why there had been no appreciable rise in the mortality rate in July, despite that month's equally scorching temperatures, he suggested that the extreme weather had taken time to wear down its victims. There was much anger among the Russian public over the authorities' handling of the heat crisis, amid suspicion that the Kremlin was trying to play down its full extent. In early August Russia media reported that doctors in Moscow were being told not to diagnose heatstroke as a cause of death. One doctor was quoted as saying the unofficial instruction being passed down was to use diagnoses that sounded "less frightening".

(www.bbc.co.uk, 8 October 2010)

Postscript

A chronology of political developments

22 September 2010.

A top Russian general has confirmed that a sale of S-300 air defence missiles to Iran will not go ahead because of UN sanctions. General Nikolai Makarov, head of the General Staff, told reporters the missiles were 'definitely' subject to new sanctions introduced in June. At the time Russia's foreign minister said the S-300 deal was not affected ... Back in June foreign minister Sergei Lavrov said a fourth round of sanctions imposed by the UN Security Council on Iran over its nuclear programme would not affect the S-300 contract. However, shortly afterwards prime minister Vladimir Putin was quoted by French media as saying the sale had been suspended ... General Makarov: ;The decision has been taken not to supply 3-300 [systems] to Iran. They are definitely subject to sanctions.'

(www.bbc.co.uk, 22 September 2010)

Russia blocked weapons sales to Iran on Wednesday [22 September] because of UN sanctions ... Armed Forces Chief of Staff General Nikolai Makarov: 'A decision has been made not to supply S-300s to Iran as they are definitely subject to the sanctions. There has been an instruction from the country's leadership to stop the deliveries, and we are obeying it' ... President Dmitri Medvedev signed a decree that prohibits: 'The transfer across Russia, including by air, the removal from Russia to Iran, and the transfer to Iran outside Russia of any combat tanks, armoured personnel carriers, large-calibre artillery systems, warplanes, attack helicopters, military vessels, missiles or missile systems as defined by the United Nations Register of Conventional Arms, S-300 surface-to-air missile systems, or materiel and spare parts used for all of the above.'

(www.cnn.com, 22 September 2010)

The [UN] Security Council's fourth round of sanctions against Iran [was] passed in June. The sanctions did not specifically include the contentious S-300 missiles, and there was confusion over whether Russia would still go ahead with its contract to sell them to Iran. The missiles would have been the backbone of a mobile, long-range air defence system that could thwart any military strike on a nuclear site in Iran ... Russian media had reported that the S-300 contract was worth $800 million. After the Security Council passed the latest sanctions, French officials said that prime minister Vladimir Putin told French president Nicolas Sarkozy that Moscow would halt delivery of the missiles ... President Dmitri Medvedev's statement on Wednesday [22 September] also banned some financial transactions with Iran and barred some Iranian nuclear and military officials from travelling to Russia.

(www.iht.com, 23 September 2010)

'Russian officials had quietly told American and French officials in June that ... President Dmitri Medvedev ... would interpret the UN sanctions against Iran as mandating that Russia should permanently halt delivery of S-300 missiles' (www.iht.com, 23 September 2010).

Poland has complained to Russia that it is dissatisfied with Russia's inquiry into the April plane crash that killed President Lech Kaczynski and ninety-four others ... [Poland] said Wednesday [22 September] that it had not received needed information about Smolensk airport ... At issue is whether the flight was civilian or military, a potentially crucial point in assigning responsibility for the decision to land. Russia considers the flight civilian ... which would make the crew or others on board responsible for the decision.

(*IHT*, 24 September 2010, p. 3)

23 September 2010.
Prime minister Vladimir Putin has rejected talks of an impending battle for control of the Arctic region's mineral resources. He told an international conference in Moscow [lasting two days] he was confident the region's resources could be exploited in a spirit of partnership. Russia believes the UN will recognize its claim to much of the Arctic seabed. The scramble for resources has been set in motion partly by improved access caused by the melting of polar ice. Russia, Norway, Canada, Denmark and the United States have all laid claims to territory in the region. Mr Putin told the International Arctic Forum on its closing day [23 September]: 'One comes across all sorts of fantastical predictions about a coming battle for the Arctic. We can see clearly that most of these frightening scenarios in the Arctic have no real foundation. I am in no doubt whatsoever that the existing problems of the Arctic, including those of the continental shelf, may be resolved in a spirit of partnership, through negotiations, on the basis of existing international legal norms' ... One quarter of the Earth's untapped energy riches are believed to be buried in the Arctic sea floor. The race for control centres on an underwater mountain ridge known as the Lomonosov Ridge. Russia, Canada and Denmark are all seeking scientific proof that the ridge is an underwater extension of their continental shelf. In 2001 Moscow submitted a territorial claim to the United Nations which was rejected because of lack

of evidence. It plans to resubmit the claim in 2010–13 after spending some 2 billion roubles ($64 million) on research ... Canada is likely to hand its file to the UN around 2013, while Denmark plans to put forward its details by the end of 2014. Under the UN Convention on the Law of the Sea, a coastal nation can claim exclusive economic rights to natural resources on or beneath the sea floor up to 200 nautical miles (370 kilometres) beyond their land territory. But if the continental shelf extends beyond that distance, the country must provide evidence to a UN commission which will then make recommendations about establishing an outer limit.

(www.bbc.co.uk, 23 September 2010)

On Wednesday [23 September] ... Russia ... announced plans to start work soon on a new atlas of the Arctic ... While Russia counts for the bulk of Arctic land, seven other states have land in Arctic territory: Canada, Denmark (Greenland), the United States (Alaska), Iceland, Norway, Sweden and Finland. No single country owns the geographic North Pole or the Arctic Ocean, which covers around one third of the total area. Under the United Nations Convention on the Law of the Sea, the eight states have jurisdiction over waters extending 12 nautical miles from their shore, and their exclusive economic zones stretch up to 200 nautical miles into the Arctic Ocean.

(www.cnn.com, 23 September 2010)

Prime minister Vladimir Putin ... called for the preservation of its 'unique nature and fragile ecosystem'. He also announced a major clean-up of rubbish left behind during communist times ... [It was announced that there would be an] expedition next month [October] to launch a floating research station in the Arctic. The station – together with an icebreaker and a research ship already in position – would gather fresh scientific evidence to bolster the Kremlin's claims to the Arctic, which Russia identified two years ago as a 'strategic economic resource' ... The conference has been dubbed 'The Arctic: Territory of Dialogue'. It brings together 300 participants, including scientists, environmental campaigners and government Arctic envoys.

(www.guardian.co.uk, 23 September 2010)

Russia on Thursday [23 September] turned over to Poland twenty new files from a probe into the 1940 Katyn massacre that could be key in proving that Soviet secret police carefully planned the killing of ... some 20,000 Polish officers and other prominent citizens ... The files contain the full list of the Polish prisoners of war executed in the Katyn forest, Russian secret police documents confirming their dispatch there as well as interrogation protocols and files confirming the burial place of the Poles ... [Russia said it is] continuing its work to fulfil Poland's request to provide more files.

(www.iht.com, 23 September 2010)

24 September 2010.

Former Soviet vice president Gennadi Yanayev ... died in a Moscow hospital aged seventy-three ... after a lengthy illness ... The twelve-member State Emergency Committee held power for only three days [in August 1991] ... President Mikhail Gorbachev was on holiday in the Crimea, in Ukraine, when the group announced it was seizing power, with Vice President Yanayev becoming president.

(www.bbc.co.uk, 24 September 2010)

Soviet government hardliners ... including the head of the KGB and the minister of defence ... seized power on 19 August 1991 ... Mr Yanayev was one of the twelve members of the so-called State Emergency Committee that announced Mikhail Gorbachev ... [who] was on a short holiday in the Crimea at the time ... was being replaced As the conspirators declared a state of emergency, Gennadi Yanayev named himself acting president ... Mikhail Gorbachev appointed him vice president in 1990 ... For three days the so-called State Committee of Emergency held control ... Mr Yanayev and the other plotters ... were arrested ... President Mikhail Gorbachev, who had been sequestered by the plotters in Crimea, now a part of Ukraine, returned to Moscow ... The plotters were imprisoned after the coup, but were released and later granted amnesty in 1994. In a 2008 interview with a Russian newspaper, Mr Yanayev denied playing a critical role in the coup plot, saying that he was pressured by more hard-line leaders to sign the documents declaring his presidency ... Mr Yanayev's hand shook visibly as he announced that he was taking over as president ... In 1993 the newspaper *Novy Vzglyad* quoted Mr Yanayev as saying that he was drunk when he signed the decree, but that he denied inebriation affected his judgement ... Mr Yanayev and his fellow plotters were arrested and jailed after the coup collapsed, but he and the others were released in 1993 and amnestied by parliament a year later ... Gennadi Zyuganov (leader of the Communist Party of the Russian Federation): 'Yanayev lived an interesting, difficult and worthy life. If they [the coup leaders] had been more decisive, they could have succeeded in preserving our country and completely turned around the difficult situation of that time.'

(www.iht.com, 24 September 2010)

26–28 September 2010.

President Dmitri Medvedev arrived in China on Sunday [26 September], amid growing energy co-operation between the two countries ... Mr Medvedev, who landed in the north-eastern port city of Dalian, visited a war memorial and met with Chinese and Russian war veterans as well as local leaders. He then flew to Beijing for meetings Monday [27 September] with prime minister Wen Jiabao and Wu Bangguo, chairman of the National People's Congress. No agenda for Mr Medvedev's three-day visit has been made public.

(*IHT*, 27 September 2010, p. 3)

China and Russia have signed a series of agreements to boost energy co-operation during a ceremony to open an oil pipeline between the countries. Leaders of the two nations agreed deals on gas supplies, energy efficiency, renewable energy and nuclear power. President Dmitri Medvedev is visiting China, where he and President Hu Jintao opened a pipeline that will supply Russian oil under a twenty-year deal ... [Russia said it was] in talks with China on plans to supply natural gas from 2015 ... In August Russia opened its section of a 625-mile (1,000-kilometre) oil pipeline from eastern Siberia to China. The pipe connects Russian oil fields with Daqing, a major oil production base in north-eastern China.

(www.bbc.co.uk, 27 September 2010)

28 September 2010.

The mayor of Moscow, Yuri Luzhkov, a dominant figure in the two decades since the Soviet collapse, was dismissed on Tuesday [28 September] after the two had engaged in an increasingly rancorous feud. The Kremlin said in a statement that Mr Medvedev has 'lost trust' in Mr Luzhkov ... Mr Luzhkov just turned seventy-four ... Mr Luzhkov recently appeared to call for Vladimir Putin to return to the presidency. Russia's president is allowed to fire public officials such as the mayor of Moscow. Mr Medvedev, who is on a visit to China, appointed deputy mayor Vladimir Resin as acting mayor.

(www.iht.com, 28 September 2010)

Yuri Luzhkov was being removed because he has lost 'the trust of the president of the Russian Federation', a presidential decree said. In recent weeks Mr Luzhkov – who has been in office since 1992 – had faced harsh criticism from the Kremlin ... Russia's constitution allows the president to fire the Moscow mayor and regional governors, and appoint successors without elections. Mr Luzhkov is one of Russia's most powerful politicians and is a senior member of the United Russia Party. Before the emergence of Vladimir Putin a decade ago, he was even tipped as a possible future president. However, the mayor has recently been the subject of a constant barrage from state-run television, which criticized him for gridlock on the capital's roads and bulldozing historic buildings. He and his billionaire wife, Yelena Baturina, have also been accused of corruption ... On Monday [27 September], after returning from a week's holiday in Austria, Mr Luzhkov said he would not stand down voluntarily.

(www.bbc.co.uk, 28 September 2010)

Yesterday [27 September] ... Yuri Luzhkov returned home [from holiday] ... He declared: 'I am not going to resign of my own accord' ... The presidential decree stated: 'Yuri Luzhkov is being relieved of his duties as Moscow mayor in connection with the Russian president's loss of confidence in him.'

(www.guardian.co.uk, 28 September 2010)

One news report detailed ways in which Yuri Luzhkov allegedly channelled funds and lucrative deals to his property developer wife, now Russia's richest woman. He was also criticized for failing to curb Moscow's notoriously bad traffic jams, and for going on a vacation during the forest fires and choking smog over the summer.

(www.cnn.com, 28 September 2010)

President Dmitri Medvedev said in Shanghai (where he is on an official visit): 'It is hard to imagine a situation in which a governor and a president of Russia, as the chief executive, can continue to work together when the president has lost confidence in the regional leader' … Legally, the Moscow mayor's position is equal in rank to a regional governor … Speculation over the future of the cap-wearing mayor had swirled in recent days, forcing him to declare on Monday [27 September] that he would not quit – an option that Medvedev's spokeswoman said the Kremlin had offered him. Luzhkov made no public comment, but in a resignation letter to United Russia, the ruling party headed by Putin, he suggested there had been an orchestrated campaign to oust him. Luzhkov said in a letter: 'Recently, being one of the party's leaders, I have been fiercely attacked by state mass media, and the attacks were related to the attempts to push Moscow's mayor off the political scene' … Luzhkov added he decided to leave the party because it 'did not provide any support, did not want to sort things out and stop the flow of lies and slander' … He helped to create … United Russia … Moscow has over 10 million people … Russia's capital sprouted gigantic construction projects … Much of that work was done by Inteko, the construction company headed by Luzkhov's wife, Yelena Baturina, who is believed to be Russia's only female dollar billionaire … During his tenure his wife has obtained much of the construction business in Moscow, becoming one of the world's richest women … Suspicions swirled constantly that corruption by Luzhkov fed his wife's wealth … Luzhkov is also disliked by preservationists for approving the destruction of historic buildings for new development. And he has sparred with gay rights groups after barring gay parades and referring to homosexuality as 'satanic' … The 2003 mayoral election [was] the last before Putin made the position by appointment only … [In July 2010] an ill-conceived repair project on the main highway to Moscow's Sheremetyevo international airport created backups that left drivers taking up to six hours to get there from the city … Controversy had brewed for years about plans to build a highway through a forest just outside Moscow that environmentalists wanted to protect. Medvedev in August ordered the project suspended, a decision that Luzhkov criticized in a newspaper article. Medvedev publicly dressed him down, telling a conference of political analysts Friday [24 September] that 'officials should either participate in building institutions, or should join the opposition' … Luzhkov, a gruff, plain-spoken politician with a fondness for keeping bees and wearing a Soviet worker's cap, came to office in 1992 … There were snarling traffic jams, soaring housing costs and cries of nepotism. But there were also allowances paid to pensioners, and a cleaner city ... Luzhkov once vied with Putin for the presidency, and he had his own power base in the capital ... In 2008 Ukraine banned ... Yuri Luzhkov ... from entering the country after he suggested the Crimean peninsula rightfully belongs to Russia, not Ukraine.

(www.iht.com, 28 September 2010)

The recession had already slowed the construction boom, but its future suddenly became an open question when President Dmitri Medvedev abruptly fired Yuri Luzhkov on Tuesday [28 September]. A day later the federal authorities announced twenty-four criminal investigations of city officials, and several cases related to construction ... The development model in this epicentre of mall and office block building blended private and public money and retained strong state control, including, in most cases, state ownership of land ... Mr Luzhkov has repeatedly denied conflicts of interest with his wife's business, and has won libel suits in city courts against news media that suggested otherwise ... As mayor of Moscow Mr Luzhkov blended populism and arm-twisting of businesses to contribute to pension funds, public works and church restorations ... One of Mr Luzhkov's deputy mayors, Alexander Ryabinin, resigned Wednesday [29 September], and later that day officials said they were investigating whether he accepted the title to a small building as a bribe from a developer ... Moscow constitutes by far the largest commercial real estate market on the continent.

(www.iht.com, 30 September 2010; *IHT*,
1 October 2010, p. 19)

Three state-controlled television channels mounted a co-ordinated attack on Yuri Luzhkov and Yelena Baturina, his billionaire wife ... Public opinion was outraged by news that the mayor's personal bee collection outside Moscow had been relocated to less hazardous climes ... The last straw was a newspaper article that Mr Luzhkov published in early September criticizing President Dmitri Medvedev's decision to suspend construction of a new road between Moscow and St Petersburg ... He [the mayor] also wrote of the need for the government to 'recover its true authority and meaning', a phrase widely interpreted as a call for Vladimir Putin to return to the presidency in 2012. Mr Medvedev's aides lost no time in accusing Mr Luzhkov of trying to drive a wedge between the president ... and the prime minister ... In 2004 Mr Putin abolished direct elections for regional posts and turned them into Kremlin appointments.

(www.economist.com, 28 September and 30 September 2010)

[In Yuri Luzhkov's] case [there was] a hint that regional elections ought to be revived. Mr Luzhkov may not be pursued by prosecutors) and his wife spends most of her time in Austria). But they have already set their sights on some in his entourage ... The Kremlin has fired or replaced all the most powerful regional leaders over the past eighteen months. It has the power to do this because it changed the law to abolish elections to these posts in 2004. Mr Luzhkov, who in 1999 was briefly a serious candidate for the presidency instead of Vladimir Putin, is by far the biggest name to have gone so far.

(www.economist.com, 30 September 2010)

On Tuesday [28 September] prime minister Vladimir Putin told reporters that he supported President Dmitri Medvedev's decision, though he did praise the mayor: 'Yuri Mikhailovich Luzhkov did a lot for the development of Moscow ... But it is clear that relations between the mayor of Moscow and the president were not working out. The mayor is subordinate to the president and not the other way around' ... Mr Medvedev ... has been clearing away a generation of older regional leaders who have long clung to power in Russia. The dismissal of Mr Luzhkov is the most pronounced step yet in this campaign.

(www.iht.com, 28 September 2010)

President Dmitri Medvedev ... has been quietly replacing a number of politically independent strongmen in sensitive local posts. They include Mintimir Shaimiev, president of the autonomous region of Tatarstan, who stood down in March [2010] after nineteen years in the job, and Murtaza Rakhimov, president of Bashkiria, who left in July [2010], having been in the post since 1993. Both Mr Shaimiev and Mr Rakhimov formally stood down voluntarily. Mr Rakhimov was even given a high state award for his services ... The ouster of Yuri Luzhkov marks the first time Mr Medvedev has used his constitutional power to fire a powerful local leader ... Mr Medvedev's spokeswoman confirmed to reporters that Mr Medvedev had informed prime minister Vladimir Putin of the decision in advance ... Officials close to Mr Putin briefed reporters that Mr Luzhkov should resign, just as officials close to Mr Medvedev did.

(*FT*, 29 September 2010, p. 7)

The conflict deepened when the federal Investigative Committee announced it was pursuing twenty-four corruption inquiries against city government officials ... Yelena Baturina is Russia's richest woman, worth an estimated $2.9 billion. She was a secretary at the city council when she met Yuri Luzhkov and founded her Inteko company in 1991, the year the couple married ... Before the financial crisis Inteko was reckoned to control 20 per cent of the capital's biggest building boom since the 1930s.

(*The Times*, 30 September 2010, p. 41)

Yuri Luzhkov has denied reports that he plans to contest his sacking ... Mr Luzhkov told a magazine he would not make an appeal nor would he stand for president at the 2012 election ... The former mayor ... was quoted by *New Times* magazine as saying although he would not appeal nor stand for president, he hoped to remain in politics ... The same magazine had published a highly critical letter from Mr Luzhkov to President Dmitri Medvedev, which he had sent to the Kremlin shortly before his sacking.

(www.bbc.co.uk, 30 September 2010)

Yuri Luzhkov ... says he is not entirely abandoning politics and intends to create an independent political movement to support democracy in Russia. Mr Luzhkov told an opposition magazine, *New Times*, in an interview published Monday [4 October]. Mr Luzhkov did not say he would set up a formal political party to challenge United Russia, which he helped lead until he was dismissed by President Dmitri Medvedev. And he did not explain what he meant by a political movement, though he did seem to suggest that he would not take part in parliamentary and presidential elections over the next two years ... Mr Luzhkov said he would not go to court to try to annul his dismissal,, maintaining that no judge would dare overrule the Kremlin. He said he had been cast aside because President Dmitri Medvedev and prime minister Vladimir Putin wanted a more obedient mayor before the national elections to help swing the vote. Yuri Luzhkov: 'They want their own person in charge' ... In the past Mr Luzhkov might have shunned *New Times*, which publishes fierce criticism of the Kremlin. But now ... he has turned to such news organizations to get across his views.

(www.iht.com, 5 October 2010)

In his first interview since being turfed out of office last week, Yuri Luzhkov said he ... planned to campaign against 'undemocratic laws' and create a reform movement similar to those that sprung up in the post-communist era of the early 1990s ... Yesterday [4 October] Mr Luzhkov named Natalia Timakova, and a Kremlin ideologist, Vladislav Surkov, as plotters of his downfall ... Yuri Luzhkov was also scathing about the United Russia Party – from which he resigned last week – calling it a spineless servant of the Kremlin.

(*Guardian*, 5 October 2010, p. 16)

Yuri Luzhkov told *New Times*: 'Our society is governed by undemocratic laws' ... He said that through the movement – which he stresses will not be a registered political party and will not take part in elections – he will 'work so that the laws of democratic society appear' in Russia ... Mr Luzhkov stepped back from earlier claims that he would challenge his firing in court ... He said: 'I do not believe that this supreme court will take a decision that would go against the president's order.'

(*The Independent*, 5 October 2010, p. 22)

Yuri Luzhkov ... has launched a stinging rebuke of the president ... Speaking in an exclusive CNN interview, Yuri Luzhkov accused President Dmitri Medvedev of overseeing 'calamities, terrorist acts, and bad harvests' during his period in power. Luzhkov said: 'When he fires or reshuffles officials, proposes projects on paper, those things are being taken quite sceptically. Any initiative is good, but it must lead to actual results, which has not been happening so far' ... In his interview with CNN Luzhkov said Wednesday

[6 October] that he believed he was fired to enable the Kremlin to tighten its grip on power. Luzhkov said: 'The presidential elections of 2012 are approaching. The authorities need the city of Moscow to support the candidate who they will propose. And they need a man from their circle as mayor of Moscow ... Mayor Luzhkov is unusual, self-sufficient, and independent. And they need someone who would follow the Kremlin's orders. That is why my career as Moscow mayor ended.'

(www.cnn.com, 7 October 2010)

29 September 2010.

President Dmitri Medvedev said Wednesday [29 September] that he planned to visit the Kuril Islands, saying they are 'a very important part' of the country and defying Japanese calls to avoid exacerbating a territorial dispute from World War II. Japanese government officials have said a visit to the region – called the Senkaku or Northern Territories in Japan and the Southern Kurils in Russia – could damage relations. Russia seized the islands at the end of World War II when Japan was defeated. The dispute over their ownership has prevented the two countries from signing a formal peace treaty.

(*IHT*, 30 September 2010, p. 6)

30 September 2010.

Kirsan Ilyumzhinov beat off a challenge from the former world champion Anatoli Karpov to win re-election as president of the World Chess Federation (Fide). Mr Ilyumzhinov has led Fide since 1995 ... The battle was marked by vicious campaigns as each candidate accused the other of intimidation ... Mr Ilyumzhinov is stepping down after seventeen years as head of the republic of Kalmykia in southern Russia.

(*The Times*, 30 September 2010, p. 41)

Anatoli Karpov's supporters described the ballot as a 'farce', and said Kirsan Ilyumzhinov' had used 'intimidation, bully-boy tactics' and even 'blatant corruption' to steamroller his way to victory ... [The] former leader of Russia's Kalmykia region claims to have been abducted by aliens ... [This year] President Dmitri Medvedev replaced Ilyumzhinov as leader of Kalmykia, a small, oil-rich, Buddhist region on the shores of the Caspian Sea. Despite toppling him from political office, the Kremlin has steadfastly backed Ilyumzhinov's bid to maintain his grip over chess's ruling body.

(*Guardian*, 30 September 2010, p. 19)

4 October 2010.

Russian President Dmitri Medvedev has launched a strong attack on President Alexander Lukashenko, who faces re-election in December ... President Medvedev accused his Belarusian counterpart of 'hysterical' anti-Russian rhetoric. He was responding to Mr Lukashenko's allegations that Russia was interfering in the election ... On Friday [1 October] he accused Russian companies of financing opposition politicians in Belarus ahead of the presidential election. He accused Mr Medvedev himself of meddling in the election, and said if he could 'concern himself more with Russia, it would be more useful' ... President Medvedev said his counterpart had broken 'not only the diplomatic rules, but the elementary rules of behaviour'. He said President Lukashenko had acted dishonourably when he promised to recognize Georgia's breakaway regions of South Ossetia and Abkhazia as independent states, but then failed to do so. He said he was astonished that in a private meeting with him, Mr Lukashenko had spoken in a negative way about former Russian presidents Boris Yeltsin and Vladimir Putin. In recent weeks state-controlled Russian television had broadcast a number of documentaries which have been critical of Mr Lukashenko – fuelling speculation that in December he will not have Moscow's support.

(www.bbc.co.uk, 4 October 2010)

Eighteen candidates have been registered to run against President Alexander Lukashenko for election in December, officials say. Mr Lukashenko is running for the top post for the fourth time, and is the favourite to win, having stifled any serious political opposition. The eighteen other names on the list are largely unknown. The central election commission has until 30 September to verify the applications. After that the candidates will have to gather 100,000 signatures in order to take part in the 19 December vote ... In 2004 a referendum was held which eliminated presidential term limits and allowed him to stand for the presidency again and again. He won the last election, in 2006, by a landslide, but it was widely condemned by international observers. The opposition remains fragmented. Two former candidates at the last presidential election – Alexander Milinkevich and Alexander Kozulin – said they would not run. Mr Milinkevich has called the election 'a farce'.

(www.bbc.co.uk, 27 September 2010)

7 October 2010. 'Russia will pay back Iran's down payment on an order for a missile system, after refusing to fulfil the contract ... Russia's state weapons exporter said it had annulled the contract and would repay Iran's $166 million payment' (www.bbc.co.uk, 7 October 2010).

'Iran's semi-official Mashreghnews cites a Russian publication reporting that China has been discussing the sale to Iran of a similar missile, and the defence ministries of the two countries have discussed the sale in secret' (www.cnn.com, 8 October 2010).

India will buy 250 to 300 advanced fifth-generation stealth fighter jets from Russia over the next ten years [India's defence ministry said] ... Fifth-generation aircraft are invisible to radar, have advanced flight and weapons control systems and can cruise at supersonic speeds ... Russia would also supply forty-five transport planes. India is a top buyer of Russian weapons and the two countries have strong ties ... The deal, which could be worth up to $30 billion, is believed to be the richest in India's military history. The agreement is expected to be signed when President Dmitri

Medvedev visits India in December ... The fifth-generation stealth fighter is currently being developed in Russia and the prototype flew for the first time this year [2010]. At the moment the United States is the only country that has a fifth-generation stealth fighter actually in service.

(www.bbc.co.uk, 7 October 2010)

10 October 2010.

United Russia ... triumphed easily in regional elections in Siberia and elsewhere in Russia on Sunday [10 October] ... United Russia said the results were evidence of the public's faith in prime minister Vladimir Putin and the leadership he has installed across Russia. But other parties said the elections were marred by fraud, and they contended that senior officials who are United Russia members illegally used law enforcement and other government agencies to suppress the opposition ... More than 30 million of Russia's 140 million people were eligible to take part in Sunday's regional elections. Preliminary results announced on Monday [11 October] ... [showed] United Russia garnering roughly 45 per cent to 70 per cent – similar to what it won in elections in other regions last March. Opposition parties made modest gains in the March local elections, but did not appear that they were able to build on those on Sunday ... Two opposition parties – the Communists and A Just Russia – had identified Novosibirsk, which is 1,800 miles east of Moscow, as a place to capitalize on this discontent. Novosibirsk is Russia's third largest city, with a relatively progressive population that some analysts suggested might be souring on Mr Putin and the ruling party. In fact, according to preliminary results, United Russia, which led Novosibirsk with roughly 45 per cent of the vote, was weaker here than in other regions. The Communists received 25 per cent, with A Just Russia garnering 16 per cent. Still, the two opposition parties said that United Russia had used underhand tactics ... [such] as deception and forgery. Local elections in Russia have regularly been faulted for malfeasance by the ruling party. After balloting in October 2009, the opposition in the federal parliament staged a walkout over the results ... A United Russia leader here [in Novosibirsk] said it was the opposition that was guilty of breaking the law to win votes.

(www.iht.com, 11 October 2010)

United Russia swept to victory in regional elections held on Sunday [10 October], but the results were marred by charges of vote rigging. According to preliminary totals, the party received an average of 60 per cent of votes across six provinces where legislatures were being elected, though votes were still being counted in thousands of mayoral and local elections across Russia. United Russia's preliminary results were up slightly from the last round of regional elections held in March [2010], which were judged to be comparatively clean by observers. The party then got about 50 per cent. On Sunday, however, opposition leaders claimed that United Russia – head by prime minister Vladimir Putin, and known informally as the 'party of bureaucrats' for its ties to the establishment – had employed dirty tactics. On Monday [11 October] the head of the central election committee in Chuvashia province resigned, saying she was put under political pressure during the election. Lyudmila Linik: 'In fifteen years of working in this election system I have always been certain that in Chuvashia the election commission system does not fall under someone's influence, and works in accordance with the law ... These last elections have made me doubt this ... [The election commission has been] guided by certain political forces' ... In Dagestan, in the war-torn Caucasus, a village mayor was shot dead in a scuffle after 4,600 ballots went missing, police said ... Vladimir Zhirinovsky, head of the opposition Liberal Democratic Party, alleged 'bribery, blackmail and threats'.

(*FT*, 12 October 2010, p. 10)

14 October 2010.

Russia has begun taking a census of its people, sending about 650,000 workers out to visit every home in the country. Population has been declining in Russia for years – though prime minister Vladimir Putin announced last year [2009] that the trend has been reversed. Demographers believe there are now about 140 million people in Russia. The census has been controversial – criticized by the Orthodox Church and the political opposition, and nearly cancelled because of the cost ... The government says the data will be used for developing social programmes and budget purposes. But opposition parties say they fear what the government will do with the information. Some have called for a boycott. The Orthodox Church was infuriated by the absence in the questionnaire of a question on faith. A spokesman for the Russian Patriarch: 'They are afraid of knowing the state of religion in our society.'

(www.bbc.co.uk, 14 October 2010)

15 October 2010.

President Dmitri Medvedev has nominated prime minister Vladimir Putin's close aide ... Sergei Sobyanin ... as the next mayor of Moscow ... Mr Sobyanin's appointment is expected to be rubber-stamped by Moscow city's legislators ... Dmitri Medvedev: 'I want to tell you that I have decided to submit your candidacy to the Moscow city government' ... The president also urged Mr Sobyanin to urgently tackle Moscow's main problems, especially corruption and the city's notorious traffic jams ... Mr Sobyanin ... served as governor of the Tyumen oblast. He moved to Moscow in 2005 to become chief of staff to the then President Putin. In 2008 he ran Mr Medvedev's successful campaign in the presidential polls. Later that year Mr Sobyanin rejoined Mr Putin's team after the latter became Russia's prime minister.

(www.bbc.co.uk, 15 October 2010)

President Dmitri Medvedev named Sergei Sobyanin, a deputy prime minister and chief of staff to prime minister Vladimir Putin, to the post ... of

Moscow mayor ... Mr Sobyanin [is] a Kremlin insider from Siberia ... Mr Sobyanin's nomination must be approved by the Moscow city council, but that is largely a formality because it is dominated by United Russia ... Mr Medvedev urged Mr Sobyanin to concentrate on issues like traffic, over-crowding and corruption.

(www.iht.com, 15 October 2010)

'The selection of Sergei Sobyanin points to how Dmitri Medvedev and Vladimir Putin are installing dependable allies in major political posts in advance of parliamentary and presidential elections over the next eighteen months' (*IHT*, 16 October 2010, p. 3).

'Sergei Sobyanin ... ran the vast oil-rich Tyumen region in Siberia for four years before being called to the Kremlin by Vladimir Putin in 2005 to serve as his chief of staff' (*FT*, 16 October 2010, p. 6).

President Dmitri Medvedev said a reason Sergei Sobyanin was nominated was that: 'Moscow should be completely integrated with federal authori-ties, so confidence can be maintained' ... Mr Sobyanin promised to work closely with the federal government ... Mr Medvedev said that among Mr Sobyanin's priorities was rooting out graft, an area in which 'very little has been done in recent times, and in several situations schemes were used that should, as a minimum, be checked for their compliance with the law'. The president also charged Mr Sobyanin with making Moscow more open and competitive for business, and addressing the cap-ital's perennial traffic problems. Mr Sobyanin was born and raised in oil-rich western Siberia.

(www.independent.co.uk, 16 October 2010)

Russia has condemned Georgia's unilateral decision to make it easier for people living in the Russian North Caucasus to travel across its border, From now on residents of the volatile republics of Chechnya, Ingushetia, Dagestan and four others will not need a visa to travel to Georgia ... The only usable land border crossing between Russia and Georgia – at Verkhny Lars, high up in the Caucasus mountains – was reopened in March [2010] for the first time in four years ... The Russian foreign ministry has con-demned what it calls an 'attempt to divide the Russian population into dif-ferent categories'.

(www.bbc.co.uk, 15 October 2010)

The Georgian parliament gave final approval on Friday [15 October] to con-stitutional amendments reducing the powers of the president and strengthen-ing the role of the prime minister after presidential elections in 2013 ... President Mikheil Saakashvili's opponents contended that the amendments were a ploy to allow him to remain the country's de facto leader – by assum-ing the role of prime minister, after the pattern of his nemesis, Vladimir Putin. Mr Putin became Russia's prime minister after his second term as president ended in 2008 ... Georgia's parliament, which is dominated by Mr

Saakashvili's party, the United National Movement, easily overcame any resistance on Friday [15 October], voting 112 to five in favour of the amendments ... Mr Saakashvili has denied that the constitutional changes are designed to keep him in control ... Under the new amendments, the president will retain control over the military as commander-in-chief, though the prime minister will gain greater influence over foreign and domestic policy-making. The changes will simplify the procedure for impeaching the president.

(www.iht.com, 15 October 2010)

The Georgian parliament on Friday approved strengthening its own powers and that of the prime minister with constitutional changes that the president's critics said would allow him to rule after his term ends in 2013 ... In 2013 President Mikheil Saakashvili's final term as president expires.

(*IHT*, 16 October 2010, p. 3)

Russia plans to help Venezuela build a nuclear power station, President Dmitri Medvedev said Friday [15 October]. The two countries signed an agreement on the construction Friday during Venezuelan president Hugo Chavez's visit to Russia. They reached the agreement in April [2010], after prime minister Vladimir Putin visited Venezuela ... Medvedev said Russia sees atomic energy co-operation as one of its international priorities and builds nuclear power stations in countries around the world. In addition to helping Venezuela build the nuclear power station, Russia will build a research reactor to produce isotopes for peaceful industry and medicine, Medvedev said.

(www.cnn.com, 15 October 2010)

Russia has agreed to help Venezuela build its first nuclear power station ... President Dmitri Medvedev announced the move [on Friday 15 October] at the end of a two-day visit to Moscow by Venezuelan president Hugo Chavez ... [who on Thursday 14 October] offered assurances that Venezuela had no interest in building a nuclear weapon and only wanted peaceful nuclear technology ... The station is likely to be built over the next ten to fifteen years ... President Dmitri Medvedev: 'I want to say specially that our intentions are absolutely pure and open ... [Russia wants Venezuela to have a] full range of energy choices' ... Chavez's visit is his ninth to Moscow and the first stop on a twelve-day European tour that includes visits to Belarus and , for the first time, Ukraine ... Russia is already building a power station in Iran and holding talks with other Latin American countries, including Brazil and Argentina.

(www.guardian.co.uk, 15 October 2010)

Russia will build two 1,200-megawatt nuclear reactors at the Venezuelan plant. Meanwhile, Rosneft, Russia's state oil giant, will buy a 50 per cent stake in German firm Ruhr Oel from Venezuelan state-owned company PDVSA. The agreement, worth $1.6 billion, was signed at the Kremlin during Venezuelan president Hugo Chavez's visit. However, the cost of the nuclear deal was not immediately revealed ... In addition to the nuclear and Rosneft deals, a shareholder in energy firm TNK-BP said that the company, which is owned by BP and Russian billionaires, would buy three of BP's assets in Venezuela by the end of the year [2010] ... While Rosneft will become an owner of a 50 per cent stake in Germany's Ruhr Oel, BP owns the other 50 per cent ... Rosneft said that the plant's capacity is ... about 20 per cent of Germany's refining capacity ... [and that] 18 per cent of Rosneft's refining capacity will be located in the heart of industrialized Europe.

(www.bbc.co.uk, 15 October 2010)

Venezuelan president Hugo Chavez announced a deal for Russia to build a nuclear power station in Venezuela, as well as more arms purchases and setting up a bilateral bank. Mr Chavez said on Friday [15 October] during his ninth visit to Moscow: 'Venezuela is on its way to getting nuclear power. I hardly need to say so, but I'll say it anyway: for peaceful purposes, of course.'

(*FT*, 16 October 2010, p. 6)

President Dmitri Medvedev said Friday [15 October] that Russia planned to build the first nuclear power plant in Venezuela ... The deal was announced during a state visit to Moscow by Venezuelan president Hugo Chavez, and is in keeping with a push by Russian businesses to expand sales of reactors and nuclear fuel around the world. Just in August [2010] Russia completed work on Iran's first nuclear power plant ... Mr Chavez was here to negotiate a variety of oil and other economic deals, in addition to the nuclear agreement. Energy officials from both countries also signed an inter-governmental agreement approving BP's plan to sell assets in Venezuela to a Russian joint venture, a sale intended to help pay Gulf spill lawsuits. Russia first offered Venezuela nuclear power in 2008, during an intense spell of anti-Western sentiment in Moscow after the war with Georgia. The agreement on Friday fleshed out that offer. It specified that the Russian state nuclear power station, Rosatom, would build one nuclear plant with two large pressurized water reactors to generate power, and one small research reactor plant to make medical isotopes and what was described as nuclear materials that could be used as pesticides for agriculture. Mr Medvedev said Friday that Russia would help Venezuela build 'an entire range of energy opportunities'. He added: 'Even an oil- and gas-rich country such as Venezuela needs new sources of energy' ... Sergei Kiriyenko, the chief executive of the Russian state nuclear company Rosatom, left open a wide range of possibilities for when Russia might begin work on a new nuclear power plant. He said: 'It could be in ten years; it could be sooner' ... He added that the smaller research reactor would be the priority for now. The deepening of Russia's nuclear co-operation with Venezuela marks only one of dozens of nuclear deals for Russia in recent years. Russia's commercial interests lie in building nuclear power reactors and selling fuel around the world. As a legacy of the Cold War, Russia has 40 per cent of the world's uranium enrichment capacity, far more than it needs for its domestic industry.

(www.iht.com, 16 October 2010)

The Russian nuclear industry has profited handsomely from building reactors in developing countries including India, China and Iran. Now it is testing the prospect of becoming a major supplier to the EU, too. At the time of the fall of communism, the Soviet nuclear industry seemed to have foisted more problems than benefits on modern Russia. The Chernobyl disaster was a fresh memory. Nuclear plants seemed just another part of the post-Soviet industrial wasteland. But the Russian industry has revived. In fact, it is on such a roll lately that officials are now talking in sweeping terms of Russia's emergence as a global player, seeking contracts wherever reactors are built, including Europe and potentially the United States. In recent months Rosatom, the state-owned nuclear company [whose chief executive is Sergei Kiriyenko, a former prime minister], completed a power plant in Iran despite a din of criticism and agreed with China to build two sophisticated new reactors that burn plutonium-based fuel. Rosatom closed a deal with Turkey for four reactors and is in talks with India for twelve. It is also preparing a bid on the second new project inside the EU, at the Temelin station in the Czech Republic, worth an estimated $8 billion … For the Czech bid, a subsidiary of Rosatom for reactor construction outside of Russia, Atomstroiexport, has teamed up with the Czech industrial giant Skoda to bid against Westinghouse, the American nuclear power plant design and construction company, and Areva of France, for two new reactors at the Temelin Nuclear Power Plant … Russia is now building a reactor in an EU country, Bulgaria … Analysts of the industry see … the Czech bid … as a test of whether the strategies that propelled Rosatom to become the world's largest nuclear plant constructor through sales in emerging markets will also succeed in the EU … The Russian say their competitive advantages will work as well in Europe as elsewhere. These include access to the country's vast military uranium enrichment facilities, and a willingness to import unwanted nuclear waste for storage and reprocessing. Russian officials point out that their industry never went into hibernation because of public disillusionment with nuclear power, as happened in the United States. The Russians tried no great leaps in technology in recent decades, but also lost no ground. Instead, they took baby steps to improve an old design, known as the VVER, the Russian abbreviation for a pressurized water reactor, their principal product on the market today … Rosatom is building fifteen reactors, ten in Russia and five abroad, out of a total of sixty reactors that are under construction worldwide, according to the Nuclear Energy Institute, a trade group in Washington. It holds signed contracts for seven units, is in negotiations for eighteen units and is participating in tenders for four units [Rosatom said] … For comparison, Westinghouse, the largest US builder of nuclear power plants, is not currently the lead contractor on any plants. But Westinghouse has built more power plants than any other company in the world, mostly in the 1960s and 1970s. The Russian have quietly rolled out safety innovations, becoming the first in the world to build core catchers, or barriers, under new reactors to catch the molten remains in a meltdown. About 40 per cent of the cost of a Russian reactor today is for safety mechanism. Outside experts generally endorse the Russian designs, saying they are fully competitive with those of US and European nuclear plant constructors. Rosatom, meanwhile, is striving to take advantage of its monopoly hold on the industry. It is a vertically integrated company, with divisions mining uranium, enriching fuel, building reactors and even decommissioning old plants ... Russia allows the importation of materials irradiated in nuclear reactors ... Russia can accept fuel for reprocessing and storage ... Russian nuclear officials say their willingness to reprocess nuclear waste, which they unfailingly call spent fuel, is a competitive advantage in negotiating for new deals around the world ... In the fuel market Russia's abundance of uranium enrichment capacity has proved an unalloyed advantage as the country competes worldwide for business in the burst of reactor construction that is sometimes called the nuclear renaissance. There are 140 reactors in advanced stages of licensing today, according to the Nuclear Energy Institute.

(www.iht.com, 11 October 2010; *IHT*, 12 October 2010, pp. 11, 13)

18 October 2010.

Ahead of a [two-day] summit meeting Monday [18 October] in France, between the leaders of Germany, Russia and France, Moscow is asking for regular participation in the EU committee that is responsible for setting the bloc's foreign policy. Vladimir Chizhov (Moscow's ambassador to the EU): 'We would like Russia and the EU to be able to take joint decisions. I do not expect to be sitting at every session of the political and security committee, but there should be some mechanism that would enable us to take joint steps. We want our relationship with the EU through the political and security committee to be formalized, to be more efficient' ... When Chancellor Angela Merkel met President Dmitri Medvedev in June [2010] near Berlin, both leaders proposed the establishment of a new entity called the EU–Russia Political and Security Committee. The new committee would consist of the foreign ministers from Russia and the EU state, as well as ... the EU foreign policy chief. The proposal, which Mr Chizhov said was initiated by Mrs Merkel ... came as a jolt to other nations in the bloc ... Analysts say Mrs Merkel has realized that the EU needs a security relationship with Russia because strengthening the Nato–Russia Council, which is supposed to discuss such issues, is going nowhere ... Mrs Merkel told Mr Medvedev in June that Germany wanted Russia to help resolve the continuing conflict in Transdniestre ... which is part of Moldova, a neighbour of the EU member Romania ... [Transdniestre] is ruled by a pro-Russian nationalist movement that has been seeking independence from Moldova. More than 1,000 Russian troops are based in the region.

(www.iht.com, 18 October 2010)

President Dmitri Medvedev awarded Russia's highest state honours on Monday [18 October] to a group of sleeper agents who were deported from the United States in a Cold War-style swap in July [2010] ... [A] Kremlin spokeswoman ... said the spies had been honoured at a Kremlin ceremony along with other members of Russia's Foreign Intelligence Service. She said: 'A ceremony took place in the Kremlin today to give the highest state awards to members of the Foreign Intelligence Service, including spies working in the United States who returned to Russia in July' ... Prime minister Vladimir Putin, who was a KGB agent in East Germany during the Soviet era, met the spies at an undisclosed location soon after they returned, sang Soviet songs with them and promised them a bright future in Russia. He said he admired what they did and warned those who betrayed their compatriots would end up paying a heavy price. The Kremlin honoured the agents despite widespread media reports that the spy ring failed to secure any major secrets. Starting in the 1990s, from Virginia to Boston to Seattle, the agents attended elite Ivy League schools to meet future power brokers, obtained influential jobs, married, had children and bought homes in upscale areas. Court documents released in the United States described how the Russian agents hobnobbed with academics and assembled data on high-end Manhattan real estate but did not accuse them of actually passing classified information to Moscow. Anna Chapman, whose glamorous pictures posted on social networking website Facebook made her a media sensation, is the only one of the ten spies to have made public appearances. She posed provocatively for a Russian magazine shoot in August and appeared at the launch of a Russian space craft earlier this month [October] as part of her new job as adviser to a bank that helps finance the space industry.

(www.iht.com, 18 October 2010)

President Dmitri Medvedev handed state honours to Russian spies deported from the United States earlier this year [2010] ... A Kremlin spokeswoman: 'A ceremony took place today [Monday 18 October] to hand top state honours to a number of Foreign Intelligence Service [SVR] employees, including the spies who were working in the United States and returned to Russia in July' ... It was not immediately clear whether the whole group received the awards ... In July prime minister Vladimir Putin revealed that he had met the ten agents, claiming they were living 'tough lives' and had been 'betrayed'. Mr Putin told journalists that he had sung Soviet-era patriotic songs with the spies.

(www.bbc.co.uk, 18 October 2010)

Anna Chapman ... re-emerged on a visit to the Baikonur cosmodrome in Kazakhstan this month for the launch of a Russian spaceship, fuelling her celebrity in Russia and abroad. Ms Chapman was in Baikonur ostensibly as the new celebrity face of a Moscow bank. FondServisBank, which works with Russian companies in the aerospace industry, said it had hired her to bring innovation to its information technologies.

(*FT*, 19 October 2010, p. 6)

19 October 2010.

President Dmitri Medvedev formally accepted an invitation to the 19–20 November meeting ... of Nato in Lisbon ... that was extended to Russia weeks ago ... President Dmitri Medvedev [on 19 October at the end of two days of talks in France with President Nicolas Sarkozy of France and Chancellor Angela Merkel of Germany]: 'I will go to the Russia–Nato summit This will further the search for necessary compromise and the development of dialogue between the Russian Federation and the North Atlantic Alliance as a whole ... We are now evaluating the idea of this proposal, but I think that Nato itself needs to understand in what form it sees Russia joining this system, what it will bring, in what manner an agreement can be reached, and how to proceed further. Only based on the evaluation of this proposal can we give an answer on how we will proceed with regard to the idea of European missile defence.'

(*IHT*, 20 October 2010, p. 3)

Russian troops have withdrawn from a Georgian town which they have occupied since a brief war between the two countries in 2008. Georgian officials said the Russian pulled out of Perevi, which is located just outside South Ossetia ... Moscow and Tbilisi agreed after the war that their troops would move back to their pre-conflict positions. Georgia had condemned Russia's military presence as a violation of the truce ... After the war Russia eventually withdrew most of its personnel, tanks and armoured vehicles to South Ossetia. But Moscow had kept a small number of its troops in Perevi, manning three checkpoints in the small town.

(www.bbc.co.uk, 19 October 2010)

20 October 2010.

A detailed report on the Smolensk air disaster in western Russia has been handed to Polish investigators in Moscow more than six months on. The report, by the Interstate Aviation Committee (Mak), which includes Russia and other ex-Soviet states, looks at the crash's circumstances. It was passed to Poland's chief investigator ... Mak said Russian, Polish and US experts had worked together to investigate the disaster ... The report's conclusions will not be revealed before Poland responds formally to the report.

(www.bbc.co.uk, 20 October 2010)

21 October 2010.

Sergei Sobyanin ... was named the new mayor of Moscow ... [He] was approved by the city legislature in a near unanimous vote ... United Russia has thirty-two of the legislature's thirty-five seats ... Only two Communists voted against Sobyanin ... Andrei Klychkov, the head of the Communist faction, blasted Russia for ignoring the city's problems ... Yuri Luzhkov has made clear he believes the true reason behind his ouster was the Kremlin's desire to have a more compliant mayor before next year's parliamentary elections ... in late 2011 ... and the 2012 presidential vote, which Vladimir Putin is widely expected to reclaim ... Luzhkov, who opposed Putin's move to cancel direct election of governors, was the lone holdover from the turbulent 1990s when regional leaders held broad sway ... He ruled over a building boom ... giving the capital a modern facelift but destroying many of its precious landmarks.

(www.iht.com, 21 October 2010)

The city council ... confirmed Sergei Sobyanin by a thirty-two to two vote ... Sobyanin takes over a city of 10.5 million ... Sobyanin said: 'The city has changed for the better and taken its rightful place as a leading global megapolis. But in recent years it is clear that many opportunities have been missed. The place of development has gradually slowed. I am deeply convinced that corruption and bureaucracy threaten to devalue many if not all of Moscow's competitive advantages. It is obvious the city needs a more open and effective system of government' ... Moscow accounts for a quarter of Russia's $1.2 trillion economy ... Sobyanin was not chosen by voters, but picked by Medvedev out of four candidates proposed by United Russia ... Yuri Luzhkov ... on Thursday [21 October] said Russians should not accept the 'dictator-type powers granted to the president' to dismiss governors ... Dmitri Medvedev named a senior United Russia official, Vyacheslav Volodin, to replace Sobyanin as deputy prime minister and chief of staff of Vladimir Putin's government, approving the candidate proposed by the government.

(www.iht.com, 21 October 2010)

'Yuri Luzhkov on Thursday [21 October] harshly criticized United Russia ... for kowtowing to the Kremlin. He said: 'This is a servile party and I quit' (www.iht.com, 22 October 2010).

Sergei Sobyanin's appointment was opposed by only three of the thirty-five deputies. The dissenting lawmakers, Communists, are the only opposition to United Russia in the council and dismissed the vote as a farce ... Andrei Klychkov [head of the Communist faction] said: 'Muscovites do not have a choice; everything has been decided behind closed doors' ... Yuri Luzhkov and his billionaire wife, Yelena Baturina, were also accused of corruption. Mr Luzhkov has denounced all the claims as 'total rubbish' ... Some Russian experts had suggested that Mr Sobyanin had suggested Mr Sobyanin would follow Vladimir Putin as the nation's president, but in the event he did not stand and instead ran Dmitri Medvedev's election campaign.

(www.bbc.co.uk, 21 October 2010)

Yuri Luzhkov [was] one of the last autonomous regional barons ... He was his own man. He behaved like an elected mayor even after Vladimir Putin scrapped elections for regional mayors and governors in 2004 ... As head of the oil-rich Tyumen province, Sergei Sobyanin was among the first governors to support Mr Putin's abolition of regional elections ... Moscow accounts for roughly 10 per cent of Russia's population and a quarter of national economic output – comparable to the oil and gas industry. Until Mr Luzhkov's sacking, the city represented the last bastion of regionalism outside the Kremlin's control. Mr Sobyanin's appointment irons out this kink. The change was executed by Dmitri Medvedev, Russia's president, but it reflects Mr Putin's choice ... [After Mr Putin] became president, he used Mr Sobyanin, a member of the upper house of parliament, to help him get rid of Yuri Skuratov, Russia's renegade prosecutor-general. In 2005 Mr Putin made Mr Sobyanin chief of the presidential administration ... If Mr Putin decides to take back the presidency in 2012, as seems increasingly likely, Mr Sobyanin will help make it happen ... Mr Sobyanin has a reputation for efficiency. Unlike his predecessor, he is free of the taint of corruption scandals. As governor of Tyumen he persuaded some oil companies to register their headquarters there and pay taxes into the local budget, which made the region one of Russia's wealthiest.

(www.economist.com, 21 October 2010; *The Economist*, 23 October 2010, p. 47)

22 October 2010.

Prosecutors on Friday [22 October] demanded that Mikhail Khodorkovsky be imprisoned for six more years if he is convicted in his politically charged second trial. Prosecutors asked for a fourteen-year prison sentence but said it should include the eight-year term that Mr Khodorkovsky is currently serving, which is due to end in October 2011. Mr Khodorkovsky has one year left to serve in the eight-year sentence imposed after a fraud-and-tax evasion trial that tarnished Russia's image during Vladimir Putin's 2000–8 presidency.

(*IHT*, 23 October 2010, p. 3)

25 October 2010.

Speculation is growing that Yuri Luzhkov is preparing to begin a new life in exile in London after he was allegedly spotted queuing up for a visa at the British embassy in Moscow. Luzhkov was seen at the embassy last week ... [an internet portal] said today [25 October] ... Friends, however, denied that ... [he] was prepared to move permanently to the UK ... Since his ignominious dismissal Luzhkov has sought to reinvent himself as a semi-opposition figure, an attempt that has provoked scorn from Russia's sceptical liberal establishment ... Few analysts, however, believe the Kremlin is planning to file corruption charges against Luzhkov, a common tactic used against fallen bureaucrats, since in the former mayor's case charges like this might lead to allegations against Vladimir Putin and Dmitri Medvedev.

(www.guardian.co.uk, 25 October 2010)

25 October 2010.

Russia said yesterday [25 October] that it would strengthen its Black Sea fleet with new warships, submarines and bomber aircraft ... The move comes months after Ukraine extended Russia's lease on its base in Sevastopol until 2042 ... Kiev's consent to the upgrade is set to be a formality under President Viktor Yanukovich ... Eighteen vessels would be added by 2010 ... Georgia said the fleet's patrols off Abkhazia were illegal.

(*The Times*, 26 October 2010, p. 38)

26 October 2010.

'Iran on Tuesday [26 October] celebrated the start of the process of loading 163 fuel rods into the core of its first nuclear reactor, putting the Bushehr nuclear power plant within months of operation' (www.iht.com, 26 October 2010).

[There is to be] a landmark ... [Nato] summit next month [November], to be attended by President Dmitri Medvedev ... [Nato] officials said several joint Nato–Russian initiatives on Afghanistan were on the table. They include the contribution of Russian helicopters and crews to train Afghan pilots, possible Russian assistance in training Afghan national security forces, increased co-operation on counter-narcotics and border security, and improved transit and supply routes for Nato forces ... With the plans yet to be finalized, officials said there was no question of Russian troops re-entering the country. A Nato spokesman said last night [25 October]: 'There are no plans to reintroduce Russian soldiers into Afghanistan – [it's] not part of Russia's intent, not Afghan, and not ours. Russians may get involved in training helicopter pilots if they provide some helicopters, but not in Afghanistan itself. In the past Russians have collaborated on training counter-narcotics police outside of the country. None of the initiatives on the table involve Russian troops in Afghanistan' ... Nato secretary-general Anders Fogh Rasmussen: 'The summit can mark a new relationship between Nato and Russia. We will hopefully agree on a broad range in which we can develop practical co-operation on Afghanistan, counter-terrorism, counter-narcotics. Russia is strongly interested in increased co-operation ... Last December [2009], when I visited Moscow, I suggested that Russia provide helicopters for the Afghan army. Since then Russia has reflected on that and there are now bilateral talks between Russia and the United States. I would not exclude that we will facilitate that process within the Nato–Russia council' ... Russian forces gained considerable experience in flying helicopter gunships during the 1979–89 Soviet occupation of Afghanistan ... An ailing Leonid Brezhnev sent troops to Kabul in December 1979 ... Mikhail Gorbachev began withdrawing troops in early 1987; the last soldiers left in February 1989.

(www.guardian.co.uk, 26 October 2010; *Guardian*, 27 October 2010, p. 17)

Nato secretary-general Anders Fogh Rasmussen: 'The summit will represent a new relationship between Nato and Russia. It will be a very substantive

Nato–Russia summit and definitely the most important event for [bilateral] co-operation since the Rome summit of 2002, when we established the Nato–Russia Council ... I would expect a decision on missile co-operation to be one of the most important outcomes of the Nato–Russia summit. Co-operation between Russia and Nato on missile defence will provide us with a very strong framework to develop a true Euro-Atlantic security architecture with one security roof. Militarily it makes sense, because co-operation between Nato and Russia will make the system more effective and give more coverage' ... Nato officials say the United States and Russia are working on a package that could see Moscow providing more than twenty helicopters to the Afghan national security forces.

(*FT*, 27 October 2010, p. 12)

Nato secretary-general Anders Fogh Rasmussen:

For historical reasons we will not see Russian boots on the ground in Afghanistan. But Russia can contribute in other ways. They can provide helicopters; they can also conduct training of Afghan security forces in Russia; we can co-operate on counter-narcotics.

(www.bbc.co.uk, 27 October 2010)

('Russia is setting out tougher terms for Nato, in return for its assistance in Afghanistan, with demands that the alliance restricts the number of troops it bases in member countries which were former members of the Warsaw Pact. Moscow has agreed in principle to supply "several dozen" military helicopters and has started training Afghan security forces. Talks are also under way for Nato to bring in arms and ammunition as an alternative to a Pakistani route, which has come under repeated Taleban attack. But Russian foreign minister Sergei Lavrov is said to have asked Nato to desist from deploying "significant military forces" to countries which joined the alliance after the break-up of the Soviet Union in 1991, maintaining that their presence would not be conducive to a relationship of trust ... Russia has complained that Nato has been slow to act on information about drug production in Afghanistan, echoing its deep concern about the heroin trade from Central Asia': *The Independent*, 28 October 2010, p. 22.)

Mikhail Gorbachev, who once supported Vladimir Putin, is voicing growing frustration with his leadership, saying that Mr Putin has undermined Russia's fledgling democracy by crippling opposition forces. Mikhail Gorbachev: 'He thinks that democracy stands in his way. I am afraid that they [Vladimir Putin and Dmitri Medvedev] have been saddled with this idea that this unmanageable country needs authoritarianism. They think they cannot do without it ... [United Russia is] a bad copy of the Soviet Communist Party' ... Mr Gorbachev was especially disparaging of Mr Putin's decision in 2004, when he was president, to eliminate elections for regional governors and the mayors of Moscow and St Petersburg ... Mr Gorbachev's criticism of Mr Putin was not new, but it appeared to turn somewhat more strident recently … Mr Gorbachev backed Mr Putin when he became president in 2000, applauding Mr Putin's efforts to stabilize the country … But in Mr Putin's second term, Mr Gorbachev began openly questioning Mr Putin's conduct.

(*IHT*, 27 October 2010, p. 3)

Mikhail Gorbachev: 'I am very concerned; we are only halfway down the road from a totalitarian regime to democracy and freedom. And the battle continues. There are still many people in our society who fear democracy and would prefer a totalitarian state' (www.bbc.co.uk, 27 October 2010).

Mikhail Gorbachev … has issued a sharp criticism of President Dmitri Medvedev and Prime Minister Vladimir Putin, saying they are 'doing everything they can to move away from democracy, to stay in power'. Gorbachev, seventy-nine, accused the two leaders of eroding civil liberties by crushing opposition parties and cancelling direct elections for regional governors.

(www.guardian.co.uk, 27 October 2010)

In its annual Corruption Perception Index, released on Tuesday [26 October], Transparency International said the United States had slipped in the rankings of 178 counties to come twenty-second, down from nineteenth last year [2009] and leaving it behind Chile and Qatar … Three-quarters of countries surveyed scored below five on a scale of zero to ten, where zero is highly corrupt and ten is least corrupt … [Scores: joint first were Denmark, New Zealand and Singapore with a score of 9.3; joint fourth were Finland and Sweden with a score of 9.2 … Ranked last was Somalia with a score of 1.1] … The index draws on thirteen surveys and country analyses by independent institutions published over the past two years. It is based on the perception of corruption in the public sector, and the countries included in the index vary slightly from year to year.

(*FT*, 27 October 2010, p. 9)

Transparency International's 2010 Corruption Perception Index is out and Russia's ranking does not look good; the country has dropped to 158th place (out of 178) and now shares a score of 2.1 with Cameroon and Tajikistan. It is also the most corrupt of the Brics … [The Bric countries are Brazil, Russia, India and China] … India came in 116th, with a score of 3.4, while China ranked seventy-eighth at 3.5, and Brazil ranked sixty-ninth with a score of 3.7 … According to Russia's interior ministry, the average size of a small business drive – bribes paid to get everyday tasks done – was 44,000 roubles in the first half of 2010, as compared with 23,000 roubles in 2009 and 20,000 roubles in 2008 … Foreign investors in Russia, used to bribes, factor the risk of corruption into almost all business transactions, something that is reflected in the risk premium they take on. It is also one reason why Russian equities are so cheap.

(www.ft.com, 27 October 2010)

Transparency International's Corruption Perception Index ... which seeks to gauge domestic public sector corruption ... is figured with data compiled from surveys of country experts and business leaders, and relies on perceptions rather than legal findings, which can differ sharply across borders, depending on enforcement. The index reflects two years of data to iron out one-time spikes ... The United States, which ranked nineteenth in 2009, fell to twenty-two, putting it behind Canada, Barbados and Chile in the Americas ... Also falling in the rankings were the Czech Republic, Greece, Hungary, Italy, Madagascar, Niger and Russia, 154 ... China ranked seventy-eight.

(*IHT*, 27 October 2010, p. 3)

Transparency International's Corruption Perception Index ... ranks countries according to 'the degree to which corruption is perceived to exist among public officials and politicians'. It defines corruption as 'the abuse of entrusted power for private gain'. Denmark, New Zealand and Singapore were tied for first place on this year's index, followed by Finland and Sweden. In last place was Somalia, followed by Myanmar and Afghanistan.

(www.baltictimes.com, 26 October 2010)

A release accompanying the 2010 Corruption Perception Index said: 'The surveys used to compile the index include questions relating to bribery of public officials, kickbacks in public procurement, embezzlement of public funds and questions that probe the strength and effectiveness of public sector anti-corruption efforts' ... Japan was seventeenth on the list with a score of 7.8, the UK was twentieth with a score of 7.6 and the United States was twenty-second with a score of 7.1 ... China was seventy-eighth with a score of 3.5 and India was eighty-seventh with a score of 3.3.

(www.cnn.com, 27 October 2010)

Transparency International ... the Berlin-based watchdog ... monitors perceived corruption and has published its annual report, based on a poll of businesses and people in 178 nations ... Transparency International's corruption index draws on thirteen different surveys of business people and governance experts conducted between January 2009 and September 2010 ... Transparency International was founded in 1993 and is a non-governmental organization that monitors corporate and political corruption ... The worst country is Somalia, followed by Burma, Afghanistan and Iraq ... In its latest report Russia is rated as among the worst for corruption, in 154th place ... The country has fallen from 146th place to 154th ... Russia tied with Tajikistan, Papua New Guinea and several African countries, and was ranked the most corrupt among the G-20 nations ... China is in 78th place.

(www.bbc.co.uk, 27 October 2010)

Russian police uncovered 35,000 cases of corruption in the first nine months of this year [2010], including alleged crimes by four deputy governors and five regional ministers. Major bribe-taking increased by 17.5 per cent from

January to September compared with the same period of 2009, the interior ministry said today [27 October]. The average size of a bribe increased 1.5 times to around $1,400 ... Police said on 21 October they were seeking the former deputy head of government in the Moscow region and his wife, believed to be in the United States, over the alleged embezzlement of $1 billion. The authorities, who have detained the region's former deputy finance chief in the same case, said they managed to recover $820 million of the misappropriated assets. Russians pay bribes totalling $300 billion a year, equivalent to almost a quarter of GDP, according to Kirill Kabanov, head of the National Anti-Corruption Committee.

(www.bloomberg.com, 27 October 2010)

Transparency International ... [released its] sixteenth annual ranking on 26 October ... The Corruption Perception Index was the first index comparing corruption globally. But it has always been controversial. As might be expected, early complaints came from poor places which felt they were being singled out by an organization that reflected the ethos of wealthy countries ... Some people take issue with the methodology based on thirteen surveys of experts and business people. Its precise working varies from country to country, and it has changed over time – so that year-on-year comparisons can be misleading.

(www.economist.com, 28 October 2010; *The Economist*,
30 October 2010, p. 76)

28–29 October 2010.

Russian and US agents have taken part in a joint operation to destroy drug laboratories in Afghanistan, the head of Russia's drug control agency says. More than a tonne of heroin and opium was seized during the raids, which took place on Thursday [28 October] close to the border with Pakistan, Viktor Ivanov announced. Mr Ivanov said the haul had a street value of $250 million and was believed to have been destined for Central Asia. Correspondents say it is the first time there has been such a joint operation. Russian officials have in the past accused coalition forces in Afghanistan of doing 'next to nothing' to tackle drug production, and thereby helping to sustain the estimated 2.5 million heroin addicts in Russia alone. Much of the heroin enters the territory of the former Soviet Union through Afghanistan's northern borders with Tajikistan and Turkmenistan. It then travels westwards across Kazakhstan before entering the central and Ural regions of Russia, where there are large numbers of addicts. Mr Ivanov said the operation involved about seventy personnel ... including four Russian counternarcotics agents ... backed up by attack helicopters. They were on the ground for several hours, destroying a 'major hub' for the production of heroin, located in a mountainous area about 5 kilometres (3 miles) from the Pakistani border near the eastern city of Jalalabad, he said. Along with ... heroin and ... morphine, a large amount of technical equipment was destroyed. Mr Ivanov said the raids were based on intelligence Russia had shared with the United States and he wanted to increase co-operation in the fight against drug trafficking. He said: 'We are ready and we want to send an additional number of our officers for posting to the international information centres functioning in Kabul, Bagram and Kandahar.'

(www.bbc.co.uk, 29 October 2010)

Russia's joint operation with the United States to destroy Afghan drugs laboratories marks the first time it has deployed security forces in the region since the Soviet military withdrew in 1989, Russia's anti-narcotics chief said Friday [20 October]. The operation in Nangarhar province in eastern Afghanistan on Thursday [29 October] was jointly conducted by the United States Drug Enforcement Agency [US DEA], the Department of Defence, Nato, the Afghan ministry of the interior and the Russian drug control agency. It involved raids on four laboratories associated with a significant drugs trafficker in the province. Approximately a tonne of heroin worth $250 million was seized, along with a smaller quantity of opium and items used in drug production, US authorities said. Viktor Ivanov (head of Russia's federal drug control agency): 'This is the first operation in Afghanistan in which Russian drug police officers took part' ... But he stressed they were not in Afghanistan as a military unit, but part of an agreement between Moscow, the Afghan government and the US DEA to share information about the flow of drugs into Russia via the southern borders with Turkmenistan, Uzbekistan and Tajikistan. He said: 'For the first time our officials handed over information about the location of drug laboratories, which was confirmed by the Afghan interior ministry and the US DEA' ... According to officials, seventy people were involved in the raid close to the Pakistani border, with helicopter gunships and Afghan police providing air and ground cover ... The Medvedev–Obama commission [is] a working group set up in 2009 by the leaders of Russia and the United States to improve communication and co-operation between the two ... Russia, estimated by the United Nations to have between one-and-a-half and 6 million addicts, has long targeted the poppy fields of Afghanistan as the source of the problem, calling on the United States and its Nato allies to do more to eradicate the opium trade. However, the strategy of destroying the poppy fields of southern Afghanistan, which yield much of the heroin flooding out of the country, is viewed as counter-productive by the US-led coalition because it drives farmers into the hands of the Taleban. Ivanov disputes this, pointing out how successful the campaign has been to eradicate the crops used to produce cocaine in Colombia, one of the world's biggest producers ... Ivanov: 'The number of laboratories is huge ... A lot of people [in Russia] have started to ask if Russia is doing the right thing in allowing Nato to use its corridors to Afghanistan, considering it presents a bigger and bigger threat to Russian society.'

(www.cnn.com, 29 October 2010)

About seventy people took part in the raid, including agents from Russia's Federal Counter-Narcotics Service, the United States Drug Enforcement Administration and Afghan drug police ... A Taleban resurgence and the return of al-Qaeda in Afghanistan could bolster Islamic extremism in Central Asia and southern Russia, where authorities continue to battle a potent Islamic insurgency in Chechnya and the surrounding region. The issue of Afghan heroin, which is derived from opium, is particularly vexing. Afghanistan is the world's largest producer of heroin, much of which seeps into neighbouring Central Asian countries and then into Russia, where it finds a ready market of over a million users. Almost 90 per cent of Russia's heroin comes from Afghanistan, according to government statistics. Injected drugs kill thousands annually and are the main driver of Russia's HIV epidemic, which is growing faster than almost anywhere else in the world ... Afghanistan's opium crop, estimated at almost 4,000 tonnes in the last year. has been the main source of financing for the Taleban and has fostered corruption among Afghan officials. But the Obama administration has called back eradication programmes, which were employed in the Bush era, out of fears that farmers would turn to the Taleban for assistance. Russia and the United States created a counter-narcotics working group last year [2009] in part to reconcile these disagreements.

(www.iht.com, 29 October 2010)

[On Saturday 30 October Afghan] President Hamid Karzai criticized the first joint operation by Russian and US agents to destroy drug laboratories in Afghanistan. Mr Karzai said Thursday's raid had taken place without his government's permission and was a clear violation of Afghan sovereignty ... Afghanistan's elite counter-narcotics force, which relies heavily on foreign training, did participate in the operation but it appears the president's office was not informed of who would accompany them ... The president said he wanted friendly relations with Moscow, but that the relationship had to be based on mutual consent. Any repetition of the operation would be met with reaction from Afghanistan, he added.

(www.bbc.co.uk, 30 October 2010)

President Hamid Karzai criticized the first joint operation by Russian and US agents to destroy drug laboratories ... Mr Karzai said he had not been informed of Russia's participation – a sensitive issue in Afghanistan ever since the Soviet occupation ended twenty-one years ago. He called it a violation of Afghan sovereignty and international law. Russia said more than a tonne of heroin and opium, with a street value of $250 million, was destroyed in the raid. Officials in Moscow have in the past accused coalition forces in Afghanistan of doing little to tackle drugs, and thereby help to sustain the estimated 2.5 million heroin addicts in Russia ... In a strongly worded statement on Saturday [30 October] President Karzai's office alleged that Russian military personnel had taken part in the 'illegal' raid. It said: 'While Afghanistan remains committed to its joint efforts with the international community against narcotics, it also makes it clear that no organization or institution shall have the right to carry out such a military operation without prior authorization and consent of the government of Afghanistan. Such unilateral operations are a clear violation of Afghan sovereignty as well as international law, and any repetition will be met by the required reaction from our side' ... A senior source in the delegation of President Dmitri Medvedev, who is currently on a visit to Vietnam, told the AFP news agency on Sunday [31 October] that Kabul's reaction to the anti-drug operation as 'simply surprising and incomprehensible' because 'the Afghan interior ministry participated in this operation' ... Afghanistan's elite counter-narcotics force did participate in the operation, but it appears that the president's office was not informed of who would accompany them. Afghanistan's interior ministry said it thought only Russian observers rather than Russian troops were to take part ... The president's national security adviser ... said Nato officials had apologized but that he wanted a public declaration.

(www.bbc.co.uk, 31 October 2010)

A raid on drug laboratories in eastern Afghanistan came under fire from the nation's president on Saturday [30 October] because Russian counter-narcotics agents had been involved, along with those from the United States and Afghanistan. In a statement sent to the news media President Hamid Karzai expressed dismay that the central Afghan government had not been told about the presence of at least two Russian agents on the raid. He called it 'a blatant violation of Afghanistan's sovereignty and of international laws' and he warned that 'any repetition of such acts will prompt necessary reaction by our country'. The Afghan ministry of counter-narcotics held a news conference on Saturday detailing the successes of the raid ... Deputy minister Mohammed Ahmad said the raid had been led by an Afghan counter-narcotics team. When he was asked directly whether Russian or other international agents had been involved, Mr Ahmad replied: 'We did not ask them where they were from, and they all look the same, and were not informed that two Russian drug specialists had also participated in this operation' ... In its statement after the raid on Thursday [28 October] the US embassy in Kabul said that the operation had been conducted by the Afghan Ministry of Interior Counter-Narcotics Police (CNP-A) Sensitive Investigative Unit and National Interdiction Unit and that the United States Drug Enforcement Administration, Nato troops and Russian personnel had played a supporting role.

(www.iht.com, 31 October 2010)

The Russian embassy in Kabul said the raid ... had been planned for three months with Afghan assistance. A source at the Russian federal anti-narcotics agency said the outburst from Kabul was 'not very understandable', while a source within the Kremlin dismissed it as 'incomprehensible' ... Afghanistan supplies more than 90 per cent of the world's opium and Afghan heroin kills more than 30,000 Russians each year ... Alexei Milovanov, representative of the Russian anti-drugs service in Kabul, said the operation was conducted by the Afghan government and Russians 'simply acted as advisers, according to an agreement between our two countries permitting the presence of Russian advisers during a drug raid'.

(www.telegraph.co.uk, 31 October 2010)

31 October 2010.

For the eighteen months that this group has been convening, nine times the city authorities [in Moscow] have refused them a permit to gather, and nine times ... they have been dispersed and herded into buses ... [But a] rally took place in Triumphalnaya Square on Sunday night [31 October] ... Ten days ago, in the seismic political rearrangement that followed the ouster of Mayor Yuri Luzhkov, the city authorities surprised many by offering to allow 200 people to attend the rally, regularly held on the last day of months that have thirty-one days, in honour of Article 31 of the constitution, which guarantees freedom of assembly. After organizers complained, they granted a permit allowing 800. The Strategy 31 movement, as it is known, represents an exceedingly narrow slice of the city's liberal elite. [A] crowd of some 1,500 showed up ... Eduard Limonov ... who leads the extreme nationalist National Bolshevik Party ... [held] his own unauthorized rally at the same spot.

(*IHT*, 1 November 2010, p. 3)

1 November 2010.

President Dmitri Medvedev is visiting the Kurils, defying Japan's warnings not to visit the disputed islands in the Pacific Ocean. Mr Medvedev arrived in Kunashir, the second largest of the four islands, where he met local residents. Japanese prime minister Naoto Kan immediately described Mr Medvedev's visit as 'regrettable'. The islands have been under Moscow's control since the end of World War II. They lie to the north of Japan's Hokkaido Island and to the south of Russia's Kamchatka peninsula. They are known in Russia as the Southern Kurils, while Japan calls them the Northern Territories ... Mr Medvedev is the first Russian leader to set foot on the Kuril Islands ... In Kunashir, known in Japan as Kunashiri, he promised greater investment in the region ... In Tokyo prime minister Naoto Kan reiterated Japan's stance on the islands. He said: 'Those four northern islands are part of our country's territory, so the president's visit is very regrettable' ... Japanese foreign minister Seiji Maehara warned that any such visit would 'hurt the feelings of the Japanese people' ... The islands have rich fishing grounds, mineral deposits and possibly oil and gas reserves. Before Russia took control of them, some 17,000 Japanese residents lived in the Kurils.

(www.bbc.co.uk, 1 November 2010)

'President Dmitri Medvedev visited the disputed Kuril Islands on Monday [1 November] ... He made the stop during an Asian tour that included a meeting of Asean over the weekend in Vietnam' (www.cnn.com, 1 November 2010).

'Japan's stance is that those four islands are part of our country's territory, so the president's visit is very regrettable,' Japanese prime minister Naoto Kan told a parliamentary panel about President Dmitri Medevev's visit, the first by a Russian [or Soviet] leader ... Japanese foreign minister Seiji Maehara, who said last month any visit by Medvedev would severely harm relations, also told parliament the visit 'would hurt the feelings of the Japanese people' ... The island that Medevdev visited lies about 10 miles (16 kilometres) from Hokkaido. But unlike the dispute with China over islands in the East China Sea, which are near potentially vast maritime oil and gas reserves, this feud with Russia has more to do with the legacy of World War II than hydrocarbon deposits. The Soviet Union occupied the four disputed islands at the end of the war and the territorial dispute has weighed on relations between Tokyo and Moscow ever since, preventing the signing of a formal peace treaty ... President Dmitri Medvedev (speaking to journalists on the island): 'It is important that there is development here; we will definitely be investing here. Life will be better here, like it is in central Russia' ... The islands are close to oil and gas production regions of Russia, but most people there live off fishing and Japan, a major fish consumer, would gain rich fishing grounds if the islands were returned ... China became Japan's biggest trade partner last year [2009], replacing the United States. Trade flows with Russia, however, are tiny in comparison. Japan's exports to Russia totalled 306.5 billion yen ($3.8 billion) in 2009, about 2 per cent of its exports to China, and its imports from Russia came to 825.5 billion yen in 2009, accounting for 1.6 per cent of Japan's total imports.

(www.iht.com, 1 November 2010)

Human rights

The government has reopened criminal investigations into the deaths of five journalists after an appeal by a media rights group that ranks Russia as one of the most dangerous countries for journalists, officials said Thursday [30 September]. The prosecutor-general's office said it had decided to reopen criminal investigations into five journalist deaths between 2001 and 2005 after receiving new information from the New York-based Committee to Protect Journalists.

(*IHT*, 1 October 2010, p. 3)

'Last year [2009] Transparency International ... placed Russia in 146th place beside Sierra Leone and Zimbabwe in its annual Corruption Perception Index of 180 countries' (*FT*, Survey, 1 October 2010, p. 2). 'Russia has more than 43 million web users, a penetration rate of about 30 per cent, and is one of the world's fastest growing internet auditoriums' (p. 4).

President Dmitri Medvedev has appointed Mikhail Fedotov, a lawyer, as the chief human rights adviser, two months after his predecessor quit over unhappiness with what she regarded as Russia's failure to engage with campaigners for more democracy. Mr Fedotov told the Interfax news agency on Tuesday [12 October] that he would focus on ridding society of positive references to Stalin … He also said he would address changes to police forces and the judicial system, as well as take up the issue of children's and family rights.

(*IHT*, 14 October 2010, p. 3)

The European Court of Human Rights said on Thursday [21 October] it had fined Russia for banning homosexual parades in Moscow … Gay rights activist Nikolai Alexeyev had lodged three cases with the court arguing that Russia had violated the European Convention on Human Rights, to which it subscribes as a member state of the Council of Europe. The Strasbourg-based court ruled that Russia had violated rights of assembly and had discriminated on grounds of sexual orientation. It ordered Russia to pay Euro 29,510 ($41,090) to Alexeyev in damages and legal fees. For years authorities had denied gays permission to hold demonstrations on the grounds they would cause a violent reaction in the country, where prejudice against gays runs deep. The court said in a statement: 'The mere risk of a demonstration creating a disturbance was not sufficient to justify its ban' … Demonstrators have sometimes been beaten by police during rallies. Moscow's ex-mayor Yuri Luzhkov called gay marches 'satanic' and said the demonstrations would endanger public health and morality … The court also said the gay community's claims were not given a fair hearing in Russia, whose constitution guarantees the right to hold demonstrations. Alexeyev has said men connected to the authorities abducted him and pressured him to drop the cases.

(www.iht.com, 21 October 2010)

The European Court of Human Rights has fined Russia for banning gay parades in Moscow … A leading activist, Nikolai Alexeyev, brought the case after the city authorities repeatedly rejected his requests to organize marches. The Moscow authorities had argued the parades would cause a violent reaction. But the court in Strasbourg said Russia had discriminated against Mr Alexeyev on grounds of sexual orientation. It said that by refusing to allow the parades, the authorities had 'effectively approved of and supported groups who had called for [their] disruption'. The court said: 'The mere risk of a demonstration creating a disturbance was not sufficient to justify its ban' … Nikolai Alexeyev: 'The authorities now have to ensure the security of peaceful gay activists, and must allow our protests to take place in Moscow or any other city in Russia. We will be applying to hold a gay pride event in Moscow in May 2011. We'll be taking the former Moscow mayor to court: he broke the law by blocking our protests. We'll also be looking to hold to account those judges who continuously came to unlawful verdicts against us' ... Some activists who have tried marching in the capital without permission have come under attack from right-wing and religious groups, or were beaten up by police ... The European Court of Human Rights said: 'The court could not disregard the strong personal opinions publicly expressed by the Moscow mayor [Yuri Luzhkov] and the undeniable link between those statements and the bans.'

(www.bbc.co.uk, 21 October 2010)

Gay rights activists said the ruling had tremendous implications for all civil society in Russia, as it states that the authorities' insistence that protesters must obtain permission to hold rallies or pickets is illegal. Currently, authorities in many Russian cities reject applications for gay marches or demonstrations of the democratic opposition, often claiming that they clash with other hastily arranged events. Russia remains largely homophobic ... Last month [September] Mr Alexeyev claimed he was abducted by plain clothes security officers from a Moscow airport and held for two days. He said he was verbally abused and told to withdraw the court case. The verdict came on the same day as Moscow got a new mayor, Sergei Sobyanin, who was inaugurated after being approved by the city's parliament.

(*The Independent*, 22 October 2010, p. 34)

Moscow's city government gave permission for an opposition demonstration to be held on Triumph Square, the site of many illegal protests by pro-democracy activists, which in the past have been broken up by police. Permission, however, was given for only 200 people ... State-controlled television channel NTV plans to run on Friday [22 October] an anti-Luzhkov documentary. The piece is a sequel to a 10 September broadcast called the 'Flat Cap Affair', which began the anti-Luzhkov media storm. The flat cap had been Yuri Luzhkov's trademark.

(*FT*, 22 October 2010, p. 9)

This year [2010] witnessed the most dramatic instance of the Russian government acknowledging Soviet crimes. Speaking [in Katyn] of the killing of thousands of Polish officers in 1940 by Soviet security police in the presence of Polish leaders, [prime minister Vladimir] Putin said: 'These crimes cannot be justified ... They have already been given the correct moral and legal assessment' ... Yet not a single perpetrator has been named, and no legal action has ever been taken. Not a single trial has ever been held in Russia in connection with an act of terror committed by the Soviet state.

(Maxim Trudolyubov, editorial page editor of *Vedomosti*, www.iht.com, 20 October 2010; *IHT*, 30 October 2010, p. 6)

Developments in Chechnya and other Caucasian republics

'Women in Chechnya are under pressure to adopt Islamic dress, according to human rights activists ... Activists in Chechnya ... said intimidation reached a peak during the fasting month of Ramadan ... Threats tapered off, they said, as Ramadan ended in mid-September' (*IHT*, 28 September 2010, p. 1).

Russian forces ... say they have blockaded two groups of rebels in Dagestan, killing fourteen of them. Nine died when security forces launched a 'special operation' in the town of Kaspiysk, and five died in another operation in Makhachkala, they said. At least eleven members of the security forces have died in militant attacks in the mainly Moslem region this month [September] ... No members of the security forces were hurt during Wednesday morning's [29 September] operations in Dagestan, Russia's Anti-Terrorist Committee (NAK) said ... Two anti-terrorist police commanders and at least four other police officers, as well as five Russian soldiers, were killed in separate attacks this month. Just days before the latest operations against the rebels, security forces reported killing a rebel leader and three of his fighters in Makhachkala.

(www.bbc.co.uk, 30 September 2010)

Islamic insurgents, including a suicide bomber, stormed Chechnya's parliament building today [19 October] leaving six people dead ... One militant set off a bomb at the gates of the parliament complex in Grozny, killing himself and wounding others ... At least two other gunmen ran into the building shouting 'Allahu akbar' – 'God is great' in Arabic – as they opened fire in the people inside ... Two police officers and one parliamentary official were killed in the attack ... The insurgents tried to get into the main parliamentary hall ... Insurgents also attacked the agriculture ministry in the same complex and shots were fired inside the office of the parliament's speaker ... Russian interior minister Rashid Nurgaliyev was in Grozny for talks with Ramzan Kadyrov ... Russia fought two wars with Chechen separatists in the 1990s before finally installing a loyal government there in 2000.

(www.independent.com, 19 October 2010)

A Chechen interior ministry official ... [said on 19 October] that the attack could have been the work of a new group, which has split off from Doku Umarov and is being led by forty-year-old Hussein Gakayev. The interior ministry source said: 'Attacking the parliament and destroying the leadership would be a way to loudly proclaim that he is the new leader, and send a message to his foreign sponsors.'

(*The Independent*, 20 October 2010, p. 23)

The militants tried to enter the main parliamentary hall, where several deputies were meeting. Unable to do so, the gunmen barricaded themselves in the ground floor of the parliament and eventually blew themselves up. All the attackers were killed. Two police officers and a civilian also died ... The situation in Chechnya remains highly volatile, despite assertions that the country is now peaceful after brutal wars in 1994–6 and 1999–2005 ... [According to] Cerwyn Moore ... a schism this summer [2010] in the insurgents' hierarchy may have contributed to the recent escalation in violence. Last week the rebel leader Doku Umarov ordered a number of commanders to renew their oath of allegiance to him. Moore said of today's assault: 'One [anti-Umarov] faction could be demonstrating its ability to carry out the attacks in Chechnya proper.'

(www.guardian.co.uk, 19 October 2010)

At least one attacker appears to have set off a suicide bomb just inside the building before others rushed inside, exchanging fire with security guards ... The official killed was reportedly the parliamentary bursar ... Deputies inside the building managed to escape by moving to an upper floor ... Russian interior minister Rashid Nurgaliyev, who was visiting Chechnya when the attack happened, held an emergency meeting with Ramzan Kadyrov.

(www.bbc.co.uk, 19 October 2010)

The three gunmen entered right through the front gates of the parliament complex, which is located in a busy section of downtown Grozny. Without uttering a word they executed two police officers standing guard at the entrance ... One of the militants then blew himself up, killing a staff member, while the others opened fire. No parliamentarians were killed in the attack.

(www.iht.com, 19 October 2010)

Seven people – four rebels, two police officers and a parliamentary official – died in the fighting. The rebels had driven right up to the assembly building, getting past security by following the car of a deputy. Chechen police said that two insurgents blew themselves up while setting off a bomb at the gates. Two more rebels ... stormed into the building and began shooting.

(*The Times*, 20 October 2010, p. 38)

Three militants who shook Chechnya by attacking its parliament on Tuesday [19 October] arrived by taxi, Russian media report. It took security forces in Grozny at least fifteen minutes to overcome the attackers, who detonated explosives and fired assault rifles. Carrying Kalashnikov assault rifles and wearing combat gear, the militants are said to have duped the driver of a Lada car. They reportedly told him they were bodyguards to an MP and 'running late'. Stopping close to the parliamentary compound, they asked the driver to 'hold on a few minutes', then waited for an MP's car to appear, the driver later told investigators. When the security gates opened to allow the vehicle in, the three jumped out and sprinted after it, opening fire on two policemen manning the checkpoint. One policeman was killed and the other seriously wounded ... Outnumbered by the bodyguards, the militants split up: two ran towards the parliamentary administration building while the third covered them by blowing himself up, killing a bodyguard and the parliamentary bursar ... According to *Kommersant*, the two gunmen kept firing until their ammunition ran out, then both blew themselves up with bombs. In all, six people including the militants were killed and seventeen injured ... No group has said it carried out the raid.

(www.bbc.co.uk, 20 October 2010)

'The Chechen population of about 1 million is mostly made up of Sunni Moslems' (www.cnn.com, 19 October 2010).

A bombing and a shoot-out caused deaths and injuries on Saturday [23 October] ... Two militants were killed and two police officers were wounded in a shoot-out in the republic of Dagestan ... A car bomb in that republic killed a police officer ... In the nearby republic of Ingushetia two militants were killed when the men opened fire at police after their car was stopped for a security check.

(www.cnn.com, 24 October 2010)

It was not possible to include coverage here of the dramatic statement by Mikhail Khodorkovsky at the end of his second trial, but interested readers can consult the postscript of the companion volume on the economy.

Bibliography

Periodicals and reports

CDSP   *Current Digest of the Soviet Press* (since 5 February 1992 *Post-Soviet*)
EBRD   European Bank for Reconstruction and Development
EIU   Economist Intelligence Unit
FEER   *Far Eastern Economic Review*
FT   *Financial Times*
IHT   *International Herald Tribune*
RET   *Russian Economic Trends*

Note the following changes of title: *Soviet Economy* to *Post-Soviet Studies*; *Soviet Studies* to *Europe-Asia Studies*.

Books and journals

Amelina, M. (1999) 'The (not so) mysterious resilience of Russia's agricultural collectives', *Transition*, vol. 10, no. 6.

Åslund, A. (1989) *Gorbachev's Struggle for Economic Reform: The Soviet Reform Process, 1985–88*, 1st edn, London: Pinter.

Åslund, A. (1991a) *Gorbachev's Struggle for Economic Reform: The Soviet Reform Process, 1985–88*, 2nd edn, London: Pinter.

Åslund, A. (1991b) 'Gorbachev, *perestroyka*, and economic crisis', *Problems of Communism*, January–April.

Åslund, A. (ed.) (1992) *The Post-Soviet Economy; Soviet and Western Perspectives*, London: Pinter.

Åslund, A. (1994) 'Russia's success story', *Foreign Affairs*, vol. 73, no. 5.

Åslund, A. (1999a) 'Russia's current economic dilemma', *Post-Soviet Affairs*, vol. 15, no. 1.

Åslund, A. (1999b) 'Russia's collapse', *Foreign Affairs*, vol. 78, no. 5.

Åslund, A. and Layard, R. (eds) (1993) *Changing the Economic System in Russia*, London: Pinter.

Bacon, E. and Renz, B. (2003) 'Return of the KGB?', *The World Today*, vol. 59, no. 5.

Balcerowicz, L. (1989) 'Polish economic reform, 1981–88: an overview' in United Nations Economic Commission for Europe (1989) *Economic Reforms in the European Centrally Planned Economies*, New York: United Nations.

Balcerowicz, L. (1993) 'Transition to market economy: Central and East European countries in comparative perspective', *British Review of Economic Issues*, vol. 15, no. 37.

Balcerowicz, L. (1994) 'Common fallacies in the debate on the transition to a market economy', *Economic Policy*, no. 19 (Supplement).

Balino, T. (1998) 'Monetary policy in Russia', *Finance and Development*, December.

Bideleux, R. and Jeffries, I. (1998) *A History of Eastern Europe: Crisis and Change*, London: Routledge.

Bideleux, R. and Jeffries, I. (2007) *A History of Eastern Europe: Crisis and Change*, 2nd edn, London: Routledge.

Bideleux, R. and Jeffries, I. (2007) *The Balkans*, London: Routledge.

Boone, P. and Fedorov, B. (1997) 'The ups and down of Russian economic reforms' in W. Woo, S. Parker and J. Sachs (eds) *Economies in Transition: Comparing Asia and Eastern Europe*, London: MIT Press.

Boycko, M. (1991) 'Price decontrol: the microeconomic case for the "big bang" approach', *Oxford Review of Economic Policy*, vol. 7, no. 4.

Boycko, M., Shleifer, A. and Vishny, R. (1994) 'Voucher privatization', *Journal of Financial Economics*, vol. 35, no. 2.

Boycko, M., Shleifer, A. and Vishny, R. (1995) *Privatizing Russia*, Cambridge, Mass.: MIT Press.

Boycko, M., Shleifer, A. and Vishny, R. (1996) 'A theory of privatization', *Economic Journal*, vol. 106, no. 435.

Broadman, H. (2001) 'Competition and business entry in Russia', *Finance and Development*, vol. 38, no. 2.

Brooks, K. (1990a) 'Soviet agriculture's halting reform', *Problems of Communism*, March–April.

Brooks, K. (1990b) 'Soviet agricultural policy and pricing under Gorbachev' in K.R. Gray (ed.) *Soviet Agriculture: Comparative Perspectives*, Ames: Iowa University Press.

Brooks, K. (1990c) 'Perestroika in the countryside: agricultural reform in the Gorbachev era', *Comparative Economic Studies*, vol. XXXII, no. 2.

Brooks, K. (1992) 'Stabilization, sectoral adjustment and enterprise reform in the agricultural sector of Russia', *American Journal of Agricultural Economics*, vol. 74, no. 5.

Brown, A., Ickes, B. and Ryterman, R. (1994) *The Myth of Monopoly: A New View of Industrial Structure in Russia*, World Bank: Policy Research Working Paper no. 1331.

Brown, D.J. and Earle, J. (1999) 'Evaluating enterprise privatization in Russia', *RET*, 1999, vol. 8, no. 3.

Buck, T., Filatotchev, I. and Wright, M. (1994) 'Employee buy-outs and the transformation of Russian industry', *Comparative Economic Studies*, vol. XXXVI, no. 2.

Business Central Europe (2001) 'A Survey of Russia and the CIS', April.

Chen, L., Wittgenstein, F. and McKeon, E. (1996) 'The upsurge of mortality in Russia: causes and implications', *Population and Development Review*, vol. 22, no. 3.

Chubais, A. and Vishnevskaya, M. (1993) 'Main issues of privatization in Russia' in A. Åslund and R. Layard (eds) *Changing the Economic System in Russia*, London: Pinter.

Cook, L. (2000) 'The Russian welfare state: obstacles to restructuring', *Post-Soviet Affairs*, vol. 16, no. 4.

Desai, P. (2000) 'Why did the rouble collapse in August 1998?', *American Economic Review*, Papers and Proceedings, May.

Desai, R. and Goldberg, I. (2000) 'Shareholders, governance and the Russian enterprise dilemma', *Finance and Development*, vol. 37, no. 2.

EBRD (1994) *Transition Report*, London: European Bank for Reconstruction and Development.

EBRD (1995a) *Transition Report Update* (April), London: European Bank for Reconstruction and Development.

EBRD (1995b) *Transition Report*, London: European Bank for Reconstruction and Development.

EBRD (1996a) *Transition Report Update* (April), London: European Bank for Reconstruction and Development.

EBRD (1996b) *Transition Report*, London: European Bank for Reconstruction and Development.

EBRD (1997a) *Transition Report Update* (April), London: European Bank for Reconstruction and Development.

EBRD (1997b) *Transition Report*, London: European Bank for Reconstruction and Development.

EBRD (1998a) *Transition Report Update* (April), London: European Bank for Reconstruction and Development.

EBRD (1998b) *Transition Report*, London: European Bank for Reconstruction and Development.

EBRD (1999a) *Transition Report Update* (April), London: European Bank for Reconstruction and Development.

EBRD (1999b) *Transition Report*, London: European Bank for Reconstruction and Development.

EBRD (2000a) *Transition Report Update* (May), London: European Bank for Reconstruction and Development.

EBRD (2000b) *Transition Report*, London: European Bank for Reconstruction and Development.

EBRD (2001a) *Transition Report Update* (April), London: European Bank for Reconstruction and Development.

EBRD (2001b) *Transition Report*, London: European Bank for Reconstruction and Development.

EBRD (2002a) *Transition Report Update* (April), London: European Bank for Reconstruction and Development.

EBRD (2002b) *Transition Report*, London: European Bank for Reconstruction and Development.

EBRD (2003a) *Transition Report Update* (April), London: European Bank for Reconstruction and Development.

EBRD (2003b) *Transition Report*, London: European Bank for Reconstruction and Development.

EBRD (2004a) *Transition Report Update* (April), London: European Bank for Reconstruction and Development.

EBRD (2004b) *Transition Report*, London: European Bank for Reconstruction and Development.

EBRD (2005a) *Transition Report Update* (April), London: European Bank for Reconstruction and Development.

EBRD (2005b) *Transition Report*, London: European Bank for Reconstruction and Development.

EBRD (2006a) *Transition Report Update* (April), London: European Bank for Reconstruction and Development.

EBRD (2006b) *Transition Report*, London: European Bank for Reconstruction and Development.

EBRD (2007a) *Transition Report Update* (April), London: European Bank for Reconstruction and Development.

EBRD (2007b) *Transition Report*, London: European Bank for Reconstruction and Development.

EBRD (2008a) *Transition Report Update* (April), London: European Bank for Reconstruction and Development.

EBRD (2008b) *Transition Report*, London: European Bank for Reconstruction and Development.

EBRD (2009a) *Transition Report Update* (April), London: European Bank for Reconstruction and Development.

EBRD (2009b) *Transition Report*, London: European Bank for Reconstruction and Development.

EBRD (2010a) *Transition Report Update* (April), London: European Bank for Reconstruction and Development.

EBRD (2010b) *Transition Report*, London: European Bank for Reconstruction and Development.

Economist survey (1992) 'Russia', 5 December.

Economist survey (1995) 'Russia's emerging market', 8 April.

Economist survey (1997) 'Russia', 12 July.

Economist survey (2001) 'Russia', 21 January.

Economist survey (2004) 'Russia', 22 May.

Economist survey (2008) 'Russia', 29 November.

Ellman, M. (1979) *Socialist Planning*, London: Cambridge University Press.

Ellman, M. (2000) 'The Russian economy under Yeltsin', *Europe-Asia Studies*, vol. 52, no. 8.

Ericson, R. (1998) 'Six years after the collapse of the USSR: the Russian economy', *Post-Soviet Affairs*, vol. 14, no. 1.

Filatotchev, I., Buck, T. and Wright, M. (1992) 'Privatization and buy-outs in the USSR', *Soviet Studies*, vol. 44, no. 2.

Filatotchev, I., Wright, M. and Bleaney, M. (1999a) 'Privatization, insider control and managerial entrenchment in Russia', *Economics of Transition*, vol. 7 no. 2.

Filatotchev, I., Wright, M. and Bleaney, M. (1999b) 'Insider-controlled firms in Russia', *Economics of Planning*, vol. 32, no. 2.

Financial Times surveys: Russia: 13 May 1992; 27 May 1993; 27 June 1994; 10 April 1995; 11 April 1996; 9 April 1997; 17 September 1997 (Moscow); 15 April 1998; 30 April 1999; 10 May 2000; 9 April 2001; 12 March 2002 (Siberia); 15 April 2002; 21 October 2002 (St Petersburg and North-West Russia); 1 April 2003; 9 October 2003 (Finance); 13 April 2004; 19 October 2004 (Investing in Russia); 5 April 2005; 11 October 2005 (Investing in Russia); 21 April 2006; 20 April 2007; 2 October 2007; 18 April 2008; 15 April 2009; 13 October 2009 (Investing in Russia); 14 April 2010.

Fischer, S. (1992a) 'Stabilization and economic reform in Russia', *Brookings Papers on Economic Activity*, no. 1.

Fischer, S. (1992b) 'Privatization in East European transformation' in C. Clague and G. Rausser (eds) *The Emergence of Market Economies in Eastern Europe*, Oxford: Blackwell.

Fischer, S. (2001) 'Ten years of transition: looking back and looking forward', *IMF Staff Papers*, vol. 48.

Fischer, S. and Frenkel, J. (1992) 'Macroeconomic issues of Soviet reform', *American Economic Review*, Papers and Proceedings, May.

Fischer, S. and Sahay, R. (2000) 'Taking stock', *Finance and Development*, vol. 37, no. 3.

Fischer, S., Sahay, R. and Vegh, C. (1996) 'Stabilization and growth in transition economies: the early experience', *Journal of Economic Perspectives*, vol. 10, no. 2.

Flemming, J. and Matthews, R. (1994) 'Economic reform in Russia', *National Institute Economic Review*, no. 149.

Freeland, C. (2000) 'To Russia with love', *The New Statesman*, 19 June 2000, p. 13).

Gaddy, C. and Ickes, B. (1998a) 'Why are Russian enterprises not restructuring', *Transition*, vol. 9, no. 4.

Gaddy, C. and Ickes, B. (1998b) 'Russia's virtual economy', *Foreign Affairs*, vol. 77, no. 5.

Gaddy, C. and Ickes, B. (2001) 'The virtual economy and economic recovery in Russia', *Transition*, vol. 12, no. 1.

Gaidar, Y. (1997) 'The IMF and Russia', *American Economic Review*, Papers and Proceedings, vol. 87, no. 2.

Gorbachev, M. (1987) *Perestroika: New Thinking for our Country and the World*, London: Collins; New York: Harper & Row.

Gregory, P. and Stuart, R. (1990) *Soviet Economic Structure and Performance*, 4th edn, New York: Harper & Row (2nd edn 1981 and 3rd edn 1986).

Gregory, P. and Stuart, R. (1994) *Soviet and Post-Soviet Economic Structure and Performance*, 5th edn, New York: HarperCollins.

Handelman, S. (1994) 'The Russian mafiya', *Foreign Affairs*, vol. 73, no. 2.

Hanson, P. (1999) 'The Russian economic crisis and the future of Russian economic reform', *Europe-Asia Studies*, vol. 51, no. 7.

Hansson, A. (1993) 'The trouble with the rouble: monetary reform in the former Soviet Union' in A. Åslund and R. Layard (eds) *Changing the Economic System in Russia*, London: Pinter.

Hellman, J. and Kaufmann, D. (2001) 'Confronting the challenge of state capture in transition economies', *Finance and Development*, vol. 38. no. 3.

Ickes, B. and Ryterman, R. (1993) 'Road block to economic reform: inter-enterprise debt and the transition to markets', *Post-Soviet Affairs*, vol. 9, no. 3.

Ickes, B. and Slemrod, J. (1992) 'Tax implementation issues in the transition from a planned economy', *Public Finance*, Supplement to vol. 47.

Ickes, B., Murrell, P. and Ryterman, R. (1997) 'End of the tunnel? The effects of financial stabilization in Russia', *Post-Soviet Affairs*, vol. 13, no. 2.

Jeffries, I. (ed.) (1981) *The Industrial Enterprise in Eastern Europe*, New York: Praeger.

Jeffries, I. (1990) *A Guide to the Socialist Economies*, London: Routledge.

Jeffries, I. (1992a) 'The impact of reunification on the East German economy' in J. Osmond (ed.) *German Reunification: A Reference Guide and Commentary*, London: Longman.

Jeffries, I. (ed.) (1992b) *Industrial Reform in Socialist Countries: From Restructuring to Revolution*, Aldershot: Edward Elgar.

Jeffries, I. (1993) *Socialist Economies and the Transition to the Market: A Guide*, London: Routledge.

Jeffries, I. (1996) *A Guide to the Economies in Transition*, London: Routledge.

Jeffries, I. (ed.) (1996) *Problems of Economic and Political Transformation in the Balkans*, London: Pinter.

Jeffries, I. (2001a) *Economies in Transition: A Guide to China, Cuba, Mongolia, North Korea and Vietnam at the Turn of the Twenty-first Century*, London: Routledge.

Jeffries, I. (2001b) 'Good governance and the first decade of transition' in H. Hoen (ed.) *Good Governance in Central and Eastern Europe: The Puzzle of Capitalism by Design*, Cheltenham: Edward Elgar.

Jeffries, I. (2002a) *Eastern Europe at the Turn of the Twenty-First Century: A Guide to the Economies in Transition*, London: Routledge.

Jeffries, I. (2002b) *The Former Yugoslavia at the Turn of the Twenty-First Century: A Guide to the Economies in Transition*, London: Routledge.

Jeffries, I. (2002c) *The New Russia: A Handbook of Economic and Political Developments*, London: RoutledgeCurzon.

Jeffries, I. (2003) *The Caucasus and Central Asian Republics at the Turn of the Twenty-First Century: A Guide to the Economies in Transition*, London: Routledge.

Jeffries, I. (2004) *The Countries of the Former Soviet Union: The Baltic and European States in Transition*, London: Routledge.

Jeffries, I. (2006) *North Korea: A Guide to Economic and Political Developments*, London: Routledge.

Jeffries, I. (2006) *Vietnam: A Guide to Economic and Political Developments*, London: Routledge.

Jeffries, I. (2006) *China: A Guide to Economic and Political Developments*, London: Routledge.

Jeffries, I. (2007) *Mongolia: A Guide to Economic and Political Developments*, London: Routledge.

Jeffries, I. (2010) *Contemporary North Korea: A Guide Economic and Political Developments*. London: Routledge.

Jeffries, I. (2010) *Political Developments in Contemporary China: A Guide*. London: Routledge.

Jeffries, I. (2010) *Economic Developments in Contemporary China: A Guide*. London: Routledge.

Jeffries, I., Melzer, M. (eds), and Breuning, E. (advisory ed.) (1987) *The East German Economy*, London: Croom Helm.

Johnson, J. (1997) 'Russia's emerging financial-industrial groups', *Post-Soviet Affairs*, vol. 13, no. 4.

Kharas, H., Pinto, B. and Ulatov, S. (2001) 'An analysis of Russia's 1998 meltdown: fundamentals and market signals', *Brookings Papers on Economic Activity*, no. 1.

Kitching, G. (1998) 'The development of agrarian capitalism in Russia 1991–97: some observations from fieldwork', *The Journal of Peasant Studies*, vol. 25, no. 3.

Light, M. (1994) 'The USSR/CIS and democratization in Eastern Europe' in G. Pridham, E. Herring and G. Sandford (eds) *Building Democracy? The International Dimension of Democratization in Eastern Europe*, London: Leicester University Press.

Light, M. (1998) 'Russia's permanent crisis', *Global Emerging Markets (Deutsche Bank Research)*, vol. 1, no. 2.

Lipton, D. and Sachs, J. (1990a) 'Creating a market in Eastern Europe: the case of Poland', *Brookings Papers on Economic Activity*, no. 1.

Lipton, D. and Sachs, J. (1990b) 'Privatization in Eastern Europe: the case of Poland', *Brookings Papers on Economic Activity*, no. 2.

Lipton, D. and Sachs, J. (1992) 'Prospects for Russia's economic reforms', *Brookings Papers on Economic Activity*, no. 2.

McFaul, M. (1995) 'Eurasia letter: Russian politics after Chechnya', *Foreign Policy*, no. 99.

McFaul, M. (1996a) 'The allocation of property rights in Russia: the first round', *Communist and Post-Communist Studies*, vol. 29, no. 3.

McFaul, M. (1996b) 'Russia's 1996 presidential elections', *Post-Soviet Affairs*, vol. 12, no. 4.

McKinnon, R. (1992a) 'Taxation, money, and credit in a liberalizing socialist economy', *Economics of Planning*, vol. 25, no. 1.

McKinnon, R. (1992b) 'Taxation, money and credit in a liberalizing socialist economy' in C. Clague and G. Rausser (eds) *The Emergence of Market Economies in Eastern Europe*, Oxford: Blackwell.

McKinnon, R. (1994) 'Financial growth and macroeconomic stability in China, 1978–92: implications for Russia and other transitional economies', *Journal of Comparative Economics*, vol. 18, no. 3.

McKinsey Global Institute (1999) *Unlocking Economic Growth in Russia*, Moscow: McKinsey Global Institute.

Malleret, T., Orlova, N. and Romanov, V. (1999) 'What loaded and triggered the Russian crisis?' *Post-Soviet Affairs*, vol. 15, no. 2.

Mitra, P. and Selowsky, M. (2002) 'Lessons from a decade of transition in Eastern Europe and the former Soviet Union', *Finance and Development*, vol. 39, no. 2.

Murrell, P. (1993) 'What is shock therapy? What did it do in Poland and Russia?' *Post-Soviet Affairs*, vol. 9, no. 2.

Nellis, J. (1999) 'Time to rethink privatization in transition economies?', *Finance and Development*, vol. 36, no. 2.

Nellis, J. (2002) 'The World Bank, privatization and enterprise reform in transition economies', *Transition*, vol. 13, no. 1).

Nikonov, A. (1992) 'Agricultural transition in Russia and the other former states of the USSR', *American Journal of Agricultural Economics*, vol. 74, no. 5.

Nolan, P. (1996) 'China's rise, Russia's fall', *Journal of Peasant Studies*, vol. 24, nos 1 and 2.

Nove, A. (1961) *The Soviet Economy*, London: Allen & Unwin.

Nove, A. (1981) 'The Soviet industrial enterprise' in I. Jeffries (ed.) *The Industrial Enterprise in Eastern Europe*, New York: Praeger.

Nove, A. (1986) *The Soviet Economic System*, 3rd edn, London: Allen & Unwin.

Sachs, J. (1992) 'The economic transformation of Eastern Europe: the case of Poland', *Economics of Planning*, vol. 25, no. 1.

Sachs, J. (1994) *Poland's Jump to the Market Economy*, Cambridge, Mass.: MIT Press.

Sachs, J. (1995) 'Consolidating capitalism', *Foreign Policy*, no. 98.

Sachs, J. (1996a) 'The transition at mid-decade', *American Economic Review*, Papers and Proceedings (May).

Sachs, J. (1996b) 'Economic transition and the exchange rate regime', *American Economic Review*, Papers and Proceedings (May).

Sachs, J. (1997) 'An overview of stabilization issues facing economies in transition' in W. Woo, S. Parker and J. Sachs (eds) *Economies in Transition: Comparing Asia and Eastern Europe*, London: MIT Press.

Sachs, J. and Woo, W. (1994) 'Structural factors in the economic reforms of China, Eastern Europe and the former Soviet Union', *Economic Policy*, no. 18.

Sachs, J. and Woo, W. (1996) 'China's transition experience reexamined', *Transition*, vol. 7, nos 3–4.

Sakwa, R. (1995) 'The Russian elections of 1993', *Europe-Asia Studies*, vol. 47, no. 2.

Sakwa, R. (2000) 'Russia's "permanent" (uninterrupted) elections of 1999–2000', *Communist Studies and Transition Politics*, vol. 16, no. 3.

Sakwa, R. and Webber, M. (1999) 'The Commonwealth of Independent States, 1991–98: stagnation and survival', *Europe-Asia Studies*, vol. 51, no. 3.

Shama, A. (1996) 'Inside Russia's true economy', *Foreign Policy*, no. 103.

Shlapentokh, V. (1993) 'Privatization debates in Russia, 1989–92', *Comparative Economic Studies*, vol. XXXV, no. 2.

Shleifer, A. (1997) 'Government in transition', *European Economic Review*, vol. 41, nos 3–5.

Shleifer, A. and Vishny, R. (1991) 'Reversing the Soviet economic collapse', *Brookings Papers on Economic Activity*, no. 2.

Siszov, A. (1993) 'Land reform developments in Russia', *Economics of Transition*, vol. 1, no. 4.

Smith, A. H. (1993) *Russia and the World Economy: Problems of Integration*, London: Routledge.

Smith, G. (1994) 'Can liberal democracy span the European divide?' in H. Miall (ed.) *Redefining Europe: New Patterns of Conflict and Cooperation*, London: Pinter.

Solnick, S. (1998) 'Gubernatorial elections in Russia, 1996–97', *Post-Soviet Affairs*, vol. 14, no. 1.

Spoor, M. and Visser, O. (2001) 'The state of agrarian reform in the former Soviet Union', *Europe-Asia Studies*, vol. 53, no. 6.

Stiglitz, J. (2002) 'On Russia's 1998 crisis: excerpts from *Globalization and its Discontents*', *Transition*, vol. 13, no. 3.

Sutela, P. (1994) 'Insider privatization in Russia: speculations on systemic change', *Europe-Asia Studies*, vol. 46, no. 3.

Sutherland, D. and Hanson, P. (1996) 'Structural change in the economies of Russia's regions', *Europe-Asia Studies*, vol. 48, no. 3.

Tompson, W. (1999) 'The price of everything and the value of nothing? Unravelling the workings of Russia's "virtual economy"', *Economy and Society*, vol. 28, no. 2.

Tompson, W. (2000a) 'Putin's power play', *The World Today*, vol. 56, no. 7.

Tompson, W. (2000b) 'Financial backwardness in contemporary perspective: prospects for the development of financial intermediation in Russia', *Europe-Asia Studies*, vol. 52, no. 4.

Treisman, D. (1996) 'Why Yeltsin won', *Foreign Affairs*, vol. 75, no. 5.

Treisman, D. (1998) 'Russia's taxing problem', *Foreign Policy*, no. 112.

Treisman, D. (2002) 'Russia renewed?' *Foreign Affairs*, vol. 81, no. 6.

Trenin, D. (2004) 'Russia and the West', *The World Today*, vol. 60, no. 4.

United Nations (2001) *World Economic and Social Survey 2001*, New York: United Nations.

United Nations (2006) *World Economic Situation and Prospects 2006*, New York: United Nations.

United Nations Economic Commission for Europe (1989) *Economic Reforms in the European Centrally Planned Economies*, New York: United Nations.

United Nations Economic Commission for Europe (1992) *Economic Survey of Europe in 1991–92*, New York: United Nations.

United Nations Economic Commission for Europe (1993) *Economic Survey of Europe in 1992–93*, New York: United Nations.

United Nations Economic Commission for Europe (1994) *Economic Survey of Europe in 1993–94*, New York: United Nations.

United Nations Economic Commission for Europe (1995) *Economic Survey of Europe in 1994–95*, New York: United Nations.

United Nations Economic Commission for Europe (1996) *Economic Survey of Europe in 1995–96*, New York: United Nations.

United Nations Economic Commission for Europe (1997) *Economic Survey of Europe in 1996–97*, New York: United Nations.

United Nations Economic Commission for Europe (1998a) *Economic Survey of Europe 1998*, No. 1, New York: United Nations.

United Nations Economic Commission for Europe (1998b) *Economic Survey of Europe 1998*, No. 2, New York: United Nations.

United Nations Economic Commission for Europe (1998c) *Economic Survey of Europe 1998*, No. 3, New York: United Nations.

Wanniski, J. (1992) 'The future of Russian capitalism', *Foreign Affairs*, vol. 71, no. 2.

Watson, J. (1996) 'Foreign investment in Russia: the case of the oil industry', *Europe-Asia Studies*, vol. 48, no. 3.

Wegren, S. (1992a) 'Private farming and agrarian reform in Russia', *Problems of Communism*, May–June.

Wegren, S. (1992b) 'Agricultural reform in the nonchernozem zone; the case of Kostroma oblast', *Post-Soviet Geography*, vol. XXIII, no. 10.

Wegren, S. (1994) 'Rural reform and political culture', *Europe-Asia Studies*, vol. 46, no. 2.

Wegren, S. (1996) 'The politics of private farming in Russia', *Journal of Peasant Studies*, vol. 23, no. 4.

Wegren, S. (1997) 'Land reform and the land market in Russia: operation, constraints and prospects', *Europe-Asia Studies*, vol. 49, no. 6.

Wegren, S. (1998) 'Russian agrarian reform and rural capitalism reconsidered', *Journal of Peasant Studies*, vol. 26, no. 1.

White, S., Wyman, M. and Oates, S. (1997) 'Parties and voters in the 1995 Russian Duma election', *Europe-Asia Studies*, vol. 49, no. 5.

Woo, W. (1994) 'The art of reforming centrally planned economies: comparing China, Poland and Russia', *Journal of Comparative Economics*, vol. 18, no. 3.

Woo, W. (1997) 'Improving the performance of enterprises in transition' in W. Woo, S. Parker and J. Sachs (eds) *Economies in Transition: Comparing Asia and Eastern Europe*, London: MIT Press.

Woo, W., Parker, S. and Sachs, J. (eds) (1997) *Economies in Transition: Comparing Asia and Eastern Europe*, London: MIT Press.

World Bank (1996) *World Development Report: From Plan to Market*, New York: Oxford University Press.

World Bank (2002) *The First Ten Years: Analysis and Lessons for Eastern Europe and the Former Soviet Union*, Washington: World Bank.

World Bank (2004) *From Transition to Development*, www.worldbank.org.ru.

Yavlinsky, G. (1998) 'Russia's phony capitalism', *Foreign Affairs*, vol. 77, no. 3.

Index

eBooks – at www.eBookstore.tandf.co.uk

A library at your fingertips!

eBooks are electronic versions of printed books. You can store them on your PC/laptop or browse them online.

They have advantages for anyone needing rapid access to a wide variety of published, copyright information.

eBooks can help your research by enabling you to bookmark chapters, annotate text and use instant searches to find specific words or phrases. Several eBook files would fit on even a small laptop or PDA.

NEW: Save money by eSubscribing: cheap, online access to any eBook for as long as you need it.

Annual subscription packages

We now offer special low-cost bulk subscriptions to packages of eBooks in certain subject areas. These are available to libraries or to individuals.

For more information please contact webmaster.ebooks@tandf.co.uk

We're continually developing the eBook concept, so keep up to date by visiting the website.

www.eBookstore.tandf.co.uk

For Product Safety Concerns and Information please contact our EU
representative GPSR@taylorandfrancis.com
Taylor & Francis Verlag GmbH, Kaufingerstraße 24, 80331 München, Germany

www.ingramcontent.com/pod-product-compliance
Lightning Source LLC
Chambersburg PA
CBHW070612270326
41926CB00011B/1668